THE WAYS OF OUR GOD

THE WAYS OF OUR GOD

An Approach to Biblical Theology

Charles H. H. Scobie

WILLIAM B. EERDMANS PUBLISHING COMPANY
GRAND RAPIDS, MICHIGAN / CAMBRIDGE, U.K.

Wm. B. Eerdmans Publishing Co.
255 Jefferson Ave. S.E., Grand Rapids, Michigan 49503 /
P.O. Box 163, Cambridge CB3 9PU U.K.

Printed in the United States of America

08 07 06 05 04 03   7 6 5 4 3 2 1

Library of Congress Cataloging-in-Publication Data

Scobie, Charles H. H.
The ways of our God: an approach to biblical theology /
Charles H. H. Scobie.
p.   cm.
Includes bibliographical references and index.
ISBN 0-8028-4950-4 (pbk.: alk. paper)
1. Bible — Theology.   I. Title.

BS543.S39   2003
230'.041 — dc21

2002073886

www.eerdmans.com

Contents

CONTENTS

Contents

CONTENTS

Preface

This book was conceived many years ago but has been a long time coming to birth. It reflects the fact that for most of my life I have lived, as it were, in two worlds. One is that of the academic study of the Bible: as a student at university in Glasgow and at a theological college (Trinity College, Glasgow), as a graduate student in a master's program (Union Theological Seminary, New York) and in a doctoral program (University of Glasgow), followed by a teaching career in a theological college (The Presbyterian College, Montreal), a university faculty of religious studies (McGill University), and a university department of religious studies (Mount Allison University). For most of that time my studies, teaching, and publications were based on the historical-critical approach that dominated the academic study of the Bible in the second half of the twentieth century. At the same time, however, I lived in another world, the world of the church and the Christian community: as a theological student, as an ordained minister, and then as a preacher, teacher, or Bible study leader often called upon to expound the message of Scripture for the contemporary Christian community, as well as a member and elder in a local Christian congregation.

The tension between these two worlds was often acute. The academic approach was based on a two-century-old tradition that had strong roots in rationalism and often led to reductionism and skepticism. Above all, it was a world in which the Old and New Testaments were two totally different areas of study; one was either an Old Testament scholar or a New Testament scholar, and never the twain shall meet. Not only was any idea of a "biblical theology" (i.e., encompassing both Old and New Testaments) assumed to be an impossibility, but so great was the emphasis on diversity within Scripture that in many quarters even the possibility of an "Old Testament theology" or a "New Testament theology" was called in question. Similarly, biblical studies on the one hand and dogmatic or systematic theology on the other very largely went their own ways. Yet, when called upon to lead a Christian congregation in worship, one was expected to read from Old Testament, Epistle, and Gospel, and then to explain how within these varied words penned long centuries ago by human authors one could hear the Word of God speaking to the congregation in the pews. For the hearers, some kind of "biblical theology" (whether they called it that or not) that enabled them to understand Scripture as an organic whole, and some kind of hermeneutical procedure (whether they called it that or not) that enabled them to connect Scripture with their lives today, was an absolute essential; if that was not possible, they might as well go home. In my experience, and I know in the experience of many others, theological colleges, at least in the so-called mainline Christian churches, provided relatively little help in bridging the huge gap between the world of the academy and the world of the Christian community.

In wrestling with this problem of the possibility and the nature of "biblical theology" and of its relation to the academic study of the Bible on the one hand and the life and work of the church on the other hand, I have been influenced and helped by numerous persons, not all of whom may even have been aware of it. As a graduate student I was already "classified" as a New Testament scholar, but at Union Theological Seminary I had the opportunity to take not only the course in New Testament theology offered by my adviser Frederick C. Grant, but also the course in Old Testament theology taught by Samuel Terrien, a course that opened up new worlds for me. In addition, I was a member of a graduate seminar led by James Muilenburg and caught something of the infectious enthusiasm of that great Old Testament scholar. My interest in Old Testament theology, especially in relation to methodology, was rekindled by participation in a seminar led by the French Old Testament scholar Edmund Jacob at the Ecumenical Institute for Advanced Theological Studies at Tantur, near Jerusalem, in 1976. My ideas for a possible methodology and structure for constructing a biblical theology began to come together during a sabbatical leave at the Institute for Ecumenical and Cultural Research at St. John's University, Minnesota, in 1983-84; my fellow residents in the institute and in particular its executive director, Patrick Henry, made helpful suggestions that I believe set me on the right track. About this time I substituted for my regular course in New Testament theology a course entitled "The Faith of the Bible" that attempted to trace major themes through both Old and New Testaments, and I am indebted to succeeding generations of students at Mount Allison University for their keen interest and probing questions. The bold idea of attempting actually to write a biblical theology took further shape during a sabbatical leave at Cambridge in 1990. Since my (admittedly hesitant and faltering) attempts to work in this area attracted little or no response from the academic community as a whole, I am particularly grateful to Bruce Winter, warden of Tyndale House, Cambridge, for his support and encouragement to proceed with publishing my preliminary studies; at the same time, Prof. Brevard Childs of Yale was good enough to read some of my material, offer constructive comments, and here again give some much needed encouragement to proceed. It goes without saying that none of those named above are responsible for the work that follows, yet without them it would not have been possible.

Teaching, administrative and publishing commitments prevented me

from undertaking the task of writing this book until after my retirement in 1998; the main draft was completed in 1999 and the first part of 2000 as my personal "millennium project."

The dawning of a new millennium has already seen a continuing and growing interest in biblical theology with the publication of a number of works, unfortunately appearing too late to be discussed in this volume. The *New Dictionary of Biblical Theology* (InterVarsity, 2000) is evidence of this interest in an approach that encompasses both testaments. After introductory articles on the history and nature of biblical theology (Part One), it follows two routes: a discussion of the theology of each of the books of the Bible in their canonical order (Part Two), followed by a thematic treatment of major biblical topics in alphabetical order (Part Three). A sign of the times, the *Evangelical Dictionary of Biblical Theology* (Baker, 1996), which also adopts a thematic approach, is now available online at http://bible.crosswalk.com/Dictionaries/BakersEvangelicalDictionary/ (free of charge). The present work argues that biblical theology is an intermediate discipline, lying between the historical study of Scripture and the appropriation of the biblical message in the life and work of the Church, including the preaching of the Word. In *Preaching the Whole Bible as Christian Scripture: The Application of Biblical Theology to Expository Preaching* G. Goldsworthy argues cogently that all true Christian preaching (not least preaching from the Old Testament) must be undergirded by a sound and comprehensive biblical theology. He relates this to proposals found in previously published works for a Christ-centered, salvation-historical approach to the whole of Scripture, and rightly laments the virtual absence of biblical theology from theological seminaries and from standard works on preaching. Finally, in *Biblical Theology: A Proposal* (Fortress, 2002), B. Childs provides in convenient and concise form a summary of his views on a "canonical approach" to biblical theology (cf. C-2.2), according to which "Biblical Theology has as its proper context the canonical scriptures of the Christian church" (11). The main goal of biblical theology is to hear the two different voices of Old Testament and New Testament in their canonical integrity, yet also to understand them as both witnesses to the one divine reality of Jesus Christ.

In researching this book I have worked in a number of libraries; the staff of the Ralph Pickard Bell Library at Mount Allison University have always been helpful, but a special thanks is due to librarians at the Atlantic School of Theology Library in Halifax, Nova Scotia, and above all at the library of Tyndale House, Cambridge, surely one of the best biblical libraries in the world. Dr. Brian Ross of Toronto read a draft version of some chapters and made helpful comments. Special thanks are due to William B. Eerdmans, Jr., for accepting a rather long manuscript for publication, and to Associate Managing Editor Jennifer Hoffman for all her help in seeing the book through to publication.

Sackville, New Brunswick, Canada   CHARLES H. H. SCOBIE
October 2002

Introduction

To attempt to write a comprehensive biblical theology is an ambitious and daunting task, and some readers may be put off simply by the size and scope of this work. Those unfamiliar with the debates regarding the possibility and nature of biblical theology may wish to skip much if not all of part I (the prolegomena) and proceed directly to the "meat" of the book in part II. Even that need not necessarily be read through from beginning to end; use of the table of contents, outline of part II, index of subjects, and cross-references will make it possible to explore particular biblical themes and topics that may be of special interest. It would be desirable, however, to read at least the second part (sections 3 through 5) of chapter E of the prolegomena, since it explains and justifies the structure of the book as a whole and the fivefold structure adopted in each of the chapters of part II in particular. Hopefully those who adopt this approach will come back in due course to part I. On the other hand, academics, especially those who doubt the possibility of a biblical theology, will want to begin with part I, where I try to address their concerns and provide a rationale for the approach adopted in part II.

Since this work attempts to deal with the whole range of biblical thought, an extensive system of cross-references has been employed. Rather than using page numbers, references are given to chapters by section and subsection (e.g., C-2.2; 4-3.2a). Abbreviations are also widely employed; these are listed on pages xv-xvii. Because of the extreme frequency with which the terms are used in this volume, OT has been used for "Old Testament," NT for "New Testament," and BT for "biblical theology."

One of the aims adopted in writing this book has been to make it accessible not just to academics but also to students, clergy, and not least to that important character, the "intelligent layperson." While constant reference has been made to the original text in researching and writing this work, Hebrew, Aramaic, and Greek words are cited, where deemed necessary, in a transliterated form, and always accompanied by an English translation. Similarly, modern works in languages other than English are cited in English translation.

For those who wish to pursue the study of BT further, fairly extensive bibliographical resources have been included. References to works cited or referred to are given in parentheses, in the text, citing the author's surname, date of publication, and page number(s), i.e., using the so-called social sciences format (e.g., Hasel 1982: 80). This has made it possible to dispense with footnotes, though it does mean placing additional material in the text; hopefully readers who are not interested will be able to skip over the references.

Even in the bibliography, the size and scope of the work has dictated being extremely selective. Only works in English are listed, though books, monographs, and articles in other languages, especially German, are well represented in translation. With the exception of a few classic studies, almost all the works cited come from the second half of the twentieth century. After some hesitation, biblical commentaries have been excluded from the bibliography and are not cited directly in the text (the occasional excursus on a topic of BT in a commentary has however been included). This is due entirely to limitations of space, and in no way to any disparagement of the value and necessity of using commentaries as an essential exegetical tool. In referring to texts where there are particular problems of translation or interpretation, I have sometimes added in parentheses the words "see commentaries"; ideally that comment should apply to all major texts or passages of Scripture referred to in this work! An attempt has been made to cite a wide range of biblical scholarship, including Protestant, Roman Catholic, and Orthodox; the criterion has not been denominational allegiance but solely the ability of the scholar concerned to shed light on the biblical text and its meaning. An attempt has also been made to indicate the range of opinions that exist in current biblical scholarship and to cite works with which I do not necessarily agree; when this has been done I have used the word "contra" (e.g., contra Collins 1990: 9-12) to indicate that the scholar concerned expresses a view different from my own. Generally speaking, the selection of works cited has been guided by my experience in advising students; many readers may regret the omission of what they consider helpful and important treatments of the various biblical themes, but I trust that if they are aware of the huge amount of literature that is available, they will appreciate the need to be highly selective.

Every effort has been made to let Scripture speak for itself, and therefore, as well as providing numerous biblical references, I have cited key passages in the text (this perhaps reflects my skepticism as to how far readers will look up Scripture references for themselves). Standard abbreviations have been used for the books of the Bible. Since it is a major contention of this work that a BT must be based only on the canonical text of Scripture, noncanonical sources have not generally been cited. However, references are given to the apocryphal or deuterocanonical books, and when this is done the reference is given in italics (e.g., *Sir* 4:1). Such references do not necessarily imply that these books are part of canonical Scripture, only that they are helpful in shedding light on

God's dealings with his people in the two centuries prior to the time of Christ; the position adopted is that they should not be used to support any doctrine that cannot be substantiated elsewhere in Scripture (see more fully, D-2.6). The symbol // has been used to indicate parallel passages, especially in the Gospels (e.g., Matt 4:1-11//Mark 1:12-13//Luke 4:1-13), though no attempt has been made to provide parallel references in every case.

The translation of Scripture used is the New Revised Standard Version, partly because it is a relatively recent, reliable translation in contemporary language, and partly because it employs inclusive language in referring to people (e.g., it does not use "man" where Scripture clearly intends to refer to people of both genders). I have employed inclusive language myself, but have not altered the wording of quotations from works written prior to this becoming general practice. On the other hand, I follow the practice of the NRSV and the majority of modern translations in referring to God as "he" and as "Father" where Scripture itself does so. Occasionally a translation other than the NRSV has been employed; this is indicated by use of the appropriate abbreviation (e.g., RSV). In some cases I have provided my own translation, indicated by AT (author's translation); this is usually a very literal rendering designed to bring out the original meaning as precisely as possible.

Abbreviations

ABD	*Anchor Bible Dictionary* (Garden City, N.Y.: Doubleday, 1992)
ASTI	*Annual of the Swedish Theological Institute*
AT	Author's translation
ATR	*Anglican Theological Review*
ATRSup	*Anglican Theological Review, Supplements*
AUSS	*Andrews University Seminary Studies*
BA	*Biblical Archaeologist*
BASOR	*Bulletin of the American Schools of Oriental Research*
BEB	*Baker Encyclopedia of the Bible* (Grand Rapids: Baker, 1988)
Bib	*Biblica*
BibT	*Bible Translator*
BJRL	*Bulletin of the John Rylands University Library of Manchester*
BRev	*Bible Review*
BS	*Bibliotheca Sacra*
BT	Biblical theology
BTB	*Biblical Theology Bulletin*
CBQ	*Catholic Biblical Quarterly*
CCen	*Christian Century*
CCris	*Christianity and Crisis*
CH	*Church History*
CEV	Contemporary English Version
CJT	*Canadian Journal of Theology*
CPDBT	*The Collegeville Pastoral Dictionary of Biblical Theology* (Collegeville, Minn.: Liturgical Press, 1996)
CQR	*Church Quarterly Review*
CT	*Christianity Today*
CTJ	*Calvin Theological Journal*
CTM	*Concordia Theological Monthly*
DB	*Dictionary of the Bible* (Edinburgh: T. & T. Clark, 1963)
DNTT	*The New International Dictionary of New Testament Theology*, 3 vols. (Grand Rapids: Zondervan, 1975, 1976, 1978)

ABBREVIATIONS

EBT	*Encyclopedia of Biblical Theology: The Complete "Sacramentum Verbi"* (New York: Crossroad, 1970, 1981)
EDBT	*Evangelical Dictionary of Biblical Theology* (Grand Rapids: Baker, 1996)
EEC	*Encyclopedia of Early Christianity* (New York: Garland, 1990)
EncJud	*Encyclopaedia Judaica* (Jerusalem: Keter, 1971)
EQ	*Evangelical Quarterly*
ET	English translation
ExpT	*Expository Times*
Fnds	*Foundations: A Baptist Journal of History and Theology*
Greg	*Gregorianum*
HBT	*Horizons in Biblical Theology*
HDB	*Hastings' Dictionary of the Bible,* 5 vols. (Edinburgh: T. & T. Clark, 1898)
HibJ	*Hibbert Journal*
HTR	*Harvard Theological Review*
HUCA	*Hebrew Union College Annual*
IB	*Interpreter's Bible,* 12 vols. (Nashville: Abingdon, 1952-57)
IBD	*Illustrated Bible Dictionary,* 3 vols. (Leicester: InterVarsity, 1980)
ICB	*Interpreter's One Volume Commentary on the Bible* (Nashville: Abingdon, 1971)
IDB	*Interpreter's Dictionary of the Bible,* 4 vols. (Nashville: Abingdon, 1962)
IDBSup	*The Interpreter's Dictionary of the Bible,* supplementary volume (Nashville: Abingdon, 1976)
IJT	*Indian Journal of Theology*
Int	*Interpretation*
IRM	*International Review of Missions*
JAAR	*Journal of the American Academy of Religion*
JBC	*Jerome Biblical Commentary* (Englewood Cliffs, N.J.: Prentice-Hall, 1968)
JBL	*Journal of Biblical Literature*
JBR	*Journal of Bible and Religion*
JEH	*Journal of Ecclesiastical History*
JES	*Journal of Ecumenical Studies*
JETS	*Journal of the Evangelical Theological Society*
JR	*Journal of Religion*
JSNT	*Journal for the Study of the New Testament*
JSOT	*Journal for the Study of the Old Testament*
JSOTSup	Journal for the Study of the Old Testament — Supplement Series
JSS	*Journal of Semitic Studies*
JTS	*Journal of Theological Studies*
KJV	King James Version
LXX	Septuagint (Greek translation of OT)
NEB	New English Bible
NIV	New International Version
NLBC	*The New Layman's Bible Commentary* (Grand Rapids: Zondervan, 1979)
NOAB	*The New Oxford Annotated Bible with the Apocryphal/Deuterocanonical*

	Books, New Revised Standard Version (New York: Oxford University Press, 1991)
NovT	*Novum Testamentum*
NRSV	New Revised Standard Version
NT	New Testament
NTS	*New Testament Studies*
OBT	Overtures to Biblical Theology
OS	*Oudtestamentische Studiën*
OT	Old Testament
REB	Revised English Bible
RelLife	*Religion in Life*
RelS	*Religious Studies*
RevExp	*Review and Expositor*
RQ	*Restoration Quarterly*
RSRev	*Religious Studies Review*
RSV	Revised Standard Version
SAJT	*Southeast Asia Journal of Theology*
SBT	Studies in Biblical Theology
SCent	*Second Century*
Scr	*Scripture*
SJT	*Scottish Journal of Theology*
SR	*Studies in Religion/Sciences religieuses*
ST	*Studia theologica*
TDNT	*Theological Dictionary of the New Testament*, 10 vols. (Grand Rapids: Eerdmans, 1964-76)
TDOT	*Theological Dictionary of the Old Testament*, 9 vols. (Grand Rapids: Eerdmans, 1974-98)
TEV	Today's English Version
Them	*Themelios*
Theol	*Theology*
ThTo	*Theology Today*
TrJ	*Trinity Journal*
TWBB	*A Theological Word Book of the Bible* (London: SCM Press, 1950)
TynB	*Tyndale Bulletin*
USQR	*Union Seminary Quarterly Review*
VT	*Vetus Testamentum*
VTSup	Vetus Testamentum, Supplements
WTJ	*Westminster Theological Journal*
ZAW	*Zeitschrift für die alttestamentliche Wissenschaft*

PART I

PROLEGOMENA TO A
BIBLICAL THEOLOGY

A. The Definition of Biblical Theology

A-1. WHAT IS BIBLICAL THEOLOGY?

The term "biblical theology" (BT) is widely used at the present time. There are encyclopedias of BT and journals devoted to BT, and people occupy chairs of BT. In the closing decades of the twentieth century there was renewed discussion of the possibility of writing a full-scale BT, a development that has given rise to hope in some but skepticism in others. Examination of the various uses of the term, however, quickly reveals widespread disagreement regarding its meaning. "Biblical theology," as J. L. McKenzie (1974) has said, "is the only discipline or sub-discipline in the field of theology that lacks generally accepted principles, methods and structure. There is not even a generally accepted definition of its purpose and scope" (15; see the extended discussion of problems of definition in J. Barr 1999: chaps. 1, 5, 6, 8, 9, 10, 12). On the other hand, there are those who have argued that "Biblical theology presents probably the most profound challenge for the Biblical scholar in the latter part of the 20th century" (Hasel 1982: 80).

If progress is to be made in the study of BT, the question of definition is clearly crucial. The term is a relatively modern one. As far as is known, it was first used in a book, *Teutsche biblische Theologie,* by W. J. Christmann, published in 1629 (no copies are known to have survived). In 1643 H. A. Diest published a volume entitled *Theologia Biblica.* The term became quite widely used in the eighteenth century, and continues to be used down to the present day. Of course, it is a fallacy to assume that what is meant by BT did not exist prior to the seventeenth century just because the term did not exist. Conversely, not everything that has been labeled "biblical theology" in the past two or three hundred years necessarily merits being thus designated.

It might seem that all that is needed is an examination of the two component parts of the term, "biblical" and "theology." "Biblical" is the adjective from the word "Bible," which in turn is derived from the Greek *ta biblia* and the Middle Latin *biblia. Ta biblia* means "the books" (*biblion,* meaning "book" or

3

"scroll," is a diminutive of *biblos,* the regular Greek word for "book"; see Arndt and Gingrich 1957: 140). Though the word is found in Dan 9:2 and *1 Macc* 12:9 referring to the sacred scriptures of the Jews, it is basically a Christian usage found first in *2 Clem* 14:2 (second century A.D.?) and eventually becoming widely employed as the standard designation of the sacred scriptures of the Christian church (A. Stewart 1898: 286). When the term passed from Greek to Latin, it also passed from a neuter plural (*ta biblia* = "the books") to a feminine singular (*biblia* = "the book"), "the transition being no doubt assisted by the growing conception of the Bible as the one utterance of God rather than as the multiplicity of voices speaking for Him" (286).

The term "Bible" can be used in a broad way as, for example, when it is said that "the Koran is the bible of Islam." And it certainly is quite common to refer to the Jewish Scriptures as "the Hebrew Bible." In order to avoid any confusion, however, the term will be used here to refer to *the books of the Old and New Testaments that constitute the Christian canon of Scripture,* i.e., the collection of those books that are recognized as normative for the faith and life of the Christian church.

"*Theology*" identifies the concern of the discipline with *theos,* "God." The term has seldom been understood in a narrow sense, however, as dealing only with the revelation of God himself, but is generally taken to include also God's relation to the world and to humankind, and related topics. There is certainly room for debate as to exactly what should be included in "theology"; for example, does it include the discussion of ethical questions, or is biblical ethics to be regarded as a completely separate discipline from BT?

"Theo*logy*" means the *logos* of *theos,* and this raises one of the most contentious aspects of any definition of BT. *Logos* (word, language, reason) in compounds of this type generally denotes the written, rational, systematic, scientific study of a given subject area (cf. bio*logy,* socio*logy,* and so on). There are those who would contend that since the biblical material is so diverse and, with its varied literary forms (history, poetry, drama, parables, and so on), actually contains very little "theology," therefore a biblical *theology* is impossible. Such a view, it may be argued, presupposes a very narrow conception of theology as rigid, systematized, doctrinal, and propositional in form. Through its diverse literary genres the Bible does give expression to an understanding (or understandings) of God in his relation to the world and to humankind. It is the testimony of the community that accepts the Bible as canonical Scripture that this understanding, though diverse and culturally conditioned, nevertheless represents the revelation of God; in and through the human words can be discerned the word of God. This understanding of God's revelation can indeed be the subject of scholarly study. Such study, as in any discipline, must be ordered in some way; what is important is that the "order" is one that arises from and is appropriate to the subject matter itself (cf. Hasel 1984: 126).

"Biblical theology" thus ought to mean something like the ordered study of what the Bible has to say about God and his relation to the world and to humankind.

It is often pointed out, however, that the term "biblical theology" can be understood in two different ways. It can be taken to mean a Christian theology that is based upon the Bible, what Ebeling (1963) called "theology that accords with the Bible, scriptural theology" (79). The problem with this is that all forms of Christian theology claim to be based in some way upon the Bible. The term might be used in a comparative sense, so that, for example, Karl Barth's theology might be said to be a "biblical theology" in comparison to Paul Tillich's, which might be characterized as more "philosophical." But this is not very satisfactory since, like both Barth and Tillich, all Christian theologians in all ages are in their own way seeking to understand what the biblical revelation and the traditional teaching of the church mean for their own day. This is better designated as "dogmatic theology" (Barth called his major work *Church Dogmatics*) or "systematic theology."

The second possible meaning of "biblical theology" is "the theology contained in the Bible, the theology of the Bible itself" (Ebeling 1963: 79), and this definition is the one that is preferred by most scholars.

Such a definition, and indeed such a way of posing the question, assumes that a clear distinction can and must be made between the teaching of the Bible itself and the way that teaching is to be understood and applied today. The Bible was written in the course of a one-thousand-year period, in times quite different from our own in many ways. Even if we accept the Bible as divinely inspired and normative for faith, it still has to be interpreted and applied in each new generation. What we may find very hard to grasp is the fact that the idea of making a clear separation between what the Bible meant in its original historical context and what it means for Christians today is a relatively modern one; it became possible with the rise of modern historical consciousness and was clearly enunciated only toward the end of the eighteenth century.

This explains why many people regard BT as a relatively modern development. Almost all discussion of the subject begins by referring to the famous inaugural address of J. P. Gabler at the University of Altdorf in 1787, entitled (in English translation of the scholarly Latin of the original) "An Oration on the Proper Distinction between Biblical and Dogmatic Theology and the Specific Objectives of Each" (see translation and commentary in Sandys-Wunsch and Eldredge 1980). Gabler is generally assumed to have advocated the strict separation of BT and dogmatics. Hence BT is taken to be a "historical concept" while dogmatics is a "normative concept" (Ebeling 1963: 79). Or, to use the distinction made in a much-quoted article by Krister Stendahl (1962) in the *Interpreter's Dictionary of the Bible,* BT is concerned with what the biblical text "meant," whereas dogmatic theology deals with what it "means" (see further below, B-7). The implication of this is that BT is a historical discipline that can be pursued quite independently of the church and the ongoing Christian community. Anyone can participate in the study, whatever their personal religious views, provided only that they have the necessary scholarly equipment (knowledge of the original languages, familiarity with the secondary literature, and so on). This is still a very widely held view of BT today. However, it poses two extremely serious problems.

Firstly, it results in the rather ludicrous view that no such thing as BT existed prior to 1787 (or thereabouts)! Surely it is obvious that from an early stage the church was concerned in some way with seeking an ordered understanding of what the Bible says about God and his relationship with the world and humankind.

Secondly, beginning in the late eighteenth and early nineteenth century, the study of BT was increasingly pursued as an independent and essentially historical discipline. As we shall see, what this led to was the *division* of BT (into OT and NT theology), the *decline* of BT (as it was absorbed by the history of religion), and finally the virtual *demise* of BT. While the development of the historical, critical study of the Bible brought great gains, unfortunately it also increasingly drove a wedge between academic biblical studies and the use of the Bible by the church. Many biblical scholars today hold that the historical study of the Bible has shown it to be so diverse in its contents that any idea of an ordered, consistent, overall "biblical theology" is a sheer impossibility. It is true that the term "biblical theology" is often used in a loose way to refer to any kind of historical study of the contents of the Bible. Thus the study and exegesis of a passage from one of Paul's letters might be referred to as an example of BT. This loose use of the term only creates confusion and should be avoided. Such a study is better classified "NT theology," or more accurately "Pauline theology."

Thus biblical scholarship today finds itself in an impasse. Students entering the field for the first time may be pardoned for scratching their heads in some bewilderment upon discovering that BT did not exist prior to 1787 and that it cannot be regarded as existing today in any strict sense of the term!

A-2. INTEGRATED, INDEPENDENT, AND INTERMEDIATE BIBLICAL THEOLOGY

The approach to BT that is advocated here is based on taking seriously both component parts of the term, "biblical" and "theology," and on recognizing that the ordered study of what the Bible says about God and his relations with the world and humankind certainly did not begin in the late eighteenth century, but has been (in one form or another) a concern of the church throughout its history up to and including the present day (cf. Robertson 1971: 65). As soon as the Gospels, Paul's letters, and other books began to be read alongside the Hebrew Scriptures in the early Christian church, and as soon as Christians began to study this twofold scriptural heritage and ask how it was to be understood and how it was to guide and direct the faith and life of the church, a form of BT came into being. It is true that no sharp distinction was drawn between the teaching of the Bible and the teaching of the church; the one was largely integrated with the other. Thus I have suggested (Scobie 1991a: 37-38) that the period prior to the eighteenth century could be characterized as a period of *integrated biblical theology.*

From the earliest stages of this period the church faced what still constitute the two greatest problems raised for Christians by the use of the Bible, the problem of unity and diversity and the problem of interpretation. As early as the second century, Christian writers are seen to be wrestling with the problem of how "the books," written over so many years by so many people, can be regarded as "the Book," or the revelation of the one God. How can the Hebrew Scriptures and the new Christian writings both be regarded as authoritative when they are so different? How is the church to deal with four Gospels that tell the story of Jesus in such diverse ways? In other words, how can unity be found in the midst of such diversity?

The other problem was that of interpretation or hermeneutics. Groups like the Gnostics had their own methods of interpretation which the church considered to be in error. How then is Scripture to be interpreted within the church?

It is true that the answers the church gave to these problems are not necessarily identical with the ones Christian thinkers would give today. And it is true also that these problems are more acute today than in the second century. Modern historical studies have emphasized the diversity of Scripture to a far greater extent. And the fact that we live between two and three thousand years after the books of the Bible were written, and in a world in which so much has changed, causes even greater hermeneutical problems. But the differences should not be overexaggerated. On reading some of the discussions of Scripture in early Church Fathers, one is often surprised at how modern the issues sound.

The rise of a new historical consciousness in the eighteenth century did certainly revolutionize the study of Scripture. The history of biblical interpretation is never simple, but it is broadly true that the dominant trend of the last two hundred years has been the drawing of a sharp distinction between the original theology of the Bible, which is to be investigated by historical methods, and the later dogmatic theology of the church. BT understood in this way is an academic discipline that can be pursued in complete independence from the church. Hence I have suggested calling this an *independent biblical theology.* For many people today this still constitutes their understanding of what BT is. Yet, as indicated at the end of the previous section, it is this approach that has led to a dead end.

The approach advocated here is not one that disparages the historical study of Scripture. It does not seek to turn the clock back to a precritical age.

But it is aware of the shortcomings of the historical-critical approach, and seeks to go beyond it to a new understanding of BT appropriate to a postcritical age. BT is not to be undertaken in independence from the life of the church, the community that recognizes the Bible as its canonical Scripture. What will be proposed here may be called *an intermediate biblical theology,* for it is seen as a bridge discipline, standing in an intermediate position between the historical study of the Bible and the use of the Bible as authoritative Scripture by the church (cf. Scobie 1991a: 49-52). BT accepts and builds on the historical study of Scripture, but it is not simply concerned with what the Bible "meant." It is also concerned with what the Bible "means" as a canonical whole, and thus cannot be separated from the process of biblical interpretation.

The issues involved in thinking through a new approach to BT are complex, and some knowledge of the history of the church's use of the Bible is a necessary precondition both for understanding the impasse in biblical studies today and for finding the way forward to a more satisfactory position.

B. The History of Biblical Theology

Various introductions to the history of biblical interpretation are available (e.g., J. D. Wood 1958; Nineham 1963; G. W. Anderson 1971; Rogerson, Lindars, and Rowland 1988; Bray 1996), and in recent years there have appeared a whole series of valuable studies of the course of BT over the past two centuries (see esp. Betz 1962; W. Harrington 1973; Hasel 1978, 1991; Smart 1979; Reventlow 1986; J. Reumann 1991: 12-19; Reventlow 1992). What can be offered here is no more than a sketch of the history of BT, focusing on the most important recurring themes and especially on the issues that still confront the study of BT today.

B-1. THE EARLY AND MEDIEVAL PERIOD

As soon as the Gospels, letters of Paul, and other Christian writings began to be used alongside the Hebrew Scriptures, i.e., long before the finalization of the canon of what came to be called the NT, these two sets of scriptures were used by the church in formulating its beliefs and in countering what it considered to be false teachings. From the outset the problem of unity and diversity raised its head. The greatest diversity is that which exists between Old and New Testaments. A radical solution to this problem was offered by Marcion (fl. ca. 140-160), who, on the basis of a thoroughgoing dualism, distinguished between the God of the Jews, regarded as a God of justice, and the God of Jesus, regarded as a God of love. Consequently he abandoned the Hebrew Scriptures entirely. It is of fundamental importance that the church rejected Marcion's views and accepted the Hebrew Scriptures in all their richness and diversity as the first (and largest) part of what came to be recognized as the Christian Bible. At the same time, the church was increasingly obliged to face the question of the relationship between the OT and the NT.

The growing acceptance during the second century of the four Gospels created another problem of unity in diversity; how could such differing accounts be considered witnesses to the one Gospel (cf. Cullmann 1956)? The discrepancies between John and the Synoptics posed an especially acute problem. Yet the church rejected both the acceptance of only one Gospel (Marcion's solution) and the combining of all four in a harmony that ironed out all the discrepancies (Tatian's solution), and instead followed Irenaeus's advocacy of recognizing the fourfold Gospel believing that Christ "gave us the Gospel under four forms but bound together by one Spirit" (*Against Heresies* 3.2.8). Thus the church again opted for a fullness of scriptural witness but with the attendant problems of diversity.

In many ways Irenaeus (fl. ca. 180) deserves the title of "first biblical theologian" (cf. Lawson 1948; Childs 1992: 30-32). In fighting off the challenge of Gnostics who claimed that their teaching was based on Scripture, Irenaeus sought to develop a Christian understanding of the OT integrated with a consistent interpretation of the Gospels and Epistles recognized as authoritative by the church. That understanding was in turn integrated with "the rule of faith," the interpretation of Christian belief preserved in those churches that claimed direct succession from the apostles (cf. Froelich 1985: 13-14).

The problem of diversity was met in the early church in part by the use of allegorization, a method of interpretation used by Greek writers and in Hellenistic Judaism, especially by Philo of Alexandria (ca. 20 B.C.–A.D. 45). Allegorization ignores the historical setting of a passage and finds in every detail a hidden meaning which may be quite different from that intended by the original author. For example, the polygamy of the patriarchs was considered an embarrassment, so Abraham's wives were allegorized as representing qualities he possessed; Abraham was wedded to "virtue" (= Sarah) and "education" (= Hagar) (Philo, *Cong.* 23; see Caird 1980: 171). Origen (ca. 185-254) argued that where there are discrepancies or impossibilities in the biblical account, this is a clue to the discerning reader that a deeper, hidden meaning is concealed in the text. The classic example of allegorization is the interpretation by Augustine (354-430) of the parable of the Good Samaritan, in which every detail is given a second level of meaning (a certain man = Adam, Jerusalem = the heavenly city, the robbers = the devil and his angels, the inn = the church, the innkeeper = Saint Paul, and so on). The method can be used to find a uniform teaching throughout Scripture, but it is obvious that where the historical meaning is bypassed, it can open the door to reading in totally different meanings so that ultimately the text means whatever the interpreter wants it to mean.

The allegorizing "School of Alexandria" was opposed by the "School of Antioch" (R. M. Grant 1984: 63-72), which took a more historical approach. Theodore of Mopsuestia (ca. 350-428), for example, interpreted most of the Psalms historically and could find only four that could be regarded as messianic prophecies. The School of Antioch anticipated many of the conclusions of modern scholarship and, significantly, found problems with the canonicity of such books as Job in the OT and James in the NT. The difference between the two schools should not be exaggerated, however; Origen recognized that most texts have a historical meaning, while the School of Antioch did allow a higher sense of Scripture which they called *theoria,* which was more akin to typology and was built on the historical sense (cf. Froehlich 1985: 85).

In the West the interpretation of Scripture eventually crystallized into rules for finding "the fourfold sense of Scripture" (see G. R. Evans 1991: 114-22). A passage could have a *literal, allegorical, moral* (or tropological), and *anagogical* meaning. A Latin couplet summarized the scheme:

> Littera gesta docet, quid credas allegoria,
> Moralis quid agas, quo tendas anagogia.

R. M. Grant (1984: 85) gives a free English translation:

> The letter shows us what God and our fathers did;
> The allegory shows us where our faith is hid;
> The moral meaning gives us rules of daily life;
> The anagogy shows us where we end our strife.

The scheme has been widely criticized in modern times, yet it recognizes that there can be different levels of meaning in Scripture, and different ways in which the Bible can function in the life of the church. It brought together into one scheme the main strands of biblical interpretation in the early church (cf. Froelich 1985: 28-29). The "letter" of Scripture is recognized and listed first. Also known as the "historical" meaning, it refers to the meaning intended by the original author. This is not necessarily "literal" in the modern sense of the word, as the original meaning may have been metaphoric or parabolic (cf. Best 1993: 66). Allegory, however misguided, was a way of seeking theological unity amidst the diversity of Scripture. The moral meaning sought to provide scriptural guidance for ethical decision making. The "anagogical" is literally that which "leads upward," which nourishes the devotional life of believers on their spiritual pilgrimage, a vital aspect of Scripture often neglected in academic study. Building on the historical meaning, the allegorical nourishes faith, the moral nourishes love, while the anagogical nourishes hope (cf. Steinmetz 1980: 30).

Modern scholars often unfairly disparage the wealth of insight contained in patristic and even medieval exegesis that in its own way often did more to nourish the faith and life of the church than has the modern historical-critical approach. Moreover, it must be remembered that the extremes of allegorization did not go unchallenged. The historical sense was championed, for example, by the twelfth-century Victorines; Thomas Aquinas (ca. 1225-74) in particular insisted on the primacy of the literal meaning and in some ways anticipated a more modern approach (R. M. Grant 1984: 87-90).

The fact remains, however, that through the medieval period no clear distinction was drawn between the teaching of the Bible and the teaching of the church; BT was integrated with dogmatics. On the principle of "the analogy of faith" *(analogia fidei)*, it was assumed that the teaching of the Bible and the doctrines of the church were one and the same. Similarly it tended to be assumed, on the principle of "the analogy of Scripture" *(analogia scripturae)*, that the teaching of the Bible was identical from Genesis through Revelation. Particularly when a Bible available only in Latin prevented the majority of believers from reading Scripture for themselves, Scripture tended to be held captive by the church so that neither its challenging diversity nor its searching criticism of all human institutions was heard as it ought to be.

B-2. THE REFORMATION

When we come to the Reformers, it is even more difficult to deny that with their appeal over the head of centuries of church tradition to the teaching of Scripture *(sola scriptura)*, they practiced a form of BT. Some scholars in fact trace the origins of BT to the Reformation (see Brueggemann 1997: 1-4; cf. Childs 1992: 43).

Martin Luther (1483-1546) scrutinized the church's beliefs and practices in the light of Scripture and was led to the conclusion that "the Church is a daughter born of the Word, not the mother of the Word" (*Lectures on Genesis*, 7:16-24, as quoted in McNeill 1952: 123). In general he rejected allegorization and insisted on seeking the grammatical and literal sense. But he was not a "literalist." If his formal principle was *sola scriptura* (knowledge of salvation is found "in Scripture alone"), his material principle was *sola fide*, "by faith alone," i.e., faith in Christ. The Bible contains both law and gospel; the law comes first, for it leads to recognition of sin; it is followed by the gospel that proclaims the salvation to be received through faith. Luther cut through the diversity of Scripture by taking "justification by faith" as his key hermeneutical concept. Thus not all Scripture is of equal value. He focused on those books that "show Christ to you" (especially John and Paul), and had problems with the canonicity of Hebrews, James, Jude, and Revelation. While this brought some very central biblical themes into sharp focus, the unity of Luther's approach was bought at the expense of ignoring or downgrading those scriptural topics that were not consistent with the theme selected as the key (cf. Niven 1953: 13-14).

The teaching of John Calvin (1509-64), especially as worked out systematically in his *Institutes of the Christian Religion*, but also in his biblical commentaries, "gave Scripture a clearer and more explicit status than Luther" (Reid 1957: 29). While one may be convinced of the truth of Scripture by the majesty of its style or the agreement of its various parts, basically believers are assured of the truth of Scripture through "the inner testimony of the Holy Spirit," i.e., by the same Spirit that inspired the prophets working in the minds and hearts of believers. "The Word must be supplemented by the operation of the Spirit before becoming effective for faith and salvation" (48). Calvin sought to ground the faith of the church in Scripture in a more comprehensive and systematic fashion than did Luther and attempted to do justice to the full range of biblical material, though even he had problems with the Song of Songs and Revelation. While the supreme revelation is found in the NT, Christ is revealed in the OT also.

Luther and Calvin were still, by modern definition, dogmatic theologians who sought to understand the meaning of the Christian faith for their day, yet Calvin in particular can in many ways be seen as the initiator of a truly biblical theology.

B-3. THE EMERGENCE OF AN INDEPENDENT BIBLICAL THEOLOGY

The fresh insights and bold discussions of the Reformers were followed all too soon by the period of "Protestant orthodoxy" (Hayes and Prussner 1984: 12-15). Scripture was held to be inspired not only in its content but in its exact wording. What emerged was a strange paradox. The Reformers had rebelled against a dogmatic system that they believed had muzzled the Word of God; Protestant orthodoxy tended to introduce its own rigid, systematized "tradition" to which Scripture in effect became increasingly subject. "Those who succeeded the Reformers lost the living reality with which Luther and Calvin had invested Scripture, so that in their hands Scripture became an external authority legalistically conceived, and adherence to the Scriptures rigid biblicism" (Reid 1957: 77).

An exception is found in the work of the Reformed theologian Johannes Cocc.eius (1603-69), who in his major work, *Summa doctrina de foedere et testamento Dei* (1648), sought to interpret the Bible as a complete and organic whole by giving central place to the concept of "covenant." Cocceius laid the basis for the influential federal or covenant theology; he also anticipated later developments in BT through his emphasis on covenant and on God's dealings with his people in a "history of salvation" (see E-1.3; McLelland 1957; McCoy 1963).

It is in the seventeenth and eighteenth centuries that three major trends are to be discerned leading to the emergence of BT as a separate discipline.

Firstly, the practice developed, especially within Lutheran orthodoxy, of compiling collections of proof texts *(dicta probantia* or *dicta classica)* in order to demonstrate the biblical basis of Protestant doctrine. These collections, sometimes referred to as *collegia biblica* (*collegium* = "collection"), were usually arranged in accordance with the standard topics *(loci communes)* of dogmatic theology. Beginning around 1560, these *collegia* flourished for about two centuries. The earliest works bearing the title biblical theology (*biblische Theologie, theologia biblica;* cf. above, A-1) were of this nature. The shortcomings of this "proof text" approach are obvious. "Its chief faults are its superficiality and its totally inadequate view of the significance of the Bible. Instead of permitting the Scripture to speak for itself, it sought, actually, to compress the Bible within the narrow confines of a dogmatic system" (Hayes and Prussner 1984: 19). Nevertheless, these collections did have the effect of turning attention back to the text of the Bible itself.

A second major trend was the movement known as Pietism, which, under the leadership of such figures as P. J. Spener (1635-1705) and A. H. Francke (1663-1727), developed as a reaction against a dry and rigid orthodoxy, and emphasized rather personal religious experience and "apostolic simplicity." Pietism turned to the Bible not as a quarry of proof texts to support orthodox doctrine (though its aim was not to depart from orthodoxy), but in order to find spiritual and devotional nourishment (Stuhlmacher 1977: 37). Spener himself contrasted "biblical theology" *(theologia biblica)* with the prevailing Protestant "scholastic theology" *(theologia scholastica)* (Ebeling 1963: 84), and in the eighteenth century several Pietists published works with the term "biblical theology" in the title (Hayes and Prussner 1984: 55).

A third and perhaps the most significant trend was the development in the seventeenth and eighteenth centuries of new critical methods of literary and historical research (see Terrien 1952: 127-32) and of what came to be known as the "historical-critical" or "grammatico-historical" approach. It is "critical" in that it refuses simply to accept traditional explanations of how the Bible came to be written, but seeks to examine and weigh the evidence. It is "historical" in that it recognizes that the Bible did not drop ready-made from heaven, but emerged from a religious community over a period of time and thus must be understood in the context of the history of that community. And it is "grammatical" in that it seeks to understand the biblical text in terms of the meaning the words had for the original writers and readers. The Reformation emphasis on the literal or plain sense of Scripture (as against the allegorical) was probably a contributing factor to the rise of the new method (cf. Best 1993: 71).

Pioneers of the new approach include Richard Simon (1638-1712), who sought to use the new methods in the service of the Roman Catholic Church, and the more radical Benedict Spinoza (1632-77), who was expelled from an Amsterdam synagogue for his critical view of Scripture (see B. F. Meyer 1989: 197). Spinoza has also been claimed (though with less justification) as "the first Biblical Theologian" (Sandys-Wunsch 1981); he certainly anticipated the independent type of BT, and combined it with a strongly rationalist approach to religion. The more moderate rationalist J. S. Semler (1725-91) argued that the books of the Bible must be studied in their original historical context as one would study any ancient book, and that this must be separated from the use of the Bible by dogmatic theology (see Hayes and Prussner 1984: 58-60). Eighteenth-century rationalism, which developed from English Deism and the German Enlightenment *(Aufklärung),* saw in this new approach an objective method by which to throw off the shackles of centuries of church dogma and penetrate back to the true teaching of the Christian faith. The rationalists sought to extract from the Bible universal and timeless truths, in accordance with reason, distinguishing them from what is merely historically conditioned and time-bound (cf. Hasel 1978: 25-28; R. M. Grant 1984: 100-109). This approach is seen in the work of K. F. Bahrdt (*Versuch eines biblischen Systems der Dogmatik,* 1769), and especially in G. T. Zachariä's five-volume *Biblische Theologie,* published between 1771 and 1786 (see Sandys-Wunsch 1980). W. F. Hufnagel, in his *Handbuch der biblischen Theologie* (1785-89), enunciated the dictum that "the proof-texts must be used to correct the theological system, not the system the proof-texts" (quoted in Dentan 1963: 20).

B-4. GABLER'S DEFINITION

This is the point at which Gabler's much-alluded-to address enters the picture (cf. above, A-1). Most discussion has focused on the *title* of the 1787 address, "An Oration on the Proper Distinction between Biblical and Dogmatic Theology and the Specific Objectives of Each." Modern studies have shown Gabler's debt to his predecessors and also questioned the extent of his immediate influence (see Sandys-Wunsch and Eldredge 1980; cf. Morgan 1987).

An examination of the address itself shows that Gabler identified himself among those "devoted to the sacred faith of Christianity," who "profess with one united voice that the sacred books, especially of the New Testament, are the one clear source from which all true knowledge of the Christian religion is drawn" (Sandys-Wunsch and Eldredge 1980: 134; page numbers in this paragraph are from this translation). In the Christian use of "the sacred books" Gabler actually distinguished three stages. The first two he subsumed under the heading "biblical theology," though he later distinguished these as "true *(wahre)* biblical theology" and "pure *(reine)* biblical theology." Stage one is the historical study of the OT and NT and of the individual authors and periods. But this was to be followed by a second stage consisting of "a careful and sober comparison of the various parts attributed to each testament" (141), with the purpose of distinguishing those opinions "which have to do with the unchanging testament of Christian doctrine, and therefore pertain to us directly," from those which "are said only to men of some particular era or testament" (142). In other words, this part of BT was not merely descriptive but very definitely also interpretive; it selected from the Bible universal and unchanging truths. These were to be "carefully collected," "suitably digested," and "cautiously compared among themselves" (142). This collection of material would then show "with unambiguous words the form of faith that is truly divine," and the result will be "biblical theology in the stricter sense of the word" (143-44). It is this "pure biblical theology" which is then to be used by dogmatic theologians and related to the thought of their own day.

It will be seen that Gabler's main interest was not in the history of religion but in Christian theology (cf. Morgan 1995: 110). He seems to have regarded "pure biblical theology" as an intermediate discipline lying between a descriptive type of BT made possible by the new historical methods on the one hand and normative dogmatic theology on the other.

Much more influential than Gabler's actual lecture was its *title* (cf. Ollenburger 1985: 42). From about the 1830s onward, it was quoted as justifying a strict separation between the dogmatic theology of the church and "biblical theology," understood solely as what Gabler had called "true biblical theology," i.e., as a purely historical and descriptive discipline. This approach that led to the history of religions school and that is so influential to this day is in fact different from what Gabler himself advocated.

Gabler's own theology soon fell out of favor. It reduced the biblical word to universal and timeless truths, failing to grasp the nature of revelation in history; it in fact eliminated a considerable amount of the biblical material as inapplicable to modern believers; and it severely limited the extent to which God may be thought of as active in both nature and history. Nevertheless, Gabler's recognition that BT cannot be simply descriptive but must form a bridge to dogmatic theology is a profoundly valid insight that can point the way toward a more satisfactory understanding of BT today.

B-5. THE RISE AND FALL OF BIBLICAL THEOLOGY

The late eighteenth and first half of the nineteenth century saw a whole series of "biblical theologies," initially by rationalist biblical scholars of varying hues who followed in the footsteps of G. T. Zachariä, and who increasingly made use of the developing historical-critical method. Generally these works were used to criticize orthodox theology. Typical of the rationalist approach were the BTs of C. F. von Ammon (*Entwurf einer reinen biblischen Theologie*, 1792) and G. P. C. Kaiser (*Die biblische Theologie*, 1813). More significant was the work of W. M. L. de Wette (*Biblische Dogmatik des Alten und Neuen Testaments*, 1813), an OT scholar who was more independent and historically oriented in his approach (see Hayes and Prussner 1984: 98-100). However, his division of the religion of the OT into Hebraism and (postexilic) Judaism, regarded as an inferior form of religion, was unfortunately to have a long-term influence. A more moderate rationalism characterized the *Biblische Theologie* (1836) of D. G. C. von Cölln (see Dentan 1963: 24-34).

The rationalists for the most part demanded that revelation submit to the bar of reason as they understood it. Diversity within Scripture was dealt with by separating out temporally conditioned ideas *(Zeitideen)* which represent an "accommodation" to the thought of people in biblical times; what is left is the essence of biblical teaching, i.e., the timeless, rational truths of religion and morality. H. E. G. Paulus's life of Jesus (*Das Leben Jesu,* 1828) is typical of the rationalist attitude to miracles: the feeding of the five thousand is explained by the crowd sharing their packed lunches, and the resurrection on the assumption that Jesus did not die on the cross but revived from a deathlike trance in the cool of the tomb. The result was the elimination of the dimension of the supernatural.

Not surprisingly, orthodox and conservative scholars stood aloof from the new BT movement. After several decades, however, the realization dawned that BT could also be written from a more conservative viewpoint. The earliest BT by a conservative scholar was L. F. O. Baumgarten-Crusius's *Grundzüge der Biblischen Theologie* (1828). While prepared to accept a historical approach, he emphasized the essential unity of Scripture. J. C. K. von Hofmann (1810-77) represents a more conservative position. In reaction to scholars who sought within Scripture a system of doctrine, he stressed that the Bible is rather the record of "salvation history" *(Heilsgeschichte)*. The meaning of this history has already been revealed in Christ, although the fulfillment of God's purpose awaits the final consummation. Hofmann's recognition of salvation history as a key element of BT was a major contribution that was to be taken up and refined by a number of twentieth-century biblical scholars.

J. L. S. Lutz's *Biblische Dogmatik* (1847) and the massive and highly influential work of H. Ewald (*Die Lehre der Bible von Gott, oder Theologie des Alten und Neuen Bundes,* 1871-76) represent a moderate conservatism (see Dentan 1963: 46-48).

By midcentury, however, the days of this type of BT were already numbered. Historical study of the Bible was revealing in ever clearer fashion the diversity of the biblical material, above all the gap that separates OT and NT when these are studied in relation to their original historical settings. The attempt to encompass both Testaments within one system of biblical doctrine was increasingly considered either a sheer impossibility or a procedure that did violence to the nature of the biblical material as it was coming to be understood.

Ahead of his time in a number of respects, the rationalist scholar G. L. Bauer, as early as 1796, had written *Biblische Theologie des Alten Testaments,* followed, quite separately, by his two-volume *Biblische Theologie des Neuen Testaments* (1800, 1802). In due course Bauer's procedure came to be accepted as the norm not only by critical scholars but even by conservatives who joined them in producing a succession of "theologies of the Old Testament" and "theologies of the New Testament." Thus from around 1870, for approximately a century, "biblical theology," in the sense of the writing of works on the theology of OT and NT together, to all intents and purposes ceased to exist.

B-6. OLD TESTAMENT AND NEW TESTAMENT THEOLOGY

For the second half of the nineteenth century and the first half of the twentieth, OT and NT theology pursued separate though generally parallel paths frequently reflecting the prevailing theological climate. Thus W. Vatke's *Die biblischen Theologie, I — Die Religion des Alten Testament* (1835) is heavily laden with Hegelian terminology. In NT studies Hegelian influence is associated with the work of F. C. Baur (1792-1860) and the Tübingen School that saw early Christianity in terms of a conflict between Jewish and Gentile Christianity, with the catholic church of the second century representing a new synthesis. Despite its flaws, this approach made a valuable contribution to biblical studies. It brought about a new awareness of the historical nature of the biblical documents and of historical development in BT. The biblical revelation was given in history, and in biblical as in all history there are growth and development, action and interaction. Here is another approach to the problem of biblical diversity.

Critical scholarship in the second half of the nineteenth century and up to the First World War tended to be dominated by an outlook that can be classified very broadly as theological liberalism, following the line that runs from F. Schleiermacher (1768-1834) to A. von Harnack (1851-1930). Typical of this view were a break with conservative orthodoxy, the rejection of many traditional church dogmas, and efforts to reconcile Christianity with modern thought.

The application of historical-critical methods revolutionized the understanding of the authorship and dating of biblical books. The Mosaic authorship of the Pentateuch was challenged and replaced by source criticism that assigned every verse to J, E, D, or P, while Psalms and Wisdom were judged to be largely postexilic. In NT studies Mark was deemed to be the earliest of the Gospels, while the Pastorals along with the minor epistles were assigned to the second century. One result was a new chronological scheme that could be used to trace the development of the theology of both Testaments.

Liberal Protestantism tended to downgrade and neglect the OT (cf. D. L. Baker 1976: 56, 79), so that the majority of OT theologies in this period came from conservative scholars such as J. C. F. Steudel (*Vorlesungen über die Theologie des Alten Testaments,* 1840), H. A. C. Hävernick (*Vorlesungen über die Theologie des Alten Testaments,* 1848), and G. F. Oehler (*Prolegomena zur*

Theologie des Alten Testaments, 1845; *Theologie des Alten Testaments,* 1873), all of whom were prepared to recognize a developing revelation in history. H. Schultz continued to regard OT religion as a divine revelation but was prepared to adopt Wellhausen's views in the later editions of his *Alttestamentliche Theologie* (1869-96). The German monopoly was broken by C. Piepenbring's *Théologie de l'Ancien Testament* (1886) and A. B. Davidson's *The Theology of the Old Testament* (1904).

Schleiermacher regarded the link between Judaism and Christianity as a historical accident and held that "the Old Testament Scriptures do not . . . share the normative dignity or the inspiration of the New" (*The Christian Faith,* 1821, p. 132, as quoted in D. L. Baker 1976: 56). Better known is Harnack's often-quoted dictum: "To reject the Old Testament in the second century was a mistake which the Church rightly rejected; to keep it in the sixteenth century was a fate which the Reformation could not yet avoid; but to retain it after the nineteenth century as a canonical document in Protestantism results from paralysis of religion and the Church" (*Marcion,* 1921, as quoted in Baker, 79).

In the field of NT studies, interest tended to concentrate on "the quest of the historical Jesus." Despite the shock waves caused by D. F. Strauss's *Leben Jesu* ("Life of Jesus," 1835-36), which held that much of the Gospels is myth, liberal scholars generally were confident of rediscovering "Jesus as he actually was," before he was buried under the dogmas of the church and the doctrines of the creeds. The "essence of Christianity" (Harnack) is thus to be found in Jesus' teaching on the Fatherhood of God, the brotherhood of man, and the infinite value of the human soul.

The classic liberal NT theology is that of H. J. Holtzmann (*Lehrbuch der neutestamentlichen Theologie,* 1896, 1897), while a moderate conservatism, not uninfluenced by liberal scholarship, is seen in the NT theologies of B. Weiss (*Lehrbuch der Biblischen Theologie des Neuen Testaments,* 1868-1903; ET, *Theology of the New Testament,* 1892) and W. Beyschlag (*Neutestamentliche Theologie,* 1891, 1892). English-speaking scholarship is represented by E. P. Gould (*The Biblical Theology of the New Testament,* 1900) and G. B. Stevens (*The Theology of the New Testament,* 1901).

Of major importance was the work of A. Schlatter (1852-1938), who sought to work out a position independent of rationalism and liberalism on the one hand and conservatism on the other. While adopting a historical approach, he emphasized the basic unity of the NT and grounded NT theology in the historical Jesus. Evidence of his stature as a biblical theologian may be seen in the 1973 publication of a key methodological essay (in Morgan 1973: 117-66); the publication of a biography by Werner Neuer (1996); and the belated translation into English of his *Theologie des Neuen Testaments* (1909-10; 2nd ed., 1921-22) in two volumes, *The History of the Christ: The Foundation of New Testament Theology* (1997) and *The Theology of the Apostles: The Development of New Testament Theology* (1999) (see also Stuhlmacher 1978).

B-7. FROM THEOLOGY TO RELIGION

Despite the continued production of OT and NT theologies, the dominant trend was leading in another direction, and in the late nineteenth and early twentieth century the study of BT virtually dissolved into the discipline known as the history of religions *(Religionsgeschichte)*.

The progress of historical research in the nineteenth century had increasingly drawn attention to diversity and to development within both OT and NT, while the newer views on authorship and dating seemed to provide a secure basis for the tracing of such development. A spate of archaeological discoveries (that continues to this day) produced a mass of material relating to the ancient Near East and the Greco-Roman world. For many, these discoveries appeared to call in question the uniqueness of biblical faith. Babylonian creation myths and law codes, Jewish apocalypticism, Hellenistic mystery religions, and pre-Christian Gnosticism were all seen as providing striking parallels to the biblical material that could no longer be studied in isolation. A climate was created that strongly favored a comparative approach in which biblical religion is but one among many.

In the OT field the history of religions approach was first manifested (despite the wording of the title) in A. Kaiser's *Die Theologie des Alten Testaments* (1886), while R. Smend's *Lehrbuch der alttestamentlichen Religionsgeschichte* (1893) inaugurated a whole series of works that were generally designated as histories of OT religion. Representative works from the field of NT studies are H. Weinel's *Biblische Theologie des Neuen Testaments* (1911) and W. Bousset's *Kyrios Christos* (1913). The influence of this approach in the English-speaking world can be seen in two works with significant titles, S. J. Case's *The Evolution of Early Christianity* (1914) and E. F. Scott's *The Varieties of New Testament Religion* (1943). No clearer characterization of the history of religions approach can be found than in W. Wrede's 1897 monograph, *Über Aufgabe und Methode der sogennante neutestamentliche Theologie* (The task and methods of so-called "New Testament theology"). This is available in English translation (Morgan 1973: 68-116) and is still worth reading, if only because its approach is still typical of many academic biblical scholars today.

Reacting against both liberals and conservatives who spoke of biblical "doctrines," *Religionsgeschichte* emphasized that the true subject matter of biblical studies is *religion*. The Bible is not a book of doctrine but the deposit of the life and religious experience of the communities of Israel and the early church. One result was a growing emphasis on the place of the *cult* in biblical religion. Thus the Psalms were interpreted in terms of a pattern of "myth and ritual" held to be common throughout the ancient Near East, while Bousset argued that NT religion centered in the worship of Jesus as "Lord" *(kyrios)* along the lines of Hellenistic cults. According to Wrede, the true subject matter of so-called New Testament theology is not theology but early Christian religion which the scholar tries to investigate "as objectively, correctly and sharply as possible. . . . How the systematic theologian gets on with its results and deals with them — that is his affair. Like every other real science, New Testament theology has its goal simply in itself, and is totally indifferent to all dogma and systematic theology" (Morgan 1973: 69). All attempts to present a systematic outline of biblical teaching are thus abandoned.

A major consequence of this approach was *the ignoring of the bounds of the canon.* "No New Testament writing," Wrede declared, "was born with the predicate 'canonical' attached" (Morgan 1973: 70). For a reconstruction of the history of early Christianity, the Apostolic Fathers are just as relevant as the minor epistles. In tracing the development of biblical religion from the OT to the NT, a study of apocryphal and pseudepigraphical literature is essential. The history of OT, Jewish, and NT religion must use all available sources, and hence the concept of the canon, imposed at a much later date, is irrelevant. With Wrede we have arrived at *a totally independent biblical theology.*

The history of religions approach was dominant up to the First World War, and it continues to this day to be a major force in biblical studies, particularly in academic circles. It is associated with the movement in Europe of a considerable portion of biblical studies from the theological seminary to the university, and also, especially in North America in the second half of the twentieth century, with the blossoming of university departments of religious studies. While it is difficult to generalize, it often seems to be an underlying assumption that such an approach, unfettered by any Christian dogmatic presuppositions, is somehow objective and neutral and thus the only one that is possible in scholarly and academic circles.

The view that the task of BT is essentially *descriptive* was given classic expression in the article "Biblical Theology, Contemporary," contributed by K. Stendahl to the *Interpreter's Dictionary of the Bible* (Stendahl 1962; cf. above, A-1). Stendahl argued that the advent of the history of religions approach meant that for the study of biblical texts, "the question of meaning was split up in two tenses: 'What *did* it mean?' and 'What *does* it mean?'" (419). BT deals with what the text "meant"; its task is to provide "a descriptive study of biblical thought" (418), whereas the question of what the text "means" (for today) belongs to the realm of theology and homiletics. One implication of this is that "in order to grasp the meaning of an OT or NT text in its own time, the comparative material, — e.g. the intertestamental literature . . . is of equal or even greater significance than some canonical material" (428). Another implication is that "this descriptive task can be carried out by believer and agnostic alike" (422).

The question may be raised as to whether such an approach can meaningfully be designated either "biblical" or "theology." When the limits of the canon are totally ignored, when the book of *Enoch* is just as much source material as the book of Isaiah, or *1 Clement* as much as 1 Corinthians, it hardly makes sense to say that the discipline is concerned with the "Bible," i.e., the canonical Scriptures of the Christian church. Ollenburger (1985) points out the irony involved in the equation of BT with the history of biblical religion: "A discipline for which the canon can play no constitutive role has become normative in a discipline which accepts the canon as in some sense decisive" (42). Similarly, when the sole concern is to describe the religion of these communities and no recognition is given to the documents as being in any way theologically normative, it is hard to see how "theology" is an appropriate designation. There is no intention here of denying the legitimacy of a history of religions approach (though whether this can ever be neutral or presuppositionless is another matter); what is being questioned is the appropriateness of retaining the terms "biblical theology," "Old Testament theology," and "New Testament theology" for such an approach.

B-8. THE REVIVAL OF THEOLOGY

The period following the First World War saw a major swing of the theological pendulum. The reaction within dogmatic theology led by Karl Barth (see Brueggemann 1997: 16-20) had its counterpart in biblical studies in a renewed interest and a return, particularly in Germany, to OT and, to some extent also, NT theology (paradoxically, Barth himself had little or no room for a separate or intermediate BT; cf. J. Barr 1999: 73).

The 1930s inaugurated what some have seen as a "golden age" of OT theology, beginning with W. Eichrodt's *Theologie des Alten Testaments* (1933, 1935, 1939), ET, *Theology of the Old Testament* (1961, 1967), an original work of great depth, power, and insight in which he sought "to understand the realm of Old Testament belief in its structural unity" as well as in "its essential coherence with the New Testament" (1961: 32). Without denying diversity and development, Eichrodt saw a basic unity in the OT and sought to present a "cross section" *(Querschnitt)* of OT thought, taking the concept of the "covenant" as his organizing principle (see Laurin 1970: 25-62; W. Harrington 1973: 41-50; Spriggs 1974; Hasel 1991: 47-51). Other German contributions included those by E. Sellin (*Theologie des Alten Testaments,* 1933), L. Köhler (*Theologie des Alten Testaments,* 1935; ET, *Old Testament Theology,* 1957), and O. Procksch (*Theologie des Alten Testaments,* 1949). The Dutch scholar T. C. Vriezen (*Hoofdlijnen der Theologie van het Oude Testament,* 1949; ET, *An Outline of Old Testament Theology,* 1958) based his OT theology on the "communion between God and man" that he believed was the key concept of NT as well as OT theology. In his *Théologie de l'ancien Testament* (1955), ET, *The Theology of the Old Testament,* the French scholar E. Jacob sought to give a "systematic account of the specific religious ideas which can be found throughout the Old Testament and which form its profound unity" (Jacob 1958: 11; see Laurin, 143-69; Harrington, 55-63).

The most influential post–World War II OT theology was G. von Rad's two-volume *Theologie des Alten Testaments* (1957, 1960), ET, *Theology of the Old Testament* (1962, 1965; see Laurin 1970: 65-89; W. Harrington 1973: 63-77; Spriggs 1974; Crenshaw 1978; Hasel 1991: 71-79). The subject of OT theology according to von Rad cannot be a systematically ordered "world of faith" (1962: 111); rather it is "what Israel herself testified concerning Jahweh," and this consists of "a continuing divine activity in history" (106). The result is a "new diachronic biblical theology" of the OT (J. Harvey 1971: 10 n. 3). This is quite different from the history of Israelite religion. In von Rad's view, modern critical historical scholarship has largely destroyed the picture of Israel's history (especially in the early period) found in the OT. There are "two pictures of Israel's history . . . that of modern critical scholarship and that which the faith of Israel constructed" (1962: 107), and it is the latter that is the subject matter of OT theology. Von Rad presents another variation of the salvation-history approach that undoubtedly represents an important aspect of OT theology, but his method is open to criticism (see Perdue 1994: 63-67), and in particular raises questions about the relationship between faith and history.

A marked feature of this period is the entry of Roman Catholic scholars into the mainstream of biblical studies. In the nineteenth century the historical-critical approach was regarded as one of the errors of "modernism," but a turning point came with the papal encyclical *Divino afflante spiritu* issued in 1943 (English text in Heinisch 1955: 433-55), which sanctioned a new approach to Scripture. The *Theologie des Alten Testaments* (1940), ET, *Theology of the Old Testament* (1955), of the Dutch Roman Catholic scholar P. Heinisch is a transitional work. A major contribution was P. van Imschoot's *Théologie de l'Ancien Testament* (1954, 1956), ET (of vol. 1), *Theology of the Old Testament* (1965).

The revival of NT theology came somewhat later and took more varied forms. The immediate post–World War II period was dominated to a large extent by the brilliant but controversial two-volume NT theology of Rudolf Bultmann (*Theologie des Neuen Testaments*, 1948, 1953; ET, *Theology of the New Testament*, 1952, 1955). In marked contrast to liberalism, and on the basis of a highly skeptical form criticism, Bultmann regarded the historical Jesus as a presupposition of NT theology rather than a part of it. The later NT was seen as an unauthentic development toward early catholicism. The core of the NT is found in the genuine Pauline epistles and in John, though even they have to be "demythologized" and reinterpreted with the help of existentialist philosophy (see Stuhlmacher 1977: 51-55). In the Bultmann tradition is H. Conzelmann's *Grundriss der Theologie des Neuen Testaments* (1967), ET, *An Outline of the Theology of the New Testament* (1969), though he adds a section on the Synoptic kerygma.

A very different approach characterizes the work of O. Cullmann (see Cullmann 1962; 1967); although he did not produce a theology of the NT as such, in a series of works he finds the key to NT theology and indeed to BT in an updated version of salvation history. With him may be compared the approach of E. Stauffer (*Die Theologie des Neuen Testaments*, 1941; ET, *New Testament Theology*, 1955), who presents a "Christocentric theology of history" with a strong emphasis on apocalyptic. F. C. Grant's *An Introduction to New Testament Thought* (1950) seeks to identify the basic unity within the variety of NT thought and summarizes it under traditional systematic headings. A broadly similar approach characterizes F. Stagg's *New Testament Theology* (1962). At the opposite pole from Bultmann stand scholars for whom the historical Jesus is the starting point of NT theology. A. Richardson's *An Introduction to the Theology of the New Testament* (1958) is based on the assumption that "Jesus himself is the author of the brilliant re-interpretation of the Old Testament scheme of salvation . . . which is found in the New Testament" (12). J. Jeremias provides an exhaustive study of the historical Jesus in his *Neutestamentliche Theologie, I: Die Verkündigung Jesu* (1971), ET, *New Testament Theology I: The Proclamation of Jesus* (1971; no further volume was published). Jeremias is confident that he can reconstruct, if not the *ipsissima verba*, then at least the *ipsissima vox Jesu*. Jesus was also the starting point for W. G. Kümmel's *Die Theologie des Neuen Testaments* (1969), ET, *The Theology of the New Testament* (1973), which deals with NT theology "according to its major witnesses, Jesus-Paul-John."

This period also sees the entry of Roman Catholic scholars into the field of NT theology, with contributions by M. Meinertz (*Theologie des Neuen Testaments*, 1950), J. Bonsirven (*Théologie du Nouveau Testament*, 1951; ET, *Theology of the New Testament*, 1963), and K. H. Schelkle, whose four-volume *Theologie des Neuen Testaments* (1968-76), ET, *Theology of the New Testament* (1971-78), follows a traditional systematic approach. "An exposition of the New Testament theology," says Schelkle (1973), "though it cannot erase the differences in the separate writings, will nevertheless have the duty, and pursue the goal, of recognizing and displaying the unity of the New Testament within its very diversity" (10).

Can this swing back to the production of OT and NT theologies in the period prior to and following the Second World War be characterized as a revival of biblical theology? It has become common to speak of a "biblical theology movement" that flourished from approximately 1945 to 1960, then collapsed (see Childs 1970; J. Barr 1988: 3-10; Hasel 1994: 211-13; Perdue 1994: 19-44). "Movement" is perhaps too strong a term, but it is clear that there were certain general trends from 1930 to 1960 that were largely developed on the Continent and flourished in Britain just as much as in North America. One can see a reaction against a purely history-of-religions approach and a return to OT and NT "theology." There is a desire to emphasize the unity of the biblical material despite its obvious diversity, and also a stress on the "uniqueness" of the Bible often expressed in terms of the uniqueness of Hebrew thought.

The BT movement came under severe criticism from a number of scholars, and for a variety of reasons. Its contention that God is revealed in historical events did not stand up well under critical analysis (see further, 3-5.1; for criticism from the conservative side, see Verhoef 1970: 12-13), while its strong emphasis on salvation history and on "the God who acts" was seen as downplaying God's activity in creation and failing to give adequate recognition to Wisdom theology. The assumption that Israelite history, especially the key event of the exodus, could be reconstructed with a fair degree of accuracy has been seriously challenged by more recent and much more skeptical approaches (cf. Perdue 1994: 40-41). The movement's claims for the "uniqueness" of biblical thought were also questioned, and its sharp contrast between Hebrew and Greek thought was criticized as oversimplified.

One of the marked characteristics of this period was the production of biblical wordbooks, beginning with the monumental *Theologisches Wörterbuch zum Neuen Testament* (1933-73), ET, *Theological Dictionary of the New Testament* (1964-76), and followed by a succession of others on a more modest scale. Though much valuable material is to be found in these volumes, they were the subject of damaging methodological criticism, especially from J. Barr (1961), and need to be used with considerable caution. Such "word study" made much of the etymology of key biblical terms; critics rightly emphasized that usage in the biblical material itself is a more dependable guide to meaning. There are limits to doing BT by means of key words; for example, there are very few occurrences of the word "faith" in the OT, but this does not mean that the reality of faith is missing (see 17-1.3).

The BT movement is considered to have faded away in the 1960s, a time of growing concern with ethical issues and protests against nuclear arms, racial discrimination, and pollution of the environment, amongst others. Many perceived the movement as failing to link BT to biblical ethics, and as having little to say on the pressing issues of the day.

Despite a general tendency to emphasize the unity of the Bible in this period (cf. Rowley 1953), perhaps the most surprising failing of the so-called biblical theology movement, yet one that is seldom commented upon, was the fact that it did not produce a single major, scholarly volume of "biblical theology."

A considerable amount of the criticism directed against this movement is valid, though by no means all of it. Much can be learned, however, from both its strengths and its weaknesses (cf. Kraftchick 1995, esp. 73-77), and its main goal of seeking a truly "biblical" theology can continue to be pursued in new ways (see C and D).

B-9. FROM THEOLOGY TO THEOLOGIES

In reviewing the latter part of the twentieth century, one can only speak of general trends. In the period following the 1960s there certainly was a significant change of emphasis. It is true that the production of OT and NT theologies did not cease. In the OT field important contributions include W. Zimmerli's *Grundriss der alttestamentlichen Theologie* (1972), ET, *Old Testament Theology in Outline* (1978); J. L. McKenzie's *A Theology of the Old Testament* (1974); C. Westermann's *Theologie des Alten Testaments in Grundzugen* (1978), ET, *The Elements of Old Testament Theology* (1982); and H. D. Preuss's two-volume *Theologie des Alten Testaments* (1991, 1992), ET, *Old Testament Theology* (1995, 1996). A more conservative-evangelical approach is represented by W. C. Kaiser's *Toward an Old Testament Theology* (1978) and W. Dyrness's briefer but useful *Themes in Old Testament Theology* (1979). W. Brueggemann's *Theology of the Old Testament* (1997) is a work of considerable power and imagination that seeks to bring a new approach to the traditional form.

On the NT side, the Oxford scholar G. B. Caird's *New Testament Theology* (1994) was published posthumously, completed and edited by L. D. Hurst (on Caird's approach, see further E-5). NT theologies have come from more conservative scholars: G. E. Ladd's *A Theology of the New Testament* (1974; Ladd 1993) is sympathetic to the *Heilsgeschichte* approach; D. Guthrie's substantial *New Testament Theology* (1981) follows a traditional systematic outline, while L. Morris's *New Testament Theology* (1986) adopts a historical, author-by-author approach in summarizing the teaching of the NT. (On the contribution of recent conservative-evangelical scholarship, see Bray 1996: 539-83.)

The first part of a projected three-volume *Biblische Theologie des Neuen Testaments* by H. Hübner was published in 1990; it deals only with Prolegomena and discusses such questions as the canon of the OT and the concept of revelation. P. Stuhlmacher's two-volume *Biblische Theologie des Neuen Testaments* (1992, 1999) is a work of major significance; reflecting Stuhlmacher's tradition-history approach (see below C-4.1), it is "open to the Old Testament." Vol. 1 deals with the proclamation of Jesus, of the early church, and of Paul; Vol. 2 deals with the remaining NT witnesses and concludes with discussion of the canon and the "centre" of Scripture. In striking contrast is G. Strecker's *Theologie des Neues Testaments* (1996). Strecker dismisses the very idea of a BT since the relation of the NT to the OT is basically one of discontinuity. He discusses the various NT witnesses in turn (beginning with Paul) but makes no attempt to find common ground since his emphasis falls entirely on their diversity.

In fact, the dominant trend in this period appears to be a renewed emphasis on diversity and development within the Bible to the point where the writing not only of BT but even of OT or NT theology is radically called in question. In some ways this represents a resurgence of the history-of-religions approach that continues to be influential in academic circles, particularly in university departments of religious studies. It reflects also the growing complexity of biblical studies resulting from the massive amounts of new material produced by archaeological investigation, as well as the proliferation of interpretive methodologies and the seemingly endless output of secondary literature. This results in ever increasing specialization, so that many no longer consider themselves even OT or NT scholars but concentrate on a narrow area of specialization; in other words, biblical scholars tend to know more and more about less and less. In this situation it is not surprising that it becomes ever more difficult to see the wood for the trees.

This is particularly true in OT studies, where one is dealing with a large body of material produced in the course of approximately one thousand years. Form criticism *(Formgeschichte)* has sought to penetrate behind the written sources to the underlying oral traditions and to discover their setting in the life of the community, while tradition history *(Traditionsgeschichte)* seeks to trace what may have been a long and complex process leading up to the final written form of the material.

Von Rad's treatment of Israel's historical traditions in his *Theology of the Old Testament* has already been mentioned (above, B-8). But von Rad wrote a second volume dealing with the prophetic traditions of the OT that really stands quite apart from the first volume. "There is a definite break," he holds, "between the message of the prophets and the ideas held by earlier Jahwism" (von Rad 1965: 3), and the prophets stand "basically outside the saving history as it had been understood up to then by Israel" (128). One criticism leveled against the two-volume theology was that it failed to deal adequately with certain types of OT material, particularly the Wisdom Literature. In volume 1 von Rad had devoted three chapters to Wisdom as part of "Israel's answer," a somewhat unsatisfactory way of treating the subject. In 1970, however, he published his *Weisheit in Israel,* ET, *Wisdom in Israel* (1972), a major study of Wisdom as yet another form of Israel's theological traditions. There is no doubt as to the magnitude of von Rad's contribution to OT theology, but one is tempted to ask: Has he given us *one* OT theology or *three* — one of the historical traditions, one of the prophetic traditions, and one of the Wisdom traditions (cf. De Vaux 1971: 55; W. Harrington 1973: 77)? Another question might be whether he has produced OT theology at all, or rather a history of Israel's theological traditions.

This trend toward the identification of OT "theologies" rather than "theology" is typical of the period, with separate studies appearing of the theology of the Yahwist, of the Deuteronomic writers, of the Priestly school, and so on. There was an explosion of interest in Wisdom as a distinctive aspect of OT thought that had been widely neglected (see Scobie 1984b). Increasingly the question was asked, "Is it possible to write a theology of the Old Testament?" and many, like P. Wernberg-Möller (1960), replied that "the possibility of a comprehensive, systematic Old Testament theology must be rejected" (29; cf. Fannon 1967: 52).

A similar renewed emphasis on diversity is to be seen in NT scholarship, even though the material is not as extensive nor produced over such a long period of time as for the OT. But form criticism and source criticism have suggested a process of handing on and shaping traditions preceding the written

Gospels. Some have even been prepared to discuss the theology of Q (the hypothetical Q sayings source used by Matthew and Luke). An influential trend in this period was *Redactionsgeschichte,* the study of the final editing process of the Gospels that tended to concentrate attention on the very different theologies of each of the four Evangelists. Similarly, numerous studies of the theologies of John, Paul, Hebrews, Revelation, and so on have also contributed to the impression of the fragmentation of the study of NT theology. Much academic study of the Bible seems to consist largely of its dismemberment (cf. L. Houlden 1986: 87).

A typical representative of this viewpoint is E. Käsemann. "The New Testament as we have it," he declared in 1973, "is a fragmentary collection of documents from the earliest period, while the bulk of the material has vanished for ever. By and large there is no internal coherence. The tensions everywhere evident amount at times to contradictions"; hence, any attempt to systematize is "a conjectural enterprise" (242). Earlier, in 1957, he had written that "a single biblical theology springing from one root and pursued in unbroken continuity, is wishful thinking and an illusion" (quoted in Schlier 1968: 33). J. Barr (1974) sums up the view held by many biblical scholars in the 1970s: "The tendency now is to say that there is no one theology, either of the Old Testament or of the New, and still less of the entire Bible" (270; cf. J. Barr 1999: 142). In an analysis of the current state of BT published in 1993, P. Pokorny argues that "we have several theologies" in both OT and NT; hence, he declares flatly, "there is not any universal Biblical Theology" (87).

Here indeed is the impasse at which modern biblical studies have arrived. Having been told that BT must be considered an objective, historical, descriptive discipline, independent from the faith and life of the church, we arrive eventually at the point where we are told that any such BT is in fact a sheer impossibility.

C. New Directions in Biblical Theology

The 1980s and 1990s saw the emergence of new trends in biblical studies, some of which give promise of opening up a way forward from the impasse reached in the 1960s and 1970s. The result was a surge of new interest in BT (cf. J. Reumann 1991; Perdue 1994: xi, 7; Hasel 1994; J. Barr 1999).

Developments in biblical studies often run parallel to developments in the study of literature, though generally with a time lag between the two. It has frequently been pointed out that literary criticism in the twentieth century focused successively on the "author," the "text," and the "reader" (Longman 1987: 18-41; W. R. Tate 1991: xvi-xviii). The widespread rejection of author-centered theories is paralleled in biblical studies by the current questioning of the historical-critical method. The focus on text-centered theories is paralleled by "the canonical approach" and by some types of literary studies of the biblical text. The various "reader-response" theories are paralleled by a renewed recognition of the church as the true "interpretive community" of Scripture. As a result, new approaches to BT have emerged, and a few scholars have actually attempted the writing of a "biblical theology."

C-1. QUESTIONING OF THE HISTORICAL-CRITICAL METHOD

Traditional literary criticism laid great emphasis on the author of a literary work; basically, a work was taken to mean what the original author intended it to mean. Historical research into the life of an author and into the circumstances in which he or she wrote was therefore a prime prerequisite of correct interpretation. The 1940s saw a major reaction against such an approach with the rise of the so-called New Criticism. The traditional emphasis on the author was dubbed "the intentional fallacy," and the focus of attention turned to the text itself as an autonomous entity.

The historical-critical approach that has dominated biblical studies for two centuries (cf. B-3) corresponds broadly to the traditional emphasis of literary criticism on the author of a work. In recent years, however, this approach too has begun to come under increasing scrutiny and reevaluation (cf. Nations 1983).

Historical criticism has been much occupied with questions relating to authorship, date, and sources of biblical books. Where these questions can be determined with a fair degree of certainty, they can be of help in understanding the text. But it should always be remembered that the results of historical criticism are far from assured, and often are highly speculative (cf. A. Wainwright 1982: 12). Acceptance of a historical approach does not mean blindly accepting whatever the "critical orthodoxy" of the day may be. Some modern critical scholars display an astonishing arrogance in asserting their own conclusions and in dismissing the views of those who do not agree with them. Biblical historical criticism ought to be characterized by a humility that recognizes the tentative nature of its theories and by a constant openness to new evidence and new interpretations.

Two aspects of historical criticism in particular have come under scrutiny in recent years.

C-1.1. "AUTHENTICITY"

Scholars employing historical criticism have frequently regarded the biblical material as data from which to reconstruct the history and religion of Israel and the early church. They have tended to look not so much *at* the biblical text as *through* the text to the history that lies behind it, to what W. R. Tate (1991) calls "the world behind the text" (3). But the results of such historical reconstruction are often far from assured. For example, there is fairly wide acceptance today of the four-source theory of Gospel origins which holds that Mark is the earliest Gospel and was used by Matthew and Luke, who also used a common sayings source designated Q along with their own sources, M for Matthew and L for Luke. But it must be remembered that this is only a theory, that it is not universally accepted and is subject to constant review and testing.

In relation to the question of authorship and the possibility of additions to books by someone other than the original author, the category of "authenticity" is often employed. Romans, it is generally agreed, was written by Paul; but there is considerable debate over the authenticity of Ephesians. The implication is that if Ephesians was not written by Paul, it is somehow "unauthentic," and as a result is frequently assigned an inferior place in theologies of the NT. Yet even if it were true that Ephesians was written by a disciple of Paul, it would still be every bit as much part of the canonical NT recognized by the Christian church as is Romans, and as far as BT is concerned, just as much part of the subject matter with which it has to deal.

Similarly in OT scholarship, material deemed to be not by the original author (e.g., the prose sections of Jeremiah) is frequently discarded as not authentic. "Material judged to be late additions or comments inserted into prophetic texts are often excised by the writers of commentaries as if the added comment were not at all important to the community of faith that preserved the whole text" (Birch 1980: 115).

Two specific examples will serve to drive this point home. Modern critical scholars have generally portrayed Amos as a prophet of doom who held out no hope for the future, and have identified Amos 9:8c-15, the so-called Appendix of Hope, as a postexilic editorial addition that is thus to be rejected as unauthentic. A second example is Bultmann's interpretation of John's Gospel, which he sees as operating with a purely realized eschatology in which there is no place for any future expectation. John is held to have demythologized conventional early Christian eschatology, thus providing a warrant for Bultmann's own program of demythologizing. What of a passage such as John 5:28-29 with its clear reference to a future resurrection of the dead? According to Bultmann, it is to be assigned to a later "ecclesiastical redactor" and hence is no part of authentic Johannine theology (see Bultmann 1955: 39). It need hardly be said that assigning material in this way to a later editor is a very easy method of disposing of passages with which the modern scholar does not agree! It should also be noted that in both these examples the modern critical interpretation has the effect of increasing the diversity within Scripture. If Amos is indeed solely a prophet of doom, he stands quite apart from the later prophets in whose message judgment and salvation were held in balance. Similarly, if John's eschatology is entirely realized, he stands quite apart from the other three Gospels, all of which (in varying degrees) display an inaugurated eschatology that still retains the hope of a final consummation.

One type of reaction to this has been J. A. Sanders's form of "canonical criticism." In his studies of the nature and function of canon (1972; 1984), he stresses that it is not just the original levels of tradition that are important but the whole process of transmitting, editing, and shaping the material up to and including its final canonical form. In this process the believing community played a vital role. Sanders points out, for example, that the earlier traditions of Israelite origins, which continued through the conquest of Palestine to the establishment of the Davidic dynasty, were cut in two and Deuteronomy was inserted to become the climax of the Torah, which then became the core of Israel's scripture. This occurred during the exile, and reflects the position of a community that lives not in the Promised Land but in the Diaspora (cf. 1972: 44-45). The canonical process was marked by both stability and adaptability; traditions were not only passed on, but were also "adapted, represented and resignified" (1984: 47).

C-1.2. HERMENEUTICS OF CONSENT

In the nineteenth century historical criticism increasingly claimed to be an objective discipline, in distinction from the church that was weighed down by centuries of tradition and dogma. But there has been growing recognition of the fact that there can be no interpretation of texts without presuppositions. Modern hermeneutical theory, especially as influenced by the work of H.-G. Gadamer (1975; see the detailed discussion in Thiselton 1980 and a helpful summary in Maddox 1985), recognizes that not only is the text historically conditioned but so also is the interpreter; we all bring to the text our own prejudgment *(Vorurteil)*. Gadamer sees interpretation as involving "the fusion of horizons" *(Horizontverschmelzung)* — the horizon of the text and the horizon of the interpreter. This does not mean that the interpreter's prejudgments go unquestioned or that they determine the interpretation of the text. On the contrary, the interpreter must remain open to the text, to its "quality of newness," and must be prepared to change his or her prejudgments (cf. Thiselton, 304f.; Maddox, 522). While interpreters bring assumptions to the text, "during the process of interpretation . . . the text itself may legitimate, deny, clarify or modify those assumptions" (W. R. Tate 1991: 212).

The underlying assumptions of many practitioners of historical criticism have frequently been rationalistic and positivistic. While claiming to be neutral and objective, many scholars have in fact ignored the most central assertions of the biblical texts themselves, those relating to the presence and activity of God in both nature and history. "The very essence of scientific and historical enquiry in modern times," writes W. Wink (1973), "has been the suspension of evaluative judgments and participational involvement in the 'object' of research. Such detached neutrality in matters of faith is not neutrality at all, but already a decision against responding. At the outset, questions of truth and meaning have been excluded, since they can only be answered participatively, in terms of a lived response" (2; cf. 37-38).

In the context of an analysis of the history of biblical scholarship that notes how easily scholars have been influenced by their philosophical presuppositions, P. Stuhlmacher (1977) has argued for what he calls "a Hermeneutics of Consent to the biblical texts" that will be marked by "a willingness to open ourselves anew to the claim of tradition, of the present, and of transcendence" (83, 85). G. F. Hasel (1982) has argued for an approach to BT "that seeks to do justice to all dimensions of reality to which the biblical texts testify" (75-76). Linked with this has been a growing awareness of the impossibility of making a rigid distinction between what a text "meant" and what it "means" (see Hasel 1984: 117-25). Such voices rightly challenge the presuppositions that underlie much of modern biblical scholarship. The call is not for a return to a precritical position, but rather for the seeking out of a new, postcritical methodology (contra J. J. Collins 1990).

C-1.3. THE CONTINUING VALIDITY
OF THE HISTORICAL APPROACH

In much contemporary literary criticism historical study of the original author of a text has been set aside as irrelevant. Whatever be the case in literature generally, in biblical studies any total abandonment of a historical-critical approach would be a major disaster that would cast the interpreter adrift on a sea of subjectivity.

The criticisms outlined above are not to be confused with a fundamentalist rejection of all historical-critical scholarship; it is not a case of "the end of the historical-critical method" (Maier 1977; cf. Stuhlmacher 1977: 66-71). Much of the criticism is coming from within, and for the most part what is being questioned is not so much the method itself as the use that has been made of it, and especially the claims that have been made for it (cf. Perdue 1994: 4-11). This is the context in which to place W. Wink's overly dramatic and much quoted assertion that "historical biblical criticism is bankrupt." By this he does not mean that the historical approach is valueless. "Biblical criticism is not bankrupt because it has run out of things to say or new ground to explore. It is bankrupt solely because it is incapable of achieving what most of its practitioners considered its purpose to be: so to interpret the Scriptures that the past becomes alive and illumines our present with new possibilities for personal and social transformation" (Wink 1973: 1-2).

In some ways the value of a historical approach to the Bible is more widely recognized than ever. As we have seen (B-8), a major change of policy in the mid–twentieth century permitted Roman Catholic scholars to adopt this approach, and since then many of them have made notable contributions. More recently an increasing number of conservative-evangelical scholars have been participating in historical-critical studies. While they are questioning many of the assumptions and conclusions of traditional historical criticism, the soundness of their scholarship has earned them a right to be heard in the current debate.

Another feature of biblical scholarship in the latter part of the twentieth century was the utilization of methods drawn from the social sciences (see Bray 1996: 511-15; Brueggemann 1997: 49-53). "The focus of these methods is not primarily on national history or the development of religious institutions or ideas as separate from other features of communal life; rather the focus is on describing the social organization of ancient Israel throughout its lengthy history" (Perdue 1994: 70). In NT studies H. C. Kee (1980) has urged the adaptation of analytical models from the social sciences "as aids to (1) historical reconstruction . . . of the development of early Christianity; and (2) interpreting the surviving evidence of the movement in a manner that is attuned to and sympathetic with the thought worlds of those who produced this material" (7-8). This is basically an extension of the historical-critical approach and represents another way of going *behind* the text. It shares the limitations of the historical-critical approach, as it tends to be based on hypothetical reconstructions of the social situations out of which the biblical texts emerged. It may be questioned to what extent, in the study of ancient communities, sufficient data are available to permit such sociological reconstruction. Nor is a sociological approach, more than any other, free from presuppositions. Sociologists tend to transfer models from other societies, and it can be questioned how valid this is in relation to biblical societies of two or three millennia ago. Nevertheless, a sociological approach can provide a different perspective and can be seen as complementing other historical methodologies.

The recognition that all biblical texts are to some degree historically conditioned means that historical study of the texts and of their background must continue to be part of the hermeneutical process, particularly as a safeguard and control against arbitrary and purely subjective interpretation (see W. R. Tate 1991: 3-60). Historical criticism, however, must recognize its limitations and moderate its claims. Above all, historical study must be recognized as a *preliminary* to true BT, the major focus of which must be on the canonical text.

C-2. THE CANONICAL TEXT

The focus of literary studies shifted dramatically from the 1940s on with the rise of the New Criticism, which urged that the object of study must be the text itself. As soon as a literary work is written down, copied, and circulated, it attains a life of its own, and can and should be studied quite independently of the historical circumstances which gave it birth. The emphasis shifted to what W. R. Tate (1991) calls "the world within the text" (61). Supporters of the New Criticism tended to claim that it was a purely objective method; anyone who expressed a subjective judgment on a text was pronounced guilty of "the affective fallacy" (cf. Keegan 1985: 76).

In literary circles the various text-centered theories have already largely given way to a reader-centered approach, if not to deconstruction. Generally speaking, however, the shift to a focus on the text itself has provided a very welcome corrective in biblical studies. In fact, the most significant form of reaction against historical criticism as it is generally practiced is seen in those who advocate *the final form of the biblical text* as the true object of study. It was in its final edited and collected form, not in any reconstructed earlier stages, that the Christian church recognized the canon of Scripture and accepted the Bible as normative for its faith and life. It was in this form also that the Bible has exerted a tremendous influence, for example, on literature and art, especially in the West.

Recent years have seen an explosion of interest in "literary approaches" to Scripture. These exhibit a wide diversity, but most agree at least in their focus on the final form of the text. Their approach tends to be synchronic rather than diachronic; they seek to look not through the text to the history which lies behind it, but at the text as it stands. Used with caution and discrimination, some literary approaches can make a significant contribution to biblical studies. The counterpart in biblical-theological studies of these text-centered theories is "the canonical approach," associated in particular with the work of B. S. Childs.

C-2.1. THE LITERARY APPROACH

As Ryken in particular has pointed out, it is quite wrong to regard a literary approach to Scripture as something new (Ryken and Longman 1993: 49; cf. Longman 1987: 13-18). It is as old as Scripture itself, and if patristic attempts at a literary approach tended to founder because of the application of Greek and Roman models, a true appreciation of the literary qualities of Scripture is to be seen in the Renaissance and in the romantic movement. R. Lowth's *Lectures on the Sacred Poetry of the Hebrews,* published in 1753, with its analysis of parallelism as a central feature of Hebrew poetry, is rightly seen as a landmark in the literary study of Scripture.

The fact remains, however, that the last third of the twentieth century saw an unprecedented explosion of interest in and a proliferation of "literary approaches" (cf. Clines 1980). On the one hand, secular literary critics "discovered" the Bible as an extremely fruitful field for literary study, and they tended to be the ones who led the way. On the other hand, biblical scholars were led to enter the field, seeing in this approach the possibility of a new and promising direction for biblical studies. Talk of a "paradigm shift" in biblical studies has become commonplace.

A major stimulus to the newer literary approaches has been the work of the great literary critic Northrup Frye. Throughout his career Frye maintained that it is quite impossible to understand English literature without a thorough knowledge of the Old and New Testaments, which are indeed, in a phrase Frye borrowed from Blake, "the Great Code of Art" (Frye 1981: xvi). Frye's own study of the Bible culminated in his major work, *The Great Code: The Bible and Literature* (1981), in which he seeks to understand the Bible as a literary whole. For this approach "higher criticism" is really irrelevant. Frye is well aware that Gen 1 is assigned by historical criticism to the late, Priestly source, but "a genuine higher criticism," he comments, "would observe that this account of creation stands at the beginning of Genesis, despite its late date, because it belongs at the beginning of Genesis" (xvii). Similarly, modern theories of authorship do not really affect the way in which the Bible is to be read and understood (202-4). Frye holds that while the Bible is "certainly the end product of a long and complex editorial process, the end product needs to be examined in its own right" (xvii).

C. NEW DIRECTIONS IN BIBLICAL THEOLOGY

Within biblical scholarship the insights of J. Muilenburg are credited with inspiring the development of "rhetorical criticism" with its focus not just on *what* the text says but on *how* it says it (cf. Brueggemann 1997: 55). It must be recognized, however, that there is no one "literary approach," but rather a bewildering array of approaches, many of which are mutually contradictory. Those seeking guidance and help for the discipline of BT must proceed with caution, aware of the pitfalls as well as the promise (see Longman 1987: 47-62; Ryken and Longman 1993: 60-68).

Some literary approaches are "academic" in the bad sense of the term; they are the work of scholars, designed for other scholars, and frequently obscurantist. For BT the proof of the pudding must be in the eating: Does any particular approach aid in the understanding and appreciation of the biblical text by the community of faith? A case in point is structuralism. This movement, which may be classified with text-centered theories, was, as W. R. Tate suggests, not so much concerned with *what* a text means as with *how* it means (1991: 187). Drawing on a number of different disciplines, literary structuralists sought to discover in texts "deep structures" that reflect conventions common to all human societies. While attempts have been made to apply structuralist analysis to biblical texts (cf. R. F. Collins 1983: 231-71; Keegan 1985: 40-72; Longman 1987: 27-37; Tate, 187-90), such attempts have not been particularly productive. We may agree with Longman's (1987) verdict on structuralism when he says that "its high level of complexity, its almost esoteric level of terminology, and its (thus far) very limited help toward understanding the text (which for many structuralists is not even a concern) have and likely will prevent the vast majority of biblical scholars from actively participating in the endeavour" (37). In fact, as far as biblical studies are concerned, structuralism clearly was a passing fad.

A marked feature of the recent upsurge of literary interest has been the focus on biblical narrative or story (see Fackre 1983; Perdue 1994: 232-47; J. Barr 1999: 345-61). Building on the work of H. Frei of Yale, "narrative theology" has quite rightly drawn attention to the fact that the Bible does not generally consist of "doctrine" stated in propositional form; much of what it has to say it says through story or narrative, what Frei characterized as "realistic narrative" or "history-like narrative." The rise of the critical approach with its strongly rationalistic presuppositions resulted in a profound skepticism regarding the historicity of the biblical accounts. As a result, narrative suffered an eclipse and scholars focused their attention on either reconstructing "what actually happened" or abstracting a symbolic or ideal meaning from the texts. Narrative theology seeks to recover the role and function of biblical narrative regardless of its historical reference. This, it has been claimed, is a way "to reassert the clear and self-interpreting sense of Scripture and give it back to the church" (R. B. Robinson 1991: 141).

This approach can be accepted only with reservations. Frequently it seems to proceed from the assumption that biblical narrative has no referential function. The popular slogan is that the Bible is not "history" but "story," and narrative is to be treated as if it were fiction; Perdue's chapter on the movement is headed "From History to Fiction" (1994: 231). Brueggemann's huge emphasis on "rhetoric" and "testimony" raises disturbing questions, especially when he declares that "one cannot go behind the narratival (liturgical?) accounts, but will have to take the word of the witnesses. . . . The hearer of this text . . . refuses to go behind these witnesses. This means that theological interpretation does not go behind the witness with questions of history, wondering 'what happened'" (1997: 206; cf. J. Barr 1999: 544, 558). To deny all reference to history would certainly undercut the basis of Christian faith, and it is vitally important for BT to maintain that "story" does *not* necessarily mean "fiction" in the sense of what is historically untrue (contra J. J. Collins 1990: 9-12). Thus Longman, while agreeing that OT prose narrative consists of "selective, structured, emphasized, and interpreted stories," contends that "a literary analysis of a historical book is . . . not incompatible with a high view of the historicity of the text" (1987: 58). The modern critical approach simply rules out any presence of God in either nature or history; to capitulate to such a presupposition is to undercut the very basis of the claims made by Scripture. Narrative typically links events by causal explanations, but as F. Watson (1997) has cogently argued, "there is no normative principle of explanation which would permit one to rule out in advance a historiographical explanation in terms of transcendence" (60; see further, C-3 and 3-5.1).

Many scholars engaged in literary study of the Bible are either indifferent or even opposed to a religious understanding of the text. Indeed, one of the attractions of the literary approach, for college students as well as university professors, seems to be the opportunity to read, study, and appreciate the Bible quite apart from any form of commitment to its message. Those who adopt this approach are of course quite free to do so, but it certainly is not in keeping with the aims of BT.

One of the striking developments in recent years, however, has been the entry into the field of a number of more conservative-evangelical scholars. Realizing that a literary approach need not be based on secular presuppositions, they have shown that literary study is quite compatible with moderately conservative presuppositions, and indeed have demonstrated that such an approach can be extremely fruitful (cf. Ryken and Longman 1993: 66). While drawing upon the insights of a wide range of scholars, they have generally avoided the more theoretical and esoteric approaches and have applied more traditional literary methods to the biblical text: the study, for example, of plot, characterization, setting, point of view, and structure in narrative, and the use of patterns, imagery, and figurative language in poetry. Foremost amongst such scholars has been Leland Ryken (cf. Ryken 1984; 1987a; 1987b), while another able exponent is Tremper Longman (cf. Longman 1987). A volume published in

1993 and edited by these two contains contributions by some of the growing number of scholars now adopting this approach (Ryken and Longman 1993).

While historical criticism has often seemed intent on dissecting the Bible into as many separate pieces as possible, one of the most important contributions of the literary approach has been to see the overarching unity of the Bible. Though the Bible consists of a multitude of originally independent units, these have been combined by a complex redactional process into an overall narrative structure that runs from Genesis to Revelation and constitutes what L. L. Thompson (1978) terms "a structure of structures" (43; see 320 n. 42). Ryken (1984) has written on "the literary unity of the Bible" (177-97), citing its narrative framework, religious orientation, recurring topics and themes, use of literary archetypes, and stylistic traits as unifying features. Frye sees typology as the key to the unity, or more exactly, the continuity of Scripture. In *The Great Code* he outlines a sequence or dialectical progression in the biblical revelation consisting of seven main phases: creation, revolution (or exodus), law, wisdom, prophecy, gospel, and apocalypse. Each phase provides a wider perspective on its predecessor and takes its place in a chain of types and antitypes (Frye 1981: 106). By looking at biblical stories and poems as literary wholes as well as locating them in their wider, literary, canonical context, this form of biblical literary criticism has the potential to make an important contribution to BT.

C-2.2. THE CANONICAL APPROACH

Of more direct interest to our main concern has been the proposal that BT be based primarily on the final form of the canonical text. This approach has been associated above all with the work of B. S. Childs, who first enunciated it in his *Biblical Theology in Crisis* (1970); worked it out in a commentary on Exodus, in introductions to both OT and NT (1979; 1984), and in his *Old Testament Theology in a Canonical Context* (1986); and finally embodied it in his magnum opus, *Biblical Theology of the Old and New Testaments* (1992).

Childs's basic thesis is that "the canon of the Christian church is the most appropriate context from which to do Biblical Theology" (1970: 99). Despite the valuable contributions it has made, historical criticism, as Childs sees it, "does not have for its goal the analysis of the canonical literature of the synagogue and church, but rather it seeks to describe the history of the development of the Hebrew literature and to trace the earlier and later stages of this history. As a result there always remains an enormous hiatus between the description of the critically reconstructed literature and the actual canonical text which has been received and used as authoritative scripture by the community" (1979: 40). What is *most* important must always be the final form of the text. "The significance of the final form of the biblical text is that it alone bears witness to the full history of revelation" (1979: 75). Thus, for example, "to distinguish the Yahwist source from the Priestly in the Pentateuch often allows the interpreter to hear the combined texts with new precision. But it is the full, combined text which has rendered a judgment on the shape of the tradition and which continues to exercise an authority on the community of faith" (1979: 76). It is clear that Childs's approach has been influenced especially by the work of Karl Barth (see C. J. Scalise 1996: 47-50) in its focus on the text as it stands, its postcritical perspective, and its emphasis on the theological nature of the canon.

This approach is quite different from the "canonical criticism" of J. A. Sanders (cf. above, C-1.1). Spina (1982) pinpoints the basic difference: "Childs believes the canonical *product* should be the object of exegesis, whereas Sanders opts for the *process*. The product is basically a literary phenomenon; the process is a historical one, since it involves an interaction between the literature and the community. This means that for Childs authority is seen to reside in the community's literature, but for Sanders it is found in the community's *use* of that literature" (185). To speak of "canonical criticism," Childs points out, would suggest that it is simply one more historical-critical technique alongside form criticism, source criticism, and so on. "Rather, the issue at stake in relation to the canon turns on establishing a stance from which the Bible can be read as sacred scripture" (Childs 1979: 82). It seems appropriate to speak of a canonical approach, though Childs has indicated a preference for the term "canonical analysis."

Childs's approach has been both welcomed and criticized. Some see his approach as anticritical (cf. J. J. Collins 1990: 5-7) or as an attempt to return to a precritical stance; in fact, few scholars have such a grasp of the historical-critical work that has been done on both OT and NT. Others are concerned that concentration on the final form of the text involves neglect of the historical context in which the traditions first arose (Birch 1980: 119-20; J. A. Sanders 1980: 186f.), or of the whole process of tradition history (D. A. Knight 1980: 145). Childs's most recent *Biblical Theology of the Old and New Testaments* should do much to allay these fears; in fact, a more valid criticism of Childs is that he focuses too much on a tradition-historical study of the prehistory of the text (cf. C. J. Scalise 1996: 61-62). Up until 1992 Childs's work had been carried out within the traditionally separate compartments of OT and NT introduction, exegesis, and theology; his 1992 volume illustrates the application of the canonical approach to biblical theology and constitutes a major breakthrough in escaping from the current impasse in biblical studies.

Childs's approach to BT, especially as manifested in his most recent volume, has affinities with the methodological discussions and proposals put forward over a number of years by G. F. Hasel, who sees BT as "not a purely historical enterprise but a theological-historical undertaking" that must be "limited by the boundaries of the Biblical canon and the canonical form of the Biblical texts" (1982: 74).

C-3. THE CHURCH AS INTERPRETIVE COMMUNITY

In recent years much of the focus in literary criticism has been neither on the author nor on the text but on the reader, on what W. R. Tate (1991) calls "the world in front of the text" (146). Arising at least in part as a reaction against text-centered theories such as structuralism, various forms of "reader-response criticism" have developed stressing that a text can be said to have meaning only as it is read and interpreted by a reader (cf. Keegan 1985: 73-91; Longman 1987: 36-41; Tate, 146-73). The fact that not only secular literary works but also the biblical texts often seem to have as many interpretations as there are readers suggests the key role played by the reader. The interpretation of the Hebrew Scriptures/Old Testament by Jewish readers is obviously quite different from that of Christian readers; each community has its own set of presuppositions which it brings to the text so that the readers determine the interpretation to be followed. While more moderate theories hold that meaning arises from the interaction between reader and text, more extreme views see meaning as something virtually created by the reader (cf. F. Watson 1997: chap. 3). At this point we are already on the slippery slope that leads to theories of "deconstruction," which in effect deny that a literary text can have "a meaning" (on deconstruction, see Longman, 41-45; Tate, 202-8).

One criticism of the so-called biblical theology movement (cf. B-8) was its irrelevance to emerging social, economic, and political issues of the 1960s. Since then, various types of "liberation theology" (Latin American, Third World, black, feminist) have sought to find a biblical-theological basis (see Perdue 1994: 73-96; Bray 1996: 516-24; Brueggemann 1997: 98-102). Some of these focus on the exodus as a key event demonstrating that God is on the side of the oppressed and downtrodden, or on the Old Testament prophets' calls for social justice. A striking example is N. Gottwald (*The Tribes of Yahweh*, 1979), whose sociological approach draws on Marxist analysis to present the early history of Israel not in terms of the traditional "conquest" but rather primarily as a peasant revolt within Canaanite society. Feminist biblical theologians may stress the thoroughly patriarchal nature of biblical society, which in contemporary hermeneutics needs to be radically reinterpreted if not totally rejected. Others, however, see a basically egalitarian approach within Scripture, in the teaching and example of Jesus and possibly in Paul (but not in the Pastorals), an approach that was smothered by reemerging patriarchalism even within the NT period itself. All forms of liberation theology combine biblical interpretation with a call to radical action in terms of contemporary social, political, and economic structures. Such "contextual theologies" are not necessarily guilty of reading contemporary concerns back into Scripture; they can serve the very useful purpose of bringing out neglected aspects of BT. Nevertheless, the obvious focus on a very limited "canon within the canon" raises serious concerns as to how adequately these approaches can serve as a basis for a truly all-biblical theology.

Emphasis on the role of the reader can be salutary for BT. One of the problems not only with the literary study of Scripture but also with biblical studies generally has been the extent to which they have been increasingly conducted in an academic setting, divorced from the life and work of the church, the very community that recognizes the Bible as its canonical Scripture. Here again it needs to be stressed that the idea of a completely neutral or detached reading of the biblical text is a myth. "The experience of doing hermeneutics is not just a scientific discipline unrelated to the task of living; it is rather a continually life-changing and life-shaping experience" (W. R. Tate 1991: 212). While there have always been scholars who have sought to bridge the gap between academic study of the Bible and its practical application in the life of the church, their voices have often been muted in a world of increasing academic specialization. There now appears to be a belated recognition by an increasing number of biblical scholars of what P. D. Hanson (1980) has called "the responsibility of biblical theology to the community of faith."

In the thought of S. E. Fish, texts have meaning only in the context of "interpretive communities" (1980: 171-72). Now it is clear that the appropriate "interpretive community" for the Bible is the church. The Bible is most truly interpreted in relation to its canonical intention not when it is dissected by historical critics, but when it is read as the Word of God by the people of God. It is the church that constitutes the true readership of Scripture (Schneider 1985), though of course the church must constantly scrutinize its faith and life in the light of the Word of God conveyed by Scripture. Hanson (1980) stresses that the biblical text *and* the contemporary life of the community of faith form the two poles of the interpretive process. "The Church needs the Bible. . . . The Bible needs the Church. Without the Church the Bible would have no community within which its message could be interpreted" (A. Wainwright 1982: 64).

The church has never stopped using the Bible in the ongoing task of dogmatic theology, in wrestling with contemporary ethical issues, in its worship (cf. the growing use of a lectionary with OT, Epistle, and Gospel readings), in countless weekly sermons, in Bible study groups, and in the personal devotional life of countless millions of Christian believers. All these must work with some kind of "biblical theology," some at least provisional view of the understanding of God in his relation to the world and to humankind as contained in the Scriptures of the Old and New Testaments. For the church, some kind of BT encompassing both Testaments is not optional, but absolutely essential (cf. D. P. Fuller 1992: 64-65). It is somewhat ludicrous that while the church throughout the world struggles on a daily basis to attain a more satisfactory form of BT, there are still many biblical scholars who maintain that there is no such thing! Fortunately the role of BT in the life of the church has won increasing recognition; witness, for example, the publication in 1996 of two dictionaries of BT, *The Evangelical Dictionary of Biblical Theology* and *The Collegeville Pastoral Dictionary of Biblical Theology*, representing evangelical Protestantism and Roman Catholicism respectively, yet both seeking to interpret biblical themes and topics in a way that makes them available to laity as well as clergy.

While literary theory generally speaks of "the reader" (in the singular), it is more helpful and accurate for the purposes of BT to speak of "the interpretive *community*." The authors of the biblical text were not isolated individuals but were members of what we may call *the biblical community*, Israel in the case of the OT and the early church in the NT. Their writings were preserved, edited, collected, and ultimately recognized as Scripture by what we may term *the canonical community*, an extension and continuation of the biblical community. Today Scripture is regarded as authoritative by what we may call the *interpretive community*, the Christian church, which itself is an extension and continuation of the canonical community. Because of this continuity the church is the community best fitted to interpret the Bible.

C-4. A REVIVAL OF BIBLICAL THEOLOGY

In our historical survey we noted the virtually complete abandonment of BT in favor of the study of separate OT and NT theologies (B-6). In the light of the trends surveyed above, it is not surprising that the latter part of the twentieth century saw a number of attempts to bridge the rigid division that has developed between OT and NT studies and return to some form of a more truly "biblical" theology.

C-4.1. TRADITION HISTORY

One such attempt can be seen in the "history of traditions" approach associated especially with the German scholars H. Gese and P. Stuhlmacher, who are influenced by the work of G. von Rad. Gese (1981a) contends that in the time of Jesus there was not yet a closed canon of the OT, and what BT deals with is "a unified process of tradition of the Old and New Testaments viewed as a whole" (15; on Gese, see J. Barr 1999: 362-77). Divine revelation is not to be located only in the earliest forms of the tradition but in the entire process, which was long and complex as traditions were continually selected, edited, and reinterpreted. Gese has, for example, traced the concept of wisdom through the OT and on into the NT where it makes a major contribution to Christology (1981b). Similarly Stuhlmacher has studied, for example, the law as a topic of biblical theology, tracing differing and developing concepts of law through both Testaments (1986: 110-33).

This approach has been hailed as a new form of BT, but it has also been subject to much criticism (see Reventlow 1986: 149-54). G. F. Hasel (1982) has asked whether this is actually BT or a "theology of tradition-building" (66). The complex development of traditions is a matter of historical reconstruction on which critical scholars frequently differ. The approach involves assumptions such as the canon of the OT not being closed in the time of Jesus which are by no means universally accepted (see further, D.2.2). The tracing of a continuous development of tradition also involves the use of noncanonical material, and in this respect the approach is more historical than canonical. Further, when revelation is located in the entire process of tradition history, it is not always clear where Christian faith is to find its norm. Despite these criticisms, however, there is much of value in this approach, not least in the attempt to bridge the gap between OT and NT scholarship.

C-4.2. BIBLICAL THEMES

Further evidence of interest in BT may be seen in the renewed study of biblical "themes" in such series as Fortress Press's Overtures to Biblical Theology, Abingdon's Biblical Encounters, and the New Studies in Biblical Theology published by Eerdmans and InterVarsity Press. Many of these studies seek to do BT by tracing themes through both OT and NT, by no means ignoring diversity but also seeking to bring out the continuity in the biblical treatment of the various themes. As a number of the titles suggest, there is also a concern to present the material in a way that will speak to the contemporary believer. "The yearning and expectation of believers," say the editors of the Overtures series, "will not let biblical theology rest with the descriptive task alone. The growing strength of Evangelical Protestantism and the expanding phenomenon of charismatic Catholicism are but vocal reminders that people seek in the Bible a source of alternative value systems. By its own character and by the place it occupies in our culture the Bible will not rest easy as merely an historical artifact" (Brueggemann 1977b: x).

Noteworthy also was the appearance of new journals in this area, such as *Biblical Theology Bulletin* (founded in 1970), *Horizons in Biblical Theology* (founded in 1970), and in Germany, *Jahrbuch für Biblische Theologie* (founded in 1986).

Such studies are certainly a form of BT that seeks to bridge the gap not only between OT and NT studies, but also between the academy and the community of faith. They are each of course limited in their scope. One of the major questions they raise concerns the relationship among the various themes and their relation to the broader structure of BT as a whole.

C-4.3. BIBLICAL THEOLOGIES

We have noted that the actual writing of BT, i.e., of works dealing with the understanding of God in both OT and NT together, came to an almost complete halt for virtually a century (B-5). The latter part of the twentieth century has seen a break in that drought and a cautious move back to attempting such an enterprise despite the many pronouncements that such a thing is an impossibility.

Two early examples come from opposite ends of the theological spectrum: M. Burrows's *An Outline of Biblical Theology* (1946a) is written from a liberal Protestant viewpoint (cf. Burrows 1946b), but is more akin to a dictionary of biblical themes than a full-fledged "theology" (see Hayes and Prussner 1984: 192-95; Scobie 1992a). *Biblical Theology: Old and New Testaments* by G. Vos (1948) is written from a strongly conservative perspective though it acknowledges a progressive revelation; it still repays reading, though unfortunately it is incomplete.

Of first importance is Samuel Terrien's *The Elusive Presence: Toward a New Biblical Theology* (1978). "The reality of divine presence," affirms the author, "stands at the centre of biblical faith. This presence, however, is always elusive" (xxvii). After an introductory chapter surveying major trends in biblical studies and discussing the modern quest of a biblical theology, Terrien proceeds to trace the theme of divine presence through the major units of the biblical canon. It is highly significant that in the second half of the twentieth century a scholar of Terrien's stature should write a volume, with the words "biblical theology" in the title, that encompasses both OT and NT and sees its task as seeking "a certain homogeneity of theological depth" that "binds the biblical books together" (33; for assessments of Terrien, see Frizzell 1980; Scobie 1992a).

In *Der Gott der ganzen Bibel* (1982) the German scholar Horst Seebass presents a sketch rather than a full BT (see Scobie 1992a). The ecumenical theologian Hans-Ruedi Weber's *Power: Focus for a Biblical Theology* (1989; see Scobie 1992a: 68-69) also attempts to sketch "the outlines of a biblical theology" (ix), focused on the theme of "power," though he concedes that what is possible is only "an ordered collection of biblical theologies which stand in tension with one another" (22). Though intended as a resource for Christian education, Gisela Kittel's *Der Name über alle Namen* (*Biblische Theologie/AT* 1989, *Biblische Theologie/NT* 1990) presents an original sketch of BT which gives an overview of Old and New Testaments in their inter-connectedness. Through the discussion of selected themes and exegesis of key passages the author shows how the God of the OT who revealed his mysterious name to Moses at the burning bush is the same God who raised Jesus from the dead and conferred on him "the name that is above every name." G. Goldsworthy's *According to Plan: The Unfolding Revelation of God in the Bible* (1991) represents a more conservative and popular attempt at outlining a BT.

The most significant BT of the twentieth century is B. S. Childs's *Biblical*

Theology of the Old and New Testaments (1992), which is the culmination of his work on "the canonical approach" to Scripture (cf. above, C-2.2). After a discussion of methodology, Childs surveys "The Discrete Witness of the Old Testament" and "The Discrete Witness of the New Testament," to use his section headings, tracing the development of traditions in each of the main units of the canon. BT proper is treated in a major section, "Theological Reflection on the Christian Bible," which discusses the biblical material related to ten major theological topics; each of these is related to contemporary theological discussion through a concluding section of "Dogmatic Theological Reflection" on each topic.

Despite the criticism that has been leveled against them, these works demonstrate that it is possible to attempt once again the writing of a truly biblical theology, and they suggest both some of the pitfalls to avoid and the approaches that are worth pursuing.

D. The Method of Biblical Theology

Our survey of the history of BT has demonstrated very clearly that the question of methodology is of fundamental importance. A way out of the present impasse in biblical studies and the development of a new approach to BT are conditional upon the working out of an appropriate methodology.

D-1. AN INTERMEDIATE BIBLICAL THEOLOGY

There can be no return to the situation of an *integrated biblical theology* that existed before the rise of the modern historical approach. Yet the pursuit of a totally *independent biblical theology* has led to an impasse. What does hold promise is an approach that sees BT as a bridge discipline, situated between the historical study of Scripture on the one hand and its use by the church in its faith and life on the other. (For the bridge metaphor, cf. Goldsworthy 1981: 43; Childs 1992: 481; Knierim 1984: 47 speaks of a "relay-station.") This may thus be termed *an intermediate biblical theology*.

The proposal advanced here may be illustrated as follows:

| Historical | → | *Biblical* | → | Faith and Life |
| Study | ← | *Theology* | ← | of the Church |

Historical-critical study of the Bible still has an important role to play (cf. above, C-1.3). The books of the Bible must be interpreted in the first instance against their historical background; questions of authorship, date, destination, purpose, and so on must be based on a critical assessment of the evidence; and study of individual books and authors must be based on painstaking exegesis that aims to understand the meaning of the text in its original setting. But the limits of historical criticism must be kept in mind. The method can generally yield only possible or probable, not certain, results. No historian is free from presuppositions; those of the biblical critic require careful scrutiny. And it is not just the (often hypothetical) original form of a tradition that is "authentic"; all levels of Scripture must be given due weight through to the final edited form.

An intermediate BT will assume and accept the findings of the historical-critical approach, but will seek to go beyond them and move from analysis to synthesis. E. A. Martens (1977) has helpfully defined BT as "that approach to Scripture which attempts to see Biblical material holistically and to describe this wholeness or synthesis in Biblical categories. Biblical theology attempts to embrace the message of the Bible and to arrive at an intelligible coherence of the whole despite the great diversity of the parts. Or, put another way: Biblical theology investigates the themes presented in Scripture and defines their inter-relationships. Biblical theology is an attempt to get to the theological heart of the Bible" (123).

A BT will still be basically concerned with "the horizon of the text," and will attempt to provide an overview and interpretation of the shape and structure of the Bible as a whole. It will seek the unity and continuity of Scripture, but without sacrificing the richness of its diversity. It will focus not on exegetical details but on the broad interrelationships between the major themes of the Bible, and above all on the interrelationship between the Testaments.

Such a BT can find an ally in some forms of the literary approach to Scripture. Especially where it deals with the biblical text in its final canonical form, such an approach can shed light on the shape and structure of the Bible, on its essential continuity, and on its use of different literary genres and of imagery and symbolism to convey its message. But care must be taken to ensure that the text is not understood in a way inconsistent with the original historical meaning.

It is clear that this cannot be done in a "neutral" or "objective" fashion. An intermediate BT is inevitably part of the interpretive process, and its presuppositions will be those of the interpretive community. No interpreter is free of presuppositions; the essential thing is to be aware of what these presuppositions are, to make them public, and to be prepared to review them continuously as one engages with the text. The presuppositions of this study include belief that the Bible conveys a divine revelation, that the word of God in Scripture constitutes the norm of Christian faith and life, and that all the varied material of the OT and NT can in some way be related to the plan and purpose of the one God of the whole Bible. Such a BT lies somewhere between what the Bible "meant" and what it "means." The issue of the nature of BT is often posed in terms of whether it is to be regarded as purely "descriptive" or also as "prescriptive." G. F. Hasel, noting J. Barr's (1988: 11-13) opposition to BT playing a normative or prescriptive role, comments that "this is exactly what a fair number of scholars are now calling for because they believe that the community of faith needs to recover the meaning of biblical theology" (Hasel 1994: 214). Bornemann (1991) points out that the view which limits BT to a purely historical, descriptive approach has a built-in presupposition, "namely, that in interpreting the biblical text one can get to its meaning without assuming that it is the word of God. Indeed, in this view it is incumbent on the biblical interpreter to assume that it is not the word of God." Against this, Bornemann rightly contends that biblical theologians do "bring to the study of the Bible the assumption that the Bible is indeed the word of God. . . . With all the difficulties and risks, the biblical theologian must be involved both with the historical witnesses of the biblical writers and the contemporary address of God" (123-24). In other words, BT is not merely a historical discipline, it is also "theology"; it is not merely descriptive, but also normative (cf. Vogels 1998: 127). As P. Stuhlmacher (1995) has urged, BT cannot read the biblical texts "only from a critical distance as historical sources but must, at the same time, take them seriously as testimonies of faith which belong to the Holy Scripture of early Christianity" (1). What is proposed here is a BT that does indeed go beyond the purely descriptive approach and that forms *part* of the process by which Scripture is read as prescriptive or normative for the Christian community of faith.

An intermediate BT provides a bridge to the faith and life of the church. If the church's norm is indeed to be found in its canonical Scriptures, then they must illuminate and direct every aspect of the church's faith and life: its theology, preaching, teaching, devotion, ethical reflection, and Christian action (on the relation between BT and preaching, see Hagner 1985). The biblical material synthesized by BT constitutes the norm that has to be correlated with the situation faced by the church today. In this process dogmatic theology plays an important role. Dogmatic theology is the final stage in the movement from the horizon of the text to the horizon of the interpreter. Professional theologians ought to be the servants of the church, continually aiding it in its thought and reflection on how biblical norms are to be applied in the contemporary situation. But there is also truth in the contention that "every Christian is a theologian"; however haltingly and however inconsistently, all believers have to have some kind of working theology, some provisional idea of how the revelation conveyed through Scripture is to be worked out in their own lives and in the life of the church. While the Christian community is the true interpreter of Scripture, it is equally true that the community must constantly scrutinize its faith and life in the light of the word of God in Scripture.

It is the task of the church to relate scriptural norms to contemporary life. Current theological and ethical concerns (e.g., ecology, feminism, human rights) do not determine or dictate the conclusions of BT, but they can prompt biblical scholars to reassess the scriptural evidence that may have been obscured or distorted by later nonbiblical prejudices and presuppositions. Thus, for example, ecological concerns can prompt the rediscovery of neglected aspects of biblical teaching on creation and stewardship, while feminist concerns have led to a thorough reevaluation of the biblical material on the role and status of women. Great care is needed, however, to distinguish between discovering and applying biblical norms to contemporary situations, and reading back contemporary social, economic, and political programs into Scripture.

D-2. A CANONICAL BIBLICAL THEOLOGY

If a BT is to be truly "biblical," then its subject matter must be the canonical Scriptures recognized by the Christian church. It is a central contention of the approach adopted here that *biblical theology is canonical theology.* As C. J. Scalise (1996) argues, "a canonical approach emphasizes that the Christian community has recognized this particular collection of books as canon — the rule which guides and tests our beliefs and actions. Christians read the Bible as *Scripture,* God's written word to the people of God" (24-25).

D-2.1. SCRIPTURE AND CANON

In order to understand how BT is canonical theology, an understanding of the nature of "Scripture" and of "canon" is essential. The concept of a canon of scripture is meaningful only in relation to a particular religious tradition. Thus Judaism and Christianity each has its own "canon," or list of books it recognizes as its own sacred scripture.

The writings that constitute what the Christian church came to call the Bible can be designated in various ways. In the NT the Hebrew Scriptures are most commonly designated simply as "the Scriptures" *(hai graphai);* see further, 1-3.5. The word "scriptures" *(graphai)* of course simply means "writings" *(graphō* = "write"), but in the NT the fifty or so uses of the word refer exclusively to the Hebrew Scriptures, the particular writings recognized as inspired and authoritative by the Jewish community. In English this can be conveniently indicated by the use of a capital letter for "Scripture" or "Scriptures."

To refer to "Scriptures" in this way involves two things that are but the two sides of the same coin. On the one hand, the implication is that the writings so designated, while penned by human authors, are not exclusively of human origin. They are also the product of divine revelation, and their writing is inspired by the divine Spirit. On the other hand, these writings are special in that they are recognized by the community of faith as authoritative and containing the norm of the community's faith and life (cf. C. J. Scalise 1996: 71).

The terms "canon" and "canonical" are widely used in modern discussion, though they were not actually used in relation to the Christian Scriptures until the fourth century. The Greek word *kanōn* derives from a Semitic root, the basic meaning of which appears to be a reed or rod (see Souter and Williams 1954: 141-43; Beyer 1965). From this, two main groups of meaning derive.

1. A *kanōn* can mean a straight edge, line, or level, employed, e.g., by masons or carpenters to check whether a piece of work is straight, level, or true. Hence comes the idea of a *standard* or *norm* by which things may be judged. The English word "ruler" or "rule" captures some of the nuances of this usage.

2. Since *kanōn* can mean a "ruler," i.e., a piece of wood on which there is a regular row of marks used for measurement, it comes also to have the meaning of a list, index, or table. From this derives the further meaning of a fixed list, or a list of limited extent.

The first meaning obviously stands in close relationship to the idea of "Scripture." Books form part of a canon, or are regarded as "canonical," if they are recognized by a community of faith as normative for the faith and life of that community.

The early church used the term *kanōn* in a variety of senses (Beyer 1965: 600-602). Synods and councils issued "canons," i.e., rules that Christians were to follow; in time church law became known as "canon law." More significantly, the phrase "the canon of the faith" (*ho kanōn tēs pisteōs* = *regula fidei* in Latin) was used to refer to a brief summary of Christian belief.

In the earliest days of the church Christians found their canon or norm not in writing, but in Christ himself, then in the gospel message that proclaimed the significance of the Christ event (cf. McDonald 1988: 164). As late as around 130, Papias the bishop of Hierapolis mentions his preference for speaking with people who could remember the apostles, for, he said, "I did not imagine that things out of books would help me as much as the utterances of a living and abiding voice" (quoted by Eusebius, *Historia ecclesiastica* 3.39; Williamson 1965: 150). As time went on, however, the church had to deal increasingly with attacks upon and distortions of its faith, and the value of having the canon or norm of faith in written form became more and more apparent. Thus, although the actual word "canon" was not applied to the Christian list of authoritative books until the fourth century, the concept of a canon or norm was inherent in Christianity from the very beginning (cf. Gamble 1985: 58).

The word "canon" implies more than a standard or norm, however, for the second meaning of the term contains the idea of *a closed list*. Both Judaism and Christianity came to adopt a "canon" in this sense also, i.e., not just a list of inspired and authoritative books but also a *closed* list of books to which, after a certain point, no additions could be made. The word "canon" has these two meanings, and Sundberg has suggested using "Scripture" to mean inspired and authoritative writings and "canon" to mean a closed list of such writings (1968: 147; 1975: 356), but unfortunately such a usage has not been generally accepted. It is thus necessary to observe carefully in which sense the term "canon" is being used.

The concept of a *closed* canon is one that causes problems for some people. Does it mean that the revelation of divine truth is entirely confined to the past? Does God not continue to guide and reveal his will to his people in succeeding generations down to and including the present day?

"Canonical criticism" has emphasized that traditions were passed on and continually reshaped to meet the changing needs of the community (cf. C-1.1), and one of its main proponents has gone so far as to say that "the overwhelming evidence points to the moment of final shaping as not particularly more important than any other" (J. A. Sanders 1980: 191). R. B. Laurin (1977) goes even further in declaring that "canonization was an unfortunate freezing of tradition growth" that was "untrue to tradition history and its contemporizing process"; he holds that "no stage, not even the New Testament, is the final or authoritative stage" (271-72). This represents a fundamental misunderstanding of the nature and role of canon. Neither Judaism nor Christianity locks God's truth into the past, but both believe, in their own way, that the supreme, unique, and final revelation of God's truth has been given in history, that this revelation is witnessed to in Holy Scripture, and that the continuing revelation of God's truth therefore consists in *interpreting and applying the canonical norm to succeeding situations and circumstances.* Thus for Christians the NT in particular witnesses to the Christ event that constitutes the norm of Christian faith and life. While that norm has to be applied in ever new situations, the revelation given in Christ cannot itself be superseded or added to, for then it would no longer be a unique and final revelation. It is precisely here that the Christian church has to part company with later sects and new religions that accept the Bible but add to it further writings of their own. If further revelation is necessary, then Christ is no longer the full and final revelation of God. Accepting a canon of Scripture does not of course mean that only those books designated as "canonical" are to be read and used by the members of the community of faith. Christians can read with much profit the writings of the Apostolic Fathers, just as they may read Augustine's *Confessions* or Bunyan's *Pilgrim's Progress* or Barth's *Commentary on Romans*. But for the Christian, neither these nor any other later books possess ultimate authority. Everything Christians read is to be judged and evaluated in the light of God's supreme self-revelation in the Christ event. And for a knowledge of that self-revelation Christians turn to those writings that they recognize as their canonical Scriptures.

D-2.2. TANAKH AND OLD TESTAMENT

Contrary to the views of Marcion (cf. B-1), the church in the second century recognized the Hebrew Scriptures as a vital component of their Bible. For the Christian community of faith the Scriptures consist of two parts, which came to be called the Old Testament and the New Testament and together constitute the Bible. The term "Old Testament" has meaning of course only within the Christian community that differentiates it from a "New Testament."

The Christian Old Testament overlaps to a considerable extent with the Hebrew Scriptures, though it is by no means identical with them in every respect. The sacred writings of Judaism, as we have seen, are referred to in the NT most commonly as "the Scriptures." Jews came to refer to them as "the Torah, the Prophets, and the Writings," or vocalizing the initial letters in Hebrew of these three terms *(Torah, Nebhi'im, Kethubhim)*, as "Tanakh." For the study of Christian BT, it is of prime importance to understand how the Tanakh came to be accepted as Scripture and especially as a closed canon, but unfortunately scholars hold quite divergent views regarding this.

1. The traditional view that was developed within Judaism and largely taken over by the Christian church is that the Hebrew Scriptures were recognized as Scripture and constituted as a closed canon in the time of Ezra, i.e., ca. 400 B.C. We can trace this view in 2 *Macc* 2:13 (first century B.C.), in 2 *Esdr* 14:37-48 (late first/early second century A.D.), and in Josephus, *Contra Apion* 1.7-8 (early second century A.D.), and it is generally assumed in the rabbinic literature. According to this view, as Childs (1979) puts it, "the canon was formed and enlarged as each new book was added. When the last book appeared, the canon was closed" (51). If this view is correct, then it would mean that the early Christian church inherited from Judaism a canon of the Tanakh that was already closed centuries before the time of Christ.

2. This traditional view was seriously questioned with the development of the historical-critical approach, and a new view emerged that, at least in broad outline, has been accepted as "critical orthodoxy" until recent years.

Historical criticism envisages a complex oral and literary development that rules out "instant canonization"; it also holds that some books such as Daniel were written later than the alleged date of the closing of the canon. The new view that emerged pictured the Tanakh as developing in three stages. Only the Pentateuch was accepted as Scripture in the time of Ezra. The Prophets were added by the second century B.C. The third group, the Writings, was the subject of dispute. The more conservative, Palestinian wing of Judaism favored a narrower canon of the Writings (the one eventually recognized by rabbinic Judaism), whereas the more liberal, Alexandrian view favored a wider canon embodied in the Septuagint (the Greek translation of the Hebrew Scriptures produced in Alexandria in Egypt) that included additional books (those later designated by Christians as the Apocrypha or deuterocanonical books). An important implication of this view is that the Jewish canon of Scripture had not yet been closed at the time of Christ. The final decision was made at a council held in Jamnia in A.D. 90, at which the Jewish authorities decided finally in favor of the shorter canon of the Writings.

3. More recently almost every aspect of "critical orthodoxy" has come under fire, though that does not necessarily mean that all such views have been

overturned (cf. Dempster 1997: 27-31). Generally speaking, contemporary scholarship emphasizes the great diversity and fluidity that prevailed in Judaism prior to the destruction of the temple in A.D. 70. At least four main positions can be discerned in relation to the canon of Scripture. Some groups such as the Samaritans and the Sadducees accepted only the Pentateuch. Others favored the "shorter canon" that eventually prevailed in rabbinic Judaism. A broader option is represented by the Septuagint, though it is not seen as an Alexandrian version but rather as simply one of a number of text types that circulated in Palestine as well as in the Diaspora. A fourth option may be represented by various groups that accepted an even wider selection of Scriptures. The Qumran discoveries show how all kinds of apocryphal and pseudepigraphal writings circulated (in Palestine!) prior to A.D. 70 (though it is not possible to determine what status they had in the eyes of the community).

The whole idea of a Council of Jamnia has been shown to be totally misleading, especially if the word "council" is thought of on the analogy of the Christian ecumenical councils of the fourth to eighth centuries (J. P. Lewis 1964). A rabbinic academy and court existed at Jamnia/Jabneh between the First and Second Revolts (A.D. 70-133), but the reference in *m. Yad.* 3:5 to a ruling on Ecclesiastes is the only evidence of a pronouncement being made at Jamnia. Debates on whether individual books "defile the hands" (i.e., are sacred scripture) are recorded both prior to and following the Jamnia period. It must be remembered that even after the idea of a closed canon had been accepted, there could still be some debate as to whether individual books were to be accepted as part of that closed canon (cf. R. C. Newman 1976).

Thus the questions of how, when, and why the Jewish canon was finally closed are still very much open ones for contemporary scholarship. For Christian BT a key question is whether Judaism had a closed canon before the time of Christ or whether the canon was finally closed only after the birth of Christianity. Quite apart from the so-called Council of Jamnia, there are still many scholars who suggest that the final closing of the canon of the Hebrew Scriptures is to be placed in the late first century A.D. (cf. J. M. Ross 1979: 185-87). Josephus, in a late work (*Contra Apion* 1.7-8; probably early second century), provides the first clear evidence of the canon that became normative in rabbinic Judaism, though he regards it as old: "for, although such long ages have now passed, no one has ventured either to add, or to remove, or to alter a syllable." On the other hand, while *Sirach* (second century B.C.) knows a threefold structure of "the law and the prophets and the others" (*Sir,* prologue), there is no clear indication that the "others" at that time consisted of a firmly fixed and closed list. Even the NT usually refers to "the law and the prophets" (Matt 11:13; John 1:45; Acts 24:14; Rom 3:21), and only once expands this to "the law of Moses, the prophets, and the psalms" (Luke 24:44), which suggests that at that point the Writings were still in a state of flux. Various reasons for closing the canon in this period have been suggested. The trauma of the Great Revolt culminating in the fall of Jerusalem and the destruction of the temple in A.D. 70 introduced a period of retrenchment and reorganization in Judaism. There was a reaction against apocalypticism (which was felt to have contributed to the tragedy) and against apocalyptic books; thus it was felt safer to backtrack to a canon without such books, and to close it to prevent any new ones being added in the future. Another suggestion is that Judaism was motivated to close its canon by the rise of the Christian church. Christians were producing new books that were being added to the Hebrew Scriptures; Judaism wanted to disassociate itself from any such move. A variant of this theory sees Judaism reacting against the claims of Christians to have received a new outpouring of God's Spirit and a rebirth of prophecy; the reaction pushed the cessation of prophecy and the production of inspired books as far back into the past as possible.

Other scholars, such as R. T. Beckwith (1980; 1985) and J. W. Miller (1994), have argued that the Jewish canon was closed as early as the second century B.C. If this be so, other motives for closing the canon must be sought. One suggestion is that only books written in Hebrew (and not in either Aramaic or Greek) could be considered canonical. There is evidence for the view that prophecy had ceased as early as *1 Maccabees* (1 Macc 4:45-46; 14:41). The strongest argument for this view is that the compilers of the Writings saw the restoration under Ezra and Nehemiah as the logical culmination of the canon.

The historical question of the origin of a closed Jewish canon has certainly not been resolved, and barring the discovery of new evidence may never be in any satisfactory way. What does seem likely is that there was no decision by a court or council but that by the late first century A.D. at least, if not earlier, a consensus had been arrived at within the Jewish community to accept the "shorter" canon and to regard it as closed.

Despite these historical uncertainties, we can speak with more confidence about how the canon of the Tanakh/OT was understood *theologically* by the developing Jewish and Christian communities. The Jewish view that came to regard the canon as being closed in the time of Ezra is clearly connected to the view that *the supreme revelation of God has been given in the Torah*. The Torah/Pentateuch forms the core of Hebrew Scripture. With the establishment by Ezra, in the postexilic period, of a community whose life is based on the Torah, the norm of the faith and life of Judaism has been finally established. In the view of the rabbis, "only the period bounded by Creation and the 'Restoration' by Ezra and Nehemiah gives rise to that which is revelatory" (Lightstone 1988: 17; cf. 62). There is thus a chronological factor associated with canonicity, since the time of Ezra is taken to constitute the cutoff point. Books such as the Song of Songs and Ecclesiastes were questioned because of misgivings over their content. Aiding their acceptance was doubtless the fact that they were linked with Solomon and were therefore dated well back into the period of inspiration. On the other hand, *Sirach*, which on the basis of content was a strong contender for inclusion in the canon, was excluded on the basis of chronology. It was clearly dated, and dated too late. The same holds true for the historical books of *1* and *2 Maccabees*.

Christians, however, look at the Hebrew Scriptures from a different perspective. They see in them the record of the period of preparation and promise that culminates in the Christ event. *It is that Christ event, and not the Torah, that constitutes the supreme revelation of God for Christians.* It follows therefore, from an NT point of view, that Jewish Scripture can be written up to the time of Christ but by definition there cannot be any Jewish Scripture *after* Christ. Thus whatever may be the case historically, *theologically* for Christians *it is the Christ event that closes the canon of the Old Testament.* In this sense chronology can be said to be a decisive factor in the Christian view of the OT canon also.

This view is not contradicted by the fact that a Jewish book almost certainly written after the time of Christ was accepted by some Christians as canonical. *2 Esdras*, which was included in the Old Latin version and in an appendix to the Vulgate (and is included, for example, in the ecumenical edition of the RSV and NRSV), was written after A.D. 70 according to most modern critical scholars. But it is ascribed to Ezra, and it was on the basis of this belief that it found a place in the Christian canon of the Vulgate.

D-2.3. THE CANON OF THE NEW TESTAMENT

The formation of the canon of the NT was also a long and gradual process. Despite lively scholarly debate in recent years, at least the main lines of development seem clear (Gamble 1985: 23-56).

Paul's letters were the first to be collected, and such a collection, at least of his main letters, was probably in existence by the end of the first century. Acceptance of the Pastoral Epistles (1 Timothy, 2 Timothy, and Titus) came later. The Synoptic Gospels (Matthew, Mark, Luke) were generally accepted by mid–second century, but doubts about John held back the acceptance of the fourfold Gospel until after 200. There was considerably more doubt and discussion about the remaining books, the so-called Catholic Epistles and Revelation.

A wide variety of literature was produced in the early Christian centuries, some of which contended for inclusion in what eventually became known as the New Testament. The Apostolic Fathers overlap the end of the NT period, and works such as *1 Clement*, the *Epistle of Barnabas*, and the *Shepherd of Hermas* actually appear in some manuscripts of the NT. Conversely, some of the minor epistles that were eventually included in the canon are lacking in some early manuscripts. A wide range of gospels, acts, epistles, and revelations, generally (falsely) ascribed to apostles, constitute what is usually termed "The Apocryphal New Testament" (Scobie 1963; Hennecke 1963).

While Paul's epistles and the four Gospels had probably won general acceptance by ca. 200, the great church historian Eusebius (ca. 260-340) could still list Christian Scriptures under three categories: books that were accepted in his day, others that were definitely not accepted, and a third category of "disputed" books on which opinions still differed (*Historia ecclesiastica* 3.25; Williamson 1965: 134). As is well known, the precise twenty-seven books that eventually constituted the canon of the NT are first listed in the Easter Letter of Athanasius in 367. The synods of Hippo (393) and Carthage (397) recognized the twenty-seven-book list, but their decisions were binding only in North Africa. By the fifth century a general consensus had developed, though doubts about individual books lingered on in certain localities for some time. Significantly, no ecumenical council made a ruling on the canon. This underlines the fact that the church did not *choose* the canon (that would have made the canon subordinate to the church); the church, over an extended period of time, *recognized* the canon that was already in existence.

Historians of the early church have looked for factors that may have influenced the development of a Christian canon. The most common suggestion points to the influence of Marcion, who arrived in Rome ca. 140 and who rejected the Hebrew Scriptures, claiming that the God of the OT was not the God revealed by Jesus (Stander 1990; J. W. Miller 1994: 8-13; on Marcion, see B-1). He issued a list of books that he considered authoritative consisting of one Gospel only, that of Luke (edited to conform with his ideas), plus ten letters of Paul. It has frequently been suggested that the actions of Marcion prompted the church to clarify which books it accepted and perhaps even to begin constructing a canon of its own. The extent of Marcion's influence is a matter of scholarly debate (see Gamble 1985: 59-62), but there can be little doubt that he did play some role in the development of an NT canon. It has also been suggested that the canon developed in reaction to groups such as the Montanists (see Groh 1990), whose claim to possess the promised Paraclete might seem to open the door to the production of new and heretical works (but see Gamble, 63-65).

From the point of view of BT, the criteria employed in admitting books to the NT canon and the motivation for closing that canon are of prime importance. Several criteria are listed in the standard works on the canon (cf. Birdsall 1980: 244). The most common is *apostolicity;* the books accepted were those ascribed to the original apostles. It is clear that this cannot be accepted as a criterion without qualification. Quite apart from the questioning of apostolic authorship of various NT books by modern critical scholarship, two of the four Gospels, those of Mark and Luke, are ascribed to persons who were definitely not apostles. (Mark, of course, was linked with Peter; Luke was linked with Paul, though with less point since Paul was not an eyewitness of the ministry of Jesus.) Moreover, many of the apocryphal and Gnostic writings were ascribed to apostles (Peter could have had a whole NT to himself); their rejection was obviously based on other criteria. It has been claimed that the books accepted as canonical were those that the church believed *to contain sound teaching*. Books produced by various Gnostic groups that were designed to promote their teachings were considered to be heretical and therefore rejected. A further suggestion is that the books that came to be accepted were those *regularly read in public worship* in the early Christian church, especially in the leading churches.

The circular nature of these criteria will readily be apparent. The books accepted as canonical were those considered to be apostolic. How does one know if they are apostolic? They are apostolic if they contain sound teaching. How does one know if they contain sound teaching? They contain sound teaching if they are regularly read at public worship. Which books are regularly read at public worship? Those which are considered apostolic!

BT is not concerned with the details of the complex process of the development of the canon of the NT. But it is vitally concerned with the *theology of the canon.* From a theological point of view it is clear that the all-important factor in the closing of the canon of the NT was the belief that *the Christ event constitutes the supreme, unique, and final revelation of God.* Only those books written within the shadow of that event and reflecting its interpretation by the earliest leaders of the Christian community could be accepted as canonical. "Apostolicity" may thus be accepted as the key criterion provided it is redefined in a broad sense. The books that were accepted were those that contained "apostolic teaching," that is, teaching in accordance with the gospel as preached by the apostles and their associates in the earliest days of the church. Here again, therefore, a chronological factor was involved; it was closeness to the unique Christ event that determined canonicity (cf. Best 1993: 42-44). While it is true that debate continued for centuries, books believed to have been written in postapostolic times were never seriously considered.

Thus, while the process of the formation of the NT canon was a long and gradual one, it can be argued that the *principle* of a closed canon was there from the beginning. The early church never simply produced additional "Scriptures" to be added to the Scriptures inherited from Judaism; it produced books testifying to a unique and unrepeatable event in history. In the Christian view God's revelation in Christ cannot be superseded, added to, or improved upon. The formation of a closed canon of Christian Scripture was thus inherent in the Christian movement from the very outset.

It is therefore *the Christ event that is decisive in determining both the canon of the OT and the canon of the NT.* It is in the light of the Christ event that Christians see the Hebrew Scriptures as the "Old Testament," a closed collection of Scriptures that documents the period of preparation and promise extending up to, but not beyond, the Christ event. It is this also which determines that the "New Testament" cannot consist of an open-ended collection of scriptures, but is a closed canon of those books that provide the earliest testimony to the unique Christ event.

D-2.4. BIBLICAL THEOLOGY IS LIMITED
TO THE CANON OF CHRISTIAN SCRIPTURE

If BT is to be truly "biblical," it will be based on the canon of Christian Scripture. This is precisely what differentiates it from the history of religion *(Religionsgeschichte)*. Historians of religion, quite legitimately in accordance with their own terms of reference, are interested in tracing the development of Judaism from its origins all the way up to the present day; they are likewise interested in tracing the origins and development of Christianity not only in the first but also in succeeding centuries. Their subject matter is religion, their approach is descriptive or phenomenological, and they seek to trace a continuous if complex process of change and development. Hence any writings produced within these communities during the periods under study are valid sources of data.

BT, however, has different aims and a different methodology. It deals only with those books recognized as normative by the Christian community. Thus it does not deal with the so-called Pseudepigrapha (such as *Enoch* or *The Testaments of the Twelve Patriarchs*), nor with the Dead Sea Scrolls, nor with the writings of Philo and Josephus, nor with the rabbinic literature, valuable though these writings may be for the historian of religion. The biblical theologian should be aware of these developments and may well note that certain trends or ideas that surface in these works are also found in the NT, but it is the theology of the canonical books alone that remains the true subject matter of BT.

Similarly with regard to the canon of the NT, it may well be that there are works belonging to the Apostolic Fathers that are earlier than the latest books included in the canon; *1 Clement* is a prime example. For the historian of religion there is no clear-cut line dividing the NT period from the post-NT period. But for the biblical theologian there is a clear line, the one recognized by the Christian church as forming the boundary of its canon of Scripture. We agree with the contention of H. Schlier (1968) that NT theology "does not enquire into the theology of the supposed sources of the NT or, at all events only does so in order to clarify the theology of the NT writings themselves. Secondly, its investigation does not extend beyond the New Testament into early Christian literature generally, or at least, does so only for the same purpose. It accepts the exclusive character of the Canon as an essential presupposition of its work" (31-32).

D-2.5. BIBLICAL THEOLOGY IS BASED
ON BOTH OLD AND NEW TESTAMENTS

A truly BT will be concerned with the entire Christian canon, that is, with both OT and NT together. Recent German discussion has focused on the possibility of *eine gesamtbiblische Theologie* (an all-biblical theology), a phrase used to indicate that what is in view is not OT theology plus NT theology, but a theology that encompasses both Testaments (cf. Scobie 1991a: 53). "Biblical theology is *biblical,* that is, concerned with the whole Christian Bible; it is more than the sum of Old Testament theology and New Testament theology, understood as separate disciplines" (F. Watson 1997: 8). Despite the by now long-standing separation of OT theology from NT theology (cf. B-6), there are signs that a growing number of biblical scholars are willing to acknowledge, as P. Stuhlmacher (1995) puts it, "that the Old and New Testaments have belonged together in a most intimate way since the beginning of the Christian Church. They belong together to such a degree that the testimony of the New Testament cannot be adequately understood without the Old and the exegesis of the Old Testament remains incomplete without taking the New into view" (2).

There are two aspects of this that must somehow be held together. On the one hand, a canonical BT must seek to do full justice to the OT. All too often the separation of BT into OT and NT theology has meant the ignoring or downplaying of the OT. A strong strain of "neo-Marcionism" (on Marcion, see B-1) runs through the work of such influential modern Protestant scholars as Schleiermacher, Harnack, and Bultmann (cf. F. Watson 1997: chap. 4). A renewed BT can play a major role in overcoming this tendency. S. Terrien (1981) has gone so far as to declare that "the Old Testament is beginning to receive for the first time in the history of the church its rightful place and modern forms of Marcionism are at last being rejected as theological anti-Semitism" (125). Terrien's own work *The Elusive Presence* is characterized by a very sympathetic presentation of the OT. Against those (e.g., H. Hübner) who hold that a NT theology should deal only with *Vetus Testamentum in novo receptum* (i.e., the OT as quoted and alluded to in the NT), NT theology, and by extension BT, must deal with *Vetus Testamentum per se* (i.e., the entire OT in and of itself; cf. Childs 1992: 77).

On the other hand, however, in a canonical BT the OT cannot be viewed on its own but only from the perspective of the Christian canon as a whole. It follows that "OT theology" as part of BT must be a Christian discipline (cf. the discussion entitled "Old Testament Theology as a Christian Theological Enterprise" in F. Watson 1997: chap. 5). It has often been noted that Jewish scholars have shown little or no interest in BT (see the discussion "Jewish Biblical Theology?" in J. Barr 1999: 286-311). While this may be due in part to historical accident (Lemke 1989: 60), it is also due to the nature of Judaism, which has been more interested in orthopraxis than in orthodoxy, which has not been so concerned with the systematization of belief, and in which the relation of Tanakh to Talmud and Midrash has been quite different from that of the OT to the NT (cf. Tsevat 1986: 36-37). In principle, however, there could be a Jewish theology of the Hebrew Scriptures, but by definition it could not be Old Testament or biblical theology. It would more properly be designated perhaps as Tanakh theology (cf. Goshen-Gottstein 1987), and its presuppositions would be different from those of OT theology. While a leading Jewish biblical scholar, J. Levenson, has written an article entitled "Why Jews Are Not Interested in Biblical Theology" (1987), paradoxically he himself has produced a number of volumes dealing with the theology of the Hebrew Scriptures (see Levenson 1985 and cf. Barr, 294). The two disciplines of Tanakh theology and Old Testament/biblical theology could exist alongside one another, could engage in dialogue and learn from each other, but they could never coalesce.

Several scholars have challenged the view that OT theology must be a Christian discipline. J. L. McKenzie claims to have written his *Theology of the Old Testament* (1974) "as if the New Testament did not exist" (319); R. P. Knierim (1984) has called for a "focus on the Old Testament in its own right" (52); and R. Rendtorff (1988) has contended that "we should examine the theology of the Hebrew Bible independently of any later religious developments, whether Jewish or Christian" (42). These scholars are reacting against a false "Christianizing" of the OT and demonstrating a commendable desire to allow the authentic voice of the OT to be heard. This is appropriate at the level of historical study of the OT, but a canonical BT as defined here is concerned with the OT along with the NT as the two parts of canonical Scripture, and hence inevitably involves Christian presuppositions. What is maintained here is that BT can *both* do justice to the OT *and* hold that, in the context of the canon, the NT is its continuation and fulfillment.

"Biblical theology," G. F. Hasel (1982) has declared, "must integrate Old Testament and New Testament Theology in a dynamic way that overcomes the present juxtaposition" (74). This means, of course, that a major concern of BT is the understanding of the theological relationship between OT and NT, a question with which the church has had to wrestle, not just in the historical-critical period, but throughout the era of "integrated biblical theology" (see further, E-2). It is worth noting that two recent German NT theologies (Hübner 1990, Stuhlmacher 1992) have revived the older title *Biblische Theologie des Neuen Testaments* ("Biblical Theology of the New Testament"); both (in somewhat different ways) see the discussion of the use of the OT in the NT as a major task of NT theology.

D-2.6. BIBLICAL THEOLOGY IS BASED ON THE CONTENT OF THE CHRISTIAN CANON

BT must be based on all the books that constitute the canon of the Old and New Testaments. In the case of the NT this does not raise any major problem. It is true that there were some lingering doubts about the book of Revelation in particular that continued in the East for several centuries after the canon had been generally accepted; but in time the East accepted the recognized canon of twenty-seven books. It is also true that Luther challenged the NT canon in a startling way and sought to downgrade four canonical books (cf. B-2). But his proposal never met with general acceptance. The surprising thing must surely be the virtual unanimity that prevails throughout the Christian church regarding the content of the NT canon.

Matters are otherwise, however, in relation to the OT. The Christian church has never been able to agree on whether to accept the "shorter canon" of the OT, i.e., the canon that corresponds in content to that finally recognized by rabbinic Judaism, or the "longer canon," i.e., that which more or less corresponds in content to the Septuagint version (see the discussion in J. Barr 1999: 563-80). There was some variation in exactly which books were included in the longer canon. (McDonald 1988: 178-79, based on Sundberg 1964: 58-59, conveniently prints eleven lists of OT books known from the early centuries of the church.) The Septuagint included the following books that are not part of the Hebrew canon:

> *1 Esdras*
> *Tobit*
> *Judith*
> *Additions to Esther*
> *The Wisdom of Solomon*
> *Ecclesiasticus (= Sirach)*
> *Baruch*
> *Letter of Jeremiah*
> *Additions to Daniel:*
>> *The Prayer of Azariah and the Song of the Three Young Men*
>> *Susanna*
>> *Bel and the Dragon*
> *Prayer of Manasses*
> *1 Maccabees*
> *2 Maccabees*

The Old Latin translation of the OT and editions of the Vulgate also include *2 Esdras*. Eastern Orthodox churches have recognized *3 Maccabees, 4 Maccabees,* and *Psalm 151*. A reliable modern translation of all the books in the longer canon (including *2 Esdras, 3 Maccabees, 4 Maccabees,* and *Psalm 151*) is available in *NOAB*. The number of these books may also vary depending on whether the additions to Esther and Daniel are counted as separate works or simply as part of these books; in some versions the *Letter of Jeremiah* is attached to *Baruch* and not counted separately.

In the early Christian centuries the OT was widely read in the Septuagint version that included the longer canon (see C. J. Scalise 1996: 60). The earliest Latin translation, the Old Latin, was made from the Septuagint and therefore also had the longer canon (including *2 Esdras*). Thus many of the leading Greek and Latin Church Fathers of the second and third centuries quote the books of the Apocrypha and appear to regard them as Scripture. However, as soon as some early Fathers such as Melito of Sardis, Origen, and especially Jerome became aware, from Jewish sources, of the shorter Hebrew canon, a distinction was made. To Jerome there seemed to be a logic to accepting the Jewish canon; after all, the Jews ought to know. In preparing the Vulgate Jerome carefully noted the additions to Esther and Daniel, and reluctantly translated *Tobit* and *Judith*. He did not oppose the reading of these books, but objected to using them to establish doctrine. Jerome's views were influential in the East, but in the West the other books of the Apocrypha were added to the Vulgate and continued to be part of the canon of the OT through medieval times.

At the time of the Protestant Reformation Luther at first accepted the wider canon but when Eck quoted *2 Macc* 12:43-45 in support of the doctrine of purgatory, Luther changed his position, recalling Jerome's doubts. In his German translation of the Bible he placed the Apocrypha (omitting *1* and *2 Esdras*) at the end of the OT, adding the notation: "Apocrypha — that is, books which are not held equal to the Holy Scriptures, and yet are profitable and good to read" (quoted in Metzger 1957: 183). All early Protestant Bibles up to and including the King James Version included the Apocrypha, usually placed separately between OT and NT, and (excluding the KJV) with a notation to the effect that they are not part of the Hebrew canon (cf. 182-88).

A reaction to what was seen as a downgrading of the Apocrypha manifested itself within the Roman Catholic Church, and at the Council of Trent (1546) those books were officially declared to be fully canonical. (However, for some reason *1* and *2 Esdras* and the *Prayer of Manasses* were not so recognized; they continued to be printed in the official text of the Vulgate, but in an appendix after the NT.) This pronouncement is authoritative for Roman Catholics to this day. Thus modern Roman Catholic translations (e.g., The Jerusalem Bible, The New American Bible) contain these books interspersed through the table of contents. In 1566 a distinction was introduced between *protocanonical* books, i.e., those received by the whole church from the beginning, and *deuterocanonical* books, i.e., those received only after doubts by some Church Fathers and some local councils (see Metzger 1991: iv).

Uncertainty prevailed for centuries in the Eastern Orthodox Church; many Greek Fathers quoted the Apocrypha while some sided with Athanasius in restricting themselves to the Hebrew canon. The Synod of Jerusalem in 1672 pronounced *Wisdom, Judith, Tobit, Bel and the Dragon, Susanna, 1* and *2 Maccabees,* and *Ecclesiasticus* as canonical. The Greek Orthodox Church has also recognized *1 Esdras, Psalm 151,* the *Prayer of Manasses,* and *3* and *4 Maccabees* (Metzger 1991: xiii). But while Orthodox churches accept the wider canon, they tend to do so on the understanding that the deuterocanonical books stand "on a lower footing than the rest of the Old Testament" (Ware 1969: 209; cf. Cronk 1982: 18).

The Church of England embodied its view in the Thirty-nine Articles (1562). Article VI lists the books of the Hebrew canon, then adds, "And the other books (as Hierome [= Jerome] saith) the Church doth read for example of life and instruction of manners: but yet doth it not apply them to establish any doctrine."

Protestants generally, however, reacted in their turn against the Council of Trent in the direction of rejecting the books of the Apocrypha altogether. The Apocrypha began to be dropped from some copies of the King James Version from 1626 onward as a result of Puritan influence. The Westminster Confession of Faith of 1646 declared that "the Books commonly called the Apocrypha, not being of divine inspiration, are no part of the canon of the scripture; and therefore are of no authority in the Church of God, nor to be any otherwise approved, or made use of, than other human writings" (I:3). The Protestant position hardened even further in the early nineteenth century and was responsible for pressuring the British and Foreign Bible Society to cease distributing Bibles with the Apocrypha. As a result, most Bibles published in Britain after that date lacked these books.

The Christian church appears to have a divided mind on this issue. What role are the books of the Apocrypha to play in BT? The primary consideration must be the attitude of the NT, though this is not as clear and simple as some imagine.

1. We have seen that from the viewpoint of BT the canon of the OT is closed by the Christ event. What lies before that is the preparation for God's supreme self-revelation in Christ. In the NT, the one great passage that gives an extensive review of salvation history, i.e., Heb 11, sees that history as continuous down to the time of Christ. Heb 11:32-38 clearly goes beyond the shorter canon and includes references to the heroes, heroines, and martyrs of the Maccabean period. In other words, the NT does not support the idea of an "intertestamental period"; it does not reflect any idea of a gap between the history of God's preparation for the Christ event and the event itself. It thus provides no prima facie reason for excluding books largely written in the second and first centuries B.C. It is on this basis that Stuhlmacher (1995: 5) argues for the use of the deuterocanonical books in constructing a BT on the grounds that they are part of the one continuous tradition process (cf. C-4.1).

2. It is clear that several NT writers knew and used books of the Apocrypha, most notably Paul, James, and the writer to the Hebrews. For example, Paul's argument in Rom 1:20-31 has too many parallels with *Wis* 13–14 for this to be a coincidence. The sayings of Jesus also contain echoes of various passages in the Apocrypha; for example, the addition of "You shall not defraud" to the commandments comes from *Sir* 4:1. (See the discussion in Metzger 1957: 158-70; and also the extensive list of citations and allusions provided in Nestle-Aland 1979: 769-73.)

3. It is a striking fact, however, that no book of the Apocrypha is cited *as*

Scripture in the NT (cf. Childs 1992: 62). It is true that the question of canonicity can hardly be settled on the basis of quotation in the NT. On the one hand, some of the books of the Hebrew canon (e.g., Judges, Esther, Ecclesiastes, Song of Songs, Ezra) are not quoted in the NT, whereas two books are quoted in Jude (the *Apocalypse of Moses* in Jude 8-9 and *1 Enoch* 1:9 in Jude 14-15) which are not in the Christian canon of the OT. Nevertheless, what the NT writers appear to be doing is citing or more often alluding to parts of deuterocanonical books with which they find themselves in agreement, but without putting these books on the same level as the (Hebrew) canon of the OT.

This suggests that these books should be read and studied for the light they shed on God's ongoing history with his people down to the time of Christ, that there is much of value in them, but that, not being on the same level as the books of the Hebrew canon, it is a wise rule not to use them in support of any doctrine that cannot be substantiated elsewhere in Scripture.

This is the view that has found support all through the centuries, from Jerome and other Church Fathers, from Luther and other Reformers, from almost all early English Bibles and from the Church of England. It thus does not represent "just an expedient compromise" (Childs 1992: 66). What has prevented the Christian church from forming a consensus around this view has been the Protestant–Roman Catholic polarization that arose in the sixteenth century and drove both sides to extremes.

In fact, more recently Protestantism has shown a willingness to modify its extremism. From the 1880s on, Protestant scholars led the way in new scholarly attitudes to the Apocrypha (Niven 1953: 21). The books of the Apocrypha have been made available with several notable modern translations of the Bible: RSV, NRSV, NEB, REB, and TEV. They have also been included in a number of commentary series, including the Cambridge Bible Commentary, the *Interpreter's One Volume Commentary on the Bible,* and the Anchor Bible. These developments do not necessarily imply acceptance of the Apocrypha as canonical Scripture, but they do recognize its importance for the study of Judaism in the second and first centuries B.C. and for the understanding of the NT.

It is more difficult to see modification of extreme views on the Roman Catholic side because of the explicit ruling of the Council of Trent. Yet Roman Catholicism was divided on the issue right up to the council, with scholars of the stature of Ximénez and Cajetan favoring the Hebrew canon. Modern Roman Catholic scholars recognize the differences of opinion that prevailed and some of the difficulties surrounding the Trent decision (Turro and Brown 1968: 523). It may be that further ecumenical dialogue will produce a softening of the Roman Catholic position, with the term "deuterocanonical" being reinterpreted to designate books which, while valuable, are not on the same level as those of the Hebrew canon.

The practice adopted here is to refer to the apocryphal/deuterocanonical books especially to shed light on the period immediately prior to the Christ event. In keeping with the view of Jerome and Luther, however, they are not used to establish any aspect of BT that does not find support in the canonical Scriptures of the OT or NT. All references to books of the Apocrypha are given in *italics* so that they may be readily identified and distinguished from the fully canonical books.

D-2.7. BIBLICAL THEOLOGY IS BASED ON THE STRUCTURE OF THE CHRISTIAN CANON

The recent "paradigm shift" of interest to the final form of the canonical text has focused attention in a new way on the *structure* of the canon, and some scholars now see this as having been in some way deliberately shaped (see the survey of scholarship in Dempster 1997: 31-46). The shape or structure of the Christian canon differs from that of the Hebrew canon in two ways that are of decisive importance for BT. Firstly, and most obviously, the Christian church added the twenty-seven books of the NT to those of the OT to constitute its Bible. But it must also be noted that the structure of the Christian OT differs significantly from that of the Jewish Tanakh, as a comparison of the two canonical lists shows:

Tanakh	Old Testament (excluding Deuterocanon)
Law *(Torah)*	
Genesis	Genesis
Exodus	Exodus
Leviticus	Leviticus
Numbers	Numbers
Deuteronomy	Deuteronomy
Prophets *(Nebhi'im)*	
Former	
Joshua	Joshua
Judges	Judges
	Ruth
Samuel	1, 2 Samuel
Kings	1, 2 Kings
	1, 2 Chronicles
	Ezra, Nehemiah
	Esther
	Job
	Psalms

                                         Proverbs
                                         Ecclesiastes
                                         Song of Solomon

Latter
    Isaiah   Isaiah
    Jeremiah   Jeremiah
                                           Lamentations
    Ezekiel   Ezekiel
                                         Daniel
    Book of Twelve   Hosea through Malachi

Writings *(Kethubhim)*
    Psalms
    Job
    Proverbs
    Ruth
    Song of Songs
    Ecclesiastes
    Lamentations
    Esther
    Daniel
    Ezra-Nehemiah
    Chronicles

The Tanakh has three major divisions — Torah (usually translated "Law"), *Nebhi'im* (Prophets), and *Kethubhim* (Writings). The Torah consists of the five books of Genesis, Exodus, Leviticus, Numbers, and Deuteronomy. The Prophets are divided into the four books of the Former Prophets, i.e., the historical books of Joshua, Judges, Samuel, and Kings, and the four books of the Latter Prophets, consisting of Isaiah, Jeremiah, and Ezekiel, plus the Book of the Twelve, the minor prophets (Hosea through Malachi). The remaining books are classified by the general term "Writings."

This order of Torah–Former Prophets–Latter Prophets–Writings has its own theological significance. It accords well with the emphasis within Judaism on Torah as the supreme revelation of God; in the Hebrew canon Torah stands at the beginning and dominates what follows. The Prophets (Former and Latter) are between the Torah and the Writings. Following directly after the Torah, they tend to be interpreted with reference to it (see Dempster 1997: 191-200). The Former Prophets illustrate what happened when Israel obeyed, or more often disobeyed, the Torah. The Latter Prophets record the efforts of those spokesmen to call Israel back to obedience to the Torah and to warn of the consequences of disobedience. The emphasis lies here rather than on prophetic visions of the future.

Jewish tradition knows two main orders for the Writings. In the Talmud (Baba Bathra 14b) the books are listed in the order of Ruth, Psalms, Job, Proverbs, Ecclesiastes, Song of Songs, Lamentations, Daniel, Esther, Ezra[/ Nehemiah], and Chronicles. It is clear that this list is based on what was believed to be the chronological order of the books (cf. J. W. Miller 1994: 140). The order that eventually prevailed within the Jewish community, however, is a different one: Psalms, Job, Proverbs, Ruth, Song of Songs, Ecclesiastes, Lamentations, Esther, Daniel, Ezra-Nehemiah, Chronicles.

This order has its own theological significance. First place is given to the Psalms, which were central to Jewish worship. Their division in their final canonical shape into five books is clearly intended to mirror the five books of the Torah, and Ps 1, which introduces the collection, pointedly commends the person who delights in and meditates upon the Torah of the Lord (v. 2). Job and Proverbs are the main representatives of Wisdom (Ecclesiastes comes later in the list), which, like Torah, provides guidance for daily living. Their position after Psalms suggests that Wisdom is not to be seen as opposed to Torah, though the inclusion of Job provides a reminder of the limits of Wisdom.

Ruth through Esther constitute the five Megilloth (scrolls), each of which, whatever its original setting and purpose, came to be associated with a Jewish festival, as follows:

Ruth: Feast of Weeks (Pentecost)
Song of Songs: Passover
Ecclesiastes: Feast of Tabernacles
Lamentations: Ninth of Ab (fast commemorating destruction of Jerusalem and of the temple)
Esther: Feast of Purim

Here, therefore, the emphasis is on the worship of the Jewish community.

Daniel is de-emphasized by its position near the end of the Writings. Its location here, rather than with the Prophets, puts the emphasis not on its eschatological features but on its call to faithfulness to God's Torah.

The placing of Ezra/Nehemiah and Chronicles at the end of the Writings, and hence at the conclusion and climax of the entire canon, emphasizes the decisive significance of the postexilic restoration with the establishment of the Torah as the norm of the community's life and the reestablishment of the temple as the focus of its worship. The order Ezra/Nehemiah and then Chronicles is at first sight surprising since it reverses the chronological order (which is followed in the Christian OT canon). J. G. McConville suggests that the order serves to de-emphasize Ezra/Nehemiah, which details the problems of the postexilic community, whereas Chronicles emphasizes the rebuilding of the temple (see 1992: 48). The order may also be intended to emphasize David's instructions to the priests and Levites in 1 Chr 23–26 (cf. J. W. Miller 1994: 135). From a more literary point of view, Chronicles is well suited to round off the canon of the Tanakh. Since it goes back and begins with Adam (1 Chr 1:1), it serves to recapitulate (albeit in sketchy and selective fashion) the whole of the Jewish Scripture from Genesis onward; "it links the entire canon together: Chronicles and Genesis almost function as book-ends for the Scriptures" (Dempster 1997: 210). Since Chronicles ends with the decree of Cyrus allowing the return and the rebuilding of the temple, it brings the story down to the postexilic restoration, which is seen as the event that closes the canon.

The absence (or de-emphasis) of eschatology in the Writings is striking. The main focus is on *the ongoing life and worship of the Jewish community* with its twin foundations of Torah and temple. Looking at the shape of this canon, one can see how it points forward to rabbinic Judaism that emerged in the early centuries of the common era, with its major emphasis on the Torah as the focus of God's revelation and its concern with the ongoing life and worship of the community.

The shape of the Christian OT differs in important ways from that of the Tanakh. It is essential for BT to recognize and appreciate the theological significance of the differences (contra J. W. Miller 1994: 173-74, who wants to reorganize the order of the Christian canon). How far the order of the Christian OT is derived from the Septuagint is a matter of debate; for one thing, the different codices of the LXX vary among themselves in the order of books. Here again, the historical question is not of prime importance for BT; what counts is the theological significance of the structure of the OT as it came to be recognized and used within the Christian community. The canonical OT begins with the Pentateuch, which is followed by a sequence of historical books, longer than that encompassed by the Former Prophets of the Tanakh. The sequence runs from Joshua through to Esther, or if the apocryphal/deuterocanonical books be included, through to the books of Maccabees. The Writings come next, in the middle rather than at the end of the canon. The Prophets constitute the last major section, with Lamentations inserted after Jeremiah, and Daniel after Ezekiel.

The addition of the NT of course shifts the central focus of God's revelation away from the Torah to the Christ event witnessed to primarily in the Gospels. The whole OT is now seen as preparing for and pointing to this event. Within the OT, therefore, the Torah, which still begins the canon, is not the primary focus; it is rather the account of human origins and the beginning of salvation history. That salvation history continues unbroken from the call of Abraham through the exile (not stopping there, as in the Tanakh), and with Chronicles, Ezra, Nehemiah, and Esther on into the postexilic period; indeed, in the apocryphal/deuterocanonical literature it continues virtually down to NT times (cf. J. A. Sanders 1992: 846). The Christian canon is more interested in a continuous history of God with his people, and this is further emphasized by the insertion of the books of Ruth and Esther at the appropriate points in the chronological sequence; they are valued as part of salvation history rather than as the basis for later festivals.

Job, Psalms, Proverbs, Ecclesiastes, and the Song of Solomon form a unit sandwiched between history and prophecy. The major emphasis is on wisdom, with three of the five (Job, Proverbs, Ecclesiastes) being Wisdom Books, and the fifth (Song of Songs) ascribed to Solomon the Wise. By being placed in this context, Psalms is separated from temple worship and presented more as a source of teaching and meditation for both individuals and community.

The Prophets, on the other hand, are given greater prominence by being placed at the end of the OT and just prior to the NT. The element of promise and of future expectation becomes much more important. It should be noted that Daniel is moved into the Prophets and given a relatively important place after the three major prophets. Since the prophets, including Daniel, are repeatedly quoted in the NT, the Prophets become part of the bridge linking the two Testaments.

The NT has its own structure that developed gradually as the main sections of the canon were brought together. Early manuscripts and references in Christian writers indicate some fluidity before the final shape of the canon was established and fully accepted.

Within the NT the four Gospels have pride of place since they are the primary witnesses to the Christ event, which is the central focus of the entire Christian Bible. The most surprising structural feature here is the way Luke's Gospel was separated from what was originally a two-volume work, Luke-Acts, and placed with the other Gospels. The problem of having four different (and sometimes differing) Gospels (cf. B-1) is addressed in the matching superscriptions added to the Gospels when they were collected into a canonical unit. They are "The Gospel according to Matthew" *(kata Matthaion)*, "according to Mark," and so on. In other words, basically the Gospel is one; each of the four Evangelists witnesses to that one Gospel (cf. Gamble 1985: 35).

It is not clear exactly what determined the order of the four Gospels in the final form of the canon (other arrangements are known in the early centuries). It is most doubtful whether the books were considered originally to have been written in the canonical order; that is more likely a conclusion that was drawn after the event. There is a logic in putting Matthew first since, of the four, it is the one that stresses the fulfillment of the OT to the greatest extent. It thus serves as a hinge between OT and NT. John's position at the end may be due to the fact that it was believed to have been written last, but it is surely due primarily to the recognition that it offers the most profound interpretation of the Christ event and brings out more fully the deeper meaning of events described in the other Gospels. If historical-critical scholars tend to regard Mark as the earliest and most historically accurate of the Gospels, theologically pride of place has always been given to John, which comes last in the sequence since it represents the climax of the fourfold Gospel (cf. Morgan 1979: 385-86).

D. THE METHOD OF BIBLICAL THEOLOGY

The book of Acts, separated from its original first volume, Luke's Gospel, now serves as a bridge between Gospels and Epistles. Originally designed to follow one of the Gospels, it readily picks up some of their main themes. As a history of the first decades of the church, it provides a context for the epistles that follow. And with its emphasis on the basic agreement of Paul, Peter, John, and James (despite differences of emphasis), it serves to underline the basic unity of the apostolic message reflected in the Epistles (cf. Gamble 1985: 78-79).

Within the Epistles themselves, those of Paul are given priority, a recognition of their theological importance. An early arrangement of Paul's epistles may have consisted of a collection of letters sent to seven churches (Gamble 1985: 42). One problem that may have been felt with Paul's writings is the way most of them obviously address quite specific local situations. By bringing together letters to *seven* churches, the idea of their universal application would be emphasized, since seven can signify completeness. The Muratorian Canon (second/third century?) states that Paul, "following the example of his predecessor John, wrote only to seven churches by name. . . . For John also, although in the Apocalypse he wrote to seven churches, nevertheless speaks to all" (translation from Gamble, 94). One thinks also of the seven letters of Ignatius of Antioch written ca. 107. Philemon and the Pastoral Epistles do not fit this scheme, but they may have been thought of as written to individuals rather than churches. The order of the Pauline Epistles was probably determined by size, with the largest coming first and letters of decreasing size following.

Hebrews is placed next probably because of the tendency to ascribe it to Paul, despite considerable doubts. As the work of an accomplished theologian and thinker, it forms a good transition between Paul's epistles and the more minor ones that follow. The so-called Catholic Epistles may owe their order to the reference to James, Cephas (= Peter), and John in Gal 2:9, again an assertion of the basic underlying unity of the apostolic message despite differences of emphasis. The book of Revelation brings the NT to a logical conclusion. While there is eschatological material in both Gospels and Epistles, Revelation is *the* Apocalypse, the most obvious reminder that while the Christ event fulfills the promises and prophecies of the OT, the final consummation of all things still lies in the future. Unlike the Tanakh, therefore, the NT concludes with a strongly eschatological orientation and outlook.

When the NT is joined to the OT, a new structure comes into being in which the Christ event becomes the main focus. This event comes not at the beginning (as with the Torah in the Tanakh) but rather in the center (not literally so, of course, since the OT is much longer than the NT). The OT proclaims what God has done, in creation and in history, and points forward in promise to the dawning of a new age. The Gospels witness to the Christ event as the fulfillment of these promises, while the Acts, Epistles, and Revelation primarily look back to the Christ event, though also forward to the final consummation.

The canonical structure of the Christian Bible thus witnesses to the centrality of the Christ event in BT. It is possible that the number of books in the canon witnesses to the same conviction. It must be borne in mind that at the time of the early church there was considerable flexibility in the method of counting the number of books in the Hebrew Scriptures. The numbers quoted seem low, but this is because the Minor Prophets (Hosea through Malachi) were grouped together as one book, the Book of the Twelve. Similarly, Ruth, Song of Songs, Ecclesiastes, Lamentations, and Esther, as already noted, were grouped together as the Megilloth and could be counted as one. Certain "double books" (1/2 Samuel, 1/2 Kings, 1/2 Chronicles, Ezra/Nehemiah) could be counted as either one or two.

Josephus refers to twenty-two books of Scripture (apparently counting the Twelve, the Megilloth, Samuel and Kings each as one). Origen knew this tradition and made the link with the twenty-two letters of the Hebrew alphabet. Christensen (1993: 51-52) has observed that this number yields a symmetrical pattern for the Christian canon:

> 22 books of the Old Testament
> 5 books (Gospels plus Acts) of a new Torah
> 22 books of epistles/Revelation.

This structure highlights the Christ event (Gospels) plus the giving of the Spirit (Acts) as the new Torah, standing between the two halves of the Christian Bible. It may be added that 22 + 5 + 22 = 49, a number significant elsewhere in Scripture in connection with the calculation of the Jubilee, which comes in the fiftieth year, after $7 \times 7 = 49$ years; the last book of the canon, Revelation, is structured on this principle, with 7 sets of 7 (= 49), followed by the concluding vision of the holy city, corresponding to the final, eschatological Jubilee (see 19-4.3). Obviously this analysis of canonical structure does not take into account the apocryphal/deuterocanonical books.

D-2.8. BIBLICAL THEOLOGY IS BASED ON THE TEXT OF THE CHRISTIAN CANON

A related question concerns the *text* of the OT to be used in the study of BT. The OT was written in Hebrew (with some Aramaic in Ezra and Daniel); the writers of the NT and most early Church Fathers, however, read the OT in the Greek LXX version that frequently diverges from the Hebrew text. The Old Latin version was based on the LXX, not on the Hebrew. Jerome's Latin Vulgate was based on the Old Latin, but Jerome recognized the importance of checking with the Hebrew original and studied Hebrew in order to do this. It is ironic that the Latin Vulgate so established itself as the Bible of the Roman Catholic Church that well into the twentieth century modern translations, such as that by Msgr. Ronald Knox (1945), were made from the Vulgate rather than from the original languages! The Protestant Reformers insisted on translations from the original languages in order to ascertain the original meaning of Scripture. In more recent years the Roman Catholic Church has fully accepted this principle.

The matter is not a simple one, however, because the LXX is more than just a translation of the Hebrew OT into Greek. As noted above (D-2.6), it contains books and material not found in the Jewish (Masoretic) text. All translation involves interpretation, and production of the LXX has to be seen as part of the ongoing process of the shaping of Scripture. Moreover, recent studies have suggested that prior to A.D. 70 there existed a plurality of texts, with the LXX representing one of a number of traditions; if this is so, the Jewish (Masoretic) text is not necessarily entirely "original," nor the LXX entirely "secondary" (see Müller 1993: 197-99).

About 80 percent of the NT citations of the OT, it has been estimated, are taken directly from the LXX. Even more significant is the fact that a number of NT quotations from the OT depend on the LXX translation for their effectiveness. For example, in Acts 15:16-18 James quotes Amos 9:11-12 in the LXX version to justify a mission to the Gentiles (see 12-2.4a; 12-3.3b).

Should BT be based on the Hebrew text of the OT or on the Greek LXX? The issue is not a new one; Jerome came to regard the Hebrew as the original, inspired text, whereas Augustine saw both the original writers and the LXX translators as inspired prophets (see Müller 1993: 194-95). Until recently Jerome has found more followers than Augustine, at least in the West.

It is interesting that at least one modern translation, the Good News Bible, lists in an appendix New Testament passages quoted or paraphrased from the Septuagint (TEV 1976: 367-70), thus recognizing the importance of the LXX as a bridge between the Hebrew OT and the Greek NT.

Once again a decision must take account of the theological factors involved. A historical-critical approach demands that the OT be translated and studied on the basis of the original Hebrew text. Yet it must also be recognized that the formation of the LXX was part of the ongoing process of preparation for the Christ event. The overwhelming use of the LXX by the writers of the NT and their dependence on the wording of the LXX in a fair number of their citations clearly indicate this. BT therefore should carefully note the Septuagint version where its citation makes a significant difference. It is not to be disregarded or set aside as an aberration or later development, but recognized as part of the scriptural tradition that the NT acknowledges as forming the preparation for the coming of Christ.

D-2.9. BIBLICAL THEOLOGY IS BASED PRIMARILY ON THE FINAL CANONICAL FORM OF THE TEXT

We have already noted the problems raised for BT by historical criticism, especially insofar as it has sought to penetrate behind the canonical text and reconstruct the "original" text or the sometimes long and complex process through which the present text evolved (see C-1.1). The longer and more complex the process (especially in the OT), the more hypothetical such reconstructions become. A more promising method is suggested by the "canonical approach" of B. S. Childs (C-2.2), and by some of the newer literary approaches (C-2.1) which hold that BT should focus primarily on the final canonical text of Scripture, i.e., the text in the form in which it was accepted as canonical by the Christian church.

The word "primarily" is important here. There is no intention of denigrating the historical-critical approach as such, though its methodology needs to be kept under critical review and its limitations recognized. As a "bridge discipline," however, BT presupposes and builds upon the historical-critical approach to Scripture. It is important to study each book of the Bible and each author in their own historical context insofar as this can be reconstructed. It is important to listen to the distinctive voice of each book and author. But BT does not stop there because the community of faith did not stop there. It brought the Hebrew Scriptures together, then it added the NT to them, thus placing each individual book in a new context, the total canonical context of the Bible. And it is this canonical context that was recognized by the church as constituting its Holy Scripture.

There may be value in source criticism of the Pentateuch or of the Gospels, though what such study produces are theories of how these works came into existence, theories that are constantly subject to challenge and review. It is important to remember, however, that the church did not canonize J, E, D, or P, nor did it canonize Q or Proto-Luke; what it accepted was the Pentateuch and the Gospels in their final form, and it is these that constitute the true subject matter of BT.

For example, as noted above (C-1.1), the final verses of the book of Amos (9:8c-15) are frequently characterized by historical-critical scholars as a later, postexilic addition to the book, the implication being that they are therefore to be disregarded in any study of Amos. Like most historical-critical judgments, of course, this view can be challenged, and in fact has been called in question by von Rad (1965: 138). But even if we grant that the "Appendix of Hope" is a later addition, the really significant thing is that *the book of Amos was not accepted as Scripture without this passage.* Perhaps the original Amos did deliver a message of judgment only without any reference to God's mercy and without any hope for the future. If this be so, the book was not deemed acceptable by the later community in that form, but only with the addition of the appendix which ensured that God's judgment and God's mercy were held in balance, as is the case in the major prophets that followed. As C. J. Scalise (1996) points out, the book of Amos "has been canonically shaped so that the messages of judgment of the historical Amos are not allowed to stand alone. . . . Inspired by God, the biblical authors and editors give us an Amos who proclaimed both God's judgment and God's mercy" (57). This does not take away from the strong note of judgment in the book that should be studied against the historical background of Israelite society in the reign of Jeroboam II, but the appendix should also be studied as part of the book and as a reminder that according to Scripture as a whole, judgment is never God's last word.

Similarly, BT will deal with John's Gospel in the present form of the text, not on the basis of hypothetical sources and redactors. We have noted (C-1.1) the influential view of Bultmann that the "original" Gospel of John had a totally realized eschatology, and that the references to the parousia in the Gospel are to be assigned to a later "ecclesiastical redactor." For Bultmann it is the reconstructed original that is the subject matter of NT theology or at least of Johannine theology. Such an "ecclesiastical redactor" is of course a purely hypothetical figure, who may or may not have ever existed. But here again, even if we concede the existence of such a redactor, the really significant thing for BT is the fact that *John's Gospel was not accepted as canonical without the references to the parousia.* Bultmann's view seeks to maximize the differences among the books of the NT: John's eschatology is totally different from Mark's, the implication being that they cannot possibly be integrated into one NT theology or one BT. But John, it may be claimed, has as many references to the parousia as Mark (cf. 14:3, 18-20, 28; 16:16, 22). Without denying many differences of style, approach, and emphasis, the fact remains that *the NT in its canonical form* is basically united in presenting an inaugurated eschatology that sees the Christ event as decisive yet also looks to the future for the final consummation.

Historical criticism has tended to look at each book of the Bible, or at least each author, *separately,* and hence to emphasize their differences. But BT deals with the writings accepted as divinely inspired and normative by the Christian church, i.e., with the Scriptures of the OT and NT *as a canonical whole.* Noting the role of historical criticism in theological education, A. Wainwright (1982) says of prospective ministers: "They are trained in the techniques which scholars have used to investigate the Scriptures. They are encouraged to take apart the sacred writings, as though they were amputating the limbs of a body. Unfortunately, when they set themselves to the task of making the Scriptures relevant for today, many of them are unable to put the pieces together again" (1). In a canonical BT the biblical texts "must be approached in a somewhat different way than is proper to their study as sources of Christian tradition. First, they must be taken together, rather than taken apart" (C. M. Wood 1981: 91). This means that the individual books and authors are to be studied not only in their original historical contexts, but also in the context of canonical Scripture as a whole. This does affect the way books are interpreted; the canonical Bible is more than the sum of the sixty-six books that it contains. The OT is read in the light of the NT, and vice versa. Each book is read in the light of the canonical whole, and "context influences understanding of text" (J. A. Sanders 1992: 843).

At least two criticisms have been leveled against this procedure. One is that it results in all books being regarded as equal in value. Thus Gamble (1985) objects that with this approach, "within the canon 2 Peter and Romans appear to have the same standing" (75). But this is not necessarily true. Romans stands at the head of the first and largest block of epistles in the NT; for BT it is obviously more important than a short letter that comes near the end of the minor epistles. OT and NT are alike the subject of BT, but are not necessarily of equal value; BT deals, e.g., with the inner dynamic of promise and fulfillment, and may recognize some kind of progressive revelation within Scripture.

Another criticism is that canonical BT obliterates the message of the individual books and authors. But this need not be the case; BT can recognize diversity as well as unity in Scripture. "A canonical reading will distinguish, but not separate, Old Testament from New, Torah from prophets, gospel from apostle" (C. M. Wood 1981: 91).

D-2.10. BIBLICAL THEOLOGY WILL REJECT A "CANON WITHIN THE CANON"

From an early period there have been those who have sought to interpret the Bible selectively, highlighting those parts most congenial to them while relegating to an inferior position (or even eliminating altogether) those portions that do not accord with their own theological presuppositions. In other words, from the broader canon of Scripture they select their own "canon within the canon." One attraction of such an approach is that it provides a way of dealing with the diversity of Scripture and of producing a more unified interpretation.

We have already noted how Marcion, as early as the mid–second century, produced his own canon consisting of Luke's Gospel (in a revised form) and ten letters of Paul. This canon was certainly more compact and more consistent than the one eventually recognized by the church, but it is highly significant that the church decisively rejected such a drastic "canon within the canon" and opted for a much more broadly based selection incorporating a considerably greater variety than Marcion was prepared to allow.

Luther may be said to have produced his own "canon within the canon" through his identification of those NT books that "show Christ," i.e., those that are consistent with his hermeneutical principle of "justification by faith." Here again, unity is purchased at a price — the devaluing of the canonical status of books such as Hebrews, James, Jude, and Revelation. It is not difficult to catch echoes of this in Bultmann's emphasis in his *Theology of the New Testament* on

Paul and John to the virtual exclusion of other books and authors (cf. Scobie 1991a: 56-57).

Liberal theologians produced a quite different "canon within the canon" by taking the teaching of the (rediscovered and reconstructed) historical Jesus as their hermeneutical key, and correspondingly devaluing Paul and the later books of the NT that were seen as representing a progressive "theologizing" and "Hellenizing" of the simple message of Jesus.

Against all such tendencies those engaged in canonical BT must make every effort to do justice to the biblical material in its totality. This is not to say that every part of Scripture is of equal value, or that the inner dynamics of the biblical material are to be disregarded. But the temptation to find a shortcut through the selection of a "canon within the canon" must be resisted. As P. D. Hanson (1982) puts it, "we are pleading for an openness to the total address of Scripture, lest we select only what reinforces our present views and exclude the possibility of growth" (4).

D-3. A COOPERATIVE BIBLICAL THEOLOGY

A major problem in recent years has been an ever increasing degree of specialization. Biblical scholars, theologians, and ethicists, for example, regard their disciplines as quite separate fields and seldom dialogue with one another. Even within these disciplines it is generally felt that no one can possibly master the whole field so that each scholar must concentrate on a very limited area. But if BT is to be truly a bridge discipline, then it has to find a way of breaking out of this unhealthy pattern of overspecialization and opening up lines of communication between the different theological disciplines. The very idea of a BT, as B. F. Meyer (1989) has affirmed, "supposes a powerful collaborative effort of scholarship" (208). An intermediate BT in other words must also be a cooperative BT.

D-3.1. OLD TESTAMENT AND NEW TESTAMENT

A truly "biblical" theology must bridge the gap that has built up between OT and NT studies, and must find ways of surmounting the view that sees these, in practice at least, as entirely separate disciplines each going its own way. In his influential article "The Meaning of 'Biblical Theology,'" G. Ebeling (1963: 96) envisaged BT as demanding the intensive cooperation of OT and NT scholars (cf. Scobie 1992a: 63-64). The cooperation between H. Gese and P. Stuhlmacher provides a good example of how an OT and NT scholar can stimulate and inform one another's work, but unfortunately such cooperation is very much the exception.

The increasingly specialized nature of biblical studies has produced a deep chasm between OT and NT studies. It is assumed that an individual must belong either to one scholarly guild or the other but never to both. The two communities are not necessarily hostile to each other, but they tend to exist in splendid isolation (cf. the discussion in F. Watson 1997: 5). Specialization of course has its place, but there must be room also for scholars who are prepared to attempt to survey and synthesize the results of both OT and NT studies. Only where this is the case will a true BT become possible. It is interesting to note that the most recent attempts to revive the writing of a "biblical theology" (above, C.4.3) have generally been undertaken by OT scholars who are also professing Christians (see Scobie 1992a: 63).

D-3.2. BIBLICAL STUDIES AND THEOLOGY

Another form of cooperation must be between biblical studies and theology. Here again overspecialization has not encouraged much dialogue between biblical scholars and dogmatic theologians. The common view that BT is descriptive but not prescriptive has led to the paradoxical situation where "theological" concerns are in effect excluded from BT (cf. F. Watson 1997: 2-4)! But if BT is to be a bridge discipline linking historically oriented biblical studies on the one hand and dogmatic theology and related fields on the other, then the bridge has to be constructed in such a way that it will carry heavy traffic, and traffic moving in both directions. As D. Jodock (1990) has said, "The relationship between theological reflection and the Scriptures ought to be understood as reciprocal. The Bible raises questions about contemporary theology, and theology raises questions about the Bible. Scriptural study contributes insights to theological reflection, and theological reflection may illumine scriptural study" (378).

One encouraging sign was the launching by SPCK in 1987 of a new series, Biblical Foundations in Theology, consisting of volumes coauthored by scholars in the fields of biblical studies and systematic theology (see the inaugural volume, Dunn and Mackay 1987). B. S. Childs has shown in his *Biblical Theology of the Old and New Testaments* how biblical theological reflection can be carried through to the point of dialogue with contemporary theology.

D-3.3. AN ECUMENICAL APPROACH

Of great importance also is cooperation among biblical scholars of different denominational and confessional backgrounds (cf. P. S. Watson 1962: 200). BT presents a continuing challenge to scholars to encompass the full range of the biblical revelation unencumbered by the blinkers of their own particular tradition. One recalls the saying that Protestantism is the religion of Paul, Roman Catholicism of Peter, and Orthodoxy of John. The truth behind this sweeping generalization is that the study of BT is so easily limited by the partial perspectives that scholars of differing Christian traditions bring to their tasks. Shortly after the summoning of the Second Vatican Council, F. J. Leenhardt published a fascinating study in which he contended that Protestantism and Roman Catholicism derive not so much from the usually assigned patron saints of Paul and Peter, but rather from "two styles of piety, two spiritualities, two mentalities" that can be traced back to Abraham and Moses respectively (1964: 61). His point is that both these spiritualities are found in Scripture. "Biblical faith, taken in its unity and integrity, incorporates these two universes and in the crucible of living experience unites them the one to the other, brings them into solidarity with each other, balances them and corrects them, the one by the other, holding them in a dialectic which is at times dramatic" (74). What is being suggested here is that scholars of different Christian traditions can help one another see more of the fullness of biblical truth.

One of the most significant developments of the twentieth century was the changed attitude of the Roman Catholic Church toward the study of Scripture that permitted Roman Catholics to enter the mainstream of biblical scholarship (cf. B-8). Equally important have been changing attitudes on the part of conservative evangelicals that resulted in a rising standard of scholarly competence and a willingness to enter into dialogue with mainline biblical scholarship. Less numerous but nonetheless welcome are contributions from the Eastern Orthodox tradition; these are available to English-speaking readers, especially through the publications of St. Vladimir's Seminary Press (see esp. Cronk 1982).

"The time is ripe," S. Terrien (1981) has contended, "for an ecumenical theology of the Bible. In Holy Scripture is found the only ground common to all the families of Christendom for the stimulus and control of theological thinking" (125). This in no way implies a desire to bring about institutional amalgamation through some kind of compromise whereby each branch of the church is required to give up some of its distinctive emphases. We are talking rather about the world of biblical scholarship and the willingness of scholars of differing traditions to work together and to listen to each other, so that together they can listen to the word of God in Scripture. In all such cooperation it is that word of God that must always remain the goal and the norm. It is in this kind of ecumenical spirit that the present work is undertaken, drawing on the studies of scholars of many nationalities and of varying Christian traditions, and with them seeking to grasp the biblical tradition in all its richness and fullness.

Cooperation between OT and NT scholars, between biblical scholars and theologians, and among scholars of different Christian traditions can be carried out in many ways — through journals and books, through meetings of societies and conferences, through personal meetings and correspondence. A final question is whether the actual writing of BT, especially the attempt to write "a biblical theology," can be carried out as a cooperative effort. G. Ebeling seems to suggest such a joint enterprise (1963: 96). Against such a view it may be observed that few major works have been produced by a committee. A. W. Walker-Jones (1989) has pointed out that biblical theologians need to "make an imaginative, synoptic theological judgment" (92). Though BT must build upon the work of countless scholars, at the end of the day an individual is required with the courage (some might say, the temerity) and the imagination to attempt the necessary synthesis, daunting as that task may be (cf. Scobie 1992a: 64-65).

D-4. A STRUCTURED BIBLICAL THEOLOGY

Is BT an activity or a literary genre? Is it a dimension of exegesis, is it part of the study of individual biblical books or themes, or can it and should it be embodied in volumes that bear the title "biblical theology"?

The first of these alternatives does not lack proponents. B. C. Ollenburger (1985) sees BT "more as an activity (helping the church to engage in critical reflection on its praxis through a self-critical reading of its canonical text) rather than as a genre of literature" (51). W. Vogels, who advocates BT "in an existential perspective," contends that "such a theology will be less concerned to make a synthesis and will try rather to answer concrete questions posed by life" (1998: 128).

Certainly the exegesis of a text can be part of BT provided the text in question is read not just in the context of the book in which it appears but also in a total biblical context. The *Believers Bible Commentary,* for example, has pointed the way here; after an exegetical study of each block of text there follow sections entitled "The Text in Biblical Context" and "The Text in the Life of the Church." Studies of individual books of the Bible or of biblical authors (the Deuteronomist, Second Isaiah, Paul, John, and so on) are often regarded as studies in "biblical theology" (cf. J. Barr 1999: 140-45). Such studies are not really "biblical" unless the study of the book or author concerned is related to the total biblical context; in practice this is rarely the case. Studies of particular themes or topics through both OT and NT (cf. C-4.2) are much more obviously a form of BT.

The question has to be raised, however, as to whether BT can remain content with such a fragmented approach, or whether all such studies of individual texts, books, or themes do not imply, implicitly if not explicitly, a broader framework or structure of some kind for understanding the canonical material as a whole. If BT is truly to be a bridge discipline, mediating the results of specialized biblical studies to the Christian community that recognizes the Bible as normative for its faith and life, then surely it must provide some kind of overall structure for understanding the complex and diverse mass of biblical material (contra J. Barr 1999: 52, who questions the value of comprehensive "OT theologies" or "biblical theologies," and who holds that "it should not be taken as axiomatic that the production of such works is the only way, or the best way, in which biblical theology can be pursued. The production of large and comprehensive volumes of this kind is not necessarily the highest goal within the discipline"). Academic scholars may be content with specialized studies ("knowing more and more about less and less"), but the believing community today, as always, shares the wish expressed by the English poet George Herbert in his sonnet "The Holy Scriptures":

> Oh that I knew how all thy lights combine,
> And the configuration of their glorie!
> Seeing not onely how each verse doth shine,
> But all the constellation of the storie.

In the period of "integrated biblical theology," the church did seek in various ways to achieve an overall understanding of the biblical revelation and to comprehend how the parts related to the whole. Of course, we may not be able today to subscribe to all the methods adopted in that period for finding a broad and underlying unity amidst all the diversity of Scripture. As we have seen (B-5), the period of "independent biblical theology" began with the writing of "biblical theologies," but as a genre these died out as the canonical context became lost and BT was interpreted as a purely historical and descriptive discipline.

The question that arises in the light of recent developments is whether the broader framework or structure essential for a full understanding of individual biblical passages, books, and themes could be provided by the writing of a new kind of BT.

The production of such a BT is indeed a daunting task, yet it can be argued that it is in fact the greatest single challenge facing biblical scholarship at the present time. Today, as for the last 150 years, the very possibility of a BT continues to be called in question by a large number of academic biblical scholars. For many the whole concept of BT is dead; but for others there are hopeful signs that in true biblical fashion it will rise again.

E. The Structure of Biblical Theology

Everyone who attempts the writing of a BT (or an OT or NT theology for that matter) must adopt a structure of some kind. This is much more than simply a question of the order of chapters in a book, or of suitable titles for these chapters; it goes to the very heart of the understanding of the nature of BT. Since a canonical BT seeks to understand the final text of the Bible as a unified whole, an essential part of this enterprise is the discerning of the basic *patterns* inherent in Scripture. "Canonical hermeneutics maintains that the process of recognizing and describing the patterns we find in the Bible is at the heart of understanding the Bible's authority in a deeper way than that afforded by the historical reconstruction of critical scholarship" (C. J. Scalise 1996: 87).

The danger to be avoided at all costs is that of imposing an alien pattern upon the biblical material; so far as is humanly possible, the structure employed should be the one that arises out of the biblical material itself.

E-1. ALTERNATIVE APPROACHES

A survey of approaches that have been adopted in the past will provide some guidance and some necessary cautions as well. It is helpful to distinguish what may be termed the "systematic," the "historical," and the "thematic" approaches, provided it is recognized that these are only general classifications; particular theologies may not always fall clearly into one or another of the categories, and certainly there are hybrid types (cf. the "Typology of Old Testament Theologies" in J. Barr 1999: 27-51).

E-1.1. THE SYSTEMATIC APPROACH

The earliest attempts to develop an independent BT were strongly influenced by the practice of Protestant orthodoxy in compiling collections of biblical proof texts or *collegia biblica* (cf. B-3). The standard practice was to arrange such texts under the principal topics or subjects *(loci communes)* dealt with in Protestant dogmatic theology. Particularly influential was the *Loci communes rerum theologicarum* (1st ed., 1521) of the reformer Philipp Melanchthon. His arrangement was partly derived from the Epistle to the Romans but was also indebted to the *Sentences* of the twelfth-century theologian Peter Lombard. The resulting scheme covered the following twenty-five subjects: God, one, triune, creation, man, man's powers, sin, fruits of sin, vices, punishment, law, promises, restoration by Christ, grace, fruits of grace, faith, hope, charity, predestination, sacraments, human orders, magistrates, bishops, condemnation, blessedness (as listed in Hayes and Prussner 1984: 16-17; see 15-19). The various *collegia biblica* produced during the seventeenth and eighteenth centuries generally followed this type of outline, with the significant addition of an opening section on Holy Scripture.

As independent BTs began to be written within Pietism and especially by rationalist scholars (cf. B-5), this traditional systematic structure was at first followed; a good example is the BT of C. F. von Ammon published in 1792. The adoption of historical-critical methods quickly gave rise to a historical approach to structure, but the systematic scheme was not entirely abandoned. Thus the BT of L. F. O. Baumgarten-Crusius (1828) combined a historical approach with a discussion of biblical concepts under the simplified systematic headings of God, man, and salvation; and a notable BT from later in the nineteenth century which retains the systematic scheme is that of H. G. A. Ewald (1871-76). In the twentieth century M. Burrows returned to this traditional scheme; despite his claim that "the outline of topics has been derived, so far as possible, from the Bible itself," his *Outline of Biblical Theology* (1946a) is clearly based on the traditional systematic categories. The ten chapters of theological reflection on the Christian Bible in B. S. Childs's *Biblical Theology of the Old and New Testaments* (1992) largely reflect the main traditional theological categories; in fact, one of the disappointments of Childs's work is his failure to tackle the key question of the appropriate *structure* for BT (cf. J. Barr 1999: 395).

With the development of OT theology as a separate discipline in the nineteenth century, the historical approach tended to dominate, though the historical and systematic approaches were combined in various ways by conservative or moderately conservative scholars such as H. A. C. Hävernick (1848), E. A. H. H. Schultz (1896), E. K. A. Riehm (1889), and C. F. A. Dillmann (1895). The English OT theology by A. B. Davidson (1904) follows a scheme of God, man, sin, redemption, and the last things (see Scobie 1991b: 167). The revival of OT theology from the 1930s onward saw a return to a systematic structure by some scholars such as L. Köhler (1935), O. J. Baab (1949), and P. van Imschoot (1954), as well as the Roman Catholic P. Heinisch (1940). E. Jacob (1958) attempted to break new ground, but his work is still largely dominated by the traditional systematic categories.

Nineteenth-century NT theologies were largely historical in structure, but the twentieth century saw a return to a systematic approach by such scholars as F. C. Grant (1950), A. Richardson (1958), and K. H. Schelkle (1971-78). A good example of a hybrid form is provided by D. Guthrie's *New Testament Theology* (1981). After weighing the pros and cons of systematic and historical approaches, Guthrie opts for the systematic for his basic structure and has major sections on God, man, Christology, the mission of Christ, the Holy Spirit, the Christian life, the church, the future, ethics, and Scripture. Not only in each major section, however, but also in each subsection the approach is historical with separate discussion (where appropriate) of the treatment of the topic in the Synoptics, the Johannine literature, Acts, Paul, Hebrews, other epistles, and Revelation.

It is clear that the systematic approach still has its defenders. In its favor it can be argued that while the system is derived from dogmatic theology, dogmatic theology largely derived it from the biblical material in the first place; that it is a natural outline corresponding to the basic questions concerning human life that arise in every age; and that it is a simple and logical scheme that is as good as any (cf. Dentan 1963: 119-20; D. Guthrie 1981: 73). Against this, however, is the objection that a systematic scheme tends to impose categories that are alien to biblical thought. "We must avoid all schemes," declares Eichrodt (1961), "which derive from Christian dogmatics — such, for example, as 'Theology-Anthropology-Soteriology,' '*ordo salutis*,' and so on. Instead we must plot our course as best we can along the lines of the Old Testament's own dialectic" (33). Similarly, a dogmatic structure is rejected by S. Terrien (1978): "It is now recognized," he asserts, "that such attempts, inherited in part from Platonic conceptual thinking and Aristotelian logic, were bound to translate the *sui generis* thrust of biblical faith into the alien idiom of didactic exposition" (34). While some traditional categories may correspond to important biblical themes, a major charge against the systematic approach is that it fails to include other themes (e.g., "the Land," which plays a significant role in OT theology and bears a capital *L* in this book to differentiate the land of Canaan or Palestine from other land mentioned in the Bible) and does not adequately accommodate significant dimensions of biblical thought, such as "Wisdom," that have been recognized in much recent work as of major importance (cf. Scobie 1984b). Those who adopt the traditional categories of systematic theology, claims Hasel (1982), "can succeed only by a *tour de force* if they seek to encompass the whole of biblical truth. The Bible does not order its material and its theology in such a way" (78).

E-1.2. THE HISTORICAL APPROACH

The advance of the historical-critical approach to the Bible in the late eighteenth and early nineteenth centuries led not only to the splitting of BT into OT and NT theology (cf. B-6), but also to the widespread adoption of a quite different method of ordering the material. The Bible began to look less and less like a textbook of systematic theology and more and more like a history book. The only order it contains, it was argued, is the historical and chronological order in which God's people (Israel and the early church) received the divine revelation and committed it to writing in the various books. It is this historical order therefore that should be followed by the biblical theologian in the presentation of the material. Such an order can be clearly seen in the BTs of W. M. L. De Wette (1813) and D. G. C. von Cölln (1836).

The separate OT and NT theologies that came to dominate the field in the nineteenth century and continued in the twentieth were mostly historical in structure. That structure tended to change with the development of historical-critical studies. Thus, for example, when as a result of Pentateuchal source criticism Gen 1 was no longer assigned to Moses but to the Priestly writer, the last of the four main sources, it came to be treated much later in the scheme. In other words, studies of OT theology came to be based not on the historical order of Jewish and Christian tradition, but on an order that was the product of scholarly reconstruction.

A similar development took place within NT theologies. The moderately conservative *New Testament Theology* of W. Beyschlag (1891) still contained a chapter entitled "Views of the First Apostles" that used not only Acts but also James and 1 Peter. As critical opinion changed, however, books like James and 1 Peter tended to be relegated to very late and very minor positions in the tables of contents. One extreme of skepticism is reached in R. Bultmann's New Testament theology (1952; 1955), which does not deal directly with Jesus at all, listing "The Message of Jesus" as a "presupposition" of NT theology. Those theologies that accept the results of more radical scholarship tend to devalue the Lucan writings, the Pastorals, the minor epistles, and Revelation. Where this is combined with skepticism about the historical Jesus, the result is an overwhelming concentration on Paul and John that may be more congenial to those of a Lutheran background but can hardly be claimed as the basis of a balanced theology of "the New Testament." In striking contrast is the historical outline of P. Stuhlmacher's *Biblische Theologie des Neuen Testaments* (1992, 1999), which begins with a major discussion of the proclamation of Jesus viewed as the foundation of NT theology; only then does he go on to discuss the proclamation of the early church, of Paul, and of the other NT witnesses.

Another approach that might be claimed as a subcategory of the historical is found in those theologies that deal with books or sections of the OT and NT more or less in the canonical order. W. E. Ward (1977) has argued that "the *structure*, or principle of *organization*, for a biblical theology should be determined by the literary units within the Old and New Testament canons" (383-84). Examples of BTs constructed on this principle are S. Terrien's *The Elusive Presence* (in the OT section at least) and G. Vos's *Biblical Theology* (though the scheme is incomplete). An OT example is G. F. Oehler's *Theology of the Old Testament* (1873), while for the NT G. E. Ladd's *Theology of the New Testament* (1993) adheres strictly to the canonical order. J. Høgenhaven proposes a structure for OT theology based on canonical units, but heads them in an unusual order: "Wisdom," "Psalmic Literature," "Narrative Literature," "Law," and "Prophecy" (1988: 111-12). Obviously, in terms of modern critical opinion, such schemes are historical only in part.

Many of these "historical" theologies are really hybrid types, since within the treatment of books, periods, or authors a systematic order of some kind is often followed. The NT theology of W. Beyschlag (1891), for example, discusses Paul under the headings of "Flesh and Spirit," "Adam and Christ," "God and World," "The Establishment of Salvation," "The Way of Salvation," "The Life in the Spirit," "The Christian Church," and "The Consummation of the Kingdom"; whereas Bultmann's section on Paul reveals his strongly anthropological approach with its two major divisions, "Man Prior to the Revelation of Faith" and "Man under Faith." Similarly, the discussion of Pauline theology in P. Stuhlmacher (1992) follows thematic subheadings. The strength of the historical approach is that it does justice to the diversity of Scripture and demonstrates the development of biblical thought. It is more suited, however, to the history of religions approach with which it is often closely connected. We have argued that a book-by-book, historical approach has its place and indeed is a presupposition of BT. But a true BT seeks to go beyond a merely historical approach and to offer an understanding of the biblical material seen as a canonical whole. Something more is needed to bridge the gap between historical-critical studies and the needs of the Christian community that seeks to find in Scripture the norm for its faith and life.

E-1.3. THE THEMATIC APPROACH

A thematic approach to BT seeks to structure its treatment around themes or topics that arise from the biblical material itself. Thus J. L. McKenzie (1974) contends that OT theology should be based on "those themes which occur most frequently and which appear to be decisive in giving Old Testament belief its distinctive identity" (24-25). In some cases there may be no hard-and-fast line separating the systematic and thematic approaches; what they have in common is the search for some form of synchronic rather than diachronic structure.

The thematic approach is in general a relatively modern one, though it should be noted that recognition of "covenant" as a key theme of BT has deep roots in the Reformed tradition, especially in the thought of Johannes Cocceius (1603-69) (see B-3). From the time of De Wette onward, certain biblical theologians sought some central organizing principle for their work. The development of the thematic approach took a new turn, however, with the publication of W. Eichrodt's impressive *Theology of the Old Testament* (1961; 1967; cf. B-8), in which he sought to present a "cross section" *(Querschnitt)* of OT thought. Rejecting both the systematic and historical options, Eichrodt took the concept of covenant as his organizing principle and arranged the main themes of the OT under the three major headings of "God and Nation," "God and World," and "God and Men." Illuminating though Eichrodt's work is, the fact remains that his structure is not altogether successful. As recent research has further underlined, "covenant" is not an all-pervasive theme in the OT, and parts of the outline are linked with it in an artificial way.

Eichrodt's work sparked a long debate, particularly among German scholars, on an appropriate "center" or "focal point" *(Mitte, Zentrum, Mittelpunkt)* for OT theology (Hasel 1991: chap. 4; D. L. Baker 1976: 377-86; Hayes and Prussner 1984: 257-60; Reventlow 1985: 125-33), in the course of which numerous suggestions have been made for a more appropriate center. For example, W. C. Kaiser takes "the promise" as an organizing principle of his *Toward an Old Testament Theology* (1978). On the other side of the argument, von Rad (1965) declared flatly that the OT "has no focal-point *(Mitte)* such as is found in the New" (362).

There has also been discussion of a "center" of the NT, often in conjunction with the question of its unity (cf. Hasel 1978: chap. 3). Many have found the center in the Christ event or in Christology, or else, in the tradition of Luther, in the concept of "justification." P. Stuhlmacher has argued that "the gospel of reconciliation" must be the center of a BT of the NT (1979: 161-90). Others have been much more skeptical about finding any center in the diverse "theologies" of the NT (cf. Best 1993: 112).

If finding one central theme for the OT and for the NT poses difficulties, this is even more the case in relation to one theme that could serve as an organizing principle for a BT that embraces both Testaments. Yet suggestions have not been lacking, one of the most common being the theme of "the kingdom of God" (see, e.g., Goldsworthy 1981). While the kingdom of God is a dominant theme in the Synoptics, the actual phrase does not occur in the OT and plays very little role in the rest of the NT; it could be argued, however, that a more general expression such as "the rule of God," "the reign of God," or "the sovereignty of God" does identify one of the major themes of the Bible.

"Covenant" has been suggested as a central theme for both Testaments (Most 1967; Fensham 1971), but covenant is even less a pervasive theme in the NT than it is in the Old. S. Terrien's *The Elusive Presence* (1978) takes as its controlling theme "the presence of God." The concept of the history of redemption or salvation history worked out in the nineteenth century by J. C. K. von Hoffman and the Erlangen School has more recently been seen as the unifying theme of BT by such scholars as G. von Rad, O. Cullmann, L. Goppelt, and G. E. Ladd. In one of the few specific proposals that have emerged from recent German discussion of the possibility of an "all-biblical theology," H. Klein has sketched out a scheme which would discuss the Old Testament under the rubric of "life" and the New under that of "new life" (see Scobie 1991b: 177-78).

It is difficult to understand the obsession with finding one single theme or "center" for OT or NT theology, and more so for an entire BT. It is widely held today that the quest for a single center has failed. Yet the debate has not been unfruitful; what it has clearly demonstrated is that there is not one but rather a number of major themes, along with more numerous minor ones, that pervade the biblical material (cf. J. Barr 1999: 343, who concedes that "whether writers of Theologies define a 'centre' or not, they will very likely have to work with some idea of one (or more?), as a simple necessity for the organization of their work"). An approach that recognizes several themes would appear to be more productive, and this seems to be the trend in a number of more recent OT theologies, including those of J. L. McKenzie (1974), W. Zimmerli (1978), W. A. Dyrness (1979), and C. Westermann (1982). E. A. Martens's *God's Design: A Focus on Old Testament Theology* (1981), on the basis of Exod 5:22–6:8, identifies four interrelated key themes: salvation/deliverance, the covenant community, knowledge/experience of God, and Land, and traces these through the OT, and suggests in a limited way how they may also be traced in the NT. While this scheme is not without its problems (cf. Scobie 1991b: 179-80), it is moving in the right direction. W. Dumbrell's *The End of the Beginning: Rev 21–22 and the Old Testament* (1985) traces through Scripture five themes that appear in Rev 21–22: the new Jerusalem, the new temple, the new covenant, the new Israel, and the new creation. Though not a fully fledged BT, this work well demonstrates the possibilities of a multithematic approach.

The above survey reveals the problems and the pitfalls of constructing a suitable structure for a BT particularly when, as here, we are concerned with a theology encompassing the totality of canonical Scripture. A systematic approach, based on categories imported from dogmatic theology, is to be rejected as tending to a certain degree to distort biblical thought, and as failing to deal adequately with all aspects of the biblical material. A historical approach tracing the development of biblical thought period by period or book by book is of course valuable, but it belongs rather to the kind of historical study of the Bible that is presupposed by, rather than part of, an "intermediate BT." The most satisfactory approach is clearly the thematic one that seeks to construct an outline based as closely as possible on themes that arise from within the Bible itself. Within this option, it is the multithematic approach that holds most promise. From a practical viewpoint, it is desirable to identify a limited number of major biblical themes, around which related minor themes could be grouped. In fact, when the numerous suggestions for a single "center" are examined, many similarities are to be observed, and the suggestions tend to fall into four major groupings. This is the basis for the multithematic approach that will be outlined below.

E-2. THE RELATIONSHIP BETWEEN
OLD AND NEW TESTAMENTS

It is of the essence of the approach proposed here that the key themes be traced through both OT and NT. The church rejected the solution of Marcion (cf. B-1) and recognized that it is the OT and the NT that together form the canon of Christian Scripture; therefore it is the two Testaments together that constitute the subject matter of BT. The Christian canon, as B. S. Childs (1986) points out, "maintains the integrity of the Old Testament in its own right as scripture of the church. However, it sets it within a new canonical context in a dialectical relation with the New Testament. In my judgment, the task of biblical theology is to explore the relation between these two witnesses" (9). The problem of the relationship between the Testaments has concerned the church from the very beginning. Over the centuries, and not least in modern times, it has generated a vast literature.

Since the majority of so-called biblical theologies have been in fact either OT or NT theologies, they generally do not offer much help in constructing a structure appropriate to a true BT. Many NT theologies tend to regard the OT simply as "background" (in fact, one background among others) to NT thought. OT theologies have on the whole shown more interest in the link between the Testaments, and a number (e.g., Vriezen 1970; von Rad 1962; 1965; Kaiser 1978; Westermann 1982) have included important discussions of the subject. The relatively few truly "biblical" theologies have of course had to deal much more directly with the issue.

It is impossible adequately to summarize the numerous solutions to this problem that have been proposed. Helpful surveys will be found in works by D. L. Baker (1976) and G. F. Hasel (1978: chap. 5), both of which provide typologies of the various theories of relationships between the Testaments that have been proposed (cf. also Reventlow 1986: chap. 2; Goldingay 1981: chap. 4).

While it may be argued that in the past there have been forms of Christianity in which the OT has been allowed to dominate the NT, there is likely to be very little support today for those approaches that Hasel characterizes as "under-emphasis of New Testament — over-emphasis of Old Testament," or Baker as "'Old Testament' solutions," as exemplified for example in K. H. Miskotte's *When the Gods Are Silent* (1967) or A. A. van Ruler's *The Christian Church and the Old Testament* (1971). There is a long history of support, however, for the opposite view, "over-emphasis of New Testament — under-emphasis of Old Testament" (Hasel) and "'New Testament' solutions" (Baker). In the present situation it is more essential than ever to avoid solutions and structures that devalue the OT, portraying it as merely a quarry of messianic proof texts, or as characterized by "law" in contrast to the New Testament, which is "gospel," or as a "history of failure" (Bultmann 1963: 50-75). The NT, it is true, sees the Christ event as the unique, final, and decisive act of God for the salvation of the world, and obviously this must be a determining factor in any BT. But the God of the NT is the same God who speaks and acts in the OT, and the Christian church recognizes not just the OT passages quoted or alluded to in the NT but the OT in its entirety as an essential component part of Holy Scripture. The true task of BT, as B. S. Childs (1986) has said, is "not to Christianize the Old Testament by identifying it with the New Testament witness, but to hear its own theological testimony to the God of Israel whom the Church confesses also to worship" (9).

In the patristic period and through medieval times, *allegorization* was the method widely used to bring theological unity to the diverse material contained in Scripture. Allegorization involves finding another, hidden, spiritual meaning (*alle* = "other"; *-gory* = "speak") beneath the literal or surface meaning of a text (cf. B-1), usually not just in the text generally but in a whole series of details each of which is assigned another level of meaning. It is important to distinguish between "allegory" and "allegorization." "Allegory" may be applied to a relatively few passages of Scripture where this clearly was the intention of the original author; the most obvious example is Paul's allegory of Hagar and Sarah in Gal 4:21–5:1. The total rejection of allegory in the parables of Jesus in favor of the view that each parable makes one point only represents the swing of the pendulum to an opposite extreme; there are certainly some allegorical elements in the parables in their canonical form (cf. Ryken 1984: 199-203). "Allegorization," on the other hand, is the allegorical interpretation of a passage by a later interpreter when this clearly was not the intention of the original author. A frequently cited example, Augustine's detailed allegorical interpretation of the parable of the Good Samaritan (cf. B-1), illustrates the fatal weakness of allegorization: the original historical context is lost and virtually any meaning can be read into a text so that the resulting interpretation becomes quite arbitrary. Allegorizing interpretation did not go unchallenged in the early church; it was widely rejected at the Reformation, especially by Luther, and is virtually totally rejected by modern critical scholarship. The guiding principle must be that a passage is to be taken allegorically only if it is clear that the original writer intended it to be. The fact remains that there is very little allegory in Scripture, and allegorization is certainly not acceptable as a means of reconciling differences, particularly the differences between OT and NT.

Clearly to be differentiated from allegory is *typology*, which has always been recognized by some as a key feature of Scripture. Though often called into question as a valid method of interpretation, much recent study, not least on the part of literary critics (see esp. Frye 1981: chap. 4), has recognized the pervasive influence of typology as one of the major factors providing continuity amid the diversity of Scripture (cf. Markus 1957). D. L. Baker's (1976) set of definitions can hardly be improved upon:

> A *type* is a biblical event, person or institution which serves as an example or pattern for other events, persons or institutions;
>
> typology is the study of types and the historical and theological correspondence between them;
>
> the *basis* of typology is God's consistent activity in the history of his chosen people. (267)

The NT constantly draws upon events, persons, and institutions from the OT as it seeks to bring out the significance of the Christ event. The fact that these are used as types does not detract from their original historical significance. Moreover, the NT use of typology is not to be viewed in terms of a mechanical fulfillment of predictions, since it has also to be recognized that the antitype generally transcends the type. The rehabilitation of typology is an important aspect of the canonical approach that leads both to a deeper appreciation of much traditional interpretation of Scripture and to a deeper understanding of the unity, or better, the continuity inherent in Scripture (see C. J. Scalise 1996: 74-76).

A category that has found more favor with modern scholars is *promise and fulfillment*. This has a solid basis in the numerous OT passages quoted in the NT and seen as prophecies that have been fulfilled in the Christ event. Modern critical scholarship has called into question a narrow proof-texting approach, but the existence of a considerable body of material that anticipates God's future action on behalf of his people is undeniable, especially in the prophetic literature which in the Christian canon forms the last part of the OT. Many modern scholars are happier designating this under the rubric of "promise" rather than "prophecy." Here again it has to be recognized that the Christ event not only "fulfills" but also transcends the original promise.

We have already noted that many scholars see *salvation history* (Heilsgeschichte) as the major theme of BT. Throughout the Bible there runs a "story line," the account of God's choice of and dealings with a people — the people of Israel in the OT and the church, seen as both the continuation and expansion of Israel, in the NT. The story of the relationship between God and people takes place within history, and from a literary point of view is reflected in the large amount of historical narrative in Scripture, especially of course in the OT. That this is *a* major biblical theme can hardly be denied, but it is not an all-encompassing one. Scripture is concerned not just with God's relation with his chosen people, but also with his relation to the entire world that he has created and to all humankind. Moreover, "*salvation* history" raises various problems. The relation of God to his people does not just involve "salvation" *(Heil);* it is also a history of disobedience and hence of judgment. The significance of salvation history for the NT is a matter of dispute, though it can be eliminated only by ignoring Luke-Acts, which after all constitutes more than a quarter of the NT. Salvation history, rightly understood, must be one category employed by BT, but only one among others.

The modern historical approach has suggested another category that has been widely employed, that of *progressive revelation*. In contrast to an ahistorical approach that sees all Scripture as of equal value, progressive revelation recognizes that God's revelation, given to a specific people within history, was given in stages. Later revelation can add to and modify what was revealed in the earlier stages. In terms of Christian Scripture, the peak of revelation is seen in Christ, who both accepted the revelation given in the OT but also at times claimed the authority to go beyond it: "You have heard that it was said to those of ancient times. . . . But I say to you . . ." (Matt 5:21-22). Virtually all interpreters of Christian Scripture accept some form of progressive revelation, but many rightly utter words of caution, and some even prefer not to use the term itself. Biblical history is a complex process, and one certainly cannot think in terms of a graph taking an absolutely regular upward climb; the relationship between God and people has many ups and downs. Nor is it to be assumed that advance to a new level of revelation abrogates what went before. The NT witnesses to the Christ event as the fulfillment of God's purposes revealed in the OT, fulfillment not in the sense of abolishing but rather of continuing and completing what went before (cf. Matt 5:17).

Connected with this is the category of *continuity*. Since the rise of the modern historical approach, it is difficult to speak of a theological unity in Scripture in the sense that the same understanding of God and his purposes is to be found uniformly throughout Scripture. But if there is not unity in this sense, it can be claimed that there is a great deal of continuity. Although the NT witnesses to the dawning of a new order, it also assumes and accepts much that is witnessed to in the OT. To give one example (a not unimportant one), it is frequently pointed out that the theme of creation does not figure prominently in the NT, especially in comparison with the amount of attention it receives in the OT. This is not because the understanding of God as creator and all that implies is unimportant to the NT; rather it witnesses to the fact that the OT view of God as creator was simply accepted as a given by the NT writers. Here, then, is an important element of continuity between the Testaments.

E-3. THE PATTERN OF PROCLAMATION/PROMISE: FULFILLMENT/CONSUMMATION

The structure that is proposed here is one in which the major themes of OT and NT are *correlated* with each other. Minor themes are then grouped around the major ones. Extensive study of key biblical themes again and again reveals a common pattern in the way these themes are developed within Scripture.

Each theme is first traced through the OT. Although on the one hand the material is discussed with an eye to the way the theme is developed in the NT, on the other hand every effort is made to listen to what the OT says on its own terms.

Within the OT there is almost always a twofold emphasis that may most conveniently be designated as *proclamation* and *promise*. While "proclamation" *(kerygma)* is a term more usually associated with NT theology, its use in connection with the OT is equally appropriate. In relation to all the major themes of Scripture, the OT *proclaims* what God has done, both in nature and in history. It proclaims God as the One on whom all living things depend, and whose order can be discerned in creation. And it proclaims God as the One who chose Israel and entered into a special relationship with her.

But if the OT *proclaims* what God has done, within every major theme there is also a strong element of *promise*. The God of the OT is "the God who makes promises" (Brueggemann 1997: 164-73; cf. Kaiser 1978, an OT theology structured on the assumption that "promise" is the "canonical theological center" of the OT). Amid the chaos and darkness caused by Israel's rebellion and disobedience, and indeed the rebellion and disobedience of all humankind, again and again the OT sees the only hope as lying in some future action of God on behalf of his people and of his world. Israel lives between past and future, between the already and the not yet, between memory and hope, between proclamation and promise. The shape of the Christian canon, with the prophetic books coming as the last section (cf. D-2.7), makes the OT an open-ended book with a strong emphasis on the promise that points to the future. Promise is to be distinguished from prediction. The OT prophets do not necessarily gaze into a crystal ball and produce an exact blueprint or scenario for the new age. Through them God promises to act for the salvation of Israel and of humankind, but often the fulfillment far exceeds the expectation. The point has been made in telling fashion by C. J. H. Wright (1992) by means of an analogy:

> Imagine in the last century a father promises his young son a horse of his own when he comes of age! In the meantime cars are invented. On his twenty-first birthday, his father therefore gives him a car instead. The promise is fulfilled, because the substantive meaning of the promise was a personally owned means of transport. It would be pointless to say that it would only be fulfilled if the son gets a horse as well, or later. That would be to take the original promise as a mere prediction which will have "failed" unless it is literally honoured. (5)

Each theme will then be discussed in terms of the NT material. The NT proclaims that in the Christ event God has acted for the salvation of his people and of all humankind. In the context of the canon this is seen as a *fulfillment* of the OT as a whole, and especially of the *promise*. Paul could be speaking for all the writers of the NT when he says that in Christ "every one of God's promises is a 'Yes'" (2 Cor 1:20). The NT proclaims that the prophecies are fulfilled and with the coming of Christ the long-promised new order and age have dawned. This has to be seen as something much more than simply the fulfillment of individual proof texts: "the final fulfillment of the promises of the Old Testament in the coming and the work of Christ can only be understood as a fulfillment of the *entire way* of promise through the Old Testament" (Westermann 1969: 222).

Yet the NT too is open-ended; it also contains a tension between the already and the not yet. It looks back to the Christ event, to the giving of the Holy Spirit, to the reconstitution of Israel, but in relation to every biblical theme it also looks forward to the final triumph of God and to the *final consummation* of his purposes.

This analysis thus provides a framework for discussing the main biblical themes. It is one that recognizes the key role played by *eschatology* (*eschaton* = "end, goal, future") in BT. Traditionally eschatology, "the doctrine of the last things," has been seen as the last chapter of books on OT, NT, or BT. But eschatology is in fact *a key dimension of every biblical theme*. Every OT theme has a future aspect to it, an aspect that is fulfilled in part in the NT, though there also is always an eschatological dimension to be reckoned with. Not only therefore is there a relationship of promise/fulfillment between OT and NT; within the OT there is tension between proclamation and promise, just as in the NT there is tension between fulfillment and final consummation.

The pattern of proclamation/promise: fulfillment/consummation thus offers a structure for discussing the main themes of Scripture in a way that will reveal their inner canonical and theological dynamic rather than just their tradition-historical development. The claim is made that this structure is in no way imposed on the basis of some outside viewpoint, but is rather the one that most naturally arises out of the nature of the biblical material itself.

E-4. THE FRAMEWORK OF A BIBLICAL THEOLOGY

The procedure that seems to offer the most promise and the least risk of distorting the biblical material is that of identifying a limited number of major biblical themes (cf. E-1.3 above), grouping around them associated subthemes, and tracing each theme and subtheme through the OT, then through the NT, following the scheme of proclamation/promise: fulfillment/consummation. The selection of themes is obviously of crucial importance. In point of fact, the major themes that are proposed here were arrived at very largely through an extensive study of the numerous proposals that have been made by biblical scholars, especially for a so-called center or focal point of BT. As was argued above (E-1.3), it is most doubtful whether the diversity and complexity of BT can be subsumed under *one* key theme, but the various proposals that have been made obviously have a lot of merit and, taken together, form the most useful guide to a multithematic approach. A survey of these proposals suggests that they tend to fall into four main groupings, and on the basis of these, four major biblical themes are proposed that are designated as "God's Order," "God's Servant," "God's People," and "God's Way." Around each of these major themes appropriate subthemes are grouped. In the outline that follows, the names of leading scholars who have suggested the themes concerned are indicated in parentheses.

E-4.1. GOD'S ORDER

To assert, as many have, that God is the center of BT (*theos* = "God") is to state the obvious; more than this is needed to form an organizing principle for a complete theology of the Bible. Similarly, neither monotheism (Hitzig), the first commandment (W. H. Schmidt), nor a single attribute of God such as holiness (Dillmann, Hänel, Sellin) or presence (Terrien) can be considered adequate, in and of itself, as a focal point. More helpful are suggestions that range from "the kingdom of God" (Baumgarten-Crusius, Steudal, Hävernick, Riehm, Schultz, Bright, Goldsworthy, Klein) to "the rule of God" (Fohrer), or "the sovereignty of God" (Jacob; cf. Calvin), or "the activity of the independent, sovereign God" (Rowley). We have already noted problems with the actual term "kingdom of God" (above, E-1.3).

But care must be taken that God's rule/reign/sovereignty/activity not be defined too narrowly. The themes of salvation or redemption (Ewald, Hirsch), or of salvation history (von Hoffmann, Cullmann, von Rad), have tended to dominate. Recognition must be given to the dialectic between creation and redemption. God is Creator and Sustainer as well as Redeemer, is active in nature as well as in history, and has a relation to all humankind as well as to Israel. "World order" is employed as a basic category of biblical thought by H. H. Schmidt (see Scobie 1991b: 188; cf. also Knierim 1981).

The major theme of "God's order" is employed here in a twofold sense. In the first place, it expresses the biblical conviction that behind the multiple, complex, and frequently puzzling phenomena of nature and history is a meaning and purpose, a pattern and order that is to be ascribed to the presence and power of the one true God. In the second place, the term is used to express the biblical distinction between the present order and the expected new order. In the NT this can be expressed by the term *aiōn*, usually translated "age" and sometimes "world." A distinction is drawn between "this *age*" and "the *age* to come" (Matt 12:32; Eph 1:21). This age is evil (Gal 1:4), being controlled by "the god of this *world*"; but believers look forward to the blessings of the new age (Mark 10:30; Luke 20:35; Eph 2:7). This distinction and this longing for the coming of a new age or a new order are deeply rooted in the OT. What is distinctive about the NT is the belief that with the Christ event the new age has already dawned (1 Cor 10:11; Heb 6:5), so that believers live in "the overlap of the ages" (see further, 1-4.1). Here the term "order" is used as the equivalent of "age," as in Tennyson's line, "The old order changeth, yielding place to new" (*The Passing of Arthur*, l. 407).

The OT *proclaims* that God, the ruler of history, has a purpose for his people, but that he is also the creator and sustainer of all things, the one whose order can be discerned in nature. Since God's purposes have not been fully realized in history and in creation, the OT *promises* the ushering in of a new age and a new order in which God will truly reign and creation itself will be renewed.

The NT proclaims the *fulfillment* of this promise: with the Christ event the new order has dawned, God's rule is inaugurated, and already there is a new creation. But the NT also holds that only at the final *consummation* will all that opposes God's will be eliminated and the present world order be replaced by a new heaven and a new earth.

Other minor themes can appropriately be considered in conjunction with this major one. One is the question of the forces that oppose God's rule. In the OT the "adversaries" belong mainly to the historical order, whereas in the NT they are largely the "principalities and powers" of the created order and the "adversary" is identified as Satan. A further subtheme that bridges the Testaments is that of the "Spirit" of God as a special mode of his being and activity. Thus under the major heading of "God's Order," the following subthemes are identified: "The Living God," "The Lord of Creation," "The Lord of History," "The Adversary," and "The Spirit."

E-4.2. GOD'S SERVANT

Christ is certainly a center, if not the center, of the NT. It is not separate elements such as the cross (Luz) or the resurrection (Künneth), important though they may be, but rather the Christ event in its totality (Reicke, Lohse) that constitutes the major theme. Numerous scholars identify Christology as the center of the NT, but this must be broad enough to encompass what is traditionally designated as both the person and work of Christ. Some put the emphasis on the results or benefits of the Christ event such as justification of sinners (Käsemann, Schrage; cf. Luther) or reconciliation (Stuhlmacher). The balance becomes distorted, however, when the main emphasis falls on anthropology (Bultmann, Braun).

The major challenge in this section is the correlation of the NT christological theme with the OT. One formula that has been proposed to link the Testaments suggests that "the Old Testament tells us *what* the Christ is; the New *who* he is" (Vischer 1949a: 7). This formula is defective in two directions. Firstly, no one clear concept of a coming Messiah emerges from the OT, but rather a variety of expectations alongside each other. Secondly, the NT does not portray Jesus as fulfilling any one concept of the Messiah; it links him in some way with virtually every form of expectation and with a variety of OT types, but equally portrays him as transcending all types and expectations.

Rather than adopt a narrow messianic proof-text approach, the method of correlation suggests comparing the means whereby God makes himself known and acts to save his people in the OT and in the NT. The controlling theme which suggests itself is that of "God's servant."

In the OT Israel is frequently addressed as God's "servant (*'ebhedh*)" (e.g., Isa 41:8). But from among his people God calls a number of individuals to be his servants, entrusted with a special task. God acts in a special way through these chosen servants: Moses supremely, but also through prophets, priests, kings, and wise persons. The failure of each of these categories generates expectations of a future servant; the NT proclaims how Jesus fulfills and transcends each of these categories.

The book of Daniel points toward a "son of man" who represents humankind as God originally intended them to be. The NT sees Jesus as the New Man; the true, representative human being; the Second Adam.

The OT can also envisage God acting not through a chosen servant but directly, through such concepts as God's glory, word, and wisdom that were developed to safeguard God's transcendence while still allowing for his activity here on earth. These concepts, along with that of Sonship, become the basis of the fully developed incarnational Christology of the NT.

The OT also knows of a suffering servant of God, particularly in the Psalms and in Isa 40–55, a servant who suffers for the sins of others but who will ultimately be vindicated. The NT links the figure of the Suffering Servant with that of the Messiah and sees his death on the cross as an atonement for the sins of the world, and his resurrection and ascension as the vindication of God's servant.

In brief, the OT *proclaims* that God makes himself known to his people either directly or through a series of servants. Since these are all imperfect, the OT *promises* the coming of a new servant, the true mediator between God and his people. The NT proclaims the *fulfillment* of the promise; Christ is the new servant who both fulfills and transcends all forms of expectation and through whom God comes in person to his people in a new way. The servant comes incognito and faces suffering and death. At the final *consummation,* however, he will come in power and glory.

The subthemes of the major section on God's servant are therefore "The Messiah," "The Son of Man," "Glory, Word, Wisdom, Son," "The Servant's Suffering," and "The Servant's Vindication."

E-4.3. GOD'S PEOPLE

Many scholars see as a key biblical theme the relationship between God and his people. This finds expression in those theologies that make "covenant" an organizing principle (Cocceius, Eichrodt, Procksch, Prussner, Payne). Others prefer to speak of "communion between God and man" (Vriezen, Fohrer), and many utilize some such formula as "Yahweh, the God of Israel . . . Israel, the people of Yahweh" (Duhm, Wellhausen, Davidson, Stade, Noth, Smend). The theme of election (Dentan, Wildberger, Preuss) highlights only one aspect of the relationship and is less satisfactory. It is clear that "God's people" is a major theme linking the Testaments (cf. Cazelles 1966; Deutsch 1972).

The OT *proclaims* that in the context of his concern for all humankind God chose a particular people to be the servant people of the Lord. The OT is also very aware of the failings and limitations of this people, and holds out the *promise* of a time when God's people will be renewed, resurrected, and reconstituted. The NT sees the *fulfillment* of these promises in the community that the Christ event brings into being, a people in continuity with Israel yet also a new community that is open to all the peoples of humankind. The church is indeed the eschatological community, though it too is imperfect and the people of God will be truly constituted only at the final *consummation.*

Several subthemes can appropriately be linked with the major theme of "God's People." The relationship of Israel to the nations of humankind needs to be explored. The destiny of God's people is closely liked with a holy land, and with its focal point, a holy city. God's people find and express their identity through worship, and are led by ministers appointed by God. Thus the subthemes for this section are: "The Covenant Community," "The Nations," "Land and City," "Worship," and "Ministry," with each of these again being traced through both OT and NT.

E-4.4. GOD'S WAY

In contrast to the previous three sections, virtually no one would claim that such themes as piety, spirituality, ethics, or ethos constitute *the* center of BT, though there is some recognition of this area as *a* major theme. For example, there has been discussion of law as a topic of BT. Biblical ethics has been a greatly neglected field, though the situation has begun to change in recent years. The separation of biblical ethics from BT has undoubtedly contributed to this neglect, yet one of the strongest conclusions to be drawn from the study of BT is that "the Old Testament portrayal of ethical behaviour is inseparable from its total message respecting Israel, that is to say, from its theological content" (Childs 1992: 676). Christians could learn here from Judaism, which has always emphasized the importance of halakah, i.e., norms of conduct derived from Scripture (see Jacobs 1971). In noting some of the many suggestions that have been made for a "center" of OT theology, J. D. Levenson (1987) comments that it is interesting to note some of the obvious candidates that do not appear on the list. "One," he says, "is humankind's duties, a theme that occupies most of the biblical materials, legal, prophetic, and sapiential alike" (299). There is a whole area here relating to the life or way of life of the people of God that is of central importance in the biblical material itself.

The pervasive biblical image of the "way" (Heb. *derekh*; Gk. *hodos*) is suggested as the term that best encompasses this broad area. "The primary image to express conduct or behaviour in the Old Testament," writes James Muilenburg (1961), "is the 'way' or 'road' *(derek)*. No other image was more rich and manifold, none more diverse in nuance and connotation" (33; cf. K. Koch 1978; Goldingay 1981: 38-65). The concept is equally at home in Torah, Prophets, and Writings: the two ways open to humankind are spelled out in Deut 30:15-20; Jeremiah reminds the people that God told them, "Walk only in the way that I command you" (Jer 7:23); while the theme of the two ways also runs through Prov 1–9 (cf. Habel 1972) and is a key term in Psalms (Crollius 1974). The call in Isa 40:3 to "prepare the way of the LORD" is applied to John the Baptist, who heralds the dawn of the new order (Mark 1:3). Jesus taught "the way of God" (Mark 12:14; cf. Navone 1973), while the early Christians were known as those who followed "the Way *(hodos)*" (Acts 9:2; etc.; on the NT usage, see McCasland 1958).

The OT *proclaims* that God has offered to Israel in the teaching of the Torah, in the preaching of the prophets, and in the way of Wisdom a lifestyle that will lead to blessing and life. Israel's repeated disobedience leads to a deepened understanding of human sinfulness, but also to the *promise* of a new quality of life in the new age. In the NT these promises find *fulfillment* in the new way of life demonstrated and communicated by Jesus, the life of the new order that believers can begin to live in the present although it will be experienced in its fullness only at the final *consummation*.

This would seem to be the most appropriate place to examine the biblical understanding of human nature as a preface to the rest of the section. Despite human sinfulness the Bible proclaims God's grace; that grace, however, calls for a response on the part of those who follow God's Way. Key elements in that response are faith and hope. The basis for biblical ethics is found in the concept of God's commandments, and the central biblical ethical imperative is "Love your neighbor." A "Way" always leads to a destination. The delineation of the two ways in Deut 30 climaxes in the appeal: "I have set before you life and death, blessings and curses. Choose life so that you and your descendants may live" (Deut 30:19). A final subtheme could thus be "life," the life that God's people enjoy here and now, as a foretaste of the future fullness of life to which God's promises point. The subthemes selected for the section on "God's Way" are therefore "The Human Condition," "Faith and Hope," "God's Commandments," "Love Your Neighbor," and "Life."

This scheme of four major themes (with the associated subthemes) is combined with the pattern of proclamation/promise: fulfillment/consummation to produce the following overall framework for a BT:

Old Testament		New Testament	
Proclamation	Promise	Fulfillment	Consummation
God's Order	A New Order	The New Order	The Final Consummation
God's Servants	A New Servant	The New Servant	The Final Consummation
God's People	A New People	The New People	The Final Consummation
God's Way	A New Way	The New Way	The Final Consummation

E-5. UNITY AND DIVERSITY

Any proposal for a BT that adopts a canonical, thematic, and structured approach faces the inevitable criticism that it will in effect impose a false unity on the biblical material, and will thereby undervalue the rich diversity of the biblical witness. It may be maintained, on the contrary, that it is precisely a canonical BT that will seek to do justice to the whole sweep of biblical thought. The structure that is proposed here allows for the surveying of the full range of the biblical material. It makes possible the identification of similarities, continuity, and even unity of thought within the Bible where these clearly exist. But it also provides ample scope for the recognition of diversity, tensions, and even paradox in biblical thought. No option is closed off in advance.

Recent years have seen an ever increasing number of studies of the dialectical or bipolar nature of much of BT (cf. Brueggemann 1985b; Birch 1984). D. A. Carson has explored the tension between divine sovereignty and human responsibility (1981). R. B. Mayers has discussed twelve major biblical themes from the perspective of "balance" (1987). G. B. Caird's *New Testament Theology* (1994) adopts an imaginative "conference table approach" that envisages all the NT writers participating in a conference (modeled on the apostolic conference in Jerusalem) and engaging in a discussion of theological matters (in effect, topics relating to the key theme of salvation); the last chapter then discusses the "theology of Jesus." The effect is to emphasize the dialogical nature of NT theology. Brueggemann makes the dialectic between "Israel's core testimony" and "Israel's countertestimony" the main structural feature of his *Theology of the Old Testament* (1997), though he supplements these with a discussion of "Israel's unsolicited testimony."

A BT need not deal in rigid "doctrines" that seek to compress all the biblical material into one mold and thus distort the true nature of the biblical witness. The structure proposed here is fully capable of incorporating recognition of the dynamic and dialectical character of much of biblical thought.

Two examples of the dialectical nature of biblical thought deserve special mention because of the important role they play in this BT.

E-5.1. CREATION AND HISTORY

The so-called biblical theology movement (cf. B-8) laid great stress on salvation history *(Heilsgeschichte)*, on "the God who acts," and on revelation in history as a unique feature of biblical thought. God's dealings with his people in history were seen as virtually the all-encompassing theme of BT. This overemphasis has more recently been questioned on several grounds, not least because it fails to give adequate recognition to the place the Bible gives to creation. One factor here has been the resurgence of Wisdom studies and the recognition that Wisdom theology is basically creation theology (cf. Scobie 1984b).

As so often in BT, it is not a case of either/or — the central theme of BT is *either* God's activity in history *or* God's activity in creation. "A balanced presentation notes that creation and history are both significant theological constructs in the Old Testament" (Perdue 1994: 150). Scripture from beginning to end reflects a dialectic between these two spheres of divine activity. This dialectic has been clearly recognized in a number of studies, for example in P. Hanson's identification within the biblical heritage of what he calls a "cosmic vector" and a "teleological vector" (1978). Similarly L. L. Thompson, in a book on the literary criticism of Scripture, speaks of the Bible's "cosmogonic mythology" and "covenantal mythology" (1978). Related to this also is C. Westermann's dialectic between "the saving God and history" and "the blessing God and creation" (1978). In particular, J. Goldingay, in an important study, *Theological Diversity and the Authority of the Old Testament* (1987), has written of "the polarity of God's involvement in the regularities of life (creation) and his acts of deliverance (redemption)." He goes on to discuss the dialectical relationship between creation and redemption under four headings: "The World God Redeems Is the World of God's Creation," "The World God Created Is a World That Needed to Be Redeemed," "Human Beings Are Redeemed to Live Again Their Created Life before God," and "The Redeemed Humanity Still Looks for a Final Act of Redemption/Re-creation." Goldingay's discussion well illustrates the exciting possibilities of a dialectical approach to BT.

The dialectic between creation and history is a key feature of this BT. The terms "creation" and "the created order" are used to refer to God's relationship with the entire world he has created and with the entire family of humankind. The terms "history" and "the historical order" are used to refer to God's dealings (in both judgment and salvation) with his people within history. Neither of these emphases is assigned the dominant position; rather there is a dialectic between them that runs through the whole of Scripture.

The recognition of God's activity in the created order and the historical order is crucial for the understanding of biblical eschatology, i.e., of what God promises to do in the future. "Apocalyptic eschatology" belongs to the created order, whereas "prophetic eschatology" is associated with the historical order. For a definition of these terms, see 1-2.1a, and for a more detailed discussion of apocalyptic eschatology, see 2-2, and of prophetic eschatology, 3-2.

E-5.2. INDIVIDUAL AND COMMUNITY

In modern thought the individual tends to occupy a central place, and to be sharply distinguished from the community and from the wider society. In the Bible no such sharp distinction is to be observed. Persons never exist solely as individuals; they are always thought of as being *incorporated* into a wider group. In the OT especially, we can distinguish four such corporate groupings that may be pictured as a series of concentric circles: persons are corporate members of (1) their own family, (2) their clan/tribal grouping, (3) the people of Israel, and (4) all humankind.

The group is thought of as a unity, something more than the sum of the individuals who currently compose it, and something that has a past and future as well as a present. H. W. Robinson (1980) spoke of the group as having a "corporate personality," and though his views have been the subject of criticism (Porter 1965; Rogerson 1970), many of his insights are still valid (cf. Fraine 1965). In the OT especially, God often deals with corporate units, and both punishments and blessings can be shared by the group as a whole. In the NT the believer exists only as part of a community that is "the body of Christ" (significantly, English words such as "corporate" and "incorporation" derive from the Latin *corpus* = "body").

Equally it is true that the group can be *represented* by and in the person of an individual. This can be an ancestor: Adam (the word *'ādhām* in Hebrew = "man") represents the whole of humankind, regarded as descended from him; Jacob/Israel represents the people of Israel, regarded as the descendants of his twelve sons. Or the individual may be a leader: a king or prophet or high priest can represent the nation as a whole. Groups can be personified as individuals, as when "daughter of Zion" stands for the city and people of Jerusalem.

Frequently references can change from the individual to the community in a way that seems strange to the modern mind. A case in point is the "I" of the Psalms, which at times does seem to be genuinely individual but at other times sounds more like a representative or personification of Israel. A similar oscillation between group and individual is to be observed in the Servant Songs of Isaiah.

E. THE STRUCTURE OF BIBLICAL THEOLOGY

Some who take an historical approach have sought to characterize collective thinking as "primitive" and restrict it to the earlier portion of the OT; with the major prophets Jeremiah and Ezekiel religion is individualized, and from then on is primarily a matter for the individual. But this picture is oversimplified and misleading. Even though Jeremiah and Ezekiel did bring about a new emphasis on the individual, the view of a person as part of a larger corporate whole was not abandoned but continues through the rest of the OT and indeed through the NT also (cf. H. W. Robinson 1980: 32-34). Theories of historical development tend to be speculative, and are based on reconstructions that can be and frequently are challenged. BT, as we have argued, is primarily concerned with the canonical text of Scripture, and in that text as it stands there is from the outset a dialectic between individual and community. At a very early stage, for example, we meet Abraham, who is presented as a real individual, with a distinctive character and personality. Yet he is also a representative figure; he is "the father of the faithful," the representative of both Israel, the group chosen by God to be his servant people, and the church, the community of those who are "children of Abraham by faith." Thus in the case of Abraham, as throughout Scripture, there is an ongoing dialectic between individual and community (cf. Fraine 1965: 18). In Eichrodt's terms the OT is characterized by "solidarity thinking," but this exists in fruitful tension with "a living individuality" that is to be understood as "the capacity for personal responsibility and for shaping one's own life" (1967: 232).

A SKETCH OF BIBLICAL THEOLOGY

CHAPTERS 1-5: GOD'S ORDER

CHAPTER 1

The Living God

Old Testament: Proclamation

1-1. IN THE BEGINNING GOD

From beginning to end the Bible speaks of God. However puzzling the events of history, however hard to understand the world in which they lived, the writers of the Bible affirm that there is an *order* in both history and creation, and that this order is known through encounter with God. The OT not only speaks of God's order, it also promises the coming of a new order. The NT proclaims that with the Christ event the new order has dawned, though its final consummation still lies in the future.

The Bible does not present a "doctrine of God" in any theoretical way; rather it provides a manifold witness to God as the ultimate reality (cf. Westermann 1979: 12-13; Brueggemann 1997: 117). He is "the living God" (Deut 5:26; 2 Kgs 19:4; Ps 42:2; etc.), the source of all life, and the one in whom alone true life is to be found. "In contrast to the living God of Israel, the gods of her neighbours are utterly lifeless and impotent, unable to save their worshippers" (Gleason 1964: 3-4).

The unity of the Bible is to be found in the first instance in its witness to this one God. "Every story," as Ryken (1984) has pointed out, "has a central protagonist, and in the Bible that protagonist is God. He is the central character, the actor whose presence unifies the story of universal history with its myriads of changing human characters" (178-79). Similarly, Patrick (1981) has argued that "the biblical God is rendered as a character and his acts are represented as part of a dramatic setting which enlists the reader's participation" (2). While the biblical God is not marked by a static "changelessness," nevertheless he does act "in character" throughout Scripture (cf. 50).

Nowhere in the Bible is the existence of God doubted. The fool who says in his heart, "There is no God" (Ps 14:1), does not doubt the existence of God in a theoretical way; rather he imagines (wrongly) that God has nothing to do with his life and that the way he lives is of no concern to God (cf. 10:4, 11). He is a practical, not a theoretical atheist (cf. von Rad 1972: 65).

1-1.1. THE LORD IS KING

In witnessing to the living God, a central biblical theme is the rule/reign/sovereignty of God. It is true that the actual phrase "the kingdom of God" does not occur in the OT (cf. E-1.3), though David can say in 1 Chr 29:11, "Yours is the *kingdom (hammamlākâh)*, O LORD, and you are exalted as head above all." Throughout the OT, however, the sovereignty of God is acknowledged, and his rule over both nature and history is expressed in manifold ways (cf. Duling 1992: 50).

God was referred to as "king" *(melekh)* from early times. Balaam says of the Israelites,

> The LORD their God is with them,
>   acclaimed as a king among them. (Num 23:21)

Resistance to the institution of the monarchy in Israel (cf. 6-1.2a) was based on the conviction that God should be the sole ruler of his people (Judg 8:23). While the earlier prophets may have been reticent in referring to God as king (Eichrodt 1961: 194-200; but note, e.g., Mic 2:13; Zeph 3:15; Jer 51:57), for 2 Isaiah God is "the King of Israel" (Isa 44:6; cf. 41:21), and in Isa 52:7 the good news to be proclaimed to a dispirited people is "Your God reigns." The conviction that God is king of the whole universe and of all nations is a characteristic emphasis of apocalyptic and is thus found particularly in Daniel:

> His kingdom is an everlasting kingdom,
>   and his sovereignty is from generation to generation.
> (Dan 4:3; cf. 5:21; 6:26).

A significant biblical symbol is that of the divine *throne (kissēʾ)* (cf. Toombs 1962a). In 1 Kgs 22:19 the prophet Micaiah had a vision of "the LORD sitting on his throne." In the midst of political change Isaiah claimed, "I saw the Lord sitting on a throne, high and lofty," and exclaimed, "My eyes have seen the King" (Isa 6:1, 5). The "mercy seat" on top of the ark of the covenant (see 14-1.1a.ii) functioned as the throne of the invisible God, though God's throne is usually depicted as being in heaven (Ps 11:4; cf. Isa 66:1).

The kingship of God is proclaimed especially in the Enthronement Psalms (B. W. Anderson 1983: 173-80; Kraus 1986: 86-91), which include Pss 29, 47, 93, and 95-99. Critical scholars have sought to link these psalms with particular liturgies or feasts celebrated at the Jerusalem temple. S. Mowinckel (1962) went so far as to reconstruct an "enthronement festival" held in the fall, and argued for translating the cultic shout *YHWH malakh* (Pss 93:1; 96:10; 97:1; 99:1) as "Yahweh has become King!" (1:106-92). Mowinckel's theory owes more to Babylonian than to biblical texts, and as Anderson points out, "the notion that Yahweh is involved in the cycles of the cosmos and must fight to win kingship anew at the turn of the year is completely alien to Israel's faith" (176). *YHWH malakh* is more properly translated "The Lord is King." The context in several of the psalms suggests that the phrase has "a polemical and confessional ring" and in effect means "*Yahweh* (and no other) is king" (Kraus, 87).

Some of these psalms envisage God enthroned in Zion and refer to his rule over Israel (Pss 97:8; 99:6-9), but much more frequent is the declaration that God is king over all the earth and over all nations:

> The Lord, the Most High, is awesome,
>   a great king over all the earth. (Ps 47:2)

> Say among the nations, "The Lord is king!
>   The world is firmly established; it shall never be moved." (Ps 96:10)

God's sovereignty is also expressed through the designation of him as "Lord" (*'ādhôn,* but frequently in the possessive form *'ªdhōnāy);* on this, see further 10-1.4.

In the OT God manifests his rule in two spheres: (a) in *the created order,* in his relationship with the world and with humankind as a whole (see chap. 2: "The Lord of Creation"); (b) in *the historical order,* in his relations with his people Israel (see chap. 3: "The Lord of History").

Who is this God who rules in both creation and history? The first part of the OT canon is the Torah, and the focal point of the Torah is God's covenant with Israel at Sinai (see 11-1.3c). The core of the covenant is found in the Decalogue, the "Ten Words" (*'ªsereth haddªbhārîm)* or "Ten Commandments" (Exod 20:1-17; Deut 5:6-21). At the outset God "introduces himself," saying, "I am the Lord (*'ānōkhî YHWH),* your God (*'ªlōheykhā),* who brought you out of the land of Egypt. . . ." The first four words then spell out the basis of the relationship between God and people. Similarly, in Deuteronomy, shortly after the second version of the Decalogue, there occurs the passage known in Jewish tradition as the Shema (from the opening word, *shªma'* = "hear"), in which God says to his people: "Hear, O Israel: The Lord our God (*YHWH 'ªlōhēnû)* is one Lord (*YHWH 'echādh);* and you shall love the Lord your God with all your heart, and with all your soul, and with all your might" (Deut 6:4-5 RSV). These key passages take us to the very core of the OT understanding of God:

> a God who is known by name,
> a God who is one, and

a God who is above all a personal God.

1-1.2. THE NAME OF GOD

a. What's in a Name?

In biblical thought a person's *name* is always closely linked with a person's *nature* and thus is regarded as highly significant (cf. Eichrodt 1967: 40; Parke-Taylor 1975: 1-3); "in Old Testament times a name expressed identification, but also identity" (Martens 1996: 297). If this is true of persons, it is even more true of God: *God's name is an expression of his essential nature.* Indeed, the frequent references to the "name" *(shēm)* of God in the OT represent virtually an alternative way of speaking of God himself (Jacob 1958: 82-85; von Rad 1962: 181-86; Eichrodt, 40-45). Thus to "love the name of the LORD" (Isa 56:6) is in effect to love God, and so on. Misusing the name of God, e.g., in swearing falsely or in attempting to use God's powers for one's own ends, is an extremely serious offense, as the third commandment underlines: "You shall not make wrongful use of the name of the LORD your God, for the LORD will not acquit anyone who misuses his name" (Exod 20:7; Deut 5:11). In the Deuteronomic writings in particular, God's name becomes a way of speaking of God's presence, especially in the temple, which is the place God will choose "as his habitation to put his *name* there" (Deut 12:5; cf. Isa 18:7; Neh 1:9). God's nature is made known not only to Israel but also throughout creation:

> O LORD, our Sovereign,
> how majestic is your *name* in all the earth! (Ps 8:1)

In both the Decalogue and the Shema, God is named in two ways: (a) by the term *ᵉlōhîm,* a word that means "God" in a general sense and can be used with reference to the whole created order to designate the "gods" of peoples other than Israel; (b) by a proper name, *YHWH,* that is used only within the historical order to denote the God who makes himself known and enters into a special relationship with his people Israel.

b. The Created Order: Words for "God"

The term *ᵉlōhîm* is by far the most common general word for "God," occurring some 2,500 times in the OT. The word is plural in form, but when used with reference to the God of Israel there is never any doubt that the reference is to the *one* God. The plural can be regarded as a "plural of majesty" or an "abstract plural" that "corresponds to our word 'Godhead' or 'divinity' and is thus suited to the task of summing up the whole of divine power in a personal unity" (Eichrodt 1961: 185). Depending on the context, however, it can be used as a true plural referring to gods worshiped by other peoples (e.g., Exod 12:12). In Jonah 1:5, for example, the non-Israelite sailors caught in a storm "each cried to his *ᵉlōhîm.*" Thus, in a general way *ᵉlōhîm* refers to a divine power who is to be worshiped and served.

Another general word for God is *ʾēl*, found in Job and Psalms and especially in Gen 12–50, where it designates the God worshiped by the patriarchs; it is used much less frequently elsewhere in the OT (see Eichrodt 1961: 178-84; B. W. Anderson 1962a: 411-14). It is significant that El was also the name of the high god or father god of the Canaanite pantheon. The OT uses the word with reference to the God of Israel, especially in such compounds as ʾĒl Shaddai = God Almighty (Gen 35:11), ʾĒl ʿElyôn = God Most High (14:18, where Melchizedek is designated "priest of God Most High"), ʾĒl ʿŌlām = God Everlasting (21:33), and ʾĒl Rᵒʾî = God of Seeing (16:13). These compound phrases suggest what the most probable etymology of the word would support: the basic idea is that of divine power and preeminence. El frequently occurs in the OT as a component part of proper names (Isra*el* = he who strives with God; Ezeki*el* = God is strong; etc.).

The use of these general names of God throughout the OT suggests that there is no absolute discontinuity between the way God is understood in Israel and among other peoples and religions. "God" designates a divine power, known, worshiped, and served by humankind. But for the God of Israel a more specific designation is required.

c. The Historical Order: The Name of Israel's God

The God of Israel is known as YHWH, the name of God revealed to Moses at the burning bush (Exod 3:13-15). This is not the revelation of a new God; rather, the same God worshiped by the patriarchs as El now reveals himself to Moses in a new way (Exod 6:2-8; cf. Eissfeldt 1956). It occurs in the Old Testament some 6,800 times. For his chosen people God "is not an impersonal force, a convenient symbol, or a conglomerate of predicates, but has a personal name (YHWH) by which he is to be worshipped" (Childs 1992: 355). In Hebrew the letters *Y H W H* represent the four consonants of the name, hence known as the Tetragrammaton (= four letters), formerly transliterated JHVH but now more accurately as YHWH. Originally Hebrew writing consisted of consonants only; signs representing the vowels were added at a much later stage. A problem arises in the case of the divine name since in time this came to be considered too holy even to be pronounced; hence the original pronunciation (and spelling) was in time lost.

Rather than pronounce the sacred name, Jews substituted another term such as *ᵃdhōnay* (often written Edonai or Adonai), meaning "my lord" or "my master." The *vowels* of this word came to be written under the *consonants* of the original name, to indicate that no attempt was to be made to pronounce the name but that "Lord" was to be substituted for it. In late medieval times the consonants of the original name were in error combined with the vowels of the substitute to produce the hybrid word "JeHoVaH" (see Parke-Taylor 1975: 9), the form of the name which became familiar to the English-speaking world especially through its use in the King James Version, even though in biblical times no such form existed (see *NOAB*, xiii).

Modern scholars generally agree that the original form of the name was probably *yahweh* = "Yahweh" (Ger. *Jahweh;* Fr. *Yahvé*). The only major modern English translation to use "Yahweh" is the Jerusalem Bible. Most others prefer to follow a tradition, going back to the LXX, that made no attempt to reproduce the sacred name but instead substituted for it the title *kyrios* = "Lord" (cf. also the Vulgate, which used the Latin *dominus* = "Lord"). Where "YHWH" occurs in the text, therefore, most modern translations render it "the LORD," using capital letters to alert the reader to the fact that this represents the divine name. This convention is adopted in this book.

There has been endless scholarly debate about the original meaning of the name (von Rad 1962: 179-87; B. W. Anderson 1962a: 410; Gleason 1964: 116-20; Parke-Taylor 1975: 46f.), although it is generally agreed that it is derived from the verb *hāyāh* = "to be." The key passage, Exod 3:13-15, where the name is revealed to Moses, has been interpreted in a number of ways. It has been suggested that by saying "I am who I am," God is in fact refusing to divulge his name, but this is unlikely, as the repeated use of the name from this point on suggests that some explanation for the name is to be found in this key passage. It has also been suggested that "Yahweh" is a causative form meaning "he who causes to be," i.e., the creator (Freedman 1960), but this meaning does not really fit the context in Exod 3. Brownlee (1977) interprets it as "the One who makes things happen." By far the most convincing explanation is that God reveals himself to Moses as the One *who is* with him and with his people. God is "I am" in the sense of "I am present," "I am with you," "I am really and truly present, ready to help and to act" (Eichrodt 1961: 190), or "I will be there (for you)" (von Rad 1962: 180; cf. G. A. F. Knight 1983: 30). This fits the general context; cf. God's assurance to Moses in v. 12, "I will be with you," i.e., from this point onward, and also the repeated assurance in Exod 33:14, "My presence will go with you." The God of the Bible, Brueggemann (1985a) has said, "is not like any other. And his strangeness is in this. He is *with his people.* He is *for his people.* His goodness is not in his great transcendental power nor in his majestic remoteness nor in his demanding toughness but in his readiness to be with and for his people" (61). S. Terrien (1978) has argued that "the reality of the presence of God stands at the center of biblical faith" (xxvii). While that presence gives meaning and purpose to life, it is also "elusive"; God's presence cannot be presumed upon or manipulated by his people.

The burning bush episode functions, we might say, as Moses' (and Israel's) "introduction" to the God of the historical order. When we are introduced to someone we have not met before, the *name* serves basically to identify the person ("This is Jane Smith"). In the course of time, however, as we get to know the person better, the "meaning" of the name is fleshed out. So the "meaning" of YHWH is to be found not primarily in etymology, but in Israel's experience of God who was indeed present with his people from this point on. Through their relationship with this God, Israel learned more and more of his true nature and purpose. It was as the LORD delivered his people from slavery, entered into covenant with them, and gave them his Torah that they came to know him as

The LORD, the LORD,
a God merciful and gracious,
slow to anger,
and abounding in steadfast love and faithfulness. (Exod 34:6)

It should be noted, however, that the LXX translates the name *ho ōn*, "the one who is," a phrase with philosophical overtones that might be represented in modern English as "the Ground of Being." Here, it is true, "the Greek version adds a metaphysical overtone absent from the Hebrew" (Barrois 1980: 28; cf. Cronk 1982: 78). But since the LXX forms part of the biblical tradition (D-2.2), it is not to be totally set aside; it serves as a reminder that the God of the historical order who is present with his people is also the God of the created order in whom all peoples "live and move and have [their] being" (Acts 17:28).

Although the name YHWH is revealed to Moses in Exod 3, it does occur earlier, the first reference being in Gen 4:26: "At that time people began to invoke the name of the LORD." Critical scholars have found in this one of the clues to the source analysis of the Pentateuch: it is the J source that regards the name Yahweh as having been used from the earliest times, while the E and P sources are careful never to use Yahweh before Exod 3. This is seen as a major discrepancy in the understanding of God. But as W. Harrington (1980) has pointed out, "The Yahwist, who undoubtedly knew of the tradition that linked the revelation of the name Yahweh firmly to Moses, has his own way of asserting that the Creator God and the God of his own Yahwistic religion were one and the same: he simply uses the name 'Yahweh' from the start" (6). From a canonical viewpoint the problem is much less serious. Whatever the case historically, the compilers of the Pentateuch allowed the name to stand in earlier contexts, as a way of affirming that the God who revealed himself to Moses was none other than the God known to the patriarchs and indeed worshiped by all humankind from an early stage.

1-1.3. THE ONE GOD

a. No Other Gods

Both OT and NT emerged from a world that was very largely polytheistic. In its historical context therefore, one of the most striking features of the biblical understanding of God is its witness to the existence of only *one* God, to what is usually termed monotheism. "For the ancient Hebrews the pressing danger and temptation was not atheism but polytheism. The question was not whether there was any God but whether there was one God or many" (Burrows 1946a: 54).

BT is not concerned with the various theories developed by historians of religion, whether an evolutionary theory that envisages a development from primitive animism through polytheism to monotheism, or the converse (which has also been maintained) of a primitive monotheism centering in a "high god" followed by a "fall" into polytheism (cf. Burrows 1946a: 54-59). BT is concerned with the witness of the canonical text, which from the outset speaks of only one God, the creator and ruler of the world, and the One who calls Israel to be his people. The first commandment constitutes a cornerstone of OT faith: "You shall have no other gods before me" (Exod 20:3). Similarly, the Shema begins, "Hear, O Israel: The LORD our God is one LORD" (Deut 6:4 RSV). Elijah called upon Israel to worship and serve the LORD and him alone (1 Kgs 18).

It has been argued that the very form of the first commandment presupposes belief in the existence of other gods; what the commandment requires is the worship of the LORD only, not of any of the other gods. Similarly in Exod 15:11 Moses can ask, "Who is like you, O LORD, *among the gods?*" while Ps 95:3 declares,

> For the LORD is a great God,
>   and a great King *above all gods.*

Such texts may witness to an early stage in Israel's faith that was characterized by "monolatry," the worship and service of one God by Israel, rather than by "monotheism," the theoretical denial of the existence of other gods (von Rad 1962: 211). Such a stage could be regarded as "practical monotheism" (Eichrodt 1961: 225), or perhaps better as "incipient monotheism": within the practical monotheism of the first commandment lay the seed that in due time would flower as the fully developed monotheism of the later biblical tradition. From a canonical point of view, however, the whole of Scripture is to be read from the viewpoint of that fully developed monotheism. "Even if it is possible in the Old Testament Scriptures to trace a development or a progressive revelation from a relatively unreflecting monolatry to a more theologically elaborated monotheism, it is quite clear that the Old Testament as a whole, in its present condition, represents a monotheistic position" (Danell 1953: 24).

It is in virtue of his position as the only God that the LORD can be said to be a "jealous" or "zealous" *(qannā')* God (Exod 20:5; 34:14; Deut 6:14-15). "Yahweh's zeal consists in the fact that he wills to be the only God for Israel, and that he is not disposed to share his claim for worship and love with any other divine power" (von Rad 1962: 207-8). This jealousy is not an irrational emotion; it is the valid response of the one God who yearns to protect his people from the dire consequences of failing to acknowledge him only. "The divine jealousy . . . is the principle of God's protection of his people" (Good 1962a: 807).

b. The Angels of God

While God is one, the Bible frequently associates with him beings generally referred to in English as "angels." Scripture no more tries to prove the existence of angels than it tries to prove the existence of God, yet angels make a significant contribution to the biblical understanding of God. They are "vehicles for vividly implementing the idea of God, and whatever value is inherent in their conception is derived solely from the service they render in assisting the believer's mind to conceive of God correctly" (Landes 1958: 20). Broadly speaking, angels function in two main ways in the OT.

Firstly, angels are *God's agents in his activity on earth*. The Hebrew *mal'ākh,* from the root *l'k* = "send," means one who is sent, a messenger. The LXX and NT Greek equivalent, *angelos,* provides the English word "angel." Most frequently mentioned is "the angel of the LORD" *(mal'ākh YHWH)*. In a number of passages it is not easy to distinguish the angel of the LORD from the LORD himself (von Rad 1962: 286-87). Thus "the angel of the LORD" appears to Hagar, but after the incident she asks, "Have I really seen God and remained alive after seeing him?" (Gen 16:7-14; cf. 31:11, 13; Exod 3:2, 4; Judg 6:11-24). Such passages see in the angel of the LORD "the operation of God himself" (Eichrodt 1961: 27). On the other hand, there are indications that "angels," i.e., divine beings, appear in human form, undistinguishable (at least at first) from a human messenger. Such angels can bear a message from God (e.g., Gen 16:10-12), but they also "carry out a variety of tasks" (Newsom 1992: 249-50); they guide, help, and support people in a number of ways (e.g., Gen 24:7, 40; 1 Kgs 19:4-8). The person who trusts in God can be sure of angelic assistance:

> For he will command his angels concerning you
> to guard you in all your ways.
> On their hands they will bear you up,
> so that you will not dash your foot against a stone. (Ps 91:11-12)

The concept of guardian angels, primarily of nations (e.g., Dan 10:13), plays a minor role in the OT.

Angels are thus a way of describing God's activity on earth and the guidance and help that he gives his people. "Angels are faithful companions of man, always reminding him of the fact that man is not living alone, abandoned and forsaken in this changing and changeable world" (Takahashi 1966: 350). The concept, however, "embodies the idea of a certain hiddenness in the nature of God: he is known only in so far as he reveals himself to man" (Landes 1958: 22).

Secondly, *angels are God's attendants in his glory in heaven.* Just as an earthly king is surrounded by a court, so God the heavenly king is surrounded by beings who constitute his heavenly court. Ezekiel sees the throne chariot of God with "four living creatures" in attendance. A rich variety of terms is used to designate such beings (Cooke 1964: 44). They are "holy ones" (Ps 89:5, 7), "mighty ones" (103:20), or "those that are on high" (Job 21:22); collectively they are the army of God (Gen 32:2) or "the assembly of the holy ones" (Ps 89:5). The main function of the heavenly court is to praise God:

> Praise the LORD! . . .
> Praise Him, all his angels,
> > praise him, all his host! (Ps 148:1-2)

They also emphasize the majesty of God (1 Kgs 22:19), and are unlimited in number:

> A thousand thousands served him,
> > and ten thousand times ten thousand stood attending him. (Dan 7:10)

Attendant angels can also function as a *heavenly council* (see H. W. Robinson 1944), a kind of deliberative assembly with whom God can take counsel and even discuss proposed courses of action (e.g., Pss 29:1-2; 82:1; 89:5-7). 1 Kgs 22:19-22 illustrates how a prophet could be admitted to the deliberations of the heavenly council. This suggests, as Landes (1958) argues, that "God's judgments are not arbitrary or despotic. They are given only after a certain amount of deliberation among the divine beings. Moreover, they are based on a full knowledge of the facts, which have been faithfully gathered and carefully reported to Yahweh by members of his council" (23).

The frequent title of God, YHWH *ts^ebhā'ôth,* "Yahweh Sabaoth," "the LORD of hosts," was originally associated with the holy war (see 19-1.5a), the "hosts" being the armies used by God to defeat Israel's enemies (e.g., 1 Sam 15:2; 17:45; Ps 24:7-10). Canonically, however, the term is used predominantly in the Prophets (247 times out of 285), where military and nationalistic connotations have been left behind and the reference is to the angelic host, as for example in the vision of Micaiah, who declared, "I saw the LORD sitting on his throne, with all the host of heaven standing beside him" (1 Kgs 22:19; see B. W. Anderson 1962b). In the LXX *ts^ebhā'ôth* is translated *pantokratôr* (almighty, all-powerful), a word that is also used to translate *shaddai* (above, 1-1.2b). Thus the epithet comes to express "Yahweh's sovereign might and majesty in history" (Anderson, 654).

Other forms of attendant angels are the "cherubim" *(kᵉrûbhîm)*, who are guardians of the divine presence (Exod 25:18-22; 1 Kgs 6:23-28), and the "seraphim" *(sᵉrāphîm)*, who appear only in Isaiah's vision (Isa 6:2-3) and function as "symbols of the consuming holiness and universally effective power of Yahweh" (Eichrodt 1967: 205).

There is little speculation in the OT regarding the nature and origin of angels; the interest is essentially practical, not philosophical. The only names of angels known to the OT are Gabriel (Dan 8:16), Michael (Dan 12:1), and Raphael (*Tob* 3:17; etc.). There is never the least suggestion that belief in angels threatens monotheism. Angels may be supernatural beings (*bᵉnē ʾēlōhîm* = "sons of God"), but they are not on the same level as God. Historically, it is quite probable that at least some of the attendant angels were pagan "gods" who were "demoted" and co-opted into the LORD's heavenly court. Thus it may well be that "Israel rather delighted in thinking of the many deities of her neighbours being reduced to powerless members of the one God's retinue or court; for Israel they were but witnesses to the one God's sovereign power" (J. A. Sanders 1972: 67).

1-1.4. THE PERSONAL GOD

The one God, who is the Lord of both creation and history, is above all else *a personal God,* who communicates with people and calls them to enter into a personal relationship with himself.

a. Anthropomorphism

So central and so vital is this aspect of its understanding of God, that the OT boldly speaks of God as having most of the characteristics that define a human person. This is generally referred to as "anthropomorphism," i.e., portraying God in the form *(morphē)* of a human being *(anthrōpos).*

Thus the main parts of the physical human body are ascribed to God: he has eyes (Amos 9:4), ears (Ps 34:15), a mouth (Lam 3:38), arms (Deut 33:27), hands (Ps 139:5), fingers (Exod 8:19), and feet (Isa 63:3) (cf. Gleason 1964: 3). Since it is through facial expressions in particular that people reveal themselves, there are numerous references to the face *(pānîm)* of God, and indeed in some texts the "face" can almost be a substitute for God himself (cf. Deut 4:37). To seek God's face means simply to seek God's presence (Ps 27:8). "The whole personality of Yahweh is concentrated in his face, his love as well as his anger, although the latter is expressed rather by the turning away or the absence of the countenance" (Jacob 1958: 77-78). Because the "face" represents God himself, that face cannot be viewed directly by human beings. Gen 32:30 may be seen as an exception that proves the rule (cf. also Isa 6:5). Exod 33:11 is not an exception, for in 33:20 God tells Moses, "You cannot see my face; for no one shall see me and live," and Moses is allowed to see only the "back" of God. It is in a metaphorical sense that worship can be spoken of as beholding God's face (e.g., Ps 42:2; Isa 1:12; cf. Eichrodt 1967: 36).

Similarly, God feels and acts like a human being. The Bible does not (like later theologians) catalogue the attributes of God. Brueggemann has argued that in the OT God is characteristically the subject of an active verb (1997: 123). Thus God sees (Gen 6:12), hears (Exod 16:12), laughs (Ps 2:4), rejoices (Zeph 3:17), hates (Deut 16:22), and repents (Gen 6:6). God is said to love (*'āhēbh;* LXX = *agapaō*) representative individuals (2 Sam 12:24) and especially his people (Deut 7:8; Jer 31:3). Above all, God speaks (Gen 1:3; etc.).

A whole range of metaphors portray God, in relation to his people, in personal terms. He is the *husband* wedded to his people (Hos 2:16), the *king* ruling his people (Ps 98:6), the *judge* acting with justice to all peoples (96:10), the *warrior* fighting for his people (Exod 15:3), the *shepherd* leading and nourishing his people (Pss 23:1; 100:3; Isa 40:11; Ezek 34). He is the *father* of his people (Ps 103:13), and especially of the king (2:7; see further, 8-1.5c), though in the OT "the father-son relationship is essentially one of respect and obedience" (McCarthy 1965: 145; but see Hos 11:1). God is addressed as "Father" in *Wis* 14:3; *Sir* 23:1. Particularly in poetry the Bible employs a rich variety of imagery in talking of God, and a literary approach can make us more sensitive to the understanding of such imagery (cf. Ryken 1984: 90-103). Inanimate objects can be used in a metaphorical way, e.g., when God is referred to as a rock (Ps 18:2; Isa 30:29; etc.). In their canonical context such metaphors suggest personal qualities; to call God a rock does not mean he is cold, hard, and impersonal, but rather that he is dependable, unvarying, and protective.

b. The Limits of Anthropomorphism

Anthropomorphism serves to emphasize the personal nature of God, but clearly there must be limits if God is not simply to be reduced to the human level (cf. Vischer 1949b: 6). God is not subject to human weaknesses and failings: he "will neither slumber nor sleep" (Ps 121:4); he does not lose his temper, "for I am God and no mortal" (Hos 11:9); and he "is not a human being, that he should lie" (Num 23:19). In three ways in particular the OT sets limits to anthropomorphism.

i. The Prohibition of Images

The second commandment absolutely prohibits the making of any visual representation of God in any form. "You shall not make for yourself an idol *(pesel)*, whether in the form of anything that is in heaven above, or that is on the earth beneath, or that is in the water under the earth" (Exod 20:4; Deut 5:8; cf. 27:15). The English words "idol" and "image" are used to translate a variety of Hebrew terms (J. Gray 1962: 673). Idols can also be referred to as "abominations" (Isa 44:19), and frequently as "worthless gods" or "nonentities" (*ĕlîl*; e.g., Lev 19:4). It is not always clear whether "idols" refers literally to material images (as in Exod 20:4) or to the deities they are supposed to represent (e.g., Ps 106:36, 38). In OT times the first and second commandments were thus very closely connected.

The commandment prohibiting images was one that Israel found hard to keep. The prototypical rebellion of the people against God involved the making of an image, the golden calf (Exod 32), a sin repeated, according to 1 Kgs 12:28-29, by King Jeroboam. Even when in exile in Babylon the Israelites found the pressure to conform to the prevailing pagan use of images or idols hard to resist.

The Decalogue offers no rationale for the prohibition of images. Deut 4:15-20, however, reminds the people that when God appeared to them at Sinai, they "saw no form." It goes on to prohibit images in human or animal form and couples this with a veto on the worship of sun, moon, or stars. The implication here is that idols represent the forces of nature and thus are utterly inadequate to represent the one true God who is the Creator of all things.

2 Isaiah employs sarcasm as a weapon against idolatry. An image is a material object; a workman fastens it with nails so that it will not wobble (Isa 41:7; cf. von Rad 1962: 217)! Isa 44:12-17 makes two basic points: idols are made by frail human beings, and they are made of common material. It has been objected that Isaiah's polemic here does not do justice to ancient religions which in fact did not worship the idols but rather the deities they represented. For ordinary people, however, that distinction may not have been clear. Pagan deities were frequently personifications of the forces of nature, and the images that represented them were themselves material objects; Israel's God, on the other hand, transcended nature. Moreover, the fact that images were of human construction easily gave the impression that the deity was at the worshipers' disposal and under human control (von Rad 1962: 217), an idea totally contrary to the biblical understanding of God.

ii. God Transcends Sexual Distinctions

The biblical God is *one* and *personal;* therefore to speak of such a God inevitably involves the use of gender. Hebrew has only two genders, masculine and feminine, and in the Bible God is always grammatically masculine. Moreover, the metaphors that portray God in personal terms (above, 1-1.4a) are predominantly masculine.

A number of scholars have argued that concentration on the male images of God has led to the neglect of what J. C. Engelsman (1979) has called "the feminine dimension of the divine." They have pointed to the use of feminine imagery in the OT, and have suggested that the biblical God transcends sexual distinctions; hence this constitutes another significant limit to anthropomorphism. Two features of the OT portrait of God have been highlighted.

(a) The Use of Gynemorphisms

When we speak of "anthropomorphism" in the OT, we are referring mainly to "andromorphisms" (picturing God in the form of a male human being). A number of studies have called attention to the fact that the OT also employs some "gynemorphisms" (picturing God in the form of a female human being) (Trible 1973: 31-34; Sakenfeld 1975: 232; Mollenkott 1983). God can be pictured as the mother of Israel; the people forget that it was God "who gave you birth" (Deut 32:18; see Trible 1978: 63). In Num 11:12 Moses speaks of God as the one who gave birth to Israel and who therefore should look after her "as a nurse carries a sucking child." God cares for Israel like a mother:

> As a mother comforts her child,
>   so I will comfort you.
>
> (Isa 66:13; cf. also Isa 46:3-4; 49:15; Hos 11:1-9)

In Isa 42:14 God's future action on behalf of his people is compared to a woman in labor:

> I will cry out like a woman in labor,
>   I will gasp and pant. (cf. Mollenkott 1983: 15)

In a variant of this imagery, God can be pictured as a midwife attending Israel at her birth (Isa 66:7-9; Pss 22:9-10; 71:6). Other scholars have called attention to the Hebrew word for "compassion" (*rachᵃmîm* and cognates), frequently used of God, that comes from the root *rchm*, meaning "womb"; they conclude that God's compassion for his people is comparable to a mother's yearning for her child (cf. 1 Kgs 3:26) (see Trible 1976: 368; 1978: chaps. 2, 3). Analogies from the animal world have also been cited: God can be likened to a mother bear (Hos 13:8), while talk of sheltering under God's wings suggests the picture of God as mother bird (e.g., Ruth 2:12; Ps 17:8; Isa 31:5).

While some of the suggested references may be questioned (see J. W. Miller 1989: 59-62), there can be no doubt that God is compared to female figures. This is brought out clearly in a text where male and female images are employed side by side:

As the eyes of servants
  look to the hand of their master,
as the eyes of a maid
  to the hand of her mistress,
so our eyes look to the LORD our God. (Ps 123:2)

Nevertheless, it is noteworthy that in almost all these references *similes* are employed; some aspect of God is *compared* to a female figure (cf. Achtemeier 1993: 19).

(b) Personified Wisdom

Particularly striking is the use of exclusively female imagery in the portrayal of personified divine Wisdom (see further, 2-1.4b; 8-1.4). In Hebrew "Wisdom" *(chokmâh)* is feminine, and in Proverbs the Wisdom that participates with God in creation is portrayed as a female figure who stations herself at the entrance to the city, "on the heights, beside the way, at the crossroads she takes her stand," and accosts the people (8:1-4). Her attendants also are female (9:3). The readers are urged to "say to wisdom, 'You are my sister'" (7:4). In later Wisdom Books she can be pictured as a mother (*Sir* 15:2) and as a bride (*Wis* 8:2). As Murphy (1994) points out, "the bold personification of Wisdom as a woman serves to crack open the culturally conditioned language that refers to the Lord in a totally masculine manner" (7).

Comparison with various goddesses of wisdom in the ancient Near East is hard to resist, and historically outside influences may have been at work in the development of the female figure of Wisdom in Israel (von Rad 1972: 152-53, 167; Eichrodt 1967: 85; Engelsman 1979: 81). Yet the striking thing about the canonical Scriptures is the total absence of any idea of a goddess or of a consort of the LORD.

The use of gynemorphisms and of feminine divine Wisdom in speaking of God's activity in creation is a reminder that the biblical God is not to be thought of in exclusively male terms. In one sense God transcends sexual distinctions, and is credited with both "male" and "female" characteristics. Yet it has to be recognized that the male imagery far outweighs the female. Moreover, while female similes are applied to God, "not once in the Bible is God addressed as mother, said to be mother, or referred to with feminine pronouns" (J. W. Miller 1989: 61).

iii. The Holiness of God

The most significant counterbalance to conceiving of God purely in human terms is found in the portrayal of the LORD as a *holy* God (cf. Gleason 1964: 18-35; Deissler and Schnackenburg 1981: 303; Brueggemann 1997: 288-93). While there are differences of emphasis in the priestly, prophetic, sapiential, and apocalyptic writings, the holiness of God is an all-pervasive theme in the OT (see esp. Gammie 1989). The root idea of holiness in the Bible (*qādhôsh* = "holy"; *qôdhesh* = "holiness") appears to be that of separation. God is holy because he is "other" than humankind. Holiness is a reminder of "the essential difference between Creator and created" (Ury 1996: 342). To come into God's presence is to encounter the holy; thus at the burning bush Moses is told, "Remove the sandals from your feet, for the place on which you are standing is holy ground" (Exod 3:5). Isaiah hears the seraphic choir singing "Holy, holy, holy is the LORD of hosts" (Isa 6:3), and is immediately conscious of his complete unworthiness to enter the presence of the holy God (6:5); it is Isaiah in particular who portrays God as "the Holy One of Israel" (1:4; etc.).

In the OT holiness can be pictured as a mysterious divine force, powerful yet also dangerous. It could almost be compared to electricity, which can be a source of light and power when used with respect but of death when misused (cf. 2 Sam 6:6-7). Yet holiness is never an impersonal power. It is God himself who is primarily holy (cf. Eichrodt 1961: 272; von Rad 1962: 205), and places, objects, or people become holy only when set apart from all common uses and dedicated to the worship and service of God. The human response to holiness must be reverence, awe, fear, and a recognition of moral inadequacy. When people do not make the right response, God's "holy name is profaned" (Amos 2:7; cf. Ezek 39:7).

1-1.5. MOSES WROTE ALL THE WORDS OF THE LORD

Modern historical scholarship stresses the oral transmission of Israel's traditions over a period of centuries. Nevertheless, canonical Scripture emphasizes the writing down of at least part of God's revelation to his people from a very early stage. Most striking is the writing of the Decalogue on two tablets of stone (Exod 24:12; Deut 4:13). After recounting the "Covenant Code" that follows the Decalogue, Exodus tells us that "Moses wrote down all the words of the LORD" (24:4). Historically, the probability of early written law codes cannot lightly be set aside. According to Deut 17:18-20, "[The king] shall have a copy of this law written for him ... and he shall read in it all the days of his life." In the Historical Books we repeatedly see how the conduct of kings was to be governed by what "is written in the book of the law of Moses" (1 Kgs 2:3; cf. 2 Kgs 14:6; 17:37; 2 Chr 23:18).

The discovery of the scroll of the law in the Jerusalem temple during renovations in the reign of King Josiah (2 Kgs 22) clearly marks an important step in the recognition of the revelation of God in written form as authoritative. "With the acceptance of the Deuteronomic laws as binding upon all Israel a great change began to take place in the nation's religion, and a written document became an authoritative rule for the conduct of its national life" (Clements 1968: 24). The public reading of "the book of the law of Moses" (the complete Torah?) by Ezra in Neh 8 marked a further stage in the acceptance of the written record of God's revelation as normative for the community. Reading was followed by interpretation: the Levites "helped the people to understand the law. . . . They gave the sense, so that the people understood the reading" (Neh 8:7-8). The OT thus testifies that from an early stage written accounts were kept of God's dealings with his people. These played an important role in preserving the faith and in proclaiming it anew to succeeding generations. A written record puts the divine revelation in a fixed form, though Deuteronomy finds it necessary to warn, "You must neither add anything to what I command you nor take away anything from it" (Deut 4:2; cf. 12:32; *Sir* 18:6).

Old Testament: Promise

1-2. A GOD WHO HIDES HIMSELF

The OT proclaims its belief in the one personal God, whose order is to be discerned in creation and in his history with his people, and the record of whose dealings with Israel was passed down from one generation to another. But faith in this God and in his order seldom came easily. To a remarkable degree the OT allows *questions* about God to come to expression (cf. Brueggemann 1997: 319-24). The psalmist confides in us that there are people who continually say to him, "Where is your God?" (Ps 42:3). In Pss 79:10 and 115:2 it is non-Israelites *(haggôyīm)* who ask this question. Elsewhere, however, it is the psalmist himself who asks the *why* questions: "Why, O Lord, do you stand far off?" (10:1). "My God, my God, why have you forsaken me?" (22:1). "Why have you forgotten me?" (42:9). "Why do you sleep, O Lord?" (44:23). "O God, why do you cast us off forever?" (74:1). If it was true that this God had manifested his rule, it was also true that there were many occasions when the people of Israel could say with Isaiah, "Truly, you are a God who hides himself" (Isa 45:15). Often what was experienced was not God's presence but his absence (cf. Wolverton 1963); in this sense too God's presence could be elusive.

1-2.1. AN EVERLASTING KINGDOM

Frequently God appears *not* to rule; tension arises between traditional belief and present experience. When this happens, the OT turns in hope and expectation to a *future* rule/reign/kingdom of God. Times of trial did not necessarily lead to an abandonment of faith, but in many ways called forth a deeper faith. Thus Isaiah can say, "I will wait for the Lord, who is hiding his face from the house of Jacob, and I will hope in him" (Isa 8:17). "God's rule is only partially and imperfectly realized. Therefore, the prophets look forward to a day when God's rule will be fully experienced, not by Israel alone but by all the world" (Ladd 1974: 46). The basic promise of the OT is that "the LORD of hosts will reign" (Isa 24:23), and "the kingdom shall be the LORD's" (Obad 21).

The expectation of a *future kingdom of God* emerges most clearly in the book of Daniel, in the great visions of Dan 2 and 7, which frame the Aramaic section of Daniel, each of which speaks of a succession of four pagan world empires that will be succeeded by a very different kind of empire, the kingdom of God.

In Dan 2 the four world empires are symbolized by parts of a great statue: its head (gold), chest and arms (silver), middle and thighs (bronze), and feet (iron/clay). The statue is destroyed when it is struck by "a stone . . . cut out, not by human hands" that "became a great mountain and filled the whole earth" (vv. 34-35). The interpretation states that with the destruction of the worldly kingdoms, "the God of heaven will set up a kingdom that shall never be destroyed," a kingdom symbolized by the stone (vv. 44-45).

In chapter 7 Daniel sees a vision of four beasts rising up out of the sea, a lion, a bear, a leopard, and a fourth "terrifying and dreadful" beast, from which emerges an arrogant, God-defying tyrant who will oppress God's people (Dan 7:8, 11, 21, 25). According to the interpretation that follows the vision, these are "four kings" who "shall arise out of the earth" (v. 17), i.e., four kingdoms or empires to which Israel will be subject. The scene switches to heaven where God is on the throne (v. 9) and where "one like a son of man" (i.e., a human being) is presented before God (on the Son of Man, see chap. 7), and

> To him was given dominion and glory and kingdom,
> that all peoples, nations, and languages should serve him;
> his dominion is an everlasting dominion, which shall not pass away,
> and his kingdom one that shall not be destroyed. (v. 14 RSV)

The interpretation indicates that this means that "the holy ones of the Most High shall receive the kingdom and possess the kingdom forever — forever and ever" (v. 18; cf. v. 27). Like each of the beasts, the "one like a son of man" is a representative figure, who stands for "the holy ones of the Most High," i.e., God's people Israel, or rather the faithful remnant of God's people. The various heathen empires are represented by beasts, for they are seen as "bestial" in nature. God's coming kingdom is represented by a human being, for it will be "humane" in nature; it will represent a restoration of Israel and of humankind to the state in which God originally intended humankind to live.

The first of the four empires of Dan 2 and 7 is clearly the Babylonian (cf. Dan 2:37, 38), but the identification of the other three is a matter of dispute. The Hebrew section of the book (Dan 8–12) contains four further visions, more detailed but also more limited in scope. The historical-critical view (based on the presupposition that prophecy, in the sense of foretelling the future, is impossible) holds that all the visions (Dan 2 and 7, as well as 8, 9, 10/11, and 12) were written in the 2nd century B.C., during the Greek (Seleucid) persecution, and are in fact "prophecy after the event" (a view espoused by the anti-Christian pagan philosopher Porphyry in the 3rd century A.D.!)

Now it is clear that the visions of Dan 8 and 10/11 cover the Medo-Persian and Greek periods (cf. Dan 8:20, 21; 11:2-4), and the arrogant tyrant they feature (Dan 8:23-25; 11:21-45) is the Seleucid king Antiochus Epiphanes, who instigated the fearful persecution of the Jews (see *1 Macc* 1:20-61) that culminated in the desecration of the Jerusalem temple in 167 B.C. Historical-critical scholars, however, also identify the *fourth* kingdom of Dan 2 and 7 with the Greek, and the "little horn" of Dan 7:8 with Antiochus. (This view causes major problems; such scholars are forced to assume that the author of Daniel invented a separate Median empire between the Babylonian and the Greek, despite the fact that he was well aware that the Medo-Persian empire followed the Babylonian and preceded the Greek — see Dan 5:28; 6:8, etc.). It may be that the faithful at the time of the Seleucid persecution felt they were living under the fourth and final empire and that the kingdom of God was at hand. While the Jews did triumph over their persecutors, and the temple was rededicated in 165 B.C., what followed in the Maccabean period was far from the kingdom of God.

It is best therefore to see the four empires of Dan 2 and 7 as the Babylonian, Medo-Persian, Greek, and Roman. Certainly from a canonical point of view this is the correct interpretation (it is also that of the Church Fathers and Calvin), for in the Gospels Jesus is identified as the "stone" of Dan 2:34, inaugurates the kingdom of God in the Roman period (see 1-3.1a), and is identified as the "Son of Man" in Dan 7 (see 7-3). Thus Dan 2 and 7 (and probably also Dan 9, a very difficult chapter) point forward to the Christ event.

From the Gospels it is clear that "the kingdom of God" became a key symbol of what on the divine side is the *promise* of the future rule of God, and what on the human side is the *hope* that God will indeed act to set things right.

a. Promise

Not only does the OT *proclaim* what God is like and what God has done; it also *promises* what he will do in the future. The subject of such promises is generally referred to in biblical studies as "eschatology," from the Greek *to eschaton* = "the end." "Eschatology" is a term that is used in a variety of ways. Here it will be used in a very broad sense with reference to any form of future expectation (cf. Vriezen 1953: 202; von Rad 1965: 114-15). Eschatology deals with what the Bible says about "the end," in the sense either of what lies ahead in history or of what will bring history itself to an end.

For discussion purposes it is convenient to make a distinction between "apocalyptic eschatology" and "prophetic eschatology," though this must not be taken to imply that in Scripture these are always clearly identifiable and rigidly separated. Ultimately, as will be seen, they are closely related, the one to the other (cf. Ladd 1974: chap. 2).

"Apocalyptic" derives from the Greek *apocalypsis*, meaning an uncovering, disclosure, or revelation. It is generally used (and is used here) to refer to a particular type of eschatology, as well as to the books in which this form of expectation is found (the "apocalyptic literature"). *Apocalyptic eschatology* operates within a cosmic and universal framework. It expects God to act in judgment and salvation in one great future event (or series of events) that will bring history as we know it to an end. The end will be brought about either by God himself or by his Messiah. Judgment will take the form of a Day of Judgment, and the new order that will then be ushered in will be radically different from the present order. Salvation will be experienced in an otherworldly or heavenly realm. This has also been termed "cosmological eschatology" or "dualistic eschatology" (Vriezen 1953: 199, 227).

Prophetic eschatology is so called because it represents the view found in the majority of the prophetic materials in the OT. It operates within the framework of salvation/judgment history. It expects God to deal with his people in judgment or salvation within the ongoing process of history. God's judgment may take the form of defeat by an enemy or exile in a foreign land; his salvation may take the form of defeat of an enemy or return from exile. The expectation is that God will act within history, and any given prophecy does not rule out the possibility that after the immediate "end" that is envisaged, God will act again and again within the ongoing historical process. This can also be termed "historical eschatology."

In brief, it may be said that while apocalyptic eschatology *looks for the end of history,* prophetic eschatology *anticipates a series of ends within history.*

It has frequently been held that OT eschatology is entirely prophetic while NT eschatology is entirely apocalyptic, thereby constituting a major discontinuity between the Testaments. But while the OT is largely prophetic in its eschatology, it has important apocalyptic elements also. In the context of a BT these deserve careful attention because they anticipate the more fully developed apocalyptic eschatology of the NT, and also because Scripture as a whole, which moves from creation to new creation, has an essentially apocalyptic framework.

OT apocalyptic eschatology will be discussed in 2-2, as it belongs to the created order, while OT prophetic eschatology will be discussed in 3-2 since it belongs to the historical order.

b. Hope

Eschatology is founded on the promise that God will act in the future. What on the divine side is given as promise, on the human side is experienced as hope.

Almost from the beginning, biblical faith not only looks back at what God has done but also has the forward look of hope.

Within the created order there are grounds for hope. Nowhere is this more clearly symbolized than in the *rainbow* after the flood (Gen 9:8-17), the sign of light shining through the storm clouds, the assurance that the cosmos will not be engulfed by chaos but that humankind does have a future that can be looked forward to in hope.

Again and again within the historical order, when God's people appear to have no future their only hope lies in God. "I will wait for the LORD, who is hiding his face from the house of Jacob, and I will *hope* in him" (Isa 8:17; cf. Pss 33:20; 130:7-8). In the midst of what appears to be the utter hopelessness of exile in Babylon, Jeremiah hears God assure his people, "I know the plans I have for you . . . plans for your welfare and not for harm, to give you a future with *hope*" (Jer 29:11).

In each chapter of this work, the second section will deal with God's promise in the OT and with the hope of God's people. On hope as part of the attitude of God's people, see 17-2.1.

As Israel looks toward the future, certain shifts occur in the understanding of God.

1-2.2. THE NAME OF GOD

While Israel looked back to the revelation of the divine personal name to Moses (1-1.2c), with the passage of time and due to reverence for the divine nature, it appears that the name came to be regarded as so sacred that it could not be spoken or pronounced. Thus with the translation of the OT into Greek (the LXX), no attempt was made either to transliterate the name into Greek characters or to provide a Greek translation. Instead the LXX substituted for YHWH the term "Lord" *(kyrios)*. Though in one sense this departed from the original sense of the name, in another it served to emphasize the basic biblical belief in the sovereignty of God. YHWH, the God of Israel, is also the one who rules over all, the one who is LORD of the future as well as the past.

1-2.3. THE ONE GOD

a. Besides Me There Is No God

If in its earlier stages the faith of Israel may have been more accurately characterized as "monolatry" (above, 1-1.3a), with the major prophets, as they discern God's activity in nature and history and especially as they hold out the promise of his acting in the future, monolatry clearly gives way before a full-fledged *monotheism*.

THE LIVING GOD

This is particularly the case with Isaiah, who has God both ask the question, "Is there any god besides me?" and provide the answer, "There is no other rock; I know not one" (Isa 44:8; cf. 44:6b). In 45:14-22 the claim is made no fewer than five times that there is no God other than the Lord (vv. 14, 18, 21, 22; cf. Scullion 1992: 1043).

b. The Angels of God

Angels play a double role in the OT promise of the coming rule of God. Firstly, in apocalyptic passages *angels mediate the vision of the end times to a prophet.* Thus an angelic figure interprets to Ezekiel his vision of the new temple and the new community in Ezek 40–48 (40:3-4). In Dan 8:16 the angel Gabriel is called to interpret Daniel's vision of the ram and goat (cf. 7:16; 10:5-6). Similarly an angel communicates a series of visions to Zechariah (Zech 1:8f.; cf. Newsom 1992: 251).

Secondly, in visions of the end time *angels may figure as God's eschatological agents.* At the end, "Michael, the great prince, the protector of your people" shall arise, evidently to assist in the deliverance of the people (Dan 12:1). The promise is that "the Lord my God will come, and *all the holy ones* with him" (Zech 14:5).

1-2.4. THE PERSONAL GOD

Anthropomorphism serves to make God more personal and therefore more real. But in one crisis after another, God's people looked for this personal God and failed to find him.

In the midst of a particularly desperate national crisis, the prophet Isaiah offered King Ahaz of Judah a sign from the Lord: "Look," he said, "the young woman is with child and shall bear a son, and shall name him Immanuel" (Isa 7:14). Immanuel (*'immānû 'ēl*) = "God with us." The meaning of the sign is apparently this: the present situation is indeed grave, and there is no evidence of God's assistance. Yet by the time of the birth of a child conceived now, the situation will have already changed sufficiently to make "God with Us" an appropriate name for the child. (Whether the child is Isaiah's, or the king's, or someone else's makes no difference to the basic meaning; see commentaries.) By the time the child is a few years old, the danger will have completely disappeared (7:15-17).

The promise and the hope that come to expression in this story are obviously not limited to the particular incident in question. However hard it is to discern God's presence in the midst of crises, OT eschatology affirms that the future will confirm that for God's faithful people, their God is indeed "God with Us" (see more fully 8-2.1).

1-2.5. BIND UP THE TESTIMONY

The promise that God would act in the future was not always immediately fulfilled, and was in fact frequently doubted. While the prophets generally delivered their message by the spoken word, the negative reaction to many of their prophecies and promises provided a particular motivation for *committing their message to writing.*

Thus Isaiah was told to write down his message

> and inscribe it in a book,
> so that it may be for the time to come
> as a witness forever. (Isa 30:8)

Cf. also 8:16, where the prophet is told, "Bind up the testimony, seal the teaching among my disciples." The idea here apparently is that the prophecy is to be committed to writing, sealed, and then preserved until the prophecy is fulfilled, at which time the written record can be reopened so that its fulfillment can be confirmed (see von Rad 1965: 41-43).

Similarly Jer 36 recounts that the prophet Jeremiah, banned from preaching in the temple, dictated his prophecies (= Jer 2–25?) to his secretary Baruch; when this scroll was burned by the king, he dictated another that presumably formed the core of the book of Jeremiah (36:32). It was important that Jeremiah's prophecies of defeat by the Babylonians, exile, and return *be committed to writing* so that when, many years later, these events did come to pass, the word he had spoken would be vindicated (cf. 2 Chr 36:22; Ezra 1:1).

In face of the apparent delay in its fulfillment, Habakkuk is told to

> write the vision;
>> make it plain on tablets,
>> so that a runner may read it. (Hab 2:2; cf. v. 3)

After receiving the great vision of Dan 7, the prophet "wrote down the dream" (7:1), and in the last chapter of the book is told to "keep the words secret and the book sealed until the time of the end" (12:4; cf. 8:26). Only with the dawning of the new order will the meaning of the vision become apparent.

New Testament: Fulfillment

1-3. IN THE FULLNESS OF TIME

Scripture is bound together by belief in one and the same God (cf. Argyle 1965: 9; Hahn 1980: 69). The God of the OT is also the God of the NT; the God of the patriarchs and prophets is also "the God and Father of our Lord Jesus Christ" (Rom 15:6). No more than the OT does the NT either doubt or attempt to prove the existence of God. It too witnesses to the reality of "the living God" (Matt 16:16; Acts 14:15; 2 Cor 3:3; Heb 3:12; Rev 7:2).

"Jesus and the primitive Church did not announce a different God from the God of the Old Testament, but they did proclaim the old God in a new way" (Deissler and Schnackenburg 1981: 309). The NT proclaims that God's promises have been fulfilled and the hopes of God's people have been realized. With the coming of Jesus the new order has dawned. At the core of the NT lies what can be termed "the Christ event." This is a convenient shorthand term for the birth, life, preaching, teaching, ministry, death, and resurrection of Jesus, seen as God's decisive act within the history of Israel and within all human history.

The NT declares that the Christ event is the climax of God's working in *the created order;* Christ is both the agent of creation and the one in whom and through whom God's purposes in creation are fulfilled. This will be discussed more fully in 2-3.

The NT also declares that Christ is the climax of God's working in *the historical order;* he represents the culmination of God's dealings with his people within history, and is God's agent in both judgment and salvation. This will be discussed more fully in 3-3.

1-3.1. THE KINGDOM OF GOD HAS DRAWN NEAR

a. The Kingdom of God

The NT fully shares the OT belief in the sovereignty of God. Despite many appearances to the contrary, God is on the throne (Matt 5:34; Heb 8:1). The persecuting Domitian may be on the throne of the Roman Empire, but John begins his vision by assuring his readers that "there in heaven stood a throne, with one seated on the throne!" (Rev 4:2; the throne of God is a recurring symbol in Revelation).

According to the Synoptic Gospels, the proclamation of "the kingdom of God" (*hē basileia tou theou*) lay at the very center of Jesus' preaching. Mark's opening summary of that message, "The time is fulfilled, and *the kingdom of God has come near (ēngiken)*" (1:15; cf. Matt 10:7; Luke 10:9), is justified by the frequency with which the term appears in the Synoptic accounts, not least in the parables of Jesus. Matthew prefers the expression "the kingdom of heaven," but no difference of meaning is intended, "heaven" being a typical Jewish reverential circumlocution for God (cf. Stein 1996: 451).

Jesus' message of the kingdom of God is grounded in the book of Daniel (see above, 1-2.1), as his preference for the title "Son of Man" clearly indicates (on "Son of Man," see further chap. 7). The frequent NT identification of Jesus as the "stone" (*lithos;* see Matt 21:42 and //s; Acts 4:11; Rom 9:32-33; and especially the collection of "testimonies" in 1 Pet 2:4-8) reflects a variety of OT texts. Among others (Ps 118:22; Isa 8:14-15; 28:16), it recalls the "stone" of Dan 2:34, 45 that brings to an end the sequence of worldly kingdoms and ushers in "a kingdom that shall never be destroyed" (2:44). The reference is clearest in Luke 20:18 where the stone "will crush anyone on whom it falls." On this view, the fourth and last worldly kingdom of Dan 2 and 7 is clearly Rome, and it is Jesus who ushers in the kingdom of God.

Despite many attempts to force Jesus' understanding of the kingdom of God into a political or territorial mold, the evidence of the Gospels makes it clear that Jesus did not share the aims of many of his contemporaries (cf. Duling 1992: 62-63 and see further, 19-3.4). In the NT the phrase "kingdom of God" refers not to a territory or a realm ruled by God, but means primarily the kingly rule or reign of God (see Ladd 1962; Marcus 1988). Jesus' view of the kingdom does build on the OT understanding of the reign of God, but to that he adds a quite unique element. There are in the Synoptics a fair number of passages that make it clear that Jesus did, in part, think of the kingdom of God in apocalyptic terms: only at the end of the present age would the forces that oppose God finally be defeated and would God reign supreme, and this future reference is found throughout the NT (see below, 1-4.1).

But the most unique and characteristic feature of Jesus' message is his proclamation that the kingdom is not only *future* but also *present;* it is already dawning in his ministry, and in his words and deeds. "This note of fulfilment is the truly distinctive element in Jesus' message which sets him apart from Judaism" (Ladd 1974: 111; cf. Bright 1953: 197; Marshall 1985: 7). The understanding of the kingdom as present is generally termed "realized eschatology," and its significance has been emphasized by a number of scholars, particularly C. H. Dodd (1936: 82). In Matt 12:28 Jesus declares, "But if it is by the Spirit of God [Luke 11:20 has 'the finger of God'; cf. Exod 8:19; Ps 8:3] that I cast out demons, then the kingdom of God has come to you *(ephthasen eph' humas)*"; in Jesus' exorcisms the power of the kingdom is already at work. Matt 11:12//Luke 16:16 regards the kingdom as present since John the Baptist. Parables such as the mustard seed (Matt 13:31-32//Mark 4:30-32//Luke 13:18-19) and the leaven (Matt 13:33//Luke 13:20-21) also imply that the kingdom is already at work, though in a quiet and unobtrusive way (cf. also the parables of the hidden treasure [Matt 13:44] and the pearl [13:45-46]). In Luke 17:20-21 Jesus says: "The kingdom of God is not coming with things that can be observed; nor will they say, 'Look, here it is!' or 'There it is!' For, in fact, the kingdom of God is among you *(entos humōn)*." This saying does not mean that the kingdom is present "in people's hearts," nor does it mean that it will appear without warning at the last day; it is to be taken to mean that the kingdom is already present "in the midst of you," i.e., in the words and deeds of Jesus. In the light of these passages, it is most natural to take Mark 1:15 to mean "the kingdom of God has arrived" (rather than "it is just around the corner"; cf. Luke 10:9, 11). Any talk of "building the kingdom of God" is utterly foreign to the NT. For Jesus the kingdom is something to which people can belong (Matt 5:3, 10; 6:33) and which people can enter (or fail to enter) here and now (Matt 21:31; 23:13; Mark 9:47; John 3:5; cf. Matt 5:3//Luke 6:20; Col 1:13), but the kingdom itself is a given (cf. Klein 1972: 403).

It is frequently asserted that there are very few references to the kingdom of God outside the Synoptic Gospels; in John's Gospel, for example, the term occurs only three times (3:3, 5; 18:36). Acts, however, does portray Philip as "proclaiming the good news about the kingdom of God" (8:12), and mentions the kingdom in summaries of Paul's message (14:22; 19:8; 20:25; 28:23, 31), something by no means impossible since there are thirteen references to the kingdom in the Pauline Epistles. Apart from that, the kingdom is mentioned five times in Revelation, twice in Hebrews, and once each in James, 1 Peter, and 2 Peter. Significantly, the majority of these passages, in keeping with Synoptic usage, refer to the kingdom as a *present* reality.

Thus Paul can say that "the kingdom of God is not food and drink but righteousness and peace and joy in the Holy Spirit" (Rom 14:17; cf. 1 Cor 4:20; Col 1:13; 1 Thess 2:12). According to Heb 12:28, "we are receiving *(paralambanontes)* a kingdom that cannot be shaken." It is one of the paradoxes of Revelation, written to a tiny persecuted community, that it so often speaks of the kingdom in *present* terms (1:6, 9; 5:10; 11:15; 12:10). If the term "kingdom" is used less frequently than in the preaching and teaching of Jesus, that is due in part to a desire to avoid misleading political overtones that might attach to the term, in part to the fact that "the emphasis shifted from the kingdom to the king himself" (Marshall 1985: 12), and in part because what is meant by "the kingdom of God" in the Synoptics comes to be expressed in other ways (see Wedderburn 1985).

Clearly there is a tension between the view of the kingdom as future and apocalyptic, and the view of it as present in Jesus' ministry and from that time forward. A BT that is truly canonical will resist the temptation to eliminate either the futurist or the realized texts as not "authentic" (cf. Bright 1953: 237; Stein 1996: 453). Rather it will show that the Gospels, consistently with the rest of the NT, witness to what is most accurately termed *inaugurated eschatology:* God's reign has already dawned in the Christ event and is operative within human history, yet only at the final consummation will it ultimately triumph and be manifested in its fullness. "God's Kingdom, his reign, will come at the end of the age in a mighty irruption into history inaugurating the perfect order of the age to come. But God's Kingdom, his reign, *has already come* into history in the person and mission of Jesus" (Ladd 1974: 144). It follows that the understanding of the kingdom of God is profoundly transformed. The kingdom is not ushered in by military force; it comes quietly and unobtrusively, and is detected and seen only with the eyes of faith. Thus Jesus can say to his disciples, "To you has been given the secret *(mystērion)* of the kingdom of God" (Mark 4:11; cf. Matt

13:11; Luke 8:10). "The mystery or secret was that the [kingdom of God] had come in the person, deeds and words of Jesus. For those with the eyes to see, things were happening, but others could easily persuade themselves that nothing of significance was happening" (Marshall 1985: 9).

b. The Gospel

At the core of the NT is the proclamation of the inauguration of the kingdom of God and of the new order in the Christ event. This is the "good news" *(euangelion)* that constitutes "the gospel," a term that is used to characterize the message proclaimed by Jesus (Matt 4:23; Mark 1:14-15; Luke 4:43) and the early church (Acts 8:12; Rom 1:16; Heb 4:6; 1 Pet 4:17; Rev 14:6), as well as the literary genre of the first four books of the canonical NT (cf. Mark 1:1). Throughout the NT this "good news" is a message that is to be preached or proclaimed. This proclamation is the *kērygma*. In Greek a *kērux* is a herald, one who bears a message from a higher authority and whose task is to proclaim it in public for all to hear; the response to the herald's proclamation is the concern of the hearers. The noun *kērygma* (proclamation) and the verb *kērussō* (to preach or proclaim) are the most frequently recurring terms in the NT to refer to the presentation of the Christian message. In an important work, C. H. Dodd (1936; see chap. 1) sought to reconstruct the primitive *kērygma* from Paul's letters and Acts; the proclamation, however, was probably not as uniform as he suggested.

The good news that the NT proclaims is of an event, of something that God has done. The stress lies entirely on *the divine initiative* in the Christ event, the source of which is to be seen in the love of God. The Gospels, in narrative form, portray the grace of God in action as Jesus constantly reaches out to offer people forgiveness, acceptance, healing, and new life. Jesus' parables are in part a defense of his conduct in reaching out to "the least, the last, and the lost." Those who see in the parable of the laborers in the vineyard (Matt 20:1-16) a gross injustice (because the laborers, who start work at different times of the day, all receive the same wage) miss the point of the parable: God's gift of the kingdom is never based on merit, but always on grace (see Jeremias 1963: 136-39). Other NT writers, especially Paul, express this more explicitly in terms of God's "grace" *(charis)*. The ministry Paul received was "to testify to the good news of God's grace *(charis)*" (Acts 20:24), and the assertion that "by grace you have been saved" (Eph 2:8; cf. 2 Tim 1:9) summarizes the very core of Paul's message (see Doughty 1973 on the centrality of grace in Paul's theology). John too recognizes that "grace . . . came through Jesus Christ" (John 1:17). Since God's grace is actualized in Christ, the NT can speak either of the grace of God (Acts 20:24; Rom 5:15; Heb 2:9; Jude 4) or of the grace of Christ (Acts 15:11; Rom 16:20; 2 Cor 8:9; Gal 1:6). The term "grace" not only speaks of the love and mercy of God; it also stresses the divine initiative, as well as the undeserved nature of the gift (the cognate term *charisma* means "gift"). Since "grace" summarizes all that God gives through Christ, it is the greatest thing one could wish for someone to know. Hence its use in the epistles in opening greetings (Rom 1:7; 1 Cor 1:3; 1 Tim 1:2; 1 Pet 1:2; Rev 1:4) and closing benedictions (Rom 16:20; 1 Cor 16:23; Heb 13:25), including the final word of Scripture: "The grace of the Lord Jesus be with all the saints. Amen" (Rev 22:21).

1-3.2. THE NAME OF GOD

Like the OT, the NT has two main ways of naming God.

a. The God Who Made the World: The Created Order

Corresponding to the Hebrew *ʾĕlōhîm* is the general Greek word for God, *theos,* which occurs some 1,340 times in the NT. It is capable of being used of other gods, the many "so-called gods *(legomenoi theoi)*" (1 Cor 8:5) of the Greco-Roman world, though predominantly it is used of the one God to whom all Scripture bears witness. This God is not unknown to the created order, however, for he is "the God who made the world and everything in it" (Acts 17:24).

b. Prepare the Way of the Lord: The Historical Order

The NT follows the practice of the LXX in designating the God who entered into a special relationship with his people Israel and revealed his name to them (1-1.2c) as *ho kyrios,* "the Lord." The NT is characterized, however, by a decisive development: *the designation "Lord" is also applied to Christ.* Thus the God who revealed himself as YHWH in the OT is seen as making himself known and being present in a unique way in the person of Jesus, who is hailed as "Lord." Particularly revealing are the instances where OT texts that use *kyrios* with reference to God are deliberately applied to Christ in the NT. For example, the call in Isa 40:3 to "prepare the way of the LORD" refers to God, whereas, as quoted in Mark 1:3, the text refers to John the Baptist preparing the way for Christ, the Lord (see further, 10-3.4).

c. You Shall Call His Name Jesus

Jesus is the divine Lord, but he is also a human being, within history, whose parents were instructed to give him a common Jewish name, Joshua (*yᵉhôshua',* the Hebrew form) or Jesus (*Iēsous,* the Greek form), meaning originally

"Jah[weh] saves." Though a not uncommon Jewish name (Josephus mentions about thirty persons who bore it), Matthew sees a deeper significance in its use in relation to Christ: "You are to name him Jesus, for he will save his people from their sins" (Matt 1:21). God's saving action in Christ now means that "there is no other name under heaven given among mortals by which we must be saved" (Acts 4:12).

It is John's Gospel in particular that underlines how the Christ event makes known the true name, i.e., the nature and purpose of God (cf. 1-1.2a). "I have made your name known to those whom you gave me from the world. . . . I made your name known to them, and I will make it known" (17:6, 26; cf. 12:28).

1-3.3. THE ONE GOD

a. There Is One God

Jesus can quote the Shema (Matt 22:37-38 and //s; cf. above, 1-1.3a), but along with the earliest Jewish Christians he assumed the OT teaching on monotheism; it was only when Christianity spread out into the wider Greco-Roman world, which generally recognized the existence of many gods, that *belief in the existence of only one God* became a necessary part of the Christian message (cf. Hahn 1980: 72).

"Paul assumes without argument the Jewish belief in only one God, even though he refers to it explicitly only rarely (e.g. Gal. 3:20). He speaks of polytheism with the same horror and sense of absurdity that we might meet, for example, in Isa. 44 (see Rom. 1:22-32)" (Ziesler 1990: 9). Paul, however, may be quoting an early Christian formula referring to belief in God and in Christ in 1 Cor 8:5-6, which begins, "Even though there may be so-called gods in heaven or on earth — as in fact there are many gods and many lords — yet for us there is one God, the Father. . . ." A somewhat similar formula appears in 1 Tim 2:5, beginning "For there is one God . . ." (cf. also Eph 4:6).

b. The Angels of God

The NT shares the OT belief in angels and associates them in a number of ways with the dawning of the new order. Angels function in the same two basic ways as in the OT.

Firstly, *angels are God's agents in his activity on earth.* They are associated with the Christ event, but only at the beginning (cf. D. F. Watson 1992; R. K. Harrison 1996: 22) and at the end. "There is no permeation of the Gospel narrative as a whole with angelic appearances of different kinds" (Kittel 1964: 84). Thus angels figure in the infancy narratives of both Matthew (1:20-24; 2:13-15,

19) and Luke (1:11-20, 26-38; 2:9-14), and they appear at the empty tomb (Matt 28:2-7; Mark 16:5; Luke 24:4; John 20:12-13) and at the ascension (Acts 1:10). But for most of the Gospels their place as agents of God is taken over by Jesus himself.

Jesus mentions angels in his teaching, for example, in Matt 18:10, which affirms belief in guardian angels (cf. Kittel 1964: 86). But the role of angels in Jesus' own ministry is virtually nil (exceptions are Matt 4:11//Mark 1:13; Luke 22:43). It is particularly striking that Jesus twice *rejects angelic assistance:* in the temptation narrative (Matt 4:5-7; Luke 4:9-12) the devil urges Jesus to throw himself off the pinnacle of the temple, citing Ps 91:11-12, a temptation Jesus rejects; at his arrest (Matt 26:54) Jesus declines to summon the aid of twelve legions of angels. Spectacular or powerful angelic aid was inconsistent with Jesus' role as the Suffering Servant.

Though angels play little part in Paul's writings, the book of Acts affirms that the early church did experience the guidance and help of God through angels. "They . . . serve the advance of the Gospel and cooperate actively in the foundation and consolidation of the Church" (Schlier 1968: 186). There is virtually no speculation in the NT regarding the origin or nature of angels. The approach is thoroughly practical; angels are "spirits in the divine service, sent to serve for the sake of those who are to inherit salvation" (Heb 1:14). Although they are clearly thought of as supernatural beings, as in the OT we may ask whether in some cases the *angelos* was a human being used by God (Mark 16:5?; Acts 5:19-20?; 12:7-11?). *Angeloi* is used of human messengers in Luke 7:24 and 9:52, and Heb 13:2 reflects the OT view that angels can at times be indistinguishable from human beings: "Do not neglect to show hospitality to strangers, for by doing that some have entertained angels without knowing it" (probably referring to Gen 18:1-8).

Secondly, angels are also *God's attendants in his glory in heaven.* According to Luke 2:13-14, "a multitude of *the heavenly host*" praises God at the birth of Christ, while Heb 12:22 can speak of "innumerable angels in festal gathering." But it is in the book of Revelation that we get the fullest picture of the heavenly worship of the angels, especially in chapters 4, 5, and 19. The "four living creatures" who surround God's throne (4:6-8) are an amalgam of Ezekiel's attendant angels and Isaiah's seraphim, and like the seraphim they sing "Holy, holy, holy, is the Lord God Almighty" (4:8 RSV). There is a close link between the heavenly worship of the angels and the earthly worship of the church, and the angelic hymns of Revelation that are strongly liturgical in form may well reflect liturgical usage with which John was familiar. Thus for John, "the Church's liturgy is a participation in the liturgy celebrated in heaven by the angels and the saints" (E. Peterson 1964: 13; cf. 14-4.5a.ii). For the book of Revelation the heavenly hosts are a further reminder to a struggling and persecuted church that despite all outward appearances, God is indeed the ruler over all. It is significant that in the NT, it is only in Revelation (with the exception of one OT allusion in

2 Cor 6:18) that God is called *ho pantokratōr,* "the Almighty" (Rev 1:8; 4:8; etc.), the word used in the LXX to translate "Sabaoth" (see above, 1-1.3b).

c. Father, Son, and Spirit

If the NT is concerned to reaffirm the monotheism of the OT, it also dares to speak of God in new ways, in the light of the Christ event and the giving of the Holy Spirit that mark the dawning of the new order. Alongside the assertion that God is one, the NT sees Christ as the Son of God and as God incarnate (see 8-3); it also sees the Holy Spirit as God present and at work in the church and in the world (see 5-3). While the issues raised by these claims are certainly not discussed in the NT in any theoretical or philosophical way, nevertheless the NT in a whole series of passages does speak of God as Father, Son, and Holy Spirit.

While it may be anachronistic to label these texts "trinitarian," it is legitimate to suggest that they reflect what may be called a "triadic formula" (cf. Childs 1992: 364; C. J. Scalise 1996: 91). Significantly, the setting of two of these is liturgical: the baptismal formula of Matt 28:19 — "baptizing them in the name of the Father and of the Son and of the Holy Spirit" — and the benediction of 2 Cor 13:13 — "The grace of the Lord Jesus Christ, the love of God, and the communion of the Holy Spirit be with all of you." Elsewhere, triadic formulae are linked with the Christian experience of justification (1 Cor 6:11), adoption (Gal 4:6), and sanctification (2 Thess 2:13; 1 Pet 1:2). These texts shade over into others that, while they may not reflect a "formula," nevertheless closely associate God with Christ as Son and with the Holy Spirit (see Luke 3:22; 10:21; John 3:34-35; Rom 5:1-5; 1 Cor 12:4-6; Jude 20-21; Rev 1:4-5).

It is in no way being suggested that these are to be seen as a parade of "proof texts," but it is legitimate and necessary to affirm that while there is no "doctrine of the Trinity" in the NT, there is the *data* from which the later doctrine was constructed (cf. Childs 1992: 364-65, 375-76).

1-3.4. THE PERSONAL GOD

Like the OT, the NT believes in one God who is above all else *a personal God.*

a. Anthropomorphism

The NT uses anthropomorphism to bring out the personal nature of God. God has arms (Luke 1:51) and a face (Matt 18:10); he feels and speaks.

As in the OT, a range of metaphors portray God in personal terms. One metaphor, however, is enhanced and comes to occupy a dominant position:

God is revealed supremely as "Father" *(patēr)*. God is "the God and Father of our Lord Jesus Christ" (Rom 15:6; Eph 1:3), but also the Father of all believers (cf. Bassler 1992: 1054-55). Clearly this derives from the usage and teaching of Jesus himself. Particularly significant is the preservation of the original Aramaic term *abba* used by Jesus himself to refer to God as "Father" (see further, 8-5.1; 17-3.5d.ii).

In the Synoptics Jesus always addresses God as "Father" in prayer, and frequently refers to God as "Father" in his teaching, especially in Matthew (5:16; 6:1, 4; etc.). In John also, Jesus prays to God as "Father" (11:41-42; 12:27-28; 17:1-26), and refers to God as "Father" in his teaching (4:21, 23). While Jesus stands in a unique Son-Father relation to God (8-3.5), nevertheless it is through Jesus that his followers come to know God as their heavenly Father (Matt 5:45; 6:9). The Fatherhood of God played an important role in early Christian belief, especially if (as many scholars believe) confessional formulae lie behind such passages as 1 Cor 8:6 ("there is one God, the Father") and Eph 4:6 ("[there is] one God and Father of all"). Paul often refers to God as "our Father" (Rom 1:7; 1 Cor 1:3; etc.). The Fatherhood of God is further affirmed in Heb 12:9; 1 Pet 1:17; 1 John 1:2-3; and Revelation (1:6; 2:28; 3:5, 21). Paul makes clear that believers are not children of God by nature, but by adoption: it is because they have been redeemed by Christ that they "receive adoption as children" and are able to call God "Abba! Father!" (Gal 4:5-6; cf. Rom 8:15-16). Similarly John makes clear that it is those who receive Christ and believe in him that receive "power to become children of God" (John 1:12); and in John 14:6 Jesus says, "No one comes to the Father except through me."

As Father, God is above all a God of love (noun — *agapē*; verb — *agapaō*). Jesus in his teaching constantly depicts God as loving, patient, and forgiving, for example, in the parable of the prodigal son (Luke 15:11-32), but he "revealed the love of God less by words than by His deeds of compassion and forgiveness" (Argyle 1965: 77). The love of God is a major theme in both Paul (Rom 5:8; 8:39; 2 Cor 13:11, 13; 2 Thess 2:16; 3:5; Eph 2:4) and John (John 3:16; 16:27; 1 John 2:15; 4:7; cf. Jude 21). The message of John is summed up in the declaration "God is love" (*ho theos agapē estin* — 1 John 4:8, 16).

"Anthropomorphism," however, takes on a new meaning in the NT with the belief that God has spoken and acted in a unique and final way in the person of a human being, Jesus of Nazareth (cf. Vischer 1949b: 9-10). It is by looking at Jesus that believers can see what God is really like: "Whoever has seen me has seen the Father" (John 14:9; cf. Matt 11:27). According to Matthew, the birth of Jesus fulfills Isaiah's prophecy that God would be Immanuel, "God with us," but obviously in a way that far exceeded the prophet's expectations (Matt 1:23 = Isa 7:14).

b. The Limits of Anthropomorphism

Despite its consistent emphasis on the personal character of God, the NT (like the OT) recognizes certain limits to the use of human imagery in relation to God.

i. The Image of God

The absolute ban on the pictorial representation of God in the form of images or idols is assumed; again, the issue really only arises as the faith spreads into the Greco-Roman world, where images are an accepted part of religious practice. Paul speaks in horror of how in pagan culture, humankind has "exchanged the glory of the immortal God for images *(en homoiōmati eikonos)* resembling a mortal human being or birds or four-footed animals or reptiles" (Rom 1:23). Christians, however, have "turned to God from idols" (1 Thess 1:9). NT references to idols *(eidōlon)* may refer to a material image (Acts 7:41), but more often denote the false gods they are supposed to represent (cf. Acts 15:29; 1 Cor 8:1; 1 John 5:21; Rev 2:14). In his discussion in Romans Paul goes to the heart of the biblical rejection of idolatry: those who employ images "exchanged the truth about God for a lie and worshiped and served the creature rather than the Creator" (1:25).

Yet, paradoxically there is another sense in which the NT proclaims that God is visible in an image, for Christ is presented as *the visible image of the invisible God*. According to Paul, Christ is "the image *(eikōn)* of God" (2 Cor 4:4) or "the image of the invisible God" (Col 1:15). The image of God in human beings, disfigured by the fall, is restored in Christ. Because of this, believers are in the process of "being transformed into the same image" (2 Cor 3:18; cf. Col 3:10), though that process will be completed only at the last day (1 Cor 15:49).

ii. Male and Female

The NT is more reticent than the OT in applying female imagery to God. Jesus does introduce women into his parables: the character of God is revealed not only in the image of the shepherd seeking his lost sheep but also in that of the woman seeking her lost coin (Luke 15:3-10; cf. also the parable of the leaven, Matt 13:33//Luke 13:20-21). In a striking image that has OT roots, Jesus pictures himself as a mother hen longing to gather her brood under her wings (Matt 23:37//Luke 13:34). Maternal imagery may be suggested by references to believers being "born of God" (John 1:12-13 — *gennaō;* cf. 1 John 4:7). According to Jas 1:18, God "gave us birth" *(apekuēsen)*. Believers can also be said to be "born of the Spirit" (John 3:6). Such passages, according to Mollenkott (1983), "encourage us to see all 'new-birth' or 'born-again' images as affirmations of the female component in the divine nature" (18). In 1 Pet 2:2-3 "the Lord" (= Christ) is likened to a nursing mother providing milk for newborn babes (Mollenkott, 22-23). Such references, however, are few and far between.

It has also been pointed out that in the NT Jesus is identified with the divine Wisdom that in the OT (cf. above, 1-1.4b.ii) is always portrayed as a female figure (see further, 8-1.4b). In the prologue to John's Gospel, for example, the author "looked at Jesus in the light of the feminine personification of Wisdom; but he fused this motif with the masculine personification of the Word." Thus, "as Sophia and Logos, the figure of Jesus combined for the primitive church the masculine and feminine elements of the human understanding of the Godhead, without allowing for the alien mythology of an androgynous deity" (Terrien 1978: 417, 473; cf. 8-3.3; 8-3.4). While OT female imagery is employed in christological statements in the NT, the female aspect tends to drop out of sight, particularly since the historical Jesus was in fact a man.

iii. The Holiness of God

Despite all it says about the personal nature of God, the NT does not abandon the OT view of the holiness of God (Argyle 1965: 16-19). Mary praises God, for "holy is his name" (Luke 1:49). Jesus addresses God as "Holy Father" (John 17:11). The angel choir of Rev 4:8 echoes the thrice-holy hymn of Isa 6:3: "Holy, holy, holy, / the Lord God the Almighty." But Christ also is "the Holy One of God" (John 6:69; cf. Luke 1:35; Acts 4:30; Rev 3:7). In the story of the unexpected catch of fish (Luke 5:1-11), Peter's reaction to Jesus is reminiscent of the prophet's reaction in Isa 6: "Go away from me, Lord, for I am a sinful man!" In the presence of holiness comes the realization of complete unworthiness. Finally, the Spirit is the "Holy Spirit" (see 5-3.5a).

1-3.5. FOR SO IT IS WRITTEN

One of the most important ways in which the NT proclaims that the new order has dawned is by its repeated insistence that the prophecies and promises recorded in the Scriptures of the OT have now been fulfilled. Wherever the NT uses the expression "the scriptures *(hai graphai)*" (e.g., Matt 21:42; Mark 12:24; Luke 24:27; John 5:39; Acts 17:2; Rom 15:4; 2 Pet 3:16), the reference is to the writings of the OT that are uniformly regarded as divinely inspired (see Gese 1981a: 10). They are "the holy scriptures" (Rom 1:2). The singular (*hē graphē,* "the scripture") generally refers to a specific passage from the OT (Mark 12:10; John 13:18; etc.). Quotations are often introduced with the formula "as it is written" (e.g., Acts 15:15). Significantly quotations often cite what Scripture "says" (*legei,* present tense), as in Rom 4:3, "What does the scripture say?" The clear implication is that God still speaks through the Scriptures, especially as these are now read in the light of the Christ event (cf. Mayer and Brown 1978: 490).

In an important study, C. H. Dodd (1952) rightly referred to the network of references to the OT as "the sub-structure of New Testament theology." The way in which the OT is interpreted — or reinterpreted — in the NT is discussed throughout the present work, especially in the third section of each chapter under the rubric "fulfillment."

The Gospels make clear that Jesus on the one hand regarded the OT as inspired and authoritative Scripture (cf. D. Guthrie 1981: 957-60), while on the other hand he saw Scripture fulfilled in his own life and ministry. In the synagogue at Nazareth he read from the prophet Isaiah, then declared to his hearers, "Today this scripture has been fulfilled in your hearing" (Luke 4:16-21; cf. Isa 61:1-2; 58:6). What "many prophets and kings desired to see" was taking place in Jesus' ministry (Matt 13:16-17//Luke 10:23-24).

It is appropriate that Matthew, standing first in the NT canon, places special emphasis on this, particularly in a special series of a dozen or so quotations each introduced with a standard formula, "All this took place to fulfill what had been spoken by the Lord through the prophet" (1:22; etc.). In the first recorded Christian sermon, Peter's first point is to link the events that have just occurred with the OT promise of the eschatological outpouring of the Holy Spirit: "This is what was spoken through the prophet Joel" (Acts 2:16; cf. also 1 Pet 1:10-12).

While the NT writers each have distinctive features in the way they employ the OT, they display a remarkable unity in their acceptance of the OT as Scripture, and in the way in which they see Scripture fulfilled in the Christ event. According to Gal 3:8, "The scripture, foreseeing that God would justify the Gentiles by faith, declared the gospel beforehand to Abraham." The classic statement of 2 Tim 3:15-17 is not an unfair summary of the understanding of the NT as a whole. "The sacred writings [i.e., the OT] are able to instruct you for salvation through faith in Christ Jesus. All scripture is inspired by God *(theopneustos)* and is useful for teaching, for reproof, for correction, and for training in righteousness, so that everyone who belongs to God may be proficient, equipped for every good work." *Theopneustos* means literally "God-breathed," or inspired by God's Spirit *(pneuma);* "it does not imply any particular mode of inspiration, such as some form of divine dictation. Nor does it imply the suspension of the normal cognitive faculties of the human authors. On the other hand, it does imply something quite different from poetic inspiration" (Mayer and Brown 1978: 491).

It is often said that the writings of the NT, while recognizing the OT as Scripture, do not claim to be Scripture themselves. But the Gospels clearly present Jesus as speaking and acting with a unique, God-given authority (Matt 7:29; 9:6; 10:1; John 5:27; 8:28; etc.), and albeit in a different sense, all of the NT authors display a God-given authority in addressing their readers in matters of belief and conduct. Specific instructions to *read* epistles to the assembled church (Col 4:16; Rev 1:3) illustrate the beginning of the process by which they came to be recognized as Scripture. Revelation is distinctive in claiming to be a work of inspired prophecy (1:3; 22:7), but 2 Pet 3:16 (whatever its authorship and date) demonstrates how at a very early stage Paul's epistles were recognized as being on the same level as "the scriptures," i.e., the OT.

New Testament: Consummation

1-4. THE BEGINNING AND THE END

While the Christ event marks the dawning of the new order, the final consummation of God's purposes still lies in the future.

1-4.1. YOUR KINGDOM COME

It is the faith of the Bible that from the very beginning to the very end God is in control of creation and of history. He is "the Alpha and the Omega [the first and last letters of the Greek alphabet], the beginning and the end" (Rev 21:6; see 1:8; cf. also Isa 44:6). In Rev 22:13, significantly, the title is transferred from God to Christ, who is "the Alpha and the Omega, the first and the last, the beginning and the end." The symbol of the divine throne permeates the NT visions of the end (Matt 19:28; 25:31; Rev 20:11-12; 21:3, 5; 22:1, 3). The time will come when God will indeed rule over history and over all creation.

While the reign of God is inaugurated with the Christ event (above, 1-3.1a), the NT also looks forward to the final consummation of all things. The kingdom of God has arrived, yet God's people are to pray, "Your kingdom come" (Matt 6:10//Luke 11:2). The kingdom lies beyond the final judgment (Matt 5:19-20; 7:21-23; Mark 9:47), and is spoken of symbolically as an eschatological banquet (Matt 8:11-12//Luke 13:28-29; Mark 14:25//Luke 22:16, 18, 29-30a; see 14-4.5b). A *future* crisis is envisaged in many of the parables such as the weeds in the wheat (Matt 13:24-30), the dragnet (13:47-50), the wise and foolish bridesmaids (25:1-13), and the pounds (Luke 19:11-27). At the last judgment the King will say, "Come . . . inherit the kingdom prepared for you from the foundation of the world" (Matt 25:34). The parables of the mustard seed and the leaven (cf. above, 1-3.1a) do *not* speak of the gradual growth of the kingdom, and still less of the triumphant progress of the church in history. They are parables not of growth, but of *contrast*, for they contrast the seeming insignificance of the kingdom at work in Jesus' ministry with its *future* coming in power and glory (cf. Jeremias 1963: 146-49). Similarly, in the parable of the seed growing secretly (Mark 4:26-29), the emphasis is not on growth but on the fact that "with the same certainty as the harvest comes for the husbandman after his long waiting," so God will "bring in the Last Judgement and the Kingdom" (Jeremias, 151-52).

Paul too can speak of the kingdom as future: "Wrongdoers will not inherit the kingdom of God" (1 Cor 6:9-10; cf. 15:24, 50; Gal 5:21; 2 Thess 1:5; 2 Tim 4:1, 18), and future references are also found in Jas 2:5, 2 Pet 1:11, and (probably) Rev 11:15.

Thus, while the reign of God is inaugurated with the Christ event (above, 1-3.1a), the NT also looks forward to the final consummation of all things; as well as the "already," there is also a "not yet." The NT maintains the distinction between "this age" and "the age to come" (Matt 12:32; Mark 10:30; Luke 20:34-35; Eph 1:21), but its characteristic position is that believers now live *in the overlap of the ages* (cf. Ewert 1980: 16-17). They are those "on whom the ends of the ages have come" (1 Cor 10:11); though still living in "the present evil age" (Gal 1:4), they have also "tasted . . . the powers of the age to come" (Heb 6:5). In one sense they are already living in "the last days" (Acts 2:17; 2 Tim 3:1; Heb 1:2; 1 Pet 1:20; 2 Pet 3:3; 1 John 2:18), but in another sense the (final, apocalyptic) "last day" still lies in the future (Matt 13:39; 28:20; Jas 5:3; 1 Pet 1:5).

Jesus' proclamation of the kingdom as present yet also to come is found not only in the Synoptic Gospels but throughout the NT, though transposed into a different key. Paul's thought, as Beker (1980) puts it, is bifocal: "With the Christ-event, history has become an ellipse with two foci: the Christ-event and the Parousia, or the day of God's final victory. The dynamic tension between the two characterizes Paul's thought" (160). If in John the emphasis is more on the already, nevertheless he too maintains the tension with the "not yet" (John 5:28-29; 6:39; 11:24; 12:48).

Thus the NT as well as the OT (above, 1-2.1) is characterized by God's promise and by the hope of God's people. On hope as an essential part of the attitude of believers, see further 17-4.1.

In the NT the future coming of God's kingdom and the final consummation of God's purposes are largely spoken of in terms of apocalyptic eschatology; these will be more fully discussed in 2-4, as they belong to the created order. But it is important to observe that there are elements of prophetic eschatology in the NT also; these will be discussed more fully in 3-4, as they belong to the historical order. Thus it is wrong to confine prophetic eschatology to the OT and apocalyptic eschatology to the NT. Both are found in both Testaments, though not to the same degree. Within the totality of canonical Scripture there is a subtle dialectic between apocalyptic and prophetic eschatology. The nature of this will be explored in the next two chapters.

1-4.2. THE NAME OF GOD

God is the one whose name (Yahweh, Immanuel) assures his people of his presence with them. Bearing the name of God and of Christ assures believers that God will be with them, and they will be with God, at the final consummation.

In Rev 3:12 the risen Christ gives this promise to the faithful believer: "I will write on you the name of my God, and the name of the city of my God, the new Jerusalem . . . and my own new name." Those thus named belong to God, and are assured of his blessing (cf. Num 6:27). In Rev 14:1 the martyrs in particular are seen as having Christ's "name and his Father's name written on their foreheads." The NT looks forward to the time when "at the name of Jesus every knee should bend . . . and every tongue should confess that Jesus Christ is Lord" (Phil 2:10-11).

1-4.3. THE ONE GOD

At the end of all things, God will reign supreme.

a. The Throne of God and of the Lamb

In the center of the new Jerusalem stands "the throne of God and of the Lamb" (Rev 22:1). At the end, all that is opposed to God is no more, and the God who has redeemed humankind through his Son shares with him the supreme sovereignty.

b. The Angels of God

Angels play a prominent role in the NT's vision of the final consummation of God's purposes, very much in accordance with their role in OT eschatological expectation (see 1-2.3b; cf. Kittel 1964: 84).

Firstly, in Revelation angels mediate the vision of the end to the prophet. Christ sent his angel to his servant John (1:1; 22:6, 16), and various parts of the revelation received by John are proclaimed by angels (10:1; 18:1, 21; 19:17).

Secondly, angels are the eschatological agents of God's salvation, and especially of his judgment. Angels are associated with the Son of Man (see 7-4), who will come "with his angels" (Matt 16:27//Mark 8:38//Luke 9:26; cf. Matt 13:41; 25:31). The angels, however, are merely agents of God, and significantly they do not know the time of the end (Matt 24:36//Mark 13:32; cf. 1 Pet 1:12). When the Son of Man comes, "he will send out the angels, and gather his elect from the four winds" (Mark 13:27; cf. Matt 24:31).

Angels represent God's presence at *the final judgment*. At the close of the age "the angels will come out and separate the evil from the righteous" (Matt 13:49; cf. 10:32-33; Luke 12:8-9). In the parable of the wheat and the weeds, "the reapers" are the angels sent to separate the evildoers from the righteous (Matt 13:39). Paul knows the same tradition: the Lord Jesus will be revealed from heaven "with his mighty angels in flaming fire" (2 Thess 1:7-8; cf. Jude 14-15). In 1 Thess 4:16 the resurrection at the last day will be preceded by "the archangel's call" (cf. Matt 24:31). In Revelation angels announce a whole series of judgments that lead up to the end (8:7, 8, 10, etc.). On the last judgment, see more fully 16-4.3.

1-4.4. WE WILL SEE HIM

The book of Revelation promises that at the consummation of all things, God's presence will be with his people, fully and directly:

> See, the home of God is among mortals.
> He will dwell with them as their God;
> they will be his peoples,
> and God himself shall be with them. (21:3)

In this life "we walk by faith, not by sight" (2 Cor 5:7), but at the final consummation faith will be replaced by sight. In fulfillment of the promise "Blessed are the pure in heart, for they will see God" (Matt 5:8), when God is revealed "we will see him as he is" (1 John 3:2). In this life it is impossible to see God's face (above, 1-1.4a), but one of God's final promises to his servants in Scripture is "they will see his face" (Rev 22:4; see also 17-4.3).

1-4.5. THE SCRIPTURES

The canonical NT is the Scripture that came to be recognized by the Christian church, along with the Scriptures of the OT, as bearing a unique witness to the Christ event and to the inauguration of the new order. Rev 22:18-19, with its warning neither to add to nor take away from the words of the book of this prophecy, echoes Deut 4:2 (above, 1-1.5) and constitutes a postscript to the book of Revelation, but because of its canonical position it also serves as a postscript to the NT, and to the Bible as a whole. Nothing is to be added to or taken away from this book; the final revelation has been given, not in the Torah but in Jesus Christ, and is not to be distorted in any way.

1.-5. THE LIVING GOD: THEOLOGICAL REFLECTIONS

1. It has been objected that the Bible does not contain a "theology," and if by that is meant a logical, rational, philosophical system of doctrine, then the ob-

jection is valid. Yet Scripture from Genesis to Revelation witnesses to the reality and activity of the living God, and BT is first and foremost "*theology*" in the sense that it deals with *theos*, with the *God* of the Bible. BT does not seek to reconstruct the history of the differing understandings of God found in successive periods of biblical history (though that is a legitimate undertaking). Rather, it focuses on the final form of the text and on the multifaceted yet ultimately unified witness that it bears to the living God.

2. For many people today BT deals with something that seems to them completely foreign. Not only does the Bible assume the existence of God, it witnesses throughout to the activity of God in both creation and history. The modern, secular, rationalist mind-set has banished God from these spheres, and tends to find "God talk" not so much untrue as meaningless. While it is the task of theologians, apologists, and preachers to communicate the biblical message to the modern mind, it is the task of BT to ensure that the essential message of the Bible is not compromised. The late twentieth century showed some signs that secularism is not all-pervasive and that in all humans there is potentially an openness to the transcendent. The scriptural understanding of angels offers an illustration. Often dismissed as outmoded mythology, there are today signs of a "rumor of angels," a renewed interest in the possibility that God, though transcendent and surrounded and worshiped by the heavenly hosts, can draw near to human beings to guide and strengthen them.

3. The biblical interest in names seems strange to most people today, who are more inclined to ask in an offhand manner, quoting Shakespeare, "What's in a name?" The biblical understanding of God's name as reflecting God's nature needs, however, to be taken seriously. The Bible names God *both* as the divine power that can be known and worshiped by all humankind *and* as the one who made himself known in a unique way to and through Israel, and who became incarnate in the Lord Jesus Christ.

4. While historically it is possible that within the OT period there was a development from monolatry to monotheism, Scripture in its canonical form witnesses throughout to belief in *one* God. What is the significance of monotheism? "It is at bottom the question whether there is any unified, any reliable control of the universe, or whether we are at the mercy of an unpredictable interplay of forces in a welter of worlds that is not a cosmos, a system, a universe at all. The polytheistic Babylonians and other Gentile peoples were in constant fear and uncertainty; Israel worshipped the one God whose ways had been made known, and whose faithfulness reached to the clouds" (Burrows 1946a: 60).

5. Alongside its witness to monotheism, the NT also speaks of God as Son and Holy Spirit (above, 1-3.3c). While "triadic formulae" can be seen as significant pointers, it is essential to remember that claims that God was uniquely present in Christ and continues to be uniquely present through the Spirit are found *throughout* the NT. Thus it is fair to see the biblical teachings about God

"as laying the foundations or preparing the way for the later development of the doctrine of the Trinity. In other words, the truth of the Bible is later more precisely specified, systematized and elaborated in the doctrinal formulations of the Trinity" (C. J. Scalise 1996: 91-92). The NT texts largely reflect a practical background of Christian worship and Christian experience, i.e., the so-called "economic" Trinity; but this, it may be argued, *implies* what came to expression in the later creeds and doctrines, i.e., the so-called "ontological" Trinity.

In the centuries that followed the NT, the church expended a huge amount of effort in trying to formulate the doctrine of the Trinity. There is much to be said for the view that these early theologians did not succeed in explaining the nature of God — something that is essentially a mystery — but what they did was rather fence off, and erect signs warning against, *wrong* views of God. In doing this they devised a technical vocabulary largely drawn from Greek philosophy but not found in the NT. This was perhaps inevitable, but it does create problems when these terms are translated into modern English. To speak of God as having one "substance" (Lat. *substantia* = Gk. *ousia*) is confusing to most people today, while to speak of God in terms of three "persons" (Lat. *persona* = Gk. *hypostasis*) is downright misleading, since in modern usage the term "persons" signifies quite separate individuals. The question of what language to use is one for theologians to deal with, but BT plays a key role in insisting that later doctrinal formulations be understood in light of the biblical evidence and not vice versa.

6. Throughout Scripture one of the most marked features of the understanding of God is that he is a *personal* God. At times this is brought home through startling anthropomorphisms, though, as we have noted, these are balanced by the prohibition of depicting God in the form of images, by making it clear that God transcends sexual distinctions, and above all by emphasizing the holiness of God. First and foremost, however, Scripture witnesses not to an impersonal "First Cause" but to "the God of Abraham, Isaac and Jacob, not of the philosophers" (Pascal). "Impersonal models, such as one finds in some versions of process philosophy, inadequately express the biblical vision of reality. In the Bible, reality, understood with historical specificity, is guided towards its goal by a divine Purposer who is not limited to the sum total of the physical substance of the universe and who therefore is best described with personal metaphors like Creator, Redeemer, and Sustainer" (Hanson 1982: 65). In the NT the personal nature of God is emphasized in a radically new way with the claim that God became a human being in the person of Christ.

7. In both OT and NT there is a strong polemic against the use of images in worship and against idolatry, a polemic that may seem remote to modern minds. In the biblical view, however, idolatry is worshiping anything less or other than the one true God. Idolatry represents the attempt to avoid the absolute claim of God on our lives. In the modern world, for example, money, power, material things, personal pleasure and gratification can all become idols.

8. One of the most controversial areas of theological discussion today relates to the question of God and sexuality. Feminist theologians have argued that the biblical view of God reflects a male-dominated society. If God is male, the argument goes, then male must be God. Therefore God should be addressed as "she" just as much as "he," and God can be designated as either "Father" or "Mother" or both. From the point of view of BT, however, there are problems with these suggestions.

a. Where God is addressed in some such way as "our Father and Mother God," or as "Father" at one time and "Mother" the next, there is a danger that biblical *monotheism* may be undermined. This problem does not arise in paganism that believes in gods and goddesses, and where a deity frequently has a consort, but any such idea is totally opposed to biblical thought that adamantly insists that God is *one* (cf. Deissler and Schnackenburg 1981: 303).

b. To address God as "Mother" strongly suggests the image of the *mother* goddess that was behind so much ancient religion with its tendency to equate the deity with the forces of nature; its attempts to control the fertility of crops, animals, and humans; and its de-emphasizing of the moral demands of religion. The tendency was well known in OT times and was vehemently opposed (see 1 Kgs 15:13; 2 Kgs 23:6; Isa 27:9; Jer 7:18; 44:15-19). It is the one God who alone is the Creator and the source of all life, but he is not to be identified with any part of creation, nor is creation to be regarded as divine (cf. Achtemeier 1993: 20-23).

c. Further problems arise in an NT context. As we have observed above (1-3.4a), one of the most characteristic features of Jesus' teaching is his naming of God as "Father." The many NT references to Jesus as God's "Son" became part of the formulation of the doctrine of the Trinity as the church sought to understand the relationship between Father and Son and Holy Spirit. Addressing God as "Mother" or "she" threatens to undermine the doctrine of the Trinity, a doctrine that, as noted above, was worked out by the church, over a period of centuries, at great cost (cf. Childs 1992: 378).

Proposals have been made to avoid gender-specific terminology, e.g., that "Father, Son, and Holy Spirit" be replaced by some such phrase as "Creator, Redeemer, and Sustainer." Such formulae, however, do not adequately express the *personal* nature of God nor the interrelationship among the persons of the Trinity. Moreover, this approach suggests that the biblical terminology is "merely" metaphor that can be changed at will, rather than the way in which God has chosen to reveal himself (cf. Childs 1992: 376-78; Achtemeier 1993: 19).

In the NT, even more than in the OT, there is no evidence to support the view that God is "patriarchal" in a negative sense. God is a caring and loving Father whose nature is most clearly seen in Jesus, who said, "He who has seen me has seen the Father" (John 14:9 RSV). The point is often made that it must be extremely difficult for persons who have suffered from an abusive father to accept God as "Father." Such persons deserve all our sympathy, but the church should not be portraying God as a projection of human fatherhood. Rather it is God who is the model of all true fatherhood, and human fathers are but imperfect reflections of "the Father, from whom every family in heaven and on earth is named" (Eph 3:14-15 RSV).

As Father, God certainly possesses "feminine" qualities of caring and nurturing, as well as "masculine" characteristics. Properly understood, the biblical portrait of God as Father provides no basis whatsoever for abuse or oppression; it does provide a model of fatherhood that is as relevant today as ever (see J. W. Miller 1989).

9. Historical-critical scholarship in the twentieth century, especially through the development of "form criticism," rightly stressed that much of the material in the Bible was originally transmitted orally within the community of faith, though this approach has at times been flawed by excessively negative presuppositions. Against this, however, is to be placed the repeated emphasis in the Bible itself on a written record, available from an early date, of God's dealings with his people and of the Torah by which they are to live. The accounts of Josiah's reformation and of Ezra's proclamation of the Torah show how God can speak to his people through the written word. The NT clearly recognizes the inspiration and authority of the OT, though it reads and interprets it as fulfilled in the Christ event. The NT canon delimits those books recognized by the church as the inspired and authoritative witness to the Christ event, and hence along with the OT as constitutive of Holy Scripture.

CHAPTER 2

The Lord of Creation

Old Testament: Proclamation

2-1. GOD CREATED THE HEAVENS AND THE EARTH

2-1.1. THE CREATED ORDER

The Bible constantly affirms that God is active and makes himself known in both the historical order *and* the created order. Unfortunately this is a truth that has not always been adequately recognized in BT, for the scriptural understanding of creation has frequently been assigned a secondary place. Particularly influential was the 1936 essay by G. von Rad, "Das theologisches Problem des alttestamentlichen Schöpfungsglaubens" (ET, "The Theological Problem of the Old Testament Doctrine of Creation" = von Rad 1984). According to von Rad, "in genuinely Yahwistic belief the doctrine of creation never attained to the stature of a relevant, independent doctrine"; it was "invariably related, and indeed subordinated, to soteriological considerations" (62; on the development of von Rad's views, see Rendtorff 1993: 94-103). This became almost an article of faith in the so-called BT movement. In an early work, B. W. Anderson (1967) went so far as to say that "in a profound sense the Bible does not really begin with Genesis but with Exodus, not with the first article of the creed . . . but the second" (35-36; contrast the more positive assessment in B. W. Anderson 1984: 1-24). Preuss still sees creation as basically subordinate to salvation history (1995: 237). Fortunately, however, the latter part of the twentieth century saw a major shift in scholarly outlook and a new willingness to recognize the central role of creation faith in BT (see esp. Brueggemann 1996; 1997: 157-64). R. Knierim (1981) has rightly contended that "our consistent systematic subordination of the Old Testament theology of creation under its theology of history seems to amount at least to a truncated view of the Old Testament's theology of creation if not to a reversal of the true relationship of the two theologies altogether" (69).

In face of the downplaying of creation in BT, it needs to be asserted that the Bible does *not* begin with Exodus but with Genesis! It is highly significant that in canonical Scripture the account of God's dealings with Israel is *preceded* in Gen 1–11 with an account of the creation of all things and of the origins and prehistory of humankind as a whole (cf. Childs 1992: 385). Similarly the Bible ends, in the book of Revelation, with a vision of a new heaven and a new earth. From a literary point of view, it is the created order that constitutes a grand "envelope structure" for the whole of Scripture with the theme of creation/new creation enclosing everything else (cf. Westermann 1972: 37). Throughout the Bible there is an ongoing dialectic between God's activity in the created order and in the historical order (cf. E-5.1, and see the discussion in P. D. Miller 1995). In some texts the emphasis is more on creation, in others it is more on history, in others again, significantly, the two concerns are juxtaposed. It is quite wrong to say that creation is subordinated to history; indeed, in canonical Scripture God's dealings with Israel in the historical order are placed in the broader context of God's concern for all humankind so that, if anything, it is history that is subordinated to creation. H. H. Schmidt, in his influential 1973 article, "Schöpfung, Gerechtigkeit und Heil: 'Schöpfungstheologie' als Gesamthorizont biblischer Theologie" (ET in Schmidt 1984), argued that creation theology should be seen as "the broad horizon of biblical theology" (102-3). In reaction to the views of von Rad, Rendtorff (1993) has argued that in the OT "faith in God the Creator was perceived and experienced as the all-embracing framework, as the fundamental, all-underlying premise for any talk about God, the world, Israel and the individual" (107-8). It is on this basis that this chapter on God as the Lord of creation is given precedence over the following chapter on God as the Lord of history.

Unfortunately, consideration of creation in the OT is often limited to Gen 1 and 2; references to God's activity in the created order are in fact found throughout the OT (cf. Westermann 1963b: 198). Four blocks of material deserve special attention.

a. Genesis 1–11

The Bible opens with the creation accounts of Gen 1 and 2. Critical analysis has assigned these accounts to the P source (1:1–2:4a) and the J source (2:4b-25) respectively, emphasizing the differences in style, theology, and order of creation. A canonical and literary approach makes it easier to see the two accounts as essentially complementing one another.

The Gen 1 story is told with consummate artistry, and is poetical, liturgical, dignified, and majestic in tone (see Ryken 1987a: 92-96). Creation is recounted in six days that follow a recurring though not monotonous pattern ("And God said. . . . Let there be. . . . And it was so. . . . And God saw that it was good. . . . And there was evening and there was morning . . ."). Literary analysis reveals a basic structure whereby days 1-3 recount the creation of the settings, while days 4-6 tell of what is created to fill them:

Day 1: Day, Night	—	Day 4: Sun, Moon, Stars
Day 2: Sky, Waters	—	Day 5: Birds, Fish
Day 3: Earth, Vegetation	—	Day 6: Animals, Humankind

The account is an orderly one, climaxing with the creation of human beings on the sixth day, followed by God's resting on the seventh day.

Gen 2 is not a retelling of Gen 1; it is a story quite different both in style and content. It focuses on human beings and their relation to the Creator. The canonical juxtaposition of Gen 1 and 2 is best seen as an example of biblical parallelism; the second account does not contradict the first but complements it (see Ryken 1987a: 96-98).

b. Psalms

Creation is a major theme in the Psalter. The category "hymns" includes songs in praise of God as the creator of all things, of which the most important are Pss 8, 95, 104, and 148. The structure of Pss 8 and 104 is clearly related to the Gen 1 account (on Ps 104, see B. W. Anderson 1984: 11-14). Significantly, a number of psalms balance God's activity in creation and in history. It is obvious that Ps 19 falls into two parts (vv. 1-6 and vv. 7-14). Critical scholars often see here two quite separate psalms, unrelated to one another (cf. McCann 1993: 28); literary-canonical analysis, on the other hand, sees the poem falling into two carefully balanced and complementary halves, praising God's revelation in creation and in the Torah. God's law as revealed in nature and in morality is a further common theme (cf. B. W. Anderson 1983: 145-48; Ryken 1987a: 192-96).

c. Second Isaiah

Creation appears as a theme in the prophets, above all in Second Isaiah (Isa 40–55). To the exiles in Babylon the prophet proclaims God as both the Lord of history and the creator of all things (Isa 40:12, 22; 42:5; 44:24; etc.). Some scholars regard creation as a strictly subordinate theme, serving only to enrich and expand the salvation-historical message (von Rad 1962: 137-39). But a passage such as Isa 45:11-13, which makes no reference to the exodus tradition, suggests that for the prophet creation faith "is not simply the supporting basis for salvation faith"; in such a passage the prophet "joyously proclaims it as part of the whole message that he wishes to bring to a people languishing in exile" (Harner 1967: 302).

d. Wisdom

The renewal of Wisdom studies in recent decades has shown again and again that *Wisdom theology is creation theology.* A number of scholars have elaborated on the insight set forth in an influential article by W. Zimmerli in which he contended that "Wisdom thinks resolutely within the framework of a theology of creation" (1964: 148; cf. Hermisson 1984; R. K. Johnston 1992: 225). Through Wisdom human beings can learn about the world and about human society because it was through Wisdom that God created all things (Prov 8), and Wisdom is, as it were, built into the structure of the universe (cf. Scobie 1984b: 44-45). The climax of the book of Job comes with God's "answer" to Job that really consists of a recital of the majesty of God's creation (Job 38–39). Creation continues to play a major role in the Wisdom Books of the Apocrypha: *Sir* 42:15–43:33 is a hymn in praise of the Creator (cf. also 16:26-30; 39:16-35), and *Wis* 13:1-9 makes an important statement on creation that influenced Paul's thought in Romans.

It is noteworthy how much OT creation theology is enshrined in *poetry:* Psalms, Second Isaiah, and the Wisdom Books are alike poetical in form, while Gen 1 can be considered "poetical prose" (cf. Westermann 1974: 36; Fretheim 1987: 21). These passages are not designed to convey scientific facts, but to praise and glorify God, the creator of all things. The cosmology of the Bible is of course a prescientific one; the universe is simply described in the way that was common in ancient times (cf. Eichrodt 1967: 93-96).

2-1.2. CREATOR AND SUSTAINER

a. In the Beginning

The Bible begins by looking *back* to God's activity in creation: "In the beginning God created the heavens and the earth" (RSV, *bᵉrēʾshîth bārāʾ ᵉlōhîm ʾēth hashshāmayîm wᵉʾēth hāʾārets*). This is preferable to taking v. 1 as a relative clause and translating "In the beginning when God created the heavens and the earth" or "when God began to create" (NRSV), as the LXX translation (part of the biblical tradition) clearly shows (cf. Eichrodt 1984).

Similarly Job 38 looks back to the origin of the universe in a creative event far removed from human ken: Were you there, the LORD asks Job, "when I laid the foundation of the earth" (v. 4)? Ps 104:5 declares that God "set the earth on its foundations." In Proverbs, Wisdom can say of God, "When he established the heavens, I was there" (Prov 8:27).

b. Continuous Creation

The biblical view of creation is not, however, a static one that relegates God's creative activity to a point in the distant past. It is also a dynamic one that sees creation as continuous. The God of the Bible is not the God of the Deists, the great Watchmaker, who created the world as a marvelous mechanism but then left it to run by itself. God is not only Creator but is also Sustainer; these two are not the same, though they are closely connected. As well as the one who created in the beginning, God is also the one upon whom all creation and all life depend here and now, and without whom they would not continue to exist. "Creation is not just an event that occurred in the beginning but is God's continuing activity of sustaining creatures and holding everything in being" (B. W. Anderson 1983: 160).

All life is sustained by God. Historically, after the settlement Israel was tempted to worship the Baals, the gods of Canaan, on the assumption that they guaranteed fertility and the productivity of crops and herds. What Israel failed to realize, says Hosea, is that it was in fact the LORD "who gave her the grain, the wine, and the oil" (Hos 2:8). As the psalmist puts it,

> The eyes of all look to you,
> and you give them their food in due season. (Ps 145:15)

"The forces of nature were not apprehended by the Hebrews as static, nor again, as mechanical; in each of their operations they are moved by the power of Yahweh" (McKenzie 1952: 29). All God's creatures depend on him for life, and were he to withdraw his breath/Spirit, they would no longer exist:

> When you send forth your spirit, they are created;
> and you renew the face of the ground. (Ps 104:30)

God is continuously active in the processes of nature:

> He covers the heavens with clouds,
> prepares rain for the earth,
> makes grass grow upon the hills. (Ps 147:8; cf. 65:9-13; Jer 5:24)

God even directs the movements of the heavenly bodies (Isa 40:26), and turns darkness into dawn and day into night (Amos 5:8; cf. also 4-1.3b).

c. Cyclic Time

The so-called BT movement strongly emphasized God's activity within history in *linear time* (cf. Cullmann 1962: 51). God's activity in the created order, however, is based primarily on *cyclic time*. The created order is structured on the basis of a *weekly cycle* and an *annual cycle* that correspond to the rhythms of nature, and in turn determine the structure of liturgical worship (cf. Knierim 1981: 80-85).

The weekly cycle is established in Gen 1 where creation itself is patterned on a seven-day week: six days of work followed by a day of rest (Gen 2:2-3). This forms the basis for the weekly celebration of the Sabbath (see further, 14-1.2).

The annual cycle is determined by the sun and the moon, created on the fourth day: God said, "Let them be for signs and for seasons and for days and years" (1:14). The seasons form the basis of the agricultural year on which harvests, and thus the life and well-being of all humankind, depend.

It is unfortunate that the issue of God's activity in the created order and in the historical order is often posed in terms of "creation" versus "covenant," for the OT speaks of *a covenant belonging to the created order* as well as God's covenant with Israel. Of the four OT covenants (see further, 11-1.3a), the first, with Noah, belongs to the created order, the other three to the historical order. It is highly significant that before speaking of the establishment of a special relationship between God and Israel, the canonical OT first speaks of God's relationship to all humankind and to all creation. Following the flood, God establishes his covenant with Noah and his descendants, i.e., with all humankind from that point on, as well as with the animal creation (Gen 8:20–9:17). God guarantees the stability of nature ("never again shall all flesh be cut off by the waters of a flood" — 9:11), and the covenant is prefaced by the promise:

As long as the earth endures,
  seedtime and harvest, cold and heat,
summer and winter, day and night,
  shall not cease. (8:22)

This covenant is echoed in the book of Jeremiah, in which the prophet refers to the LORD's "covenant with day and night and the ordinances of heaven and earth" (33:25): God will no more break the Davidic covenant than he will break his covenant with creation (33:20-21, 25-26). In the covenant of the created order God guarantees the stability of creation and in particular the succession of the seasons in cyclic time that is essential for the continuation of human life (cf. 5:24; 31:35-37).

The annual cycle forms the basis for the liturgical year (see 14-1.3). Though annual feasts came to be associated with events of salvation history, their agricultural significance was not forgotten; in its worship Israel celebrates the God of both creation and history.

d. Creation and Chaos

In Gen 1 God creates by divine fiat: "God said, 'Let there be light'; and there was light" (v. 3).

The discovery from the mid–nineteenth century onward of Babylonian and other ancient Near Eastern creation accounts prompted some scholars to suggest that the OT (especially in Job, Psalms, and Isaiah) drew on the very different view that portrays creation in terms of a *conflict* or *combat* among the gods, or between one of the gods and the *waters of chaos* and/or a *beast/monster of chaos;* see further, 4-1.3 (also Gunkel 1984). Echoes of this, it is claimed, can be seen even in Gen 1 in the references to "the deep" (*teḥôm* — v. 2) and the "waters" *(māyim)* that God separates in order to create the dry land (vv. 6-10).

It is true that throughout the Bible there is a recognition of "powers" that oppose God (see the discussion in 4-1.3), but nowhere is there any suggestion of a conflict among deities. Canonically Gen 1 has first place, and later passages are to be read in the light of its strongly nondualistic orientation. There may be later references to a dragon or sea monster or serpent, but Gen 1:21 makes it clear that "God created the great sea monsters." As Childs (1992) puts it, "There is no question of a primordial dualism, but there remains the threat of non-being which resists the world pronounced good by God" (386).

The basic thrust of the OT understanding of creation is that *God exists prior to and independently of all created things.* One result of this is that "the realm of nature, which ancient people regarded as sacred, was desacralized, or emptied of divinity" (B. W. Anderson 1967: 31). On the biblical view, nature "is not divine but divinely created" (Cronk 1982: 33). Another result is the strong prohibition of images of God (Exod 20:4). Images of God are prohibited in part because an image has to be based on the representation of something within the created order, whereas a God who is completely other than the created order cannot be so represented (see 1-1.4b.i).

e. *Ex Nihilo?*

Closely connected with the above is the question of creation *ex nihilo.* Later theology has been very concerned with a correct philosophical understanding of the biblical view of creation. Did God create the world and all that it contains as, say, a sculptor creates a statue, i.e., by changing the form of preexisting material? Or did he create in a more radical sense by bringing the material itself into existence (*creatio ex nihilo,* "creation out of nothing")?

Here again it has been claimed that in both Gen 1 and 2 there are traces (borrowed from earlier, non-Israelite accounts) of the idea that God worked with preexisting material. Thus in Gen 1 (the so-called "wet account") "the deep" and "the waters" represent a preexisting watery chaos with which God wrestles to bring order; and in Gen 2 (the so-called "dry account") the existence of the earth as a dry, waterless desert forms the starting point. On this view, in Genesis "God is content to mould matter without creating it" (Jacob 1958: 143).

But it is most unlikely that either of the Genesis accounts has this type of philosophical question in mind at all (cf. McKenzie 1952: 27). Such questions were only raised, after contacts with Greek thought, very late in the OT period. As soon as the question was raised, it was clearly answered in terms of *creatio ex nihilo,* in 2 *Macc* 7:28: "Look at the heaven and the earth and see everything that is in them, and recognize that God did not make them out of things that existed," or (Syriac, Vulgate, NRSV footnote) "God made them out of things that did not exist" (contrast, however, *Wis* 11:17).

While too much weight must not be placed on the vocabulary used, it is noteworthy that the word for "create" in Gen 1 is *bārā'*, which in the OT is used exclusively of divine activity. Certainly in terms of the total canonical context, God's work of creation is unique. He, and he alone, brings all things into being and sustains them by his mighty power. "Nothing can exist independently or outside of God's being and will. God is not merely a divine artist or craftsman, but the absolute Creator and ground of all being" (Cronk 1982: 32).

f. God Saw That It Was Good

A fundamental assertion of the OT is that creation, as the work of God, is *basically good.* There is no trace of any idea that the physical universe, or matter, or human life, or the human body is inherently inferior or evil. "However deeply Israelite thought was conscious of the gulf between the worlds of God and man, it never attempted to explain this gulf in terms of the material character of Nature, as if this in and of itself gave rise to an imperfect kind of existence" (Eichrodt 1967: 108).

The Gen 1 account of creation is punctuated six times by the recurring refrain, "And God saw that it was good" (vv. 4, 10, 12, 18, 21, 25), and climaxes in the final verdict, "God saw everything that he had made, and indeed, it was very good" (v. 31). "This sentence which runs through the chapter, that the works of Creation are good, will not disappear just because in the eyes of man there is much in the works of Creation that is not good, much that is incomprehensible, much that appears savage and senseless. This sentence is pronounced despite such negative experience and judgement of the world and despite the never-ending questions after the why, after the meaning" (Westermann 1974: 61).

2-1.3. LET THEM HAVE DOMINION

a. Humankind as the Crown of Creation

In its understanding of the created order, the OT sees humankind as *the crown of creation*. This is the central theme of both Genesis creation accounts (von Rad 1962: 150). The climax of the Gen 1 account is the creation of humankind on the sixth day (vv. 26-27). The second creation account in Gen 2 is framed by the creation of man at the beginning and of woman as the climax at the end. Ps 8 says of human beings:

> You have made them a little lower than God,
>   and crowned them with glory and honor. (v. 5)

b. The Relation of Humankind to Creation

The relation of humankind to creation in the Bible has frequently been misunderstood or misrepresented. It can be characterized in a twofold way, in terms of *celebration* and of *dominion:* God intends human beings both to *enjoy* and to *use* creation.

The Bible begins with a hymn of praise celebrating creation. As already noted, the OT typically responds to creation in *poetical* fashion. Job is invited to contemplate the marvels and mysteries of God's creation (Job 38–39). Proverbs is intrigued with every detail of the natural world, and marvels at the wisdom of even the smallest of God's creatures: ants, badgers, locusts, and lizards (30:24-28). The 104th Psalm stresses that all of God's creative activity is directed toward the enjoyment of his creatures:

> You cause the grass to grow for the cattle,
>   and plants for people to use,
> to bring forth food from the earth,
>   and wine to gladden the human heart,
> oil to make the face shine,
>   and bread to strengthen the human heart. (vv. 14-15)

The regular movements of the sun and the stars (Ps 19:1-6) and the fearsome phenomenon of a thunderstorm (Ps 29) alike excite in human beings a "wondering reverence" for creation (Eichrodt 1967: 155).

It is important to highlight the response of celebration before turning to those passages that speak of humankind being given dominion over creation. In Gen 1:26 God says, "Let us make humankind in our image, according to our likeness; and let them have dominion *(rādāh)* over the fish of the sea, and over the birds of the air, and over the cattle, and over all the wild animals of the earth, and over every creeping thing that creeps upon the earth." In 1:28 the first humans are told, "Be fruitful and multiply, and fill the earth and subdue *(kābhash)* it." The second account offers a similar understanding, though differently expressed, especially in the story of humankind naming the animals (Gen 2:19-20). Humankind's dominion over creation is also echoed in the Psalms:

> You have given them dominion *(māshal)* over the works of your hands,
> you have put all things under their feet. (8:6)

> The heavens are the LORD's heavens,
> but the earth he has given to human beings. (115:16)

Thus "the whole demythologized world can become man's environment, his space for living, something which he can mould" (Wolff 1974: 162).

Few aspects of biblical thought have come under closer scrutiny and fiercer attack in recent years than these references to human "dominion" over creation. Gen 1:28 has become for many the "major proof text for the environmental guilt of Christianity" (Froelich 1971: 269). It is essential therefore to understand these passages in their broader context. *"Dominion" does not mean "domination."* The concept is used in two significant ways in the OT. Firstly, it is *God* to whom dominion is ascribed (e.g., Pss 103:22; 145:13; Dan 6:26). All dominion belongs to God in the first place, but he delegates responsibility to human beings, who are thus to treat the earth as God himself would treat it, i.e., as stewards of God's creation. Humankind is made "the responsible representative of the divine cosmic Lord" (Eichrodt 1967: 127). Secondly, in the OT dominion is ascribed to the *king* (e.g., Ps 72:8). But the king is never to be a tyrant; he is the shepherd of his people, always caring for their best interests (Ps 72:4; cf. 6-1.2c). It is by subduing his enemies (2 Sam 8:11) that the king makes it possible for his people to live in peace (1 Kgs 4:24). "These pieces of evidence suggest that 'to subdue and have dominion' is not at all a charter for abuse, but rather a command to order, maintain, protect and care for — i.e., to exercise control in the best interests of — the subject, in our case, 'nature'"; what Gen 1:28 asserts is that humankind has been appointed "king in the kingdom of things" (Brueggemann 1969: 1166). This conception of kingship is thoroughly in keeping with the teaching of Jesus (Mark 10:42-44); human beings are not to "lord it over" God's creation or God's creatures.

In the OT there are many examples of the responsible care that human beings must exercise over creation (cf. Sauer 1974: 429-32). The story of Joseph provides an example of responsible control over the earth: the bumper harvests of the fat years are saved to provide for the lean years (Gen 41). The provision for fields to lie fallow in Sabbatical and Jubilee Years (Lev 25) safeguards against depletion of natural resources. Other passages show concern for everything from not cutting down trees (Deut 20:19-20) to treatment of water pollution (2 Kgs 2:19-22).

"Dominion" means responsible stewardship. "The truth is that the world was given to us by God, and we were given to the world by God. Therefore, in the final analysis the world is not ours to possess; it is ours only to be enjoyed, shared, and then passed on to others. Our world is the gift, *par excellence,* and whenever we forget that fact both it and our souls are endangered" (Schumaker 1980: 26).

c. In the Image of God

Humankind's place in creation is defined further when humans are said to be created "in the image of God" *(imago Dei).* This is asserted in three passages:

(1) "Then God said, 'Let us make humankind in our image *(b^etsalmēnû),* according to our likeness *(kidh^emûthēnû);* and let them have dominion. . . .' So God created humankind in his image *(b^etsalmô),* / in the image of God *(b^etselem ^elōhîm)* he created them; / male and female he created them" (Gen 1:26-27).

(2) "When God created humankind, he made them in the likeness of God *(bidh^emûth ^elōhîm).* Male and female he created them. . . . When Adam had lived one hundred thirty years, he became the father of a son in his likeness *(bidh^emûthô),* according to his image *(k^etsalmô)*" (5:1-3).

(3) "Whoever sheds the blood of a human, / by a human shall that person's blood be shed; / for in his own image *(b^etselem ^elōhîm)* God made humankind" (9:6).

Two different Hebrew words are used, *tselem* = "image" (LXX *eikōn;* cf. Eng. "icon") and *d^emûth* = "likeness" (LXX *homoiōsis, idea);* while these have different shades of meaning, they are used in parallel and refer to the same thing (cf. J. Barr 1968: 24). There is no biblical basis for the later patristic attempts to draw a distinction between the two Hebrew words (contra Cronk 1982: 36).

There has been endless debate as to what these terms mean (see Childs 1992: 567-69). The context indicates that the "image" is something unique to human beings that distinguishes them from the animals (Horst 1950: 259). Clearly it does not mean a physical resemblance (Creager 1974: 104), but indicates a similarity to God with which human beings are endowed. One procedure has been to ask, what differentiates humans from animals? Answers have included mind, reason, intellect, self-consciousness, spirituality, creativity, free will, moral consciousness, and immortality (cf. *Wis* 2:23). A safer approach is to stick closely to what the biblical texts say.

(a) The image of God in humankind is linked closely to their being given *dominion* over creation (Gen 1:26; cf. above, 2-1.3b, and see also *Sir* 17:3-4). Humans are capable of a close personal relationship with the God who is above all a personal God (1-3.4), and are called to share with him the responsibility of caring for the creation he has entrusted to them.

(b) The image is linked with the creation of humans as male and female (Gen 1:27; 5:1-2), i.e., as capable of close interpersonal relationships with other humans.

(c) Because of the possession of the image of God, human life is infinitely precious, and the greatest crime is thus the taking of another human life (Gen 9:6).

What the three above-quoted passages, taken together, suggest is that the image of God in humankind is to be understood primarily in terms of *personhood:* human beings are created for personal relations with God and with other humans, and it is because of their worth as persons that murder is so strongly condemned. A person "has a share in the personhood of God; and as a being capable of self-awareness and of self-determination he is open to the divine address and capable of responsible conduct" (Eichrodt 1967: 126; cf. Porteous 1962a: 684). "Man is a person, is the image of God, insofar as he can be man who hears the Word of God, who speaks with God in prayer, who obeys him in service"; as a consequence, "in whatever measure God is no longer for man really God, in that measure man ceases really to be man, and ceases therewith to take himself and others seriously as human beings" (Horst 1950: 266-67).

With the fall (below, 2-1.5a) humans cease to live in a right relationship with God and hence with each other, but the references to the image in Gen 5 and 9 make it clear that "the essence of the divine image was not lost in the fall. It was damaged but not destroyed — defaced but not effaced" (Creager 1974: 117).

2-1.4. CREATION THEOLOGY

a. The Heavens Declare the Glory of God

BT has frequently denied that there is any revelation of God in nature; God is known only in salvation history, through his special revelation to his chosen people (cf. Westermann 1963b: 200). But the OT frequently testifies to creation as revealing at least something of the nature of God. Many texts suggest that "the experienced world itself gives knowledge of Yahweh" (Brueggemann 1997: 157).

Contemplation of the universe discloses God's majesty:

> O Lord, our Sovereign,
>   how majestic is your name in all the earth! (Ps 8:1)

Ps 19 proclaims:

> The heavens are telling the glory of God;
> and the firmament proclaims his handiwork. (v. 1)

Ps 104, in celebrating the created order (cf. above, 2-1.3b), focuses on "the existing cosmos as evidence and manifestation of the divine beneficence" (J. Barr 1993: 84) and makes no reference to God's relationship with Israel. According to Ps 148, all parts of creation join in a doxology of praise to the LORD. Isaiah calls on his hearers to "lift up your eyes on high and see: / Who created these?" (Isa 40:26), while for Jeremiah, the "fixed order" of nature testifies to the Creator (Jer 31:35-36).

b. Creation and Culture

It is OT Wisdom theology, however, that testifies most clearly to a knowledge of God that is available to all humankind through the created universe (see J. Barr 1999: 476-78). Wisdom is based on *observation* and *experience,* and it seeks to discern the *order* that undergirds both the physical universe and human society (cf. Hermisson 1984: 119). Thus the divine Wisdom, implanted in creation (above, 1-1.4b; cf. 8-1.4b), inspires arts and crafts (Exod 28:3; 31:3; 35:35), agriculture (Isa 28:23-29), medicine (*Sir* 38:1-15), and politics (Deut 34:9; 1 Kgs 3; Prov 8:15-16). Wisdom also provides the basis for what can be claimed as the beginning of *science* (cf. J. Barr 1972: 31-32). Ps 104 and Job 38, with their catalogues of many features of creation, can be seen as examples of "science by lists" (cf. von Rad 1972: 123). As well as composing proverbs and songs, it is said of Solomon that "he would speak of trees, from the cedar that is in Lebanon to the hyssop that grows in the wall; he would speak of animals, and birds, and reptiles, and fish" (1 Kgs 4:32-33); in other words, he did biology by classifying the various species. The author of the deuterocanonical *Wisdom of Solomon,* while strongly condemning the human tendency to idolatry, nevertheless affirms the possibility of knowing God through the beauty of nature, for God is "the author of beauty" (13:3):

> For from the greatness and beauty of created things
> comes a corresponding perception of their Creator. (13:5)

Historical studies confirm what Scripture itself indicates: that Israelite Wisdom has close affinities with an international wisdom movement. While Solomon's wisdom is said to have "surpassed the wisdom of all the people of the east, and all the wisdom of Egypt" (1 Kgs 4:30), there is nothing to suggest that the wisdom of those areas was invalid. Strikingly absent from Wisdom are any references to exodus, covenant, Torah, or any of God's dealings in history with his people Israel. Proverbs incorporates material of non-Israelite origin in Prov 30 and 31:1-9 (reading "of Massa" in 30:1 and 31:1); it is now known that the "Words of the Wise" in Prov 22:17–23:34 show many parallels with the Egyptian wisdom of Amen-em-ope. It is significant that Job is not an Israelite (Job 1:1). Even *Sirach,* which identifies Wisdom and Torah, recognizes that God created Wisdom and

> poured her out upon all his works,
> upon all the living according to his gift. (1:9-10)

Thus, as R. K. Johnston (1992) affirms, "there is found in wisdom an appreciation for truth whenever it may be found" (236). Of course, Israel's borrowing from international wisdom involved selection and modification of material, yet we may agree with Eichrodt that Wisdom provides a basis for recognizing a *revelatio generalis,* a "general revelation" to all humankind, as well as the *revelatio specialis,* the "special revelation," vouchsafed to Israel (1967: 91). Similarly Brueggemann (1997) says of OT Wisdom material, "As 'natural theology,' this deposit of sustained reflection is indeed revelatory: it reveals and discloses the God who creates, orders and sustains reality" (681).

c. Every Living Thing

Not only human beings but all living things are created and cared for by God. Fish, birds, and animals figure in the creation accounts as part of what is declared to be "good" (Gen 1:25), and as part of creation, animals praise God (Ps 148:1, 10). While Scripture clearly differentiates between animals and humans, it also sees them as closely related, sharing in "the community of the sixth day of creation" (Birch and Vischer 1997: 2; cf. Gen 1:24-31). God's covenant with Noah and his descendants also includes the animal world: "I am establishing my covenant with you . . . *and with every living creature*" (Gen 9:9-10). The animal creation is cared for by God:

> For every wild animal of the forest is mine,
>   the cattle on a thousand hills.
> I know all the birds of the air,
>   and all that moves in the field is mine.
> (Ps 50:10-11; cf. Job 38:39; Pss 145:15-16; 147:9; Jer 8:7)

As with creation generally, the relation of human beings to animals is defined in terms of both *celebration* and *dominion.* Many poetical passages celebrate the animal creation. Ps 104 regards storks, wild goats, badgers, and other wild animals with a sense of wonder. Job is asked by God,

> Do you give the horse its might?
>> Do you clothe its neck with mane?
> Do you make it leap like the locust?
>> Its majestic snorting is terrible. (Job 39:19-20)

Here the horse is not regarded for its usefulness to humankind, but as an object of awe, wonder, and admiration. In Wisdom the animal kingdom provides lessons from which humankind can learn (e.g., Prov 6:6-11). From the perspective of Wisdom in particular, "God made the creatures and delights in them for their own sake. Mystery is allowed for; intrinsic value affirmed. We can but wonder" (R. K. Johnston 1992: 230).

Against these passages have to be balanced those that assert humankind's dominion, specifically over the animal creation (Gen 1:26; Ps 8:6-8). Animals stand in the service of humankind. In the OT "dominion" clearly includes the right to use animals for food (cf. Gen 9:3), though the laws of clean and unclean animals in the Torah specified which animals could and which could not be eaten.

Any idea that "dominion" means either cruelty or ruthless exploitation is ruled out by many passages that speak of the need for humans to respect and care for animals. This is a special concern of Deuteronomy (see 22:1-4, 6, 7, 10; 25:4). Animals are specifically included in the Sabbath rest (Exod 20:10//Deut 5:14). A similar attitude is found in Wisdom:

> The righteous know the needs of their animals,
>> but the mercy of the wicked is cruel. (Prov 12:10)

Here too, in relation to animals, "dominion ought to be understood in terms of stewardship, of giving thanks for, tending, and nurturing what is first and always God's" (J. D. Jones 1981: 269).

2-1.5. THE CORRUPTION OF CREATION

While the OT proclaims that creation is essentially good, it also recognizes that it is a good thing gone wrong. Humankind's rebellion against and alienation from God, traced especially in Gen 1–11, result in a disorder that pervades not only *human society* but also even *the physical universe*. God's response is expressed in terms of a tension between *judgment* and *salvation*. Because he is holy, God cannot tolerate the existence of sin and evil; but because he is a God of mercy, his aim is not the destruction but the salvation of humankind.

a. Human Society

The canonical position of Gen 3–11 is highly significant. Following the initial creation accounts, these chapters offer not one but four pictures of humankind's rebellion against and alienation from God (see von Rad 1962: 154-65). "Genesis 1–2 describes the relationship between God, man and nature *as it was originally intended to be;* while Gen 3–11 presents that relationship *as it is* — corrupted and subverted by man's sinful rebellion against the love and will of God" (Cronk 1982: 29).

i. Gen 3 is the classic account of "the fall." From a literary point of view, it can be seen as "the prototypical biblical tragedy," with pride, the putting of oneself in the place of God, as the fatal "tragic flaw" (Ryken 1984: 84). The basic temptation is to "be like God" (Gen 3:5). Pride leads to disobedience. God commanded Adam not to eat from "the tree of the knowledge of good and evil" (2:17; cf. 2:9), but the serpent urges the first couple to do precisely this, and they disobey God's command. Biblical usage suggests that "knowing good and evil" means something like knowing all things or sharing in divine wisdom (cf. 2 Sam 14:17), or "the knowledge of that which is useful or harmful to man" (Westermann 1974: 93). One theme in the chapters that follow is the growth of technology. But with this comes the realization that knowledge can be used for good or evil. Bronze and iron can be used for tools, but also to make weapons to wound and kill (Gen 4:22-24); the baking of bricks makes possible the building of a city, but also of a tower that reaches to the heavens (11:3-4).

Rebellion against God and disobedience of his commands result in alienation from God, symbolized by the expulsion from the garden. The human couple are not punished by death immediately, but they are cut off from access to the tree of life and thus condemned to die eventually (cf. 20-2.2). Moreover, the immediate result of their actions is portrayed as "*the enslavement of all life to the hostile powers of death* — suffering, pain, toil, struggle — by which it is worn out before its time" (Eichrodt 1967: 406).

ii. Gen 4 graphically illustrates how alienation from God produces alienation from one's fellow human beings. The story of the first two human brothers, Cain and Abel, is not a story of brotherly love but of brotherly hatred, and of the first recorded murder. Lamech exemplifies the human thirst for unlimited revenge.

iii. The longer story of the flood (Gen 6–8) represents God's righteous judgment on a creation that has become corrupt. "The LORD saw that the wickedness of humankind was great in the earth, and that every inclination of the thoughts of their hearts was only evil continually" (6:5). The waters below and above the earth threaten to return all things to the primeval chaos (cf. B. W. Anderson 1984: 160). But by saving Noah and his family God makes possible a new beginning for the human race, and for all creation.

iv. The story of the Tower of Babel (Gen 11) is a variant on the theme of human beings wishing to put themselves in the place of God, with disastrous results. Humankind is fragmented into different languages and nations; yet among these are the ancestors of Abram through whom God will begin to work out his plan for the salvation of the human race.

These four stories speak powerfully of "the solidarity with which all men are bound together in sin" (Eichrodt 1967: 404). But they also point forward to God's plan of salvation.

In their present canonical form, the first eleven chapters of Genesis clearly display an overall design, "a dramatic movement from the original harmony of creation, through the violent disruption of that order and the near return to chaos, and finally to a new creation under the rainbow sign of the everlasting covenant" (B. W. Anderson 1978: 39).

b. The Physical Universe

The Bible sees the corruption and disorder that result from human rebellion and alienation as pervading not only human society but also *the physical universe*. Here again, recent interest in ecology and concern over the environment have focused attention on a neglected dimension of biblical thought.

The disorder that results from the fall affects humankind's relationship with the earth: "Cursed is the ground because of you" (Gen 3:17). God brought his people "into a plentiful land to eat its fruits and its good things," but, Jeremiah charges,

> When you entered in you defiled my land,
> and made my heritage an abomination. (Jer 2:7)

When God's people disobey him, nature itself goes into mourning:

> Swearing, lying, and murder,
> and stealing and adultery break out;
> bloodshed follows bloodshed.
> Therefore the land mourns,
> and all who live in it languish;
> together with the wild animals
> and the birds of the air,
> even the fish of the sea are perishing. (Hos 4:2-3; cf. Dyrness 1992: 269)

In Joel 1:2-12 also, the divine punishment on sin and disobedience extends to nature.

Old Testament: Promise

2-2. NEW HEAVENS AND A NEW EARTH

Experience is very far from suggesting that God rules over all the earth. The writer of Ps 10 prays,

> Break the arm of the wicked and evildoers;
>   seek out their wickedness until you find none.
> The LORD is king forever and ever;
>   the nations shall perish from his land. (vv. 15-16)

What the psalmist appears to be saying here is not so much that "the LORD is king," as that the Lord ought to rule over all humankind but appears not to. Zech 14:9 anticipates a time when "the LORD *will become king* over all the earth."

Within the created order the promise and hope of God's future action to establish a new order takes the form of *apocalyptic eschatology.*

2-2.1. APOCALYPTIC ESCHATOLOGY: THE END OF HISTORY

a. The Place of Apocalyptic in the Old Testament

OT apocalyptic eschatology (see 1-2.1a) has been held by some scholars to be insignificant, or even nonexistent. Gowan (1986) contends that "the OT does not speak of the end of the world, of time, or of history," and that "the OT vision of the future deals throughout with the world in which we now live" (2). While he rightly emphasizes the ethical implications of OT eschatology, and especially the obligation of humankind to care for the earth, Gowan's view does not do justice to the cosmic dimension of OT eschatology, and it sets aside features such as the resurrection of the dead (see 20-2.4b) and the final judgment (see 2-2.3; 16-2.3). Apocalyptic material is in fact to be found, most notably in Isa 24–27 ("The Isaiah Apocalypse"); parts of Isa 56–66; parts of Ezekiel; Dan 2, 7, 12 (in part); Joel 2 and 3; and Zech 9–14. It is true that in these books prophetic and apocalyptic material cannot always be clearly separated; one often tends to blend into the other.

Historical-critical scholarship frequently sees apocalyptic as a late, postexilic development in the history of Israelite religion, reflecting the influence of Persian thought (see Patrick 1981: 112). Others, while still seeing it as late, stress more its development from classical prophecy on a trajectory that runs through 2 Isaiah, 3 Isaiah, 2 Zechariah to Daniel (see Hanson 1971, and in more detail Hanson 1979; cf. also D. S. Russell 1964: 92-96). Its lateness is then frequently advanced as a reason for rejecting it as a nonessential part of OT faith. Probably most of the apocalyptic material is exilic or later, though at times a circular argument is employed: All apocalyptic material comes from the postexilic period. But what about Isa 24–27? It must be a later insertion. How do we know that? Because all apocalyptic material is postexilic!

A canonical BT, however, is not concerned with disputed questions of origin and date, but with the role apocalyptic plays within the final form of the OT and of Scripture as a whole. In the OT apocalyptic materials are not large quantitatively, but they do occur spread out through the prophetic books, interspersed among the more dominant prophetic eschatology. Moreover, they become more significant when seen in relation to NT eschatology, and particularly in relation to the structure of canonical Scripture as a whole.

b. Characteristics of Apocalyptic Eschatology

Apocalyptic eschatology, as we have seen (1-2.1a), operates within the framework of the created order (see Ladd 1974: chap. 3). "Salvation history" fades from view (cf. von Rad 1965: 304), and God's workings are portrayed on a cosmic scale. The eschaton or "end" anticipated by apocalyptic does not consist of future events within history, but rather of the end of history itself as we know it. It also tends to work within a dualistic framework in which God is opposed by powers of evil that for the time being seem to control the world. The only hope therefore lies in the defeat of evil and the judgment of the wicked in a final cosmic event; hence the sharp demarcation between this age and the age to come. Apocalyptic tends to focus on the evil and corruption of the present world order, and to be pessimistic about attempts to ameliorate the situation by human means. Hence one finds little or no concern for social action in apocalyptic (cf. Schmithals 1975: 40-47). Only God can put matters right, and all that God's faithful people can do is watch and pray for the coming of the end. Typically, "apocalyptic writings foster hope in situations of crisis for those despairing of help from earthly sources" (Hanson 1987: 27).

Apocalyptic makes extensive use of visions of the future, often conveyed to the seer through the mediation of an angel. Hence the use of imagery and symbolism that clearly are not designed to be taken with a grim literalness. Similarly we do not find a rigid consistency of outlook in the various visions of the future, and caution must be exercised in any attempts to harmonize the various elements in the picture of the end, or to draw up an "eschatological timetable." All that can be done is to sketch out the main features of apocalyptic expectation.

2-2.2. SIGNS OF THE TIMES: COSMIC UPHEAVALS

Though apocalyptic holds out the hope of the ultimate cosmic triumph of God's purposes, it does not see this as an easy victory. The end will be preceded by various disasters and cosmic upheavals that will be the birth pangs of the new order:

> The heavens will vanish like smoke,
>> the earth will wear out like a garment. (Isa 51:6)

Long ago God created the earth and the heavens:

> They will perish, but you endure;
>> they will all wear out like a garment. (Ps 102:26)

Isa 24:1-20 presents a remarkable picture of the *reversal of creation* (see Hanson 1987: 93-103). In a terrifying vision Jeremiah sees God's coming judgment accompanied by cosmic upheavals:

> I looked on the earth, and lo, it was waste and void;
>> and to the heavens, and they had no light.
> I looked on the mountains, and lo, they were quaking,
>> and all the hills moved to and fro. (Jer 4:23-24)

This reversal of the process of creation is reflected also in Zeph 1:2-3 (cf. also 1:15):

> I will utterly sweep away everything
>> from the face of the earth, says the LORD.
> I will sweep away humans and animals;
>> I will sweep away the birds of the air
> and the fish of the sea. . . .
> I will cut off humanity
>> from the face of the earth.

In Joel's vision the Day of the Lord (below, 2-2.3) is preceded by cosmic signs: "I will show portents in the heavens and on the earth, blood and fire and columns of smoke. The sun shall be turned to darkness, and the moon to blood, before the great and terrible day of the LORD comes" (Joel 2:30-31; cf. 3:14-15; Amos 8:9). As the end draws near, the cosmic powers opposed to God will grow stronger; see more fully, 4-2.4.

2-2.3. THE DAY OF THE LORD: COSMIC JUDGMENT

The end will be the occasion for God's judgment of the entire world. It will be the time when the Lord comes "to judge the earth" (Ps 96:13). That judgment will extend to all peoples:

> He will judge the world with righteousness,
>   and the peoples with equity. (Ps 98:9)

> By fire will the LORD execute judgment,
>   and by his sword, on all flesh. (Isa 66:16; cf. 66:24)

As we shall see (3-2.3), an important theme in the prophetic literature is the coming "day of the LORD" *(yôm YHWH)*, sometimes referred to in short-hand fashion as "the day" (e.g., Ezek 7:7; cf. Isa 34:8), a day when God's judgment will fall not only on his enemies but also on disobedient Israel. While the majority of references envisage God's judgment within history, in some cases the immediate judgment becomes a window through which may be viewed God's final apocalyptic judgment.

Thus the prophet Joel declares:

> Blow the trumpet in Zion. . . .
> Let all the inhabitants of the land tremble,
>   for the day of the LORD is coming, it is near. (Joel 2:1; cf. 1:15)

The agent of God's judgment is a plague of locusts (1:2-7; 2:4-9), something clearly in the realm of prophetic eschatology. *Through* this immediate judgment, however, Joel sees God's final judgment, preceded by cosmic signs (2:10, 30-31; 3:14-15). Similarly in Isa 13 the prophet sees the Day of the LORD in terms of the downfall of Babylon, but *through* that he also sees the cosmic day of judgment (vv. 9-10) when God says,

> I will punish the world for its evil,
>   and the wicked for their iniquity. (v. 11)

The last judgment is described in more detail in *Wis* 4:20–5:23; it will be a time when the wicked

> will come with dread when their sins are reckoned up,
> and their lawless deeds will convict them to their face. (4:20)

The end will be marked by the final defeat not just of Israel's historical enemies, but of the cosmic powers of sin and disorder (see more fully, 4-2.5). For a further discussion of final judgment, see 16-2.3.

2-2.4. ALL THINGS NEW: COSMIC SALVATION

In apocalyptic eschatology visions of cosmic upheavals and cosmic judgment are balanced by visions of cosmic salvation — of a renewal of the created order, and ultimately of a new creation.

a. Paradise Restored

Many prophetic pictures of the new age envisage the renewal of creation and the miraculous fertility of the land. God will give waters in the wilderness (Isa 41:18-20; 43:19-21).

> The wilderness and the dry land shall be glad,
>   the desert shall rejoice and blossom. (35:1; cf. 35:7; Lev 26:3-13)

The land will produce prodigious crops:

> The time is surely coming, says the LORD,
>   when the one who plows shall overtake the one who reaps,
>   and the treader of grapes the one who sows the seed;
> the mountains shall drip sweet wine,
>   and all the hills shall flow with it. (Amos 9:13)

Similar prophecies of future fertility are found in Ps 72:16, Isa 30:23-24, Ezek 34:26-29, Joel 2:18-24, 3:18, and Zech 8:12. Hos 2:18-23 envisages a new covenant between God and Israel that will include a new relationship to the created order and an abundance of "the grain, the wine and the oil" (cf. Dyrness 1992: 269-71).

Taken literally, such prophecies might seem to belong more to prophetic eschatology than to apocalyptic. But it is clear that what these passages envisage is nothing less than the reversal of the curse upon the ground of Gen 3:17-19 that was the result of human sin (see above, 2-1.5b). "Since the curse pronounced upon the land by God consisted in its subsequent failure to produce crops without the backbreaking toil of man, the prediction that the soil will become abundantly fertile is then equivalent to a prediction that the divine curse will be removed from the soil" (DeGuglielmo 1957: 310). The ground was cursed with "thorns and thistles" (Gen 3:18), but in the new age "thorns and briers" will become "a fruitful field" (Isa 32:13, 15; cf. 55:13). The theme of paradise restored becomes explicit in Isa 51:3:

> For the LORD will comfort Zion . . .
> and will make her wilderness like Eden,
>   her desert like the garden of the LORD,

and in Ezek 36:35, where the prophet declares that "this land that was desolate has become like the garden of Eden" (cf. Jer 31:12). The vision of the restored land in Ezek 47:1-12 echoes the creation accounts of Gen 1 and 2 at a number of points (see further, 13-2.3). What is involved here is far more than a literal longing for bumper crops. In the new age the consequences of human sin will be reversed, and creation itself will be renewed.

b. The Wolf and the Lamb

The paradise restored theme is further seen in the promise that the transformation of creation will encompass the animal kingdom. The threat of wild animals will be removed (Isa 35:9; Ezek 34:28), and God will make a new covenant of peace between humankind and the animal kingdom (Hos 2:18; Ezek 34:25), thus reversing the enmity that was another result of the fall. Isaiah goes further and envisages an eschatological reconciliation among beasts, as well as between animals and humans:

> The wolf shall live with the lamb,
>   the leopard shall lie down with the kid,
> the calf and the lion and the fatling together.
>
> (Isa 11:6, see vv. 7-8; cf. 65:25)

"It is only in the Messianic End-time that the relationship of the animals to one another, as well as the relation between man and beast, will no longer be marked by domination and conflict, but by peaceful play" (Wolff 1974: 248 n. 13; cf. Schumaker 1980: 14).

c. New Heavens and a New Earth

In a few passages we find the anticipation of a full-blown, apocalyptic, radically new order:

> For I am about to create new heavens
>   and a new earth;
> the former things shall not be remembered
>   or come to mind. (Isa 65:17; cf. 66:22)

Isa 30:26 envisages a time when "the light of the moon will be like the light of the sun, and the light of the sun will be sevenfold," but Isa 60:20 and Zech 14:7 suggest a return to the original state, even before the creation of day and night, when the LORD himself is the light.

The basic principle of these visions of cosmic salvation is the correspondence between the beginning and the end, between creation and new creation, a theme especially emphasized by the work of H. Gunkel, *Urzeit und Endzeit* (= primordial time and end time). "Ktisiology and eschatology, the beginning and the end, are co-ordinate" (Lindeskog 1953: 8). The end will be a return to the beginning, to creation as God originally intended it to be, though the end will also bring something more (cf. Jacob 1958: 142). In the descriptions of a renewed earth, "almost every sentence is related to creation and corresponds to something in the primal history, Genesis 1–11. No one can fail to see that here primal time and end time correspond to each other. The end time is described as creation made whole again" (Westermann 1972: 19).

2-2.5. THE TIME OF THE END

Generally in OT apocalyptic visions the time of the end is not specified; the apocalyptic events will come to pass "on that day" (Zech 14:4, 6, 8, 20).

The book of Daniel is generally classified as apocalyptic, but as we shall see (3-2.5), most of Daniel's visions are prophecy, i.e., they anticipate events that are to happen in the course of history. Only in the visions of the final coming of the kingdom of God in Dan 2 and 7 (see 1-2.1), and then in 12:1-4, does the book look beyond history to the apocalyptic end of history.

While this is true, there is no justification in the text for the view of "Bible Prophecy" advocates who insert into the visions of Dan 2, 7, and 9 a gap of at least 2000 years and then find in the concluding verses of each vision evidence of an elaborate "end-times" scenario. The visions of Daniel are content to anticipate the final triumph of the kingdom of God without going into details and without attempting to forecast the time of the end.

It is in an apocalyptic context that the power opposed to God is said to prevail for "a time, times and half a time" (7:25; 12:7 NIV). Historical-critical scholars generally interpret this to mean three and a half years, and they link it with the 1,150-day period of the desecration of the sanctuary in Dan 8:14, and with the references to 1,290 days (Dan 12:11) and 1,335 days (Dan 12:12). These references, however, belong to the realm of prophetic eschatology and evidently reflect varying understandings of the period 168 to 165 B.C. (see further 3-2.5). But in the context of apocalyptic eschatology, "a time, times and half a time" is best taken to refer to a long and indefinite period.

Thus when Daniel asks the angel, "What shall be the outcome of these things?" he is told, "Go your way, Daniel, for the words are to remain secret and sealed until the time of the end" (12:9); in other words, the time of the final consummation is *not* revealed to Daniel. While prophetic eschatology may involve specific predictions of historical events (as in 8:14; 12:11-12), apocalyptic eschatology recognizes that the end of all things cannot be predicted, for that is something that lies entirely in the hand of God.

New Testament: Fulfillment

2-3. A NEW CREATION

2-3.1. THE GOD WHO MADE THE WORLD

The NT assumes and accepts the basic OT proclamation of God as Creator and Sustainer of all things (cf. Maly 1975: 104; Childs 1992: 391).

Jesus refers to creation as a past event (e.g., Mark 10:6; 13:19) in a way that assumes his hearers share this basic belief. God's sustaining care has a more direct place in his teaching, and his parables frequently draw their illustrations from the natural world (cf. Stuhlmacher 1987: 4). God makes his sun rise and sends rain (the essentials for life and growth) on all humankind (Matt 5:45). He feeds the birds of the air (6:26-30) and cares for the sparrow (10:29).

Acts depicts the early church acknowledging God as Creator both in its liturgy (4:24) and in its missionary preaching (14:15; 17:24). Paul likewise assumes the OT faith in the Creator (Rom 1:20; 11:36; 2 Cor 4:6; Eph 3:9), as does the writer to the Hebrews (1:10-12). Passing references are found in the other epistles (Jas 1:17; 2 Pet 3:5). In Revelation God is to be praised, "for you created all things, / and by your will they existed and were created" (4:11; cf. 10:6; 14:7).

Only in the Pastorals is there evidence of encounter with a view that doubts or denies the biblical understanding of creation by forbidding marriage and demanding dietary restrictions, so that it becomes necessary to counter the false teachers by reaffirming that all foods are created by God "to be received with thanksgiving by those who believe and know the truth. *For everything created by God is good,* and nothing is to be rejected, provided it is received with thanksgiving" (1 Tim 4:1-5). Here, as in the OT, creation is to be *enjoyed* by humans and *used* in the way that God intends.

The NT also makes explicit what is already found in *2 Macc* 7:28 (above, 2-1.2e), that is, that creation is to be understood in terms of *creatio ex nihilo* (creation out of nothing). Thus Paul in Rom 4:17 refers to the God "who gives life to the dead and calls into existence the things that do not exist" *(kalountos ta mē onta hōs onta).* Similarly Heb 11:3 affirms that by faith we understand that the worlds were created by God's word, "so that what is seen was not made out of visible things" (NRSV footnote; *eis to mē ek phainomenōn to blepomenon gegonenai).*

2-3.2. THE COSMIC CHRIST

a. All Things Were Made by Him

While the NT accepts and reaffirms the OT understanding of creation, it does add a very significant new dimension to that belief through its proclamation of *the creation of all things through Christ.* As we shall see (8-3), by identifying him with the divine Word and Wisdom, the NT presents Christ as God's agent in creation.

Thus Paul, in 1 Cor 8:6, refers to the "one Lord, Jesus Christ, through whom are all things and through whom we exist." Col 1:15-20 (regarded by many scholars as a pre-Pauline hymn) devotes most of its first stanza to Christ's role in creation, "for in him all things in heaven and on earth were created."

The prologue of John's Gospel explicitly identifies Christ with the divine Logos/Word: "He was in the beginning with God. All things came into being through him, and without him not one thing came into being" (1:2-3; cf. 1:10).

Heb 1:1-4 (perhaps also based on an earlier hymn) speaks of Christ as God's Son "through whom he also created the worlds *(epoiēsen tous aiōnas),*" and refers to him as the one who "sustains all things by his powerful word." Rev 3:14 calls Christ "the origin of God's creation *(hē archē tēs ktiseōs tou theou).*"

The emphasis on Christ as the agent of creation is not seen as detracting in any way from God's role in creation. But over against the OT view, it does shed new light on *the purpose and goal of creation.* All things were created not only *through* Christ but also *for* him (Col 1:16). In other words, *Christ is the clue to creation.* For the NT, "the activity of creation could no longer be conceived of apart from Jesus Christ because redemption lay at the heart of creation from the outset" (Childs 1992: 372). In him God's activity in the historical order and in the created order coalesces, for he is the mediator of both creation and redemption.

b. Christ Who Is the Image of God

The NT also reaffirms the OT view that "man . . . is the image *(eikōn)* and reflection *(doxa)* of God" (1 Cor 11:7), but it both builds on the OT view and radically reinterprets it by declaring that Christ is "the image *(eikōn)* of God" (2 Cor 4:4; cf. F. Watson 1997: 281). "He is the image *(eikōn)* of the invisible God, the firstborn *(prōtotokos)* of all creation" (Col 1:15). Similarly in Heb 1:3 Christ is called "the reflection *(apaugasma)* of God's glory and the exact imprint *(charaktēr)* of God's very being."

The allusion to the creation narrative is apparent, and the meaning is clear. The image of God in humankind, defaced at the fall, is restored in the person of Christ. As a result of what God has done in Christ, the divine image can be restored in believers (2 Cor 3:18; Col 3:9-11) so that they are "conformed to the image of his [God's] Son" (Rom 8:29; cf. 1 Cor 15:49).

Thus the full meaning of "the image of God" in humankind (cf. above, 2-1.3c) is revealed in Christ, and "we learn from Jesus what it is to be human" (F. Watson 1997: 283). Unlike humankind, Christ did not rebel against and disobey God, but entered into the closest personal relationship with him and perfectly obeyed him, and thus truly shares his Lordship over all creation: to be human means not establishing an autonomous existence, but living in a right relationship with God. In his life, Christ through his love and care for all people became the model of true interpersonal relationships: to be truly human is also to live in a right relationship with others. As the True Man, Christ's life was indeed infinitely precious, yet he gave his life for the sins of the world: willingness to forget self and give all in the service of others is the highest mark of true humanity.

c. To Reconcile All Things

Christ is not only the mediator of creation, but as the true image of God, and through his death and resurrection, he is also the mediator of redemption, a redemption that embraces all creation (cf. DeWitt 1991: 25-44).

Through Christ "God was pleased to reconcile to himself all things *(ta panta)*, whether on earth or in heaven, by making peace through the blood of his cross" (Col 1:20). This sweeping statement clearly affirms that Christ's atoning death avails not just for individual believers but for the whole of creation. Similarly, in Heb 1:2 it is said that God appointed Christ "heir of all things" *(klēronomon pantōn)*. Paul further affirms the cosmic scope of redemption when he says that "in Christ God was reconciling the world *(kosmon)* to himself" (2 Cor 5:19). Similarly, John 3:16 declares that it was because "God so loved the world *(ton kosmon)* that he gave his only Son."

2-3.3. IN THE THINGS THAT HAVE BEEN MADE

For the NT God is revealed supremely in the Christ event, but like the OT it does also acknowledge that God can be discerned within the created order. In Rom 1:19-20 Paul declares that *God can be known through the world he has made:* "For what can be known about God is plain. . . . Ever since the creation of the world his eternal power and divine nature, invisible though they are, have been understood and seen through the things he has made." However, this view that God's nature is made plain in creation is modified in two ways. (a) What can be known about God in this way appears to be limited: creation reveals only God's "power" *(dynamis)* and "divine nature" *(theiotēs)*. (b) Paul goes on to evaluate humankind's response to God's self-revelation in creation in very negative terms (Rom 1:21, 25). At this point Paul's thought is closely parallel to *Wis* 13 (see above, 2-1.4b; cf. J. Barr 1993: 58, 67), and it is difficult to avoid the conclusion that he has been influenced by it.

In Rom 2:14-15 Paul speaks of a further way in which God can be known through the created order: *his moral law can be known through conscience* (see further, 18-3.3e.ii).

In Acts Paul is depicted as appealing in more positive terms to a knowledge of God available through the created order. In his address at Lystra in 14:15-17, Paul appeals to the bounty of nature as a "witness" to God. In his famous address in 17:22-31, Paul is portrayed as finding a point of contact with his Athenian audience by speaking of "the God who made the world and everything in it" (v. 24) and quoting a Greek poet to the effect that "in him we live and move and have our being" (v. 28). Some scholars have found here a more positive evaluation of natural theology than is found in Romans, and have seen in the Acts passages a reflection of Luke's own theology, not Paul's. The differences between the two sets of passages, however, can be exaggerated (cf. J. Barr 1993: 39-57). Both find a place within the canonical NT (cf. J. Barr 1999: 469), and together they affirm that there can be some knowledge of God through creation, though both agree on the need to go on to proclaim the full Christian message.

2-3.4. THE CORRUPTION OF CREATION

While the NT shares the OT view of creation as essentially good, it also shares and in fact deepens its insights into the corruption of creation. Creation is indeed a good thing gone wrong. The "world" *(kosmos)* is God's creation and the object of his love and care, but from another viewpoint it is the sphere of humankind's rebellion and the territory occupied by powers opposed to God (see 4-3.3a). Not only the world of human beings but even the physical universe is out of joint.

In a remarkable passage (Rom 8:19-23) Paul sees the corruption of the created order as extending even to the physical universe so that, like humankind, it too longs for the final redemption: "We know that the whole creation has been groaning in labor pains until now" (v. 22). Thus "as long as man refuses to play the part assigned to him by God, so long the entire world of nature is frustrated and dislocated" (Moule 1964: 12).

2-3.5. REALIZED ESCHATOLOGY: A NEW CREATION

The NT picks up the OT promise that the corruption of creation will be overcome, and expresses it largely in terms of apocalyptic eschatology. After all, the Christ event did not bring world history to a close or transform the physical universe. Yet the NT also claims that the Christ event is of cosmic significance, and with it, albeit in a hidden and paradoxical way, *the new creation has already begun.* NT apocalyptic for the most part takes the form of futurist eschatology, but there are also elements of a realized apocalyptic eschatology.

a. We Have Seen His Star

In the Gospels the Christ event is depicted as the climax of God's activity in the created order and is therefore accompanied by *cosmic signs*. Jesus' birth is heralded by a star that summons non-Jews to worship the newborn king (Matt 2:1-12). At Christ's death darkness covers the land (Matt 27:45//Mark 15:33), the sun's light fails (Luke 23:44), and the earth shakes (Matt 27:51). On the Sunday morning there is a great earthquake (Matt 28:2). In other words, *the signs of the end appear within history,* signaling that the Christ event is the climax of God's activity in the created as well as the historical order.

b. With the Beasts

For Jesus the animal creation is under God's continuing care (Matt 6:26//Luke 12:24; Matt 10:29-31//Luke 12:6-7), and he knows of the importance of humans caring for animals (Matt 12:11-12; Luke 13:15). During his temptation in the wilderness Jesus was "with the wild beasts" (Mark 1:13) but suffered no harm. Thus with Christ the eschatological reconciliation of humanity and the animal kingdom (cf. above, 2-2.4b) is anticipated. "Jesus comes for the sake of humans. He is *the* human being created as God intended, and therefore his relationship with the animals accords with God's original design. What the creation narrative has to say about the relationship between humans and animals becomes reality in Jesus' presence. The 'community of the sixth day' is restored" (Birch and Vischer 1997: 16).

c. Even Wind and Sea Obey Him

The cosmic significance of Christ is portrayed especially in the "nature miracles." In all his "mighty works" Jesus is concerned to help people through the power of God. But whereas he usually mediates God's healing power, in this special group Jesus mediates God's power over the forces of nature.

One group of nature miracles depicts Jesus protecting people from danger by mediating God's power to subdue the forces of chaos, represented in biblical symbolism by the sea. This group includes the stories of the stilling of the storm (Matt 8:23-27; Mark 4:35-41; Luke 8:22-25) and of Jesus walking on the water (Matt 14:22-33//Mark 6:45-52//John 6:16-21). A second group depicts Jesus providing for people's bodily needs by mediating God's power over the creative forces of nature. It consists of the feeding of the multitude found in six versions (Mark 6:32-44 and //s), the miraculous catch of fish (Luke 5:1-11; cf. John 21:1-11), and the changing of water into wine (John 2:1-11).

All attempts to rationalize the nature miracles are modernizations that completely miss the point of the narratives as they stand in the canonical accounts. The focus of the Evangelists is on their meaning and significance. Negatively, they are not spectacular events designed to compel belief, a temptation that Jesus rejected (Matt 4:3-4//Luke 4:3-4). This is confirmed by the fact that in all or most cases the nature miracles were not public events, but were perceived as demonstrations of divine power only by the disciples (see R. H. Fuller 1963: 37). Positively, the events are interpreted in the light of the OT understanding of God. Underlying the first group is the proclamation of the Creator's victory over the powers of chaos represented by the sea (see further, 4-1.3b). The main teaching of the stilling of the storm and the walking on the water is that "Jesus shares the power of God as the Lord of the mysteries of creation" (A. Richardson 1941: 90). Underlying the second group is the proclamation of God as the continuing source of the earth's bounty. The basic purpose of these narratives is therefore to assert that the God who comes to humankind in Jesus is the God who is the Creator and Sustainer of all things.

d. Behold the New Has Come

The giving of the Spirit, which inaugurates the new age, is accompanied by the cosmic signs foretold by Joel according to Acts 2:19-20 (see further, 5-3.3b). Although Paul can picture creation itself still longing for the final consummation, nevertheless he can also see in the Christ event the beginning of the promised new creation. Christ's death accomplishes the creation of a new humanity (Eph 2:15). "So if anyone is in Christ, there is a new creation *(kainē ktisis):* everything old has passed away; see, everything has become new!" (2 Cor 5:17). "Neither circumcision nor uncircumcision is anything; but a new creation is everything!" (Gal 6:15). Thus, according to Paul, "believers must live in the world and be a sign of hope that the expected New Creation has already begun" (Stuhlmacher 1987: 11). "This term ['new creation'] is rich in connotations, implying both the ongoing character of God's involvement with the human family and the indivisibility of the creative and redemptive sides of God's activity. Adumbrated in the life of communion with God which the disciples shared with Christ was the fellowship intended by God from the dawn of human civilisation" (Hanson 1982: 112).

The Fourth Gospel opens with the same words as the creation account of Gen 1: "In the beginning . . ." *(en archē(i)* = Gen 1:1 LXX); John also thereby presents Christ as the agent both of the original creation and of the new creation.

New Testament: Consummation

2-4. NEW HEAVENS AND A NEW EARTH

Just as the Bible begins in Genesis with creation and with the relation of the created order to God, so it ends in Revelation with a vision that sees the final goal of the whole created order and of the whole of human society. As in the rest of the NT, Christ is seen as the clue to God's purposes in the created order.

2-4.1. APOCALYPTIC ESCHATOLOGY: THE END OF HISTORY

The apocalyptic eschatology of the NT has been the subject of grave misunder-standing and misinterpretation over the centuries (on the history of scholarship, see K. Koch 1972). Rationalists and liberals were embarrassed by apocalyptic and dismissed it as a shell from which the true essence of Christian faith can be extracted. A century ago J. Weiss and A. Schweitzer shocked the world of biblical studies with their advocacy of "thoroughgoing eschatology," contending that both Jesus and the earliest Christians, including Paul, believed the apocalyptic end of all things was imminent. The twentieth century saw renewed efforts to eliminate or minimize apocalyptic eschatology either by putting all the emphasis on "realized eschatology" (C. H. Dodd) or by regarding it as outmoded first-century mythology that has to be "demythologized" and reinterpreted existentially (R. Bultmann). However, in an influential article published in 1960, E. Käsemann argued that apocalyptic is "the mother of all Christian theology" (Käsemann 1969), and much discussion since then has underlined what C. D. Myers (1995) has called "the persistence of apocalyptic thought in New Testament theology" (cf. Ladd 1981; Buzzard 1992).

Apocalyptic eschatology resists all efforts to eliminate it from the NT. Apocalyptic material is found not only in the so-called Synoptic "Little Apocalypse" (Matt 24; Mark 13; Luke 21) and in the book of Revelation; it is a key element in Paul's writings (cf. Beker 1980) and is in fact found in all parts of the NT.

The study of NT apocalyptic, however, is still vitiated by the continuing acceptance of the assumption that Jesus, Paul, and the early Christians all expected that the apocalyptic end of all things was imminent. Since the world did not come to an end, on this key issue they were, to put it bluntly, mistaken and in error (see, e.g., C. D. Myers 1995: 212). No doubt there were early Christians who, especially in times of crisis and persecution, hoped and prayed and indeed expected that the end might be near. But as shall be argued below (2-4.5), the consistent teaching of all of Scripture is that the time of the final consummation of all things is known only to God.

Apocalyptic has also been misunderstood through the failure to recognize the presence in the NT (as well as in the OT) of *prophetic eschatology*. As will be shown in chapter 3, the NT looks forward to various events that will happen *within* history prior to the *end* of history.

Finally, apocalyptic has been misunderstood by those who think that a detailed blueprint or scenario of the end-time events can be derived from Scripture. No such timetable is to be found in the NT, not even in the book of Revelation since, according to its method of "recapitulation," it continually oscillates between present and future and thus does not set out future events in linear fashion (cf. Cronk 1982: 251-52). The main events of the final consummation include:

> the parousia (second coming) of Christ (see 7-4)
> the final defeat of the powers of evil (see 4-4.5)
> the resurrection of the dead (see 20-4)
> the final judgment (see 16-4.3)
> a new heaven and a new earth (see below, 2-4.4)

Attempts to place these events in an exact sequence, however, involve imposing that sequence *on* the NT, not deriving it *from* the NT.

2-4.2. SIGNS OF THE TIMES: COSMIC UPHEAVALS

In keeping with the apocalyptic tradition, the NT envisages the final consummation as being preceded by disasters and calamities that will constitute the birth pangs of the new age. Before the end comes there will be massive disruptions of the natural order.

> But in those days . . .
> the sun will be darkened,
>   and the moon will not give its light,
> and the stars will be falling from heaven,
>   and the powers in the heavens will be shaken.
>
> (Mark 13:24-25 and //s; note the reversal
> of the scenario of Gen 1)

2 Peter expects the dissolution of the universe before the ushering in of the new order: "The heavens will pass away with a loud noise, and the elements will be dissolved with fire, and the earth and everything that is done on it will be disclosed [var.: burned up]. Since all these things are to be dissolved in this way, what sort of persons ought you to be in leading lives of holiness and godliness, waiting for and hastening the coming of the day of God, because of which the heavens will be set ablaze and dissolved, and the elements will melt with fire?" (3:10-12).

Throughout the period between the first and second advents of Christ there will be other signs that nature itself is out of joint. "There will be great earthquakes," warned Jesus, speaking of the time that will precede the end, "and in various places famines and plagues" (Luke 21:11 and //s). The third and fourth "Horsemen of the Apocalypse" (Rev 6:5-8) represent famine and pestilence, and Revelation speaks repeatedly of earthquakes that characterize the period before the end (6:12; 8:5; 11:13, 19; 16:18).

2-4.3. THE DAY OF THE LORD: COSMIC JUDGMENT

The NT takes up the OT expectation of a "Day of the Lord" *(hē hēmera tou kyriou)* but understands it entirely in an apocalyptic sense (1 Cor 5:5; 1 Thess 5:2; 2 Pet 3:10; etc.; 2 Pet 3:12 and Rev 16:14 speak of "the day of God"). This is clearly identified with the final day of judgment, and because of the role of Christ in that judgment and its close association with his parousia, it can also be called "the day of our Lord Jesus Christ" (1 Cor 1:8; 2 Cor 1:14; cf. Phil 1:6; 2:16). Elsewhere it can simply be identified as "the day" (1 Cor 3:13; 1 Thess 5:4) or "that day" (Matt 7:22; 2 Tim 1:12, 18). For a fuller discussion of the future judgment in the NT, see 16-4.3.

2-4.4. ALL THINGS NEW: COSMIC SALVATION

a. New Heavens and a New Earth

The NT offers symbolic visions of the final consummation that will mark the end of human history and inaugurate a radically new order.

Just as in the beginning "God created the heavens and the earth" (Gen 1:1), and just as OT apocalyptic looked for the creation of "new heavens and a new earth" (Isa 65:17; cf. 2-2.4c), so at the end, "in accordance with his promise, we wait for new heavens and a new earth, where righteousness is at home" (2 Pet 3:13).

Throughout Scripture the sea or the great waters symbolize the powers in the universe opposed to God (see further, 4-1.3b). It is only with the final vision of Revelation that all that is opposed to God will be eliminated: "I saw a new heaven and a new earth; for the first heaven and the first earth had passed away, and the sea was no more" (21:1).

b. Paradise Restored

In keeping with the apocalyptic principle of *Urzeit/Endzeit*, and with the prophetic promise of paradise restored (2-2.4a), the new order is pictured in part in terms drawn from the original creation accounts. Jesus refers to the final consummation as the time of "the renewal of all things" (Matt 19:28); creation itself will be "reborn" (*palingenesia* = "rebirth, regeneration"; cf. 17-4.4). In Acts 3:21 Peter links the parousia of Christ with "the time of universal restoration" (*achri chronōn apokatastaseōs pantōn*).

While the garden is replaced by the holy city in Rev 21–22 (see further, 13-4.2), other features of the Garden of Eden appear such as the river (Rev 22:1; cf. Gen 2:10) and the tree of life (Rev 22:2; cf. Gen 2:9).

In the new order there will be no sun or moon (Rev 21:23; 22:5), for God himself will be the source of light, as at the beginning of Gen 1, before the creation of sun and moon on the fourth day of creation, and as in the promise of Isa 60:20 and Zech 14:7.

At that time "the creation itself will be set free" (see Rom 8:18-22). God's ultimate purpose is "to gather up all things in him [Christ]" (Eph 1:10; cf. Col 1:20).

2-4.5. THE TIME OF THE END

There are indications in the NT that at least some in the early church believed that the final, apocalyptic end of all things was at hand and would occur soon, or at least within their own lifetime. Among Jesus' hearers were some who "supposed that the kingdom of God was to appear immediately" (Luke 19:11). That Paul may have shared this view is suggested by 1 Thess 4:15. Yet one of Paul's aims in the Thessalonian correspondence is clearly to dampen expectation of an imminent end, an expectation that had led some even to give up working (1 Thess 5:14; 2 Thess 3:11), and in 1 Thess 5:2 he quotes the most common NT saying on the subject to the effect that the end will come "like a thief in the night," i.e., suddenly and unexpectedly (see below). Moreover, elsewhere Paul certainly envisages his death occurring before the end of all things (Phil 1:21-24; see 20-4.4a). A common explanation is that Paul changed his mind with the passing of time, but this is not certain since historical scholarship cannot be sure of the dating of each of Paul's letters.

Scholars who argue that Jesus, Paul, and the earliest Christians expected an imminent apocalyptic end (cf. above, 2-4.1) focus on a few texts, especially Mark 9:1 (cf. Matt 16:28; Luke 9:27), "Truly I tell you, there are some standing here who will not taste death until they see that the kingdom of God has come with power," and Mark 13:30 (near the end of the Little Apocalypse), "Truly I tell you, this generation will not pass away until all these things have taken place" (cf. Matt 24:34; Luke 21:31-32). In Matt 10:23 Jesus tells his disciples, "You will not have gone through all the towns of Israel before the Son of Man comes."

It is remarkable that the Gospel writers, from their later vantage point, did not simply eliminate these sayings. Clearly they understood Jesus to be speaking not of the ultimate apocalyptic end, but of more immediate events that would occur within the lifetime of some of Jesus' hearers. One such event was the death and resurrection of Jesus and the giving of the Holy Spirit that could certainly be seen as a further stage in the coming of the kingdom "with power." The other event that the Gospel writers understand Jesus referring to is the fall of Jerusalem, seen as a manifestation of God's judgment; this, however, belongs to the category of prophetic eschatology, not apocalyptic eschatology (see further, 3-4).

In the final, canonical form of the NT, the more typical view is that while certain prophetic eschatological events may happen in the foreseeable future, "the end is not yet" (Matt 24:6//Mark 13:7//Luke 21:9). The time of the final end of all things is known only to God. In a key text that could not have conceivably been invented by the early church, Jesus acknowledges even *his* ignorance: "But about that day or hour no one knows, neither the angels in heaven, nor the Son, but only the Father" (Mark 13:32-37//Matt 24:36; cf. Matt 24:42, 44, 50; Luke 12:46). In Acts 1:6-7, in response to the apostles who ask about an imminent consummation, Jesus says, "It is not for you to know the times or periods that the Father has set by his own authority."

The NT teaching on the final end is not that it will come *soon,* but that when it does come it will come *suddenly and unexpectedly.* This is clear for example from the picture of "the thief in the night" (Matt 24:43-44; cf. 24:36-42; Luke 12:39-40; 1 Thess 5:2, 4; 2 Pet 3:10; Rev 3:3). Precisely the same point is made in the parable of the wise and foolish bridesmaids (Matt 25:1-13; cf. Luke 12:35-38).

2 Pet 3:3-10 illustrates how early Christians were advised to counter those who mocked their belief in the coming of the end: the destruction of the world by the flood is cited as a precedent (vv. 5-7); God's timescale is quite different from ours (v. 8, quoting Ps 90:4); the delay of the end allows for the spread of the gospel (v. 9); and the end will come "like a thief." In other words, the end is not imminent, nor is it calculable by human beings, but it is certain.

2-5. THE LORD OF CREATION: THEOLOGICAL REFLECTIONS

1. For several decades in the mid–twentieth century BT stressed God's dealings with his people in "salvation history" to the point where creation theology was reduced almost to an appendix to "revelation in history" and was thus seriously undervalued. The preoccupation with history led to the neglect of "Yahweh's relationship to and presence in the order of the world" (Knierim 1981: 63). Here we note the three main arguments that were advanced for this subordination: it

was held, firstly, that the OT material on creation was a relatively *late* feature of Israel's faith; secondly, that creation theology was *not unique* to ancient Israel; and thirdly, that creation faith has very little place *in the NT*.

a. The "lateness" of Israel's creation faith is based on the critical view that two of the main loci of creation faith in the OT, Gen 1 and Isa 40–55, come from the Priestly source and "Second Isaiah" respectively, both of which, it is claimed, are to be dated to the time of the Babylonian exile. Historically it can well be argued that Israel recognized God as creator long before the exile (cf. B. W. Anderson 1984: 4), but the most important point to be made is that a canonical BT is not based on historical reconstructions, but on the Bible in its completed canonical form. As argued above, what is most significant is that canonical Scripture begins and ends with God's concern for all creation and all humankind, and places everything else within that overall framework.

b. As is well known, one of the major challenges to biblical faith in modern times arose from the discovery in 1853 and publication in 1876 of a Babylonian account of creation. This was followed by other finds, including a Babylonian version of the flood story, and subsequently by further discoveries, including Ugaritic texts. The assessment of these finds was influenced by H. Gunkel's important study, *Schöpfung und Chaos in Urzeit und Endzeit* (1895; shortened ET in Gunkel 1984). Gunkel argued for the priority of the Babylonian creation myth, a version of which he contended lies behind the OT accounts, though he did concede that considerable modifications were made in the process. Scholars have refined Gunkel's theory in the light of later finds, and as a result there is a widespread popular perception that the comparative material from the ancient Near East has undermined the uniqueness of the biblical accounts. The "BT movement" shied away from creation partly because it believed God's activity in creation was not unique to Israel while his activity in history was.

In response to this, it must be said first of all that BT should not really be concerned with what is or what is not unique to Israel. H. H. Schmidt (1984) has rightly argued for the importance of creation theology in the OT, but he does so by contending that the OT shares with all ancient Near Eastern cultures a belief in a divinely ordained order in the universe. Once again, however, it needs to be emphasized that *BT should be concerned with the canonical text,* and comparisons, favorable or unfavorable, with other cultures are not its primary concern.

Secondly, it needs to be said that whatever the historical relationship of the biblical and ancient Near Eastern accounts, the differences are far more significant than the similarities. For example, the other accounts are all polytheistic, whereas Scripture speaks only of the one true God; the Babylonian myth grounds creation in the slaying of the chaos monster (Tiamat) by one of the gods (Marduk), whereas the biblical account is basically nondualistic; in the Babylonian account the flood is sent at the whim of the gods, whereas the biblical account is based on a moral interpretation.

Finally, it can be said that if there are points of contact (e.g., the universe is not eternal but has a divine origin; nature reveals a divinely implanted order), that does not contradict but in fact accords well with the biblical witness to a "general revelation" in creation (see next section) by which all humankind can attain a partial though imperfect knowledge of God.

c. While it is true that the NT lacks both the creation narratives and the magnificent creation poetry of the OT, it has been shown above that the entire NT from the teaching of Jesus to the book of Revelation accepts and reaffirms what the OT says about creation. The downgrading of creation theology on the basis of its absence from the NT is a serious error that stems from a basic misunderstanding of the NT and a failure to read it in its total canonical context.

A symptom of the neglect of creation in the Christian tradition is the absence of a celebration of creation in the traditional Christian liturgical year. The three main Jewish festivals were originally rooted in the cyclic time of the created order (cf. 14-1.3). The North American tradition of "Thanksgiving" is one attempt to fill this gap, as are various forms of "harvest thanksgiving" celebrations.

2. The downgrading of creation in BT is certainly closely related to what has been called "the eclipse of creation" in much modern Protestant theology. In his presidential address to the American Theological Society in 1971, G. S. Hendry analyzed the theological and philosophical factors responsible for this eclipse (Hendry 1971). It is clear that in much modern Christian thought, the retreat from theology to anthropology has left theologians mute regarding God's activity in the created order (cf. Westermann 1974: 3).

Connected with this is the issue of so-called "natural theology" and the debate as to whether "by nature, that is, just by being human beings, men and women have a certain degree of knowledge of God and awareness of him, or at least a capacity for such an awareness . . . prior to the special revelation of God made through Jesus Christ" (J. Barr 1993: 1). Against Brunner, the Barthian position sought to deny any possibility of a natural theology. There continues to be strong opposition by some biblical scholars to seeing any support for "natural theology" in the Bible, especially for the view that a knowledge of God can be attained through human reason (see F. Watson 1997: 242-67). The evidence examined above, however, makes it very difficult to maintain the Barthian position. There are passages in both OT and NT which proclaim that God can be known through creation. While this knowledge has limitations, and has to be supplemented by the revelation of God in the Christ event, nevertheless it provides a point of contact on which the fuller revelation can build. It would be more accurate, however, to use the terminology of "general revelation" and "special revelation." There is no "natural" knowledge of God in the sense that it originates on the human side. What is known of God in creation is known because God reveals himself through the created order to all humankind. To this general revelation must be added, according to the NT, the special revelation given through Christ.

There is still today widespread interest in and appreciation of nature (witness, e.g., the popularity of landscapes in art, of travel to view the beauties of nature, of geographical societies and magazines, of bird-watching, etc.). Such activities are not of course specifically Christian, but on the basis of BT they do provide a point of contact for the Christian message.

3. The biblical understanding of the created order, and especially the stories of Gen 1–11, has unfortunately constituted one of the main battlefields in the "war" between "science" and "the Bible," particularly since the publication of Charles Darwin's *The Origin of Species* in 1859. The theory of evolution along with new views of the origin of the universe, the age of the earth, and so on were perceived as being in direct conflict with the biblical accounts. Attempts to harmonize the biblical and scientific views (the "concordist" theory; cf. Pinnock 1989: 144-45), for example by interpreting each of the six "days" of creation as a thousand years (on the basis of Ps 90:4), proved to be a dead end. Apart from the fact that science sees the earth as thousands of millions of years old, it was noted long ago that the creation of the sun on day 4 while day and night begin on day 1 hardly suggests that this is a scientific account. As a result, a polarization developed that persists in some quarters to this day. On the one hand, "evolutionism" dismisses Gen 1–11 as little better than primitive superstition and looks only to science to provide information on the nature and origin of the universe and humankind's place in it. On the other hand, "creationism" insists on a rigidly literal interpretation of the biblical texts, and if science disagrees, so much the worse for science (see Berry 1982).

Both these views reject the first principle of interpretation of a biblical text: the correct identification of its literary genre. Much of what the Bible says about creation is in the form of *poetry*. In Gen 1–11 truth is conveyed in *story* form. The intention of these stories is to convey theological truth, not "scientific" truth (cf. Cronk 1982: 27-29). To expect the biblical stories to correspond to the current scientific theory is patently ridiculous. Apart from anything else, scientific theories constantly change; the current theory is quite different from that held fifty years ago, and doubtless a quite different theory will have emerged fifty years from now. It so happens that the current "big bang" theory of the origin of the universe appears to accord much better with the biblical account than earlier theories of "continuous creation" (cf. B. W. Anderson 1984: 16-17); but it would be highly unwise to link the biblical text with any particular scientific theory that could change overnight. "Creationists" are just as much at fault as "evolutionists" in insisting that the only possible interpretation of Gen 1–11 is a literal one; both views depend on the thoroughly modernistic, rationalistic presupposition that the only kind of truth is literal, scientific truth. Because of this, both groups fail to let the texts speak on their own terms.

The biblical accounts, it has been argued, convey truth in story form; R. W. Berry (1982) speaks of "stories of ultimate meaning" (250). It has become common to characterize these accounts as "myth," but that term has been avoided here for two reasons. Firstly, even in academic circles the term frequently designates what is regarded as untrue, whereas the purpose of the Genesis stories is precisely to convey truth about God, the world, and humankind. Secondly, the term "mythology" is frequently applied to the polytheistic myths, e.g., of Greece and Rome, and to those of the ancient Near East that differ markedly from the biblical accounts. Compared with the Babylonian myth, the Genesis account, argues Pinnock (1989), "thoroughly demythologizes nature and sees it as the creation of the one true God"; in this sense it is "not myth but antimyth" (149).

A true understanding of the nature of the biblical texts allows us to see that there is no necessary conflict between the Bible and science. Indeed, the creation theology of the Bible based on wisdom encourages a positive assessment of science. On this view a scientific understanding is possible precisely because it was through wisdom that God created all things and endowed the universe with a divine order, and equally because God endowed human beings with wisdom to discern that order: "human discovery and divine disclosure stand in a complementary relationship" (Crenshaw 1977: 365). On this view scientists are indeed "thinking God's thoughts after him." At the same time, it is wise to recall the biblical view that wisdom has its limits. Science can teach us much about the marvels of the universe in which we live, but it cannot answer the most basic questions of human life. If science is regarded by many today with considerable suspicion, this is due to a renewed comprehension of an obvious truth: from a moral and spiritual viewpoint, science (and its ally technology) is essentially neutral and can be used for good or ill. Hence the need today as never before to hear what the biblical texts have to say on the most basic questions of human life.

4. The issue of the relation of the biblical viewpoint to modern science and technology was brought to the fore by the ecological crisis of the second half of the twentieth century. Worldwide concern over depletion of nonrenewable resources; acid rain; pollution of land, sky, and sea; global warming; disposal of nuclear waste; and other examples of what C. B. DeWitt (1991) calls the "degradations of creation" (13) have made the ecological crisis one of the burning issues of our time (cf. Dumas 1975: 24-31). The hunting of wild animals, trapping for furs, the extinction of certain species, the use of animals in sport and entertainment, modern methods of raising animals for food, the use of animals in medical experimentation, and the cloning of animals are all examples of serious areas of concern regarding humankind's relation to the animal kingdom (see Linzey and Regan 1988: 147-94).

The fact that the rise of the science and technology that made possible the horrendous exploitation of nature took place in the West, i.e., in a society strongly influenced by the biblical tradition, has been seen by some as more than a coincidence. Thus in a seminal article published in 1967, L. White suggested that "by destroying pagan animism, Christianity made it possible to exploit nature in a mood of indifference to the feelings of natural objects" (1205); Christianity bears a large burden of guilt for the ecological crisis, though in a figure like Saint Francis of Assisi it also provides a potential patron saint of ecologists. White's thesis is certainly an oversimplification: the factors giving rise to modern science and technology were complex and included the influence of Greek science (cf. J. Barr 1972: 27). On the other hand, the views of White and those who have followed him cannot be brushed aside, and they constitute a challenge Christians cannot ignore (cf. Santmire 1985; R. K. Johnston 1992: 228-30).

It need not be a case of seeking to "make the Bible relevant" by relating it to current concerns and in the process sacrificing essential Christian beliefs in order to find common ground with contemporary post-Christian culture (cf. F. Watson 1997: 242). The ecological crisis is an example of how a contemporary problem can encourage the recovery of aspects of biblical faith that have indeed been neglected (cf. Childs 1992: 409).

The question for BT is whether the modern exploitation of nature is rooted in the Bible or represents a misunderstanding and distortion of the biblical view of creation. That the latter is the case is suggested by the biblical emphasis on the celebration of creation, and by its understanding of "dominion" not as domination but as responsible stewardship (cf. Froelich 1971: 271-75; Dumas 1975: 32-35). Indeed, as Dyrness (1992) has argued, "the problems we face with our environment are not ultimately between the human creation and the rest of the natural order — debates limited to this horizon are far too restrictive. Our problem relates to our fundamental estrangement from our creator" (274). BT can help the church find more satisfactory answers to our environmental problems, because it can provide a more radical analysis of these problems. At root, humankind has a wrong relationship to creation because it has a wrong relationship to the Creator.

Christianity, with a few exceptions like the Celtic saints and Francis of Assisi, does not have a great track record on the treatment of animals; here too BT has an important role to play in providing a specifically Christian motivation for respect and reverence for the animal creation (see Linzey and Regan 1988: chap. 4; Birch and Vischer 1997: 36-81).

5. In the Bible God's activity in the created order is located not just in the past and in the present, but also in the future. Apocalyptic expectations, while more prominent in the NT than in the OT, are an essential part of the overall framework of biblical thought.

An important key to BT lies in recognizing the distinction between prophetic and apocalyptic eschatology; these are often closely related, but they are also quite distinct. The Bible often looks forward to events that will occur within history (see further, chap. 3), but when it speaks of the final consummation and the *end* of history, its consistent view is that the time of the end is known only to God.

Apocalyptic eschatology has had a rough ride in the history of the Christian church (see Schmithals 1975: 213-48). It has frequently been rejected or ignored (cf. the resistance in the East to recognizing Revelation as canonical). In modern times numerous ways have been sought to "reinterpret" or "demythologize" it. At the other extreme have been recurring revivals of apocalyptic enthusiasm, expecting the end of the world and claiming to be able to predict when this will occur, a procedure which, as well as being quite unbiblical, constantly brings Christian and biblical thought into disrepute (see Hanson 1987: 39-57).

A canonical BT has an important role to play in seeing apocalyptic in its proper perspective, and in striking a correct balance between prophetic and apocalyptic expectation.

CHAPTER 3

The Lord of History

Old Testament: Proclamation

3-1. I WILL CALL TO MIND THE DEEDS OF THE LORD

God is not only the ruler of creation; he is also the ruler of history. The OT proclaims that God has acted and spoken within human history in a unique way by calling a people to be his people and entering into a special relationship with them. Through this people God works out his plan for the salvation of humankind. We refer to this as God's activity within "the historical order."

3-1.1. SALVATION HISTORY

Biblical scholars have long recognized that a considerable part of the OT consists of "historical books." At first glance these books recount the history of the Israelite people from their origins in the patriarchal era to the Persian period, following their return from exile in Babylon, or, if the deuterocanonical history is included, down to the Maccabean period in the second and first centuries B.C. But study of these books quickly reveals that this is not history in the generally accepted, modern sense of the word, for OT "history" assumes the one thing that modern historiography excludes, i.e., the presence and activity of God in the events of history. It recounts the history of God with his people.

Because a major theme of this history is the way God saved his people from slavery and guided and protected them over the centuries, the German term *Heilsgeschichte* has frequently been employed, being translated into English as "redemptive history" or, more commonly, "salvation history." "Israel's history is a history of salvation; a history in which and through which God brings help and salvation into the world" (Kraus 1958: 19). In the OT salvation is primarily this-worldly; it is salvation *from* one's enemies, with the exodus deliverance being the prime example: "The LORD saved Israel that day from the

Egyptians" (Exod 14:30). But of course, salvation is not only "from," it is also "for." In the case of Israel, they are saved "from" Egypt "for" life in the Land (see 13-1), a life lived in accordance with God's Way and marked by peace, healing, blessing, and joy (see 20-3). God can therefore be called the "God of our salvation" (Pss 65:5; 79:9) and given the title "Savior" (see more fully, 10-1.5). It has quite rightly been pointed out, however, that because of their rebelliousness and disobedience, God often disciplines and judges his people, as well as saving or redeeming them, so that there is a history of judgment as well as redemption, of damnation as well as salvation (cf. Hanson 1978: 52). As well as a history of salvation *(Heil)*, there is also a "history of disaster *(Unheil)*" (Cullmann 1967: 91). Yet God's ultimate purpose is always to bring salvation to Israel and to all humankind.

It is a basic contention of the OT that God is a righteous *(tsāddîq)* God, a God of righteousness *(ts^edhāqâh)*. As such, he can be pictured as a judge:

> The heavens declare his righteousness,
> for God himself is judge. (Ps 50:6; cf. 9:8; Isa 58:2; Jer 11:20)

Modern study has shown, however, that basic to the biblical understanding of righteousness is the concept of relationship (cf. von Rad 1962: 370-83; Ziesler 1972: 38-39). "Yahweh's righteousness is his fulfilment of the demands of the relationship which exists between him and his people Israel, his fulfilment of the covenant which he has made with his chosen nation" (Achtemeier 1962b: 82). People are righteous basically when they fulfill the demands of their relationship with God and with their fellow human beings (see further, 18-1.4). Unlike Israel, which does not always live up to its obligations, God in his righteousness remains faithful and always ready to save and deliver his people. In the Bible God's righteousness is not an abstract quality; when the relationship between God and his people has gone wrong, God *acts* to put things right. Thus Brueggemann (1997) defines God's righteousness as "Yahweh's ready capacity to be present in situations of trouble and to intervene powerfully and decisively in the interest of rehabilitation, restoration and well-being" (130). Samuel reminds the people of "all the saving deeds (*tsidhqôth*, lit. 'righteousnesses') of the LORD" (1 Sam 12:7). God is "a righteous God and a Savior" (Isa 45:21). "Righteousness" can be used in parallel with "salvation" (Ps 71:15), and can even be translated "deliverance" (22:31), or "vindication" (Isa 62:1-2). If God has to judge and discipline his people, it is only because he wishes to restore them to a right relationship with himself. This is what he seeks to do through "salvation history." When we speak of God as the Lord of history and of God's activity in "the historical order," it is to this that we are referring.

a. Linear Time

While God's activity in the created order is based on *cyclic* time (2-1.2c), his activity in the historical order is based on *linear* time. Although the OT as a whole does not follow a strictly chronological order, the historical books do, and the prophetic books can be slotted into that linear, chronological sequence. "Narrative by its very nature is sequential and chronologically framed; that the biblical narrative should possess these traits is not surprising. What is noteworthy about the Old Testament narrative is the drive toward a single, all-embracing story line and chronological framework" (Patrick 1981: 102).

b. Historical Sequences

Within the canon of the OT, the historical books are arranged in two or, with the deuterocanonical books, three historical sequences, as follows:

Sequence I	Sequence II	Sequence III
Gen 12–50		
Exodus		
Leviticus		
Numbers		
Deuteronomy	1 Chronicles	
Joshua		
Judges		
<Ruth>		
1 Samuel		
2 Samuel		
1 Kings	2 Chronicles	
2 Kings		
	Ezra	*Tobit*
	Nehemiah	*Judith*
	<Esther>	
		1 Maccabees
		2 Maccabees

Sequences I and II overlap to a considerable degree. Sequence I covers the period from Abraham to the exile. Sequence II is largely the work of "the Chronicler": 1 Chronicles covers the period from Abraham to David, albeit in very sketchy form and almost entirely by means of genealogies. 2 Chronicles covers the same period as 1 and 2 Kings (David to the exile), but the books of Ezra and Nehemiah go beyond the exile and recount the return and immediate postexilic period. The books in Sequence III belong to the Apocrypha/Deuterocanon, which in most modern Protestant translations is placed between OT and NT. The Roman Catholic Jerusalem Bible follows the Vulgate in placing them in Sequence II between Nehemiah and Esther. *Tobit* and *Judith* are set in the postexilic period (though there are problems of chronology). *1* and *2 Maccabees* pick up where Ezra and Nehemiah leave off and continue the story of God's people through the Hellenistic period.

Sequence I begins with the Torah (Genesis through Deuteronomy) and continues with what in the Jewish canon is termed "the Former Prophets" (Joshua–2 Kings). The books of Sequence II, however, are found in the Jewish canon in the Writings, and of course, *Tobit, Judith,* and *1* and *2 Maccabees* find no place in that canon at all. By way of contrast, therefore, the Christian canon of the OT lays considerably more stress on linear time, with the two (or three) sequences following one after the other emphasizing the continuous history of God's dealings with his people leading toward its climax in the Christ event. This sequential concern is further emphasized by the placement in the Christian canon of the books of Ruth and Esther (which in the Jewish canon are in the Writings) in what is taken to be their correct point in the chronological sequence (cf. D-2.7).

The prophetic books from Isaiah through Malachi are each grounded in a particular historical situation (or situations), but they are *not* arranged in chronological order. Their canonical order appears to depend on size and importance, with the four "major" prophets coming first: Isaiah, Jeremiah, Ezekiel, and Daniel, followed by the twelve minor prophets grouped together in Jewish tradition as "the Scroll of the Twelve." Some of the prophetic books incorporate some historical material as an aid to relating them to their historical setting (e.g., Isa 36–39 = 2 Kgs 18:13–20:19; Jer 52 = 2 Kgs 24:18–25:30), and they contain many references to historical persons and events. Thus they can generally be assigned to a place in the history that forms the subject of the historical books, though not without problems and difficulties in individual cases.

c. Historical Summaries

In addition to the actual narrative sequences, at intervals there occur various summaries that provide a précis of God's activity in history. Von Rad called attention to these brief summaries that he believed functioned as Israelite "creeds," particularly to the so-called Little Credo of Deut 26:5-10, the words of which, he held, are "out and out a confession of faith" (1962: 122). The "Little Credo" does not mention the Sinai events (124), but as Huffmon (1965) has argued, it may well have functioned as the prologue to a ceremony of covenant renewal (cf. the summary of Josh 24:1-13; on covenant renewal, see 11-1.3d). From the point of view of BT, it is of little consequence whether these creedal statements came first, with the narratives being developed as expansions of them, or whether they are secondary summaries of the narrative (cf. Clements 1968: 56). From a canonical and literary point of view, they serve the purpose of reminding the reader of "the story so far" and of further emphasizing the activity of God in the events of history.

In addition to Deut 26:5-10, such summaries are found in Deut 7:17-26; 8:2-4; Josh 24:1-13; Judg 6:8-10; 1 Sam 8:8; 12:6-11; 2 Sam 7:8-11; 1 Kgs 8:9, 16-21; Neh 9. In the Deuterocanon, a summary is found in *Jdt* 5:5-21, while the longest of all the summaries appears, in poetical form, in *Sir* 44–50. This poem focuses on the main characters in salvation history: "Let us now sing the praises of famous men . . ." (44:1). Beginning with Enoch, Noah, and Abraham, the survey continues through Nehemiah (49:13) and concludes with praise of the high priest Simon (probably ca. 225-200 B.C.), thus bringing the sequence quite close to the writer's own time (ca. 180 B.C.).

d. Salvation History Psalms

God's activity in the historical order is not only narrated and summarized; it is also the subject of songs of praise. The deliverance of the Israelites at the crossing of the sea was celebrated in the songs of Moses and Miriam (Exod 15:1-18, 21), and the victory over Sisera in the Song of Deborah (Judg 5). Many historical scholars consider these to be among the oldest parts of the OT.

God's care for his people in history is celebrated especially in the "Salvation History Psalms." Pss 105 and 106 retell in poetic fashion the history of God's people from the time of Abraham to the entry into the Promised Land. Ps 78 tells of

> the glorious deeds of the LORD, and his might,
>> and the wonders that he has done (v. 4),

and carries the story down to the time of the choice of David and of the Jerusalem sanctuary. Pss 135 and 136 likewise recount the mighty deeds of the LORD who is also the Creator.

These psalms "recite events fundamental to Israel's self-understanding as a people and essential to Israel's knowledge of who God is" (B. W. Anderson 1983: 55). "In them Israel is *commemorating* everything that Yahweh has done and that has supported and determined the life and being of the people of God" (Kraus 1986: 60). While they extol what God has done for his people, they can be very honest in recounting also the people's faithlessness to their LORD; the story is one of judgment as well as salvation (Pss 78:21-22, 31-33; 81:12; 95:10-11), and is obviously intended to point a lesson for future generations. A further group of psalms proclaim in a more general fashion the way in which God created and cares for his people (66:1-12; 100; 114; 149). Others again combine the praise of God the Lord of creation and God the Lord of history (33; 103; 145; 146).

3-1.2. THE STORY LINE

The OT story of God's dealings in history with his people moves through a sequence of fairly well defined periods (cf. Cronk 1982: 57-75).

a. The Patriarchal Period: God Calls the Ancestors of His People

Chapters 12–50 of Genesis tell how God called the ancestors of his people. The call of Abraham in 12:1-9 is pivotal (cf. 11-1.1), and the threefold promise of descendants, blessing, and Land runs like a thread through these narratives (see von Rad 1962: 167-75). They are in many ways a suspense story: time and again the promise is threatened, but God finds a way of preserving and renewing it. While the period is structured genealogically by three generations: Abraham (father), Isaac (son), and Jacob/Israel (grandson), from a literary viewpoint it is structured around three cycles of stories: the Abraham cycle (12–25:18), the Jacob cycle (25:19–36), and the Joseph cycle (37–50). A small amount of material relating to Isaac is found in 26–27. The story of Joseph and his family is a long connected narrative or novella that serves to link the patriarchal period with the story of the exodus by explaining how the Israelite tribes came to reside in Egypt.

b. The Exodus Event: God Delivers His People

The books of Exodus through Deuteronomy tell the story of the bondage of the Israelites in Egypt, the call of Moses, God's mighty act of deliverance of the tribes from Egypt at the exodus, the concluding of the covenant and the giving of the Torah at Mount Sinai, and the forty years of wandering in the wilderness. Deuteronomy recapitulates both the narrative and the laws of the preceding books. Ryken (1987a) has characterized this block of material as an "epic" — a long narrative telling of the birth of a nation, possessing a unifying hero (Moses), and employing an exalted style (130-35; cf. Cross 1983). Yet Ryken also points out "anti-epic motifs": rather than glorifying the hero, it depicts him as a reluctant leader, and rather than glorifying the nation, it continually stresses their failings. Despite God's deliverance of his people and constant care for them, they repeatedly "murmur" (Exod 15:24; etc.) and rebel against him. Even while Moses is still atop Mount Sinai, the people under Aaron make a golden calf (Exod 32), while accounts of revolts against the authority of Moses are found, e.g., in Exod 17:1-7 and Num 12 and 16 (see Wilcoxen 1968).

The core of the epic is the exodus event. The book of Exodus opens with the Israelites in slavery, completely powerless to save themselves. The emphasis is strongly on divine initiative and divine intervention, manifested in the ten plagues and the dramatic parting of the sea that allows the Israelites to escape but destroys the pursuing Egyptians. The central importance of the exodus event in the OT is shown by the repeated references back to it in the Historical Books: "The LORD brought us out of Egypt with a mighty hand and an outstretched arm" (Deut 26:8; cf. Josh 24:5-7; Judg 6:8-9; 1 Sam 12:6-8; 1 Kgs 8:53); in the Psalms:

> I will call to mind the deeds of the LORD;
>> I will remember your wonders of old. . . .
> Your way was through the sea,
>> your path, through the mighty waters
>> (Ps 77:11, 19; cf. 66:5-6; 78:12-13;
>> 105:23-38; 106:8-12; 114; 135:8-9; 136:10-15);

and in the Prophets: "You brought your people Israel out of the land of Egypt with signs and wonders, with a strong hand and outstretched arm, and with great terror" (Jer 32:21; cf. Isa 11:15-16; Ezek 20:6, 9; Hos 11:1; Amos 2:10; Mic 6:4).

c. The Entry: God Settles His People in the Land

The book of Joshua tells how the Israelites under Moses' successor Joshua conquer the central, southern, then northern parts of the Land (Josh 1–12), which is then apportioned to the various tribes (Josh 13–21). The book concludes with Joshua's farewell and a covenant ceremony at Shechem. The book of Judges modifies any impression of a sudden and complete conquest. For some two centuries the Israelite tribes had to fight for their lives against both the inhabitants of the land and new invaders. Chapters 3–16 tell the story of thirteen "judges," temporary military commanders raised up by God to deliver his people. A sixfold stereotyped literary pattern is used to convey a theological interpretation of history (cf. 3:7-11, the account of the first judge):

1. The people did evil in the sight of the LORD and served other gods.
2. The LORD was angry and sold them into the hands of X.
3. The people cried to the LORD.
4. The LORD raised up a deliverer, Y.
5. The deliverer defeated the enemy.
6. The land had rest for Z years.

As soon as the cycle is completed, the narrative returns to point 1, and then starts all over again (see von Rad 1962: 327-34; L. L. Thompson 1978: 106).

Judg 17–21 contain supplementary stories that do not fit this pattern. Ruth is an independent story placed after Judges because it is set in this period of history.

Politically, during this period the Israelites form at best a loose confederation of tribes. The at-times anarchic political, social, and religious conditions are attributed to the fact that "in those days there was no king in Israel; all the people did what was right in their own eyes" (Judg 21:25).

d. The Monarchy: God Rules His People through Kings

1 and 2 Samuel and 1 and 2 Kings form a continuous historical narrative. The figure of Samuel acts as a bridge between the periods of the judges and the establishment of the monarchy, for he is instrumental in the selection of Saul as the first king and then, after Saul's fall from grace, in the anointing of David. David's reign is narrated in detail, and 2 Sam 9–20 plus 1 Kgs 1–2 constitute a vivid and probably eyewitness account of the last days of David; historical scholars term this the "Succession Narrative," as its main interest lies in showing that Solomon was the true heir to the throne.

1 and 2 Kings recount the reign of Solomon, the division of the kingdom upon his death into the northern kingdom of Israel and the southern kingdom of Judah. The history alternates between North and South until the fall of the North to Assyria in 722 B.C., then continues the story of the South to the time of the exile in 586. Deuteronomy through 2 Kings is frequently referred to as the "Deuteronomic History" because the narrative is controlled by the theology propounded in Deuteronomy, sometimes referred to as the "piety-prosperity equation." God assigns rewards or punishments *within history* (see esp. the blessings and curses of Deut 28). Faithfulness to the LORD and obedience to his commands by king and people will bring prosperity and victory over one's enemies; unfaithfulness and disobedience will bring disaster and defeat. Typical of the history is the classification of rulers into "good kings" and "bad kings," the latter being in the majority. Jeroboam, the first ruler of the North, is the prototypical rebel (1 Kgs 12:25-33), and a typical verdict, e.g., on King Baasha of Israel is, "He did what was evil in the sight of the LORD, walking in the way of Jeroboam and in the sin that he caused Israel to commit" (1 Kgs 15:34). In other words, what we have is a thoroughly theological interpretation of history. Both the fall of the North to the Assyrians and of the South to the Babylonians are interpreted as justly deserved punishments. Typical also are the frequent references to prophetic predictions followed in due course by a note of the fulfillment of the prophecy (e.g., 1 Kgs 21:19 > 1 Kgs 22:37-38 and 2 Kgs 9:30-37; cf. von Rad 1962: 340 and L. L. Thompson 1978: 126, where twenty-six examples from 1 and 2 Kings are listed).

1 and 2 Chronicles constitute a separate historical sequence beginning with the genealogy of Adam and continuing through to the end of the exile, though a detailed account begins only with the reign of David (see von Rad 1962: 347-56). These books draw on Samuel and Kings, but also on other sources, and tell the story from a distinctive viewpoint that tends to glorify the Davidic dynasty and shows a special interest in the worship of the temple but rejects messianic expectation (R. North 1963; Goldingay 1975). They also bring out even more clearly the connection between Israel's sin and God's judgment on the nation (North, 372-74; Goldingay, 122).

e. The Exile: God Disciplines His People

2 Kgs 24 and 25 tell of the fall of Jerusalem to the Babylonians in 597 and the deportation of some of the population; then of a second fall in 586, the destruction of the temple, and a further deportation. The Babylonian exile was a traumatic experience for the Jewish people. Next only to the exodus in significance in OT history, it is an event which, paradoxically, produced some of the deepest and most profound insights into the relationship between God and his people. It is anticipated in the book of Deuteronomy, e.g., in 4:23-31, 30:1-5, though Deuteronomy also holds out the hope of repentance and return (cf. Brueggemann 1968: 393). The survival in Babylon of King Jehoiachin, heir to the Davidic throne (2 Kgs 25:27-30), allows the Deuteronomic History to end with a glimmer of hope. Jeremiah and Ezekiel furnish further information on this period and interpret the exile as a punishment for Israel's unfaithfulness, but also as a period of disciplining from which God's people may emerge and make a fresh start. The prophecies of Isa 40–55 in particular hold out this hope.

f. The Return: God Restores His People

2 Chronicles, while containing no account of the exile, concludes on an optimistic note with the decree of King Cyrus of Persia, who had defeated the Babylonians, permitting the return of God's people and the rebuilding of the temple in Jerusalem. The books of Ezra and Nehemiah recount the return to the Land in successive stages, and emphasize the rebuilding of both the temple and the walls of Jerusalem, and the rebuilding of the religious community under the leadership of Ezra and Nehemiah. (Problems of chronology and theories of textual dislocation are not the concern of BT; for the literary structure of these books, see L. L. Thompson 1978: 135-37.) The book of Esther is placed after Nehemiah since it is set in the Persian period. The prophetic books of Haggai and Zechariah (chaps. 1–8) are set in the immediate postexilic period.

g. The Maccabees: God Again Delivers His People

In the Deuterocanon, *1* and *2 Maccabees* are independent accounts of God's people in the Hellenistic period. They focus on the persecution of God's people and the desecration of the temple in 168 B.C. under the Greek (Seleucid) king Antiochus and the successful rebellion that resulted in Jewish independence under the rule of the Maccabees (or Hasmonean dynasty) from 165 to 63. While the narratives furnish historically valuable accounts of this period, these books continue the OT tradition of the theological interpretation of history. Freedom is regained and God's people are ruled by Judas Maccabeus, his brothers, and their successors, but in and through these events it is God who delivers his people. Salvation history, the history of God's dealings with his people, continues down to NT times.

3-1.3. GOD ACTS IN HISTORY

That Scripture portrays God as active in history is beyond question. The nature of that activity, however, merits careful analysis. In what follows, six ways in which the OT looks at God's activity in history are suggested, though without wishing to give the impression that they necessarily fit neatly into watertight compartments.

a. Divine Intervention

Probably the most common view of "the God who acts" is that of the God who intervenes dramatically in history to deliver his people from suffering and oppression. The classic case is the exodus (above, 3-1.2b), which undeniably is an event of major proportions in the first narrative sequence (see von Rad 1962: 175-79). It is portrayed as an act of God's power (Exod 15:6), accompanied by a series of "miracles" — the ten plagues, the parting of the sea, the pillar of cloud/fire, the provision of water/manna. The events are said to occur in public, with the plagues and the parting of the sea witnessed by the Egyptians as well as the Israelites. They serve not only to deliver the Israelites but also to afflict and slaughter their enemies. In this tradition, "The LORD is a warrior (*'îsh milchāmâh)*" (Exod 15:3). "We can say that Yahweh proceeds step by step to procure the freedom of his people. Few scripture narratives are so dominated and structured by divine intervention" (Patrick 1981: 83).

Into this category we might also place the deliverance of Jerusalem at the time of Sennacherib's invasion (Isa 36–37), and the deliverance of Daniel from the lions' den (Dan 6). These divine interventions to deliver those in distress exhibit the same characteristics as the exodus: they are acts of God's power, publicly demonstrated, involving the defeat and death of Israel's enemies.

The fact remains that the exodus is the main, and most important, example of this category. Minor examples occur later but only occasionally, in crisis situations, when the very existence of God's people is at stake.

b. Divinely Inspired Leadership

In the model of "divine intervention," deliverance is credited solely to God by means of miraculous events, though in the exodus narrative, of course, God does use a human agent, Moses, to lead and direct his people. In other historical narratives, however, the emphasis falls much more on God raising up a deliverer who leads his people to victory. This is the case with the thirteen judges and with kings such as David and Solomon; the same pattern reemerges in the time of the Maccabees, where Judas and his brothers are divinely inspired military leaders. The prophets constitute another class of divinely inspired leaders capable of influencing the course of history. For example, the encounter of the prophet Ahijah with Jeroboam, in which Ahijah tore his garment in pieces, was not merely a prophecy of the breakup of Solomon's kingdom; it undoubtedly helped bring that event about (1 Kgs 11:26-39; cf. 1 Kgs 12).

c. Judgment/Salvation

In the Historical Books and the Prophets, God works for the most part within the flow of history, using nation-states as his agents (cf. von Rad 1962: 67). Thus the Assyrians or the Babylonians are used as agents of judgment against Israel and Judah, while the Persians are used as agents of God's salvation in delivering God's people from exile.

This view is characteristic especially of the "Deuteronomic History" (Deuteronomy through 2 Kings; see above, 3-1.2d), one of the main purposes of which is to show that the destruction of Jerusalem "came about, not because of God's arbitrariness, but because of Israel's long history of disobedience" (Brueggemann 1968: 387).

There are marked differences here from *(a)* above. God's judgment does not fall on Israel's enemies but on Israel herself. Even when God acts to save his people, salvation lies on the far side of judgment and suffering. Although God uses world powers, he does so without their being aware of it; in Isa 45:5 God says of Cyrus, "I arm you, though you do not know me." In Isa 10:5 God refers to Assyria as "the rod of my anger." God can call King Nebuchadrezzar of Babylon "my servant" (Jer 25:9). Thus, although these are historical events, they are not *public* demonstrations of God's power in the same sense as in *(a)*. Finally, the accounts do not envisage God "intervening," and generally there are no "miracles." God works within the historical process in ways that could be otherwise explained. God "overrules" rather than "intervenes."

d. Providence

Another mode of divine activity may be discerned in OT narrative, with the Joseph narrative and the Succession Narrative providing the best examples. In these accounts God does not "intervene" at all, nor does he employ world powers as his agents; there are no theophanies and no miracles. The action focuses on certain notable though decidedly human individuals who believe in God but who basically employ their own talents and their own powers. God's activity is implied rather than stated, and is seen primarily in how, in the long run, events turn out in a way that conforms with God's purpose.

The Joseph narrative (Gen 37–50) tells in dramatic fashion of Joseph's escape from death at the hands of his brothers and his eventual rise to a position of power in Egypt that enables him to ensure the survival of his family. Nowhere does God figure directly in the narrative, yet the point of the story is to show that "man's evil designs cannot thwart God's well-laid plans" (Fritsch 1955: 29). This may raise the question: If God controls events, are the characters in the story simply marionettes that he manipulates (cf. Redford 1970: 74)? Yet the characters are real people who make real choices (cf. Ackerman 1982: 112). In a paradoxical way God *overrules* human motives and events so that at the end of the story Joseph can say to his brothers, "Even though you intended to do harm to me, God intended it for good, in order to preserve a numerous people" (Gen 50:20).

The Succession Narrative (2 Sam 9–20; 1 Kgs 1–2) deals with the last part of David's reign, and focuses on the question of who will succeed him to the throne (see von Rad 1962: 311-17). It is a unified literary masterpiece, and the story is told with vivid detail and great psychological insight (see Whybray 1968: 19-47). While "the Lord initiates action guaranteeing the Davidic dynasty . . . his activity occurs more subtly and less directly than in most biblical narrative" (L. L. Thompson 1978: 110). Although the actual term does not appear in the biblical text, it is appropriate to speak here of God's "providence" (cf. von Rad, 51-52), for in these stories the narrator sees God at work behind the scenes. The Joseph story, as Eichrodt (1967) points out, "is the classic expression of a morally profound belief in Providence" (169).

These narratives also stand in a close relation to OT Wisdom theology. Joseph is an example of wisdom in action (Fritsch 1955: 33; von Rad 1966; but see also Coats 1973). The Succession Narrative could almost be an illustration of the teaching of the book of Proverbs (cf. Whybray 1968: 56-95); Brueggemann (1972) has shown how it exemplifies a Wisdom teaching that is "profoundly secular in that it presents life and history as a human enterprise" (82).

The book of Esther is notable as the only book in the Bible that does not mention God. The narrative, however, hints that the averting of tragedy is due to divine providence (see Ryken and Longman 1993: 218), for example, in Mordecai's question to Esther, "Who knows? Perhaps you have come to royal dignity for just such a time as this" (4:14). What is implicit in the Hebrew text is made explicit in the LXX version, which has additional material with prayers to God by Mordecai and Esther. Mordecai's dream and its interpretation, in particular, "emphasize God's providential care for the people Israel in a universally hostile world" (*NOAB*: AP: 41).

e. Blessing

Another model of divine activity concerns God's "blessing." Westermann (1982) in particular has drawn attention to the OT's witness not only to "the saving God and history" but also to "the blessing God and creation" (35-84, 85-117). God is present not just in *"saving events,"* but equally in the resulting *state* of health, wholeness, *shalom*.

> *Blessing is a working of God which is different from saving* insofar as it is not experienced as the latter in individual events or in a sequence of events. It is a quiet, continuous, flowing, and unnoticed working of God which cannot be captured in moments or dates. Blessing is realized in a gradual process, as in the process of growing, maturing, and fading. The Old Testament does not just report a series of events which consists of the great acts of God. The intervals are also part of it. In them God gives growth and prosperity unnoticed in a quiet working, in which he lets children be born and grow up, in which he gives success in work. The saving God is also the blessing God. . . . The entire Old Testament thus speaks of *God's continuous action in addition to the acts which occur once* in his saving and judging deeds. (103)

Blessing in this sense also has links with Wisdom theology, and brings together God's activity in the created as well as the historical order. The too-easy correlation of blessing with piety leads to problems in the OT. Serious questions are raised, especially in the book of Job (cf. 16-1.5c), which also point the way toward the recognition that blessing can be found even in the midst of suffering. On "blessing," see further 20-1.4.

f. Suffering Love

Study of metaphors and anthropomorphic language applied to God in the OT suggests yet another model of divine activity in which a loving God is involved in the suffering of his people. In later Christian theology Patripassianism (from the Latin words for "Father" and "suffer") was seen as a heresy, so the biblical evidence must be carefully scrutinized. In an important study entitled *The Suffering of God*, T. E. Fretheim (1984) points out how in the OT God suffers *because* his people reject him; human wickedness and rebellion "grieve" God's heart (Gen 6:6; Ps 78:40). God also suffers *with* his people, for he "knows," i.e., experiences, their suffering (Exod 3:7), and can say,

> For the hurt of my poor people I am hurt,
> I mourn, and dismay has taken hold of me. (Jer 8:21)

We can also say that in the OT God suffers *for* his people, allowing himself to be "burdened" (Isa 43:24) and to be "weary" (7:13) with their sins. "In all their affliction he was afflicted" (63:9 RSV). God can be spoken of as a mother in labor pains (42:14). And while the Suffering Servant of 2 Isaiah is not God, he may well be seen as a mirror of God's own attitude and experience. Such passages thus point to yet another model for God's activity in which God is deeply involved in the world and suffers because of, with, and for his people.

From this survey it is apparent that to speak of all acts of God as "interventions" is misleading. The OT sees God as present and active in history in a broad range of ways. In fact, it emphasizes more God's ongoing "activity" than his isolated "acts."

3-1.4. GOD SPEAKS IN HISTORY

The OT certainly sees God as present and active *in history,* in his dealings with his people. As has been noted, the so-called BT movement laid great stress on "the God who acts" and who reveals himself through historical events. We have argued that this emphasis on God acting in the *historical* order has to be balanced by the equally biblical emphasis on God acting in the *created* order (see E-5.1; 2-1.1).

Emphasis on God's revelation of himself to his people through *historical events* poses other problems, however. God not only reveals himself by *acting* in events of history; he also reveals himself by *speaking* to and through individuals.

a. Receiving God's Revelation

We noted above that one model of God's activity in history can be described as "divinely inspired leadership." God calls Abraham (Gen 12:1-3), he calls Moses (Exod 3), he calls the great prophets (Amos 7:15; Isa 6; Jer 1; etc.), and he does this basically by *speaking* to them. Moreover, he continues to guide them, to reveal more of himself to them, and to give them a message that they in turn are to deliver to the people. In these cases God reveals himself not in *public* events of history but in *private* experiences of individuals (cf. C. J. Scalise 1996: 33). Such events constitute a very important part of God's dealings with his people (see Dyrness 1979: 25-38, which takes "the self-revelation of God" to the patriarchs and Moses as the foundation of OT theology).

202

God's self-revelation can of course take various forms. He "appears" to individuals (see 8-1.1). In some cases the revelation is *visual* rather than *auditory*. God reveals himself in *dreams* (e.g., Gen 40:5-19; 1 Kgs 3:5; Dan 2), and especially in the case of the prophets, through *visions* (e.g., Amos 7:1–9:4; Zech 1:7–6:15). But even in these cases, when the individuals communicate the message to others they do so by words, so we can legitimately refer to God *speaking* through them.

b. Recognizing God's Activity

That God speaks to individuals, and through them to his people, is particularly significant because historical events are recognized as acts of God only where a person such as Moses or one of the prophets is inspired to interpret and to proclaim the meaning of these events in terms of divine activity. In this sense it is misleading to speak of God revealing himself through acts in history. The revelation is given not just in the events, but in the God-given interpretation of the events. The "God who acts" is recognized only because he is the "God who speaks." The exodus is recognized as a mighty act of the LORD only because, through Moses, God proclaims it as such, just as God's activity in the disaster of the Babylonian exile is recognized only when Jeremiah proclaims God's word which interprets the meaning of that event.

Moreover, as Cullmann (1967: 90) points out, the person who speaks God's word can operate only within the context of the community of God's people, and only if at least some of them respond in faith and accept the proclamation. It is because the Israelites accept Moses' interpretation of what might simply have been seen as a series of natural disasters that they follow his lead and participate in the exodus. It is only because some of the exiles accept Jeremiah's interpretation that they take heart and keep their faith and are prepared one day for a return from exile. OT history is history interpreted by faith (J. J. Collins 1979: 191).

A corollary of this is that "There is no event within the Old Testament tradition which by its very nature must inevitably be interpreted as an 'act of God'" (Davidson 1966: 103). For example, following the first deportation to Babylon, the "prophet" Hananiah proclaimed that this was but a temporary setback and within two years the exiles would return. Jeremiah, on the other hand, proclaimed that Israel would spend many years under the iron yoke of Babylon (Jer 28). The same historical situation provoked two quite different interpretations, and at the time only faith could discern who was speaking the word of God.

Further, the proclaimed interpretation of historical events and the response of the community thereto take place within the context of an ongoing tradition, of a "confessional heritage" (Hanson 1978: 32). Knowledge of how God has acted in the past provides guidance for discerning his action in the future. The God who delivered the Israelites at the exodus can be expected to lead his people in a new exodus. On the other hand, the tradition of what God has done in the past may be modified and reinterpreted by new divine activity. The recognition therefore that God *speaks* in history, through individuals to his people, is essential to understanding how God "acts" in history.

3-1.5. REMEMBER THE FORMER THINGS

In relation to God's activity in the historical order, a special role within the community is played by *memory.* God's people are constantly called to *remember* what God has done for them in the past: "Remember what the LORD your God did to Pharaoh and to all Egypt, the great trials that your eyes saw, the signs and wonders, the mighty hand and the outstretched arm . . ." (Deut 7:18-19). The psalmist declares:

> I will call to mind the deeds of the LORD;
>   I will remember your wonders of old. (Ps 77:11)

The verb *zākhar* (remember, call to mind), cognate nouns, and the opposite (*shākhach* = "forget") are used in the OT in a theologically significant way, particularly in Deuteronomy and Psalms, with a wider range of meaning than is usually associated with "remember" in English (Childs 1962: 30). "In Scripture . . . memory is typically constitutive of identity and determinative of conduct" (Verhey 1992: 667).

Deuteronomy in particular is concerned with how future generations will relate to the redemptive acts of the past; the great majority of references to "remembering" refer to the exodus/covenant/wilderness complex of events (Blair 1961: 45). Tradition preserves the memory of these acts of God, but in the OT this is never simply a recalling of the past, a "mere remembering." "Present Israel has not been cut off from redemptive history, but she encounters the same covenant God through a living tradition. Memory provides the link between past and present" (Childs 1962: 55). Thus "memory functions as an actualization *(Vergegenwärtigung)* of the decisive event" in Israel's tradition (53). By "actualization" Childs means "the process by which a past event is contemporized for a generation removed in time and space from the original event" (85). Through memory, in the biblical sense, "the past is brought into the present with compelling power" (Blair 1961: 43; cf. Clements 1968: 85). Memory thus results in action. Israel is to "remember the sabbath day, and keep it holy" (Exod 20:8), and to remember God's commandments to obey them (Deut 8:11).

It is clear that in OT times the *cult* played an important role in this special kind of "remembering." "Israel celebrated in her seasonal festivals the great redemptive acts of the past both to renew the tradition and to participate in its power" (Childs 1962: 75). This is seen particularly in the celebration of Passover (cf. 14-1.3). The day of the exodus deliverance is to be "a day of remembrance *(zikkārôn)* for you. You shall celebrate it as a festival to the LORD" (Exod 12:14). "The happenings at Sinai, especially the direct utterance of God to his people and his claim upon them, are brought back to the memory of Israel in the liturgy of the feast as that event upon which the life of the people rests, and by which its character is determined" (Kraus 1958: 25); in the annual Passover ritual "the Exodus ceased to be a fact of the past and became a living reality" (Jacob 1958: 191). Similarly the feasts of Purim (Esth 9:26-28) and Hanukkah (*1 Macc* 4:59) commemorate great deliverances of God's people (cf. 14-1.3).

Remembering can take place, however, in settings other than cultic ones. Ps 42 provides a good example: the psalmist is cut off from the temple (v. 6), but what revives his downcast soul is the memory of corporate worship (v. 4), and indeed of God himself (v. 6; cf. G. H. Davies 1962b: 345). In a number of individual laments we see how memory works in a noncultic and more individual setting (see Childs 1962: 60-65).

Memory functions in a more dialectical way in 2 Isaiah. On the one hand, in line with the Deuteronomic approach, the prophet hears God say,

> Remember this and consider,
>> recall it to mind, you transgressors,
> remember the former things of old. (Isa 46:8-9a)

Isa 43:18-19a therefore comes as a surprise:

> Do not remember the former things,
>> or consider the things of old.
> I am about to do a new thing.

Whatever God has done in the past, and however important the memory of it is for Israel's present, it pales in comparison with the "new thing" that God is to do in the future.

Old Testament: Promise

3-2. I WILL RESTORE THE FORTUNES OF MY PEOPLE

3-2.1. PROPHETIC ESCHATOLOGY: THE END IN HISTORY

Despite the proclamation of God as the ruler of history, the actual course of events frequently made this hard to believe (cf. von Rad 1962: 391-401). The interpretation of history set forth especially in Deuteronomy, and worked out in the Deuteronomic History (above, 3-1.2d), based on the "piety-prosperity equation," became increasingly problematical with the fall of the Northern Kingdom to Assyria. An event that must particularly have strained belief in God as the ruler of history was the death of King Josiah in battle in 609 B.C. After David and Hezekiah, he is the prime example of a king who "did what was right in the sight of the LORD" (2 Kgs 22:2). His program of religious reform in accordance with God's Torah showed that he was truly God's anointed one. How can one make sense of the death of God's messiah? For many, the fall of Jerusalem to the Babylonians, the destruction of the temple, and the ensuing exile constituted "the focal, exemplar case in which Yahweh failed in defense of Yahweh's own dynasty, temple, city, and people" (Brueggemann 1997: 321; see also Brueggemann 1995). Even after the seemingly miraculous return from exile, Judah found herself ruled not by a king of the LORD's appointing but by a series of pagan empires — Persian, Ptolemaic, Seleucid, and finally Roman.

Israel's agonizing over the question of whether God really does rule in history finds vivid expression in the poetry of "lament" or "complaint," found especially in the psalms of lament and in the book of Lamentations.

a. The Psalms of Lament

About one third of the Psalms, the largest single category, may be classified as psalms of lament. A broad, recurring pattern may be identified in these psalms, though the pattern is far from rigid (cf. Brueggemann 1974: 6; B. W. Anderson 1983: 76-77). Common features are (1) *a cry to God:* however much the author may be moved by doubt or despair, the psalm is not a cry into the void of the universe, but a plea addressed to God; (2) *the lament/complaint:* describing the situation faced by the psalmist from which God seems to be absent; (3) *petition:* an appeal to God to act in this situation and set matters right; (4) *expression of trust in God:* the psalmist reaffirms faith in God as the one who is in control despite appearances to the contrary; this may include a review of God's past mighty acts; (5) *vow to praise God:* the psalm may conclude with a vow that the psalmist will, in the future, praise God and testify to what he has done.

A broad distinction may be drawn between individual laments (the larger group) and community laments, though because of the individual/community dialectic the distinction should not be pressed too far. It is in the community laments that generally envisage situations faced by the nation (famine, disease, enemy attack, defeat, exile), that God's activity in history is most clearly questioned. Community laments include Pss 12, 44, 80, 85, 90, and 94. While one or two envisage a specific historical situation (e.g., Ps 137 reflects the Babylonian exile), these psalms usually employ general terms so that they could fittingly be turned to in any time of national emergency (cf. B. W. Anderson 1983: 71). Historically they probably did not have a fixed place in the liturgical calendar, but were available for use in times of crisis, in conjunction with a national fast and call to repentance (cf. Westermann 1980: 30-31). The psalms of lament give full and frank recognition to the fact that so often God appears to be absent from history. Yet despair is never their last word. "Israel characteristically met the hurtful dimensions of existence head-on, of course viewing them as faith crises, times of wondering about God and his fidelity, but also as faith opportunities" (Brueggemann 1974: 4). These psalms also affirm faith in the God who has acted in the past, and above all they are directed toward the future in expectation and hope.

b. The Book of Lamentations

Seldom in the OT does the cry of despair find more moving expression than in the book of Lamentations, an anthology of five poems that attempt to come to terms with the fall of Jerusalem to the Babylonians and the destruction of the temple in 586 B.C., "the point in Israel's life where the tension between history and faith is, for the first time, most sharply posed" (Gottwald 1962: 51). The alphabetic acrostic form used in four of the five poems may be designed to underline the completeness of Jerusalem's desolation and of the poet's despair. Poems 1, 2, and 4 are modeled on the funeral dirge, and the dominant theme is the contrast between the former state of Jerusalem and her present situation. The personified figure of Zion asks,

> Is it nothing to you, all you who pass by?
>   Look and see
> if there is any sorrow like my sorrow. (1:12)

The poems provide God's people with a way of pouring out their anguish and despair, and may well have been composed for use in communal worship. Running through them is the implied question, How could God have allowed this to happen? The answer that these events are divine punishment for the sins of the people (1:5; 2:1-6; 4:6) is put forward but does not seem to be entirely adequate.

Lamentations has a somewhat symmetrical structure; standing between the laments of 1 and 2 and 4 and 5, the pivot of the collection is poem 3, which in 3:19-39 introduces a "theology of hope" in the midst of despair (Gottwald 1962: chap. 5). An individual speaks for the nation:

> But this I call to mind,
>   and therefore I have hope:
> The steadfast love of the LORD never ceases,
>   his mercies never come to an end. (3:21-22)

As we have already noted, a solution to the problem of whether God really does rule was increasingly sought in *eschatology,* in the promise and the hope that present conditions would not continue indefinitely but that God would act in the future to put things right.

Prophetic eschatology, as we have seen (1-2.1a), operates within the framework of salvation/judgment history. It expects that God's judgment or salvation will be actualized in events that will occur within the ongoing historical process. Prophecies of judgment are based on Israel's failures to keep the covenant and obey the Torah, but prophetic eschatology is more optimistic than apocalyptic eschatology. Some is conditional in nature; if the people amend their ways, they will be spared (cf. Jer 7:5-7), but if not, judgment will follow. There is thus a strong emphasis on the importance of social action. For prophetic eschatology evil resides basically not in cosmic powers but in people; therefore it is people who need to repent and change their ways.

3-2.2. SIGNS OF THE TIMES: A TIME OF ANGUISH

As the OT looks to the future within history, it does so not with an easy optimism but rather with unflinching realism. "Many are the afflictions of the righteous" (Ps 34:19), and though the OT sees light at the end of the tunnel, it does not minimize the intervening darkness. The forces that oppose God will not simply wither away. Indeed, opposition to God and to his people may be expected to intensify; on this, see more fully 4-2.2.

The book of Daniel speaks of the many trials God's people will undergo within history as they are subject to a whole series of pagan empires. The ultimate in pagan oppression is the abolition of the temple sacrifices and their replacement by "an abomination that desolates" (LXX *bdelygma tōn erēmōseōn;* Dan 11:31; 12:11). This happened several times: the temple was desecrated and destroyed by the Babylonians in 586 B.C., was descrated by Antiochus Epiphanes in 167 B.C., and finally descrated and destroyed by the Romans in 70 A.D. Whichever of these events is envisaged by the Daniel references, they all fall within the sphere of prophetic eschatology and refer to events within the course of history (see further 3-2.5).

3-2.3. JUDGMENT IN HISTORY

One aspect of prophetic eschatology arises from the promise and the hope that wickedness will not prevail indefinitely but that God will judge those who persistently disobey him and flout his authority. In the early stages of Israel's history, it is primarily on Israel's enemies that God's judgment is expected to fall, the classic case being that of Pharaoh and the Egyptians at the time of the exodus (cf. above, 3-1.3a). The major prophets continued to foresee God's judgment falling on world powers that oppress God's people (see 4-2.3). For example, Jeremiah was commanded to write "in a scroll all the disasters that would come on Babylon. . . . When you finish reading this scroll, tie a stone to it, and throw it into the middle of the Euphrates, and say, 'Thus shall Babylon sink, to rise no more'" (51:60, 63-64).

More typically, however, the prophets backed their searching analyses and condemnation of all aspects of the life of the nation by announcing that *it is on God's own people that judgment will fall.* As noted above (2-2.3), an important theme in the prophets is that of "the day of the Lord" *(yôm YHWH).* While a few references (e.g., Lam 1:12; 2:1) are to God's *past* judgments within history (cf. Everson 1979), most refer to a *coming* day when God will act. The earliest reference, in Amos, assumes that the term is well known and refers to God's judgment that will fall on his enemies (5:18). It is indeed in this sense that the term is used of the judgment that will fall, within history, e.g., on Babylon (Isa 13), on Edom (Isa 34), and on Egypt (Jer 46:3-12; Ezek 30:1-9).

Amos, however, turns the conventional expectation upside down when he declares that the Day of the Lord will be "darkness, not light" (5:18-20), i.e., it will be a day of judgment on Israel! This theme is picked up, e.g., in Ezek 7 where the message, "The time has come, the day is near" (vv. 7, 12), is spoken "to the land of Israel" (v. 2), and in Zeph 1 where God says, "I will stretch out my hand against Judah . . . for the day of the Lord is at hand" (vv. 4, 7).

Amos's prophecies were directed against the northern kingdom of Israel. After pronouncing God's judgment on the surrounding nations (1:3–2:5), Amos turns on his immediate audience and declares,

> For three transgressions of Israel,
>   and for four, I will not revoke the punishment. (2:6; see 2:6-16)

Because of their sins, the people will be carried off into exile (4:2-3; cf. 7:11). Similarly in Hosea, God says of the northern Israelites:

> They shall return to the land of Egypt,
>   and Assyria shall be their king,
>   because they have refused to return to me. (11:5)

The classic case of God's judgment falling on his own people within history is found in the fall of the southern kingdom of Judah and the destruction of the temple in 586 B.C. The prophet Jeremiah persistently foretold the judgment that would fall on Judah unless the nation underwent a radical reformation of its national life (e.g., in the Temple Sermon, Jer 7; 26). Prophecies of judgment are directed not only against God's people as a whole, but also specifically against the Land (cf. 13-1.2c), the city of Jerusalem (cf. 13-1.4d), and the temple (cf. 14-1.1b.v).

3-2.4. SALVATION IN HISTORY

Beyond judgment lie the promise and hope of restoration and salvation. Jeremiah's prophecies of doom and destruction are not his last word. The "Book of Comfort" (Jer 30–31) paints a hopeful picture of a future that God will provide beyond the punishment of exile: "For behold, days are coming, says the LORD, when I will restore the fortunes of my people" (30:3 RSV). 2 Isaiah's message is one of comfort (Isa 40:1), and the emphasis shifts from God's judgment to God's mercy:

> For a brief moment I abandoned you,
>   but with great compassion I will gather you.
> In overflowing wrath for a moment
>   I hid my face from you,
> but with everlasting love I will have compassion on you,
>   says the LORD, your Redeemer. (54:7-8)

Since it is Israel's sins that brought down God's judgment, future salvation must include deliverance from sin:

> Help us, O God of our salvation,
>   for the glory of your name;
> deliver us, and forgive our sins,
>   for your name's sake. (Ps 79:9)

In prophetic eschatology salvation takes the form of restoration within history. It includes return from exile to the Land, and the rebuilding of the city of Jerusalem (see 13-2), as well as the ingathering of Israel and the reunion of North and South (see 11-2.5).

God's action in history provides two basic typologies for envisaging his future saving acts.

a. A New Exodus

First and foremost, the exodus event is seen as a type of God's coming deliverance.

Hosea sees God's coming judgment as a return to the land of Egypt (11:5); but just as the exodus showed God's love for his people (11:1; cf. 13:4-5), so God will again deliver them (11:11) and lead them through the wilderness (2:14-20; 12:9).

Isaiah foresees a deliverance comparable to the crossing of the sea (10:26), and transfers the pillar of cloud by day and fire by night to the future Zion (4:5).

It is in 2 Isaiah, however, that the new exodus emerges as a major theme (cf. B. W. Anderson 1962d: 177-95; Bruce 1969: 33). Here the antitype will far exceed the type; this time the Israelites will not go out "in haste," "for the LORD will go before you" (52:12). As the LORD saved his people at the crossing of the sea, so now he promises, "When you pass through the waters, I will be with you" (43:2). As he led his people through the wilderness, so now God promises, "I will make a way in the wilderness" (43:19). God will build a superhighway across the desert for the new exodus (40:3-4; 49:11), and as through Moses he gave the Israelites water from the rock (Exod 17:1-7), so he will lead his people "by springs of water" (Isa 49:10; cf. 41:17-18). As God led the Israelites into the Land and eventually gave them the city of Jerusalem,

> So the ransomed of the LORD shall return,
>   and come to Zion with singing. (51:11)

For Jeremiah, too, God's coming deliverance and the return of God's people to their own Land will be patterned on the exodus (16:15; 23:7-8). Similarly, Ezekiel foresees a time when God will act to deliver his people "with a mighty hand and an outstretched arm" (20:33-34; cf. Deut 5:15; Ps 136:12).

b. The Restoration of the Davidic Kingdom

In some passages what is envisaged is the restoration of the Davidic kingdom. "On that day I will raise up the booth of David that is fallen" (Amos 9:11). This expectation is, of course, linked with that of a future king of David's line (see 6-2.2). In the portrait of the messianic king in Isa 9:2-7, it is said of him that

> His authority shall grow continually,
>   and there shall be endless peace
> for the throne of David and his kingdom. (v. 7)

Jer 17:25 envisages a future in which God's people will be ruled by "kings who sit on the throne of David" (cf. 23:5; 30:9; 33:17; see also Ezek 34:23-24; 37:24-25; Hos 3:5; Zech 12).

3-2.5. THE TIME OF THE END

Prophetic eschatology expects God to act in the future but within the ongoing flow of history. Sometimes God's future acts of judgment or salvation can be spoken of without specific time reference, as, e.g., in Hos 3:5: "*Afterward* (*'achar*) the Israelites shall return and seek the LORD their God, and David their king; and they shall come in awe to the LORD and to his goodness *in the latter days (bᵉ'achᵃrîth hayyāmîm).*"

Elsewhere, however, prophetic eschatology can be much more specific. Thus Jeremiah predicted that the Babylonian exile would last seventy years: "Only when Babylon's seventy years are completed will I visit you, and I will fulfill to you my promise and bring you back to this place" (29:10; cf. 25:11-12). Jeremiah's prophecy was in fact remarkably accurate (cf. Ezra 1:1, and see commentaries for details).

It is characteristic of prophetic eschatology that after a prophecy has been fulfilled, the course of history continues. As already noted (2-2.5), much of the book of Daniel consists of prophetic eschatology: the various visions anticipate the succeeding Babylonian, Medo-Persian, Greek, and Roman empires. Here again, prophetic eschatology can be specific, as in the reference in Dan 8:14 to the 2,300 evenings and mornings (= 1,150 days) interval before the restoration of the temple in 165 B.C.; the references in Dan 12:11 (1,290 days) and 12:12 (1,335 days) are best seen as "end-notes" inserted just before the conclusion of the book, reflecting differing understandings of the length of this period. Such specific historical predictions, however, are not to be confused with prediction of the time of the final consummation, something that is nowhere found in the Bible.

New Testament: Fulfillment

3-3. WE ARE WITNESSES TO ALL THAT HE DID

The NT proclaims the Christ event as the climax of salvation history, and also as the event by which God's salvation *(sōtēria)* is offered to all humankind. When Simeon sees the infant Jesus he praises God, saying,

> My eyes have seen your salvation, . . .
> a light for revelation to the Gentiles
>   and glory to your people Israel. (Luke 2:30, 32)

What the early Christian preachers took to the world was "the message of this salvation" (Acts 13:26).

The NT also speaks of God's "righteousness" in a way that develops from, though also modifies, the OT understanding. The Greek word *dikaiosynē* (in LXX = *tsᵉdhāqâh*) has a rich and varied range of meaning in the NT (see Achtemeier 1962a). It can be translated into English as "righteousness," "justice," or "justification." While "justification" is the appropriate translation in only one or two cases, the verb *dikaioō* predominantly carries the meaning "justify." As in the OT, "righteousness" has to do with right relationships. It is through the Christ event that God acts to put things right, i.e., to bring sinful and rebellious humanity back into a right relationship with himself. Christ therefore shares with God the title of Savior (see more fully, 10-3.5). At the outset of the Epistle to the Romans Paul links righteousness closely with salvation. "I am not ashamed of the gospel," he says, "it is the power of God for *salvation. . . .* For in it the *righteousness* of God is revealed" (1:16-17). In a key passage, 3:21-31 (see W. Reumann 1966), Paul argues that a right relationship with God is never something that can be earned or merited. But the righteousness of God has now been disclosed in the Christ event, especially in his atoning death (3:25). As a result of this, people can only be "justified by his grace as a gift" (3:24), a gift that has to be accepted through faith (see 17-3.3). Since faith is the only precondition for salvation, Jews and Gentiles have equal access to the gospel. Thus the climax of salvation history inaugurates the time when God's salvation/righteousness is offered to all humankind (see further, 12-3.4).

3-3.1. THE CLIMAX OF SALVATION HISTORY

In the NT there are elements of both continuity and discontinuity with the account of God's history with his people recorded in the OT. The continuity with OT salvation history is underlined particularly in two NT summaries, in Acts 7 and Heb 11. Though differing in theological emphasis, they nevertheless exhibit a not dissimilar basic pattern:

Acts 7	Heb 11
	Abel
	Enoch
	Noah
Abraham	Abraham
	Sarah
Isaac	Isaac
Jacob	Jacob
Moses	Moses
Joshua	
	Judges
David	David
Solomon	
	Samuel
the prophets	the prophets
	others, including
	Maccabean martyrs
the Righteous One	Jesus

213

The survey of salvation history in Acts 7 is cut short by the angry reaction of the crowd (Acts 7:54); it is the Heb 11 survey in particular that sees salvation history continuing, without a break, up to the Christ event (cf. D-2.6).

It is the claim of the NT, however, that the Christ event is not simply another stage in the ongoing history of God with his people, but is rather *the climax of salvation history*. In this event God has spoken and acted within history in a unique, final, and decisive fashion. Through this event God brings into being a new people, the church, and the NT tells of God's dealings with this people in the first decades of their history.

3-3.2. THE STORY LINE

Though dealing with a much more limited period of time, the NT story of God's dealings with his people also moves through a sequence of well-defined stages. The narration of the Christ event in the four Gospels is central, a fact that is underlined in the canonical arrangement of the NT: the four Gospels are grouped together (Luke having been detached from Acts) and are placed in a block as the first part of the canon, the NT equivalent of the Torah in the OT (cf. D-2.7).

The Christ event is *preceded* by the account of *John the Baptist*, who constitutes a link between the two Testaments. In him the NT reaches backward to link up with the story of God and his people in OT times.

The Christ event is *followed* by the story of *the early church*, primarily in the book of Acts, though the Epistles and the book of Revelation each have their own historical setting in this story. In these books the NT reaches forward and points to the continuing history of God with his people.

a. John the Baptist

All four Gospels link the Christ event with the ministry of John the Baptist (Matt 3; Mark 1:2-9; Luke 3:1-22; John 1:6-9, 19-36). John is a real figure in history (from a historical point of view, his ministry is independently attested by the Jewish historian Josephus; see Scobie 1964: 17-22). In the Gospels he is portrayed primarily as a prophet whose ministry thus marks the eschatological rebirth of prophecy. He calls the people to repentance (cf. Scobie, 117-30) in view of the imminent advent of the "Coming One." The Synoptics recognize him as the returning Elijah and forerunner of the Messiah (Mark 1:2; Matt 11:10//Luke 7:27), though according to John 1:21, John himself declined any titles. Each in its own way, the Gospels show him as the person who historically prepared the way for Jesus.

b. The Christ Event

The presentation of Jesus' life and ministry in the NT is found almost entirely in the four Gospels. A few of Jesus' sayings are echoed in Acts and the Epistles, plus a few brief allusions to his ministry. While Matthew and Luke have "infancy narratives" (Matt 1–2; Luke 1–2), the main interest of these narratives is in the theological significance of Jesus. Apart from these and the prologue of John's Gospel (1:1-18), the Gospels deal entirely with the ministry of Jesus that constituted approximately the last three years of his life. Despite distinctive theological and literary features, all four Gospels share a basic common outline that gives prominence to the passion narrative, and follows it with accounts of resurrection appearances.

From a literary viewpoint the Gospels are not "biographies" in the modern sense. They are thoroughly theological documents, written to elicit faith in Jesus as the Messiah and Son of God (Mark 1:1; John 20:31). But they also deal with a real person in history, and the fact that they are theological in nature does not mean that they are not also historical.

c. The Early Church

The book of Acts is the one NT book that deals with the history of the early church. Clearly it was originally the second volume of a two-volume history of Christian origins, the first volume of which was the Gospel of Luke (cf. Luke 1:1-4; Acts 1:1-2). In its canonical position it serves as a bridge between the Christ event as presented in all four Gospels and the early Christian community (cf. D-2.7). Inevitably it is highly selective; it recounts "acts of apostles" (there is no definite article in either case), primarily the acts of Peter in the first part and the acts of Paul in the second. But in another sense, what it recounts is "the acts of the Holy Spirit"; history is divinely directed, and a major theme is the extension of the gospel to the Gentiles under divine leading, with the approval of Peter, and under the leadership of Paul.

Paul's letters are an extremely valuable source of information on the early church. Historical-critical scholars do not agree on the dating of the letters or on their relationship to some of the events recounted in Acts, though some scholars are undoubtedly overly skeptical regarding the historicity of Acts. While it has become widely recognized that Luke was a "theologian," this does not mean that he was not also a "historian"; indeed, as Marshall (1970a) has argued, "his view of theology led him to write history" (52). Since Luke-Acts constitutes some 27 percent of the NT, Luke has to be regarded as a major theological witness, alongside John, Paul, and the writer of Hebrews, and not less important than any of them. In a canonical BT his theology must be given due weight and held in balance with the other major witnesses.

The other letters also contribute to our understanding of the early church, despite some uncertainties regarding authorship, date, and location. The book of Revelation sheds a vivid light on Christians as a persecuted minority in the province of Asia probably in the last decade of the first century.

3-3.3. GOD ACTS IN HISTORY

The NT shares with the OT the belief that God has acted within human history, though it tends to be dominated by one event, the Christ event, that is seen as the climax of God's activity not only in the historical order but also in the created order.

Just as the exodus was seen as a type of God's future deliverance (3-2.4a), so the Christ event is presented as the antitype of the exodus event, with Christ, the new Moses, the deliverer not just of Israel but of all humankind (see further, 6-3.1). Isaiah's proclamation of a new exodus through the wilderness (Isa 40:3) is applied to John the Baptist as the herald of the Christ event (Mark 1:3//Matt 3:3; Luke 3:4-6).

The clearest use of exodus typology in the Gospels comes in Luke 9:31, where the actual word is used: at Jesus' transfiguration Moses and Elijah were speaking to him "of his departure *(exodos),* which he was about to accomplish at Jerusalem." "For the instructed Christian reader of the Gospel that could mean nothing less than the repetition of God's mighty acts of redemption in His [Jesus'] death and resurrection at Jerusalem" (Nixon 1963: 16-17).

As the exodus climaxed in a meal, commemorated in the Passover, so the Christ event climaxed in the Last Supper, commemorated in the Eucharist (see 14-3.5c). It is significant that Paul starts his sermon at Antioch in Pisidia by recounting the exodus deliverance (Acts 13:17-19), "obviously because he sees in it the first instance in which the coming of Christ announces itself" (Piper 1957: 9; cf. Bruce 1969: 37). For the same reason, the exodus event occupies a large portion of Stephen's speech (Acts 7:17-44; see Nixon 1963: 22-23). Paul underlines the exodus typology when he refers to Christ as "our paschal lamb" (1 Cor 5:7). He further elaborates it in 1 Cor 10:1-15, where he draws a parallel between the believers of his day and the Israelites who "passed through the sea, and . . . were baptized into Moses in the cloud and in the sea. . . . they drank from the spiritual rock that followed them, and the rock was Christ" (vv. 1-4). These exodus events, says Paul, "occurred as examples *(typoi)* for us" (v. 6; cf. v. 11), that is, "as anticipations of the full salvation God was to bring" (Piper, 11). These passages show that Paul "knew that he belonged to the new eschatological Exodus under Jesus, the Messiah" (Sahlin 1953: 84).

John similarly draws on the exodus event for types of Christ: the manna prefigures Christ as the bread of life (John 6:25-35) while the rock prefigures Christ as the source of living water (7:38). More so than any NT book, Hebrews looks to the exodus typology (tabernacle, priesthood, sacrifice) as foreshadowing the person and work of Christ. Revelation makes extensive use of exodus imagery. The present experience of God's people is interpreted in terms of the exodus deliverance (see Piper 1957: 14-15); e.g., they are sustained by the hidden manna (Rev 2:17). In Rev 8 and 9 John has a vision of a series of plagues that will form part of God's judgment on the wicked. These partly echo the plagues that preceded the exodus (hail and fire, Rev 8:7 = Exod 9:23-24; water turned to blood, Rev 8:9 = Exod 7:20; darkness, Rev 8:12 = Exod 10:21; cf. Talbert 1994: 41), and partly represent the cosmic upheavals that precede the final consummation (see 2-4.2). In Rev 15:3 the martyrs sing the Song of Moses (see 6-4.1).

Apart from specific references, it is clear that the broad pattern of the exodus event influences much of the NT understanding of the Christ event and its consequences. The church is seen as the new Israel, chosen by God, delivered from slavery (to sin), traveling through the wilderness of this age, toward the promised rest.

Despite its more limited time frame, the NT's understanding of God's activity does not necessarily follow a simple pattern. In various degrees the six modes of divine activity identified in the OT (3-1.3) are also reflected in the NT.

a. Divine Intervention

Exodus typology suggests the model of divine intervention. But clearly there are major differences from the exodus narrative of the OT. The Christ event is a demonstration of God's power, only in a very paradoxical sense. It is accompanied by "miracles," but while some of these such as the exorcisms and healings are performed in public, others such as the virginal conception, the nature miracles, and the resurrection are not truly "public" events (see 2-3.5c). Moreover, at a crucial point Jesus specifically refuses to call upon divine intervention in the form of legions of angels (Matt 26:53). Most striking of all, in the NT it is not God's enemies but God's agent who is put to death.

A few traces of the deliverance view survive in the early church, e.g., the deliverances from prison in Acts 5:19-20 and 16:26. Against this, however, are many occasions when followers of Jesus are not delivered but face imprisonment, suffering, and death.

b. Divinely Inspired Leadership

In the NT Jesus does function as a divinely inspired leader, and he is related typologically to the various forms of leadership in the OT (cf. chap. 6). But here again there are major differences. Jesus is a far cry from Gideon, David, or Judas Maccabeus; he does not defeat his enemies but dies forgiving them. In the early church God raises up leaders. Some of these hold a unique and unrepeatable position — members of Jesus' family and especially the apostles, foremost of whom are Peter and Paul; others, especially "bishops," "elders," and "deacons," exercise forms of leadership that would become continuing "offices." On these, see more fully 15-3.2 and 15-3.3.

c. Judgment/Salvation

National and international events are less important in the NT. God's people are the church, a small community that is not a nation and hence not a player on the world stage.

Herod and Pilate, however, do represent national and international governments; without them being aware of it, God uses them to accomplish his predestined plan (Acts 4:27-28).

d. Providence

Although the NT recognizes that "all things work together for good for those who love God" (Rom 8:28), nothing in the style of the Joseph narrative or the Succession Narrative is found in the NT, which would have difficulty in thinking of Jesus or any members of the early church exercising the degree of independence and responsibility for their own actions, or the reliance on their own talents and wisdom, that is found in these narratives. Both Jesus and the early Christians seek God's guidance through *prayer*. Moreover, a major new factor in the more direct mode of divine activity that characterizes the NT is the work of *the Holy Spirit*.

e. Blessing

In the NT also, God is active in blessing, "giving you rains from heaven and fruitful seasons" (Acts 14:17; cf. Matt 5:45), and providing the necessities of life (Matt 6:25-33). He "gives to all mortals life and breath and all things" (Acts 17:25), and is the source of every perfect gift (Jas 1:17). But in the NT blessing is also profoundly transformed, since it comes above all through Christ. Moreover, there is a tendency to focus on "spiritual blessing in the heavenly places" (Eph 1:3). On blessing, see more fully 20-3.4.

f. Suffering Love

This category, more peripheral in the OT, moves to central position in the NT. The supreme instance of divine activity in history is found in the Christ event. In Jesus, God is deeply and personally involved in human history, not in the sense of a rescue mission by means of outside intervention but by participation in the sin and suffering that characterize human existence. To transpose Fretheim's categories, in Christ God suffers *because* his people reject him, *with* his people when they suffer, and *for* his people through the death of Christ. The ideal of the Suffering Servant becomes reality in the person of Jesus (cf. 9-3.1).

God, in Christ, through the Spirit continues to be involved in the ongoing history of the church and thus continues to be involved in suffering. When God's people are unfaithful, they "grieve the Holy Spirit of God" (Eph 4:30) and crucify the Son of God over again (Heb 6:6). The NT focuses on a great act of divine deliverance, parallel to yet also profoundly different from the exodus deliverance, for the Christ event is above all the supreme manifestation of God's suffering love in action.

3-3.4. GOD SPEAKS IN HISTORY

In the NT, as in the OT, when discussing God's dealings with his people, it is essential to recognize that God not only *acts* in history but also *speaks* in history.

As noted above, for the NT God has acted uniquely and decisively in the Christ event. In Christ, however, word and act fuse in a unique way. As Hebrews puts it, "Long ago God spoke to our ancestors in many and various ways by the prophets, but in these last days *he has spoken to us* by a Son" (1:1-2). According to John, Jesus is "the Word" incarnate (see 8-3.3). The Gospels provide an account not only of what Jesus *did* but also of what he *said*, and it is through both his deeds and his words that the supreme revelation of God is given.

That God *speaks* to individuals and through them to his people is, in the NT also, an essential condition of recognizing that God has acted in history. The events of Jesus' life and death are ambiguous. In the first century, as in the twenty-first, the "life of Jesus" was capable of being understood in many different ways. Jesus could be seen as a martyred prophet or as a political troublemaker. That he is seen in the NT as the Son of God incarnate who died to atone for the sins of the world, is due to the fact that God calls the apostles and others, and that he speaks to them and through them, interpreting the meaning of the Christ event. That interpretation is accepted by a *community* that relates it to its "confessional heritage," seeing it as the climax and fulfillment of God's *acting* and *speaking* to his people in history prior to and down to the time of the Christ event.

As in the OT, God can communicate through dreams (Matt 1:20; 2:12; etc.)

or visions (Luke 1:22; Acts 9:10; 18:9; 2 Cor 12:2). In Revelation, John constantly oscillates between visions and auditions, between "I heard" (1:10; etc.) and "I saw" (1:12; etc.), but here again, since in communicating his vision the prophet expresses his message in words, we are justified in referring to God *speaking* to and through the prophet.

Thus in the NT we have not only a record of the Christ event, and of the earliest days of the Christian church, we also have the *inspired interpretation* of these events. It is as *the community of faith* accepts this interpretation that the Christ event is recognized as God's unique act in history for the salvation of all people.

3-3.5. DO THIS IN REMEMBRANCE OF ME

In the NT, as in the OT, the great saving act of God in history is *remembered* by the community. Christians are called to "remember *(mnēmoneue)* Jesus Christ, raised from the dead, a descendant of David" (2 Tim 2:8; cf. Rev 3:3). One of the functions of the Holy Spirit is to remind believers of all that Jesus said (John 14:26). Quite apart from specific references to "remembering" (*mnēmoneuō* = "remember, call to mind"), the whole tradition that came to be embodied in the four written Gospels is the product of the early communities' *memories* of the words and works of Jesus (cf. G. H. Davies 1962b: 345). As in the OT, it is through memory that "the past is brought into the present with compelling power" (see 3-1.5).

In the NT, again as in the OT, *liturgy* plays an important role in the process of remembering and of the "actualization" of past events. The Eucharist (see 14-3.5c), like the Passover, does not merely reenact the great redemptive event to which the community looks back, it makes that event contemporary for the worshipers who thus participate in its power (see Verhey 1992: 669). The Pauline version of the Words of Institution concludes (1 Cor 11:25) with "Do this, as often as you drink it, *in remembrance of me (eis tēn emēn anamnēsin)*." The fact that *anamnēsis* occurs five times in the LXX, translating various forms of the root *zkr*, suggests that OT usage provides significant background for this key NT text. Thus "the celebration of the Eucharist as a 'memorial' is the releasing of Christ's power and personality afresh" (Sykes 1960: 117; for differing interpretations of this text, cf. Bartels 1978: 243-45). As year by year God's people "looked back to the release from Egypt as the great saving act of the Living God on behalf of his chosen people, so now they would remember the body broken and the blood poured out . . . the great, new saving act of God in Christ for all mankind" (D. Jones 1955: 188).

New Testament: Consummation

3-4. THE END WILL NOT FOLLOW IMMEDIATELY

3-4.1. PROPHETIC ESCHATOLOGY: THE END IN HISTORY

It has already been argued (1-4.1; 2-4.2) that in the NT apocalyptic and prophetic eschatology are both present and must be held in balance. There certainly is the expectation of a final, apocalyptic end of all things, but the NT also foresees an interval of unknown duration, a period of ongoing history between the Christ event and the final end. In addition to *apocalyptic* eschatology, there is also *prophetic* eschatology in the NT. Certain events are foreseen as happening in the future, within the ongoing flow of history, events that may be regarded as anticipations of God's final judgment and salvation. Each of these events may be regarded as a "window" through which a glimpse may be caught of the final end, but they themselves are not that end.

Jesus' teaching on the future is found especially in the so-called Apocalyptic Discourse of Mark 13 (the same material with minor variations is found in Matt 24 and Luke 21; scholarly discussion has focused mainly on Mark 13). Careful analysis of this chapter in its canonical form does not support the common view that it deals entirely with the apocalyptic end of history, an event that Jesus expected to occur soon, at least within the lifetime of his hearers, the corollary to this being that Jesus was mistaken.

The context of the discourse is the question of the temple, which Jesus prophesies will be destroyed (vv. 1-4; on the temple, see 14-3.1). The discourse proper falls into four clearly defined sections.

a. Vv. 5-23 deal with *prophetic* eschatology, i.e., events that will take place within history. Significantly, Jesus begins with a warning against being led astray by those who claim the end is near (vv. 5-6). In vv. 7-13 he envisages a continuing period within history that will be marked by wars, earthquakes, famines, the worldwide preaching of the gospel, and the persecution of Jesus' followers. These events are *not* signs that the final consummation is imminent; on the contrary, these verses are "intended to dampen down wild enthusiasm which saw any disaster as the prelude to the Last Days" (Hooker 1982: 84). In vv. 14-23 Jesus reverts to the coming desecration of the temple that will see a repetition of the "desolating sacrilege *(to bdelygma tēs erēmōseōs)*" of Dan 9:27; 11:31; 12:11 (see above, 3-2.2; Matt 24:15 specifically refers to Daniel). He goes on to speak of the sufferings Palestinian believers will experience, a prophecy fulfilled in the terrible events of the Great Revolt of A.D. 66-70. These events, however, are but a foretaste of what the church will experience throughout the whole period before the final consummation. Significantly this section ends with another warning against false prophets who declare the end is near (vv. 21-22), and with a warning to be alert (v. 23).

b. Vv. 24-27 deal with *apocalyptic* eschatology, i.e., the events of the final consummation consisting of cosmic upheavals, the parousia of the Son of Man, and the ingathering of the elect. This is in fact the only section of the discourse that is "apocalyptic" in the strict sense of the term (cf. D. Wenham 1982).

The remaining sections of the discourse deal with the timing of the events previously mentioned.

c. Vv. 28-31 deal with *prophetic* eschatology, and look back in particular to the prophecy of the coming destruction of the temple and the judgment that will fall on God's people (vv. 1-2 and 14-23). The parable of the fig tree (v. 28) suggests that these events will happen within history in the not too distant future: judgment will fall on Jerusalem within the present generation (v. 30).

d. Vv. 32-37, on the other hand, deal with *apocalyptic* eschatology, and the events of the final consummation described in vv. 24-27. Here the matter of timing is totally different: no one knows when the end events will take place, not even Jesus himself, and constant watchfulness is therefore enjoined. As already noted (see 2-4.5), Mark 13:32 is a remarkable verse that would never have been invented by early Christians. In relation to *prophetic* eschatology Jesus confidently predicts events that will take place within the lifetime of some of his hearers, but in relation to *apocalyptic* eschatology and the final end of all things, Jesus confesses his own ignorance. As far as the final consummation is concerned, "Jesus' assurances about God's promises do not include a binding timetable for God; at least he does not know one, and neither do the angels" (Tiede 1990: 72).

Strictly speaking, it would be more accurate to term Mark 13 "The Prophetic-Apocalyptic Discourse" (cf. Hooker 1982: 79-80). The same verdict applies, broadly speaking, to the book of Revelation. It is difficult to chart John's eschatology because of the way he continually oscillates between earth and heaven, and between present and future. The events of the final apocalyptic end occur mainly in chapters 19–22, though they are anticipated in earlier passages. Chapters 2–18 deal for the most part with events that will happen in history before the end, i.e., strictly speaking, with prophetic rather than apocalyptic eschatology.

3-4.2. SIGNS OF THE TIMES: TRIALS AND TRIBULATIONS

In Matt 16:1-3 Jesus accuses Pharisees and Sadducees who come to question him of being able to forecast the weather but not being able to "interpret the signs of the times." Since the phrase "signs of the times" is frequently understood to mean signs that the apocalyptic end of the world is near, it is important to examine the NT understanding of "signs" (see Ewert 1980: 37-38). The word "sign" (*sēmeion*) is ambiguous; it is used both in a bad and a good sense. If people are looking for a spectacular stunt that will compel belief, then "no sign will be given to this generation" (Mark 8:12; cf. Luke 17:20). But to those whom he accused of failing to interpret the signs of the times, Jesus did say that no sign would be given them "except the sign of Jonah" (Matt 16:4 and //s). As Jonah was a preacher of repentance, so it is Jesus' call to repentance that is the sign to the present generation (Luke 11:30). Thus interpreting the signs of the times means basically discerning what God is doing in the *present*. This is made even clearer in the Lucan version of the "weather forecast" saying: "Why do you not know *how to interpret the present time?*" (Luke 12:56).

This accords with the more favorable use of "sign" in John's Gospel, where Jesus' seven mighty works are "signs" (2:11; etc.), not in the sense of spectacular stunts, but indications that God is present in the works Jesus performs here and now. Similarly the life of the early church was often marked by "signs," indications that God is at work in the *present* (Mark 16:17, 20; Acts 2:43; 4:30; 5:12; Rom 15:19; 2 Cor 12:12; Heb 2:4).

While the term "signs" is used in Luke 21:25 of the cosmic signs that will precede the apocalyptic end, overwhelmingly for the NT interpreting the signs of the times means not speculating when the end of the world will come (cf. the warnings in Mark 13:4-5, 22), but discerning what is happening in the *present* and what will continue to happen *within history*, however long it may last.

As it looks to the future within history, the NT does not offer any easy optimism. In this period God's people will experience "tribulation" (*thlipsis*, lit. "pressure," hence "oppression," "distress," "affliction"; see Schippers 1975: 807). Jesus warned his disciples, "They will hand you over to be tortured *(eis thlipsin)* and will put you to death" (Matt 24:9); "in the world you have tribulation" (John 16:33 RSV; cf. Mark 4:17). Paul and Barnabas warned their converts that "it is through many persecutions *(dia pollōn thlipseōn)* that we must enter the kingdom of God" (Acts 14:22). The author of Revelation assures his readers that he shares their tribulation (1:9), and he warns the church at Smyrna: "for ten days you will have tribulation" (2:10 RSV). Revelation goes on to warn of many terrible events that will characterize the period before the end. The various catastrophes listed in the vision of the seven seals in Rev 6, including the "Four Horsemen of the Apocalypse" (vv. 2-8) — invasion, civil war, famine, and pestilence — closely parallel the tribulations of the Synoptic apocalypse (see Talbert 1994: 34-35). On the NT understanding of suffering, see further 16-3.5.

The setting for the tribulations of the faithful is a world that will not automatically get better and better, but rather where the struggle between good and evil will intensify (on this, see further 4-4). Not only will there be cosmic upheavals (above, 2-4.2), but there will be continuing conflicts in the historical order.

While the present age lasts, the church will face pressure of two kinds — from within and without.

a. Within the church *false teachers* will arise. Jesus warned against false messiahs and false prophets who would "lead astray, if possible, the elect"

(Mark 13:22; cf. 13:5-6 and //s), a warning that is echoed in such passages as 1 Tim 4:1-2, 2 Pet 2:1-3, and Rev 2:14-15 and 2:20-23, written to communities for whom false teaching was already a problem.

b. From without, the church will be subject to *persecution*. Jesus clearly anticipated the time when his followers would be "persecuted for righteousness' sake" (Matt 5:10-12), and warned of what those who "will be hated by all because of my name" can expect (Mark 13:9, 11-13, and //s). "If they persecuted me, they will persecute you" (John 15:20). In a similar vein 2 Tim 3:12 warns that "all who want to live a godly life in Christ Jesus will be persecuted."

The book of Acts and the Epistles testify, each in their own way, to the many trials and tribulations faced by the earliest Christians. The NT clearly warns that this will be the pattern as long as history lasts.

3-4.3. JUDGMENT IN HISTORY

Just as the OT prophets foresaw and foretold the judgment of God that would operate within the historical process and would fall either on Israel or on foreign nations, so the prophetic eschatology of the NT looks for the coming judgment of God within history. It does so in two main areas.

a. Judgment on Jerusalem

Jesus' mission to Israel and to its capital city of Jerusalem (cf. 13-3.4a) stands in the OT prophetic tradition. Indeed, the parallels between Jesus and Jeremiah are particularly close. Like Jeremiah, Jesus calls the people and city to repentance, and like Jeremiah, he too warns that failure to heed God's call will bring divine judgment. Jesus' sayings on Jerusalem "are heavily weighted with the phrases of the dire words Jeremiah spoke before the first destruction of Jerusalem" (Tiede 1990: 53): Matt 23:38, for example, echoes Jer 22:5; Luke 19:43 echoes Jer 6:6; and according to Matt 21:13//Luke 19:46, Jesus quotes Jeremiah's condemnation of the temple (Jer 7:11). For Jesus too, neither the Holy City nor the temple is immune from God's judgment, and he in fact foretells the destruction of both (cf. 13-3.4b; 14-3.1a). Where Jesus refers to critical events that will happen in the lifetime of his hearers, the main reference is to the fall of Jerusalem and the destruction of the temple, events that did in fact take place in A.D. 70, and thus within the lifetime of many who heard Jesus speak. These events are not the apocalyptic end, though they may be seen as anticipations of the final judgment.

b. Judgment on Rome

Judgment on Jerusalem will be carried out by the armies of Rome. But as the early church grew and expanded, it came into conflict with Rome. By the time Revelation was written, Christians were liable to persecution and Rome had come to represent "the kingdoms of this world," and to be identified as the beast that symbolized the powers of evil (Rev 13). Just as Isaiah foretold the fall of the great pagan city of Babylon ("Fallen, fallen is Babylon" — Isa 21:9), so John in the book of Revelation foresees the eventual downfall of Rome, which he refers to, using the code word "Babylon": "Fallen, fallen is Babylon the great!" (18:2). Rev 18 is an extended dirge that anticipates the fall of Rome, climaxing in a vision of an angel who "took up a stone like a great millstone and threw it into the sea, saying, 'With such violence Babylon the great city / will be thrown down'" (v. 21, echoing Jer 51:63-64).

3-4.4. SALVATION IN HISTORY

Just as the OT prophets foresaw and foretold the salvation of God that would operate within the historical process, so the prophetic eschatology of the NT anticipates a continuing saving activity of God in history, in the period between the first and second advents of Christ. It does this in two main ways.

a. Worldwide Preaching of the Gospel

One development that is foreseen as taking place within history is the worldwide preaching of the gospel; this will be a major feature of the period between the Christ event and the final consummation. Within the Synoptic apocalypse, as part of the first section that deals with prophetic eschatology (cf. above, 3-4.1), Jesus discourages belief in an imminent end by declaring that "the good news must first be proclaimed to all nations" (Mark 13:10; cf. Matt 24:14: "this good news of the kingdom will be proclaimed throughout the world, as a testimony to all the nations; and then the end will come"). The preaching of the gospel is "one of the events that must take place before the End: only when the proclamation of the gospel is completed — that is, when it has been preached to *all* the Gentiles — can the disciples expect the End of all things" (Hooker 1982: 89). This understanding of the delay of the final end is echoed in 2 Pet 3:9: "The Lord is not slow about his promise, as some think of slowness, but is patient with you, not wanting any to perish, but all to come to repentance." The longer the final end is delayed, the more people will get the chance to hear and respond to the message of salvation.

b. The Millennium

The relationship between prophetic and apocalyptic eschatology is critical for the understanding of the meaning of the millennium. The sole source for this belief is Rev 20:1-7. It is not mentioned elsewhere in the NT, and attempts to find a place for it in other eschatological passages are unwarranted (cf. Ewert 1980: 106-7; D. Guthrie 1981: 872-74). In this passage John sees an angel coming down from heaven who seizes and binds Satan and throws him into the bottomless pit for a thousand years. The martyrs then come to life and reign with Christ for a thousand years, thus participating in the "first resurrection." This may sound like the final apocalyptic victory of good over evil, but after the thousand years are over, Satan escapes from prison and rallies the forces opposed to God for one last battle. Only then is the devil thrown into the lake of fire and the way cleared for the last judgment (20:11-15) and the final vision of the new heaven and the new earth (21:1–22:5).

A period of a thousand years *(chilia etē)* is mentioned six times in this short passage, and is generally referred to as "the millennium" (from the Latin *mille* = "one thousand"; *annus* = "year"). Historically it is probable that the idea derives from the Jewish apocalyptic tradition that could include apocalyptic timetables in which each "day" of a "week" represented a thousand years, and some of which envisaged a two-stage eschatology with a messianic age of limited duration here on earth prior to the final defeat of evil and the final consummation beyond history (see Rist 1962b: 381; J. M. Ford 1992: 832). The concern of BT is not with origins but with how the millennium functions within the present canonical context.

So little is said about the millennium in the short passage that various options are left open. There are two main problems. Firstly, does the millennium occur on earth or in heaven? The constant oscillation in Revelation between earth and heaven makes this a difficult question to decide, though in most interpretations the millennium has been pictured as taking place here on earth. Secondly, what is the relation of the millennium to the second coming (parousia) of Christ? The problem here is that there is no certainty that Revelation recounts all the eschatological events in order; the writer also oscillates between present and future, and many of his visions overlap. Historically, three main interpretations of the millennium have been held, conveniently labeled depending on the relation between millennium and parousia (see Clouse 1977; Ewert 1980: 111-15).

Premillennialism ("pre" = before) expects that the parousia will occur before the millennium, which has generally been pictured as a thousand-year reign of Christ on earth. This view was favored by many in the early church (also referred to as *chiliasts* from the Greek word for one thousand), who often pictured the period in very literalistic terms, filling out the details by arbitrarily drawing on passages from the OT prophets (see Bietenhard 1953). Similar interpretations have been held in later centuries down to modern times, generally by smaller and more sectarian groups within Christianity, and often by groups that are socially and economically underprivileged. Daniélou (1970) expects the millennium to follow the parousia and interprets it in terms of paradisical and messianic symbolism. This view claims that Rev 19:11-16 (which precedes the millennium passage) refers to the parousia, hence the parousia precedes the millennium. Against this it must be pointed out firstly that it is not clear that Rev 19:11-16 does refer to the parousia; along with the following verses (19:17-21), it describes the victory of Christ over the forces of evil. Secondly, even if 19:11-16 does refer to the parousia, it is precarious to fit it into an exact timetable since John's visions cannot be assumed to be presented in chronological order. A variation of premillennialism is associated with "dispensationalism," a view that arbitrarily assigns numerous OT prophecies, literally interpreted, to a millennial kingdom following the "rapture" of the faithful and the parousia of Christ.

Postmillennialism ("post" = after) expects the parousia to follow the millennium. This suggests much more a period within history prior to the final apocalyptic events, and postmillennialists have generally portrayed the millennium in this-worldly terms. Some have identified the millennium with the triumph of the church. With the establishment of Christianity in the Roman Empire in the fourth century, it could be argued that the power of Satan (formerly operative in the persecuting empire) was bound, and the martyrs were vindicated. Since the fourteenth century it has been less easy to accept a literal millennium with this starting point. Others have thought more in terms of a gradual conversion of the world to Christianity, and this view has acted as a stimulus to Christian missions and service in the world.

Amillennialism ("a" = not) ought strictly to mean rejection of any belief in a millennium, but in practice it is used to refer to those who do not take the idea literally but seek to interpret it symbolically. The millennium is seen as an eschatological symbol that refers to the whole period from the historical Jesus to the final consummation, a period in which the powers of evil may for a while be held in check though they may also break out again at any time. As Jesus' saying about "tying up the strong man" (Matt 12:29 and //s) suggests, the coming of Jesus inaugurated the period in which, to a degree, Satan is bound and restrained (cf. C. Brown 1976: 702; Clouse 1977: 162-64). Study of the book of Revelation suggests that its use of numbers is symbolic rather than literal, and on balance the amillennial view commends itself as the most satisfactory interpretation (cf. D. Guthrie 1981). On this view, the thousand-year period is "symbolic of Christ's reign in and with his Church during the indefinitely long period between his first and second advents" (Cronk 1982: 266). It is on this basis that discussion of the millennium has been included within the framework of prophetic eschatology.

However literally or nonliterally the thousand-year period is taken, it does function as an important symbol that points toward two basic biblical truths.

Firstly, it does suggest that within human history *the forces of good can win at least limited victories.* Unlike all-out apocalyptic, the NT does not totally abandon the world and the remainder of history to Satan and the powers of evil. Christians are not left, as in apocalyptic, with no option but to despair totally of this world and simply watch and pray for the final consummation. Christians are called to combat evil and to work for good in the world, in the assurance that at least limited gains are possible.

Secondly, the other side of the coin is that prophetic eschatology is balanced by apocalyptic, so that it has to be realized that *no historical victory is ever final,* for the powers of evil are extremely resilient. The NT does not support any belief in automatic or inevitable progress. Social action has to be tempered by realism, and the recognition that as long as history lasts there will be a struggle between the forces of good and evil. There are no grounds for complacency; just when it seems that evil has been defeated on one front, it may be ready to reappear on another.

The concept of the millennium therefore witnesses to the dialectic between the prophetic and apocalyptic eschatologies that characterizes the total biblical view.

3-4.5. THE TIME OF THE END

Prophetic eschatology is concerned with events that will happen within history, before the final consummation.

In the case of the fall of Jerusalem, the Gospels present Jesus as seeing this as an event that cannot be long delayed, and will certainly happen within the lifetime of some of his hearers. Other events are placed on a more open-ended timescale. We have already argued that neither Jesus himself nor the NT as a whole knows how long history will last. The end will come suddenly and unexpectedly, but it need not come soon (see 2-4.5).

3-5. THE LORD OF HISTORY:
THEOLOGICAL REFLECTIONS

1. The so-called biblical theology movement laid great emphasis on "the God who acts"; the central and unique claim of the Bible is that God reveals himself through his mighty acts in history. BT is thus basically "a theology of recital" (G. E. Wright 1952: 38). This position quickly came under fire for a number of reasons (cf. B-8).

Though history is clearly important, it was questioned whether *all* the biblical material could be brought under the heading of "the acts of God in history" (J. Barr 1963; Davidson 1966: 100; Lemke 1982).

Others contended that an emphasis on divine activity in history was not unique to ancient Israel, as, e.g., G. E. Wright (1952: 39-41) had claimed (contrast Perdue 1994: 39). For example, the Moabite Stone (discovered in 1868), which dates from ca. 840 B.C., reveals that the Moabite king Mesha attributed the oppression of Moab by the Israelites to the fact that his god, Chemosh, was angry with the land; similarly he attributed his victories over his enemies to the fact that Chemosh delivered him from his oppressors. To give another example, the Persian ruler Cyrus, who Isaiah proclaimed was used by the LORD to restore his people, himself attributed his success and especially his conquest of Babylon to Marduk, the patron deity of Babylon (Davidson 1966: 103). The position taken in this work is that whether or not a belief is unique to the Bible is not a primary concern of BT, the focus of which should be on the canonical biblical text.

A further criticism of the BT movement is that it assumed that at least the basic outline of events narrated in the Bible is historical. Skepticism regarding the Bible's historicity, particularly of the earlier part of the OT, is nothing new, but one trend in the second half of the twentieth century was a growing skepticism regarding the historical reliability not just of the earlier part of the OT but of much of the rest of it, as well as of the Gospels and Acts (cf. Lemke 1982: 44-46). It might be held that what really matters is the *theological significance* attributed to the various narratives as this is embodied in the traditions transmitted within the community, but this is hardly a satisfactory position (cf. Davidson 1966: 101; contra J. J. Collins 1979: 197-98). What significance can the exodus have if the event never happened (cf. Marshall 1970a: 35)? For BT it is not crucial whether the exodus occurred in the fifteenth or thirteenth century B.C., but BT can hardly proceed without assuming at least the basic historicity of the biblical narratives. Over against the skeptics there are other scholars who contend that the study of nonbiblical sources, the discoveries of archaeology, and the evidence of papyri and inscriptions do show that where the biblical narratives can be checked they are basically historically reliable. In the NT, the two-volume work by Luke, i.e., Luke-Acts, "the first Christian history," constitutes a crucial test case. We argued above (3-3.2c) that Luke's role as a theologian does not preclude him from being regarded also as a historian (cf. the discussion in C-2.1).

A further searching critique of the "God who acts" position was made in a 1961 article by L. Gilkey, "Cosmology, Ontology, and the Travail of Biblical Language" (see also O. C. Thomas 1983: 5-6). Gilkey contended that traditional orthodoxy took quite literally biblical accounts of the mighty acts of God, and of God speaking to individuals. Liberalism rejected this on the grounds that "the orthodox belief in special revelation denied the reign of causal law in the phenomenal realm of space and time" (194); at best, "the divine activity became the continual, creative, immanent activity of God" (195). The proponents of the BT movement reacted against liberalism and sought to reinstate revelation through history. But, Gilkey argued, they did not set aside the modern assumption of a causal order within history; they rejected the miraculous, and on close inspection it becomes clear that they in fact did not believe that most of the events happened. Though asserting that God "acted" and "spoke," such language has in fact become equivocal. According to Gilkey, the BT movement scholars in practice virtually limited the so-called mighty acts of God to the exodus, and even here saw the narratives not so much as literal accounts of what happened as "creative interpretations" (197).

Gilkey's article was considered by some as having demolished the whole idea of revelation through history; others saw it as a challenge to rethink what Scripture says about God's activity in the historical order and to seek to understand it in a more satisfactory fashion (cf. the essays collected in O. C. Thomas 1983).

Related to Gilkey's critique was yet a further criticism: the idea of a God who basically stands outside this world of sin and suffering but occasionally intervenes to rescue his favorites was more and more regarded as both theologically unacceptable and in fact unbiblical.

2. The approach adopted here is that much of the biblical material is concerned with God's activity in the historical order — but by no means all of it. To focus only on God's activity in history is to distort the overall biblical picture. Hence, in this work a constant effort is made to *balance* God's activity in *the created order* and in *the historical order.*

While the exodus is undoubtedly a key event in the OT, it is very far from the only example of God's activity in history. For the Bible, God acts in history in calling a people to serve him; hence "salvation history" (including "judgment history") begins with the call of Abraham and continues down to the time of Christ; in the NT it continues further, though transposed into a new key, in God's dealings with the church, the new Israel. As argued above (3-1.3f), it is more appropriate to speak of God's ongoing "activity" in history than of isolated "acts." In a sense we could say that the Bible speaks of one ongoing "master act" of God, stretching from creation to consummation (cf. Kaufman 1968), though this must not preclude recognizing certain events as having a special significance.

Over against those who conceive of God's activity largely or even solely in "interventionist" terms, it is important to note the range of ways in which Scripture sees God as active in history (above, 3-1.3; 3-3.3). Direct "intervention" is rare, though it *is* claimed at a few crucial points in salvation history, especially at the exodus. But more frequently God acts through the leadership of inspired individuals, or within the events of history. Recent studies of providence and blessing provide a helpful corrective in seeing God as active "behind the scenes" in the ongoing events of everyday life. In particular, the understanding of God as active in suffering love, which is rooted in the OT and comes to full flower in the NT, provides a highly significant counterbalance to views focused on "outside intervention."

Recognition of God's activity in history, whether in biblical times or today, is always a matter of faith (cf. above, 3-1.4), and it is therefore essential to recognize that God not only *acts* in history but also *speaks* in history: through inspired spokespersons he provides the interpretation of events. All history involves interpretation. History can never simply be a matter of seeking to establish "what actually happened"; the way in which events are selected and presented always involves interpretation that depends on the presuppositions one brings to the study of history. Even those who are most skeptical about the historicity of the biblical narratives or about God's activity in history are presenting an interpretation based on their own particular presuppositions. In today's secular world many people find it no easier to believe that God is active in history than to believe that he is active in creation (cf. Kaufman 1968: 175-79). Such a view is based on secular presuppositions that can and should be challenged.

The Bible presents an alternative view: God *speaks* through prophets and apostles, challenging the community to recognize events of history, above all the Christ event, as "saving events." If God is the Creator and Ruler of all that is, we cannot assume that he is locked out of history by rigid laws of cause and effect. The Bible sees God at work in history in a variety of ways, calling a people to serve him and dealing with them in judgment and salvation, as he works out his purpose for all humankind.

3. Focus on the canonical accounts of God's activity in history runs the risk of imprisoning God in the past. One important consideration here is the biblical understanding of memory (above, 3-1.5; 3-3.5). The events of salvation history are never merely past events. For the community of faith they can be repeatedly "actualized" or contemporized through the reenactment of past events in liturgy, which serves as both an inspiration to the community and a spur to action.

The biblical understanding also suggests ways in which God may continue to be seen as active in our contemporary world. In the OT especially, God's people were a national unit and thus God's dealings with them were closely bound up with the history of Israel. In the NT and subsequently, God's people are a community of faith drawn from all nations, whose dealings with God are therefore separate from the history of any one nation. For Christians, therefore, the activity of God in history is to be discerned primarily in his dealings — in judgment and in mercy — with his people, the church.

4. The distinction between prophetic and apocalyptic eschatology is a crucial one. The OT, especially the prophetic books, sees God as active *within history*, not just in the past but also in the future. God will act in history and calls

on his people to cooperate with him in the carrying out of his purposes, even though eventually (at a time known only to God) history itself will come to an end.

The NT alters the emphasis somewhat, but not the basic pattern. The expectation of a final consummation is brought into clearer focus, but short of that God continues to work out his purposes *within* history. God's people are called to cooperate with him, and in the view of the NT the primary task of the church, so long as history lasts, is to witness to the gospel by word and deed.

The symbol of the millennium (above, 3-4.4b) brings to a focus the biblical balance between prophetic and apocalyptic eschatology, between social action and realism. It suggests *both* that God's people must be involved in working for a better world *and* that no final victory over evil is possible this side of the final consummation.

5. The NT sees a period of indefinite length stretching out between the Christ event and Christ's return at the final consummation. This period is portrayed with an unflinching realism; throughout it, those who are faithful to God may expect to encounter trials and tribulations (above, 3-4.2).

Rev 7:14 (RSV) uses the phrase "the great tribulation," and some have seen this as a reference to a final period of trial immediately preceding the final consummation. The view propounded by John Darby and widely circulated by proponents of so-called biblical prophecy, that believers will be "raptured" (i.e., taken up to heaven) *prior to* the great tribulation (usually identified with the events of Rev 4–18), not only has no basis in the NT, but totally contradicts the main thrust of NT teaching that believers will *not* be spared tribulation (see Ewert 1980: 51-53, 85-86; cf. 7-5.6; 20-4.4a). As long as history lasts, the church can expect opposition and suffering. Believers are not told that they will be exempt; rather they are exhorted to "be patient in suffering" (Rom 12:12), knowing that neither tribulation, nor distress, nor persecution, nor famine, nor nakedness, nor peril, nor sword can separate them from the love of Christ (8:35).

CHAPTER 4

The Adversary

Old Testament: Proclamation

4-1. OUR ADVERSARIES

4-1.1. WHAT THWARTS GOD'S PURPOSES?

The Bible is a book of faith: it discerns meaning and order in both creation and history, and associates these with the purposes of God. But the Bible is also a thoroughly realistic book: it acknowledges that God's purposes often seem to be thwarted, and that in both history and creation it is *disorder* rather than order that often seems to prevail.

What is it that thwarts God's purposes and promotes disorder? On the historical level a major answer to this question is: the faithlessness of God's people and their failure to be the kind of community God called them to be. One side of biblical history is the chronicle of Israel's rebellion, disobedience, and folly, and hence, as we have seen (3-1), it can become "judgment history" just as much as "salvation history."

But the Bible also recognizes other sources of opposition: God and his people frequently encounter *adversaries* or enemies. The most common terms are *tsar* = "enemy" and *'ōyēbh* = "enemy"; less common but more important theologically is *sāṭān* = "adversary, accuser" (see Hamilton 1992: 985-86).

In the historical order these "adversaries" are generally foreign nations who oppose, attack, or enslave Israel. It becomes clear also, however, that even within Israel the righteous must be prepared to face opposition from personal enemies, people who flout God's will.

The question then arises: Are these adversaries that are constantly encountered in history and society self-originating and self-sustaining, or are they the agents of an adversary or adversaries that pervade the whole created order, i.e., a cosmic power, or powers, of evil and disorder? If strict monotheism is to be maintained, then the problem is how to account for the presence and power of evil and disorder in the world. If the existence of powers opposed to God is recognized, in the created as well as the historical order, then the problem is how to reconcile the resulting dualism with biblical monotheism. A few OT passages that stress mono-theism come close to making God the author of evil as well as good:

> I form light and create darkness,
>> I make weal and create woe;
>> I the LORD do all these things. (Isa 45:7; cf. Deut 32:39; Job 5:18)

But elsewhere the OT moves in the direction of recognizing the existence of powers opposed to God.

4-1.2. THE HISTORICAL ORDER

a. Historical Adversaries

Throughout the OT God's people face adversaries in the form of other peoples and nations. Pharaoh and the Egyptians constitute the classic case of an enemy opposing God's purposes and oppressing his people. Pharaoh orders all the newborn male Hebrew children put to death (Exod 1:22), though despite this, Moses providentially survives. The enslavement of the Israelites seems to thwart God's promise and purpose for his people. The exodus event is a mighty deliverance from these adversaries:

> Your right hand, O LORD, glorious in power —
>> your right hand, O LORD, shattered *the enemy*. (Exod 15:6; cf. vv. 9-10)

The Israelites face further opposition in their wilderness wanderings (e.g., the Amalekites — Exod 17:8-16), but these are only a foretaste of the adversaries to be encountered when Israel enters the Land. On his deathbed Moses prays to God for Judah:

> Strengthen his hands for him,
>> and be a help against his *adversaries*. (Deut 33:7)

If the book of Joshua dwells largely on the defeat of the adversaries who oppose Israel's occupation of the Land (cf. Josh 10:25; 23:1), the book of Judges balances that with a picture of continuing struggle against adversaries. Only under David and Solomon were God's people granted rest from their enemies (though see 1 Kgs 11:14; cf. v. 23).

The period that begins with the monarchy, however, sees new opposition on a vaster scale: the rise of major empires, the Assyrian and then the Babylonian, that threaten the very existence of God's people. After the exile and the return, Israel is subject to Persians, Ptolemies, and Seleucids (and after the Maccabean period to the Romans). World empires as adversaries of God's people constitute a major theme of the book of Daniel: Dan 2 and 7 foresee, in symbolic form, a succession of four pagan world empires to which God's people will be subject (see 1-2.1).

The Psalter contains numerous references to "enemies" (*'ōyēbh* occurs about eighty times, *tsar* about twenty times, *sātān* four times), and the identity and nature of these "enemies" has been the subject of much debate (cf. G. W. Anderson 1965; B. W. Anderson 1983: 82-87). Some of the references are clearly to national enemies, enemies of God's people; this is the case in the Royal Psalms (see further, 6-1.2b) that speak of "the king's enemies" (45:5; cf. 2:1-3; 18:47; 21). At his coronation the king is invited by God to

> sit at my right hand
> until I make your enemies your footstool. (110:1)

Of course, the king's enemies are also the enemies of God's people.

Enemies also figure in community laments (see 3-2.1a). Ps 44, for example, is a prayer for deliverance of the nation from enemies at whose hands they have received a humiliating defeat. Other examples include Pss 74, 79, 80, 123. In "Hymns" we also find praise to God for the defeat of national enemies, for example, in 66:3, 7; 98:1-3; 135:10-11.

> If it had not been the LORD who was on our side . . .
>   when our enemies attacked us,
>   then they would have swallowed us up alive. (124:1-3)

The enemies of the nation, of course, are also the enemies of God:

> Remember this, O LORD, how the enemy scoffs,
>   and an impious people reviles your name. (74:18)

Here again we see a tension between belief in God as king of the whole earth and the reality of many nations who flaunt God's laws and live as enemies of God and his people.

b. Personal Adversaries

Other references to "enemies" in the Psalms bring us closer to home, and refer to personal adversaries within society (3:7; 6:10; 7:5; 9:3; etc.). The context in most cases sheds light on the nature of these "enemies": they are "the wicked"

(3:7), who "pursue" those faithful to God (7:1), mock them (35:19-20), and falsely accuse them (27:12). They are insolent (86:14) and hateful (38:19). Metaphorically, they can be described as a hostile army (27:3), hunters seeking their prey (35:7), or wild beasts (22:12-13) (cf. Kraus 1986: 130-31).

Scholars have speculated on the original setting of these psalms, and assigned them to various historical periods. Some (Mowinckel, Birkeland) have detected references to magical practices (cf. Kraus 1986: 135-36). But in their canonical form the references to enemies are cut free from any particular historical setting. Readers can "fill in the blanks" and identify the "strong bulls" and "roaring lions" with whatever adversaries they face in their personal lives (cf. G. W. Anderson 1965: 29). "By using conventional language," these psalms "portray a situation that is *typical* of every person who struggles with the meaning of life in the concrete situations of tension, hostility and conflict" (B. W. Anderson 1983: 86-87).

The stress on personal enemies in the Psalter underlines an important aspect of biblical faith. God's people are called upon not to retreat from society but to live out their faith in society. This inevitably means that they will provoke opposition.

c. Treatment of Enemies

Nowhere does the OT specifically *command* hatred of enemies. It does command hatred of evil, as, e.g., in Amos 5:15: "Hate evil and love good," and it records *expressions* of hatred of adversaries as evildoers and opponents of God:

> Do I not hate those who hate you, O LORD?
>   And do I not loathe those who rise up against you?
> I hate them with perfect hatred;
>   I count them my enemies. (Ps 139:21-22)

The tendency to seek vengeance on one's enemies is deeply rooted in human nature. In the ancient song preserved in Gen 4:23-24, Lamech boasts of exacting not just sevenfold but seventy-sevenfold vengeance on his enemies (compared with this, the *lex talionis* of Exod 21:23-24 is a considerable advance; cf. 18-1.2a.v). A series of "imprecatory" psalms call out to God for vindication, and sometimes for vengeance against enemies (see B. W. Anderson 1983: 87-93). Ps 137, for example, is a terrible cry for vengeance against the Babylonians. Clearly these psalms must be treated with caution and seen in their total canonical context (see 4-3.2b; cf. Hobbs and Jackson 1991: 26-28).

Yet in tension with this within the OT is another attitude toward enemies. It is quite wrong to make the oversimplified contrast that is frequently drawn between the OT and NT in terms of hatred of enemies versus love of enemies (cf. J. A. Sanders 1962: 101). In Torah, Prophets, and Writings there are some passages that enjoin if not love of enemies, at least an attitude quite different from hatred.

Joseph showed a remarkable spirit of forgiveness toward his brothers who had sought to kill him (Gen 50:15-21). According to Exod 23:4-5, "When you come upon your enemy's ox or donkey going astray, you shall bring it back. When you see the donkey of one who hates you lying under its burden and you would hold back from setting it free, you must help to set it free." This is not merely a question of "kindness to animals" (though that is not excluded; cf. 2-1.4c). An animal was an important economic asset, and its loss would be a severe blow to its owner. The Torah therefore enjoins extending positive help to one in need even when a personal enemy.

Amid the many wars that characterize the Historical Books, Elisha's treatment of the Aramean army affords a remarkable instance of feeding one's enemies rather than slaughtering them (2 Kgs 6:8-23). In his letter to the exiles in Babylon, the prophet Jeremiah advocated an attitude to the Babylonians, the enemy who had conquered Judah and destroyed both city and temple, that many must have considered revolutionary: "Seek the welfare of the city where I have sent you into exile, and pray to the LORD on its behalf, for in its welfare you will find your welfare" (Jer 29:7). Instead of hating their enemies, God's people are to pray for them!

Prov 25:21-22 advises:

> If your enemies are hungry, give them bread to eat;
>   and if they are thirsty, give them water to drink;
> for you will heap coals of fire on their heads,
>   and the LORD will reward you.

By showing kindness to an enemy, the hope is that the enemy will feel remorse (cf. Wolff 1974: 190-91), and the way will thus be opened for a reconciliation.

In the Deuterocanon we find this advice:

> Forgive your neighbor the wrong he has done,
>   and then your sins will be pardoned when you pray. (*Sir* 28:2)

4-1.3. THE CREATED ORDER: POWERS OF CHAOS

a. Creation and Conflict

The Gen 1 account, as has been noted (2-1.2d), portrays God creating all things by divine fiat. A contrast is frequently drawn between this biblical account and other accounts from the ancient Near East that generally took the form of a conflict between the creator god and another deity or a beast/monster representing the powers of chaos. These hostile powers were defeated and restrained but not entirely eliminated. The cosmos is constantly threatened by the powers of chaos, and a central feature of religion is an annual ceremony, with appropriate ritual, that celebrates the enthronement of the victorious deity and guarantees the continued restraint of the powers that threaten life.

The OT knows nothing of a conflict between deities, and reconstructions of an analogous annual festival are highly speculative and go well beyond the biblical evidence. Nevertheless, in the OT there is another tradition that portrays creation in terms of God's victory over chaos and that employs two sets of powerful symbols, the *waters* of chaos and a *beast/monster* of chaos.

b. Here Shall Your Proud Waves Be Stopped

Ps 104:6-9 refers to creation in the following terms:

> The waters stood above the mountains.
> At your rebuke they flee;
>   at the sound of your thunder they take to flight. . . .
> You set a boundary that they may not pass,
>   so that they might not again cover the earth.
> (cf. Pss 24:1-2; 46:1-3; 65:7; 136:6; 148:4-6)

A similar statement is found in the account of Wisdom's role in creation in Prov 8:28-30:

> When he made firm the skies above,
>   when he established the fountains of the deep,
> when he assigned to the sea its limit,
>   so that the waters might not transgress his command,
> when he marked out the foundations of the earth,
>   then I was beside him.

"According to this passage, wisdom was older than the primeval waters of chaos, and attended Yahweh in the successive works of creation, including his assigning a limit to the unruly waters of chaos" (B. W. Anderson 1967: 73). In Job 38:8-11 God asks Job:

> Or who shut in the sea with doors
>   when it burst out from the womb? —
> when I made the clouds its garment,
>   and thick darkness its swaddling band,

and prescribed bounds for it,
    and set bars and doors,
and said, "Thus far you shall come, and no farther,
    and here shall your proud waves be stopped"?

Creation on this view involved the restraint of the waters and the fixing of boundaries. What happened in the flood was the temporary removing of these restraints (Gen 7:11). Such a view is not necessarily inconsistent with Gen 1, though it does represent a different emphasis. The Genesis account begins with a reference to darkness covering "the face of the deep *(t^{e}hôm)*," and to the Spirit of God sweeping "over the face of the waters *(hammāyîm)*" (1:2). Creation involves a separation of the waters (1:6-7), and the earth emerges only when the waters are gathered together into one place to form the seas (1:9-10).

Moreover, in keeping with the OT understanding of "continuous creation" (2-1.2b), God is the one who constantly restrains the waters of chaos. According to Ps 65:7,

You silence the roaring of the seas,
    the roaring of their waves,
    the tumult of the peoples.

In a similar vein Ps 89:9 says,

You rule the raging of the sea;
    when its waves rise, you still them.

God's continuing restraint of the waters is part of his rule over the cosmos celebrated in the Enthronement Psalms (see 1-1.1):

The LORD sits enthroned over the flood;
    the LORD sits enthroned as king forever. (Ps 29:10)

Ps 93 is devoted to this theme:

The floods have lifted up, O LORD,
    the floods have lifted up their voice;
    the floods lift up their roaring.
More majestic than the thunders of mighty waters,
    more majestic than the waves of the sea,
    majestic on high is the LORD! (vv. 3-4)

These psalms proclaim that "God is enthroned triumphantly over the powers that threaten to plunge human history into meaningless disorder and chaos"

(B. W. Anderson 1983: 178). God's control over the hostile waters is seen in the graphic description of a storm at sea in Ps 107:23-30, where in response to the sailors' cry of despair,

> He made the storm be still,
> and the waves of the sea were hushed. (v. 29)

In this passage strong overtones of the victory over the primeval waters of chaos carry over into God's ability to control the waters of an actual storm at sea.

Similarly God's power over water manifested in the historical order, especially in the parting of the sea at the time of the exodus, also reflects his victory over the waters of chaos; the Lord of the created order is also the Lord of the historical order (cf. Bruce 1969: 42). There are clearly cosmic overtones in the Song of Moses:

> At the blast of your nostrils the waters piled up,
> the floods stood up in a heap;
> the deeps congealed in the heart of the sea. (Exod 15:8)

In reference to the exodus event, Ps 77 says,

> When the waters saw you, O God,
> when the waters saw you, they were afraid;
> the very deep trembled. . . .
> Your way was through the sea,
> your path, through the mighty waters;
> yet your footprints were unseen. (vv. 16, 19)

In similar fashion God parted the waters of the Jordan in Josh 3:7-17, while in the battle against Sisera cosmic powers were involved and God used the waters of a river in flood to defeat the enemy:

> The stars fought from heaven,
> from their courses they fought against Sisera.
> The torrent Kishon swept them away,
> the onrushing torrent, the torrent Kishon. (Judg 5:20-21)

The historical enemies of God's people can be spoken of in terms of waters that will be vanquished by God. Here "the enemies are manifestations of the intransigent elements which had to be quelled by Yahweh before creation could begin, and which must ever be defeated by him as he continues his activity in history" (H. G. May 1955: 11).

> Ah, the thunder of many peoples,
> > they thunder like the thundering of the sea! . . .
> The nations roar like the roaring of many waters,
> > but he will rebuke them. (Isa 17:12-13)

"It is easy to perceive underneath these figures the theme of the chained, rebellious sea" (Jacob 1958: 141). On a more personal level, Psalms often speaks of troubles that threaten individuals as "waters" (69:1-2, 14-15, etc.). What these passages suggest, therefore, is that behind both the national enemies and the personal adversaries that God's people confront (above, 4-1.2a, b) lie more sinister cosmic powers of evil (cf. Kraus 1986: 134-36).

God is depicted as triumphing over these powers. At creation they were subject to his "rebuke *(gᵉʿārâh)*" (Job 26:11; Pss 18:15; 104:7). At the exodus God "rebuked *(wayyigʿar)* the Red Sea" (Ps 106:9). "Rebuke" (verb *gāʿar*, noun *gᵉʿārâh*), however, is clearly too tame a translation; what the term signifies is "the exercise of power over the forces that stand in the way of the fulfilment of God's purpose" (Kee 1968: 237).

c. You Broke the Heads of the Dragons

Especially in Psalms, Job, and Isaiah, the powers opposed to the God of creation can be pictured as a "dragon" or "sea monster" (*tannîn*; cf. Ps 74:13; Isa 27:1; Job 7:12), or "serpent" (*nāchāsh*; cf. Isa 27:1; Job 26:13). Specifically, such a creature can be called either "Rahab" *(rahab)* or "Leviathan" *(liwᵉyāthān)*. Since the picture is one of some kind of sea monster, the connection with the "waters" imagery is a close one:

> You rule the raging of the sea;
> > when its waters rise, you still them.
> You crushed Rahab like a carcass,
> > you scattered your enemies with your mighty arm.
> > > (Ps 89:9-10; cf. Job 9:13; 26:12-13; Isa 30:7; 51:9)

Historically, the figure of Leviathan may reflect an ancient and widespread myth of a dragon of chaos or evil (Gordon 1966: 1-4). At creation Leviathan was destroyed by the LORD:

> You divided the sea by your might;
> > you broke the heads of the dragons in the waters.
> You crushed the heads of Leviathan;
> > you gave him as food for the creatures of the wilderness. (Ps 74:13-14)

Similarly Isa 51:9 speaks of God's destruction of Rahab and the dragon.

A more common view is that Leviathan was subdued rather than destroyed. Ps 104:26 describes the sea "and Leviathan that you formed to sport in it." Here "The monster *Leviathan* . . . has become, for this author, merely a harmless, sportive creature of God" (*NOAB*, OT: 763).

Do the waters and the monsters represent powers of evil opposed to God, and if so, where did they come from? The Bible does not directly answer such questions. Gen 1 does make clear that "God created the great sea monsters" (v. 21). Nevertheless, they do symbolize powers that are at least apparently opposed to God, and that God apparently is prepared to tolerate within certain limits. Note especially the portrait of the two creatures Behemoth and Leviathan in Job 40 and 41 (cf. also 2 *Esdr* 6:49-52). These are far more than the hippopotamus and the crocodile; clearly they relate to the dragon tradition. Their strength and fierceness are emphasized, yet God created them and God controls them. In fact, God has Leviathan, as it were, on a leash (Job 41:1-5), which suggests that the powers of evil are never beyond God's control (see 16-1.5c).

4-1.4. THE CREATED ORDER: POWERS OF EVIL

The OT has a few, but only a few, references to powers or spirits of evil and disorder at work in the world (see the detailed discussion in Langton 1949: 35-52; Kuemmerlin-McLean 1992).

The few references to *demons* connect them particularly with wilderness areas. Azazel, who figures in the Day of Atonement ceremony, is apparently a demon living in the wilderness (Lev 16:8f.). Lilith appears in Isa 34:14 as a demon haunting desolate places, while *sheʿîrîm*, probably = "hairy ones," are perhaps goatlike demons living in desert places (Lev 17:7; 2 Chr 11:15). *Shēdhîm*, "demons," are mentioned in Deut 32:17 and Ps 106:37. "Demonology lies out on the periphery of the Old Testament. The comparative dearth of Old Testament references to demonology is all the more striking in view of the great importance of the subject in the religions of other peoples of antiquity" (B. W. Anderson 1967: 150; cf. Ling 1961: 3; Eichrodt 1967: 223). The strongly monotheistic belief of the OT leaves little room for such demonic powers.

The same viewpoint is even more clearly reflected in the few OT references to *evil spirits*. In 1 Sam 16:14-23 the Spirit of the LORD departs from Saul, and he is possessed by an evil spirit that causes a mental disorder; yet what the writer says is that "an evil spirit *(rûach rāʿāh) from the LORD* tormented him." 1 Kgs 22:19-23 boldly speaks of the LORD putting a "lying spirit" *(rûach sheqer)* in the mouth of the prophets of Israel; the spirit volunteers for the job (v. 21), but is completely subservient to the LORD (vv. 22-23). Nothing shows more clearly the basically *nondualistic* character of the OT; even an evil or lying spirit does not operate in independence from the LORD.

A marked change occurs, however, in the late OT period, as the book of

Tobit dramatically illustrates. In that book Sarah is oppressed by "the wicked demon Asmodeus" (3:8), who had killed seven husbands in succession before they had been able to consummate their marriage. Tobit's son Tobias, with the help of the angel Raphael, banishes the demon that is then bound by Raphael (8:1-3). The Synoptic Gospels witness to a widespread belief in demons or evil spirits that must have developed especially in the second and first centuries B.C.

4-1.5. THE CREATED ORDER: THE ADVERSARY

In the late OT a significant change of emphasis begins to take place: there commences a development toward the recognition of the existence of *a personal power of evil.* Behind the various adversaries that thwart God's purposes there begins to emerge the figure of *"the adversary,"* or "the Satan" *(hassāṭān;* LXX = *ho diabolos).* Used with the definite article, "the Satan" is not a name but a title, meaning "the adversary" or "the accuser." "Satan" can be used of historical adversaries (e.g., 1 Sam 29:4; 1 Kgs 11:14, 25) and in the sense of an accuser (Ps 109:6). In Num 22:22, 32 the angel of the LORD acts as an "adversary" to Balaam as he sets out to curse the Israelites; in this case "the angel is both adversary to and accuser of Balaam, and is dispatched on his mission by Yahweh" (Hamilton 1992: 986). The word begins to acquire a new significance in three OT passages.

a. In *the prologue to Job* (1:6–2:7), "the Satan" is among "the sons of God" (1:6), i.e., apparently a member of the heavenly council (cf. 1-1.3b), although he has come from "going to and fro on the earth" (1:7). On two occasions God and the Satan enter into a dialogue concerning Job. The Satan asks for, and receives, permission to try Job's faith by inflicting various trials upon him. The Satan is thus the adversary of Job; he unjustly accuses him and is the agent of his sufferings, though only because God allows this to happen. The Satan is more than Job's accuser; he is also "calumniator and above all *tempter,* who has a double end to pursue: to make men rebel against God and to destroy them" (Prager 1981: 809). Even in Job, "the traits which will develop into the kind of character which he possesses in New Testament times can already be dimly discerned" (Ling 1961: 6).

b. In the heavenly court scene of *Zech 3* (see M. E. Tate 1992: 463-64), "the Satan," still apparently a member of the heavenly council, acts as accuser and prosecutor in the trial of the high priest Joshua. Significantly, the Satan is "rebuked" (verb *gāʿar).* "The angel of the LORD" stands by Joshua, who is cleansed of his sin and reinstated. Thus both the prosecuting and the defending counsel are pictured as angels of God, each with their own duty to perform.

c. In *2 Sam 24* David is condemned for holding a census of the people, and the text boldly states that "the anger of the LORD was kindled against Israel, and he incited David against them, saying, 'Go, count the people of Israel and Judah'" (v. 1). In retelling the story, 1 Chr 21:1 makes a significant change; it asserts that "*Satan* stood up against Israel, and incited David to count the people of Israel." "Satan" is used here without the definite article, in reference to a figure who definitely incites David to do what is contrary to the will of God. "This shows that by the fourth century in Israel the concept of a supernatural adversary had solidified into a quite definite, sharply delineated figure" (Eichrodt 1967: 206; contra M. E. Tate 1992: 465-66).

Historical-critical scholarship is virtually unanimous in holding that the serpent that appears in the story of the fall in Gen 3 was not originally identified with Satan or with an evil power. Serpents were thought of as wise or cunning, and in the story the serpent may have originally been intended only to represent a possibility that entered into the mind of the woman. But serpents could also symbolize chaos and evil (see Joines 1975: 8-9), and Eichrodt (1967) is right when he says that "the superhuman informedness about the tree of knowledge, and the demonic hostility toward God, which burst out in the serpent's words, are an unmistakable sign that a deliberate anti-God power is here at work; and the interpretation of this figure by the Church in terms of Satan was an absolutely correct intuition of its real character, even though the development of the actual Satan concept may belong to a much later period" (405; cf. also 207).

It is in *Wisdom* that the serpent is for the first time explicitly identified as Satan or the devil *(diabolos):*

> For God created us for incorruption,
> and made us in the image of his own eternity,
> but through the devil's envy death entered the world. (2:23-24)

Historically, what we see throughout the Bible as a whole is a growing awareness of the existence of a personal power of evil in the world. Canonically, it is legitimate and indeed necessary to read Gen 3 in the light of that later development and to recognize that here at the outset of human history battle is joined between the forces of good and the forces of evil.

Note: Isa 14:4-21, one of a series of oracles against foreign nations (Isa 13–23), is a mock funeral dirge addressed to the king of Babylon, who thought himself an equal of the gods but who will be laid low in death. In v. 12 he is addressed:

> How you are fallen from heaven,
>   O Day Star *(hêlēl)*, son of Dawn *(ben shāhar)!*
> How you are cut down to the ground,
>   you who laid the nations low!

The reference to the king as "Day Star" or "Morning Star" may reflect a Canaanite myth of a minor deity who sought to become equal with the High God (see commentaries). The Vulgate translated "Day Star" as "Lucifer" (lit.

"light-bearer"), and some Church Fathers linked this figure with Satan, regarded as a rebellious angel cast out of heaven before creation (cf. below, 4-3.3b). However, there is no hint of a connection with Satan in the biblical text, and such patristic speculations fall outside the province of BT (cf. Elwell 1988d: 2:1907). In the NT it is Christ, not Satan, who is identified as the "Morning Star" (2 Pet 1:19; Rev 22:16).

Old Testament: Promise

4-2. WRATH TO HIS ADVERSARIES

4-2.1. INTENSIFICATION OF OPPOSITION AND FINAL VICTORY

Whatever adversaries thwart God's purposes in the historical or the created order, it is the faith of the Bible that they will ultimately be overcome. This faith is not based, however, on an easy optimism, and it is never associated with anything like a modern doctrine of progress. Indeed, in biblical eschatology the main emphasis falls on the expectation of *an intensification of the opposition* to God and to his people before the final victory is attained. Simply put, biblical eschatology expects that things will get worse before they get better.

4-2.2. THE HISTORICAL ORDER: INTENSIFICATION

In the earlier historical books Israel is promised victory over her adversaries, in particular, over the Egyptians at the exodus and over the inhabitants of Canaan at the conquest. And some spectacular victories are recorded: the destruction of the Egyptian army at the sea, the fall of Jericho, Gideon's victory over the Midianites.

But the situation changes as Israel is brought to realize that God is not automatically "on our side." God can and does use Israel's enemies to punish and to discipline her (cf. 3-1.3c). Thus, if the major prophets saw light, it was only at the end of a long and dark tunnel. One of the main things that separated them from "false prophets" was their refusal to preach a popular but deceiving message of easy victory. A classic example is the confrontation between Jeremiah and Hananiah in Jer 28.

In Dan 7 the last of the four beasts is the most terrible of all (v. 7); it is "terrifying and dreadful and exceedingly strong" (v. 7), and it launches an all-out attack on God's people (v. 21).

4-2.3. THE HISTORICAL ORDER: VICTORY

Despite this, the OT believes that ultimately God's adversaries will be overcome.

a. Their Dominion Shall Be Taken Away

However long and hard the struggle, the historical adversaries of Israel will finally be defeated. Isaiah declares:

> According to their deeds, so will he [God] repay;
>> wrath to his adversaries, requital to his enemies. (59:18)

Echoing God's "rebuke" of the waters of chaos, 17:13 declares:

> The nations roar like the roaring of many waters,
>> but he [God] will rebuke them, and they will flee far away.
>>> (cf. 50:2; Nah 1:4)

In Ps 110 the anointed king of David's line is exalted by God and assured of victory over his enemies. An oracle is declared, probably by some official of the temple:

> The LORD [God] says to my lord [the king],
>> "Sit at my right hand
> until I make your enemies your footstool." (v. 1)

At the "Day of the Lord" (cf. 3-2.3), God will judge and punish Israel's enemies such as Babylon (Isa 13:6-16), Edom (34:8), and Egypt (Jer 46:10).

b. They Shall Be Put to Shame

Similarly, however strong the opposition of personal adversaries, the OT generally holds that sooner or later they will get their just deserts.

> All my enemies shall be ashamed and struck with terror;
>> they shall turn back, and in a moment be put to shame. (Ps 6:10)

The fact that this is not always the way things work out in life raises serious problems; see 16-2.5.

4-2.4. THE CREATED ORDER: INTENSIFICATION

In the created order also, the power of evil will intensify before it is finally defeated. The four beasts of Dan 7 may represent historical adversaries in the form of world empires (above, 4-2.2), but they emerge from "the great sea" and take the form of "four beasts." "The origin of these beasts out of the sea, the locus of the chaotic, undoubtedly signifies that the historical evil manifest in the empires is rooted in a radical opposition to God's purpose which couches deep in his creation" (B. W. Anderson 1967: 139). They represent therefore an intensification of evil not only in the historical order, but also in the created order.

Ezek 38–39 speaks of a final threat to a restored Israel posed by an invasion from the north led by "Gog, of the land of Magog" (38:2). The prophecy may well have had a historical basis; traditionally, invading armies came from the north (cf. Jer 1:13f.). "Gog" (*gôg*) may represent Gyges, king of Lydia in the seventh century B.C. (A "Magog" is listed in Gen 10:2 in a context that suggests western Asia Minor.) Yet the enemy host will be met by God himself (Ezek 38:18f.), to the accompaniment of cosmic signs (38:20, 22). The eschatological context, the mystery surrounding the name of the enemy, and divine participation all suggest a symbolic *final battle* with the forces opposing God. "The description which began on the nebulous fringes of history has been elevated into the trans-historical, into an arena beyond direct relation to contemporary reality. Gog has become the representative of the cosmic powers of the returned chaos which Yahweh destroys in the latter days, powers which cannot be described as historical, although presented partly in historical dress" (Childs 1959: 196).

4-2.5. THE CREATED ORDER: VICTORY

The OT affords at least glimpses of the final victory over the cosmic powers of evil and disorder.

In Daniel's vision the fourth beast "was put to death, and its body destroyed and given over to be burned with fire" (Dan 7:11; cf. 7:26).

In Ezek 39 the forces of Gog and Magog will be defeated in a last great battle: "You shall fall upon the mountains of Israel, you and all your troops and the peoples that are with you; I will give you to birds of prey of every kind and to the wild animals to be devoured. . . . I will send fire on Magog and on those who live securely in the coastlands; and they shall know that I am the LORD" (vv. 4-6). The enemies' weapons will be destroyed (vv. 9-10) and the slain will be buried (vv. 11-16). Victory will be celebrated in a great sacrificial feast (v. 17) that will be followed by a final restoration.

Victory in the created order will involve the overthrow of the hostile powers represented by the beasts. "On that day the LORD with his cruel and great and strong sword will punish Leviathan the fleeing serpent, Leviathan the twisting serpent, and he will kill the dragon that is in the sea" (Isa 27:1). This oracle seems to be based on a belief that "the chaos monster, who was defeated and chained at the beginning, would break loose from his fetters and, making his last challenge, would be decisively overcome" (B. W. Anderson 1967: 134). The Isaiah apocalypse foretells the defeat not only of Israel's historical enemies ("the kings of the earth"), but of cosmic powers of evil:

> On that day the LORD will punish
>   the host of heaven in heaven. . . .
> Then the moon will be abashed,
>   and the sun ashamed. (Isa 24:21-23; see Gowan 1986: 115-16)

The final eschatological battle is also portrayed in Zech 14. "All the nations" shall attack Jerusalem, but then "the LORD will go forth and fight against those nations" (vv. 2-3) and strike them down (vv. 12-15). In this case we seem to be on the borderline between prophetic and apocalyptic eschatology.

New Testament: Fulfillment

4-3. OUR ADVERSARY, THE DEVIL

The theme of adversaries who thwart God's purposes continues in the NT, but with a markedly different emphasis from that found in the OT. While Jesus and the church confront opposition within the historical order from political authorities and personal opponents, the real source of opposition is now seen to lie in the created order, in evil spirits and cosmic powers that are in fact agents of a personal and powerful adversary, Satan or the devil. The basic monotheism of the OT is not abandoned, but it is *modified* by the fuller recognition of the cosmic powers of evil (cf. Rist 1962a).

4-3.1. D-DAY AND V-DAY

On the surface it appears that after the Christ event nothing has changed. The world did not come to an end. Sin and death, evil and disorder are still rampant. Yet a major claim of the NT is that with the dawning of the new order, *Satan has been defeated* and *the powers of evil and disorder are doomed*. There is certainly tension if not paradox here: Satan has been defeated, but at the same time he is not yet finally defeated, for that will happen only at the final consummation of all things.

Many have found helpful O. Cullmann's analogy drawn from the Second World War (1962: 84, 141). The Christ event may be compared to D-Day (the name given to the Allied invasion of Europe, the turning point of the war); the *decisive battle* against Satan has been fought and won, and evil is defeated in principle. But still ahead lies "V-Day" ("Victory Day," marking the final surrender of the Nazi forces and the end of the war in Europe); the *final victory,* while assured, will come only at the last day.

4-3.2. ADVERSARIES IN THE HISTORICAL ORDER

a. Historical Adversaries

In the NT God's Servant and God's people encounter historical adversaries. Herod the Great, the antitype of Pharaoh (above, 4-1.2a), orders all the children under two years of age in the Bethlehem area to be put to death; despite this, Jesus providentially survives (Matt 2:1-18). John the Baptist runs afoul of Herod Antipas, who sends him to his death (Mark 6:17-29).

The Synoptic Gospels frequently refer to conflicts between Jesus and various adversaries (*antikeimenos* = "opponent, adversary"), particularly representatives of the scribes and Pharisees (see the list of passages in Hultgren 1979: 26-27). Typically some saying or action of Jesus (or his disciples) provokes a hostile reaction, but an authoritative word or deed of Jesus usually silences the opposition. For example, the Lucan account of the healing of a woman with a spirit of infirmity concludes: "All his opponents were put to shame" (Luke 13:17). Mark 2:1–3:6 contains no fewer than five "conflict stories"; the final one concludes on a sinister note — "The Pharisees went out and immediately conspired with the Herodians against him, how to destroy him" (3:6). While it may well be the case that these stories served certain functions in the early church, there are no good grounds for doubting their basic historicity (contra Hultgren, 198). The Pharisees are frequently listed as opponents, but it must be remembered that of all the groups within contemporary Judaism, Jesus probably came closest to the Pharisees; his encounters with them were more in the nature of a "family quarrel," and obviously they do not reflect any kind of anti-Judaism.

In John's Gospel too, Jesus meets opposition, especially on the part of *hoi Ioudaioi,* usually translated "the Jews." (For a survey of modern scholarship, see von Wahlde 1982: 34-41.) They question Jesus (2:18; 8:57; 10:24), accuse him (8:48, 52), plot against him (from as early as 5:18), and engineer his death (18:12, 31, etc.). Although *Ioudaioi* in Acts and Paul means "Jews" (in distinction from "Gentiles"), in John the term is frequently (though not always) used in a special, narrower sense. Clearly it does *not* mean the Jewish people as a whole; for example, several times people who are ethnically Jews are said to be in fear of "the Jews" (7:13; 9:22; 20:19). Historically it stands in a close relation to the Pharisees and the chief priests, and refers to the Jewish authorities who opposed Jesus. Since these are almost always associated with Jerusalem and the surrounding area of Judea *(Ioudaia)*, there probably is a geographical element in the term (see 7:1; cf. Cuming 1949; Lowe 1976). Many historical-critical scholars think the particular Johannine usage reflects hostility between church and synagogue in the author's day (cf. Bratcher 1975: 402-3).

Theologically the term *Ioudaioi* represents "the opposition," and symbolizes any persons who cling to their own traditions and privileges and refuse to be open to the inbreaking of new truth. A more sinister note is struck in John 8:44: behind the historical adversaries of Jesus and everything he stands for lies the figure of the devil, whose agents they are.

Above all, in the passion narrative, Jesus is opposed by the representatives of government, Herod Antipas, the ruler of Galilee and Peraea, and Pontius Pilate, the representative of Rome. The early liturgy of Acts 4:24-30 quotes Ps 2:1-2:

> The kings of the earth took their stand,
>   and the rulers have gathered together,
>   against the Lord and against his Messiah,

and goes on to explain the reference: "For in this city, in fact, both Herod and Pontius Pilate, with the Gentiles and the peoples of Israel, gathered together against your holy servant Jesus . . ." (vv. 27f.).

The early church continued to experience opposition from the Jewish authorities (Acts 4:3-22; 5:17-41; 6:12-15; 8:1-3). Herod Agrippa further harassed the church and executed the apostle James (12:1-2). Paul constantly encountered opposition (13:50; 14:19; 16:19-39; 17:5-9; 18:12-17; 19:23-41). His active career culminated in his arrest, various hearings including those before the Roman procurators Felix and Festus, his appeal to Caesar, and his journey to Rome (Acts 21–28). It was from personal experience that Paul knew that "many live as enemies *(tous echthrous)* of the cross of Christ" (Phil 3:18). Jas 4:4 asks, "Do you not know that friendship with the world is enmity with God? Therefore whoever wishes to be a friend of the world becomes an enemy of God." In the book of Revelation the adversary is the power of Rome (13:1-10), as embodied in the authorities enforcing emperor worship in the province of Asia (13:11-18), both of them portrayed by the now-familiar biblical symbol of a "beast."

b. Treatment of Enemies

Jesus took up and developed further the OT teaching on the treatment of enemies (above, 4-1.2c). In the antitheses of the Sermon on the Mount, he moves beyond the *lex talionis* of the Torah and calls on his followers not to retaliate against those who mistreat them (Matt 5:38-42). "You have heard," he continues, "that it was said, 'You shall love your neighbor and hate your enemy.' But I say to you, Love your enemies and pray for those who persecute you" (vv. 43-44). In response to Peter's question, "Lord, how often shall my brother sin against me, and I forgive him? As many as seven times?" Jesus replies, "I do not say to you seven times, but seventy-seven times" (Matt 18:21-22 RSV; see commentaries). While this figure really constitutes a call to infinite forgiveness, it also represents a total reversal of Lamech's seventy-sevenfold vengeance (Gen 4:23-24; cf. above, 4-1.2c). This is one of the most striking cases where Jesus' teaching was matched by his example, for according to Luke 23:34, Jesus prayed for those who crucified him, "Father, forgive them; for they do not know what they are doing." Luke underlines in a telling way how Jesus' followers are to take him as their example when he recounts the words of the dying Stephen, the first Christian martyr: "Lord, do not hold this sin against them" (Acts 7:60). Willingness to forgive those who have wronged them is of course based on the forgiveness believers have received from God, as the parable of the unforgiving servant so forcefully illustrates (Matt 18:23-35; see Blomberg 1990: 240-43).

Paul discusses relations with enemies in Rom 12:14-21, advising believers to "bless those who persecute you" and "do not repay anyone evil for evil." While the teaching of Jesus clearly underlies this passage, it is interesting that Paul clinches his argument with a quotation from the OT: "If your enemies are hungry, feed them . . ." (Rom 12:20 = Prov 25:21-22).

4-3.3. THE CREATED ORDER: SATAN

Beyond the historical adversaries encountered by Jesus and the early church lie powers of evil that belong to the created order. These are spoken of in three main ways: as Satan or the devil, as evil spirits or demons, and as "powers" of evil.

a. That Ancient Serpent Who Is the Devil and Satan

The NT gives a prominent place to a personal and powerful adversary and enemy, the leader of the cosmic forces of evil. No doubt it reflects developments that had taken place within Judaism (cf. Gaster 1962b: 225-26), though BT is concerned only with the material that appears in the biblical text.

Echoing the OT usage, this figure can be called "the adversary *(antidikos)*" (1 Pet 5:8). Other terms include "the enemy *(echthros)*" (Luke 10:19; cf. Matt 13:39), "the evil one *(ponēros)*" (Matt 13:19), "the tempter *(peirazōn)*" (Matt 4:3; 1 Thess 3:5), and "the god of this world *(ho theos tou aiōnos toutou)*" (2 Cor 4:4). The names Beelzebul (Mark 3:22; see Bietenhard, Brown, and Wright 1978: 469,

472) and Beliar (2 Cor 6:15) are drawn from Jewish tradition. The most common terms are "Satan" *(satan)* and "the devil" *(diabolos)*. In Rev 12:1-6 Satan appears as "a great red dragon" who threatens God's people and God's Messiah. Rev 12:9 and 20:2 draw together and identify the various traditions of a leader of the powers of evil with their references to "the great dragon . . . that ancient serpent, who is called the Devil and Satan, the deceiver of the whole world." Retroactively it is recognized that Satan has been at work in the world since the beginning, being identified with the serpent of Gen 3 (cf. 2 Cor 11:3) as well as the dragon/sea monster symbol of the powers of evil.

On the basis of the NT, the figure of Satan cannot be lightly set aside. He is a master of deception, "a liar and the father of lies" (John 8:44), and is quite capable of disguising himself as an angel of light (2 Cor 11:14). His power is shown particularly in the narrative of the temptations (Matt 4:1-11//Mark 1:12-13//Luke 4:1-13); "their evil quality," remarks Ling (1961), "was in each case hidden beneath a superficial attractiveness capable of momentary appeal even to Jesus" (62-63). Satan enters into Judas (Luke 22:3; John 13:27) and fills the heart of Ananias (Acts 5:3).

The NT not only recognizes the reality of Satan but acknowledges that, for the time being, he holds sway in this world. In the temptation narrative he is able to offer Jesus "all the kingdoms of the world" (Matt 4:8-9). Hence he can be called "the ruler of this world *(ho archōn tou kosmou toutou)*" (John 12:31; 14:30; 16:11), and according to 1 John 5:19, "the whole world lies under the power of the evil one." Such passages suggest that in the NT, "this age is viewed as an age in which Satan has been permitted in the sovereign purpose of God to exercise a tragic sway over men" (Ladd 1974: 119). They also help to explain an otherwise perplexing ambiguity in the use of the term "world" *(kosmos)* by Paul, and especially by John. On the one hand, the *kosmos* is God's creation (Rom 1:20); God created it through Christ (John 1:10), and God loves it (John 3:16). On the other hand, *kosmos* can also be used in a very negative sense. The wisdom of the world is opposed to the gospel (1 Cor 1:20), and believers "have received not the spirit of the world" (2:12). In John especially, the *kosmos* did not know Christ (John 1:10), and indeed hates him (7:7) and his followers (17:14). 1 John 2:15-16 warns readers not to love the *kosmos,* "for all that is in the world — the desire of the flesh, the desire of the eyes, the pride in riches — comes not from the Father but from the world." In these contexts *kosmos* clearly "stands for a system directly opposed to God" (D. Guthrie 1981: 132). The broader canonical context makes it clear that there is no thought of a Gnostic-type dualism; "the world" is not inherently evil, it is evil only insofar as it rebels against God and allows Satan to take control.

The NT does not speculate as to the origin of Satan, though it is clear that the devil's power is exercised only within the sovereignty of God.

b. I Saw Satan Fall

The inbreaking of the new order is associated with a severe conflict between Jesus, the new Servant of God, and Satan. This conflict climaxes in a decisive victory, though Satan's power will not be finally destroyed until the final consummation. "The New Testament portrays the Messiah, the Anointed of God, standing at the very storm centre of the cosmic conflict between the kingdom of God and the kingdom of Satan" (B. W. Anderson 1967: 162; cf. Prager 1981: 811).

Jesus joins battle with Satan in the temptations. In the contest Jesus holds his own and "the devil left him" (Matt 4:11), but not for good. Luke 4:13 significantly concludes, "When the devil had finished every test, he departed from him until an opportune time." According to Matthew and Mark, Jesus sees in Peter's rebuke (in the Caesarea Philippi incident) a further temptation from Satan, to which he responds sharply, "Get behind me, Satan!" (Mark 8:33). For Luke the "opportune time" comes when Satan enters into Judas and prompts him to betray Jesus (Luke 22:3; cf. 22:6). The conflict continues in 22:31, where Satan seeks control over Peter. Though Satan is not explicitly mentioned in the Gethsemane narrative, the temptation theme clearly echoes the earlier temptation. The theme of conflict with Satan during Jesus' ministry is equally strong in John's Gospel, which also knows the tradition of Satan entering into Judas (6:70; 13:2, 27); as he prepares to go to his death, Jesus says that "the ruler of this world is coming" (14:30).

If the Gospel tradition concentrates on the theme of conflict with Satan, it does not leave the reader in doubt as to the final outcome of the struggle. In Luke 10:17-18 the returning seventy disciples report, "Lord, in your name even the demons submit to us!" to which Jesus replies, "I watched Satan fall from heaven like a flash of lightning." This verse has been the subject of much comment and controversy. Traditionally it has been taken as a reference back to an expulsion of Satan from heaven before creation, an event that is not recorded in Scripture. The context in Luke suggests rather that the defeat of the demons is seen as an anticipation of the overthrow of Satan, either provisionally at the cross or ultimately at the final consummation (cf. Caird 1956b: 31).

Satan does not figure directly in the Synoptic passion narratives, but in John Jesus anticipates the passion by declaring, "Now is the judgment of this world; now the ruler of this world will be driven out" (12:31; cf. 16:11, 33). "The world is judged because One has come who does not yield to the tyranny of Satan, but comes to break his tyranny" (Ling 1961: 35).

The later NT looks back to the Christ event as marking the decisive defeat of Satan. Christ partook of human nature "so that through death he might destroy the one who has the power of death, that is, the devil" (Heb 2:14). The purpose of Christ's coming was "to destroy the works of the devil" (1 John 3:8). Rev 12 portrays a scene of war in heaven with Michael and his angels fighting the dragon/serpent/devil/Satan and his angels. "The great dragon was thrown down . . . to the earth, and his angels were thrown down with him" (v. 9). Here again there is no indication of a premundane fall of Satan; this fall of Satan is most naturally understood as the counterpart in the heavenly realms of Jesus' victory through his cross and resurrection.

Note: In Rev 8:10-11 and 9:1-11 there are references to a star fallen from heaven; these have sometimes been connected with Satan. The "star" of 8:10-11 called "Wormwood" is simply an angel who brings one of a series of plagues (cf. Jer 9:15). The "star" of Rev 9:1-11 is no doubt an evil angel, who opens the bottomless pit and releases a terrible plague of locusts. His name is Abaddon *(abaddōn)* or Apollyon *(apollyōn),* meaning "destroyer." The text does not connect him with Satan; he is an evil angel given (limited) powers by God to inflict a plague upon the earth.

c. The Devil Prowls Around

While Jesus has won the decisive battle against Satan, the war is not yet over. Christians have to be on guard against the power and the wiles of the devil. Indeed, in a sense Satan is now more active than ever. The period between the Christ event and the final consummation is the period in which Satan has his final fling. In Rev 12 Satan, having been thrown down from heaven, persecutes the church (vv. 13-17), although in fact his days are numbered (v. 12).

Throughout the NT, especially but by no means exclusively in the Pauline Epistles, repeated warnings against the devil are to be found (1 Cor 7:5; 2 Cor 2:11; 4:4; 6:15; 11:14; 2 Thess 3:3). Clearly Paul took the threat of Satan extremely seriously; "The conception of Satan which emerges from these Pauline references is that of a spirit characterized by an insatiable appetite for power and self-aggrandisement; to his power over them men themselves contribute, because both the weakness of their fallen nature, and the plausibility of his offers of apparent good render them unable to resist his pressures" (Ling 1961: 42). Paul finds his work being countered by Satan (2 Cor 12:7; 1 Thess 2:18). In Acts 26:18 Paul is sent to the Gentiles, "to open their eyes so that they may turn from darkness to light and from the power of Satan to God." Christians are advised to "put on the whole armor of God, so that you may be able to stand against the wiles of the devil" (Eph 6:11). Jas 4:7 counsels, "Resist the devil, and he will flee from you." 1 Pet 5:8 warns, "Like a roaring lion your adversary the devil prowls around, looking for someone to devour." In the letters to the seven churches, the readers are frequently reminded of the activity of Satan (Rev 2:9, 13, 24).

4-3.4. THE CREATED ORDER: DEMONS

In the Synoptic Gospels the existence of demons or evil/unclean spirits is simply assumed. The contrast with the OT is striking, and historically no doubt reflects developments especially in the second and first centuries B.C. (cf. above, 4-1.4; and see Langton 1949: 105-45).

a. All Who Were Possessed with Demons

In the Synoptics, especially in Mark, Jesus is constantly confronted by "demons" (*daimonion* = "demon"), "evil spirits" (*pneuma to ponēron* = "evil spirit"), or "unclean spirits" (*pneuma to akatharton* = "unclean spirit," used particularly in Mark), who possess people. The symptoms of demon possession described in the Gospels are generally of what would today be classified as various forms of mental illness. In some cases physical symptoms are described (the Gadarene demoniac in Mark 5:1-20 had violent outbursts, howled, and injured himself; the boy healed in Luke 9:38-43 and //s exhibited the symptoms of epilepsy), but these appear to be outward manifestations of mental derangement. The narratives of exorcisms are separate from the accounts of healing the sick, i.e., those who are lame, blind, deaf, paralyzed, and so on (see 20-3.3), and the Gospels distinguish between healing the sick and casting out demons (e.g., Mark 1:32; 6:13; 16:17-18).

Apart from the Synoptics, demons appear only very rarely in the NT. In John's Gospel Jesus' opponents accuse him of having a demon (7:20; 8:48; 10:20), i.e., of being mad, but there are no accounts of exorcisms; John seems to emphasize Satan as the opposing power, to the exclusion of demons (cf. Ling 1961: 31), and it may be that his selection of only seven major "signs" leaves no place for minor works such as exorcisms (cf. M. Perry 1990: 106). Paul connects demons with pagan idols (1 Cor 10:20-22; cf. Rev 9:20), while 1 Tim 4:1 warns against "paying attention to deceitful spirits and teachings of demons."

Though demons/evil spirits are generally mentioned on their own, they appear to be thought of as agents of Satan; in Mark 3:22-23 Beelzebul (= Satan) is called "the ruler of the demons" (cf. Schlier 1961: 16).

b. They Fell Down before Him

Exorcisms, or the casting out of demons/evil spirits/unclean spirits, are a major feature of Jesus' ministry in the Synoptics (though not after the passion narratives commence). The accounts are remarkable for their simplicity. Usually the evil spirit is cast out by a simple word of command on Jesus' part. Exorcism is never linked with forgiveness of sin; demons represent an evil power over which the victim has no control. Specific exorcisms are narrated, and Jesus' power over the demons is attributed to his "authority" (*exousia* — e.g., Mark 1:27).

Exorcisms have a twofold significance. Firstly, they demonstrate Jesus' care and compassion for individuals, and his concern to bring healing and wholeness not just of body but also of mind and spirit. Secondly, on a more theological level, Jesus' conflict with the demons runs parallel with his conflict with Satan. Jesus' opponents could not deny his exorcisms, but they did accuse him of being in league with the ruler of the demons. The absurdity of this charge was promptly pointed out by Jesus: "How can Satan cast out Satan? . . . No one can enter a strong man's house and plunder his property without first tying up the strong man" (Mark 3:22-27; cf. Caird 1956b: 71). Jesus' casting out of the demons manifests the presence of the kingdom: "If it is by the Spirit of God that I cast out demons, then the kingdom of God has come to you" (Matt 12:28; cf. Luke 11:20; see 1-3.1a). "The success of Jesus' assaults indicated that the head of that evil kingdom had already been bound, making possible the spoiling of his domain. On that basis demons were cast out of people and individuals were liberated from Satan's oppression in order to become participants in the blessings of God's kingdom" (D. G. Reese 1992: 141; cf. R. H. Fuller 1963: 40-41). The exorcisms do not merely *prepare* for the coming of the kingdom (contra Hiers 1974); they demonstrate that the powers of the kingdom are already present. Paradoxically, as supernatural powers, the demons recognize Jesus' true identity but are sharply commanded to keep quiet (Mark 1:24-25; 3:11; 5:7; cf. A. Richardson 1941: 72).

Significantly, in the Synoptics Jesus is said to "rebuke" the evil spirits (Mark 1:25; 9:25; Luke 4:39; cf. also Jesus' "rebuke" of the storm in Mark 4:39 and //s). This clearly recalls both God's rebuke of the powers of chaos at creation (above, 4-1.3b) and his promised rebuke of his foes in the new age (4-2.3a; the NT word *epitimaō* in the LXX = *gā'ār*). Here again, however, "rebuke" is too weak a translation; Jesus' "rebuke" is "the word of command by which God's agent defeats his enemies" (Kee 1968: 244). Jesus is no mere wonder-worker like a Hellenistic "divine man," nor is he a dealer in magic; he is the one through whom God is even now defeating the powers of evil and inaugurating the kingdom.

c. He Gave Them Authority over Unclean Spirits

While Jesus has won the decisive battle against the demons, the war is not yet over. Jesus authorized his disciples to participate in the ongoing struggle against these powers of evil and disorder. In the charge to the Twelve, Jesus "gave them authority over unclean spirits, to cast them out" (Matt 10:1 and //s). Though not mentioned in their charge, the Seventy mention exorcism in their report: "Lord, in your name even the demons submit to us!" (Luke 10:17).

There is some evidence that a ministry that included exorcism continued in the early church. Philip cast out unclean spirits (Acts 8:7). Paul is credited with casting out evil spirits in 19:12 (cf. also 16:16-18, where he casts out a "spirit of divination" from a slave girl).

4-3.5. THE CREATED ORDER: POWERS

a. The Spiritual Forces of Evil

The NT frequently uses the language of power, employing a variety of terminology, including among others such words as *archontes* (rulers), *exousiai* (authorities), and *dynameis* (powers). The vocabulary is fluid and can be translated into English in various ways (see Schlier 1961: 11-12; Wink 1984: 3-35).

In many texts the reference is clearly to human persons and institutions, "the powers that be" who exercise power and authority in this world. Jesus refers sarcastically to "the so-called rulers *(hoi dokountes archein)* of the Gentiles" (Mark 10:42 AT), and warns his followers that they will be brought before "the rulers *(tas archas)*, and the authorities *(tas exousias)*" of the synagogues (Luke 12:11). The beast of Rev 13:2 that is given power *(dynamis)*, a throne *(thronos)*, and great authority *(exousia)* is in fact the Roman Empire. Clearly the NT is well aware of the reality of power in the world.

Elsewhere, however, especially in the Pauline Epistles, this language is used to refer to spiritual powers, generally regarded as forces opposed to God. The classic reference is in Eph 6:12 — "For our struggle is not against enemies of blood and flesh, but against the rulers *(tas archas)*, against the authorities *(tas exousias)*, against the cosmic powers *(tous kosmokratoras)* of this present darkness, against the spiritual forces of evil in the heavenly places." In several texts it is not immediately clear whether the reference is to this-worldly or spiritual powers. 1 Cor 2:6-8 refers twice to "the rulers *(archontes)* of this age." Since they "crucified the Lord of glory," they are apparently human rulers, religious and political authorities, "the chief priests and leaders *(archontes)*" who "handed him over to be condemned to death and crucified him" (Luke 24:20). But the fact that they are called the rulers "of this age" *(tou aiōnos toutou)* strongly suggests spiritual powers, agents of "the god of this world *(tou aiōnos toutou)*" (2 Cor 4:4). The obvious solution is that the "rulers" are both human and spiritual; behind the powers and authorities of this world "stand invisible powers, infinitely more dangerous, of whom the visible human 'rulers' are the mere agents" (MacGregor 1954-55: 23; cf. Caird 1956b: 17; Berkhof 1977: 20). The NT repeatedly refers to these spiritual powers, although "in general, it is noteworthy that there is no clearly defined hierarchy among these angelic powers. Various titles of independent origin are used in a manner which seems intended simply to convey an impression of superhuman power" (Ling 1961: 65). The *stoicheia,* or "elemental spirits," of Gal 4:3, 8-9 (cf. Col 2:8, 20) may also refer to such spiritual powers (but see commentaries, and Wink 1984: 67-77).

In the NT there is no speculation regarding the origin of these powers. Historically, NT usage may have been influenced by Jewish apocalyptic (Berkhof 1977: 16-17) or by Hellenistic belief in astral deities (cf. MacGregor 1954-55: 19-21); BT, however, is concerned not with origins but with how the powers are understood in the NT. There can be no room for an ultimate dualism, for Col 1:16 clearly asserts of Christ that "in him all things in heaven and on earth were created, things visible and invisible, whether thrones *(thronoi)* or dominions *(kuriotētes)* or rulers *(archai)* or powers *(exousiai)*" (cf. Schlier 1961: 37). All power and authority is ultimately God-given and is good if used as God intends. This explains why Rom 13:1-7 directs believers to be subject to "authorities" *(exousiai)* and "rulers" *(archontes)* when they act as God's servants by upholding law and order (cf. Titus 3:1; and see 19-3.4). But in all other cases the powers are regarded as hostile to God; the obvious conclusion is that "when a particular Power becomes idolatrous, placing itself above God's purposes for the good of the whole, then that power becomes demonic" (Wink 1984: 5; cf. Berkhof, 28-35). The powers are not directly associated with Satan, though indirectly Eph 2:2 suggests a link with its reference to "the ruler *(archōn)* of the power *(exousia)* of the air" (cf. also John 12:31).

b. Triumphing over Them

In face of these rebellious powers that were responsible for the death of Christ and that threaten the early Christians, the NT unambiguously proclaims their decisive defeat by Christ. As he approaches the cross, Jesus declares, "Now is the judgment of this world; now the ruler *(archōn)* of this world will be driven out" (John 12:31). At the cross Christ "disarmed the rulers *(tas archas)* and authorities *(tas exousias)* and made a public example of them, triumphing over them in it" (Col 2:15). Through his resurrection and exaltation to God's right hand, Christ shows himself to be the messianic king of whom God says in Ps 110:1,

> Sit at my right hand
> until I make your enemies your footstool. (cf. above, 4-2.3)

Ps 110:1 is quoted or alluded to numerous times in the NT (see 10-3.4b). Christ's victory over the powers is stressed in two such passages. According to Eph 1:20-22, God raised Christ from the dead "and seated him at his right hand in the heavenly places, far above all rule *(archē)* and authority *(exousia)* and power *(dynamis)* and dominion *(kyriotēs)*. . . . And he has put all things under his feet." 1 Pet 3:21-22 similarly speaks of the risen Christ who is now "at the right hand of God, with angels, authorities *(exousiai),* and powers *(dynameis)* made subject to him."

c. Who Shall Separate Us?

While Jesus has won the decisive battle against the powers, the war is not over; the "already–not yet" tension applies here also, and V-Day lies only at the final consummation (see below, 4-4.5a). The Christ event means that the rulers of this age "are doomed to perish" (1 Cor 2:6). In the present, however, there is always the danger of slipping back under the control of the elemental spirits (Gal 4:9). Believers are called to take a stand against the rebellious powers of this world, not through the use of violence but by using spiritual weapons, "the whole armor of God," consisting of truth, righteousness, the gospel of peace, faith, salvation, and "the sword of the Spirit, which is the word of God" (Eph 6:10-11, 13-17). Despite the formidable foes at both a human and spiritual level, believers can engage in this conflict knowing that ultimately they will be "more than conquerors," and convinced "that neither death, nor life, nor angels, nor rulers *(archai)*, nor things present, nor things to come, nor powers *(dynameis)*, nor height, nor depth, nor anything else in all creation, will be able to separate us from the love of God in Christ Jesus our Lord" (Rom 8:37-39).

New Testament: Consummation

4-4. THE ANTICHRIST

4-4.1. INTENSIFICATION OF OPPOSITION AND FINAL VICTORY

The NT ends on a note of triumph: ultimately all the adversaries of God and his people will be defeated and eliminated. But as in the OT (cf. 4-2), even more in the NT is there an emphasis on an *intensification* of opposition before the final victory. To outward appearances at least, Satan will continue to dominate this world; he will even have a kind of final fling before his eventual defeat. So, far from a gradual progress toward a just and humane society, as long as history lasts there will be conflict between good and evil, and in keeping with one of the basic principles of biblical eschatology (cf. 2.2.2), things will get worse before they get better.

4-4.2. THE HISTORICAL ORDER: INTENSIFICATION

Jesus and the first Christians faced a variety of adversaries in the historical order (above, 4-3.2). Contrary to the views of much contemporary biblical scholarship, it has been argued that the NT does *not* expect the imminent end of all things but envisages a period of unknown duration stretching between the Christ event and the final consummation (see 2-4.5).

Both Jesus himself and the writers of the NT are under no illusion that this period will be one of gradual progress and improvement. On the contrary, they are very blunt in warning that, if anything, opposition to the gospel will intensify. Believers must be prepared to face trials and tribulations, and in particular, opposition and persecution.

For a fuller discussion, see 3-4.2.

4-4.3. THE HISTORICAL ORDER: VICTORY

The NT declares that however much the historical powers that oppress God's people appear to have the upper hand, eventually they will be judged by God within history.

Very much in the OT prophetic tradition, Jesus called God's people to repentance and faith but also warned them that persistent opposition to God's message would eventually bring judgment on the nation and especially on Jerusalem and the temple.

As the church spread outward in the course of the first century, it increasingly found itself opposed by the authorities of the Roman Empire. No matter how powerful that empire might appear, the book of Revelation foretells its eventual downfall.

For a fuller discussion, see 3-4.3.

4-4.4. THE CREATED ORDER: INTENSIFICATION

a. The Antichrist

In addition to a general expectation that evil will be rampant up until the final consummation, the NT also presents, in a variety of forms, the expectation that evil will be focused in a person (or series of persons) who will be the eschatological agent(s) of Satan and who must be defeated or eliminated before the final end comes.

Such a figure is frequently referred to as an anti-Messiah or as "the Antichrist." The term "Antichrist" is of Christian origin, though in the NT it occurs only in the Johannine Epistles. Historians of religion, however, generally hold that a figure of this type played a role in Jewish apocalyptic, probably under the influence of Persian eschatology, though its roots are to be found in the monster of chaos of ancient Near Eastern mythology (cf. Rist 1962a: 141; D. S. Russell 1964: 276).

The Antichrist can be conceived of as a monster that will be slain by the

Messiah as part of the final apocalyptic events. Advocates of "Bible Prophecy" interpret the "little horn" of Dan 7:8 and "the prince who is to come" of Dan 9:26, 27 as references to a future Antichrist (part of their projection of the closing verses of Daniel's visions into the "end-times"; cf. 2-2.5). These references, however, are to figures of history, though it may be argued that the apocalyptic appearance of the Antichrist can be *anticipated* by specific historical figures (Nebuchadnezzar, Antiochus Epiphanes, Emperor Domitian) in whom evil is, as it were, incarnated.

The term "Antichrist" can be used as a convenient label for an eschatological adversary provided we do not associate with it preconceived notions of the nature and role of such a figure but are prepared to examine the NT evidence carefully before drawing any conclusions. A figure of this type occurs in three main passages of the NT.

i. In 2 Thess 2:1-12 Paul seeks to dampen expectation that the final consummation is imminent by teaching that before the end comes, there must first occur an eschatological rebellion *(apostasia)* that will involve the coming of a figure referred to in the passage as "the lawless one" *(ho anthrōpos tēs anomias, ho anomos),* or "the one destined for destruction" *(ho huios tēs apōleias),* who puts himself in the place of God. This figure is presently being "restrained," but when he is revealed the Lord Jesus will destroy him. The passage poses a series of difficult exegetical problems (see commentaries). "The lawless one" is certainly an apocalyptic Antichrist figure, yet the passage also suggests that this figure is in the world now, doing the work of Satan, though under restraint (according to v. 7, "the mystery of lawlessness is already at work"). Who, then, is the restrainer? The most probable explanation (which goes back to Tertullian) is that the Roman Empire is seen as a force for law and order that thus restrains evil (see Whiteley 1964: 237-40; cf. Caird 1956b: 27). Less likely is the view championed by Cullmann (1962: 164-66) that the restraining power is the preaching of the gospel, with "the one who now restrains" (v. 7) being Paul himself.

The reference in v. 4 to the one "who exalts himself above every so-called god or object of worship, so that he takes his seat in the temple of God, declaring himself to be God" is reminiscent of Antiochus Epiphanes desecrating the temple in 167 B.C., of Pompey's capture of Jerusalem in 63 B.C., and also, much closer to the time of the letter, of the emperor Caligula's order to erect a statue of himself in the temple in A.D. 40. This suggests that the Antichrist figure represents the power of evil at work in the world, focused from time to time in particularly evil individuals who flout God's law.

ii. In 1 John 2:18 the writer declares, "It is the last hour! As you have heard that antichrist is coming, so now *many antichrists (antichristoi polloi) have come.*" These antichrists are the false teachers, who have been leading the church astray (cf. 1 John 2:22; 4:3; 2 John 7). Here we seem to have a form of almost completely realized eschatology. Antichrist is not an apocalyptic figure who will appear in the future, but a power currently at work in the world and in the church. The designation of such persons as "antichrists" suggests that they are agents of a satanic power. The realized nature of the eschatology is not inconsistent, however, with the view that there may be a final manifestation of that power at the end of time.

iii. Rev 13 presents a vision of two beasts, "a beast rising out of the sea," a composite of the beasts of Dan 7, signifying the Roman Empire, and "another beast that rose out of the earth," to be identified with the organization propagating and enforcing emperor worship in the province of Asia (see Schlier 1961: 76-89; Talbert 1994: 51-59). Rev 13 thus confirms the identification of the fourth beast of Dan 7 with the Roman Empire. These are seen as incarnations of evil, as the by-now-familiar images of the "beast" and the "sea" show. The number of the beast, 666 or 616 (Rev 13:18), most probably represents the words "Nero Caesar" (see commentaries). "The whole chapter reveals that evil assumes the form of a demonic parody of God, of Christ, and of divine revelation, with the intention of subverting the truth and corrupting men's minds" (Yates 1974: 45). The beast thus manifests itself within history, though it will be defeated only at the final consummation (Rev 20:10).

A certain common pattern can thus be seen in all three passages, despite their differences. They all speak of a personal power of evil at work in the period preceding the final end, a power that can apparently become incarnate in specific individuals who are particularly evil or lawless. Once again these passages warn against a facile optimism or belief in automatic progress. "The doctrine of Antichrist is a reminder to us to take seriously the power of sin and Satan in human history" (Ewert 1980: 78; cf. Stauffer 1955: 213). As long as history lasts, evil is never far away and may break out at any time.

b. Satan Will Be Loosed

In the three passages just considered, Satan is referred to only in 2 Thessalonians where "the coming of the lawless one" is said to be "apparent in the working of Satan" (2:9). All the various Antichrist figures, however, may be thought of as agents of Satan.

It is only when we near the end of the apocalyptic scenario and the last great struggle is at hand that Satan puts in a personal appearance. In Rev 20 the dragon/serpent/devil/Satan is seized by an angel from heaven and shut up in a pit for a thousand years, i.e., for the duration of the millennium (see 3-4.4b). The significant point is that when the thousand years are ended, Satan makes a jailbreak; he "will be released from his prison" and will gather the forces of Gog and Magog, Ezekiel's symbols of the forces of evil, who will wage one last battle against God's people (above, 4-2.5). Here we have a powerful symbolic representation of the persistence of the power of evil. If the millennium symbolizes the fact that there can be some progress in history, the escape of Satan symbolizes the fact that evil is still a force to be reckoned with, and even if temporarily restrained, may break out again at any time short of the final consummation.

4-4.5. THE CREATED ORDER: VICTORY

Only at the last day will Satan and all the powers of evil be finally defeated and destroyed. Just as God's adversaries in the created order are depicted in a variety of ways in the NT, so there are a variety of pictures of the final victory over them. Basically each of these pictures conveys the same message, and it would be a mistake to attempt to put them in some kind of sequence or slot them into an apocalyptic timetable.

a. Victory over the Powers

While the rebellious powers have already been defeated in principle, they will be eliminated only at the final consummation. Paradoxically, while Ps 110:1 is quoted in connection with the victory over God's enemies won through Christ's resurrection and exaltation to God's right hand (above, 4-3.5b), it is also alluded to in connection with the final apocalyptic victory.

Thus, in speaking of the final consummation, Paul says, "Then comes the end, when he [Christ] hands over the kingdom to God the Father, after he has destroyed every ruler *(archēn)* and every authority *(exousian)* and power *(dynamin).* For he must reign until he has put all his enemies under his feet" (1 Cor 15:24-25). It would be precarious to make Christ's "reign" into an interim period in an apocalyptic timetable; basically it is the time of the final campaign in the war against evil.

Similarly, Heb 10:12-13, referring to Christ's exaltation to God's right hand, states that "since then [he] has been waiting 'until his enemies would be made a footstool for his feet.'"

b. Victory over the Antichrist

The NT speaks of several "Antichrist" figures, representing a personal power of evil within history (above, 4-4.4a). These, however, are but anticipations of a figure who will be manifested, but then destroyed, at the final consummation.

The "Antichrist" figure of 2 Thessalonians will be destroyed by Christ: "Then the lawless one will be revealed, whom the Lord Jesus will destroy with the breath of his mouth, annihilating him by the manifestation of his coming" (2:8). The Beast of Rev 13 reappears in 16:12-16, linked with the dragon (= Satan, from whom he derives his authority — 13:2) and with another figure, "the false prophet," constituting, as it were, an unholy trinity. From these come unclean or demonic spirits who assemble "the kings of the whole world" for the eschatological battle "at the place which is called in Hebrew Armageddon *(harmagedōn)*" (16:16 RSV). While the name is sometimes interpreted as "Mount Megiddo" and linked with the city of Megiddo, a location that saw a number of decisive battles in OT times, there is no mountain at Megiddo (cf. Talbert 1994: 75). The location is uncertain, though it may refer to Mount Zion, thought of as the scene of the final, apocalyptic events (cf. 20:9, and see J. W. Bowman 1962: 227).

The battle is described in 19:11-21 where the armies of heaven, led by Christ, capture the beast and the false prophet and throw them into the lake of fire.

c. Victory over Satan

The final eschatological battle and the final victory over Satan himself are portrayed in Rev 20:7-10. Having been released after the thousand years and having gathered the forces of Gog and Magog (above, 4-4.4b), Satan and his cohorts surround "the camp of the saints and the beloved city" (v. 9). Fire comes down from heaven and consumes them, and finally the devil is thrown into the lake of fire.

d. No More Sea/Night

Only when human history has come to an end, at the final apocalyptic consummation, will there be a state when no adversary is left to oppose God and his people. Even the very symbols of evil will then disappear.

From the beginning of the Bible the *sea* had symbolized the forces of chaos and disorder, the powers of evil and all that is opposed to God. But in the Bible's final vision John observes that "the sea was no more" (Rev 21:1; cf. Bruce 1969: 50; Gowan 1986: 119).

Similarly, the inhabitants of the heavenly city will find that "there will be no more night" (Rev 22:5); despite the absence of sun and moon (21:23), darkness will be completely banished, "for the Lord God will be their light, and they will reign forever and ever" (22:5).

4-5. THE ADVERSARY: THEOLOGICAL REFLECTIONS

1. Few people today are likely to quarrel with the Bible's recognition that the purposes of God are frequently thwarted by human adversaries, nor with its ac-

knowledgment that when individuals stand up for what is right and just and humane, they must expect opposition from within society. But what distinguishes the biblical view of the adversaries of God's reign is the recognition of their spiritual dimension. Building on views incipient in the OT, the NT witnesses clearly to an array of supernatural powers of evil, loosely linked to the dominant figure of Satan. Behind all earthly manifestations of evil lie cosmic powers opposed to God. For the NT these powers are real. They have been defeated by Christ in the decisive battle of the war between good and evil, though they will be totally eliminated only at the final consummation.

From the seventeenth or eighteenth century onward belief in Satan, demons, and evil powers has met growing skepticism even among professing Christians. This is due to a number of causes: a decline in belief in the supernatural, reaction against excesses such as witch-hunting, and belief that "human beings must accept full responsibility for their lives and stop trying to foist it off on some nonexistent others" (Hinson 1992: 475; cf. J. M. Ross 1954).

The events of the twentieth century, however, have given rise to second thoughts. For many, what happened under the Nazis could only be called "satanic" or "demonic." "Auschwitz, Dachau, Buchenwald, Hiroshima, Nagasaki, to say nothing of Hitler and Stalin, will not let modern men and women dismiss or sidestep or ignore the question: Why do human beings who are in and of themselves good do unimaginably horrid things? Where in the world does such destructiveness come from?" (Hinson 1992: 475). The biblical view that the powers of evil will not diminish but rather intensify before the final consummation can be graphically illustrated from the twentieth century, which, for example, has seen more people killed in wars than in the previous five thousand years combined (figures are quoted in Wink 1992: 221).

2. The fact that *Satan* often figures in jokes, even among Christians, is an indication of the inroads of skepticism. What many, of course, reject is not the biblical Satan, but later caricatures — a figure dressed in red, with a tail and a pitchfork in hand. When he is not taken seriously and is dismissed in this way, doubtless no one is more pleased than the devil himself.

While recognizing the pervasive presence of evil in the world, many people prefer to regard Satan merely as a personification of evil. Wink (1986) defines Satan as "the symbol of the spirit of an entire society alienated from God" and "the real interiority of a society that idolatrously pursues its own enhancement as the highest good" (24-25). It may be questioned whether such definitions really do justice to the biblical view that sees Satan as a grim reality, who is both powerful and personal and is "the archadversary and archdeceiver of humankind" (Hinson 1992: 475). Modern theology has generally grossly underestimated the cunning and the capabilities of Satan (cf. Eisenhower 1988). The clear witness of the NT, and the evidence of history and experience, confirm that Satan cannot be dismissed as "myth" or "metaphor," or relegated to the periphery of the Christian faith (cf. Rae 1955: 214-15).

A common objection is that belief in Satan as leader of the powers of evil and as tempter undercuts human moral responsibility; "the devil made me do it" becomes an acceptable excuse. Nothing in the NT would encourage such a view, and "we must insist that a belief in Satan and his activity is no excuse for quitting the moral struggle" (M. Perry 1990: 110). Belief in Satan means taking evil seriously, and it means being summoned to resist evil. It is the knowledge that Satan has been defeated in principle which assures believers that he can therefore be defeated in their lives and in their society.

3. Belief in *rulers/powers/authorities* as supernatural forces of evil was for long "a neglected emphasis in New Testament theology" (J. S. Stewart 1951), but the second half of the twentieth century saw a series of important studies of this topic (including MacGregor 1954-55; Caird 1956b; Schlier 1961; Berkhof 1977; Wink 1984; 1986; 1992).

Many feel that here, if anywhere, there is a case for "demythologizing" (see MacGregor 1954-55: 27). Wink (1984) has proposed an elaborate reinterpretation according to which "the Powers are simultaneously the outer and inner aspects of one and the same indivisible concretion of power" (105); they do not really have a separate existence, for "we encounter them primarily in reference to the material or earthly reality of which they are the innermost essence" (107). While the emphasis on the powers being encountered in earthly institutions is helpful, the question has to be again raised as to whether this does justice to the biblical view. If the powers were originally created through Christ, have been defeated by him, and will be eliminated at the final consummation, then they exist apart from their specific manifestations on earth.

Here again, belief in such powers does not encourage complacency. Their operation may be seen in all the structures of human society: national states, governments, political parties, multinational corporations, financial institutions, trade unions, governing boards, ecclesiastical organizations, etc. All such structures are God-given for the preservation of human life and society, yet when the "powers" behind them rebel and claim ultimate authority for themselves, then to varying degrees these structures can become demonic. Perceiving how and when this happens involves what Paul calls "the discernment of spirits" (1 Cor 12:10). "The Holy Spirit 'shrinks' the Powers before the eye of faith. They may well have inflated themselves into omnipotent total value systems, but the believer sees them in their true proportions" (Berkhof 1977: 48-49). Wink sees the powers at work in what he calls "the domination system" that pervades so much of our society today, a system that is characterized by exploitation, dehumanization, and violence (1992: 13-49). The church's task is not only to "unmask" but also to "engage" the powers, using nonviolent means. While this may indeed involve social, political, and economic action, according to the NT the main weapons of the Christian are those listed in Eph 6:13-17.

4. The NT material on *demons/evil spirits* poses special problems (cf. Michl 1981a: 195; see also the discussion of healing in 20-3.3 and 20-5.3). The

symptoms of those possessed by demons are only too well known in our world, but the modern reaction is to send for a psychiatrist, not an exorcist (or to employ some form of group therapy). Belief in demons and the practice of exorcism were widespread in the ancient world and were by no means unique to Jesus or to early Christianity (see J. M. Hull 1976: 313; cf. Matt 12:27; Mark 9:38; Acts 19:13). In modern Western society, virtually no one believes in demons. Many Christians therefore accept the argument that if the incarnation was real, it involved Jesus' acceptance of the first-century explanation of mental illness (the theory of "accommodation"; cf. M. Wilson 1975: 293; Best 1993: 120-21; contra Langton 1949: 159-61; D. Guthrie 1981: 128-29; Elwell 1988d: 612). Allowance has to be made for cultural change, and Christians today should welcome and accept modern psychiatry as a God-given means of healing appropriate to our time. Modern methods of healing should be seen not as replacing, but rather as supplementing prayer to God, the true source of all healing (see Mark 9:29).

The situation may be different, however, in certain parts of the world where belief in demons is still a reality. Moreover, in the closing decades of the twentieth century an increasing number of cases of demon possession were reported in modern Western society, and today interest in the subject is far from dead. It may be that where persons believe they are possessed, exorcism is appropriate; some churches (including Anglican and Roman Catholic) retain a liturgy of exorcism but generally use it with extreme caution, and only after other possibilities have been eliminated (cf. the discussion in Wink 1986: 58-64). M. Perry (1990) suggests that "a formula of personal exorcism is appropriate (if at all) only in cases where Satan is seen to be in (improper) possession of a person, and that person has been knowingly trafficking in the things of Satan in such a way and to such an extent that he has lost control of himself. . . . Exorcism is a rarely-needed remedy, appropriate only in conditions of unusual severity" (110).

5. The figure of *Antichrist* has fascinated many over the centuries. Some have sought to identify the Antichrist with specific figures in history ranging from Nero or Domitian in NT times, through Muhammad and various popes, down to Stalin or Hitler in modern times (cf. Rist 1962a: 143; Ewert 1980: 75-79). Making such identifications as part of a scheme to show that the time of the end is near has no warrant in Scripture, which consistently holds that only God knows the time of the end. On the other hand, it is quite consistent with the biblical view to see the power of evil or the Antichrist at work in certain historical figures (such as Hitler) who seem to be monsters of iniquity. Such persons can be seen as foreshadowing the last outbreak of evil before the parousia and the final victory of Christ.

6. The NT has much to say about Satan and the various forms in which the powers of evil manifest themselves. But no more than the OT does it speculate on the *origin* of God's adversaries. This stands in striking contrast to the Jewish tradition that developed various theories of fallen angels (Langton 1949: 107-

39), and to Christian tradition that took up and even further elaborated this explanation. On this view, God created angelic beings and, in order that they might truly serve him, endowed them with free will. Some angels, led by Satan, rebelled against God and were cast out of heaven prior to creation (alternatively the fall of the angels is connected with Gen 6:1-4). In the English-speaking world the most elaborate presentation is found in John Milton's *Paradise Lost,* which significantly devotes two whole books to describing events that have little or no basis in the Bible whatsoever!

In Job 1 and 2 and Zech 3 "the Satan" is an angelic being (4-1.5), and therefore presumably created by God. According to Col 1:16, the various "powers" were all created through Christ. Since Satan and the powers are portrayed as opposed to God, it is a fair assumption that they are thought of as having rebelled against God. Jude 6 (cf. 2 Pet 2:4) merely hints at a belief in fallen angels (see, however, Prager 1981: 809-10). John 8:44 says the devil "was a murderer from the beginning," and 1 John 3:8 says "the devil has been sinning from the beginning"; "from the beginning *(ap' archēs)*" could suggest a rebellion before creation. The NT references to the fall of Satan from heaven (Luke 10:17-18; John 12:31; Rev 12:9; see 4-3.3b), on the other hand, all seem to refer to the consequences in the heavenly realm of the victory won by Christ through his life, death, and resurrection. Later speculation that linked Satan, as a fallen angel, with Isa 14:4-21 (see above, 4-1.5) and Rev 8:10-11 and 9:1-11 (see 4-3.3b) goes well beyond the biblical evidence.

The Bible provides little incentive to speculation regarding the origin of Satan and the powers of evil. It does take them with the utmost seriousness, assuring believers that they are defeated in principle even if they will not be eliminated until the final consummation, in the meantime exhorting believers to be ever vigilant and to take heart, knowing that the decisive battle has already been won.

CHAPTER 5

The Spirit

Old Testament: Proclamation

5-1. THE SPIRIT OF THE LORD

In the overall canonical context, one way of speaking of God's activity is particularly significant: it is in and through his Spirit that God brings order to both creation and history, and it is also through his Spirit that he inaugurates the new order.

5-1.1. WHITHER SHALL I GO FROM YOUR SPIRIT?

a. Wind, Breath, Spirit

The Hebrew *rûach* (feminine; LXX predominantly *pneuma*, neuter) can mean, depending on context, "wind," "breath," or "spirit" (see Maertens 1966: 13-26; Heron 1983: 3-10). In the NT the Greek *pneuma* carries the same three basic connotations.

The *wind*, though itself invisible, is regarded in the Bible as a mysterious force, powerful in its effects, and is often closely linked with God (cf. Exod 10:13; 14:21; 15:8, 10; Jonah 1:4). The wind can also be destructive and the agent of God's judgment (Isa 27:8; Hos 13:15; see R. Koch 1981b: 870).

The human *breath* (also *neshāmâh;* cf., e.g., Isa 42:5), though in itself invisible, is linked in the closest fashion with the mysterious force of life itself; it is a matter of simple observation that when a body stops breathing it is dead, and the connection between breath and life was widespread in the ancient world (Jacob 1958: 122). The source of breath/life is God himself. Adam was a lump of clay until God "breathed into his nostrils the breath of life" (*nishmath chayyîm;* Gen 2:7). Though the giver of life, God also has the power to destroy "all flesh in which is the breath of life *(rûach chayyîm)*" (Gen 6:17).

These usages shed light on those passages where *rûach* means "spirit," either human or divine. Human beings have a spirit, the life force that animates them (see further, 16-1.1b). Here we are concerned with the Spirit of God, which may be defined in preliminary fashion as the unseen yet life-giving power of God at work in creation and in history.

b. God as Spirit

The OT can speak of God and his Spirit virtually interchangeably. To say that the Israelites "rebelled and grieved his holy spirit" (Isa 63:10) simply means that they grieved God. God's Spirit is synonymous with his presence, as in Ps 139:7:

> Where can I go from your spirit?
>> Or where can I flee from your presence? (cf. Ps 51:11; Hag 2:5)

God is spoken of as Spirit particularly in his activity; "it can therefore be said that the spirit is God himself in creative and saving activity" (Jacob 1958: 124).

The OT does not speculate on God's nature as "spirit." The nearest it comes to this is in Isa 31:3:

> The Egyptians are human, and not God;
>> their horses are flesh, and not spirit.

But the main point here is the contrast between human weakness and divine power.

c. His Holy Spirit

Since human beings have a "spirit," God's Spirit is occasionally distinguished as "the Holy Spirit," i.e., the Spirit which is separate or different from that of humans. This usage, however, is found in only two passages in the OT, Ps 51:11 and Isa 63:10-11. It occurs twice in the Deuterocanon (2 *Esdr* 14:22; *Wis* 9:17).

5-1.2. THE CREATED ORDER: CREATION

God is active through his Spirit in creation (cf. Koenig 1978: 22-25; Heron 1983: 10-12). In the midst of the primeval chaos, "the Spirit of God was moving over the face of the waters" (Gen 1:2 RSV; some translations, e.g., NRSV, read "a wind from God . . ."). Creation through God's Spirit can be closely associated with creation through God's word:

By the word of the LORD the heavens were made,
    and all their host by the breath *(rûach)* of his mouth.

(Ps 33:6; cf. Job 26:13; Wis 1:7; Jdt 16:14)

Specifically it is through his *rûach* that God creates human life. "The LORD God formed man from the dust of the ground, and breathed *(nāphach =* 'breathe, blow') into his nostrils the breath *(nᵉshamah)* of life" (Gen 2:7).

Just as God is not only Creator but also Sustainer (cf. 2-1.2b), so all living things continuously depend on the divine Spirit for their existence:

If he should take back his spirit *(rûchô)* to himself,
    and gather to himself his breath *(nishmāthô),*
all flesh would perish together,
    and all mortals return to dust. (Job 34:14-15; cf. 33:4)

When you take away their breath *(rûchām),* they die. . . .
When you send forth your spirit *(rûchᵃkhā),* they are created.

(Ps 104:29-30)

5-1.3. THE CREATED ORDER: WISDOM

God's Spirit is also linked with the gift of wisdom by which God enables people to discern his truth in the created order (cf. 2-1.4b). When Pharaoh was advised to "select a man who is discerning and *wise,* and set him over the land of Egypt," he asked, "Can we find anyone else like this — one in whom is *the spirit of God?*" (Gen 41:33, 38). Daniel is described as "a man . . . endowed with a spirit of the holy gods," for "enlightenment, understanding, and *wisdom* like the wisdom of the gods" were found in him (Dan 5:11; cf. 4:8-9, 18; 5:14; cf. *Wis* 9:17). According to Job 32:8, "it is the spirit in a mortal, / the breath of the Almighty, that makes for understanding."

In keeping with the broad understanding of wisdom in the OT (2-1.4b), the gift of artistic ability can also be ascribed to the Spirit of God. Thus God says of Bezalel, the master craftsman, "I have filled him with the Spirit of God, with . . . knowledge and all craftsmanship" (Exod 31:3 RSV; cf. 35:31); this suggests that the Spirit "works in man not only mighty deeds of deliverance, but along with these, aids in shaping lovely objects that will speak of God's own beauty and assist in worship" (Dyrness 1979: 203). In *Wis* 1:6-7, wisdom is virtually identified with "the spirit of the Lord," while in 7:7 Solomon declares, "I called on God, and the spirit of wisdom came to me." The context in such passages suggests that when someone is endowed with the Spirit of God, which is "the spirit of wisdom," there is no sense of a sudden or occasional possession by an outside power; rather, the Spirit works quietly and continuously in the lives of the wise. Nevertheless, it seems that this spirit is conferred only on a few exceptional people.

5-1.4. THE HISTORICAL ORDER: DIVINE CARE

God is active through his Spirit in the historical order in his care for his chosen people. A few passages speak of God's Spirit as active in salvation/judgment history in the deliverance and guidance of God's people. At the time of the exodus of the Israelites from Egypt, God "put within them his holy spirit" (Isa 63:11), and the Spirit of the LORD led them in the wilderness (63:14; Neh 9:20). "Here . . . the spirit is the medium through which God's presence in the midst of his people becomes a reality" (Eichrodt 1967: 61).

Through his Spirit God continues to guide his people (cf. Ps 143:10; Hag 2:5; Zech 4:6), though often that guidance is rejected:

> Woe to the rebellious children . . .
>   who carry out a plan, but not mine;
> and who make a league, but not of my spirit. (Isa 30:1 RSV)

The predominant emphasis in the OT, however, is on the Spirit as the means by which God confers special powers and gifts on the *leaders* of his people.

5-1.5. THE HISTORICAL ORDER: HUMAN LEADERSHIP

In the OT God's Spirit is referred to particularly in connection with the bestowing of special gifts on those who are the *leaders* of God's people.

a. Ecstasy

In early times the Spirit was thought of as a mysterious and quasi-physical power that broke in from the outside and took possession of a person, though only for a short period of time. "The power of the spirit emerges like a volcanic eruption, now here now there, sudden and unmediated, and then disappears again according as God calls his own to particular deeds" (Eichrodt 1967: 52). Thus "the spirit of the LORD rushed on" Samson, endowing him with extraordinary physical strength (Judg 14:6, 19). When Saul met up with a band of prophets, the Spirit came upon him so that he fell into "a prophetic frenzy," being "turned into a different person" (1 Sam 10:6; cf. 11:6; 19:23-24). Elijah was physically transported from one place to another by the Spirit (1 Kgs 18:12; 2 Kgs

2:16). Ezekiel was transported by the Spirit, but Ezek 8:3 and 11:24 make it clear that this occurs "in visions." The reaction of those who said that "the prophet is a fool, / the man of the spirit is mad!" (Hos 9:7) suggests that even in Hosea's day prophecy could still be accompanied by ecstatic phenomena. In such cases (frequently paralleled in the history of religions) "the Spirit of God is experienced in ways that exclude all rational thought and action; the person seized by the Spirit is no longer aware of what he is doing" (Schweizer 1980: 10).

b. Prophecy

In the history of God with his people, the Spirit confers powers of leadership. Num 11:17, 25 assume that Moses is endowed with God's Spirit, which is linked with the gift of prophecy. Judges such as Othniel (Judg 3:10), Gideon (6:34), and Jephthah (11:29) were endowed with the Spirit in their capacity as military leaders; in such cases the Spirit represents "a supernatural power or force which makes possible the accomplishment of things beyond man's normal capabilities" (Maertens 1966: 29). Of the kings (apart from Saul, see *(a)* above), only David is linked with the Spirit. When Samuel anointed him, "the spirit of the Lord came mightily upon David from that day forward" (1 Sam 16:13; cf. 2 Sam 23:2).

But it is particularly with the *prophets* that the Spirit is associated. The Spirit of the Lord spoke to Micaiah (1 Kgs 22:24). Micah can say,

> But as for me, I am filled with power,
>   with the spirit of the Lord. (Mic 3:8)

The Spirit entered into Ezekiel (Ezek 2:2; 3:24; etc.).

Some scholars detect a certain reserve on the part of the major prophets in claiming the inspiration of God's Spirit (cf. Amos 7:14, and see Jacob 1958: 125). The older association of the Spirit with abnormal and ecstatic behavior was generally foreign to the major prophets, and their emphasis is overwhelmingly on the *word* of God that addressed them, and that constituted the message they were commissioned to deliver to God's people. In Isa 59:21 God speaks of "my spirit that is upon you, and my words that I have put in your mouth." This type of inspiration by God's Spirit does not bypass human reason but rather employs it.

Nevertheless, even in the major prophets the sense is retained of a mysterious power, freely conferred by God on those he chooses, and ecstatic elements are not entirely lacking, as can be seen especially in the case of Ezekiel (cf. the discussion in Williams 1974). Zechariah can look back on his predecessors and refer to "the words that the Lord of hosts had sent by his spirit through the former prophets" (Zech 7:12; cf. Neh 9:30).

c. Transferring of the Spirit

There are three notable cases of the transfer of the Spirit which reflect a hope that the Spirit could be passed on to others.

Moses took some of the Spirit that was upon him and put it upon the seventy elders (Num 11:24-25; on the difficulty of controlling the Spirit, see vv. 26-29); Joshua "was full of the spirit of wisdom, because Moses had laid his hands on him" (Deut 34:9); and Elisha's request for a double share of Elijah's spirit, though "a hard thing," was granted (2 Kgs 2:9-10, 15). However, there is no word of the elders, Joshua, or Elisha transmitting the Spirit to others in their turn.

The Spirit of God is thus an important way of speaking of God in the OT. Though invisible, God's life-giving and powerful Spirit can work in creation and in history. Through his Spirit God confers gifts, especially upon leaders of his people. Yet the dominant impression is that such endowment with the Spirit is an exceptional occurrence. In the history of Israel only a relatively few individuals receive the Spirit, and even they probably for only limited periods of time. Moses' exclamation in Num 11:29, "Would that all the LORD's people were prophets, and that the LORD would put his spirit on them!" appears to be a pious but vain hope.

Old Testament: Promise

5-2. I WILL POUR OUT MY SPIRIT

The Spirit of God plays an important role in the promises of the dawning of a new order.

5-2.1. BY THE SPIRIT OF THE LORD

Frequently it is God's Spirit that inspires visions of the future. In his prayer Ezra recalls how God warned the people of the future consequences of their disobedience "by your spirit through your prophets" (Neh 9:30). The Spirit plays a major role in the visions of Ezekiel (e.g., Ezek 2:2; 3:12, 14; 37:1). It is through "the spirit of the holy gods" that Daniel is able to interpret the prophecy contained in the writing on the wall (Dan 5:14 RSV).

In the NT the role of the Spirit in inspiring the OT prophets is recognized. The prophets, according to 1 Pet 1:10-12, "made careful search and inquiry, inquiring about the person or time that the Spirit of Christ within them indicated when it testified in advance to the sufferings destined for Christ and the subsequent glory. It was revealed to them that they were serving not themselves but you, in regard to the things that have now been announced to you through those who brought you good news by the Holy Spirit sent from heaven" (cf. Acts 1:16; Heb 10:15; 2 Pet 1:21).

5-2.2. THE PROMISE OF THE SPIRIT

The giving of the Spirit in the OT is an exceptional occurrence; a relatively few individuals receive the Spirit, usually for limited periods of time. The OT also reflects a longing for a fuller outpouring of God's Spirit, and promises that this will indeed take place when the new order dawns.

The psalmist prays that God would put "a new and right spirit within me" (Ps 51:10). Isaiah sees the need for God's people to be cleansed "by a spirit of judgment and by a spirit of burning" (Isa 4:4); they must suffer God's judgment "until the Spirit is poured out upon us from on high," bringing a rich harvest of justice and righteousness (32:15-17 RSV).

5-2.3. THE SPIRIT AND GOD'S PEOPLE

One of the major marks of the new age will be the outpouring of God's Spirit upon his people (cf. Heron 1983: 17-20). In Isa 44:3 God promises, "I will pour my spirit upon your descendants, / and my blessing on your offspring," like life-giving water on thirsty ground. Ezekiel develops the idea: God promises that when the exiles are restored, he will "put a new spirit within them" (Ezek 11:19), thus enabling them to walk in his ways. In 36:25-27 God declares, "I will sprinkle clean water upon you, and you shall be clean from all your uncleannesses. . . . A new heart I will give you, and a new spirit I will put within you. . . . I will put my spirit within you." The day is coming when "I will never again hide my face from them, when I pour out my spirit upon the house of Israel, says the Lord GOD" (39:29).

The future outpouring of God's Spirit is dramatically portrayed in Ezekiel's vision of *the valley of dry bones* (37:1-14). The present state of "the whole house of Israel" (v. 11) is like that of a people who are not only dead but whose bones lie dried out and unburied on the slopes of a valley; they are cut off from life and their hope is lost. The only hope for the resurrection of God's people lies with God. The prophet is instructed to promise such a resurrection, employing the various interlocking meanings of *rûach* (cf. Maertens 1966: 36). God says to the bones, "I will cause *breath* to enter you, and you shall live" (v. 5); only the breath of God (Gen 2:7) can confer life. The prophet is to summon this breath "from the four *winds*" (v. 9) that will blow across the valley revitalizing the corpses. This breath/wind is none other than the *Spirit* of God: God will raise his people from the grave of exile, restore them to the Land, and "I will put my spirit within you, and you shall live" (v. 14). "*Ruach* in the book of Ezekiel was related most closely to a messianic people, a people renewed by the Spirit to fulfil the purpose of God in history" (Moody 1976: 22). Ezekiel's dry-bones prophecy can be thought of as having been fulfilled to some extent in the return from exile in Babylon. Yet insofar as that return fell short of expectations, Ezek 37:1-14 is to be seen as containing a "surplus" of meaning referring to a still-future eschatological event.

The prophet Joel introduces his vision of the new age (Joel 2:28–3:21) with a prophecy of the future outpouring of God's Spirit:

> Then afterward
> I will pour out my spirit on all flesh;
> your sons and your daughters shall prophesy,
> your old men shall dream dreams,
> and your young men shall see visions.
> Even on the male and female slaves,
> in those days, I will pour out my spirit. (2:28-29)

This is linked with the cosmic portents that will precede the Day of the LORD (2:30-31; cf. 2-2.3). Three points relating to this passage should be noted. Firstly, the emphasis is on the future reception of the Spirit by *all* God's people (v. 32a), without distinction of sex (sons/daughters, male/female slaves), age (old men/ young men), or social status (male/female slaves, i.e., in addition to free persons). Secondly, the outpouring of the Spirit is linked with the gift of prophecy. Thirdly, the outpouring of the Spirit is an eschatological event, occurring "afterward," and linked to cosmic signs and the Day of the Lord.

In the Prophets, therefore, we find the anticipation of "a new era in which the Spirit will work among a greater number of individuals and different kinds of people to create a more faithful community of men and women serving God" (Blomberg 1996: 345).

5-2.4. THE SPIRIT AND GOD'S SERVANT

In the new order God's Spirit will be poured out not only on God's people but also especially on the Servant of God who will lead that people (see chap. 6).

The future king who will come from David's line will be uniquely endowed with the Spirit:

> The Spirit of the LORD shall rest on him,
> the spirit of wisdom and understanding,
> the spirit of counsel and might,
> the spirit of knowledge and the fear of the LORD. (Isa 11:2)

As Maertens (1966) suggests, "this proliferation of names for the spirit of God serves only to indicate the stupendous wealth of spiritual gifts which will proceed from that divine source" (40). It should be noted that the LXX version of this text adds a seventh gift of the Spirit, "piety" *(eusebeia).*

Of the Servant, chosen by God (see 9-1), God says, "I have put my spirit upon him" (Isa 42:1), while the speaker in Isa 61:1-3, probably also to be identified with the Servant, declares, "The spirit of the Lord GOD is upon me" (v. 1; cf. Zech 12:10).

Thus in Isaiah, Ezekiel, and Joel we find the promise of an eschatological outpouring of God's Spirit. While the future Servant of God will be uniquely endowed with the Spirit, the emphasis falls, in contrast to the old order where the Spirit is bestowed occasionally on exceptional individuals, on the reception of the Spirit by *all* God's people. What for Moses was only a pious hope — that all God's people would receive God's Spirit (above, 5-1.5c) — in the new age will become a glorious reality.

5-2.5. THE SPIRIT AND A NEW CREATION

Just as God's Spirit was active in the work of creation, so will the same Spirit be active in bringing about a new creation.

Isa 32:15 speaks of the devastation of nature that will occur

> until the Spirit is poured upon us from on high,
>   and the wilderness becomes a fruitful field. (RSV)

New Testament: Fulfillment

5-3. ALL FILLED WITH THE HOLY SPIRIT

The NT testifies to the giving of God's Spirit as a major sign of the dawning of the new order; the Spirit was uniquely operative in the Christ event, and through Christ, after his death and resurrection, was bestowed upon the church. It is essential that everything the NT says about the Spirit be read in the light of the OT promise that in the new age God's Spirit would be poured out upon his people (above, 5-2). The NT claims that the OT promises of an eschatological outpouring of God's Spirit have been fulfilled; God's people have received "the promised Holy Spirit" (Eph 1:13; cf. Luke 24:49; Acts 1:4; Gal 3:14). In keeping with the "already–not yet" tension so characteristic of the NT, the presence of the Spirit not only is evidence that the new order has dawned, but also points forward to the final consummation of God's purposes (cf. Fee 1994: 803-

26). As in the OT (cf. above, 5-1.1a), the Greek *pneuma* can mean wind, breath, or spirit (human or divine).

5-3.1. THE PROMISE OF THE SPIRIT

On the threshold of the new age, Spirit-inspired prophecy is reborn, and a great prophet reiterates the promise of the Spirit.

a. The Lucan Infancy Narrative

In Luke 1 and 2 "the whole environment of Jesus is imbued with the Holy Spirit" (Maertens 1966: 111), and the Spirit inspires several of the supporting characters in the drama to hail the dawn of redemption (see Ewert 1983: 32-35). *Elizabeth* was "filled with the Holy Spirit" and hailed Mary as the mother of the Lord (1:41-43); *Zechariah*, "filled with the Holy Spirit," blessed God for visiting and redeeming his people (1:67-68); *Simeon*, in fulfillment of a revelation by the Holy Spirit, went into the temple, and when "the Holy Spirit rested on him," he gave thanks for seeing God's salvation (2:25-32).

b. John the Baptist

As the last representative of OT prophecy (3-3.2a), John the Baptist is "filled with the Holy Spirit" (Luke 1:15) and reiterates the promise that the new order will be marked by an outpouring of God's Spirit (see Dunn 1970: 8-22).

An important part of John's message was the contrast between his preparatory baptism and that of the Coming One: "I baptize you with water for repentance, but one who is more powerful than I is coming after me. . . . He will baptize you with the Holy Spirit and fire" (Matt 3:11//Luke 3:16; Mark 1:8 omits "and fire"). Thus, according to Matthew and Luke, John ascribed to the Coming One a twofold baptism: on the wicked he will pour out a fiery river of judgment, but on God's people he will pour out the blessings of God's Holy Spirit (cf. Scobie 1964: 67-73). The version of this saying in John's Gospel identifies Jesus as the one who will baptize with the Holy Spirit (1:33-34). The risen Christ repeats this promise (Acts 1:5), and Acts tells of its fulfillment on the Day of Pentecost (Acts 2).

5-3.2. JESUS AND THE SPIRIT

There is relatively little in the teaching of Jesus concerning the Holy Spirit; the Synoptics concentrate on portraying Jesus as the new Servant, uniquely endowed with the Spirit, in fulfillment of the OT promises. "Jesus does not speak *about* the Spirit but rather acts and speaks *in* the Spirit" (Schweizer 1980: 48).

a. The Teaching of Jesus

i. *The Help of the Spirit*

In the eschatological discourse Jesus tells his disciples not to be anxious when brought to trial but to "say whatever is given you at that time, for it is not you who speak, but the Holy Spirit" (Mark 13:11//Matt 10:20; Luke 12:12). Here believers are assured of the Spirit's help especially when they face persecution. Luke's Gospel lays particular emphasis on the Spirit. In 11:13 Jesus declares that if imperfect earthly parents give good gifts to their children, "how much more will the heavenly Father give the Holy Spirit to those who ask him!"

ii. *The Blasphemy against the Holy Spirit*

Jesus gave a special warning concerning blasphemy against the Holy Spirit that comes in two forms. In Mark 3:28-29 Jesus says, "Truly I tell you, people will be forgiven for their sins and whatever blasphemies they utter; but whoever blasphemes against the Holy Spirit can never have forgiveness *(ouk echei aphesin eis ton aiōna)*, but is guilty of an eternal sin *(enochos aiōniou hamartēmatos)*." Matthew and Luke preserve a slightly different form of the saying: "And everyone who speaks a word against the Son of Man will be forgiven; but whoever blasphemes against the Holy Spirit will not be forgiven" (Luke 12:10; Matt 12:32 adds, "either in this age or in the age to come").

It is important to recall that the NT, and not least Jesus himself, speaks frequently of God's forgiveness; what is referred to here is a special case. It is hardly satisfactory to explain the saying as an exaggeration meaning "it is a very serious sin to speak against the Holy Spirit" (cf. O. E. Evans 1957: 242-43). The best key to interpretation is found in the context in Mark and Matthew. Jesus casts out demons by the Spirit of God (Matt 12:28), but his opponents are so blinded that they call white black and black white; they observe the power of God at work and call it the power of Satan (Mark 3:22). "By attributing what was obviously a good act to the power of Satan, his critics were blunting their own faculty of distinguishing between right and wrong and running the risk of being unable thereafter to recognize goodness when they met it. To blaspheme against the Holy Spirit by calling His works evil is to deprive oneself of a standard of judgement for one's own life, and thus to become incapable of repentance" (Caird 1994: 116-17). What the Pharisees witnessed was the inbreaking of the new order *(aiōn);* by declaring this to be the work of Satan they cut themselves off from any chance of forgiveness in the new order and were guilty of the sin against the new order (see A. Richardson 1958: 108).

b. The Spirit of the Lord Is upon Me

All the Gospels reflect a tradition that *the Spirit was uniquely operative in the life of Jesus,* the new Servant. "The Evangelists have no doubts that Jesus was the wholly unique Man of the Spirit" (Kamlah, Dunn, and Brown 1978: 697), and they make it clear that "from his miraculous conception onwards, Christ is under the influence of the Spirit of God" (R. Koch 1981b: 878; cf. Ewert 1983: 47-61).

The Holy Spirit effects the virginal conception of Jesus by Mary (Matt 1:18, 20; Luke 1:31-35; see 8-3.5b). The climax of Jesus' baptism is the descent of the Holy Spirit (Matt 3:16; Mark 1:10; Luke 3:22; cf. John 1:32-33; Acts 10:38; see Barrett 1947: 39). In his ministry Jesus is led and empowered by the Spirit (Mark 1:12//Matt 4:1//Luke 4:1; Matt 12:28; Luke 4:14; 10:21; John 3:34).

In particular Jesus is identified with *the Spirit-filled Servant.* Matthew quotes and applies to Jesus Isa 42:1-4 (Matt 12:17-21). Luke describes Jesus as reading Isa 61:1-2 in the synagogue at Nazareth ("The Spirit of the Lord is upon me . . .") and claiming that "today this scripture has been fulfilled in your hearing" (Luke 4:16-21). It is through God's Spirit that Jesus casts out the demons (Matt 12:28).

Finally, in the NT the Spirit is linked with Jesus' resurrection. Christ, says Paul (probably quoting a primitive confessional formula), was "declared to be Son of God with power according to the spirit of holiness by resurrection from the dead" (Rom 1:4). He was "put to death in the flesh, but made alive in the spirit" (1 Pet 3:18, perhaps quoting an early hymn). Similarly 1 Tim 3:16 (clearly a hymn) says of Christ:

> He was revealed in flesh,
>   vindicated in spirit.

What this portrayal of the working of the Spirit in the life of Jesus emphasizes is that "Jesus himself, all that he says and does, is God's presence. In him the age of God's salvation is dawning. His life and proclamation is the event of God's presence, fulfilling all prophetic expectations. That is the life of the Holy Spirit" (Schweizer 1980: 57).

During his ministry the Spirit rests on Jesus alone. Only when his mission is accomplished, after his death and resurrection, is the Spirit given to his followers (John 7:39; Acts 1:4-5; see Bruce 1963: 166-67).

5-3.3. THE GIVING OF THE SPIRIT

After Jesus' death and resurrection, the NT declares, the Spirit was given by God in a new way and was received by the new people of God as a sign of the inauguration of the new order. Throughout the NT it is assumed that the church is a Spirit-endowed community (Horn 1992: 266, 269). On the Day of Pentecost, at the conclusion of the first Christian sermon, Peter declares to his hearers, "Repent, and be baptized every one of you . . . and *you will receive the gift of the Holy Spirit*" (Acts 2:38). Acts constantly portrays the Spirit as guiding and empowering the church; so much so that it has been suggested that an equally suitable title for the book would be "The Acts of the Holy Spirit." In Acts, "it is by the Spirit that the Church's expansion through evangelism is inspired, directed, and confirmed at every stage" (Moule 1978: 37; cf. Maertens 1966: 55).

The Spirit figures prominently in the NT epistles and in the book of Revelation. Believers are those who "have tasted the heavenly gift, and have shared in the Holy Spirit" (Heb 6:4); they are those who have been "sanctified by the Spirit to be obedient to Jesus Christ" (1 Pet 1:2). It is "worldly people" who are "devoid of the Spirit" (Jude 19). The fullest treatment of the Holy Spirit is found in the Pauline Epistles, though for an account of the *giving* of the Spirit we turn to two other sources: the book of Acts and the Gospel of John.

a. All Were Given the One Spirit to Drink

Paul says nothing of the giving of the Spirit as a past event, but he assumes that all believers have received the Spirit. "For in the one Spirit," he says, "we were all baptized into one body . . . and we were all made to drink of one Spirit" (1 Cor 12:13; cf. 2 Cor 1:21-22; Titus 3:6). Conversely, "Anyone who does not have the Spirit of Christ does not belong to him" (Rom 8:9). "The teaching that the Spirit has been given to all Christians as such can be regarded as the fundamental teaching upon which all St. Paul's other utterances concerning the Spirit are based" (Whiteley 1964: 125; on the Spirit in Paul, see Beker 1958; Maertens 1966: 69-94; P. W. Meyer 1979; Heron 1983: 44-51; Horn 1992: 271-76; Fee 1994, who provides a detailed exegetical study of all the relevant passages).

Since he is writing to relatively new converts, it is not surprising that Paul links the Spirit with the beginning of the Christian life and with the rite of baptism: "You were washed, you were sanctified, you were justified . . . in the Spirit of our God" (1 Cor 6:11); "in the one Spirit we were all baptized into one body" (1 Cor 12:13; cf. Titus 3:4-7). It is only by the Holy Spirit that someone can confess that "Jesus is Lord" (1 Cor 12:3). It is through the Spirit that believers are set free and are adopted as children and heirs of God (Rom 8:14-17; cf. Gal 4:6-7), and it is through the Holy Spirit that "God's love has been poured into our hearts" (Rom 5:5). It is with the help of the Spirit that prayer is possible (Rom

8:26-27; cf. Jude 20). Fee well sums up the role of the Spirit for Paul as "God's empowering presence" (1994: 5-9; cf. also D. Guthrie 1981: 553-62).

The Spirit delivers believers from the powers that threaten humanity, the powers of "sin," "death," and "the flesh *(sarx)*" (Rom 8:1-4), and frees them to love and serve God (Gal 5; cf. Rom 8:6). Christians do not live "according to the flesh," i.e., on a purely human level as if God did not exist, but "according to the Spirit," and they therefore "set their minds on the things of the Spirit" (Rom 8:5). For Paul "*sarx* [flesh] designates the earthly, human, and creaturely, *pneuma* [spirit] the divine presence which encounters us in Jesus Christ, and into which we are drawn by him" (Heron 1983: 45; see further, 16-3.1b).

b. The Rush of a Mighty Wind

The giving and receiving of the Spirit plays a key role in the theology of Luke-Acts.

i. Luke 24:49, where Jesus tells the Eleven, "And see, I am sending upon you what my Father promised; so stay here in the city until you have been clothed with power from on high," paves the way for a central event in Luke-Acts, *the giving of the Spirit on the Day of Pentecost* (Acts 2; see Ewert 1983: 101-15). Luke presents this as a precisely datable event, occurring in sequence after Jesus' resurrection and ascension, on the feast of Pentecost, fifty days after Passover. "When the day of Pentecost had come, they were all together in one place. And suddenly from heaven there came a sound like the rush of a violent wind, and it filled the entire house where they were sitting. Divided tongues, as of fire, appeared among them, and a tongue rested on each one of them. All of them were filled with the Holy Spirit and began to speak in other languages, as the Spirit gave them ability" (Acts 2:1-4). The coming of the Spirit is likened to the rushing of a violent *wind,* in keeping with the OT view of the Spirit and possibly alluding to the summoning of the winds in the vision of Ezek 37. Peter declares that "this is what was spoken through the prophet Joel," and Joel 2:28-32 is quoted verbatim in Acts 2:17-21, thereby underlining the fact that what his hearers have just witnessed is nothing other than the promised eschatological outpouring of the Holy Spirit; with the dawning of the new age God's Spirit is poured out on *all* who believe regardless of age, sex, or social status. The passage from Joel includes reference to cosmic signs (Acts 2:19-20 = Joel 2:30-31; cf. 2-2.2). Pentecost was not the final cosmic catastrophe, but Luke regards the signs as having been fulfilled. "Wonders" *(terata)* and "signs" *(sēmeia)* were seen on earth in Jesus' ministry (Acts 2:19 = Acts 2:22); "fire" *(pyr)* did appear when the Spirit was given (Acts 2:19 = Acts 2:3); and the sun was turned into darkness at Jesus' crucifixion, where Luke alone adds the comment, "while the sun's light failed" (Acts 2:20 = Luke 23:45). By these connections Luke proclaims that Pentecost is a central event in God's working not only in the historical order, but also in the created order. It is a unique happening that marks the culmination of the Christ event and the inauguration of the new age (cf. Hoekema 1972: 16-17).

Joel's prophecy of the gift of the Spirit to all God's people without distinction (Joel 2:28-29 = Acts 2:17-18) is picked up in Acts 2:38, where all the hearers are offered the gift of the Spirit on condition of repentance and baptism, and Peter declares that "the promise is for you, for your children, and for all who are far away, everyone whom the Lord our God calls to him" (v. 39; cf. Isa 57:19).

The Spirit confers the gift of speaking "in other languages" or "tongues" (*lalein heterais glōssais,* Acts 2:4), so that the Jews from all over the Diaspora heard them speaking in their own native language (2:6, 8). The relation of this to Paul's references to the gift of "tongues" raises difficult problems (see below, 5-3.4b). Although the Pentecost audience would all know Greek and/or Aramaic, Luke clearly intends the "tongues" to mean a miraculous ability to speak a variety of foreign languages. He thereby interprets Pentecost as *the reversal of Babel* (Gen 11:1-9; see 2-1.5a; cf. Stendahl 1977: 126; Moule 1978: 87-88). Humanity's prideful reaching up to the heavens and making a name for themselves results in confusion of language, inability to communicate, and the scattering of people over the face of the earth; the sending down of the Spirit from heaven restores communication and points forward to the uniting of people from all over the earth. Although the audience is confined to Jews and proselytes (Acts 2:10), the "tongues" of Pentecost anticipate the ingathering of the Gentiles that is about to begin (cf. A. Richardson 1958: 119-20; Beare 1964: 237).

ii. There are several references in Acts to the giving of the Spirit in connection with baptism (see Bruce 1963: 174-77). Unlike John's baptism (Matt 3:11; Luke 3:16), Christian baptism confers the gift of the Spirit (contra Parratt 1971: 233). Peter's appeal in Acts 2:38 sets forth the general rule: "Repent, and be baptized . . . and you will receive the gift of the Holy Spirit." 19:2 also suggests that normally the gift of the Spirit is linked with baptism. But there are exceptions, in both directions. In the case of Cornelius the gift of the Holy Spirit *precedes* baptism: it is the obvious fact that he and his family and friends have received the Spirit that prompts Peter to authorize their baptism (10:44-48; cf. 15:8). On the other hand, in 8:12-17 the gift of the Spirit *follows* baptism, after an interval. Though baptized by Philip, the Samaritans did not receive the Spirit (vv. 12, 16); this occurred only when Peter and John arrived, prayed, and laid hands on them (cf. the case of Paul in 9:17-18, and of the disciples of John at Ephesus in 19:1-7). This is narrated as an exceptional case, and there is no indication here, or elsewhere in the NT, that a second, superior "baptism with the Spirit" is necessary for all believers (see Dunn 1970: 55-72, 226; Blomberg 1996: 347).

The point that Luke makes in these narratives is that the Spirit blows where he wills, and cannot be controlled by human beings. Although normally baptism and the gift of the Spirit are linked, God's power to confer the Spirit is not limited by the restricted vision of his church, nor does the mere performance of a rite by the church of itself confer the Spirit. The church baptizes, but it is God who bestows the Holy Spirit.

c. Receive the Holy Spirit

A distinctive view of the giving and receiving of the Holy Spirit appears in the Johannine literature. John can say that "God is spirit" (John 4:24), but for him, as for Paul and Luke, the emphasis is on the eschatological giving of God's Spirit that is closely linked to the Christ event, culminating in the cross and resurrection (7:39). In particular, "in John's writings the Spirit is the continuity between the earthly life of Jesus and the Christ of faith" (Benjamin 1976: 42).

i. The Paraclete

In a series of five related passages in the farewell discourses, Jesus promises the gift of the Spirit, which is identified by three different terms that John clearly understands as equivalent:

(1) 14:16-17	Paraclete	Spirit of Truth	—
(2) 14:26	Paraclete	—	Holy Spirit
(3) 15:26-27	Paraclete	Spirit of Truth	—
(4) 16:7-11	Paraclete	—	—
(5) 16:13-15	—	Spirit of Truth	—

In addition, the term "Paraclete" is used in 1 John 2:1, where it is applied not to the Spirit but to Christ: "We have an advocate *(paraclēton)* with the Father, Jesus Christ the righteous."

BT is not concerned with possible origins of the term *paraclētos* (see Barrett 1950: 8-12; R. E. Brown 1967: 119-26; G. Johnston 1970: 80-118), but with its canonical usage. The derivation of the term is of limited help (see Brown, 115-19), as it suggests a fairly broad range of meanings. *Parakaleō* means literally to call to one's side, hence to summon to one's aid; but also to exhort, encourage, or comfort. A *paraclētos* in the passive sense is thus "one who is called to someone's aid" (Lat. *advocatus;* Eng. "advocate"), hence a defense attorney; or in a more active sense a helper, mediator, intercessor, supporter, or patron (see Grayston 1981), as well as exhorter, encourager, or comforter ("comforter" is the KJV rendering; for a defense of this meaning, see J. G. Davies 1953). In 1 John 2:1 the context favors "intercessor" or "advocate"; Christ intercedes with the Father for sinners. Paul ascribes a similar function to the Spirit who "intercedes" for us (Rom 8:26-27). In John's Gospel, however, the Paraclete is not portrayed as an intercessor.

The best indication of the meaning of the Spirit-Paraclete in John is found in the fact that the term "Paraclete" *(paraclētos)* is also used of Jesus in 1 John 2:1, while in John 14:16 Jesus says to the disciples, "I will ask the Father, and he will give you *another* Paraclete," clearly presupposing that *Jesus is a Paraclete in the first place.* As Maertens (1966) explains, "hitherto Jesus himself has been their paraclete, sustaining and guiding them. Henceforth they are to have a 'new paraclete'" (122). In the Johannine literature there is thus a tandem arrangement in which *both* Christ *and* the Spirit are thought of as Paracletes. The Spirit-Paraclete will come only after Jesus departs (John 16:7); when Jesus' physical presence is withdrawn, the Spirit-Paraclete takes his place. "The Paraclete is the presence of Jesus when Jesus is absent" (R. E. Brown 1967: 128). Unlike the OT, where God's Spirit is given only intermittently and to isolated individuals, Jesus assures his disciples that the Father will give the Paraclete "to be with you forever" (John 14:16). Broadly speaking therefore, the Spirit means for the disciples everything that Jesus meant for them while he was with them in the flesh.

Having said that, it is the case that in the five passages in John 14–16 two main functions of the Paraclete are emphasized. One is guidance: the Spirit will teach the disciples all things, bringing to remembrance all that Jesus said (14:26); he will guide them into all truth "because he will take what is mine and declare it to you" (16:14). As Benjamin (1976) puts it, "the Spirit is the continuation of Christ speaking in the believer" (47). In John "the function of the Paraclete is not that of an intercessor or pleader for the disciples before God . . . but that of a helper towards their discernment of the self-revelation of the Father in his own human-divine person" (Caird 1994: 211). It is in this sense that the Paraclete is also "the Spirit of Truth" *(to pneuma tēs alētheias),* a term that is also peculiar to John. It is important, however, to note that "the Holy Spirit does not reveal any new truths to the disciples, but reminds them of the teaching of Christ . . . which hitherto they have not understood" (R. Koch 1981b: 882). The unique and final revelation of God has been given in Christ; the Spirit guides the church in applying that revelation in new situations and circumstances, but it does not bring a new revelation.

The Spirit's other function in John relates to the world. The Paraclete testifies to Christ (15:26) and convicts the world of sin: "When he comes, he will prove the world wrong about sin and righteousness and judgment" (16:8-11); the Spirit is thus a prosecutor, not merely the defending counsel. There is a similarity here to the Synoptic passages that promise the Spirit's help in time of persecution (5-3.2a.i); the authorities judge and condemn believers, but the authorities are themselves judged by the Spirit.

Thus, in relation to the disciples the Paraclete is to be with them as Jesus was in his earthly life and in particular to guide them in applying the teaching of Jesus in new situations. In relation to the world the Paraclete testifies to Christ and condemns the world for its unbelief. "The Paraclete's primary function in John is to continue the revelatory work of Jesus in the disciples and before the world, and to maintain that communion of knowledge and love between the Father, the Son and the disciples" (Forestell 1975: 196).

The coming of the Paraclete does not take place in a vacuum; G. Johnston (1970) helpfully suggests that the Spirit-Paraclete is "an active divine power that becomes embodied in certain outstanding leaders within the catholic Church: the exegete, the teacher and evangelist, the prophet, the consoler out of sorrow, and the witness for the defence in times of persecution" (119).

ii. He Breathed on Them

John is as clear as Luke-Acts that the Spirit can be given only after Jesus' death and resurrection (John 7:39). John differs from Luke as to the mode and timing of the giving of the Spirit. On the evening of Easter Sunday, Jesus appears to the disciples, greets them, and commissions them (John 20:19-23). "When he had said this, he breathed on them and said to them, 'Receive the Holy Spirit'" (v. 22). Technically known as "insufflation," Jesus' breathing on the disciples *(enephusēsen)* reflects Gen 2:7 where God breathed into humankind the breath (spirit) of life; this is John's way of saying that the Spirit brings about a new creation (cf. Beare 1958: 98-99). It also recalls God's promise to his people in Ezek 37:5 (cf. vv. 9-10): "I will cause breath to enter you, and you shall live" (cf. Grassi 1964-65: 164). As in creation, the Spirit is the life-giving power of God (John 6:63; cf. Rom 8:11; 2 Cor 3:6; see Moule 1978: 27-29).

John 20 stands in tension with Acts 2; they appear to describe basically the same event, but from quite different perspectives. From a canonical standpoint the giving of the Spirit to the Eleven in John 20 can be seen as a foreshadowing and anticipation of the Acts 2 giving of the Spirit on a much larger scale (see D. Guthrie 1981: 533-34; Ewert 1983: 91-94).

iii. Worship in Spirit

In John the Spirit is also closely linked with *worship* (cf. Barrett 1950: 6-7, 15). The true worshipers are those who worship the Father "in spirit and truth" (John 4:23-24). John connects receiving the Spirit with becoming a Christian; being born anew/from above *(anōthen)* is equated with being born "of water and Spirit" (3:3-8; see further, 17-3.2b). Like Paul and Luke, John thus links the gift of the Spirit with *baptism,* though here too this is not something that is subject to human control. The Spirit is like the wind, that mysterious force that "blows where it chooses" (3:8). "God allows his Spirit to act with sovereign freedom, as in nature so also in the person who opens himself to the guidance of the Spirit" (Schweizer 1980: 71). At the climax of Jesus' discourse on the bread of life in John 6 that has strong *eucharistic* overtones, Jesus says, "It is the spirit that gives life. . . . The words that I have spoken to you are spirit and life" (v. 63).

5-3.4. THE GIFTS OF THE SPIRIT

The gifts of the Spirit, received by believers, empower God's people for love and service.

a. Varieties of Gifts

Throughout the NT the Spirit confers a wide variety of gifts on believers. "God did not establish the church and then leave it to its own resources. By his Spirit he equips his children to fulfill their calling" (Ewert 1983: 262).

The book of Acts portrays these gifts in narrative form. The Spirit, for example, confers the gift of prophecy (2:17-18; 11:28; 20:23; 21:4). The Spirit is the source of wisdom (6:3, 10), faith (6:5; 11:24), comfort (9:31), joy (13:52), and above all guidance (8:29; 10:19; 11:12; 13:2, 4; 15:28; 16:6-7; 19:21). Heb 2:4 says the Christian message was testified to by "signs and wonders and various miracles, and by gifts of the Holy Spirit, distributed according to his will." The idea of the manifold gifts of the Spirit probably underlies a surprising text, Rev 1:4-5, where in a "trinitarian" type of reference John confers grace and peace from God, from Christ, and from "the seven spirits who are before his [God's] throne" (cf. 3:1; 4:5; 5:6). Since seven is symbolic of completeness, John most probably thinks of "the spirit of God in its all-encompassing form" (Horn 1992: 276), but he may also have in mind the sevenfold gifts of the Spirit in the LXX version of Isa 11:2 (above, 5-2.4).

The most important references to spiritual gifts, however, are found in the Pauline Epistles. The context of these references suggests that Paul, broadly speaking, thought of two types of gifts. In some texts he has in mind gifts that the Spirit bestows on *all* believers. In 1 Thess 1:5 Paul emphasizes to all to whom he writes that the Spirit must be the dynamic of their new way of life. Urging the Galatians to "walk by the Spirit," Paul warns against "the works of the flesh" and then continues: "The fruit of the Spirit is love, joy, peace, patience, kindness, generosity, faithfulness, gentleness, and self-control" (Gal 5:22-23); the lives of those who live by the Spirit will be marked by these qualities (on the nine "graces" in Gal 5:22-23, see Moody 1976: 113-15; Ewert 1983: 240-43). A shorter list of qualities appears in 1 Cor 13 in the context of Paul's discussion of gifts bestowed by the Spirit: faith, hope, and love, of which the greatest is love (*agapē*) (v. 13).

Elsewhere, however, Paul has in mind more specialized gifts that relate particularly to the conduct of public worship and to the leadership of the community. This is especially the case in 1 Corinthians where he is addressing problems that had arisen in that particular situation (see commentaries). Here Paul employs two terms: usually *charisma* (plural, *charismata*; also used in 1 Pet 4:10), meaning "a freely bestowed gift" (*charis* = "grace"), and less frequently *pneumatika* (plural only), meaning "things [bestowed by] the Spirit" (*pneuma* = "spirit"). Both terms suggest that the qualities listed are not natural endowments but are bestowed by God's grace through his Spirit (Martin 1992: 1016).

In 1 Cor 12:8-10 Paul gives a list of such gifts: wisdom, knowledge, faith, gifts of healing, working of miracles, prophecy (i.e., proclaiming God's word), discernment of spirits, tongues, interpretation of tongues. With this may be compared the list of gifts *(charismata)* in Rom 12:6-8. In 1 Cor 12, in the context of the same discussion, a further list is given, not of gifts but of what might be called "functions" (at this early date they are hardly "offices"): apostles, prophets, teachers, deeds of power, gifts of healing, forms of assistance, forms of leadership, tongues, interpretation of tongues. With this may be compared the list of functions in Eph 4:11.

In the discussion of such gifts in 1 Cor 12–14, Paul's main point is that "there are varieties of gifts, but the same Spirit" (12:4; on this passage, see Blomberg 1996: 348). All believers have received some "manifestation of the Spirit" (12:7), and the important thing is that all cooperate in deploying their gifts "for the common good." Paul drives his point home by the extended analogy of the body and its members (12:12-27; see further, 11-3.4b), by means of which he stresses that "all the members have a special *charisma*, but one does not have all the *charismata*, and some *charismata* are not universally available" (Martin 1992: 1017).

Paul further seeks in 1 Cor 13 to see these specialized gifts in true perspective by contrasting them with the gifts the Spirit bestows on *all* believers, of which the greatest is love *(agapē)* (cf. Stendahl 1977: 124; Koenig 1978: 148-56). Gifts such as prophecy, tongues, and knowledge (all mentioned in the 1 Cor 12:8-10 list) will come to an end, for they serve a limited purpose in governing the life of the church, whereas "love never ends" (13:8-10).

b. The Gift of Tongues

One gift calls for special consideration. In both lists of the gifts of the Spirit in 1 Cor 12 Paul mentions "various kinds of tongues," "the interpretation of tongues," and speakers in "various kinds of tongues," and in 1 Cor 14 he discusses their place in worship. The phenomenon is frequently referred to as *glōssolalia* (*glōssa* = "tongue"; *laleō* = "speak"), though this term does not appear in the NT. As in English, so in Greek the word "tongue" *(glōssa)* can mean both the physical organ and the sounds it produces, i.e., speech, language. Paul does not define what he means by "tongues" since the phenomenon is well known to his readers. But it appears that speaking in tongues is unintelligible (14:9); it involves the emotions, not reason (14:14), and gives the impression of people being out of their minds (14:23). What the passage clearly indicates is a religious experience, a form of prayer and praise (cf. Tugwell 1973), involving emotional ecstasy and resulting in the production of unintelligible sounds, akin to that experienced in Pentecostal and neo-Pentecostal churches today.

The relation of the gift of tongues in Paul to that described in Acts raises problems. As we have seen (5-3.3b), Luke presents the "other tongues" of Acts 2 as foreign languages. (He records two further instances of speaking with tongues, in Acts 10:46 and 19:6; it may be that he understands these to refer to foreign languages also, though there is no indication of this in these two passages; see D. Guthrie 1981: 539.) Employing the principle that Scripture is its own interpreter, some scholars, following the Reformers, interpret Paul in the light of Acts 2, arguing that Paul also refers to speaking in actual foreign languages, a position that still finds supporters today (so Gundry 1966). Some further argue that this was a special miraculous gift, confined to the earliest days of the church.

But it is a sounder approach to interpret Acts 2 in the light of Paul, since the evidence of 1 Corinthians so clearly points to ecstatic utterance. In fact, the reaction of the crowd in Acts 2:13 ("Others sneered and said, 'They are filled with new wine'"), which indicates that speaking in tongues could be confused with drunkenness, strongly suggests that the phenomenon was in fact the same as that reflected in 1 Corinthians, i.e., unintelligible, ecstatic utterance (cf. Beare 1964: 238; D. M. Smith 1974: 313-14, 318; Best 1993: 138; Blomberg 1996: 350). Luke has retold the story to give it a powerful symbolic significance. (That two quite different phenomena are referred to, ecstatic utterance in 1 Corinthians and foreign languages in Acts 2, is a less likely option; but see Lindsell 1975: 677.)

Paul does not deny the validity of speaking in tongues; indeed, he claims the gift himself (1 Cor 14:18). But while it may build up the faith of an individual, it does not edify the church (14:4). Therefore he discourages its use in public worship; if it is permitted, it must be accompanied by "interpretation." Paul's advice in 1 Cor 14 embodies four basic principles that should govern public worship (cf. Martin 1992: 1017-18): intelligibility (v. 19), the effect on outsiders (vv. 23-25), upbuilding of the community (v. 26), and order (v. 40). On the basis of these criteria, Paul rates prophecy as the most important of the specialized gifts for public worship (v. 1).

Paul stresses that the more sensational and abnormal gifts are not the most important ones. It is noteworthy that in both lists in 1 Cor 12, "speaking with tongues" is placed last. Some kind of order of importance is suggested in 12:28. All gifts do have their place, and what counts most of all is that all members of the church work together for the good of the whole body (cf. 12:7). Those who are "helpers," working quietly in the background, are inspired by the Spirit just as much as a preacher proclaiming an eloquent message.

c. Testing the Spirits

The gift of the Spirit, while a tremendous source of life and power for God's people, was also a source of problems and controversy. There were those who for reasons of prestige, power, or even financial gain claimed to be endowed by the Spirit when they in fact were not. An important but difficult task for the NT church was that of "testing the spirits."

i. Test Everything

Paul is aware of the fact that "the spirit of the world" is at work as well as "the Spirit that is from God" (1 Cor 2:12); thus one of the gifts of the Spirit is in fact "the discernment *(diakrisis)* of spirits" (12:10). Paul suggests criteria for discernment. In 12:1-3 it is suggested that the Spirit is truly at work only when he leads people to confess the Lordship of Christ. If a "different gospel" is preached, then it must be the work of a "different spirit" (2 Cor 11:4). In 1 Thess 5:19-22 Paul advises, "Do not quench the Spirit. Do not despise the words of prophets, but test everything; hold fast to what is good; abstain from every form of evil."

ii. Give Me This Power

The story of Simon the magician in Acts 8:9-24 is designed to serve as a warning. When he saw how Peter and John conferred the Spirit, Simon offered them money, saying, "Give me also this power." No doubt he would regard the cash payment as an investment that would soon be recouped by use of his new powers. The point of the story is that the power of the Spirit can never be controlled or manipulated by humans, and anyone who wishes or claims to use the Spirit for personal gain is a fraud.

iii. Do Not Believe Every Spirit

A major purpose of the Johannine Epistles is to counter a false teaching being propagated by persons who claimed to be inspired by the Spirit. John therefore counsels his readers: "Do not believe every spirit, but *test the spirits* to see whether they are from God" (1 John 4:1). In 1 John two tests are recommended, one doctrinal and one ethical. The false teaching was probably a form of Docetism that denied the reality of the incarnation (Christ only appeared to be human; from *dokeō* = "seem, appear"). No form of teaching that denies that Christ was both fully divine *and* fully human is inspired by God's Spirit: "By this you know the Spirit of God: every spirit that confesses that Jesus Christ has come in the flesh is from God, and every spirit that does not confess Jesus is not from God" (1 John 4:2; cf. 2:22-23; 2 John 7). After warning against such false teaching (1 John 4:1-6), John goes on (4:7-21) to discuss an equally important test: the presence or absence of God-inspired love *(agapē)* that translates into practice. "Whoever does not love does not know God. . . . Those who say, 'I love God,' and hate their brothers or sisters, are liars. . . . Those who love God must love their brothers and sisters also" (4:8, 20-21).

5-3.5. SPIRIT, SON, AND FATHER

a. The Holy Spirit

In striking contrast to the OT (above, 5-1.1c), in the NT the Spirit is frequently referred to as "the Holy Spirit" (cf. Moule 1978: 22-23); the phrase occurs about 90 times spread throughout the NT (except for Revelation). The largest number of usages occurs in Luke-Acts (53), reflecting the strong stress on the Spirit especially in Acts (40). Paul uses "Holy Spirit" 15 times, and it appears also in Matthew (5), Mark (4), John (3), the Pastorals (2), Hebrews (5), 1 Peter (1), 2 Peter (1), and Jude (1). This appellation reflects *continuity* in the biblical understanding of the Spirit. The Holy Spirit of the NT is the same Spirit of God proclaimed as active in creation and history and promised as an eschatological gift in the OT. But it also reflects the distinctive NT emphasis on God, active as Holy Spirit, in a new and fuller way, as the climax of the Christ event.

b. Spirit of God/Spirit of Christ

While the NT recognizes throughout that the "Holy Spirit" is the Spirit of God, yet the giving of the Spirit as part of the inauguration of the new order is closely associated with the person of Jesus as the new Servant of God. As Beker (1958) observes, "in Christian experience the Spirit is inseparably connected with the Messiah, i.e. with the historical event of Jesus Christ" (5).

Paul regards the Spirit as "the Spirit of God" (1 Cor 2:11; Rom 8:9, 11) that God has bestowed (Rom 5:5; 1 Cor 2:12), although he can think of the Spirit as distinguished from God (Rom 8:26-27). Yet he can also speak of "the Spirit of Christ" (Rom 8:9), of God sending "the Spirit of his Son" (Gal 4:6), and of receiving "the help of the Spirit of Jesus Christ" (Phil 1:19). In 2 Cor 3:17-18 Paul goes so far as to say that "the Lord is the Spirit," but this has to be read in the context of his discussion of the true interpretation of the OT. It does not in fact constitute an outright identification of Christ with the Spirit, and it is noteworthy that in the very same verse Paul refers to "the Spirit of the Lord." Paul, suggests Whiteley (1964), "would have said that the Father acts *in* the Son and *as* the Spirit" (127). Since God has acted fully and finally in Christ, the Spirit that is at work in God's people is both the Spirit of God and the Spirit of Christ. That Paul closely identified yet also distinguished Father, Son, and Spirit is suggested by the references to the "same Spirit," "same Lord," and "same God" in 1 Cor 12:4-6, and by the threefold formula in 2 Cor 13:13: "The grace of the Lord Jesus Christ, the love of God, and the communion of the Holy Spirit be with all of you."

Acts 2 separates the giving of the Spirit from the historical Jesus, yet Peter's sermon declares, "Being therefore exalted at the right hand of God, and having received from the Father the promise of the Holy Spirit, he [i.e., Christ] has poured out this that you both see and hear" (Acts 2:33). Here it is clearly Jesus who at his exaltation received the promised Spirit as well as the power to pour it out upon the church (see the discussion in M. M. B. Turner 1982). This accords with the saying of John the Baptist, preserved in all four Gospels, that Jesus will baptize with the Holy Spirit (above, 5-3.1b). For Luke, as for Paul, the Spirit can be spoken of as "the Spirit of Jesus" (Acts 16:7).

In John the Paraclete is sent *from* the Father (John 14:26) and "comes from" (*ekporeuetai* = "proceeds from") the Father (15:26), but John brings the giving of the Spirit into even closer association with Christ by placing the event on Easter evening and having Jesus himself (resurrected but not ascended; cf. 20:17) exercise the divine prerogative of breathing breath/life/spirit into the new people of God (20:22; cf. 1:33; cf. above, 5-3.3c.ii). Thus John can also say that Jesus sends the Spirit (15:26; 16:7).

New Testament: Consummation

5-4. HIS SPIRIT AS A GUARANTEE

While the NT overwhelmingly refers to the Spirit as a present reality in the life of the church, and in the life of the believer, the Spirit also has a role to play in passages that look forward to the final consummation.

5-4.1. I WAS IN THE SPIRIT

As in the OT, the Spirit inspires visions of the final consummation. The Spirit inspires prophecy that includes foretelling of future events as in the prophecies of Agabus (Acts 11:28; 21:10-11; see Bruce 1963: 181), and in the case of the disciples at Tyre (Acts 21:4). This is especially the case in the book of Revelation. The message given to John to transmit to the churches concerns both present and future: "Write what you have seen, what is, and what is to take place after this" (1:19). John claims to write "prophecy" (1:3), and this is closely linked with his claim to be inspired by the Spirit. At the outset he tells of how he "was in the Spirit on the Lord's day" (1:10), and this claim is emphasized throughout the work (4:2; 14:13; 17:3; 21:10; 22:17). The recipients of each of the seven letters are urged to "listen to what the Spirit is saying to the churches" (2:7; etc.). John bears his testimony through "the spirit of prophecy" (19:10).

5-4.2. HE HAS GIVEN US HIS SPIRIT

The Spirit does not figure *in* visions of the end; but as a present reality in the life of the church and of the believer, the Spirit is seen as anticipating and guaranteeing the final consummation; "it is the proleptic realization of the kingdom of God in history pointing to the completion of our salvation" (Beker 1958: 6). Heb 6:4-5 says of those who have been "enlightened" and "have shared in the Holy Spirit," that they "have tasted the goodness of the word of God and *the powers of the age to come.*" For Paul in particular, "the Spirit is the power of the new age already broken into the old, not so as to bring the old to an end or render it wholly ineffective, but so as to enable the believer to live in and through the old age in the power and in the light of the new" (Kamlah, Dunn, and Brown 1978: 701). Possession of the Spirit is a ground of *hope* for the future: in Gal 5:5 Paul says that "through the Spirit, by faith, we eagerly wait for the hope of righteousness," and in Rom 15:13 he prays that the Roman Christians "may abound in hope by the power of the Holy Spirit" (cf. 5:5).

5-4.3. THE SPIRIT AS THE FIRST INSTALLMENT

In three passages the Spirit is referred to as an *arrabōn,* a word translated into English in a variety of ways (see Ewert 1983: 285-88). As a business term it means a first installment, deposit, or down payment "that pays a part of the purchase price in advance and so secures a legal claim to the article in question, or makes a contract valid"; it is "a payment that obligates the contracting party to make further payments" (Arndt and Gingrich 1957: 109). Whereas a pledge may be returned to the owner when full payment is made (cf. Gen 38:20, 23), a first installment is "earnest money" which "represents a real part of the object of contract, given in advance both to insure final payment and also to contribute to it" (Ahern 1947: 182).

In 2 Cor 1:22 Paul says God gave us "his Spirit in our hearts as a first installment." In 5:1-5, in the context of a discussion of the future life, Paul declares that "he who has prepared us for this very thing is God, who has given us the Spirit as a guarantee"; the life the believer now experiences in the Spirit anticipates and guarantees the greater gift of life beyond death (cf. Rom 8:11). Eph 1:13-14 refers to "the promised Holy Spirit," which is "the guarantee of our inheritance" (RSV); here, in more general terms, the Spirit anticipates and guarantees the inheritance *(klēronomia)* that awaits believers, i.e., the coming kingdom (Eph 5:5).

Thus "the Spirit whom God has given them is for Christians the guarantee of their full future possession of salvation" (Behm 1964: 475). The experience of the Spirit in the life of believers and in the life of the church is both a foretaste of the coming kingdom and a guarantee of the certainty of its coming. "This Christ-like relation with God, this sonship brought by the Spirit, this beginning of membership in the family of God, was a guarantee that ultimately the process would be completed and God's design for man's glorious destiny would be achieved" (Moule 1978: 34).

The understanding of the Spirit as a guarantee also serves as a reminder of the imperfections of the present life. "The Spirit itself warns us to be modest in our claims. Even the most Spirit-filled community is not yet in heaven but only in a threatened, groaning and dying world. The fulfilment will come only when God does away with all our affliction, suffering and death" (Schweizer 1980: 110). But the gift of the Spirit is supremely a ground for hope: it testifies to the dawning of the new order and provides a foretaste of the triumph of that order at the final consummation.

5-4.4. THE SPIRIT AS THE FIRST FRUITS

A similar thought is expressed by Paul using the OT idea of the "first fruits" *(aparchē)*, the offering of the first portion that represents the whole harvest (see Ewert 1983: 288-90; Fee 1994: 807). "We ourselves," says Paul in Rom 8:23, "who have the first fruits of the Spirit, groan inwardly while we wait for adoption, the redemption of our bodies." Here again the present possession of the Spirit is for believers the first installment and guarantee of redemption which is in part a present experience but in part still a future hope. It may be noted that the OT offering of the first fruits was linked with the feast of weeks (Pentecost), which for Christians was associated with the giving of the Spirit (cf. Murray 1975: 167).

5-4.5. THE SPIRIT AS A SEAL

Receiving the Spirit can also be referred to as being "sealed" *(sphragizō* = "to seal, mark as a means of identification"). In 2 Cor 1:21-22, Eph 1:13, and 4:30 believers are said to be marked with the seal of the Spirit. "Tombs, documents, books, etc., were sealed as a means of attestation and security, so God gives the seal of the Spirit as assurance of ownership and future inheritance" (Moody 1968: 103). Each of the three texts clearly has *future* reference: "those who have the Spirit belong to God and have the deep assurance that when God brings in the final stage of redemption he will acknowledge them" (Ewert 1983: 282; cf. Fee 1994: 807-8).

Early Church Fathers often speak of baptism as a "seal," and it is possible, though by no means certain, that these texts have baptism in mind in view of the close links between baptism and receiving the Spirit (see Ewert 1983: 282; contra Parratt 1971: 268-70).

5-5. THE SPIRIT: THEOLOGICAL REFLECTIONS

1. The theme of the Holy Spirit is a central one for BT. It is a *biblical* theme, for the Spirit who occupies such a central place in the NT is the same Spirit witnessed to in the OT. That Spirit was experienced only in a limited way in the OT, for the Spirit would be poured out in full measure on God's people only in the new age. The NT proclaims that this promise has been fulfilled; the Spirit rested uniquely on Christ as the new Servant of God, and was then poured out on the new people of God, following his death and resurrection, as the culmination of the Christ event that inaugurated the new age. All the main NT witnesses agree that everyone who has faith and is incorporated into the new people of God receives the gift of the Spirit. It is the Spirit who guides and empowers the church.

2. Western theology has tended to emphasize the role of the Spirit in the historical order, and in God's relations with his people (cf. Heron 1983: 59). It is important, however, to remember the witness of the OT to the operation of God's Spirit in the created order (cf. 5-1.2 and 5-1.3). It is through his Spirit that God creates and sustains and gives life to all things, and it is through his Spirit that God confers gifts such as wisdom and artistic ability. "Western theology has tended to confine the activity of the Creator Spirit to the redemptive realm of the church, but Eastern Orthodoxy, which employs Psalm 104 in daily worship, has vigorously challenged this confinement and contended for both a creative and a redemptive work of the Spirit. At least on this point the West can learn from the East, for creation cannot be excluded as a realm in which the Spirit works" (Moody 1968: 28).

3. The saying on the blasphemy against the Holy Spirit (5-3.2a.ii) has long been an exegetical, theological, and pastoral problem (see McKnight 1996). The NT consistently portrays God as more than willing to forgive sin, but it does recognize that repentance is a prerequisite for receiving that forgiveness. What Jesus is referring to therefore is the situation where a person has become incapable of repentance. By calling the works of God's Spirit the works of the devil, Jesus' opponents did precisely that. "To call good evil in this way is to deliberately pervert all moral values, and to persist in such an attitude can only result in a progressive blunting of moral sensibility, the ultimate conclusion of which will be to become so hardened in sin as to lose for ever the capacity to recognize the value of goodness and to be attracted by it. To reach such a state is to be incapable of repentance; the sinner has shut himself out, irrevocably and eter-

nally, from the forgiving mercy of God" (O. E. Evans 1956-57: 244). It follows that people of tender conscience who worry and even agonize over whether they might have committed the sin against the Holy Spirit need to be assured that their very anxiety is proof that they have not committed it (cf. Moule 1978: 33).

4. Within the biblical material, and especially the NT, there is a dialectic between two major emphases that may conveniently be labeled by the phrases "Do not quench the Spirit" and "Test the spirits"; this dialectic is found *within* both Paul and John, as well as elsewhere in the NT.

a. *Do not quench the Spirit.* On the one hand, the NT stresses again and again the central role of the Spirit. "No one can say 'Jesus is Lord' except by the Holy Spirit" (1 Cor 12:3), and Acts, the Epistles, and Revelation alike portray the Spirit as the dynamic, driving force within the church. Historically, when the Spirit has not been given this central place within the church, the living body has withered away to dry bones. One tendency has been to tie the gift of the Spirit to baptism, so that through an extreme sacramentalism the church seeks to control and dispense the Spirit (cf. Dunn 1970: 224). Pentecostalism in the early twentieth century and the various forms of "neo-Pentecostalism" or the "charismatic movement" (even within the Roman Catholic Church) in the later twentieth century can certainly be seen as reactions against both a Protestantism and a Roman Catholicism that had become institutionalized and not sufficiently open to the winds of the Spirit. Over against those who have argued that the gifts of the Spirit were confined to the apostolic age, "there is no exegetical warrant for claiming that any of the gifts have ceased" (Blomberg 1996: 351). All Christians who accept Scripture as normative should agree that "there is nothing that the church needs more today than to be filled with the Spirit of God. Such fulness is the most important key to victorious Christian living and a radiant Christian witness" (Hoekema 1972: 79).

b. *Test the spirits.* On the other hand, much of the NT material betrays an awareness of abuses and excesses against which the church must be on guard.

i. Anyone can claim to be inspired by the Spirit and can even seek, like Simon Magus, to benefit financially from such claims. The gift of discernment is required, and the canonical NT furnishes important guidelines (5-3.4c). The Spirit will indeed guide believers into all truth, but it cannot be at variance with the truth that has already been fully and finally revealed in the Christ event. This criterion is as valid today as ever in evaluating those who claim new revelation through the Spirit.

ii. The NT provides no basis for requiring a "second blessing" or subsequent "baptism with the Spirit," as required by many Pentecostal/neo-Pentecostal groups. *All* believers receive the gift of the Spirit when they become Christians and continue to be guided and empowered by the Spirit throughout their lives (see Dunn 1970; Hoekema 1972; Koenig 1978: 121; Moule 1978: 85; Ewert 1983: 43-45).

iii. While the Spirit is an energizing and inspiring force, the Bible warns against an unbalanced approach that overemphasizes the emotional and even the irrational aspects of Spirit possession. Ecstatic phenomena are known to the OT, but in the Prophets especially, inspiration does not bypass human reason but employs it. While Paul is loath to criticize any manifestation of the Spirit, he strongly commends those characterized by intelligibility, edification, and order (1 Cor 14). It is difficult to see how a particular ecstatic manifestation such as "speaking with tongues" can be considered an essential and indispensable proof of reception of the Spirit. This is precisely what Paul denies (cf. Sweet 1967: 240, 256-57); he does not regard it as a gift appropriate to all believers (1 Cor 12:30), and twice puts it at the end of lists of spiritual gifts (cf. Hoekema 1972: 30-54). On the other hand, he does concede that it can be of value to some individuals (cf. the discussion in Best 1993: 126-47). The gift that tops the list in 1 Cor 13 is love, which in the NT is always the supreme test of possessing the Spirit: "ultimately, it is not the gifts themselves that count, valuable as they are, but the love towards others for which they equip believers" (Koenig 1978: 117).

5. The NT identifies the Holy Spirit experienced in the life and worship of the early church with the same Spirit of God recognized in the OT as active in both the created order and the historical order. The NT, however, links the Spirit, especially as poured out at Pentecost, in a unique way with the Christ event. It does not enter the field of theological speculation, but it recognizes the Spirit as both the Spirit of God and the Spirit of Christ (cf. above, 5-3.5b). The baptism of Jesus in particular can be seen as a manifestation of the triune God, as the voice of the Father identifies Jesus as the beloved Son and the Spirit descends upon him in the form of a dove (cf. Cronk 1982: 134). As already noted, the NT, especially in a series of "triadic formulae" (see 1-3.3c; 1-5.5), links the Holy Spirit closely with God as Father and with Christ as the Son. These formulae are pointers to the key role of the Spirit throughout the NT, and to the fact that after the Christ event the church continued to experience the presence of God, incarnate in Christ, in and through the Holy Spirit. Here again, therefore, it may fairly be claimed that the NT does provide the data from which the doctrine of the Trinity was constructed as, over a period of time and under the guidance of the Holy Spirit, the church was led to summarize the testimony of Scripture and to formulate its understanding of the one God as Father, Son, and Holy Spirit (cf. Heron 1983: 46-48, 56-57, 60; Fee 1994: 831-42).

A SKETCH OF BIBLICAL THEOLOGY

CHAPTERS 6-10: GOD'S SERVANT

CHAPTER 6

The Messiah

Old Testament: Proclamation

6-1. THE LORD'S MESSIAH

Though God is wholly other than the created world and the world of human history, nevertheless he is active and works out his purpose in the world. He does this primarily through those he chooses to be his "servants." The word "servant" (*'ebhedh*) occurs frequently in the OT, where it can mean a slave or servant, a subject of a king, or a worshiper of a god (see C. R. North 1962: 292; Michel 1978: 608-10). The LXX translates *'ebhedh* either by *pais* (which can also mean boy, youth, or son) or by *doulos* (slave).

In the first instance it is the people of Israel who are called to be "the servant of the LORD":

Remember these things, O Jacob,
and Israel, for you are my servant. (Isa 44:21)

On Israel as God's servant, see more fully 11-1.2.

From within the people of Israel, however, God chooses a series of individuals, men and occasionally women, to be his servants. Moses is the servant of the LORD par excellence; the title is ascribed to him some forty times (see esp. Num 12:7). But kings, especially David, can also be called God's servant (2 Sam 3:18), as can priests (Ps 134:1), prophets (Amos 3:7), and the hero of a Wisdom Book, Job (Job 1:8). These servants play a role in God's purposes in the OT, but they have their limitations, and in time they become the basis for expectations of a future Servant of the LORD. The NT proclaims that Jesus both fulfills and transcends these expectations.

In the OT a person chosen to serve God in a special way can be called an "anointed one." The Hebrew term for "anointed one" is *māshîach*, from *māshach* = "anoint" (see D. S. Russell 1964: 304-7; Roberts 1992: 39-41; Kaiser

1995: 15-17). The Greek translation *christos* (hence "Christ") is an exact equivalent, derived from the verb *chriō* = "anoint." Anointing with oil was a ceremony by which a person was recognized and designated as one chosen by God to serve him in a specific way. In the OT we read of the anointing of *priests* (Exod 29:7, 29), including "the high priest who was anointed with the holy oil" (Num 35:25; cf. Lev 4:3, 5, 16); *prophets* (1 Kgs 19:16; cf. Ps 105:15); and especially *kings* (1 Sam 10:1; 16:13; 1 Kgs 1:32-40). The king in particular is frequently referred to as "the anointed of the LORD" (*mᵉshîach YHWH*) or "the Lord's messiah" (e.g., 1 Sam 24:6; 2 Sam 19:21; Lam 4:20).

The most surprising use of the term in the OT is found in Isa 45:1:

> Thus says the LORD to his *anointed,* to Cyrus,
>   whose right hand I have grasped
> to subdue nations before him.

Here a non-Israelite, the Persian king Cyrus, is described as God's anointed one. This is, however, quite in accordance with the basic biblical meaning: a "messiah" is an individual chosen by God to serve him in a specific way. Cyrus was the particular instrument chosen by God to deliver his people from exile.

"Messiah" thus refers in the first instance to *specific historical persons* chosen by God as his instruments: David is God's messiah, the high priest is God's messiah, Cyrus is God's messiah. These and other similar persons are chosen by God in the present, in history, and *not* as an ideal future figure. That development came later and is discussed in 6-2.

The OT proclaims that God makes himself known and leads his people through selected individuals, so that in this sense there are many "messiahs" in the OT. Here we employ the term *in a very general sense* and examine the various types of persons chosen by God to be his servants in the OT. In each case they form the basis for the *promise* of a future ideal figure (6-2), and in each case the NT claims that Jesus is the fulfillment of these hopes and promises (6-3). It is essential that the NT claim that Jesus is the promised "Messiah" or "Christ" be seen not just in the light of a relatively few OT "messianic prophecies," but against the broader background of God's dealings with his people through a variety of servants or mediators (cf. Gese 1981a: 142).

The scheme adopted here utilizes the three "offices" traditionally recognized as present in the OT: *king, priest,* and *prophet.* These are preceded by a study of *Moses,* who constitutes a very important messianic type, and are expanded by adding the *wise,* a badly neglected category in traditional BT.

6-1.1. GOD'S MESSIAHS: MOSES

Towering above the other servants of God in the OT is the figure of Moses. Historical scholars seek to separate out the portraits of Moses in the four hypothetical sources J, E, D, and P, emphasizing the *differences* among these portraits (see von Rad 1962: 289-96) and exhibiting various degrees of skepticism as to how much can be known about the Moses of history. BT does not deal with hypothetical reconstructions but with the composite picture of Moses found in the canonical text, however that may have come into being. While differences of emphasis may be detected, Moses emerges in the canonical text as a powerful and commanding figure. Even those who consider much of the material on Moses legendary acknowledge that "his character shines through" (S. B. Frost 1963: 48, 51; cf. Rendtorff 1968: 20). It is this composite, canonical character that influenced the NT and is thus the true subject of BT (cf. Parnham 1972).

In some ways unique and defying classification (cf. Eichrodt 1961: 289), Moses in other respects combines, to varying degrees, the other four messianic categories of prophet, priest, king, and sage.

Moses shares many of the features of the office of *prophet* (see Eakins 1977: 463-64), and is specifically designated as such: "By a prophet the LORD brought Israel up from Egypt" (Hos 12:13; cf. Deut 18:15, 18). In fact, later generations saw Moses as "Israel's prophet par excellence" (Rhodes 1977: 111). Like a prophet he experiences a call (Exod 3:1–4:17; see J. Baker 1965); speaks on behalf of God, prefacing his message with "Thus says the LORD" (Exod 5:1; etc.); performs signs and wonders (Deut 34:11-12; *Sir* 45:3); and prophesies in virtue of his possession of the Spirit (Num 11:16-29). His ministry is characterized by "selfless and persistent intercession" for his people (McBride 1990: 234; cf., e.g., Exod 32:31-32). Yet he is also regarded as superior to all other prophets: "Never since has there arisen a prophet in Israel like Moses" (Deut 34:10; cf. Num 12:6-8).

Moses also has a *priestly* role. He is of the tribe of Levi (Exod 2:1), and in the covenant ceremony of Exod 24 he builds an altar and officiates at the sacrifice. It is from the Mosaic legislation that the whole system of priesthood and sacrifice is derived, though it is with his brother Aaron that the Israelite priesthood finds its origin. In Ps 99:6 it is said that "Moses and Aaron were among his [God's] priests."

Nowhere in the canonical Scriptures is Moses specifically designated as *king,* though he performs royal functions in guiding, providing for, and judging the people (cf. Eakins 1977: 464-65). The question of the Hebrew in Exod 2:14, "Who made you a prince *(sar)* and a judge over us?" (RSV), is an example of dramatic irony; this is in effect what Moses became.

Similarly Moses has certainly some of the attributes and exercises some of the functions of a *sage;* he is the wise teacher of his people. He was brought up in the Egyptian court, one of the locations in which the international wisdom tradition flourished; Acts 7:22 probably reflects later Jewish tradition when it alludes to the fact that "Moses was instructed in all the wisdom of the Egyptians."

But as the exodus is a unique event in Israel's history, so Moses has three unique and unrepeatable roles: as *deliverer* of God's people from oppression, as *covenant mediator* (Deut 5:22-27), and above all as *lawgiver* (see further, 18-1.2a). "The LORD spoke to Moses" (Lev 16:1; Num 1:1; 9:1), and Moses conveyed the divine directions to the people. In contrast to founders of other religions, no laws or even "sayings" are attributed to Moses himself (cf. Eichrodt 1961: 295). He stands in a unique relationship to God; he alone is said to have communed with God "face to face" (Deut 34:10).

Despite all this, Moses is consistently recognized as a human figure (cf. McBride 1990: 230). He was guilty of the murder of an Egyptian (Exod 2:11-14). Because of a failure to trust God, he was not permitted to enter the Promised Land (Num 20:12; 27:12-14; Deut 32:51). There is never any suggestion that he is more than a human figure. The closest one comes to this is in the Deuterocanon, in the verses in praise of Moses in *Sir* 44:23–45:5, where it is said that

> He [God] made him [Moses] equal in glory to the holy ones,
> and made him great, to the terror of his enemies. (45:2)

No tomb of Moses was known (cf. Deut 34:6), and there is no sign of a cult of Moses. His greatness arises from the unique task with which he was entrusted by God.

The figure of Moses dominates Exodus through Deuteronomy. Surprisingly few references to Moses are found in the remaining books of the OT (cf. McBride 1990: 239); in them his foundational role is assumed rather than elaborated upon.

6-1.2. GOD'S MESSIAHS: KINGS

The OT understanding of kingship is fraught with ambiguity. Israel was surrounded by nations ruled by kings. One deeply rooted line of thought opposed the establishment of a monarchy: Israel is to be a *theocracy,* ruled by God alone (cf. J. Becker 1980: 14-17). Another line of thought saw the political and military necessity of *kingship,* presented the establishment of the monarchy as divinely directed, and developed a *royal theology.* The dialectic between these two approaches is finally resolved by the emergence of the expectation of the coming of a future, ideal king (cf. Brueggemann 1997: 600-621).

a. The Monarchy

In the narratives that lead up to the establishment of the monarchy, the strong tension between monarchic and antimonarchic views is evident (cf. Eichrodt 1961: 441-42). The "judges" were not kings, but military commanders with only temporary authority over the tribes. After the resounding victory over the Midianites, under the leadership of Gideon (Judg 6–8), "the Israelites said to Gideon, 'Rule over us, you and your son and your grandson also; for you have delivered us out of the hand of Midian'" (8:22). Gideon firmly turns down the proposal to establish a hereditary monarchy on the grounds that "I will not rule over you, and my son will not rule over you; the LORD will rule over you" (8:23). On this theocratic view the kingship of the LORD excludes any human monarch. The story of Gideon's son Abimelech (Judg 9) illustrates the dangers of a dictatorial monarch, and Jotham's fable (9:8-15) has been characterized as "the most forthright anti-monarchical poem in world literature" (von Rad 1962: 59).

In 1 Sam 8 it is the people who take the initiative and request the establishment of a monarchy, a request that displeases God, who tells Samuel, "They have not rejected you, but they have rejected me from being king over them" (v. 7; cf. 10:17-27; 12). These passages act as a counterbalance to the promonarchic view that comes to dominate.

After cataloguing the apostasy and anarchy of the period, the book of Judges pointedly remarks, "In those days there was no king in Israel; all the people did what was right in their own eyes" (17:6; 21:25; cf. 18:1; 19:1). In 1 Sam 9 and 11 it is God who takes the initiative in appointing Saul as the first king. Saul, of course, falls from grace, but with the appointment of David as king the promonarchic view triumphs. In the key passage, 2 Sam 7 (see J. Becker 1980: 25-31; Kaiser 1995: 77-83), David's request to build a "house" *(bayith),* i.e., a temple, is turned down, but he is granted a "house" in another sense. God reaffirms his choice of David as king and says to him through the prophet Nathan,

> Moreover the LORD declares to you that the LORD will make you a house. When your days are fulfilled and you lie down with your ancestors, I will raise up your offspring after you, who shall come forth from your body, and I will establish his kingdom. He shall build a house for my name, and I will establish the throne of his kingdom forever. I will be a father to him, and he shall be a son to me. When he commits iniquity, I will punish him with a rod such as mortals use. . . . But I will not take my steadfast love from him. . . . Your house and your kingdom shall be made sure forever before me; your throne shall be established forever. (vv. 11-16)

A royal dynasty is thereby established, descended from David (cf. Jer 33:17) and hence from the tribe of Judah, a development foreseen in Jacob's blessing of his son Judah: "The scepter shall not depart from Judah" (Gen 49:10), and also in Num 24:17 where Balaam prophesies:

> A star shall come out of Jacob,
>   and a scepter shall rise out of Israel.

b. The Royal Theology

Around the Davidic monarchy there developed what is best described as a "royal theology." Based on 2 Sam 7 and 23, it finds its fullest expression in the Royal Psalms (Pss 2; 18; 20; 21; 45; 72; 89; 101; 110; 132; 144), which were designed for use in the Jerusalem temple and originally referred to the existing king of Israel (cf. von Rad 1962: 318-24; Durham 1984: 425-29; Kaiser 1995: 83-90, 92-135).

According to the royal theology, the king as the LORD's "anointed" enjoys a special status. He is divinely chosen (Ps 89:3, 19), and God and king are bound together in a special *covenant* relationship. Looking back to the episode of 2 Sam 7, 2 Sam 23 interprets the relationship between God and the king in terms of covenant: "For he has made with me an everlasting covenant *(berîth 'ôlām)*" (v. 5; cf. 11-1.3a.iv). In Ps 89 God says,

> I have made a covenant with my chosen one,
>   I have sworn to my servant David:
> "I will establish your descendants forever,
>   and build your throne for all generations."
> (vv. 3-4; cf. 1 Kgs 8:23-24; Pss 72:5, 15; 132:11-12)

Isa 55:3 repeats the divine promise of an "everlasting covenant"; like Ps 89, 2 Isaiah speaks of "the inviolable promises of grace which Yahweh once made to David" (Eissfeldt 1962: 199). The Davidic covenant receives special emphasis in Chronicles (see 2 Chr 7:18; 13:5; 21:7). The king can be spoken of as God's son (cf. 2 Sam 7:14), but by adoption, not by nature (cf. Ps 2:7). See more fully, 8-1.5c.

In the royal theology the king is assured of victory over his enemies (Num 24:15-24; Pss 2:1-3; 89:23; 110:1, 5-6), and of universal dominion; as God's viceroy, he is said to rule the whole world (Pss 2:8; 72:8, 10-11). He virtually shares God's throne (Ps 110:1; see B. W. Anderson 1983: 190). The king will always be strengthened and supported by God (2 Sam 7:15; Ps 89:21). But the king is by no means an absolute ruler (cf. Brueggemann 1997: 606-14). He is expected to obey God's Law (Deut 17:14-20; 1 Kgs 9:3-9; Ps 89:30-34), and ideally his reign is one of justice, peace, and prosperity (Pss 72:1-7; 45:4, 6-7). The king has legal functions, acting in place of a court of appeal (cf. 1 Kgs 3:16-28); Ps 72:1-2 makes clear what is meant by the king "judging" the people (cf. Kraus 1986: 119):

> Give the king your justice, O God,
>   and righteousness to a king's son.
> May he judge your people with righteousness,
>   and your poor with justice.

In the OT king and people are closely bound together. In terms of the individual/community dialectic, the king represents the people: for example, he leads them in worship (1 Kgs 8:62) and intercedes for them (2 Chr 30:18-19). Through the king both divine blessing and divine punishment may be channeled to the people (see Fraine 1965: 152-69).

c. The Shepherd-King

The OT king may sound like an absolute ruler, but modern antimonarchical sentiment can easily blind us to the biblical ideal of kingship. The true king is above all the *shepherd* of his people, protecting them, caring for them, spending himself in their service (cf. G. E. Wright 1939; Thomson 1955). Of course, it is God himself who is the true Shepherd of Israel (Gen 49:24; Pss 23:1; 28:9; 80:1; cf. 1-1.4a), but "Moses, David and all the others to whom the task of governing His people is entrusted are under-shepherds, responsible to Him" (Bruce 1969: 101). In keeping with the OT understanding of the term "Messiah" (above, 6-1), God can even say of the Persian king Cyrus, "He is my shepherd, / and he shall carry out all my purpose" (Isa 44:28).

It is *David* who is the shepherd-king of Israel par excellence. The fact that as a boy David was a shepherd (1 Sam 16:11; 17:15) and knew what it was like to risk his own life to save his sheep (17:34-36), reinforces the sheep-shepherd metaphor.

> He [God] chose his servant David,
> and took him from the sheepfolds;
> from tending the nursing ewes he brought him
> to be the shepherd of his people Jacob,
> of Israel, his inheritance.
> With upright heart he tended them,
> and guided them with skillful hand. (Ps 78:70-72)

The tribes of Israel recognized that God had said to David: "It is you who shall be shepherd of my people Israel, you who shall be ruler over Israel" (2 Sam 5:2).

Significantly, the greater number of OT references are to the kings who *failed* to be shepherds of their people. Jeremiah condemns the rulers of Judah, shepherds "who have scattered my flock, and have driven them away, and have not attended to them" (Jer 23:1-2). In the first section of an extended sheep-shepherds allegory (Ezek 34), Ezekiel is even more outspoken in condemning "you shepherds of Israel who have been feeding yourselves!" (v. 2). In the absence of leadership,

> the people wander like sheep;
> they suffer for lack of a shepherd. (Zech 10:2)

Zechariah also condemns the leaders of the people (10:3; 11:4-17), including a shepherd "who does not care for the perishing, or seek the wandering, or heal the maimed, or nourish the healthy" (11:16), thus illustrating in reverse the functions of a true shepherd-king. In a stern word of judgment God says,

> "Awake, O sword, against my shepherd,
> against the man who is my associate,"
>   says the LORD of hosts.
> Strike the shepherd, that the sheep may be scattered. (13:7)

Here again, it is the failings of the actual leaders of Israel that pave the way for the expectation of a messianic shepherd-king.

d. Decline and Fall

The northern monarchy did not survive the fall of Samaria in 722 B.C. In the south the Davidic dynasty was maintained until the exile, despite the negative verdict pronounced on so many of the kings by the Deuteronomic Historian. The king at the time of the Babylonian assault, Jehoiachin, was carried off to exile. Nevertheless, 2 Kings concludes on what is obviously intended to be a note of hope: "In the thirty-seventh year of the exile . . . King Evil-merodach of Babylon . . . released King Jehoiachin of Judah from prison; he spoke kindly to him" (25:27-28). Despite the catastrophe that had befallen God's people, nevertheless the Davidic dynasty still survived and there was still hope that a descendant of David would once again sit upon the throne (cf. McKenzie 1974: 285-86).

The narratives that relate the postexilic period provide an astonishing anticlimax. Though the book of Ezra mentions two persons of royal descent, Sheshbazzar (1:8, 11; 5:14) and Zerubbabel (3:2, 8; 5:2; cf. Hag 2:2-4, 20-23; Zech 4:6-10), in the immediate postexilic period, thereafter the monarchy simply disappears. (The Maccabean dynasty that lasted approximately a century in the second and first centuries B.C. was not of Davidic descent.) Over against the promise of a continuing Davidic monarchy, there stands the reality of a dynasty that had come to an end.

6-1.3. GOD'S MESSIAHS: HIGH PRIESTS

a. The High Priest

The Torah provides for a hereditary priesthood in Israel. The role of regular priests in ministering to the people will be discussed in 15-1.2; here we are concerned only with the high priest, who plays a major role in the relationship between God and people in the OT.

This servant of God is referred to as *hakōhēn hagādhôl*, "the high priest" (lit. "the great priest"), less often as *hakōhēn hārō'sh*, "the chief priest" (lit. "the head priest"), or quite often simply as *hakōhēn*, "the priest." The LXX uses the term *archiereus*, "high priest," only five times in the OT (forty-one times in the Deuterocanon), but this is the term used in the NT.

The office was established under the Mosaic Law. Aaron, the brother of Moses, was the first high priest, and all subsequent holders of the office had to trace their descent from him. Moses was directed to consecrate Aaron in a ceremony that involved sacrifice, washing with water, robing with special garments, and anointing with oil (Exod 29:1-9). Because anointing was an essential part of this ritual, the high priest could be referred to as *hakōhēn hamāshîach*, "the anointed priest" (lit. "the priest, the anointed one" or "the priest, the messiah"). In Lev 21:10 he is referred to as "the priest who is exalted above his fellows, on whose head the anointing oil has been poured."

The high priest played a major role in the ritual of the Day of Atonement (Lev 16) when, as the representative of God's people, he once a year made atonement for their sins. The high priest was subject to additional restrictions to avoid ritual defilement (21:10-15), yet there is frank recognition of the fact that the high priest himself is a sinful human being; hence on the Day of Atonement he has first of all to offer a sin offering for himself (16:6, 11; cf. 4:3-12).

In the earlier period the high priest's duties were religious only, but in the postexilic period the office assumed a new importance. After the return the high priest Jeshua and the Davidic Zerubbabel appear alongside each other as joint leaders of the restored community (Ezra 3:2); they are "the two anointed ones" of Zech 4:14. With the disappearance of the monarchy, "the high priest . . . acquired much of the dignity that had formerly belonged to the king" (Abba 1962b: 878). Under Persian, then Greek rulers, and in NT times under the Roman Empire the high priest acted as representative of the people and was the closest the Jews had to a head of state. As such he presided over the Sanhedrin, the Jewish council that was allowed limited powers by the Romans.

b. Melchizedek

The OT speaks of another major priestly figure earlier than and quite unconnected with the priesthood established under Moses.

In Gen 14:17-24 Abram is met by "King Melchizedek of Salem," who is "priest of God Most High." Melchizedek blessed Abram, and received a tithe from him.

In the Royal Psalm 110, probably a coronation liturgy (cf. Kraus 1986: 112), the king is told:

The LORD has sworn and will not change his mind,
  "You are a priest forever according to the order of Melchizedek." (v. 4)

David evidently claimed the right to exercise priestly as well as kingly functions (cf. 2 Sam 6:13-14; 8:18); by his conquest of Jerusalem he had become the successor of the ancient priest-kings of the city (cf. Ringgren 1956: 15). Similarly, Solomon "blessed all the assembly of Israel" (1 Kgs 8:14) and "offered sacrifice before the LORD" (8:62; cf. 3:4), combining priestly with royal functions.

6-1.4. GOD'S MESSIAHS: PROPHETS

A prophet (Heb. *nābhî'* probably = "one who calls, declares, proclaims"; Gk. *prophētēs* = "one who speaks on behalf of another," i.e., God) is one who declares a message from God. "The prophets" are a varied group, but they and their message constitute a major component part of the OT (see von Rad 1965; Winward 1969; J. M. Ward 1991; Sawyer 1993; Brueggemann 1997: 622-49).

Two main groups of prophets appear in the OT: the earlier prophets who figure in the Historical Books (known in the Hebrew canon as the Former Prophets), and the so-called writing prophets, i.e., those who have a book named after them (known in the Hebrew canon as the Latter Prophets). The earlier prophets are known to us primarily through narratives, though accounts of messages they delivered are also preserved. The books of the writing prophets consist mainly of the words of the prophets, though they also contain some historical, biographical, and even autobiographical material. The term "writing prophets," though commonly used, is misleading; while prophets may occasionally have written down (Isa 30:8) or dictated (Jer 36) their message, they were first and foremost preachers whose words were recorded, compiled, and eventually formed into books by their disciples (cf. Isa 8:16; see Winward 1969: 23-26).

The earlier prophets include Samuel (1 Sam 3:20; Acts 13:20), Nathan (2 Sam 7; 12), Ahijah (1 Kgs 11:29-39), and Micaiah (22:5-28). But the outstanding examples are the ninth-century prophets Elijah (who came to be thought of as the prototypical prophet) and Elisha; both of these are the subject of narrative cycles (Elijah in 1 Kgs 17–2 Kgs 2 and Elisha in 2 Kgs 2–8). They are colorful characters whose ministries are characterized not only by fearless proclamation of the word of the LORD, but also by the working of miracles (cf. Winward 1969: 18). Elijah is credited with seven miracles, and Elisha, who inherited a double portion of his master's spirit (2 Kgs 2:9-12), with fourteen (cf. *Sir* 48:12-14). These mighty works included healing the sick (2 Kgs 5), feeding the hungry (1 Kgs 17:8-16; 2 Kgs 4:42-44), and raising the dead (1 Kgs 17:17-24; 2 Kgs 4:32-37).

The writing prophets are divided into the Major Prophets — Isaiah, Jeremiah, Ezekiel, and Daniel — and the twelve Minor Prophets, or "the Book of the Twelve" (Hosea through Malachi). Historical scholarship plays an important role in seeking to reconstruct the original setting of these prophets and of their message.

Historically these prophets were preceded by individuals known as "seers" (*rō'eh; rā'āh* = "to see"), who figured earlier in Israel's history (cf. Eichrodt 1961: 296-303); according to 1 Sam 9:9, "the one who is now called a prophet was formerly called a seer." They also stand in some relation to earlier bands of prophets, a movement labeled by Eichrodt as "Nabism" (1961: 309-38) and characterized by possession of the Spirit (cf. 5-1.5a), ecstatic behavior, and religious dance. After his anointing Saul was directed to a certain location: "There . . . you will meet a band of prophets coming down from the shrine with harp, tambourine, flute, and lyre playing in front of them; they will be in a prophetic frenzy. Then the spirit of the LORD will possess you, and you will be in a prophetic frenzy along with them and be turned into a different person" (1 Sam 10:5-6; cf. v. 13, which indicates that the phenomenon was short-lived; cf. also 19:20). We hear also of cultic prophets attached to local shrines, and royal prophets who functioned at the court (on these, see further 15-1.3).

What is often called "classical prophecy" emerged from these earlier movements but went on to become something distinctive (see Eichrodt 1961: 338-91; von Rad 1965: 6-14 stresses the discontinuity with these earlier movements). Ecstatic elements became much less important, and the main emphasis shifted to the *word* of God declared by the prophet and then written down and preserved for future generations. That word was received by the prophets sometimes in the form of "visions" (e.g., the five visions of Amos 7:1–9:4, the eight visions of Zech 1:7–6:15), but also in the form of "auditions" in which the prophet heard the words of the message he was to declare. Thus Amos, for example, says both "This is what the Lord GOD *showed* me" (Amos 7:1) and "Then the LORD *said* to me" (8:2). Prophetic oracles are generally poetic in form. Literary study of the various forms of prophetic speech has greatly enhanced our understanding of their message (see Patterson 1993; Sawyer 1993: 26-41).

The great prophets were essentially individuals (Eichrodt 1961: 343) who experienced a *call* from God in the form of a radical irruption of the divine into their lives (von Rad 1965: 53-69). According to Amos 7:15, "the LORD took me from following the flock"; Isaiah heard God's call while worshiping in the Jerusalem temple (Isa 6). The calls described in most detail are those of Jeremiah (Jer 1) and Ezekiel (Ezek 1–3). With these we may compare the call of Moses (Exod 3:1–4:17). The call narratives exhibit a common form (Baltzer 1968: 568-70), and in each case the call leads into a *commissioning* of the prophet to declare God's word.

The prophets' task was seldom an easy one, and they frequently faced unpopularity and opposition (e.g., 1 Kgs 22:27; Jer 38:1-13). In calling Jeremiah God told him, "I . . . have made you today a fortified city, an iron pillar, and a bronze wall, against the whole land" (Jer 1:18). Their life was made even more difficult at times by the existence of "false prophets," who typically told their hearers what they wanted to hear, as in the cases of the four hundred prophets who assured King Jehoshaphat of victory (1 Kgs 22:6) and Hananiah, who promised a quick return from exile (Jer 28).

Their primary task was to declare "the word of the LORD" (*d⁰bhar YHWH*) to his people in particular historical situations. The prophets are authoritative messengers sent from God to his people (cf. J. F. Ross 1962). "These uncredentialed, authoritative speakers do not utter universal truths, but speak concretely to a particular time, place and circumstance" (Brueggemann 1997: 624). The phrase "the word of the LORD came to *X*" occurs more than 120 times in the OT (von Rad 1965: 87). They delivered oracles that typically began either "Hear the word of the LORD" (Isa 1:10; etc.) or "Thus says the Lord GOD" (7:7; etc.). While their message was primarily directed to Israel, they also proclaimed God's word to other nations.

Their words could at times be made more forceful by the use of "prophetic symbolism." Thus, for example, Ahijah tore a new garment into twelves pieces to symbolize the coming breakup of the united kingdom (1 Kgs 11:29-31), and Jeremiah shattered an earthenware jar to symbolize the coming destruction of Jerusalem (Jer 19). These acted-out messages were no doubt thought of not just as forecasting events but in a sense as actually setting the events in motion.

Prophets stood in a close relationship with God's people, identifying with them in their sinfulness (Isa 6:5; Ezek 4:4-6) and sharing in their suffering (Jer 4:19-20). "Everywhere there is evident a sincere and sympathetic identification between the divine messenger and the members of the Chosen People" (Fraine 1965: 171). Another aspect of their ministry was intercession on behalf of the people (e.g., Amos 7:2-3; Jer 7:16; 27:18). The prophets "entered into real dialogue with Yahweh, sometimes even to the point of expostulation and argument. At times their intercessions were the occasion for Yahweh to change plans out of compassion, but this does not mean that they controlled Yahweh; God listened and was affected" (Rhodes 1977: 125).

It is true that in a sense the prophets introduced neither a new doctrine of God nor a new ethic (Eichrodt 1961: 352). Rather they brought the demand of the God of the covenant to bear on every aspect of the life of the nation, shattering the complacency of those who assumed that "God is on our side" or that God can be worshiped in the cult regardless of the moral standards of individuals or of society.

It has long been fashionable among modern historical scholars to declare that the prophets "were not foretellers, but forthtellers." This may have been a helpful corrective if prophecy was thought of purely in terms of prediction; the prophets were indeed deeply concerned with the contemporary social, political, economic, and religious life of Israel. But prediction remains a major element in the OT prophets. In the Historical Books prophecy/fulfillment is an important literary feature (see L. L. Thompson 1978: 126-27; Sawyer 1993: 16-18). See, for example, Elijah's prophecies of the deaths of Ahab (1 Kgs 21:19) and Jezebel (21:23), which are followed in due course with accounts of their deaths as prophesied (22:37-38; 2 Kgs 9:30-37). Whether or not the word spoken by a prophet takes place or proves true is the criterion for distinguishing a true from a false prophet (Deut 18:22; see, however, 13:1-6). In the prophetic books future prophecies play a major role. Such prophecies can be broadly classified as oracles of judgment and oracles of salvation. "The form of the prophets' message is the word of God to Israel, and its substance is God's righteous judgment and gracious redemption" (J. M. Ward 1991: 18; cf. Winward 1969: 31-33). Oracles of judgment are frequently preceded by a searching analysis of the conditions of society; on the ethical teaching of the prophets, see 18-1.2b. Conditional prophecies are found that say, in effect, *if* you mend your ways, then you will be spared (e.g., Jer 7:5-7). But when it became clear that the people would not repent, prophetic oracles simply proclaimed future judgment. Such prophecies, however, are balanced by oracles of salvation; the prophets saw "light at the end of the tunnel" in the form of a coming new age.

6-1.5. GOD'S MESSIAHS: THE WISE

The traditional classification of "prophet, priest, and king" omits an office that is important in BT, namely, "the wise," those who are the teachers of the Wisdom tradition (see also 15-1.4). Anyone in Israel who exhibited certain qualities could be deemed "wise," but many references to "the wise" point to something more than this — to a specific class or group whose function was to study and propagate "Wisdom." Attention is often drawn to the threefold classification in Jer 18:18: "For the law shall not perish from the *priest*, nor counsel from the *wise*, nor the word from the *prophet*" (RSV; cf. Ezek 7:26). Here "the wise" appears as a category alongside priests and prophets (cf. Crenshaw 1981: 27-28). *Sir* 38:24–39:11 clearly points to "the scribe" who studies Wisdom as a separate class. Recent biblical scholarship has done much to recover the significance of OT Wisdom and the role of "the wise" (cf. the discussion "The Sage as Mediator" in Brueggemann 1997: 680-704). A marked feature of this tradition is the existence of wise women as well as wise men; on this see 15-1.5b.ii.

Wisdom appears to have flourished in a variety of settings in Israel, though information about the bearers of this tradition is not as detailed or as specific as we might wish (see Clements 1992: 20-26). Traditionally Wisdom is associated with King Solomon (1 Kgs 3:3-28; 4:29-34; 10:1-10), and hence also with the royal court. Government officials were educated and literate and thus equipped to collect and codify Wisdom material. Royal counselors (e.g., Ahithophel, 2 Sam 16:23) were reckoned as wise. Some Wisdom material suggests a court setting (Prov 14:28; 16:12; etc.), though not necessarily a royal origin (Eccl 4:13; 10:20). Historically this is almost certainly the channel by which Egyptian Wisdom influenced Israel.

There is also evidence of a whole other area of popular, folk, clan, or family Wisdom in which traditional teaching was passed down from one generation to the next (see Morgan 1981: 39-41, 54). 1 Sam 24:13, for example, cites an "ancient proverb" that says, "Out of the wicked comes forth wickedness" (cf. 10:12; 1 Kgs 20:11; Ezek 18:2 for further examples of traditional proverbs). "The father of a clan instructs his children, especially his sons, about mastering life. His counsel is authoritative, backed by a father's authority and an appeal to past experience" (Crenshaw 1976: 955; cf. 1981: 33). This is supported by the way Wisdom teaching is often addressed to "my son" (Prov 1:8, 10, 15, etc.; Eccl 12:12), and by the emphasis on parental instruction:

> Hear, my child, your father's instruction,
>> and do not reject your mother's teaching. (Prov 1:8)

Such teaching was passed down from one generation to another (4:3-4; *Sir* 8:9).

The Wisdom tradition continued in the postexilic period, though of the setting for this we know very little. Some scholars suggest the existence of Wisdom schools, but the arguments for this are largely based on inference. The clearest indication is found in *Sir* 51:23:

> Draw near to me, you who are uneducated,
>> and lodge in the house of instruction. (see Crenshaw 1981: 36)

Along with kings, priests, and prophets, the wise constitute an important group through whom God sought to lead and guide his people.

Old Testament: Promise

6-2. THE COMING OF A MESSIAH

The OT promises that God will usher in the new order through a new Servant or Anointed One, modeled on one or more of the categories of persons employed by God in the past. While the actual term "Messiah" is not used in the OT of a future, eschatological agent through whom God will usher in the new order, the term was clearly used in this sense by NT times (cf. D. S. Russell 1964: 307). It is true that some forms of eschatological expectation lacked a messianic figure (cf. J. Becker 1980: 79), but the NT witnesses to a variety of messianic expectations in contemporary Judaism. Different forms of expectation are found based on each of the "messianic" categories.

6-2.1. A SECOND MOSES

Considering the standing of Moses as man of God and servant of the Lord, it is not surprising that he came to serve as a model for God's eschatological agent. As God had acted in the past to deliver his people by Moses at the time of the exodus, so he would act in the future by means of a second Moses, or a figure like Moses.

Toward the end of his life, anticipating a time when his leadership would be no longer available, Moses assured the people: "The Lord your God will raise up for you a prophet like me from among your own people; you shall heed such a prophet. . . . 'I will raise up for them a prophet like you from among their own people; I will put my words in the mouth of the prophet, who shall speak to them everything that I command'" (Deut 18:15, 18).

Most critical scholars believe that in its original context in Deuteronomy, the passage envisages a succession of future leaders, i.e., the main prophets of the OT (cf. Clements 1968: 64). Nevertheless, the passage does speak of the coming of a Moses-like "prophet" in the singular; and especially with the cessation of prophecy within Israel (cf. below, 6-2.4), this passage would naturally be seen as pointing to an eschatological role for a Moses-like figure (cf. Kaiser 1995: 57-61; Allison 1993: 73-84). Samaritans looked for a messianic figure of this type, and such an expectation is reflected by the remarks of the Samaritan woman in John 4.

6-2.2. A KINGLY MESSIAH

The dialectic between promonarchic and antimonarchic views, between the need for strong leadership and the failings of actual leaders, between the promise of an "everlasting covenant" and the failure of the Davidic line, led to the expectation of the coming of an ideal, future ruler who would bring the benefits of kingship without the weaknesses of the all-too-human kings Israel had experienced in the past. Despite God's promises to the Davidic line (Ps 89:1-37), the shortcomings of actual kings raised serious questions (89:38-52) about God's support of the monarchy (cf. Eissfeldt 1962: 201-2; Clifford 1980: 201-2). The accession of a new king would naturally be a time when people hoped for better things. But as each new king failed to live up to these expectations, the tendency grew to project the ideal into the future (cf. Ringgren 1956: 23). The story line of 1 and 2 Kings might appear to indicate the failure of the monarchy and of God's promises, yet even in these books, "although God punishes with complete justification the sins of David's descendants, the hope remains that there will yet be a 'son of David' through whom the nations will experience God's favour" (T. D. Alexander 1998: 209).

This tendency would be strengthened by the use of the Royal Psalms in worship. "The poets of the psalter described an *anointed one* Israel needed but never got" (Durham 1984: 430). The more imperfect the actual existing king, the more worshipers would see the Royal Psalms as prayers to God to send an ideal ruler in the future. No king, not even the Deuteronomic "good kings," ever lived up to the ideal set forth in the Royal Psalms. "Since the type was not perfectly embodied in any of the Davidic kings, it is understandable that in the course of time, especially after the collapse of the Davidic monarchy in 587 B.C., these psalms were interpreted to refer to *the* 'Anointed One' (Messiah) of the future, who would come in the fullness of time to rule over God's kingdom on earth" (B. W. Anderson 1983: 191; cf. Obersteiner 1981: 577). The failure of the monarchy after the exile meant that the portraits of the ideal king inevitably were taken as promises of a future king whom God would one day send to save and rule his people (cf. Ringgren 1956: 38; R. E. Brown 1994: 159; contra McKenzie 1974: 288-89). It is particularly significant that long after the monarchy ceased to exist the Royal Psalms were retained in the final canonical form of the Psalter (note especially the prominent position of Ps 2). It is clear that these psalms "were treasured in the Psalter . . . as a witness to the messianic hope which looked for the consummation of God's kingship through his Anointed One" (Childs 1979: 517).

Over the centuries the figure of David tended to be idealized, and so expectation generally centered on a future descendant of David. The coming of a Davidic, messianic king is an important theme in Isaiah (see von Rad 1965: 169-75; J. M. Ward 1991: 57-59). Isa 9:1-7 comes from a period of crisis when the Northern Kingdom had fallen to the Assyrians. The prophet promises a future restoration of the North and the defeat of the enemies of God's people.

> For a child has been born for us,
>   a son given to us;
> authority rests upon his shoulders;
>   and he is named
> Wonderful Counselor, Mighty God (*'ēl gibbôr*),
>   Everlasting Father, Prince of Peace.
> His authority shall grow continually,
>   and there shall be endless peace
> for the throne of David and his kingdom.
>   He will establish and uphold it
> with justice and with righteousness. (vv. 6-7)

Isaiah may have originally delivered the oracle upon the birth of an heir to the throne or the accession/coronation of a new king (cf. J. Becker 1980: 45), but in its canonical context it expresses the hope that a future king of David's line will usher in a new age of peace and justice.

Isa 11:1-5 sketches a portrait of the ideal ruler of God's people, empowered by God's Spirit. Vv. 6-9, with their vision of a renewed creation, provide a context that is clearly eschatological.

> A shoot *(chōṭer)* shall come out from the stump of Jesse,
>> and a branch *(nētser)* shall grow out of his roots.
>>> (v. 1; v. 10 refers to "the root *(shōresh)* of Jesse")

The metaphor of a tree is used to refer to the Davidic dynasty; a descendant of Jesse (the father of David) will be a branch of this tree. Just as a fresh shoot may spring up from the stump of a tree that has been felled, so a new king will spring from David's line (see Kaiser 1995: 164). A series of important passages in other prophetic books see David as the prototype of a future ruler. It may be that historically some of these passages reflect a postexilic movement that Becker (1980) labels "restorative monarchism" (see 48-63), but the longer the postexilic community lasted without an actual monarch, the more these passages would be seen as referring to a future ideal king. Amos 9:11 looks for a restoration of the fallen booth of David (cf. Hos 3:5). In Mic 5:2-4 the future king will come from Bethlehem, the home of Jesse:

> But you, O Bethlehem of Ephrathah,
>> who are one of the little clans of Judah,
> from you there shall come forth for me
>> one who is to rule *(môshēl)* in Israel,
> whose origin is from of old,
>> from ancient days. (v. 2)

Jeremiah picks up the imagery of the tree in Jer 23:5-6 and 33:14-16; it is evident that "the Branch" has become a title of the future messianic king (see also 30:9, 21). Passages such as the blessing of Judah (Gen 49:10), and Balaam's oracle (Num 24:17; see above, 6-1.2a), that originally pointed forward to the Davidic monarchy could also be seen as prophecies of a future Messiah of David's line.

A distinctive note is struck in Zech 9:9-10:

> Rejoice greatly, O daughter Zion!
>> Shout aloud, O daughter Jerusalem!
> Lo, your king comes to you;
>> triumphant and victorious is he,
> humble and riding on a donkey. . . .
> He will cut off the chariot from Ephraim
>> and the war horse from Jerusalem;
> and the battle bow shall be cut off,
>> and he shall command peace to the nations;
> his dominion shall be from sea to sea,
>> and from the River to the ends of the earth.

While there is no mention here of Davidic descent, other features of the royal theology are prominent: victory over enemies, a reign of peace and universal dominion. The unique feature of this portrait is that the king is "humble" and rides a lowly ass, not a warhorse. "The entire context underlines the peaceful, unwarlike character of the messiah, even though he is coming as a victorious king. Yet his victory is God's victory in the apocalyptic establishment of his eternal kingdom" (Gese 1981a: 150).

In the new age God will be the shepherd of his people:

> He will feed his flock like a shepherd;
>   he will gather the lambs in his arms,
> and carry them in his bosom,
>   and gently lead the mother sheep. (Isa 40:11; cf. Zech 9:16)

Both Jeremiah and Ezekiel follow their condemnations of unfaithful shepherd-kings with promises that God himself will "gather the remnant of my flock out of all the lands where I have driven them" (Jer 23:3; cf. 31:10), and will "feed them with good pasture" (Ezek 34:11-16). This is not inconsistent, however, with God working through a Davidic messianic shepherd-king, and so Ezek 34:23 (cf. 37:24) promises: "I will set up over them one shepherd, my servant David, and he shall feed them" (see Kaiser 1995: 194-97). The messianic king in Mic 5 "shall stand and feed his flock in the strength of the LORD" (v. 4).

Despite a certain amount of idealization, the figure of a Davidic Messiah belongs essentially to the realm of prophetic eschatology. "There is no clear evidence that the Messiah was thought of as a transcendental figure whose mission would go beyond the realities of history" (R. E. Brown 1994: 159).

6-2.3. A PRIESTLY MESSIAH

It is generally held that there is not a lot of evidence of the expectation of a priestly messiah in pre-Christian Judaism (Higgins 1953: 321, 325).

We have seen, however, that priest and king could be linked in the person of Melchizedek (above, 6-1.3b). When the Royal Psalms are interpreted with reference to a messianic king, then Ps 110:4, in which the king is told, "You are a priest forever according to the order of Melchizedek," can be interpreted as pointing to a Messiah figure who will be both king and priest. The way Jesus quotes Ps 110:1 in disputing the teaching of the scribes (Mark 12:35-37 and //s) clearly assumes that the psalm was interpreted messianically in Jesus' day (see Higgins 1953: 335).

The vision of Zech 4:11-14 speaks of two "anointed ones" or messiahs, Zerubbabel (a Davidic king) and Joshua (a high priest). By applying the title "anointed" to the high priest, this text also paved the way for the expectation of a priestly messiah figure. In 3:8 Joshua, the high priest, is told, "You and your colleagues . . . are an omen of things to come: I am going to bring my servant the Branch." Here the messianic "Branch" is a *priestly* figure, modeled on the person of the high priest (see Kaiser 1995: 211-13; and cf. Zech 6:9-15).

6-2.4. AN ESCHATOLOGICAL PROPHET

By late OT times it was believed that prophecy had ceased. Referring to the death of Judas, *1 Macc* 9:27 says, "There was great distress in Israel, such as had not been *since the time that prophets ceased to appear* among them" (cf. Ps 74, and see Young 1949: 291). Belief that the new age would be marked by a rebirth of prophecy (Joel 2:28-29; cf. 5-2.3), however, paved the way for the hope of a prophetic eschatological figure (Cullmann 1963: 14-23).

This could be expressed in general terms as in *1 Macc* 4:45-46; when the people did not know what to do with the stones of the old altar at the rededication of the temple, they "stored the stones . . . *until a prophet should come* to tell what to do with them." Similarly, in 14:41 "the Jews and their priests . . . resolved that Simon should be their leader and high priest forever, *until a trustworthy prophet should arise.*"

Belief in a coming prophet like Moses (above, 6-2.1), based on Deut 18:15, 18, can be seen as a more specific form of prophetic expectation. When a delegation from Jerusalem asked John the Baptist, "Are you the prophet *(ho prophētēs)?*" (John 1:21), they had in mind the eschatological, Moses-like prophet (cf. 6:14; 7:40).

Similarly Elijah, as an outstanding OT prophet, also served as the type of a coming prophet (see Keown 1987). In Mal 4:5-6 God promises, "Lo, I will send you the prophet Elijah before the great and terrible day of the LORD comes. He will turn the hearts of parents to their children and the hearts of children to their parents, so that I will not come and strike the land with a curse." Here the promised "messenger" of Mal 3:1-3, who is to prepare the way of the Lord (i.e., God) and who has a purifying role, is identified with the eschatological Elijah, who is to restore intergenerational harmony before the Day of the Lord. The Malachi passages are the basis for *Sir* 48:9-10, which says of Elijah:

> At the appointed time, it is written, you are destined
>> to calm the wrath of God before it breaks out in fury,
> to turn the hearts of parents to their children,
>> and to restore the tribes of Jacob. (v. 10)

A similar belief in the eschatological role of Elijah underlies *2 Esdr* 6:26.

The NT reflects a further development of this belief in contemporary Judaism, although the evidence outside the NT itself is not extensive (see

Faierstein 1981). The disciples on one occasion asked Jesus, "Why do the scribes say that first Elijah must come?" (Matt 17:10 RSV//Mark 9:11). Here Elijah is apparently expected to prepare the way not merely for God and the coming judgment, but specifically for the coming of the Messiah (cf. John 1:21). The function ascribed to him in Malachi and *Sirach* of restoring harmony within God's people would be appropriate to one preparing the people to receive a Messiah.

6-2.5. AN ESCHATOLOGICAL TEACHER

OT eschatological expectation sees the need for people to be *taught* in the new age. One strand of thought sees this as a function of God himself, especially in relation to the ingathering of the Gentiles (see 12-2.4). Many nations will flock to Zion, to the house of the God of Jacob, "that he may teach us his ways" (Isa 2:3). God says of the Gentiles, "I am surely going to teach them . . . my power and my might" (Jer 16:21).

In Isa 11:2, however, the messianic king has wisdom attributes, for he will be endowed with "the spirit of wisdom and understanding," and this suggests teaching as one of his functions. Isa 30:20-21 promises that despite a time of adversity and affliction, "yet your Teacher will not hide himself any more, but your eyes shall see your Teacher." While some scholars see God as the Teacher (Gowan 1986: 87), more probably the reference is to a messianic figure who will guide God's people in the new age, saying to them, "This is the way; walk in it" (see Kaiser 1995: 172-73).

In anticipation of the new age, Joel 2:23 calls on the people of Zion to rejoice in the LORD, "for he has given you the teacher for righteousness (*'eth-hammôreth lits^edhāqâh*)" (NIV). Here too the reference is to an eschatological teacher of righteousness (see Kaiser 1995: 139-42).

John 4:25 seems to presuppose an expectation that the coming Messiah will teach God's people: "When he comes, he will show us all things" (RSV). The verb *anangellō*, here translated "show" (NRSV "proclaim"), means to disclose, announce, or teach (Arndt and Gingrich 1957: 50).

New Testament: Fulfillment

6-3. YOU ARE THE MESSIAH

The NT is unanimous in its claim that Jesus is the Christ or Messiah. The Gospels portray Jesus as claiming to be the promised Messiah but as being remarkably reticent about making such a claim in public. In the central scene of the Synoptic Gospels, Peter's confession at Caesarea Philippi, Peter confesses that

Jesus is the Messiah, but in his response that confession is immediately modified by Jesus in two very significant ways: by switching from the title "Messiah" to that of "Son of Man," and by linking that title with his forthcoming suffering and death (Matt 16:13-23; Mark 8:27-33; Luke 9:18-22). Similarly in another key scene, the trial before the high priest, Jesus does acknowledge that he is the Messiah (so Mark 14:61-62; in Matt 26:64 and Luke 22:67-68 he is noncommittal), but again immediately switches to the title "Son of Man." The context connects the saying closely with his imminent suffering and death. In John Jesus makes messianic claims more freely and earlier than in the Synoptics (cf. 4:25-26).

The NT equally makes it clear that after Jesus' death and resurrection, when the possibility of misunderstanding was greatly reduced, early Christians freely and openly proclaimed that Jesus was the promised Messiah. In addressing Jewish audiences they would, like Paul, testify that "the Messiah was Jesus" (Acts 18:5; cf. 17:3; 18:28). Mark, considered by most scholars to be the earliest Gospel, concerns "the good news of Jesus, *Messiah* and Son of God" (1:1 AT); John, considered by most to be the latest Gospel, claims to have been written "so that you may come to believe that Jesus is the *Messiah,* the Son of God" (20:31). Beyond the Gospels we find Jesus confessed as Messiah/Christ throughout the canonical NT. Obviously the earliest Christians re-interpreted the title, retaining the connotations of fulfillment but excluding any political, nationalistic, or military associations (cf. Ziesler 1990: 29). Thus, in ascribing the title "Messiah" to Jesus, the Gospel portrait of the person and work of Jesus considerably modifies the understanding of "Messiah."

As Christianity spread out into the Greco-Roman world, the term "Christ" would have little meaning, and what was originally a *title* came to be used simply as a *name.* Even Paul, surprisingly enough, though he knows that "Christ" is a title (Rom 9:5), tends to use it as a name (5:1).

In addition to identifying Jesus by the actual title "the Messiah" *(christos),* the NT associates him with each of the main categories of messianic expectation. According to the NT, *Jesus fulfills each of the messianic types,* but equally *he transcends them all.* The process is a dialectical one: each category sheds light on the Christian understanding of Jesus while the understanding of Jesus reinterprets the categories. Moreover, the reinterpreted messianic categories themselves must be understood in relation to the categories of Son of Man, Son of God, and Suffering Servant (see chaps. 7, 8, and 9).

6-3.1. AS HE RAISED UP MOSES

Moses is mentioned more often in the NT than any other OT figure (R. F. Johnson 1962: 449; Meeks 1976: 605), and is widely recognized and revered as the mediator of God's revelation and the shepherd and representative of God's people (cf. Hay 1990: 245-51). Nothing was more natural than that the writers of the NT should turn to the figure of Moses as they sought to articulate their understanding of the person of Jesus. The broader background of Moses Christology is the recognition of the exodus and associated events as a type of the salvation event of the new order (see 3-3.3). Several NT writers recognize Moses as a type of Christ; they are also aware of the limitations of the typology and they all, to varying extents, proclaim the superiority of Christ to Moses. At the transfiguration (Mark 9:2-8 and //s) Moses (along with Elijah) is a *witness* to Jesus. Peter's proposal to make booths for all three is mistaken because in essence it would put all three on the same level (Hay, 241).

a. The Second Moses

The most striking parallels to Moses are found in Matthew's Gospel, which comes close to presenting Jesus as a second Moses (see L. L. Thompson 1978: 233; Allison 1993).

The massacre of the innocents (Matt 2:13-18) parallels the massacre of the Hebrew male children in Exod 1:15-22, with Herod seen as an antitype of Pharaoh. Like Moses, Jesus is called from Egypt to return and lead his people (Matt 2:15, 19-21). The forty days and nights of the temptation (Matt 4:2 only) recall the similar period Moses spent on Mount Sinai (Exod 34:28). The Sermon on the *Mount* (Matt 5:1) recalls the giving of the Torah on *Mount* Sinai. It has long been recognized that Matthew presents five major blocks of Jesus' teaching, which parallels the five books of Moses. The ten miracles of Matt 8–9 (cf. R. H. Fuller 1963: 77-82) recall the ten mighty works of the exodus story. Like Moses (Deut 34:1), Jesus makes his final appearance on a mountain (Matt 28:16).

Matthew nowhere quotes Deut 18:15, and he does not present Jesus as the Moses-like prophet. He utilizes Moses typology, but only as one element among several in his Christology. Jesus is a second Moses, but also one far greater than Moses (cf. Allison 1993: 267).

Moses typology is found in Luke also. When it is said that Jesus' mighty works were done by "the finger of God" (11:20), one is reminded of the same expression in Exod 8:19 where Moses and Aaron are agents of the power of God. It is in Luke 9:31 that Jesus speaks of his coming "departure *(exodos)*" (cf. 3-3.3).

b. The Prophet like Moses

Another strand of thought does see Jesus as the prophet like Moses, in fulfillment of Deut 18:15. The transfiguration narrative presents a series of parallels with the Exod 24 account of Moses ratifying the covenant on Mount Sinai (Teeple 1957: 84), while the voice from the cloud which says, "listen to him *(akouete autou)"* (Mark 9:7 and //s), echoes Deut 18:15, "him shall you heed (LXX: *autou akouesthe)."*

In particular it is Luke-Acts that identifies Jesus as the Moses-like prophet with explicit quotations of the Deuteronomy text in Acts 3:22 and 7:37 (perhaps the texts alluded to in Luke 24:27). Critical scholars tend to see these texts as preserving a very primitive form of Christology (cf. R. H. Fuller 1969: 169-73).

c. Superior to Moses

In Hebrews, John, and Paul the emphasis falls more on the superiority of Jesus to Moses.

In Heb 3:1-6 (possibly refuting a Moses Christology) the writer draws a parallel between Moses and Jesus (v. 2), but immediately goes on to underline an even more striking contrast: "Moses was faithful in all God's house as a *servant*" (v. 5, quoting Num 12:7), but Christ "was faithful over God's house as a *son*" (v. 6). Moses' main function was to "testify to the things that would be spoken later" (v. 5), but there is no real comparison between the two figures (cf. E. L. Allen 1956: 105).

John "shows a remarkable ambivalence toward the Moses traditions" (Meeks 1976: 606). Several passages in John suggest a link between Jesus and "the prophet," by which is meant the prophet like Moses (4:25; 6:14; 7:40, 52). John the Baptist denies he is "the prophet" (1:25), thus clearing the way for that title to be ascribed to Jesus. John appears to regard it as applicable to Jesus but inadequate (Glasson 1963: 29). But the main emphasis is on contrast: "The law indeed was given through Moses; grace and truth came through Jesus Christ" (1:17). In contrast to Moses, who gave the Israelites manna and water from the rock, Christ is the true "bread of life" (6:35) and the source of "living water" (4:10) (see Glasson, chaps. 6, 7). John 6 is replete with Passover and exodus typology: the feeding of the crowds prompts the people to hail Jesus as "the [Moses-like] prophet who is to come into the world" (v. 14), while the miraculous crossing of the sea that follows (vv. 16-21) is a reenactment of Israel's passing through the Red Sea (cf. Cronk 1982: 175).

The few Pauline references stress the contrast even more. In 2 Cor 3:7-18 Moses is linked with the old covenant that has now been replaced. According to Gal 3:19-20, the Law was given through an intermediary *(mesitēs)*, i.e., Moses; the implication is that in Christ God has acted more directly.

Thus, while Moses typology provides important clues to the identity of Jesus, there is never any question of the two figures being on the same level; the antitype far exceeds the type.

6-3.2. THE KING OF ISRAEL

Repeatedly in the NT Jesus is presented as the royal Messiah, descended from David. Yet in so doing, the NT profoundly reinterprets the meaning of "king."

All four Evangelists, writing from their own perspectives, present Jesus as a king, though not the king of popular expectation. Both Matthew and Luke in their genealogies show Jesus' descent from David, an essential qualification for the Davidic Messiah (Matt 1:6, 17; Luke 3:31-32). Matthew's genealogy (Matt 1:1-17) is highly stylized, with three sets of fourteen generations preceding the birth of Jesus: vv. 2-6 represent an age of waiting, vv. 6-11 an age of kings, vv. 12-16a a second age of waiting, while v. 16b announces the birth of the messianic king. In 2:3-6 Herod is told that the Messiah must be born in Bethlehem and Mic 5:2 is explicitly quoted. In Luke 1:32 Mary is told by Gabriel that she will bear a son who "will be great, and will be called the Son of the Most High, and the Lord God will give to him the throne of his ancestor David"; this declaration echoes the announcement of the Davidic covenant in 2 Sam 7 (cf. Rogers 1993: 465). In the Synoptics Jesus is hailed as "Son of David" (Matt 9:27; 15:22; Mark 10:47; Luke 18:38). Matthew's account of the triumphal entry is the most explicit in portraying Jesus as fulfilling the prophecy of a peaceful messianic king in Zech 9:9 (quoted in Matt 21:5b), and in having Jesus hailed as "Son of David" (Matt 21:9; cf. Mark 11:10). In John 1:49 Nathanael declares Jesus to be "the King of Israel," though in the same breath he also uses the title "the Son of God." After the feeding of the multitude, John portrays Jesus as withdrawing since he saw that the people "were about to come and take him by force to make him king" (6:15). Jesus' words to Pilate in John 18:36 are not inappropriate as a summary of the viewpoint found in all four Gospels: "My kingdom is not from this world." Paradoxically, in all the Gospels the theme of Jesus' kingship surfaces most clearly in the passion narrative. Jesus is mocked by the soldiers as if he were a king, complete with robe, scepter, and crown, and on the cross he hangs under the title "Jesus of Nazareth, King of the Jews" (Matt 27:37; Mark 15:26; Luke 23:38; John 19:19). The narratives make powerful use of dramatic irony: Jesus is king, but he is crowned with a crown of thorns and rules from a tree.

Apart from the use of the title "king," Jesus is portrayed in the Gospels as the true shepherd-king of God's people. "When he saw the crowds," we are told, "he had compassion for them, because they were harassed and helpless, like sheep without a shepherd" (Matt 9:36; cf. Mark 6:34; see Num 27:17; 1 Kgs 22:17; Ezek 34:5; Zech 10:2). The words of Zech 13:7 about striking the shepherd and scattering the sheep are applied to Jesus in Matt 26:31 and Mark 14:27. Jesus is the shepherd-king who will die for his flock, but will return to care for them after his resurrection.

John gives a more elaborate portrayal in the allegory of the Good Shepherd in 10:1-18 (on the connection with Ezek 34, see Thomson 1955: 414). Jesus is contrasted with thieves, bandits, strangers, and hired hands, like the false shepherds of Jeremiah, Ezekiel, and Zechariah. By claiming to be "the Good Shepherd," Jesus was "identifying himself as the Messiah and associating his ministry with the activity of God" (Cronk 1982: 181). The supreme mark of the Good Shepherd is that he "lays down his life for the sheep" (John 10:11). This understanding of Jesus as the messianic shepherd-king is reflected in the titles applied to him: "the great shepherd of the sheep" (Heb 13:20) and "the shepherd and guardian of your souls" (1 Pet 2:25).

In his sermon at Antioch in Pisidia, Paul cites Jesus' Davidic descent as a qualification of Israel's Savior (Acts 13:22-23), and he identifies Jesus with the "Son" of the Royal Psalm 2 (v. 7). But Luke is very aware of the perception that Christians act "contrary to the decrees of the emperor, saying that there is another king named Jesus" (Acts 17:7), and the whole of Luke-Acts is in one sense an early Christian "apology," demonstrating that Christianity is not a subversive movement (cf. Luke 23:1-4).

In his epistles Paul recognizes that Jesus was "descended from David according to the flesh" (Rom 1:3; cf. 2 Tim 2:8), but generally he avoids the royal category, probably because of the danger of political misunderstanding. The royal function tends to be subsumed under the title "Lord" (see 10-3.4).

In establishing Christ's unique position as the Son of God, the writer to the Hebrews draws on the royal theology, quoting in 1:5 Royal Psalm 2 (v. 7) and in 1:8-9 Royal Psalm 45 (vv. 6-7), and again in 1:5 Nathan's oracle of 2 Sam 7:14.

Paradoxically, recognition of Christ as the royal Messiah reemerges in the book of Revelation. It is because Christ, "the Lion of the tribe of Judah, the Root of David," has conquered that he can open the scroll with seven seals and reveal the meaning of history (5:5; cf. 22:16).

Thus, although he fulfills the promise of a royal, Davidic Messiah, in the NT this is completely divorced from the political and military connotations that no doubt dominated popular expectation. The kingship of Christ has to be seen in the broader canonical context: Jesus is the Messiah, but he is also the Suffering Servant; he is "the Lion of the tribe of Judah," but he is also "the Lamb that was slaughtered" (Rev 5:5, 12).

6-3.3. A GREAT HIGH PRIEST

In the NT priestly functions are ascribed to Christ. Like a priest, he intercedes for the people. John 17 has been seen as Jesus' "High Priestly prayer" (A. Richardson 1958: 200; Cronk 1982: 190); at the Last Supper Jesus "prayed for himself, his disciples, and then for those who would believe through the disciples' message. Each of these acts had priestly implications" (Shoemaker 1996: 632). References in Paul to Christ having secured "access" *(prosagōgē)* to God use priestly terminology (Rom 5:2; Eph 2:18; 3:12). But any attempt in the early church to interpret Jesus in terms of a priestly Messiah would immediately encounter the objection that Jesus' descent was traced not from the priestly tribe of Levi but from the royal tribe of Judah.

The Epistle to the Hebrews has a unique Christology, the main element of which is the presentation of Jesus as priestly Messiah (see 2:17; 3:1; 4:14; 5:5; cf. Shoemaker 1996: 632). Hebrews meets the objection regarding Jesus' descent head-on in 7:14: "For it is evident that our Lord was descended from Judah, and in connection with that tribe Moses said nothing about priests." The writer solves this problem by finding the true type of Christ not in the Mosaic high priesthood but in the priest-king Melchizedek; Christ is a priest "according to the order of Melchizedek" (5:6, quoting Ps 110:4; cf. Heb 5:10; 6:20–7:22). Melchizedek was a priest (and king) before the institution of the Aaronic priesthood under Moses. He is the type of a superior priesthood and foreshadows the priesthood of Christ.

Nevertheless, the high priest of the Mosaic legislation is also seen as a type of Christ, the messianic high priest. Hebrews, however, underlines the *contrast* rather than the *comparison*. In contrast to the OT priests who hold office on the basis of physical descent, Jesus became high priest "through the power of an indestructible life" (7:16). In contrast to the OT priests who die and are succeeded by others, Christ's priesthood is eternal (7:23-24). In contrast to the high priest of the OT who had to lead the Day of Atonement ritual "year after year," Christ has made the once-for-all sacrifice for sin (9:25-26). Above all, in contrast to the OT which "never so much as contemplated a sinless High-priest" (R. A. Stewart 1967: 126), in Christ we have "a high priest, holy, blameless, undefiled," totally unlike the high priest of Lev 16 who had to offer sacrifices "first for his own sins, then for those of the people" (Heb 7:26-27).

A priest mediates between God and people. As the sinless Son of God, Christ represents God to humankind. But as the perfect priest, Christ also represents humankind to God since he is also *fully human*: "For we do not have a high priest who is unable to sympathize with our weaknesses, but we have one who in every respect has been tested as we are, yet without sin" (Heb 4:15; cf. 2:17-18; 5:1-2, 7-9).

There comes a point where the typology breaks down, for in Hebrews Christ is not only the perfect high priest, he is also the perfect sacrifice (see further, 9-3.4b). "The Epistle to the Hebrews is saturated with the double figure of Christ as sinless High-priest, and Christ as spotless Calvary victim — the two strands are sometimes separated, sometimes interfused, but they permeate virtually every chapter" (R. A. Stewart 1967: 134).

6-3.4. A PROPHET MIGHTY IN DEED AND WORD

The Gospels portray both John the Baptist and Jesus as *prophetic* figures. It is essential to remember that by NT times prophecy had been dead for centuries, and the rebirth of prophecy was regarded purely as an eschatological phenomenon (cf. above, 6-2.4). "In Jesus' day there were no Jewish prophets. For the Jew the return of the prophetic spirit was inextricably related to messianic times. No Jew could use the phrase 'just another prophet' as so many modern scholars do. The next prophet would be one of two individuals: Elijah (or the forerunner of the Messiah) or the Messiah himself" (Young 1949: 297).

The Gospels indicate that John was widely regarded as a prophet (Matt 14:5; Mark 11:32 and //s), his garb (Mark 1:6) was that traditionally associated with prophets (cf. Scobie 1964: 128), and his message with its warning of coming judgment and call for repentance was truly in the prophetic tradition. According to John 1:20-23, John modestly declined all titles: he was neither the Messiah, Elijah, nor the (Moses-like) prophet. He did claim to be the "voice" of Isa 40:3, i.e., the one who announces the dawning of the messianic age.

In the Synoptics, however, Jesus identifies John as a prophet, and "more than a prophet"; he is the "messenger" of Mal 3:1 (Matt 11:9-10; Luke 7:26-27) and "Elijah who is to come" (Matt 11:14). In terms of the contemporary belief in a returning Elijah as the forerunner of the Messiah cited by the disciples, Elijah has already come in the person of John, who met a prophet's fate (Matt 17:10-13; Mark 9:11-13). The Gospel writers themselves underline John's role as the eschatological Elijah and forerunner of the Messiah (cf. the conflation of Mal 3:1 and Isa 40:3 in Mark 1:2-3; Luke 1:17).

By casting John the Baptist in the role of the eschatological Elijah, Jesus was at least indirectly casting himself in the role of the Messiah. Yet in the Gospels Jesus himself is also, in part, interpreted in prophetic categories.

In portraying Jesus as the "prophet like Moses," Luke-Acts and John employ a type of prophetic Christology. But quite apart from parallels with Moses, Jesus is presented in the Gospels as a prophet. Certainly the Evangelists do not hesitate to show others hailing Jesus as a prophet, "like one of the prophets of old" (Mark 6:15). In the Caesarea Philippi incident, Jesus asks the disciples who people believe he is, and they report, "John the Baptist; and others [say], Elijah; and still others, *one of the prophets*" (Mark 8:28 and //s; cf. Matt 21:11, 46; Luke 7:16; John 4:19; 9:17). In Luke 24:19 the two disciples on the walk to Emmaus refer to "Jesus of Nazareth, who was a prophet mighty in deed and word before God."

While Jesus nowhere directly claims the title, he does accept it indirectly when he says, "Prophets are not without honor except in their own country and in their own house" (Matt 13:57//Mark 6:4//Luke 4:24//John 4:44). When he says it is impossible for a prophet to be killed outside of Jerusalem, he clearly puts himself in that category (Luke 13:33-34; cf. R. H. Fuller 1969: 127; Toon 1984: 75). More importantly, Jesus is portrayed in the Gospels as a prophetic figure (cf. Dodd 1930; Higgins 1946; Fuller, 125-29). His baptism corresponds to a prophetic call. He is conscious of being "sent" by God (Mark 9:37; Matt 15:24). He proclaims God's coming judgment on nation, city, and temple (see 13-3.4a; 14-

3.1a), and God's coming salvation in his preaching of the kingdom of God. His fearless denunciation of King Herod Antipas as "that fox" (Luke 13:32) is in the true prophetic tradition. Events such as the cursing of the fig tree (Mark 11:12-14, 20-24) can be seen as examples of prophetic symbolism.

The Gospels portray Jesus as the antitype of several major OT prophetic figures in addition to Moses.

Since *Elijah* can be the representative of the prophets (e.g., at the transfiguration — Mark 9:4 and //s), an Elijah typology might be expected (cf. Mark 6:15; Luke 4:25-26). In the Synoptics this is generally ruled out by the identification (noted above) of John the Baptist as Elijah, the forerunner of the Messiah. In John's Gospel, however, since the Baptist does not claim that role, it may be that the title is thereby cleared for Jesus (cf. Martyn 1976). In John, for example, Jesus performs seven miracles or signs, the same number credited to Elijah.

What in fact appears more clearly in the Gospels is an *Elisha* typology (cf. R. E. Brown 1971). Some of Jesus' miracles are more similar to Elisha's than Elijah's. Jesus' cures of lepers recall the story of Elisha and Naaman (2 Kgs 5); in Luke 4:27 Jesus refers specifically to Elisha, while the healing of the ten lepers in Luke 17:11-19 presents a series of parallels to the Naaman story (see Brown, 90). John's version of the feeding of the crowds (6:1-14) is closely modeled on Elisha's multiplication of loaves, even to the mention of "barley" loaves (2 Kgs 4:42-44). The raising of the widow of Nain's son from the dead in Luke 7:11-17 parallels Elisha's raising of the son of the Shunammite woman in 2 Kgs 4:18-37 (but cf. also 1 Kgs 17:17-24).

What this suggests is that the relationship between John the Baptist and Jesus is patterned on that between Elijah and Elisha. Elisha took over from Elijah and received a double portion of his spirit in a scene set by the Jordan (2 Kgs 2:6-15); so Jesus takes over from John after his baptism in the Jordan and his receiving of the Spirit (Mark 1:9-11 and //s; cf. R. E. Brown 1971: 88).

According to Matthew's version of the Caesarea Philippi incident, some of the people identified Jesus with *Jeremiah* (16:14), and there are also a number of striking parallels between Jesus and Jeremiah. Like the great OT prophet, Jesus calls the people to repentance, but also prophesies the capture of Jerusalem and the destruction of the temple. In cleansing the temple Jesus quotes Jeremiah's words about "a den of robbers" (Mark 11:17 and //s = Jer 7:11).

While prophetic typology is thus a component part of the portrait of Jesus in the Gospels, far more so than in the case of John the Baptist, Jesus is "more than a prophet." He does not merely announce the dawning of the new age, as John did; in his life, death, and resurrection he inaugurates it. Jesus does not merely revive OT prophecy; he fulfills it (cf. Dodd 1930: 66). It is significant that in John 4 the Samaritan woman begins by saying to Jesus, "Sir, I see that you are a prophet" (v. 19), but is led to see that he is also the promised Messiah (vv. 25-26, 29), and indeed "the Savior of the world" (v. 42). Taken by itself, the title "prophet" is quite inadequate to express Jesus' true identity; taken in conjunction with other titles and ways of understanding Jesus, it contributes to the overall picture (cf. Cullmann 1963: 43-50).

6-3.5. A TEACHER COME FROM GOD

A considerable part of Jesus' ministry was devoted to *teaching*. He is frequently called a *didaskalos* (= "teacher"; Luke also uses the term *epistatēs*). Both these Greek words probably translate "rabbi" (from Heb. *rabbî*, lit. "my master"), which is strictly a term of address, though it was used as an honorary designation for teachers of the Torah (on contemporary Jewish usage, see R. H. Fuller 1969: 49-50). The term "rabbi" is also applied directly to Jesus (Mark 9:5; John 1:38; 4:31; etc.). In John 3:2 Nicodemus says to Jesus, "Rabbi, we know that you are a teacher *(didaskalos)* who has come from God." Jesus has some of the characteristics of contemporary rabbis (cf. Dodd 1930: 53-56): he gathers a group of disciples around him, transmits his teaching to them so that they in turn can pass it on to others, and engages in debates on the interpretation of Torah. Jesus was also, to some extent, a teacher in the Wisdom tradition (on this, see 8-3.4 and 18-3.2b.iv).

Yet Jesus is also sharply contrasted with contemporary teachers, particularly because of the "authority" *(exousia)* he claimed and displayed in his teaching. Those in the synagogue at Capernaum "were astounded at his teaching, for he taught them as one having authority, and not as the scribes" (Mark 1:22). Jesus never quoted authorities (one of the marks of the rabbinic literature); he claimed to reveal the will of God directly. This authority is seen particularly in Jesus' claim to bring the definitive interpretation of Torah: "You have heard that it was said to those of ancient times. . . . But I say to you" (Matt 5:21-22, 27-28, 31-34, 38-39, 43-44).

Jesus is thus far from being "a rabbi." He is *the* eschatological teacher of righteousness who brings the full and final revelation of the will of God and of the true meaning of Torah.

New Testament: Consummation

6-4. THE KINGDOM OF HIS MESSIAH

During his lifetime Jesus' messiahship was discernible only through faith; at the final consummation it will become manifest to all. The kingdom of the world will be "the kingdom of our Lord and of his Messiah" (Rev 11:15).

While the messianic categories apply almost entirely to Christ's work on earth, they can be associated with the exalted and returning Christ as a reminder that the one who will come at the final consummation is the same one who was God's unique agent here on earth.

6-4.1. THEY SING THE SONG OF MOSES

The coming one is the Christ who is the second and greater Moses. In Rev 2:17 the risen Christ promises: "To everyone who conquers I will give some of the hidden manna." According to Exodus, Moses commanded Aaron to put some of the manna in a jar that was to be placed "before the LORD" and "before the testimony" (16:33-34 RSV), i.e., the ark of the covenant. According to the story preserved in 2 *Macc* 2:4-8, the ark was one of the objects concealed by Jeremiah in a cave at the time of the exile, only to be disclosed at the last day. The reference in Rev 2:17 assumes that the manna was hidden with the ark. Jesus as the new Moses promises that his faithful people will receive the manna with which the Israelites were fed in the time of Moses; in the new age they will be fed with the true bread.

In Rev 15:3 the victorious martyrs "sing the song of Moses, the servant of God." What follows in 15:3-4 is not the Song of Moses in Exod 15:1-18, but like it, it is a song of praise celebrating the great and amazing deeds God has accomplished not through Moses but through Christ, the second Moses.

6-4.2. KING OF KINGS

The one whose royal attributes were paradoxically seen in a life of humble service and in suffering and death will finally be universally recognized as "King of kings and Lord of lords" (Rev 19:16; cf. 17:14). He will triumph over all "the kings of the earth" (19:19). Already in 1:5 Christ is recognized as "the ruler of the kings of the earth."

The triumphant notes with which Christ's kingship is sounded in the eschatological visions of Revelation are in striking contrast to the more restrained and paradoxical ascriptions of kingship to Christ in the Gospels and Acts. "It is easy to see why the name is not more freely used. The title was politically dangerous. Further, in view of their favourable attitude to the Empire, it is naturally avoided by St. Paul and the author of I Peter, just as, for the contrary reason, it is thrown out as a challenge by the Seer John" (V. Taylor 1953: 77).

The coming one is also the shepherd-king who will truly care for his people. Peter promises the presbyters who faithfully care for their flock, "when the chief shepherd appears, you will win the crown of glory that never fades away" (1 Pet 5:4). John, employing what Thomson calls "a bold mixture of metaphors" (1955: 415), says of the martyrs in heaven:

The Lamb at the center of the throne will be their shepherd,
and he will guide them to springs of the water of life. (Rev 7:17)

6-4.3. CLOTHED WITH A LONG ROBE

The risen and returning Christ also retains priestly features. In the composite vision of Rev 1:12-16, Christ is "clothed with a long robe and with a golden sash across his chest." Both the robe and the girdle were priestly garments (see, e.g., Exod 28:4).

6-4.4. HE WHO HAS THE SHARP TWO-EDGED SWORD

The future Christ likewise has prophetic features. In particular he proclaims God's word. According to Rev 1:16 (cf. 2:12), "from his mouth came a sharp, two-edged sword." Recalling Isa 11:4, the "sword of the Spirit" is identified with "the word of God" in Eph 6:17, while in Heb 4:12 the word of God is described as "living and active, sharper than any two-edged sword." The risen Christ remains a prophetic figure, proclaiming the word of God.

6-4.5. THEN I WILL KNOW FULLY

Though Jesus was the supreme teacher during his lifetime, there are matters that will be revealed only at the final consummation. "For now we see in a mirror, dimly, but then we will see face to face. Now I know only in part; then I will know fully" (1 Cor 13:12).

6-5. THE MESSIAH: THEOLOGICAL REFLECTIONS

1. There is no question that for the NT the Christ event is absolutely central (cf. E-4.2). Traditionally Christian theology has found it convenient to draw a distinction between "the person of Christ" and "the work of Christ," between "Christology" and "atonement," between the study of who Jesus is and the study of what he accomplished, especially through his death. These topics, however, cannot be treated in isolation. The significance of Jesus' death cannot be separated from the NT proclamation of his resurrection and exaltation, nor can it be considered in isolation from the question of who Jesus is. While chapters 6–8 of this study deal with matters traditionally classified as "Christology," chapter 9 with the death of Jesus, and chapter 10 with his resurrection and exal-

tation, this division is made primarily for reasons of convenience; the biblical material itself witnesses to the close connection between these topics, and this must always be kept in mind.

2. The Christ event is central not just for the NT but for the entire Bible, as is clearly shown by a study of the canon of both OT and NT (see D-2.3; D-2.4), and especially by a study of the *structure* of canonical Scripture as a whole (see D-2.7). A true BT must thus examine the Christ event in its total biblical context.

Traditionally this has frequently been done in terms of individual OT texts that are seen as "prophecies" of Christ's coming — in other words, as messianic proof texts. There is some merit in this approach, for the NT does frequently quote specific OT texts and link them with the Christ event. But the linkage between the Christ event and the OT is much more broadly based than any mere proof-text approach would indicate. In many ways "promise" is a more satisfactory category than "prophecy," and the second section of the preceding discussion, which takes up the theme of promise, indicates how the OT, in a much broader way, points forward to the coming of a new Servant of God. As has been indicated, many texts that referred originally to a specific historical situation came, in time, and under divine guidance, to be understood as pointing to a future fulfillment. This is not to be dismissed as finding a "double meaning" in Scripture; rather it is part of the dynamic process of progressive revelation (contra Kaiser 1995: 18-19, 31-32). Moreover, it must constantly be remembered that in this area of BT above all others there is a tension between continuity and the inbreaking of the radically new. Jesus does fulfill the hopes and expectations of the OT, but he also transcends them in a way that has the writers of the NT straining to find language and categories that will adequately express the significance of Christ.

3. The NT witnesses to the fact that one of the earliest confessions of faith was "Jesus is the Christ." The importance of this confession is seen in the fact that at a relatively early stage the followers of Jesus were called "Christians" (*christianoi* — Acts 11:26; 26:28; 1 Pet 4:16), and before long the movement was called "Christianity" (*christianismos,* used first in Ignatius in the early second century). "Christology" deals with the question, "Who is Jesus?" BT's primary concern is with the answer given to this question in canonical Scripture, and this has formed the subject matter of the above chapter. Historical-critical scholarship has sought to penetrate behind the canonical text and raise the question of "Jesus' messianic self-consciousness," i.e., to ask the question, "Who did Jesus think he was?" as distinct from the question, "Who did the Gospel writers think Jesus was?" It has pursued several quests for "the Jesus of history" as distinct from "the Christ of faith."

Some scholars have considered this an impossible task since we have no direct access of any kind to Jesus' self-consciousness. Others have boldly sought to disentangle from the Gospel material what is "authentic" and goes back to the historical Jesus, as distinguished from material that is the product of the early Christian community. The "Jesus Seminar" is but one manifestation of this approach that has a two-hundred-year history behind it. BT is not primarily concerned with such historical considerations, but it cannot totally ignore them. One strand of historical-critical scholarship has held that the ministry of the historical Jesus was nonmessianic: Jesus made no claims to be Messiah, and such claims were introduced only by the early church. Mark believed Jesus to be the Messiah, but he inherited traditions which were originally nonmessianic and sought to deal with them by inventing the literary device of "the messianic secret."

Such a position, if true, would seriously undermine the claims of the entire NT that Jesus was the promised Messiah, for it would introduce a fatal discontinuity between the Jesus of history and the Christ of faith. It is essential that there should be, not necessarily an identity, but at least a continuity between the claims, both explicit and implicit, made by Jesus for himself and the claims made for him by the early church. In the question of Jesus' messianic self-consciousness, a strong case can in fact be made for the basic historicity of the Gospel material. Not only sayings material but also narrative must be taken into consideration; as Cronk (1982) suggests, Jesus' "threefold work of preaching, teaching and miracle-working was, in effect, an enacted or performative announcement of his identity" (140). Historically the reticence with which Jesus refers to himself as the Messiah (especially in the Synoptic Gospels) makes good sense. Open claims to be the Messiah would have at best given rise to misunderstanding, and at worst encouraged armed rebellion against Rome. The Gospels themselves clearly indicate that while Jesus claimed to be Messiah, he radically reinterpreted the popular understanding of the term. The NT witness to Jesus as the Christ has a solid historical basis in Jesus' life and ministry, but allowance has always to be made for the fact that every book of the NT was written after Jesus' death and resurrection when it was abundantly clear that Jesus was not a military or political messiah, and when the term could thus be freely used in a way that was impossible in Jesus' lifetime. John's Gospel emphasizes that Jesus' own disciples recognized the true nature of his claims only after his resurrection (see 2:22; 12:16).

4. The NT expresses the significance of Jesus in the first instance in terms drawn from salvation history, from God's dealings with his chosen people in the OT. The significance of Christ is universal, but part of "the scandal of particularity" is that Jesus became incarnate as a Jew, as part of the particular tradition used by God to prepare for his coming. The NT portrait of Jesus as the new Moses, and as messianic king, priest, prophet, and wise teacher, has to be understood in the first instance against the background of this particular tradition. The task of the contemporary theologian will be to transpose these categories into ones that are meaningful to people today, but without compromising the claims made for Jesus in the biblical material.

5. Most important of all, though the NT presents Jesus as the promised "Messiah," that title is qualified in three fundamentally important ways. First of all, as demonstrated above, in the case of each of the five messianic categories, while the type points forward to and illuminates the identity of Jesus as the Christ, nevertheless in each case the antitype far exceeds the type, and thus all the categories are themselves radically reinterpreted through their application to Jesus. Secondly, the category of "Messiah," however defined, is seen as inadequate on its own to define the identity of Jesus. One must combine it with the title "Son of Man" (see chap. 7), and above all "Son of God" (see chap. 8), to see the full picture of who Jesus is. Thirdly, Jesus is not only "Messiah" but also "Suffering Servant" (see chap. 9). Herein lies the truly new and revolutionary basis of NT Christology, which undoubtedly goes back to Jesus himself. Christ is indeed the messianic king who will one day triumph over all the enemies of God, but his triumph comes only through suffering and death: before the crown comes the cross.

CHAPTER 7

The Son of Man

Old Testament: Proclamation

7-1. SON OF MAN, I SEND YOU

In addition to the different categories of "servant" discussed in chapter 6, the title "Son of Man" is used in Scripture to designate God's people, or at least the faithful remnant thereof, as God's servant, and especially to designate an apocalyptic Servant of the Lord who will bring God's judgment and salvation at the time of the end.

7-1.1. THE SON OF MAN PROBLEM

In 6-3 we noted that in two key scenes in the Synoptic Gospels, Peter's confession at Caesarea Philippi (Mark 8:27-33 and //s) and the trial before the high priest (Mark 14:61-62 and //s), Jesus seems reluctant to take the title "Messiah" *(christos)* on his lips and immediately switches to the expression "Son of Man" *(ho huios tou anthrōpou;* while the basic meaning of this term is a "human being," the English phrase "Son of Man" is employed here as a literal translation of the Hebrew, Aramaic, and Greek originals). It is clear that this was Jesus' own title of choice. It occurs frequently in the Gospels (in John as well as the Synoptics), in all the sources identified by critical scholars (Mark, Q, M, and L), and always on Jesus' own lips. On the other hand, it hardly ever appears outside of the Gospels, the only exceptions being Acts 7:56 and Rev 1:13 and 14:14.

The "Son of Man problem" has been exhaustively discussed by scholars. Studies have focused both on the origin and meaning of "Son of Man" in Judaism (in the OT, intertestamental literature, and nonbiblical sources) and on the use of the term by Jesus. The results have often been confusing and frequently negative. No agreement has been reached on the origin and meaning of the term, and many critical scholars deny that Jesus uttered some or all of the sayings. More than one scholar has asked the question, "Is the Son of Man problem really insoluble?" (Hooker 1979).

BT focuses primarily on the canonical text, though it cannot ignore historical problems completely. For the purposes of BT, it is wise to take our basic orientation from the Gospels and to begin with that of which we can be reasonably certain.

1. In the Gospels "Son of Man" appears as a title (correctly reproduced in virtually all English translations with a capital, or capitals, as either "Son of man" or "Son of Man"). The term is not only accepted by Jesus and applied to himself, but it appears to have been the title he preferred.

2. In the Gospels no attempt is made to explain the origin or significance of "Son of Man." The conclusion is thus inescapable that Jesus assumed that the basic meaning of the term was already known to his hearers (cf. Maddox 1968: 48). This could be the case only if "Son of Man" circulated and had meaning in at least some part of contemporary Judaism. Jesus does, however, modify the term in a significant way (by associating it with suffering and death). There is a close analogy with Jesus' use of "kingdom of God"; here too the term must have been familiar and meant something to his hearers, though Jesus goes on to modify and interpret it in a unique way.

3. Despite the fact that the Greek expression for "Son of Man," *ho huios tou anthrōpou*, represents an underlying Aramaic expression that means basically "a human being," this is clearly *not* what it means in the Gospels. It does *not* designate Jesus as a mere human being, but on the contrary is an exalted title that portrays Jesus as an authoritative figure in his earthly life and identifies him as an apocalyptic figure, presently in heaven, who will come as God's agent of judgment and salvation at the end of history.

4. Some of Jesus' sayings clearly echo Dan 7, and this is thus an important text that is part of the background of the NT usage. But on its own, Dan 7 does not explain Jesus' use of the term, and therefore we must assume that some further development took place after Dan 7 but before the time of Jesus.

5. That the title was preserved in the earliest Christian communities and reproduced in all four Gospels is a tribute to the historicity of the Gospels and their fidelity to their sources, since it is clear that "Son of Man" did not last long as a christological title in the early church. It is not used by Paul (though, as we shall see, it reappears in Paul in a new form). The logical explanation is that the term was abandoned as soon as Christianity spread into the Greco-Roman world, where there was little knowledge of Jewish apocalyptic and where the term in Greek made little or no sense to those unaware of the Aramaic original.

Taking these points as our basic orientation, we shall examine the use of the term in the OT in 7-1, then its use in Dan 7 and the development of the term between Dan 7 and NT times in 7-2.

7-1.2. ADAM AND HUMANKIND

In the OT the English phrase "son of man" translates the Hebrew *ben 'ādhām* (the Aramaic equivalent is *bar nāsh* or *bar 'enāsh;* for a summary of the philological problems, see Hahn 1969: 15-17). The Hebrew *ben* (Aram. *bar*) means "son of."

The Hebrew *'ādhām* is a frequently occurring word in the OT (562 times), usually translated "man." More correctly, *'ādhām* is usually a collective noun meaning "humankind" or "humanity," i.e., human beings, as distinct from God or animals (cf. Gen 2) but without reference to sex, race, or other distinction (Fraine 1965: 135-36). The collective nature of the term is shown by the fact that it is never used in the plural, e.g., Isa 31:3, "The Egyptians are human (*'ādhām*), and not God." *'ādhām* is often used of individuals, always in the sense of human beings, and hence should be translated "person" or "one"; e.g., "Blessed is the person *('ādhām)* to whom the Lord imputes no iniquity" (Ps 32:2 AT).

Gen 1 and 2 speak of the creation of *'ādhām*, and 1:27-28 makes it clear that the term includes both male and female: "So God created *'ādhām* in his own image . . . male and female he created *them*. And God blessed *them*." In the second creation account (2:18-25), *'ādhām* is differentiated into male and female, man and woman, and the common terms *'îsh* (man, male, husband) and *'ishshâh* (woman, female, wife) are introduced. "Only after the appearance of the *'ishshâh* did he [Adam] function as an *'îsh*" (Bratsiotis 1974: 227). Although *'îsh* is generally used in the sense of man/male/husband, it is important to note that, depending on the context, it too can be used in the general sense of "humankind"; see, e.g., Isa 2:9, Jer 2:6 where it is used in parallelism with *'ādhām*. The same is true of another less common word, *'enôsh*, that means "man" but is equally capable of signifying "humankind" (e.g., Ps 8:4). In Gen 4 and 5 and in a few later references (e.g., 1 Chr 1:1; Job 31:33; and of course in the NT), "Adam" is used as a proper name to denote the first man in distinction from the first woman, Eve *(chawwâh)*.

The corresponding term, *'enāsh*, in biblical Aramaic usually has the general sense of human beings/humankind (e.g., Dan 2:10; 3:10; 5:5).

A common biblical idiom links the Hebrew *ben* (Aram. *bar*), meaning "son" or "child," with a noun to denote the class or type to which a person belongs, e.g., "a son of peace" = a peaceful person. Thus the expression *ben 'ādhām* (Aram. *bar nāsh* or *bar 'enāsh*) means a human being, a member of the human race, and the plural *benê 'ādhām* means "human beings," "all those who make up the human race or share the human situation" (Fraine 1965: 140-41), as in, e.g., Ps 115:16:

The heavens are the LORD's heavens,
  but the earth he has given to *human beings*.

$b^e n\hat{e}$ '*îsh* can be used in the same sense (Ps 62:9), as can the Aramaic $b^e n\hat{e}$-
'^{a}nāshā' (Dan 2:38).

The context will determine what aspect of human nature is being referred
to. The story of the fall in Gen 3 underlines the weakness and sinfulness of
'*ādhām*, but other passages such as Ps 8:4 emphasize humankind's God-given
dignity:

> What are human beings *('^{e}nôsh)* that you are mindful of them,
> mortals *(ben-'ādhām)* that you care for them?

7-1.3. ANGEL OR HUMAN BEING

In order to speak to his people, God often uses a human being. In some cases
the human figure is not clearly differentiated from an angel (cf. 1-1.3b).

In Josh 5:13 the "man" *('îsh)* who stood before Joshua is evidently a supernatural figure, the "commander of the army of the LORD," but in Gen 18:1–19:16
and Judg 13 it is not clear whether the "men" are supernatural beings (or even
God himself) or are to be thought of as human beings used by God as "angels"
(mal'ākîm) in the sense of "messengers."

7-1.4. MEN AND WOMEN OF GOD

On numerous occasions in the OT God speaks to and through human beings,
men and occasionally women. In 6-1 we examined in detail the various categories of persons used by God. Here we note the fairly frequent phrase "man of
God" *('îsh '^{e}lōhîm)*.

Some passages refer to a "man of God" who remains anonymous (1 Sam
2:27; 1 Kgs 13:1-31; 20:28; 2 Kgs 23:16-17; 2 Chr 25:7, 9). The title is applied specifically to Moses (Deut 33:1; Ps 90:1; etc.), Samuel (1 Sam 9:5-14), David (2 Chr
8:14; Neh 12:24, 36), Elijah (1 Kgs 17:18, 24; 2 Kgs 1:9-13), Elisha (2 Kgs 4:7-16),
and others. A "man of God" is thus a person specially chosen by God to serve
him.

There is no corresponding phrase "woman of God," although women do
figure in two of the categories of God's servants, those of "prophet" and "wise
person" (see 15-1.5b).

7-1.5. O SON OF MAN

Ninety-three times in the book of Ezekiel the prophet is addressed as *ben
'ādhām*, usually translated "son of man," in the sense of "human being" or "hu-

man one." Thus God says to Ezekiel, "Son of man, stand upon your feet, and I will speak with you" (2:1 RSV; cf. 2:3; 2:8; etc.).

The term seems to have a twofold significance. In contrast to the overpowering experience of the divine presence in Ezek 1, the prophet is a mere human being. Yet the phrase also sounds like a title, conferring a certain dignity and authority. Out of all humankind this human being is the individual chosen by God for this particular situation; this individual is the recipient of God's Spirit (2:2) and God's Word (2:8–3:3) (cf. A. Richardson 1958: 128; D. S. Russell 1964: 341).

Once only is Daniel addressed in similar fashion. When the angel Gabriel approaches him, Daniel falls on his face and hears Gabriel say, "Understand, O son of man *(ben 'ādhām)*, that the vision is for the time of the end" (Dan 8:17 RSV).

Thus, while it is true that *'ādhām*, "humankind," is in rebellion against God (2-1.5a; 16-1.2), it is also true that God, in carrying out his purpose of salvation, employs *bᵉnê 'ādhām*, "human beings," "individuals." Despite their human nature, it is through such persons that God's message of judgment and of salvation is proclaimed to his people and to all humanity.

Old Testament: Promise

7-2. ONE LIKE A SON OF MAN

As God has acted and spoken in the past through select human beings, so he will bring in the new order through a person of his choosing, a "son of man" or "human one."

7-2.1. WITH THE CLOUDS OF HEAVEN

This expectation originates in Dan 7, which we have already noted as a key OT passage (1-2.1; on Dan 7 see T. W. Manson 1950b: 173-75; Hooker 1967: 11-30; Nickelsburg 1992: 137-38; it should be noted that Dan 7 is in Aramaic, not Hebrew). After the vision of the four beasts representing successive world empires, Daniel sees a vision of God sitting in judgment on the kingdoms of this world. Daniel sees "in the night visions,"

> and behold, with the clouds of heaven
> > there came one like a son of man *(kᵉbhar 'ᵉnāsh)*,
> and he came to the Ancient of Days
> > and was presented before him.

And to him was given dominion
    and glory and kingdom,
that all peoples, nations, and languages
    should serve him. (7:13-14 RSV)

Daniel is then given the interpretation of the vision. The four beasts are four kings who shall arise out of the earth, "but the holy ones of the Most High shall receive the kingdom and possess the kingdom forever — forever and ever" (7:18). In 7:27,

The kingship and dominion
    and the greatness of the kingdoms under the whole heaven
    shall be given to the people of the holy ones of the Most High.

Just as each beast symbolizes a world empire, so the "one like a son of man" is *a collective figure* symbolizing "the holy ones of the Most High," i.e., God's faithful people, and specifically, in the context of the book of Daniel, the faithful remnant, those of his people who remain true to God despite suffering and persecution (cf. Bruce 1982: 55). There is no indication in the text of Dan 7 that the "one like a son of man" was understood as referring to an individual figure, whether the Davidic messiah, personified Wisdom, or an angel (see Dunn 1980: 69-74; contra Chilton 1996: 36-37).

The passage delivers a word of hope to God's faithful people: Despite their present trials, a day is coming when the situation will be reversed. The persecuting empire will be destroyed and God's people will inherit a universal kingdom. Suffering will be replaced by vindication.

7-2.2. THE ADAM CONNECTION

Why is the figure representing God's faithful people in Dan 7 depicted as "one like a son of man"? Some scholars have seen here the influence of ancient Near Eastern speculations regarding an "original man" or "heavenly man" as reconstructed by the history of religions school (cf. D. S. Russell 1964: 345-50). Be that as it may, BT is concerned not with the origin of the phrase but with its meaning in the context of canonical Scripture.

A number of features of Dan 7 recall the opening chapters of Genesis and suggest a connection between the first human being and the "one like a son of man."

a. The vision of the winds stirring up "the great sea," and of the "four great beasts" that "came up out of the sea," recalls "the deep" and "the waters" of Gen 1:2, and also the beast or dragon (cf. 4-1.3) that symbolizes the powers of chaos and disorder, restrained by God in the process of creation.

b. The description of the fourth beast in particular emphasizes that the world empires are "bestial" in their cruelty and savagery; the coming kingdom, by contrast, will be "human" or "humane," representing human beings as God intended them to be when he first created them.

c. The "dominion" *(sholṭān)* given to the one like a human being in Dan 7:14 recalls the dominion over the beasts granted to humankind in Gen 1:28 (cf. 2-1.3b).

d. The strongly universal note struck in Dan 7:14 suggests the basic apocalyptic understanding of the end as a restoration of the beginning (cf. 2-2.4). "All peoples, nations, and languages" will serve the one like a son of man, thus restoring the basic unity of humankind, symbolized by *'ādhām* but marred by the fall and the fragmentation of humankind into different peoples (Gen 10) and languages (Gen 11).

The fact that "the holy ones of the Most High" are symbolized by "one like a son of man" is far from accidental; in the coming age, all that is "inhuman" will be done away with and God's people will be the representatives of humanity and of the human race as God intended them to be.

7-2.3. AN INDIVIDUAL ESCHATOLOGICAL FIGURE

Between the figure of the Son of Man in Dan 7 and the title "Son of Man" in the Gospels there is obviously a considerable gap. In Daniel the "one like a son of man" is a collective figure, symbolizing the faithful remnant of God's people; in the Gospels the Son of Man is an individual figure. In Daniel the "one like a son of man" comes with the clouds of heaven *to* God, from whom he receives the kingdom; in the Gospels the Son of Man comes with the clouds of heaven *from* God to judge the wicked and bring God's salvation to the righteous.

The obvious conclusion to draw would be that in the period between Daniel and the NT the term "son of man" had been individualized and had developed into an apocalyptic, Messiah-type figure. This is in fact the view held by many scholars (e.g., Cullmann 1963: 140-42; R. H. Fuller 1969: 36-42; Nickelsburg 1992: 138-42), though also disputed by others (e.g., Dunn 1980: 67-82; Borsch 1992: 131-35). The debate has raged to and fro (cf. Leivestadt 1972; Lindars 1975) without any universally accepted conclusion.

Even if there were no literary evidence of this development, Jesus' use of the term in the Gospels would require us to assume that some such reinterpretation had taken place. In fact, however, there is evidence that in some quarters within Judaism, the "one like a son of man" of Dan 7 had developed into an individual apocalyptic figure, the agent of God's judgment and salvation at the end of days (see D. S. Russell 1964: 327-34).

One place where there is evidence of this is in the Similitudes of Enoch (= *1 Enoch* 37–71), which formed one segment of a quite extensive Enoch literature (see T. W. Manson 1950b: 176-89; Hooker 1967: 33-48; Nickelsburg 1992: 138-40). In this work that clearly echoes Dan 7, the phrase "that son of man" does refer to an individual apocalyptic figure, equated with "the Elect One," "the Righteous One," "the Righteous and Elect One," and "the Lord's Messiah," who will be God's eschatological agent of judgment and salvation. Of the wicked it is said:

> And they shall be downcast of countenance
> And pain shall seize them,
> When they see that son of man
> Sitting on the throne of his glory. (1 Enoch 62:5)

On the other hand, the elect "shall be saved on that day," and "with that son of man they shall eat and lie down and rise up for ever and ever" (62:14). Several passages in the Similitudes suggest that this work came from a group that "did not expect a political Messiah who would defeat the enemies of Israel in an earthly war and establish a political kingdom, but the supernatural, heavenly 'Son of Man' . . . the pre-existent heavenly being who lives in heaven from the beginning of time until he comes to earth at the end of time" (Cullmann 1963: 142). Here again, some historical scholars have seen the influence of belief in a divine "original man." Another conception of the Son of Man is also found in the Similitudes: in other passages he is apparently identified with Enoch, an outstanding example of a pious human being (Gen 5:18-24), now exalted to heaven (Gen 5:24; 1 Enoch 71; cf. Lindars 1975: 59).

The use of Enoch, however, is fraught with problems for BT. Scholarly controversy rages regarding the origin, dating, and significance of the various parts of the Enoch literature. There is no clear evidence that the Similitudes existed prior to the time of Jesus (cf. Dunn 1980: 77). They have not been found among the Dead Sea Scrolls, though it would be precarious to draw any inference from this (contra Leivestadt 1972: 246). On the other hand, it is clear that they are a typical Jewish apocalyptic work that almost certainly reflects traditions originating before the time of Jesus.

Moreover, Enoch is not part of canonical Scripture and so cannot be used directly in BT (interestingly enough, however, it is accepted as canonical by the Ethiopian Church).

7-2.4. LIKE THE FIGURE OF A MAN

We are on firmer ground when we turn to 2 Esdras (see Tödt 1963: 24-27). It is true that in its present form this is a Christian work, or at least has undergone Christian revision, but chapters 3–14 incorporate a Jewish apocalypse of the late first century A.D. that in turn almost certainly draws on earlier, traditional, apocalyptic material. It can therefore shed light on apocalyptic beliefs that circulated in NT times.

Moreover, 2 *Esdras* was regarded as of value by early Christians and circulated in a wide number of versions, including the Old Latin. Following the Council of Trent it was included as an appendix to the Vulgate, under the title the Fourth Book of Esdras, so it has had some measure of canonical recognition in part of the Christian tradition. Few if any would argue today that it should be regarded as canonical Scripture, but it is of value in tracing the development of Jewish apocalyptic beliefs that shed light on the NT.

In 2 *Esdr* 13 Ezra describes a dream: "And lo, a wind arose from the sea and stirred up all its waves. As I kept looking the wind made something like the figure of a man come up out of the heart of the sea. And I saw that this man flew with the clouds of heaven" (vv. 2-3). After this "an innumerable multitude of people were gathered together from the four winds of heaven to make war against the man who came up out of the sea. And I looked and saw that he carved out for himself a great mountain, and flew up on to it" (vv. 5-6). The multitude approached, but the figure "sent forth from his mouth something like a stream of fire" that destroyed the attackers. "After this I saw the same man come down from the mountain and call to himself another multitude that was peaceable" (v. 12). An interpretation of the vision is then granted, according to which the man "is he whom the Most High has been keeping for many ages, who will himself deliver his creation" (v. 26). The figure is also identified as "my Son" in vv. 32, 37, 52, who will appear on Mount Zion (v. 35) to judge the nations.

While the references to "that man" and "the clouds of heaven" obviously echo Dan 7, here the "man" has become an individual, preexistent, apocalyptic figure who will defeat the enemy in the final apocalyptic battle and deliver God's faithful people.

7-2.5. THE IDEAL HUMAN BEING

One further development that sheds light on certain NT passages remains to be noted. Mention of the figure of Adam generally conjures up pictures of the fall of Gen 3 and its consequences. In the late OT period, however, a tendency arose in some quarters to stress the perfection of Adam and to portray Adam not so much as the originator of human sin but rather as an exalted figure, the ideal human being (see Scroggs 1966: 21-22).

The main section of *Sirach's* hymn "In Praise of Famous Men" concludes:

> Shem and Seth and Enosh were honored,
>   but above every other created living being was Adam. (*Sir* 49:16)

The hymn on Wisdom in history in *Wis* 10–12 begins:

Wisdom protected the first-formed father of the world,
        when he alone had been created;
    she delivered him from his transgression,
and gave him strength to rule all things. (10:1-2)

This understanding of Adam sheds light on the use of the term "son of man" in Dan 7 where, as we have seen (above, 7-2.2), it signifies a "humane" kingdom, representing human beings as God first intended them to be.

It also sheds light on the individual apocalyptic Son of Man of *2 Esdras.* Adam as the ideal human being (rather than the originator of human sin) is an appropriate type of a future apocalyptic figure who will bring salvation not only to God's people but to all humankind.

New Testament: Fulfillment

7-3. BEHOLD, THE SON OF MAN

All four Gospels identify Jesus with the figure of the "Son of Man." The phrase *ho huios tou anthrōpou* is virtually impossible in Greek, but it makes perfect sense as a very literal translation of an underlying Aramaic expression (*bar ʾenāsh*, or in the emphatic form, *bar ʾanāshā*; alternate forms are *bar nāsh*, emphatic *bar nāshā*), i.e., "son of man" or "the son of man." The Gospels presuppose that the expression meant something to Jesus' hearers, and it has been shown above that there is evidence that "Son of Man," while having its origins in Dan 7, developed into a term designating an individual apocalyptic figure, the agent of God's judgment and salvation at the end of days. Jesus builds on this understanding of the term, though he also significantly modifies it. Outside the Gospels "Son of Man" occurs only in Acts 7:56 and Rev 1:13 and 14:14; evidently it quickly dropped out as a christological title. The basic meaning of the title, however, resurfaces in Paul: as Adam was the founder of the human race which is subject to sin and death, Jesus is the Second Man, the eschatological Adam, the one in whom and through whom a new humanity is being created.

7-3.1. THE SON OF MAN IN THE SYNOPTIC GOSPELS

Jesus is associated with the title "Son of Man" in all four Gospels, but since the Johannine usage has distinctive features, it is best, initially at least, to consider the material in the Synoptics and in John separately.

The title occurs sixty-nine times in the Synoptics. It is common and convenient to divide the Synoptic sayings into three main groups on the basis of their content (cf. the discussion in Hahn 1969: 28-42).

Group A: Sayings that speak of *the present activity and authority of the Son of Man.* These sayings all associate the title with Jesus in the course of his earthly ministry. When Jesus says, "The Son of Man came eating and drinking" (Matt 11:19//Luke 7:34), he is obviously referring to himself and to his practice of dining with tax collectors and sinners in contrast to the asceticism of John the Baptist.

The application of the title to Jesus in his ministry is very far from indicating that Jesus is a "mere man." As Son of Man, he has a God-given mission to proclaim the message of the kingdom (Matt 13:37) and to seek and to save the lost (Luke 19:10). He has a unique authority to forgive sins (Mark 2:10 and //s) and to act as lord of the Sabbath (2:28 and //s), prerogatives that in Jewish thought belonged to God alone.

Group B: Sayings that speak of *the rejection, suffering, death, and resurrection of the Son of Man.* In response to Peter's confession, "You are the Messiah," Jesus immediately "began to teach them that the Son of Man must undergo great suffering, and be rejected by the elders, the chief priests, and the scribes, and be killed, and after three days rise again" (Mark 8:31//Matt 16:21; Luke 9:22). This saying is repeated in broadly similar terms in Mark 9:31 (//Matt 17:22-23; cf. Luke 9:44), and yet again in Mark 10:33-34 (//Matt 20:18-19; Luke 18:32). Despite his divine mission and authority, the Son of Man is treated with contempt (Mark 9:12) and rejected (Luke 17:25). Not only does he face opposition from enemies, the Son of Man is betrayed by one of his own followers (Mark 14:21 and //s; 14:41 and //s; Luke 22:48).

Critical scholars make much of the fact that no group B sayings are found in the hypothetical Q source. In response to this, it can be pointed out that the Q sayings include some that refer to the Son of Man's rejection. There are those who speak against the Son of Man (Matt 12:32//Luke 12:10), and who hate and revile his followers (Luke 6:22; cf. Matt 5:11). The Son of Man has nowhere to lay his head (Matt 8:20//Luke 9:58). Secondly, if the Q hypothesis is valid, it was a sayings source that lacked a passion narrative; as such, its aims were limited and it must have been intended to supplement other material (oral or written) that did speak of Jesus' suffering, death, and resurrection (cf. Hooker 1967: 194).

Group B constitutes the bridge between groups A and C. How could the Jesus of the earthly ministry be the Son of Man at God's right hand waiting to come at the end of days as God's agent of judgment and salvation? The unique answer Jesus gave to this question was that the path to the apocalyptic status of the Son of Man lay through rejection, suffering, and death. While group B sayings speak only of the Son of Man rising from the dead, the broader context strongly implies his exaltation to God's right hand.

Group C: Sayings that speak of *the Son of Man's future coming as God's agent of judgment and salvation.* These sayings are all set in an apocalyptic context. The final consummation can be referred to as "the days of the Son of Man" (Luke 17:22) or "the day that the Son of Man is revealed" (17:30). The coming of the Son of Man will be sudden and unexpected (Luke 12:40//Matt 24:44; Luke 17:24//Matt 24:27). In these sayings the Son of Man is an exalted figure, currently "seated at the right hand of the Power," who at the end of the age will come "with the clouds of heaven" (Mark 14:62 and //s; cf. Matt 24:30). While the reference to coming with the clouds of heaven clearly quotes Dan 7:13, the Son of Man is here not a collective figure but an individual who will come at the end of days. He will be *the agent of God's judgment* (Matt 13:41-42; 16:27), so that "those who are ashamed of me and of my words . . . of them the Son of Man will also be ashamed when he comes in the glory of his Father with the holy angels" (Mark 8:38//Luke 9:26; cf. Matt 10:32-33; Luke 12:8-9). He will be *the agent of God's salvation*, gathering in the elect from the ends of the earth (Mark 13:27 and //s), and welcoming the righteous into the kingdom (Matt 25:34) and bestowing on them eternal life (25:46). On this group, see further below, 7-4.2.

In all three groups it is clear that the Evangelists intend that the reader identify Jesus with the Son of Man. Indeed, in a few texts it seems that either the Evangelists or their sources used "Son of Man" and "I" on Jesus' lips interchangeably. Where Mark 8:27 has "Who do people say that I am?" Matt 16:13 has "Who do people say that the Son of Man is?" Conversely, where Luke 6:22 has "Blessed are you when people hate you . . . on account of the Son of Man," Matt 5:11 reads "Blessed are you when people revile you . . . on my account." While this means there may be doubt about the original form of a few sayings, it does confirm the strong early tradition that Jesus used "Son of Man" as a self-designation (cf. Bruce 1982: 52).

Yet, curiously, in none of these texts does Jesus identify himself directly with the Son of Man. This is in contrast to Jesus' use of the term "Messiah"; despite his reticence about claiming this title in public (cf. 6-3), at least in Mark 14:61-62, when the high priest asks Jesus, "Are you the Messiah?" he answers, "I am." *Never,* however, does anyone ask Jesus, "Are you the Son of Man?" or does Jesus answer, "I am." The Synoptic usage constitutes, therefore, what must be termed *indirect identification.*

This observation sheds light on the sayings of group C, for in these sayings Jesus actually speaks of the Son of Man in the third person: "Those who are ashamed of me . . . of them the Son of Man will also be ashamed when *he* comes in the glory of *his* Father" (Mark 8:38). Some scholars have concluded from this that Jesus here speaks of the Son of Man as someone other than himself, and that therefore he did not identify himself as the Son of Man (so Bultmann 1952: 29; cf. Chilton 1996: 39, 46). An examination of these sayings in their canonical context, however, shows quite clearly that the Evangelists understood Jesus to be speaking of himself. We have here an extension of the *indirect identification* found in the other groups. It is as if Jesus did not want directly to claim identity with the Son of Man figure, but wanted his hearers to make that identification for themselves. In relation to group C, therefore, we can speak of an *implied identification* of the earthly Jesus with the coming apocalyptic Son of Man.

7-3.2. THE SON OF MAN IN JOHN'S GOSPEL

John's Gospel agrees with the Synoptics that Jesus spoke of himself as the Son of Man, though it preserves an independent tradition consisting of twelve Son of Man sayings (1:51; 3:13, 14; 5:27; 6:27, 53, 62; 8:28; 9:35; 12:23, 34; 13:31; see Higgins 1964: 153-84; D. Guthrie 1981: 282-90; Nickelsburg 1992: 146-47).

In John "Son of Man" is not merely a variation for "Son of God" or "Son" (contra Freed 1967). The Son of Man sayings are distinctive, and despite some typical Johannine terminology, are for the most part in striking agreement with the Synoptic tradition. As Borsch (1992) remarks, "What is, on any explanation, so remarkable about these sets of traditions is that they say many of the same things about the Son of Man in quite distinctive language" (142).

As in the Synoptics, there is no doubt that the title applies to Jesus, though here too we must speak of indirect identification. The one possible exception is John 8:28, where Jesus says, "When you have lifted up the Son of Man, then you will realize that I am he." Yet even here we may see a variation of what was noted in relation to Mark 8:38: in Jesus' lifetime Jesus' identity with the Son of Man is *implied,* and it is only after his death and resurrection that the church makes this identity explicit (cf. Smalley 1969: 295).

Most of the Johannine sayings can be classified in accordance with the three Synoptic groups, though in John there is in some cases a tendency for sayings to overlap more than one group.

Group A: Some Johannine sayings speak of the present activity and authority of the Son of Man. In his teaching the Son of Man presents a God-given message (John 8:28), and invites people to believe in him (9:35, a text which however has no direct Synoptic parallel). 1:51 may be classified here: in an obvious reference to the story of Jacob's ladder (Gen 28:11-22), Jesus declares, "Very truly, I tell you, you will see heaven opened and the angels of God ascending and descending upon the Son of Man." Just as God revealed himself to Jacob/Israel, so in the ministry that is about to begin the disciples will come to see that God's supreme revelation is given in Jesus.

Group B: As in the Synoptics, the Son of Man meets opposition and death, but is vindicated and raised up by God. The eucharistic saying, John 6:53, with its reference to the Son of Man's flesh and blood, alludes to his death. John is distinctive in speaking of the Son of Man being "lifted up" (3:14; 8:28; 12:34). This is a typical Johannine double meaning; it refers both to Jesus being raised up on the cross *and* to his being exalted to heaven (cf. Cullmann 1963: 185; Smalley 1969: 291). A similar double meaning attaches to the saying that the Son of Man will be "glorified" (12:23). Where John goes beyond the Synoptics is in speaking of the Son of Man's vindication by God not in terms of resurrection but of exaltation (something that is implicit but not directly stated in the Synoptics). Hence the references to the Son of Man "ascending" into heaven (3:13; 6:62).

Group C: There are also Johannine sayings that speak of the Son of Man as God's agent of judgment and salvation. God has given the Son of Man authority to execute judgment (5:27). The Son of Man is the one who confers eternal life (3:14-15; 6:27; cf. 6:53; cf. Matt 25:46), though here, typically of John, eternal life may be thought of as both present and future (cf. Smalley 1969: 293).

The one feature of the Johannine sayings that is not paralleled in the Synoptics is the reference to the Son of Man's "descending" from heaven (John 3:13; cf. 6:62). This allusion to the Son of Man's preexistence is in accordance with John's emphasis on this theme.

7-3.3. THE THEOLOGICAL PROCLAMATION

BT's prime concern is with the view of Jesus as the Son of Man presented in the canonical Gospels. What does it mean that they portray Jesus as the Son of Man?

a. Jesus Is the Inclusive Representative of God's People

Some of the Gospel sayings clearly allude to Dan 7, where the Son of Man, as we have seen (7-2.1), represents God's people, or rather the faithful remnant. (Note especially the references to the Son of Man's "coming on the clouds of heaven," e.g., Matt 24:30 = Dan 7:13; cf. Mark 14:62.) Thus, while the Gospels clearly presuppose that the Son of Man is an individual, apocalyptic figure, the collective interpretation of Dan 7 is not completely left behind. In terms of the biblical community/individual dialectic, an individual "Son of Man" can represent God's people Israel as God intended them to be. Jesus is in effect the faithful remnant of God's people reduced to one person; he alone is truly faithful, and truly fulfills the role that God intended his chosen people to play in the historical order (cf. Cullmann 1963: 156).

The Bible portrays a progressive narrowing down of God's people that may be represented diagrammatically:

```
\   I   S   R   A   E   L   /
 \                        /
  \   R E M N A N T      /
   \                    /
    \  THE TWELVE      /
     \               /
      \   JESUS     /
```

Although God called Israel as a people to serve him, in practice only a remnant remained faithful (see 11-2.2a). Jesus' twelve disciples represent a further narrowing down, though with the intention of forming the core of a new Israel. But at the supreme crisis in Jesus' ministry, they too prove unfaithful. Finally, on the cross, Jesus alone is the Danielic Son of Man, the sole inclusive representative of God's people Israel (cf. the allusion to Jacob/Israel in John 1:51; see above, 7-3.2). The classic statement of this view is found in T. W. Manson's *The Teaching of Jesus* (1935). Manson argued that Jesus' mission was "to create the Son of Man, the Kingdom of the saints of the Most High, to realise in Israel the ideal contained in the term. This task is attempted in two ways: first by public appeal to the people through the medium of parable and sermon and by the mission of the disciples: then, when this appeal produced no adequate response, by the consolidation of his own band of followers. Finally, when it becomes apparent that not even the disciples are ready to rise to the demands of the ideal, he stands alone, embodying in his own person the perfect human response to the regal claims of God" (227-28). Thus "Jesus embodies the Israelite ideal and embodies Israel" (T. W. Manson 1950b: 192).

While this interpretation has merit and helps us understand what the NT means by identifying Jesus as "the Son of Man," it is not the whole truth. It does not include the universal and cosmic elements in the Son of Man title, and it does not fully explain the expectation of the Son of Man as the apocalyptic agent of God at the end of days. It does, however, help us understand the references in group B to it being "written" that the Son of Man must suffer (Mark 9:12; Mark 14:21//Matt 26:24; Luke 18:31). As a future apocalyptic figure, the Son of Man was certainly not expected to suffer. But Jesus' own unique contribution lay in his combining the type of figure portrayed in Dan 7 and the type of figure portrayed in 2 *Esdras*. As the inclusive representative of Israel, the one who is truly obedient to God, Jesus suffers as all God's faithful servants have; but it is because of his perfect obedience that he expects to be vindicated as the future Son of Man.

b. Jesus Is the Inclusive Representative of Humanity

Even in Daniel the Son of Man has broader connotations; as we have seen (7-2.2), he echoes the figure of Adam, representing all humankind. So Jesus is the inclusive representative not only of Israel, God's people, but also of all humanity. He is the culmination of God's saving activity not only in the historical order but also in the created order.

Luke's genealogy traces Jesus all the way back to Seth as "son of Adam, son of God" (Luke 3:38); and undoubtedly "Luke's purpose in tracing the ancestry of Christ to Adam is to emphasize the Lord's solidarity with the entire human race" (Cronk 1982: 132). In Gen 3 humankind fell to the temptation of the ser-

THE SON OF MAN

pent; in his temptations Jesus, representing humankind, resists the temptation of Satan. The vision of the sheep and the goats in Matt 25:31-46 sheds further light on the understanding of Jesus as representing all humanity. "When the Son of Man comes in his glory," he presides over the judgment, and tells those who serve their fellow human beings, "Truly I tell you, just as you did it to one of the least of these who are members of my family, you did it to me." To help a fellow human being is to help the Son of Man, because he represents and is indeed present in all humanity; "the Son of Man comprehends *all* men" (Cullmann 1963: 158). We catch an echo of the same understanding of Jesus in John 19:5 where Pilate says of Jesus, "Here is the man!" *(idou ho anthrōpos)*. Jesus, as a human being perfectly obedient to God, represents not the Adam whose rebellion and disobedience brought sin and death into the world, but Adam as the ideal human being (above, 7-2.5), the one who typifies what God intended human beings to be.

c. The Son of Man Has Authority

The Son of Man/Human One is presented in the Gospels as an authoritative figure, the very opposite in fact of a "mere man." He has the authority to forgive sin (Mark 2:10), a prerogative normally preserved for God; "in this respect . . . the Son of Man has been invested with the authority of God himself, and he acts as God's representative and with his power" (Hooker 1967: 90). He declares himself to be "lord even of the sabbath" (Mark 2:28), placing himself above one of the commandments of the Decalogue. And yet, paradoxically, this authority is exercised by one who has nowhere to lay his head (Matt 8:20//Luke 9:58). Thus "the majority of Son of Man sayings can be seen as forming one pattern in which the general theme of authority, its rejection and its vindication, is expressed" (Marshall 1970b: 81).

d. The Path to Glory Leads through Suffering

This is stressed particularly in the Synoptic group B sayings. The overall pattern of this group is strongly reminiscent of the Suffering Servant of 2 Isaiah, who is rejected, suffers for the sins of others, is put to death, but is raised up and vindicated by God. Basically the same theme is also apparent in the paradoxical Johannine references to the Son of Man's "lifting up" and "glorification" (John 3:14; 8:28; 12:23; 13:31). At this point the title Son of Man reflects what is in fact the central paradox of the NT. Jesus is a "son of man" in the original sense: he is a real human being, subject to all the ills that beset the human race. He stands in the succession of "men of God" (above, 7-1.4) and servants of God such as the prophet Ezekiel, who was addressed as "son of man" (above, 7-1.5), and like such servants he faces opposition and hence suffering. Yet he is also the Son of Man in the exalted sense of the title, the one who speaks with God's authority and will be the agent of God's judgment and salvation at the final consummation. What the group B sayings make clear is that "the link between the earthly Jesus as the Son of Man and the Son of Man as the heavenly, universal judge is the crucifixion of Jesus, after which he is raised from death and exalted to heaven" (Maddox 1968: 73). The most distinctive feature of NT Christology is its combining of the apocalyptic Son of Man figure with the humble Suffering Servant; on this, see further 9-3.1.

7-3.4. THE SECOND ADAM

a. Christ and Adam

It is surprising that Paul does not speak of Jesus as the Son of Man. Because of the background of the term in Jewish apocalyptic, he evidently preferred to present Christ in ways that would be more readily understood in his predominantly Gentile, Hellenistic churches.

Yet Paul must surely have known of the pre-Gospel tradition that linked Jesus with the Son of Man, since he knows and utilizes other aspects of the very early Christian apocalyptic tradition. A study of Pauline theology reveals that he has in fact transposed the Son of Man tradition into a new key in those passages where, in his own way, he draws a parallel between Adam and Christ (cf. Shed 1964: 151-73; Ziesler 1990: 52-57; Borsch 1992: 140-41; H. N. Wallace 1992: 64).

There can be no doubt that Paul had pondered deeply the story of the creation and fall of Adam/humankind in Gen 1–3. In Rom 5:12-21 Paul draws a parallel between Adam and Christ (cf. Cullmann 1963: 170-73): "sin came into the world through one man," i.e., Adam/humankind, and death through sin. But the situation is no longer hopeless; it has been reversed through "the one man, Jesus Christ" (v. 15). In this way, according to Paul, Adam is "a type *(typos)* of the one who was to come," i.e., of Christ. Both Adam and Christ are *representative figures;* Adam represents humanity in rebellion against God, while Christ represents the new humanity. As is often the case in BT, the correspondence between the two figures is one of contrast more than comparison: "the free gift is *not* like the trespass" (v. 15). Adam is characterized by his disobedience of God, Christ by his obedience; what Adam did led to death, what Christ did led to life; what Adam did led to condemnation, what Christ did led to justification (cf. Barrett 1962: 15-16; Scroggs 1966: 76-82).

In 1 Cor 15:21-22, 45-49 Paul elaborates on this understanding of the Adam/Christ typology (cf. Cullmann 1963: 167-70; Scroggs 1966: 82-89). "For since death came through a human being [*anthrōpos,* i.e., Adam/humankind], the resurrection of the dead has also come through a human being [*anthrōpos*, i.e., Christ]; for as all die in Adam, so all will be made alive in Christ" (vv. 21-22). Hence Christ can be called "the last Adam *(ho eschatos adam)*" (v. 45). Adam was "the first man" *(ho prōtos anthrōpos)* who was "from the earth"; Christ is "the second man" *(ho deuteros anthrōpos)* who is "from heaven" (v. 47). Here again, while this may be termed "Adam typology," it is the *contrast* between the two figures that is emphasized.

Whereas in Romans the emphasis is more on life in the present, in 1 Corinthians the Second Man brings resurrection life. "In his body of glory Christ is true humanity, the realization of that existence that the Christian will himself have one day. Christ is also the mediator of that nature" (Scroggs 1966: 92). These passages show that "Paul believes that the eschatological age has been inaugurated by a man who embodies God's intent for all men — an intent thwarted by the first Adam, fulfilled by the Last" (ix).

At this point the traditional distinction between Christology and atonement breaks down. It is the recognition that Christ as Son of Man is the inclusive representative of all humankind, and as the Last/Second Adam represents the new humanity, that forms the foundation for one of the most important ways of understanding the meaning of Christ's death and resurrection in the NT. See 9-3.4c, "Identification/Incorporation."

b. The Christ Hymn of Philippians 2

Adam-Christ typology is also present in the great christological hymn of Phil 2:6-11 (see Cullmann 1963: 174-81). Historically it is likely that Paul quotes here from an early Christian hymn, in which case this type of Christology must have existed from a very early stage. Canonically it comes to us as part of the Pauline corpus, though in contrast to the passages reviewed above, here the Adam/Christ typology is implicit rather than explicit.

The statement that Christ was in the "form" *(morphē)* of God recalls the creation of Adam/humankind in the "image" of God (Gen 1:26). Unlike Adam (Gen 3:5), Christ

> did not regard equality with God
> as something to be exploited. (Phil 2:6)

Christ reverses the process; instead of displaying pride, the essence of which is the desire to be like God, Christ displayed humility, and despite the divine nature that was already his, he humbled himself and was born in the likeness of human beings *(en homoiōmati anthrōpōn genomenos)* and as a man *(hos anthrōpos)*. Whereas Adam/humankind disobeyed God with tragic consequences for the human race, Christ became obedient (cf. Rom 5:19) even unto death. Adam's disobedience led to the fall and the loss of lordship over creation; Christ's obedience led to his exaltation (Phil 2:9) and the acknowledgment of his Lordship (2:10-11) over all creation (cf. Barrett 1962: 16-17).

While the hymn does reflect Adam/Christ typology, it is important that the parallelism not be pushed too far (contra Bakken 1968: 74-76). According to Phil 2:6, Christ did not regard equality with God as a *harpagmos*. It has long been recognized that this Greek word is ambiguous. It could mean "something to be snatched at" *(res rapienda)*. On this basis some have contended that the Christ hymn begins with Jesus (like Adam) as an ordinary man. Adam in his pride snatched at equality with God and thus fell; Christ in his humility obeyed God even unto death and was rewarded by being exalted to a heavenly status. This may be good parallelism, but it is not what the passage in its present form says. *Harpagmos* can also mean "something to cling on to" *(res rapta)*, and this is the meaning that the canonical context requires. Christ originally had divine status, for he was "in the form of God" (2:6), but in humility he took on human form in the incarnation. The hymn thus follows the basic canonical NT pattern of preexistent divine status/incarnation/exaltation to divine status (see 8-3.1, and cf. Barrett 1962: 70-72).

c. The Son of Man in Hebrews

Although commentators are divided (see P. Giles 1975: 329), a strong case can be made for the presence of the Son of Man tradition in Hebrews. Ps 8:4-6 is quoted in Heb 2:

> What is man that thou art mindful of him,
>   or the son of man, that thou carest for him?
> Thou didst make him for a little while lower than the angels,
>   thou hast crowned him with glory and honor,
>   putting everything in subjection under his feet. (vv. 6-8 RSV)

The chapter then goes on in v. 9 to identify "the son of man" with Jesus, who in his incarnation "for a little while was made lower than the angels," but now is "crowned with glory and honor because of the suffering of death." The pattern of humiliation/glorification is suggestive of the Johannine Son of Man sayings in particular (cf. Cullmann 1963: 188), though the understanding of Jesus as the inclusive representative of humanity also seems to be in view (cf. Giles, 330). Jesus is the divine Son and the exalted Son of Man, but only because he was also fully identified with humanity in his incarnation (cf. vv. 17-18).

7-3.5. THE EXALTED SON OF MAN

The Son of Man/Second Adam who lived in humility on earth and who suffered and died, following his resurrection has been exalted to heaven (on the ascension, see further 10-3.2).

In Acts 7:55-56 the dying Stephen gazes into heaven where he sees "Jesus standing at the right hand of God," and says, "I see the heavens opened and the Son of Man standing at the right hand of God!" A unique feature of this vision is that Stephen sees the Son of Man *standing (hestōta);* reflecting Ps 110:1, the NT generally pictures the exalted Christ *sitting* at the right hand of God (cf. 10-3.3). The *standing* Son of Man probably envisages the exalted Christ as Stephen's advocate or intercessor before the Father (cf. Cullmann 1963: 183), or alternatively as rising to welcome the first Christian martyr (see commentaries). Bruce points out that when Stephen sees the exalted Son of Man, "he has just acknowledged Jesus before the Sanhedrin; now he in turn is acknowledged by the Son of Man, standing at God's right hand as advocate on Stephen's behalf" (Bruce 1969: 28; see Mark 8:38; and cf. above, 7-3.1, "Group C").

In the opening vision of Revelation (1:12-16) John sees the Son of Man who is to come at the final consummation (below, 7-4.3), presently in heaven: "In the midst of the lampstands I saw one like the Son of Man" (v. 13). The picture is a composite one, with features drawn from a variety of OT sources (see commentaries). The most striking part of the description is v. 14: "His head and his hair were white as wool, white as snow," a clear allusion to the description of the Ancient One in Dan 7:9 (see Lindars 1975: 63). Here, as in John 3:13; 6:62, we have the climax of the revelation of the Son of Man: he is indeed a human figure, but at the same time he is fully divine.

New Testament: Consummation

7-4. ONE LIKE A SON OF MAN

The future coming of Christ is a major element in the NT picture of the final consummation (cf. above, 6-4). While the NT does not provide a timetable of the eschatological events (cf. 2-4.1), the future coming of Christ is associated with the final defeat of the powers of evil, and especially with the resurrection and the final judgment.

In Dan 7 the figure of the "one like a son of man" plays a key role in the ushering in of the new order; to him is given the universal and everlasting kingdom. So in the NT it is above all as Son of Man that Christ is expected to return. This event is usually referred to as the parousia, from the most frequently used NT word for Christ's "coming" at the end of the age. There are, however, other references to the future coming of Christ that do not employ the terms "Son of Man" or "parousia"; these are considered here also.

7-4.1. THE PAROUSIA

The Greek word *parousia* is the term most frequently used in the NT to refer to the coming of Christ in power and glory at the final consummation. *Parousia* means presence; and then coming, advent, or arrival (Arndt and Gingrich 1957: 635), e.g., the coming or arrival of someone who has been absent (2 Cor 7:6-7; Phil 1:26). It is the official term for the visit of a person of high rank, and was used especially of kings and emperors visiting a province. *Parousia* comes to be used in the NT virtually as a technical term for "the visible coming of Christ at the end of the age" (A. Richardson 1958: 54).

An essential element is the belief that the future coming will be in a visible fashion, in power and glory (cf. 8-4.2), in contrast to the first coming when Jesus' true nature was veiled and hidden. The parousia "establishes, once and for all, the public vindication and glorification of Jesus" (Riggans 1995: 16). Thus Christ's return can also be spoken of as his future "revelation" *(apokalypsis);* believers "wait for the revealing of our Lord Jesus Christ" (1 Cor 1:7; cf. 2 Thess 1:7; 1 Pet 1:7). A similar thought is expressed in the Pastorals when they speak of Christ's future "appearing" or "manifestation" *(epiphaneia).* This term is used of Christ's *first* coming in 2 Tim 1:10, a text that speaks of "the appearing of our Savior Christ Jesus, who abolished death and brought life and immortality to light through the gospel." In 1 Tim 6:14, however, the reference is future: the readers are urged "to keep the commandment . . . until the manifestation of our Lord Jesus Christ" (cf. 2 Tim 4:1, 8). Titus 2:11-13 uses this terminology in reference to *both* of Christ's advents: "For the grace of God *has appeared (epephanē),* bringing salvation to all . . . while we wait for . . . the *manifestation (epiphaneian)* of the glory of our great God and Savior, Jesus Christ."

Because of the role of the returning Christ in the final judgment, the parousia can also be referred to as "the day of the Lord" (1 Cor 5:5; 2 Pet 3:10; etc.) or "the day of the Lord Jesus" (2 Cor 1:14; cf. Phil 1:6), or even simply as "the day" (1 Cor 3:13; 1 Thess 5:4). On this terminology, and on the future judgment, see more fully 2-4.3; 16-4.3.

7-4.2. THE PAROUSIA IN THE TEACHING OF JESUS

As already noted, in Synoptic group C Jesus talks about the future coming of the Son of Man (above, 7-3.1). Though not explicitly stated, implicit in these sayings is the identification of Jesus himself with the Son of Man (cf. Elwell 1988b: 1919).

The climax of the Synoptic apocalypse is the parousia of the Son of Man. Mark 13:1-23 deals with events that will characterize the period between Christ's first and second advents, but then vv. 24-27 look beyond that to the final consummation (see 3-4.1). "Then they will see 'the Son of Man coming in clouds' with great power and glory" (Mark 13:26//Matt 24:30; Luke 21:27; cf. Mark 8:38 and //s; 14:62 and //s). Matthew and Luke have additional sayings that emphasize the sudden and unexpected nature of the parousia: "For as the lightning comes from the east and flashes as far as the west, so will be the coming of the Son of Man" (Matt 24:27//Luke 17:24; cf. Matt 24:37-41//Luke 17:26-35).

In the new age the Son of Man will be "seated on the throne of his glory" (Matt 19:28), and he will be the agent of God's judgment (13:36-43; cf. Luke 18:8; 21:36). A person's attitude toward Jesus now will determine how he or she is judged by the Son of Man (Mark 8:38//Luke 9:26; cf. above, 7-3.2). The vision of the sheep and the goats sets forth the criteria for judgment that will be applied "when the Son of Man comes in his glory, and all the angels with him" (Matt 25:31).

As noted above (7-3.2), John's Gospel shares with the Synoptics belief in the Son of Man as the coming judge: the Father "has given him authority to execute judgment, because he is the Son of Man" (5:27). In 14:3 Jesus promises the disciples, "I will come again and will take you to myself, so that where I am, there you may be also" (cf. 21:22).

A particular problem has always been felt with a few sayings of Jesus that appear to assert the imminent coming of the Son of Man; since this did not take place, an obvious conclusion is that Jesus was in error (on these passages, see Moore 1966: 125-46, 175-90). This is part of the more general problem of "the time of the end," on which see 2-4.5. After speaking of the coming of the Son of Man in Mark 13:26, in v. 30 Jesus says, "Truly I tell you, this generation will not pass away until all these things have taken place." As already noted, however (3-4.1), the so-called Apocalyptic Discourse deals with both *prophetic* eschatology, i.e., the fall of Jerusalem and the destruction of the temple (vv. 1-23), and *apocalyptic* eschatology, i.e., the coming of the Son of Man (vv. 24-27). Vv. 28-37 then address the question of the timing of these events: vv. 28-31 suggest that the fulfillment of the prophetic forecast will occur within the present generation, whereas in relation to the final apocalyptic events, "about that day or hour no one knows" (cf. Moore 1966: 134). Mark 9:1 (especially if linked with the preceding verse, 8:38) and especially Matt 10:23 do pose problems (on the interpretation of Matt 10:23, see Sabourin 1977). The fact that these sayings were faithfully preserved and recorded by the Evangelists decades after the time of Jesus shows that *they* did not understand them as referring to an imminent parousia. The coming of the kingdom of God with power and the coming of the Son of Man may have been understood as referring in these texts to the transfiguration, or more likely to Jesus' resurrection and ascension and to the outpouring of the Holy Spirit.

7-4.3. THE PAROUSIA IN THE CHURCH'S EXPECTATION

While Paul does not designate Jesus as Son of Man, he does speak of the future coming *(parousia)* of Christ; in fact, "nearly every letter of the Pauline corpus witnesses to the parousia expectation" (McArthur 1962a: 659). When Paul wrote 1 Thess 4:13-17, he appears to have anticipated the parousia in his own lifetime: "We who are alive, who are left until the coming of the Lord, will by no means precede those who have died" (cf. Plevnik 1975: 203). Paul continues, "For the Lord himself, with a cry of command, with the archangel's call and with the sound of God's trumpet, will descend from heaven" (according to Joel 2:1, a trumpet signals the coming of the Day of the Lord; see 2-2.3). In 2 Thess 2:1-12, on the other hand, Paul clearly discourages expectation of an imminent parousia; a series of events involving the intensification of evil and the annihilation of "the lawless one" (cf. 4-4.4a) must take place first. And in a text such as Col 3:4 he refers to a time when "Christ who is your life is revealed," without giving any indication that he thinks of this event as imminent (cf. 2-4.5). In 1 Thess 4:13-17 Paul does link the parousia closely with the future resurrection of believers, and in Phil 3:20-21 he speaks of "expecting a Savior" who will "transform the body of our humiliation" (cf. also 1 Cor 15:23).

Although to some degree Acts de-emphasizes imminent eschatological expectation, it by no means eliminates the promise of Christ's coming; indeed, the opening scene depicting Christ's ascension climaxes in the angelic assurance, "This Jesus, who has been taken up from you into heaven, will come in the same way as you saw him go into heaven" (1:11; cf. 3:20-21; 10:42; 17:31).

Hebrews asserts that Christ "will appear a second time" (9:28). 1 Pet 1:7 speaks of the day "when Jesus Christ is revealed." 2 Pet 3:1-13 discusses the problem of the delay of the parousia (see 2-4.5). James counsels patience "until the coming of the Lord" (5:7; cf. 5:8). 1 John 2:28 counsels readers to abide in Christ so as not to be "put to shame before him at his coming"; 3:2 declares that when Christ "is revealed, we will be like him, for we shall see him as he is."

Revelation opens with the vision of the exalted Son of Man (above, 7-3.5). In the letters to the seven churches the risen Christ speaks of his coming in judgment to the churches: "I will come to you *(erchomai soi)* and remove your lampstand from its place" (2:5; cf. 2:16; 3:3, 11). Here, however, we are dealing with prophetic rather than apocalyptic eschatology. What is in mind is a series of judgments that will fall on these individual Christian congregations in the near future, not at the final consummation. The counterpart of these warnings of judgment is the promise of 3:20: "If you hear my voice and open the door, I will come in *(eiseleusomai)* to you." In accordance with the principles of biblical eschatology, however, these "comings" foreshadow the final coming of Christ.

In keeping with John's technique of overlapping visions, the parousia is portrayed at various points in the book. The theme is first introduced almost at the outset in 1:7: "Look! He is coming with the clouds . . . ," a text that combines references to Dan 7:13 and Zech 12:10.

In the final vision of the fourth heptad (Rev 14:14-20), John sees "a white cloud, and seated on the cloud was one like the Son of Man, with a golden crown on his head, and a sharp sickle in his hand!" (v. 14). The sickle is used by the Son of Man to reap the eschatological harvest. As Jesus' parable of the wheat and the weeds reminds us (Matt 13:24-30), that harvest has a twofold object: the gathering of the wheat into the barn and the destruction of the weeds. The harvest of Rev 14:15 and 16 represents the ingathering of the faithful; the martyrs in v. 4 are the "first fruits" of this harvest. When the metaphor shifts, however, to cutting clusters of grapes to be thrown into "the great wine press of the wrath of God" (v. 19), we are clearly dealing with the judgment of the wicked. This is confirmed by the presence of "the angel who has authority over fire," fire being a frequent biblical symbol of judgment. In 16:15 there is a further reference to the parousia with the reminder that Christ will come "like a thief," i.e., suddenly and unexpectedly.

Many see a further portrayal of the parousia in the second vision of the seventh heptad (19:11-16), though the scene is actually one version of the final battle against the forces of evil which assumes that the parousia has already taken place. Here Christ's title is not Son of Man but "The Word of God" (v. 13), though in being called "Faithful and True" (v. 11) and depicted as having eyes "like a flame of fire" (v. 12), he matches exactly the description of the Son of Man in chapters 1–3 (see 3:14; 1:14; 2:18). The returning Christ rides a white horse and leads the armies of heaven against the enemies of God, whose judgment is again portrayed with the metaphor of the winepress (19:15). The portrait of the victorious Christ is enhanced by features of the royal Messiah.

It is understandable that in the first flush of enthusiasm, or later in times of severe trial and persecution, some Christians would hope and pray that the parousia and accompanying apocalyptic events would happen soon. But that is *not* the view of Paul or of any other NT writer. The overall consistent view of the NT is that the end will come suddenly and unexpectedly, but the time of the end lies entirely in God's hands.

7-4.4. FIRST AND SECOND COMING

The term *parousia* is not used in the NT in reference to the "coming" of Christ in his incarnation, with the possible exception of 2 Pet 1:16: "For we did not follow cleverly devised myths when we made known to you the power and coming *(parousia)* of our Lord Jesus Christ." While the reference could be to teaching on the future parousia of Christ, the context, with the clear reference to the transfiguration, favors a reference to Jesus' "first coming." *Parousia* was used in this double way fairly soon after the NT. Justin Martyr, ca. 150, was the first to speak of "the first coming" *(hē protē parousia)* and "the second coming" *(hē deutera parousia)* (cf. McArthur 1962b: 261). If an explicit verbal reference to "the second coming" of Christ is lacking in the NT, Heb 9:28 does come very close to this mode of expression when it says that "Christ, having been offered once to bear the sins of many, will appear a second time *(ek deuterou . . . ophthēsetai),*" and according to John 14:3, Jesus said, "I will come again *(palin erchomai)."*

7-4.5. EVEN SO, COME

In the NT the church eagerly anticipates the coming of the Lord. Here we have another example of the "already–not yet" tension that runs throughout the NT. The NT looks forward in *hope* to the parousia of the Lord Jesus Christ; that hope is, however, grounded in the belief that the Christ event, to which believers can look back in time, is God's decisive intervention in human history (cf. Cullmann 1956: 142-44). This is why the future hope of the NT is not just belief that the forces of evil will eventually be destroyed or belief that the kingdom of God will finally come in its fullness, but specifically belief in the second coming of Christ. The one who will come in power and glory at the end of days is the same Son of Man who lived here on earth, who went through suffering and death, and who is exalted at God's right hand.

The Aramaic expression *māranā' thā',* meaning "Our Lord, come!" was probably a prayer in use in the church from the earliest times. It is found in the NT in 1 Cor 16:22, and probably also lies behind Rev 22:20, "Come, Lord Jesus!" It is a prayer for Christ to come in a double sense. As we have seen (above, 7-4.3), Christ can come within history either in judgment or to be with his people. These comings anticipate the final parousia when Christ will come as the agent of God's judgment and salvation.

"Maranatha!" ("Our Lord, come!") has this double sense. If, as has often been suggested, it was used as a prayer in the Eucharist (cf. Dunn 1997: 45), it would have the twofold meaning: come at the final consummation, and come be present with us now in the Eucharist in anticipation of that final consummation (cf. 14-3.5c; 14-4.5b). On this view "the real presence of the Lord at his table is a promise and foretaste of his presence when he comes in glory" (Elwell 1988b: 1922).

7-5. THE SON OF MAN: THEOLOGICAL REFLECTIONS

1. From the second century onward, the title Son of Man *(ho huios tou anthrōpou)* was widely understood as referring to Jesus' humanity: the ortho-

dox view was that Jesus is both divine (Son of God) and human (Son of Man) (cf. Dunn 1980: 65; Callan 1996: 939). Modern biblical scholarship has rendered a great service by showing that this is not the biblical understanding of the term; it is in fact a christological title, one of the most exalted to be applied to Jesus, though one that in fact combines Jesus' divinity and his humanity.

2. BT is concerned primarily with the canonical text, and that has been the focus of the above study. There can be no doubt that the four Evangelists identify Jesus as the Son of Man and believe that Jesus himself accepted the title. This view, however, has been widely challenged by modern scholarship. Whether Jesus did think of himself as Son of Man, and if so, what he meant by the title, has been the subject of endless debate.

Conservatives generally accept all three groups of Synoptic sayings (above, 7-3.1) and the Johannine sayings (7-3.2) as basically historical (see, e.g., D. Guthrie 1981). Critical scholars have held a wide variety of views (see Guthrie's summary, 270-71). Many of them dismiss the Johannine sayings as unhistorical because they echo typically Johannine emphases. With regard to the Synoptics, a common critical view (e.g., Bultmann 1952: 30; Tödt 1963; Higgins 1964: 185-209) is that groups A and B are not historical (Jesus could not have identified himself with an apocalyptic figure; Jesus could not have foretold his suffering, death, and vindication by God). Only group C is authentic, but here Jesus speaks of the Son of Man as someone different from himself. On this view Jesus is at best a forerunner of the Son of Man, not the final eschatological figure, a view that involves enormous difficulties (cf. Hooker 1967: 189). Others, more skeptical, reject the historicity of all three groups: the Son of Man sayings are all the creation of the early church (see Teeple 1965; W. O. Walker 1972; 1983). Others again, who favor the purely realized eschatology advocated by C. H. Dodd, reject group C but are prepared to accept all or some of groups A and B; in other words, expectation of a future coming of Jesus as Son of Man has no basis in the historical Jesus but is an invention of the early church (see the critique of this position in Moore 1966: 49-79). Finally, there are some critical scholars who are prepared to defend the historicity of at least some of the sayings in all three groups (cf. Hooker 1967: 191, 193; Lindars 1975). These contradictory views highlight the often arbitrary nature of much historical-critical scholarship, and suggest that scholars' presuppositions (often concealed) have much to do with the conclusions reached (cf. Guthrie, 271).

As has been repeatedly argued, BT cannot depend on the vagaries of historical-critical scholarship; it must be based primarily on what is said in the canonical text, and that is the procedure that has been followed above. On the other hand, it cannot be oblivious to the historical problems. The Gospel writers do not merely repeat accounts of the words and deeds of Jesus; on their own admission they interpret these words and deeds in the light of the church's postresurrection faith and developing understanding. The key question is whether that development was a legitimate one. BT cannot be concerned with discussing the historicity of each individual saying. But if the early church seriously distorted Jesus' teaching or ascribed to him claims that have no basis in his own self-understanding, then the foundation of BT collapses. It is necessary therefore to look briefly at the historical problems.

The view that the early church invented the Son of Man sayings and ascribed them to Jesus encounters major obstacles. Son of Man sayings occur in all four sources identified by source critics: Mark, Q, M, and L; to reject their historicity is therefore to violate the criterion of "multiple attestation." Jesus' use of the term "Son of Man" is markedly different from that current in contemporary Judaism, and also from what became the church's view; to reject the sayings therefore also violates the criterion of "dissimilarity." If the early church created the sayings, it is impossible to give an adequate explanation of why the title appears only on Jesus' own lips while all the evidence suggests that it quickly dropped out as a title in the early church (cf. Bruce 1969: 28). Since many scholars accept some sayings but reject others, it is necessary briefly to consider each of the groups of sayings in turn.

Group A: the sayings that speak of *the present activity and authority of the Son of Man.* At least two attempts have been made to explain away this group. First, it has been suggested that in these sayings the "Son of Man" simply means "mankind" or "human beings." The context, however, is totally against this; it makes no sense to say that humankind can forgive sins or is lord of the Sabbath. The sayings regard these as functions unique to Jesus. Second, following up on the work of earlier scholars (cf. Bultmann 1952: 30), G. Vermes in 1967 argued that *ho huios tou anthrōpou* reflects an Aramaic usage that is the equivalent of "I." It was not a title at all, but an oblique way by which a speaker referred to himself. By saying "the Son of Man has authority on earth to forgive sins" (Mark 2:10), Jesus was saying nothing more than "I have power to forgive sins" (Vermes 1967). This proposal provoked widespread debate (see Borsch 1992: 132-35) and has been strongly contested (see Jeremias 1971: 261 n. 1). All the Evangelists, however, take the term to be a title, and it is hard to believe that this tradition which is so widespread, and is independently attested in the Synoptics and John, is based on a misunderstanding in translation from Aramaic into Greek (cf. Marshall 1970b: 71; Hooker 1979: 157-58).

Group B: those sayings that speak of *the rejection, suffering, death, and resurrection of the Son of Man.* Many critical scholars have doubted that Jesus uttered these sayings. None of them appear in the Q source (see, however, above, 7-3.1), and it is held that they are the product of the later reflection of the church. Behind this is the feeling that it would have been either impossible or out of character for Jesus to have foretold his own future in this way; they are "prophecies after the event" (cf. Bultmann 1952: 30). Such skepticism is surely unwarranted; even if we did not believe that this was a God-given insight, it could be argued that with the fate of John the Baptist before him, it would not be difficult for Jesus to see that his ministry was taking him on a path that would inevitably lead to suffering and death, beyond which he looked for God's vindication.

Group C: those sayings that speak of *the Son of Man's future coming as God's agent of judgment and salvation.* As noted above (7-3.1), this group of sayings poses a special problem. In them Jesus appears to refer to the Son of Man *in the third person,* and thus many critical scholars hold that he was speaking of someone other than himself (cf. Callan 1996: 938). Such scholars therefore hold that at best Jesus considered himself to be a herald or forerunner of the apocalyptic Son of Man (cf. Borsch 1992: 130-31); it was only in the early church that Jesus was *identified* with the Son of Man. This extremely radical view in effect denies that Jesus was the unique and final agent of God, and implies that later Christian belief regarding Jesus has no secure historical basis. As argued above, a more satisfactory view is one that may be labeled *"implied identification."* In these sayings Jesus implies that he is the future, apocalyptic Son of Man; "he makes a distinction not between two different figures, but between his present and the future state of exaltation" (Jeremias 1971: 276). Behind such a saying as Mark 8:38 lies Jesus' claim to be God's unique representative ushering in the new order. He says in effect: "Your reaction to me and to my message decides your eternal destiny." But he leaves his hearers to draw the conclusion: Jesus himself must be the coming apocalyptic Son of Man.

There is no good reason to doubt that groups A and B are basically historical in preserving the memory that Jesus did at times identify himself with the Son of Man. Group C may be understood as preserving the memory that Jesus was nevertheless reticent in making outright claims.

Historical scholars have also expressed skepticism regarding the Johannine sayings, mainly because of their difference from the Synoptics. Whether or not they have undergone changes in transmission, the most striking aspect of the Johannine sayings is surely the degree to which they reflect a tradition closely akin to that found in the Synoptics: they depict Jesus as using the term "Son of Man" and applying it to himself, and they agree that the term does not mean simply a human being but rather is one of the more exalted christological titles, signifying God's eschatological agent in judgment and salvation. There is thus no sound reason for denying that John uses an independent source that ultimately goes back to Jesus himself (cf. Smalley 1969: 301).

We may affirm, therefore, that what the NT says of Jesus as Son of Man is in basic continuity with the claims made by Jesus himself, even though the NT is written from a postresurrection point of view.

3. While the term "Son of Man" was central to Jesus' self-understanding, after his death and resurrection its use in the early church was severely limited. Its use by Stephen in Acts 7:56 suggests that it was a feature of the theology of the Hellenists (cf. Ciholas 1981: 19). The references in Rev 1:13 and 14:14 may well depend on early Palestinian prophetic-apocalyptic traditions. The fact that Son of Man sayings appear in all four Gospels and all their sources, clearly indicates

that the earliest communities valued and passed on these traditions (cf. Jeremias 1971: 266). But the absence of "Son of Man" from Paul's letters shows that as soon as Christianity spread into the wider Greco-Roman world, the term faded away as a meaningful christological title in communities ignorant of the Jewish apocalyptic background, and for whom the literal translation of the original Aramaic produced a strange and meaningless Greek expression.

4. It is the task of contemporary theology to reflect the far-reaching claims made by the NT in designating Jesus as Son of Man and the Second Adam. Jesus represents the culmination of God's activity in the whole created order. God's purposes for humanity are most clearly revealed in the figure of Jesus.

5. As Son of Man, Jesus is accorded a major role in the final consummation of all things. The parousia or "second coming" of Christ is witnessed to throughout the NT, from Gospels to Revelation. "The Parousia hope belongs to the very fabric and substance of the New Testament, in all its parts, and to the very fabric and substance of Jesus' own thought and teaching in so far as it is possible to reconstruct this" (Moore 1966: 4-5; cf. Riggans 1995: 14; Dunn 1997: 42). It cannot be de-eschatologized or demythologized to mean something else. Scholars such as T. F. Glasson (1945) who eliminate the parousia completely from the teaching of Jesus, regard it as an invention of the early church, and replace NT eschatology with a belief in "a world-wide triumph of the Gospel" (232) are clearly influenced by their liberal theological presuppositions.

The NT refers to the parousia using a variety of language and imagery (see Plevnik 1975: 133-272; Dunn 1997: 46-51). "Some of it is borrowed from the Old Testament, some from Jewish apocalyptic, some from the political world in which the writers lived, or from ordinary life. All of it, however, has been employed by the biblical writers, under the inspiration of the Spirit, to portray the triumph of our Lord at the end of the age" (Ewert 1980: 90). The language employed in speaking of the parousia may be figurative and symbolic, but it points toward a future reality. In this world Christians can acknowledge Jesus as the Son of Man only through faith. At the final consummation the truth of such claims will be made manifest. For Christians, belief in the parousia means that "the future will not come to us as a total surprise. For the God we encounter at the end of time will be the God who encounters us at the mid-point of time, God in Christ" (Dunn, 56).

6. Christ's parousia is closely linked with the other events that constitute the final consummation, especially the resurrection and the final judgment, though nowhere does the NT offer an exact timetable of these final events. What has already been said about NT apocalyptic (2-4.5; 2-5.5) therefore applies equally here: the Bible nowhere provides any basis for calculating the time of the parousia (cf. Cullmann 1956: 141). "Keep awake therefore, for you do not know on what day your Lord is coming" (Matt 24:42).

In particular, there is no basis in the NT for the view introduced by John Darby and widely propagated today that postulates *two* appearances of Christ at the end of this age, one (based in 1 Thess 4:13-17) involving the "rapture" of the saints, followed by a seven-year tribulation, followed by another appearing involving the final defeat of evil. There is nothing in 1 Thess 4:13-17 to indicate other than that it refers to Christ's parousia and the resurrection at the end of the age (cf. 20-4.4a.i; and see Elwell 1988b: 1918-19). As we have already noted, the idea of a pretribulation "rapture" not only has no basis in the NT, but also directly contradicts NT teaching that God's faithful people will *not* be spared tribulation but are called to endure to the end (see 3-5.5; 20-4.4a; cf. Ewert 1980: 85).

7. From a theological point of view it is particularly important that the title Son of Man not be considered in isolation. While it is convenient and traditional to separate discussion of the person and work of Christ, the separation is artificial, particularly in relation to the understanding of Christ as the inclusive representative of humanity since this is also closely bound up with a major way of understanding the meaning of Christ's death (see 9-3.4c).

As a title, "Son of Man" has to be seen in relation to the other titles ascribed to Jesus. We noted in chapter 6 Jesus' reluctance to claim the title Messiah, especially in public. Such reluctance is easily understandable in light of the fact that, for the majority of people, "Messiah" would have strong political and military connotations. It is equally understandable that Jesus would prefer the title Son of Man that denoted a messianic type of figure, but one that, since it came from the apocalyptic tradition, was free of political and military connotations.

Though Jesus accepted the title Son of Man, as we have seen he profoundly modified it by combining it with the figure of the Suffering Servant (see further, chap. 9). Between the earthly activity of the Son of Man and his future eschatological role lie his suffering, death, and resurrection.

The title Son of Man has also to be taken in conjunction with the testimony of all four Gospels to Jesus as the Son of God. This connection is brought out more clearly in John's Gospel with its references to the Son of Man descending from heaven. Jesus is not only the one who exercises God's authority here on earth, who suffers, is rejected, dies and rises again, and will come again in power and glory at the final consummation; he is also the glory, word, and wisdom of God, and the Son of God (see chap. 8), the one who is not only fully human but also fully divine.

CHAPTER 8

Glory, Word, Wisdom, Son

Old Testament: Proclamation

8-1. BY YOUR WORD AND BY YOUR WISDOM

The NT does not rest content with portraying Jesus as God's Servant who fulfills each of the messianic categories and as the Second Adam or Son of Man, the inclusive representative of a new humanity. It proclaims that Jesus is not only fully human but also fully divine. Jesus' divinity is associated especially with the recognition of him as "Son" or "Son of God," a term that has its roots in the OT though it is used in a profoundly new sense in the NT. There is, however, a strong link between NT claims for the divinity of Christ and the way the OT speaks of God himself appearing to human beings, and especially the way the OT portrays God as present and acting within the world, through his "glory," "word," and "wisdom." Another mode of God's relating to Israel and to humankind is expressed in father-son terms. These categories form the foundation for the expectation of the activity of God in the new age, an expectation that the NT sees as fulfilled in the person of Christ.

8-1.1. GOD APPEARS TO PEOPLE

The OT speaks of God himself appearing to people. Although employing two very similar terms, Westermann (1965) conveniently distinguishes two different types of divine appearances: *epiphanies* in which God appears from afar and intervenes to help his people, and *theophanies* in which God appears to individuals "in order to reveal himself, and to communicate with his people through a mediator" (99; cf. also Jeremias 1962).

a. Epiphanies

The Greek term *epiphaneia* (from *epiphainō*, passive = "show oneself, make an appearance") means an appearance, and in a religious context specifically, "a visible manifestation of a hidden deity, either in the form of a personal appearance, or by some deed of power by which its presence is made known" (Arndt and Gingrich 1957: 304). In Westermann's classification, it refers to poetical passages where "Yahweh appears in order to help his people and to destroy his foes" (1965: 96). Judg 5:4-5 is a typical example:

> LORD, when you went out from Seir,
>> when you marched from the region of Edom,
> the earth trembled,
>> and the heavens poured,
>> the clouds indeed poured water.
> The mountains quaked before the LORD, the One of Sinai,
>> before the LORD, the God of Israel.

Other examples include Ps 18:7-15 (cf. also Pss 29; 114), Mic 1:3-4, Nah 1:3-6, Hab 3:3-15. In most cases reference is made back to the exodus events, including the crossing of the sea. "That first occasion on which God came to the aid of his people was experienced anew in God's saving deeds. In this way it became a part of the songs of victory, and is heard again in a variety of contexts where God's helping and saving acts for his people are told or sung" (Westermann 1965: 97).

Epiphanies generally follow a threefold pattern consisting of: (1) God is said to come or go forth from such and such a place (Teman, Seir, Zion, etc.); (2) cosmic disturbances accompany God's appearance (earth/mountains quake, thunder, lightning, darkness, etc.); (3) God intervenes for Israel/against her enemies.

b. Theophanies

More typical are various appearances of God to individuals. While "theophany" (*theophaneia,* from *theos* = "God"; *phainō* = "become visible, appear") is the standard term, it must be remembered that in these encounters, strictly speaking, God is not *seen;* the Bible holds that "no one has ever seen God" (John 1:18; cf. Terrien 1978: 69). There may be accompanying phenomena, but typically in a theophany God is *heard* rather than seen.

Divine appearances are typical of the *patriarchal narratives* (see Terrien 1978: 63-95). God appears to Abraham to call him (Gen 12:1-3), and to enter into covenant with him (Gen 15); in Gen 18 one of the "three men" who visit him turns out to be the LORD (v. 13). Jacob's encounter with God at Bethel (Gen 28:10-22) comes in the form of a dream, but the mysterious figure with whom he wrestles at the ford of Jabbok (32:22-32) turns out to be none other than God himself (v. 30).

Particularly striking are the direct personal appearances of God to *Moses* at or near Mount Sinai/Horeb. In the call of Moses (Exod 3:1–4:17) the LORD speaks to him from the burning bush. On that occasion, we are told, "Moses hid his face, for he was afraid to look at God" (3:6). Elsewhere, however, Moses comes closest to being the exception that proves the rule: in 33:17-23 Moses is not allowed to see God's face but does see his back, and in Num 12:8 God says of Moses, "With him I speak face to face . . . and he beholds the form of the LORD" (cf. Deut 34:10).

Somewhat set apart from these is the great theophany at Sinai (Exod 19–24; see Jeremias 1962: 897; Terrien 1978: 119-38). This is portrayed with the use of thunderstorm and volcano imagery (19:16, 18). While basically it is a theophany to Moses, who acts as mediator between God and people, according to 24:9-10, "Moses and Aaron, Nadab, and Abihu, and seventy of the elders of Israel went up, and they saw the God of Israel."

God appears to *Elijah* at Horeb (1 Kgs 19), and this theophany is remarkable in its disassociation of God from the cosmic imagery of the epiphanies or the Sinai theophany (cf. Terrien 1978: 230-36). The LORD was not in the wind, the earthquake, or the fire, but in "a sound of sheer silence (*qôl dᵉmāmâh daqqâh*)" (vv. 11-12). The encounters of the prophets with God generally take the form of visions or auditions (Isa 6:1; Amos 9:1; Ezek 1).

In addition to these accounts of the direct appearances of God, the OT speaks of various forms of divine self-manifestation by which God is related to the world indirectly rather than directly. As we have already seen, *angels* are a means of God's communication with human beings (1-1.3b), and God can be present and active through his *Spirit* (5-1). Here we consider three other important forms of God's self-manifestation, and of his presence and activity in the world: his *glory, word,* and *wisdom.*

A variety of terminology has been employed. In the context of a comparative study, Ringgren discusses "the hypostatization of divine qualities and functions," and quotes two definitions of "hypostasis": a "quasi-personification of certain attributes proper to God, occupying an intermediate position between personalities and abstract beings" (Oesterley-Box), and "a personification of qualities, functions, limbs etc. of a higher god" (Mowinckel) (Ringgren 1947: 8). "Hypostasis," however, has such a complex history in Christian trinitarian theology that it is better to avoid the term (cf. von Rad 1972: 147; Balchin 1982: 207). It is preferable to speak of different *modes of God's self-manifestation* (cf. Jacob 1958: 73-85; Eichrodt 1967: chap. 12) or of "divine agency" (Hurtado 1988: 17).

8-1.2. THE GLORY OF THE LORD

An important way in which the OT portrays God's presence and activity here on earth is by speaking of his "glory."

a. The Meaning of "Glory"

The Hebrew word for glory (*kābhôdh;* LXX, NT *doxa;* Lat. *gloria;* see C. C. Newman 1992: 17-24) denotes in the first instance that which is heavy or weighty; then it comes to mean wealth or position of honor, "what adds to a person's standing, what increases a person's position and influence" (Molin 1981a: 295). Applied to people, it can mean fame, reputation, honor, prestige. Applied to God, especially in the phrase "glory of the LORD" *(kābhôdh YHWH),* it refers to God's power and majesty, to the self-revelation of the transcendent God, and in particular means "the visible brightness of the divine presence" (A. Richardson 1958: 65), "the reflected splendour of the transcendent God" (Eichrodt 1967: 32). God's glory can be linked with a "cloud" as a symbol of the divine presence (see esp. Exod 24:15-18; cf. 16:10; 40:34-35; Num 16:42; 1 Kgs 8:11; Ezek 10:4). The visual imagery is not self-contradictory, for a cloud can be suffused with light. What the combined images do symbolize, however, is that glory simultaneously reveals and conceals the divine presence. "The *kᵉbod Yahweh* is therefore not God himself in his true and unrecognizable essence, but *God insofar as he allows men to recognize him*" (Molin, 296).

b. The Historical Order: God's Presence with His People

Glory is a way of speaking of God's presence with his people in the historical order. As soon as the Israelites entered the wilderness, they became aware of this presence; they "looked toward the wilderness, and the glory of the LORD appeared in the cloud" (Exod 16:10). Here God's glory is linked with the "pillar of cloud by day" and the "pillar of fire by night" by which God led his people in the wilderness (13:21-22). At the decisive meeting between God and people, "the glory of the LORD settled on Mount Sinai, and the cloud covered it for six days. . . . Now the appearance of the glory of the LORD was like a devouring fire" (24:16-17).

God's glory is associated especially with the tent (see 14-1.1a.ii). When its construction was complete, "the glory of the LORD filled the [tent]" (40:34), and in this way God's presence went with his people as they traveled. The other side of the picture, however, is that God's glory, like his holiness (cf. 1-1.4b.iii), is mysterious and even dangerous: "Moses was not able to enter the tent of meeting because the cloud settled upon it, and the glory of the LORD filled the tabernacle" (40:35; cf. 1 Kgs 8:11; 2 Chr 7:2). This aspect of God's glory is graphically illustrated in the story of Exod 33:18-23, where Moses' request, "Show me your glory," is denied. Moses' face has to be shielded from God's glory; it is through his name that God's true nature is revealed (cf. McConville 1979: 153-54). God's glory was also associated with the ark of the covenant, so that when the ark was captured by the Philistines the wife of Phinehas named her son Ichabod, saying, "The glory has departed from Israel" (1 Sam 4:21-22). The ark was the dwelling place of "the King of glory" (Ps 24:7-10; on the ark, see 14-1.1a.ii).

With the building of Solomon's temple, God's presence was transferred there: "The glory of the LORD filled the house of the LORD" (1 Kgs 8:10; cf. 2 Chr 7:1-2). Thus the psalmist can say,

> O LORD, I love the house in which you dwell,
> and the place where your glory abides. (Ps 26:8)

God enters the temple as "the King of glory" (24:7-10). In the light of all that God has done for them, the people are called to

> sing the glory of his name;
> give to him glorious praise. (66:2)

Ezekiel is *the* prophet of the glory of God: the book opens with his great vision of the throne chariot of God. Though the vision comes to a climax with what might be taken as a description of God (1:26-28), Ezekiel is careful to specify that what he saw was in fact "the *appearance* of the *likeness* of the *glory* of the LORD" (v. 28); in other words, Ezekiel sees God, but only, as it were, at three removes. Ezekiel's prophecies of judgment on Israel come to a climax with the vision of the departure of the glory (10:18f.; 11:23), when God's glory is airlifted out of the city by the cherubim!

c. The Created Order: God's Presence in the Universe

Glory is also a way of speaking of God's presence in the created order.

> The heavens are telling the glory of God;
> and the firmament proclaims his handiwork.
>   (Ps 19:1; cf. 97:6; 145:10-11)

The psalmist sees God's glory in the might and majesty of nature (Ps 29). Isaiah, in his great vision, heard the seraphim calling,

> Holy, holy, holy is the LORD of hosts;
> the whole earth is full of his glory. (Isa 6:3)

"The holiness of Yahweh transcends cultic edifices, for his glory fills the earth in its entirety instead of being confined to a sanctuary" (Terrien 1978: 249).

The psalmist calls on God's people to "declare his glory among the nations" (Ps 96:3; cf. 138:4-5), and in 97:6 "all the peoples behold his glory," though only through "clouds and thick darkness" (v. 2; see McConville 1979: 157).

8-1.3. THE WORD OF THE LORD

The OT also portrays God's activity and self-manifestation on earth by speaking of his word.

a. The Meaning of "Word"

To understand the meaning of "word" *(dābhār)* in the OT, we must set aside modern notions of the spoken word as "a mere word." In the OT "a spoken word is never an empty sound but an operative reality whose action cannot be hindered once it has been pronounced, and which attained its maximum effectiveness in formulae of blessing and cursing" (Jacob 1958: 127-28; cf. T. W. Manson 1963: 144-47). The story of Jacob cheating his brother Esau out of his father's blessing provides a vivid example; once the words are uttered, there is no way they can be recalled (Gen 27). The spoken word is effective and cannot be changed.

If this is true of a human word, even more so is it the case that *God's* word is powerful and effective. Once a prophet utters God's word entrusted to him, it has a life of its own. God's word "is like a projectile shot into the enemy camp whose explosion must sometimes be awaited but which is always inevitable, and these explosions are the events of history" (Jacob 1958: 131). Referring to the death of the Egyptian firstborn at the exodus, *Wis* 18:15-16 declares:

> Your all-powerful word leaped from heaven, from the royal throne,
> into the midst of the land that was doomed,
> a stern warrior carrying the sharp sword of your authentic command.

In such passages God's word is understood "as bearer of divine power, obviously separate from God and yet belonging to him" (L. Dürr, quoted in Ringgren 1947: 157).

b. The Historical Order: God Speaks to His People

The word is the major means by which God communicates with individuals and with his people.

The Torah consists of the words of the LORD. The so-called Ten "Commandments" are in fact the Ten *Words* (Decalogue): "Then God spoke all these *words* . . ." (Exod 20:1; 34:1; Deut 4:13; etc.). After receiving the Covenant Code, "Moses came and told the people all the *words* of the LORD" (Exod 24:3). In Deuteronomy especially, the commandments are referred to as God's "words" (*dᵉbhārîm*; 4:10; 5:5; 12:28; etc.). Collectively they constitute God's "word." "The whole life of God's people is based on the word of God, in which is summed up the clear and unambiguous will of their sovereign Lord" (Eichrodt 1967: 72). It is in God's word that true life is to be found: "One does not live by bread alone, but by every word that comes from the mouth of the LORD" (Deut 8:3). It is this word of which the psalmist says,

> Your *word* is a lamp to my feet
>   and a light to my path. (Ps 119:105)

Above all, God communicates his word to, and through, the prophets. "Now the word of the LORD came to me saying . . ." (Jer 1:4; cf. 1:9; Hos 1:1; Joel 1:1; Jonah 1:1; Mic 1:1; Zeph 1:1; Hag 1:1; Zech 1:1; Mal 1:1); "the word of the LORD came to the priest Ezekiel" (Ezek 1:3). Prophetic oracles are typically introduced by one of two formulae: "Hear the *word* of the LORD" (Isa 1:10; etc.) or "Thus says the Lord" (Isa 7:7; etc.) (see 6-1.4).

In contrast to finite humanity, "the word of our God will stand forever" (Isa 40:8; cf. 59:21). God's word is frequently a word of judgment (e.g., Hos 6:5), but it can also be a word of salvation and of healing: "He sent out his word and healed them" (Ps 107:20; cf. *Wis* 16:12).

c. The Created Order: God Creates and Sustains

It is also through his word that God creates and sustains all things.

The Bible opens with a powerful portrayal of God's creative word which, once spoken, is immediately effective: "Then God said, 'Let there be light'; and there was light" (Gen 1:3). As the psalmist puts it:

> By the word of the LORD the heavens were made,
>   and all their host by the breath of his mouth. . . .
> For he spoke, and it came to be;
>   he commanded, and it stood firm. (Ps 33:6, 9; cf. also 147:15)

God's word continues to be active in creation, not only in the more unusual phenomena of nature such as the thunderstorm (Ps 29), but also in the regular rhythm of the seasons on which fertility and life depend:

> He sends out his command to the earth;
> > his word runs swiftly.
> > > (Ps 147:15-18, here v. 15; see also 148:8; *Sir* 42:15; and cf. 2-1.2b)

8-1.4. THE WISDOM OF THE LORD

The OT also portrays God's presence and activity in the world by speaking of his wisdom.

a. The Meaning of Wisdom

Wisdom *(chokhmâh)* is a faculty possessed by human beings; it can mean wisdom, skill, or shrewdness. The teachings of Wisdom are not based on direct divine revelation but rather on observation and experience of the world and of human society. Yet Wisdom does ultimately come from God; it was through Wisdom that God created all things, and divine Wisdom is thus built into the structure of the universe (see further, 1-1.4b.ii; 2-1.4b). The revival of Wisdom studies in recent decades has highlighted the major role of Wisdom in the OT, particularly if the Deuterocanon is taken into account (cf. Cady, Ronan, and Taussig 1986: 16).

b. The Created Order: God's Presence in Creation

In the Wisdom Literature we find a special understanding of divine Wisdom (sometimes referred to as "speculative" or "theological" Wisdom). Wisdom is spoken of in personal terms and, as has been already noted (1-1.4b.ii), always as a female person (see von Rad 1972: 144-76; Crenshaw 1981: 96-99). Prov 8 is a key passage: in vv. 1-11 Wisdom makes her appeal to human beings:

> Does not wisdom call,
> > and does not understanding raise her voice?
> On the heights, beside the way,
> > at the crossroads she takes her stand;
> beside the gates in front of the town,
> > at the entrance of the portals she cries out:
> "To you, O people, I call,
> > and my cry is to all that live." (vv. 1-4; cf. vv. 20-33; 3:13-18)

In vv. 12-21 she sets forth her claims. The figure of Wisdom preexists creation:

The LORD created me *(qānānî)* at the beginning of his work. . . .
Ages ago I was set up,
   at the first, before the beginning of the earth.
When there were no depths I was brought forth *(chôlāl^{e}tî* = "was born").
(vv. 22-25)

Wisdom functioned as God's agent in creation:

When he established the heavens, I was there,
   when he drew a circle on the face of the deep . . .
when he assigned to the sea its limit . . .
when he marked out the foundations of the earth,
   then I was beside him, like a master worker;
and I was daily his delight,
rejoicing before him always.
(vv. 27, 29-30; see commentaries for variant readings in v. 30)

The above translation (NRSV) reads *'āmûn,* "master worker," rather than *'ummān,* "a little child" (cf. Ringgren 1947: 103). This accords with the understanding of Wisdom as "the fashioner *(technitēs)* of all things" in *Wis* 7:22 and 8:6. It is in line with this that the psalmist exclaims:

O LORD, how manifold are your works!
   In wisdom you have made them all. (Ps 104:24; cf. 136:5; Jer 51:15)

It is because God created all things through his Wisdom that the wise can find God's truth in creation (cf. 2-1.4b).

The Wisdom hymn of Job 28 emphasizes the inaccessibility of Wisdom, but it too links Wisdom with creation (vv. 23-27). "As a result wisdom occupies a mediating position between God and the creation; wisdom mediates God to the world" (Gese 1981a: 192).

The portrait of Wisdom is considerably enlarged in the Deuterocanon. *Sir* 24 is a poem, based on Gen 1 (see Gese 1981a: 196), in praise of Wisdom, who tells the heavenly council of her origin:

I came forth from the mouth of the Most High,
   and covered the earth like a mist.
I dwelt in the highest heavens,
   and my throne was in a pillar of cloud. . . .
Before the ages, in the beginning, he created me,
   and for all ages I shall not cease to be. (vv. 3-4, 9)

Wisdom sought a resting place on earth, and God made her dwell among his people Israel (v. 8), and especially in Jerusalem (vv. 10-11).

Wisdom receives an even more extended treatment in *Wisdom of Solomon*. In 6:12-25 the reader is assured that she "hastens to make herself known to those who desire her" (v. 13). In *Wis* 7–9 Solomon speaks of his quest for Wisdom and his desire to know her as bride and teacher. Wisdom is here portrayed as "God's chief agent" (Hurtado 1988: 43). 7:22-23 enumerates twenty-one attributes of Wisdom:

> There is in her a spirit that is intelligent, holy,
> unique, manifold, subtle,
> mobile, clear, unpolluted,
> distinct, invulnerable, loving the good, keen,
> irresistible, beneficent, humane,
> steadfast, sure, free from anxiety,
> all-powerful, overseeing all,
> and penetrating through all spirits
> that are intelligent, pure, and altogether subtle.

The description continues:

> For wisdom is more mobile than any motion;
> because of her pureness she pervades and penetrates all things.
> For she is a breath of the power of God,
> and a pure emanation of the glory of the Almighty;
> therefore nothing defiled gains entrance into her.
> For she is a reflection *(apaugasma)* of eternal light,
> a spotless mirror of the working of God,
> and an image of his goodness. (vv. 24-26)

Since Wisdom shares God's throne (9:4, 10), she is "the direct expression of God's nature and purposes" (Hurtado 1988: 50). Yet another poem on Wisdom appears in *Bar* 3:9–4:4. Unlike the earlier poems, this one stresses the difficulty of finding Wisdom; she can be found only by those to whom God sends her.

It is frequently pointed out that these descriptions of Wisdom are reminiscent of what is said regarding a goddess of wisdom in other cultures (Ringgren 1947: 128-49; Dunn 1980: 169; cf. 1-1.4b.ii). This was not possible in Israel; Wisdom is not a separate divine being but a form of self-manifestation of the one God. Some scholars speak of Wisdom as a "personification" of a divine attribute (Dunn, 176), but others argue rightly that Wisdom is something more than a mere personification. "It is obvious that Wisdom is here not an abstraction or a purely poetic personification but a concrete being, self-existent beside God" (Ringgren, 104; cf. Jacob 1958: 118; Gese 1981b: 30). Though originating from God, and a form of divine self-manifestation, Wisdom is spoken of in strongly personal terms, as a female figure, separate from both God and the created order.

c. The Historical Order: Wisdom and Torah

Wisdom theology is basically creation theology, but in the late OT period Wisdom is brought into association with God's word and Spirit and in particular with the Torah, God's word spoken to his people in the historical order (on Torah, see more fully 18-1.2a).

In *Sirach* Wisdom and Torah are brought into a close relationship:

> The whole of wisdom is fear of the Lord,
>> and in all wisdom there is the fulfillment of the law. (19:20)

Sir 1:1-30 is a poem on Wisdom that identifies her with "the fear of the Lord." The hymn in praise of Wisdom in *Sir* 24 concludes:

> All this is the book of the covenant of the Most High God,
>> the law that Moses commanded us. (v. 23)

In *Wis* 10–12 Wisdom is integrated into an account of salvation history, beginning with a sequence of illustrations of how Wisdom saved seven wise men, Adam, Noah, Abraham, Lot, Jacob, Joseph, and Moses. It was through Wisdom that Moses delivered God's people from Egypt and protected them in the wilderness, giving them water from the rock (10:15–11:9).

The strongest statement of this view is found in *Baruch;* it in effect overturns the earlier emphasis on the international and universal appeal of Wisdom:

> She has not been heard of in Canaan,
>> or seen in Teman. (3:22)

No one knows the way to Wisdom (3:31), but God

>> gave her to his servant Jacob
>> and to Israel, whom he loved.
> Afterward she appeared on earth
>> and lived with humankind. (3:36-37)

In other words, Wisdom is again identified with Torah:

> She is the book of the commandments of God,
>> the law that endures forever. (4:1)

In this way God's activity in the created and historical orders is brought together.

d. Wisdom, Word, and Spirit

Wisdom is not rigidly separated from the other forms of God's self-manifestation.

Their common role in creation naturally brings Wisdom and word together:

> O God of my ancestors and Lord of mercy,
> who have made all things by your *word*,
> and by your *wisdom* have formed humankind. (*Wis* 9:1-2; cf. *Sir* 24:3)

On the links between Wisdom and Spirit, see 5-1.3 (cf. also Rylaarsdam 1946: chap. 5).

8-1.5. SONS OF GOD

God's relation to his people and to humankind can also be expressed in terms drawn from the father-son relationship (see Hengel 1976: 21-23; D. Guthrie 1981: 301-3).

a. The Sons of God: Angels

Angelic beings can be designated "sons of God" in the sense of "divine beings" (see 1-1.3b), e.g., in Gen 6:2, 4; Deut 32:8. The "sons of God" form the divine council (Job 1:6; cf. Ps 82:6). In Dan 3:25, in the story of the fiery furnace, the king sees not three but four figures in the fire, "and the appearance of the fourth is like *a son of the gods*" (RSV). In v. 28 the fourth figure is interpreted as God's "angel," a special divine messenger sent to deliver God's faithful servants.

b. The Son of God: Israel

God's people Israel are frequently referred to, collectively, as God's son, especially in connection with the exodus event: "You are the sons of the LORD your God," the Israelites are told in Deut 14:1 (RSV). "Yahweh was father to Israel, his 'first-born,' because of the gracious and faithful nature of Yahweh. . . . They were Yahweh's son, the object of his special favour; by virtue of the acts of Yahweh the foundations of their history as a people — election and covenant — were laid. These were the grounds of their favoured status with Yahweh" (Cooke 1961: 217). Moses is to say to Pharaoh, "Thus says the LORD: Israel is my firstborn (*bᵉkhōr*, LXX *prōtotokos*) son" (Exod 4:22). In Hos 11:1 God declares:

> When Israel was a child, I loved him,
>> and out of Egypt I called my son. (cf. Jer 3:19)

"In all these texts the title 'Son of God' expresses both the idea that God has chosen this people for a special mission, and that his people owe him absolute obedience" (Cullmann 1963: 273). Israel, however, is frequently a rebellious and disobedient son; see, e.g., Isa 1:2, Jer 3:22.

c. The Son of God: The King

The king is regarded as God's son (cf. 6-1.2b). In Nathan's oracle God declares, with reference to David's son who will succeed to the throne, "I will be a father to him, and he shall be a son to me" (2 Sam 7:14). According to Ps 89:26:

> He [the king] shall cry to me, "You are my Father,
>> my God, and the Rock of my salvation!"

At his coronation the king declares:

> I will tell of the decree of the LORD:
> He said to me, "You are my son;
>> today I have begotten you." (Ps 2:7)

This shows that the king is not regarded as divine by nature (as in ancient Egypt, for example; cf. Kraus 1986: 113). "The royal psalms, despite their dependence upon the court poetry of the ancient world, do not confer divinity upon the king" (B. W. Anderson 1983: 187). He is God's son *by adoption,* "begotten" by God on the day of his coronation. Similarly in Ps 89:27 God says of David:

> I will make him the firstborn,
>> the highest of the kings of the earth.

Despite the high-sounding language, there is no trace in the Royal Psalms of veneration of the king (Kraus 1986: 111).

Just as the people of Israel are God's son, so too is the king as the inclusive representative of the people. "The king too is 'son' as one specially chosen and commissioned by God. . . . The king is son of God because the nation is" (Cullmann 1963: 273). "Yahweh had chosen Israel, entered into covenant with him, and called him his first-born son. Yahweh had also chosen David and his 'house,' entered into covenant with them, and called the Davidic king his first-born son" (Cooke 1961: 225).

d. The Sons of God: The Righteous

Occasionally, in the late OT period, righteous persons can be referred to as sons of God. The righteous man "boasts that God is his father. . . . For if the righteous man is God's son, he will help him" (*Wis* 2:16, 18 RSV); cf. *Sir* 4:10:

> Be a father to orphans,
>   and be like a husband to their mother;
> you will then be like a son of the Most High,
>   and he will love you more than does your mother.

Old Testament: Promise

8-2. THE LORD WILL COME

8-2.1. THE COMING OF THE LORD

Corresponding to the conviction that God can be directly involved in this world and with his people are the promise and hope that at some point in the future God himself will act to put things right.

In some forms of eschatology the expectation is that God himself will act to usher in the new order (cf. Jeremias 1962: 898). 2 Isaiah looks for a future appearing of God: "See, the Lord GOD comes with might" (Isa 40:10).

> The LORD has bared his holy arm
>   before the eyes of all the nations;
> and all the ends of the earth shall see
>   the salvation of our God. (52:10)

Isa 64:1f. is a prayer for God himself to return as the divine warrior in a future epiphany: "O that you would tear open the heavens and come down" (cf. 42:13). In 2 Isaiah, "it is not a deliverer-king of the lineage of David who will bring about the new ordering of all things, but God himself. He himself will be the king of his people" (Kraus 1958: 67). Zech 9:14 and 14:3 similarly depict God himself appearing to save his people.

Isa 7 contains a significant prophecy that God himself will be with his people. The original historical context is the grave threat posed to Judah by the alliance of Israel and Syria. Though King Ahaz of Judah declines to seek a sign from God, the prophet Isaiah declares: "Therefore the Lord himself will give you a sign. Look, the young woman is with child and shall bear a son, and shall name him Immanuel. He shall eat curds and honey by the time he knows how to refuse the evil and choose the good. For before the child knows how to refuse the evil and choose the good, the land before whose two kings you are in dread will be deserted" (vv. 14-16). The word translated "young woman" (*'almâh*) normally means a young woman of marriageable age (the Hebrew word for "virgin," *b^ethûlâh*, is not used). The young woman is not identified; she may be the prophet's wife, the king's wife, or any Israelite woman. The oracle is basically one of assurance: by the time a child conceived now is born, i.e., nine months from now, the situation will have changed sufficiently to justify the optimistic name Immanuel (*'immānû 'ēl*), meaning "God with us." Before the child reaches the age of moral discretion, prosperity will have returned and Judah's enemies will be no more.

Although originally linked to a very specific historical situation, this oracle was preserved and ultimately became part of canonical Scripture because it is paradigmatic for the faith of Israel. However dark and difficult a situation may be, God will not desert his people; the time will come when those who have faith in the LORD will be able to affirm that indeed "God is with us!"

In the LXX translation of Isaiah, a significant reinterpretation of the passage takes place: v. 14 is rendered "Behold, a virgin (*parthenos*) will conceive. . . ." This translation suggests a dimension of the miraculous in some future act of God in history. The LXX text, it should be recalled, is quoted as Scripture in the NT and hence is part of the canonical tradition (cf. D-2.8).

While one form of OT expectation looks for a future coming of God himself, other forms expect a future manifestation of God's glory, word, or wisdom, or for the coming of a future king as Son of God.

8-2.2. THE GLORY OF THE LORD SHALL BE REVEALED

In a world in which God's glory seemed to be more often concealed than revealed, his people were sustained by the promise that in the future it would be fully revealed (see G. H. Davies 1962a: 402).

a. The Historical Order

The Babylonian exile formed the original background for promises of the future manifestation of God's glory in Isaiah and Ezekiel. In a sense they can be considered as having been fulfilled with the return, but since that return fell far short of expectations, they can also be viewed as promises awaiting fulfillment.

Isaiah envisages the restored Jerusalem being blessed by God's presence portrayed in terms of the cloud/fire of the wilderness period, while "over all the glory there will be a canopy" (4:5). 2 Isaiah envisages the triumphant return of the exiles; a superhighway will be constructed for them in the desert,

then the glory of the LORD shall be revealed,
    and all people shall see it together. (Isa 40:5)

Still thinking of that journey, Isaiah assures the people that

Your vindicator shall go before you,
    the glory of the LORD shall be your rear guard. (58:8)

In 35:2 it is said of the returning exiles, "They shall see the glory of the LORD" (cf. 59:19; 60:2, 19). 60:1-2 dramatically proclaims,

Arise, shine; for your light has come,
    and the glory of the LORD has risen upon you.
For darkness shall cover the earth,
    and thick darkness the peoples;
but the LORD will arise upon you,
    and his glory will appear over you.

In these verses "the prophet describes a grand and glorious world theophany, a revelation of KABHODH which will reverse the circumstances of Israel and Judah, transform society, human beings and nature, and reassert the reign of Yahweh" (C. C. Newman 1992: 63).

For Ezekiel also, the coming restoration will manifest God's glory: "And I will display my glory among the nations" (Ezek 39:21). After his vision of the new temple (Ezek 40–42), the prophet sees the return of God's glory: "And there, the glory of the God of Israel was coming from the east . . . and the earth shone with his glory. . . . As the glory of the LORD entered the temple by the gate facing east, the spirit lifted me up, and brought me into the inner court; and the glory of the LORD filled the temple" (43:2, 4-5; cf. 44:4).

In a similar vein Zechariah looked for the restoration of Jerusalem and was given the promise, "For I will be a wall of fire all around it, says the LORD, and I will be the glory within it" (Zech 2:5).

b. The Created Order

Although the OT sees God's glory in the created order (8-1.2c), it also looks for a future universal manifestation of the divine glory.

At some time in the future, "all the earth shall be filled with the glory of the LORD" (Num 14:21). The psalmist expresses a hope that has still to be fulfilled when he sings:

Blessed be the LORD, the God of Israel . . .
    may his glory fill the whole earth. (Ps 72:18-19; cf. 57:5, 11; 108:5)

In 2 Isaiah's vision of the future, God will gather all nations, "and they shall come and see my glory" (Isa 66:18; cf. 35:1). Habakkuk is confident that the day will come when

> the earth will be filled
> > with the knowledge of the glory of the LORD,
> > as the waters cover the sea. (Hab 2:14)

According to 2 *Macc* 2:8, Jeremiah promised that in the new age "the glory of the Lord and the cloud will appear."

8-2.3. SO SHALL MY WORD BE

While the OT speaks frequently of God's self-manifestation through his word, in the later OT especially there is a sense of the scarcity of God's word. Amos had already prophesied:

> The time is surely coming, says the Lord GOD,
> > when I will send a famine on the land;
> not a famine of bread, or a thirst for water,
> > but of hearing the words of the LORD. (Amos 8:11)

It is in this context that the OT promises that God will again send his word. 2 Isaiah promises that God's powerful and effective word will once again go forth:

> For as the rain and the snow come down from heaven,
> > and do not return there until they have watered the earth, . . .
> so shall my word be that goes out from my mouth;
> > it shall not return to me empty,
> but it shall accomplish that which I purpose,
> > and succeed in the thing for which I sent it. (Isa 55:10-11)

The eschatological Torah (see 18-2.2a) can be referred to as God's word:

> For out of Zion shall go forth the law,
> > and the word of the LORD from Jerusalem. (Isa 2:3//Mic 4:2 RSV)

8-2.4. THE SPIRIT OF WISDOM AND UNDERSTANDING

Wisdom is among God's eschatological gifts. According to Isa 33:5-6, "The LORD . . . will fill Zion with justice and righteousness . . . abundance of salvation, *wisdom,* and knowledge" (RSV). In Isa 11:2 the messianic king will be endowed with the Spirit of the LORD, which is "the spirit of *wisdom* and understanding." *Sir* 24:32-33 foresees a future outpouring of divine wisdom:

> I will again make *instruction* shine forth like the dawn,
>   and I will make it clear from far away.
> I will again pour out *teaching* like prophecy,
>   and leave it to all future generations.

8-2.5. I WILL MAKE HIM THE FIRSTBORN

We have already seen how the expectation arose, especially after the disappearance of the monarchy following the exile, of a future, ideal king (6-2.2). With their continuing use in worship, the Royal Psalms are to be seen as pointing forward to a future king who would be God's adopted son (Pss 2:7; 89:26-27).

New Testament: Fulfillment

8-3. THE WORD BECAME FLESH

In the first chapter of the NT, Matthew sets the tone for what is to follow by linking the story of the birth of Christ with the prophecy of Isa 7:14. Jesus is indeed "Emmanuel," "God is with us" (Matt 1:23). "The coming of Jesus is the LORD radically and powerfully with his people in times of distress to rescue them" (Brueggemann 1985a: 71). In the OT God himself appears to his people (above, 8-1.1); in the NT God appears in a unique way in the person of Christ. As Jacob (1958) observes, "a line not always straight, but none the less continuous, leads from the anthropomorphism of the earliest pages of the Bible, to the incarnation of God in Jesus Christ" (32).

While the NT refers back to OT theophanies (Acts 7:30-34 = Exod 3:1-10; Heb 12:18-21 = Exod 19), "in reality there are no true theophanies in the NT, for their place is taken by the manifestation of God in Christ" (G. H. Davies 1962a: 4:620). Thus 2 Tim 1:10 looks back to "the appearing *(epiphaneias)* of our Savior Christ Jesus" (cf. Titus 2:11; 3:4; and see 7-4.1). In the NT "the fundamental affirmation is that God's decisive self-disclosure occurred in Jesus" (Alsup 1962: 898).

8-3.1. PREEXISTENCE AND INCARNATION

Closely linked with the conviction that in the person of Jesus God himself entered human history is belief in what came to be termed the "preexistence" and "incarnation" of Christ (on what follows, see esp. Marshall 1982).

Two of the fundamental convictions of the NT concerning Jesus are that (1) he lived as a man on earth and met his death by crucifixion, and (2) he was raised from the dead to "God's right hand," where he shares in the divine nature and status.

Some reconstructions of NT Christology assume that whatever divine status Jesus had was conferred upon him at his exaltation. This may be represented as follows:

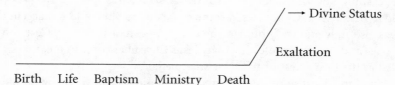

Such a pattern represents an "adoptionist" Christology. A variant of this sees Jesus being adopted as Son of God at his baptism.

But the view represented in the canonical NT as a whole is *not* that Jesus received divine status at his baptism or exaltation, nor even that Jesus as a person came into being with his conception and birth by Mary; his divine status not only *followed* but also *preceded* his earthly life. This may be represented in the following way:

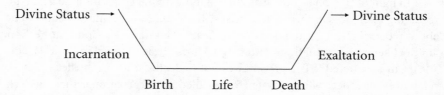

The fully developed NT Christology thus has three main stages:

1. Preexistence ("pre" = before, + "exist"): Christ existed and had divine status prior to his life on earth.
2. Incarnation: Christ, though divine, became "incarnate" ("in" + Latin root *carn-* = "flesh"), i.e., became "flesh," fully and truly human.
3. Exaltation: After his death and resurrection Jesus was exalted to a position of divine status.

In the NT Christ's preexistence and incarnation are presented most clearly in the Johannine literature. Christ as the divine Word or Logos existed "in the beginning" (John 1:1; see below, 8-3.3). In 8:58 Jesus declares, "Before Abraham was, I am." In this text we see the close connection between preexistence and the full divinity of Christ; it is one of a series of "I am" sayings, e.g., 6:20, "It is I (*egō eimi* = 'I am'); do not be afraid" (cf. 8:24, 28; 13:19; 18:5; see also 6:35; 8:12; 10:11;

11:25; 14:6; 15:1; and Matt 14:27), that echo the divine name in the OT (Exod 3:14), and a common formula of divine self-manifestation, e.g., "I am the LORD, and there is no other (LXX — *egō eimi, kai ouk estin eti*)" (Isa 45:18; cf. 41:13; 43:25). In other words, this idiom presents Jesus speaking as does the LORD in the OT (see R. E. Brown 1966).

The counterpart of preexistence is incarnation: "The Word became flesh" (John 1:14). The Johannine community may well have encountered a form of false teaching known as Docetism (*dokeō* = "to seem, appear") that was prepared to believe that Christ was in some sense divine but could not accept that he was also fully and truly human (he only "appeared" to be so). Certainly in 1 John 4:2 and 2 John 7, confessing that "Jesus Christ has come in the flesh" is regarded as the litmus test of true Christian belief.

Belief in Christ's preexistence and incarnation, however, is by no means confined to the Johannine literature. The Christ hymn of Phil 2:6-11 (considered by many scholars to be pre-Pauline and therefore very early) is structured precisely on the threefold pattern of preexistence (v. 6), incarnation (vv. 7-8), and exaltation (vv. 9-11) (see the discussion in 7-3.4b). The same conviction underlies Paul's claim that though Christ "was rich, yet for your sakes he became poor" (2 Cor 8:9), as well as his assertion that in Christ "the whole fullness of deity *(pan to plērōma tēs theotētos)* dwells bodily *(sōmatikōs)*" (Col 2:9).

In light of the Johannine insistence that the divine Logos became flesh, the recurring references in the NT to Christ's "flesh" are significant: Christ brought about reconciliation "in the body of his flesh" (Col 1:22 AT); God sent his Son "in the likeness of sinful flesh" (Rom 8:3); Christ "was revealed in flesh" (1 Tim 3:16); Christ suffered (1 Pet 4:1) and was put to death (3:18) "in the flesh." These references all reflect what may fairly be called an incarnational theology (cf. Marshall 1982: 11).

Belief that Jesus was fully divine as well as fully human is expressed in the NT in a variety of ways. So, far from importing ideas from the Hellenistic world, the NT draws on key themes from the OT to depict Jesus in terms of the divine glory, word, and wisdom. The title "Son of God" also has OT roots, though in the NT it is radically reinterpreted in the light of the experienced reality of Christ. The claim of the virginal conception of Christ is yet another way of asserting that God was uniquely active in the Christ event.

8-3.2. BEHOLDING THE GLORY OF THE LORD

The NT follows the OT in speaking of the glory of God (Luke 2:9; Acts 7:2, 55; Rev 15:8; etc.). What is distinctive in the NT, however, is the linking of God's glory with the person of Jesus and seeing in him *the unique and final manifestation of God's glory,* i.e., God's own presence on earth. "It is in Christ that the glory of God is made known, in Him God's presence is apprehended" (Brockington 1945: 24).

While fulfilling the prophecies of the eschatological manifestation of the glory of God, the NT understanding of glory becomes even more paradoxical than that of the OT. To outward appearances Jesus is a poor and homeless prophet and teacher who ends up being executed as a criminal, yet in such a person the NT sees nothing less than the glory of God!

Throughout the Synoptic Gospels the glory remains veiled save at one point where the veil is briefly lifted: the accounts of Jesus' *transfiguration* in Matt 17:1-9//Mark 9:2-10//Luke 9:28-36 (on the transfiguration, see Trites 1994). "It is the one occasion in which the bright beams of His divine glory blazed through the sackcloth covering of His humanity" (S. L. Johnson 1967: 133). In all three accounts the mountaintop setting, the transformed appearance of Christ, the shining garments, and the cloud symbolic of the divine presence recall the revelation of God's glory on Mount Sinai. Matthew's comment that "his face shone like the sun" (Matt 17:2) recalls Moses' experience on Sinai when "the skin of his face shone" after being in the presence of the LORD (Exod 34:29-35). Moses and Elijah were the two people in the OT who encountered God's presence on the mountaintop; so at the transfiguration they appear as witnesses to the divine presence manifested in Jesus (cf. Terrien 1978: 422-28). The theme of the glory is made explicit in Luke, who refers to the appearance of Moses and Elijah "in glory" and tells of how the three disciples "saw his [Christ's] glory" (9:31-32). Peter's proposal to build three tents (Mark 9:5) recalls the tent of the wilderness wanderings that was the shrine of the divine glory (above, 8-1.2b); Jesus' rejection of the proposal was due to the fact that "it was quite out of order to give Moses and Elijah a permanent position on the mount of revelation. There was no need for three tabernacles, nor even for one. For Jesus was Himself the new tabernacle of the Divine glory" (Caird 1956a: 293). The reference to the transfiguration in 2 Pet 1:17-18 recalls the time when Christ "received honor and glory from God the Father" and heard the voice from "the Majestic Glory." This revelation of Christ's glory is but a brief lifting of the veil, and an anticipation of the glory that is still basically eschatological. Luke's version of the transfiguration in particular sees it as an anticipation of Jesus' resurrection, ascension, and parousia (Caird, 292).

It is clear that a glory Christology is an important component in Pauline theology (see G. H. Davies 1962a: 2:402-3; C. C. Newman 1992: 157-247). In 2 Cor 3:7–4:6 Paul contrasts the revelation of God's glory at Sinai with "the greater glory" of the revelation in Christ when he says that believers, "seeing the glory of the Lord as though reflected in a mirror, are being transformed into the same image from one degree of glory to another" (3:18). Unbelievers have been blinded by the god of this world "to keep them from seeing the light of the gospel of the glory of Christ" (4:4), for "it is the God who said, 'Let light shine out of darkness,' who has shone in our hearts to give the light of the knowledge of the glory of God in the face of Jesus Christ" (4:6). Thus "as God's glory used to be manifest in Israel in the tabernacling Presence . . . so now it is manifest in Christ" (Davies, 2:402). The divine glory manifested in Christ was "veiled from men without faith" (A. Richardson 1958: 66). The "rulers of this age" also failed to recognize him, "for if they had, they would not have crucified the Lord of glory" (1 Cor 2:8). From these and other texts it is clear that Paul "identifies Jesus as the one who mediated the eschatological glory of God: parallel to and in the sequence of God's past revelations of Glory, the coming, life, death and resurrection of Jesus mediated Glory" (Newman, 245).

In Hebrews Christ is presented as "the reflection of God's glory and the exact imprint of God's very being" (1:3; cf. *Wis* 7:25).

John's Gospel shares this "glory" Christology, but has its own distinctive emphases. There is no account of the transfiguration because John "regards the whole of Christ's incarnate life as an embodiment of the *doxa* of God. . . . The Christ of the Fourth Gospel is the locus, so to speak, of the tabernacling presence or *doxa* of God" (A. Richardson 1958: 65; cf. Caird 1956a: 294; Beck 1962b: 686). Jesus' glory is paradoxical here also, however; it can be discerned only by those who believe (cf. Molin 1981a: 297). By his first sign Jesus "revealed his glory; and his disciples believed in him" (John 2:11). The paradox strains almost to the breaking point when Jesus' death on the cross is spoken of as his "glorification" (cf. 7:39; 12:16, 23, 27-28; 13:31-32). As he approaches death, Jesus says, "So now, Father, glorify me in your own presence with the glory that I had in your presence before the world existed" (17:5). Here the implication of Christ's sharing and manifesting the glory of God is clearly brought out.

The prologue of John's Gospel (1:1-18) is a key christological passage. As Gese (1981a) in particular has demonstrated, "the relationship of the prologue to the Old Testament is extensive and intimate. Even in its apparent critique of the Old Testament and its emphasis on the lack of fulfilment and completion, the prologue is oriented to the Old Testament tradition with its references to the provisional nature of all present reality and its movement toward the eschatological goal" (222; see the detailed analysis of the prologue in this essay). The prologue in fact presents Jesus as the eschatological glory, word, and wisdom, as well as the only Son of the Father. The incarnate Son is presented as the embodiment of the divine glory in the key verse, 1:14: "And the Word became flesh and lived among us, and we have seen his *glory*, the *glory* as of the Father's only Son, full of grace and truth."

8-3.3. THE WORD BECAME FLESH AND DWELT AMONG US

Christ does not merely speak God's word, he *is* the divine Word *(logos)* who became flesh (cf. above, 8-3.1).

The number of passages in which this christological term occurs is few, but they are key passages. The prologue of John's Gospel identifies Christ as the preexisting Logos (1:1 [three times] and 1:14). While the actual term *Logos* does not occur after 1:14, nevertheless the prologue provides the key to understanding the whole Gospel, much as Mark 1:1-13 does for Mark's Gospel (see Hooker 1974). 1 John 1:1 probably refers back to the prologue: "what was from the beginning . . . concerning the word of life *(peri tou logou tēs zōēs)*." In Rev 19:13 it is said of the rider on the white horse, "his name is called The Word of God" *(ho logos tou theou)*.

It should also be noted that apart from the actual identification of Christ with the *logos*, the language of speaking and of the word is frequently linked with the Christ event. Thus Heb 1:2 says, "In these last days he [God] has spoken to us by a Son." Both Jesus' own message (Mark 2:2; Luke 5:1; 8:11) and the message of the early church (Acts 13:26; 20:32; 1 Cor 1:18; 2 Cor 5:19; Eph 1:13; 2 Tim 2:9; Heb 4:12; Rev 1:9) are often referred to as "the word" *(logos)*.

The background of *logos* as a christological term is debated. The history of religions school stressed the background in Greek philosophy and Philo (see T. W. Manson 1963: 138-41; D. Guthrie 1981: 321-23), and many scholars see this as at least part of the background. More recently, however, there has been a swing back to OT/Jewish background (cf. Ladd 1993: 274, 277). BT reads the *logos* passages in the light of the canonical Scriptures. "The designation of Christ as the Logos in John 1 is just as firmly connected with the Old Testament conception of the Word as it is sharply opposed to the Hellenistic concept of the Logos; for it knows nothing either of a cosmic mind in the pantheistic, or of a redemptive idea in the idealistic and mystical sense, but sees the universal and sovereign will of the personal God incarnate in all its dynamic momentum in the life of a human person" (Eichrodt 1967: 80; cf. Gese 1981a: 197). The NT clearly has the OT understanding of God's Word in mind, and uses it in explaining the meaning and the significance of the Christ event. At the same time, the Christ event modifies the OT understanding of God's Word.

"Logos" is the dominant category applied to Christ in the prologue to John's Gospel. The opening verse emphasizes the preexistence of the Logos. "In the beginning" (1:1-2) echoes Gen 1:1 and places the Logos with God before creation (see Gese 1981a: 177). The Logos stands in the closest possible relationship with God. The REB seeks to catch the nuances of John 1:1: "The Word was in God's presence, and what God was, the Word was." The Logos is the agent of creation, for "all things came into being through him" (1:3). He is the source of light, life, and truth, terms that frequently recur in John's Gospel (cf. 1 John 1:1-2). Recalling the various OT uses of "the word of God" (cf. above, 8-1.3), Buckwalter (1996) well summarizes what the NT references imply by identifying Jesus with the Logos: "[T]he NT understands Jesus as the ultimate means through which God created, revealed, and personified himself to creation. Jesus as the word of God discloses God's saving plan for and to creation, makes God better known to creation, is known firsthand to creation, has come for the saving good of creation, and is equal to the Father as supreme authority over all creation" (830).

The most distinctive affirmation of the NT is that the Logos became a human being in the incarnation: "And the Word became flesh *(ho logos sarx egeneto)* and lived among us" (John 1:14; cf. 1 John 1:1-2: "We have heard . . . seen . . . touched . . . the word of life"). "Such an affirmation would amaze and refute all Hellenistic philosophical and gnostic dualisms that separated God from his world. . . . John wished to emphasize that it was God himself in the Word who entered human history, not as a phantom, but as a real man of flesh" (Ladd 1993: 278; cf. D. Guthrie 1981: 328; Marshall 1982: 2-4). In John the Logos in effect takes the place of the Torah as the supreme revelation of God: "The law indeed was given through Moses; grace and truth came through Jesus Christ" (John 1:17).

8-3.4. CHRIST, THE WISDOM OF GOD

We have already seen that in the Gospels Jesus is portrayed as the authoritative eschatological teacher of Wisdom (6-3.5). But the NT goes beyond this in identifying Jesus with the figure of Wisdom. A number of recent studies have shown that Wisdom, the mediatrix of creation and salvation, is a major christological category.

Luke reports that as Jesus grew up he "increased in wisdom" (Luke 2:52), and later the people of his hometown were astounded at his wisdom (Matt 13:54). But a series of passages in Matthew and Luke bring Jesus into closer relationship with the figure of Wisdom. "The queen of the South . . . came . . . to listen to the wisdom of Solomon, and see, something greater than Solomon is here!" (Matt 12:42//Luke 11:31); "compared to the king of Wisdom," comments Gese (1981a), "to whom all wisdom tradition goes back, the proclamation of Jesus appears as the greater, i.e. the pristine and final revelation of wisdom" (42).

There is some difference of emphasis between Matthew and Luke. Recent studies have shown that while Luke portrays Jesus as the eschatological envoy of Wisdom, Matthew makes a direct equation of Jesus with Wisdom. As Suggs (1970) notes, "The Jesus who meets us in Q as *sophos* and 'child of wisdom' brings truth to men; he is the mediator of divine revelation. The Jesus who meets us in Matthew retains his function as teacher and revealer, but is no longer merely a prophet (albeit the last and greatest) of Sophia. He is Wisdom and that means, as well, that he is the embodiment of Torah" (127; cf. Hamerton-Kelly 1973: 83; Dunn 1980: 198; J. M. Reese 1981: 44-45).

For example, in Luke 11:49 Jesus says, "Therefore also the Wisdom of God said [quoting a lost Wisdom Book?], 'I will send them prophets and apostles, some of whom they will kill and persecute.'" In Matthew's version (23:34) Jesus says, "Therefore *I* send you prophets . . . ,'" thus speaking as, and directly identifying himself as, Wisdom (see Conzelmann 1976: 958).

In Matt 11:28-30 Jesus speaks very much in the tones of Wisdom: "Come to me, all you that are weary and are carrying heavy burdens, and I will give you rest. Take my yoke upon you, and learn from me; for I am gentle and humble in heart, and you will find rest for your souls. For my yoke is easy, and my burden is light." It is difficult not to hear in this echoes of *Sir* 51:23, 25-27:

> Draw near to me, you who are uneducated,
>> and lodge in the house of instruction. . . .
>> Acquire wisdom for yourselves without money.
> Put your neck under her yoke,
>> and let your soul receive instruction. . . .
> See with your own eyes that I have labored but little
>> and found for myself much serenity.

As long ago as 1914 H. Windisch declared that "the pre-existent Christ of the New Testament, especially of Paul, is the divine wisdom of the Jews" (quoted in von Roon 1974: 207). Recent studies have confirmed and extended this insight (for summary and bibliography, see Dunn 1980: 176-96), though it has not gone unchallenged (von Roon 1974).

The context of Paul's remarks on Wisdom in 1 Cor 1–2 is his polemic against those who follow "the wisdom of the world" (1:20), in contrast to which the preaching of a crucified Messiah rates as "folly" (1:21; see Conzelmann 1976: 959). Nevertheless, perhaps taking up the language of his opponents (Dunn 1980: 177), Paul identifies Christ as "the power of God and the wisdom of God" (1:24), "who became for us wisdom from God" (1:30); he is the manifestation of preexistent Wisdom, and the agent through whom God's predetermined plan of salvation, "God's wisdom, secret and hidden" (2:7), has come into effect. Col 2:2-3 refers to "Christ . . . in whom are hidden all the treasures of wisdom" (cf. Goldsworthy 1987: 27-28).

The reference in 1 Cor 8:6 to "one God, the Father, from whom are all things and for whom we exist, and one Lord, Jesus Christ, through whom are all things and through whom we exist" strongly recalls the relationship between God and preexistent Wisdom through whom God created all things (Prov 3:19), and who is "an associate in his works" (*Wis* 8:4; cf. 8-1.4b). Particularly striking are the Wisdom motifs and terminology found in the Christ hymn of Col 1:15-20: Christ is the "image *(eikōn)* of the invisible God" (v. 15), as is Wisdom (*Wis* 7:26), who existed before all things, through whom all things were created, and in whom all things hold together — all assertions about Wisdom that are here applied to Christ (cf. J. M. Reese 1981: 46; Balchin 1982: 214-17). When Paul says in 1 Cor 10:4 that the rock from which the Israelites drank in the wilderness was Christ, he is ascribing to Christ the role played by Wisdom in *Wis* 11:4-8 (see above, 8-1.4c).

The category of Wisdom also underlies the prologue of John's Gospel. The combination of Word and Wisdom is not surprising since we have already seen them linked in *Wis* 9:1 (cf. 8-1.4d); thus, "in presenting Jesus as the incarnation (or 'enfleshment') of the divine Logos, John is telling us that the Wisdom and Word of God has entered into union with human nature" (Cronk 1982: 161). While Christ is primarily designated as the Logos in the prologue, recent studies have demonstrated just how deeply the christological terminology and concepts of the prologue are indebted to Wisdom. Tobin (1992) tabulates the parallels, and summarizes them: "Both the *logos* of the hymn in the Prologue and wisdom in Jewish wisdom literature are with God in the beginning; both are involved in the creation of the world; both seek to find a place among humankind; both are within a Jewish tradition of speculation about the deeper meaning of the early chapters of Genesis. In addition, many of the parallels between the *logos* in the hymn and the figure of wisdom are found in passages which like the hymn are poetic in character (Prov 8:22-31; Sir 24). The parallels are not simply conceptual but also stylistic" (354). "Just as according to Sirach 24:7 cosmic wisdom wills to take up its dwelling in the world as the revelation of Torah in salvation history, so also does the Logos in John 1:10, 11" (Gese 1981a: 202). "In the prologue of John," Gese declares, "we see Old Testament wisdom theology in full maturity adopted and led to completion" (54; cf. Brueggemann 1997: 345). "Although the hymn hails the incarnation of the Logos (v. 14), it is the figure of Wisdom that is thus evoked in the key elements of the four strophes" (Terrien 1978: 418). The Johannine prologue "both exploits and surpasses the hymns about Lady Wisdom" (J. M. Reese 1981: 47). Jesus' presentation of himself as the bread of life (John 6:25-59) recalls Wisdom, who invites people to "Come, eat of my bread" (Prov 9:5; cf. *Sir* 15:3), though unlike Wisdom (*Sir* 24:21), Christ truly satisfies (John 6:35; see Terrien, 467-70).

We have already noted the linking of Christ with God's glory in Heb 1:3 (above, 8-3.2). The prologue to the epistle also resonates with the language of Wisdom with its reference to the Son, through whom God "also created the worlds. He is the reflection of God's glory and the exact imprint of God's very being, and he sustains *(pherōn)* all things by his powerful word" (vv. 2-3). The term "reflection" *(apaugasma)* is exactly the same word that is used of Wisdom in *Wis* 7:25.

The latter part of the twentieth century saw a significant shift in NT studies. With the relatively small amount of attention paid to Wisdom in standard works on Christology, we may compare the book by J. D. G. Dunn, *Christology in the Making,* which has a major section entitled "The Wisdom of God" (Dunn 1980: 163-212), one of the main conclusions of which is that "the doctrine of the incarnation began to emerge when the exalted Christ was spoken of in terms drawn from the Wisdom imagery of pre-Christian Judaism" (259; cf. J. W. Montgomery 1962: 57; Hamerton-Kelly 1973: 241).

8-3.5. THE SON OF GOD

In the NT one of the most important designations of Jesus is "Son of God" or "Son." (There does not appear to be any significant difference between the two terms; see Marshall 1967: 87-88; Pinto 1974: 76; D. Guthrie 1981: 304-5; contra Hahn 1969: 279.)

Jesus is termed "Son of God" or "Son" in all four Gospels. In light of the tendency of some critical scholars to see the ascription of a divine nature to Christ as a late development, it is significant that while John's Gospel (commonly held to be the latest) claims to have been written "so that you may come to believe that Jesus is the Messiah, *the Son of God*" (20:31), Mark's Gospel (commonly held to be the earliest) begins with an almost identical claim that what follows is "the good news of Jesus, Messiah, *Son of God*" (1:1 AT).

Son of God/Son is an important designation in Paul and Hebrews. It is much less common in the general epistles (it does not appear in James or Jude), with the notable exception of the Johannine Epistles. Nor is it prominent in Acts, though significantly Paul's message is said to center in the proclamation of Jesus as the Son of God (Acts 9:20; cf. 13:33). Christ is called "the Son of God" only once in Revelation (2:18). It is significant that the title has such a central place (in addition to its use in the Synoptics) in the three major theological witnesses of the NT — Paul, John, and Hebrews.

While there is no denying the widespread occurrence of the title in the canonical NT, the question of what it means demands careful study, especially in the light of the various meanings of "son of God" in the OT (above, 8-1.5). A variety of meanings have been suggested (cf. Dunn 1980: 13-22; Elwell 1988g).

i. It might mean simply "a righteous person" as in *Wis* 2:16, 18 and *Sir* 4:10 (above, 8-1.5d). NT usage clearly means far more than this, though when the centurion at the cross says, "Truly this man was son of God" (Mark 15:39//Matt 27:54 AT — there is no definite article), historically it may be that this is what the centurion meant (cf. Luke 23:47); clearly, however, Mark and Matthew see a much deeper significance in the remark.

ii. An important feature of Jesus' teaching was the Fatherhood of God (see 1-3.4a). It has been held that the NT sees Jesus as a "son of God" in the same sense that anyone (or at least any believer) may be regarded as a child of God; at most, Jesus' relationship of sonship to God would differ from that of his disciples in degree but not in kind. Study of the relevant texts in the Gospels, however, reveals that Jesus never identifies his sense of Sonship with that of his followers. As Marshall points out, Jesus never linked his disciples with himself in saying "our Father" (1967: 90; cf. John 20:17, where Jesus distinguishes "my Father" from "your Father").

iii. In light of the designation of the king in the OT as (adopted) "son of God" (above, 8-1.5c), it has been claimed that "Son of God" as applied to Jesus in the NT should be seen as a messianic title, the equivalent of "Messiah" (*christos*), and thus not implying a divine nature; like David or Solomon, Jesus would be a fallible mortal, chosen by God to carry out a specific task. On this view "Messiah" and "Son of God" in Mark 1:1 and John 20:31 would be precisely equivalent terms (cf. Matthew's version of Peter's confession in 16:16, where "the Christ" and "the Son of the living God" could be seen as parallel terms; and also Matt 26:63//Mark 14:61). Historically the evidence of the Dead Sea Scrolls indicates that "Son of God" was a messianic title (see R. H. Fuller 1969: 32; Dunn 1980: 15-16); but we have already seen that while the NT identifies Jesus as the promised Messiah, it also portrays him as transcending all the messianic categories (cf. 6-3). In the total canonical context, it is clear that "Son of God" does not merely reiterate "Messiah" but complements it, pointing to a deeper and fuller understanding of Jesus' identity (cf. D. Guthrie 1981: 305-6).

iv. "Son of God" can be understood as meaning that Jesus was not a "mere man" but was divine by nature, something that would at least imply preexistence and incarnation (cf. above, 8-3.1). Orthodox Christianity (as expressed in the creeds) has always understood the title to mean that while Jesus was fully human, he was also fully divine, and it is clear that this is what the title signifies in the canonical NT, as the identification of Jesus with God's glory, word, and wisdom strongly corroborates. (Of course, it is possible to recognize this while holding that such a view was a late development within early Christianity, and that it has no basis in the historical Jesus; on the historical question see below, 8-5.1.)

a. My Beloved Son

The Synoptic Gospels, with minor differences of emphasis, present Jesus as the Son of God (this is a special emphasis in Matthew; cf. Dunn 1980: 48-50; Verseput 1987). Important references occur at two crucial events in Jesus' ministry: at the baptism Jesus hears a voice from heaven saying, "This is my Son, the Beloved" (Matt 3:17//Mark 1:11//Luke 3:22), and at the transfiguration a voice from the cloud says of Jesus, "This is my Son, the Beloved" (Matt 17:5//Mark 9:7; cf. Luke 9:35). The powers of evil recognize their enemy when they see him: in the temptation narrative the devil twice addresses Jesus beginning, "If you are the Son of God . . ." (Matt 4:3, 6//Luke 4:3, 9), and when Jesus exorcises demons they cry out, "You are the Son of God!" (Mark 3:11//Luke 4:41; Matt 8:29//Mark 5:7//Luke 8:28).

Jesus himself claims to be the Son of God. Even as a boy he affirms a unique relation to God as his Father (Luke 2:41-51; cf. R. E. Brown 1994: 127). This claim is reflected in sayings of Jesus such as Matt 24:36//Mark 13:32, and particularly in Matt 11:27 (//Luke 10:22): "All things have been handed over to me by my Father; and no one knows the Son except the Father, and no one knows the Father except the Son and anyone to whom the Son chooses to reveal him." In the parable of the vineyard Jesus implicitly identifies himself with the son (Matt 21:37-39 and //s), and in Mark 14:61, when the high priest asks, "Are you the Christ, the Son of the Blessed One?" Jesus responds, "I am," an answer that immediately calls forth a charge of blasphemy.

In the Gospels the language of Sonship is most fully developed in John's Gospel, which contains numerous references to Jesus as the "Son of God" or simply "the Son." Many of these texts speak of the relationship between the Father and the Son. There is a certain dialectic between identity (10:30; 14:10) and differentiation (3:16), between communion (5:20; 14:31) and subordination (5:30). As Son of God, Jesus is "sent" by the Father (5:37; 6:44) and shares two of the supreme prerogatives of God: to give life (5:21) and to judge (5:22; cf. Pinto 1974: 88).

The prologue identifies Jesus as the preexisting divine Logos who became incarnate. 1:14 and 18 with their references to "the only *(monogenēs)* Son" (see commentaries on text and translation) form the transition from the Logos doctrine of the prologue to the body of the Gospel where Sonship predominates. *Monogenēs* is characteristic of Johannine Christology (1:14, 18; 3:16, 18; 1 John 4:9) and means "only or "unique" (Arndt and Gingrich 1957: 529); it underlines the otherwise obvious fact that for John "Son" involves full divinity (for a fuller discussion of Johannine usage, see Dunn 1980: 56-59; D. Guthrie 1981: 312-16).

In Paul "Son of God" is an important christological title, used of the preexistent one, "sent" by God (Rom 8:3; Gal 4:4), the agent of creation (1 Cor 8:6; Col 1:16, 18), the agent of reconciliation through his death (Rom 5:10; cf. 8:32; Gal 2:20), and the one who renders filial obedience to God (Rom 5:10; 8:32; Gal 2:20; cf. Col 1:13f.). The proclamation of Jesus as God's Son is the very heart of the gospel (Gal 1:15-16). Nowhere does Paul argue for the divine Sonship of Christ; it appears as a basic Christian belief shared by Paul and his readers (for a fuller discussion of Pauline usage, see Hengel 1976: 7-15; Dunn 1980: 36-46; D. Guthrie 1981: 317-19).

Sonship is also an important category in Hebrews (see Hengel 1976: 85-88): in contrast to the "many and various ways" in which God has spoken in the past, "in these last days he has spoken to us by a Son" (1:1-2). Any thought that Jesus might be some kind of angelic messenger, rather than the true Son of God, is dismissed (1:5-14). Particularly striking is the contrast with Moses, the greatest servant of God in the OT. Jesus belongs to quite a different category: "Moses was faithful in all God's house as a servant. . . . Christ, however, was faithful over God's house as a son" (3:5-6). The central importance of this belief is shown by the fact that apostasy involves spurning the Son of God (10:29; cf. 6:6 and also 4:14, which implies that acknowledgment of Jesus as Son of God was part of the basic Christian confession).

b. The Virginal Conception

Another way in which the NT proclaims that God himself is uniquely active in the Christ event is in the accounts of the virgin birth, or more accurately, the virginal conception. (The NT says nothing about Mary's status after the birth of Jesus; on Jesus' brothers and sisters, see 15-3.2b.i.) The virginal conception is affirmed in the infancy narratives of both Matthew and Luke. Despite their major differences, these narratives do agree in calling Mary a virgin (*parthenos*, Matt 1:23; Luke 1:27); in affirming that nevertheless a child will be born to her (*gennaō*, passive, Matt 1:20; Luke 1:35); in denying that Joseph and Mary had sexual relations before Jesus' birth (use of *ginōskō*, Matt 1:25; Luke 1:34); in ascribing conception to the agency of the Holy Spirit (Matt 1:18, 20; Luke 1:35); and in annotating the genealogies to anticipate possible objections (Matt 1:16; Luke 3:23). Though many efforts have been made to detect other references (e.g., Mark 6:3; John 1:12-13, 45; 6:42; 8:41; Rom 1:3; Gal 4:4), nowhere else in the NT is there any clear and unambiguous mention of the virginal conception (cf. Machen 1930: 244-68; but see also the discussions in H. E. W. Turner 1956: 12; Cranfield 1988: 178-80).

Seen in a canonical setting, the infancy narratives certainly echo OT stories of the birth of servants of God in special circumstances, i.e., when the mother was advanced in years (Isaac) or barren (Samson, Samuel). In none of these stories, however, is there any question of a virginal conception. Thus what stands out is not the similarities to these OT stories but the fundamental contrast. This is most clearly brought out in Luke, where the infancy narratives of John the Baptist and Jesus are juxtaposed. John's birth is special in the OT sense because his parents are advanced in years and his mother is barren (1:7, 18, 25, 36); Jesus' birth is special because Mary is not yet married and has not yet had sexual relations with a man (cf. Moody 1962: 790-91).

Matthew concludes his account of the virginal conception by affirming that "all this took place to fulfill what had been spoken by the Lord through the prophet" and quoting Isa 7:14. The Isaiah prophecy finds a twofold fulfillment in the birth of Jesus. Firstly, in accordance with the original meaning of the passage, it is a renewed assurance that however dark and difficult the situation, God does not desert his people. After centuries of waiting, the Christ event enables them to recognize that "God is with us" in a new and unique way. Secondly, in accordance with the extended meaning in the LXX version of Isa 7:14 (above, 8-2.1), this event is initiated not by any human action but by a unique act of God himself.

The infancy narratives do not appear to be making theological statements concerning either the sinlessness of Mary nor the status of virginity as such (cf. R. E. Brown 1973: 38-40). Rather, both narratives are concerned to stress the divine initiative in the Christ event. "The birth narratives have as their centrepiece the entrance of the supernatural into ordinary human life. Something is about to happen at God's initiative, unprecedented in the history of the world" (Buckwalter 1996: 800). Jesus is not just a rare human being who emerged from within human history through, as we might say, a chance combination of heredity, environment, and the opportune time. The Christ event represents God's unique action within history; it is the work of God's Holy Spirit bringing about a new creation. The virginal conception "indicates that God himself made a new beginning in the course of the history of his creation by coming himself in person and becoming part of that history. He himself originated this particular human life by a new act of creation. Jesus Christ is not a saviour arising out of the continuity of human history, but God in person intervening in it, coming to the rescue" (Cranfield 1988: 189; cf. Piper 1964: 141-48). It is Luke who makes explicit the connection between the virginal conception and Jesus' divine Sonship: "The child to be born will be holy; he will be called Son of God" (Luke 1:35).

c. Is Jesus God?

While the NT recognizes Jesus as divine as well as human, it prefers to call him "Son of God" rather than "God." A number of texts might be read as designating Jesus as "God," though a fair number involve problems of text and/or translation (John 1:18; Acts 20:28; Rom 9:5; Gal 2:20; Col 2:2-3; 2 Thess 1:12; Titus 2:13; 2 Pet 1:1; 1 John 5:20; see V. Taylor 1962; R. E. Brown 1994: 177-85; on translation see esp. V. Perry 1976). John 1:1 asserts that "the Word was God *(theos ēn ho logos),*" but it also distinguishes the Logos from God: "the Word was with God *(ho logos ēn pros ton theon)*" (see commentaries on the difficulties of this text). One clear example, however, is John 20:28 where Thomas hails Jesus as "My Lord and my God!"

   If there is a reluctance directly to call Jesus "God," it is important to note that the NT does not hesitate to quote a number of OT texts that originally referred to God and apply them to Jesus (e.g., Rom 10:13 = Joel 2:32; Phil 2:10 = Isa 45:23). A particularly striking example is Heb 1:8-9, which quotes the words of Ps 45:6-7 but applies them to Christ: "But of the Son he says, 'Your throne, O *God,* is forever and ever. . . .'" What Ziesler (1990) says about Paul is true of the NT as a whole: "God's powers and reign are exercised through Christ as God's plenipotentiary representative, but Christ is not identical with God. Things traditionally said about God may now be properly said about Christ but not that he *is* God, for the element of subordination remains" (39-40). This, however, is to be understood "not in the sense of later so-called 'subordinationism,' but in the sense that Jesus Christ is God only in the revelation of himself" (Cullmann 1963: 306).

New Testament: Consummation

8-4. WITH GREAT POWER AND GLORY

8-4.1. THE REVEALING OF THE LORD

Everything the NT says about Jesus in terms of divine glory, word, and wisdom, and divine Sonship, is fraught with paradox. In the present time this paradox must be accepted through faith; only at the final consummation will faith be replaced by sight. In this period of the overlap of the ages, "we see in a mirror dimly, but then face to face" (1 Cor 13:12 RSV). Only at the parousia, the second coming of Christ, will every eye see him (Rev 1:7) and, by implication, recognize him for what he truly is (cf. 1-4.4; 17-4.3). As already noted (7-4.1), in the Pastorals the parousia is spoken of as the future manifestation *(epiphaneia)* of Christ.

8-4.2. WHEN HE COMES IN HIS GLORY

The paradox of incarnation is nowhere greater than in the NT presentation of Jesus in terms of the glory of God. That glory was, and still remains, veiled; only at the final consummation will the veil be lifted and the glory of the Lord finally revealed (see Ewert 1980: 161-63).

At his parousia the Son of Man will be "seated on the throne of his glory" (Matt 19:28; cf. 25:31). 1 Pet 5:1 speaks of "the glory to be revealed" (cf. 4:13). Believers will also share in the eschatological glory. James and John beg Jesus, "Grant us to sit, one at your right hand and one at your left, in your glory" (Mark 10:37), but to aspire to this they must be prepared to share Christ's sufferings (see Hill 1967: 284-85). Jesus says, "Those who are ashamed of me and of my words, of them the Son of Man will be ashamed when he comes in his glory and the glory of the Father and of the holy angels" (Luke 9:26; cf. Mark 8:38; Matt 24:30//Mark 13:26//Luke 21:27).

For the present, Christ within believers represents "the hope of glory" (Col 1:27), as they wait for "the manifestation of the glory of our great God and Savior, Jesus Christ" (Titus 2:13), but "when Christ who is your life is revealed, then you also will be revealed with him in glory" (Col 3:4). Paul speaks of the believers' "hope of sharing the glory of God" (Rom 5:2; cf. 8:17-18; 2 Cor 4:17; Col 3:4; 2 Thess 2:14; Heb 2:10).

In Revelation John hears the heavenly choir glorifying God in hymns which swell to a mighty chorus at the final consummation:

Hallelujah!
For the Lord our God
    the Almighty reigns.

Let us rejoice and exult
   and give him the glory. (19:6-7)

When the holy city comes down out of heaven from God, "it has the glory of God" (21:11). The city needs neither sun nor moon, "for the glory of God is its light" (21:23).

8-4.3. THE NAME BY WHICH HE IS CALLED IS THE WORD OF GOD

In his incarnation Christ is the Word made flesh. The full revelation of the Word awaits the end time. In Rev 19:11-16 Christ is depicted as leading the armies of heaven against the forces of evil, and the name by which he is called is "the Word of God *(ho logos tou theou)*." The Logos who according to John's Gospel was "in the beginning" with God, will come at the end to fulfill God's purposes for all humankind.

8-4.4. ALL THE TREASURES OF WISDOM

Wisdom is linked with the final consummation in two ways. On the part of believers, wisdom is required for a true understanding of the events that will precede the end. Interpreting both the number of the beast and the symbolism of the seven heads of the beast "calls for wisdom" (Rev 13:18; 17:9). In the total canonical context this means the divine wisdom, incarnate in Christ.

At present faith is centered in "Christ . . . in whom are hidden all the treasures of wisdom and knowledge" (Col 2:2-3; cf. 8-3.4). These treasures will not remain forever hidden. The heavenly worship of God and of the risen and exalted Christ anticipates the full and final revelation:

Worthy is the Lamb that was slaughtered
   to receive power and wealth and wisdom. . . . (Rev 5:12)

8-4.5. WITH MY FATHER

In the present believers recognize Jesus as the Son of God; they are called by God "to wait for his Son from heaven" (1 Thess 1:10).

After destroying all that opposes God, Christ will deliver the kingdom to the Father: "Then comes the end, when he [Christ] hands over the kingdom to God the Father, after he has destroyed every ruler and every authority and power" (1 Cor 15:24; see vv. 24-28).

8-5. GLORY, WORD, WISDOM, SON:
THEOLOGICAL REFLECTIONS

1. Once again, BT is concerned primarily with the canonical text and with its witness to the divine nature of Christ. Historical problems, however, are more acute in this area than in any other aspect of Christology, and these problems cannot be totally ignored by BT. A crucial question is how far Christology began with Jesus, and how far it began only after Easter (cf. Marxsen 1969a: 1-21). If the witness of the NT books to the divinity of Christ has no basis in the historical Jesus, then the foundation of Christian belief collapses.

No one denies that in John we find a full-blown incarnational theology. But there are critical scholars who see this as a later and unauthentic development. A wide range of views has been held.

i. Some scholars deny that Jesus ever thought of himself as divine or as Son of God. According to Harnack's famous dictum, "The Gospel, as Jesus proclaimed it, has to do with the Father only and not with the Son." Scholars who stand in the Bultmann tradition see Jesus merely as a prophet who proclaimed the kingdom of God; only after Easter did "the proclaimer become the proclaimed."

ii. Another view is that Jesus became aware of his divine Sonship only at his baptism. This would favor an "adoptionist" Christology in which Christ was not preexistent or divine by nature, but only by adoption; this can be combined with the view that "Son of God" simply means (a human) "Messiah" (above, 8-3.5). The main basis for this view is the quotation from Ps 2:7 in the heavenly voice at Jesus' baptism (Matt 3:17 and //s), but it is highly significant that the words "today I have begotten you" from Ps 2:7 are *not* spoken by the voice. The designation "beloved" *(agapētos)* strongly suggests a unique relationship to God, akin to the Johannine *monogenēs* (above, 8-3.5a; see Pinto 1974: 78; D. Guthrie 1981: 309).

iii. Another view is that Jesus was hailed as Son of God by the early church only after and as a result of his resurrection and exaltation; this can be seen as a variant form of adoptionist Christology. The favorite proof text here is Rom 1:4, which states that Christ "was declared to be Son of God with power according to the Spirit of holiness by resurrection from the dead" (cf. also Acts 2:36; 13:33). In the context of the Pauline letters as a whole, however, there is no basis here for adoptionism. The emphasis in Rom 1:4 is on the fact that the resurrection declared Jesus as Son of God "with power *(en dynamei)*," the clear implication being that he was Son of God before that, but in his earthly life was in apparent weakness (on these texts see Marshall 1967: 101-2; contra Dunn 1980: 33-46).

iv. A yet more radical view that continues to be propagated is that belief in the divinity of Christ had no place at all in the earliest Christian communities. It is Hellenistic in origin (cf. Hahn 1969: 298), and entered Christianity only after it left Palestinian soil and spread into the wider Greco-Roman world in which heroes of Greek mythology as well as Oriental rulers (see Acts 12:22) could be termed "sons of God" (cf. Dunn 1980: 14-17), and a miracle worker could be seen as a "divine man *(theios anēr)*." Hengel has shown that most of the alleged Hellenistic parallels are far from convincing (see 1976: 23-41). In any case, since Paul clearly identifies Jesus as the Son of God, this leaves only approximately twenty years (ca. A.D. 30-50) for this alleged development to have taken place, a very small window of opportunity for such a major belief not only to penetrate but also to become dominant in the various Christian communities. If, as many critical scholars hold, some of Paul's formulations reflect early Christian tradition (e.g., Rom 1:3-4), the gap becomes impossibly short.

Against all these views it can be maintained that there is good historical evidence that Jesus saw himself as standing in a unique relationship to God (cf. Marshall 1967: 90-98). There are Synoptic passages that cannot easily be dismissed as nonhistorical. It is perverse to reject all the Johannine sayings as unauthentic and then to dismiss Matt 11:27//Luke 10:22 as a "bolt from the Johannine blue"! Matt 24:36//Mark 13:32, "But about that day and hour no one knows, neither the angels of heaven, nor the Son, but only the Father," is a text the early church could hardly have invented. Further strong evidence of Jesus' sense of Sonship is found in his distinctive use of *abba* in address to God (cf. 1-3.4a). The original Aramaic term is quoted in Mark 14:36, and was preserved in the early church (Rom 8:15; Gal 4:6). *Abba* was used as a familiar term within the family circle, but never in Jewish liturgical practice. It witnesses to the fact that "before his Father Jesus sees himself as 'the Son' in an exceptional intimacy" (Pinto 1974: 84; cf. Dunn 1980: 26-28; D. Guthrie 1981: 304). Thus we may agree with Marshall (1967) that "the roots of the NT designation of Jesus as the Son of God lie in his own consciousness of being uniquely related to the Father" (103).

Furthermore, in addition to the *explicit* claims made by Jesus, there is considerable evidence that *implicitly* he claimed to be doing what only God himself could do. Thus he claimed the right to forgive sins, something that is clearly a divine prerogative (e.g., Mark 2:5-11). He claimed the right to supersede the Torah and reveal God's will directly (e.g., 10:2-9). In reaching out to the outcasts of society, he embodied the grace of God. In claiming to inaugurate the kingdom of God (e.g., Matt 12:28), he was again doing what only God could do.

It is clear that as the early Christians reflected on the meaning of the Christ event, their understanding of that event matured and developed especially in relation to the preexistence of Christ. What can be claimed is that the development of Christology within the NT legitimately and necessarily made *explicit* what was *implicit* in the words and deeds of the historical Jesus.

The above study has shown how the basic understanding of Jesus as divine in nature has its roots in the OT understanding of God's glory, word, and wisdom, and not in ideas imported into Christianity after it expanded beyond Palestine.

One further consideration favors the view that Christ was recognized as divine from the earliest days of Christianity. Both France (1982) and Hurtado (1988) have drawn attention to the significance of the fact that from an early date Jesus became an object of devotion, something that involved "an unprecedented reshaping of monotheistic piety to include a second object of devotion alongside God" (Hurtado, 100). Thus Jesus is the subject of early Christian hymns (e.g., Phil 2:6-11; Col 1:15-20); prayer can be directed to Jesus (Acts 7:59-60; 9:14, 21; 22:16; 1 Cor 1:2; note that to "call on the name of the Lord" is an OT expression for worship offered to God; see France, 30); Christ's name is invoked in baptism; the Lord's Supper sets forth his redemptive death; he is "confessed"; and prophecy is claimed as the words of the heavenly Christ (Rev 1–3) (cf. Hurtado, 101-14). What this shows is that "already in the earliest post-Easter period Christians were learning to think and speak of Jesus in much the same way as they thought and spoke of God" (France, 32).

2. Attention was drawn above (8-3.4) to the recognition in recent scholarship of the widespread influence of the OT understanding of Wisdom on NT Christology. The identification of Christ with "Lady Wisdom" has appealed especially to feminist theologians. Yet the fact remains that the bulk of the references to Wisdom are implicit rather than explicit. What accounts for the "muted status" (Cady, Ronan, and Taussig 1986: 50) of Sophia in the NT? Two reasons may be suggested. One is that Jesus as a matter of historical fact was *male*. The functions of Wisdom could be ascribed to him, but not so readily the feminine term *sophia* (cf. J. M. Reese 1981: 45). The second factor is the clear OT tradition that Wisdom was *created* by God (albeit prior to the creation of the universe; see 8-1.4b). Although the full implications of this did not emerge until the Arian controversy, John at least was already concerned to affirm that there never was a time "when the Son was not"; "*in the beginning* was the Logos, and the Logos was with God, and the Logos was God."

3. The virginal conception of Christ has often been dismissed as marginal and of very little importance in the NT as a whole. Canonically, however, it comes in a very prominent position in the first chapter of the NT, and is independently attested to in Luke's Gospel. Moreover, as Piper (1964) points out, "the composition of Matthew and Luke makes manifest that in their eyes the Virgin Birth, far from being an isolated event, illumined the whole ministry of Jesus" (143). Although it is not mentioned elsewhere in the NT, nothing outside of the two infancy narratives "can be found . . . which is opposed to the possibility or the actuality of the virgin birth" (Kürzinger 1981: 940).

The question of historicity, of whether the virginal conception is "literally true," has occupied much of the modern discussion (see V. Taylor 1920; Machen 1930, esp. chap. 9; Piper 1964: 137-40; J. S. Wright 1978: 662-63). Many modern scholars have distinguished in some way between the literal truth of the event and its spiritual/theological/symbolic/poetic/demythologized meaning, abandoning the former while still seeking to salvage something of the latter (cf.

Pittenger 1969). Rejection of historicity is almost always based on modern "scientific" presuppositions that rule out in advance God acting within history and deny the possibility of miracle. Science works only with general laws based on observation of as many cases as possible. The NT, however, presents the virginal conception as a unique event, the only one of its kind in human history (cf. Buckwalter 1996: 799). The biblical view is well expressed in the Lucan narrative: "For nothing will be impossible with God" (Luke 1:37).

Often this rejection of historicity has been coupled with allegations that the belief was derived from pagan, Greek mythology, though careful study of the biblical evidence shows that the NT accounts are quite distinct from such pagan ideas. Stories "about how Zeus begat such persons as Hercules, Perseus, and Alexander constitute nothing more than mythological fornication. . . . The yawning chasm between these pagan myths of polytheistic promiscuity and the lofty monotheism of the virgin birth of Jesus is too wide for careful research to cross" (Moody 1962: 791; cf. Machen 1930: 324-39; A. Richardson 1958: 172-73; Kürzinger 1981: 943-44; R. E. Brown 1973: 62; Elwell 1988g: 2124). The alleged pagan "parallels" are not real parallels at all; "in none of them is there any question of a truly virginal conception; rather it is a matter of physical intercourse between a god and a mortal woman from which a birth results" (Cranfield 1988: 181).

It has also been objected that belief in the virginal conception is incompatible with the genealogies, both of which trace Jesus' descent through Joseph (Matt 1:1-17; Luke 3:23-38). Obviously this worries modern critics far more than it worried Matthew and Luke, both of whom saw no problem in combining virginal conception and genealogy in one Gospel. Both include notes (Matt 1:16; Luke 3:23) which indicate that they were perfectly aware of what they were doing, and both clearly felt that while Joseph was not biologically Jesus' father, he was his father in every other way: legally, socially, and personally (cf. Cranfield 1988: 180).

A further objection raised against the virginal conception is that it in effect denies the full humanity of Jesus, but of this there is no trace in the NT. Jesus was born, lived, and died as a fully human person. As far as Luke is concerned, "it is significant that in the same passage in which the supernatural birth of Jesus is so strongly indicated, a statement is included about the human growth of Jesus (Lk. 2:40), about his obedience to his earthly 'parents' (note the plural, Lk. 2:51) and about his increase in wisdom (Lk. 2:52). Clearly the relating of the virgin birth was not intended to deny the true humanity of Jesus" (D. Guthrie 1981: 367).

Many people today are reluctant to regard belief in the virginal conception as an essential of Christian faith. Nevertheless, Machen's (1930) verdict still holds true: "even if belief in the virgin birth is not necessary to every Christian, it is certainly necessary to Christianity. And it is necessary to the corporate witness of the Church" (396).

4. In 1 Cor 8:5-6 Paul declares that "even though there may be so-called gods in heaven or on earth . . . yet for us there is one God, the Father, from whom are all things and for whom we exist, and one Lord, Jesus Christ, through whom are all things and through whom we exist." Apropos of this text Hurtado (1988) rightly points out that "early Jewish Christians . . . apparently felt thoroughly justified in giving Jesus reverence in terms of divinity and at the same time thought of themselves as worshipping one God" (1). This remark applies to the NT as a whole: nowhere is there any indication that the various ways outlined above of expressing the divine nature of Christ are thought of as undermining the monotheism inherited from the OT. The same can be said regarding the NT witness to the Holy Spirit as God active on earth and present with his people (cf. 5-3.5 and 5-5.5).

As already discussed (1-3.3c and 1-5.5), it was the task of post-NT Christian theology to work out an understanding of God as one, but also as Father, Son, and Holy Spirit. The orthodox doctrine of the Trinity represents the church's attempt to do this insofar as the mystery of the Godhead can be stated in human language.

CHAPTER 9

The Servant's Suffering

Old Testament: Proclamation

9-1. DESPISED AND REJECTED

9-1.1. THE SUFFERING SERVANT

As we have seen, many of the leading figures of the OT are referred to as "servants" of God, and in the NT are seen as types of Christ (see the discussion in chap. 6). The position of God's servant was not one of privilege, prestige, or power. The lives of these individuals were frequently marked by anguish and suffering: the call to be a servant of the LORD (*'ebhedh YHWH*) was also a call to face suffering and perhaps even death.

Particularly in their acceptance of unjust suffering, these servants can be seen as anticipating the suffering of Christ in the NT. H. Wheeler Robinson published a series of studies entitled *The Cross of Job* (1916), *The Cross of the Servant* (1926), and *The Cross of Jeremiah* (1926) that were later collected and published in one volume with the significant title *The Cross in the Old Testament* (1955). The book of Job shows how one whom God calls "my servant Job" (1:8) may nevertheless be faced with the most agonizing suffering (on Job and the problem of suffering, see 16-1.5c). The ministry of Jeremiah presents a number of parallels with the later ministry of Jesus, and in his case we have a unique insight into the anguish involved in being true to his call to serve the Lord, particularly in the so-called "confessions of Jeremiah" (see 17-1.3d).

In the OT there emerges what we may call a "profile" of the ideal servant of God. While embodied to varying degrees in specific historical individuals, the "Suffering Servant" is portrayed especially in certain psalms and in the "Servant Songs" of Isaiah.

9-1.2. THE SERVANT PSALMS

a. The Psalms of the Servant

The psalms of lament frequently portray an individual who is God's servant yet undergoes suffering. For example, Ps 69 consists of a plea, "Do not hide your face from your *servant*" (v. 17). The psalmist is in distress,

> for the waters have come up to my neck.
> I sink in deep mire,
>   where there is no foothold;
> I have come into deep waters,
>   and the flood sweeps over me. (vv. 1-2)

Although he confesses that he has done wrong (v. 5), nevertheless he claims:

> It is zeal for your house that has consumed me;
>   the insults of those who insult you have fallen on me. (v. 9)

He is reproached and insulted by enemies:

> Insults have broken my heart,
>   so that I am in despair.
> I looked for pity, but there was none. . . .
> They gave me poison for food,
>   and for my thirst they gave me vinegar to drink. (vv. 20-21)

These and other similar psalms may appropriately be termed "Servant Psalms." While each is a distinctive poem, as a group they reflect a common profile of a suffering servant of God that is also reflected in a number of other psalms even when the actual term "servant" does not appear.

Some psalms of this type are ascribed to David, one of the great examples of a servant of God; Ps 18, for example, is "a Psalm of David the servant of the LORD" and is a thanksgiving for deliverance rather than a petition.

Ps 22 is also ascribed to David, and while it does not contain the term "servant," it follows very closely the patterns and motifs of the Servant Psalms. The first part of the psalm (vv. 1-21) alternates between expressions of despair (vv. 1-2, 6-8, 12-18) and hope (vv. 3-5, 9-11, 19-21). In the opening verse the psalmist cries out in distress, "My God, my God, why have you forsaken me?" He is "scorned by others, and despised by the people" (v. 6), mocked (v. 7), and surrounded by ravening beasts (vv. 12-13, 16, 20-21). He is so weak and emaciated (vv. 15, 17) that he is given up for dead, and people already divide up his few belongings:

> They divide my clothes among themselves,
> and for my clothing they cast lots. (v. 18)

Yet against all the odds the psalmist clings to faith, sustained by the memory of God's care for his people (vv. 3-5) and God's care of him from his mother's womb (vv. 9-11). In this powerful psalm God's suffering servant appears as the representative of suffering Israel and of suffering humanity (cf. Tostengard 1992: 167). In these verses "there is much to remind us of the suffering servant of the Lord" (Zimmerli and Jeremias 1957: 55-56).

b. The Suffering of the Servant

The Servant Psalms exhibit a common pattern, though of course not every feature of the pattern is necessarily found in every psalm (see B. W. Anderson 1983: 75-77).

The psalmist is frequently (though not always) described as God's *servant* (Pss 18 [in heading]; 69:17; 86:2, 4, 16; 143:2, 12; 116:16). He is threatened by a situation often portrayed in vivid metaphors, e.g., in terms of deep waters (69:1-2) or wild beasts (22:12-13, 16, 20-21). He is betrayed by his friends (41:9), despised and mocked (69:20-21; 22:6), and comes close to death (18:4-5; 22:15; 86:13; 116:3; 143:3). The servant cries out to God (22:1; 69:17; 86:2; 116:4; 143:2, 11), who hears and delivers him (18:6; 22:4). He praises and thanks God (18:46-50; 69:30-36; 116:8), and acknowledges God's salvation in public worship (22:22, 25; 116:12-19).

Whatever the historical origin of these psalms, in their canonical form and context they reflect a broadly based insight into human life: those who undertake to serve the Lord — whether a great figure like Moses, or those called to be prophets or kings, or ordinary members of the people of God — cannot expect to be spared suffering. Service and suffering go hand in hand, though the servant who cries out to God for help may hope for ultimate deliverance and salvation.

9-1.3. THE SERVANT SONGS

a. The Songs of the Servant

Since the work of Duhm (1875, 1892), it has become common to isolate four passages in 2 Isaiah, to refer to them as "the Servant Songs" (Duhm's term was *Ebed Jahwe-Lieder* = "Servant of Yahweh Songs"), and to refer to their subject as "the Suffering Servant" (see von Rad 1965: 250-62). Scholars do not agree on the exact extent of these songs (cf. Lindhagen 1956: 279), though generally they are identified as follows (for problems of text and translation, see commentaries):

Song I: Isa 42:1-7 or 9 or 12
Song II: Isa 49:1-6 or 7 or 13
Song III: Isa 50:4-9 or 11
Song IV: Isa 52:13–53:12

Some critical scholars regard the author of the songs as different from the author of Isa 40–66, and/or regard them as later interpolations into the text. The evidence for this is not convincing, however (see C. R. North 1962: 292; von Rad 1965: 251), and in any case a canonical BT will take the songs as they stand as part of the book of Isaiah.

Though the isolation of the four songs is helpful in drawing attention to the importance of their content, it should be noted that the word "servant" (*'ebhedh*) occurs in only three of the songs (*not* in Song III), while the term *does* appear a dozen times elsewhere in 2 Isaiah. In Isa 53:11 the figure is given another title, "the righteous one." If the criterion is not simply the occurrence of the term "servant" but the similarity in content, then other passages, particularly 61:1-3, have a high claim to be considered Servant Songs also (cf. Bruce 1969: 84-85). Therefore, while retaining the by-now traditional identification of four songs, we seek to understand them in their broader canonical context, noting especially the striking similarities between the servant of the Isaiah songs and the figure portrayed in the Servant Psalms.

In these passages the servant is portrayed as one chosen by God (Isa 42:1; 49:1, 7) for a specific task (bringing forth justice — 42:1; and salvation — 49:6) and equipped by God for that task (42:1; 49:2; 50:4-5, 7-9). He will work quietly and patiently until the task is accomplished (42:3-4).

b. The Suffering of the Servant

The most characteristic feature of the servant is the fact that he suffers, though this emerges progressively in the songs. He is "deeply despised" (49:7) and subject to "insult and spitting" (50:6). He is "a man of suffering and acquainted with infirmity" (53:3), and is "oppressed" and "afflicted" (53:7). The exact nature of his suffering is not clear; "as in the psalms of lament, multiple competing images give us oblique indication" (Zimmerli and Jeremias 1957: 33).

The servant's suffering is interpreted in *sacrificial* terms: 53:10 speaks of the LORD making his life "an offering for sin (*'āshām*; LXX — *peri hamartias*)," and *'āshām* is the term used for the "sin offering" that atoned for sin (see 14-1.5b.ii). The servant's suffering is *vicarious*, because he does not suffer for his own sins but for the sins of others: "surely he has borne our infirmities" (53:4), "he was wounded for our transgressions" (53:5). And clearly it is *substitutionary*, for the servant accepts the penalty that by rights should fall on others: "The

LORD has laid on him the iniquity of us all" (53:6). This vicarious and substitutionary suffering is also *redemptive:*

> Upon him was the punishment that made us whole,
>   and by his bruises we are healed. (53:5)

The benefits of the servant's suffering and death extend to "many" *(rabbîm): many* are astonished at what he does (52:14); he bears the sin of *many* (53:12) and makes *many* righteous (53:11). What is meant by "many" is indicated in 52:15, which speaks of the effect of the servant's mission on "many nations." In keeping with the broader context of 2 Isaiah, the servant's mission is directed not just to Israel (49:5-6) but also to all nations (42:1, 4; 49:6). Accordingly, the "we," "us," and "our" of 53:1-6, while it includes Israel, is not to be limited to them but embraces all humankind.

c. Proposed Identifications

In the canonical text the servant is an anonymous figure (see W. M. W. Roth 1964: 171), and from before NT times there has been much debate regarding his identity (cf. Lindhagen 1956: 280-83; C. R. North 1962: 293). Four main types of identifications have been proposed (with various subtypes).

i. Individual

It has been held that the portraits are based on an individual historical person. The numerous proposed candidates include Moses, Isaiah, Jeremiah, Ezekiel; kings such as Hezekiah, Josiah, Jehoiakin, Zerubbabel; others such as Job or Cyrus. Indeed, as H. W. Robinson (1980) has pointed out, "the identifications with outstanding individuals almost parallel Ben Sirach's catalog of the famous men of Israel, or the roll call of the heroes of faith in Hebrews 11" (39 n. 60). The large number of such identifications suggests two conclusions: firstly, it is most unlikely that any one historical figure is intended, and secondly, many outstanding individuals in Israel's history embodied the servant ideal to a certain extent. Under this heading must also be noted the view that the servant was the prophet himself, an identification at least as old as Acts 8:34, where the Ethiopian asks Philip, "About whom, may I ask you, does the prophet say this, about *himself* or about someone else?"

ii. Collective

A strong case can be made for a collective interpretation, specifically for identifying the servant with Israel. In Song II "my servant" is in fact equated with "Israel" (Isa 49:3).

iii. Ideal

Others have argued that the portrait is not of any one individual or group but rather depicts the ideal servant of God. This need not conflict with the first two views since the ideal could be embodied, to varying degrees, in outstanding individuals and in the people of Israel.

iv. Messianic

The songs have been seen as prophecies referring to an individual, messianic figure who will come in the future. This has been the traditional view of the Christian church, which has seen these prophecies fulfilled in the person of Jesus.

d. The Identity of the Servant

The fact that these solutions have all been argued with great conviction suggests that they are not necessarily mutually exclusive but that elements of truth will be found in each of them.

The starting point must be the recognition that it is in the first place *Israel* that is called to be the servant of the Lord. As noted above, this identification is specifically made in Song II:

> And he [God] said to me, "You are my *servant*,
>   *Israel*, in whom I will be glorified" (49:3),

and it is consistent with the repeated identification of Israel as God's servant not only in 2 Isaiah (41:8-9; 42:19; 43:10; 44:1-2, 21; 45:4; 48:20; 49:3) but also elsewhere in the OT (e.g., Ps 136:22; Jer 30:10; 46:27-28; see 11-1.2b). The LXX understands Song I in this sense, for it inserts "Jacob" and "Israel" in Isa 42:1. Historically this makes good sense, for the original setting of the prophet's message is the period near the end of the Babylonian exile, a time of suffering and distress for God's people.

However, an outright identification of the servant with all Israel is blocked by Song II, which speaks of *the servant's mission to Israel*:

> And now the LORD says,
>   who formed me in the womb to be his *servant*,
> to bring *Jacob* back to him,
>   and that *Israel* might be gathered to him, . . .
> "It is too light a thing that you should be my *servant*
>   to raise up the tribes of *Jacob*
>   and to restore the survivors of *Israel*." (49:5-6)

This suggests that the servant is not Israel as a whole but rather a group within Israel, specifically the faithful remnant (see 11-2.2a). Historically the reference would be to those Israelites in exile in Babylon who remained steadfast in their faith. On this view the servant is narrowed done to a smaller group.

The songs, however, envisage an even further narrowing down of the servant to an individual; within them there is clearly a progression from a collective toward a more individual understanding of the servant, especially in Song IV.

When we bear in mind the typically biblical dialectic of community/individual, we realize that it is not necessary to make an either/or decision between a collective and an individual interpretation (cf. Lindhagen 1956; Fraine 1965: 190-91). The most satisfactory solution is one that sees in the Servant Songs what might be called a "job description" of the ideal servant of the Lord. Israel as a people was called to be God's servant and ought to have been God's servant, but the OT again and again shows how it failed to fulfill this role (cf. Cazelles and Mussner 1970: 840). Outstanding individuals within Israel certainly did embody the ideal to varying degrees. Since Israel as a whole appeared to have failed, the prophet saw the servant's role falling on a smaller group. In the immediate historical context he is no doubt thinking of the faithful remnant among the exiles in Babylon. Yet in Song IV especially, we see a more individual interpretation. If even the remnant fails adequately to embody the servant ideal, then the only hope lies in the coming of a true servant of God in the future (see further below, 9-2).

9-1.4. THE DEATH OF THE SERVANT

Being a servant of God involves suffering; it may also involve risking and perhaps even losing one's life.

a. The *Servant Psalms* can speak of the threat of death. In Ps 18:4 the psalmist says, "the cords of death encompassed me," and in 22:15, "you lay me in the dust of death." When the psalmist either anticipates or gives thanks for deliverance from death, the reference seems to be not to a resurrection following actual physical death but rather to being snatched away from the jaws of death and thus avoiding actual physical death.

b. The fourth *Servant Song* speaks much more explicitly of the death of the servant, who is compared to "a lamb that is led to the slaughter" (Isa 53:7). He was "cut off from the land of the living" (v. 8) and "poured out himself to death" (v. 12), so that it could be said of him that

> they made his grave with the wicked
> and his tomb with the rich. (v. 9)

While it is not impossible to interpret this as metaphorical language, in distinction from the Servant Psalms the fourth Servant Song does appear to contemplate the servant's death, though also his ultimate vindication (and therefore resurrection).

9-1.5. MARTYRDOM

The historical narratives of the OT certainly contain examples of how God's servants were called upon not only to suffer but even to lay their lives on the line. According to 1 Kgs 19:10, King Ahab slew God's prophets with the sword, while Jer 26:20-23 recounts the death of the prophet Uriah. Jeremiah himself came close to losing his life at one point in his career (38:1-13). 2 Chr 24:20-22 tells of the death of the priest Zechariah. The summary of salvation history in Neh 9 declares that the people of Israel rebelled against God and "killed your prophets" (v. 26).

It is only at the very end of the OT period, however, that we can see a *theology of martyrdom* beginning to emerge. In the period of persecution under Antiochus Epiphanes (*1 Macc* 1), many Jews gave their lives as martyrs. "Many in Israel stood firm. . . . They chose to die rather than to be defiled by food or to profane the holy covenant; and they did die" (1:62-63). 2:37-38 tells the dramatic story of how many Jews allowed themselves to be killed rather than fight on the Sabbath. The most detailed accounts are the prototypical martyrologies of Eleazar in *2 Macc* 6:18-31 and of the mother and her seven sons in *2 Macc* 7. In the latter story the death of the seven brothers is seen as atoning for the sin of Israel (7:37-38). With this we may compare the words of the three men thrown into the fiery furnace, according to the *Prayer of Azariah* (part of the LXX version of Daniel), which speaks of their anticipated death as an atoning sacrifice (Dan 3:39-40 LXX).

While these references are in deuterocanonical books, the tradition of the martyrdom of God's faithful servants belongs within BT since it is clearly alluded to in the NT. Matt 23:35 (//Luke 11:51) refers to "the righteous blood shed on earth, from the blood of righteous Abel to the blood of Zechariah son of Barachiah." Here Abel is seen as a prototype of later martyrs; Zechariah (see above) is mentioned as the last example in Scripture of a martyr (apparently assuming that 2 Chronicles is the last book in the OT canon). In the parable of the wicked tenants (Mark 12:1-11), some of the servants sent by the owner of the vineyard are beaten and killed (v. 5).

Zech 12:10–13:1 apparently refers to the martyrdom of a servant of God, probably a prophet or king (cf. *NOAB*, OT: 1230). "And I will pour out a spirit of compassion and supplication on the house of David and the inhabitants of Jerusalem, so that, when they look on the one whom they have pierced, they shall mourn for him, as one mourns for an only child" (12:10). The Hebrew reads "when they look on *me* whom they have pierced," suggesting that in attacking God's servant people are attacking God himself (see commentaries).

Extensive national mourning for the martyred servant will be followed by divine forgiveness and cleansing (13:1).

Old Testament: Promise

9-2. MANY SHALL BE ASTONISHED

Does the OT promise the coming of an ideal servant of God in the future, one who will be called to suffer and perhaps even to die? This question has been the subject of considerable debate.

According to Luke 24:45-46, the risen Christ, speaking to his disciples, "opened their minds to understand the scriptures, and . . . said to them, 'Thus it is written, that the Messiah *(ton Christon)* is to suffer and to rise from the dead.'" In 1 Cor 15:3 Paul quotes a very early Christian formula to the effect that "Christ *(Christos)* died for our sins in accordance with the scriptures." Thus in the early church, not only was it claimed that Jesus combined the roles of Messiah *(Christos)* and suffering/dying servant, but also that the combination of these two roles was "in accordance with the scriptures" (i.e., of the OT).

That the OT Scriptures do envisage the possibility of such a combination has been widely challenged in modern biblical scholarship. It is frequently asserted that in Jesus' day, on the one hand, the figure of the Suffering Servant of Isa 53 was identified with Israel (but never with the Messiah), while on the other hand, the figure of a Messiah was identified with a triumphant Davidic-type king (but never with the Suffering Servant). In other words, Messiah and Servant were mutually exclusive categories. On this view the two categories were brought together for the first time by Jesus himself, or on a more radical view, by the early church.

This problem of whether a combination of Messiah and Servant can be thought of as being "in accordance with the scriptures" can be approached from two directions. We can ask what evidence there is that a future Servant was identified with the Messiah (below, 9-2.1). Or we can look at some of the main types of "messianic" expectation (in the broad sense, see 6-2) and ask whether such figures might have been understood as servants of the Lord, destined to suffer; below we consider whether this might be so in the case of a Mosaic Messiah (9-2.2), a royal Messiah (9-2.3), a prophetic Messiah (9-2.4), and the Son of Man (9-2.5).

9-2.1. A MESSIANIC SERVANT?

We have argued above (9-1.3c, d) that the OT portrait of the Suffering Servant constitutes a "job description" of the ideal servant of God, an ideal embodied (but only imperfectly, and in varying degrees) in Israel and in outstanding individuals. In Song IV especially, the Servant is understood as a *future* individual who will be the true Servant of the Lord.

It is true that in postbiblical Judaism the Servant was almost always interpreted as referring to Israel, though one interesting exception is the Targum on Isa 53 that does identify the Servant with the Messiah but significantly transfers the suffering to either Israel or Israel's enemies (see Rowley 1950b: 106; Cullmann 1963: 58-59)!

The Septuagint translation, however, which, we have argued, forms part of the biblical tradition and was used by most NT writers, witnesses to a different understanding. Although it starts out in Song I by identifying the Servant with Israel, in Song IV the translation points to the expectation of a *future* Suffering Servant. In Isa 52:14-15 the verbs are changed to *future:* "Many *shall* be astonished at him . . . ," etc. In 53:2 where the Hebrew text has "For he grew up before him like a young plant *(yônēq),*" the LXX reads *paidion,* the word for "child," and the same word it uses in the messianic prophecy of 9:6:

> For to us a *child* is born,
> to us a son is given.

These changes in translation suggest that the LXX tradition was prepared to identify the Servant of the songs with a future Messiah.

It should also be noted that the speaker in Isa 61:1, who closely resembles the Servant (above, 9-1.3a), declares that "the LORD had anointed *(māshach)* me," and "is thus in some sense a Messiah" (Bruce 1969: 85).

9-2.2. A SUFFERING MOSAIC MESSIAH?

Some scholars associate the figure of the Servant with *Moses* (cf. Lindhagen 1956: 300; von Rad 1965: 261-62), and see the songs as either modeled on the historical Moses or looking forward to a Messiah of the "second Moses" type (see 6-2.1). While Deut 18:15, 18 thinks of the coming prophet like Moses primarily as a teacher, in the OT Moses is the servant of the Lord par excellence and well fitted to be the type of a suffering Messiah figure.

In the Pentateuch Moses is portrayed as a "suffering mediator" (von Rad 1962: 294). In Exod 32:30-34 Moses told the people, "You have sinned a great sin. But now I will go up to the LORD; perhaps I can make atonement for your sin." Moses offered to take the penalty for the people's sins upon himself: "But now, if you will only forgive their sin — but if not, blot me out of the book that you have written." Like the Servant of Isa 53:10 who will give his life as "an offering for sin," Moses was prepared to give his life as an atonement for the sins of the people; "it is a substitution of life for life through a total surrender of self" (Gese 1981a: 96). Such a role can hardly have been excluded from the expectation of an eschatological Moses or prophet like Moses.

9-2.3. A SUFFERING ROYAL MESSIAH?

Others see in the Servant a *royal* figure. Recognition of this need not depend on theories (proposed especially by Scandinavian scholars) of influence from the ancient Near Eastern Tammuz cult with its drama of a ritually humiliated, dying and rising king (see Lindhagen 1956: 301-2). The kingly Messiah figure is addressed by God as "my servant" in a few texts (Ezek 34:23-24; 37:24-25; Zech 3:8), though without specific reference to suffering or death. David, the prototype of the royal Messiah, may have suggested to many a great warrior and a conquering king, but historically David faced opposition and knew much suffering, especially at a personal and family level. He is frequently called God's servant (2 Sam 3:18; etc.), and the canonical association of David with some of the Servant Psalms (including Ps 22) directs our attention to "David the Royal Sufferer" (S. B. Frost 1962: 111). In Isaiah's visions of the future, the reaffirmation of the "everlasting covenant" with David (Isa 55:3) follows closely upon the portrait of the Servant in Isa 53.

9-2.4. A SUFFERING PROPHETIC MESSIAH?

In the OT the prophets are repeatedly called God's "servants," and both the historical and the prophetic books show again and again how acceptance of God's call to be a prophet could entail suffering. "The prophet, to the extent that he obeyed his call, lived a life of agony" (J. A. Sanders 1972: 54). Ezekiel is told that briers and thorns will be with him, and he will sit upon scorpions (Ezek 2:6). Micaiah was flung into prison with "reduced rations of bread and water" (1 Kgs 22:27). The classic case is Jeremiah, for in addition to the record of the sufferings he endured, a series of autobiographical "confessions" survive which give a unique insight into the mental and spiritual anguish of a great and sensitive soul (Jer 11:18-23; 15:10-21; 17:14-18; 18:18-23; 20:7-18; see 17-1.3d).

In the light of this, the expectation of an eschatological prophet (6-2.4) might well suggest a figure who would be expected to suffer. Jesus himself envisaged the inevitability of a suffering prophet when he warned his followers to expect persecution: "for in the same way they persecuted the prophets who were before you" (Matt 5:12; cf. 23:29-35).

9-2.5. A SUFFERING SON OF MAN?

We have seen that in Jesus' day the title "Son of Man" could signify an individual, supernatural, eschatological figure who will come at the final consummation as God's agent to judge the wicked and bring God's salvation to the righteous (see 7-2.3, 4). Acting in that capacity, the Son of Man could scarcely be identified with a Suffering Servant of God.

We have also seen, however, that the Son of Man figure originates in Dan 7 (7-2.1), where the title stands for the faithful remnant of God's people. For Daniel that remnant must be prepared to suffer for their faith: "Some of the wise shall fall, so that they may be refined, purified, and cleansed, until the time of the end" (Dan 11:35). Insofar as the Dan 7 reference does not drop out of sight, the Son of Man can be seen *both* as one who, as the embodiment of Israel/the remnant, must expect to suffer *and* as one who will be vindicated by God and appointed the future Judge/Savior.

Messianic expectation in Jesus' day was marked by considerable variety and fluidity (cf. 6-2). The crowds in John 6:15 who threatened to take Jesus "by force to make him king" and the crowds who hailed Jesus' entry into Jerusalem shouting, "Hosanna to the Son of David!" (Matt 21:9), no doubt were typical of a widespread popular expectation that looked for a triumphant Messiah who would deliver Israel from subservience to Rome and restore the glories of David's kingdom.

The LXX, however, shows that at least in one strand of Judaism the Suffering Servant could be identified with the Messiah, while there is also much scriptural evidence that "messianic" expectations, whether of the Mosaic, royal, prophetic, or Son of Man types, were by no means inconsistent with a figure who could be expected to suffer and die, though of course also ultimately be vindicated by God. The NT understanding of Jesus as a Messiah who also suffers and dies is a startling and paradoxical one, but it is not altogether without some OT precedent.

New Testament: Fulfillment

9-3. HE HUMBLED HIMSELF

9-3.1. JESUS THE SERVANT

The NT portrays Jesus supremely as the servant who suffers and dies for others.

a. The Category of Servant

There can be no doubt that "servant" is a key category in the NT understanding of Jesus. Its importance is not to be measured simply by the number of occurrences of the word "serve" *(diakoneō)* or "servant" *(diakonos, doulos, pais),* or by the number of quotations and allusions to the Servant Psalms and Servant Songs, significant though these are. It is seen above all in the manifold ways in which Jesus accepted and incarnated "the servant pattern."

b. References to the Servant Psalms

The passion narrative is permeated by quotations from and allusions to the Servant Psalms; their influence in fact is more marked than that of the Servant Songs (cf. J. H. P. Reumann 1974: 39-43; Tostengard 1992: 170). In particular, Ps 22 is echoed in the passion narratives of all four Gospels, so much so that S. B. Frost (1962) calls the psalm "the fifth Gospel" (113, 115). The following table lists the quotations and allusions to the psalm in the Gospel accounts:

Ps 22:1 (My God, My God, why have you forsaken me?)	Matt 27:46 (quote) Mark 15:34 (quote)
Ps 22:7 (mocking, shaking heads)	Matt 27:39, Mark 15:29, Luke 23:35
Ps 22:8 (Let God deliver you)	Matt 27:43
Ps 22:15 (my mouth is dried up)	John 19:28
Ps 22:16 (they have pierced my hands and feet)	Matt 27:35, Mark 15:24, Luke 23:33, John 19:23
Ps 22:18 (they divide my clothes, they cast lots)	Matt 27:35, Mark 15:24, Luke 23:34, John 19:24 (quote)

Historically, it may be that Jesus' quotation of Ps 22:1 prompted the early church to discover other references to Jesus' suffering and death in the psalm (cf. Reumann, 49). Mark's passion narrative also shows the influence of Pss 41 (Ps 41:9 = Mark 14:18) and 69 (Ps 69:9 = Mark 15:32; Ps 69:21, "they gave me vinegar to drink" = Mark 15:23, 36). Cf. also Pss 37:32, 54:3, 86:14 with Mark 14:1; Ps 38:11 with Mark 14:50; Pss 27:12, 35:11 with Mark 14:56; Pss 38:13-14, 39:9 with Mark 14:61; Ps 55:12-14 with Mark 14:66-72. These correspondences are not a parade of proof texts (cf. Kraus 1986: 189-90); rather they have a cumulative effect in demonstrating how closely Jesus conforms to the OT pattern of the Suffering Servant of God portrayed in the Psalms (cf. Reumann, 58).

Particularly striking is Jesus' quotation of Ps 22:1 in the "Cry of Dereliction" (Matt 27:46//Mark 15:34). It is quite possible, of course, as is often suggested, that Jesus went on to recite the whole psalm (which he would certainly know by heart), including therefore the "happy ending" of vv. 22-31. But great care must be taken to avoid "explaining away" the Cry of Dereliction. "The Godforsakenness of Jesus cannot be taken to be a charade of helpful metaphor but must be taken absolutely seriously. The depth of the forsakenness of the psalmist serves as a proper background for the depth of the experience of the cross" (Tostengard 1992: 170). On the cross Jesus, as the Suffering Servant, shares and takes upon himself the suffering of God's people and of all humanity. Jesus "not only identifies himself with all the suffering that finds expression in the Psalms uttered in the presence of God, but also he alone is the servant of God, in whose life and death are fulfilled all the sufferings of all those who cry out in prayer. He alone is able to take upon himself the indescribable totality of what it means to be forsaken by God and to be far from his presence" (Kraus 1986: 189).

The author of Hebrews declares that "it was fitting that God . . . in bringing many children to glory, should make the pioneer of their salvation perfect through sufferings," and goes on to quote Ps 22:22: "I will proclaim your name to my brothers . . ." (Heb 2:10-12). Jesus in his suffering and death was identifying himself as the brother of all humankind, but his sufferings were for their sake, in order to "bring many children to glory."

c. References to the Servant Songs

The NT undoubtedly identifies Jesus with the Suffering Servant of 2 Isaiah (see Kesich 1965: 6), though the exact extent of the references to the Servant Songs and specifically to Isa 53 in the NT is a matter of dispute among biblical scholars.

The heavenly voice heard by Jesus at his baptism (Mark 1:11 and //s) echoes both Ps 2:7 ("You are my Son, the Beloved") and Isa 42:1 ("With you I am well pleased"; cf. Matt 12:18), thus indicating that in Jesus the figures of Davidic Messiah and Suffering Servant are combined (see R. Wallace 1981: 22). In his inaugural address in the synagogue at Nazareth, Jesus quotes in reference to himself Isa 61:1-2, a passage that probably would be taken as referring to the Servant (cf. above, 9-1.3a; and see France 1968: 42-43; Michel 1978: 612). The Evangelist Matthew, who typically sees Jesus as fulfilling OT prophecy, quotes Isa 53:4 in Matt 8:16-17 and Isa 42:1-4 in Matt 12:15-21, both in relation to Jesus' healing ministry. John 12:38 quotes Isa 53:1 in the context of the lack of response to the signs performed by Jesus.

On two key occasions Jesus points to the significance of his own death by alluding to Isa 53's claim that the death of the Servant is for the sake of "many" (cf. above, 9-1.3b; see Childs 1992: 509). In the "ransom saying" Jesus combined Servanthood with a vicarious death "for many": "The Son of man came not to be served but to serve *(diakonēsai),* and to give his life as a ransom *for many (anti pollōn)*" (Matt 20:28//Mark 10:45). At the Last Supper Jesus took the cup of wine, the symbol of his impending death, and said, "This is my blood of the covenant, which is poured out *for many (hyper pollōn)*" (Mark 14:24//Matt 26:28; see Kesich 1965: 56-57; R. Wallace 1981: 27). Also in the context of the Last Supper, according to Luke 22:37 Jesus said, "For I tell you, this scripture must be fulfilled in me, 'And he was counted among the lawless'"; in the light of his impending death, this is a highly significant quotation of Isa 53:12 (cf. Culpepper 1966: 56; France 1968: 30-32).

The book of Acts and the Epistles clearly witness to the identification of Jesus with the Suffering Servant. In the story of Philip and the Ethiopian, Isa 53:7-8 is quoted in full, and the story assumes that Philip went on to apply this passage to Jesus (Acts 8:35). Reflected in Acts 3 and 4 is a Christology that identifies Jesus as God's *pais*. While this could mean "son," it is more probably to be translated "servant," as in 3:13, God "has glorified his servant Jesus" (cf. 3:26; 4:27, 30). The title "Righteous One" *(ho dikaios)*, given to Jesus in Acts 3:14, 7:52, 22:14, and 1 John 2:1, recalls "the righteous one" of Isa 53:11 (see Menard 1957). The Christ hymn of Phil 2:6-11 identifies Jesus as the one who took the form of a servant *(doulos)*. Paul quotes Isa 53:1 in Rom 10:16 and Isa 52:15 in Rom 15:21 (though neither text refers to suffering and death). On the other hand, it is hard not to believe that in several of his references to Jesus' suffering and death, Paul had Isa 53 in the back of his mind (see, e.g., 1 Cor 15:3-4; 2 Cor 5:21); in particular, references to Christ being "given up" *(paradidōmi* = "hand over, deliver") by God (Rom 4:25; 8:32; cf. Gal 1:4; Eph 5:2; Titus 2:14) reflect Isa 53:6, 12, where the same verb is used in the LXX (cf. Hengel 1981: 35-36). A series of references to Isa 53 is found in 1 Pet 2:21-25, while Heb 9:28 is a clear echo of Isa 53:12.

d. The Servant Pattern

Here, however, as often in BT, a narrow "word study" approach can miss the broader picture. Quite apart from specific quotations or allusions to the Servant Psalms and Songs, the narratives of the Gospels are full of parallels between Jesus and the broader "servant pattern" laid down in the OT. Jesus is called and chosen by God and is obedient, fulfilling his God-given mission. He is misunderstood and mocked, suffers and dies; yet he is vindicated by God, and his death and resurrection have profound significance both for Israel and for the nations.

In all the Gospels, much of the dramatic power of the narrative comes from the fact that Jesus chooses the way of the cross with his eyes wide open; according to Luke 9:51, "When the days drew near for him to be taken up, he set his face to go to Jerusalem." Following the account of Peter's confession, the Synoptic narrative is punctuated by a series of three "passion predictions" in which Jesus speaks of his coming suffering, death, and resurrection:

1. Matt 16:21//Mark 8:31//Luke 9:22
2. Matt 17:22-23//Mark 9:31//Luke 9:44
3. Matt 20:18-19//Mark 10:33-34//Luke 18:31-33

(On these see Kesich 1965: 13-20; D. Guthrie 1981: 438-39.) The disciples are depicted as finding it difficult or impossible to accept these predictions of Jesus' suffering and death. Significantly in Mark, the three passion predictions are enclosed within two healings of the blind (8:22-26; 10:46-52), suggesting that Jesus was seeking to open the eyes of his disciples to the necessity of his suffering and death (cf. Kesich, 20). Jesus further alludes to his coming death in the parable of the vineyard (Matt 21:39 and //s). In John also, Jesus speaks of his coming death (3:14). The "hour" of his passion is anticipated (2:4) and in due course arrives (12:23; 17:1; see Guthrie, 450). In Gethsemane (Luke 22:40-46 and //s) Jesus sweated blood as he agonized over the decision whether or not to accept the cup of suffering.

9-3.2. WHY DID JESUS DIE?

It is obvious that the death of Jesus holds a central place in the NT. Foulkes (1996) argues that in the NT Jesus' death (and resurrection) is central in Christian preaching, in the worship of the church, and for the meaning of Christian discipleship. Each of the four Gospels culminates in a "passion narrative," and there is truth in Kähler's famous dictum that Mark's Gospel is really "a passion narrative with an extended introduction." Numerous passages in Acts, the Epistles, and Revelation refer to Christ's death or his "blood" and assign supreme significance to it. References to Jesus' "cross," frequent in the narrative of the Gospels, are particularly characteristic of Paul (cf. also Heb 12:2; 1 Pet 2:24; and see Cousar 1990: 21 on the language of crucifixion).

In the light of the far-reaching claims made for Jesus by the early church, one of the most pressing questions the early communities must have had to answer was: Why did Jesus die?

Although in one sense the NT may see Jesus as following in the footsteps of the martyrs of the OT (see above, 9-1.5), and may even see him as in some sense a suffering prophetic Messiah (9-2.4), the NT does not employ martyr as a major interpretive category in its understanding of Jesus' death. In the parable of the wicked tenants (Mark 12:1-12), a clear distinction is made between the owner's servants who are killed (= prophets) and the "beloved son" (cf. Hengel 1981: 41; on the parable, see Blomberg 1990: 247-51). The Greek word *martys* means primarily "witness," though in the NT one can see the transition to the sense of "martyr," i.e., those who witness to their faith to the point of death (see Acts 22:20 with reference to Stephen, and Rev 2:13 with reference to Antipas). Only in Rev 1:5 and 3:14 is the term applied to Jesus, but almost all translations render it "witness." For the NT Jesus is not one in the succession of Jewish martyrs who have given their lives for the faith; the true successors of the Maccabean martyrs are Stephen, Antipas, and "the martyrs *(tōn martyrōn)* of Jesus" (Rev 17:6 RSV). Rather, the death of Jesus is a unique event, with cosmic significance.

In seeking to answer the question, Why did Jesus die? the New Testament presents broadly two types of answers, *narrative* and *kerygmatic.*

There can be no doubt that the death of Jesus and its significance was a key element in the church's kerygma or proclamation from the very beginning, and in both biblical and theological studies attention has focused on what we have termed the "kerygmatic" answers to the question, Why did Jesus die? This has obscured the undoubted fact that also from the very earliest days of the church Christian believers sought to answer the same question in a *narrative* fashion, i.e., by recounting, in some detail, the sequence of events that led up to Jesus' death. These accounts, preserved initially in oral tradition, and probably used in the worship services of the early church, became the basis of the passion narratives of the Gospels. The historical-critical approach to the passion narratives has sought to peel off the layers of later interpretation in order to isolate what can be considered historical. Redaction criticism and some of the newer literary approaches have more helpfully focused on the canonical texts and on how the four Evangelists, each in his own way, present the traditions of Christ's passion and interpret them for the Christians of their day (cf. Conzelmann 1970; Haenchen 1970). Thus, while the Gospels tend to provide narrative answers and the Epistles kerygmatic answers to the question of why Jesus died, we must be careful not to make too rigid a distinction, because of course, the passion narratives do also offer theological explanations of what happened. It is not that the Gospels are nontheological while the Epistles are theological; it is rather that the Gospels present their theology primarily in a narrative mode while the Epistles present theirs in a kerygmatic mode.

The most important emphasis in the Gospel accounts is the sinlessness of Jesus. What the passion narratives make clear is that Jesus did not deserve to die; he was guilty of no crime and was in fact the last person to deserve to be put to death as a common criminal. Conversely, the narratives reveal the greater and lesser sins of a whole cast of characters involved in the chain of events that led to the crucifixion of Jesus. The cast includes:

Judas, who betrayed his master
the Pharisees, who opposed Jesus on religious grounds
the Sadducees, who felt their position threatened
the false witnesses, who lied for money
Caiaphas, who was quite prepared to sacrifice a man's life
Pilate, who allowed himself to be blackmailed
the crowd, whose allegiance changed so quickly
the disciples, who forsook Jesus and fled
the Roman soldiers, who were only doing their duty

Thus it was a whole combination of factors that led to Jesus' death. Put in another way, his death was caused by sinful human nature, by a variety of people who were all first and foremost looking out for themselves.

It has been suggested that from a literary point of view the Gospels could be classified as tragedy (see Ryken 1984: 83-85). One does get the sense of events moving inexorably toward a tragic conclusion. Yet two features of the narrative make this a less than appropriate designation for the Gospels as a whole. One is of course the fact that the Gospels end with resurrection accounts that turn tragedy into triumph, or perhaps one could say, into comedy. The other is the complete absence of a major feature of tragedy: the existence in the protagonist of a "tragic flaw." The sins of the supporting cast throw into even clearer relief the sinlessness of Jesus.

9-3.3. GOD SO LOVED THE WORLD

Jesus' death has a central place in the NT kerygma not because it is seen as the outcome of various human forces, but because it is viewed in the light of the overall plan and purpose of God. Behind the historical events the NT sees a profound theological meaning. "The Son of Man *must (dei)* undergo great suffering . . . and be killed" (Mark 8:31); "there is a compelling divine necessity about this 'must' . . . the hand of God is in it" (Morris 1965: 27). According to Peter's sermon at Pentecost, Jesus was delivered up "according to the definite plan and foreknowledge of God" (Acts 2:23). In the context of a reference to Christ's death as a ransom, 1 Pet 1:20 claims that "he was destined before the foundation of the world, but was revealed at the end of the ages for your sake." What these typical texts assert is that "redemption through Christ was not a sudden whim of God, but was planned *before the foundation of the world*" (*NOAB*, NT: 338).

That the death of Jesus was in accordance with God's purpose is emphasized above all by presenting it as happening *in fulfillment of OT Scripture* (see Foulkes 1996: 157-58). Jesus believed that "it is written" that the Son of Man must suffer (Mark 9:12; cf. 14:21 and //s; cf. Matt 26:54, 56; Luke 18:31). According to Luke 24:26-27, the risen Christ taught two of his disciples that it was necessary that the Christ should suffer, and "beginning with Moses and all the prophets, he interpreted to them the things about himself in all the scriptures." A basic claim of the very early form of Christian kerygma quoted by Paul was that "Christ died for our sins *in accordance with the scriptures*" (1 Cor 15:3; cf. Acts 3:18). If the inauguration of the new order happens in fulfillment of Scripture (1-3.5), this is to be seen particularly in regard to Christ's death. The Gospels relate numerous details of the passion narrative to corresponding OT passages (cf. above, 9-3.1).

John 3:16 is frequently and rightly cited as a summary of the purpose of God that the whole NT sees lying behind the total Christ event: "For God so loved the world that he gave his only Son, so that everyone who believes in him may not perish but may have eternal life." For the NT the Christ event is grounded in the love of God (see V. Taylor 1956: 30, 92-93). Jesus' death in particular is a result and expression of that love. "Behind the drama of the self-giving Christ is the self-giving love of God" (Cousar 1990: 26). The picture presented by some later theories of the atonement of Jesus changing the attitude of God toward sinners is inconsistent with the NT data. "God did not send the Son into the world to condemn the world, but in order that the world might be saved through him" (John 3:17); "God proves his love for us in that while we still were sinners Christ died for us" (Rom 5:8). Thus "salvation is not something wrung from an unwilling God by the desperate intervention of a compassionate Son who took pity on those subject to His Father's destroying wrath. Salvation proceeds rather from the loving heart of God the Father himself" (Morris 1965: 154).

In the cross the NT sees God acting for the salvation of humankind. What Christ did in his death, he did "for others"; i.e., his death was a vicarious one. Language expressing this pervades all main sections of the NT. Paul says Christ died "for us" (Rom 5:8), or more personally "for me" (Gal 2:20), or more broadly "for all" (2 Cor 5:14), or more specifically "for the ungodly" (Rom 5:6). John says Christ, the Good Shepherd, died "for the sheep" (John 10:11) and for the people (11:50); in 6:51 Jesus gives his flesh "for the life of the world." In a telling example of irony (cf. Ryken and Longman 1993: 419), John sees in Caiaphas's politically expedient advice, "it is better . . . to have one man die for the people than to have the whole nation destroyed," a deeper truth: Jesus dies "for the nation [i.e., Israel], and not for the nation only, but to gather into one the dispersed children of God [i.e., Gentiles]" (11:50-52). Through his death "the Son gave himself for the world, shedding the life substance, his blood, instituting the new covenant, sanctifying the new Israel, yes, the entire world" (Gese 1981a: 116). Hebrews asserts that he died "for everyone" (2:9). According to 1 John 3:16, "He laid down his life for us."

In the NT Jesus' death is presented as a historical event. The Gospels furnish considerable historical details that pin the event down to a specific place and a specific time. Early Christian preaching linked Jesus' death especially with the Roman procurator Pontius Pilate (Acts 3:13). On the other hand, Jesus' death is never presented as a mere historical event. It is a unique and unrepeatable act of God for the salvation of humankind. Jesus "has no need to offer sacrifices day after day . . . ; this he did *once for all* when he offered himself" (Heb 7:27). This aspect of the Christ event is expressed by saying that Christ died "once" *(hapax)* or "once for all" *(ephapax;* cf. Heb 9:12, 26, 28; 10:10; as well as Rom 6:10; 1 Pet 3:18).

The NT claims that in the death of Christ something happened that is of momentous significance for humankind. Later theological discussion of the atonement has distinguished between its *objective* and *subjective* aspects. This terminology is of course foreign to the NT, but what the terminology signifies is not.

What appears to be a very early basic formula, "Christ died for our sins" (1 Cor 15:3; see Hengel 1981: 37-38) or "Christ died for us" (Rom 5:8), combines the two aspects of Christ's death in the most concise form: the *objective* event

("Christ died") and its *subjective* appropriation ("for us"). The two aspects can be distinguished but belong closely together: in all NT references to Christ's death *there is a dialectic between the objective and subjective aspects.* Later theories of the atonement have gone astray when they have emphasized one aspect at the expense of the other (cf. Culpepper 1966: 127). The NT speaks of both "the saving deed of Christ, and . . . the appropriation of his work by faith, both individual and communal. These two *together* constitute the Atonement" (V. Taylor 1956: 88).

In our treatment of the various ways in which the NT speaks of Christ's death, we will endeavor to respect the dialectic between objective and subjective, between what the NT claims *happened* at the cross and what *happens* when God's people experience and appropriate its benefits. These two aspects are expressed in the *double headings* employed in the following section.

9-3.4. CHRIST DIED FOR US

The NT speaks of the meaning of Christ's death using a wide variety of images and metaphors that complement and illumine each other, revealing different facets of the significance of the cross (see further, 9-5.5). For the purpose of discussion we group these under four broad headings, though it must be stressed that these are not watertight compartments.

a. Victory/Liberation

Christ's death is presented in the NT as the decisive battle in the conflict with the forces that enslave and oppress humankind (Satan/demons/evil powers), a victory by which humankind is redeemed/saved/delivered/set free/liberated.

This is the view that dominates the Gospels and Acts, and is also reflected in the Epistles and Revelation. The theme of Jesus' conflict with the adversaries of the created order, the cosmic powers of evil, has already been discussed in 4-3. The understanding of Jesus' death in terms of victory/liberation predominated in the theology of the Church Fathers but was neglected by later interpreters, especially in the West, though in the twentieth century its significance was reaffirmed by G. Aulén (*Christus Victor*, 1969; see R. Wallace 1981: 28-31; Childs 1992: 516-18).

This interpretation does not rest merely on a series of specific texts. What has often been overlooked is that the Christ event in the Gospels and Acts is structured in terms of *a drama of conflict.* Humankind on its own fights a losing battle against Satan and the forces of evil. With Christ's appearance the battle is joined in earnest, and in his ministry Jesus engages the demons who are agents of Satan. The final battle is joined at the cross, and Christ's resurrection represents victory over all the forces of evil. In Cullmann's analogy (4-3.1) D-Day, the decisive battle, now lies in the past, but V-Day, the final victory, still lies in the future. As a result of this decisive victory, believers are said to be redeemed, saved, delivered, set free, liberated from the power of sin and death.

Another way of expressing this is in terms of "ransom" (see Morris 1965: 52-55; D. Guthrie 1981: 440-41). "For the Son of Man came not to be served but to serve, and to give his life a *ransom (lytron)* for many" (Mark 10:45//Matt 20:28). The "for many" strongly suggests Isa 53. Barrett (1972a: 20-26) sees a reference to Moses' willingness to give his life to free the people from the penalty of their sin in Exod 32:30 (see above, 9-2.2). Such references are not necessarily mutually exclusive. Similar terminology is found in 1 Cor 6:20, in the Pastorals (1 Tim 2:5-6; Titus 2:14), and in 1 Peter: "You know that you were ransomed *(elytrōthēte)* from the futile ways inherited from your ancestors, not with perishable things like silver or gold, but with the precious blood of Christ" (1:18). A ransom is a sum paid, or something of value given, in order to secure the release of someone held captive. In NT times "slaves could be 'redeemed' by paying a suitable ransom price; so too could prisoners of war" (Tuckett 1992: 520; cf. Morris, 52-53). Similarly believers are said to have been "bought" (*agorazō* — 1 Cor 6:20; 7:23; Rev 5:9) or "bought back" (*exagorazō* — Gal 3:13; 4:5). Christ's death can set people free from sin (Titus 2:14) and from the bondage of their past (1 Pet 1:18). Unlike later patristic speculation, the NT does not push the metaphor to the point of asking to whom the ransom was paid.

Liberation is also spoken of in the NT in terms of "redemption *(apolytrōsis)*," a word related to "ransom." The OT tells of how God "redeemed" his people by liberating them from slavery in Egypt (see 11-1.2). In the NT God "redeems" a new people by liberating human beings from sin, death, and all the powers of evil. Whether or not the Last Supper was an actual Passover meal, Jesus' institution of the Eucharist linked his approaching death with exodus typology (see 3-3.3); his sacrificial "blood of the covenant" (see next section) will effect a deliverance and a redemption of cosmic proportions. Thus, in Christ believers have "redemption through his blood" (Eph 1:7); they have been rescued "from the power of darkness and transferred . . . into the kingdom of his beloved Son, in whom we have redemption, the forgiveness of sins" (Col 1:13-14; cf. Heb 9:15).

b. Sacrifice/Reconciliation

Christ's death is presented throughout the NT as a sacrifice (on terminology, see Horvath 1979: 6-19) that atones for the sins of the world and reconciles humankind to God (cf. Culpepper 1966: 68-70; Tuckett 1992: 518-20; contrast Käsemann 1971: 42-43, 45). The numerous OT references and allusions see the OT sacrificial cult as a type of Christ's sacrifice, but also strongly imply that as a result of what Christ has accomplished by his death, the cult is not only fulfilled but also superseded (cf. Hengel 1981: 53).

At the outset we must recall that the NT identification of Jesus with the Suffering Servant of Isa 53 carries strong sacrificial connotations, for the servant is said to give his life as a "sin offering" (*'āshām;* cf. above, 9-1.3b).

Sacrifice is implied in the numerous references to the "blood" of Christ that echo the OT sacrificial cult, e.g., Acts 20:28, Rom 5:9, Rev 1:5, and Matt 26:28//Mark 14:22-24, where "this is my blood of the covenant" refers back to the sacrifice that sealed the Sinai covenant (Exod 24:8; cf. also 1 Pet 1:2, where the reference to being "sprinkled" with blood also alludes to Exod 24; see commentaries). Just as in the OT the sacrificial blood had cleansing power (Lev 16:19), so as the result of his sacrificial death "the blood of Jesus . . . cleanses us from all sin" (1 John 1:7), and in the striking and paradoxical imagery of Rev 7:14, the redeemed are those who "have washed their robes and made them white in the blood of the Lamb."

According to Eph 5:2, "Christ loved us and gave himself up for us, a fragrant offering *(prosphora)* and sacrifice *(thusia)* to God." It is in Hebrews that the death of Christ as a sacrifice is worked out in greatest detail (see Morris 1965: 284-302; Horvath 1979: 66-70). Not only is Christ the great high priest (on this, see in more detail 6-3.3), but he is also the sacrifice: "He has appeared once for all at the end of the age to remove sin by the sacrifice of himself" (Heb 9:26). In Hebrews the ritual of the Day of Atonement constitutes a type of Jesus' atoning death (9:11-14, 25), but the author also links Jesus' death with the inauguration of a new covenant and thus thinks also in terms of covenant sacrifice (7:22; 8:6; 9:15-22; cf. Tuckett 1992: 520).

OT sacrificial imagery is further reflected in texts that use the *hilaskomai/ hilastērion/hilasmos* word group, generally translated either "propitiation" or "expiation." According to Heb 2:17, Christ's work as high priest was "to make expiation *(hilaskesthai)* for the sins of the people" (RSV). In 1 John 2:2 and 4:10 Christ is said to be the *hilasmos:* "propitiation" or "expiation" for our sins. In Rom 3:25 it is said that God put forward Christ as a *hilastērion* by his blood. In the LXX *hilastērion* translates the word *kappōreth,* which means the "mercy seat," or lid of the ark, that was sprinkled with blood by the high priest on the Day of Atonement. Some interpreters, following the lead of Dodd, take that to be the reference here. "God has put [Christ] forth as a *new* mercy seat, a new locus of reconciliation, a new meeting place for God and men" (Swain 1963: 136; cf. Abba 1962a: 201), but this interpretation has also been subject to severe criticism (see Brown, Link, and Vorländer 1978: 151-54).

References to Jesus as a/the Lamb all imply sacrifice. In John's Gospel the Baptist identifies Jesus as "the *Lamb* of God who takes away the sin of the world" (1:29, 36). Paul asserts that "our *paschal lamb (to pascha),* Christ, has been sacrificed" (1 Cor 5:7). 1 Pet 1:18-19 talks of believers being ransomed "with the precious blood of Christ, like that of a *lamb* without defect or blemish."

"The Lamb" is used frequently in Revelation as a title of Christ, but whereas John and 1 Peter use the term *amnos* for "lamb," Revelation uses *arnion* (on Revelation, see further 9-4.2). The image of a/the Lamb is grounded in a number of not necessarily mutually exclusive OT ideas (cf. Barrett 1955: 210).

i. Undoubtedly the *Passover lamb* is a type of Christ, as the 1 Cor 5:7 reference explicitly affirms. That the references in John point in the same direction is suggested by the fact that "the Johannine passion narrative represents Christ as the true passover" (Barrett 1955: 211). In John 19:29 the reference to "hyssop" recalls the Passover ritual (Exod 12:22); in John 19:36 the quotation, "None of his bones shall be broken" (Exod 12:46; Num 9:12), deliberately parallels Jesus with the Passover lamb; and according to John's chronology, Jesus dies on the cross at the same time the Passover lambs are being slain in the temple (see Kesich 1965: 59).

ii. The figure of the Lamb also echoes the *Suffering Servant* who in Isa 53:7 is compared to "a lamb that is led to the slaughter."

iii. There may also be a reference to the *scapegoat* of Lev 16 (despite the difference between sheep and goats). The fact that the sins of the Israelites were transferred to the animal that was to "bear on itself all their iniquities to a barren region" (Lev 16:22) suggests a connection with "the Lamb of God who takes away *(ho airōn)* the sin of the world" (John 1:29).

iv. There is almost certainly also a reference to the story of *the binding of Isaac* (Gen 22), the central point of which is the assurance that "God himself will provide the lamb for a burnt offering" (v. 8). References to that story are just below the surface at a number of places in the NT.

OT references thus provide a particularly rich background for the designation of Jesus as a/the Lamb, whose death constitutes a sacrifice for the sins of Israel and of all humankind.

What is said about Christ's death as a sacrifice is not to be separated from the rest of the Christ event. Christ's sacrificial and reconciling death is closely linked with his incarnation and life; what Jesus offers to God is his whole life of obedience.

The interpretation of Jesus' death as a sacrifice is complicated by the question of the meaning of sacrifice in the OT; this is dealt with more fully in 14-1.5b (see also D. Guthrie 1981: 432-36). Modern discussion has tended to polarize around the question of whether sacrifice is to be interpreted in terms of "propitiation" or "expiation" (see Brown, Link, and Vorländer 1978: 151); is it a propitiatory offering that averts the anger of a personal deity or an expiatory offering that nullifies the effects of sin (cf. Tuckett 1992: 519)? The two views affect the translation of key NT texts. In Rom 3:25, according to KJV God set forth Christ "to be a propitiation *(hilastērion)* through faith in his blood," whereas according to RSV God put forward Christ "as an expiation by his blood." In 1 John 2:2 (cf. also 4:10), according to KJV Christ "is the propitiation *(hilasmos)* for our sins," whereas in RSV "he is the expiation for our sins." Some more recent translations avoid the propitiation/expiation dichotomy: both NRSV and NIV translate Rom 3:25 as "a sacrifice of atonement" and 1 John 2:2 as "the atoning sacrifice for our sins."

These translations reflect a modern turning away from "propitiation" that is often linked with the idea of "appeasing" the deity. In Abba's (1962a) view, for example, propitiation "as a religious term expresses pagan conceptions of appeasing the Deity and is inappropriate to the religion of Israel"; correspondingly, "there is no idea in the NT of the wrath of God being propitiated by the sacrifice of Christ" (3:920-21). On this view, in the NT the work of Christ is represented "not as a propitiation by the Son of the Father's wrath, but as the divine act of 'covering' or 'blotting out' sin" (2:201).

While expiation may be an element in sacrifice, it is not by itself an adequate category to explain the meaning of sacrifice in either OT or NT. As will be argued more fully in 14-1.5b.iii, the Bible sees God as a just and holy God who cannot ignore sin, but must pass judgment on it. In OT sacrifice the sins of the worshiper are transferred to the sacrificial victim whose death pays the penalty of sin. God, however, is not only just but also merciful, and the essence of the biblical understanding of sacrifice is that *God himself* provides the means of atoning for sin (cf. Brown, Link, and Vorländer 1978: 150). In the OT sacrificial system he does this in a partial and preparatory way; in the NT, through the cross of Christ, he makes full atonement for the sins of humankind. Provided this context is kept fully in mind, Christ's death can be referred to not just as an expiation, but also as a propitiation for sin. This is underlined by the NT emphasis on the *sinlessness* of Christ. What he offers is a life of perfect obedience; 1 Pet 1:19 refers to "the precious blood of Christ, like that of a lamb without defect or blemish."

As noted above, where it is the Passover lamb that is the type of Christ, the benefits of Christ's sacrifice are more akin to the "liberation" model. The link with exodus typology is obvious: the Passover lamb originates with the killing of the lambs whose blood was instrumental in sparing the Israelites from death at the time of God's great act of salvation of his people. Christ's sacrificial death delivers not only Israel but all humankind from the bondage of sin and death.

In other cases, however, the effect of Christ's sacrificial death is atonement for the sin that separates human beings from a holy God. The most comprehensive way of expressing the result of this for believers is to say that they are "reconciled" with God (see Childs 1992: 485-86); even though the actual terminology of "reconciliation" is found only in Paul, this understanding lies behind most NT references to Christ's death as a sacrifice.

It is *Paul* who develops the terminology of *reconciliation* (*katallassō, apokatallassō* = "reconcile"; *katallagē* = "reconciliation"; see Brown, Link, and Vorländer 1978: 166-74; D. Guthrie 1981: 487-92; R. Wallace 1981: 33-37) that is effected through Christ's death (Rom 5:10), his cross (Eph 2:16), his blood (Eph 2:13), or "the blood of his cross" (Col 1:20). Sin results in estrangement from and hostility to God (Col 1:21; cf. Rom 11:28), whereas the removal of the barrier of sin results in the reconciliation of human beings to God. God does not need to be reconciled to human beings. The texts consistently say that "we were reconciled to God through the death of his Son" (Rom 5:10; cf. 5:11; Col 1:22); "in Christ God was reconciling the world to himself" (2 Cor 5:19). "It is God who effects reconciliation. He is the subject, mankind the object. God takes the initiative; only he can act in this situation of estrangement" (Blackman 1962: 17; cf. Cousar 1990: 81-82). Reconciliation is grounded in the love of God (Rom 5:8).

Paul can say that in Christ God was reconciling "the world" (2 Cor 5:19), or even "all things" (Col 1:20), to himself. But reconciliation is effective for those who respond in faith, and all Paul's texts are addressed to believers. Christ's death has not only reconciled sinful human beings to God, it has brought Jews and Gentiles together into one new humanity; by both being reconciled to God, they have been reconciled to one another (Eph 2:11-16). In 2 Cor 5:18-20 Paul speaks of believers being entrusted with "the ministry of reconciliation." While Christians are certainly to work for reconciliation among their fellow human beings (Matt 5:23-24; 1 Cor 7:11), the primary meaning here is preaching the gospel and entreating others to be reconciled to God (2 Cor 5:20).

A similar understanding of Christ's death, if not the actual vocabulary of "reconciliation," is found in Hebrews, where it is the ritual of the Day of Atonement (14-1.3) that constitutes the type (9:25). Just as, on that occasion, sacrifice was made for the sins of the nation, so Christ's sacrifice removes sin (9:26, 28) once and for all *(hapax)*. As a result, believers can enter into God's presence "in full assurance of faith" (10:22; cf. 4:16). What Hebrews declares in the kerygmatic mode — that Christ entered the Holy Place of the heavenly temple with his own blood (9:11-12) — Matthew and Mark state in the narrative mode: at Jesus' death the curtain of the temple was torn in two (Matt 27:51//Mark 15:38). Both make essentially the same point: Jesus' death removes the barrier of sin and makes possible access to a holy God (cf. Hengel 1981: 42). Very similar are those texts that speak of the result of Christ's work as "access" (*prosagō* = "bring to"; *prosagōgē* = "approach, access") to God for believers (Rom 5:2; Eph 2:18; 3:12; 1 Pet 3:18).

Paul also links Christ's sacrificial and atoning death with the terminology of "righteousness"/"justification" (cf. 3-3); this is one of a number of ways that Paul speaks of the benefits of Christ's death, though it is found mainly in Galatians and Romans (see Gal 2–3; Rom 3–6; cf. also 1 Cor 6:11; Phil 3:2-11). Actually, when Paul talks about "justification," he more often uses the verb *(dikaioō)* than the noun *(dikaiosynē)*. Through Christ's "sacrifice of atonement by his blood" God "justifies" believers, i.e., accepts them and receives them back into a right relationship with himself. Typically Paul emphasizes both that justification is a gift of God's grace (Rom 3:24) and that it can be received only through faith (3:26); cf. Paul's assertion in Acts 13:39 (AT): "In this man [Christ] everyone who believes is justified."

It is frequently alleged that "justify" *(dikaioō)* is a legal word (cf. Morris 1965: 241), and hence that when people are justified they are "declared righteous," as if a verdict were being delivered in a court (the problem being that people are not in fact righteous before God). But "the Septuagintal use of 'justify' *(dikaioō)* for the Hebrew verb *ṣdk* shows that the legal or forensic reference is only one among several, all of which concentrate on the restoration of healthy relationship within the family or tribe or nation, often including the relationship with Yahweh" (Ziesler 1990: 88). To say that "justify" means "to make righteous" is no more satisfactory; that is certainly not what happens instantly when a person is justified. It is more accurate to say that in justification God *accepts the sinner into a right relationship with himself.* This acceptance has two aspects. In relation to the past it involves forgiveness of sins, as Rom 4:6-8 shows. Paul generally says very little about forgiveness; for him it is included in justification. In regard to the present and future, the believer is brought into a new, dynamic, personal relationship with God, in Christ, through the Spirit. In the context of Paul's theology justification is a personal experience, but it also has a corporate aspect, for the person justified is incorporated into the church, the body of Christ. Although justification is primarily a present experience, in terms of the already–not yet dialectic it can also be spoken of as future (Gal 5:5): "the justification experienced in the present establishes the hope and certainty of justification in the final judgment" (Stuhlmacher 1994: 63). On the role of faith in justification see 17-3.3, and on the relation of law to justification see 18-3.3b.

c. Identification/Incorporation

Another understanding of Christ's death is found in an important group of Pauline and Petrine texts that echo themes also found more widely in the NT. The most important texts are Rom 8:1-4; 2 Cor 5:14-15, 21; 8:9; Gal 3:13-14; 1 Pet 2:24; 3:18. These passages tend to have a basic twofold structure, proclaiming (a) what Christ has done in and through his death and (b) the benefits of his death for believers. For example:

A For our sake he [God] made him [Christ] to be sin who knew no sin,
B so that in him we might become the righteousness of God. (2 Cor 5:21)

A Though he was rich, yet for your sakes he became poor,
B so that by his poverty you might become rich. (2 Cor 8:9)

(Cf. the common theme in patristic theology that

A Christ became what we are
B so that we might become what he is.)

Further consideration shows that this understanding of Christ's death implies a broadly based NT pattern that may be outlined and then discussed as follows:

A. *What Christ has done*   B. *Benefits for believers*
  A-1 Identification   B-1 Incorporation
  A-2 Substitution   B-2 Participation

A-1 *Identification*. The basic presupposition of this understanding is that Christ through his incarnation *identified* himself with humankind. As the Son of Man, Christ is the inclusive representative of Israel, and of humanity (7-3.3); as the Second Man and Last Adam (7-3.4a), in terms of the biblical individual/community dialectic, he represents in himself all humankind. The Gospels assert this in the narrative mode: Jesus, though himself sinless (Matt 3:14), accepted "a baptism of repentance for the forgiveness of sins" (Mark 1:4) because he stood shoulder to shoulder with sinful Israel (Matt 3:15), thereby being "counted among the lawless" (Luke 22:37 = Isa 53:12; cf. Cronk 1982: 135). His ministry was marked by identification with the outcasts of society such as prostitutes and tax collectors, with whom he shared table fellowship, despite the criticism of the Pharisees (Mark 2:15-17 and //s; Luke 7:36-39; 19:1-10). The Cry of Dereliction (9-3.1b) marks his total identification with suffering and despairing humanity. Christ, the eternal Word made flesh (John 1:14), came "in the likeness of sinful flesh" (Rom 8:3) and was found "in human likeness" (Phil 2:7). He "became like his brothers in every respect" (Heb 2:17), with the one key qualification that he did not share human sin (2 Cor 5:21; Heb 4:15).

A-2 *Substitution*. Christ, in his death, bore on behalf of humankind the penalty for human sin. The basic presupposition here is the understanding of human existence found in Gen 1–3 (cf. 2-1.5; 20-2.2). All human beings are "in Adam," bound together in the solidarity of humankind. Adam's sin and disobedience brought upon him and all humankind the penalty of death. Humankind is separated from God and under the dominion of death, for "the wages of sin is death" (Rom 6:23). Paul works this out especially in Rom 5:12-19 as he contrasts the two representative figures, Adam and Christ (cf. 7-3.4a). In this key passage he begins with the reminder that "sin came into the world through one man [i.e., Adam], and death came through sin, and so death spread to all because all have sinned" (v. 12), but then goes on to show that "everything which happened to man in Adam is parallelled, or rather reversed, by what happened to man in Christ" (Hooker 1978: 465). Thus, "just as one man's [i.e., Adam's] trespass led to condemnation for all, so one man's [i.e., Christ's] act of righteousness leads to justification and life for all" (v. 18). On the cross Christ, though innocent, bore the penalty due to sinful humanity (2 Cor 5:21). In him, the representative human being, all humankind died: "One has died for all; therefore all have died" (5:14). This basic Pauline understanding of Christ's death is also affirmed in 1 Pet 2:24: Christ "bore our sins in his body on the cross."

The very early Christian confession, received by Paul and passed on to the Corinthians, "Christ died for our sins *(hyper tōn hamartiōn hēmōn)*" (1 Cor 15:3), is echoed in a whole series of NT passages all of which use the same preposition: "Christ died *for* the ungodly" (Rom 5:6), Christ became a curse "*for* us" (Gal 3:13), the righteous suffered "*for* the unrighteous" (1 Pet 3:18), etc. While *hyper* can mean "on behalf of," the context in these references strongly favors the meaning "in place of" (cf. D. Guthrie 1981: 465-67, 474; Cousar 1990: 55-56).

Although the word is not used in the NT, it is legitimate here to say that Christ died as the *substitute,* i.e., in place of humankind whom he represented (so D. Guthrie 1981: 465-70; cf. Cousar 1990: 79; contra Whiteley 1964: 130-32; V. Taylor 1956: 30; Käsemann 1971: 43; Hooker 1994: 28, 36). "Christ also suffered for sins . . . the righteous for the unrighteous" (1 Pet 3:18), i.e., as a substitute for the unrighteous. Substitution is also implied by Paul's statements that God, by "sending his own Son in the likeness of sinful flesh and for sin *(peri hamartias),* . . . condemned sin in the flesh" (Rom 8:3 RSV), and "for our sake he [God] made him [Christ] to be sin *(hamartian epoiēsen)* who knew no sin" (2 Cor 5:21). In these texts *hamartia* carries the additional sense of "a sin offering." Here again this ties in with the NT identification of Christ as the servant of Isa 53 who is to give his life as "an offering for sin" (LXX *peri hamartias*) and whose sacrifice is clearly vicarious and substitutionary (cf. above, 9-1.3b; and see Morris 1965: 32-33). Substitution is further implied by Paul's statement that Christ became a curse for us (Gal 3:13). According to Deut 21:23, one who hangs upon a tree is under a curse, i.e., being punished by God. Christ's death by crucifixion posed a major problem for early Christians, and doubtless this text deeply perplexed them (see Hooker, 10-11). Paul declares that Christ accepted the penalty of sin in order to free humankind from that penalty. These texts support the view that "Christ suffered what in some sense sinful man should have suffered" (Guthrie, 470). The term "substitution" may thus fairly be applied to these texts, but it must not be separated from the associated themes of "incorporation" and "participation."

B-1 *Incorporation.* Believers receive the benefits of Christ's incarnation and atonement when through repentance and faith they experience a new birth, and through baptism are incorporated into Christ and become members of the new Israel and the new humanity of which he is the Head. This process of incorporation involves making a radical break with the past, dying to the old life and rising to the new life in Christ (see more fully, 17-3.2). The slogan "The pain was all his, the gain all mine" does not accurately represent the NT understanding of atonement. "Christ shares our humiliation — but if we are to share his glory, then we must share *his* humiliation. This refers not simply to the symbolic rite of baptism, but to the Christian's attitude to life. . . . Christ identifies himself with the human situation, and shares human experience, even to the point of death; the Christian, however, is able to share Christ's resurrection (and all that this means) only if he is willing to identify himself with Christ's death" (Hooker 1978: 474, 479).

Incorporation means that from being "in Adam," believers are now "in Christ Jesus" (Rom 8:1; Gal 3:14), "in Christ" (2 Cor 5:17), or "in him" (5:21). For each believer this is a personal matter, but it also and at the same time has a strongly corporate aspect. "To be in Christ is therefore both personal, because it requires personal faith and relation to Christ, and also corporate, because there is a new unity of mankind in him" (Ziesler 1972: 165). To be "in Christ" is to be in the body of Christ, the church, that constitutes the new Israel and is the core of a new humanity (see 11-3.4c). Just as it was through the sacrificial "blood of the covenant" (Exod 24:8) that Israel became the covenant people of God, so it is by Christ's "blood of the covenant" (Mark 14:24) that believers are called to enter the new covenant as members of the new Israel. It is only as believers are transferred from one corporate entity (sinful humanity) to another (the corporate Christ, the new Israel) that they pass from the old order to the new (see 2 Cor 5:17). Christ's "death and resurrection are the bridge between the old age and the new, since those who are baptized into Christ share his death to the old age, and begin again in the new" (Hooker 1994: 42).

B-2 *Participation*. It is in virtue of being "in Christ," incorporated into the new humanity, that believers participate even now in Christ's life and righteousness, in anticipation of the final consummation. "In Christ Jesus" we are set free "from the law of sin and death" (Rom 8:2). "In him we . . . become the righteousness of God" (2 Cor 5:21), "so that, free from sins, we might live for righteousness" (1 Pet 2:24). Because Christ absorbed the curse of sin, in him the blessing comes to the Gentiles (Gal 3:14). The bread and wine of the Lord's Supper "proclaim the Lord's death" (1 Cor 11:26), but reception of them inevitably involves a "sharing *(koinōnia)*" or communion not only with Christ but with "the many" who constitute the "one body" and the one community (10:16-17). In other words, "just as we are united in our common humanity by our weakness and sin and subjection to death, so now we can be united in a new humanity — one that is marked by power, by righteousness and by life" (Hooker 1994: 37).

In principle, by Christ's death humankind's debt was paid. "One man's act of righteousness leads to justification and life *for all*" (Rom 5:18); "as all die in Adam, so *all* will be made alive in Christ" (1 Cor 15:22). Christ "is the atoning sacrifice for our sins, and not for ours only but also for the sins *of the whole world*" (1 John 2:2). But such texts must not be taken out of their total canonical context. Christ died for all, but the benefits of his death are only for those who are incorporated into him and who participate in his risen life. Those who accept the message of the cross are those "who are being saved," but those who reject it are "those who are perishing" (1 Cor 1:18; cf. 2 Cor 2:15-16).

d. Example/Following

Finally, Christ's death is also presented in the NT as an *example* that inspires believers to *follow* him. While this is not a major theme, it is present in the NT. Here again this understanding of Christ's death must not be separated from the others outlined above.

In the Gospels Jesus serves as an example: "It is enough for the disciple to be like the teacher, and the slave like the master" (Matt 10:25//Luke 6:40). But in particular, in his sufferings and death he sets an example that his disciples may be called upon to follow. "If any man would come after me, let him deny himself and take up his cross and follow me" (Matt 16:24 RSV and //s). Though in one sense, as we have seen, Jesus' death is unique, in another sense the NT recognizes that it represents an example that believers may have to follow: "the path of the master is to be the path of his followers, and that path is the way of the cross" (Hanson 1982: 80). Mark's Gospel in particular "underlines the link between the death of Christ and the cost of discipleship" (Hooker 1994: 51). Perrin draws attention to a significant set of parallels among John the Baptist, Jesus, and Christian believers in Mark: John the Baptist "preached" (1:7) and then "was delivered up"; Jesus "came preaching" (1:14) and was "delivered to men" (9:31; also to priests and Gentiles in 10:33); Christians are to preach (13:10) and will be delivered to councils (13:9) or delivered up (13:11) (Perrin and Duling 1982: 238). Jesus' disciples are called to follow in the footsteps not only of Jesus' forerunner, but also of Jesus himself.

Christ's suffering does not mean that believers are spared suffering, a fact amply illustrated by Paul's life as a Christian; if they hope to be glorified with Christ, that hope is valid only if they follow the pattern he set and in this life "suffer with him" (Rom 8:17; see Cousar 1990: 170-75). This approach is set forth with special clarity in 1 Pet 2:21: "For to this you have been called, because Christ also suffered for you, leaving you an example, so that you should follow in his steps." On Jesus as an ethical example, see further 18-3.2.

9-3.5. THE DESCENT OF THE SERVANT

The discussion of what happened to Jesus between his death on "Good Friday" and his resurrection early the following Sunday is based largely on two passages in 1 Peter that are difficult to understand and have been the subject of varying interpretations.

A. 1 Pet 3:18-20 declares:

For Christ also suffered for sins once for all, the righteous for the unrighteous, in order to bring you to God. He was put to death in the flesh, but made alive in the spirit, in which also he went and made a proclamation *(ekēruxen)* to the spirits in prison, who in former times did not obey, when God waited patiently in the days of Noah, during the building of the ark.

B. 1 Pet 4:6 asserts:

For this is the reason the gospel was proclaimed *(euēngelisthē)* even to the dead, so that, though they had been judged in the flesh as everyone is judged, they might live in the spirit as God does.

The context of A is the death of Christ; it was after this that he preached to the spirits in prison/the dead.

At least some early Christians must have raised the question of what happened to Jesus between his death and resurrection. The general Jewish view was that the dead go to Sheol, the equivalent of the Greek Hades (see further, 20-2.3), a shadowy underworld that is the abode of the departed but not a place of punishment. In Acts 2:24-31 Peter proclaims Jesus' resurrection and quotes Ps 16, including v. 10, as a Davidic prophecy of the resurrection:

For you will not abandon my soul to Hades,
    or let your Holy One experience corruption. (Acts 2:27; cf. v. 31)

The implication is that at his death Jesus descended to Sheol/Hades, and that it is from there that he was raised from the dead. Eph 4:9 says Christ "descended into the lower parts of the earth *(ta katōtera merē tēs gēs)*"; this probably also refers to Christ's descent to Sheol/Hades, though some take it as a reference to the incarnation (see commentaries). This became the basis for the phrase in the Apostles' Creed that is misleadingly translated "he descended into hell."

What is the meaning of Jesus' "descent into Hades"? (See especially the detailed treatment in Selwyn 1969.)

a. It affirms the reality of Christ's death (see J. M. Robinson 1962a: 826). John 19:31-35 recounts the procedure used by the Romans to check that a victim of crucifixion really was dead. By asserting that Jesus descended into Hades (Acts 2) and went to the place of the dead (1 Peter), the NT is asserting the reality of Christ's death and ruling out any idea that he only swooned or lapsed into a coma from which he later revived.

b. The two passages in 1 Peter clearly mean more than this. They claim that Jesus preached/announced the good news to the spirits in prison/the dead. The verbs used are those normally employed of proclaiming the Christian message *(kērussō, euangelizō)*. To whom did Jesus preach during his sojourn among the dead? While B refers simply to "the dead," A mentions the spirits who did not obey in the days of Noah. This could refer to the wicked generation that prompted God to send the flood or the evil angels referred to in Gen 6:1-4.

If the evil angels are in view, then these passages mean that Christ proclaimed to the powers of evil their own defeat (Luther's view). But this is hard to square with the preaching of "good news."

The more likely interpretation, therefore, is that these passages attempt to answer the difficult question: If salvation depends on the Christ event, what happens to all those who died before the coming of Christ? From an early period these texts were taken to mean that Christ brought salvation to the righteous of OT times (cf. Matt 8:11; Heb 11:39-40). But what 1 Pet 4:6 says is that Christ went to the place of the dead and preached the gospel to "the dead," without further qualification. 1 Pet 3:18-20 indicates that he preached even to the wicked generation that preceded the flood, and perhaps even to the evil angels. What these passages proclaim, therefore, is that Christ preached to *all* who had died up to his time. This is not to say that all people will be saved, but it does claim that all people get a chance to hear the Christian message, if not in this life, then beyond it, and that they will be judged depending on their reaction to the gospel. In other words, the "descent into Hades" is a way of declaring the universal scope and significance of the Christ event.

New Testament: Consummation

9-4. THE LAMB WHO WAS SLAIN

After his resurrection and even at the final consummation, God's Servant still bears the marks of his suffering and death.

9-4.1. THE MARK OF THE NAILS

In John 20:25 Thomas declares, "Unless I see the mark of the nails in his hands, and put my finger in the mark of the nails and my hand in his side, I will not believe." According to 20:27, after his resurrection Jesus still bore the marks of his passion.

9-4.2. A LAMB STANDING AS THOUGH IT HAD BEEN SLAIN

In Revelation the exalted and returning Christ is frequently referred to as "the Lamb." Some have suggested that this title derives from a Jewish tradition found in the Testaments of the Twelve Patriarchs and Enoch in which a lamb is an apocalyptic figure that triumphs over God's enemies (see Talbert 1994: 29). One text that might accord with this interpretation is Rev 17:14, where the ten kings "will make war on the Lamb, and the Lamb will conquer them."

Such an interpretation, however, misses the main point. Jesus is a conquering figure in Revelation, but only because he suffered and died as a sacrifice for sin (see R. Wallace 1981: 49-50). That the Lamb is sacrificial is shown by the references to "the Lamb that was slaughtered" (5:12; 13:8; cf. 5:6) and to "the blood of the Lamb" (7:14; 12:11). The paradox appears at its sharpest in 5:5-6, where in two adjacent verses Jesus is referred to both as a lion and a lamb, both a conquering and a sacrificial figure. Even as the victorious, exalted, and returning Lord, Jesus remains the sacrificial Lamb.

9-4.3. EVERY EYE WILL SEE HIM

According to Rev 1:7, when Christ comes at the final consummation as Son of Man,

> every eye will see him,
> even those who pierced him;
> and on his account all the tribes of the earth will wail.

Though not an exact quotation, this is a clear allusion to the mourning over a martyred servant of God in Zech 12:10 (cf. above, 9-1.5). This passage is also alluded to in the reference to the parousia in Matt 24:30; at the coming of the Son of Man, "all the tribes of the earth will mourn." (In John 19:37 the Zechariah passage is quoted following the account of the soldier piercing Jesus' side.)

The Christ who returns as Son of Man is the Christ who was pierced, who suffered and died. At the final consummation everyone will see him, including those responsible for his death. Their mourning and wailing has been interpreted in terms of their realization of what they have done and therefore of the fate which awaits them, but more probably their tears are tears of penitence (see commentaries). What John's vision suggests is that at the parousia even those who sent Jesus to his death will get a chance to mourn for their sins and to repent.

9-5. THE SERVANT'S SUFFERING: THEOLOGICAL REFLECTIONS

1. Two thousand years of familiarity have blunted if not totally obscured the astonishing nature of the claims the NT makes in relation to the death of Jesus. A survey of possible analogies simply underlines the uniqueness of these claims. There have been individuals who have met an unjust death with dignity; Socrates would be a prime example. As Hengel has shown (1981: 4-18), in the Greco-Roman world it was considered a noble thing to die for a friend (cf. John 15:13;

Rom 5:6), and especially for one's city or country (cf. Horace's line *dulce et deco-rum est pro patria mori* = "it is sweet and becoming to die for the fatherland"). The ancient world was also familiar with human sacrifice (voluntary or invol-untary) to propitiate the imagined wrath of the gods in order to secure deliver-ance from enemies (Hengel, 19-28). This practice was not unknown among Is-rael's neighbors (2 Kgs 3:26-27), and even in Israel itself (16:3; 17:17), although it is strongly condemned in the OT (see Jer 7:31). Within Judaism the Maccabean martyrs may be said to have died for the Torah (cf. *1 Macc* 1:56-57; 2:50; *2 Macc* 13:14), and there is some evidence that their death could be regarded as an aton-ing sacrifice (above, 9-1.5). All these examples of dying in a good cause refer to *specific situations* where *the benefits of the death are confined to a very limited group of people.* The NT, however, claims that Jesus' death has *cosmic* signifi-cance; he died for the sins of the world and of all humankind!

Moreover, most of the analogies relate to dying in a good cause or for a good friend. Paul can envisage that on rare occasions someone might give his or her life for a righteous person, but what distinguishes Jesus' death is that while we still were sinners, Christ died for us (Rom 5:6). Christ's death is seen as being on behalf of those who are totally *un*deserving!

Furthermore, we have to realize that after long centuries of recognizing the cross as a central symbol of Christianity, it is virtually impossible for us today to appreciate the shocking effect of a message that centered in a figure who, so far from being a triumphant Messiah or a national hero, died as a common criminal and experienced the most agonizing and degrading form of execution known in the Roman world (cf. Käsemann 1971: 36-37; Hooker 1994: 8; Sandnes 1994: 20).

To most people in the first century, therefore, the message of the cross, with its unprecedented claims on behalf of the Son of God who died a shameful death for the sins of all humankind, was pure folly; only believers could see in it the wisdom of God (cf. 1 Cor 1:18–2:5).

2. In discussing the death of Jesus it is essential to remember that the NT does not view that death in isolation. It is part of "the Christ event" — the in-carnation, life, teaching, deeds, death, resurrection, and exaltation of Christ. For the purposes of discussion we deal separately with the death of Jesus, but its close relationship to the other aspects of the Christ event must never be allowed to drop out of sight. "The incarnation, life, death, and resurrection of Jesus must be treated as a unity and as all essential parts of the saving event of God in Jesus Christ" (Culpepper 1966: 134). For example, the Western (and especially Lutheran) tendency to focus on Jesus' death and see all Christian theology as basically a "theology of the cross" (see Käsemann 1971: 34, 47-48; cf. Cousar 1990: 7-9) needs to be balanced by Orthodox Christianity's emphasis on the in-carnation (cf. Childs 1992: 529). Theologically, Christ's death can be understood only in terms of who he is: atonement cannot be separated from incarnation. We have noted above how, especially in the identification/incorporation model, belief in Christ as the inclusive representative of Israel and of humanity is es-

sential for understanding this interpretation of Jesus' death. Equally of course, all NT reflection on the meaning of Jesus' death presupposes his resurrection; the two belong together and cannot be separated (cf. Cousar, 103-8). "By raising Jesus from the dead God revealed himself as the one who vindicates the Crucified" (Viering 1970: 142). Without the resurrection Jesus would only be a martyred prophet, not the Savior of the world.

3. In keeping with the aims of a canonical BT, we have sought to understand how the writers of the NT interpret the sufferings and death of Christ. Here once again, however, historical questions cannot be completely ignored. It is essential to ask whether the church's understanding of Jesus as the Suffering Servant has a basis in the life and teaching of Jesus himself. BT cannot discuss the authenticity of each individual text, but it does have to be concerned with whether or not there is a basic continuity between the historical Jesus and the NT's understanding of the cross.

Some critical scholars (see esp. Hooker 1959) have questioned whether Jesus saw himself as the Suffering Servant of 2 Isaiah. It is argued that references to the Servant are few and of doubtful authenticity, and those that are most likely to be genuine do not refer to vicarious suffering (for a critique of such views, see esp. France 1968).

In response to this, three points need to be made. Firstly, there are a number of Gospel texts that do have a strong claim to historicity, in particular Luke 22:37 (= Isa 53:12) and the two "for many" sayings (Mark 10:45; 14:24 and //s), that clearly allude to Isa 53 and the Servant's vicarious and redemptive suffering and death (see V. Taylor 1956: 16-17; France 1968: 32-39; cf. Stagg 1962: 51; Cazelles and Mussner 1970: 843). Secondly, this question cannot be limited to Isa 53 or even to the four Servant Songs; the Servant Psalms need to be taken into account, and there are no grounds for doubting Jesus' quotation of Ps 22:1 in the cry of dereliction on the cross. Thirdly, the question should not be limited to whether Jesus quoted or alluded to certain OT texts. The evidence of the Gospels and especially of the passion narratives makes it abundantly clear that the acceptance of the "servant pattern" (above, 9-3.1d) was a deliberate choice made by Jesus himself.

In identifying himself as "Messiah" and "Son of Man" (albeit indirectly), Jesus certainly rejected popular triumphalist expectations; to the dismay of his disciples and no doubt many of the people of his day, he interpreted both these titles in terms of the Suffering Servant (see 6-5.5; 7-5.7). While this may have been contrary to popular expectation, it was not without basis in the OT (see above, 9-2), so that Jesus' combination of Messiah/Son of Man and Suffering Servant may indeed be seen as "in accordance with the Scriptures."

It has also been doubted whether Jesus forecast his own sufferings and death (cf. above, 9-3.1d); the three passion predictions especially have been seen as "prophecies after the event." This view often seems to be based on a rationalistic rejection of the possibility of any prophecy. Yet even on a human level, there are no good grounds for doubting that Jesus, aware of the fate of many of the prophets (see 9-2.4, and cf. Luke 13:33), and in particular with the fate of John the Baptist before him (see Stauffer 1955: 98-100), could have spoken both of his coming sufferings and death and of his hoped-for vindication by God (see V. Taylor 1956: 14-15; D. Guthrie 1981: 438-39).

4. Closely connected with the above is the question of how Jesus understood his coming sufferings and death. This is a topic that must be approached with reserve and reverence. We cannot know what went on in Jesus' mind; our only clue to this lies in the sayings preserved in the Gospels. Obviously, after Jesus' death and resurrection the early church looked back and reflected on the significance of the cross and saw in it ever deeper levels of meaning. For BT the key question is not whether the NT's understanding of the cross is *identical* with that of the historical Jesus, but whether it is in *continuity* and *consistent* with it. In contradistinction to Bultmann's exclusion of the historical Jesus from NT theology, Stuhlmacher (1986) rightly contends for the essential historicity of the Gospels' portrait of Jesus as "messianic reconciler," and thus for the essential continuity of the early church's proclamation with Jesus' own understanding of his ministry: "Jesus worked and suffered as the incarnation of God's word about reconciliation, and for that very reason he was already proclaimed as reconciler by the kerygma of the pre-Pauline community," hence "Jesus' words and deeds are to be incorporated into a theology of the New Testament as a presentation of his mission as the messianic reconciler, which is what he himself wanted to be and what through his death and resurrection he for faith once and for all became" (12).

There is no doubt that Jesus interpreted his ministry in terms of a struggle with Satan and his minions, the demons (see 4-3.3; 4-3.4); the victory/liberation model thus has a firm basis in the historical Jesus. The sacrificial interpretation of Jesus' death has deep roots not only in the early Christian community but also in Jesus' own self-understanding (contra Horvath 1979: 85, who holds that "the sacrificial interpretation of Jesus' achievement is rather a late development in the theology of the early Church"). Moreover, Jesus' identification of himself as the Servant (above, 9-3.1; 9-5.3) who will give his life as a ransom "for many" clearly alludes to Song IV, where the Servant's death constitutes a "sin offering" (above, 9-1.3b), thus providing a basis for the sacrifice/reconciliation model and for the more elaborate identification/incorporation model. Antwi (1991) has shown that Jesus' action in forgiving sins (Mark 2:5-11; Luke 7:47-49) in effect amounted to a claim to replace the sacrificial system and the temple cult. "By pronouncing forgiveness of sins . . . Jesus was declaring that he embodied in himself that which constituted the means of atonement hitherto known to the people only through the cult. . . . It can thus be said that the roots of NT soteriological interpretation of the death of Jesus can be traced back to Jesus himself" (27-28). Sandnes (1994) supports this view and draws attention to the "cleansing of the temple" as an act of eschatological symbolism by which Jesus "attacked the sacrificial system and indicated a replacement of its atoning function" (22; cf. 14-3.1a). In addition, at the Last Supper Jesus clearly spoke of his approaching death in sacrificial terms (Matt 26:28//Mark 14:24). The example/ following model is grounded in Jesus' own call to his followers to take up their cross and follow him (Matt 16:24).

5. The NT does not present any carefully thought out or systematic doctrine of the atonement. It affirms that "Christ died for our sins" (1 Cor 15:3), but it does so using a wide range of picture language. It was left to later Christian theologians to work out various "theories of the atonement" based to a greater or lesser degree on the biblical evidence. The task of BT is to set forth the biblical material, not in the form of competing theories but as parallel and complementary understandings of the meaning of Christ's death. It is important therefore that theological reflection hold in balance the four main NT ways of understanding the death of Christ outlined above. Focusing on only one of the views and making it dominant to the exclusion of the others will inevitably distort the biblical teaching. "Almost all of the historical views of the atonement give expression to important biblical truths, but many of them fail in their purpose because they seize upon an important aspect of the subject and set it forth as if it were the whole" (Culpepper 1966: 137).

This is particularly the case with the example/following model, especially if it is made to provide the basic understanding of the cross to the exclusion of the other three, as frequently happens in a "moral" or "exemplarist" theory of the atonement. Such a view, which still flourishes in some liberal theological circles today, fails to take human sin and the consequences thereof seriously, and in effect holds that "man must find his own way to salvation by his good works executed in the imitation of the example of Christ" (McGrath 1985: 212; cf. D. Guthrie 1981: 508). While in the NT "the death of Christ is an example for the Christian," yet "in no place in the NT is the example of Christ's suffering and death presented without the emphasis also being on what was done in his death 'for us'" (Foulkes 1996: 159). It is significant that the clearest reference to Christ's sufferings as an example is found in 1 Peter (2:21), the letter that also provides unambiguous evidence for identifying Jesus as the Servant of Isa 53 (2:21-25), the one who ransoms believers (1:18), who died as a sacrificial lamb (1:19), and who "bore our sins . . . on the cross" (2:24). It is those who have been set free from the powers of evil, reconciled to God and incorporated into a new humanity through the blood of Christ, who are then called to accept suffering by following the example of Christ.

6. For all the richness and variety in the NT understanding of the atonement, the various models (especially the first three), taken together, do have a number of key points in common (cf. Morris 1965: 364-419). They assume that human beings are in a position in which they are powerless to save themselves: they are imprisoned by the powers of sin and death, alienated from God through their sin, and members of a humanity that is doomed to death. The cross both reveals humanity's plight and declares that what they could not do

for themselves God in his love has done for them in and through the death and resurrection of Jesus (cf. Käsemann 1971: 40, 45).

All the models regard the cross as a real event within history, but an event with an eternal significance that they attempt to understand and explain with a variety of metaphors and imagery. This significance is primarily linked with the problem of human sin that separates God and humankind. Christ's death is vicarious; he died for others. One of the biggest ongoing debates revolves around the question of whether his death may also be called "substitutionary." This is linked closely with the question of whether in the first instance the OT sacrificial system, and then the sacrificial death of Christ, are to be understood in terms of "expiation" or of "propitiation." We have argued that in neither case can ideas of propitiation and therefore of substitution be eliminated (see esp. the discussion in Morris 1965: 404-19). Substitution is widely rejected today, even by many biblical scholars and Christian theologians, because for them it conjures up a picture of a capricious and vindictive deity arbitrarily inflicting suffering and death on an innocent person (cf. Placher 1999: 6-7). The Bible, however, takes human sin with the utmost seriousness. Far from being arbitrary, a holy and just God *must* judge sin, and both OT and NT do not hesitate to speak of the wrath and the judgment of God (see 16-3.3); sin cannot simply be dismissed or overlooked. Yet the astounding paradox of the biblical view is that God himself makes provision for atonement, in a preparatory way in the OT and fully and finally in Christ! It is God himself, by totally identifying himself with sinful humanity in Christ and voluntarily accepting the just penalty of sin, who makes it possible for humans to be liberated, reconciled, and incorporated into a new humanity. "The pain that God endures on the cross is the price love pays for taking sin seriously but refusing to stop loving" (Placher, 17; cf. Viering 1970: 145; Childs 1992: 520; Trotter 1996b: 44).

7. Finally, all four models speak not just of what Christ has done for humankind through his death but also of the benefits his death brings to believers: victory results in liberation, sacrifice in reconciliation, identification/substitution in incorporation/participation, example in following. These benefits, of course, have to be appropriated by believers; the Christ event calls for a *response* in terms of faith and commitment (see the discussion in 17-3). Some understandings of Jesus' death (especially some of those that center in substitutionary atonement) run the risk of so emphasizing what Christ has done for believers that they neglect to emphasize what believers are called upon to do and be in response. This easily becomes a form of "cheap grace." While the cross of Christ is unique, Christians are called to take up their cross daily (Matt 16:24 and //s). In a daring phrase Paul talks about his own sufferings as "completing what is lacking in Christ's afflictions" (Col 1:24). For the NT, faith in the cross does not mean an individualistic and inward-looking glorying in the fact that "I've been saved"; it means incorporation into a community whose members are called to a life of service and often of suffering.

CHAPTER 10

The Servant's Vindication

Old Testament: Proclamation

10-1. THEY SHALL NOT PREVAIL AGAINST YOU

God's servants are called upon to suffer and perhaps even to die, yet they are sustained by the promise that ultimately they will be vindicated by God. This pattern of suffering/vindication is found throughout the OT, and forms the background to what the NT says about the suffering and vindication of God's Servant, Jesus. Pamment (1981) has suggested that one reason Moses and Elijah appear with Jesus at his transfiguration (immediately following the first passion prediction — Mark 8:31; 9:4), is that they are major OT examples of servants of the Lord who both suffer and are vindicated. "These two figures have been rejected by the people and vindicated by God. Their presence serves to confirm the validity of Jesus' prediction. God had allowed both Moses and Elijah to suffer before their vindication and Jesus' fate would be no different" (339).

10-1.1. ASSURANCE OF FINAL TRIUMPH

a. The Servant Psalms

Typically in the Servant Psalms, God's servant is delivered, praises God, and acknowledges God in public worship. Thus Ps 22, which begins with an anguished cry at the apparent absence of God, turns in vv. 22-26 to praise and to testimony "in the midst of the congregation" to God's vindication of his servant:

> He has not hid his face from him,
>   but has heard, when he cried to him. (v. 24 RSV)

Similarly in Ps 69 the mood changes abruptly in vv. 30-36 to praise of God, presumably for a favorable answer to the psalmist's plea. The writer is now able to affirm that

> the LORD hears the needy,
>> and does not despise his own that are in bonds. (v. 33)

Since such transitions are common in the psalms of lament, scholars have suggested that "the transition from sorrow to rejoicing, from lament to thanksgiving, was occasioned by something that occurred in the setting of worship within which these psalms had their place. There is reason to believe that at a certain moment in the service a member of the Temple personnel, a priest or sometimes a prophet, pronounced an 'oracle of salvation' which assured the suppliant of God's grace and favour" (B. W. Anderson 1983: 77). While such oracles have not been preserved, they do seem to be alluded to in such passages as Pss 12:5, 22:22, 85:8, 91:14-16.

Whether used in the context of public worship or of private devotion, these psalms express the strong conviction that God's faithful servants, whatever trials and sufferings they may have to endure, will ultimately be vindicated by the Lord and delivered out of their distress.

Some of these psalms speak of the threat of death, as in the case of the Davidic Ps 18:

> The cords of death encompassed me;
>> the torrents of perdition assailed me;
> the cords of Sheol entangled me;
>> the snares of death confronted me. (vv. 4-5)

When the psalmist goes on to praise God for answering his cry (v. 6), we must suppose that the reference is to deliverance from death in the sense of removal of the threat of death rather than to the resurrection of the dead (cf. Kraus 1986: 166-67; cf. also Ps 56:13).

b. The Servant Songs

In the Songs also, the Servant is ultimately vindicated. In Song II the Servant, though despised and abhorred by the nations, will at some point in the future be vindicated by God in the eyes of the rulers of the world (Isa 49:7). In Song III, despite the suffering he faces, the Servant can say,

> The Lord GOD helps me; . . .
>> and I know that I shall not be put to shame;
>> he who vindicates me is near. (50:7-8)

We have noted that in Song IV, 53:7-9, 12 refer to the death of the Servant (9-1.4b); v. 10, "he shall see his offspring, and shall prolong his days," and v. 12, "I will allot him a portion with the great," speak of the Servant's vindication in terms that, in context, imply a resurrection from the dead.

10-1.2. GOD WHO RAISES THE DEAD

God's servants look to him for vindication because they acknowledge him as the one who created life in the first place, and who is capable of bringing life out of death. God is the one who created all life (Gen 1–2). He created his people "from one person [Abraham], and this one as good as dead" (Heb 11:12). He raised up his people from the death of slavery in Egypt. And he raised up his people from the death of exile; in the book of Jonah, being swallowed by the great fish symbolizes the death of exile, and Jonah's regurgitation signifies the resurrection of the return. In the book of Daniel, in face of certain death in the fiery furnace or the lions' den, God's servants discover that "our God whom we serve is able to deliver us" (3:17; cf. 6:16, 20).

10-1.3. GOD TOOK HIM

In two exceptional cases the OT records that God vindicated his servants not by raising them from the dead but by receiving them directly into his presence.

a. Enoch

After a brief note on Enoch and his family, Gen 5:24 simply records, "Enoch walked with God; then he was no more, because God took him." The repeated assertion that Enoch "walked with God" (5:22, 24) indicates a life of close communion with and obedience to God (cf. 6:9, where the expression is used of Noah). The phrase "God took *(lāqach)* him" indicates that God received Enoch into his presence in a way that bypassed the normal death process (cf. the use of the same word in Ps 49:15; 73:24).

b. Elijah

The account of Elijah's departure is found in 2 Kgs 2. Accompanied by his successor Elisha, he crossed the Jordan where they exchanged some final words. "As they continued walking and talking, a chariot of fire and horses of fire separated the two of them, and Elijah ascended *(wayya'al,* LXX *anelēmphthē)* in a whirlwind into heaven. Elisha kept watching and crying out, 'Father, father! The chariots of Israel and its horsemen!'" (2:11-12; cf. 2:1).

10-1.4. THE VINDICATING GOD: LORD

God's servants look to him for vindication because they acknowledge him as "Lord," the one who reigns over all and who therefore ultimately cannot let wrong prevail (cf. 1-1.1; see B. W. Anderson 1962c). In Ps 35, for example, God's servant (v. 27) cries out, "How long, O LORD, will you look on?" (v. 17), and prays, "Vindicate me, O LORD, my God" (v. 24).

The most common OT word for "lord" is '*ādhôn* (Aram. *mār;* Gk. *kyrios*), or *'ªdhōnay* (plural of majesty, lit. "my lord") especially when referring to God. The word can be used in a secular context, referring to, e.g., the master of a servant (Gen 24:12) or a king in relation to his subject (1 Sam 24:8), but it is most frequently used of God.

In the LXX *kyrios* is used to translate *'ªdhōnay,* but even more significantly, as the divine name *YHWH* dropped out of use from motives of reverence, *kyrios* was used as a substitute for *YHWH* (see 1-2.2).

In meaning, therefore, *'ªdhōnay* approximates closely to calling God "King" (see 1-1.1). While God can be addressed as "Lord" in a personal way (as in Ps 35, cited above), he is also "Lord of all the earth" (Josh 3:11; cf. Ps 97:5; Zech 4:14).

10-1.5. THE VINDICATING GOD: SAVIOR

God's servants also look to him for vindication because they acknowledge him as "Savior," the one who can and will deliver them.

In the OT God is a God who saves (*yāsha',* Hiph. = "deliver, save"), the author of salvation (*yēsha', yªshû'â* = "deliverance, salvation"), and can therefore be called "Savior" (*môshîa'*). Indeed, as we have seen (3-1.1), God's dealings with his people can be characterized as "salvation history," though God is a God who judges as well as saves.

The supreme example of God saving his people in the OT is the exodus event. In Ps 106:21 the Israelites are condemned because

> they forgot God, their Savior,
>   who had done great things in Egypt.

After the settlement God continued to save and deliver Israel from their enemies. While God is the true author of salvation, he can use his servants as saviors of his people. Thus both *judges* (Judg 3:9, 15; Neh 9:27) and *kings* (2 Kgs 13:5) are called "saviors."

In response Israel praises God as their Savior. In 2 Sam 22:2-3 David declares: "The Lord is my rock, my fortress, . . . my savior," while in Ps 17:7 God is "savior of those who seek refuge from their adversaries." "Savior" is particularly prominent as a title of God in Isaiah, where "the term is used to emphasize his uniqueness. God alone is seen as Saviour in contrast to foreign gods and idols" (Elwell 1988f: 1912):

> I, I am the Lord,
>> and besides me there is no savior. (43:11; cf. 45:15; Hos 13:4)

In Isaiah also, "Savior" is associated not only with proclamation but also with promise. The day will come when Israel will know that "I, the Lord, am your Savior" (60:16); indeed,

> all flesh shall know
>> that I am the Lord your Savior. (49:26)

Old Testament: Promise

10-2. A PORTION WITH THE GREAT

The final triumph of God's servants will come in the new order.

10-2.1. GOD'S PEOPLE WILL RISE

The OT looks for a future resurrection of God's people. In Hos 6:1-2 the people say,

> Come, let us return to the Lord;
>> for it is he who has torn, and he will heal us;
>> he has struck down, and he will bind us up.
> After two days he will revive us;
>> on the third day he will raise us up,
>> that we may live before him.

In Ezek 37 the vision of the valley of dry bones clearly refers to a hoped-for national resurrection. See further 11-2.2b.

While texts such as these originally applied to particular situations in the life of God's people, they could be reapplied in new situations and thus became part of the general eschatological hope.

10-2.2. GOD'S SERVANTS WILL RISE

Toward the end of the OT there begins to develop the belief that God's faithful servants will live beyond death. This belief takes the form of a future resurrection. See the more detailed discussion in 20-2.

New Testament: Fulfillment

10-3. GOD HAS HIGHLY EXALTED HIM

The NT not only tells of the suffering and death of the Servant, it also proclaims his vindication by God. The Servant's humiliation was temporary; it was followed by his exaltation. This is expressed in the NT in a variety of ways that at times seem to overlap or even merge, yet each makes a distinctive claim:

- Jesus was raised from the dead
- he ascended into heaven
- he sits at God's right hand
- he rules as Lord and Savior

10-3.1. RESURRECTION

a. The New Testament Proclamation

That God raised Jesus of Nazareth from the dead is one of the most fundamental affirmations of the NT; indeed, in a sense it is the most fundamental. In the Gospels, Acts, the Epistles, and Revelation it has a key place, and there is scarcely a page of the NT that does not directly or indirectly reflect faith in Jesus' resurrection.

The other NT writers would agree with Paul in regarding the resurrection as the keystone; take that away and the whole edifice would collapse: "If Christ has not been raised, then our proclamation has been in vain and your faith is in vain" (1 Cor 15:14). "The crucifixion without its sequel in resurrection would not have revealed God, effected our salvation, and brought into existence the Church" (O'Collins 1993: 25).

The NT proclamation assumes two basic forms:

i. Narrative Proclamation

The four Gospels proclaim the resurrection in the narrative mode through the stories of the empty tomb and of the appearances of the risen Lord. The accounts are found as the last section in each Gospel, in Matt 28, Mark 16, Luke 24, and John 20–21. Opinion is divided as to whether or not Mark's Gospel originally concluded with 16:8, the point at which it breaks off in some of the best manuscripts (see Wilckens 1978: 31-35); that verse has the women fleeing the tomb in "terror and amazement" but stops short of recounting resurrection appearances. At a very early stage both a "shorter ending" and a "longer ending" (16:9-20) were supplied (see translations, commentaries); the latter was generally accepted by the church as part of canonical Scripture, and should continue to be regarded as such. It draws in part from the endings of the other Gospels and in part, presumably, from surviving oral tradition. What is really significant is that Mark's Gospel was accepted as canonical only with the addition of vv. 9-20; the Gospel is not complete without an account of resurrection appearances (cf. R. E. Brown 1973: 97-98; Childs 1984: 94-95, 206). Again, while John 21 may be an appendix added to the original Gospel, this in no way detracts from its status as part of canonical Scripture.

The accounts have many features in common but also differ on details, e.g., the figures encountered at the tomb, the observers of the appearances, the order of the appearances, the words spoken by Jesus (see Jeremias 1971: 300-303; Jeremias attempts to separate primary and secondary material). The most serious discrepancy relates to the place of Jesus' appearances: Matthew locates these in Galilee (28:7, 10, 16); Mark appears to support this tradition (14:28; 16:7); Luke confines the appearances to Jerusalem (Luke 24); while John combines Jerusalem and Galilean appearances (John 20–21).

Historically, elaborate attempts have been made to reconcile every single detail of the accounts (see Childs 1984: 201-2), but forced harmonizations serve no useful purpose. The differences in detail do not justify skepticism regarding the historical basis of the accounts (contra Bater 1969; Marxsen 1970: 72-74). In fact, the differences tend to throw into stronger relief the main features that the accounts have in common: the discovery of the empty tomb, the appearances to women, and the appearances to disciples (cf. J. A. T. Robinson 1962: 46).

ii. Theological Proclamation

That God raised Jesus from the dead was a key element in the kerygma proclaimed by the early church. Examples are provided in the sermons of Acts, and in the Epistles frequent references are made back to the message originally proclaimed to the recipients. In distinction from the narrative form of the Gospel accounts, kerygmatic references are concise. As a general rule, "Paul proclaimed the *fact* of Jesus' resurrection, but not the *accompanying circumstances*" (Kepler 1963: 112), an observation that holds true for all NT writers other than the four Evangelists.

One important passage constitutes something of an exception as it combines kerygmatic and narrative elements: this is the early tradition cited by Paul in 1 Cor 15:3-8:

> For I handed on to you as of the first importance what I in turn had received: that Christ died for our sins in accordance with the scriptures, and that he was buried, and that he was raised on the third day in accordance with the scriptures, and that he appeared to Cephas, then to the twelve. Then he appeared to more than five hundred brothers and sisters at one time, most of whom are still alive, though some have died. Then he appeared to James, then to all the apostles. Last of all, as to one untimely born, he appeared also to me.

(On this passage see R. H. Fuller 1971: chap. 2; R. E. Brown 1973: 81-86; Wilckens 1978: 6-16.) The tradition that Paul received (from the Jerusalem church?) and passed on to the Corinthians proclaims Christ's death, burial, and resurrection, then recounts appearances to Cephas (Peter), the Twelve, more than five hundred believers, James, "all the apostles," and finally to Paul himself (Paul's own addition to the early tradition).

b. The Significance of the Resurrection

According to the NT, the resurrection is:

i. An Act of God

First and foremost the resurrection is presented as something that God has done (cf. Stauffer 1955: 135; Wilckens 1978: 16-18). The most common NT formula makes God the subject of the verb and Christ the object: "God raised him up" (Acts 2:24; cf. 5:30; 10:40; etc.; Rom 4:24; 8:11; 1 Cor 6:14; Gal 1:1; Eph 1:20; Col 2:12; 1 Thess 1:10; 1 Pet 1:21). In some cases a passive is used, but this is the Jewish "reverential passive," designed to avoid mentioning God. Thus Matt 28:6 declares that "he has been raised" (not "he has risen" as in KJV, RSV; cf. Luke 24:34; Rom 8:34). The implication of these texts is that Christ was raised, i.e., by God. "The act of resurrection is always an act of God. . . . The power behind it was the power of God" (D. Guthrie 1981: 390).

The understanding of the resurrection as an act of God is underlined by the fact that it is declared to be "in accordance with the scriptures" (1 Cor 15:3). It was not a desperate, last-minute expedient, but part of the divine plan. Luke 24:46 and 1 Cor 15:4 both mention Jesus' resurrection "on the third day" in connection with the fulfillment of OT Scripture. Many have found a problem here as there is no obvious OT text that predicts a resurrection *on the third day*. One NT passage does point to such a text: Matt 12:38-42 gives a version of Jesus' saying on the sign of Jonah (compare and contrast Luke 11:29-32) that includes the words "For just as Jonah was three days and three nights in the belly of the sea monster, so for three days and three nights the Son of Man will be in the heart of the earth" (Matt 12:40). Jonah was a typical servant of the Lord whose task involved suffering, yet who was snatched from death by divine intervention. His story also symbolizes Israel undergoing the death of exile and being raised to life again by the return. The text is thus appropriately applied to Jesus as the servant of God par excellence, and as the representative head of Israel. Suggestions for other texts that Luke and the Pauline tradition might have had in mind include Hos 6:2 and Exod 19:10-11 (see A. Richardson 1958: 190-92; Wilckens 1978: 10-11).

The fact that the church had difficulty finding OT texts that pointed to a resurrection on the third day strongly supports the historicity of the Gospel accounts. The story of the discovery of the empty tomb on the Sunday was not invented to fulfill OT prophecy; rather the church had to do the best it could in finding a text which would agree with the fact that the tomb was found empty "on the third day."

ii. The Climax of the Christ Event

The resurrection cannot be viewed separately from Jesus' life and death, nor they from it. The resurrection vindicates the claims of Jesus. As an essential part of the Christ event, it marks the inauguration of the new order: "the resurrection of Jesus, along with his exaltation and his giving of the Spirit, constitute an eschatological event — the beginning of the end time" (R. E. Brown 1973: 125). "The bodily resurrection of Christ is important theologically because it attests the cosmic significance of God's act in raising Christ from the dead"; Christ's resurrection is "the resurrection of humanity, the new Adam. It is the beginning of the new creation of the latter days" (A. Richardson 1958: 197).

iii. A Challenge to Faith

The Gospels, it can be argued, have a threefold structure. Firstly, in the accounts of Jesus' ministry they present Christ as one who makes unique and far-reaching claims. Secondly, in the passion narratives they describe Jesus' death that radically calls these claims into question. Thirdly, the resurrection narratives reinstate the claims of Jesus. They in no way prove them, but they re-present the claims in a new way that again challenges the hearer/reader to respond in faith. For the NT the cross cannot possibly be understood apart from the resurrection, nor the resurrection apart from the cross (see Wilckens 1978: 27).

Here, as always, faith stands in tension with doubt (cf. 17-3.3). Only the first witnesses see the empty tomb and meet the risen Christ; thereafter belief in the resurrection is entirely a matter of faith. But even for these first witnesses a strong element of faith was involved. Significantly, Matthew's account states that although the eleven disciples worshiped the risen Christ on the mountain in Galilee, "some doubted" (28:17). The classic case of doubt is Thomas (John 20:24-29). Although he is depicted as being convinced by one of the most "physical" of the resurrection appearances, the real punch line of the story is v. 29, "Have you believed because you have seen me? *Blessed are those who have not seen and yet have come to believe.*" The context recognizes the clear possibility of doubt, yet calls for faith. In the longer ending of Mark, the disciples' lack of faith after the resurrection is mentioned no fewer than three times (16:11, 13, 14), and Jesus declares, "The one who believes and is baptized will be saved; but the one who does not believe will be condemned" (16:16).

iv. A Call to Commitment

In each of the narrative accounts those who are recipients of a resurrection appearance also receive a commission. Matt 28:18-20 constitutes "The Great Commission" (see Wilckens 1978: 48-50); the others are Mark 16:15-18 (part of the longer ending), Luke 24:47-48, John 20:21-23, and Acts 1:8. These are all commissions to a group. One commission is to an individual: in John 21:15-19 it is Peter who receives a commission. As Stählin (1956) points out, the appearance accounts have two basic motifs, "He lives!" and "He sends!" (288). Belief in the resurrection is never theoretical or philosophical; it entails decision and commitment, and hence also risk.

v. A Guarantee of the Resurrection of Believers

For the NT it is Jesus' resurrection and victory over death that assures the resurrection of believers. Matthew makes this connection when he recounts how, at Jesus' death, "the tombs also were opened, and many bodies of the saints who had fallen asleep were raised. After his resurrection they came out of the tombs and entered the holy city and appeared to many" (27:52-53). Jeremias (1971: 309) regards this as a very early interpretation of the meaning of Jesus' resurrection. On the link between the resurrection of Christ and the resurrection of believers, see more fully 20-4.3c.

c. The Easter Event

One of the most remarkable features of the NT is that *it nowhere attempts to describe the actual resurrection of Jesus;* this is hidden by the veil that descends from Friday evening until early Sunday morning. (This is best appreciated by comparing the reverent silence of all four Gospels with the account given in the apocryphal *Gospel of Peter.*)

What the NT does recount are the consequences of the Easter event, i.e., the discovery of the empty tomb and the resurrection appearances. To the extent that these are described in some detail, interest in "what actually happened" is therefore not totally lacking.

i. The Empty Tomb

The discovery that the tomb in which Jesus' body had been laid was empty figures prominently in all four Gospel accounts but surprisingly is not directly mentioned anywhere else in the NT. The 1 Cor 15 tradition declares that Christ "was buried" (cf. the reference to Jesus' burial in Col 2:12), then "he was raised on the third day"; this almost certainly assumes an empty tomb, since for first-century Jews a resurrection must be a resurrection of the body (cf. J. A. T. Robinson 1962: 45-46; D. Guthrie 1981: 380). "It would have been absurd for Paul, whose roots of faith were in the Old Testament, to have preached of the raising of Christ, when he believed that Christ's dead body was decaying in the tomb" (Mánek 1957: 278).

While the Gospels are content to bear a clear and consistent witness to the fact that the tomb was found empty, they do not offer this as a proof that Jesus was raised from the dead (cf. Stählin 1956: 285-86). Indeed, according to Mark the reaction of the women to the discovery of the empty tomb was "terror and amazement" and fear (16:8); in Luke the apostles dismiss the story as "an idle tale" (24:11); in John Mary Magdalene seeks a rational explanation of her own ("They have taken the Lord out of the tomb, and we do not know where they have laid him") and stands weeping (20:2, 11, 13). Only Matthew mentions joy (at the angel's message) as well as fear (28:8).

In the Gospels the women and the disciples do not believe in Christ's resurrection because of the empty tomb; they believe because of their encounters with the risen Christ. "In the genesis of resurrection faith it was the appearance of the glorified Lord that first brought his disciples to believe; and this belief, in turn, interpreted the empty tomb. Having seen the risen Jesus, they understood that the reason why the tomb was empty was because he had been raised from the dead" (R. E. Brown 1973: 127).

Why, then, is the empty tomb so prominent in the Gospel narratives? The accounts reflect the fact that for first-century Jews, while *an empty tomb does not prove the resurrection, a tomb with Jesus' body in it would certainly disprove such a resurrection.* A resurrection without an empty tomb would have been incredible. "A bodiless resurrection, or the notion that a man might be 'spiritually' raised while his body lay on in the tomb, would have seemed to the Jew an absurdity. In whatever form the Resurrection was first proclaimed by the apostles, it must have implied an empty sepulchre" (J. A. T. Robinson 1962: 46). Thus, while an empty tomb did not *prove* that Jesus had been raised from the dead, it did constitute what O'Collins calls a "negative confirmatory sign" (1993: 17).

ii. The Appearances

Accounts of appearances of the risen Christ are a major feature of the Gospel narratives. These accounts make it clear that it was the appearances, not the empty tomb, that led to faith in the risen Christ.

The very early tradition preserved by Paul in 1 Cor 15:5-8 (above, 10-3.1a.ii; cf. Saunders 1976: 740) can be related, in part, to the Gospel accounts, although the appearance to James that it lists has no equivalent at all in the Gospels. Like the Gospel accounts, the Pauline tradition constitutes an appeal to eyewitnesses, some of whom were still alive at the time Paul wrote (15:6). The tradition specifies an event that occurred "on the third day," thereby revealing "the historical nature of the event, which was not a private, subjective experience but one that occurred in actual time and was attested by Cephas, the Twelve, and five hundred people" (Adams 1996: 678). A major objection raised against this list is that it contains no women, whereas women play a prominent role in the Gospel narratives. This can be accounted for if the 1 Cor 15 list was shaped by early disputes between Christians and Jews and appealed only to male witnesses in accordance with Jewish law.

Matt 28:16-20, Mark (implied in 16:7), and John 21 tell of appearances in Galilee, while Matt 28:9-10, Luke, and John 20 tell of appearances in Jerusalem. These traditions need not be mutually exclusive, though Luke 24:49 does constitute a problem, and Luke apparently did not know of Galilean appearances (cf. Moule 1968: 4-5). The kerygmatic proclamation in Acts and the Epistles does not list appearances, but this is no reason for supposing that they represent a later development (contra W. O. Walker 1969).

iii. The Nature of Christ's Resurrection Body

The accounts of the empty tomb and of the appearances raise the difficult question of the nature of Christ's resurrection body.

Caution has to be exercised in laying too much stress on the vocabulary of "appearance." The most common term translated "appeared" is *ōphthē* (Luke 24:34; Acts 9:17; 13:31; 1 Cor 15:5, 6, 7, 8), the passive of *horaō*, which could mean either "he was seen" or "he appeared." In the LXX it is used of appearances of God and of angels, so it does not necessarily imply the appearance of a human physical body. Witnesses are said to "see" the risen Christ *(horaō)* (Mark 16:7; Matt 28:17; Luke 24:37, 39; John 20:18, 25, 29), but again the verb leaves an ambiguity as to what type of "seeing" is meant.

The Gospel accounts of the nature of Christ's risen body are marked by a tension between elements of continuity and discontinuity with his precrucifixion body. Some passages seem to speak of a continuing physical existence. In Luke 24:39 Jesus says, "Look at my hands and my feet; see that it is I myself. Touch me and see; for a ghost does not have flesh and bones as you see that I have." In John 20:27 the risen Christ invites Thomas to touch him, and in 21:9-13 he shares a meal of bread and fish with disciples (cf. Luke 24:42-43).

On the other hand, some passages suggest a different form of existence, no longer bound by the limitations of space and time; "Christ did not come from the grave, like Lazarus . . . in his previous body, but in a new one, to which the laws of gravity and mortality no longer applied" (Stauffer 1955: 135). In Luke 24:16 the risen Christ is not immediately recognizable (cf. John 20:14; 21:4), while in Luke 24:31 he vanishes from sight. In John 20:17 Christ tells Mary not to hold him, while in 20:19, 26 he appears though the doors are locked. The tension is not between one Gospel and another but within both Luke and John. Taken as a whole, the evidence suggests that the risen Christ was recognizable to those who had known him before the crucifixion, and that there was a continuity between his risen form and his previous physical body; but also that his risen form was different and not subject to physical restrictions.

Paul's discussion in 1 Cor 15 sheds light on the nature of Jesus' resurrection. While primarily discussing the resurrection of believers, implicit in Paul's argument is a parallel between the resurrection of believers and the resurrection of Christ (cf. Phil 3:21). Though Paul speaks of believers being raised in a "body" *(sōma),* it is clear that he does not mean simply a physical body. "Flesh and blood *(sarx kai haima)* cannot inherit the kingdom of God," he declares (1 Cor 15:50). Resurrection involves the transformation of the physical body into a spiritual body *(sōma pneumatikon)* (v. 44); see further, 20-4.4b. It is fair to infer from this that Paul conceived of Jesus' risen body not as a resuscitated corpse, but as a new form of existence in a spiritual or glorious body (Phil 3:21) provided by God (cf. Mánek 1957: 278-80).

While a strong element of mystery regarding the resurrection must always remain, the testimony of the Gospel accounts and the kerygmatic proclamation do fit a reasonably consistent pattern. Both agree that the physical body of Jesus was raised from the tomb, and was transformed by God into a glorious or spiritual body that had elements of both continuity and discontinuity with the previous physical body (cf. Moule 1968: 9-10). On the one hand, it was not subject to the limitations of space and time, and it was at least closely analogous to the body in which believers would be raised. But on the other hand, it was recognizable, and according to Luke and John at least, still possessed certain physical characteristics. The resurrection appearances, according to the NT, were not merely visions. This is underlined by the encounter of the risen Christ not only with individuals but with groups, especially the five hundred of 1 Cor 15:6 to whom Paul clearly appeals as surviving eyewitnesses (cf. R. E. Brown 1973: 91).

10-3.2. ASCENSION

The NT agrees that after his death Christ was exalted to heaven to a position of power and authority.

a. The New Testament Proclamation

In some passages Jesus' resurrection from the dead and his ascension into heaven are not clearly differentiated. In Peter's speech in Acts 2:32-33, for example, resurrection and exaltation are closely connected. Eph 1:20 declares that God "raised him [Christ] from the dead and seated him at his right hand in the heavenly places." In passages that mention only Jesus' exaltation (e.g., Phil 2:9-11; Heb 1:3), it may well be that "the resurrection is silently taken for granted" (Wilckens 1978: 67).

In other passages, however, Jesus' ascension is viewed as a separate event. John's Gospel, in its account of Jesus' appearance to Mary, has Jesus say, "I have not yet ascended *(oupō gar anabebēka)* to the Father" (20:17); here the resurrection is past but the ascension is still future. The longer ending of Mark presents a similar view. After recounting a series of appearances, it then states, "So then the Lord Jesus, after he had spoken to them, was taken up *(anelēmphthē)* into heaven and sat down at the right hand of God" (16:19). The clearest separation of the two events is found in Luke-Acts, which also contains the only actual accounts of the ascension. It is going too far, however, to speak of a "twofold ascension" (R. Koch 1981a: 39-40); the references in the Epistles are concerned with theological proclamation, not with chronological exactitude.

The ascension plays a key role in Luke-Acts; indeed, for Luke it is the climax of the Christ event (cf. Franklin 1970: 194). Luke 24 concludes its account of the first Easter Sunday: "Then he led them out as far as Bethany, and, lifting up his hands, he blessed them. While he was blessing them, he withdrew from them and was carried up *(anephereto)* into heaven" (vv. 50-51; the last phrase is missing in some manuscripts). Acts 1 speaks of appearances over a period of forty days (v. 3) and recounts Jesus' last words to his disciples: "When he had said this, as they were watching, he was lifted up *(epērthē)*, and a cloud took him out of their sight. While he was going and they were gazing up toward heaven, suddenly two men in white robes stood by them. They said, 'Men of Galilee, why do you stand looking up toward heaven? This Jesus, who has been taken up *(analēmphtheis)* from you into heaven, will come in the same way as you saw him go into heaven'" (vv. 9-11; cf. v. 2). The following verse — "Then they returned to Jerusalem from the mount called Olivet" — implies that the incident narrated in the previous verses took place on the Mount of Olives.

The Luke-Acts accounts pose problems. Luke 24 appears to date the ascension on Easter Sunday evening; Acts 1 dates it precisely forty days after Jesus' death. Luke 24 locates it at Bethany; Acts 1 at the Mount of Olives. Luke and Acts appear to embody variant traditions (see Moule 1957: 205-7; Stempvoort 1958; Toon 1984: 10-12). John and the longer ending of Mark seem to imply an ascension shortly after the resurrection, though they are not strictly incompatible with the forty-day interval of Luke.

b. The Significance of the Ascension

Regardless of the variant forms of the tradition, the ascension of Christ does play a significant role in the theology of the NT.

i. It brings to an end the series of Jesus' resurrection appearances. During these appearances Jesus was still localized; he appeared at only one place at a time, either in Jerusalem or in Galilee. In the ascension Christ's glorified, risen body in which he appeared to his followers was taken from this earth (cf. Luke 24:51). The blessing Jesus bestows on his disciples (24:50) is his final blessing, after the manner of OT farewell blessings (cf. Wilckens 1978: 68). In Luke-Acts especially, the ascension "is described as a decisive and deliberate withdrawal from sight, to be distinguished from the mere 'disappearance' in the Emmaus story" (Moule 1957: 208; cf. Luke 24:31). Thus "the ascension completes the Resurrection" (Toon 1984: 17; cf. Argyle 1955: 240; Stempvoort 1958: 41).

ii. The ascension asserts that following Jesus' death and resurrection God received him into his nearer presence in heaven. As in the case of the resurrection, the emphasis is on the initiative of the Father: "This Jesus *God* raised up" (Acts 2:32; cf. Argyle 1955: 241). The cloud of Acts 1:9 is symbolic of the divine presence (cf. Exod 13:21; 40:34; etc.). Jesus is said to be taken up to heaven (Mark 16:19; Acts 1:10-11; Heb 4:14), to share God's glory (Luke 24:26; 1 Tim 3:16); John speaks of Jesus being "glorified" (John 7:39; 17:1). The Johannine references stress that Jesus ascended to where he was before (John 3:13; 6:62; 8:14), or to the Father (20:17; cf. 16:5, 28); thus "they portray Christ in the descent-ascent motif of his journey from and to his Father" (Gulley 1992: 472). Put another way, the ascension confirms that Jesus' resurrection was no mere resuscitation from the dead: "the resurrection was conceived not as the return of Jesus after his death on the cross to earthly life, but as his elevation into his position of power *in heaven* as the Son of God to whom all powers had been delegated" (Wilckens 1978: 23).

iii. The ascension signifies that Jesus' presence is no longer limited in space or time. The ascension frees Jesus to be present anywhere, at any time. Jesus' continuing presence with believers was promised in the concluding words of the Great Commission: "I am with you always, to the end of the age" (Matt 28:20). With the ascension the relationship between Jesus and those who believe in him changes; from that point on they do not see Jesus physically, but they know him in and through the Holy Spirit (cf. McKim 1992: 37). Both Acts

(1:4-5; 2:33) and John (7:39) emphasize that the giving of the Spirit takes place only after Jesus' ascension (cf. 5-3.3). "When he ascended, he sent the Spirit, and with the Spirit, by the Spirit, he is God with us for ever" (Haroutunian 1956: 280). The ascension does *not* mean that Jesus' activity on earth comes to an end (cf. O'Toole 1979: 112); on the contrary, he can be present with his people, through the Spirit, at all times and in all places (cf. MacRae 1973: esp. 160-61).

iv. The accounts of Jesus' ascension are reminiscent of the OT ascensions of Enoch and Elijah (above, 10-1.3). The parallels are closest with Elijah (see Wilckens 1978: 72); the same Greek word (passive of *analambanō* = "to be taken up") that is used of Elijah (2 Kgs 2:11 LXX) is used of Jesus being "taken up" into heaven in Mark 16:19 and 1 Tim 3:16. Both ascensions precede a giving of the Spirit (2 Kgs 2:9, 15; Acts 1:1-5). Compared with the Elijah story with its chariot and horses of fire, however, the Acts account is much more restrained. Stauffer (1955) claims that "what is quite unmistakable in all the accounts is a reference by analogy or antithesis to the old biblical reports of ascents to heaven" (137). Analogies there are, but ultimately the antithesis is the more significant. Jesus' ascension is fundamentally *different* from these OT prototypes: while it was granted to Enoch and Elijah to bypass death, Jesus' ascension came only on the far side of suffering and death.

10-3.3. AT GOD'S RIGHT HAND

a. The Claims of the New Testament

How is Jesus' existence subsequent to his resurrection and ascension conceived of in the NT? The most common answer is to say that Jesus is "at God's right hand." According to Mark 14:62//Matt 26:64, Jesus himself told the high priest:

> "You will see the Son of Man
> seated at the right hand of the Power,"
> and "coming with the clouds of heaven."

(Luke 22:69 omits the reference to coming with the clouds, and reads "But from now on the Son of Man will be seated at the right hand of the power of God.") In Acts 2:33, following a mention of Jesus' resurrection, Peter refers to Christ as "being therefore exalted *(hypsōtheis)* at the right hand of God." In Rom 8:34 Paul speaks of Jesus "at the right hand of God," while Heb 1:3 says that "when he had made purification for sins, he sat down *(ekathisen)* at the right hand of the Majesty on high." Acts 7:55 is unique in describing a vision of Jesus as the Son of Man "*standing (estōta)* at the right hand of God"; on the meaning of this, see 7-3.5.

b. Theological Significance

In ancient times the right hand of a king or emperor was the position of greatest power and authority in the kingdom. "'The right hand of' is a metaphor for a position of honor, bliss, authority, power and glory" (Toon 1984: 16; cf. McKim 1992: 36).

The source of the expression in the NT is certainly Ps 110:1, a passage quoted or alluded to no fewer than nineteen times in the NT:

> The LORD says to my lord,
>   "Sit *at my right hand*
> until I make your enemies your footstool."

In this Royal Psalm, originally the speaker would be a priest/cultic prophet who declares that God (the LORD) says to the king (my lord), "Sit at my right hand." But after the collapse of the monarchy, Ps 110 was recognized as messianic, pointing forward to a coming king/priest (cf. 6-2.3). In identifying Jesus as the messianic king and priest, the early Christian tradition found in Ps 110:1 appropriate language in which to express what happened to Jesus at his exaltation.

According to Mark 12:35-37 and //s, Jesus himself quoted Ps 110:1 in what appears to be polemic directed against the idea that the Messiah will be simply an earthly king, descended from David. Sharing the assumptions that were made about the psalm in his own day, Jesus takes the speaker in the psalm to be David, so that the "my Lord" (= the Messiah) to whom David refers must be someone greater than David.

The session at God's right hand is theologically significant in a number of ways.

i. It signifies that Jesus is as closely related to God as possible short of outright identification. In quoting Ps 110:1, Heb 1:13 emphasizes that this is a status far greater than that of an angel.

ii. It symbolizes the defeat of the enemies of Christ, i.e., of death and the powers of evil. God raised Christ from the dead "and seated him at his right hand in the heavenly places, far above all rule and authority and power and dominion. . . . And he has put all things under his feet" (Eph 1:20-22; cf. 1 Pet 3:22). Christ's session at God's right hand "is a figurative symbol of His victory over the power of evil, whose essential doom was sealed by the Cross and resurrection" (Argyle 1955: 241). See more fully, 4-3.5; 9-3.4a.

iii. For Hebrews especially, Jesus' ascension inaugurates his heavenly priestly ministry, for the exalted Christ is a "minister *(leitourgos)*" in the heavenly sanctuary (8:1-2). Christ's sacrifice is complete only when he enters the heavenly sanctuary (9:24-26); "thus the ascension becomes an essential part of the atonement, allowing the historical Jesus who is now the reigning Priest/King to finish in heaven . . . the sacrificial work necessary to accomplish our redemption" (Trotter 1996a: 39). Jesus' heavenly ministry also involves interces-sion: the writer to the Hebrews says of those who approach God through Christ, that "he always lives to make intercession *(eis to entunchanein)* for them" (7:25). Similarly, in Rom 8:34 Paul refers to "Christ Jesus, who died, yes, who was raised, who is at the right hand of God, who indeed intercedes *(entunchanei)* for us." In the OT the high priest gained access to the Holy of Holies, i.e., to God's presence, briefly, once a year; in contrast, the exalted Christ is constantly in God's presence, interceding for believers (cf. D. Guthrie 1981: 399-400).

iv. God's right hand is the position from which Jesus will come at the final consummation. See 10-4.

10-3.4. JESUS CHRIST IS LORD

One of the most exalted titles accorded Jesus in the NT, "Lord" *(kyrios),* is very closely linked with his resurrection/ascension/exaltation (cf. Cullmann 1963: 195). At the conclusion of the first recorded Christian sermon, Peter refers to Christ's exaltation to the right hand of God, quotes Ps 110:1 ("The Lord said to my Lord, 'Sit at my right hand . . .'"), and proclaims: "Let the entire house of Is-rael know with certainty that God has made him both Lord *(kyrion)* and Mes-siah" (Acts 2:33-36). In the christological hymn of Phil 2 (see 7-3.4b; 8-3.1), the last stanza says of the servant who suffered on a cross:

> Therefore God also highly exalted him
>> and gave him the name
>> that is above every name,
> so that at the name of Jesus
>> every knee should bend,
>> in heaven and on earth and under the earth,
> and every tongue should confess
>> that Jesus Christ is *Lord,*
>> to the glory of God the Father. (vv. 9-11)

Such passages show that in the early church, following his resurrection/ascen-sion/exaltation, Jesus was recognized as the divine "Lord," the one to whom be-lievers owe worship, loyalty, and obedience.

It is important to realize, however, that in NT times "Lord," *kyrios* (and its underlying Aramaic equivalent, *mār*), had a wide range of meanings. In secular usage *kyrios* could refer to the master or owner of a slave (e.g., Matt 18:25; Acts 16:19). As a form of address *(kyrie)* it could signify respect, or even mere polite-ness, much like the English "Sir."

Kyrios could also, however, mean "Lord" in the sense of "God," since, as noted above (10-1.4), it not only translated the Hebrew word for "Lord" (*'ᵃdhōnay*), but even more significantly was used in the LXX to represent the divine name *YHWH*. This usage carries over into the NT, where *kyrios* still frequently means God (e.g., Matt 1:20; Luke 1:9; Rev 4:11; etc.). In the wider Greco-Roman world, *kyrios* also carried a clear connotation of divinity, for it was frequently used of the many deities of Hellenistic religion, and of the various mystery cults (e.g., Isis, Serapis, Osiris). In 1 Cor 8:5 Paul comments sarcastically that indeed, "there are many gods and many lords." *Kyrios* was also widely applied to rulers in the Greco-Roman world. It was employed as a title of the Roman emperor (see Cullmann 1963: 197-99), and according to Suetonius, the emperor Domitian (ruled A.D. 81-96) claimed to be *dominus et deus,* "lord and god." Surprisingly the title is also attested in relation to the Jewish rulers Herod the Great, Agrippa I, and Agrippa II, all of whom are mentioned in the pages of the NT (see Bietenhard 1976b: 511).

The Gospel writers, of course, fully believed in the Lordship of Christ, and so from their later perspective can refer to Jesus as "Lord" (e.g., Luke 10:1; John 6:23; on *kyrios* as an "auxiliary christological title" in Matthew, see Kingsbury 1975). But they also report that the historical Jesus was frequently addressed as "Lord." When this is done by outsiders (e.g., the leper in Matt 8:2 or the centurion in 8:6), it may have merely signified politeness or respect. However, when the disciples address Jesus as "Lord," something more than politeness or respect is implied. Not only did they look to Jesus for guidance (Luke 11:1), but those who addressed Jesus as "Lord, Lord" were clearly making a commitment to follow him (Matt 7:21-23; cf. John 13:13). As "Lord," Jesus is a figure of authority; he is "lord of the sabbath" (Matt 12:8). For the disciples, therefore, calling Jesus "Lord" meant at least recognizing him as an authoritative teacher and as a master to be followed.

However, Thomas's confession in John 20:28 — "My Lord and my God!" — makes it clear that it was only after Jesus' resurrection that the full meaning of "Lord" dawned on the disciples: to call Jesus *kyrios* is to acknowledge his divine nature and divine authority. "Lord" went on to become one of the major titles of Christ. No doubt this was especially so as the church spread beyond Palestine: titles such as "Messiah"/"Christ" and "Son of Man" became less intelligible, whereas "Lord" was a familiar term in the wider Greco-Roman world that well expressed what the church believed about Christ. Particularly significant is the tendency in the NT to take OT texts that call *God* "Lord" and apply them to Christ (e.g., Mark 1:3 = Isa 40:3; Heb 1:10-12 = Ps 102:25-27).

In the NT Christ is called "Lord" in three contexts. Firstly, he is *the Lord of individual believers.* Pauline texts such as 2 Cor 4:5 ("We proclaim Jesus Christ as Lord") and Rom 10:9 ("If you confess with your lips that Jesus is Lord and believe in your heart that God raised him from the dead, you will be saved") strongly suggest that "Jesus (Christ) is Lord" was an early Christian confession of faith that Paul inherited (cf. Caird 1994: 338). Thomas's confession is in many ways the climax of John's Gospel; despite his doubts, Thomas is led to accept Christ as "*my* Lord and *my* God!" (John 20:28). In the early church believers were baptized "in the name of the Lord Jesus" (Acts 19:5). Thus, when *individuals* heard and believed the message of the gospel, they became Christians by accepting Christ as Lord.

Secondly, *Christ is Lord of the church.* In the NT, conversion to Christianity always involves incorporation into the Christian *community* of which Christ is the Lord. Only seldom do NT believers speak of "*my* Lord" (John 20:13, 28; Phil 3:8); overwhelmingly they say "*our* Lord" (Acts 15:26; Rom 1:4; 1 Cor 1:7; Eph 1:3; 1 Tim 1:2; Heb 13:20; Jas 2:1; 1 Pet 1:3). In 1 Cor 1:2 Paul writes to the church of God in Corinth, but he reminds his readers that they have been called "together with all those who in every place call on the name of our Lord Jesus Christ, *both their Lord and ours.*" Christ is Lord of the whole church, and the church is the sphere in which he is acknowledged as Lord. Thus believers are chosen in the Lord (Rom 16:13), they meet on the Lord's Day (Rev 1:10), they share in the Lord's Supper (1 Cor 11:20), they greet one another in the Lord (Rom 16:22), they rejoice in the Lord (Phil 3:1), and so on (see Bietenhard 1976b: 517).

Thirdly, *Christ is Lord of the cosmos.* As *kyrios,* Christ is the one who created all things (1 Cor 8:6) and who merits the worship of all creation (Phil 2:9-11). Peter, in saying that Christ "is Lord of all" (Acts 10:36), "asserts the universality of Jesus' Lordship over all men" (MacRae 1973: 155). Despite the claims of the emperor Domitian, it is Christ who is "King of kings and Lord of lords" (Rev 19:16). Here, of course, we have the typical NT paradox. In one sense Christ is Lord of all creation, but in another sense this will not be manifest until the final consummation. Cullmann (1963: 224-31) speaks of the "two lordships" of Christ. Between his first and second comings, Christ is Lord of both the church and of all creation: the crucial difference is that for the time being only in the church is Christ's Lordship recognized and acknowledged.

To call Christ "Lord" has two basic implications. It signifies a *confession,* a statement of belief regarding who Christ is. But calling Christ "Lord" also very strongly implies a *commitment.* "Lord" may be defined as the one to whom ultimate loyalty is due. NT usage was no doubt to some extent polemical. It is not the emperor nor the gods of the various Hellenistic cults who are Lord: only Christ bears that title and deserves the ultimate loyalty and obedience it claims. In calling Jesus *kyrios,* "Paul is thinking of one to whom the Christians belonged, one whom they served, and one who gave shape, significance, and a centre to their lives" (Ziesler 1990: 36). Jesus himself emphasized that commitment must involve obedience: "Not everyone who says to me, 'Lord, Lord,' will enter the kingdom of heaven, but only the one who does the will of my Father in heaven" (Matt 7:21). Because *kyrios* is a divine title, Christ as Lord is the object of the church's prayer and worship (1 Cor 12:3). Christians pray to the Lord (2 Cor 12:8) and *to* God *through* Christ the Lord (Rom 7:25).

10-3.5. THE SAVIOR OF THE WORLD

In the NT Christ is also called "Savior" *(sōtēr)*, and to some extent this title is parallel to "Lord," though there are significant differences. In the Gospels Jesus never claims the title "Savior," nor is it applied to him by others. It is used far less frequently than "Lord," and mainly (but not exclusively) in the later books of the NT.

Like "Lord," "Savior" was a word rich in meaning in the world of NT times. First and foremost it appeared in the LXX as a title of God himself (see above, 10-1.5), and in the NT God continues to be called "Savior" (e.g., Luke 1:47; 1 Tim 4:10; Titus 1:3). It was also commonly used as a title of gods (such as Zeus) who would deliver people from danger or peril, or from illness (it was used especially of Asklepios, the god of healing). In the Hellenistic world *sōtēr* was a favorite title of kings who were frequently accorded divine honors. In particular, the Roman emperor could be addressed as *sōtēr*. "The term *sōtēr tēs oikoumenēs,* saviour of the (inhabited) world, was first applied to Caesar . . . and *sōtēr tou kosmou,* saviour of the world, is attested from the time of Hadrian, but is probably older" (Schneider and Brown 1978: 217).

Paul uses *sōtēr* a couple of times only, although in a way that suggests it may already have been in use as a title (Phil 3:20; Eph 5:23). It appears in Luke-Acts (Luke 2:11; Acts 5:31; 13:23) and also in John 4:42, where it is the Samaritans who acknowledge that "this is truly the Savior of the world." The title really seems to have come into its own in the late NT period. Like "Lord," the church found "Savior" well suited to convey to the Greek world the divine nature and authority of the risen and exalted Christ. It is significant that it is in the Pastoral Epistles that *God* is most frequently called "Savior" (1 Tim 1:1; 2:3; 4:10; Titus 1:3; 2:10; 3:4) and that *Christ* is most frequently given the same title (2 Tim 1:10; Titus 1:4; 2:13; 3:6) (cf. Cullmann 1963: 238-39)!

Like "Lord," "Savior" may have been employed, at least in part, in a polemical way: it is Christ, not the Roman emperor, nor Asklepios, who is the true Savior (cf. Bauer 1981c: 813). Despite its predominantly late use, the title is solidly grounded in the basic NT conviction that it is through Christ that God brings salvation to his people (Matt 1:21; Acts 5:31), and indeed to all humankind. Whereas in the OT God is the Savior who delivers people from their enemies and from oppression, in the NT God, in Christ, saves people from sin (Matt 1:21) and from death (2 Tim 1:10). Thus, "like *Kyrios,* the title *Soter* presupposes the completion of Jesus' earthly work and its confirmation in his exaltation" (Cullmann 1963: 241).

New Testament: Consummation

10-4. OUR LORD, COME!

Christ's present position as the risen, ascended, exalted Lord and Savior is discerned only through the eyes of faith. At the final consummation it will become evident to all.

10-4.1. JESUS WILL COME IN THE SAME WAY

Jesus' resurrection/ascension/exaltation inaugurates the period that extends from the Christ event to the parousia.

In the Acts account of the ascension, the two angelic figures tell the apostles, "This Jesus, who has been taken up from you into heaven, will come in the same way as you saw him go into heaven" (1:11; cf. 3:21). When Paul reminded the Thessalonians of their call to serve God "and to wait for his Son from heaven" (1 Thess 1:10), "he undoubtedly implies a previous Ascension into heaven" (Argyle 1955: 241).

10-4.2. *MARANA THA*

As noted above (10-3.4), Christ's Lordship over all is confessed by the church but will become manifest to all only at the final consummation. At present Christ's Lordship over the cosmos is a matter of faith. God's people look forward to the day when Christ will come as "King of kings and Lord of lords" (Rev 19:16; cf. 17:14; 1 Tim 6:15), and his Lordship will be universally acknowledged. As it waits, the church prays *marana tha,* "Our Lord, come" (1 Cor 16:22; cf. Rev 22:20, which probably reflects the same Aramaic phrase; see also 7-4.5).

10-4.3. WE AWAIT A SAVIOR

Similarly, while the church acknowledges Christ as Savior in the present, the work of salvation will be complete only at the final consummation (cf. Bauer 1981c: 812). It is from heaven, says Paul, that "we are expecting a Savior, the Lord Jesus Christ" (Phil 3:20), while Titus 2:13 speaks of believers waiting "for the blessed hope and the manifestation of the glory of our great God and Savior, Jesus Christ." As has frequently been observed, the NT speaks of salvation in three tenses. Insofar as it depends on the finished work of Christ, Paul can say "we were saved (*esōthēmen* = aorist)" (Rom 8:24). Believers appropriate salvation in the present and thus can be referred to as "those who are being saved (*hoi sōzomenoi* = present participle)" (2 Cor 2:15). But as Christ's work as Savior will not be completed until the final consummation, Paul can also say "we [will] be saved (*sōthēsometha* = future)" (Rom 5:9).

10-5. THE SERVANT'S VINDICATION: THEOLOGICAL REFLECTIONS

1. It is impossible to doubt the centrality of the resurrection for the NT, and for the Christian faith. If Jesus' death had been the end of the story, he might have been revered as a martyr or remembered as a teacher, but there would have been no NT and no Christian church. Kepler (1963) is reflecting the view of the NT itself when he declares that "without Jesus' resurrection there would have been no early Church, no New Testament, no religion called Christianity" (7).

2. As presented in the NT, the resurrection of Jesus is the supreme miracle, the supreme instance of divine intervention in human history. Not surprisingly, therefore, many, especially in modern times, reject belief in the resurrection. From a historical point of view, the central place of the resurrection in the self-understanding of the early church cannot be doubted; therefore those who doubt that the resurrection actually occurred are obliged to provide some explanation of how the belief arose among the earliest Christians. This has given rise to an incredible variety of rationalizations. In the case of the empty tomb, it has been suggested that Jesus did not really die on the cross but only swooned, or fell into a coma from which he later revived; that the disciples removed his body (cf. Matt 28:11-15); that the Jewish authorities removed his body; that the Roman authorities removed his body; that Joseph of Arimathea removed the body; that criminals removed the body; that an earthquake was responsible for the body's disappearance; or that the women went to the wrong tomb. In the case of the resurrection appearances, the other half of the swoon theory is that having revived in the tomb, Jesus left it and later encountered some of his disciples. The hallucinations theory suggests that the women, tired and distressed, imagined their encounters with Christ, such hallucinations being due to wishful thinking. A variant of this regards the appearances as "visions," possibly sent by God to the disciples. The ultimate in absurdity is the view that Jesus had a twin brother and that it was he who was seen after Jesus' death. On close scrutiny, most such rationalizations prove to be so far-fetched that many find them more difficult to believe than that Jesus was raised from the dead.

3. It is not only nonbelievers, however, who in modern times have doubted that the resurrection was in any sense a historical event: this view has been put forward by some who still claim to be Christians (see, e.g., Whitaker 1970), even by some who have been appointed to high office in the church. For those who reject the historicity of the resurrection, Easter must be explained solely in

terms of the revival of the disciples' faith. The classic expression of this view is found in Bultmann's essay "New Testament and Mythology" (1953): "The real Easter faith is faith in the word of preaching which brings illumination. If the event of Easter Day is in any sense a historical event additional to the event of the cross, it is nothing else than the rise of faith in the risen Lord, since it was this faith which led to the apostolic preaching. The resurrection itself is not an event of past history" (42). A similar view is found in Marxsen (1970), for whom what "Jesus is risen" really means is that in spite of his death on the cross, "the activity of Jesus goes on" (77). The real miracle is that "Jesus evokes faith even after his death" (138). This faith was expressed in various ways by the early church, and in particular "the notion of the resurrection of the dead was ready to hand. So one made use of it" (138; cf. Marxsen 1990: 73). In other words, the stories of the empty tomb and the appearances have no historical basis but were created in the early church as an "interpretation" of present experience.

Bultmann's view was opposed by Barth, who argued that the resurrection was a real event, though not one that could be verified or proved by the methods of historical scholarship. Pannenberg has argued for the historicity of the resurrection and has pointed, for example, to 1 Cor 15:3-7 as a passage that preserves a very early tradition, and in effect appeals to surviving eyewitnesses (on the modern discussion, see Geyer in Moule 1968: 105-35; Crawford 1972; Migliore 1976). Since the resurrection was a unique event, this means it is not open to the usual means of historical verification; but it does not mean that the event did not happen. The NT, with great clarity and conviction, proclaims that the resurrection was an event that occurred *prior to and apart from the disciples' faith in that event* (see O'Collins 1993: 2-11; cf. Miethe 1987: ix).

4. At the opposite extreme from Christians who doubt the historicity of the resurrection are those who not only believe it happened, but believe it is possible to *prove* that it happened. There is an ongoing debate on the historical evidence for and against the resurrection (see Miethe 1987, which documents a debate held in 1985 between Habermas and Flew on the topic "The Historicity of the Resurrection: Did Jesus Rise from the Dead?"). Opponents denounce the evidence as late and contradictory, though frequently their objections are more philosophical in nature. Proponents point to 1 Cor 15:3-7 as very early eyewitness testimony, and appeal to such things as the revival of the disciples' faith, the existence of the church, the existence of the NT, and the remarkable and very early change in the day of worship from the Jewish Sabbath to the Christian Sunday.

It must be very seriously questioned, however, whether historical evidence could by itself ever compel faith in the resurrection. Nowhere does the NT itself attempt to do this. It presents the resurrection as an act of God, the climax of the Christ event, that is *proclaimed* by the church (Acts 17:18); and it summons those who hear the proclamation to respond in *faith* (on the role of faith in the resurrection, see above, 10-3.1b.iii). Therefore, while it is certainly possible to prove that the earliest Christians believed in the resurrection, it is not possible, simply on the basis of historical evidence, to prove that Jesus rose from the dead. There are those who concede that belief in the resurrection is primarily a matter of faith yet who also hold that historical arguments may play a secondary and supporting role (cf. O'Collins 1993: 31-35).

5. The ascension and session at God's right hand have provoked less discussion than the resurrection, though they are regarded by many modern critics as nothing more than relics of an outworn mythology. It is true that these accounts do employ symbolic language in speaking of events that lie beyond our present experience, but truth may be powerfully conveyed by symbolism, and both these events assert important theological truths.

The ascension and session complete the Christ event. They underline forcefully that the resurrection of Jesus was not merely the resuscitation of a corpse. In the cases of Jairus's daughter, the widow of Nain's son, and Lazarus (see further, 20-4.3b), all of whom were raised by Jesus from the dead, we are left to assume that they resumed their normal life here on earth, only to face death again in due course. Jesus' triumph over death is of a totally different order (cf. Saunders 1976: 739), though it does guarantee the ultimate resurrection of believers. God not only raised Jesus from the dead; he also took him to be with him in the highest position of power and authority. To believe in Christ's ascension and session at God's right hand is therefore to believe that the Christ event is God's final and decisive act within human history for the salvation of humankind. The ascension and session complete the full NT pattern of preexistence/incarnation/exaltation (see 8-3.1). Thus, "so far from being incredible, the Ascension is an indispensable part of the Christian message, without which that message would not be complete or intelligible" (Argyle 1955: 241; cf. D. Guthrie 1981: 391).

6. In modern times it has become popular in some branches of the church to equate conversion to Christianity with "accepting Christ as Savior and Lord." While these terms are certainly scriptural, and while God is called both Savior and LORD (= *YHWH*) in the OT (e.g., Isa 43:3; 45:21; Hos 13:4; *Sir* 51:1), it should be noted that in the NT the combined phrase "Lord and Savior" as applied to Christ occurs only four times, all in 2 Peter (1:11; 2:20; 3:2, 18; cf. Cullmann 1963: 238).

As noted above (10-3.4), "Lord" *(kyrios)* is a very frequent NT title, and one that ascribes to Christ divine nature and authority. Some scholars, following Bousset (1970), hold that the earliest church did not confess Jesus as the divine Lord. *Kyrios* became a christological title only when Christianity spread into the Greco-Roman world; it was adopted on the analogy of the many "lords" worshiped in Hellenistic cults (see the critique of Bousset's position in Cullmann 1963: 205-15; cf. also S. E. Johnson 1962: 151). Against this, however, the very early use of the title is attested by the Aramaic expression *marana tha*, meaning "Our Lord, come"; "the ascription of lordship to Christ in this Aramaic formula indicates that Jesus was already called Lord in Palestinian Christianity at an early date" (Bietenhard 1976b: 515). Reference to James as "the Lord's brother" (Gal 1:19; cf. 1 Cor 9:5) probably also reflects a very early usage.

Moreover, there are no good grounds for doubting that Jesus was called Lord by his disciples, even if the full meaning of the term became apparent to them only after Jesus' resurrection, ascension, and exaltation. In postresurrection/exaltation usage, *kyrios* takes on new depths of meaning, but there is a real *continuity* with the preresurrection/exaltation usage on the part of the disciples. "The same disciples who during Jesus' lifetime had expressed only their role as followers with the address 'my Lord' — these disciples encountered him after his death as the exalted Christ who was present in the Church's worship and who demanded absolute devotion of his people" (Cullmann 1963: 202).

"Savior" *(sōtēr),* on the other hand, is not a title that goes back to the historical Jesus; it is used much less frequently than "Lord," and comes into its own mainly in the Pastorals and 2 Peter.

Nevertheless, the two titles together do sum up both the finished work of Christ and the response that is called for on the part of believers. To accept Christ as Lord and Savior is to recognize that the claims he makes upon the lives of believers are the claims that only God can make, and to respond by offering him the worship, the allegiance, and the service that are his due.

A SKETCH OF BIBLICAL THEOLOGY

CHAPTERS 11-15: GOD'S PEOPLE

CHAPTER 11

The Covenant Community

Old Testament: Proclamation

11-1. MY PEOPLE ISRAEL

A major theme of BT is God's creation of a *people* to serve him (cf. E-4.3). "When God, the Father of our Lord Jesus Christ, began to act in our world so that he could be recognized, he acted toward and within *a people*" (Westermann 1963c: 259; cf. Watts 1956: 232; Marks 1972; Shaw 1990: vii). Recognition of "the people of God" as a major biblical theme does not depend in any narrow way on the use of a particular terminology, but rather in the broadest possible way on the fact that the "story line" of salvation history (see chap. 3) is largely the account of relations between God and Israel in the OT and God and the church in the NT. In the OT Israel is referred to as a "people" (*'am;* LXX *laos),* chosen by God from among the nations *(gôyîm;* LXX *ethnē).* The actual phrase "people of God" occurs only eleven times, but phrases such as "my people," "your people," and "his people" are frequent (ca. 300 times).

11-1.1. THE CONGREGATION OF ISRAEL

The story of God's activity in the historical order begins with *the call of Abraham.* Gen 12:1-3 is a key passage: inseparable from God's call of Abraham as an individual is his promise to him: "I will make of you a great nation . . ." (12:2; cf. the repetition of the promise in 22:17-18). In contrast to 11:4 where the peoples say, "Let us make a name for ourselves," God promises Abraham, "I will make . . . your name great" (12:2; see Dumbrell 1984: 60-61). "After the chaos described in the first eleven chapters of Genesis, the initiative of God sets in motion the story of the people of Israel" (D. J. Harrington 1980: 4-5). As Goldingay (1987) points out, "It is not even that God makes an already existent people his own; he brings a people into being. They only exist as a people because of an act of God" (62). God's promise is continued to Abraham's son Isaac (Gen 26:4) and grandson Jacob (28:14). A special importance attaches to Jacob since it is his new name, Israel, that is to be borne by God's people. Alternate accounts of the giving of the new name are found in 32:22-32 and 35:9-15. From Jacob's twelve sons are descended the twelve tribes of "Israel," and it is these "children of Israel" *(beᵉnê yisrāʾēl)* who collectively constitute God's people.

Israel, as God's people, is frequently referred to in the OT by means of two closely related and often overlapping terms. *Qāhāl,* translated as "congregation" or "assembly," means basically a group of people gathered together for a particular purpose, e.g., an army assembled for battle (1 Sam 17:47). It is used of Israel, especially as assembled at Mount Sinai to enter into the covenant and receive the Torah, or as assembled to worship God (Ps 22:22). In almost one hundred instances the LXX translates *qāhāl* as *ekklēsia,* though it also uses a variety of other terms. Closely linked with *qāhāl* is *ʿēdhāh,* which also has the meaning of an assembly or gathering though it stresses more the idea of corporate unity. In the LXX it is generally translated by *synagōgē* (never by *ekklēsia*).

11-1.2. A CHOSEN PEOPLE

The story of Israel is based on the belief that from out of all the nations of the world God has, in his grace, chosen Israel to be his own people. "The community of faith in the Bible is the people *called*" (Hanson 1986: 467). In theological terms this is belief in the "election" of a particular group of people. BT in the twentieth century made an important contribution in rediscovering the importance and the true meaning of the biblical understanding of election; see especially the classic study by Rowley (1950a). Election is embedded in the biblical narrative from the account of the call of Abraham onward. God, in fact, continues to make choices: Isaac, not Ishmael; Jacob, not Esau. Election is a lived reality rather than an abstract doctrine, though it is true that in the book of Deuteronomy especially, "Israel's privileged position before God is made the subject of careful reflection" (Clements 1968: 45). "For you are a people holy to the LORD your God; the LORD your God has chosen *(bāchar)* you out of all the peoples on the earth to be his people, his treasured possession" (Deut 7:6; cf. 14:2). While it is primarily Israel that is chosen, God also calls individuals to serve him in and through his people (see 6-1 on the special individuals chosen by God to serve him). The prophets in particular experienced a divine call, and according to Jer 1:5, Jeremiah was consecrated as a prophet even before his birth.

While election is traced back to the call of Abraham, God's call of Israel to be his people is realized above all in the exodus deliverance (see 3-1.3a; cf. Rowley 1950a: 19-21; Shaw 1990: 25-26). This is the event by which God "redeemed" his people: "I am the LORD, and I will free you from the burdens of the

Egyptians and deliver you from slavery to them. I will *redeem* you with an outstretched arm and with mighty acts of judgment. I will take you as my people, and I will be your God" (Exod 6:6-7).

The basic meaning of "redeem" (Heb. *gāʾal, pādhāh*) is to secure the release of someone or something through the payment of a price. In Hebrew law a "redeemer" *(gōʾēl)* is a person whose duty is to, e.g., buy back the forfeited property of a family member (cf. Ruth 4:1-12) or purchase a family member's release from slavery (Lev 25:47-49). When God is said to have "redeemed" Israel (Exod 15:13; Deut 7:8; 2 Sam 7:23; Ps 106:10; Isa 43:1; etc.) or is given the title "Redeemer" (esp. in Isaiah, e.g., 41:14; 44:24), the emphasis is on God delivering his people so that they may live in an intimate relationship with him, rather than on the payment of a price (Dentan 1962: 22). While individuals may look to God to "redeem" them from various troubles (esp. in the Psalms, e.g., 49:15; 69:18), throughout the Bible redemption is primarily corporate: it is his people whom God chooses and redeems.

A natural modern reaction to election is that it is fundamentally unfair: God is playing favorites. But three basic emphases in the biblical material must always be kept in mind.

a. Election Is by Grace

Israel is not chosen because she deserved to be, or for any merit of her own, but solely out of God's grace (cf. Brueggemann 1997: 414-17). Therefore she can bring no claim against God.

Election is constantly referred back to God's choice of Abraham and his promises to the patriarchs. But in Gen 12 the choice of Abraham is totally unexpected and unexplained; it depends entirely on divine initiative, divine grace, and divine love. "He loved your ancestors," Israel is told, and "he chose their descendants after them" (Deut 4:37). Thus election "in no sense presupposes any prior quality on the part of the men concerned or in their relationship with God" (Molin 1981b: 955). "It is God's sovereignty, not human initiative, that brings the people of God into existence" (Bush 1992: 100). Similarly, the account of Israel's redemption insists "that the deliverance from Egypt resulted from *God's grace alone.* God took the initiative. He made them His people by His deliverance" (Watts 1956: 234).

Election by grace finds classic expression in Deut 7:7-8: "It was not because you were more numerous than any other people that the LORD set his heart on you and chose you — for you were the fewest of all peoples. It was because the LORD loved you and kept the oath that he swore to your ancestors." Here election "is forcefully described as a free act of divine grace" (Clements 1968: 47; cf. D. J. Harrington 1980: 9). Similarly the gift of the Land is not due to any righteousness possessed by Israel, but is a gift from God (Deut 9:4-6). That the choice of Israel derives "solely from the mysterious and inexplicable love of God" (Childs 1992: 426) is a major theme of the Deuteronomic reflection on the meaning of election.

b. Election Is for Responsibility

Although Israel constantly found this difficult to remember and accept, the main thrust of the biblical understanding of election is that it is not for privilege but for responsibility: "the notion of a people selected by God is never a claim to superiority but rather a call to service" (Shaw 1990: 8). In Gen 12:2 Abraham is told, "I will bless you . . . so that you will be a blessing." While, as we have seen, individuals are called to be God's servants (6-1; 9-1), basically it is Israel, the people of God, that is called to be the servant of the Lord. Moses tells the Israelites that what the LORD requires of them is "to serve the LORD your God with all your heart and with all your soul" (Deut 10:12). In the context of a warning against the worship of idols, God says to his people in Isa 44:21:

> Remember these things, O Jacob,
>   and Israel, for you are my servant;
> I formed you, you are my servant.

The "suffering servant" of 2 Isaiah is in the first place the people of Israel, or at least the faithful remnant (Isa 49:3), even though the Servant Songs also think of an ideal future individual (see 9-1.3d). Israel is to be God's priest in relation to the rest of humankind: "Now therefore, if you obey my voice and keep my covenant, you shall be my treasured possession out of all the peoples. Indeed, the whole earth is mine, but you shall be for me a priestly kingdom and a holy nation" (Exod 19:5-6). The prophets were constantly to remind Israel of the responsibility entailed by election, and spell out what that responsibility meant in specific circumstances (see Rowley 1950a: 45-68).

c. Election Implies a Higher, Not a Lower, Standard of Judgment

Being God's chosen people does not mean that he will judge them less severely. On the contrary, since God's will has been more clearly revealed to them and they have been chosen to serve God in a special way, their failures will bring greater condemnation. The prototypical rebellion of Israel against God through the worship of the golden calf (Exod 32) resulted in the slaughter of three thousand of the people (v. 28) and in the sending of a plague (v. 35). In Num 21 the Israelites' rebellious complaints resulted in an attack by poisonous serpents as a result of which many died (v. 6).

Israel is not spared divine judgment because they are God's people; indeed, it is precisely because they *are* the covenant community that God disciplines them. This pattern continues throughout the OT: as already noted (3-1.1), God's dealings with his people constitute not only a history of salvation *(Heilsgeschichte)* but also a history of judgment. Election and covenant are the basic presuppositions of the prophets' messages of judgment (see below, 11-1.3e). Nowhere is this more forcefully put than in Amos 3:2, where God says to Israel:

> You only have I known
>   of all the families of the earth;
> *therefore* I will punish you
>   for all your iniquities.

"The Election is the often unexpressed but always evident basis of every prophecy of judgment; it heightens the claim on Israel, and results in a correspondingly harder punishment" (Danell 1953: 31).

Election thus has to be understood in the full canonical context. "The Old Testament relates for us a very remarkable story. God, it tells us, has of his own free grace directed his special attention to one small people — a people of no particular importance in the great general history of the world. This people God has called, chosen, delivered, and endowed with many gifts of his favour and of his presence. But this people he has also judged and smitten more than any other people upon earth" (Kraus 1958: 9).

11-1.3. THE COVENANT COMMUNITY

God and his people are bound together in a special relationship brought into being by God's call of Abraham and his deliverance of his people from slavery in Egypt. While the terminology is not all-pervasive in the OT, the most important way of understanding this relationship is in terms of "covenant" (cf. E-4.3). Some critical scholars (Wellhausen, Perlitt) have argued that covenant was a late innovation, not introduced until the seventh century B.C. Historically this view is speculative and highly improbable, but in any case, BT must be based on the canonical understanding of "covenant" (cf. Childs 1992: 413-20; Brueggemann 1997: 296-97, 418; for a survey of scholarly discussion, see Nicholson 1986: 3-117).

a. The Four Covenants

In its present canonical structure the OT speaks of four successive covenants: one in the *created* order and three in the *historical* order. The first three occur in

Genesis and Exodus, and in the canonical form of these books covenant is an important structuring concept (see Rendtorff 1989).

i. The Covenant with Noah (Gen 9:1-17; see Dumbrell 1984: 11-43)

It is highly significant that before speaking of the establishment of a special relationship between God and Israel, the canonical OT first speaks of God's relationship to all humankind. Following the deliverance from the flood, God establishes his covenant with Noah and his descendants (Gen 9:9), i.e., with all humankind from that point on. The sign of this covenant is the rainbow (9:13).

ii. The Covenant with Abraham (Gen 15; 17; see Dumbrell 1984: 47-77)

This marks the beginning of the special relationship between God and his people, for through this covenant God promises Abraham many descendants and possession of the land. Gen 15 and 17 represent alternate accounts. The sign of this covenant is circumcision.

iii. The Sinai Covenant (Exod 19–24; see further below, 11-1.3c)

The promises to Abraham are fulfilled when God delivers Israel from slavery and enters into covenant with them at Mount Sinai. Moses acts as mediator of this covenant, which is sealed with a sacrifice (Exod 24:4-8) and a shared meal (24:11).

iv. The Covenant with David (2 Sam 23:5; Ps 89:3, 28; 1 Kgs 8:23-24; Jer 33:21)

Unlike the others, there is no narrative of the establishment of this covenant; it is referred to in the above passages and assumed in many others (see further, 6-1.2b).

b. The Meaning of "Covenant"

The Hebrew word for covenant is *bᵉrîth*, but it is doubtful how much light modern critical studies of the etymology of the word can shed on the OT understanding of covenant (see Nicholson 1986: 13-20, 94-103). Moreover, there are certainly passages in the OT that refer to the "covenant relationship" between God and people even when the actual term *bᵉrîth* is not employed. Much modern discussion of the covenant has been dominated by comparisons with the ancient Near Eastern "suzerainty treaties" (Mendenhall 1962: 714-15, 719; Hillers 1969: 29; Dumbrell 1984: 94-99; Nicholson 1986: 56-82) that were imposed by a powerful nation (the "suzerain") upon less powerful vassals. The suzerain offered protection and expected in return compliance with the conditions of the treaty. There are striking parallels between such treaties and the Sinai covenant in particular (also with the book of Deuteronomy), though there are also significant differences. Historically there may be some connection.

Considerably more significant for the biblical understanding of covenant is the way the term is used in the OT itself. Apart from the specifically religious usage, it can refer to *treaties* between nations (Gen 21:25-32; Josh 9:3-27; 1 Kgs 5:12), to a bond of *friendship* between individuals (1 Sam 18:1-3), and to *marriage* (Mal 2:14). Primarily covenant is to be understood in terms of the canonical OT accounts of the four covenants. The use of the term in relation to treaties, friendship, and marriage confirms what the canonical accounts make clear: a covenant involves an agreement between two parties. "Even though the burden is most unequally distributed between the two contracting parties, this makes no difference to the fact that the relationship is still essentially two-sided" (Eichrodt 1961: 37). By "covenant" the OT means "an enduring commitment by God and his people based on mutual vows of loyalty and mutual obligation through which both parties have their lives radically affected and empowered" (Brueggemann 1985a: 10).

As used in the OT, the term "covenant" denotes:

- an agreement between two parties
- that establishes a special relationship between them
- with mutual but not necessarily equal obligations,
- sealed by a special ceremony.

The extent to which biblical covenants in fact involve mutual obligations has been the subject of dispute. Some scholars identify the Sinai covenant as *conditional,* with the Torah representing the conditions that Israel must keep in order to remain within the covenant relationship. The other three are viewed as *unconditional,* with God making a promise in each case but demanding nothing in return; in these cases "covenant" is viewed more as a solemn oath on the part of God. Noah is promised that a flood will never again destroy the earth; Abraham is promised that his successors will be a great nation; and David is promised a royal dynasty. These take the form of *promises* that God undertakes not to revoke. The contrast, however, is more a matter of degree than of kind (cf. Brueggemann 1997: 419-21; contra Dumbrell 1984: 31-32). While the Torah does indeed represent Israel's side of the bargain in the Sinai covenant, there is some obligation stated or implied in the other three covenants also: Noah and his descendants have to follow the "Noahide laws," faith and obedience are required of Abraham (cf. Bush 1992: 101-2), and faithfulness to God's Torah is required of David and his successors (contra Mendenhall 1962: 718).

In the LXX *b^erîth* is translated not by the more exact equivalent *sunthēkē* but by *diathēkē*, which can mean a person's last will and testament. This suggests a more one-sided understanding of covenant, with all the emphasis on the gracious promise and gift of God (though *diathēkē* need not be entirely unilateral, as in Greek though a will can bind both the testator and his heirs; see Eichrodt 1961: 66).

c. The Sinai Covenant

The conclusion of the covenant between God and people at Sinai is the pivotal point of the Torah, and indeed of the whole OT (see Hillers 1969: 48-54; Dumbrell 1984: 80-104).

The narrative framework is designed to provide the context of the event and to underline its significance. It follows the account of the exodus/Red Sea deliverance and of God's protection in the wilderness (Exod 1–18). These are pointedly recalled in 19:4: "You have seen what I did to the Egyptians, and how I bore you on eagles' wings," and in 20:2: "I am the LORD your God, who brought you out of the land of Egypt, out of the house of slavery."

As an agreement between two parties, the covenant must include the people's consent. God takes the initiative, but the people's consent is asked for (19:5) and given: "Everything that the LORD has spoken we will do" (19:7-8).

The covenant involves obligations on the part of both God and people. God's contribution has in a sense already been fulfilled in the exodus deliverance, though God also promises Israel his continued presence and protection. The people's obligation is found in the Decalogue (Exod 20:1-17; Deut 5:6-21; cf. 4:13), in the Book of the Covenant (Exod 20:22–23:33), and in the rest of the Torah through to the end of Deuteronomy (cf. 18-1.2a). Thus "in the covenant the people learned what it meant to be 'the people of God'" (Watts 1956: 236).

The covenant establishes a special relationship between God and Israel: "Now therefore, if you obey my voice and keep my covenant, you shall be my treasured possession out of all the peoples . . . a priestly kingdom and a holy nation" (Exod 19:5-6). This relationship is frequently referred to in Scripture, even when the actual term "covenant" is lacking, by means of what may be termed a "covenant formula." Thus in Exod 6:7 the LORD declares: "I will take you as my people, and I will be your God." At the conclusion of the Holiness Code in Lev 26:11-12, God promises, "I will place my dwelling in your midst, and I shall not abhor you. And I will walk among you, *and will be your God, and you shall be my people*" (cf. Ps 95:7).

d. Covenant Renewal

While the Sinai covenant is a unique event, it also inaugurates an ongoing relationship between God and people. In Deut 29:14-15 the LORD tells the assembled Israelites, "I am making this covenant . . . not only with you who stand here with us today . . . but also with those who are not here with us today." The OT also recognizes that the covenant relationship between God and people is one that can and must be periodically renewed. The covenant never belongs to the past; it is the ever present reality in the life of God's people.

i. Specific Renewals

Seven specific renewals of the covenant are narrated in the OT: one in the land of Moab near the end of the wilderness wanderings (Deut 29–30); one at Shechem, under Joshua, after the entry into Palestine (Josh 8:30-35), in fulfillment of instructions given in Deut 27–28; a further renewal at Shechem near the end of Joshua's life (Josh 24:1-28); one under the direction of the priest Jehoiada (2 Kgs 11:17-18); one that formed part of Josiah's reformation (2 Kgs 23:1-3); one under the direction of Ezra (Ezra 10:1-5); and another under Ezra (Neh 8–10). These renewals take place at certain key points in salvation history.

ii. A Covenant Renewal Festival

Many biblical scholars have argued for a regular, annual covenant-renewal ceremony in ancient Israel, most probably in connection with the feast of tabernacles (cf. Eichrodt 1961: 123; von Rad 1962: 192-93; and see 14-1.3). While such reconstructions go beyond the evidence, it should be noted that Deut 31:9-13 does prescribe the public reading of the Torah every seven years at the feast of tabernacles.

e. Covenant in the Prophets

The actual term "covenant" does not occur frequently in the earlier prophets (for the reasons, cf. Eichrodt 1961: 51-52; Nicholson 1986: 24-27; Hos 6:7; 8:1 are notable exceptions). This is a good example, however, of the limitations of the "word study" approach to BT. Even when the actual term "covenant" is lacking, the prophetic message has as one of its basic presuppositions the special relationship between the LORD and Israel, based on the exodus event, a relationship that is portrayed through a rich variety of images (cf. L. L. Thompson 1978: 188-89; Dumbrell 1985: 80-81). As L. C. Allen (1992) points out, "the prophetic books use a network of terms, formulas, and motifs that point to a relationship that may be conveniently summed up in terms of covenant" (150). The prophets assume Israel's obligations under this relationship in the form of the Torah, and this is the basis of their indictment of the people who have failed to obey the Lord (Hillers 1969: 120-41). The covenant relationship, frequently expressed through the covenant formula (Jer 24:7; 30:22; 31:33; 32:38; Ezek 36:28; 37:23, 27), is also the basis for many of their future promises.

f. Covenant Love

God's choice of Israel as his people is an act of divine *love* (cf. above, 11-1.2a). Having entered into covenant with his people, God binds himself to them by a special kind of love denoted by the Hebrew word *chesedh*. The older translation, "loving-kindness," does not fully convey the original meaning; RSV and NRSV use "steadfast love." Another suggestion is "covenant love." "The covenant love of Yahweh is . . . a faithful love, a steadfast unshakeable maintenance of the covenantal relationship" (Good 1962b: 167); it is related to "tenacious fidelity in a relationship, readiness and resolve to continue to be loyal to those to whom one is bound" (Brueggemann 1997: 217).

Ideally, of course, both sides in the relationship should show covenant love. Israel frequently fails to do this:

> They have broken my covenant,
>   and transgressed my law. (Hos 8:1)

Nevertheless, God's *chesedh* remains constant.

> Many times he delivered them,
>   but they were rebellious in their purposes. . . .
> Nevertheless he regarded their distress. . . .
> For their sake he remembered his covenant,
>   and showed compassion according to the abundance
>   of his steadfast love. (Ps 106:43-45)

Even in the aftermath of the incident of the golden calf (Exod 32), God reveals himself not only as a God of judgment (34:7b) but as

> The Lord, the Lord,
> a God merciful and gracious,
> slow to anger,
> and abounding in steadfast love and faithfulness *(rabh-chesedh we 'emeth)*
>   (34:6),

and goes on to renew the covenant (34:10-28). As Bush (1992) remarks, "here we have a theology of grace unsurpassed in the OT" (108). A recurring refrain in the Psalms is:

O give thanks to the LORD, for he is good;
for his steadfast love endures forever. (Pss 106:1; 107:1; 118:1; etc.)

11-1.4. GOD AND PEOPLE

While the relationship between God and people is most frequently referred to in terms of "covenant," it can also be expressed in a variety of ways using a range of images and metaphors.

God can be spoken of as a *father* and Israel as his *children* (Exod 4:22-23; Isa 1:2, 4; Hos 1:10; 11:1; see 8-1.5b). God can be spoken of as a *husband* with Israel as his *wife* (Isa 54:5) or *bride* (Jer 2:2). In the light of this image Israel's forsaking of the LORD in favor of other gods is referred to as "playing the harlot" (RSV); see the extensive discussion of this theme in Ortlund 1996. Israel's "marital" unfaithfulness is condemned, e.g., in Exod 34:16; Lev 20:5; Judg 2:17; Jer 3:6-10; Ezek 16, and in the shocking allegory of Oholah and Oholibah, the two whores, in Ezek 23. The accusation is taken up by Hosea: "The land commits great whoredom by forsaking the LORD" (1:2; cf. 2:7; 4:10). The "whoredom" was both metaphorical and literal, as the cult of Baal was characterized by low moral standards and sacred prostitution. Yet, just as Hosea continued to love his unfaithful wife Gomer, so God continues to love his unfaithful spouse:

How can I give you up, Ephraim?
How can I hand you over, O Israel? . . .
My heart recoils within me;
my compassion grows warm and tender. (Hos 11:8)

God is also spoken of as a *shepherd* and his people as *sheep* throughout the OT.

He will feed his flock like a shepherd;
he will gather the lambs in his arms. (Isa 40:11)

It is he that made us, and we are his;
we are his people, and the sheep of his pasture. (Ps 100:3)

Isaiah pictures the relationship in terms of *master* and *animal* (1:3). In yet another image Israel is a *vine* planted by God (Ps 80:8; cf. Jer 2:21). In Isaiah's parable of the vineyard (5:1-7),

the vineyard of the LORD of hosts
is the house of Israel (5:7);

when the vines no longer produce good grapes, they invite judgment, a theme picked up in Ezek 15 (cf. Jer 2:21).

11-1.5. UNITY AND DIVERSITY

One would expect that, as a people created and called into being by God himself, and as a "family" tracing their descent from the twelve sons of the one father Jacob/Israel, the *unity* of God's people would be a given. The narrative of the OT, however, reveals that this was very far from the truth. Within the lifetime of Jacob/Israel, his sons conspired to murder or at least get rid of their brother Joseph (Gen 37)!

There is tension between the canonical account and much of the modern historical-critical reconstruction of Israel's origins that tends to envisage a complex process with various tribes infiltrating into Palestine over a number of centuries. Noth propounded the view that the twelve tribes came together in a tribal confederation or amphictyony only under Joshua. Be that as it may, the canonical account makes it clear that there were differences and tensions among the tribes from the beginning. Two major groupings are to be discerned in those tribes descended from Jacob's two wives Leah and Rachel, with the descent of lesser tribes being traced to the two concubines Bilhah and Zilpah. In particular, a major division between North and South runs throughout biblical history. This is evident in the reign of David (cf. 2 Sam 19:41–20:2), and it comes as no surprise when these differences bring about the division of the kingdom after the death of Solomon in 922 B.C. (1 Kgs 12). The divided kingdoms of Israel in the north and Judah in the south reflect not only tribal and political rivalries but also theological differences (cf. Scobie 1976: 89-90). The schism is underlined by the fact that the Northern Kingdom arrogated to itself the name "Israel," though after the fall of the North "Israel" was used as a self-designation by the continuing community of Judah. With the Assyrian conquest and the fall of Samaria in 722, the Northern Kingdom of Israel ceased to exist and disappeared from history. The account in 2 Kgs 17 represents a southern point of view that does not regard the population remaining in the North as true Israelites. In NT times the continuing northern population was represented by the Samaritans.

If unity is defined in terms of an integrated political unit, then the twelve tribes were unified only during the reigns of David and Solomon (and even then with considerable internal stresses). Prior to that, some kind of loose confederation seems to have been the norm; after that, God's people remained basically disunited.

Old Testament: Promise

11-2. THE ISRAEL OF GOD

11-2.1. THE END OF THE STORY?

The account of God's people in the OT is a suspense story. Time and again it seems, from a human point of view, that the story is about to come to an end. But by God's grace a new beginning becomes possible and the story continues. There are four major crises.

a. The *enslavement in Egypt* of the descendants of Jacob/Israel radically calls in question God's promises of a people to the patriarchs and the very existence of Israel. The exodus comes as a miraculous deliverance.

b. The *fall of the Northern Kingdom* to the Assyrians eliminates the greater part of God's people, and the survival of Judah in the south appears highly precarious. Yet Judah does survive.

c. The *Babylonian exile,* following the traumatic events of the capture of Jerusalem and the destruction of the temple, seems to indicate that the South had only a temporary reprieve and that now it too would disappear from history. Again the return from exile under the Persian ruler Cyrus seemed nothing short of a miracle.

d. The Deuterocanon tells of the *persecution under Antiochus,* a vicious religious persecution that once again threatened the very existence of God's people. The success of the Maccabean revolt and the recovery of independence is seen as another divine deliverance.

In each of these cases, by God's grace a new beginning becomes possible and the story continues. It is this record of God's gracious dealings with his people that inspires hope as the OT looks toward the future of God's people.

11-2.2. YOU ARE MY PEOPLE

The history of God's dealings with his people is one of both judgment and salvation. Because of Israel's repeated rebellion and disobedience, for a number of the prophets "the idea of Israel being the people of God becomes future prospect, not present reality" (Goldingay 1987: 74). Even in the midst of their pronouncement of judgment on a people who break God's law and disregard the covenant, some prophets continue to hold out hope for the future of God's people. While Amos can say, "The end has come upon my people Israel" (8:2), his long litany of judgment is balanced by God's assurance that "I will not utterly destroy the house of Jacob" (9:8). The verdict implied by Hosea's naming of his son "Not My People" will surely be reversed (1:10; 2:23). While God's great act of redeeming his people lies in the past (above, 11-1.2), Isaiah sees the promised return from exile as a new act of redemption (50:2; 52:3; cf. Mic 4:10); the time will come when Israel will again be called "The Holy People, / The Redeemed of the LORD" (Isa 62:12). In the Psalms we find prayers to God for a future redemption of his people (25:22; 44:26); Israel is called to hope in the LORD, for "it is he who will redeem Israel / from all its iniquities" (130:8).

The promise of a future for God's people takes two main forms.

a. The Faithful Remnant

Since God's people as a whole has proved disobedient, one form of the promise looks for the survival of a faithful "remnant" (*sheʾar;* on this and cognate words, see Hasel 1972: 386-88). Although this hope emerges most clearly in the major prophets, its roots go back much earlier. The flood represents God's judgment on humankind, yet God's ultimate purpose is salvation, so he chooses Noah and his family as a remnant. "This remnant which survived the great flood constitutes the nucleus of mankind in which mankind's future existence was secured" (Hasel, 389). Under Queen Jezebel it appears that all Israel has forsaken the LORD and a despairing Elijah complains, "I alone am left" (1 Kgs 19:14); he considers himself a remnant of one. Elijah is told of the judgment that will fall upon Israel, but not on all, for in fact God says, "I will leave seven thousand in Israel, all the knees that have not bowed to Baal" (19:18). Here it is clear that "the remnant will constitute the kernel of a new Israel faithful to Yahweh and his covenant requirements; it will be saved primarily as an act of the grace of God" (Hasel, 391).

The expectation of the survival of a faithful remnant is an important aspect of prophetic eschatology; as L. C. Allen (1992) argues, "the prophetic notion of a remnant builds a bridge between the outworking of divine judgment and the possibility of salvation" (163; cf. J. C. Campbell 1950). Amos envisages only a small minority escaping the coming judgment (3:12), yet he also expresses the hope that the LORD may yet be gracious "to the remnant of Joseph" (5:15). The remnant is a special emphasis in the prophet Isaiah (see Rowley 1950a: 73-75), who gave his son the symbolic name *Sheʾar Yāshûbh,* meaning "a remnant shall return" (7:3). Like Amos, a prophet of judgment, Isaiah nevertheless held that a "holy seed" would survive (6:13; cf. 4:2-4). The remnant "will be called 'holy' not because of any qualification of its own but because of God's mercy" (Hasel 1972: 396). Isaiah declared that "though your people Israel were like the sand of the sea, only a remnant of them will return" (10:22; cf. also 11:11, 16; 28:5; 37:31). Mic 5:7-9 envisages the remnant after the exile showering blessings on "many peoples" but also treading upon their adversaries. In Jer 23:3 God promises, "I myself will gather the remnant of my flock out of all the lands where I have driven them."

In the postexilic period the returning exiles are seen as a remnant that has remained faithful to the LORD (Ezra 9:8; Hag 1:12, 14), but the prophetic hope remains that at some point in the future God will act to restore his people, or at least a faithful remnant of them.

b. Death and Resurrection

A more radical view of the situation sees no remedy short of a death and resurrection of God's people (cf. 10-2.1). This hope is given classic expression in Ezekiel's vision of the valley of dry bones (37:1-14). The scattered bones symbolize a people that is totally dead; the only hope lies in a miraculous resurrection brought about by the power of God's Spirit. "The creative, awakening voice of God brings a dead people back to life. This word, and this alone, is to be the source of Israel's life. Through death and resurrection God brings about deliverance" (Kraus 1958: 68-69).

11-2.3. A NEW COVENANT

God remains faithful to the covenant he has made with his people; his *chesedh* endures forever (cf. Lev 26:44-45; Ezek 16:59-60). But God's people continually break the covenant and imperil its continued existence. Because of the conditional nature of the Sinai covenant, the possibility existed from the outset that it might be annulled by God because of the people's unfaithfulness (Exod 32:10). A way out of this impasse is seen in the prophetic literature with the hope and promise of *a new covenant* (cf. Payne 1961).

As part of Ezekiel's vision of the new age, God says of his people, "I will make a covenant of peace *(bᵉrîth shālôm)* with them; it shall be an everlasting covenant" (37:26; cf. 16:60; 34:25). The assurance of God's presence and the covenant formula of Lev 26:11-12 are then repeated in this eschatological context: "My dwelling shall be with them; and I will be their God, and they shall be my people" (Ezek 37:27; cf. 11:20; 36:28).

Similarly in 2 Isaiah God promises his people, "I will make with you an everlasting covenant" (Isa 55:3; 61:8; cf. 54:9-10). Israel is to be "a covenant to the people" (42:6; 49:8).

It is Jeremiah, however, who gives classic expression to this expectation by speaking explicitly of a "*new* covenant" in 31:31-34, part of the "Book of Comfort" (Jer 30–31; cf. also 32:38-40; see B. W. Anderson 1969a: 229-38; von Rad 1965: 212-17; Dumbrell 1985: 86-95). "The new community he anticipates is not to be derived from the old shattered one. It depends only and singularly on a new move from God" (Brueggemann 1994: 47). "The days are surely coming, says the LORD, when I will make a new covenant with the house of Israel and the house of Judah. It will not be like the covenant that I made with their ancestors when I took them by the hand to bring them out of the land of Egypt — a covenant that they broke, though I was their husband, says the LORD" (Jer 31:31-32). According to Jeremiah, the Sinai covenant, which has been broken by Israel, will be replaced by a new kind of covenant that will have three main characteristics.

a. An Inward Torah

In contrast to the law that was given at Sinai and inscribed on tablets of stone (Exod 31:18), God promises that under the new covenant, "I will put my law within them, and I will write it on their hearts" (Jer 31:33). In the Shema Israel is commanded to "love the LORD your God with all your heart," and this is followed by the command to "keep these words that I am commanding you today in your heart" (Deut 6:5-6; cf. 10:16; 11:18). But again and again the people of Israel failed to keep the words of the Torah in their hearts. It is the awareness of this that leads the psalmist to pray:

> Create in me a clean heart, O God,
>   and put a new and right spirit within me. (Ps 51:10)

Under the promised new covenant, God does not call for greater efforts in obeying the Torah; he promises God's people a clean heart and a new and right spirit.

b. Universal Knowledge of God

The new covenant will also be marked by a knowledge of God on the part of all his people: "No longer shall they teach one another, or say to each other, 'Know the LORD,' for they shall all know me, from the least of them to the greatest" (Jer 31:34). No doubt in the original historical setting there was here "a veiled but unmistakable reference to the shortcomings of those who had previously been charged with transmitting the Mosaic law to the people" (Swetnam 1974: 112-13; cf. Jeremiah's complaint in Jer 8:7-9). But in the new age God's people will not only know his Torah, they will know *(yādhaʿ)* God himself; i.e., they will enter into a close personal relationship with him.

c. Forgiveness of Sins

Since Israel's sin and disobedience have disrupted the original covenant relationship, a new covenant will be possible only when God forgives his people. "For I will forgive their iniquity, and remember their sin no more" (Jer 31:34; cf. also 32:40).

Both Jeremiah and Ezekiel frequently promise a new God/people relationship even when the term "covenant" is not specifically used; see Jer 24:7, 30:22, 31:1, 32:38; cf. also Zech 8:8. In Ezek 11:19-20 God promises: "I will give them one [or, a new] heart, and put a new spirit within them; I will remove the heart of stone from their flesh and give them a heart of flesh, so that they may follow my statutes and keep my ordinances and obey them. Then they shall be my people, and I will be their God" (cf. 36:26-28). These passages echo Jeremiah's "law in the heart" theme, and conclude with the familiar covenant formula.

Thus, as Eichrodt (1961) puts it, in Jeremiah, Ezekiel, and 2 Isaiah the covenant relationship "has become a description of the great good lying in the future, and the Sinai covenant is for them but the shadow cast by the coming consummation" (63).

11-2.4. GOD AND PEOPLE

The OT expresses in a variety of ways the promise that the broken relationship between God and people will be restored. The theme of Hos 1–3 is the future reconciliation of the estranged husband (the LORD) and wife (Israel). Israel's adulterous relationship with the Baals will come to an end and "husband and wife" will be reconciled (2:16-20). The judgment that declared Israel "Lo-ammi" (Not My People) will be reversed,

and I will say to Lo-ammi,
"You are my people";
and he will say, "You are my God." (2:23; cf. 11:8-9)

This promise is placed in the context of a new covenant with the beasts and birds of the created order (2:18), a theme echoed in Ezek 34:25 (cf. 2-2.4a and b). Jer 31:20 pictures the wayward son (Ephraim) being reconciled with his loving and forgiving parent.

11-2.5. UNITY AND DIVERSITY

The various catastrophes that overtook God's people led partly to their dispersion outside the Holy Land, and within the Land to the division of the kingdom and the fall of the North. Part of the promise of a new order is the prophecy of *the restoration of the unity of God's people*. This takes two forms:

a. The Ingathering of Israel

In the new age all God's scattered people will be gathered together and their unity restored (cf. Brueggemann 1997: 442-44). They will be brought back from east, west, north, and south (Isa 43:5-6; cf. Ps 107:3). Isa 49:8-13 envisages the ingathering of God's people, probably from both Egypt and Babylon (see commentaries):

> Lo, these shall come from far away,
>> and lo, these from the north and from the west,
>> and these from the land of Syene. (v. 12)

11:1-16 foresees a similar ingathering brought about by a new exodus. Ezek 34 expresses the same hope by means of an extended allegory: God who is the true shepherd will recover his scattered sheep (cf. Mic 2:12). In Ezek 36:24 God declares, "I will take you from the nations, and gather you from all the countries, and bring you into your own land."

b. The Reunion of North and South

The original unity of the twelve-tribe people of God, torn by the defection and defeat of the North, will be restored (see Scobie 1976: 90-93). While Jeremiah does not overlook the sins of the North, he speaks of God's continuing care for her (3:12). The "Book of Comfort" (Jer 30–31) assures the North of God's love (31:2-6) and promises the restoration of the northern tribes. It is with Judah (the South) and Israel (the North) jointly that God will enter into the new covenant (31:31). "The imposition of the New Covenant will mean the healing of the breaches long since existing between the two kingdoms. It will give expression to the prophetic conviction that there can only be, and has only ever been, one unified people of God" (Dumbrell 1985: 89; cf. B. W. Anderson 1969a: 238).

Ezekiel proclaims the same promise with a vivid instance of prophetic symbolism that follows the vision of the valley of dry bones. In the oracle of the two sticks (37:15-23), the reunion of God's people, Judah and Joseph (= North), is symbolized. The prophet is told to take two sticks, marking one "For Judah, and the Israelites associated with it" (i.e., the South) and the other "For Joseph (the stick of Ephraim) and all the house of Israel associated with it" (i.e., the North). He is told to "join them together into one stick, so that they may become one in your hand" (vv. 15-17). In the accompanying oracle God declares, "I will take the people of Israel from the nations among which they have gone. . . . I will make them one nation in the land" (vv. 21-22). In Ezekiel's vision of a restored land, all twelve tribes will be involved and each will receive a new and equal allotment of territory (47:15–48:35). The prophecies of Jeremiah and Ezekiel are echoed in Zech 10:6-12 (though Zech 11:4-14 represents a puzzling reversal of the prophecy).

New Testament: Fulfillment

11-3. THE NEW ISRAEL

The Bible is concerned throughout with the relationship between God and people. That relationship continues in the NT with the story of the origins and early development of the Christian church (see 3-3.2c). With the birth of Christ God comes to his people Israel in a new way and fulfills the promises made to Abraham and his descendants (Luke 1:54-55). The NT understanding of the church as "the people of God" is based even less than in the OT on the occurrence of the actual phrase. In 2 Cor 6:16 Paul quotes the OT covenant formula, "I will be their God, / and they shall be my people *(laos)*," and applies it to the church. In Rom 9:25-26 he sees Hosea's prophecy of the restoration of "my people" (Hos 2:23) as fulfilled in the church (see also Rom 15:10; cf. Worgul 1982: 24-25). Only in 1 Pet 2:10 is the Christian community directly told, "now you are God's people." The church as the continuation of the people of God and as the new Israel, however, is a central reality of the NT. Christ fulfills God's purposes in *the historical order* by incorporating believers into the new Israel. Christ fulfills God's purposes in *the created order* by opening Israel to all humankind and by incorporating believers into the new humanity.

11-3.1. I WILL BUILD MY CHURCH

a. Church and Synagogue

Matthew's Gospel has been called "the Gospel of the church" because it has a major interest in the community that continues after Jesus' death. A canonical BT will find it significant that it was this Gospel that was given first place in the canon of the NT. In a key passage in the Gospel, Peter says to Jesus, "You are the Messiah, the Son of the living God," and Jesus, as part of his response, declares, "You are Peter, and on this rock *I will build my church,* and the gates of Hades will not prevail against it" (16:16-18; see 15-3.2a.ii). The word translated "church" is *ekklēsia* (see G. Johnston 1943: 35-45). In Greek this means an assembly, especially "a regularly summoned political body" (Arndt and Gingrich 1957: 240), and it is used in this sense in Acts 19:32, 39, 41. In Acts 7:38 and Heb 2:12 (quoting Ps 22:22) it is used of the congregation of Israel in the OT. But overwhelmingly it is the word used to refer to the early Christian community, most frequently in the sense of a church as a local congregation (e.g., Matt 18:17; Acts 5:11; Phil 4:15), such as "the church of God that is in Corinth" (1 Cor 1:2) or "the churches [plural] of Judea" (Gal 1:22), but also in the sense of the one universal church to which all believers belong (e.g., Matt 16:18; Acts 9:31; 1 Cor 12:28; Eph

1:22). Thus the one universal church is present and manifest in each local community (cf. Schlier 1968: 205-6).

Although there are only one or two direct references in the NT to the congregation of Israel in the OT, the adoption of the term *ekklēsia*, used in the LXX to translate the Hebrew *qāhāl* (cf. above, 11-1.1), strongly suggests that the church saw itself as the people of God in continuity with "the congregation in the wilderness" (Acts 7:38; cf. Caird 1994: 214; contra J. Y. Campbell 1948; Marshall 1973: 363). The term *ekklēsia* is used "with the deliberate intent to identify the church as the people of God, continuous with the faithful people of God in pre-Pentecost and Old Testament times" (Bender 1962: 5). The choice of *ekklēsia* rather than *synagōgē* (generally used to translate *'ēdhāh*) is readily explained by the desire of the church to distance itself from the Jewish "synagogue," the term *synagōgē* being in general use for local Jewish assemblies or the building in which they met (see Marshall, 363). The exception that proves the rule is the use of *synagōgē* in Jas 2:2 either for a Jewish synagogue that Jewish Christians continued to attend or for a local Christian assembly that was content, for whatever reason, to retain the Jewish terminology.

b. Did Jesus Intend to Found a Church?

In the NT the church is frequently referred to as "the church of God" (1 Cor 1:2; Acts 20:28; etc.), but Paul can also refer to "all the churches of Christ" (Rom 16:16). While it is God who brought the church into being, this is inseparably linked with the Christ event. Critical scholars, however, have frequently questioned whether Jesus himself ever intended to found a church. While BT is concerned primarily with the canonical text, the link between the church and Christ is of profound theological significance, and thus the historical question cannot be set aside. Much depends, of course, on what is meant by the term "church." If it conjures up pictures of the Crusades or the Inquisition, of a hierarchical institution or a high-powered organization, then no one is going to argue that the church goes back to the historical Jesus. However, historically it can be argued that if the question really is, Did Jesus foresee and intend that a community begun by him should continue after his death? then the answer is a decisive yes (see Martin 1979: 17-21).

i. Jesus and the Ecclesia

Doubts have been expressed because only two passages in the Gospels credit Jesus with using the term *ekklēsia:* Matt 16:18, quoted above, and Matt 18:17. Despite doubts, a strong case can in fact be made for the historicity of these sayings: both passages have strong Semitic features, and *ekklēsia* could represent an original *qāhāl,* or else the Aramaic word *kᵉnîshtā'*. Nevertheless, the view that the church goes back to the historical Jesus in no way stands or falls on the historicity of these two texts, but is much more broadly based. Important though the term *ekklēsia* is, the early Christian community can be referred to in the NT in many different ways (see further, 11-3.4).

ii. Jesus and the Eschaton

Another frequent objection is that Jesus could not have foreseen or made any provision for the church because of his belief in the imminent end of all things. We have already pointed out that the Gospels in their canonical form do not assert this, and argued that while Jesus made certain prophetic predictions regarding the relatively near future, he declined to speculate on the time of the final consummation (see 2-4.5).

iii. Jesus and the People of God

On the positive side, the Gospels clearly portray Jesus directing his mission to God's people Israel. Jeremias (1971) goes so far as to say that "the *only* significance of the whole of Jesus' activity is to gather the eschatological people of God" (170). Matthew in particular shows Jesus' concern for "the lost sheep of the house of Israel" (10:6; 15:24). Jesus' intention was not to create a narrow, particularist sect within Judaism. To the very end he appealed to the nation as a whole, as his last journey to Jerusalem (as depicted in the Synoptics) clearly shows. Nevertheless, the component of judgment in his message, and the growing opposition he faced, made it clear that not all would respond (see B. F. Meyer 1965). The Gospels picture a *community* of "disciples *(mathētai)*" forming around Jesus, with Jesus in a position of leadership (cf. T. W. Manson 1950a: 3-7). Thus, "when Israel *as a whole* did not accept Jesus' message, the circle of his disciples acquired a new function. It received the task of representing *symbolically* what really should have taken place in Israel as a whole: complete dedication to the Gospel of the reign of God, radical conversion to a new way of life, and a gathering unto a community of brothers and sisters" (Lohfink 1984: 34). From this broad and loosely defined group of disciples Jesus "appointed *twelve,* whom he also named apostles, to be with him, and to be sent out to proclaim the message, and to have authority to cast out demons" (Mark 3:14-15//Luke 6:13). The number twelve is clearly intended to recall the twelve patriarchs and the twelve tribes that constituted God's people Israel. By this *"symbolic prophetic action"* (Lohfink, 10) we see Jesus creating the nucleus and the leadership of a renewed Israel (cf. Matt 10; Mark 6:7-13; Luke 9:1-6). "When Jesus chose the Twelve, their number implied that they represented the faithful remnant of the old Israel who would also be the foundation of the new" (Bruce 1969: 62); cf. Luke 12:32, where, by calling his disciples a "little flock," Jesus is designating them as the faithful remnant of Israel. Jesus spent much of his time teaching and training the Twelve, and it was at his last supper with them, anticipating his own imminent death, that he inaugurated the eschatological new covenant (1 Cor 11:25; see 11-3.3). Hence "there was a continuity in personnel between Jesus' disciples before his death and those who bore witness to him after the resurrection" (D. J. Harrington 1980: 28).

iv. Jesus' Ethical Teaching

Jesus taught an ethic for the people of God that was not an *Interimsethik* designed for a brief interval before the end, but rather a set of guidelines for daily living that assume the continuation of life here on earth and the continuation of a community of his followers.

Granted that the church does go back to Jesus, the question has often been raised as to when precisely it came into being (cf. T. W. Manson 1950a: 1; R. Smith 1952: 21-22). Was it with the call of the first disciples, who formed the nucleus of the new Israel? Was it with Peter's confession at Caesarea Philippi, which can be seen as the origin of a believing, confessing community? Was it at the Last Supper when Jesus inaugurated the new covenant? Was it with Jesus' death and resurrection? Or was it with the giving of the Spirit on the Day of Pentecost?

There is of course truth in all these suggestions. The church is firmly anchored in the ministry of the historical Jesus. Yet the church as an ongoing community does not really come into existence until the completion of the Christ event. "Before there could be a 'Messianic' community Jesus the suffering Messiah had first to die"; it was only after Jesus' death and resurrection, and the giving of the Spirit at Pentecost, that the disciples "became the Church *through the baptism of the Spirit*" (G. Johnston 1943: 56; cf. D. J. Harrington 1980: 27). Acts, the Epistles, and Revelation all testify to the fact that the church is the "community of the Spirit" (Elwell 1988a: 459; for the role of the Spirit in the church, see 5-3). It is the completion of the Christ event with the giving of the Spirit that inaugurates the new age and brings into being the eschatological community of the church.

11-3.2. A NEW PEOPLE

Through the Christ event God brings a renewed Israel into being, a community that stands in continuity with the Israel of the OT but is also new insofar as it fulfills the promises for a new people of God in the new age.

a. The New Israel

Historically the Christ event brought into existence a new community, the Christian church. Theologically that community is presented in the NT as the fulfillment of the promises of a new Israel (11-2). It is "Israel" insofar as it stands in continuity with the OT people of God; it is "new" insofar as it is the eschatological community, the community of the new age that has now dawned, the nucleus of a new humanity (Eph 2:15).

Christ as the Son of Man is the inclusive representative of God's people (7-3.3a). In his death and resurrection, Israel dies and rises again to new life. With the giving of the Spirit at Pentecost the dry bones are brought back to life (above, 11-2.2b; cf. 5-3.3b).

b. Election and Predestination

Like Israel in the OT, the church in the NT is conscious of being a chosen people. Christians are said to be "called" (*kaleō* = "call"; *klētos* = "one who is called") by God (e.g., Rom 1:7; Eph 4:1; 1 Pet 5:10) and "chosen" (*eklegomai* = "choose"; *eklektos* = "one who is chosen") by him (e.g., Rom 11:5; 1 Pet 2:9). 2 Pet 1:10 combines the two terms by counseling its readers to "confirm your call and election." Another frequent term for believers is "saints" *(hagioi)*, i.e., holy ones, a people set apart in the service of God (e.g., Rom 1:7; Heb 13:24), a term that has strong ethical implications (see 18-3.1a). By adopting this self-designation, "the church understood itself to be the sacred people of God's possession, a people with a pattern for life which differed from that of the world" (Lohfink 1984: 131). The promises of a future redemption (*lutrōsis* = "redemption"; *lutroō* = "redeem") of God's people (above, 11-2.2) have been fulfilled (Rom 3:24; 1 Cor 1:30; Gal 4:5). Just as God in his grace redeemed Israel through the exodus event, so the new Israel is redeemed by the Christ event (Bauer 1981b: 740), especially by the death of Christ (Mark 10:45; Eph 1:7; Heb 9:15; 1 Pet 1:18-19; see further, 9-3.4a). It is Christ who "gave himself for us that he might redeem us from all iniquity and purify for himself a people of his own" (Titus 2:14; cf. Ps 130:8).

Even more so than in the OT, the emphasis is very consciously on election by grace. The initiative lies entirely with God, who acts through Christ. "You did not choose me," Jesus tells his disciples, "but I chose you" (John 15:16). "In both the Old and New Testament idea of the people of God, the essential is that God chooses and creates his people, and that they become his people by responding to his gracious acts" (Bender 1962: 14). As in the OT (see 11-1.2a), election is in no way based on merit; as Paul puts it, "God chose what is weak in the world to shame the strong; God chose what is low and despised in the world, things that are not, to reduce to nothing things that are" (1 Cor 1:27-28).

The divine initiative is stressed by speaking not just of election but also of predestination: God "chose us in Christ before the foundation of the world to be holy and blameless before him in love" (Eph 1:4). "Those whom he [God] foreknew he also predestined [*proorizō* = 'decide upon beforehand, predestine'] to be conformed to the image of his Son . . . and those whom he predestined he also called" (Rom 8:29-30). While it is primarily the church that is chosen and predestined, this language can also be used of individuals: Paul (echoing Jeremiah) can assert that God set him apart before birth (Gal 1:15-16; cf. Jer 1:5). Predestination emphasizes even more than election that salvation depends entirely on grace — on what God does, prior to and apart from anything human beings can do. The Pauline language makes it difficult to explain predestination simply by saying that God foreknows those who will accept the gospel and it is these who are preordained to salvation (contra Cronk 1982: 205).

Talk of predestination raises two problems. Firstly, if belief in Christ is predestined, what place is there for human choice? Secondly, if some are predestined to believe in Christ, does it follow that others are predestined not to believe ("double predestination")?

While the NT asserts that believers are predestined, both Acts and the Epistles make it abundantly clear that the gospel is a message that is proclaimed, and that people who hear the message choose either to receive it or reject it (see, e.g., the varied reactions to Paul's sermon in Athens in Acts 17:32-34). Within one chapter of making his strongest statements on divine election (Rom 8), Paul speaks of the proclamation of the word of faith, which some believe and obey and some do not (Rom 10). In other words, the NT in general and Paul in particular assert *both* divine predestination *and* human responsibility (cf. Caird 1957: 324), and leave the paradox unresolved.

Advocates of "double predestination" find their chief proof texts in Rom 9. If God chooses some, it must mean he does not choose others. "The radiance of predestining grace casts a shadow of rejection" (Caird 1957: 325). Thus Isaac is chosen, not Ishmael; and Jacob, not Esau (9:7, 13). Paul defends the right of a sovereign God to make such choices, and he illustrates this by the analogy of the potter and the clay (9:20-24). The potter has every right to make out of the same lump of clay "one object for special use and another for ordinary use" (v. 21). It is important to note, however, that in Rom 9–11 Paul is discussing God's choice of a *people* to serve him. In the OT God chose the descendants of Jacob/Israel to be his servant people; this does not mean he ceased to care for Ishmael or Esau (see Gen 21:15-21; 36:31-43). Now God has chosen a new people from both Jews and Gentiles (Rom 9:24). This observation puts Paul's remarks in perspective but does not entirely resolve the problem. Individuals also decide for or against the gospel, and if believers are at the same time predestined to believe, the implication is that nonbelievers are predestined not to believe. This is both a paradox and a mystery beyond human understanding; at the conclusion of his discussion Paul appropriately exclaims, "O the depth of the riches and wisdom and knowledge of God! How unsearchable are his judgments and how inscrutable his ways!" (11:33).

There remains a tension between election and predestination on the one hand and free will on the other, but it is not a tension that the NT discusses in any philosophical way. It is content to affirm the paradox of believers who decide for the gospel yet who come to recognize that it is God who has chosen them long before they reacted in any way.

c. The Church and Israel

The church is the new people of God because it has been brought into existence by God's unique and decisive action in the Christ event; but it is also in continuity with the Israel of OT times. The question of the precise relationship between the church and Israel is a difficult and delicate one. When Paul asks God's peace and mercy "upon the Israel of God" (Gal 6:16), the traditional interpretation has been that this refers to the *church,* which has *replaced* the Jewish people as "Israel," the people of God.

In favor of such a view, the NT clearly proclaims that God's eschatological promises to his people (set out in 11-2 above) have been fulfilled. The church is the community of the new covenant (below, 11-3.3). The prerogatives of Israel are now the prerogatives of the church, as in 1 Pet 2:9-10 where Christians are told, "You are a chosen race, a royal priesthood, a holy nation," quoting Exod 19:6. With the Christ event, "Israel" is radically redefined insofar as now is the time for the eschatological ingathering of the Gentiles (see more fully, 12-3). Membership of the new Israel is no longer based on ethnicity but on faith: "New members come through being elected by God and confessing their faith in him, not through birth. The New Israel is not the physical seed of Abraham . . . but a community of those who have experienced God's saving act in Christ" (Huffmon 1969: 74). As Paul puts it in Gal 3:7, it is "those who believe," i.e., those who respond in faith to God's grace in Christ, who "are the descendants of Abraham" (cf. 3:29; Rom 4:16-18). The NT already witnesses to the growing separation of Jewish and Christian communities (e.g., 2 Cor 11:24; Gal 1:13; 3:7; 1 Thess 2:14; on the term "the Jews" in John, see 4-3.2a). This view is reinforced by texts which suggest that God has turned from ethnic Israel to the Gentiles (Acts 28:28), and thus called into being a new people that replaces the old Israel (Matt 21:43 and //s).

Later Christian thought held the Jewish people as a whole responsible for Jesus' death, citing especially the words used by the crowd to pressure Pilate into passing the death sentence: "His blood be on us and on our children!" (Matt 27:25). The destruction of the temple and of the city of Jerusalem, foretold by Jesus (see 14-3.1a; 13-3.4b) and carried out by the Romans in A.D. 70, has traditionally been seen by Christians not simply as a divine judgment on the Jewish people, but as a sign of their final rejection as the people of God.

It is far from clear, however, that in portraying the church as the people of God the NT also asserts God's final judgment and rejection of the Jewish people. It is doubtful if "Israel" in Gal 6:16 refers without remainder to the church (on problems of translation and interpretation, see commentaries and P. Richardson 1969: 74-84; Shaw 1990: 189-90). Careful study suggests that it was not until the middle of the second century that Christians applied the term "Israel" specifically and exclusively to themselves (see Richardson, 9). The passion narratives as a whole make it clear that the responsibility for Jesus' death lay partly with Pilate and partly with a small group of Jewish leaders, *not* with the people at large. Jesus no doubt saw the coming destruction of the temple and the city of Jerusalem as a divine judgment, but there is nothing to indicate that he saw these as representing a final rejection of the Jewish people, any more than Jeremiah's prophecy of the destruction of the temple and city in the sixth century B.C. represented a final judgment. In the NT there is a strong emphasis on the *continuity* of the people of God. The church does not *replace* the Israel of OT times; it *is* Israel, renewed and reconstituted as the eschatological people of God. Believers in Christ are joined with the heroes and heroines of faith from OT times (Heb 11).

The most thorough and searching discussion of the relationship between the church and Israel is found in Rom 9–11 (see Shaw 1990: 192-95). In this passage Paul explores a number of approaches to what for him is obviously a heart-wrenching problem. Recalling the promises of God in the OT that even if his people as a whole do not respond there will always be a *remnant* who remain faithful, Paul quotes Isaiah's promise that "a remnant of them will return" (Rom 9:27 = Isa 10:22; cf. Rom 9:29 = Isa 1:9), and also cites the case of Elijah and the seven thousand who did not bow the knee to Baal (Rom 11:2-4; cf. above, 11-2.2a). "So too at the present time," he maintains, "there is a remnant, chosen by grace" (11:5). Since Israel as a whole has not responded to the Christ event, God chooses for the time being to work through the church that constitutes the faithful remnant.

The understanding of the church as the remnant would be appropriate in the earliest days of the church when all the first Christians were Jews. It was not as appropriate as soon as Gentiles began to enter the church. Paul takes account of this when he goes on to employ an agricultural metaphor in the allegory of the olive tree (11:17-24). Israel is an olive tree; Gentile believers are shoots that have been grafted on to the tree; Jews who do not believe in Christ are branches that have been broken off (though Paul allows the possibility that they may be grafted in again). On the one hand this illustration stresses the continuity of the church with Israel, but on the other hand it excludes nonbelieving Jews from God's people. Paul, however, also insists that God has not rejected his ancient people (11:1-2), and he resists what might appear to be the logical conclusion of the olive tree illustration, and goes on to assert his belief that ultimately "all Israel will be saved" (11:26). Thus in Rom 9–11 Paul insists "that Israel, even in the rejection of the Gospel, is beloved of God and that her survival vis-à-vis the Church is somehow — beyond human understanding — caught up in the mystery of divine election" (B. W. Anderson 1969a: 226).

d. Take Heed

Election gives no grounds for complacency. Repeated ethical admonitions and warnings throughout the NT make it clear that membership in God's people, the church, is no automatic guarantee of salvation. It is possible to fall from grace, and believers are not exempt from God's judgment any more than were the Israelites of OT times who rebelled against God and persistently broke his laws.

Thus in 1 Cor 10:1-13 Paul does not hesitate to cite the precedent of the various judgments that fell on Israel in the wilderness (see above, 11-1.2c), and warns, "So if you think that you are standing, watch out that you do not fall" (v. 12). The principle is also illustrated by a specific case of immorality in 5:1-5. The unrepentant sinner is to be excommunicated, though there appears to be hope that such strict discipline may lead to the person being saved at the last day (see commentaries). The letters to the seven churches in Rev 2–3 afford another striking example. Membership in the Christian community is of no avail to those who deliberately rebel and disobey God: "Repent, and do the works you did at first. If not, I will come to you and remove your lampstand from its place" (2:5; cf. 2:16; 2:22-23; etc.).

11-3.3. THE NEW COVENANT

The word "covenant" *(diathēkē)* occurs only thirty-three times in the NT, as against almost three hundred times in the OT; statistics can be misleading, however, and the covenant is more important in the NT than these figures might suggest (cf. O. Becker 1975: 369). It does occur in a number of key passages.

a. The Institution of the Lord's Supper

In the words of institution of the Lord's Supper, Jesus sees his impending death as the sacrifice that inaugurates the new covenant promised by Jeremiah. In the version preserved in Matt 26:28//Mark 14:24 Jesus, as he takes the cup, says, "This is my blood of the covenant," clearly referring to the sacrifice that inaugurated the Sinai covenant in Exod 24:8. The version preserved in 1 Cor 11:25 and Luke 22:20 (the longer reading) speaks of "the new covenant in my blood," clearly echoing the Jer 31 promise of a new covenant (on the Lord's Supper, see more fully 14-3.5c). The Christ event, focused in Jesus' death on the cross, inaugurates the promised new covenant, a new relationship between God and people.

b. Covenant in Paul

While not a major theme in Paul, the apostle does see the Christians as the true inheritors of the covenant God made with Abraham (Gal 3:15-18). In 2 Cor 3:5-6 he echoes Jeremiah's vision of a new covenant written not on stone but on the heart when he declares that God has qualified Christians to be "ministers of a new covenant, not of letter but of spirit; for the letter kills, but the Spirit gives life" (see Bruce 1969: 54-55; Dumbrell 1985: 107-13; cf. also the reference to "two covenants" in Gal 4:24, on which see more fully 13-3.5a). And in Rom 11:26-27 he expresses the hope that Jews who presently do not accept Jesus as the Christ will eventually be included in the new covenant of Jer 31.

c. Covenant in Hebrews

The theology of the new covenant is most fully developed in Hebrews, which sees Jesus as "the guarantee of a better covenant" (7:22) and quotes the Jer 31:31-34 passage in full (Heb 8:8-12) as part of a discussion showing how the new covenant is better than the old and makes the old obsolete. As in the Last Supper tradition, the new covenant is linked with the sacrificial death of Christ, who is the mediator of the new covenant. The author drives home this point by playing on the double meaning of *diathēkē* in Greek: as well as translating the Hebrew *bᵉrîth*, it can also mean "testament" in the sense of a "last will and testament." Thus, just as "a will takes effect only at death" (9:17), so the new covenant takes effect only through the death of Christ (see Bruce 1969: 56-57).

These three key sets of references assert that in Christ "the covenant with Israel was fulfilled, transformed and transcended" (Cronk 1982: 80).

11-3.4. CHRIST AND PEOPLE

The new people of God is founded by Christ and bound to God in a new covenant relationship brought into being by Christ's sacrificial death. Christians are incorporated into Christ as the inclusive representative of the new Israel and of the new humanity. "To be in Christ is to be in the church, and to be in the church is to be united in Christ" (Bender 1962: 37). In a multitude of ways the NT expresses its understanding of the relationship between Christ and the church.

a. Images of the Church

The nature of the church is expressed in the NT in a rich variety of images. Minear, in his book *Images of the Church in the New Testament* (1960), finds no fewer than ninety-six "analogies" of the church.

One of the most significant images is that of *the family* (see Lohfink 1984: 39-44). This understanding of the church is grounded in the ministry of Jesus, who said, "Whoever does the will of my Father in heaven is my brother and sister and mother" (Matt 12:50). While disciples have to make sacrifices, perhaps even leaving their natural families, they gain a new family of "brothers and sisters, mothers and children" (Mark 10:28-30). Believers are "those of the family of faith *(tous oikeious tēs pisteōs)*" (Gal 6:10); they are children of God, their Father, and thus brothers and sisters of one another. "Brothers" *(adelphoi)* is in fact the most frequent designation of Christians in the NT; the term "sister" *(adelphē)* is also used, though less frequently (Rom 16:1; 1 Cor 7:15; Jas 2:15). Collectively the church can be spoken of as "the brotherhood" *(adelphotēs,* 1 Cor 6:5-6; 1 Pet 2:17; 5:9). Paul carries the analogy a step further in referring to Christ as "the first-born among many brethren" (Rom 8:29 RSV); he is the elder brother in the family of the church. Paul also uses family images in speaking of his own relationship to his churches: he dealt with the Thessalonians, he says, "like a father with his children" (1 Thess 2:11), and he regarded Timothy as a "son" (Phil 2:22).

Another image is that of *the temple of God:* "We are the temple of the living God," Paul tells the Corinthians (2 Cor 6:16). Under the new order God's presence and worship are no longer localized in the Jerusalem temple, but are located wherever the new community of the church is to be found (see more fully, 14-3.1b).

The OT marital metaphor is continued in the NT; unfaithful Israel is condemned by Jesus as "an evil and adulterous generation" (Matt 12:39; 16:4; Mark 8:38). But while in the OT the LORD was the husband and Israel the (often unfaithful) wife (11-1.4), in the NT *Christ* is the bridegroom (Mark 2:19; John 3:29), and the *church* is the bride (see Ortlund 1996: chap. 6). In Eph 5:22-31 Paul draws out an extended parallel between the love of husband and wife and Christ's love for the church. 2 Cor 11:2-3, however, strikes a note familiar from the OT: though promised in marriage "as a chaste virgin to Christ," the danger is of the church being led astray from "a sincere and pure devotion" to her husband, Christ.

b. The Body of Christ

Characteristic of Pauline theology is the understanding of the church as the body of Christ *(sōma christou).* The major exposition is found in 1 Cor 12:12-30;

Rom 12:4-8 represents a more condensed version. The origin of this concept, a question that has provoked much discussion, is not a direct concern of BT (see Barth 1958: 137-42; Käsemann 1971: 103; Worgul 1982: 25-26; Ziesler 1990: 59-60); even if Paul borrowed the illustration, what counts is what "the body of Christ" means in its canonical context. For Paul, the church is the body of Christ and all the individual members of the church constitute its members: "You are the body of Christ and individually members of it" (1 Cor 12:27). Individual believers are incorporated into the body through baptism and receive the gift of the Spirit (12:13). As so often, the main point of Paul's discussion is practical and pastoral. "It is noteworthy that most of Paul's discussions of the 'body of Christ' are found in the context of the discussion of divisions in the church and the need for unity" (Bender 1962: 37). The metaphor of the body and its members speaks of diversity within unity. As in a human body, so in the church; the various members have different functions, but all are necessary and all must work together for the common good. This is developed at some length in 12:14-26. Thus various members of the church have different functions, but none should vaunt themselves against the others (12:27-30; Rom 12:6-8). Implied rather than stated in the metaphor is an understanding of the church as continuing the work of Christ here on earth, the work that Christ carried out in his human body during his incarnate life (preaching, teaching, healing, and so on). "The name 'body of Christ' . . . describes the right of Christ to rule the church and to use it as his own instrument" (Barth, 146). Talk of the church as an "extension of the incarnation" has to proceed with caution, however, for the NT is only too aware of the faults and failings of the church.

The metaphor of the body and members is carried a stage further in Colossians and Ephesians. Unlike 1 Corinthians and Romans where Paul is addressing a local church, here it is the universal church Paul has in mind. Moreover, here the church is equated with the body of Christ (Col 1:24; Eph 5:30), but Christ is said to be the "head" of the body (Col 1:18; Eph 1:22-23; see Worgul 1982: 26-27). This defines more sharply the relationship between Christ and the church. Christ is in control: as the human body obeys the commands of the brain, so the church ought to live and act in conformity with the will of Christ.

c. "In Christ"

Paul frequently speaks of believers as being "in Christ" (Rom 12:5; 1 Cor 3:1; 2 Cor 5:17; Gal 3:28; etc.). In fact, the expression almost functions in place of the absent adjective and noun "Christian." Believers are "those who are in Christ Jesus" (Rom 8:1). The phrase points to a close personal relationship between the believer and Christ (see 17-3.4), but the context of many of the "in Christ" references shows that Paul is thinking just as much in corporate as in individualistic terms. "For Paul, this is not just an individual experience, a kind of mystical union between the believer and Christ. For in a real sense, to be 'in Christ' is at the same time to be in the church" (Elwell 1988a: 460). To be "in Christ" and to be a "member" of "the body of Christ" are thus very closely linked: "the two belong together in that they mutually interpret one another" (Käsemann 1971: 106).

d. Images of the Church in John's Gospel

The absence of the term *ekklēsia* from John's Gospel (it is found in 3 John 6, 9, 10) in no way indicates a lack of interest in the church in the broader sense (see Martin 1979: 86-96). In the Gospel Jesus speaks of the community of his disciples that will continue after his death in a number of vivid images. In the allegory of the Good Shepherd (10:1-18), Jesus uses sheep-shepherd imagery to talk of his relationship to his followers. The OT image of Israel as a vine (above, 11-1.4) is picked up in the allegory of the vine and the branches in 15:1-11; the branches all come from a common root, Christ, who is "the true vine," and they live and bear fruit only insofar as they "abide" in the vine. Jesus' purpose is to "gather into one the dispersed children of God" (11:52) and to draw all people to himself (12:32). In his farewell discourses (13:31–17:26), Jesus prepares his disciples to lead the community that will continue after his death.

11-3.5. UNITY AND DIVERSITY

According to John 17:21, Jesus, shortly before his death, prayed for his disciples, "that they may all be one." One would expect the *unity* of the new Israel, as a community bound together by a common allegiance to "one Lord, one faith, one baptism, one God and Father of all" (Eph 4:5-6), to be a given.

The NT does see the new community of the church, at least to some degree, as fulfilling the OT eschatological promises of the ingathering of Israel, the reunion of North and South, and the uniting of all humankind through the ingathering of the Gentiles. *All* believers are united in fellowship with God and with one another. But that is only one side of the picture. The evidence of Acts and the Epistles makes it clear that from the very beginning of the church, its ideal unity fell far short of being actualized.

a. The Ingathering of Israel

Jesus' mission was primarily one of reaching out to all sections of Israelite society to bring God's people together into God's kingdom. Historically Jesus' ministry was almost entirely confined to Palestine and to the Jewish people. According to Matt 10:5-6, he directed his disciples, during his lifetime, to follow his own example: "Go nowhere among the Gentiles, and enter no town of the Samaritans, but go rather to the lost sheep of the house of Israel." In Acts 2:5-11 the first Christian preaching was directed to an all-Jewish audience, many of them drawn from throughout the Diaspora. Paul, in his travels through the Diaspora, is depicted as going first to the local synagogue (13:14; 14:1; etc.). In these ways Jesus and his earliest followers sought to bring about the ingathering of God's own people (above, 11-2.5a) as the new age dawned.

b. The Reunion of North and South

The old division between North and South is symbolically overcome through the incorporation of Samaritans (who represented the northern tradition) into the new Israel.

Jesus' attitude to the Samaritans is strikingly different from that which prevailed in his day. Luke's Gospel highlights Jesus' favorable attitude in three passages: 9:51-56, where Jesus refuses to call down fire from heaven on a Samaritan village; 10:25-37, where a Samaritan is the hero of one of Jesus' most famous parables; and 17:11-19, where the one leper who returns to give thanks is a Samaritan. John's Gospel exhibits an even stronger interest in the Samaritans (historically this may indicate a link between the Johannine community and Samaria). John 4 depicts Jesus as visiting Samaria, conversing with a Samaritan woman, and declaring the word so that "many Samaritans . . . believed in him" (v. 39; cf. v. 41). In his acceptance of and mission to Samaritans, Jesus inaugurates the eschatological reunion of North and South.

In Acts the Christian movement is depicted as expanding in three stages as the gospel is proclaimed to (1) Jews, (2) Samaritans, and (3) Gentiles (see further, 12-3.3a). It is significant that when the Hellenists were forced to leave Jerusalem after the death of Stephen, the first place they made for was Samaria. Acts 8 recounts a mission (the first Christian mission in fact) to the Samaritans, led by Philip. The Christian acceptance of and mission to the Samaritans fulfill the OT promise of the eschatological reunion of North and South (above, 11-2.5b). Representatives of the old Judah and the old Israel are brought together in a new, reunited Israel.

c. One New Humanity

Not only does the church represent a reunited Israel, but through the incorporation of the Gentiles it represents a new humanity (Eph 2:15). For a fuller treatment, see 12-3.

d. The Meaning of Community

In the church believers are bound together in fellowship with God in Christ, and in fellowship with one another. Lohfink points to "togetherness" as a key characteristic of the Christian community by calling attention to the frequent use in the Epistles of the reciprocal pronoun *allēlōn,* meaning "one another." Believers are to "live in harmony with one another" (Rom 12:16), "have the same care for one another" (1 Cor 12:25), "bear one another's burdens" (Gal 6:2), etc. (see Lohfink 1984: 99-100, where twenty-three examples are cited!).

The meaning of Christian community is illuminated in particular by the frequent use in the NT of words from the *koinōn-* root (see Martin 1979: 34-45). The adjective *koinos* means "common" or "that which is shared," while the verb *koinōneō* means "to share or participate in." Particularly frequent is the noun *koinōnia,* meaning "sharing, fellowship, communion." The basic idea behind these words is that of sharing or having something in common (see Bender 1962: 44). This essential element of sharing within the Christian community depends entirely on the divine initiative: "it is not a random coming together of men because they share a common interest; it is the coming together of those whom God has called into *koinōnia* with Himself through His Son and in him with one another" (Panikulam 1979: 140). Believers are called to respond to that initiative, and that response is effected within them through the working of the Spirit (141).

Christians have *koinōnia,* fellowship or communion with God (1 John 1:6), through Christ (1 Cor 1:9; 1 John 1:3), in the Spirit (2 Cor 13:13; Phil 2:1). One way this is symbolized is through the Lord's Supper, where the "cup of blessing" is "a sharing" *(koinōnia)* in the body and blood of Christ (1 Cor 10:16); the common meal is one of communion with the risen Lord. Believers must be prepared also to share in the sufferings of Christ (Phil 3:10; 1 Pet 4:13).

The Christian community is marked by fellowship and sharing (1 John 1:3). Christians share God's grace (Phil 1:7), the gospel (1:5), their faith (Phlm 6; Titus 1:4), salvation (Jude 3), the divine nature (2 Pet 1:4), and the coming glory (1 Pet 5:1). They also share in the work of the gospel, and Paul can describe Titus as his "partner" *(koinōnos)* (2 Cor 8:23). Christian fellowship is symbolized by "the right hand of fellowship" (Gal 2:9), and by greeting one another "with a holy kiss *(en philēmati hagiō(i))*" (Rom 16:16; 1 Cor 16:20; 2 Cor 13:12; 1 Pet 5:14).

Christian *koinōnia* is not just something spiritual; it has to be expressed in concrete ways. Believers are expected to "share what you have" (Heb 13:16; cf. Rom 12:13; 1 Tim 6:18). The earliest community in Jerusalem was marked by a voluntary sharing of resources; "all who believed were together and had all things in common *(hapanta koina)*" (Acts 2:44). Some of Paul's churches "entered into partnership" with him (Phil 4:15 RSV), i.e., helped support him financially. Paul's great collection of money for the famine-stricken church in Jerusalem is referred to as a "contribution *(koinōnia)* for the poor among the saints at Jerusalem" (Rom 15:26 RSV).

The church is thus a caring and sharing community, a "life-sustaining fellowship" (Hanson 1986: 501), in which the members of the body of Christ receive their life from God, and comfort, encourage, and support one another.

e. No Divisions among You

While the NT has much to say about the *unity* of the church, it appears, paradoxically, that most of the appeals were occasioned by actual divisions and disunity within the early Christian communities. Thus the question of unity and disunity preoccupied Christians from the beginning (Schlier 1968: 193). As early as Acts 6 we hear of a division between Hebrews and Hellenists, a division that clearly reflected not just linguistic or organizational differences but also differing theological viewpoints (see Scobie 1976: 94-96). The question of the admission of the Gentiles produced major differences, including a confrontation between Paul and Peter (Gal 2:11-14), that were only partly resolved by the Jerusalem Council of Acts 15 (see 12-3.3). Many of the Pauline churches were wracked by divisions based on anything from a conflict of individual personalities (Phil 2:4) to cliques that clearly represented different interpretations of the faith (1 Cor 1:12). In the later epistles and Revelation, divisions were created by the activities of "false teachers." 1 John counters a group that denied the fundamental Christian belief in the incarnation, and that "went out from us" (2:19), thus initiating the first (but not the last!) recorded schism of the church.

In the NT the unity of the church is grounded in what God has done through Christ (see Schlier 1968: 194-200). By his sacrificial death Christ has reconciled human beings to God and to each other (cf. 9-3.4b), gathered the dispersed children of God into one (John 11:52), and broken down "the dividing wall" that separated Jews from Gentiles (Eph 2:14-16). In baptism believers are incorporated through the Spirit into the one body (1 Cor 12:13), the life of which is nourished by the Lord's Supper, in which "we who are many are one body, for we all partake of the one bread" (10:17); hence there can be only "one body and one Spirit" (Eph 4:4-5). Since the church is the body of Christ, it is unthinkable that it should be divided. "Has Christ been divided?" Paul cries passionately. "Was Paul crucified for you? Or were you baptized in the name of Paul?" (1 Cor 1:13). There can be only one gospel (Gal 1:6-7); when false teachers deny any basic component of that gospel, that unity is threatened.

New Testament: Consummation

11-4. THE TWELVE TRIBES OF ISRAEL

11-4.1. THE END OF THE STORY

It is difficult for modern readers whose thought is so conditioned by individualism to realize the extent to which the biblical vision of the end and goal of creation and history is envisaged in essentially corporate terms. The story line of the Bible concerns God's relationship with a people, and the end of this story is a vision of that people, embracing those of every race and nation together worshiping and praising God, the Lord of creation and of history.

On the relatively few occasions when Jesus refers to the world to come, he generally pictures it in corporate terms. "Many will come from east and west and will eat with Abraham and Isaac and Jacob in the kingdom of heaven" (Matt 8:11); in this vision God's people of the old and new orders will be united in the fellowship and joy of the new age. The community of the final consummation will still stand in continuity with God's people Israel: "When the Son of Man is seated on the throne of his glory, you who have followed me will also sit on twelve thrones, judging the twelve tribes of Israel" (Matt 19:28//Luke 22:28-30).

Paul's vision of the future is likewise strongly corporate in nature. Though God's people have been redeemed through the Christ event (above, 11-3.2b), in keeping with the already/not yet dialectic, redemption is still a future hope (Rom 8:23-24); at the present time the Holy Spirit is "the pledge of our inheritance toward redemption as God's own people" (Eph 1:14). According to 1 Thess 4:13-18, God's people — both the living and the dead — will participate together in the new existence.

The whole of Revelation presents a picture of heaven and of the final consummation described in strongly corporate terms. The vision of the 144,000 servants of God (7:4; 14:1), 12,000 from each of the twelve tribes of Israel (7:5-8), is in fact "a proleptic vision . . . of the redeemed church" (Talbert 1994: 60). The number 144,000 is not to be taken literally, since these people are identified with the "great multitude that no one could count" of 7:9; they are those who "have been redeemed from the earth" (14:3). In keeping with John's numerical symbolism, 12 signifies the people of God and 1,000 a large but indefinite number (144,000 = 12 × 12 × 1,000); what the vision means is that "the Church of history contains an indefinitely large number of Old Testament saints as well as countless Christians who have lived since the time of Christ" (Cronk 1982: 258).

11-4.2. MY PEOPLE

With the final consummation God's purpose in election is fulfilled, and God takes his people to himself (Rev 18:4). The unfaithfulness of God's people will finally be at an end (cf. 21:8), and the eschatological banquet that is also "the marriage supper of the Lamb" (19:9) will be celebrated, with God's faithful people finally recognized as "the bride, the wife of the Lamb" (21:9; see Ortlund 1996: 161-69).

11-4.3. THE COVENANT FULFILLED

The ultimate goal is a new order in which the promises of Lev 26:11-12 (cf. 11-1.3c) and Ezek 37:27 (cf. 11-2.3) will finally be fulfilled, when "the home of God is among mortals" and when, in terms of the old covenant formula,

> He will dwell with them;
> they will be his peoples,
> and God himself will be with them. (Rev 21:3)

11-4.4. GOD AND CHRIST AND PEOPLE

Other ways of expressing the relationship between God and people, and Christ and people, find their fulfillment in the vision of the final consummation. The parent-child relationship between God and people will be fully enjoyed: "Those who conquer will inherit these things, and I will be their God and they will be my children" (Rev 21:7).

11-4.5. UNITY AND DIVERSITY

It is only at the final consummation that all divisions and differences will be reconciled and God's people will find their true unity. Jews and Gentiles will partake together of the eschatological banquet (see 14-4.5b).

In John's vision of the final consummation, the holy city has twelve gates, three each on the north, south, east, and west sides (Rev 21:12-13). This echoes Ezekiel's vision (Ezek 48:30-34), but whereas for Ezekiel the gates are "exits," for John they symbolize "abundant access" (Talbert 1994: 101) to the city (cf. Rev 21:25). The new Jerusalem symbolizes the true Israel, incorporating believers who come from all points of the compass and from every land and nation, and who live in unity because all that is opposed to God is excluded from the city (see also 13-4.2).

11-5. THE COVENANT COMMUNITY: THEOLOGICAL REFLECTIONS

1. A full appreciation of the biblical understanding of the people of God is of the first importance for the Christian church, both as it looks back and assesses the twentieth century and as it moves forward into a new millennium. While many have been prepared to recognize the importance of "the people of God" for the OT (so much of which is clearly concerned with God's relationship to Israel), in the nineteenth and twentieth centuries the NT was frequently interpreted in a much more individualistic fashion (cf. Shaw 1990: 10). Evangelicals emphasized a personal and individual "decision for Christ," while liberals following Harnack saw Christianity as a matter "of God and the soul, of the soul and its God" (cf. Lohfink 1984: 1-5), or following Bultmann saw faith as bringing a new self-understanding to the individual. Opinion polls (at least in Europe and North America) reveal that many still claim to believe in God and even to accept the basics of the Christian faith without attending a church or being affiliated with an organized Christian body. Today there are more exponents than ever before of "Christianity without the church."

The closing decades of the twentieth century saw a growing disenchantment with the organized and institutional churches, many of the reasons for which are not hard to find. People may point to historical blots on the church's reputation such as the Crusades or the Inquisition, but more often they focus on contemporary failings, ranging from abuse of children in church homes to financial fraud by TV evangelists. Another standard criticism focuses on the disunity of the churches and sees Christianity, like other religions, as a divisive rather than a reconciling force (e.g., Roman Catholics versus Protestants in Northern Ireland). It was denominational rivalry on the mission field, especially during the great missionary expansion of the nineteenth century, that stimulated Christian cooperation and led, with the founding of the World Council of Churches in 1948, to the modern ecumenical movement. The second half of the twentieth century saw both the rise of this movement but then also its failure to maintain its original momentum and to resolve the deep-seated differences among churches. In the second half of the twentieth century also, the horrific results of anti-Semitism, especially following the Holocaust, raised with a new urgency the question of the relationship of the Christian church to the ongoing Jewish community. In the discussion of all these issues, BT ought to play a leading role.

2. Modern BT has shown that for *both* OT *and* NT "the people of God" is a theme of the first importance. Sociologically, that people takes many forms in the Bible, ranging from the seminomadic tribes of the patriarchal period all the way to the small persecuted communities of the book of Revelation. Nevertheless, a strong continuity runs through Scripture: God calls not merely individuals but a people to serve him. In the NT the preaching of the gospel does call for

individual decision and faith, yet also and equally for the incorporation of the believer into the Christian community, the body of Christ (cf. Martin 1979: 14-17). Modern individualism seriously distorts the biblical perspective. In such a view "the church is ultimately only a gathered group of saved individuals, an organizational reunion of the regenerate, a spiritual fellowship in human hearts, and inherently separate from all external forms. 'Being saved' is fundamentally differentiated from the communal. This hyper-individualistic concept of salvation does not fit well with biblical perspectives and leads to serious theological, ecclesial, and ethical distortions" (M. E. Tate 1994: 475). Against such distortions it is essential to emphasize that for the NT the idea of an individual Christian, or of a person who becomes a Christian prior to or apart from belonging to the church, is unthinkable; there is no place in the NT for a doctrine of "solitary salvation" (Cronk 1982: 215; cf. Lohfink 1984: 26-28).

Most human institutions are based on either common inherited characteristics such as race or language or on common interests. The church is radically different from either type. In the OT God does choose to work through one particular people, the Israelites, but his purpose always was to use them as his servant in mediating salvation to all humankind. With the dawning of the new age in the Christ event, God's people is opened up to all human beings without any preconditions (see further, chap. 12).

The NT speaks of the church using a rich diversity of images (see above, 11-3.4). One of the most significant and all-encompassing is that of the family. Martin (1979) is certainly being true to the NT when he argues that "the church at its best reflects all that is noblest and most worthwhile in human family life: attitudes of caring and mutual regard; understanding of needs, whether physical or of the spirit; and above all the sense of 'belonging' to a social unit in which we find acceptance without pretence or make-believe" (124).

The biblical portrait of the people of God underlines that the covenant community does not consist of its leadership (priesthood/clergy), nor of its institutional structure, nor of buildings. It consists of a *community* called by God that seeks to serve him in response to that call. The twentieth century saw a renewed emphasis on the *laity,* and it should be remembered that "laity" comes from *laos,* meaning (the whole) people (of God). The recognition of "the people of God" as a central theme of BT "captures the historical, 'on-the-move' character of the church and rescues it from lifeless and static thinking" (D. J. Harrington 1980: 1). As chapter 13 will show, there is a constant tension in Scripture between the rootedness of God's people in the Land and their call to be a pilgrim people. The view that comes to dominate in the NT is that of God's people as "sojourners and pilgrims" (see 13-3.3b). The title of Käsemann's 1984 study of the Epistle to the Hebrews could well be applied to God's people through much of Scripture: they are *The Wandering People of God* (cf. also Shaw 1990: 210-14).

3. The church is a community called into existence purely by the grace of

God. Election by grace is spelled out again and again in both OT and NT. God's people come into existence solely by divine initiative. The church as a community, and individuals as part of that community, are chosen by God. There is much to be said for Hanson's view that "perhaps the single most important source of renewal for contemporary communities of faith lies in the rediscovery of their identity as 'the people called'" (1986: 467).

Predestination emphasizes that membership in the people of God and the body of Christ is due not to any merit or initiative on the part of those concerned but solely to God's grace in Christ. For the Christian, belief in predestination tends to be retroactive. One may go through years of searching and doubt, one may agonize over the decision whether or not to respond to the gospel, but *after* coming to faith one may look back and conclude that this was God's purpose all along. Nevertheless, the fact that the NT asserts *both* divine election/rejection *and* human choice remains a paradox. Problems arise in later theology when one or the other of the poles of the paradox is denied.

4. Critics of the church who point to its many failings will find in Scripture much that is familiar. The Bible is nothing if not realistic, and it amply documents the unfaithfulness of God's people in OT times. The same holds true for the NT. If Acts tends to accentuate the positive and perhaps even to some degree idealize the very early church, the Epistles (including the letters to the seven churches in Revelation) more than compensate for that with their documentation of the many failings of the early Christian communities.

A BT of the church must reject all forms of ecclesiastical complacency and triumphalism. God's people are not exempt from God's judgment, as Scripture amply demonstrates, and membership in the covenant community is no automatic guarantee of salvation (cf. above, 11-1.2c and 11-3.2d).

5. One of the greatest failings of the church is its lack of unity. Just as ideally Israel was one people but in practice was more often than not divided (11-1.5), so in the NT the huge potential of the church to heal ancient wounds (11-2.5b; 11-3.5b) and to unite all people into one new humanity in Christ (11-3.5c) is far from being realized in practice. The divisions of the church within the NT were amplified in later church history with divisions first between East and West, then in the West between Protestantism and Roman Catholicism, and finally within Protestantism into a multitude of denominations and sects.

The biblical appeal for unity still needs to be heard. Basically the NT teaches that the church is and only can be one; hence the appeal to churches (plural) is essentially: "Become what you are," i.e., one people of God. Scripture also recognizes, however, the importance of recognizing *diversity* within *unity*; this is one of the main points, for example, of the metaphor of the one body and the many members. Moreover, in the Bible unity is not grounded in a hierarchy nor in institutional uniformity; Solomon's bureaucratic centralization of authority merely contributed to the schism between north and south. The books of the NT suggest a variety of Christian communities — Pauline,

Petrine, Johannine, and so on — held together not by an overall organizational structure but by a common acceptance of "one Lord, one faith, one baptism."

With some exceptions, movements to bring about organic union of churches across denominational lines have not been very successful, particularly in the late twentieth century. Indeed, the demand for organizational unity sometimes leads to further divisions. On the other hand, transdenominational organizations such as the Bible societies and Christian groups bringing aid to refugees and victims of natural disasters have proved remarkably successful in achieving their (admittedly limited) aims. A model that seeks to bring churches together in some kind of loose federation might not only be more practical and realistic, but also more in keeping with the biblical norm.

6. The relationship between Israel, the people of God in the OT, and the church, the people of God in the NT, is an important topic for BT, but also a difficult and delicate one. In the light of the treatment of Jews by Christians over the centuries, and especially in the light of the Holocaust, this theme became a pressing but also controversial issue in the latter part of the twentieth century.

Jesus, his apostles, and the very earliest members of the church were all Jews. With the success of the Gentile mission, however, and the failure of the majority of Jews to accept the Christian mission, the composition of the church changed. By the second century the church was composed overwhelmingly of persons of Gentile background, and the church began to see itself as "Israel," and as having totally displaced the Jews as the people of God.

The NT, however, as we have seen (11-3.2), emphasizes the *continuity* of Israel. In Paul's analogy the church is still the original olive tree, though with some branches added and some removed. Certainly the people of God in OT times belong in God's kingdom (Matt 8:11; Heb 11), and while only a remnant continue in the eschatological Israel, Paul's hope is that ultimately "all Israel will be saved" (Rom 11:26). This suggests that in some mysterious way God's ancient people continue to have a place in God's plan, and will have a place at the final consummation. Christians therefore cannot speak, on the basis of the NT, of any final or total rejection of the Jewish people (cf. Hanson 1986: 540-44).

Christians today must approach Jews first of all with deep contrition for the ways Jews have been treated over the centuries in so-called Christian countries. While they will continue to bear witness before all humankind to their belief in the significance of the Christ event, they will also recognize the special relationship of the Jewish people to the one God whom they also serve. In addition, they will recognize how much Jews and Christians have in common, and how much they can learn from each other.

CHAPTER 12

The Nations

Old Testament: Proclamation

12-1. AMONG THE NATIONS

The choice of Israel as the people of God inevitably raises the question of her relationship to the other peoples of humankind. Israel is chosen from among the nations, but she must also live among the nations. If God has chosen Israel as his people, then what is their relationship to the other peoples of the earth?

12-1.1. THE GOD OF THE NATIONS

From the very outset the Bible declares that God is not only the God of Israel but also the God of all the nations. Indeed, it is the latter truth that is proclaimed first in the canonical form of the OT. God's concern with the whole created order precedes his concern with Israel in the historical order. Gen 1–11 portrays God as the creator and sustainer of all life. All humankind are the descendants of Adam, and of Noah (cf. Brueggemann 1997: 494). In schematic fashion all nations are depicted as descended from the three sons of Noah (Gen 10).

 The call of Abraham, which marks the beginning of God's election of a special people (see 11-1.1), is immediately linked with the blessing of the nations. "I will make of you a great nation," God promises Abraham, "and I will bless you, and make your name great, so that you will be a blessing. I will bless those who bless you . . . and in you all the families of the earth shall be blessed" (Gen 12:2-3; cf. Isa 19:24; *Sir* 44:21). This text can be read to mean "by you all the families of the earth shall bless themselves" (RSV), but it certainly came to be understood as meaning that through Abraham and his descendants God's blessing would be channeled to all humankind (see LXX of Gen 12:3; *Sir* 44:21; Acts 3:25; Gal 3:8; cf. Rétif and Lamarche 1966: 21-22; Muilenburg 1965). "Here it becomes clear that the whole history of Israel is nothing but the continuation of God's dealings with the nations, and that therefore the history of Israel is only to be understood from the unsolved problem of the relation of God to the nations" (Blauw 1962: 19).

Although the salvation/judgment history that occupies a great deal of the OT is mainly concerned with God's dealings with Israel, God's concern for all nations never drops out of sight. Because God cares for Israel, that does not mean that he does not care for other nations. This point is driven home in Amos 9:7, where God says:

> Are you not like the Ethiopians to me,
>   O people of Israel? says the LORD.
> Did I not bring Israel up from the land of Egypt,
>   and the Philistines from Caphtor and the Arameans from Kir?

12-1.2. THE SINS OF THE NATIONS

In tension with the theme of God's care for all nations lies the theme of the sinfulness of the non-Israelite nations.

The sinfulness of all nations is stressed in the story of the flood, where "the LORD saw that the wickedness of humankind was great in the earth" (Gen 6:5), and in the story of the Tower of Babel (Gen 11). The holy war against the Canaanites is justified on the grounds of their wicked and abhorrent religious and moral practices: it is "because of the wickedness of these nations that the LORD is dispossessing them before you" (Deut 9:4; cf. Exod 23:33; Deut 7:1-6, 16). Despite the harshness of the provisions for holy war, "Deuteronomy was not preaching a hatred of Gentile nations, but a hatred of false religious teachings and practices" (Clements 1968: 36).

12-1.3. THE STRANGER WITHIN YOUR GATES

Although in the OT Israel is defined primarily as an ethnic group, the descendants of the twelve sons of Jacob/Israel, it is important to note that the division between the people of God and the nations of the world was never a watertight one. At all stages in Israel's history provision was made for the incorporation into Israel of people of non-Israelite descent.

a. A Mixed Crowd

The important northern tribes of Ephraim and Manasseh were descended from Joseph and Asenath, the daughter of an Egyptian priest (Gen 41:50-52). The biblical text relates that non-Israelite as well as Israelite elements participated in the exodus deliverance. "The Israelites journeyed from Rameses to Succoth. . . . A mixed crowd *('ērebh rabh)* also went up with them" (Exod 12:37-38; cf. Num 11:4; Lev 24:10; Ezek 16:3). Moses married a Midianite wife (Exod 2:21), and he did not hesitate to invite Hobab, a Midianite, to accompany Israel, promising him that "if you go with us, whatever good the LORD does for us, the same we will do for you" (Num 10:29-32).

Incorporation of non-Israelites into Israel continued after the settlement. After the fall of Jericho, Rahab and her family were "adopted" as Israelites (Josh 6:25). Numerous non-Israelites found positions in David's kingdom (2 Sam 11:3; 15:19-23). Even as late as the return, some of the returnees were unable to prove that they were of Israelite descent (Ezra 2:59-63).

b. The Stranger/Resident Alien

Throughout the OT there is recognition of the existence and rights of the "stranger" or "resident alien" *(gēr)*, the foreigner who for whatever reason is resident within Israel. The duty to deal kindly with the stranger is clearly laid down in the Torah: "You shall not oppress a resident alien; you know the heart of an alien, for you were aliens in the land of Egypt" (Exod 23:9; cf. Deut 14:28-29; 16:11-14).

c. A Classic Case: Ruth

While a number of different themes intertwine in the book of Ruth, the closing section (4:13-22) provides the key to its main emphasis. Ruth, a foreigner, is not only incorporated into Israel, she is also the great-grandmother of King David! The fact that she is a Moabite is stressed throughout the story: 1:4, 6, 15, 22; 2:2, 6, 10, 21; 4:3, 5, 10. Moab was the traditional enemy of Israel. After the exile Nehemiah forbade intermarriage with Moabites (Neh 13:23-27), while Ezra went further and broke up such mixed marriages (Ezra 9:1-2; 10:44). Deuteronomy decrees that "no Ammonite or Moabite shall be admitted to the assembly of the LORD. Even to the tenth generation, none of their descendants shall be admitted to the assembly of the LORD" (23:3). This would of course disqualify King David himself, the great-grandson of a Moabitess! The book of Ruth stands in tension with these tendencies and represents another strand of OT thought that is open to the incorporation of people of other nations into the community of Israel (see R. L. Hubbard 1988: 41).

12-1.4. PROSELYTES

In the later OT period and down into NT times the OT view of the "resident alien" *(gēr)* developed into that of the "proselyte," the person of non-Israelite descent who in a more formal way could "convert" to Judaism (on proselytes, see Braude 1940; Pope 1962a; Kuhn 1968; McKnight 1990). The term "proselyte" derives from the Greek *prosēlytos,* which is used in the LXX to translate *gēr.* The word means literally "one who approaches" or "comes forward" (from *proserchomai*). While much remains unclear about the development of Jewish proselytizing, the practice does seem to have flourished among many Jews from about the second century B.C. to A.D. 70, with a marked decline thereafter (but see McKnight, 117). The zeal of at least some Pharisees is alluded to in Matt 23:15, where they are said to "cross sea and land to make a single convert *(prosēlytos)*"; Rom 2:17-23 may also refer to the practice (cf. Jeremias 1958: 12).

In the NT two groups are distinguished. Proselytes proper were those who accepted circumcision (in the case of males) and the full obligations of the law. In addition to Matt 23:15 (above), there are three other references in the NT, all to persons from the Diaspora (Acts 2:10; 6:5; 13:43). Other Gentiles attached themselves to synagogues and participated in their life and worship without accepting circumcision and the full obligations of the law, i.e., they were a type of "adherent" of Judaism (see McKnight 1990: 113). These are termed "God-fearers" *(sebomenoi ton theon* — Acts 13:50; 16:14; 17:4, 17; 18:7 — or *phoboumenoi ton theon* — 10:2, 22; 13:16, 26).

Proselytism, even when it took the form of an active seeking out of converts to Judaism, had certain clear limitations, and it can hardly be described as a "mission" to the nations of humankind. For one thing, it was far from universally recognized within Judaism; it was apparently the work of a relatively few enthusiasts, with many others being indifferent or even hostile. Moreover, proselytizing "meant nothing less than naturalization, becoming a Jew" (Jeremias 1958: 17). Finally, the practice was not linked with what the next section will show as a major element in the OT's understanding of the relationship between Israel and the nations: the concept of the eschatological ingathering of the Gentiles.

12-1.5. EXCLUSIVISM

A contrary and narrowly exclusivist view is also evident in the OT that advocates the strictest separation between Israel and other nations and in particular opposes mixed marriages. This tendency seems to have operated at certain times of crisis when the faith of Israel was in danger of being swamped by foreign influences, particularly following the settlement in Canaan and in the postexilic period. Thus Joshua, in his farewell address, admonishes the Israelites to "do all that is written in the book of the law of Moses . . . so that you may not be mixed with these nations left here among you" (Josh 23:6-7; cf. also above, 12-1.3c, on the book of Ruth). In the postexilic period Nehemiah forbade intermarriage with foreigners such as Moabites (Neh 13:1-3, 23-30), and Ezra went further and actually broke up mixed marriages (Ezra 9–10; see Bossmann 1979).

The separation of Israel from other nations was the main purpose of the food laws of the Torah (Lev 11; Deut 14:3-21). These laws divide all creatures into clean (which may be eaten) and unclean (forbidden as food). For example, "any animal that has divided hoofs and is cleft-footed and chews the cud — such you may eat" (Lev 11:3); this allows the cow but forbids the pig. Various suggestions have been advanced for the elaborate set of distinctions (see G. J. Wenham 1981: 6-9; Childs 1986: 84-86). A popular explanation is that the laws are based on hygiene. While there may be some truth to this, it is essentially a modern explanation. Others have held that the unclean animals are carnivorous, eating flesh with blood in it, something forbidden to Israel by the Torah. This fits some cases but not all. Noting that in the OT all life is sacred, and any eating of meat was a concession made after the flood (Gen 9:3-4), Milgrom (1963) contends that the food laws were given for the Jew "to discipline his appetites further by narrowing down the permitted animals to a few" (291). A likelier explanation is that the unclean animals were associated with non-Israelite religions (cf. Isa 65:4). This does not explain all cases, but there may have been associations with other religions the evidence for which has not survived. Wenham favors a symbolic interpretation developed by M. Douglas that is based on the biblical recognition of three main types of creatures (birds, fish, land animals). The creatures that conform to these pure types are clean; those that in some way cross the boundaries between the types are unclean. Because of the close relationship between humans and animals, the food laws "expressed an understanding of holiness, and of Israel's special status as the holy people of God. The division into clean (edible) foods and unclean (inedible) foods corresponded to the division between holy Israel and the Gentile world" (Wenham, 11). Whichever explanation be adopted, it is clear that the main purpose of the laws is to keep Israel separate from other peoples. This is confirmed by the only rationale supplied by the text itself in Lev 11:44: "For I am the LORD your God; sanctify yourselves therefore, and be holy, for I am holy" (cf. 20:26). This became true particularly in the Diaspora where Jews lived as a minority among Gentiles. One of the main forms of social contact with others is sharing a meal, and it is precisely this form of mixing that is made difficult if not impossible by a strict observance of the food laws.

Old Testament: Promise

12-2. ALL THE NATIONS SHALL COME

Although the ambiguity of the OT's understanding of the relationship between Israel and the nations is carried forward into the promises of a new order, the most significant understanding of the relationship is that which finds expression in the expectation of *the eschatological ingathering of the Gentiles.*

12-2.1. THE GOD OF THE NATIONS

While prophetic eschatology (based on the historical order) generally looked for a restoration of a Davidic kingdom of Israel, the more apocalyptic eschatology (based on the created order) began to look for a universal rule of God. Thus in the key vision of Dan 7 we read of one like a son of man who is presented before God:

> To him was given dominion
>   and glory and kingship,
>   that *all peoples, nations, and languages*
>   should serve him. (v. 14)

In Isaiah also, we find a vision of God's rule extending over all humankind: God's law and justice will go forth "for a light to the peoples. . . . The coastlands wait for me" (51:4-5).

12-2.2. THE JUDGMENT OF THE NATIONS

The other side of the coin is God's judgment on the nations that forms part of the OT's vision of the future (cf. 2-2.3; 16-2.3; 16-4.3). God's coming judgment on the nations for their wickedness is a frequent refrain in the message of the prophets (see Brueggemann 1997: 502-18); thus Amos catalogued and condemned the sins of each of the surrounding nations in turn (1:3–2:3). In the main prophetic books various "Oracles against the Nations" are usually collected into a block (Isa 13–23; Jer 46–51; Ezek 25–32; Obad 1-18). The nationalistic and bitter tone of many of these passages has to be understood against the background of defeat, exile, and continual subjection to one empire after another. God's judgment on the nations is usually envisaged in terms of prophetic eschatology. A final apocalyptic judgment encompassing all peoples is envisaged in Dan 12:2-3.

12-2.3. THE ESCHATOLOGICAL REVERSAL

Because Israel was subjected to one foreign empire after another, some of her visions of the future look for a turning of the tables. At the present time Israel is humiliated and her God despised by the nations; she has been defeated and enslaved; she has been ravaged and despoiled. In the new order matters will be reversed and Israel will be compensated for the wrongs she has suffered.

> Because their shame was double,
>> and dishonor was proclaimed as their lot,
> therefore they shall possess a double portion. (Isa 61:7)

Several themes intertwine in this form of expectation.

a. The Homage of the Nations

In a startling reversal of the present situation, the nations shall come to acknowledge Israel as God's people.

> Then my enemy will see,
>> and shame will cover her who said to me,
> "Where is the LORD your God?" (Mic 7:10)

Similarly Isaiah declares:

> The descendants of those who oppressed you
>> shall come bending low to you,
> and all who despised you
>> shall bow down at your feet.
>
> (60:14; see Scobie 1992b: 290; see also
> Isa 40:5; 45:14; 49:7; 52:10; 55:5; Zeph 2:11)

b. The Service of the Nations

Just as Israelites have been enslaved by foreigners, so in the new age foreigners will come and serve Israel. This eschatological reversal motif is evident in passages such as Isa 45:14: "They shall come over in chains and bow down to you," and 61:5:

> Strangers shall stand and feed your flocks,
>> foreigners shall till your land and dress your vines.
>
> (see also Ps 72:11; Isa 60:10)

c. The Tribute of the Nations

Israel was repeatedly plundered by invading armies and forced to pay tribute to foreign empires. Here too there will be an eschatological reversal:

> Nations shall come to your light,
>> and kings to the brightness of your dawn. . . .
> The abundance of the sea shall be brought to you,
>> the wealth of the nations shall come to you. . . .
> They shall bring gold and frankincense. (Isa 60:3, 5, 6; cf. 18:7; 60:11; 61:6)

Ps 72:10 says of the messianic king:

> May the kings of Tarshish and of the isles
>> render him tribute,
> may the kings of Sheba and Seba bring gifts.

In a reversal of the plundering of the Jerusalem temple and removal of its precious vessels, in the new age the tribute of the nations will be directed to the temple. "For thus says the LORD of hosts: . . . I will shake all the nations, so that the treasure of all nations shall come, and I will fill this house with splendor, says the LORD of Hosts" (Hag 2:6-7).

> Because of your temple at Jerusalem
>> kings bear gifts to you. . . .
> Let bronze be brought from Egypt;
>> let Ethiopia hasten to stretch out its hands to God.
>> (Ps 68:29, 31; cf. *Tob* 13:11)

12-2.4. THE INGATHERING OF THE NATIONS

The motif of the eschatological reversal serves to introduce a major theme of the OT promise, one that comes to fullest expression in a much more positive way in the theme of *the eschatological ingathering of the Gentiles* (see Rowley 1945: chap. 2; Jeremias 1958: 57-60).

Many of the eschatological reversal passages speak of, or imply, a movement of the nations to Israel; they will "come" and "bring" gifts. Several of the passages specify the exact destination: "my holy mountain Jerusalem" (Isa 66:20), "Mount Zion" (18:7), "your temple at Jerusalem" (Ps 68:29; cf. Hag 2:7). Here we see a development of the Zion theology (see 13-1.4c) in which not only will the Holy City and the temple be restored to Israel, they will also be the center and goal for the nations of humankind. Just as the Jews of the Dispersion come in pilgrimage to Zion, so in the new age shall *all nations participate in that pilgrimage.*

Three aspects of this theme deserve careful attention.

a. Every Knee Shall Bow

In a series of passages that envisage the ingathering of the nations, the nationalistic overtones fade into the background and much higher motives for the pilgrimage are adduced.

i. The Instruction of the Nations

The nations will come to learn about God and his Torah. This is the keynote of one of the earliest and most important oracles of the ingathering, found in both Isa 2:2-4 and Mic 4:1-4 (see Martin-Achard 1962: chap. 4; Brueggemann 1997: 501-2):

> In days to come
>> the mountain of the LORD's house
> shall be established as the highest of the mountains,
>> and shall be raised above the hills;
> all nations shall stream to it.
>> Many peoples shall come and say,
> "Come, let us go up to the mountain of the LORD,
>> to the house of the God of Jacob;
> that he may teach us his ways
>> and that we may walk in his paths."
> For out of Zion shall go forth instruction *(tōrâh),*
>> and the word of the LORD from Jerusalem. (Isa 2:2-3)

The veil of ignorance of God will be lifted from the nations,

> And he [God] will destroy on this mountain
>> the shroud that is cast over all peoples,
>> the sheet that is spread over all nations. (25:7; cf. Jer 16:21; Isa 60:3)

ii. The Worship of the Nations

Isa 19:19-22 envisages even the old enemy Egypt offering sacrificial worship to the LORD. 2 Isaiah expects that the nations will come to worship God.

> And the foreigners who join themselves to the LORD . . .
> these I will bring to my holy mountain,

> and make them joyful in my house of prayer;
> their burnt offerings and their sacrifices
>   will be accepted on my altar;
> for my house shall be called a house of prayer
>   for all peoples. (Isa 56:6-7; cf. Ps 86:9; Isa 60:7; Zech 14:16)

Jeremiah stresses repentance as the condition for such worship by the nations: "At that time Jerusalem shall be called the throne of the LORD, and all nations shall gather to it, to the presence of the LORD in Jerusalem, and they shall no longer stubbornly follow their own evil will" (3:17; cf. 16:19; Zeph 3:9; *Tob* 14:6).

iii. The Salvation of the Nations

At the center of this promise is the expectation that the nations will come to participate in God's salvation.

> Turn to me and be saved,
>   all the ends of the earth!
>   For I am God, and there is no other.
> By myself I have sworn,
>   from my mouth has gone forth in righteousness
>   a word that shall not return:
> "To me every knee shall bow,
>   every tongue shall swear." (Isa 45:22-23; cf. 51:5)

The nations will share God's salvation because they will become part of God's people: "Many nations shall join themselves to the LORD on that day, and shall be my people" (Zech 2:11). As part of God's salvation, the nations along with Israel shall enjoy the blessings of peace (9:10; cf. Isa 2:4//Mic 4:3; Jer 12:16).

The older, more nationalistic ideas could even be reinterpreted in the light of this higher vision. Thus Amos 9:11-12 speaks of a revival of the house of David,

> in order that they may possess the remnant of Edom
>   and all the nations who are called by my name.

I.e., in the coming age Israel would settle old scores, especially against her traditional enemy Edom. The LXX, however, interprets the text in the light of the eschatological ingathering of the Gentiles and translates:

> that the rest of mankind may seek after the Lord,
> and all the nations upon whom my name is invoked.
>
> (cf. Rétif and Lamarche 1966: 49)

b. A Blessing in the Midst

The eschatological pilgrimage to Zion indicates that it is *through Israel* that God will bring the nations to learn his Torah, to worship him, and to share in his salvation. A number of important passages emphasize this mediating role of Israel.

A remarkable oracle in Isa 19:16-25 concerns Egypt and Assyria, two great empires, rivals of one another and oppressors of Israel. The prophet foresees a time when "the Lord will make himself known to the Egyptians" (v. 21), who will come to know and worship the Lord. Not only so, the ancient enemies will be reconciled and will worship together: "On that day there will be a highway from Egypt to Assyria, and the Assyrian will come into Egypt, and the Egyptian into Assyria, and the Egyptians will worship with the Assyrians" (v. 23). Israel, a geographically small country situated between the two giants, will nevertheless play a mediating role: "On that day Israel will be the third with Egypt and Assyria, *a blessing in the midst of the earth,* whom the Lord of hosts has blessed, saying, 'Blessed be Egypt my people, and Assyria the work of my hands, and Israel my heritage'" (vv. 24-25). "This passage, which promises the heathen the knowledge of Yahweh and his blessings, on the same terms as Israel, is beyond all question one of the peaks of the revelation of universalism" (Rétif and Lamarche 1966: 54).

The mediating role of Israel is featured in another striking picture of the ingathering in Zech 8:20-23.

> Thus says the Lord of hosts: Peoples shall yet come, the inhabitants of many cities; the inhabitants of one city shall go to another, saying, "Come, let us go to entreat the favor of the Lord, and to seek the Lord of hosts; I myself am going." Many peoples and strong nations shall come to seek the Lord of hosts in Jerusalem, and to entreat the favor of the Lord. . . . In those days *ten men from nations of every language shall take hold of a Jew, grasping his garment and saying, "Let us go with you, for we have heard that God is with you."*

c. Nations Shall Come

Despite these numerous passages on the ingathering of the Gentiles, *there is no indication of any real missionary outreach on the part of Israel in the OT period.* This is so for three important, interlocking reasons.

i. The Ingathering of the Nations Is an Eschatological Event

The nations will come "in that day" (Mic 7:12; Zech 2:11), "at that time" (Jer 3:17; Zeph 3:9), "in days to come" (Isa 2:2//Mic 4:1).

ii. The Ingathering Will Be the Work of God, Not of Israel

It is God who promises, "These will I bring . . ." (Isa 56:7), "I am coming to gather all nations" (66:18; cf. 25:6; Hag 2:7; Zeph 3:9).

iii. The Nations Will Come to Israel, Not Israel to the Nations

The movement will be from the nations of the earth to the center, represented by Jerusalem/Mount Zion/the temple (cf. Jeremias 1958: 60). The verb that is used repeatedly is "come": "nations shall *come* to your light" (Isa 60:3); "all flesh shall *come*" (66:23; cf. 45:14; 60:5, 14; Mic 7:12; *Tob* 13:11). This movement, essentially from the periphery to the center, has been described as *centripetal* (Jeremias, 60 n. 2, ascribes this terminology to an article published by B. Sundkler in 1936).

12-2.5. A LIGHT TO THE NATIONS

Despite the general lack of a theology of mission, nevertheless a missionary role for Israel is at least glimpsed in three OT books.

a. Isaiah

In the Servant Songs of Isaiah (see 9-1.3), the Servant's task is not restricted to Israel but includes the nations who are to share in God's salvation. Thus in 42:6 God says to the Servant:

> I have given you as a covenant to the people,
>> *a light to the nations.*

Similarly in 49:6 God says,

> I will give you as *a light to the nations,*
>> *that my salvation may reach to the end of the earth.* (cf. also 52:15)

Nevertheless, here too it has to be said that "Israel saw itself as bearing witness and being 'a light to the nations' (Isa. 42:1-7, 49:1-6), but only through example from Jerusalem or Zion, the centre of the world, not through active outreach" (Hogg 1988: 242).

b. Jonah

A missionary role for Israel is also glimpsed in the book of Jonah, a story that makes masterly use of satire (Ryken 1987a: 337-40) to poke gentle fun at the attitude represented by the pouting prophet. The object of the satirical attack is "the kind of nationalistic zeal that made God the exclusive property of Israel and refused to accept the universality of God's grace" (337).

In the opening scene the sailors provide a foil to the fleeing prophet (Hedlund 1991: 121). Gentiles they may be, but they do pray to their gods while Jonah sleeps; and their concern for Jonah's welfare (1:13) is in direct contrast to Jonah's lack of concern for Gentiles throughout the story. Jonah is theologically orthodox: he fears "the LORD, the God of heaven, who made the sea and the dry land" (1:9); he knows that the LORD is "a gracious God and merciful, slow to anger, and abounding in steadfast love" (4:2; see Exod 34:6; etc.), but he refuses to draw the logical conclusion from these theological premises.

The dominant note of the book is a universal one. God's presence is universal; the idea that Jonah could escape from God even at the ends of the earth is gently ridiculed. God's love and care are universal; they extend to the people of pagan Nineveh, even to children and animals (4:11)! But does it suggest that the mission of God's people is universal? Is it "a missionary tract" (Hedlund 1991: 126)? Does it call on Israel to "take up her task of proclaiming the true God to the nations, however distasteful that may be" (Bright 1953: 161)? Seen in its canonical context, this is less certain.

The book of Jonah portrays an attitude in tension with the dominant OT view, but historically this did not lead to missionary outreach (cf. Blauw 1962: 33-34). That had to await the dawning of the new age and the mission of Jesus, whose preaching of repentance is portrayed as "the sign of Jonah" (Luke 11:29).

c. Psalms

A strongly universal note runs through the book of Psalms (see Senior and Stuhlmueller 1983: chap. 5). God is the creator of the whole earth (see 2-1.1b on creation psalms) and the ruler of the whole earth (see 1-1.1 on enthronement psalms); therefore all the peoples of the earth are called upon to worship him (33:8; 66:4; 67; 86:9; 96:9; 98:4; 138:4; 148:11), for he is "the hope of all the ends of the earth" (65:5).

Some of the Royal Psalms speak of the universal dominion of the messianic king "in extravagant language and with surprising boldness" (Kraus 1986: 120). God says to the king at his coronation:

> Ask of me, and I will make the nations your heritage,
>   and the ends of the earth your possession. (2:8)

Ps 72 prays for the king:

> May he have dominion from sea to sea,
>> and from the River to the ends of the earth. . . .
> May all kings fall down before him,
>> all nations give him service. (vv. 8, 11)

Historically these psalms may reflect the period when David and Solomon ruled a considerable empire (cf. Kraus, 121), but after the collapse of the monarchy they refer to the coming messianic king who, as God's vice-gerent, will rule over the whole earth.

The Servant Psalm 22 (cf. 9-1.2a) moves from lament to praise to a concluding hymn (vv. 27-31) with a "remarkable eschatological vision in which all peoples of the earth worship the Lord" (Hogg 1988: 240-41):

> All the ends of the earth shall remember
>> and turn to the LORD;
> and all the families of the nations
>> shall worship before him. (v. 27)

New Testament: Fulfillment

12-3. MAKE DISCIPLES OF ALL NATIONS

A major feature of the new order is the incorporation of Gentiles into the new people of God. From a very early stage the emerging Christian church engaged in extensive missionary activity. Historically the rapid growth and expansion of Christianity in the Greco-Roman world in the first century of its existence is a truly remarkable phenomenon (cf. Scobie 1984a: 47). This important development was not based on an extension of the practice of proselytizing, but on the theological conviction that since the new age had dawned with the Christ event, the time for the ingathering of the Gentiles, promised in the OT Scriptures, had now arrived.

12-3.1. SERVANT TO THE CIRCUMCISED

While the postresurrection missionary outreach of the early church is beyond dispute, the attitude of Jesus to a Gentile mission has been the subject of much discussion and debate (see D. W. Allen 1959; T. W. Manson 1964; Hahn 1965: 26-28).

a. Condemnation of Pharisaic Proselytizing

The only recorded remark of Jesus concerning proselytizing condemns the practice: "Woe to you, scribes and Pharisees, hypocrites! For you cross sea and land to make a single convert, and you make the new convert twice as much a child of hell as yourselves" (Matt 23:15). We may agree that here "Jesus was condemning a superficial proselytizing . . . his saying was aimed at the smug self-righteousness of the Pharisees and the fanaticism of their converts" (Jeremias 1958: 17).

b. Jesus' Mission to Israel

The Gospels make it clear that within his lifetime Jesus directed his mission and that of his disciples primarily to the people of Israel. According to Matt 10:5-6, Jesus instructed his followers: "Go nowhere among the Gentiles, and enter no town of the Samaritans, but go rather to the lost sheep of the house of Israel." And in 15:24 he declares, "I was sent only to the lost sheep of the house of Israel."

While Jesus certainly had contacts with Gentiles, the Gospels make no mention of his deliberately seeking them out (D. W. Allen 1959: 157-59).

This is strikingly confirmed by Paul in Rom 15:8, where he states that "Christ became a servant to the circumcised" (RSV). In the context of a discussion of the unity of Jews and Gentiles, Paul is unable to appeal to any tradition of contact between Jesus and Gentiles, "valuable as such an argument would have been in this connexion" (Jeremias 1958: 37).

c. The Eschatological Ingathering

Jesus, however, did proclaim the entry of the Gentiles into the kingdom and the equality of Gentiles as an eschatological event. In doing so, he rejected all narrower and more nationalistic views and went back instead to the best thought of the OT.

In Matt 8:5-13 the faith of a Gentile centurion prompts Jesus to declare, "I tell you, many will come from east and west and will eat with Abraham and Isaac and Jacob in the kingdom of heaven" (v. 11; the Lucan version has "people will come from east and west, from north and south, and will eat in the kingdom of God" — 13:29; cf. also Mark 13:27). The context makes it abundantly clear that the reference is to the ingathering of the Gentiles (in Matt 8:12 they are contrasted with "the heirs of the kingdom"). This is so despite the fact that the OT passages echoed in the saying (Isa 43:5-6; 49:12; Ps 107:3) originally referred to the ingathering of Israel (see 11-2.5a), though the Isa 49:12 reference comes directly after the Servant Song that designates the Servant/Israel as "a light to the nations" (49:6). What Jesus does is to redefine the eschatological Israel to include the Gentiles.

According to Jesus, Gentiles will participate equally in the eschatological events of resurrection and judgment. The men of Nineveh (who repented at the preaching of Jonah) and the queen of the south (who came to hear the wisdom of Solomon) "will rise up at the judgment with this generation and condemn it" (Matt 12:41-42//Luke 11:31-32). In the woes pronounced on the Galilean towns of Chorazin and Bethsaida, their fate at the judgment is compared unfavorably with Tyre, Sidon, and Sodom (Matt 11:21-24; cf. Luke 10:13-15; see also Matt 10:15//Luke 10:12). In the great judgment scene of Matt 25:31-46, "all the nations" come before the Son of Man; those who meet the criteria "inherit the kingdom."

The cleansing of the temple (Matt 21:12-13//Mark 11:15-19//Luke 19:45-48//John 2:13-17) is to be seen primarily in this context. This is not merely a dramatic way of calling attention to abuses in the operation of the temple; if that were so, Jesus would be simply a reformer within Judaism. But the merchants and money changers operated in *the Court of the Gentiles*. According to the Synoptics, as well as quoting Jer 7:11 (which refers to abuse of the temple), Jesus quoted Isa 56:7, "My house shall be called a house of prayer / for all peoples," a text that refers to the eschatological ingathering of the Gentiles. This provides the essential clue to the meaning of the incident, along with the saying about destroying the temple and rebuilding another not made with hands (Matt 26:61//Mark 14:58//John 2:19). Jesus foresees a new, eschatological temple (cf. 14-2.1a), in the worship of which the Gentiles will fully share.

Thus Jesus clearly envisaged Gentiles participating fully in the kingdom of God. His own task, however, was to gather together the lost sheep of the house of Israel. The ingathering of the Gentiles would be an eschatological event, something that lay on the other side of his approaching death.

d. Jesus' Acceptance of Gentiles

However, since for Jesus the new order is not only future but also breaking in here and now, in his words and deeds Jesus accepted Gentiles as well as Jews and gave them a share in the dawning salvation.

In the account of the healing of the centurion's servant (Matt 8:5-13//Luke 7:1-10), Jesus extends his ministry to a Gentile and comments, "Truly I tell you, in no one in Israel have I found such faith" (Matt 8:10//Luke 7:9). "It is not just at the end time that Gentiles will be received on equal terms with Jews; that happens in Jesus' ministry" (Scobie 1984a: 60; cf. W. Manson 1953a: 263-64). Similarly, Jesus' encounter with the Syrophoenician woman (Matt 15:21-28//Mark 7:24-30) evoked the comment, "Woman, great is your faith!" The healing of the Gerasene demoniac (Mark 5:1-20//Luke 8:26-39; cf. Matt 8:28-34) occurs in a preponderantly Gentile area. In John 12:20-22 Jesus learns from Philip and Andrew that "some Greeks" *(hellēnes tines)* who had come to Jerusalem to worship at the feast wish to see him. "Greeks" here means Gentiles (cf. 7:35), though they may have been God-fearers. There is no indication whether Jesus actually met with them, but vv. 24f. anticipate Jesus' death and resurrection and the implication seems to be that only the completed Christ event signals the Gentile mission (cf. v. 32).

The later Gentile mission thus has a firm basis in the ministry of the historical Jesus.

e. Universal, Not Nationalistic

In keeping with Jesus' affirmation and anticipation of the eschatological ingathering of the Gentiles was his rejection of any form of narrow and nationalistic expectation. He cites examples of the favorable treatment of Gentiles in the OT (Luke 4:25-27: the widow of Zarephath, Naaman the Syrian), and in particular prefers the more universal apocalyptic tradition. Jesus, it is rightly said, "removes the idea of vengeance from the eschatological expectation" (Jeremias 1958: 41-46). Jesus' preference for the term "Son of Man" reflects his reluctance to claim the title "Messiah" that would suggest to many a military/political figure who would restore a nationalistic kingdom of David (cf. 6-3.2); instead it recalls the vision of Dan 7 with its references to a son of man to whom is given a kingdom, "that all peoples, nations, and languages should serve him" (v. 14).

For Jesus, Jewish descent plays no role at the judgment. A universal criterion will be applied when "all the nations" are gathered before the Son of Man (Matt 25:32).

12-3.2. KEEP THE LAW OF MOSES

The NT witnesses to the fact that there were different views within the earliest Christian communities concerning the nations and their relationship to the new people of God. According to Acts 11:2 (RSV), "the circumcision party *(hoi ek peritomēs)*" opposed Peter's acceptance of Gentile converts, and specifically his eating with them, something that would break the Jewish food laws. In 15:1 some men from Judea go to Antioch and teach "unless you are circumcised according to the custom of Moses, you cannot be saved." At the ensuing "Jerusalem Council," it is "some believers who belonged to the sect of the Pharisees" who argue that Gentile converts must be circumcised and keep the law of Moses (15:5).

Paul's letter to the Galatians reflects the activities of a similar group whom modern scholars for convenience label "Judaizers." In the account of his second visit to Jerusalem (= Acts 15?), Paul refers to "false believers secretly brought in, who slipped in to spy on the freedom we have in Christ Jesus" (Gal 2:4). Despite agreement with the Jerusalem leaders, the controversy resurfaced with Peter's visit to Antioch. Peter ate with Gentile converts until "certain people came from James," apparently identified with "the circumcision party *(tous ek peritomēs)*" (Gal 2:12; cf. Acts 11:2, above). Acts thus suggests that Peter was sympathetic to this point of view.

It is important to note that those who belonged to this group did not object to Gentiles becoming members of the church. But they thought of the church as a direct continuation of Israel, and they followed the view that Gentiles could be incorporated into Israel only as *proselytes,* through circumcision and acceptance of the entire law. This view failed to grasp the significance of the Christ event as inaugurating the new order (cf. Dobbie 1962: 282-83).

12-3.3. A DOOR OF FAITH TO THE GENTILES

The view that pervades most of the NT is that Gentiles are to be accepted as members of the people of God on the basis of faith in the proclamation of the gospel, but without circumcision or the requirement to observe the entire law.

a. The Origins of the Gentile Mission

Traditionally this view is connected above all with the figure of *Paul.* His letters provide many glimpses of his missionary travels and methods, and they also reveal the key role played by the acceptance of Gentiles in his thought and theology. Moreover, the second part of Acts provides information on his missionary activities, at least in the later part of his ministry, with a strong emphasis on his mission to Gentiles.

Acts goes out of its way to emphasize *Peter's* acceptance of Gentile converts before recounting any missionary outreach by Paul (Acts 10–11). The Cornelius episode (10:1–11:18) strongly underlines the role of divine guidance and the giving of the Spirit in the conversion of the first Gentiles (cf. Best 1984: 11-12). Peter's basic acceptance of a Gentile mission is witnessed to in Gal 2:1-10, even if Paul does go on to charge Peter with some inconsistency (cf. Lotz 1988: 201-7).

Acts, however, also preserves traditions from the early days of the church which make it clear that the Gentile mission originated neither with Paul nor with Peter, but with the *"Hellenists."* 6:1 points to a division in the earliest Christian community in Jerusalem between "Hebrews *(hebraioi)*" who spoke Aramaic and "Hellenists *(hellēnistai)*" who spoke Greek. Traditions relating to Stephen (Acts 6–7), however, indicate that the Hellenists were distinguished not just by language, but by their theological viewpoint that included a radical attitude to both Torah and temple (cf. Scobie 1984a: 50). Enough evidence survives to indicate that the Hellenists, following their expulsion from Jerusalem (8:1), went on to conduct a mission in three stages.

i. They went first to *Jews,* probably largely Hellenistic Jews. 6:8-9 alludes to Stephen's ministry in Jerusalem. According to 11:19, the Hellenists who were scattered after Stephen's death "traveled as far as Phoenicia, Cyprus, and Antioch, and they spoke the word to no one except Jews."

ii. Secondly, the Hellenist Philip undertook a mission among the *Samaritans* (8:4-13; see 11-3.5b).

iii. Thirdly, the Hellenists went on to preach to *Gentiles.* According to 11:20, "Among them were some men of Cyprus and Cyrene who, on coming to Antioch, spoke to the Greeks also, proclaiming the Lord Jesus" (adopting the reading *hellēnas* rather than *hellēnistas;* see commentaries). Regardless of which is the correct reading, the context clearly indicates that Gentiles are meant. It is at Antioch that Paul later comes on the scene and becomes the enthusiastic proponent of the Gentile mission. It is thus the Hellenists who "form the historical link between the earliest Jerusalem community and Paul" (Scobie 1984a: 49).

b. The Development of the Gentile Mission

Acts presents Antioch as the first center of the Gentile mission. Barnabas and Saul were associated with Antioch (11:22, 25-26), and it is from there that they set out on a missionary journey (Acts 13–14) that was directed in the first instance to Jews (13:5, 14), but in the course of which they turned also to Gentiles (13:46). On their return to Antioch Paul and Barnabas "related all that God had done with them, and how he had opened a door of faith for the Gentiles" (14:27).

According to Acts, the challenging of the policy of the Antioch church by Judaizers led to the "Council of Jerusalem" of Acts 15. The account raises some historical problems, especially when compared with Paul's letters, above all with Gal 2:1-10, if this is indeed an account of the same meeting. However, the basic point on which both accounts agree is that Paul and the leaders of the Jerusalem church endorsed the acceptance of Gentiles without requiring circumcision and observance of the entire law. According to Acts 15:16, James, in his summing up, referred to the promise of the ingathering of the Gentiles in Amos 9:11-12 (in the LXX version; see above, 12-2.4a.iii).

One of the major barriers to accepting Gentiles was the Jewish food laws, the main function of which was to keep Jews separate from Gentiles (cf. 12-1.5). Hence the divine vision that convinced a reluctant Peter to accept Gentiles took the form of a declaration that all animals are clean (Acts 10:9-16; cf. 11:5-10; 15:7-

9). The Council of Jerusalem agreed to accept Gentiles without requiring observance of the ritual laws of Judaism. It was Peter's failure to follow through on this agreement that caused a problem in Antioch; along with others he withdrew from table fellowship with Gentile Christians (Gal 2:11-14), thus failing to acknowledge that with the dawning of the new age the food laws were abolished so that Israel might be open to all who believe.

Historically the Christian gospel was preached first to Jews, then to Samaritans, then to Gentiles. This sequence is also reflected (without the Samaritan element) in Paul's practice of preaching first to Jews and only thereafter to Gentiles. Paul lays down the basic principle that underlies this in Rom 1:16, where he states that the gospel is "the power of God for salvation to everyone who has faith, to the Jew first and also to the Greek" (cf. 2:9-10). This is consistent with Paul's procedure as portrayed in Acts (see 13:14, 46; cf. 3:26; 15:16-18).

12-3.4. THAT EVERY KNEE SHOULD BOW

The Gentile mission launched by the Hellenists, accepted with reluctance by Peter and with enthusiasm by Paul, must be seen in the total context of BT. The mission is firmly rooted in the OT, and in the message and ministry of Jesus.

a. The Theology of Mission: A Light to the Gentiles

While the NT theology of mission depends on the OT promise of the ingathering of the Gentiles, one cannot simply speak of the "fulfillment" of the OT promises. As so often happened, the new reality brought into being by the Christ event exceeds the expectations of the OT, and even to some extent reverses them. Once again we see that BT is frequently a theology of surprise. This is seen especially in relation to the three aspects of OT expectation that prevented an active missionary outreach in OT times (see 12-2.4c).

i. Present Rather Than Future

In the OT the ingathering of the Gentiles is an eschatological event. There is no outreach in the present because the Gentiles will find their place in God's purpose only at some point in the future. The Judaizers, and James and Peter initially, appear to have subscribed to this view. But the dominant NT understanding is paradoxical with its reference to both the "already" and the "not yet." The new order has dawned, so now is the time for the ingathering of the Gentiles, though this will be fully accomplished only at the final consummation. "The new age, or new creation, of which the prophets in the past had spoken, and for which the saints of Israel had longed . . . was no longer a purely future thing which had to be prepared for, but a reality of the present which was to be received and entered into" (W. Manson 1953b: 390; cf. Cullmann 1961: 45-46).

This fundamental theological point is well brought out by the Great Commission of Matt 28:18-20, where the risen Christ tells his disciples: "All authority in heaven and on earth has been given to me. Go therefore and make disciples of all nations, baptizing them in the name of the Father and of the Son and of the Holy Spirit, and teaching them to obey everything that I have commanded you. And remember, I am with you always, to the end of the age." Historical-critical scholars have debated the "authenticity" of this saying, noting in particular the "trinitarian" baptismal formula (see B. J. Hubbard 1974; Matthey 1980; Arias 1991). Alternate forms of the missionary command are found in Mark 16:15 (part of the longer ending), Luke 24:47 (see Peters 1972: 172-98), and John 20:21, where the risen Christ says to the disciples, "As the Father has sent me, so I send you." In Acts 1:8 the risen Christ commands the apostles to witness "to the ends of the earth"; they are to fulfill the role of the Isaianic servant (cf. 12-2.5a) by being "a light to the nations, / that my salvation may reach to the end of the earth" (Isa 49:6, also quoted by Paul in Acts 13:47). Theologically, what is significant is that the command is not ascribed to the historical Jesus but to the risen Christ. It is *the completion of the Christ event* that signals the inauguration of the new order and thus the time for the ingathering of the Gentiles (cf. Jeremias 1958: 39).

As already noted (11-3.5b), the Hellenist mission to Samaria represents, in symbolic form, the fulfillment of the promise of the eschatological union of North and South. It is not surprising that the Hellenists went on to take the next logical step and inaugurate the eschatological ingathering of the Gentiles. While much is unclear historically, it appears that the Hellenists were more in line with the teaching and outlook of Jesus. Jesus had proclaimed the eschatological ingathering of the Gentiles, and anticipated it in his acceptance of Gentiles. The Hellenists were the first to realize a basic principle of BT, that with the Christ event the new order has been inaugurated and the time for the fulfillment of the eschatological events has arrived, even if the final consummation still lies in the future. B. F. Meyer notes Stephen's reference to the Son of Man (Acts 7:56) and Philip's reference to the Servant (8:32-35) as significant allusions to sources that strike the note of universalism (1989: 181). The connection of the Gentile mission with the Hellenists reminds us that this mission was not a late development but was rooted in a group that belonged to the very earliest community and that in fact stood most clearly in continuity with Jesus himself.

The Christ hymn of Phil 2:6-11, widely recognized as pre-Pauline, constitutes an early witness to this theological viewpoint. The purpose of the Christ event, climaxing in the exaltation of Christ, is:

> so that at the name of Jesus
>> every knee should bend,
>> in heaven and on earth and under the earth,

> and every tongue should confess
>> that Jesus Christ is Lord,
>> to the glory of God the Father.

This utilizes (though it also adapts) the language of Isa 45:23b, one of the most striking texts that speaks of the eschatological participation of the nations in God's salvation (above, 12-2.4a.iii).

The basis of the Gentile mission in inaugurated eschatology is further underlined by the role of the Holy Spirit in the missionary theology of the NT, for the giving of the Spirit is a major sign of the dawning of the new order (cf. 5-3). Acts especially emphasizes the role of the Spirit in guiding and empowering the Christian mission (see esp. 1:6-8; cf. Cullmann 1961: 45-46).

ii. The Church Rather Than God

In the OT the ingathering of the Gentiles is the work of God, not of Israel. Here we have a reversal also, though one that may be able to claim some support in the OT. The Gentile mission, inaugurated by the Hellenists, is taken up by many in the church, including Paul. It is willed by God, inaugurated by the Christ event, and empowered by the Holy Spirit, but it is undertaken by members of the Christian community.

The church assumes the role of the Isaianic Servant. According to Acts 13:46-47, Paul justified his turning to the Gentiles by quoting the climax of the second Servant Song in Isa 49:6 and applying it to the church ("us" — v. 47):

> I have set you to be a light for the Gentiles,
>> so that you may bring salvation to the ends of the earth.

iii. Centrifugal Rather Than Centripetal

In the OT the ingathering of the Gentiles involves the nations coming to Israel, not Israel going to the nations. Here the reversal is even more striking: the basically *centripetal* movement of the OT is replaced by the *centrifugal* movement of the NT (cf. Scobie 1984a: 52). The OT "come" (12-2.4c.iii) is replaced by the NT "go": "*Go* therefore and make disciples of all nations . . ." (Matt 28:19); "*Go* into all the world and preach the gospel to the whole creation" (Mark 16:15).

Whereas in the OT the nations were to come *to* Zion, Luke portrays the church "beginning *from* Jerusalem" (Luke 24:47) but spreading outward in ever widening circles (Acts 1:8). Thus Jerusalem does have a key place in the Gentile mission, but as the starting point, not as the final goal.

Although the centrifugal pattern dominates the NT, there are a few echoes of the centripetal pattern of the OT, specifically of the theme of the tribute of the nations (12-2.3c; cf. Scobie 1992b: 302-5).

The Magi of Matt 2:1-12 come "from the East" and are clearly non-Jews, representatives of the nations. 2:11 echoes Isa 60:5-6:

> the wealth of the nations shall come to you. . . .
> They shall bring *gold* and *frankincense,*

with the significant addition of "myrrh." (The later tradition of the "kings" probably reflects Isa 60:3.) At the outset of his Gospel, with this symbolic account of the Gentiles coming *to* Jesus, Matthew anticipates the closing of the Gospel with its commission to go *to* the Gentiles.

Paul's collection of money from his Gentile churches (see 1 Cor 16:1-4; 2 Cor 8–9; Rom 15:22-29; Acts 24:17) also echoes this theme. While this was certainly intended as a manifestation of Christian charity and Christian unity, it was also a symbolic enactment of the eschatological tribute of the Gentiles, as the various non-Jewish representatives gathered the money and brought it to Jerusalem (see Nickle 1966: 139; contra Best 1984: 22). See also 12-4.5 on Rev 21:24-26.

b. The Pauline Theology of Mission

The Gentile mission plays a key role in Paul's understanding of his own call and ministry, and of the message he is called to proclaim (see Hahn 1965: 95-110; Senior and Stuhlmueller 1983: 161-90; Scobie 1970; Bowers 1987). The purpose of Paul's call through God's Son was "so that I might proclaim him among the Gentiles" (Gal 1:16), and he could speak of himself as "an apostle to the Gentiles" (Rom 11:13; cf. Acts 9:15).

Acceptance of Gentiles on the basis of faith, without the requirement of circumcision and observance of the whole law, is one of the key interlocking pieces in Pauline theology. Both the success of the Gentile mission and the opposition he encountered led Paul to theological reflection on the theology of the Gentile mission. In Galatians we see his struggle with the Judaizers who would accept Gentiles as Christians only if they were circumcised and obeyed the whole Jewish law (above, 12-3.2). Romans represents Paul's more mature reflection, though even here his thought is far from systematic.

Paul sees the Gentile mission in part in the light of the OT proclamation that the God of the created order is the God of all nations. Thus in Rom 3:28-30 he asks: "Is God the God of Jews only? Is he not the God of Gentiles also? Yes, of Gentiles also, since God is one" (cf. D. G. Miller 1961: 72-74); and in 10:12 he asserts, "There is no distinction between Jew and Greek; the same Lord is Lord of all and is generous to all who call on him."

A study of Galatians and Romans, however, shows that basically Paul's understanding was a *salvation-historical* one, and that he recognized three periods in the history of God's dealings with his people.

1. The first period, *from Abraham to Moses,* is the period of *promise.* Referring back to the key passage in Gen 12:1-3, Paul affirms that God's purpose in calling Abraham and thus choosing Israel as his people was always, from the start, a *universal* one. "The scripture, foreseeing that God would justify the Gentiles by faith, declared the gospel beforehand *(proeuēngelisato)* to Abraham, saying, 'All the Gentiles shall be blessed in you' [= Gen 12:3]" (Gal 3:8; cf. Rom 4). In Gal 3:6-9, "The point is clear: the original promise is to be offered to those originally in view in it and on the original terms — to the Gentiles, by faith. The covenant promise was not intended solely for Jews" (Dunn 1990: 247-48). Abraham's acceptance into a right relationship with God through faith reveals God's ultimate purpose for humankind. In two passages Paul uses a *chronological* argument. In Rom 4:10-12 he points out that Abraham was accepted into a right relationship with God through faith (Gen 15:6) *before* he was circumcised (17:24). In Gal 3:15-18 he points out that Abraham lived several hundred years *before* the giving of the Torah. "My point is this: the law, which came four hundred thirty years later, does not annul a covenant previously ratified by God, so as to nullify the promise" (v. 17). The whole of salvation history is to be seen in the light of its beginning, and in the light of God's original promise which, once given, cannot be revoked but represents his ultimate purpose for humankind.

2. The second period is *the period of the law,* from Moses to Christ. God chose to work through the people of Israel in order, ultimately, to bring the message of salvation to all humankind. This period is evaluated positively by Paul, provided that one realizes that it is not the final stage of salvation history. Paul writes of his fellow Jews: "They are Israelites, and to them belong the adoption, the glory, the covenants, the giving of the law, the worship, and the promises" (Rom 9:4). Note that "the giving of the law" is included; the law is God-given and has an important role in God's purposes in this period of salvation history (see further, 18-3.3b).

3. For Paul the key point is that with the Christ event the new age promised in the OT has dawned, and thus *the third stage of salvation history has begun,* characterized, among other things, by the eschatological giving of the Spirit and the eschatological ingathering of the Gentiles. The second stage, the stage of the law, has come to an end; and all people, Jews and Gentiles, are now accepted into a right relationship with God, by God's grace in Christ, solely on the basis of their faith. No one can be justified by "works of the law," by which Paul means primarily circumcision and the food laws (cf. 18-3.3b), for there can be no preconditions to receiving the gift of God's grace. The era of the law has passed, and Jews and Gentiles are now accepted into God's people on an equal basis: Christ "has abolished the law . . . that he might create in himself one new humanity in place of two" (Eph 2:15). Paul's claim is that

> the advent of Christ has introduced the time of fulfilment, including the fulfilment of his purpose regarding the covenant. From the beginning, God's

eschatological purpose in making the covenant had been the blessing of the nations. . . . So, now that the time of fulfilment had come, the covenant should no longer be conceived in nationalistic or racial terms. No longer is it an exclusively Jewish *qua* Jewish privilege. The covenant is not thereby abandoned. Rather it is broadened out as God had originally intended — with the grace of God which it expressed separated from its national restriction and freely bestowed without respect to race or work, as it had been bestowed in the beginning. (Dunn 1990: 197)

Thus with the Christ event, God's original promise to Abraham begins to be fulfilled. The gospel is offered to Jew and Gentile alike, as a gift of God's grace to be received by faith. It is those who respond to the gospel in faith, whether Jew or Gentile, who are the true descendants of Abraham (Rom 9:8; Gal 3:29). Thus in this new, third, and final stage of salvation history, "neither circumcision nor uncircumcision is anything; but a new creation is everything!" (Gal 6:15).

Paul came to see the church's mission in worldwide terms; his goal apparently was the preaching of the gospel, as far as humanly possible, through the entire inhabited earth (cf. Knox 1964).

c. Theologies of Mission

While Paul is *the* theologian of the Gentile mission, the other main writers of the NT, with minor differences of emphasis, also recognize that the Christ event inaugurates the eschatological ingathering of the Gentiles.

Mark (see Hahn 1965: 111-20; Senior and Stuhlmueller 1983: 211-32; Scobie 1984a: 54-55) emphasizes Jesus' contacts with Gentiles during his ministry and his excursions into Gentile territory, and it may be argued that the climax of his Gospel comes with the words of the Gentile centurion at the foot of the cross: "Truly this man was God's Son!" (15:39; see Kiddle 1934). Mark anticipates the Gentile mission which, however, will come only after Jesus' death (13:10; 14:9).

Matthew (see Hahn 1965: 120-28; Senior and Stuhlmueller 1983: 233-54; Scobie 1984a: 55-56) combines a strong emphasis on the restriction of Jesus' mission to Jews in his lifetime (10:5-6) with an equally strong emphasis on the Great Commission (see above, 12-3.4a.i), the command to preach the gospel to all nations (28:18-20; cf. Clark 1947).

Luke (see Hahn 1965: 128-36; Senior and Stuhlmueller 1983: 255-79; Kiddle 1935; S. G. Wilson 1973; Scobie 1984a: 56-57) shows how the threefold OT expectation of the restoration of Israel, the reunion of North and South, and the eschatological ingathering of the Gentiles is anticipated in Jesus' ministry by his portrayal of Jesus as the one who fulfills God's promises to Israel (1:54-55), who favors Samaritans (cf. 11-3.5b), and who sends out the Seventy (10:1-12), the traditional number of the Gentile nations (see Wilson, 45-47). The same threefold pattern is used to structure the book of Acts (see Acts 1:8; cf. Scobie 1992b: 299). The crucial role of the Holy Spirit at each stage of the realization of the eschatological pattern is emphasized by the prominence given to the Jewish Pentecost (Acts 2), the Samaritan Pentecost (Acts 8), and the Gentile Pentecost (Acts 10).

It is sometimes alleged that interest in missionary outreach, including outreach to the Gentiles, is totally lacking in the Johannine literature (see Davey 1961; Hahn 1965: 152-63; Senior and Stuhlmueller 1983: 280-96; Scobie 1984a: 58-59; the most comprehensive study is Okure 1988). Though mission is not a dominant theme, John does underline the universal nature of the gospel; Christ is "the Savior of the world" (John 4:42; cf. 3:16; 1 John 2:2). There are no accounts of contacts with Gentiles, but the request of the Gentile "Greeks" in John 12:20-22 to see Jesus foreshadows the Gentile mission *after* Jesus' death and resurrection (cf. v. 24), as also does the reference in 10:16 to gathering in "other sheep that do not belong to this fold." Moreover, an important theme in John, that of "sending," expresses a strong sense of "mission" (see May 1959: 27; DuBose 1983). As the Father sent the Son (7:28-29; 8:42), so the Son sends his disciples (20:21) into the world (17:18), and "whoever receives one whom I send receives me; and whoever receives me receives him who sent me" (13:20). The Father sends the Holy Spirit to aid the church in its mission (cf. Winn 1981: 88-101).

12-3.5. DO THE WORK OF AN EVANGELIST

The NT reflects a variety of situations and methods in relation to outreach to the Gentiles (see Senior and Stuhlmueller 1983: 332-39). The role of the apostles as those "sent out" was a key one (cf. 15-3.2a). Their role was to proclaim the significance of the Christ event. Peter (and the rest of the Twelve?) confined their apostolic ministry almost entirely to Jews. Paul claimed to be an apostle (Gal 1:1), and specifically "an apostle to the Gentiles" (Rom 11:13).

The designation "evangelist" *(euangelistēs)* occurs only three times in the NT, in Acts 21:8 (with reference to Philip), in the list of gifts in Eph 4:11, and in the advice to Timothy to "do the work of an evangelist" in 2 Tim 4:5. Evangelists are distinguished from apostles in Eph 4:11, but it is doubtful that the term signifies a formal office (see Shepherd 1962; V. Becker 1976: 114). It refers rather to a function, that of "proclaiming the good news about the kingdom of God and the name of Jesus Christ" (Acts 8:12). The activity of Philip in Acts 8 suggests that an evangelist was an itinerant preacher, but the fact that Philip settled down in Caesarea (8:40; 21:8) and Timothy settled in Ephesus (1 Tim 1:3) shows that "the work of an evangelist properly belongs to the local church leader in the exercise of his normal duties" (A. Campbell 1992: 128).

In addition to verbal communication, the power of example is extremely important (see "The Modalities of Mission" in Senior and Stuhlmueller 1983: 332-39). This is strikingly demonstrated in the advice given in 1 Pet 3:1: "Wives

. . . accept the authority of your husbands, so that, even if some of them do not obey the word, they may be won over *without a word* by their wives' conduct."

The greater part of the NT material on missionary methods relates to Paul (Acts, the Epistles). While his primary task was to preach the gospel (1 Cor 1:17; etc.) and to "win" (9:19) people, his concern was not just with "saving souls." "For Paul . . . conversion meant incorporation. Baptism is baptism into the body of Christ. The new believer implicitly becomes a believer-in-community" (Bowers 1987: 187). Hence Paul was very much concerned with founding and nurturing Christian communities. "Paul repeatedly displays commitment not only to founding but also to upbuilding, not only to begetting but also to rearing, not only to planting but also to nurturing" (188-89). Through return visits, through a team of helpers, and of course through his letters Paul continually sought to build up these communities.

New Testament: Consummation

12-4. A GREAT MULTITUDE FROM EVERY NATION

The NT's vision of the ultimate goal of creation and of history is breathtaking in its scope. It gives a central place to the people of God, but this is a community that consists of people "from every tribe and language and people and nation" who have been ransomed by the blood of Christ (Rev 5:9).

12-4.1. THE GOD OF THE NATIONS

From beginning to end the Bible sees God as the ruler of all nations. The writer of Revelation is told that he must prophesy "about many peoples and nations and languages and kings" (10:11). Christ is destined "to rule all the nations" (12:5), and a share in that rule is promised to believers who persevere in their faith (2:26).

12-4.2. THE NATIONS RAGE

As the NT looks to the future, on the one hand it sees the nations as powers that will continue to oppose God and his kingdom. From the vantage point of the final consummation the elders can say,

> The nations raged,
>   but your wrath has come. (Rev 11:18; cf. Ps 46:6)

In keeping with the coming intensification of evil (4-4.2), the nations will make war on each other, and on God's people. The power of Rome in particular is seen as ranged against the church.

12-4.3. TO ALL THE NATIONS

On the other hand, the time between now and the end is also the time for the preaching of the gospel to all nations (cf. 3-4.4a; see J. W. Thompson 1971). Before the end comes, "the good news must first be proclaimed to all nations" (Mark 13:10). "And this good news of the kingdom will be proclaimed throughout the world, as a testimony to all nations; and then the end will come" (Matt 24:14; cf. also Matt 26:13//Mark 14:9, which presuppose a worldwide preaching of the gospel).

Such a worldwide mission is also in view in 2 Pet 3:9, where one of the reasons given for the delay of the parousia is: "The Lord is not slow about his promise, as some think of slowness, but is patient with you, not wanting any to perish, but all to come to repentance."

In Rev 14:6-7, as part of his visions of the end events, John sees "another angel flying in midheaven, with an eternal gospel *(euangelion)* to proclaim to those who live on the earth — to every nation and tribe and language and people." Earlier, in 5:9, the twenty-four elders are pictured praising Christ as the Lamb and singing,

> You were slaughtered and by your blood you ransomed for God
> saints from every tribe and language and people and nation.

In other words, the benefits of Christ's atoning death are available to all. Thus, in addition to the worldwide mission conducted by the church within history, Rev 14:6-7 envisages *a final eschatological proclamation of the gospel* which will ensure, not that all humankind will be saved, but that all will receive, if not in this life, then at the final consummation, an opportunity to hear and to respond to God's gracious offer of salvation through Christ.

12-4.4. THE JUDGMENT OF THE NATIONS

Ultimately all the powers opposed to God will be defeated (see more fully, 4-4.3) and all humankind must face the final judgment (see more fully, 16-4.3).

12-4.5. THE FINAL INGATHERING OF THE NATIONS

Although with the dawning of the new order the eschatological ingathering of the nations has begun, that process will be completed only at the last day. As we have seen (12-3.1c), Jesus envisaged Jews and Gentiles sharing in the kingdom of God at the final consummation. The time will come when "every creature in heaven and on earth and under the earth and in the sea, and all that is in them" will join in ascribing blessing and honor and glory to God (Rev 5:13).

In John's vision of the final consummation, the holy city has no need of sun or moon, "for the glory of God is its light, and its lamp is the Lamb. The nations will walk by its light, and the kings of the earth will bring their glory into it. . . . People will bring into it the glory and honor of the nations" (Rev 21:23-24, 26). Here is the final fulfillment of the promise of the eschatological tribute of the nations (above, 12-2.3c). Though fulfilled in a symbolic way by the gifts of the Magi and the Pauline collection (above, 12-3.4a.iii), only at the end will all the kings of the earth bring their riches to (the heavenly) Jerusalem. Only then in a complete way will

> nations . . . come to your light,
>   and kings to the brightness of your dawn,

bringing with them "the wealth of the nations" (Isa 60:3, 5). All that is best and finest in human society and human culture is not abandoned, but is redeemed and brought in to share the life of the kingdom of God. All that is unclean and false is of course excluded (Rev 21:27; cf. 22:3; see Scobie 1992b: 304-5).

The holy city is envisaged as a diverse community into which will be incorporated peoples of all nations, languages, and cultures. All national rivalries will be abandoned and hurts healed in the eschatological community in the center of which stands the tree of life, for "the leaves of the tree are for the healing of the nations" (22:2).

12-5. THE NATIONS: THEOLOGICAL REFLECTIONS

1. The relation between God's people and the other peoples of humankind is a major issue dividing Judaism and Christianity. In the OT Israel consists of the descendants of Abraham and especially of the twelve sons of Jacob/Israel. There was always provision for the incorporation of non-Israelites, and by NT times this had crystallized into recognized procedures for the acceptance of proselytes. However, despite some evidence of Pharisees seeking proselytes (cf. Matt 23:15), Judaism was — and remains — basically a nonmissionary religion. Christianity, on the other hand, virtually from the outset, embarked on a vigor-

ous program of missionary outreach, the main features of which are clearly delineated in Acts and the letters of Paul.

The contrast, however, as a biblical-theological approach clearly shows, is not simply one of OT versus NT. An important feature of OT expectation is the ingathering of the Gentiles. Despite glimpses of interest in a missionary role for Israel in Isaiah, Jonah, and Psalms, Jewish missionary outreach was minimal because of the belief that the ingathering would be an eschatological event, would be the work of God, and would consist of a centripetal pilgrimage of the nations to Zion (cf. 12-2.4c). Once again the distinctive feature of the NT proclamation is that with the Christ event the eschaton has broken into history: *now* is the time for the eschatological ingathering of the Gentiles. To this conviction the NT adds a startling reversal of OT expectation in two respects: (a) the mission to the Gentiles is not only the work of God, for he has entrusted the task to his people, the church; (b) the centripetal movement of OT expectation is replaced by a centrifugal movement, "beginning from Jerusalem" and reaching to the ends of the earth.

2. In the period therefore between the Christ event and the parousia, *mission* is a major mandate of the church. The good news is to be shared as far as possible with all humankind. This in no way implies a hope or expectation that all will respond positively. The church's task is to proclaim the gospel: it is a fact of history, already well attested in NT times, that some respond and some do not. While Paul may have seen his missionary travels as an effort to reach as many as possible before the parousia, other NT passages think of the huge task of worldwide evangelization as one of the reasons for the delay of the end (cf. 3-4.4a). The church today still lives in this interim period, and the proclamation of the gospel to all humankind remains one of its greatest tasks and challenges.

3. Missionary zeal has varied over the centuries. After the amazing expansion of the early centuries and the gradual conversion of most of Europe, in medieval times interest in evangelism faded. Because Christendom was hemmed in by Islam, the opportunities for missionary outreach were severely limited; that attitude continued in early Protestantism. The situation changed dramatically, however, with the discovery of new worlds, and it was the Roman Catholic Church that was the first to launch a renewed missionary outreach. It was only with the evangelical revivals of the eighteenth century that Protestant outreach began and eventually developed, especially in the nineteenth century, into a huge global enterprise.

4. Worldwide discovery and exploration, along with the whole process that culminated in the "global village" of the late twentieth century, have also brought the Christian West up against other cultures and other world religions. Many within the Christian church have reacted strongly against any view that regards these religions as representing error, with all truth being vested in Christianity. That "all religions lead to God" is a widely held view. Many today reject any form of direct evangelization, and limit "mission" to various forms of

humanitarian aid, or at most to providing assistance to indigenous churches. The confusion of religious and cultural (including economic) outreach has rightly come under particularly strong condemnation.

BT suggests that Christianity must take a dialectical attitude toward other religions. The OT strongly condemns native Canaanite religion because of its polytheism, its idolatry, and its immoral practices such as child sacrifice and cultic prostitution. The NT takes a similar attitude to the pagan religions of the Greco-Roman world. On the other hand, the recognition by BT that God works in the created order as well as the historical order does not support the view that God's people are in sole possession of all truth. The God of the Bible "desires everyone to be saved and to come to the knowledge of the truth" (1 Tim 2:4). All peoples can know something of God and of his will for them (cf. 2-1.4a and b), especially through creation and conscience (2-3.3). In the NT it is in Acts in particular that a bridge-building missionary strategy is commended. In his address at Athens (Acts 17), Paul's attitude toward the existing religion of his hearers is a dialectical one: he is outraged by the city's idolatry, yet he is also able to find common ground with his hearers before going on to urge the distinctive claims of the Christian faith. Therefore, a Christian attitude to other religions, based on biblical principles, will seek to be discriminating and will take Christ as the norm. It is foolish to hold that all religions lead to God; some religions deny the existence of God! Nor can Christians accept as equally true religions (including sects and cults) that advocate and encourage practices that are clearly immoral by biblical standards. (Of course, Christians are to be judged by biblical standards also!) Biblical principles, on the other hand, do allow Christians today to affirm what is true and what is best in other faiths, while at the same time seeking to share the good news of what God has done uniquely in and through the Christ event.

A more speculative question, often raised today, concerns the fate of adherents of other faiths (in previous centuries, or at the present time) who have never had a chance to hear the Christian message (see the thorough treatment of this issue in J. A. Sanders 1991). This is not a problem for those who believe in "universalism," in the sense that all people will ultimately be saved. Such a view, however, can be held only by ignoring the biblical evidence (not least in the teaching of Jesus) of a final judgment and a final separation (see the discussion in 16-4.3d.i, and cf. Sanders, 81-128). The opposite position is that salvation is confined to those who hear and accept the Christian gospel (see Sanders, 37-79). This view appeals broadly to the teaching of the NT that salvation is by grace alone and that God's grace is manifest in the Christ event. It also appeals to specific texts, especially Jesus' words in John 14:6: "I am the way, and the truth, and the life. No one comes to the Father except through me," and Peter's declaration in Acts 4:12 that "there is no other name under heaven given among mortals by which we must be saved." It holds that while people may attain some knowledge of God through general revelation (see 2-1.4; 2-3.3), that knowledge is only enough to make them deserving of God's condemnation but not suffi-cient for salvation (cf. Sanders, 68-70). This raises a serious problem for many believers: How could a just and loving God condemn all those who lived before Christ, and the billions who have lived since Christ but have never had a chance to hear the gospel? Is such a God the God of the Bible, and specifically the God whom Jesus called "Father"? The Bible, it is true, does not deal directly with this speculative question, though it may be held that in at least three places it points toward an answer. Firstly, in its treatment of those who lived *before* Christ, the Bible affirms that a person can be saved without actually knowing the name of Christ. Such was the case with Abraham (Rom 4), and indeed with all those on "the roll call of faith" in Heb 11. Of course, salvation is always a gift of God's grace to be received by faith. By analogy, it is possible for others who have not heard the name of Christ to respond in faith to God's grace. Secondly, Rev 14:6-7 (above, 12-4.3) speaks of a final, eschatological proclamation of the gospel that will give all peoples a chance to respond. Thirdly, as already noted (9-3.5), the belief that Christ preached to the dead (the descent into Hades; see 1 Pet 3:18-20; 4:6) suggests that all people get a chance to hear the Christian message, if not in this life then beyond it, and are judged depending on their reaction to the gospel (see Sanders, 177-214). Affirming this possibility, however, in no way detracts from the biblical summons to witness to Christ as the supreme revela-tion of God and to seek to share the good news with all humankind.

5. The NT provides glimpses of specific missionary methods (cf. 12-3.5). While the focus tends to be on the apostles and other individuals, including some who are occasionally described as "evangelists," the NT also suggests that mission is a function of the whole people of God. Verbal proclamation of the gospel is essential, but this can be seriously jeopardized unless it is matched by Christian example.

CHAPTER 13

Land and City

Old Testament: Proclamation

13-1. THE LAND THAT I WILL SHOW YOU

The biblical account of Israel as the people of God is closely bound up with the relationship between Israel and "the Land."

13-1.1. LAND AND CITY

It is a commonplace that the OT is a book of *history;* much less attention has been paid to the large role played in the OT by *geography.* "The Land" is an important theme in BT, especially OT theology, though one that was for long largely neglected (cf. W. D. Davies 1974: 4-5; Brueggemann 1977b: 3; Martens 1981: 97; Orlinsky 1986: 41). In 1943 von Rad published an important article entitled "Verheissenes Land und Jahwes Land im Hexateuch" (ET, "The Promised Land and Yahweh's Land in the Hexateuch," in von Rad 1966: 79-93), in which he asserted that "in the whole of the Hexateuch there is probably no more important idea than that expressed in terms of the land promised and later granted by Yahweh, an idea found in all the sources, and indeed in every part of each of them" (79). Von Rad noted that this key OT theme was so far largely unexamined; his own article claimed to be no more than a brief survey, and in any case was confined to the Hexateuch. In due course the theme was taken up by a number of scholars, most notably by Davies in his *The Gospel and the Land* (1974) and by Brueggemann in his *The Land* (1977b). These were welcome correctives (that have been followed up by other scholars), though Brueggemann certainly goes too far in claiming that "land is central, if not *the central theme* of biblical faith" (3). Similarly, E. A. Martens has an excellent discussion of the Land in his *God's Design: A Focus on Old Testament Theology* (1981), but he can make "Land" one of the four major themes of OT theology (cf. E-1.3) only by

541

including material under that heading, such as the Wisdom Literature, that does not have any particular link to the Land in the biblical text (cf. von Waldow 1974: 493).

Discussion of this theme has been clouded at times by a failure to distinguish clearly between "land" and "the Land" (Alfaro 1978 does not make a clear enough distinction). "Land" can mean "the good earth," created by God and graciously given by him to all humankind as a source of sustenance, prosperity, and well-being. The God of the Bible is not just concerned with "spiritual" matters and with the salvation of people's "souls," but with their total well-being, and in this concern "land" plays an important role. This is an aspect of God's activity in *the created order,* and as such was discussed in 2-1.

But "land" in the Bible can also mean one specific geographical area, the land of Canaan or Palestine, "the Land" (with a capital *L*), "the Promised Land," "the holy land" (Zech 2:12; *Wis* 12:3; *2 Macc* 1:7), the Land of Israel (*'erets yisrā'ēl,* not common, but see 1 Sam 13:19; 1 Chr 22:2; Ezek 40:2; Matt 2:20), that figures prominently in God's dealings with his people in *the historical order* (on terminology, see von Rad 1966: 80-82; W. Janzen 1992: 143-45). It is this understanding of the Land that is the concern of this chapter.

Various descriptions of the *extent* of the Land are given in the OT (see esp. Num 34:1-12; Deut 11:24; cf. W. Janzen 1992: 145-46). The exact boundaries are of little significance to Christian BT, though they can be crucial in relation to the claims of some modern Zionists that the whole of "the Land of Israel" rightfully belongs to the Jews (see below, 13-5.4).

"The Land" is a biblical theme that is marked by deep-rooted tensions and ambiguities. The center and focus of the Land is the city, and the themes of Holy Land and Holy City are closely related.

13-1.2. THE HOLY LAND

In the course of salvation history God's people alternate between living in the Land and living outside it. "Israel," as Brueggemann (1977b) says, "is always on the move from land to landlessness, from landlessness to land" (14). To be more precise, biblical history can be divided into six periods, in three of which Israel is "landless," and in three "landed." In the OT there are two landless periods and two landed; in the NT (see 13-3) there is one landed and one landless period.

In the OT, *landless period I* extends from the call of Abraham to the settlement in Canaan. The patriarchs lived but did not settle in the Land. As Heb 11:9 well summarizes it, Abraham "stayed for a time in the land he had been promised, as in a foreign land, living in tents." The long years of slavery in Egypt and the wanderings in the wilderness were spent entirely outside the Land.

From the settlement to the exile constitutes *landed period I,* though the division of the kingdom and the fall of the North in 722 B.C. reduced the area occupied by God's people.

The Babylonian exile is *landless period II,* when not all God's people, but the most important part, were forced to live far from the Land.

The return, from 538 B.C. onward, marks *landed period II,* though the "Land" was then an even smaller area around the Holy City and temple.

a. The Land as Gift and Goal

In the OT the Land can be evaluated positively. While they live in it, it is a gracious *gift,* bestowed by God, for his people to enjoy. In their landless periods it is a future *goal* to which God's people can look forward in hope and anticipation.

The Land as goal is a central element in God's promise to Abraham in Gen 12:1-9 (cf. B. W. Anderson 1995: 146-48). Even before the promise of descendants, Abraham is told, "Go . . . to the land that I will show you" (12:1); and when he reaches Canaan God promises, "To your offspring I will give this land" (12:7). The promise is renewed in 13:14-17, in the covenant of 15:18-21: "To your descendants I give this land, from the river of Egypt to the great river, the river Euphrates," and again in 17:8 where Abraham and his descendants are promised the Land as "a perpetual holding."

Abraham only sojourns in the Land (17:8), though he does acquire one small portion as a token of the whole, the family burial place at Machpelah (Gen 23). The promise of the Land is continued to Abraham's descendants: to Isaac (26:3) and to Jacob, who is promised, "The land that I gave to Abraham and Isaac I will give to you, and I will give the land to your offspring after you" (35:12). The enslavement of the Israelites in Egypt appears to make the Land an impossible goal, but the promise is renewed to Moses (Exod 3:8, 17; 6:8; cf. Deut 1:8). The exodus deliverance revives the hope, and Israel journeys toward the Promised Land. The story of the spies (Num 13) underlines both the greatness of God's gift and the people's reluctance to accept it in faith. The promise of the Land is also echoed in later summaries of salvation history (1 Chr 16:15-18; Neh 9:8; Ps 105:11).

Since God is the creator of the whole earth, the Land is first and foremost God's Land (March 1994: 60-61). The Land belongs to God, but he has granted the use of it to Israel; "for the land is mine; with me you are but aliens and tenants" (Lev 25:23). The Land is "the LORD's land" (Josh 22:19). "Israel can claim nothing. Instead, her existence, livelihood, and security depend completely on her God, the true owner of the land" (von Waldow 1974: 496). The gift of the Land is a major theme of Deuteronomy (cf. P. D. Miller 1969; W. Janzen 1992: 147-48; Habel 1995: 39-41). Although Israel is going to have to wrest the Land from existing inhabitants, the emphasis falls on the Land as a gift of God's grace. It is God who will defeat the Canaanites (Deut 7:1) and bring his people "into the land that he swore to your ancestors, to Abraham, to Isaac, and to Jacob, to give you — a land with fine, large cities that you did not build, houses filled with all sorts of goods that you did not fill, hewn cisterns that you did not hew, vineyards and olive groves that you did not plant" (Deut 6:10-11). Constantly it is stressed that "the LORD your God is bringing you into a good land" (8:7), "a land flowing with milk and honey" (6:3; etc.) that is the "inheritance" or "allotment" *(nachªlâ)* of Israel (4:21; etc.; see Habel, 33-35). With the settlement in the Land, God's promises to the Israelites were fulfilled (Josh 23:14) and God "gave them rest *(yānach)*" (21:44).

The book of Joshua is almost entirely concerned with the Land, its conquest (Josh 1–12) and its division among the twelve tribes (Josh 13–22). The allocation of territory by lot (14:2, etc.) demonstrates that it is the LORD who is granting the land to the tribes and families of Israel (cf. von Rad 1966: 85; Martens 1981: 105; Habel 1995: 54-74).

If there is some evidence in the OT of a "royal ideology" according to which the king controls and uses the Land as he pleases (Habel 1995: 17-32), this runs quite counter to the dominant biblical view. Nowhere is this seen more clearly than in the story of 1 Kgs 21 where King Ahab wishes to acquire Naboth's vineyard but Naboth refuses to part with his "ancestral inheritance," i.e., the land originally allotted to his tribe and family. The moral of the story is that the king is not a law unto himself but must obey God's Torah and must respect God's allotment of the Land to his people.

b. The Land as Challenge

The Land is not only evaluated positively as gift and goal; it can also be evaluated ambiguously, as a *challenge* to which Israel may or may not be able to rise. This too is an important emphasis in Deuteronomy: as well as blessings, the Land also brings certain dangers.

i. There is the danger of forgetting that the Land is a gift from the LORD, and of relying on self rather than on God. "Take care that you do not forget the LORD your God. . . . When you have eaten your fill and have built fine houses and live in them, and when your herds and flocks have multiplied, and your silver and gold is multiplied, and all that you have is multiplied, then do not exalt yourself, forgetting the LORD your God. . . . Do not say to yourself, 'My power and the might of my own hand have gotten me this wealth.' But remember the LORD your God, for it is he who gives you power to get wealth" (Deut 8:11-18; cf. also 6:10-11; 9:4-5).

ii. There is the danger of being seduced by the gods of the Land and of worshiping them rather than the LORD. "Take care, or you will be seduced into turning away, serving other gods and worshiping them, for then the anger of the LORD will be kindled against you . . . then you will perish quickly off the good land that the LORD is giving you" (Deut 11:16-17; cf. 6:14).

iii. There is the danger of failing to live in the Land in accordance with God's commandments. The gift of the Land demands a specific lifestyle (cf. Martens 1981: 108-10), and in many ways the Torah constitutes God's guidelines for living in the Land (cf. von Rad 1966: 90-91; Brueggemann 1977b: 60; W. D. Davies 1984: 51-52; Habel 1995: 43-47). "These are the statutes and ordinances that you must diligently observe in the land that the LORD . . . has given you" (Deut 12:1). "Thus the land was conceived as a sacred trust, granted to Israel on condition that it remain faithful to the laws of the God who had given it" (Clements 1968: 51). Ps 37 sees trust and obedience as conditions for retaining the Land:

> Trust in the LORD, and do good;
>> so you will live in the land, and enjoy security. (v. 3)

It is the meek (*ʿanāwîm* = "poor, afflicted, humble") who "shall inherit the land" (v. 11; cf. also vv. 9, 22, 29). Disobedience, on the other hand, pollutes the Land (Lev 18:27; Num 35:33; Deut 21:23; Ps 106:35).

iv. There is the danger of not being content with God's gift but of expanding beyond the boundaries of the Land. The conquest of Palestine proper was not completed until the time of David. But David did not stop there; he embarked on what were clearly wars of conquest against neighboring states: Edom, Moab, Ammon, and Syria (2 Sam 8). Solomon inherited this empire which constituted "the land of his dominion" (1 Kgs 9:19).

c. Loss of the Land

There is a constant tension between the understanding of the Land as an unconditional gift promised to the descendants of Abraham (Gen 13:15; 17:8; Ps 105:9-11; on this see esp. Orlinsky 1986) and as a gift granted only on condition of Israel's continued faithfulness to the covenant and obedience to the Torah (cf. von Rad 1966: 91). The Israelites do not have a "right" to the Land; as March (1994) correctly points out, "from the biblical perspective . . . land rights are quite subordinate to land responsibilities" (56). Deut 28:63 warns that if the Israelites do not diligently obey the Torah, they will be "plucked off the land" (cf. 4:25-26; 30:15-20). Throughout the Deuteronomic history of Joshua–2 Kings there is an increasing emphasis on the conditional nature of the gift (see Josh 23:16; 1 Kgs 9:6-7; 14:15; 2 Kgs 21:8), and it is the people's persistent disloyalty and disobedience that leads the prophets to foretell the loss of the Land (on the Land in the prophets, see esp. Zimmerli 1985).

Thus Amos proclaims to Amaziah, the religious leader of the Northern Kingdom:

> Your land shall be parceled out by line;
> you yourself shall die in an unclean land,
>   and Israel shall surely go into exile away from its land.
>
> (7:17; cf. 4:2-3; 5:27)

The predictions of Amos were fulfilled with the fall of the northern kingdom of Israel to the Assyrians in 722 B.C. (2 Kgs 17:23).

It is Jeremiah who most clearly foretold the loss of the southern kingdom of Judah. Through the worship of false gods, social injustice, and alliances with foreign powers Israel has defiled the Land (cf. Habel 1995: 80-84):

> I brought you into a plentiful land
>   to eat its fruits and its good things.
> But when you entered you defiled my land. (2:7)

Because of the people's disobedience, God will bring up the Babylonians against them: "I will bring them against this land and its inhabitants. . . . This whole land shall become a ruin and a waste" (25:9, 11). Jeremiah's predictions became reality with the fall of the Land to the Babylonians in 597 and 586, and the subsequent exile of many of the people from the Land.

13-1.3. LIVING WITHOUT THE LAND

Paradoxically, the Land also receives a much more negative evaluation in the OT. As Jansen (1973) points out, in the OT "the land is a sacred plot by virtue not of any inherent sacredness but of God's choice of it as an instrument towards his purposes. If these purposes are thwarted he will lay aside that instrument" (175). God's people can live without the Land; indeed, in some ways they are better off when they are landless than when they are landed.

a. Salvation History outside the Land

Many key persons and events of salvation history are located outside the Holy Land. The patriarchs only sojourned there; their faith was not tied to any specific location (cf. von Rad 1962: 7). The great foundational events of Israel's faith — the exodus deliverance, the concluding of the covenant, and the giving of the Torah — all take place outside the Land. Moses, the greatest leader of God's people in the OT, never entered the Land.

b. Grace in the Wilderness

It would be going too far to say that the Pentateuch as a whole, or Deuteronomy in particular, sees the wilderness period as the ideal. The wilderness period is "an ambiguous place and time" (Cohn 1981: 14; cf. W. D. Davies 1974: 75-90; von Rad 1962: 280-89). After all, the wilderness is the place of Israel's murmuring and rebellion. But for Jeremiah it was the place of Israel's honeymoon with the LORD (2:2); Israel found "grace in the wilderness" (31:2). God, they discovered, is present even there, and is able to provide for his people in marvelous ways (water from the rock, manna, quail).

Similarly, when Israel lost the Land at the time of the exile, this was not the unmitigated disaster so many feared it would be. In fact, the exile saw the ministry of Israel's three greatest prophets — Jeremiah, Ezekiel, and 2 Isaiah. Once again Israel found God outside the Land, and indeed it was in exile that she learned some of her greatest lessons. Jeremiah in particular, though foretelling an eventual return (29:10), encouraged the exiles to settle down in the land of Babylon, for they could live and serve God there as well as in the Land of Israel (29:7). In 2 Isaiah Israel's faith achieved a more universal dimension; it is in and through the exile that God's people come to realize that their God is Lord of the lands and not just Lord of the Land. Von Waldow (1974) declares that "to be a great nation, Israel needs a land — there can be no great nation without land" (505); but in and through the exile, when she was not great in any political or military sense, Israel discovered that it is not necessary to be "a great nation" in order to know and love and serve God. Thus the exile drew the people back to the wilderness narratives as "a paradigm of their own experience" (Cohn 1981: 23; cf. Jer 2:2-3; 31:1-3; Hos 2:14; 9:10).

c. The Dispersion

Even after the return of some of the exiles, others chose to continue living outside the Land. From then until NT times, for various reasons the Dispersion, or *Diaspora*, grew, and groups of Jews settled in various locations, most notably in Alexandria in Egypt.

Such books as Esther and Daniel deal with the perils of the Diaspora, though they also strongly express the conviction that God cares for and protects his people outside the Land.

In the late OT period it is evident that the Torah rather than the Land is becoming the focal point for Israel's faith. By NT times large numbers of Jews had long been living in "the Dispersion among the Greeks" (John 7:35).

13-1.4. THE HOLY CITY

The Pentateuch looks forward to the entry of Israel into the Promised Land, but it is really only with the settlement that interest develops in a holy city as well as a holy land. Deuteronomy, however, anticipates the significance of what it terms "the place that the LORD your God will choose" (12:5; etc.). With the settlement it was only natural that interest should turn to finding some focal point in the Land that could serve as a religious and political center.

a. Shechem

The earliest contender for such a center was Shechem, a city and sanctuary located some forty miles north of Jerusalem in a strategic pass between Mount Gerizim and Mount Ebal (see B. W. Anderson 1957). In the context of the promise, Gen 12:6 states that Abraham "passed through the land to the place (*māqôm*; LXX *topos*) at Shechem." In accordance with Moses' commands (Deut 27:2-8), it was there that Israel renewed the covenant (Josh 8:30-35). And Josh 22–24 makes clear that Shechem was the first Israelite center after the settlement. It was only after the advent of the monarchy that Shechem came to be identified as a northern rather than a national center (cf. 1 Kgs 12:1). While the city retained its prestige as a religious center during the divided monarchy, it lost its political significance with the establishment of Samaria as the northern capital on a more defensible site.

b. Jerusalem

Jerusalem was not captured at the time of the settlement but only two centuries later in the time of David. According to 2 Sam 5:6-9, "David took the stronghold of Zion." David obviously saw the military, political, and religious possibilities of the site, and chose it as a focus of unity among the Israelite tribes (cf. McConville 1992: 23). Its choice as capital is closely linked both with the royal theology (6-1.2b) and the Jerusalem temple (14-1.1a.iv) (see Weinfeld 1983). The transfer there of the ark (2 Sam 6) helped increase its prestige (see Cohn 1981: 66-69). "With the forging of a link between Sinai and Zion . . . Jerusalem is assimilated to the ancient covenantal theology" (McConville, 26; cf. Roberts 1973: 343). So closely is the city connected with David that it can be called "the city of David" (2 Sam 6:12, 16, etc.). It is here that Solomon built the temple. With the division of the kingdom, Jerusalem became the capital of Judah only, but then with the fall of the North it became the sole focal point of the Land. With the centralization of all worship in the Jerusalem temple by Josiah (see 14-1.1a.v), the city received a further boost to its prestige.

Jerusalem thus came to be seen as the Holy City, the city chosen by the LORD. Whatever the original historical meaning of Deuteronomy's references to "the place that the LORD your God will choose," within the context of the canon they are to be taken as referring to Jerusalem. Shechem could claim to be a much older center. The biblical story has many twists and turns in its plot; it is full of surprises, and one of them is the choice of Jerusalem as Holy City despite the fact that it was one of the last parts of the Holy Land to be acquired by Israel.

As the center and focus of the Land, Jerusalem could stand for the Land and people as a whole. Especially when personified as the daughter of Zion (Ps 9:14; Isa 1:8; Jer 4:31; etc.), "Jerusalem typifies Israel as God's chosen people" (Porteous 1967: 97).

c. The Zion Theology

OT history and theology can be seen as revolving around two mountains, Mount Sinai and Mount Zion (cf. Levenson 1985: 89-96). Yet despite the central significance of covenant and Torah, the actual site of Sinai has no ongoing significance. It is Zion that becomes the center and symbol of OT faith, and the focus of what is aptly termed a "Zion theology" (see Gowan 1986: 6-9).

Jerusalem may have made a late appearance in the story of Israel, but along with the city David inherited ancient traditions attached to the site (Hayes 1963; but see Roberts 1973). There are traces of the belief that Jerusalem was located at the center of the world, at "the navel of the earth *(ṭabbûr hā'ārets;* LXX *omphalos tēs gēs)*" (Ezek 38:12; cf. 5:5); a similar claim was probably also made for Shechem; see Judg 9:37 (cf. W. D. Davies 1974: 6-9; Weinfeld 1983: 106-7; but see Sperling 1976; Talmon 1977). Historical-critical scholars believe that Mount Zion was equated with the Mount Zaphon of Canaanite mythology (cf. Ps 48:2). If there was borrowing of this type, then as always there was considerable adaptation also. BT is not concerned with origins, but with the way the Zion theology functions in the canonical text. Almost certainly the ancient "Salem" ruled by the priest-king Melchizedek (Gen 14:18-20) is intended to be identified with Jerusalem, which provided a link between the Holy City and the father of God's people.

The great prophet of the Holy City is Isaiah (cf. von Rad 1965: 155-69; Dumbrell 1985: 5-20). For him it is the place God has chosen and will protect (Isa 10:12-13; 26:1). He calls on the people to

Look on Zion, the city of our appointed festivals!
    Your eyes will see Jerusalem,
        a quiet habitation, an immovable tent,
    whose stakes will never be pulled up,
        and none of whose ropes will be broken. (33:20)

The Zion theology in fact received its biggest boost when Isaiah encouraged King Ahaz to hold on in face of the invasion of the Assyrians under Sennacherib in 701 B.C. All the signs pointed to Judah suffering the same fate as the Northern Kingdom had twenty years earlier. The country was devastated, but miraculously the besieged city of Jerusalem did not fall to the enemy (Isa 36–37). Zion emerged with a greatly enhanced reputation as the focal point of the Land, the place chosen and protected by the LORD. Canonically, however, Isa 1–39 is balanced by Isa 40f., which presupposes the fall of the city and the Babylonian exile (cf. J. G. McConville 1992: 34).

The Zion theology receives its most remarkable expression in the "psalms of Zion" (Pss 46; 48; 76; 84; 87; 121; 122; 132), in which "the reader encounters remarkable concepts, descriptions and expressions by which Zion or Jerusalem is praised and glorified" (Kraus 1986: 78). Zion is the location chosen by God as his dwelling place (132:13); it is "the city of God" (46:4; 48:1; 87:3), "the holy habitation of the Most High" (46:4). Since Zion was built on a hill, it can be spoken of as "his holy mountain" (48:1); in the OT mountains are symbols both of God's presence and of permanence and security (see Cohn 1981: 25-41). God's presence within the city guarantees protection from enemies from both the created order (46:3) and the historical order (2:1-6; 46:6; 48:4-7; 76). According to 46:4, "There is a river whose streams make glad the city of God." Since no river actually flows from Zion, critical scholars see here the influence of ancient Near Eastern traditions of the source of the primeval waters as the dwelling place of the god El (cf. Hayes 1963: 423; Kraus, 80); in its present context water represents the supreme symbol of life.

The Zion theology must be seen in its canonical context that serves to modify the glorification of Zion in two ways. Firstly, as against the ancient Near Eastern mythology that may have had some influence on this tradition, "in the Israelite view, Zion was not a holy hill from primeval times; rather, at a particular point in history, in the time of David, it became sacred, the place where Yahweh chose to be present in the midst of his people" (B. W. Anderson 1983: 193-94). Secondly, Zion did not prove to be invincible after all; at a particular point in history it did fall to its enemies, and "no almighty divine power intervened to save Jerusalem from Nebuchadnezzar's armies" (Gowan 1986: 8). Isa 1–39 and the Zion psalms have to be read in the light of that fact.

d. Loss of the City

Not surprisingly the history of the city closely parallels that of the Land. In their proclamation of judgment on a faithless and disobedient nation, the prophets foretell the loss of the city as well as the Land.

The prophet Micah thundered:

> Zion shall be plowed as a field;
> Jerusalem shall become a heap of ruins. (3:12)

Ezekiel employed symbolic actions to foretell the coming siege of Jerusalem (4:1-3). But it was Jeremiah in particular who fearlessly declared the impending doom of the city (see J. G. McConville 1992: 37-40). In a striking example of prophetic symbolism, Jeremiah smashed a potter's earthenware jug in the presence of some of the elders and priests, and proclaimed God's message: "So will I break this people and this city. . . . I am now bringing upon this city . . . all the disaster that I have pronounced against it" (19:10, 15).

These prophecies were fulfilled with the capture of Jerusalem and the destruction of the temple in 586.

13-1.5. LIVING WITHOUT THE CITY

God's people learned in exile to survive without the city, as they did without the Land. Daniel prayed with his windows open toward Jerusalem (Dan 6:10), yet it was in Babylon that he was called to serve God (cf. *Jdt* 9:1).

Old Testament: Promise

13-2. A LAND OF DELIGHT

13-2.1. RESTORATION AND REBUILDING

The Babylonian exile taught God's people that they could live apart from the Holy Land and the Holy City. Nevertheless, the great prophets of the exile did announce a return to a restored Land and a rebuilt city; these themes play a prominent role especially in the prophecies of Ezekiel and 2 Isaiah.

Yet the actual return, begun in 538, fell short of expectations, to put it mildly. The restored Land, an area surrounding the city of Jerusalem, was but a fraction of the area promised to the patriarchs or ruled by David and Solomon. The city was rebuilt, with difficulty, but not on the grandiose scale that had been hoped for.

The promises of the exilic and postexilic prophets relating to the Land and the city tended therefore to become part of *the eschatological hope*. They naturally were associated with *prophetic* eschatology: a restored kingdom would be located in a restored Land with a restored city as its focal point. Yet *apocalyptic* elements also appear, and these led to a new evaluation of the place of Land and city in biblical faith.

13-2.2. THE HOLY LAND: RETURN TO THE LAND

The prophets who foretold exile from the Land as a punishment for Israel's sins also foretold an eventual return to the Land.

Thus the book of Amos, despite all its words of doom, concludes with the promise:

> I will plant them upon their land,
>   and they shall never again be plucked up
>   out of the land that I have given them. (9:15)

Hosea envisaged a new entry into the Land (2:15). In Jer 16:15 God says of his people, "I will bring them back to their own land that I gave to their ancestors" (cf. 24:6; 30:3, 18; 31:17). Jeremiah symbolized his faith in the future of the Land by redeeming a piece of family property at Anathoth, thus dramatizing the Lord's promise: "Houses and fields and vineyards shall again be bought in this land" (32:6-15; cf. 3:18). His prophecy mentioned a specific time frame: "When Babylon's seventy years are completed will I visit you, and I will fulfill to you my promise and bring you back to this place" (29:10; cf. 25:12). With the return this prophecy was fulfilled, as 2 Chr 36:22 and Ezra 1:1 point out (see J. G. McConville 1992: 44; see also Ezek 20:42; 34:13; 36:24; etc.). In Ezekiel God promises the exiles in Babylon: "I will gather you from the peoples, and assemble you out of the countries where you have been scattered, and I will give you the land of Israel" (11:17; cf. 34:13). 2 Isaiah paints a glowing picture of the return and of the renewed Land (Isa 49:8-13; cf. 32:15-20). Deuteronomy anticipates both the exile and a return conditional on obedience (30:1-5).

13-2.3. THE HOLY LAND: PARADISE RESTORED

It is Ezekiel who provides the most vivid and detailed picture of the restored Land, one in which prophetic and apocalyptic elements blend in bewildering fashion. His vision may have inspired hope in the exiles, but it was so far removed from the reality encountered by the returnees that it could only be seen as a promise of a still-future restoration and transformation of the Land. The Lord promises the exiles, "You shall live in the land that I gave to your ancestors" (36:28; cf. 37:25). "The land that was desolate shall be tilled, instead of being the desolation that it was in the sight of all who passed by. And they will say, 'This land that was desolate has become like the garden of Eden; and the waste and desolate and ruined towns are now inhabited and fortified'" (36:34-35).

The restored Land is described as part of the vision of Ezek 40–48 (see 45:1-8; 47:13–48:29). In a sense, what is envisioned is a reallocation of the Land to the twelve tribes, but one that is not only completely different from the original allocation under Joshua but also completely defies the geography of Palestine (contra Greenberg 1984: 200-201). Brueggemann (1977b) is incorrect in saying that "the land distribution proceeds as the original one" (142). Each tribe is to receive an equal portion consisting of a strip of land running east/west; seven of these are north of a central strip and five are south of it. The boundaries are approximately those of Num 34:1-12, excluding any territory originally allocated in Transjordan as well as "the conquests of the monarchy" (Greenberg, 200), so that the imperialist ambitions of David and Solomon are rejected and God's people are isolated, as far as possible, from foreign influences. The vision powerfully symbolizes the reconstitution of God's people and the principle of equal treatment (see Zimmerli 1985: 258), but since geographically and politically it was incapable of ever being translated into practice, it is to be seen as part of the eschatological hope.

Eschatological symbolism becomes even more dominant in the vision of Ezek 47, in which the prophet sees a stream flowing from the new temple eastward through the Land, increasing as it goes to a great river that flows into the Jordan valley, then south into the Dead Sea, where it makes the water fresh and brings new life, with trees growing on either bank. This is hardly a literal, geographical map of a restored Land; it is a vision of paradise restored. The river recalls the river of Gen 2:10, flowing out of Eden; the living creatures that swarm, and the fish, recall the creation account of Gen 1:20-21; and the trees that bring life and healing recall the tree of life in Gen 2:9. The Land is restored through the God-given, cleansing, healing, life-bringing stream that flows from the sanctuary.

An idealized picture of the restored Land is also found in some of the postexilic prophets. Both Joel and Zechariah pick up on Ezek 47. In Joel's new age,

> a fountain shall come forth from the house of the LORD
>   and water the Wadi Shittim (3:18),

while according to Zechariah's apocalyptic vision of a transformed nature, "living waters shall flow out from Jerusalem, half of them to the eastern sea and half of them to the western sea; it shall continue in summer as in winter" (14:8). Mal 3:10-12 pictures the blessing of the new age: "Then all nations will count you happy, for you will be a land of delight, says the LORD of hosts."

A fully apocalyptic picture is found in 2 *Esdr* 7:26, which speaks of a time when "the land that now is hidden shall be disclosed."

13-2.4. THE HOLY CITY: THE ESCHATOLOGICAL JERUSALEM

In the context of the Babylonian exile, there are prophecies of a rebuilt city parallel to those of a restored Land. Prophetic and apocalyptic elements blend with no clear dividing line between the two.

According to Isa 35:10,

> The ransomed of the LORD shall return,
>   and come to Zion with singing,

and 1:26 declares that Zion "shall be called the city of righteousness, / the faithful city" (cf. 44:26; 51:3).

The modest nature of postexilic Jerusalem, however, paved the way for a development in which "late biblical and post-biblical Judaism made the idealised image of that historical Jerusalem the cornerstone of their hopes for a national and religious renaissance and ultimately perceived in it the prototype of the New Jerusalem, the very pivot around which turned their eschatological aspirations" (Talmon 1971: 307-8).

In the vision of Ezek 40–48 the city is located in the "holy district," that is, part of the central strip of territory separating the tribal allocations (45:6; 48:15-20). The most striking feature is the separation of the temple from the city (45:1-6). The city is described as a square, with three exits or gates on each of the four sides, each one linked with the name of one of the twelve tribes (48:30-35). Another striking feature of Ezekiel's prophecy is that the holy city is never called "Zion" or "Jerusalem"; rather the vision of the new community (and also the book of Ezekiel) concludes with the promise that "the name of the city from that time on shall be, The LORD is There" (*YHWH shāmāh,* 48:35). Thus "God will be present in the Temple, but also among the lay cross-section of all Israel who reside in the city. Holy place and holy people will be realized in the future restoration" (Greenberg 1984: 202). The city serves as the focal point of the restored community of God's people living in the Land, with God himself dwelling in their midst. Similarly, Isa 4:2-6 envisages a cleansed and purified Zion with God's presence (cloud by day, fire by night) within it (cf. Zeph 3:14-18). And, in an apocalyptic context in Joel, God declares:

> You shall know that I, the LORD your God,
>   dwell in Zion, my holy mountain.
> And Jerusalem shall be holy. (3:17)

What virtually constituted a city in ancient times was the wall that surrounded and protected it; the rebuilding of the walls under Nehemiah was the key to the postexilic restoration of Jerusalem. Yet in Zech 2:1-5 the prophet is granted a vision of a restored Jerusalem that is clearly much more symbolic than literal. "Jerusalem shall be inhabited," Zechariah is assured, "like villages *without walls.* . . . For I will be a wall of fire all around it, says the LORD." It is God himself who will be the all-sufficient protection for the eschatological Jerusalem.

In the new age Zion will be the central point to which the Gentiles will flock in the eschatological pilgrimage (Isa 2:2-4; Mic 4:1-3; Zech 8:20-23; etc.; see more fully, 12-2.4). Here the more inward-looking and nationalistic Zion theology has been transformed into a hope that encompasses all the nations of the world.

Isa 54:11-14 presents a vision of the new Jerusalem as a city constructed out of precious stones, a vision that is continued in *Tob* 13:16-17:

> The gates of Jerusalem will be built with sapphire and emerald,
> and all your walls with precious stones.
> The towers of Jerusalem will be built with gold,
> and their battlements with pure gold.
> The streets of Jerusalem will be paved
> with ruby and with stones of Ophir. (v. 16)

Isa 65:17-25 presents an idealized picture of Jerusalem as part of the new creation:

> For I am about to create Jerusalem as a joy,
> and its people as a delight. (v. 18)

13-2.5. THE HOLY CITY: THE HEAVENLY JERUSALEM

In the late OT period the idealization of the Holy City leads to belief in an ideal and heavenly Jerusalem, of which the earthly city is but a poor counterpart. The *present* Jerusalem can be contrasted not only with the *future* Jerusalem, but also with the Jerusalem *above* (cf. Gowan 1986: 17).

The heavenly Jerusalem will be revealed at the last day, "for indeed the time will come . . . that the city that now is not seen shall appear" (2 *Esdr* 7:26). "And Zion shall come and be made manifest to all people, prepared and built, as you saw the mountain carved out without hands" (13:36; cf. 10:25-59).

New Testament: Fulfillment

13-3. TO THE END OF THE EARTH

13-3.1. LANDS AND CITIES

From one point of view the NT can be seen as a continuation of the OT account of God's people alternating between land and landlessness (13-1). In the NT two periods can be distinguished:

i. A *landed* period, continuing landed period II of the OT and consisting of the ministry of Jesus and the earliest period of the church, both of which are located in the Holy Land and associated to a considerable extent with the Holy City.

ii. A *landless period,* from the time of Stephen's death onward, when God's people are exiled from Land and city and dispersed throughout much of the known world.

The landless period of the NT is, however, *radically different from the two landless periods of the OT.* It is not seen as a period of waiting and hoping for a return to the Land, but rather as *the real goal of salvation history.* It is in accordance with God's plan and purpose that there is a clear movement in the NT

from the Land to the lands, and
from the City to the cities.

13-3.2. THE LAND IN THE GOSPELS

a. Jesus and the Land

In the teaching of Jesus there is little or no concern with the Land as such. His conception of the kingdom of God (cf. 1-3.1a) is quite divorced not only from political and nationalistic interests (cf. W. D. Davies 1974: 336-54), but also from geographical considerations. Jesus may echo Ps 37:11 in pronouncing "Blessed are the meek, for they will inherit the earth/land *(tēn gēn)*" (Matt 5:5), but the kingdom of heaven, the adherents of which are portrayed in the Beatitudes, is a kingdom that can be embodied anywhere on the earth's surface (cf. Chapman 1992: 134). The Gentiles will be gathered in (Matt 8:11; see 12-3.1c) not to the Holy Land, but to the kingdom of God (cf. Chapman, 137-39). If some of the disciples still thought in terms of the restoration of a (territorial) Jewish kingdom, their views were brushed aside by Jesus (Acts 1:6; cf. Luke 24:21; see Chapman, 148-51). It is difficult therefore to agree with Brueggemann (1977b) when he contends that "Jesus' actions are also to be understood as the return of the dispossessed to the land from which they had been driven," and still less when he says that "the action, the preaching, and the person of Jesus, all attest to new land now being given" (173-75; cf. Martens 1981: 147, 252-53; Wilken 1992: 48).

b. The Scene of Jesus' Ministry

The Gospels are certainly interested in the Holy Land as the scene of Jesus' ministry. Jesus is a real person — in geography as well as history — and all four Gospels are careful to record the principal geographical locations connected with his ministry — Bethlehem, Nazareth, Capernaum, Caesarea Philippi, Bethany, Gethsemane, Calvary, and so on. It is just possible that some of these places had already become the object of reverence and even of pilgrimage within the NT period; that certainly became the case post-Constantine. It may be that some such interest underlies John's references to the "place *(topos)*" associated with various events of Jesus' ministry (John 6:10, 23; 18:2; 19:17, 20, 41; cf. 11:48).

A number of scholars have explored the question of geographical symbolism in the Gospels. R. H. Lightfoot, following up the work of E. Lohmeyer, suggested that Mark, and to a lesser extent Matthew, while viewing Jerusalem as the place of rejection, regarded Galilee as the place of salvation, the true Holy Land for Christians (Lightfoot 1937). His work was further developed by Marxsen, with modifications (1969b). The interpretations of both Lightfoot and Marxsen depend on theories of the existence of a Galilean Christianity, theories that are speculative and uncertain (cf. Stemberger 1974). In any case, the geographical distinction within Mark is far from clear. Jesus meets opposition and rejection in Galilee (2:6, 16, 24; 3:2, 6) and attracts followers from Judea and Jerusalem (3:8). Moreover, the whole point of 6:1-6 is that Jesus was rejected in his own Galilean hometown of Nazareth! It is very possible that Mark embodies Galilean traditions, but we may agree with W. D. Davies (1974) when he concludes that the Gospels of Mark and Matthew "lend little, if any, support to the view that preoccupation with Galilee had led to its elevation to *terra Christiana*" (243). Conzelmann (1960) has discussed the treatment of geography in Luke, but it is doubtful whether or how far Luke attaches theological significance to geographical locations (cf. Davies, 244-52); he does, however, have a special interest in the city of Jerusalem (see below, 13-3.4).

Lightfoot drew attention to John 4:44-45, which passage suggests that in John's Gospel Jesus' "own country" *(patris)* that rejects the prophet is Judea or Jerusalem and not Galilee as in the Synoptics. Jesus is rejected by "his own" (cf. 1:11) in Judea, but is received and welcomed in Galilee. Lightfoot's views were taken up by W. A. Meeks, who concluded that "the geographical symbolism of John is not dominated by Jerusalem to the exclusion of Galilee, but is shaped by the apparently deliberate dialectic between Jerusalem, the place of judgment and rejection, and Galilee and Samaria, the places of acceptance and discipleship" (1966: 169). R. T. Fortna underlines the contrast between Judea on the one hand and Galilee, Samaria, and Perea on the other. But against such theories it must be pointed out that although Jesus gets a predominantly hostile reception in Judea, John's Gospel also locates believers there, while Jesus does encounter opposition in Galilee and Perea; only in Samaria does he appear to meet with unqualified success (see Scobie 1982: 79). What does appear to be significant is that in John Jesus visits all areas of the Holy Land — Judea, Samaria, Galilee, and Transjordan; in every area his coming provokes a crisis that reveals those who do and those who do not belong to the *true* Israel (cf. W. D. Davies 1974: 321-31).

Particular geographical areas have no special significance. This accords with Davies' demonstration that in John there is a deliberate "replacement of 'holy places' by the Person of Jesus" (334; cf. Alfaro 1978: 61). In narratives that refer to Bethel (1:51), Jacob's well (4:6), the pool of Bethzatha (5:2-9), and the pool of Siloam (John 9), the person of Christ replaces each of these OT holy places. Similarly, as the true source of living water (7:37-38), Jesus takes the place of the eschatological Jerusalem (Zech 14:8; see above, 13-2.3). In the new age that is dawning, worship is no longer bound geographically either to the Samaritan holy place, Mount Gerizim, or to the Jewish holy place in Jerusalem; worship is now in spirit and in truth, and the source of the Spirit is Christ (John 4:20-26).

13-3.3. FROM THE LAND TO THE LANDS

a. From the Land

The Land plays no significant role in the theology of the early church as this is reflected in the NT. Rather, interest turns from the Land to the lands of the nations.

The book of Acts shows a number of striking parallels in reverse to the book of Joshua: it thinks in terms of conquest, not of the Land but of the whole world; not by the sword, but by the gospel (see Chapman 1992: 152-53). Unlike Jeremiah, who bought a field to symbolize his faith in the future of the Land (Jer 32:9; see above, 13-2.2), Barnabas sold a field (Acts 4:37), symbolizing his faith that the future lay not in the Land but in the new community. Stephen's speech in Acts 7 deals almost entirely with the first landless period: this is where almost all the key events of salvation history take place (vv. 2-44). What happens after the settlement is given a very negative evaluation (vv. 45-53; cf. W. Janzen 1992: 151). References to the Land in Paul are conspicuous by their absence (cf. W. D. Davies 1974: 164-220). "Once Paul had made the Living Lord rather than the Torah the centre in life and in death, once he had seen in Jesus his Torah, he had in principle broken with the land" (220). Paul does let slip a remarkable comment in Rom 4:13, where he says that "the promise that he would inherit *the world* did not come to Abraham . . . through the law." Now in Gen 12, what Abraham was promised was not "the world *(kosmos)*" but the land of Canaan! This suggests that for Paul the Land is "a great advance metaphor for the design of God that his people should eventually bring the whole world into submission to his healing reign. God's whole purpose now goes beyond Jerusalem and the Land to the whole world" (N. T. Wright 1992: 67; cf. B. W. Anderson 1995: 154). For the most part, Paul's interest turned away from Palestine to the lands of the Roman Empire. One of the last glimpses we have of him as a free man shows him planning to carry the gospel to Spain, at the very opposite end of the known world from the Holy Land (Rom 15:28).

b. Sojourners and Pilgrims

What reemerges in the NT is the sense of God's people as sojourners and pilgrims; while history lasts, it is God's intention that his people live throughout the inhabited world in a dispersion/diaspora. On the death of Stephen the Hellenists are "scattered" *(diesparēsan)* throughout Judea and Samaria (Acts 8:1, 4; cf. 11:19). "When the church was addressed as 'exiles of the dispersion' (James 1:1, 1 Peter 1:1), the authors did not have in mind the absence of Christians from Palestine but from the heavenly city" (Minear 1983: 28; cf. below, 13-3.5). Believers are "aliens" *(paroikoi)* and "exiles" *(parepidēmoi)* (1 Pet 2:11). The theme of "God's pilgrim people" is brought out particularly in the letter to the Hebrews: the "Roll Call of Faith" concentrates very largely on the first landless period (11:4-29), skips over the two landed periods in a few verses, and ends with a reference to the faithful of Maccabean times who "wandered in deserts and mountains" (11:38). In particular, though it alludes to the Land promised to Abraham (11:9), it characterizes the patriarchs as "strangers and foreigners *(xenoi kai parepidēmoi)* on the earth" who desired "a better country, that is, a heavenly one" (11:13, 16). Here, as W. Janzen (1992) remarks, "the land realism of the OT is totally dissolved, not only for the NT era, but even retrospectively for Abraham" (151).

13-3.4. FROM THE CITY TO THE CITIES

The NT is more interested in the Holy City than in the Holy Land.

a. O Jerusalem, Jerusalem!

The Gospels present Jesus as taking his mission and message to Jerusalem as the historic center of Israel and the location of the leaders of God's people. The Synoptics (apart from the Lucan infancy narrative) tell of only one visit of Jesus to Jerusalem, at the very end of his life. John supplements their account by telling of earlier visits that seem to be presupposed by Jesus' lament over the city in Matt 23:37//Luke 13:34: "Jerusalem, Jerusalem, the city that kills the prophets and stones those who are sent to it! How often have I desired to gather your children together as a hen gathers her brood under her wings, and you were not willing!" Jerusalem is a place of danger (cf. Luke 13:33), yet Jesus' message must be heard there despite the likely reaction.

In all four Gospels Jerusalem is the place of Jesus' rejection and crucifixion (cf. Matt 16:21; Luke 9:31), and of some of his resurrection appearances. For Luke, however, Jerusalem holds a unique place. His Gospel *opens* in Jerusalem (see Luke 1–2), and for him "the beginnings of the life of Jesus are intertwined inextricably with the age-long centre of Jewish hope" (W. D. Davies 1974: 253). There are twice as many references to Jerusalem in Luke as in each of the other Gospels, and unlike the others, Luke also *ends* in Jerusalem, for the disciples are told to "stay here in the city" (24:49). From a literary viewpoint therefore, the Holy City provides a frame for Luke's account of Jesus' life and ministry.

b. The Fall of Jerusalem

In true prophetic fashion (reminiscent especially of Jeremiah; cf. above, 13-1.4d), Jesus takes his message to the Holy City, but when it is largely rejected, prophesies judgment in the form of a coming siege and destruction (Mark 13:14-20; Luke 19:43-44; 21:20, 24). We have noted this in 3-4.3a as an example of prophetic eschatology. With the fall of Jerusalem to the Romans in A.D. 70, Jesus' prophecy was fulfilled within the lifetime of some of his hearers.

c. Witnesses in Jerusalem

In Acts Jerusalem functions as the launchpad from which the church takes off on its universal mission. Anticipating this, in Luke 24:47 the risen Christ tells the disciples that "repentance and forgiveness of sins is to be proclaimed . . . to all nations, *beginning from Jerusalem.*" In Acts 1:8 (a verse that serves as a table of contents for the book of Acts) Christ tells his disciples, "You will be my witnesses *in Jerusalem,* in all Judea and Samaria, and to the ends of the earth." Acts 1–7 portrays the life of the earliest Christian community in Jerusalem. Even after the church has begun to expand outward, the Jerusalem community functions as the "mother church."

Paul also recognizes the place of Jerusalem in the history of salvation when he speaks of having proclaimed the gospel "*from Jerusalem* and as far around as Illyricum" (Rom 15:19). In 11:26-27 he quotes an anthology of OT texts to prove that the message of deliverance and forgiveness comes "out of Zion" (see N. T. Wright 1992: 65-67). Although there were ambiguities in Paul's relationship to the Jerusalem community, it is clear that he never ceased to regard it as the mother church (cf. Bruce 1968), as is shown in particular by the collection of money from his Gentile churches for the church at Jerusalem (cf. 12-3.4a.iii).

d. From Jerusalem to Rome

In its centrifugal expansion (12-3.4a.iii) the early church moves from the City to the cities of the Roman world, from Jerusalem to Caesarea, Damascus, Antioch, Philippi, Athens, Corinth, Ephesus, and eventually Rome.

Acts begins where Luke's Gospel leaves off, in the city of Jerusalem (Acts 1–7), but significantly it closes in another city, the city of Rome. Jerusalem does not disappear in Acts (the Council of Jerusalem in Acts 15 is a key event), but clearly for Luke, "Christianity is a Way which began in Jerusalem, but passes through it" (W. D. Davies 1974: 260). The primary concern of Acts is the spread of the Christian faith "to the ends of the earth" (1:8). The book closes in Rome, the capital of the empire, and obviously not only did all roads lead to Rome, they also led from Rome to the ends of the earth. By beginning in the city of Jerusalem, Acts stresses the continuity of Christianity with Judaism in the historical order; by ending in Rome it stresses God's universal purpose in the created order.

13-3.5. THE JERUSALEM ABOVE

In the NT the city of Jerusalem ceases to be the focal point for God's people; in its place, Christians look to the Jerusalem that is above.

a. Galatians 4:21-31

This passage is an allegory in which Paul contrasts Hagar, the slave woman who bore Abraham a son (Ishmael) according to the flesh, and Sarah, the free woman who bore Abraham a son (Isaac) according to the promise. In a turnaround that would shock his Jewish contemporaries, Paul identifies Hagar with the Sinai covenant and contends that she "corresponds to *the present Jerusalem,* for she is in slavery with her children. But the other woman corresponds to *the Jerusalem above;* she is free, and she is our mother" (vv. 25-26). The Judaism centered in Jerusalem persecutes the infant church (cf. the death of Stephen) "just as at that time the child who was born according to the flesh [Ishmael] persecuted the child who was born according to the Spirit [Isaac]" (v. 29). The Jews, of course, claimed to be descended from Isaac, but Paul connects them with Ishmael and hence with "slavery"! They are, in Paul's view, enslaved to the Law because they fail to realize that the Christ event has shattered the old order based on the Law and ushered in the new age in which Jew and Gentile alike are being gathered into the eschatological community on the basis of faith alone. Thus "in these verses Paul sees the Land, and its focal point Jerusalem, as both in theory and in practice relativized by the death and resurrection of the Messiah" (N. T. Wright 1992: 69). In Paul's view the faith of the new people of God is focused not on any geographical center but on "the Jerusalem above," on a city that already exists not on earth but in heaven. "Those who live by faith in Christ *already* live the life of the new Jerusalem; they are already citizens of heaven" (W. D. Davies 1974: 197).

b. Hebrews 12:18-24

This passage contrasts how God's people approach their God under the old covenant and under the new. In contrast to the Israelites, who could approach Mount Sinai only in fear and trembling, Christian believers, the writer tells his readers, "have come to Mount Zion and to the *city* of the living God, *the heavenly Jerusalem,* and to innumerable angels in festal gathering, and to the assembly of the firstborn who are enrolled in heaven" (vv. 22-23). The faith of Christians is focused not on the earthly Jerusalem but on a new community symbolized by the heavenly city. "In order to belong to this city, one must be prepared to leave the earthly city behind, out of the reckoning, taking as one's model the suffering of Jesus outside the city wall. The present Jerusalem (and therefore the Temple and the Land) belong to the created things that will be shaken; the new community to which Christians belong is of the order of things that cannot be shaken, the Kingdom prepared for God's people (12:26-8)" (N. T. Wright 1992: 71).

Both these key passages assume that the *heavenly Jerusalem* is a present reality and that it *replaces* the earthly city of Jerusalem as the focus for the faith of God's people.

New Testament: Consummation

13-4. THE HOLY CITY, NEW JERUSALEM

13-4.1. A NEW EARTH

In the NT pictures of the final consummation, *a holy land plays no part at all.* The focal point of the Christian hope is not a territory but a community — a community imperfectly realized at present, located in many lands, partially realized now in the heavenly realms, but to be fully realized only when heaven and earth are replaced by a totally new order. The symbol of this community is not a holy land but a holy city.

Heb 11:15-16 speaks of the saints of the OT as people who were seeking "a better country, that is, a heavenly one," but significantly it comments that what God has prepared for them is "a city."

13-4.2. THE HOLY CITY

While the NT speaks of a heavenly Jerusalem to which Christians can look at the present time, it also expects that at the last time a city will come down from heaven and be revealed.

This present/future tension is most clearly seen in Hebrews; in addition to speaking of the heavenly Jerusalem (above, 13-3.5b), Heb 13:14 declares, "Here we have no lasting city, but we are looking for the city that is to come." Thus the epistle looks both to a city above and to a city that is to come.

It is in Revelation that the two cities coalesce. The church in Philadelphia is promised, "If you conquer, . . . I will write on you the name of my God, and the name of the city of my God, the new Jerusalem that comes down from my God out of heaven" (3:12). This promise is then taken up and elaborated in the great final vision of 21:1–22:5 that is so rich in imagery and symbolism. Here the heavenly city and the future city are revealed as essentially one, for John declares, "I saw the holy city, the new Jerusalem, *coming down out of heaven from God*" (21:2; cf. 21:10).

The vision is the fulfillment of the OT prophecies of the eschatological and the heavenly Jerusalem (above, 13-2.4; 13-2.5), especially the prophecies of Ezekiel, but with significant modifications. The city represents the community of God's people, the church (cf. Dumbrell 1985: 1), as is clear from the identification with "the bride" (21:2, 9). The major emphasis is on the fact that God is fully and completely present with his people in the city:

> See, the home of God is among mortals.
> He will dwell with them;
> they will be his peoples,
> and God himself will be with them. (21:3)

Thus will be fulfilled Ezekiel's promise of a city whose name is "The LORD is There" (Ezek 48:35).

The city, like that of Ezekiel (48:30-34), will have twelve gates, three in each of the four walls, inscribed with "the names of the twelve tribes of the Israelites" (Rev 21:12). But there are two differences from Ezekiel's city. Firstly, in Ezekiel's vision the gates function as "the exits of the city" (Ezek 48:30); the tribes may enter and leave the city through them to return to their tribal allocations, so that the main emphasis in Ezekiel is on the Land. In Revelation the Land has disappeared altogether, and the eschatological community of God's people is constituted by the city. "The holy city becomes co-extensive with the redeemed society as a whole" (Minear 1983: 27). Secondly, in Ezekiel the twelve gates are identified with the twelve tribes of Israel by name. In John's vision the twelve tribes are not named and the "Israelites" who enter by the gates are the people of the new Israel, drawn from all nations, as Rev 21:24, 26 make clear (cf. 11-4.5). In addition, unlike all ancient cities, the gates of the new Jerusalem are never closed (21:25).

To Ezekiel's prototype John adds twelve foundations on which are "the twelve names of the twelve apostles of the Lamb" (Rev 21:14; 15-4.1). The twelve foundations are each identified with a precious stone (21:19-20), "the twelve gates are twelve pearls . . . and the street of the city is pure gold, transparent as glass" (21:21; cf. 21:11, 18). Here the imagery both alludes to the twelve stones, one for each of the tribes of Israel, on the priestly breastplate (Exod 28:15-21) and also echoes Isa 54:11-14 and *Tob* 13:16-18 (cf. 13-2.4); the most beautiful and precious things known on earth are but pointers to the glories of the heavenly city.

The city is described as having a wall that is measured by the angel who is showing the city to John (Rev 21:17). This may seem strange in the light of Zechariah's vision of the eschatological Jerusalem that was to be without a wall (cf. 13-2.4), but the solution lies in the statement that "the wall is built of jasper" (Rev 21:18), jasper being particularly associated with the divine presence (4:3). That presence is further emphasized by the description of the city as a perfect cube (21:16), thus identifying it with the Holy of Holies, the place where God dwells in the midst of his people (cf. 14-4.1).

On the *Urzeit/Endzeit* principle one might expect the vision of the final consummation to correspond to the Garden of Eden. In accordance with the visions of the restored Land in Ezekiel, Joel, and Zechariah (13-2.3), two features of the garden do reappear in the city: "the river of the water of life" of Rev 22:1 (echoing the river of Gen 2:10) and "the tree of life" of Rev 22:2 (Gen 2:9; cf. Rev 2:7, where the tree is located "in the paradise of God"). Yet the final goal of human history, as of salvation history, is not a garden nor a land but a city, a community of peoples from all nations, living together in the presence of God.

13-5. LAND AND CITY: THEOLOGICAL REFLECTIONS

1. Our study has shown that Land and city are indeed major, interlocking themes of BT. The biblical understanding of these themes is complex, and it is extremely important to look at all the relevant biblical material in the total canonical context. The alternating landless and landed periods highlight the Bible's dialectical approach: OT faith is frequently focused on the Holy Land and the Holy City, but is not necessarily tied to them. The NT view is not discontinuous with the OT; rather it picks up on one aspect of the OT approach, that of living without the Land and without the city. For the NT and hence for Christians, Land is telescoped into city and the city becomes the heavenly/eschatological Jerusalem, a vision of God dwelling with his people that can guide believers in the present and constitutes the goal of both human history and salvation history. The idea of a Christian "Holy Land" is not found in the NT or in the early church, but developed only in the Byzantine period (see Wilken 1988; 1992). The attempts of the Crusaders to recover the "Holy Land" by force of arms may have parallels in the holy war of the OT or the Muslim conception of jihad, but they have no basis in the NT.

2. For Christians therefore, Land and city are primarily significant as the scene of the main events of salvation history: the story of Israel, the ministry of Jesus, the beginnings of the Christian church. As such they have been the subject of much study during the course of Christian history; the development of biblical archaeology in the late nineteenth and twentieth centuries has reinforced the rootedness of the scriptural accounts in history, and has often shed new light on the meaning of the Bible. For Christians the Land can be the goal of pilgrimage, as has been the case over the centuries. Such pilgrimage may or may not be spiritually profitable; it is in no way obligatory on Christians. "A visit to Palestine may help the Christian to appropriate more fully and to clarify as to detail the geographical images of sacred history which he carries with him. While the possibility cannot be excluded that such a trip may in itself become for him an act or sign of God's leading, there is no more guarantee that this will happen than on many another trip" (Jansen 1973: 178). The Land clearly does not hold the same significance for Christians as it does for most Jews, and still less can a Christian's visit to Jerusalem be put in the same class as a Muslim's pilgrimage to Mecca.

3. This does not mean that the only option for Christians is a disembodied spirituality or otherworldliness (cf. Minear 1983: 29). For one thing, "land" is still entrusted to the stewardship of believers as to all humankind (cf. 2-5). Moreover, the Bible does suggest how different geographical locations can be invested with special meaning, and so it can be for Christians today. "That man is little to be envied," wrote Dr. Samuel Johnson, "whose piety would not grow warmer among the ruins of Iona" (*Journey to the Western Isles,* 580). For many Iona is a holy place, but it need not be for all. Worship is not required at either Gerizim or Jerusalem; it is to be in spirit and in truth (John 4:21, 23). "These words," maintains Jansen (1973), "do not take faith off the map; they redeem it from static attachment to certain holy places alone, so that the whole map can now become potential territory for God's election towards his ends." However, "the claim that God can choose any place as the place of his self-manifestation should not be inverted into an assertion of divine immanence everywhere" (178).

4. "The Land" became a major world issue in the second half of the twentieth century (cf. Klatzker 1983) because of the Zionist movement, the establishment of modern Israel, and the Arab-Israeli conflict. That conflict has deep religious roots since both groups claim the Land on the basis of the promise to Abraham, the Jews tracing their claim through Abraham's son Isaac and the Arabs through his son Ishmael (the Muslim claim to Jerusalem is also linked to the "Night Journey" of Muhammad). The question is extremely complex, and numerous arguments can be advanced on behalf of each of the competing parties (cf. Harkness and Kraft 1976: 200-202; Ellisen 1991: 145-66; March 1994: 65-81). It should also be noted that the understanding of the Land in modern Judaism is far from uniform (see Gowan 1986: 29-30). What light, if any, does a BT of Land and city throw on this vexed question?

Some conservative Christians regard the OT prophecies of a return (13-2.2) to the Land as a vital part of biblical "prophecy," i.e., as part of an apocalyptic timetable. The establishment of Israel in 1948 is seen as a sign that the end times are near. These prophecies, however, are primarily an example of *prophetic* eschatology, and they were largely fulfilled with the return of 538 B.C. onward (cf. Woods 1991: 10; March 1994: 68-70). It is true that Ezekiel and other prophets present a more idealized picture of a still-future paradise restored, but in the light of the NT these prophecies coalesce with those of the heavenly/eschatological Jerusalem that become the focus of faith in the present and the future goal for believers, a goal that lies beyond history. The NT gives no support for including a literal return to Palestine by the Jewish people as part of any eschatological timetable. For Christians it is important to recognize that in the NT the hopes associated with Land and city are refocused on Christ. "Such a recognition releases us from the need to try to interpret literally a passage like Ezekiel 40–48 . . . which in my view [was] never meant to be taken so . . . but whose essence is a promise of God's presence (Ezk. 48:35b). For Christians, this translates very well into the presence of God with his people the Church in Christ" (J. G. McConville 1992: 50; cf. N. T. Wright 1992: 73-74; Chapman 1992: 130-66, 255-67).

Christians are bound to feel a special sympathy for the Jewish people in the light of the biblical heritage they share. They must also feel a deep penitence for the way Jews have been treated in so-called Christian countries over the past two thousand years. But they cannot share the view that Jews have an inalienable right to the whole of the Holy Land. Sympathy for the Jewish view has to be balanced by a concern for an equally biblical principle, that of justice; Christians must therefore encourage the search for a solution that will be a just one for both Jews and Arabs (see March 1994: 83-98).

CHAPTER 14

Worship

Old Testament: Proclamation

14-1. O COME, LET US WORSHIP

In the Bible worship is absolutely central in the life of God's people. It is an essential part of their response to God that is made possible by God himself. "Acceptable worship under both covenants is a matter of responding to God's initiative in salvation and revelation, and doing so in the way that he requires" (D. Peterson 1992: 19).

God's people respond to him, and express their identity and unity by meeting together for public worship. Public worship, or "cult" (see McKenzie 1974: 37-38), involves the assembling of God's people at specific places and at specific times, to worship God in a specific manner. Here we deal with public worship; for private prayer and devotion, see 17-1.5, 17-3.5.

14-1.1. WHERE GOD IS WORSHIPED

The OT portrays God's people worshiping him at specific locations from the earliest time. "Although it was always clear that God dwelt in heaven (Gen. 11:5; Ex. 19:11 and 1 Kings 8:27), God did choose particular places where he would meet with his people" (Dyrness 1979: 146; cf. Eichrodt 1961: 102). There are frequent references to the "place" where God is worshiped, and the word for "place," *māqôm* (LXX *topos*), functions as a technical term for a sanctuary, e.g., "the place at Shechem" (Gen 12:6; cf. 28:19; etc.).

There is a tension running through the OT between two competing understandings of where God is to be worshiped. One view is that God may be worshiped in many places: "In every place *(māqôm)* where I cause my name to be remembered I will come to you and bless you" (Exod 20:24). The other view is that God is to be worshiped in one place only: "But you shall seek the place *(māqôm)* that the LORD your God will choose out of all your tribes as his habitation to put his name there. You shall go there, bringing your burnt offerings and your sacrifices" (Deut 12:5-6).

a. The Story of Where God Is Worshiped

i. The Patriarchs

The patriarchs are pictured as worshiping God, in the course of their wanderings, at a variety of places. Many of these locations may have been preexisting Canaanite sanctuaries, but if so they were invested with new meaning as the sites of encounters between the patriarchs and their God. Thus Abraham "passed through the land to the place at Shechem, to the oak of Moreh. . . . Then the LORD appeared to Abram . . . so he built there an altar to the LORD" (Gen 12:6-7; cf. 13-1.4a). Jacob's dream at Bethel (28:11-22) is a classic case: "He came to a certain place and stayed there for the night. . . . Taking one of the stones of the place, he put it under his head and lay down in that place" (v. 11). In his dream Jacob saw a ladder or stairway *(sullām)* "set up on the earth, the top of it reaching to heaven; and the angels of God were ascending and descending on it" (v. 12). God then renewed the patriarchal promise, and Jacob awoke, saying, "Surely the LORD is in this place — and I did not know it! . . . How awesome is this place! This is none other than the house of God, and this is the gate of heaven" (vv. 16-17). Jacob took the stone, set it up for a pillar, and called the name of the place "Bethel" *(bêth* = "house of"; *'ēl* = "God"). A sanctuary is a place where God dwells, and where there can be communication between earth and heaven. Other patriarchal sites are Mamre, near Hebron (13:18), and Beersheba (46:1-5). Most of these sites went on to become Israelite sanctuaries after the settlement.

ii. The Wilderness Period

Following the exodus, in the period of the wilderness wanderings, the Israelites worshiped God with the help of a portable sanctuary, the tent, and a portable shrine, the ark, both of which are constructed following directions given by God, through Moses.

A. The tent. Two terms are used for the portable sanctuary, each of which reflects an understanding of its function. (1) *Mishkān,* usually translated "tabernacle," comes from the root *shākhan,* meaning to "abide" or "dwell"; it is thus the place where God dwells or is present in the midst of his people (Exod 29:45). (2) *'ōhel mô'ēdh* means "the tent of meeting." It is the place of which God can say, "I will meet with the Israelites there" (29:43). Specifically it is the place where God speaks through Moses to the people (33:7-11; Num 7:89; 11:16-17).

Historical-critical scholars claim to detect two different traditions that were later blended, but the text in its present, canonical form understands both terms to refer to one structure, as in Exod 40:34: "Then the cloud covered the tent of meeting *('ōhel mô'ēdh),* and the glory of the LORD filled the tabernacle *(hammishkān)."* The LXX generally uses *skēnē* (tent) to translate both expressions. The importance attached to the tent may be gauged by the fact that Exod 25–31 consists of detailed instructions for its construction, while Exod 35–40 recounts its being made. Following the ratification of the covenant in Exod 24, the appropriate response of the people is worship (cf. Dumbrell 1985: 43-44). That worship, however, is to be carried out as God directs, and thus Moses is told, "In accordance with all that I show you concerning the pattern of the tabernacle and of all its furniture, so you shall make it" (25:9; cf. 25:40). "It belongs to God alone to decide in which manner he shall be served" (Barrois 1980: 30).

The tent is essentially a *movable* structure; God's presence is not tied down to one particular place but moves with his people. "As long as Israel is not definitely settled in Canaan, God's house is not a house of stones, but the tent . . . which is carried from station to station while the people is on the march" (Barrois 1980: 33). Worship consisted primarily of animal sacrifice, and the tent was provided with an altar and other appropriate furnishings and vessels.

After the settlement the tent was set up in Shiloh (Josh 18:1; 19:51), then apparently moved to the sanctuary at Gibeon (1 Chr 16:39; 2 Chr 1). According to 1 Kgs 8:4, at the time of the building of Solomon's temple, along with the ark, "the tent of meeting, and all the holy vessels that were in the tent," were brought up (i.e., to Jerusalem). But the text mentions only the ark being placed in the Holy of Holies. The tent is thus linked with the temple, but is also replaced by it.

B. The ark. *'ārôn* (LXX *kibōtos*) means a chest or box, and the ark is described as a chest of acacia wood, overlaid with gold; precise directions were given through Moses for its construction (Exod 25:10-22; cf. 37:1-9; Deut 10:1-3). Here again critical scholars seek to separate varying early traditions (cf. Kraus 1966: 125-28; Terrien 1978: 162-75), but BT is concerned with the material in its final, canonical form. The two principal features of the ark reflect its two main functions. Firstly, on top of the chest was the "mercy seat" *(kappōreth;* LXX *hilastērion),* flanked by two cherubim, that served as the throne of the invisible presence of God (Exod 25:17; cf. 1-1.1) and the place where atonement was made for sin. Thus the ark symbolized the presence of the sovereign God with his people (cf. Lev 16:2). On the Day of Atonement (see below, 14-1.3) sacrificial blood was sprinkled on the mercy seat (16:14). Secondly, inside the chest were placed the stone tablets given by God to Moses with the Decalogue inscribed on them (Deut 10:1-2). They are referred to as "the tablets of the covenant" (9:9), hence the expression "the ark of the covenant" *('ārôn beerîth* — Num 10:33; Deut 10:8; Josh 3:3). Here again an essential feature was the shrine's portability (cf. H. Davies 1967: 39-42); it had two pairs of rings attached for poles that were used to carry it without actually touching the holy object.

The ark accompanied the Israelites during their wilderness wanderings (Num 10:33), was carried before them as they entered the Land (Josh 3), and after the settlement was housed first at Shechem (Josh 8:33), then at Shiloh (1 Sam 4:3). Carried into battle in a time of national crisis (4:3-9), it was captured by the Philistines (4:11), though after a severe plague it was returned to the Israelites and lodged in relative obscurity at Kiriath-jearim. From there David had it brought to his new capital of Jerusalem (2 Sam 6:1-15), an event probably commemorated in Ps 24, and on the completion of Solomon's temple it was placed in the Holy of Holies (1 Kgs 8:6). The ark is thus primarily the symbol of God's presence with his people (see H. Davies 1967: 42-45). "The ark becomes the palladium of the nation; God leads his own as they journey toward the Promised Land" (Barrois 1980: 32). Along with the tent, it witnesses to "the distant God who yet condescends to be really present in the midst of his people and enables them to participate in the divine life" (Eichrodt 1961: 112). But equally the ark is a reminder that God cannot be manipulated. Carrying the ark into battle did not guarantee victory over the Philistines. Linked with this is the function of the ark as a reminder of God's Law. The "ark of the covenant" served as a continuing reminder to the people of their covenant obligations, and in particular of the Decalogue. This is the aspect on which Deuteronomy focuses in particular (Deut 10:1-5).

iii. The Settlement

With the settlement of the tribes in the Land a situation returns in which God's people worship at many different locations, often associated with stories of the patriarchs and hence with the earlier history of God's people. The location of the tent and ark at Shiloh made it a particularly important sanctuary (1 Sam 1–3), but at some point it came under God's judgment and was destroyed (Ps 78:60; Jer 7:12; 26:6, 9). A variety of sanctuaries continued in use in the North until the fall of Samaria in 722 B.C., and in the South until the centralization of all worship in the Jerusalem temple under Josiah in 621. Special importance was attached to the northern shrines at Dan and Bethel after the separation of the kingdoms (1 Kgs 12:29-30).

iv. The Jerusalem Temple

The construction of what came to be the preeminent temple was of course not possible until the relatively late capture of Jerusalem by David. According to 2 Sam 7, it was the desire of King David to build a temple in Jerusalem, the city he had captured and designated as the capital of the newly united kingdom (cf. 13-1.4b). This passage plays upon three senses of the term *bayith*, meaning "house." David now lives in a house (v. 2 = royal palace), and wishes to build a house for God to dwell in (v. 5 = a temple). The prophet Nathan denies God's request; it is David's son who will build the temple, but David is promised a house (v. 11 = a dynasty). The passage may reflect a tension between the older view of the God who moves with his people and the view of a God who dwells in a permanent structure (v. 6; cf. Barrois 1980: 50), but more significant is "the rejection here of the sufficiency of any human initiative in the matter of temple building" (Dumbrell 1985: 49). The erection of the altar is associated with David, though the choice of the site is divinely directed (2 Sam 24:18-25; 1 Chr 22:1). But God chooses Solomon as the builder of the temple. Its construction is narrated in 1 Kgs 5–7, and the account of its dedication is given in 1 Kgs 8. Chronicles tends to emphasize David's role more than does Kings (cf. 1 Chr 22), and it identifies the site chosen by David with "Mount Moriah" (2 Chr 3:1), the site where Abraham was to sacrifice Isaac (Gen 22), thus linking the temple with the early patriarchal traditions. The temple is seen as the successor to the tent in Pss 15, 27, and 61 (see Rabe 1967).

In its design the temple had a series of enclosures leading to the Holy of Holies. It was designed for sacrificial worship with an altar and appropriate furnishings and vessels, on a lavish scale; but it was also a center for teaching, a place for the administration of justice, and the goal of pilgrimage (cf. Baltzer 1965: 264).

Having been constructed by Solomon, the temple naturally functioned both as a royal and a national sanctuary, a kind of Westminster Abbey of Israel, but no conflict was seen between this and the continued existence of various local places of worship. The division of the kingdom left Judah in possession of the Jerusalem temple. The failure of the Assyrians to capture Jerusalem in 701 B.C. boosted the prestige of the Jerusalem temple and encouraged a close integration of the understanding of the temple with the "Zion theology" (see 13-1.4c).

v. Reformation and Centralization

A profound change in the place of the temple occurred with the reformation under Josiah following the discovery of "the book of the law" in the temple (2 Kgs 22:8). It has long been recognized that the scroll must have been a copy of Deuteronomy (in whole or in part) with its law requiring all worship to be conducted at "the place *(māqôm)* that the Lord your God will choose out of all your tribes as his habitation to put his name there" (12:5). Josiah proceeded to cleanse the Jerusalem temple of all pagan influences (2 Kgs 23:4-14) and to close down all sanctuaries other than the Jerusalem temple, thus centralizing all worship at that location (23:15-20), a move that would make it possible "to maintain the closest vigilance over the operation of the cult, and to ensure its orthodoxy" (Clements 1968: 77).

vi. Destruction and Rebuilding

With the capture and destruction of Jerusalem by the Babylonians in 586, the temple also perished, while its vessels were carried off by the Babylonians

(2 Kgs 25:8-17). A prime motivation for the return was the desire, by at least some, to rebuild the temple. This took place ca. 520-515 and is described in Ezra 3–6. The rebuilding was encouraged by the prophets Haggai and Zechariah (cf. Dumbrell 1985: 60-63). This structure is generally referred to as the Second Temple in distinction from the First Temple, that of Solomon; clearly it was not comparable to the magnificent structure that had preceded it.

vii. Desecration and Rededication

The Jerusalem temple remained a focal point of worship during the postexilic period. It was not until the time of the Seleucids that it faced its next crisis. *1 Macc* 1:21-24 tells of the desecration (though not destruction) of the temple under the persecuting Greek king Antiochus Epiphanes. With the success of the Maccabean revolt under Judas Maccabeus, the temple was cleansed and rededicated, an event commemorated in the feast of Hanukkah (4:42-59). The temple was largely rebuilt under Herod the Great, and the massive reconstruction continued into NT times (John 2:20).

b. The Understanding of Where God Is Worshiped

i. In the OT a sanctuary is thought of basically as *a place where God dwells*, a Beth-El, a house of God, where God's people could meet with him (cf. Hannay 1950: 279). "The God of Israel was not a captive Deity, but he could be sought out and would appear at appointed times and places" (J. O. Lewis 1977: 541). The location of the ark, which symbolized God's presence with his people, first in the tent and then in the temple, reinforces this understanding. The OT is well aware of the tension to which this gives rise. Indeed, in the classic passage it is Solomon himself who says, "But will God indeed dwell on the earth? Even heaven and the highest heaven cannot contain you, much less this house that I have built!" (1 Kgs 8:27). Yet Solomon proceeds to dedicate the temple! This passage tackles the problem by regarding the temple as "the place of which you said, 'My name shall be there'" (8:29-30); it is not God himself but God's "name" (*shēm*) that is located in the temple (see 1-1.2a). Alternatively, it can be God's "glory" (*kābhôdh*) that dwells in the temple (cf. 8-1.2). In addition, a striking feature of tent and temple is the complete absence of any image of the deity; God may be thought of as present, but his presence is a spiritual one, not tied to any material object housed in the sanctuary. In these ways a dialectic is maintained between the transcendent Creator and the God who deigns to dwell with his people.

ii. The sanctuary acts as *a buffer zone between the Holy God and a sinful world.* The ground plans of tent and temple are broadly similar; they are constructed on the principle of *gradation* (see Zehr 1981: 142-44), i.e., with a series of courts that are regarded as of increasing holiness. An outer court was for Is-raelites only; then came a court for male Israelites only, a court for priests only, and finally the innermost shrine, the Holy of Holies where God was present and that could be entered, only very briefly, by the high priest, once a year on the Day of Atonement. In Herod's temple there was also an outer Court of the Gentiles representing the interface with the outside world.

iii. The sanctuary served as *the focal point of Israel's worship*. The tent was placed in the center of the camp (Num 2:2). The temple was placed in the center of the Land; there sacrifice was offered on behalf of the people (Deut 12:5-14). To the temple God's people went to attend the festivals from across the Land, and later from all over the Diaspora.

iv. The Jerusalem temple in particular could inspire *a love and devotion to the sanctuary*. Psalms of the sanctuary overlap with the psalms of Zion (see 13-1.4c); it is a pilgrim to Zion who declares,

> My soul longs, indeed it faints
>   for the courts of the LORD. (Ps 84:2)

The temple is a place of refuge (5:7), the place where God answers prayer (18:6), a place to meditate on God's love (48:9), a place where true satisfaction is to be found (65:4). Pilgrims made brief occasional visits to the temple; for some there could be no greater joy than to reside permanently in God's house:

> One thing I asked of the LORD,
>   that will I seek after:
> to live in the house of the LORD
>   all the days of my life,
> to behold the beauty of the LORD,
>   and to inquire in his temple.
>   (27:4; cf. 84:3-4, and see Terrien 1978: 304-12)

v. The prominence accorded all sanctuaries and especially the Jerusalem temple is balanced by *the prophetic critique* of the value of buildings apart from the people's obedience to God (cf. the discussion of the tension between a theology of glory and a theology of the name in Terrien 1978 passim). It is Jeremiah, especially in his Temple Sermon (Jer 7; 26), who forcefully attacks the complacency bred by the presence of the temple in Jerusalem and the assumption that God will protect it and the city regardless of how the people behave. The crowds may chant, "This is the temple of the LORD, the temple of the LORD, the temple of the LORD" (7:4), but Jeremiah reminds them that the presence of a sanctuary did not save Shiloh (7:12); neither does the presence of the temple in Jerusalem automatically guarantee exemption from God's judgment. The temple is divinely appointed as a place of worship and as an aid to worship, but no building is indispensable. Ezekiel also pronounced God's coming judgment on the temple (Ezek 7:22). It was the prophetic interpretation of the destruction of the temple by the Babylonians as God's judgment on a disobedient people (cf. 3-2.3) that helped make some sense of what otherwise would have been an un-mitigated disaster. As the exiles went on to discover, God can be worshiped apart from and in the absence of a temple.

vi. The OT does not completely resolve the tension between many sanctu-aries and one sanctuary, or between a movable sanctuary and a fixed temple. The advantage of one sanctuary is that it can serve as a focus for the unity of God's people. This is doubtless why the rival northern sanctuaries at Bethel and Dan are viewed with such disfavor in 1 Kgs 12. But a fixed place of worship has its disadvantages, especially when God's people are scattered abroad during and after the exile. The late OT period saw the development of a different place of worship, *the synagogue*. The word "synagogue *(synagōgē)*" signifies an "assem-bly" of a group of God's people, and only secondarily a building to house such an assembly (in the LXX *synagōgē* translates *'ēdhāh* = the "congregation" of Is-rael; see 11-1.1 and 11-3.1a). Historically the exact origins of the synagogue are obscure (see Sonne 1962: 478-80; Rowley 1967: 213-29; R. A. Stewart 1971: 38-40), though the institution may well go back to the exile. Certainly by NT times syn-agogues were widespread not only in the Diaspora (Acts 9:2; 13:5, 14; 14:1; etc.), but also in the Land of Israel (Luke 4:16, 33, 44; Acts 6:9; 24:12). Though neces-sarily not a place of sacrifice, the synagogue is a place of worship, study, and in-struction (see Martin 1974: 23-27), and with its many locations it harks back to the older tradition of many sanctuaries, emphasizing that God's presence is not restricted to any geographical location, but that he can be worshiped and served anywhere. Rather than being a place where God dwells, it is a place where God's people meet (cf. D. Peterson 1992: 112).

vii. The temple is usually interpreted in terms of salvation history, and of the historical order. The linking of both tent and ark with Solomon's temple (despite their absence from the Second Temple) emphasizes the continuity with Israel's historical traditions and connects Zion with Sinai. Yet the sanctuary also witnesses to *the God of the created order*. The prohibition of images of the deity in worship in no way prevented extensive use of decorative and symbolic architecture and art in the tent and the temple. The artistic talents of those em-ployed in construction and decoration were thought of as the product of wis-dom, conferred by God's Spirit (see Exod 31:1-11; cf. 5-1.3). From the descrip-tions given, it is clear that most of the decoration in the temple was related to the created order rather than the historical order. Most of the decorated motifs were drawn from nature, in the form of either flora (pomegranates, lilies, gourds, palms) or fauna (oxen, lions). Features such as the two great pillars (1 Kgs 7:15-22) and the huge bronze "sea" (7:23-26) were probably "symbols of Yahweh's cosmic dominion" (McKenzie 1974: 52).

14-1.2. WHEN GOD IS WORSHIPED: THE SABBATH

The time of worship is determined both by the cyclic time of the created order (see 2-1.2c) and by the linear time of the historical order (see 3-1.1a). The *weekly* cycle, associated with creation in Gen 1–2, provides the basis for the weekly observance of the Sabbath. BT is concerned not with the contradictory and unproductive efforts to find a non-Israelite origin of the Sabbath (cf. Kraus 1966: 81-87; Andreasen 1974: 454-55), but with the biblical material.

The importance of the Sabbath (*shabbāth,* from *shābhath* = "rest") is underlined by its inclusion in the Decalogue, in which it constitutes the longest of the commandments, although the observance of a Sabbath is already mentioned in Exod 16; variant versions are found in Exod 20:8-11 and Deut 5:12-15. The Sabbath is to be observed primarily by all members of the community abstaining from work: "Remember [Deut 5:12 — 'observe'] the sabbath day, and keep it holy. Six days you shall labor and do all your work. But the seventh day is a sabbath to the LORD your God; you shall not do any work" (Exod 20:8-10; Deut 5:12f.). Surprisingly little is said in the OT about worship on the Sabbath (cf. Wolff 1972: 500), although Isa 1:13 assumes that it was a day to worship at the temple, Num 28:9-10 prescribes a special burnt offering to be made on the Sabbath (cf. also Lev 24:8), and Ps 92 is classified as "A Song for the Sabbath Day." The seriousness with which the Sabbath was viewed is indicated by the provision of the death penalty for breaches of its observance (Exod 31:14; cf. Num 15:32-36). Observance of the Sabbath is grounded in both the created order and the historical order (cf. Slane 1996: 697-98).

The Exodus version links the Sabbath with *the created order:* "For in six days the LORD made heaven and earth, the sea, and all that is in them, but rested the seventh day; therefore the LORD blessed the sabbath day and consecrated it" (20:11). According to Genesis, humankind rest on the first day of their lives; they look back on the great work God has done before starting their own work. "The day of rest is to remind man forcefully, at least every seven days, that he has been put into a world provided with all that he needs, and what is more, a world richly endowed with many, many beautiful things. The Sabbath is thus an invitation to rejoice in God's creation" (Wolff 1974: 501). The Sabbath also establishes one form of cyclic time. Life is not to be a meaningless succession of working days, but an alternating rhythm of work and rest. Just as in the Sabbatical Year (19-2.3b) "man desists from utilizing the land for his own business and benefit, so on the sabbath day he desists from using that day for his own affairs. . . . On one day out of seven the Israelite is to renounce dominion over his own time and recognize God's dominion over it" (Tsevat 1972: 454-55). In the OT "rest" is evaluated positively. According to Exod 31:17, "The LORD made heaven and earth, and on the seventh day he rested, and was refreshed *(wayyinnāphash)*" or "renewed his being" (Terrien 1978: 393). "Rest" is also used in a special sense referring to the settlement in the Promised Land (33:14; Deut

12:9; Ps 95:11), and hence to an existence free from want, oppression, and war (Josh 23:1; cf. von Rad 1966: 94-97).

The Deuteronomy version associates the Sabbath with *the historical order:* "Remember that you were a slave in the land of Egypt, and the LORD your God brought you out from there with a mighty hand and an outstretched arm; therefore the LORD your God commanded you to keep the sabbath day" (5:15). The Sabbath is thus a celebration of liberation: liberation from the forces that oppress humankind, and liberation from a life of endless and meaningless drudgery. It is essentially a joyful occasion (Isa 58:13-14; cf. 56:2), and the commandment takes special care to safeguard the rights of all members of society — the family, servants, aliens, and even animals (cf. Tsevat 1972: 450; Bloch 1978: 3-4) — to enjoy the day of rest. "The sabbath commandment is a shining example of the fact that the basic commandments given to Israel are all benefits. They are not really demands; they are a liberation from demands. They are permissive, not oppressive" (Wolff 1974: 137).

As with all religious rites, there was always the danger of people simply going through the motions of observing the Sabbath. Amos 8:4-6 is a damning indictment of merchants who outwardly observe the Sabbath but inwardly cannot wait to get back to cheating their customers (cf. Isa 1:13). In the postexilic period attempts were made to enforce Sabbath observance. Neh 13 recounts how after warning and remonstrating with those who broke the Sabbath, Nehemiah ordered the city gates closed on the Sabbath, thus effectively closing down business activities. In this development inward motivation tended to be replaced by external compulsion.

14-1.3. WHEN GOD IS WORSHIPED: THE FESTIVALS

As well as the weekly cycle there is also an annual cycle, a "liturgical year" marked by a series of "appointed festivals of the LORD" (Lev 23:2, 4; see Garrett 1996). "The fact that the year was marked by a whole series of festivals is a reminder of the extent to which celebration, praise and thanksgiving were at the heart of Israelite religion" (D. Peterson 1992: 37). The main festivals are legislated in the Torah; like other aspects of Israel's worship, they are divinely appointed. Historical-critical scholars, however, generally see these festivals as the end product of a long process of development, the intricacies of which they try to reconstruct (on the history of scholarly study, see Kraus 1966: 1-25). Some postulate a "myth and ritual" pattern common throughout the ancient Near East and hold that the OT festivals were derived from Canaanite and/or Babylonian prototypes. The existence in Israel of a "new year festival," a "Yahweh enthronement festival," and a "covenant renewal festival" has been suggested, even though such festivals are not specifically mentioned in the OT! Undoubtedly Israelite worship had a certain amount in common with the cultic practices of the surrounding peoples. But the Israelite festivals are to be kept "to the LORD *(laYHWH)*" (Deut 16:10), and celebrating a festival consists of appearing before the LORD God, the God of Israel (Exod 34:23); in their canonical form they are unique because they are inseparably linked to the worship of the LORD. BT is concerned not with hypothetical theories of origins, but with the OT material in its final canonical form, and with its theological significance.

The Torah contains a number of cultic calendars (Exod 23:10-19; 34:18-24; Lev 23; Num 28–29; Deut 16:1-17; on these see Kraus 1966: 26-45). At the core of all of them stand the three major annual feasts or festivals: "Three times in the year all your males shall appear before the LORD God" (Exod 34:23; cf. Deut 16:16). The annual cycle is grounded in God's action in both the *created* and the *historical* orders. It is a common view that originally the festivals belonged to the created order. When God creates sun and moon, he says, "Let them be for signs and for *seasons* and for days and years" (Gen 1:14). The main festivals are related to the seasons of the Palestinian agricultural year, and specifically to the various harvests. In time, it is held, they came to be associated also with events of salvation history, and so linked to the historical as well as the created order. What is significant for BT, however, is that when the festivals were linked to historical events, their original anchorage in the created order was not forgotten (cf. Eichrodt 1961: 120). In their canonical form therefore, the festivals celebrate the presence and activity of God in *both* creation *and* history.

The festival of *Passover* (*pesach*: Lev 23:5; Num 28:16; Deut 16:1-2), celebrated on 14 Nisan along with the festival of *unleavened bread* (*matstsôth*: Lev 23:6-14; Num 28:16-25; Deut 16:3-8), celebrated on 15-22 Nisan (March/April), marks the barley harvest (Lev 23:9-10: created order) and the exodus deliverance when the LORD struck down the firstborn of Egypt but "passed over" the houses of the Israelites (Exod 12: historical order; on Passover see Kraus 1966: 45-55; Elder 1977; Otto and Schramm 1980: 10-22).

The festival of *weeks/Pentecost* (*shābhu'ôth*: Lev 23:15-21; Num 28:26-31; Deut 16:9-12), celebrated on 6 Sivan (May/June), marks the wheat harvest (Lev 23:16: created order). The historical reference of this festival is less obvious, though in postbiblical times it was associated with the giving of the Law at Mount Sinai (see Bloch 1978: 185). However, the instructions for observing the festival in Deut 16:9-12 conclude with the admonition: "Remember that you were a slave in Egypt, and diligently observe these statutes," and the dating of the arrival of the Israelites at Mount Sinai in the third month (Exod 19:1), the date of the festival of weeks, is probably intended to connect the festival with the Sinai event (see Kraus 1966: 58-61).

The festival of *booths or tabernacles* (*sukkôth*: Lev 23:34-43; Num 29:12-16; Deut 16:13-15), celebrated on 15-21 Tishri (September/October), marks the grape and olive harvest (Lev 23:39: created order) and commemorates the wilderness wanderings when the Israelites lived in booths or tents (Lev 23:42-43: historical order).

Thus, in addition to celebrating God's goodness in creation, the festivals also celebrate the different phases of the exodus event and God's deliverance of his people (cf. 3-1.2b). In their historical significance these festivals not only recall what God has done for his people in the past; they bring the past into the present (see more fully, 3-1.5).

Festivals, of course, are capable of becoming outward observances unrelated to serving God in daily life. When this happens they become the target of outspoken criticism by the prophets. According to Amos 5:21, God declares:

> I hate, I despise your festivals,
>   and I take no delight in your solemn assemblies. (cf. Isa 1:14)

The OT also requires the observance of an annual event, the *Day of Atonement (yôm hakkippurîm)*, that is not a feast but a fast (Lev 16; cf. Exod 30:10; Lev 23:26-32; Num 29:7-11; Acts 27:9). This is a day of repentance, and of sacrifice for the sins of the nation. The prescribed ritual involved the selection of two goats, one of which was sacrificed as a sin offering; Aaron was to lay his hands on the head of the live goat "and confess over it all the iniquities of the people of Israel," and then drive it into the wilderness, symbolically bearing away the sins of the people (Lev 16:20-22).

The Day of Atonement is associated with the celebration of the new year in an unnamed feast mentioned only in Num 29:1-6 and Lev 23:24-25, known in postbiblical Jewish tradition as Rosh Hashanah, literally "the head of the year" (see Bloch 1978: 13-25). The main feature of this day in the biblical references is the blowing of trumpets.

In the postexilic period two new festivals were added. Based on the account in the book of Esther of a great deliverance of the Jews from their enemies, the feast of *Purim (pûrîm* = "lots") is a celebration of freedom from persecution; see Esth 9:23-28. The feast of *Hanukkah (hānukkâh* = "dedication") commemorates the rededication of the temple in 164 B.C.; see 1 *Macc* 4:36-59; 2 *Macc* 10:5-8. It is the "Feast of Lights" (so called by Josephus; see Bloch 1978: 61), commemorating the rekindling of the light of religious freedom after the darkness of persecution. Both Purim and Hanukkah belong to the historical order (see Kraus 1966: 88-92). Postbiblical Judaism continued to develop and add to the liturgical year (see Bloch 1978), but BT is concerned only with the canonical material.

14-1.4. HOW GOD IS WORSHIPED: PREPARATION

In addition to the place and time, the way God is to be worshiped is also prescribed in the Torah and described in many narrative passages in the OT. Here again historical-critical study seeks to trace the evolution and development of modes of worship over the centuries. For BT the primary emphasis must be on the modes of worship in their final, canonical form.

A major problem underlies the OT understanding of worship: How can sinful human beings come before a holy God? In order to participate in worship one has to be a member of God's people and in a state of purity before God. The symbol of admission to God's people is *circumcision*. Purity is maintained or recovered by rites of *purification*.

a. Circumcision

Circumcision, the surgical removal of the foreskin of the male genital organ, is the outward sign of the covenant and signifies membership in the people of God (Gen 17:14; cf. 34:14-16; Exod 12:43-48). The OT traces this rite back to God's covenant with Abraham: every male descendant of Abraham is to be circumcised on the eighth day (Gen 17; 21:4; cf. Luke 2:21). The requirement is embodied in the Torah (Lev 12:3). Circumcision was a family duty, generally carried out by the father, not by a priest. While it can be administered to adults who join God's people, e.g., to slaves (Gen 17:12) or foreigners (Exod 12:48), it is normally administered to infants. Those who are born into a family that is part of God's people are within the covenant, and this is recognized by circumcision. Though circumcision is an outward act, both the Torah and the Prophets speak of a spiritual circumcision, a circumcision of the heart (Lev 26:41; Deut 10:16; 30:6; Jer 4:4; 9:25), of the ear (Jer 6:10), or of the lips (Exod 6:12, 30).

b. Purification

In the OT a holy God can be approached only by those who are "clean" and free from any impurity that would bar them from the divine presence. At Mount Sinai the Israelites were required to wash their clothes before approaching God (Exod 19:10, 14). Ps 24:3-4 is an entrance liturgy, specifying who is fit to enter the temple:

> Who shall ascend the hill of the LORD?
>   And who shall stand in his holy place?
> Those who have clean hands and pure hearts.

No formal distinction is made between what we would term "ritual" and "moral" impurity, though both are recognized in the OT. Rites of cleansing involving water are prescribed largely for what we would classify ritual or ceremonial impurity.

Uncleanness is associated in particular with anything to do with pagan cults, certain types of food, blood, childbirth, menstruation, certain diseases, and especially death. "The primary purpose for the laws of purity was to set the people apart to the Lord" (Dyrness 1979: 152). Uncleanness can be removed by following a prescribed ritual involving water, though it may also involve the elapse of a specified period of time. The main regulations are found in Lev 11–15, 19. Cleansing as a means of healing is graphically portrayed in the story of Naaman washing in the waters of the Jordan (2 Kgs 5). Typically, in the Prophets there is an emphasis on spiritual and ethical cleansing:

> Wash yourselves; make yourselves clean;
>> remove the evil of your doings
>> from before my eyes;
> cease to do evil,
>> learn to do good. (Isa 1:16-17; cf. 6:5)

14-1.5. HOW GOD IS WORSHIPED: COMING BEFORE THE LORD

While there is much material in the OT relating to worship, there is not a lot in the way of specific description of worship practices. Nevertheless, the main elements of worship can be identified, and of these, sacrifice plays a leading role.

a. Elements Of Worship

i. Prayer

The most basic element of public worship is prayer (cf. Eichrodt 1961: 172-76). Typically an individual prays to God on behalf of the people; in the temple prayer was probably led by a priest, but it appears that anyone could lead the prayers of the synagogue (cf. Matt 6:2, 5). Many examples of public prayer are found in the OT, and in particular the Psalter can be seen, in one sense, as the "prayer book" first of the temple, and later of the synagogue. The main types of prayer may be classified as follows:

Adoration. The most basic purpose of the cult is to

> ascribe to the LORD the glory of his name;
>> worship the LORD in holy splendor. (Ps 29:2; cf. 95:6; 99:5; etc.)

Prayer reflects the adoration, reverence, and awe with which worshipers must approach God (Rowley 1967: 257-59).

Prayers of *confession* are an essential part of coming before the Lord. The penitential psalms (Pss 32; 38; 51; 130) furnished material with which all worshipers could identify. Ezra 9:6-15 is an example of a public prayer of confession.

In prayers of *petition* the people bring their requests before God; such requests figure prominently in the psalms of lament.

In prayers of *thanksgiving* the people offer their thanks to God. The psalms of thanksgiving (B. W. Anderson 1983: chap. 4; cf. Rowley 1967: 260-61) are examples of such prayers that enable worshipers to "give thanks to the Lord, for he is good" (Ps 136:1).

Prayers of *intercession* are prayers on behalf of others. Prayers, e.g., by Abraham (Gen 18:16-33), Moses (Exod 32:11-14, 31-34), and Samuel (1 Sam 12:23) provide models (cf. Rowley 1967: 263).

ii. Praise

In public worship God's people praise him in song and in music (on music, see Rowley 1967: 203-12).

> O come, let us sing to the Lord;
>   let us make a joyful noise to the rock of our salvation! (Ps 95:1)

The Psalter can also be seen as the "Book of Praise" for temple and synagogue. The Psalms testify to the extensive use of music in worship, and give us a glimpse of the temple orchestra (Ps 150). Ezra 3:10-11, describing the laying of the foundation of the Second Temple, mentions the use of trumpets and cymbals to praise the Lord; "and they sang responsively, praising and giving thanks to the Lord." The passage quotes Ps 136 and indicates that the people joined in the response, "for his steadfast love endures forever." Praise could also be expressed through the medium of dance; when the ark was brought to Jerusalem, "David danced before the Lord with all his might" (2 Sam 6:14, 16; cf. Pss 149:3; 150:4).

iii. Scripture Reading

The reading of Scripture in some form was probably a part of public worship from an early period; the reading of the Torah, for example, was an essential part of covenant renewal liturgies (see 11-1.3d). Neh 8:1-3 tells of how Ezra read "the book of the law of Moses" to the people. By NT times the law and the prophets were read in synagogue worship (cf. Luke 4:16-20; Acts 13:15); a lectionary ensured the reading of the whole Torah over a specific length of time (cf. Rowley 1967: 235; Otto and Schramm 1980: 107).

iv. Preaching

What might be termed "preaching" also had a place in public worship. At least some of the prophetic preaching took place in the context of public worship, in the courts of the temple. In synagogue worship the reading of Scripture was followed by preaching (cf. Luke 4:21; Acts 13:15-16).

v. Almsgiving

While care of the poor is commended in the OT, it was evidently only in the synagogue that almsgiving was incorporated into worship (cf. Matt 6:2-4).

b. Sacrifice

Public worship in the OT is characterized above all by the practice of sacrifice.

i. The OT Accounts

The OT recognizes sacrifice as a means of approach to God in use by humankind from the earliest times; cf. the sacrifices of Cain (cereal) and Abel (animal) in Gen 4:3-4; of Noah (8:20); and the various accounts of the patriarchs building altars and offering sacrifices (12:7; etc.). The use of sacrifice by other peoples in the ancient world is also recognized. BT is not concerned with the various theories regarding the origin of sacrifice (see Abba 1977: 123-31), but with the understanding of sacrifice reflected in the canonical text. The Torah gives detailed regulations for a whole system of sacrificial worship, and sacrifice figures in many narratives (see von Rad 1962: 250-72).

ii. Types of Sacrifice

Broadly, three main types of sacrifice can be distinguished (cf. Kraus 1966: 113-22).

Gift offerings consist of something valuable offered to God, generally as a token of thanksgiving or consecration, or in fulfillment of a vow. They can be termed *minchâh,* which means gift, tribute, or offering (especially of grain or cereal), or *ʿōlâh,* meaning whole burnt offering (lit. "that which goes up"), where an animal was entirely burned as a way of offering it to God. Such offerings were to be made in the sanctuary every day. Thank offerings *(tôdhâh)* could be offered at any time as a token of gratitude to God (Lev 7:12-13; Ps 50:14; Jer 17:26). The first fruits *(bikkûrîm)* of the harvest were offered to God in recognition of the fact that the whole harvest comes from God and really belongs to him (Exod 23:19; 34:26; Num 15:17-21; Deut 15:19-23).

Peace offerings (*shelem*; cf. *shālôm* = "peace"; see 20-1.2) consist of a sacrifice that is partly burned on the altar and partly eaten as a kind of fellowship meal by worshipers and priests. Examples of this type include the sacrifice at the Sinai covenant (Exod 24:5, 11), the covenant renewal ceremony of Josh 8, the ceremony marking the bringing of the ark to Jerusalem (2 Sam 6:16-19), and the dedication of the temple (1 Kgs 8:62-64). This type of sacrifice symbolized fellowship and communion with God, and solidarity, harmony, health, and wholeness within the community. Sacramental meals of this type were "concerned with the real presence of the deity and that personal union with him from which all life and strength derive" (Eichrodt 1961: 157).

Sin offerings are termed *chaṭṭā'āth*, "sin offering," or *'āshām*, "guilt offering." These sacrifices are said to make atonement for sin, and make possible the restoration of a right relationship between the worshipers and God. They are accompanied by confession of sin and prayer (Lev 5:5). The belief that a sin offering could atone for the sins of persons who have died is found in only one passage in the Apocrypha/Deuterocanon (2 *Macc* 12:39-45).

While these broad types can be distinguished, in practice they may have tended to merge, especially in the later OT period. Probably all sacrifices were thought of as gifts to God, and equally as having an atoning significance (cf. C. R. North 1950: 206).

iii. The Meaning of Sacrifice

Although the OT describes the sacrificial system in detail, it says much less, directly at least, about how sacrifice is to be understood. It may at one time have been thought of in terms of nourishing or feeding the deity, but in the OT such ideas have been almost completely left behind. God, the Creator of all, does not *need* the offerings of human beings (Ps 50:9-11; cf. Kraus 1966: 114). "The idea of God smelling the sweet savour of the offering . . . serves to express the belief that he has heeded the sacrifice and is graciously pleased to accept it" (Eichrodt 1961: 143-44).

The above brief survey of types of sacrifice suggests that it was thought of in a variety of ways and had a variety of meanings. Broadly speaking, it may be said that sacrifice served to *maintain or restore a right relationship between God and his people.* Sacrifices were "visible and tangible expressions of the relationship of God's people with Himself" (Webber 1982: 26). A key point is that the whole system was provided by God himself. "The apparatus of sacrifice is itself a gift graciously vouchsafed by the covenant God as God's gift to man" (Eichrodt 1961: 164).

Sacrifice involves offering something precious to God. Although cereal offerings are prescribed in some cases, what is most commonly involved is animal sacrifice. Cattle and sheep were among the most valuable things people might possess. In the context of BT as a whole, special interest focuses on the most common type, the sin offerings, that involved the sacrifice of an animal. Such offerings are said to "atone" for sin, i.e., for the sin of God's people that separates them from a holy God. The OT terms for "atone" come from the root *kpr* (*kipper* = "atone"; LXX *exilaskomai*). The term *kappōreth* (LXX *hilastērion*) is used for the "mercy seat" on top of the ark, where the blood of the sin offering was sprinkled on the Day of Atonement (Lev 16:15). The root meaning of *kpr* may be to "cover," or perhaps to "wipe away," but etymology is an uncertain guide to meaning that is best derived from what the OT texts say.

Animal sacrifice involves the shedding of blood and hence the offering of a life to God. The clearest explanation of sacrifice is found in Lev 17:11, where God says, "The life of the flesh is in the blood; and I have given it to you for making atonement for your lives on the altar; for, as life, it is the blood that makes atonement." There can be no doubt that human sacrifice, and specifically child sacrifice, was practiced by Israel's neighbors, and on occasion within Israel (e.g., 2 Kgs 16:3; 21:6; Jer 7:31). This practice is specifically outlawed in the Torah (Lev 18:21; Deut 12:31), and the story of Gen 22 at one level teaches that God does not demand human sacrifice but accepts animal offerings as a valid substitute (Eichrodt 1961: 150).

Modern discussion has tended to polarize around the question of whether sacrifice is to be interpreted in terms of "propitiation" or "expiation" (cf. Abba 1977: 133; see also 9-3.4b). The difference is indicated by the grammatical construction: one propitiates God, but one expiates sin: a propitiatory offering averts the anger of a personal deity, while an expiatory offering nullifies the effects of sin.

"Propitiation," it is held by many modern scholars, conjures up a picture of a capricious God who must be appeased and whose wrath must be turned aside by one means or another. Such a view, many argue, is unworthy of the God of the Bible. "Expiation" is felt to be more acceptable; it recognizes that reparation has to be made for sin, but this is done by the worshiper giving up something of value as a kind of compensation that "covers" the sin.

The OT frequently repeats the instruction that worshipers are to lay their hands on the sacrificial animal (Lev 1:4; 3:2; etc.), a practice that has been variously interpreted (see Gese 1981a: 104-6; Childs 1992: 504-5). On the propitiation model this symbolizes the transfer of guilt, so that the penalty of sin falls not on the worshiper but on the sacrifice. On the expiation model it simply identifies the offering as belonging to and coming from the worshiper.

As already noted, the shedding of blood is a key feature of animal sacrifice. On the propitiation model, sin against God demands the life of the sinner, but the life of the sacrificial animal is substituted for the human life. On the expiation model the animal simply represents a valuable possession of the worshiper, and its death is the means of offering it to God.

While OT sacrifice may well be thought of in part as expiating sin, expiation by itself is not an adequate category. The Bible certainly does not think of sacrifice as "appeasing" a capricious God or getting God to change his mind. But neither does the Bible think of sacrifice as a kind of commercial transaction with God at best a spectator on the sidelines. In the Bible sin is never thought of impersonally; it is always a disruption of the right relationship between God and human beings. God is a just God and therefore cannot condone sin, but must pass judgment on it. God, however, is also a merciful God who in the OT provides a partial and preparatory system for atoning for sin, and who in the NT, through Christ, makes full atonement for the sins of humankind (see 9-3.4). Herein lies the basic difference between pagan and biblical understandings of sacrifice: the biblical emphasis is not on changing the deity's mind by man-made sacrifices, but on *God himself* providing the means of atonement. Provided this context is understood, sacrifice can fittingly be spoken of in terms of "propitiation."

This explanation accords best with the worshiper laying hands on the victim, a practice that suggests "not simply identification or ownership, but that the victim was a vicarious substitution for the donor himself, or that the worshipper's sins were symbolically transferred to the animal" (D. Peterson 1992: 40). In the OT laying on of hands signifies a transfer from one person to another; in this case "the hands conveyed guilt to the victim which was otherwise innocent" (Dyrness 1979: 154). This ties in with the requirement that sacrifices be "without blemish" (Exod 12:5; 29:1; Lev 1:3; etc.). It also accords best with the Lev 17:11 explanation that "as life, it is the blood that makes atonement." OT usage shows that "blood" is generally a way of referring to death (of a person or animal), and the basic idea behind atonement is the death of the victim (cf. Morris 1952). Thus Moses offers to make atonement for Israel through his own death (Exod 32:30-34). Through its death, the sacrificial animal pays the penalty for the sins transferred from the worshiper (cf. D. Guthrie 1981: 433).

Finally, this explanation accords best with the reference to the Suffering Servant giving his life as a sin offering (*'āshām*) in Isa 53:10 (see 9-1.3b). In Isa 53 it is clear that "our" sins are transferred to the Servant ("the LORD has laid on him the iniquity of us all" — v. 6), so that the Servant voluntarily accepts the punishment for sins not his own ("he was wounded for our transgressions" — v. 5; cf. Dyrness 1979: 158-59).

Sacrifice was intended primarily to atone for what we would regard as ritual sins, and also sins of inadvertence (Lev 4:27; Num 15:22-31). "But whoever acts high-handedly . . . affronts the LORD, and shall be cut off from among the people" (Num 15:30; cf. Ps 19:13). A passage such as Lev 6:1-7, however, shows that sacrifice could also atone for what we would term moral offenses: deception in matters of deposit or security, robbery, oppressing one's neighbor, finding what is lost and lying about it, and swearing falsely. This law prescribes restoration of the amount concerned plus one-fifth, and a guilt offering. Thus sacrifice is not a substitute for making reparation but a concomitant of it (cf. Brueggemann 1997: 667). The restoration reestablishes a right relationship between the persons concerned, while the sacrifice reestablishes a right relationship with God (cf. Job 42:8; see Eichrodt 1967: 447). Moreover, the sacrificial ritual of the Day of Atonement was designed to remove "all the iniquities of the people of Israel, and all their transgressions, all their sins" (Lev 16:21).

iv. The Prophetic Critique of Sacrifice

The prophets strongly denounced a dependence on sacrificial worship that was not matched by faithfulness to the Lord and obedience to obligations of the covenant. A series of passages appear to state that God does not desire sacrifice: see Amos 5:21-24, Isa 1:11-13a, 66:3, Mic 6:7-8, and Jer 7:21-26 (note esp. v. 22 — "In the day that I brought your ancestors out of the land of Egypt, I did not speak to them or command them concerning burnt offerings and sacrifices"). In Hos 6:6 God says, "I desire steadfast love and not sacrifice." The prophetic critique is matched in certain psalms, e.g., Ps 51:16-17:

> For you have no delight in sacrifice;
> if I were to give a burnt offering, you would not be pleased.
> The sacrifice acceptable to God is a broken spirit. (cf. 40:6)

Despite these strongly worded attacks, what the prophets attacked was the abuse of the sacrificial system and not the system itself (see von Rad 1962: 279; Otto and Schramm 1980: 961; Brueggemann 1997: 678; cf. McKenzie 1974: 58-61). Their criticism was directed against "the smug self-confidence of the whole cultic machine and those who operated it" (Eichrodt 1961: 366). Sacrifice is not effective unless "accompanied by appropriate religious-ethical dispositions" (Daly 1978: 99). It must not be forgotten that the criticism of a prophet like Jeremiah was criticism from within; he himself was "of the priests who were in Anathoth in the land of Benjamin" (Jer 1:1).

Old Testament: Promise

14-2. ALL PEOPLE SHALL COME TO WORSHIP

The destruction of the temple in 586 B.C. and the Babylonian exile had a traumatic effect, not least on Israel's worship. Prophetic voices spoke of a return from exile and a renewal of traditional worship. But visions of a restored and reformed worship merge with eschatological expectations of a radically new form of worship appropriate to the coming new order, however that may be conceived.

14-2.1. WHERE GOD IS WORSHIPED

a. The New Temple

i. Prophetic Visions of a Rebuilt Temple

The absence of a temple during the period of the exile provided the setting for prophecies of the building of a new temple following the return. Initially these fall within the realm of prophetic eschatology and simply look forward to a rebuilt Jerusalem temple. Thus in Isa 44:28 God says of the temple, "Your foundation shall be laid." The prophecy of Haggai is largely concerned with encouraging the returnees to rebuild the temple, though his assurance that "the latter splendor of this house shall be greater than the former" (2:9) was hardly fulfilled in the building that was constructed in 520-515. Similarly Zechariah hears the Lord declare: "I have returned to Jerusalem with compassion; my house shall be built in it" (1:16).

ii. Apocalyptic Visions of an Eschatological Sanctuary

With Ezekiel's extensive description of the new temple that is part of his vision of the restored community (Ezek 40–48), we cross the boundary from prophecy to apocalyptic. The plan of this new temple is divinely revealed, through an angel. On the face of it the detailed specifications for the temple suggest a blueprint to be used by those who return from exile. But this new temple has some striking differences from Solomon's temple, not least in its separation from both the city and the prince; the temple envisaged by Ezekiel "would no longer be the seat of a royally controlled institution, but of the restored theocracy, free now from all human compromises" (Barrois 1980: 64). The site of the new temple is "a very high mountain" (Ezek 40:2), but it is not specifically identified with Zion/Jerusalem, so that here too we have a major discontinuity with Solomon's temple (cf. Dumbrell 1985: 57).

The question has to be raised, however, as to whether Ezekiel's vision ever really constituted a building plan for the returning exiles. It is a striking fact "that no instructions are given to the prophet to build the temple. The only instruction he receives is to tell the people about the heavenly temple" (Hamerton-Kelly 1970: 5). Just as Ezekiel's vision of the restored Land (13-2.3) is ideal and apocalyptic rather than practical and historical, so it is with his vision of the future temple. Historically, when the Jerusalem temple was rebuilt ca. 520-515, it was neither according to the plan nor on the scale envisaged by Ezekiel. What this suggests therefore is that Ezekiel presents "a vision of the heavenly temple which would be manifested on Zion, in the eschatological age" (Hamerton-Kelly, 5), i.e., an apocalyptic sanctuary not constructed by human hands but established by God himself.

The book of *Tobit* confirms that even during the period of the Second Temple, at least some of God's people continued to look for an ideal future sanctuary. The dying Tobit prophesies the exile, the return, and the rebuilding of the temple, "but not like the first one until the period when the times of fulfillment shall come" (14:5). Just as this book's vision of the new Jerusalem is clearly apocalyptic (cf. 13-2.4), so Tobit goes on to envisage, beyond a merely rebuilt Jerusalem sanctuary, a new house of God that will be rebuilt "with a glorious building for all generations for ever, just as the prophets [Ezekiel?] said of it" (14:5 RSV), i.e., an eschatological temple. Tobit envisages the eschatological sanctuary as a new tent rather than a new temple:

> Give thanks worthily to the Lord . . .
> that his tent *(skēnē)* may be raised for you again with joy. (13:10 RSV)

b. The Heavenly Temple

Parallel with the expectation of a new temple is the belief in a heavenly temple that already exists and is the prototype of the earthly one. Such a belief is already witnessed to in Exod 25–31, where Moses is given instructions for the construction of the tent and is told to follow the "pattern *(tabhnîth)*" revealed by God (25:9, 40). The LXX translates *tabhnîth* as *paradeigma* and *typos* (cf. Eng. "paradigm," "type"). In other words, the earthly structure is to be patterned on an already existing heavenly model (cf. Hamerton-Kelly 1970: 5-6). Similarly, in 1 Chronicles David passes on to his son Solomon the detailed plan for the temple that God had revealed to him (28:19). Visions of God on a throne, surrounded by angelic hosts (1 Kgs 22:19; Isa 6:1-3; Dan 7:9-10), also suggest a heavenly dwelling place of God that corresponds to the temple on earth.

Belief in a new temple and a heavenly temple need not be seen as incompatible or even competing visions. The revelation to Ezekiel, by an angel, of the God-given eschatological temple (40:4) would accord well with the view that the future temple (like the tent of old) already has a heavenly prototype.

A variant form of eschatology is found in *2 Maccabees,* which recounts a tradition that prior to the destruction of the temple the prophet Jeremiah was divinely directed to take the tent and the ark and the altar of incense to the mountain from which Moses had viewed the Promised Land. There he concealed them in a cave, the location of which was not divulged. The same tradition speaks of an eschatological restoration. Jeremiah says, "The place shall remain unknown until God gathers his people together again and shows his mercy. Then the Lord will disclose these things, and the glory of the Lord and the cloud will appear" (*2 Macc* 2:4-8; contrast, however, Jer 3:16-17).

14-2.2. WHEN GOD IS WORSHIPED: THE SABBATH

The coming new age will be characterized by a pure worship of God, and this will include faithful observance of the Sabbath. In Ezekiel's vision of the new community the priests are to "keep my sabbaths holy" (44:24), as are the people (46:3).

More significantly, in 2 Isaiah the Sabbath is brought into association with the ingathering of the Gentiles (cf. 12-2.4). The "foreigners" who "join themselves to the LORD" in the new age will keep the Sabbath (Isa 56:6). The book of Isaiah concludes with a vision of how

> From new moon to new moon,
>   and from sabbath to sabbath,
> all flesh shall come to worship before me,
>   says the LORD. (66:23)

14-2.3. WHEN GOD IS WORSHIPED: THE FESTIVALS

Ezekiel's vision also speaks of the observance of the "appointed festivals" in the new age (44:24; cf. 45:17; 46:9). Isaiah calls the Zion of the messianic age "the city of our appointed festivals" (33:20).

It is important to remember that in the postexilic period the various festivals continued to be celebrated. Passover commemorates God's great act of deliverance from oppression in Egypt; Purim and Hanukkah are likewise festivals of deliverance. Especially while God's people continued to live under foreign domination (Persian, Ptolemaic, Seleucid, Roman), these feasts would have an eschatological as well as a historical orientation; not only did they look back to past deliverances, they also looked forward to the day when God would again act to deliver his people, and when all oppression would cease.

14-2.4. HOW GOD IS WORSHIPED: PREPARATION

The new order will be marked by a new and pure form of worship. According to Zech 14:20-21, everything in Jerusalem will be "Holy to the LORD." In the new age offerings will be "pleasing to the LORD as in the days of old" (Mal 3:4). Thank offerings will be made to the LORD (Jer 33:10-11; cf. vv. 17-18), and Israel's pure worship will be accepted by God (Ezek 20:40-41).

Jeremiah denounces the sins of Jerusalem and asks,

> How long will it be
> before you are made clean? (13:27)

Ezekiel goes further and speaks of a future cleansing: "I will sprinkle clean water upon you, . . . and a new spirit I will put within you" (36:25-26). With this may be compared Ezekiel's vision of a cleansing, life-giving stream flowing from the temple in Ezek 47.

14-2.5. HOW GOD IS WORSHIPED: COMING BEFORE THE LORD

Some visions of the future assume the continuation of sacrificial worship. Here too this is expanded to include the Gentiles who will bring their offerings to the eschatological temple (Isa 56:6-7; Zeph 3:10). Isa 19:19-22 envisages even the old enemy Egypt offering sacrificial worship to the LORD (cf. 12-2.4a.ii).

Other visions of the new age include *an eschatological feast,* which can be a symbol either of *judgment* or of *joy* (see G. Wainwright 1981: 20-21; Priest 1992: 236). In Zeph 1:7-9 judgment falls on the members of the royal house who will be the sacrificial victims at the feast. Similarly in Jer 46:10, "the Lord GOD of hosts holds a sacrifice," this time with the Egyptians as victims. In Ezek 39:17-20 the birds and the beasts are called to gather for "a great sacrificial feast on the mountains of Israel," with the victims being the forces of Gog. In 29:3-5 and 32:2-8 the victim is Pharaoh, pictured as the "dragon." In these cases the feast is modeled on the peace offering in which the worshipers participated, but it is used primarily as a symbol of judgment.

Joy is the theme in Isa 25:6, which forms part of the "Isaiah Apocalypse" (Isa 24–27). In the new age,

> On this mountain the LORD of hosts will make for all peoples
> > a feast of rich food, a feast of well-aged wines,
> > of rich food filled with marrow, of well-aged wines strained clear.

A great eschatological feast, symbolizing fellowship, joy, and nourishment, will be held on Mount Zion (cf. Ezek 39:17, "on the mountains of Israel"). The reference to the feast being "for all peoples" links it with the eschatological ingathering of the Gentiles (see 12-2.4). The prototype of this eschatological feast is probably the covenant meal in Exod 24:9-11, when Moses and his companions went up Mount Sinai where "they beheld God, and they ate and drank" (cf. Priest 1992: 234-35).

New Testament: Fulfillment

14-3. WORSHIP IN SPIRIT AND IN TRUTH

As in the OT, so also in the NT worship is an important and essential mark of God's people. As OT worship is rooted in the exodus event, so NT worship is rooted in the Christ event (cf. Webber 1982: 30).

14-3.1. WHERE GOD IS WORSHIPED

a. Jesus and the Temple

The Gospels depict Jesus showing an ambivalent attitude toward the temple. On the one hand he accepts it as part of the existing, God-given order; on the other hand he proclaims its destruction as part of God's coming judgment and its replacement by a new temple in the new age.

The Lucan infancy narrative stresses the element of continuity with the OT order: Jesus is presented at the temple (2:22-39), and as a boy finds it natural that he should be in his Father's house (2:49; see commentaries). A saying such as Matt 5:23-24 accepts the temple as part of the present order.

But Jesus also claims to be "something greater than the temple" (Matt 12:6), and in the light of the coming new age he pronounces judgment on the temple: "Not one stone will be left here upon another" (Mark 13:2 and //s). This is dramatized in the incident of the "cleansing of the temple" (Matt 21:12-13; Mark 11:15-19; Luke 19:45-48; John 2:13-22). In part Jesus can be seen as a reformer, taking action against abuse of the temple courts, burning with zeal for God's house (John 2:17 = Ps 69:9). But beyond this, the incident is clearly an act of eschatological symbolism (cf. Hiers 1971; B. F. Meyer 1993: 235-36). In denouncing those who have made the temple "a den of robbers" (Mark 11:17 and //s), Jesus echoes Jeremiah, who pronounced God's judgment on the temple and foretold its coming destruction (Jer 7:11; note the context). In quoting Zech 14:21 (John 2:16-17), Jesus justifies expelling the merchants as the required cleansing foretold for the messianic age (reading "traders," not "Canaanites," in Zech 14:21; see C. Roth 1960: 178-81). In quoting Isa 56:7, "My house shall be called a house of prayer / for all peoples," Jesus envisages, beyond the destruction of the present temple, the establishment of the eschatological temple that will be the focal point of the ingathering of the Gentiles (see 12-3.1c; and cf. Lohmeyer 1962: 38-42; McKelvey 1969: 61-67).

Jesus' saying on the temple is found in Matt 26:60-61, Mark 14:57-59, John 2:18-22 (cf. also Acts 6:13). In Matthew and Mark the saying is quoted by "false witnesses" at Jesus' trial; we must suppose that they distorted or misinterpreted the saying in some way, for John's version confirms that Jesus *did* speak both of the destruction of the existing temple and of the raising up of a new one, i.e., an eschatological temple (cf. McKelvey 1969: 67-72; Hahn 1973: 6, 27; and see next section on John 2:13-22).

According to Matt 27:51, as Jesus dies the curtain of the temple is torn in two; for the new community God's presence is no longer to be found in the Holy of Holies, but in the person of Christ and in the church that is his body. For Luke God's "glory" no longer resides in the temple but in the person of Christ (Luke 9:32; 21:27; see Baltzer 1965: 275-77; and cf. 8-3.2).

b. The Church as the New Temple

While the early church did not initially break completely with the Jerusalem temple, the NT proclaims that the new community, the Christian church, constitutes the new temple.

The early chapters of Acts depict the Jerusalem community meeting for prayer within the courts of the temple (2:46; 3:1-11; 5:12, 42; cf. Luke 24:53), although there is no mention of any participation in the sacrificial cult (see Hahn 1973: 43). Even Paul is depicted in Acts, at a relatively late stage in his career, as participating in a temple ceremony (21:26).

On the other hand, the Hellenists, led by Stephen, clearly held a much more radical view (Acts 7:47-50). Stephen was accused of "saying things against this holy place" (6:13), and in his defense (7:2-53), while referring favorably to "the tent of testimony in the wilderness" (7:44), he virtually portrays Solomon's building of the temple as an act of rebellion (7:47-53). Isa 66:1-2 is quoted (Acts 7:49-50) as part of the antitemple polemic. This view appears to have been more in line with the eschatological dimension of Jesus' attitude to the temple.

It is in the Pauline Epistles that we see the outcome of the Hellenists' recognition that the new age has dawned. "Do you not know," Paul asks the Corinthians, "that *you are God's temple* and that God's Spirit dwells in you (*en humin* — plural)? If anyone destroys God's temple, God will destroy that person. For God's temple is holy, and you are that temple" (1 Cor 3:16-17). Here Paul understands the Christian community ("you," plural) as constituting the temple. God's presence is not in the Holy of Holies; God now dwells in his people, through his Spirit (see McKelvey 1969: 98-102). Similarly in 2 Cor 6:16 Paul declares, "We are the temple of the living God." The same view is present in 1 Cor 6:19-20: "Do you not know that your body is a temple of the Holy Spirit within you . . . ?" Though certainly referring to the physical body of the individual, the corporate understanding of the church as the body of Christ, indwelt by the Holy Spirit, also lies behind this passage, for the bodies of believers "are members of Christ" (v. 15; cf. McKelvey, 102-6). In Eph 2:20-22 the metaphor of the temple as a building is applied to the church that is depicted as "built upon the foundation of the apostles and prophets, with Christ Jesus himself as the cornerstone. In him the whole structure is joined together and grows into a *holy temple* in the Lord; in whom you also are built together spiritually into a dwelling place for God." A not dissimilar metaphor is found in 1 Pet 2:4-10, where the church is referred to as a "spiritual house" (see McKelvey, 125-32). The temple is where God's presence dwells and where he is truly worshiped. With the dawning of the new age, God's presence and worship are no longer localized as they were in relation to the Jerusalem temple; they are located wherever the new community that is the body of Christ is to be found.

A similar approach is found in John's Gospel, though transposed into a different key. Jacob's dream at Bethel is the background of 1:51, where Jesus says, "You will see the heaven opened and the angels of God ascending and descending upon the Son of Man." Earthly sanctuaries are no longer necessary, for it is in the person of Christ that "the house of God and the gate of heaven" are now to be found (W. D. Davies 1974: 298). In 2:13-22 the cleansing of the temple and the saying on the temple are brought together. When the Jews challenge the cleansing and demand a sign, Jesus answers, "Destroy this temple, and in three days I will raise it up" (v. 19). The Jews object that the present building has been under construction for forty-six years. John comments that Jesus "was speaking of the temple of his body. After he was raised from the dead, his disciples remembered that he had said this; and they believed the scripture and the word that Jesus had spoken." There is a typical Johannine double meaning here. At one level Jesus refers to his own body, and thus to his coming death and resurrection. But at another level Jesus speaks of the destruction of the Herodian temple and the creation of a new temple, i.e., the church which is his body. This interpretation accords well with the understanding of worship presented in John 4, where in response to the Samaritan woman's question regarding the rival claims of Mount Zion and Mount Gerizim, Jesus declares, "The hour is coming when you will worship the Father neither on this mountain nor in Jerusalem. . . . But the hour is coming, and is now here, when the true worshipers will worship the Father in spirit and truth. . . . God is spirit, and those who worship him must worship in spirit and truth" (vv. 21, 23-24). The temple worship of both rival sanctuaries is now being replaced by a spiritual form of worship that is not confined to one geographical location but, rather, is focused in the person of Jesus and in the community of his followers. John's "emphasis is on Jesus as the New Temple, the new point of contact and the one to whom divine homage must now be directed . . . the glory theophany associated with the temple/tabernacle in the OT is now manifested in Jesus" (Dumbrell 1985: 68-69). The verb used in 1:14, which says the Word lived *(eskēnōsen)* among us, comes from the same root as *skēnē*, meaning tent or tabernacle. The verse could be translated "The Word became flesh and tabernacled among us." Thus in the NT "Jesus replaces the temple of Jerusalem as the source of life and renewal for the world and as the centre for the ingathering of the nations. He does this because he is the ultimate meeting point between God and humanity" (D. Peterson 1992: 101-2; cf. Hannay 1950: 284; Cronk 1982: 83).

c. The Heavenly Temple

Alongside the understanding of the church as the new temple is found a parallel tradition of a heavenly temple (cf. above, 14-2.1b).

Stephen highlights the fact that "the tent of testimony" was made after the pattern of a heavenly prototype (Acts 7:44). According to Hebrews, the worship of the earthly sanctuary is but "a sketch and shadow of the heavenly one" (8:5), which is seen as "the greater and more perfect tent" that Christ entered after his sacrificial death (9:11-12). Christ the High Priest now ministers in "the sanctuary and the true tent that the Lord, and not any mortal, has set up" (8:2). As the terminology indicates, for the writer to the Hebrews the heavenly sanctuary corresponds to the tent of the Pentateuch rather than to the Jerusalem temple.

John's visions in Rev 4–20 picture heaven in part in terms of a temple, though this merges with the picture of a divine palace (see McKelvey 1969: 155-76). In 7:15 it is said of the martyrs in heaven, that

> they are before the throne of God,
>   and worship him day and night within his temple.

Both the tent and the ark figure in the heavenly sanctuary. 15:5 refers to "the temple of the tent of witness *(ho naos tēs skēnēs tou martyriou)* in heaven," and according to 11:19, "God's temple in heaven was opened and the ark of the covenant was seen within his temple." This recalls the tradition of the hiding of the tent and the ark until they are revealed again at the last day (above, 14-2.1b). Here, however, the tent and the ark are in heaven and function as symbols both of God's presence with his people here and now and of the eschatological worship of God.

d. Your Synagogue

According to Luke 4:16, Jesus "went to the synagogue on the sabbath day, as was his custom." Many of the earliest Christians came from a background of synagogue worship. Christian worship in its early stages was closely linked with the synagogue, but in time a separation took place. In his missionary endeavors Paul followed a policy of taking his message first to the local synagogue (Acts 9:20). The letter of James refers to the congregation to which he writes as a "synagogue" (*synagōgē* — 2:2); this could reflect an early stage when a Christian group still worshiped in a Jewish synagogue, or the use of the term "synagogue" to refer to an entirely Christian assembly (see 11-3.1a). John's Gospel foresees a time of open conflict and warns believers that a time will come when "they will put you out of the synagogues" (16:2).

e. The Church in Your House

As the church gradually realized its own identity and separated from both temple and synagogue, local Christian congregations generally met in the house of one of their members. Christianity was centered not in a land or a city or a temple but in a Person, and in the community that formed around that Person; nevertheless, the community required a place of some kind where it could meet for regular worship, and initially at least, the only space available was in the homes of some of its better-off members. In the Gospels we see Jesus teaching in private homes (Mark 2:1; 7:17; 9:33; 10:10), accepting hospitality and participating in meals (Luke 5:29); he himself presided over his last meal with his disciples in an upper room of a home in Jerusalem (Mark 14:15). In his mission charge to his disciples, he assumes that in any given place they will make a private home their base of operations (6:10). Acts portrays believers meeting in private homes from the earliest time (2:46; 5:42; 20:7-12). The NT records the names of specific individuals in whose homes Christian congregations met: Mary (Acts 12:12), Prisca and Aquila (Rom 16:3-5; 1 Cor 16:19), Philemon (Phlm 2), Nympha (Col 4:15), and Gaius, who Paul says "is host to me and to the whole church" (Rom 16:23). In his study of "the house church," Branick (1989) argues that for about the first century of the church, "the private dwelling shaped the Christians' community life, forming the environment in which Christians related to each other, provided an economic substructure for the community, a platform for missionary work, a framework for leadership and authority, and probably a definite role for women" (14-15).

14-3.2. WHEN GOD IS WORSHIPED: THE SABBATH

Although in practice Jesus accepted the Sabbath as part of the existing order, he consistently put human need before strict observance of the Sabbath law, thus precipitating a series of confrontations with the Pharisees (Mark 2:23-28; 3:1-6; Luke 13:10-17; 14:1-6; John 5:1-18; 9:14; see W. Stott 1978: 408-9; Slane 1996: 698). "The sabbath was made for humankind," he declared, "not humankind for the sabbath" (Mark 2:27). What follows, however, is a more far-reaching claim: "The Son of Man is lord even of the sabbath" (2:28). Even the Mosaic Law has now to be understood and interpreted in the light of the unique authority claimed by Jesus. True rest is to be found in Jesus himself (Matt 11:28-30). Yet Jesus does not seek to abolish the Sabbath, but rather to restore its original meaning and intention (cf. Leitch 1966: 428, Otto and Schramm 1980: 103; contra Rordorf 1968: 63).

The Sabbath, however, also marks the transition from the old to the new order. After his death Jesus' body lies in the tomb on the Sabbath; only when the Sabbath is over is Jesus raised to life, so it is "after the sabbath" that the women go to the tomb (Matt 28:1 and //s).

Christian preaching begins within the old order, and Paul is pictured on several occasions as preaching in a synagogue on the Sabbath day (Acts 13:14; 16:13; 17:2; 18:4). But as part of the old order the Sabbath is no longer binding on Gentile Christians (Col 2:16; cf. Rom 14:5-6; Gal 4:8-11).

The NT speaks of Christians gathering for worship on "the Lord's day" (*hē kyriakē hēmera;* see Trafton 1996: 488). The actual expression is found only in Rev 1:10, where John says, "I was in the Spirit on the Lord's day *(en tē(i) kyriakē(i) hēmera(i))*." This reference is to be understood in connection with two other passages that speak of Christians gathering for worship on the first day of the week: Acts 20:7, where "on the first day of the week *(en de tē(i) mia(i) tōn sabbatōn)* . . . we met to break bread," and 1 Cor 16:1-4, where Paul tells the Corinthians to put aside a contribution for the collection "on the first day of every week *(kata mian sabbatou)*" (see W. Stott 1978: 412). The wording of these passages echoes the resurrection accounts of the women going to the tomb "on the first day of the week" *(te(i) mia(i) tōn sabbatōn* — Mark 16:2 and //s) and makes clear that the determining factor in Christians worshiping on this day was Jesus' resurrection. It is significant that in John's Gospel, after the initial resurrection appearances on Easter Sunday, Jesus' next appearance to his disciples is exactly a week later and therefore again on a Sunday (20:26; cf. Stagg 1962: 295).

14-3.3. WHEN GOD IS WORSHIPED: THE FESTIVALS

Jesus was brought up in a family that observed the festivals (Luke 2:41-42), and he himself went up to Jerusalem for Passover (John 2:13, 23; 11:55) and for an unnamed feast (5:1). With the possible exception of one occasion in Paul's career (Acts 20:16), however, the early church did not observe the OT festivals. Paul is concerned because the Galatians observe "special days, and months, and seasons, and years" (Gal 4:10; cf. Col 2:16-17). This is doubtless related to Paul's strong opposition to requiring Gentile converts to observe the ceremonial laws of the Torah as a precondition of salvation. In Rom 14:5-6 he leaves the observance of "days" (unspecified) to each believer to decide. His real objection, however, to the observance of the OT festivals seems to have been that "these are only a shadow of what is to come, but the substance belongs to Christ" (Col 2:17).

With the dawning of the new order, the OT system of feasts is no longer required of Christians, because the meaning of each of the feasts has found its fulfillment in Christ. Christ's death is interpreted in terms of the Passover sacrifice (1 Cor 5:7b-8) and hence replaces the Passover (cf. 9-3.4b). Similarly an important theme of John's Gospel is the fulfillment of the OT feasts by Jesus (see W. D. Davies 1974: 296). In Hebrews the existing Day of Atonement ritual is superseded by the sacrifice of Christ.

14-3.4. HOW GOD IS WORSHIPED: PREPARATION

As in the OT (14-1.4), worship in the NT raises the question of how sinful human beings can come before a holy God. In the NT the rite of circumcision is replaced by baptism, which is a sign of admission to membership in the people of God and of cleansing from sin.

a. Circumcision

Insofar as he was brought up within the existing order, Jesus was circumcised as required by the Torah (Luke 2:21), and in a particular set of circumstances Paul had Timothy circumcised (Acts 16:3). Yet Paul fiercely defended the position that circumcision was not to be required of Gentile converts (Gal 5:2-3; on Paul's attitude to the Law, see 18-3.3b).

b. Baptism

Numerous narrative accounts in Acts and more incidental references in the Epistles witness to the fact that from the earliest days all believers were admitted to membership of the church through baptism. There are far more references to baptism in the NT than to the Eucharist (cf. Moule 1961: 47).

The Gospels indicate a link between Christian baptism and that of John the Baptist. John's baptism had a threefold significance: it symbolized cleansing from sin conditional on repentance; it symbolized admission to the eschatological people of God; and it foreshadowed the coming messianic baptism (cf. Scobie 1964: 67-73, 110-16). In accepting baptism at the hands of John, Jesus both identified himself with the existing people of God (Mark 1:5) and provided the pattern for the new people of God to follow (1:9; Matt 3:15). Christian baptism, however, as the rite of admission to the new people of God, was not possible until after the completion of the Christ event. No command to baptize is attributed to the historical Jesus; it is to the risen Christ that Matthew ascribes the command: "All authority in heaven and on earth has been given to me. Go therefore and make disciples of all nations, *baptizing them* in the name of the Father and of the Son and of the Holy Spirit, and teaching them to obey everything that I have commanded you" (28:18-20; on this see Martin 1974: 94-97).

The NT provides only brief glimpses of the church's baptismal practice. Baptism is not self-administered; people are baptized by a representative of the church. The rite is carried out in water, most probably by immersion (cf. Matt 3:16//Mark 1:10; Acts 8:38). Traces of an emerging baptismal liturgy may be detected in Acts 8:38 (especially in the Western text that adds a baptismal confession, "I believe that Jesus Christ is the Son of God"; cf. Cullmann 1950: 75). The laying on of hands is associated with the gift of the Spirit after baptism in 8:17 and 19:6.

The central importance of baptism in the NT is seen from the way it can be linked with each of the major themes of the NT: the new order, the new Servant, the new people, and the new way.

Christian baptism differs fundamentally from that of John (although it fulfills John's prophecy of a coming baptism with the Holy Spirit) because it is related to *the new order* that has been inaugurated by the Christ event. In baptism believers pass from the old order to the new; this is a passage from death to life, and thus in effect a rebirth (John 3:3). It can also be viewed as a passage from darkness to light (Eph 5:7-14; Heb 6:4; 1 Pet 2:9, in all of which the context is probably baptismal). Repeatedly baptism is linked with the gift of the Spirit (1 Cor 12:13; Titus 3:5; John 3:5; cf. also 5-3.3b.ii), which is the outstanding sign of the new age.

Baptism is thus linked in the closest possible way with Christ, who is *the new Servant* of God. Baptism is in the name of Christ or of the Lord Jesus (Acts 19:5), and persons are said to be baptized "into Christ" (Gal 3:27; Rom 6:3-4) or to "put on Christ" (Gal 3:27 RSV). For Paul especially, this means nothing less than a participation by the believer in the Christ event, i.e., in the dying and rising of Christ, an understanding that may have been made more vivid by the practice of baptism by immersion, the going down into the water symbolizing death to the old life and the coming up out of the water symbolizing rising to the new life (Rom 6:3-4). John expresses the connection of baptism with the Christ event in his own way (see Lindars 1976: 52-58): the water that issues from Christ's side (John 19:34) is a symbol of baptism that links it with his sacrificial death (cf. 1 John 5:8).

Baptism also marks the entry of believers into *the new people* of God: "In the one Spirit we were all baptized into one body" (1 Cor 12:13). Links with the old Israel are established through seeing the waters of the flood and of the Red Sea as types of the waters of baptism by which God adds persons to the new Israel (10:1-2; 1 Pet 3:20-21). Paul draws a parallel between circumcision, the rite of admission to God's people in the OT, and baptism, the rite of admission to God's people under the new order that he calls "a spiritual circumcision" (Col 2:11-12). Baptism unites believers with Christ, and hence also with each other. It thus ought to be a bond of unity (Eph 4:4-5), though even in the NT it is clear that the reality fell short of the ideal (1 Cor 1:10-16).

Baptism has profound implications for *the new way* to be followed by believers. Like John's baptism, it signifies cleansing from sin, conditional on repentance (Acts 2:38, etc.), and it has strong ethical consequences (see Moule 1961: 57). In Rom 6 Paul stresses that the new life to which the baptized rise is to be marked by a clean break with the sins of the past (cf. also 1 Cor 6:9-11; see Otto and Schramm 1980: 175-77). "Those baptized are pardoned, cleansed and sanctified by Christ, and are given as part of their baptismal experience a new ethical orientation under the guidance of the Holy Spirit" (Lazareth 1982: 2). The implications of baptism for Christian living are spelled out especially in 1 Peter (historically, the epistle may be based on a sermon to the newly baptized; see R. E. O. White 1996: 52).

The question of infant baptism is not raised directly in the NT. Certainly it is true that "baptism upon personal profession of faith is the most clearly attested pattern in the New Testament documents" (Lazareth 1982: 14); there are obvious reasons for this. However, references to the baptism of a "household (*oikos* = 'house, household, family')" (Acts 16:15, 31, 33-34; 18:8; 1 Cor 1:16) probably imply infant baptism, since children were certainly considered part of the "household." The preservation and transmission of the story of Jesus blessing the children (Mark 10:13-16 and //s) may well have been designed to answer questions about the role of infants in Christian congregations, and specifically whether or not they should be baptized. The contemporary question, however, cannot be resolved by citing proof texts, nor by any purely historical study; theological considerations are inevitably involved.

14-3.5. HOW GOD IS WORSHIPED: COMING TOGETHER

The NT speaks of the early Christian communities "coming together" or "gathering" (Acts 4:31; 1 Cor 11:17; Heb 10:25) for worship on a regular basis, yet there are no detailed descriptions of how God was worshiped in the early church; at best, we have a series of glimpses of worship in the narrative of Acts and in references in the Epistles.

With the dawning of the new age in the Christ event, animal sacrifice was rejected and the concept of sacrifice was spiritualized. The basic elements of nonsacrificial worship can be identified; these indicate clearly the influence of the synagogue. In addition, a new form of worship, the Lord's Supper or Eucharist, emerges and assumes a place of central importance.

a. Sacrifice

Nothing shows more clearly the transition to the new order than the NT view of sacrifice. Jesus' parents complied with the Torah and offered the prescribed sacrifice after his birth (Luke 2:22-24, 27). If the Last Supper was a Passover meal, then it would involve the sacrifice of a lamb in the temple (Mark 14:12). The earliest Christians met in the temple for prayer (Acts 3:1), but there is no mention of participation in the sacrificial cult. We know of one occasion when Paul, relatively late in his career, participated in a temple ritual that involved sacrifice (21:26).

But the church, from a very early date, came to understand Jesus' death as a sacrifice that atones for the sin of the world and reconciles humankind to God (see more fully, 9-3.4b). A practical consequence of this was the abandonment of participation in the sacrificial cult by the new community. The OT sacrificial system was seen as pointing forward to the sacrifice of Christ, but with the coming of the antitype the need for the type was abolished. The entire teaching of Hebrews is designed in fact to make it clear "that the inauguration of the new covenant by Jesus means the fulfilment and replacement of the whole pattern of approach to God established under the Mosaic covenant" (D. Peterson 1992: 228).

With the dawning of the new order, a major reinterpretation of sacrifice becomes possible. As all believers constitute "a holy priesthood," their task is to "offer spiritual sacrifices *(pneumatikas thysias)* acceptable to God through Jesus Christ" (1 Pet 2:5). Thus Paul calls on the Romans to "present your bodies as a living sacrifice, holy and acceptable to God, which is your spiritual worship *(logikēn latreian)*" (Rom 12:1). For Paul this means basically the offering of oneself, perhaps even the offering of one's life (Phil 2:17; cf. 2 Tim 4:6), in the service of Christ.

While this may be referred to as a "spiritualization" of sacrifice, it must be noted that it is interpreted in the NT in the most concrete and down-to-earth fashion. Heb 13:15 thinks of Christian worship as a form of sacrifice — "let us continually offer a sacrifice of praise to God, that is, the fruit of lips that confess his name" — but immediately goes on to say, "Do not neglect to do good and to share what you have, for such sacrifices are pleasing to God" (13:16). The gifts that the Philippian church sent to Paul in support of his ministry are referred to as "a fragrant offering, a sacrifice acceptable and pleasing to God" (Phil 4:18). Paul may regard Christian sacrifice as "spiritual worship" (Rom 12:1), but "the apostle is not simply considering some form of inner consecration here, but the consecration of ourselves as a whole, able to express our obedience to God in concrete relationships within this world" (D. Peterson 1992: 177). In fact, the whole of Rom 12:2–15:13 may be seen as spelling out what this "spiritual worship" means in practical terms (cf. Daly 1978: 101-2).

b. Elements of Worship

The NT gives us no detailed description of early Christian worship; we are afforded only a few glimpses.

One such glimpse is 1 Cor 14, where Paul discusses worship at Corinth (see Otto and Schramm 1980: 166-73). Some claim this chapter shows that the earliest Christian worship was entirely "charismatic," with members of the community contributing prophecy, praise, prayer, and speaking in tongues as the Spirit moved them. Such a conclusion goes far beyond the evidence. For one thing, we do not know how typical the situation at Corinth was; worship at Jerusalem, for example, may have been much more "liturgical" in nature. Moreover, in 1 Cor 14 Paul is seeking to *restrain* the type of worship that prevailed in Corinth. In response he sets down guidelines for worship: it must be intelligible (vv. 7, 19), appealing to the mind as well as the emotions (v. 15), making for the upbuilding of the community (v. 26), and ordered (vv. 33, 40).

Liturgical scholars frequently assume that the Eucharist was celebrated at every service of Christian worship in NT times, but this is by no means certain. The discussion in 1 Cor 14, for example, says nothing about the Eucharist. Hahn (1973) is therefore probably right when he asserts that "the separate existence of a worship service consisting of word of God and prayer can hardly be disputed" (72; cf. Otto and Schramm 1980: 166).

The worship of the NT is characterized by the same elements that originated in the OT period and were developed in the synagogue (14-1.5a). The influence of the synagogue on early Christian worship was undoubtedly strong (cf. Rowley 1967: 242; Webber 1982: 51-52).

i. Prayer had a central place (see Martin 1974: 28-38). The first Christians devoted themselves to "the prayers" (Acts 2:42), probably at the time of the temple prayers (cf. 3:1; see D. Peterson 1992: 158); both Acts and the Epistles witness to the importance of public prayer. Such prayers must have been led by an individual, but the community as a whole responded with "Amen" (see 1 Cor 14:16; cf. Martin 1974: 37). No doubt all the main types of prayers were represented (cf. 14-1.5a), though the evidence is much less extensive than in the OT.

Adoration. In Acts 4:24 God is addressed in prayer as "Sovereign Lord, who made the heaven and the earth, the sea, and everything in them." Revelation provides many examples of what are basically prayers of adoration (4:11; 5:9-10, 12-13; 7:12; 15:3-4).

Confession. John assures his readers that "if we confess our sins," we will receive forgiveness and cleansing (1 John 1:9), while Jas 5:16 shows that confession of sin was part of prayers for healing.

Petition. In Phil 4:6 Paul commends prayers of petition, and 1 Tim 2:1 mentions "supplications" (*deēsis* = "supplication, entreaty"). In Acts 4:29 the church's petition is, "grant to your servants to speak your word with all boldness."

Prayers of *thanksgiving* were also part of Christian worship (Phil 4:6; Col 4:2; 1 Tim 2:1; 4:4-5; for an example see Rev 11:17).

1 Tim 2:1 commends prayers of *intercession,* and 2:2 mentions specifically prayers "for kings and all who are in high positions." Acts 12:5 shows the church praying for the imprisoned Peter.

ii. Praise was undoubtedly an important element in the corporate worship of the community. Unlike the OT, there is no mention of musical instruments, though Eph 5:19 (RSV) does speak of "addressing one another in psalms and hymns and spiritual songs, singing and making melody to the Lord with all your heart" (cf. Col 3:16; 1 Cor 14:26; Jas 5:13). While the terms should not be pressed too far, "psalms" *(psalmoi)* suggests that the church followed the synagogue in using the Psalter in worship (cf. 1 Cor 14:26), while "hymns" *(hymnoi)* and "songs" *(ō(i)dai)* suggest specifically Christian compositions. Several NT passages are poetic in form and are regarded by many scholars as examples of early Christian hymns; they include John 1:1-18; Phil 2:6-11; Col 1:15-20; Rev 4:8, 11; 5:13; 7:12; 11:17-18; 15:3-4.

iii. Scripture reading doubtless had a place also, as 1 Tim 4:13 indicates. This would certainly mean the reading of the Hebrew Scriptures. Most of the epistles of the NT were probably designed originally to be read before the congregation assembled in worship (cf. Col 4:16; 1 Thess 5:27; Rev 1:3).

iv. There would also be preaching that might be based on a Christian interpretation of OT passages, or theological proclamation and ethical exhortation similar to what is found in many of the epistles. The "prophecy" discussed by Paul in 1 Cor 14:1-5 comes close to being what today would be termed preaching; it involves speaking to the congregation "for their upbuilding and encouragement and consolation" (v. 3; but see D. Peterson 1992: 196-97). The speeches of Acts are missionary sermons, but in both style and content they may suggest something of the nature of preaching within Christian communities.

v. Again following the synagogue tradition, there would be some place for almsgiving. 1 Cor 16:2 witnesses to the practice in Pauline churches of contributing money at the weekly meeting for worship; in this case it was saved up to be sent as part of Paul's collection for the Jerusalem church.

c. The Lord's Supper

The essentially new element in the worship of the NT is what Paul refers to as the Lord's Supper *(kyriakon deipnon,* 1 Cor 11:20). The term "eucharist" does not occur in the NT, though it is derived from the verbal form *eucharistēsas* = "having given thanks," which does appear in the NT accounts (Matt 26:27; Mark 14:23; Luke 22:17, 19; 1 Cor 11:24). The earliest references are those embedded in 1 Cor 10:16-21, 11:23-26 (see Klauck 1992: 363-65). With this is to be taken the account of the institution of the rite at Jesus' last supper with his disciples; one form of this tradition is found in Mark 14:22-25 and (with minor variations) Matt 26:26-29, while a variant tradition is found in Luke 22:15-19 (where there is both a "shorter reading" and a "longer reading" to be reckoned with; see commentaries). John's Gospel has an account of the Last Supper but makes no reference to the Eucharist. This does not mean that John is "antisacramental"; rather "John presupposes the institution and brings out its full meaning in various places" (Toon 1996: 493). In particular 6:52-58, part of the Bread of Life Discourse, clearly contains eucharistic teaching (see Cullmann 1953: 93-102; Delorme 1964: 143-56; Cronk 1982: 177).

Jesus' "Last Supper" with his disciples is to be understood in part with reference to the meals he shared during his ministry, especially with the outcasts of society (cf. Hahn 1973: 18-19), and to the story of the feeding of the crowds. From a historical point of view, there is a discrepancy between John and the Synoptics regarding the timing of the Last Supper. The Synoptics regard it as a Passover meal, whereas John places it one day before the Passover (see Higgins 1952: 17-20; Delorme 1964: 21-67). Possible ways of reconciling the discrepancy are not the concern of BT. From a theological point of view the difference is irrelevant; Jesus' death took place at the Passover season, a fact that did affect the way it was understood by the early church (contra Higgins, 13).

At first the Lord's Supper was probably part of a full meal shared by early Christian congregations; this is most clearly seen from 1 Cor 11:20-22, 33-34. The Lucan term "breaking of bread *(hē klasis tou artou)*" (Acts 2:42, 46; 20:7, 11; cf. Klauck 1992: 366; D. Peterson 1992: 155-57), and perhaps also the term *agapē* in the sense of "love feast" (Jude 12; see Arndt and Gingrich 1957: 6), probably both refer to actual meals that also included a form of Eucharist.

Basically the Lord's Supper has a threefold reference. It looks back to the *past* in grateful remembrance and thanksgiving for the Christ event, especially for Christ's death and the new covenant between God and his people that is thereby established. All the accounts mention Jesus giving thanks during the meal, though it is only in the Pauline form (and the longer reading in Luke) that Jesus specifically commands his followers, "Do this in remembrance of me" (Luke 22:19b; cf. 1 Cor 11:25). In accordance with the biblical understanding of memory, the Eucharist makes the past event contemporary for the worshipers (see more fully, 3-3.5). Paul adds that by participating in this meal believers "proclaim *(katangellete)* the Lord's death" (1 Cor 11:26). The Passover setting of the Last Supper (irrespective of whether Jesus and disciples shared an actual Passover meal or not) is extremely significant. Passover celebrates the great saving event that brought salvation to God's people Israel; the Lord's Supper celebrates the great saving event accomplished through the death and resurrection of Christ that brings salvation to all humankind. Thus the Passover events are seen as "symbolic foreshadowings of the holy eucharist" (Cronk 1982: 61). Christ sees his approaching death in terms of an atoning sacrifice (Higgins 1952: 51); as the "Lamb of God," he is the antitype of the Passover lamb (see 9-3.4b). The phrase "This is my blood of the covenant" (Mark 14:24; Matt 26:28) echoes "the blood of the covenant" which was an essential element in the sacrificial rite that sealed the Sinai covenant (Exod 24:8; see Jeremias 1966: 94-95). The Pauline form has "This cup is the new covenant in my blood" (1 Cor 11:25, so also the longer reading in Luke); this is a reminder that Christ's death inaugurates the new covenant prophesied by Jeremiah (see 11-2.3). Matthew and Mark also refer to the blood as being poured out for "many," echoing Isa 53:11-12 and suggesting that Jesus' death is related to the Isaianic prophecy of the Suffering Servant (cf. 9-1.3).

In the *present* the Lord's Supper, like the peace offerings of the OT, symbolizes the communion of believers with their risen Lord and with one another. In the meal the presence of the Lord is central; so Paul can refer to "the Lord's supper" (*kuriakon deipnon* — 1 Cor 11:20), "the cup of the Lord" *(potērion kuriou),* and "the table of the Lord" *(trapeza kuriou* — 10:21), and talks of "communion" (*koinōnia* — 10:16; cf. 11-3.5d) with Christ. As believers are drawn closer to Christ, they are naturally also drawn closer to one another. This aspect of the meal is brought out especially in 10:17 (AT): "Because there is one loaf *(artos),* we who are many are one body, for we all partake of the one bread." Sharing in the one loaf of bread symbolizes and realizes the unity of believers in the body of Christ.

The Lord's Supper has a *future* reference also, for all the texts have some form of eschatological saying; on this see 14-4.5b.

New Testament: Consummation

14-4. THEY FALL DOWN AND WORSHIP

In the NT view of the end and goal of creation and history, worship plays a central role. In the final vision of the Bible, it is said that at the end God will come to dwell with his people, "and his servants will worship him" (Rev 22:3).

14-4.1. I SAW NO TEMPLE

It seems paradoxical that the climax of the BT of the temple is a vision of the holy city in which there is no temple: "I saw no temple in the city, for its temple is the Lord God the Almighty and the Lamb" (Rev 21:22). The prototype of the community of God's people at the final consummation is not the holy temple but the holy city (cf. 13-4.2). The contrast with Ezekiel's vision of the new community with the new temple in its midst is striking, the more so as John uses so much of Ezekiel's imagery.

On closer inspection, however, it can be seen that Rev 21–22 is "replete with temple imagery," so that the temple is in effect an "absent presence" (Dumbrell 1985: 35). In his vision of the final consummation, John hears a voice saying,

> See, the home (*skēnē*, lit. 'the tent') of God is among mortals.
> He will dwell *(skēnōsei)* with them. (21:3)

Only at the end will the basic purpose of tent and temple be fulfilled; in John's vision the members of the covenant community "dwell in God's presence and

God tabernacles with them in the fullest sense of the word" (Zehr 1981: 169). The holy city itself is envisioned as a perfect cube (21:16), just as was the Holy of Holies in the temple (Elwell 1988h: 2028). There is no temple in the city because the city itself is now the Holy of Holies, where God and the Lamb dwell. There is no longer any need for a holy place set apart in an unclean world, a buffer zone between a holy God and a sinful world (cf. 14-1.1b.ii), for all that has been unclean has been eliminated (21:27; 22:3; cf. Zech 14:20-21). In effect, therefore, at the final consummation the heavenly temple (14-3.1c) merges with the holy city.

14-4.2. UNCEASING PRAISE: THE SABBATH REST

At the final consummation God's people move beyond the rhythm of work and rest that characterizes life here on earth and enjoy an eternal Sabbath of unceasing praise to God (cf. Ewert 1980: 167-69).

Just as the Israelites looked forward to the "rest" of the Promised Land (above, 14-1.2), so the author of Hebrews interprets the final consummation in terms of rest. In one of his frequent exhortations (3:7–4:11), he cites Ps 95:7-11 as a reminder that rebellion and unfaithfulness on the part of the Israelites put their entering into the "rest" in peril. Just as the exodus is a type of deliverance through the Christ event, so entering the Promised Land and finding rest is a type of the final consummation. Christians look forward to a "Promised Land": thus "a sabbath rest still remains for the people of God" (Heb 4:9). Hebrews links this with God's own rest on the first Sabbath, so that the goal of Christians is to "enter God's rest" (4:10). "This rest is an eschatological expectation, a fulfilment of the prophecies of redemption, an entering into that rest which there has always been, from the beginning, with God. In the fulfilment of this hope the whole purpose of creation and the whole purpose of redemption are reunited" (von Rad 1966: 102).

In Rev 14:13 the martyrs are assured that they will "rest from their labors."

14-4.3. UNCEASING PRAISE: NO NEED OF SUN OR MOON

Just as there is no need for a temple at the final consummation, so there is no need for times or seasons of worship. In Gen 1 a major purpose of the creation of sun and moon is to regulate sacred time (1:14; cf. 14-1.3). But the new age lies beyond both the cyclic time of the created order and the linear time of the historical order. There is no need of annual feasts, and hence no need for sun or moon (Rev 21:23). The new age will be marked by the continuous worship of God by his people.

14-4.4. THEY HAVE WASHED THEIR ROBES

Purity is a condition for entering into God's presence. In his parable of the wedding banquet, Jesus warned that those without a "wedding robe" would not gain admission to the eschatological banquet (Matt 22:11-14). Thus in Revelation it is those who "have washed their robes and made them white in the blood of the Lamb" who are "before the throne of God, and worship him" (7:14-15).

14-4.5. HIS SERVANTS SHALL WORSHIP HIM

The praises of the church here on earth are both an echo of the heavenly liturgy (cf. 1-3.3b) and an anticipation of the worship of the end time.

a. Elements of Worship

The various elements of worship find a place in visions of the future.

i. The Prayers of the Saints

Earth is even now linked to heaven as the heavenly hosts bear "the prayers of the saints" to the Lamb (Rev 5:8), and the prayers of God's people rise like incense to the heavenly realm (8:3-4).

ii. The Songs of the Redeemed

The visions of Revelation are characterized throughout by angelic songs of praise (e.g., 4:8, 11; 5:8-14; 7:12; 11:17-18), and in this worship all creation joins (5:13; cf. Piper 1951: 10-13). The praises of the church here on earth have a strongly *eschatological* character: to sing "Hallelujah! / For the Lord our God the Almighty reigns" (19:6) is a colossal act of faith; it mirrors both the present worship of heaven and the future triumph song of the final consummation (19:1-8). The hymns and doxologies of Revelation, whether or not they reflect the liturgy of the church in John's day (cf. 1-3.3b; and see Piper, 17-20; O'Rourke 1968; Hahn 1973: 80-81), certainly served as a model for later Christian worship (cf. D. Peterson 1992: 275-78).

iii. The Reading of the Scroll

The vision of the reading of a scroll in Rev 5 symbolizes the final revelation of God's purpose in history.

iv. The Proclamation of the Word

Rev 14:6-7 envisages a final eschatological preaching of the gospel to all peoples (see 12-4.3).

b. The Marriage Supper of the Lamb

The NT vision of heaven and of the final consummation is a corporate rather than an individual one. One way of expressing this is through the picture of an *eschatological feast* (cf. above, 14-2.5). In all cases but one, the feast is a symbol of *joy;* it is a great meal or eschatological banquet in which God's people will participate.

One of the most common images used by Jesus in speaking of the final consummation is the eschatological feast (see G. Wainwright 1981: 26-27). In the saying on the eschatological ingathering of the Gentiles, Jesus declares, "Many will come from east and west and sit at table *(anaklithēsontai)* with Abraham, Isaac, and Jacob in the kingdom of heaven" (Matt 8:11 RSV//Luke 13:29; *anaklinō* = "recline," the customary position at feasts). Picturing the kingdom of God in terms of a feast was clearly common among Jesus' contemporaries; when Jesus dined with a leader of the Pharisees, it was one of the dinner guests who exclaimed, "Blessed is anyone who will eat bread in the kingdom of God!" (Luke 14:15). In Luke 22:28-30 Jesus promises his disciples that they will "eat and drink at my table in my kingdom"; here Jesus pictures himself as Messiah presiding at the eschatological feast that is referred to by some scholars as "the Messianic Banquet."

These sayings provide a context for the references to feasts in the parables of Jesus; see especially the parables of the wise and foolish bridesmaids (Matt 25:1-13), the wedding feast (22:1-14), and the great dinner (Luke 14:15-24). Each of these has an eschatological orientation and an implied reference to the Messianic Banquet.

In the NT the Lord's Supper has a strongly eschatological element; each celebration is a foretaste of the Messianic Banquet (on this see G. Wainwright 1981, esp. 147-54). The accounts of the institution of the Eucharist all have some form of "eschatological saying." In the Synoptics Jesus says, "Truly I tell you, I will never again drink of the fruit of the vine until that day when I drink it new in the kingdom of God" (Mark 14:25; Matt 26:29 has "in my Father's kingdom"; Luke 22:18 has "until the kingdom of God comes"; see also vv. 15-16 in Luke). Jesus knows his death is imminent; the next time he drinks wine will be at the Messianic Banquet when he drinks it in the new age with his disciples. In 1 Cor 11:26 Paul comments, "For as often as you eat this bread and drink the cup, you proclaim the Lord's death *until he comes*"; the Eucharist is to be celebrated up until the time of the parousia, for it is an anticipation of the end. These eschatological sayings, especially the Synoptic version, give the Lord's Supper a *future* reference. As well as looking back to the Christ event in the *past* and symbolizing communion with Christ in the *present* (above, 14-3.5c), each time the meal is shared believers anticipate the *future* joy and fellowship of the final, eschatological feast.

Appropriately, there is one final reference to the Messianic Banquet in the book of Revelation. In 19:6-8 John hears a mighty chorus that already anticipates the final consummation:

> Hallelujah!
> For the Lord our God
>   the Almighty reigns.
> Let us rejoice and exult
>   and give him the glory,
> for the marriage of the Lamb has come,
>   and his bride has made herself ready;
> to her it has been granted to be clothed
>   with fine linen, bright and pure.

The "fine linen" is explained as "the righteous deeds of the saints." John is then instructed, "Write this: Blessed are those who are invited to the marriage supper of the Lamb" (19:9). Christ is the Bridegroom and the church is the bride at the eschatological wedding banquet, which has obvious echoes of the wedding feasts in Jesus' parables, and especially of Matt 22:11-14, where the guest without a wedding robe is cast into outer darkness. It is the righteous deeds of the saints that constitute the "fine linen" (cf. Rev 7:14) that in turn guarantees their place at the eschatological feast.

The one exception to this pattern is Rev 19:17-18, a text that echoes the eschatological feast of Ezek 39:17-20 with its theme not of joy for the righteous, but of judgment on God's adversaries. The birds of the air are summoned, "Come, gather for the great supper of God," and are called to devour the flesh of captains and kings.

14-5. WORSHIP: THEOLOGICAL REFLECTIONS

An overview of the biblical material confirms the centrality of worship in the life of the community of faith, all the way from Abraham's response of building an altar to the God who calls him (Gen 12:7) to the triumphant, heavenly worship of the book of Revelation. Despite this strong common theme, differences between OT and NT pose a major challenge to Christian interpreters who seek a BT of worship. Historical criticism has tried to unravel the long and complex development of worship practices in the OT and the more sketchy material of the NT (cf. Hahn 1973), typically employing sometimes quite speculative hypotheses to explain the origin and different stages of the cult. Where amid all this diversity, and particularly amid the striking differences between worship in the OT and in the NT, is the Christian community to find a norm or standard for worship?

1. *Where God Is Worshiped.* In the OT one gets the general impression of a worship located primarily in one centralized building, the temple in Jerusalem. The temple is foreshadowed in the Torah by the tent, it figures prominently in the historical and some of the prophetic books, while Psalms appears to have originated as what Christians might term its combined service book and hymnbook. In the NT, on the other hand, we find a worship, separated from the temple, that has apparently no place for sacred buildings and regards the community of faith as the true temple. Unlike Jewish apocalypses that focused on an eschatological or a heavenly temple, the holy city of the Christian apocalypse is one in which there is no temple (Rev 21:22).

Closer study, however, reveals within the Bible a striking dialectic between the *value* of sacred buildings and the *danger* of sacred buildings. Moreover, this dialectic is not an OT-NT one; it is very much found within the OT itself. On the one hand, tent and temple are built at God's command and to a divinely revealed plan. The best and most skilled craftspersons and builders are employed, and worship is enriched by the best art and music available. On the other hand, there is an awareness that even the highest heavens cannot contain God, much less a house built with human hands (1 Kgs 8:27; words spoken by Solomon at the dedication of the temple!). God's presence cannot be captured or controlled by means of a building, hence the prophetic critique of temple worship. The destruction of the temple results in Israel learning that just as it can live without the Land and city, so it can live without the temple.

The NT evidence has to be read in the light of the historical context: circumstances ruled out any construction of sacred buildings by the earliest Christian community. The existence of house churches, however, shows that from the outset Christians required some building in which to meet for worship and fellowship; unable to construct buildings designed for the purpose, they simply used existing houses. As early as the second half of the second century, such buildings were modified (internally) in order better to function as "churches" (see Branick 1989: 15). Moreover, the absence of a temple from the final vision of Revelation is not due to a Christian aversion to buildings as such, but to the vision of a holy city that is itself the Holy of Holies and in which God and his people enjoy a perfect communion that is only foreshadowed by worship here on earth. A Christian theology of worship must draw on both OT and NT. On biblical grounds it will see the value of buildings dedicated to the worship of God and enriched by the best of art and music, while at the same time always remaining alert to the dangers of confining God and the worship of God to any earthly structure.

2. *When God Is Worshiped.* The relationship between the OT Sabbath and the Christian Lord's day raises difficult questions for BT (on the hermeneutical issues, see Swartley 1983, esp. 90-95). Observance of the Sabbath is of major importance in the OT, where it is grounded both in the historical order and in the created order. The NT, however, witnesses to a startling change in the day of worship from the *last* to the *first* day of the week, to the "Lord's day" that commemorates Christ's resurrection from the dead. From the very beginning the Christian church has faced three options (see Swartley 1983: 65-90).

i. One is to regard the OT Sabbath as an eternal and divine ordinance still binding on Christians. The Sabbath is ordained in creation, was commanded in the Decalogue, and was observed by Jesus and the earliest Christians. This view is maintained by some (e.g., Seventh-Day Adventists) to this day, but is rejected by most Christians as failing to do justice to the radically new character of the Christ event and to the NT witness to the Lord's day.

ii. A second, widely held option (see Rordorf 1968; Carson 1982) is that the Lord's day supersedes the Sabbath. Jesus, it is argued, attacked the Sabbath itself. In Col 2:16-17 Paul classifies the Sabbath with the ceremonial laws of the old covenant, applicable to Jews only, not with the moral laws that remain binding on Gentiles who are incorporated into the new Israel. For the first three centuries the church observed Sunday as the day of worship, but *not* as a day of rest, and the identification of Sabbath and Sunday is relatively late (cf. Rordorf 1968: 296, 297).

iii. The third option is to hold that the OT *principle* of a weekly day of rest was, with the Christ event, *transferred* from Saturday to Sunday, the Lord's day (see Beckwith and Stott 1980). Jesus did not abolish the Sabbath, but sought rather to restore its original meaning and purpose. In the NT the Decalogue continues to be binding on Christians; Church Fathers who rejected Sabbath observance of any kind sought to dispose of the fourth commandment either by spiritualizing it (rest from sin) or by referring it solely to the eschatological consummation, but neither of these devices is very convincing. During the first three centuries Christians were powerless to observe or legislate a day of rest, but as soon as this became possible, under Constantine, legislation was enacted making it possible to observe Sunday as a day of rest and worship.

If one seeks to do justice to the totality of the biblical material, a strong case can be made for option iii., i.e., for transferring the principle of a day of rest and linking that day of rest to Sunday, not in any legalistic way but as a key element of the Lord's day that is primarily a day of worship but also a day of freedom, fellowship, and recreation of body, mind, and spirit (cf. Leitch 1966: 430-32). Such a day is not to be seen as "a hindrance to a full and free life, but on the contrary as providing periodic escapes from all the things that crowd in on life and threaten its fulfillment" (Andreasen 1974: 453). A day of worship and rest is not something to be enforced on others, least of all if Christians are a minority in a pluralistic society, though Christians will rightly want to urge on society the value of a day of rest. Rather, for believers, the Lord's day is to be observed voluntarily and gladly, recognizing it as a gift from God for the liberation of his people and of all humankind.

Unlike the attention paid to Sabbath/Lord's day, Christians have paid relatively little heed to the well-developed cycle of annual feasts in the OT. The Christian church in time developed its own liturgical year, and how far this was modeled on the Jewish pattern or how far it represents an independent development is a matter for liturgical scholars to determine. Theologically, however, a correspondence can be noted. The Christian Easter is the equivalent to Passover, both feasts commemorating God's decisive act in redeeming his people. Christianity celebrates Pentecost but with a transformation in its meaning. Lent and especially Holy Week can be seen as an equivalent of the Day of Atonement with its emphasis on the people's confession and repentance. All Saints' Day might correspond loosely to Purim and Hanukkah with their memories of the courage of God's people in the face of persecution and martyrdom. The most glaring gap in this kind of scheme is any Christian equivalent to the feast of booths/tabernacles. Our study has shown how the OT festivals maintain the typical biblical dialectic between God's activity in the created order and in the historical order (see 2-1.2c). The Christian year is based entirely on the historical order and ignores the harvest/agricultural aspect of tabernacles and the other OT festivals, something that is symptomatic of the relative neglect of the created order in Christian theology and liturgy. Some branches of the church have sought to remedy this by the introduction of a harvest festival or thanksgiving festival at harvest time, or by the introduction of a liturgical season of "Creation" in the fall, prior to Advent. This certainly serves to bring the liturgical year more into line with its biblical basis.

3. *How God Is Worshiped.* In the OT circumcision is the rite that marks admission to the people of God. Under the new order, that people is reconstituted on a new basis. Circumcision, as Paul emphasized so strongly, is no longer required. Instead baptism is administered to all who through God's grace are incorporated into the new Israel. The fact that baptism is equally available to males and females underlines this universal aspect.

The impossibility of settling the question of infant baptism merely by citing proof texts has been noted above (14-3.4b). Paul's parallel between baptism and circumcision (Col 2:11-12) is relevant to such a discussion, however, for it serves as a reminder of the biblical understanding of corporate solidarity (cf. 1 Cor 7:14; 10:1-2). Also relevant is the strong biblical theme of the priority of divine grace and of the divine initiative involved in anyone becoming part of God's people. Although those who respond to the preaching of the gospel make a conscious decision, it is also true that "you did not choose me but I chose you" (John 15:16; cf. Cullmann 1950: 31). The differing positions on infant baptism and adult baptism reflect varying views on the relative importance of divine grace and human response. Infant baptism is based on the conviction that, as in the OT, the children of believers belong to the covenant community (see Marcel 1953, significantly titled *The Biblical Doctrine of Infant Baptism: Sacrament of the Covenant of Grace*). Adult, or more accurately "believers," baptism is based on the conviction that in the NT baptism presupposes a prior decision in relation to the gospel (see Brooks 1987, significantly titled *Baptism in the New Testament: The Drama of Decision*).

Perhaps the greatest discontinuity between worship in the OT and in the NT is the centrality of animal sacrifice in the OT and its total absence from the NT. Yet the prophetic critique of sacrificial worship helped pave the way for the development of the worship of the synagogue with its focus on God's word in Scripture and praise and prayer detached from animal sacrifice, a development that in turn paved the way for one aspect of Christian worship. The radical NT reinterpretation of sacrifice paved the way for the other. The NT sees Christ's death as a sacrifice that renders the OT sacrificial system obsolete. That sacrifice is commemorated in the Lord's Supper, which forms the second focal point of Christian worship. The NT does not provide a detailed eucharistic theology; it does see the Lord's Supper as an essential form of worship that *ought* to express the unity of God's people. It is a tragedy that in later Christian history, disputes over the meaning of the Eucharist have divided Christians. In contemporary ecumenical dialogue it is essential that later traditions "be confronted critically with the witness of the NT" (Klauk 1992: 371).

Post-NT Christian liturgical practice underwent a long and complex process of development. At the time of the Reformation, and again in more modern times, under the impetus of various "liturgical reform" movements, efforts have been made to return worship to its pristine purity. The fact remains, however, that at the present day Christian worship includes a huge range of options. One of the most basic divergences is between a more informal, charismatic approach, employing extempore prayers and emphasizing various manifestations of the Spirit, and a more ordered, liturgical approach, employing a common "prayer book" and traditional prayers (there may, of course, be many intermediate positions). The danger of using 1 Cor 14 as a norm has been noted above (14-3.5b), and if, as seems very likely, early Christian worship was basically modeled on the synagogue (with the addition of the Lord's Supper), then the norm is more likely to have been an ordered service with lectionary readings and at least some set prayers. This would not, however, exclude the possibility of smaller gatherings for prayer where the worship was more informal.

Overall, therefore, BT points toward considerably more continuity between OT and NT in the theology of worship than is often supposed, while at the same time acknowledging the radically new elements brought about by the Christ event that inaugurates the new age and anticipates the final consummation.

CHAPTER 15

Ministry

Old Testament: Proclamation

15-1. THE MINISTERS OF THE LORD

Studies of "ministry" in BT have tended to focus mainly on the NT. Yet the OT too recognizes the need for the regular oversight, guidance, and care of God's people, and makes provision for it.

In the OT ministry is grounded in the nature of God himself and his relationship to his people (see Wharton 1981: 22-36). God calls the whole people to serve; in the first instance it is Israel who is the servant of the LORD (Ps 136:22; Isa 41:8-9; Jer 30:10; see 11-1.2b). Despite their many failures, God continues to love and care for his people, and minister to them. He does this by calling individuals and groups from within his people as a whole. Such persons are called to minister to the ministering people, and to be servants of the servant people of the LORD.

The basic meaning of "ministry" is the service of others (Lat. *ministrare* = "to serve"; *minister* = "one who serves"). The OT speaks of those who are called to serve others. The Hebrew verb *shārath* = "to serve" is used in a variety of contexts, not all of them specifically religious. Joseph served (NRSV "attended") his master Potiphar (Gen 39:4); Joshua is described as Moses' servant (Exod 24:13); the queen of Sheba, visiting Solomon, was amazed by "the attendance of his servants" (1 Kgs 10:5). The word is used most of the time, however, of those who minister or serve as priests. Aaron's job is to minister (Exod 28:35); he and his sons "minister in the holy place" (28:43). Even when applied to priests, the word does not lose its basic meaning of "to serve." "The secular uses show that the Hebrew word was not in itself a priestly thing, though priesthood was one form of ministry" (G. Johnston 1963: 661).

Broadly speaking, God calls two types of persons to be his servants/ministers. We have already noted that from time to time in the OT God chose *exceptional individuals* as leaders of his people (6-1). Moses, the kings, the high priests, the major prophets, and the wise ministered to the people, and indeed they can be taken as models for ministry. They were largely national figures, and it was through them that God revealed himself to his people in salvation history.

In addition to these outstanding individuals, however, the OT knows of a larger number of persons who ministered to the people *on an ongoing basis* and *at the grassroots level.* While the two groups overlap and cannot be rigidly distinguished, it is convenient to deal here with those engaged in the more regular forms of ministry. Ongoing ministry implies some form of "order," i.e., structure and organization, with persons holding some form of "office," and with provision for the perpetuation of these offices. Those engaged in regular ministry in the OT may be conveniently classified as "elders," "priests," "prophets," and "teachers." These "offices" are found throughout most of the OT, though it is important to note that they were characterized by considerable flexibility and were adapted to a variety of situations over the centuries.

15-1.1. ELDERS

The oldest and most enduring form of biblical ministry is the eldership. The Hebrew *zāqēn* in the OT and the Greek *presbyteros* in the NT have a double meaning, designating a person either as "old" or as the holder of a special office. The LXX usually translates elders *(z^{e}qēnîm)* as *presbyteroi,* though in Deuteronomy the term *gerousia* (= council of elders) is preferred. *Presbyteros* is actually the comparative and can be used in this sense in the NT (e.g., Luke 15:25 — "the elder son"), but the comparative sense has largely faded so that it more usually means "old" (e.g., Acts 2:17; 1 Tim 5:1). The link between the two meanings is found in the widely held view that the elderly have experience and wisdom that qualifies them to give advice, act as leaders, and represent the social group to which they belong (cf. Job 12:12; *Sir* 25:3-6). The qualification of old age is not necessarily retained, however; wisdom can be found in younger persons, and the emphasis tends to fall more on possession of the necessary qualifications for the office, regardless of age; in the Bible an elder "must be thought of as the holder of an office, not the representative of a particular age group" (Conrad 1980: 123). Elders are not peculiar to the biblical tradition but are found in many cultures in the ancient Near East (McKenzie 1959: 529-32; Conrad, 126-27); cf. the references to "elders of the land of Egypt" (Gen 50:7), "elders of Midian" (Num 22:4), etc.

No account is given of the origin of elders in the OT; they simply appear as an existing class in Exod 3:16 when Moses is told to "go and assemble the elders of Israel" (cf. Bornkamm 1968: 655). In the Pentateuch there are frequent references to "the elders of Israel" (e.g., Exod 24:1) and the "elders of the people" (e.g., Num 11:24); these function generally as leaders and representatives of the people as a whole. In Exod 19:7-8 Moses summons "the elders of the people" and sets before them the terms of the covenant, but it is "the people" who respond.

Two passages refer to a special group of seventy elders. In Exod 24:1 Moses is instructed to bring "seventy of the elders of Israel" up Mount Sinai in the context of the ratification of the covenant. In Num 11:16-25 Moses is told to select "seventy of the elders of Israel" and bring them to the tent. Then the Lord "took some of the spirit that was on him and put it on the seventy elders; and when the spirit rested upon them, they prophesied" (v. 25). Here elders are called and commissioned; they share with Moses both the responsibility of leadership and empowerment by the Spirit. In Deuteronomy they are assigned some judicial functions (see 21:1-9; 25:5-10). After the conquest elders continue to function as representatives of the whole people (e.g., Josh 7:6; 1 Sam 8:4-5; 1 Kgs 8:1), but also as leaders of local communities; e.g., Josh 20:4 refers to "the elders of that city." Ezek 7:26 sees the giving of counsel as a function of the elders. During the exile Jeremiah wrote from Jerusalem to Babylon to the "elders among the exiles, and to the priests, the prophets, and all the people" (29:1); it is noteworthy that the elders come first in this list. "Indeed, in exile, when all other political forms have been shattered, the elders take on enhanced significance as those who exercise limited self-government on behalf of the people" (Bornkamm 1968: 658). *Susanna*, which is set in Babylon, gives a prominent role to elders who may be appointed as judges (*Sus* 5), and as late as *1 Macc* 1:26 we continue to hear of local elders.

In the late OT period and down into NT times, two important developments occur. Firstly, the old council of seventy elders reemerges as the Sanhedrin, "a clearly delineated supreme ruling body of the Jews with its seat in Jerusalem" (Bornkamm 1968: 658), accorded limited judicial powers by the Romans. This body appears in the NT as the *synedrion*. It may be that all members of the Sanhedrin were originally referred to as elders (Bornkamm, 659), and in the NT the Sanhedrin is twice referred to as the *presbyterion* (Luke 22:66; Acts 22:5). The term "elders," however, came to designate the lay members only (drawn from leading families), as distinct from priests and scribes. The expression "the elders, the chief priests, and the scribes" (Mark 8:31; 11:27; Acts 4:5) describes exactly the membership of the Sanhedrin in Jesus' day.

Secondly, local synagogues (cf. 14-1.1b.vi) were headed by elders. Thus in Luke 7:3-5 the centurion at Capernaum sends to Jesus "some Jewish elders" who can testify that "he loves our people, and it is he who built our synagogue for us."

Despite the high regard in which they were held, elders had their failings (Isa 3:14; 9:15; Ezek 8:11-12). The elders of the Sanhedrin were among those who opposed Jesus (Matt 16:21; 21:23; etc.) and the early church (Acts 4:5; 5:21).

15-1.2. PRIESTS

In OT ministry a central role is played by the priesthood.

a. Non-Mosaic Priesthood

Priesthood was widely found in the ancient world, and the existence of a non-Israelite priesthood is clearly recognized in the OT: in Gen 14, for example, Abraham pays a tithe to Melchizedek, "priest of God Most High" (v. 18; cf. 6-1.3b), while Moses' father-in-law Jethro is said to be a Midianite priest (Exod 3:1). Within Israel priestly functions are ascribed to the patriarchs such as Abraham (Gen 22) and Jacob (31:54), both of whom offered sacrifice. Even after the time of Moses, David appears to have exercised priestly functions (2 Sam 6:13-14), and probably also Solomon (1 Kgs 8:62-64).

At a different level, there is a sense in which the whole people of Israel could be regarded as priests. In Exod 19:6 (RSV) God tells Israel, "You shall be to me a kingdom of priests and a holy nation."

b. Mosaic Priesthood

Priesthood in the OT, however, refers primarily to the system revealed by God, through Moses, and embodied in the legislation of the Pentateuch. Modern critical-historical scholarship has attempted to reconstruct a complex process of development of the priesthood. A cornerstone of Wellhausen's position was that the distinction between priests and Levites, though found in Exodus, Leviticus, and Numbers, is in fact postexilic in origin. Wellhausen's view has of course been criticized from a conservative perspective as well as by scholars offering other critical reconstructions (see the summary in Childs 1986: 145-49). A BT of the priesthood cannot be concerned with hypothetical reconstructions but must be based on the canonical text.

The canonical account affirms that God, through Moses, established an organized priesthood in Israel that was intended to be the sole valid priesthood from that time on. The system was a hereditary one, and provision was made in the legislation for support of the priesthood; e.g., certain portions of the sacrifices were given to the priests.

Priests were to be descended not only from the tribe of Levi but also from Aaron, the brother of Moses: "But you shall make a register of Aaron and his descendants; it is they who shall attend to the priesthood, and any outsider who comes near shall be put to death" (Num 3:10). Distinguished from the priests are the Levites, who belong to the tribe of Levi but are not descended from Aaron (3:5-13).

The purpose of the priesthood was to mediate between a holy God and a sinful people. The main duties of the priests were to administer the whole system based on purity and on sacrifice, and also to instruct the people (Deut 33:10). This is well summed up in Lev 10:10-11: "You are to distinguish between the holy and the common, and between the unclean and the clean; and you are to teach the people of Israel all the statutes that the LORD has spoken to them through Moses."

The Levites carried out minor cultic duties, and in Chronicles especially are linked with the ministry of music in the temple. "King Hezekiah . . . commanded the Levites to sing praises to the LORD. . . . They sang praises with gladness" (2 Chr 29:30).

The OT recognizes with great honesty the frequent failures of the priesthood. In fact, the prototypical rebellion, the worship of the golden calf (Exod 32), was led by Aaron, the father of the priesthood! Aaron's sons Nadab and Abihu were struck dead for their sin (Lev 10:1-2). Another rebellion against Moses was led by Korah, a Levite (Num 16). In 1 Sam 2:12-17 we find the sons of the priest Eli condemned for their wickedness. Solomon deposed Abiathar and made Zadok high priest; thereafter all priests had to be of Zadokite descent. The narrative may well reflect power struggles within the priesthood. According to 1 Chr 24:3, Zadok was descended from Aaron through his son Eleazar. Mal 1:6–2:9 constitutes a damning indictment of the priests of Malachi's day.

There is thus considerable tension in the portrayal of priesthood in the OT. On the one hand, a priesthood is necessary to operate the whole system whereby Israel is maintained in or restored to a right relationship with God. The hereditary principle is necessary to ensure a regular succession of qualified and trained priests. On the other hand, priests occupy a powerful and privileged position, and this frequently leads to corruption.

15-1.3. PROPHETS

The "earlier prophets" of the OT (e.g., Samuel, Elijah, Elisha) and the so-called writing prophets (those represented by a book in the canon) were exceptional individuals through whom God spoke to his people and revealed himself and his will to them. They have been discussed in 6-1.4.

The OT also speaks of an ongoing ministry of full-time, professional prophets, organized in groups or "prophetic guilds." In 1 Sam 10 Saul encountered "a band of prophets *(chebhel n^ebhî'îm),*" possessed by the Spirit of the LORD, who were in "a prophetic frenzy." In 19:20 he met a similar group referred to as "the company *(lah^aqâh)* of the prophets." A royal official, Obadiah, saved the lives of a hundred "prophets of the LORD" when they were threatened by Jezebel (1 Kgs 18:4, 13). The most frequent designation for such groups is "the sons of the prophets *(b^enê hann^ebhî'îm)*" (1 Kgs 20:35; 2 Kings 2:3; etc.; NRSV translates "the company of prophets"). Prophets appear as leaders of the exiles in Babylon, along with elders and priests (Jer 29:1). As late as the time of Nehemiah we read of the appointment of "prophets" in Jerusalem (Neh 6:7).

Such ongoing groups could not function in a vacuum, and in most cases they were attached either to sanctuaries or the court, where they functioned as "cultic prophets" or "royal prophets," respectively.

a. Cultic Prophets

The band of prophets in 1 Sam 10 came "from the shrine" at Gibeath-elohim (v. 5). "Sons of the prophets" are associated with sanctuaries at Bethel (2 Kgs 2:3), Jericho (2:5), and Gilgal (4:38). Jer 26:7 and 35:4 suggest the presence of prophets in the Jerusalem temple.

b. Royal Prophets

The most outstanding example of a royal prophet is Nathan, who held an official position in the court of David (2 Sam 7; 12). In 1 Kgs 22:6 King Ahab assembles four hundred of his prophets to ask their advice. (1 Kgs 18 shows that under the influence of Jezebel, prophets of Baal and Asherah had found their way into the royal court.)

These guilds seem to have operated in some respects like "monastic orders," living a common life and united by their devotion to the LORD. One of their main functions was to speak God's word, and people would "inquire" of the prophets, seeking to know God's will (1 Kgs 22:5). They probably delivered something akin to a sermon at local shrines and the Jerusalem temple, and may well have played some role in the leadership of worship.

As in the case of the priesthood, there is tension in the portrayal of the prophetic guilds in the OT. On the one hand, they are recognized as God's spokespersons, inspired by his Spirit, but on the other hand, their failings are only too evident. While Nathan could speak out courageously against King David (2 Sam 12:1-7), the temptation was great to deliver a message the king wanted to hear, as in the case of the prophets of Ahab (1 Kgs 22). Significantly, the failings of prophets and priests are often mentioned together: Isaiah complains that "the priest and the prophet reel with strong drink" (28:7); Micah complains that priests and prophets accept bribes (3:11); Jeremiah complains that priests and prophets lack courage (4:9) and mislead the people (5:31); according to Lam 4:13, Jerusalem fell because of "the sins of her prophets / and the iniquities of her priests."

It is noteworthy that the great individual prophets of the OT (see 6-1.4) are disassociated from the prophetic guilds. Thus Amos, while he experienced a call to be a prophet, declared, "I am no prophet, nor a prophet's son" (7:14); i.e., he was not a professional prophet or a member of a prophetic guild. If he spoke in the sanctuary at Bethel (7:13), that was not because he was a cultic prophet but because there he could address pilgrims to the sanctuary; the same applies to Jeremiah (Jer 7:1-4).

15-1.4. TEACHERS

In the OT various groups shared the responsibility of teaching the people. We have noted that the priests had the task of teaching people the Torah. In the Wisdom tradition, teaching took place in court, clan, and family settings (cf. 6-1.5). After the exile these traditions blended and emerged in new forms. Two terms are employed to designate these postexilic teachers.

a. Scribes

A scribe *(sōphēr, saphar* = "count, recount"; LXX, NT *grammateus)* was originally a literate person or secretary, usually a government official (e.g., 2 Kgs 22:3; Isa 36:3). After the exile, however, the term came to be used of those who *study* and *teach* the Torah.

"Ezra is the type par excellence of these earliest post-exilic doctors of the law" (Black 1962: 246). Though a priest, he is also called "the scribe of the law of the God of heaven" (Ezra 7:12), who "had set his heart to study the law of the LORD, and to do it, and to teach the statutes and ordinances in Israel" (7:10). Ezra's work was a natural continuation of the priestly teaching function, but the "scribes" who followed him also drew on the Wisdom tradition.

Sir 38:34–39:11 portrays the ideal scribe who

> . . . devotes himself
>   to the study of the law of the Most High!
> He seeks out the wisdom of all the ancients,
>   and is concerned with prophecies.
>
> > (38:34–39:1; note the correspondence to
> > Law/Writings/Prophets, the main
> > divisions of the Hebrew canon)

Such a scribe "will be filled with the spirit of understanding" and "will pour forth words of wisdom of his own" (39:6).

Scribes appear frequently in the Gospels, often in association with the Pharisees (on the relation between the two, see Black 1962: 247-48). By this time the office was no longer confined to priests; laypersons could become scribes. A measure of their importance is the fact that they were represented on the Sanhedrin (cf. Matt 26:57; Mark 14:43; Luke 22:66; Acts 23:9).

In the Gospels Jesus frequently clashes with the scribes (Matt 9:2-8; Mark 7:1-8; Luke 6:6-11), especially over the interpretation of the Torah. He also exposes their failings: they are hypocrites who "do not practice what they teach" (Matt 23:3); they "do all their deeds to be seen by others" (23:5; cf. Mark 12:38-40); they are concerned with the minutiae of legal observance but "have neglected the weightier matters of the law: justice and mercy and faith" (Matt 23:23).

b. Rabbis

The term "rabbi" (Heb. *rabbî*; Aram. *rabbûnî*) means literally "my great one" or "my master." In NT times it was used as a title of respect applied to a religious teacher. As such it is used once of John the Baptist (John 3:26) and frequently, by a variety of people, of Jesus (Matt 26:25; Mark 9:5; John 1:38; etc.; in the form "rabbouni" in John 20:16).

With the reorganization of Judaism after A.D. 70, "scribes" evolved into "rabbis," and the term came to denote a specific office associated with the synagogue. The beginnings of the transition can already be seen in the NT. John's Gospel says "rabbi" means "teacher" (1:38; cf. 20:16). Gamaliel I (known in Jewish tradition by the variant title rabban rather than rabbi) was a noted Jewish teacher; he taught Paul (Acts 22:3), and in Acts 5:33 is described as "a teacher of the law *(nomodidaskalos)*."

Once again Jesus draws attention to the failings of this class: scribes, he says, "love to have . . . people call them rabbi" (Matt 23:7); i.e., they love honorific titles.

15-1.5. MINISTRY AND GENDER

a. Married Ministers

Since the offices of priest and Levite were hereditary, it was important that holders of these offices should be married, and this is simply assumed in the OT. Some prophets were certainly married (Isa 8:3; Ezek 24:15-18; on Jeremiah see 19-1.2c). Given their position as respected leaders of the community, we may assume that elders would be married also; there is nothing in canonical Scripture to indicate otherwise.

b. Women Ministers

Women play a very limited role in the ministry to God's people in the OT. As far as we know, they were totally excluded from the *eldership* and from the *priesthood*. There is no indication in canonical Scripture that women served as elders. The limitation of the priesthood to men has been challenged on the basis of the references in Exod 38:8 and 1 Sam 2:22 to "the women who served at the entrance to the tent of meeting"; significantly, neither of these references is reproduced in the LXX, and at best they constitute a very minor exception. Reasons for the exclusion of women from the priesthood include the suggestion that the responsibilities of motherhood made acceptance of priestly duties impractical, the OT belief that women are socially inferior to men, the belief that according to the Torah menstruation and childbirth render women ritually unclean, and the desire to be different from ancient Near Eastern religions that usually employed priestesses (see Hayter 1987: 63-73). Whatever the reason, the system established in the Torah is that of a hereditary priesthood in which the office descends solely through the male line.

While the law of Exod 23:17 requires that all men attend the three main pilgrim festivals, this does not mean that women were excluded, though family duties might often have made it difficult for them to attend. Women do attend worship (Deut 29:11), and make vows (Num 6:2). In terms of participation in the cult (as distinct from priestly ministry), women are neither excluded nor regarded in principle as inferior (cf. Otwell 1977: 152-78).

The situation, however, is quite different when we come to *prophets* and *wise persons*. Unlike the priesthood, there is no indication that these offices were hereditary. They are to be regarded rather as "charismatic"; they depend on a gift *(charisma)* granted by God. A prophet was one who had the gift of prophecy and was called by God to prophesy. A wise person was one recognized as having the gift of wisdom. While women by definition were excluded from an office that descended on the hereditary principle through the male line, it is clear that women could receive the gifts of prophecy or wisdom and thus participate in these forms of charismatic ministry.

i. Prophets

Several persons are designated by the term "prophetess" (*nᵉbhî'â*; cf. P. J. Scalise 1986: 9-10). *Miriam*, the sister of Moses and Aaron (Num 26:59), is termed a prophetess in Exod 15:20-21, where she "and all the women" are inspired to celebrate in dance and song the victory at the sea (on Miriam, see R. J. Burns 1987). Mic 6:4 ranks her along with Moses and Aaron as the divinely commissioned leaders of Israel, but Num 12:1-15 records some kind of power struggle in which she is punished for challenging the unique authority of Moses (critical scholars see in this the reflection of a later power struggle, perhaps in the period of the monarchy). The narrative, however, does not question the claim that God spoke through Miriam as well as through Moses (cf. Otwell 1977: 156). *Deborah,* who is designated as a prophetess (Judg 4:4), was a major political, judicial, and religious leader (cf. Eichrodt 1961: 298-99). She "judged" Israel (4:5) and chose Barak as the commander of the Israelite forces (4:6). Small wonder that she was remembered and revered as "a mother in Israel" (5:7). The Song of Deborah (Judg 5) celebrates the victory over Sisera (critical scholars regard it as one of the oldest parts of the OT). At the time of Josiah's reformation, it was the prophetess *Huldah* who was consulted by the king's advisers and who declared God's word to king and country (2 Kgs 22:12-20). The narrative implies "that she held some official capacity in Jerusalem at the time" (Burns, 44; cf. Otwell, 158). Ezek 13:17-23 indicates that false prophets could be women as well as men. A prophetess, Noadiah, is mentioned as an opponent of Nehemiah in Neh 6:14. It is noteworthy that all these narratives "make no effort to explain the phenomenon of prophetesses or to indicate that the appearance of prophetesses was regarded in any way as exceptional" (Burns, 46).

ii. The Wise

In the OT the gift of wisdom transcends distinctions of gender (cf. Scobie 1984b: 46); there are wise women as well as wise men (cf. P. J. Scalese 1986: 10). In 2 Sam 14:1-20 "Joab sent to Tekoa and brought from there a wise woman (*'ishshâh chᵃkhāmâh*)" who persuaded King David to permit the return of Absalom. In 20:14-22 it is a "wise woman" who negotiates with Joab, the commander of the besieging army, and saves the city of Abel Beth-maacah from destruction. Though not termed "wise" in the narrative of 1 Sam 25, Abigail was "of good understanding" (*ṭôbhath-sekel,* 25:3 RSV), and had "discretion" (*ṭaʿam,* 25:33 RSV), both synonyms for wisdom, as her quick action and persuasive speech clearly demonstrate. Though Prov 31:1-9 is entitled "The Words of King Lemuel," it is actually the wise advice of the king's mother. In none of these passages is there any hint of surprise that women should be among "the wise."

Old Testament: Promise

15-2. THEY SHALL MINISTER TO ME

As we have seen in 6-2, the ministry of outstanding individuals — Moses, kings, high priests, prophets, the wise — forms the basis for the expectation of an eschatological figure who will be a new servant of God or Messiah. He will lack the imperfections of the earlier servants and will truly lead God's people.

The failures and shortcomings of existing forms of regular ministry form the background for the hope and the promise that in the new age there will be a reformation or renewal or transformation of the regular ministry to God's people.

15-2.1. ELDERS

Isaiah's vision of the new age includes a place for elders. In a strongly apocalyptic passage the prophet says:

> For the Lord of hosts will reign
>   on Mount Zion and in Jerusalem,
> and before his *elders* he will manifest his glory. (24:23)

15-2.2. PRIESTS

Ezekiel's vision of the restored Israel includes a renewed and reformed priesthood: "The levitical priests, the descendants of Zadok . . . shall come near to me to minister to me" (44:15). What appears to be envisaged is a renewal and reformation of the existing priestly system, and detailed regulations are provided in 44:15-31.

In the context of the eschatological ingathering of the Gentiles, it is said to Israel:

> You shall be called priests of the Lord,
>   you shall be named ministers of our God. (Isa 61:6)

Here all God's people are priests (cf. Exod 19:6), insofar as it is through them that the Gentiles will have access to God in the new age (cf. Best 1960: 276). Isa 66:21 goes even further and envisages non-Israelites ministering in the temple: "And I will also take some of them as priests and as Levites, says the Lord."

15-2.3. PROPHETS

In the late OT, prophetic guilds disappear from the scene, as do individual prophets, no doubt because of the belief that prophecy had ceased (see 6-2.4). This clears the way for belief that in the new age prophecy will be reborn: "Your sons and your daughters shall prophesy" (Joel 2:28-29). Joel, however, does not have in mind a special office of prophet; it is all God's people who will prophesy in the new age (cf. 5-2.3).

15-2.4. TEACHERS

There will be a need for God's people to be taught in the new age. For Ezekiel this will be a task for the priests: "They shall teach my people the difference between the holy and the common, and show them how to distinguish between the unclean and the clean" (44:23).

15-2.5. MINISTRY AND GENDER

a. Married Ministers

Ezekiel's vision of the future includes regulations for the marriage of priests: "They shall not marry a widow, or a divorced woman, but only a virgin of the stock of the house of Israel, or a widow who is the widow of a priest" (44:22).

b. Women Ministers

One of the striking features of Joel's promise of the eschatological outpouring of the Spirit and the rebirth of prophecy is the way it refers to both sexes. "Your sons and your daughters shall prophesy," he says, and the Spirit will be poured out "even on the male and female slaves" (2:28-29).

New Testament: Fulfillment

15-3. MINISTERS OF CHRIST

As in the OT, so in the NT God calls a people to serve him; in the first instance it is the whole church that is called to ministry, to the humble and loving service of others (see Lazareth 1982: 20-21). Christians are to "serve one another" (1 Pet 4:10). All the Corinthians are "called to be saints" (1 Cor 1:2), which "means essentially to be set apart or 'dedicated' to the service of God" (Furnish 1981: 131). All believers are slaves/servants of God (1 Pet 2:16; Rev 2:20), and are called to serve Christ (Rom 14:18; Col 3:24). Within the church, however, certain persons are called to minister in a special way to the rest of God's people.

The most important NT terms for ministry are the verb *diakoneō* = "serve," and cognate words (*diakonia* = "service, ministry"; *diakonos* = "servant, minister, or deacon"). Rarely used in the LXX, these words had a humble origin in everyday life where they referred to serving others in a practical way, e.g., by serving at table (cf. John 2:5, 9). They carry "no overtones of rule or officialdom" (Steele 1986: 3). They are used frequently of Christ himself, and then pass into general use for the ministry and service that characterizes the life of the whole people of God (see Hess 1978: 546-49). The noun *diakonos* begins to take on a special connotation and to refer to the office of deacon, though it is hard to say exactly when the transition takes place. Also significant is the term *doulos,* often translated "servant" but more exactly "slave," and the verb *douleuō* = "perform the duties of a slave, serve, obey." Paul identifies himself as the slave or servant of Christ (Rom 1:1; Gal 1:10), and the apostles are so designated in Acts 4:29 (cf. 16:17).

The key to the understanding of ministry in the NT is the ministry of Christ himself. In him the various ministries of the OT find their fulfillment, and from him the various ministries of the church proceed. It is important to distinguish in the NT between what may be called "special ministers" and "regular ministers." Special ministers are a unique group that bridge the gap between the historical Jesus and the emerging regular ministries of the church. They consist primarily of the apostles, but also of members of Jesus' family. Their ministry is noncontinuing, and with the death of the apostles and the brothers and mother of Jesus the category ceases to exist. Regular ministers emerge in the NT and form the basis for the ongoing ministry of the church.

15-3.1. THE MINISTRY OF CHRIST

In chapter 6 we saw how God's choice of exceptional individuals to minister to Israel (Moses, kings, high priests, major prophets, and the wise) generated expectations of the future coming of a second Moses, a kingly Messiah, a priestly Messiah, an eschatological Prophet and an eschatological Teacher; and how Jesus both fulfilled and surpassed these expectations. In similar fashion we may say that the more regular ministries of the OT, outlined above, are fulfilled but also superseded by the ministry of Christ. Even more significant is the NT belief that the OT portraits of various servants of the LORD, and especially the expectation of a "Suffering Servant," find their true fulfillment in the person of Christ (see chap. 9).

a. The Minister

The NT depicts Jesus as the one who came to minister and to serve God's people. The motto for Jesus' own ministry could well be "The Son of Man came not to be served but to serve" (Mark 10:45). Without him God's people are lost, "like sheep without a shepherd" (Matt 9:36//Mark 6:34).

Christ as the new Servant sets the pattern for ministry. "Whoever wishes to become great among you must be your servant" (Mark 10:43). Jesus could say to his disciples, "I am among you as one who serves" (Luke 22:27). John's Gospel lacks the Synoptic sayings on "serving," but in the account of the washing of the disciples' feet (13:1-11), the meaning of humble and loving service of others is portrayed in the most striking fashion (see D. M. Smith 1981: 219-20). The incident in fact recalls the words of Jesus recorded by Luke: "The kings of the Gentiles lord it over them; and those in authority over them are called benefactors. But not so with you; rather the greatest among you must become like the youngest, and the leader like one who serves. For who is greater, the one who is at the table or the one who serves? Is it not the one at the table? But I am among you as one who serves" (22:25-27). By both teaching and example Jesus presents a view of leadership and authority radically opposed to that which prevails in the world.

b. The Disciples

By word and deed Jesus called all who would follow him to a life of service. But he also called some to serve the wider community of which they were part. We noted in 11-3.1b.iii that one indication of the fact that Jesus did expect a new community to survive his death was the care with which he selected and trained an inner group of his disciples to form the basis of ministry in the new people of God.

The Gospels speak frequently of those who became Jesus' "disciples." *Mathētēs* means a learner, pupil, or disciple. "It is plain that 'disciple' in this sense does not include everyone whom Christ has called to communion with Himself and to participation in the Kingdom of God; it applies only to those whom He invested with a special mission within the eschatological community" (Riesenfeld 1953: 112). The term can be used of a quite broad group of Jesus' followers; Luke 6:17, for example, speaks of "a great crowd of his disciples." It can also be applied to the inner group of twelve whom Jesus called in a special way to special tasks and responsibilities (Matt 10:1).

15-3.2. SPECIAL MINISTERS

Certain persons, who minister to God's people in the NT, hold a unique and unrepeatable position. They mediate between the ministry of Jesus himself and the later regular ministry of the church that we see beginning to emerge in the NT. Their positions were not directly perpetuated after their death.

a. The Apostles

i. All the Apostles

Within the leadership of the early church the NT makes clear that the apostles played a key role (for a summary of modern critical scholarship, see Reumann in Barrett 1972b: vi-xvi). The term *apostolos* (*apostellō* = "to send out") means one who is sent out, a messenger, ambassador, or delegate. Whether or not it represents the rabbinic term *shālîach* (Rengstorf) is a matter of conjecture; BT is concerned with the understanding of apostle presented by the biblical text. It may be that historically speaking the term "apostle" was not employed until after Jesus' death and resurrection, although the Gospels tell of how Jesus "sent out" *(apesteilen)* his disciples on a particular mission during his own ministry (Matt 10:5 and //s; see also Luke 6:13). In any case, the occasional use of the term "apostle" in the Synoptic Gospels has a theological validity; the Evangelists, by using the term, are recognizing that apostleship goes back to Jesus himself. John's Gospel does not use the actual term "apostle," but the NT understanding of apostleship lies close to the surface at a number of points: as the Father has sent the Son, so the Son "sends" his closest disciples into the world (17:18; 20:21). In the NT the term "apostle" is used in three basic senses.

Firstly, the term can be equated with and restricted to an inner group of Jesus' disciples, known as "the Twelve," who were chosen and specially trained by him, and sent out after his death and resurrection as the authorized leaders of the new people of God. The number twelve is highly significant; it recalls the twelve patriarchs and twelve tribes of Israel, and confirms Jesus' intention that a community, the new Israel, should continue after his death (cf. 11-3.1b), a community led by the Twelve (cf. Rev 21:14; see Reid 1955: 8). The Synoptics enshrine a strong tradition that Jesus chose this special group of twelve (Mark 3:13-19; Luke 6:12-16); John refers to "the twelve" (6:67-71; 20:24), though he does not list their names. Jesus instructed them and sent them out on a mission during his own ministry (Matt 10; Mark 6:7-13, cf. 3:14-15; Luke 9:1-6). Paul also knows a very early tradition that refers to "the twelve" as recipients of a resurrection appearance (1 Cor 15:5). Lists of the names of the Twelve are found in each of the Synoptics (Matt 10:2-4; Mark 3:16-19; Luke 6:14-16), and also in Acts 1:13. (The names are not exactly the same; the lists may reflect divergent traditions, or some of the Twelve may have been known by more than one name.) It is Luke in particular who equates this group with the "apostles." In Acts 1:21-22 Peter identifies two essential qualifications for being an apostle: he must have been a follower of Jesus during his lifetime, and he must be a witness of the resurrection. Following Jesus' ascension Acts narrates how the place on the Twelve made vacant by the suicide of Judas was filled (1:15-26). Matthias was appointed through drawing lots (a procedure that would not be thought of as pure chance but as divinely guided). Significantly no attempt was made thereafter to fill vacant places (e.g., on the death of the apostle James, the son of Zebedee, in 12:2). The office is unique and unrepeatable and dies out with the deaths of its first holders.

Secondly, the NT also embodies a different tradition according to which the apostles were a wider group than the Twelve. In 1 Cor 15:5-7 (where Paul is probably quoting an early tradition), "all the apostles" are listed as a group separate from "the twelve." James, the Lord's brother, is called an apostle in Gal 1:19. 1 Cor 9:5-6 appears to assume that Barnabas is an apostle. Rom 16:7 says Andronicus and Junia "are prominent among the apostles"; the most natural way to read the verse is to see Paul as designating these two persons as apostles (see commentaries, and Omanson 1986: 17). Less certain is the reference to Silvanus and Timothy in 1 Thess 1:1. Then, of course, there is Paul himself, who time and again insists that he is an apostle (Gal 1:1; 1 Cor 1:1; Rom 1:1; etc.). References to false apostles (2 Cor 11:13; Rev 2:2) further suggest the existence of true apostles who traveled from place to place.

Thirdly, in a few cases the term "apostle" is used in a much more general sense to mean simply an authorized delegate or messenger of a Christian congregation. Referring to the delegates of his churches involved in gathering the collection for the Jerusalem church, Paul says, "As for our brothers, they are messengers *(apostoloi)* of the churches" (2 Cor 8:23). Similarly in Phil 2:25, Paul refers to Epaphroditus as "your messenger *(apostolos)* and minister to my need." These cases stand quite apart from the first two categories and refer to people entrusted with a specific task and dispatched from their local church in order to carry out that task.

ii. Peter

Among the apostles a special position is held by Peter; in the Gospels and in Acts he is generally portrayed as the leader and spokesman for the Twelve. In a number of episodes in the Gospels we find him speaking for the group. Two separate narratives suggest that Jesus conferred on Peter a unique position of leadership and authority in the church.

Following Peter's confession in Matt 16:17-19 (on this passage, see R. E. Brown et al. 1973: 83-101), Jesus declares, "You are Peter *(petros)*, and on this rock *(petra)* I will build my church. . . . I will give you the keys of the kingdom of heaven, and whatever you bind on earth will be bound in heaven, and whatever you loose on earth will be loosed in heaven." This passage, found in Matthew only, has been the subject of endless debate, particularly because of its later use in relation to the claims of the papacy. The historicity of the passage has been seriously questioned, but a series of Semitic features argues in favor of a very early Aramaic tradition underlying the passage. This includes the pun in Aramaic on the name "Peter" meaning "rock." To suggest that the rock is Peter's faith or his confession of Jesus as Messiah does not do full justice to the play on the name; it is Peter/the Rock who is given a foundational position in the new community. The authority to bind and loose (a rabbinic expression) means power to lay down rules for the community. This is hardly an arbitrary authority, however; such decisions would surely have to be made in accordance with the teaching of Jesus and the guidance of the Spirit. Moreover, it is highly significant that the same authority is given to *all* the disciples in Matt 18:18.

In John 21:15-19 Peter is reinstated; after his threefold betrayal he has the opportunity of reaffirming his faith three times and then receives the threefold commission "Feed my lambs. . . . Tend my sheep. . . . Feed my sheep." Here the emphasis is more on pastoral responsibility than on authority to make rulings.

In the accounts of resurrection appearances Peter is listed first among the disciples (cf. Mark 16:7; 1 Cor 15:5). In the early chapters of Acts Peter is the major figure and acts as the leader and spokesman for the early Jerusalem community. Several of his speeches or sermons are recorded, including the first Christian sermon on record, preached on the Day of Pentecost (Acts 2). The Cornelius episode (10:1–11:18) shows Peter (albeit reluctantly) supporting the Gentile mission (cf. 15:7-11).

Against this however have to be balanced some passages that suggest limits to Peter's authority. Despite his leadership role, the Gospels frankly record his failure to stand by Jesus after his arrest, and his threefold denial of his master. The evidence of both Acts and Galatians shows that Peter did not retain his position of leadership in the Jerusalem church; that was taken over by James, with Peter becoming a roving missionary to Jewish communities. Gal 2:11-14 gives us a glimpse of a confrontation between Peter and Paul on the question of eating with Gentile converts to Christianity in which Paul declares that Peter was clearly in the wrong. In John's Gospel as a whole (as distinct from the appendix, chap. 21), Peter is portrayed as in no way superior to the Beloved Disciple.

It would therefore appear that while Peter was given a position of leadership and authority in the early church, that position was by no means absolute but was shared with the other apostles and with Paul. The NT evidence accords well with early Christian tradition in placing Peter in Rome at the end of his life, but not in making Peter the founder of the church at Rome. The question of whether Peter's authority could be passed on, e.g., to the bishop of Rome, is not raised in the NT.

iii. This Ministry and Apostleship

The basis of apostleship, as far as we can tell from the NT, was a direct call from Christ himself. That call was based on grace, not on merit, as the narrative of the call of Peter in Luke 5:1-11 vividly shows. Peter's reaction is one of awareness of his own sin and unworthiness; hence "it is of the grace of Christ's call that he enters 'the ministry,' not of his own merit" (W. D. Davies 1962b: 236-37; cf. Smart 1960: 33).

Essentially the apostles were called *to share, to continue, and to extend Jesus' own ministry.* In sending them out during his own ministry, Jesus instructed them, "As you go, proclaim the good news, 'The Kingdom of heaven has come near.' Cure the sick, raise the dead, cleanse the lepers, cast out demons" (Matt 10:7-8). After Jesus' death and resurrection, they continued to carry out this commission. As far as we know, they became primarily preachers of the word (Acts 6:2, 4). Peter, Paul, and Barnabas certainly became itinerant missionaries; the exception is James, who remained as head of the mother church in Jerusalem.

In their preaching the apostles testified, as no one else could, to the Christ event. "It is a simple historical fact that no one in all time has stood in the same relation with Jesus Christ as the original apostles. Nor is their function as apostles transferrable. Their gospel, their faith, their ministry, can and must be shared by any church that is to be truly Christian, but not their apostleship" (Smart 1960: 34). It is true that not all the apostles in the wider sense met the qualifications laid down in Acts 1:21-22. Paul (as far as we know) never met the historical Jesus, and James was not a follower of Jesus during his ministry. Significantly, however, both Paul (1 Cor 9:1) and James (15:7) were recipients of resurrection appearances, and they and their message received the approval of those who had stood closest to the historical Jesus (Gal 2:9). It is as the primary witnesses to the Christ event that the apostles can be said to be the foundation of the church (Eph 2:20; Rev 21:14). According to 1 Cor 12:28, "God has appointed in the church first apostles" (cf. Eph 4:11). The message they proclaimed became the norm for the faith and life of the developing church (2 Pet 3:2), and indeed became the basis for the canon of the NT (see D-2.3).

b. Jesus' Family

Another form of unique and unrepeatable leadership in the early church is found in the members of Jesus' own family.

i. The Brothers of the Lord

Jesus' brothers and sisters are mentioned as a group in the Gospels (Matt 13:55-56//Mark 6:3). The brothers are termed *adelphoi,* the normal Greek word for "brothers," and the Gospels do nothing to suggest that they were other than younger brothers (and sisters) of Jesus, i.e., children of Mary (the Helvidian theory). Later Christian tradition found a problem with this and, noting that *adelphoi* can refer to broader forms of relationship, suggested that they were sons of Joseph by a former wife, i.e., stepbrothers of Jesus (the Epiphanian theory), or sons of Mary's sister, i.e., cousins of Jesus (the Hieronymian theory).

In the Gospels the brothers are not followers of Jesus and indeed try to restrain him (Mark 3:21, 31-35). Similarly in John 7:6-8 Jesus rebukes his brothers, and it is clearly stated that "not even his brothers believed in him" (v. 5). The brothers do appear with Mary in Acts 1:14 as members of the early Jerusalem community, thus implying a radical change of attitude toward Jesus. That they played some role as itinerant missionaries is suggested by the tantalizingly brief reference in 1 Cor 9:5, where Paul claims that he has the right to be accompanied by a wife, "as do the other apostles and *the brothers of the Lord* and Cephas." There is no further mention of the brothers and no evidence that as a group they exercised any leadership role in the church.

Among the brothers a unique role is played by James. Although not a follower of Jesus in his lifetime, the tradition preserved in 1 Cor 15:7 makes him the recipient of a special resurrection appearance: "then he appeared to James." In Acts we find him taking over the leadership of the Jerusalem community from Peter and presiding over the Council of Jerusalem (Acts 15). Paul confirms this switch of positions; in Gal 1:18-19 James appears to be subordinate to Cephas (Peter), whereas by the time of the visit recorded in 2:9 James is listed ahead of Cephas and John. The unique place held by James was presumably due to his family relationship to Jesus. The NT is silent about the later part of his career. Later tradition associates the Epistle of James with him, though this is not claimed by the epistle itself. (Later Christian tradition, as well as Josephus, records his death at the hands of the Jewish authorities in the early sixties.)

ii. Mary, the Mother of Jesus

Mary is mentioned in Acts 1:14 in a way which implies that she was a member of the earliest Christian community. She is not credited with any leadership role in the church, however, and indeed is not mentioned again either in Acts or any of the epistles. Paul never mentions Mary by name and knows nothing of any participation by her in the life of the church. While Mary played an essential role in the birth of Christ, there is nothing in the NT to indicate that her presence was essential for the birth of the church (D. F. Wright 1989: 18).

Mary is mentioned, however, in all four Gospels in a way which suggests that she did hold a special place for many early believers. Assessment of the place of Mary in the NT is made more difficult both by the role of Marian theology and devotion in the Roman Catholic Church and by the Protestant reaction to this and neglect of the figure of Mary. The differing portraits of Mary in each Gospel, highlighted by critical scholarship (see R. E. Brown et al. 1978), must be taken into account, but BT will seek to assess Mary in the total canonical context.

Matthew presents Mary as the virgin who will bear the Savior of God's people (Matt 1:21). It is in Luke, however, that we get the fullest portrait of Mary, for in the infancy narrative of Luke 1–2 it is Mary who plays the leading role. She is the recipient of the annunciation by the angel Gabriel telling her that she will bear "the Son of the Most High" (1:32). The Magnificat (1:46-55; assuming with the best manuscripts that it is to be attributed to Mary) echoes the Song of Hannah (1 Sam 2:1-10) and gives Mary a key role in salvation history. The birth stories of John and Jesus run parallel to one another, and Elizabeth acts as a foil to highlight the importance of Mary.

These references have to be balanced by the somewhat more negative portrait found in Mark's Gospel. In 3:20-35 Jesus' family *(hoi par' autou)* try to seize him because they believe "he has gone out of his mind" (v. 21). In vv. 31-35 Jesus is very brusque in referring to his family; it is whoever does the will of God that is his brother, sister, or mother. Equally pointed are the references to his family in 6:1-6: "Prophets are not without honor," says Jesus, except "among their own kin" (v. 4). It is noteworthy that these more negative references are missing in both Matthew and Luke.

Mary appears in only two scenes in John's Gospel. At the wedding at Cana (2:1-11) Mary apparently asks for a miracle and, though Jesus grants her request, his response, "What have you to do with me?" (v. 4 RSV), suggests at least a mild rebuke. That Mary is pictured as interceding with Jesus on behalf of others or acting as a mediator is unlikely (R. E. Brown et al. 1978: 193). At the cross Mary is entrusted to the care of the Beloved Disciple (19:26-27).

In the Gospel material as a whole, Mary is presented as one who played a unique role in God's purposes and in the history of salvation. Matthew and Luke stress the divine initiative in the selection of Mary as the one who will bear the Savior, a point underlined by the angelic announcements (Matt 1:20-21; Luke 1:26-38). As the "favored one *(kecharitōmenē)*" (Luke 1:28), Mary is in a unique way the recipient of God's grace (recipient, not dispenser). The Magnificat in particular relates the birth of Mary's child to God's purposes in salvation history.

It is also true that Mary is presented as an outstanding representative of God's people and of the faithful remnant. Both infancy narratives breathe an atmosphere of piety and faithfulness to the God of Israel. Mary is depicted as belonging to a group of people, which includes Simeon and Anna, who are "righteous and devout, looking forward to the consolation of Israel" (Luke 2:25). It is not certain that Luke intended to connect Mary with the "virgin daughter" of Israel/Zion of various OT passages (cf. G. A. F. Knight 1966; Thurian 1963: 13-19). Nor is there any clear indication that the "woman" of Rev 12 is to be identified with Mary; rather she is a personification of Israel/the church (R. E. Brown et al. 1978: 239; Ruether 1979: 25; D. F. Wright 1989: 15).

Mary is presented as one whom future believers will call "blessed." After being blessed by Elizabeth (Luke 1:42), Mary herself says, "From now on all generations will call me blessed" (1:48). Mary was not blessed by material prosperity (1:52-53), nor by being spared suffering (2:35; cf. John 19:26), but by knowing that she has been chosen by God to serve him in a unique way.

The Lucan material in particular presents Mary as an example and a role model for believers to follow. Faced with a perplexing, threatening, and seemingly impossible task, she responds in humility and obedience: "Here am I, the servant of the Lord; let it be with me according to your word" (Luke 1:38). She acts as a true servant *(doulē)* of the Lord. The Orthodox understanding that "Mary's voluntary submission to the will of God — her freely willed agreement with the divine plan announced by the angel — was a fundamental and necessary condition of the union of God and man in Christ" is in accordance with the biblical evidence (Cronk 1982: 128-29). Her obedience does not need to be seen as totally passive; for example, it is Mary who takes the initiative in going to visit Elizabeth for three months (Luke 1:39-40, 56). While the Matthean narrative gives chief place to Joseph, Luke focuses on Mary. As a canonical whole the birth narratives do not present a picture of one partner dominant over the other; both Mary and Joseph have a role to play.

iii. Who Are My Mother and My Brothers?

The presence of Jesus' mother and brothers in the early church, and especially the role of James as the head of the mother church in Jerusalem, might suggest the possibility of a continuing leadership role for members of Jesus' family, a kind of "caliphate." Historically Eusebius, on the authority of Hegesippus, states that James, after his martyrdom, was succeeded as head of the Jerusalem church by Simeon, who is described as the son of Jesus' uncle Cleophas, and hence a cousin of our Lord (*Ecclesiastical History* 4.22). But after this there is no more evidence of a leadership role for members of Jesus' family, nor is there anything in the NT to suggest such a possibility.

Jesus' mother and brothers do play a significant role in the early church, in some ways akin to that of the apostles. Their presence in the church (in the case of James, for three decades) helps guarantee the authenticity of the material that came to be written in the Gospels, and the essential continuity between the message of Jesus and the message of the early church.

15-3.3. REGULAR MINISTERS: MINISTERIAL FUNCTIONS

Acts and Paul's letters (apart from the Pastorals) indicate the leading role played by the apostles and by Jesus' family in the early days of the church; they have less to say about other forms of leadership or about the type of organization that would continue when the unique special ministries ceased to exist. The NT does have much to say about ministry, but its primary interest is in *functions* rather than in *order* or *offices* (cf. Barrett 1985: 32). The principal functions of the ministry include oversight, preaching, prophecy, teaching, the conduct of worship, and pastoral care.

a. Oversight

The NT suggests that from the outset the earliest Christian communities were under the care and oversight of leaders who exercised a form of authority. The term *episkopoi* (below, 15-3.4 b.ii) refers literally to those who have "oversight." From one point of view, most of the NT epistles (including the letters to the seven churches in Rev 2–3) illustrate the nature of this oversight: they are addressed to Christian congregations, and the authors clearly write on the assumption that they have both the authority and the responsibility to speak to the communities as they do. 1 Cor 12:28 lists "forms of leadership" *(kybernēseis):* this involves giving guidance and direction (Bourke 1968: 501) and suggests a form of oversight like that of *episkopoi.* 1 Thess 5:12 refers to "those who labor among you, and have charge of *(proistamenous)* you in the Lord" (cf. Rom 12:8). Similarly Heb 13:7 exhorts the recipients to "remember your leaders *(hēgoumenoi)."*

b. Preaching

An essential function of Christian ministers is the proclamation or preaching of the gospel. Christ sent his disciples out to "proclaim the good news" (Matt 10:7). The church was founded on the preaching of the apostles (Acts 5:42; 10:42), and in the speeches of Acts we have examples of the preaching of Stephen, Peter, and Paul. Acts 13 suggests a close link between Christian preaching and the synagogue sermon: in the synagogue at Antioch in Pisidia, after the reading of the law and the prophets, Paul is invited to give a "word of exhortation." He begins with the Scriptures (referring to the passages that had been read? — see commentaries), but then proclaims their fulfillment in the Christ event and calls for a response (vv. 16-41). Paul saw his primary task as the preaching of the gospel (1 Cor 1:17; 9:16). The apostles committed this task to their successors: thus a bishop must be able "both to preach with sound doctrine and to refute those who contradict it" (Titus 1:9), and elders are to "labor in preaching" (1 Tim 5:17).

c. Prophecy

Prophecy was an important form of ministry in the OT (above, 15-1.3); though it died out in late OT times, it was expected to be reborn in the new age (above, 15-2.3). The ministry of John the Baptist, herald of the Coming One, constitutes precisely this rebirth, while Jesus himself fulfills the expectation of an eschatological prophet (see 6-3.4). Prophecy, however, continues in the early church, and Peter sees the outpouring of the Spirit at Pentecost as a fulfillment of Joel's prophecy that in the new age all God's people shall prophesy (Acts 2:17-18 = Joel 2:28-29). Prophets appear in the book of Acts (11:28; 13:1; 15:32; 21:9-10) and Paul's letters (Rom 12:6; 1 Cor 12:10, 28-29; 13:2, 9; 14:6, 22, 29, 37; Eph 4:11; 1 Tim 1:18; 4:14). The book of Revelation sheds much light on NT prophecy, since the author refers to his work as a "prophecy" (1:3; 19:10; 22:7, 10, 18-19) and produces a book with many similarities to the prophetic books of the OT (see Hill 1972: 415).

In the NT prophecy is inspired by the Spirit (Acts 11:28; 21:11; Eph 3:5; Rev 1:10) and is based on God-given revelation (1 Cor 13:2; 14:30; Eph 3:5; Rev 1:1, 9). John frequently links prophecy with "the testimony of [or, to] Jesus" (Rev 1:2, 9, etc.; on the meaning of this, see Hill 1972: 411-12). As in the OT, Christian prophets addressed God's word primarily to the present situation of God's people (cf. Hill, 416), in order to build up the community (Acts 15:32; 1 Cor 14:3-4), but the present is seen in the light of God's future (as throughout Revelation), and prophecy therefore includes a predictive element in some cases (Acts 11:28; 21:11; cf. Bourke 1968: 499-500). From this it is apparent that there was a considerable overlap between "preaching" and "prophecy."

Throughout the NT there are references to "false prophets" (cf. E. E. Ellis 1976: 701). Jesus warned his disciples, "Beware of false prophets, who come to you in sheep's clothing but inwardly are ravenous wolves" (Matt 7:15). False prophets are to be expected throughout the period that extends to the end of history (Mark 13:22). Specific NT examples include the "Jewish false prophet, named Bar-Jesus" (Acts 13:6), and "that woman Jezebel, who calls herself a prophet" (Rev 2:20). Examples could be multiplied if we assume that most "false teachers" (see 3-4.2) claimed to be prophets. It was the existence of such false prophets that made necessary the "testing of the spirits" (see 5-3.4c).

Prophecy may have been available in principle to all God's people, but generally it is regarded as a gift bestowed only on certain believers (Rom 12:6; 1 Cor 12:28; Eph 4:11). Some scholars see "prophets" as an office in the early church (cf. Acts 13:1; 1 Cor 12:28; Rev 11:18; 18:24), but this is to go beyond the evidence. Historically prophets did not go on to constitute a separate form of regular ministry (cf. below, 15-3.4), perhaps because of the many problems with false prophets (cf. E. E. Ellis 1976: 701), and it is best to regard prophecy as a *function,* later absorbed by *presbyteroi* and *episkopoi.*

d. Teaching

"Teachers" are mentioned by Paul in Rom 12:7, 1 Cor 12:28-29, and Eph 4:11. 1 Tim 2:7 and 2 Tim 1:11 use the term of Paul himself, while in 1 Tim 3:2 a bishop is to be a teacher (cf. also 2 Tim 2:24). From one point of view Paul's letters can be regarded as "teaching instruments" (Furnish 1981: 112), and so can the other epistles. Romans and Hebrews contain the most systematic instruction and offer the best examples of teaching in the NT period. The Pastoral Epistles emphasize the importance of "sound teaching" (1 Tim 1:10), i.e., the teaching passed on by the apostle Paul (vv. 10-11). Teaching is to be based on Scripture (i.e., the OT), understood as "the sacred writings that are able to instruct you for salvation through faith in Christ Jesus" (2 Tim 3:15). Timothy is not only to teach sound doctrine but also to entrust the Christian message "to faithful people who will be able to teach others as well" (2:2). According to Heb 5:12, the recipients of the letter ought by this time to be teachers, though in fact they need to relearn the ABCs of the faith.

e. Conduct of Worship

The NT has surprisingly little to say about who led the public worship of the early Christian communities. 1 Cor 14 shows that anyone inspired by the Spirit could pray and prophesy, but we cannot assume that this was the norm in all congregations. *Baptism,* it has been claimed (cf. W. D. Davies 1962b: 243), was administered by the apostles (Acts 2:38-41), by Philip (8:12), by Ananias (9:18), and by Peter (10:47-48), though there is nothing in any of these accounts to preclude the actual baptizing being done by others. Paul certainly baptized, but only on occasion (1 Cor 1:14-16). We are left to assume that normally baptism was administered by the leaders of local congregations. Particularly surprising is the absence of any indication as to who presided at the *Lord's Supper* (cf. Lazareth 1982: 22; Barrett 1985: 33).

f. Pastoral Care

The term "pastors" appears only in the list of Eph 4:11, but pastoral care was certainly a major feature of ministry in the NT. "Pastor" *(poimēn)* means literally a shepherd, and Christ as the Good Shepherd (John 10:11) and "the great shepherd of the sheep" (Heb 13:20) is the model for pastoral ministry. Just as Jesus is the shepherd-king (6-3.2), so those assigned the task of ministry are called to be shepherds of their flock. Jesus' charge to Peter was to feed/tend the lambs/sheep (John 21:15-17; cf. Matt 10:6). The elders *(presbyteroi)* are charged in 1 Pet 5:2-3 to "tend the flock of God that is in your charge," and are warned, "Do not lord it over those in your charge, but be examples to the flock." In the light of the OT background, "the shepherd cares, seeks out, feeds, comforts, strengthens, heals, defends and provides" (Steele 1986: 26). The Pauline Epistles are full of insights into the pastoral ministry of Paul, and 1 Corinthians, for example, "is concerned from first to last with problems of pastoral care" (Gilmour 1963-64: 396; see especially the fine discussion of Paul as pastor in Furnish 1981). Pastoral care aims particularly at "building up" the Christian community (cf. 2 Cor 10:8; 13:10).

15-3.4. REGULAR MINISTERS: MINISTERIAL OFFICES AND STRUCTURES

Although the NT's main interest is in ministerial *functions,* it also testifies to the emergence of church *order* and ministerial *offices.*

a. Priesthood

The most remarkable discontinuity between OT and NT ministries is the total absence of the office of priest in the early Christian church. The term "priest" *(hiereus)* does occur in two contexts.

i. The person and work of Christ himself, as we have seen (6-3.3), is interpreted in terms of priesthood, especially in the Epistle to the Hebrews.

ii. The belief that *all* God's people should be "a kingdom of priests and a holy nation" (Exod 19:6 RSV; cf. Isa 61:6) is taken up and applied to the church as a whole in the NT. The readers of 1 Peter are told, "You are a chosen race, a royal priesthood, a holy nation, God's own people" (2:9); they are to be "a holy priesthood, to offer spiritual sacrifices . . . to God through Jesus Christ" (2:5). John tells his readers that Christ has "made us to be a kingdom, priests serving his God and Father" (Rev 1:6). We have already seen (14-3.5a) that Christians can be said to offer "spiritual sacrifices," and priestly language is frequently applied to believers in the NT (cf. Best 1960: 280-94). In Revelation the martyrs have a priestly function: "You have made them to be a kingdom and priests serving our God" (5:10; cf. 20:6). Thus, while there is no priestly office in the NT, there is a "general priesthood" of all believers (cf. Best, 297).

b. The Emerging Offices

Within the NT we can see three offices in process of emerging.

i. Presbyters/Elders (presbyteroi)

In the NT Jewish elders appear as leaders of local synagogues and as members of the Sanhedrin (cf. above, 15-1.1). Elders *(presbyteroi)* are also found in the early Christian communities, and (as in the OT) they simply appear without any explanation of their origin. They are associated with the mother church in Jerusalem in Acts 11:30 and 21:18. According to 14:23, Paul and Barnabas appointed elders in each of the churches they had established. In Acts 15 the Jerusalem Council consisted of "the apostles and the elders" (vv. 2, 4, 6, 22, 23; 16:4). In 20:17-35 Paul addresses the elders of the church at Ephesus; their task is "to shepherd the church of God" (v. 28). Jas 5:14 mentions "the elders of the church" who can be summoned to pray for the sick; and in 1 Pet 5:1-4 "the elders" are exhorted to "tend the flock of God that is in your charge." In all these cases the conclusion is inescapable that early Christian congregations simply took over the Jewish practice of local synagogue elders (cf. Lemaire 1973: 146-47; Schweizer 1961: 47, 71, 200). Harvey (1974: 326) prefers to emphasize the influence of LXX references to *presbyteroi*; it is not necessary to make an either/or decision between the two options.

Despite the references in Acts that link Paul with elders, one of the puzzles of the NT is that nowhere in his epistles (outside the Pastorals) does Paul mention *presbyteroi* by name. But then he shows very little interest in organization or office, and focuses rather on gifts bestowed for ministry and on the functions of those who minister. Paul does refer in a general way to "those who . . . have charge *(proistamenous)* of you in the Lord" (1 Thess 5:12; cf. Rom 12:8); precisely the same word is used of elders in 1 Tim 5:17.

The Pastorals reflect a more developed form of church government with presbyters, bishops, and deacons. Here a *presbyteros* is one who has been ordained to a specific office. 1 Tim 5:19-21 deals with disciplining elders. Although not much is said regarding duties, 5:17 affords an important insight: "Let the elders who rule well be considered worthy of double honor, especially those who labor in preaching and teaching." Here one function of the elders is to "rule" *(proistēmi* = "be at the head of, rule, direct, manage"). The "honor" bestowed on them refers to financial compensation (see v. 18); presumably elders are paid by the church so that they can devote their full time to their duties. "Especially those who labor in preaching and teaching" suggests that two types of elders are envisaged, one group that "rules" and another that also engages in preaching and teaching.

ii. Bishops/Overseers (episkopoi)

The term *episkopos* in secular use meant an overseer, superintendent, or guardian (*epi-skopeō* literally means to "over-see"). In such passages as Acts 20:28 and Phil 1:1, it may be that it should be translated in some such way. But in the Pastoral Epistles there can be no doubt that *episkopos* is used of an office, usually translated "bishop." 1 Tim 3:1 speaks of the one who "aspires to the office of bishop"; vv. 2-7 outline the qualifications for the job, but unfortunately not its duties.

A key question is how *presbyteroi* and *episkopoi* were related. The NT evidence clearly indicates that the two terms were originally used virtually interchangeably (cf. Schweizer 1961: 85; Bourke 1968: 506; Coenen 1975: 199; Barrett 1985: 52). In Titus 1:5-9 the writer begins by speaking of "elders," but in v. 7 he slides over into talking about "a bishop." In Acts 20:17 Paul meets with the Ephesian elders, but in v. 28 he urges them to watch over the flock "of which the Holy Spirit has made you *episkopoi*" (some prefer to translate as "overseers" rather than "bishops"). In 1 Pet 5:1-2 elders are urged to tend the flock of God "exercising the oversight" *(episkopountes)*. This equation of elders and overseers/bishops helps to explain the one text in which Paul does appear to refer to church officials, Phil 1:1, where he writes to the saints at Philippi, with the *episkopoi* and *diakonoi*: "bishops and deacons" (if offices are referred to) or "overseers and helpers" (if the reference is more to functions). Either way, it is possible to see the *episkopoi* as referring to local elders on the synagogue model.

The NT, however, also suggests a form of differentiation between *presbyteroi* and *episkopoi*. It is noteworthy that in the Pastorals, while "elders" are referred to in the plural, "bishop" is always singular; this suggests that within the council of elders, one emerged with special authority and responsibility for oversight. We noted above the evidence of 1 Tim 5:17 that *presbyteroi* "rule" like synagogue elders, but some have the responsibility of preaching and teaching. Thus in the NT we have two understandings of *presbyteroi*: as a group of local church leaders on the model of the Jewish synagogue, and as emerging individual leaders who take over the functions of the apostles as these fade from the scene. This is borne out by 2 John 1 and 3 John 1, where the author identifies himself as "the elder" but is clearly an individual in a position of authority who can give directions to Christian congregations the members of which he regards as his "children" (3 John 4).

iii. Deacons/Servants (diakonoi)

As we have already seen (15-3), *diakonos* means a servant or minister and can be used in a quite general way. Here again the question has been raised in regard to Paul's reference to *diakonoi* in Phil 1:1 as to whether an office is in mind ("deacons") or simply people who were "helpers" (*NOAB*, NT: 280). In Rom 16:1 Paul commends "our sister Phoebe, a deacon *(diakonos)* of the church at Cenchreae." Although some take *diakonos* here to mean simply "servant" or "minister," the term more probably indicates an office, or at least is in transition to indicating an office (see Gryson 1976: 3-4; contra Daniélou 1961: 8).

There can be no doubt that when we come to 1 Tim 3:8-13, *diakonoi* refers to "deacons" as a specific office in the church. Here again this passage lists the qualifications for office but does not define the duties of deacons. That they looked after the finances of local congregations and organized poor relief is suggested by the fact that the word *diakonos* generally has a strong practical connotation, and by the warning that they must not be "greedy for money" (v. 8).

Acts 6:1-6 recounts the appointment of the seven (see Barrett 1985: 49-50). Although the term *diakonos* is not used, the passage does refer to "the daily distribution *(diakonia)* of food" to the needy members of the Jerusalem community, and the seven persons chosen were assigned the duty of serving *(diakonein)* tables (vv. 2-3). This strongly suggests that Luke intends the narrative to indicate the origin of the office of deacon. It is true that Stephen goes on to preach and teach, but this is not incompatible with his having served originally as a "deacon."

The NT does not see deacons as what they later became: a preliminary stage in the process of becoming a presbyter/priest. They are distinct from those to whom is committed the ministry of the Word (Acts 6:2, 4); they are called, on behalf of the whole community, to the very practical ministry of caring for those in need.

c. Conciliar Structures

The NT also supplies evidence of ministry being exercised by groups, in conciliar fashion, rather by individuals. As noted above, in the Pastorals "elders" are always mentioned in the plural, a fact which suggests that early Christian communities, like Jewish synagogues, were headed by a council of elders. That this was so is confirmed by 1 Tim 4:14, where Timothy is told, "Do not neglect the gift that is in you, which was given to you through prophecy with the laying on of hands by the council of elders *(presbyterion)*" (so NRSV; translating as "the elders" obscures the reference to a corporate body; cf. the use of the term with reference to the Sanhedrin, above 15-1.1).

If local congregations were ruled by a council, there also is evidence of conciliar government at the highest level. The single most important policy decision in the early church, the question of whether and on what conditions Gentiles may be admitted (see 12-3.3b), was decided not by any individual but by the "Council of Jerusalem" (Acts 15; on the relation of this to Gal 2:1-10, see commentaries). According to Acts 15, the council was composed of "the apostles and the elders" and was presided over by James. After an open debate with contributions by Peter, Paul, and Barnabas, James summed up the consensus and formulated the written decree to be issued by the council. While the decree was issued in the name of the apostles and elders (v. 23), the decision to send delegates to Antioch was taken "with the consent of the whole church" (v. 22). It has been claimed that "in this instance the *apostoloi* and the *presbyteroi* are patterned after the Jewish Sanhedrin . . . and not just the synagogue council" (Bornkamm 1968: 663; cf. Coenen 1975: 199). But there is no evidence of the council as an ongoing body, and it is more likely that it was patterned on the Jewish synagogue model but was regarded as having greater authority by virtue of being the ruling body of the mother church in Jerusalem. The "elders" are clearly differentiated from the "apostles"; and there is no justification for identifying them (contra A. Campbell 1993: 516-27).

These witnesses to a corporate understanding of church order form an important counterbalance to the view that in the NT authority is exercised by individuals, whether apostles or bishops.

d. Appointment to Office

The NT gives some indications as to how persons were chosen and appointed to office. In Acts 6 the seven were chosen not by the apostles but by "the whole community" (vv. 2-3); the apostles, however, appointed them (v. 3) and "prayed and laid their hands on them" (v. 6; see commentaries on variant reading). In 14:23 Paul and Barnabas appointed the local elders, and "with prayer and fasting they entrusted them to the Lord." The word "appoint" *(cheirotoneō)* means to "choose" or (literally) "elect by raising hands" (cf. 2 Cor 8:19), but here the meaning is clearly "appoint," not "elect." Later *cheirotonia* became the technical term for ordination, but the verb cannot be pressed to mean "ordain" here.

In the Pastorals a presbyter is ordained by the laying on of hands by the members of the *presbyterion,* or council of elders (1 Tim 4:14). Titus is instructed to "appoint elders in every town" (Titus 1:5), though Timothy is warned, "Do not ordain anyone hastily" (1 Tim 5:22). In 2 Tim 1:6 Paul reminds Timothy "to rekindle the gift of God that is within you through the laying on of my hands." To reconcile this with 1 Tim 4:14, it would be necessary to suppose that Paul acted as a member of the *presbyterion* (but note that 5:22 suggests rather ordination by an individual).

15-3.5. MINISTRY AND GENDER

a. Married Ministers

No passage in the NT directly addresses the question of whether or not the ministers of God's people should be married. There is evidence that the majority, following the OT pattern, were indeed married; but there is some evidence also for voluntary celibacy on the part of a few.

i. Marriage

Peter was married, as the reference to his mother-in-law in Mark 1:30 shows. 1 Cor 9:5 indicates that not only Peter but several other apostles were married: "Do we not have the right to be accompanied by a believing wife, as do the other apostles and the brothers of the Lord and Cephas?" (but see commentaries). In the Pastoral Epistles a bishop is required to be "married only once. . . . He must manage his own household well, keeping his children submissive and respectful in every way — for if someone does not know how to manage his own household, how can he take care of God's church?" (1 Tim 3:2, 4-5). Similarly 3:12 instructs: "Let deacons be married only once, and let them manage their children and their households well." It is not simply a case of bishops and deacons being permitted to marry; what is urged is the positive value of the example of the family man.

ii. Celibacy

A couple of NT passages suggest that while celibacy is not required, it can be of value in certain circumstances. In Matt 19:10-12 Jesus sets forth the option of renouncing marriage for some of his followers "for the sake of the kingdom of heaven." In 1 Cor 7 Paul, though not directly discussing the ministers of the community, does suggest that the unmarried person is free from family responsibilities and anxieties and thus is free to "please the Lord" (see vv. 32-35). It is clear that Paul, who presumably saw himself in this situation, is stating a personal preference, not a general rule.

b. Women Ministers

The question of the place of women in the church's ministry is linked with the question of the status of women generally and their role in society; on this see further, 19-3.3c.ii.

There is evidence in the NT that women did play a role in leadership and ministry in the early church. That role was not comparable in extent to that of men, but given the social conditions of the time, it was in fact quite remarkable.

While Jesus chose only men as members of the Twelve, women do play a considerable role in the accounts of his ministry. Jesus was quite prepared to teach women as well as men (Luke 10:39). He defied convention by speaking to women in public and accepting them as persons (John 4:7-42). "By any reading of the Gospels Jesus' attitude toward women was revolutionary" (Omanson 1986: 16). A group of women ministered to Jesus, providing for him out of their own means (Luke 8:1-3); they followed him to the cross when his male followers deserted him (Mark 15:40-41).

Women play a key role in the resurrection narratives, and become the first to proclaim the good news of Jesus' resurrection. Although the leadership of the early church was largely male, a surprising number of women were involved in various types of ministry. According to Acts 21:8-9, Philip had four daughters, all of whom "had the gift of prophecy." In the husband-wife team of Priscilla and Aquila, the wife appears as in no way inferior (Acts 18:24-26) and is referred to by Paul as a "fellow worker" (Rom 16:3 RSV); it is noteworthy that she is said to have taught Apollos. In Phil 4:2-3 (RSV) two women, Euodia and Syntyche, are said by Paul to have "labored side by side with me in the gospel." The persons greeted in Rom 16 include no fewer than eight women, including Phoebe, who is termed a *diakonos* (above, 15-3.4b.iii), and Junia, who is termed an apostle (15-3.2a). There is thus considerable evidence that in relation to ministry Paul was prepared to put into practice the basic principle that in Christ there is neither male nor female (Gal 3:28; on this text, see more fully 19-3.3c and 19-5.3.d; cf. also Hayter 1987: 133-39). It is clear that "Paul was able to carry out his extensive missionary and church-developing activity only by full and generous participation of women, as well as men, in the urban centres where he took up residence" (Kee 1992-93: 231; cf. MacHaffie 1986: 23-26). Women are mentioned particularly in connection with house churches (see 14-3.1e). The early church met in the house of Mary (Acts 12:12); Priscilla (Prisca) and her husband Aquila had a church in their house (Rom 16:3-5; 1 Cor 16:19); Apphia is linked with Philemon and Archippus in the reference to their house church in Phlm 2, while Nympha presided over a church in her home in Laodicea (Col 4:15).

The Pastorals envisage a more limited role for women, probably because of changed circumstances. In 1 Tim 3:11, however, following the reference to deacons in vv. 8-10, "women" *(gynaikas)* are counseled to be "serious, not slanderers, but temperate, faithful in all things." While the reference could be to the wives of deacons, it is more natural to take it as referring to female deacons (so Schweizer 1961: 86 n. 334).

Two passages create a special problem, particularly in the light of this evidence of the participation of women in the church's ministry. In 1 Cor 14:33-35 Paul declares, "As in all the churches of the saints, women should be silent in the churches. For they are not permitted to speak, but should be subordinate, as the law also says. If there is anything they desire to know, let them ask their husbands at home. For it is shameful for a woman to speak in church." Some have questioned whether Paul could have written this, and there is some evidence of textual dislocation (cf. Hall 1974: 50; Cleary 1980: 81). However, these verses can be seen as part of Paul's letter, and certainly they are part of the canonical text; it is just too easy to dispose of a difficult text by pronouncing it a later interpolation. They must be read, however, in the light of another passage in the same letter, 11:2-16. Admittedly this is a difficult passage (see commentaries, and the discussion in Hayter 1987: 119-27). On the one hand, Paul seems to be following Jewish tradition in requiring women to have their heads covered in worship, yet in vv. 11 and 12 he asserts the essential equality of men and women "in the Lord." Moreover, the whole discussion assumes that women *do* pray and prophesy in the worship of the church at Corinth (cf. Daniélou 1961: 9). There is no indication in the text that Paul is thinking of public worship in one passage but not the other. The most satisfactory solution therefore is that in 1 Cor 14 Paul is not talking about women leading in worship, but rather expressing his concern about disturbances during worship created by women in the congregation abusing their newfound freedom in Christ to interrupt or question those giving prophetic leadership (cf. Stouffer 1981: 258; Omanson 1986: 20-21; Hayter, 127-31).

1 Tim 2:11-14 directs: "Let a woman learn in silence with full submission. I

permit no woman to teach or to have authority over a man; she is to keep silent. For Adam was formed first, then Eve; and Adam was not deceived, but the woman was deceived and became a transgressor." The question of authorship is not decisive for BT; the text, whether written by Paul or not, is part of canonical Scripture. It is generally assumed that the context is public worship and that what is being discussed is the role of men and women in worship and in church leadership. Traditionally v. 12 has been interpreted, and continues to be interpreted, by women as well as by men (see A. L. Bowman 1992), to mean that women can neither lead in public worship nor be ordained. While fashions in hair style and costume jewelry (v. 9) may be culturally conditioned, the appeal to Gen 2 and 3 in vv. 13-14 indicates, it is argued, an unchanging principle. The writer appeals to the story of Adam and Eve: "The unstated application of his argument, then, is that just as in creation the final authority rested with man, so in the church this order should be maintained" (Bowman, 205).

The passage has been the subject of intensive study in recent years; while some writers support the traditional view, many others, from a wide range of theological viewpoints, have questioned that interpretation. Spencer (1974) points out that allowing women to learn (v. 11) was itself a major advance on contemporary Jewish practice. The reference to Eve cannot be taken in isolation; in Rom 5:12 and 1 Cor 15:22 Paul lays all the blame on Adam (cf. Stouffer 1981: 256)! Many scholars have called attention to v. 12, where women are not permitted "to teach or to have authority over a man." The word translated "to have authority" *(authentein)* occurs only here in the NT and is comparatively rare in Greek. It could certainly mean "have authority," but it could also mean something like "domineer" (so NEB, contra G. W. Knight 1981: 260). Hence the background could again be one in which some women were abusing their new-found freedom in Christ by teaching men in a domineering fashion in public worship. In that particular situation, the writer finds such behavior intolerable, but he is not giving a ruling on women in ministry valid for all time.

One particular group of women exercised a special ministry in the early church. The plight of *widows* in ancient times could be a desperate one, and the church at an early stage sought to help this disadvantaged group (Acts 6:1-7; Jas 1:27). 1 Tim 5:3-16 shows that in certain circumstances widows were supported financially by the church (in v. 3 "honor" indicates this; cf. v. 17); in return they dedicated themselves to a life of prayer and service. The fact that they were "put on the list" or "enrolled" (v. 9 — *katalegein*) and took a "pledge" (v. 12 — *pistin*), along with the context of the passage (directions for bishops, deacons, elders), justifies our speaking of an "order" of widows (cf. Daniélou 1961: 13-14; Stählin 1974: 455-58; Thurston 1989: 36-55). 1 Timothy assumes the existence of such an order; while it spells out qualifications (age, marital status, good deeds — vv. 9-10), unfortunately it does not list duties. It is implied, however, that "widows" engaged in pastoral visitation (cf. v. 13) and cared for the sick and needy. The story of Dorcas in Acts 9:36-43 may give us a glimpse of the order in embryonic form (Thurston, 31-35). The order of widows (that continued in the early church) allowed a particular group of women to exercise God-given gifts in a form of ministry, recognized by the church, though one that had strict limitations.

New Testament: Consummation

15-4. THE TWELVE APOSTLES OF THE LAMB

As we have already seen, the biblical vision of the final consummation is a corporate one. While there will no longer be a need for ministry, nevertheless, in the vision of the end recognition is given to the special ministry of the apostles and to the regular ministry of the elders.

15-4.1. THE APOSTLES

According to Matt 19:28//Luke 22:30, Jesus promised his twelve disciples that, "at the renewal of all things, . . . you who have followed me will also sit on twelve thrones, judging the twelve tribes of Israel." At the final consummation the role of the Twelve as the leaders of the new Israel will be fully recognized.

A similar recognition is accorded the apostles in Rev 21:14, which says "the wall of the city has twelve foundations, and on them are the twelve names of the twelve apostles of the Lamb" (cf. also 18:20).

15-4.2. THE PRESBYTERS

In the book of Revelation a notable part is played by the twenty-four elders. In his vision John sees around the divine throne "twenty-four thrones, and seated on the thrones are twenty-four elders, dressed in white robes, with golden crowns on their heads" (4:4). The elders worship God and sing his praise (4:10-11; cf. 7:11-12; 11:16-17; 19:4). In 5:8 they join with the four living creatures in offering to God the prayers of the saints. In 7:13-14 one of the elders addresses John and identifies for him those who are robed in white. The presence of elders in the eschatological Jerusalem recalls the vision of Isa 24:23 (see 15-2.1). A link with the twenty-four divisions of the priesthood (1 Chr 24:4) has been suggested, but it is much more likely that "twelve of the elders represent the patriarchs of the twelve tribes of ancient Israel as well as the entire body of Old Testament saints; and the other twelve elders stand for the people of the new covenant, nurtured on the faith of the twelve apostles" (Cronk 1982: 255-56).

15-5. MINISTRY: THEOLOGICAL REFLECTIONS

1. The relationship between a BT of ministry and the understanding and practice of ministry in later centuries and today raises a host of complex and difficult questions. Modern historical studies have strongly emphasized *diversity*
and *development* in the various forms of ministry found in the OT and NT.
Most biblical scholars hold that "there is no such thing as *the* New Testament
Church order" (Schweizer 1961: 11). The implication is that it is impossible to
find a norm for church government today in Scripture. Since "the Church in
the New Testament can assume many forms, and is not limited to any one particular form which is peculiarly the expression of its very being," any attempt
"to squeeze the Body of Christ into conformity with any single, fixed and necessary mould or form" must be opposed (W. D. Davies 1962b: 217). Proof of this is
often seen in the fact that, historically, quite different church orders — congregational, presbyterial, episcopal, papal — have all claimed scriptural support
(though often by focusing on some parts of the NT at the expense of others).
Historical scholars also emphasize that what we have in the NT is a series of
very partial and imperfect glimpses of a developing and evolving church order.
It is a common view, for example, that there seems to have been a general movement within the NT from an earlier period when there was much fluidity in organization and when the chief interest lay in the functions of church leaders, to
a later period when a form of organization was beginning to emerge and interest began to turn to various offices held by the church's leaders. These approaches are sometimes referred to as "charismatic" and "noncharismatic ministries." Moody suggests "charismatic" and "official," corresponding to the
Greek terms *charismata* (gifts) and *cheirotonia* (choice, ordination) (1965: 175).
Moreover, it is clear that this development continued and can be traced
through the second and third centuries and beyond with the emergence of the
"threefold order" of bishop, priest, and deacon, to be followed later, especially
in the West, by a more elaborate hierarchy. Most historical scholars see this as a
continuous development in relation to which the boundaries of the canon are
quite irrelevant. To many this suggests that the NT material is descriptive but
not prescriptive.

While some branches of the Christian church claim to find their norm
solely within Scripture, advocates of the monarchical episcopate usually concede that this order is not found in fully developed form in the NT, and hence
they find their norm not solely in Scripture but to some degree also in ongoing
and developing church tradition. Knox (1957), for example, argues that the
norm for church government is not to be found in the NT but rather in the situation that the church had reached around A.D. 200; but if the norm is not
found in Scripture, why stop at one particular point in church history rather
than another?

In response, BT must take the limits of the canon seriously. This means on the one hand that the basic norms for ministry are to be found within the canon, not beyond it. Scripture obviously does not provide a blueprint for church order complete with job descriptions, but it can be argued that there are basic principles within Scripture that can guide the ordering of the church and of its ministry today. If we believe in the inspiration and authority of Scripture, we will not regard the point at which the canonical NT cuts off as purely fortuitous but will recognize what is contained in Scripture as sufficient to guide the church in any age.

A canonical approach also means that BT must take into account *all* the canonical material. The fact that differing approaches are represented and have been enshrined side by side in the canon suggests that each has something to contribute. For example, some interpreters emphasize the Pastoral Epistles as embodying the most fully developed church order within the NT and as pointing forward to the later threefold ministry and the monarchical episcopate. Others focus on 1 Corinthians with its emphasis on the gifts of the Spirit and lack of formal organization as the earliest NT emphasis. A canonical BT must not choose between these two emphases, but must seek to do justice to both. If the norm is to be found in Scripture, there must be a balance between Spirit-inspired enthusiasm and doing all things decently and in order. Steele (1986) makes the same point with reference to the Pauline and Palestinian communities: "the church needs the official aspect of authority to keep in line the charismatic tendency toward unchecked spontaneity, a lesson learned by the early Pauline churches. It needs the charismatic authority to keep the office holder continually responsible for the way in which one exercises one's gift, a lesson learned by the Palestinian church" (17).

2. Throughout canonical Scripture, in both OT and NT, there is a recognition of the need for both inspired leadership and organizational structure. Some have seen any form of organized ministry as a late and nonessential development in early Christianity. According to this line of thought, "the individual existed before the local congregation, and the local congregation before the universal church." In the earliest stages the church was led by the Spirit, and it was only with the continued delay of the parousia that a need was felt for organized leadership. When ecclesiastical offices did develop, they "were regarded as purely peripheral to Christianity, and were concerned solely with administrative duties and the maintenance of order" (Riesenfeld 1953: 97). Such a view fails to grasp the main thrust of the BT of ministry. Just as modern individualism obstructs a clear view of the church as the new people of God, so it also obscures the essential role of ministry within God's people.

OT and NT agree on the corporate nature of faith and on the need for the oversight and care of God's people. In the OT, in addition to the exceptional leadership of Moses, kings, high priests, major prophets, and the wise, provision for regular, ongoing ministry by elders, priests, and prophets existed from the very beginnings of the life of Israel as God's people. In the NT ministry is not a late innovation, but is grounded in the ministry of Jesus himself. The "special ministries" of the apostles and of Jesus' family bridge the gap between the historical Jesus and the "regular ministries" that developed in the emerging church. The need for oversight and leadership was *not* something that developed later in the life of the church. There was much that was spontaneous in the earliest Christian congregations, but it is also true that "Church life in the New Testament was from the first ordered" (W. D. Davies 1962b: 220), and that "the Church has never been without persons holding specific authority and responsibility" (Lazareth 1982: 21).

3. The NT sees ministry and order as essential features of the new people of God, the church, but first, last, and all the time it grounds ministry in the teaching, example, and command of Jesus. Thus "the prototype for the ministry is our Lord himself" (Reid 1955: 1; cf. Smart 1960: 19). W. D. Davies (1962b) is accurately summarizing the NT view when he says, "since the Church is the Body of Christ, it is called upon to perform His work: the Church is the continuation of the life of Jesus, the Messiah. But what was the nature of that life? It can be summed up in one word — ministry *(diakonia)*" (235). The special ministry of the apostles and then the regular ministries that developed within the Christian church are "simply the ministry of Jesus Christ being continued, expanded and carried ever further afield in the world as Jesus Christ lives and speaks and acts redemptively through his ministers" (Smart, 37).

The NT understanding of ministry means putting oneself in the lower place (cf. above, 15-3.1a). As Wharton (1981) points out, the technical opposite of ministry is "magistry" or "mastery": "a relationship in which the will of a 'greater' (magis) is imposed upon a 'lesser' (minus) person as determined by relative rank or power. The modes of mastery are command, coercion, or inducement" (20). Unfortunately, over the centuries many of those called to Christian ministry have often been more interested in mastery. "The Church has often set up leaders who were lords and princes. Then it has tried to baptize this lordship by calling it 'service.' But the ministry that is a ministry of service does not seek power for itself. Rather it uses power to empower others" (Ruether 1979: 69).

The basic NT understanding of ministry does not of course in and of itself provide any blueprint for church order, but it does qualify everything else the NT does say about ministry and order, and it stands in judgment on all later forms of ministry and order that fail to live up to the norm.

4. After its fundamental emphasis on the *nature* of ministry, the NT has most to say about the *functions* of ministry. The basic functions of oversight, preaching and prophecy, teaching, conduct of worship, and pastoral care (above, 15-3.3) were exercised firstly by the apostles, then by the developing regular ministries, and they continue to provide normative direction for the exercise of ministry today.

The NT, however, provides guidance on more than the functions of ministry; it provides at least a basic framework for church order. It is difficult to see how any form of order that does not contain the NT offices of *presbyteros, episkopos,* and *diakonos* can claim to be biblical. The NT also suggests that no system can seen as biblical without a significant conciliar element. At the same time, however, Scripture itself provides ample warrant for adopting and adapting these offices and structures to changing times and circumstances. For those who accept Scripture as normative, it is equally difficult to see how any developments that took place *after* the NT, such as the monarchical episcopate or the papacy, can be regarded as of the *essence* of the church (cf. W. D. Davies 1962b: 238); that is to make tradition superior to Scripture.

The most difficult and controversial questions of church order revolve around the origin and place of "bishops." There are two main theories: one sees monarchical bishops as evolving upward from the local councils of elders, the other sees them as appointed downward by the apostles. The first view, championed by Lightfoot, remains the most convincing one in the light of the NT evidence: *presbyteroi* and *episkopoi* were originally the same, but the single *episkopos* or bishop emerged from the council of elders over a period of time, either because he came to preside at the Eucharist or because a person was needed to speak for the community, or to ensure unity, or for some such reason. Jay points out that this view was held as late as the time of Jerome (ca. 342-420), who wrote that "a presbyter . . . is the same as a bishop, and before ambition entered into religion . . . the churches were governed by the council of presbyters, acting together. But after each began to think that those whom he had baptised were his, not Christ's, it was unanimously decreed that one of the presbyters should be elected and preside over the others, and that the care of the Church should wholly belong to him, that the seeds of schism might thus be removed" (Jerome, *Commentary on Titus* 1.6-7, quoted in Jay 1981: 159; cf. 159-61).

The second view begins with the undoubted fact that the apostles, such as Peter and Paul, traveled and had authority over a wide area. It claims that these apostles appointed bishops as their successors in the main cities of the eastern Roman Empire. During the second century when the church was threatened by Gnosticism and other forms of "false teaching," the church sought to defend itself by compiling lists of bishops in the main sees, tracing them back to the original bishop appointed by an apostle. This "apostolic succession" was held to guarantee and provide the norm for sound doctrine: the true faith was that championed by the bishops in the main sees who belonged within the apostolic succession. This theory has two main weaknesses. Firstly, a chain is only as strong as its weakest link, and the weakest link in this case is the first one: there is no evidence in the NT that the *episkopoi* of which it speaks were appointed by the apostles. Timothy is not called an *episkopos* in the NT, and while in 2 Tim 1:6 Paul speaks of laying hands on Timothy, 1 Tim 4:14 makes it clear that he was ordained by a council of elders! Secondly, church history provides ample proof that a mere mechanical succession is no guarantee that the holders of the office of bishop will always be supporters of orthodox doctrine. The NT is interested in a form of "apostolic succession"; not in the mechanics of a chain of office-holders, but in the faithful transmission of the apostolic proclamation and interpretation of the Christ event. It is the *message* preached by the apostle Paul that Timothy is to "entrust to faithful people who will be able to teach others as well" (2 Tim 2:2). Continuity of the later Christian church with the earliest Christian communities, with the apostles and indeed with the ministry of Christ himself, is obviously essential to the church, but it is of no value unless it is accompanied by faithfulness to the gospel. The later church, whether led by bishops or employing other forms of church order, has frequently strayed from the gospel and found itself in need of reformation. The only norm and criterion on which such ongoing reformation can be based is the apostolic proclamation and interpretation of the gospel that is recorded in the NT. The true Christian church must thus be both "catholic" and "reformed" and must find its norm both of doctrine and of order within canonical Scripture.

5. One of the most difficult and controversial issues today is the role of women in ministry. Opponents of the ordination of women often argue that a male God can be served only by male ministers, but we have seen that in the Bible God transcends sexual distinctions (see 1-1.4b.ii; 1-3.3b.ii), and we may agree with Hayter (1987) when she says that "intelligent Christian thinkers would do well, therefore, to abandon once and for all the argument that the ultimate reason for the maleness of Judaistic and Christian priesthoods is the maleness of the God whom they represent, with its corollary that the acceptance of women priests would turn Christianity into a different, non-biblical religion" (74). Biblical evidence is frequently quoted in favor of both the subordination and the equality of women in ministry, and it is obvious that this is an issue where nothing can be settled by quoting isolated proof texts: e.g., citing 1 Cor 14:33-35 as the basis for women to be silent in church, when 11:5, 13 (and Acts 21:8-9) clearly show that women functioned as prophets; or citing 1 Tim 2:11-14 as the basis for excluding women from teaching when Acts 18:26 clearly shows that Priscilla taught Apollos. The key hermeneutical issue is where the NT is setting forth a principle valid for all time and where it is giving advice only for a specific historical situation (see the discussion in Hayter, 146-67; and cf. Packer 1991: 18).

There can be no doubt that in the OT the role of women was severely limited, especially through their exclusion from the priesthood that was organized on the hereditary principle. Given the social conditions of the time, it is all the more remarkable that where ministry depended not on the hereditary principle or on social convention, but on divine charisma, i.e., in the case of the prophets and the wise, then women as well as men were definitely capable of receiving the divine gift. The attitude of Jesus was truly revolutionary; he accepted women as equal. When the Holy Spirit was poured out at Pentecost, it is significant that the key text from Joel 2:28-32 quoted by Peter emphasizes that the eschatological gift of the Spirit is bestowed regardless of sex (Acts 2:17-21, "sons and daughters," "slaves, both men and women"). The Spirit equipped the members of the body of Christ for ministry, and there can be no doubt that the basic *principle* is that "there is no longer male and female; for all of you are one in Christ Jesus" (Gal 3:28; cf. 19-3.3c.ii). It has been argued that this principle means that while women are equal "in the eyes of God," in the organization of the church they must accept a subordinate place. But that is not the way Paul interpreted the principle that in Christ there is neither Jew nor Greek; he was adamant that this equality must be real and must be expressed in the life and practice of the church, and he spent much of his ministry fighting for this position. For a variety of historical reasons, he did not push the principle so strongly in the case of slave and free, or male and female.

Putting the revolutionary principle of equality into practice in the social conditions of NT times was fraught with difficulty, and it seems clear that "the church of the post-apostolic age began to move away from an egalitarian structure toward a hierarchical, patriarchal structure which was reflective of contemporary society" (Omanson 1986: 15). Just as advocating the total abolition of slavery was unrealistic and impractical given the social conditions of the period, so granting women complete equality in ministry would also have been impractical and probably counterproductive. The amazing thing is the degree of participation of women in ministry, particularly in the Pauline churches, including Corinth (cf. P. J. Ford 1975). 1 Tim 2:11-14 (as noted above) is a very difficult text; insofar as it does advocate a reduced role for women, this text obviously reflects not the basic NT principle of equality but a specific historical situation in which it seemed best for the time being to conform to the norms of the surrounding society.

The distinction between basic principle and specific practice is a crucial one. The task of the church today is to ask how the basic principle is to be applied in very different social circumstances from those that prevailed in NT times.

A SKETCH OF BIBLICAL THEOLOGY

CHAPTERS 16-20: GOD'S WAY

CHAPTER 16

The Human Condition

Old Testament: Proclamation

16-1. WHAT ARE HUMAN BEINGS?

God's people are called to walk in his way (on the biblical understanding of "the way of the Lord," see the discussion in E-4.4). As background to considering the way of life appropriate to the members of the people of God, we look first at the biblical understanding of human nature and especially of the individual human being.

16-1.1. HUMAN NATURE

Many biblical scholars are quick to point out that the provision of an analysis of human nature is not a primary purpose of Scripture. Nowhere, it is claimed, does the Bible present a systematic, theoretical discussion of anthropology, or of what traditionally was termed a "doctrine of man" (cf. Childs 1992: 566; Schultz 1996: 602). While there is some truth in this claim, nevertheless in its canonical form Scripture does present an understanding of the human condition. "Systematic" it is not, and still less is it "theoretical." But the Bible is concerned from start to finish with human beings, and offers in a variety of literary forms a consistent though also developing understanding of the human condition.

It is not insignificant that in its final canonical form Scripture begins in Gen 1–11 with a prologue that does present the basic biblical understanding of human nature, albeit largely in story form (see below, 16-1.2a). It is also noteworthy that in the NT Paul begins his letter to the Romans, containing the most systematic exposition of the gospel he produced, with an analysis of human nature in Rom 1–3.

a. Characteristics of Old Testament Anthropology

A traditional approach in BT has been to study the "anthropological terms" employed in the OT. Such a study can help clear the ground. For example, it is useful and important to know that OT terms usually translated as "soul" and "heart" do not necessarily mean in the OT what they signify in modern usage. But as a major avenue of approach to this subject, the "word study" method has severe limitations (cf. Childs 1986: 197).

The OT does employ a wide range of terms in talking about human beings, but attempts to give precise definitions of these terms and to grasp the understanding of human nature they express are fraught with dangers. "Stereotyped translation of Hebrew words is not wise or possible" (Schultz 1996: 602). One has to be very wary of imposing a modern understanding (i.e., misunderstanding) on the biblical material. Some preliminary cautions are therefore in order.

The OT generally thinks of human beings in a very concrete way; it finds it difficult if not impossible to think of individuals apart from their physical bodies.

The various words used cannot be rigidly defined and pigeonholed. It is noteworthy that terms used for different parts of a person are frequently used in poetic parallelism. Thus Ps 84:2 says:

> My *soul (naphshî)* longs, indeed it faints
>   for the courts of the LORD;
> my *heart* and *flesh (libbî ubh^esārî)* sing for joy
>   to the living God.

This does not mean that the psalmist equates the three terms, but it does suggest an overlap of meaning and warns against a too rigid separation of the terms.

Terms that are used for parts of a person can frequently be used to refer to the whole person, and can in fact be replaced by personal pronouns. Thus Prov 2:10-11 says:

> For wisdom will come into your *heart,*
>   and knowledge will be pleasant to your *soul;*
> prudence will watch over *you;*
>   and understanding will guard *you.*

In a text such as this, speaking about your "heart" and "soul" seems to be almost another way of speaking about "you."

Most of all, the OT thinks of a human being as a *unity.* It does not make a twofold division into "body" and "soul," nor a threefold division into "body," "mind," and "spirit." Rather, *each of the major anthropological terms describes the whole person from one particular aspect.* As Whiteley (1964) puts it, "the anthropological language of the Biblical writings is aspectival, not partitive" (36).

b. The Main Anthropological Terms

The *physical body* is created by God and is something to be admired, especially when it is strong and beautiful. Great height brings respect (1 Sam 9:2), though God does not judge human beings by their size (Prov 25:6). Women such as Sarah (Gen 12:11, 14), Rebecca (24:16), and Bathsheba (2 Sam 11:2-3) are noted for their beauty, and male beauty is admired also, e.g., Joseph (Gen 39:6) and David (1 Sam 16:12, 18). The fullest descriptions of human beauty are found in the type of poem in the Song of Songs classified as a "wasf" or an "emblematic blazon" (Ryken 1987a: 283-85); three of these catalogue in detail the attractive features of a woman (4:1-5; 6:4-7; 7:1-5), and one of a man (5:10-15). The effect of these descriptions is to "evoke a strong feeling of the worth of the person" (Ryken, 285). But the OT also recognizes that beauty can be dangerous and deceptive (Prov 11:22; 31:30).

Hebrew has no word for "body" as such, but the human body as a whole can be referred to as "flesh" (*bāsār;* the word can refer to the flesh of animals as well as humans; e.g., Lev 4:11). Flesh is something all humans share, and the expression "all flesh" (Isa 40:5-6 RSV) simply means all human beings (NRSV translates "all people"). But it is the aspect of a human being that is most obviously "subject to attack, injury, damage, and to decay" (Kraus 1986: 144).

> All *flesh* is grass,
> and all its beauty is like the flower of the field.
> (Isa 40:6 RSV; cf. Ps 103:15-16)

The flesh is subject to weakness and faints without water (Ps 63:1). For this reason the term is never used of God. *Bāsār* characterizes human beings from the perspective of their weakness, frailty, and mortality. As Childs (1986) puts it, "man is not a semi-divine creature striving to realize some ideal by which to fulfil a destiny, but rather a short-lived mortal, born in a family, given a community, and greatly restricted in time and place" (199). It should be noted, however, that the OT never suggests that flesh in and of itself is evil, or the source of evil (cf. Schultz 1996: 603).

Closely related to flesh is blood *(dām),* which is generally regarded as "the seat of the vital physical life per se" (Wolff 1974: 60). When the blood ebbs away, so does life. Thus "the life of every creature is the blood in it" (Lev 17:14 RSV). Because of this, blood must be treated with special respect. The Torah prohibits the tasting of blood (Gen 9:4), and the shedding of human blood is a crime against God (9:4-6). In sacrifices the blood must be poured out or sprinkled on the altar; it is a precious gift to be offered back to God (Lev 17:3-6).

The term *nephesh* is usually translated "soul," though this is seldom a really appropriate equivalent. The word appears to be connected with the throat, the part of the body that takes in food and that breathes. It is with their *nephesh* that human beings long, desire, strive, or yearn (cf. Wolff 1974: 15). Thus *nephesh* "does not denote an inner soul, but rather the whole person as the seat of human desires and emotions" (Childs 1992: 572). However, "it also represents the seat and the process of spiritual feelings and inner conditions" (Kraus 1986: 145), in which case "soul" can occasionally be an appropriate translation (e.g., Pss 35:9; 43:5). Since it is connected with vital needs, it can virtually mean life itself (Lev 24:17; Ps 30:3). In some cases it simply means a person, an individual (Lev 17:10). Thus it is not so much that a person *has* a *nephesh* as that he or she *is* a *nephesh*. It can also be used of persons referring to themselves, so that "my *nephesh*" simply means "I" (1 Kgs 20:32). Only in a few rare cases is the term used of God (Isa 1:14; Jer 12:7).

We have already seen that the OT has much to say about the Spirit of God (5-1). Human beings have a spirit, a *rûach,* also. The word is closely connected with the breath (also *n⁰shāmâh*) that signifies life and the vital powers conferred on a person by God. It is associated with a range of feelings perhaps because of the rise and fall of breath; one's spirit can be bitter (Gen 26:35) or jealous (Num 5:14), but also steadfast and generous (Ps 51:12). It can also be used of "energetic actions of the will" (Wolff 1974: 38). It is through their *rûach* that human beings have an affinity for God.

Lēv is the "heart," but this is not always an accurate English equivalent. It is true that it can be associated with the feelings (1 Sam 1:8; Prov 15:13; Deut 20:8), and also with wishes and desires (Ps 21:2). But "in by far the greatest number of cases it is intellectual, rational functions that are ascribed to the heart — i.e. precisely what we ascribe to the head and, more exactly, to the brain" (Wolff 1974: 46). Thus it is linked with insight or understanding (Isa 42:25; Job 34:10), with memory (Dan 7:28), and with thinking (1 Sam 27:1). In some cases it can also be linked with the will, and with the seat of decision making. The heart can be inclined either toward evil or toward good. Deep in the hearts of the wicked there is no fear of God (Ps 36:1). When the heart is "hardened," it is closed to God and to obedience to him. On the other hand, a requirement for worshiping God is a pure heart (Ps 24:4) or a "whole heart" (9:1). Thus "the wholeness and integrity of a person are dependent on the clear direction and the wholeness of the 'heart'" (Kraus 1986: 146). The heart lies deep within a person, but God "knows the secrets of the heart" (Ps 44:21). "Heart" and "spirit" can overlap in meaning (cf. 51:10). The OT does speak of the heart of God, always in connection with God's relationship to human beings.

In the OT strong emotions are connected not so much with the heart as with the internal organs such as *mē̆ʿim* ("the bowels, intestines"; e.g., Jer 4:19; Isa 16:11) and *k⁰lāyôth* (the kidneys). For example, Ps 73:21 (NEB) reads:

When my heart was embittered,
I felt the pangs of envy.

The second line means literally, "I was pierced in my kidneys."

16-1.2. SIN

a. Creation and Fall

As noted above (16-1.1), while the OT has little or no systematic or theoretical discussion of anthropology, one section of Scripture does constitute something of an exception to this general rule: Gen 1–11, and especially the accounts of creation and fall in Gen 1–3, does set forth the basic biblical understanding of the human condition. Regardless of the origin and date of these chapters, their present canonical position gives them the status of a prologue not only to the OT but to the whole of Scripture. Throughout the Bible their understanding of human nature is sometimes elaborated upon but is everywhere to be assumed. Though set in "prehistory," these narratives are basically "etiologies" (cf. Sabourin 1973: 64), i.e., they provide an understanding of human nature as it exists to this day; "these are the stories of Everyman and Everywoman" (Bergant, Fischer, and Halstead 1996: 449).

The OT understanding of human nature is grounded in its belief in God as creator (cf. Porteous 1962b: 243; on creation, see the fuller discussion in chap. 2). Gen 1 and 2 depict human beings as the crown of God's creation (cf. 2-1.3a), and this never ceases to amaze the writers of the OT:

What are human beings that you are mindful of them,
mortals that you care for them?
Yet you have made them a little lower than God,
and crowned them with glory and honor.
You have given them dominion over the works of your hands;
you have put all things under their feet. (Ps 8:4-6)

Further, the OT acknowledges that God is the creator not just of "humankind" but of each individual human being. Thus the psalmist can say:

For it was you who formed my inward parts;
you knit me together in my mother's womb (139:13),

while Job acknowledges: "Your hands fashioned and made me" (Job 10:8). "Not only the creation of mankind as a whole but also the evolution of the individual

— indeed of one's own life — is traced back to Yahweh as being a work of art fashioned by his hands" (Wolff 1974: 98).

As Gen 1 and 2 affirm, human beings, including their physical nature, are basically part of God's *good* creation. It is immediately after the account of the creation of humankind in Gen 1:26-30 that v. 31 declares, "God saw everything that he had made, and indeed, it was very good" (cf. 2-1.2f).

Moreover, human beings, unlike the rest of creation including the animals, are made in the "image" of God; i.e., they are endowed with personhood and are created with the ability to live in a personal relationship with God (see the fuller discussion in 2-1.3c).

But if human nature as created by God is basically good, the Bible sees it as a good thing spoiled, and what has spoiled it and continues to spoil it is human sin. The basic nature of human sin is vividly portrayed, with amazing psychological insight, in the account of the fall in Gen 3, and in the stories of Cain and Abel, the flood, and the Tower of Babel that follow (see the fuller discussion in 2-1.5a). In Gen 3 Adam is a representative figure ("Adam" = humankind) who is portrayed as the ancestor and representative of all humankind; the story thus portrays the universality of sin and the solidarity of all human beings in sin (see Gelin and Descamps 1964: 10-12). The effects of sin as illustrated in these stories are "alienation from God, from others, from oneself, and from creation" (Doriani 1996: 736).

b. All Have Sinned

Regardless of whether or not specific terms for "sin" are employed, the understanding of human nature found throughout the OT, and indeed Scripture as a whole, is characterized by a frank and honest recognition of the nature and pervasiveness of human sinfulness. As Childs (1986) points out, "Although the Old Testament has not developed a fully-fledged doctrine of sin such as one finds in Paul and in rabbinic Judaism, there is everywhere recognition of disruption, alienation and falsehood within human society, and above all in relation to God" (200). Basically the OT agrees with Paul's verdict that "all have sinned and fall short of the glory of God" (Rom 3:23). It is true that the OT refers to some people as "righteous" and can portray a figure like Job as "blameless and upright" (Job 1:1). Such expressions, however, are to be seen as signifying "an overall orientation of life which is pleasing to God" rather than "impeccable perfection" (Eichrodt 1967: 395).

It is often pointed out that there is very little reference back to Gen 3 in the rest of the OT. This is, however, in no way indicative of a failure to recognize the reality of human sin. As von Rad (1962) points out, "The Old Testament is chock-full of references to sins which have been committed at some particular place, at some particular time, and by some particular person. But we seldom find theological reflexion on 'sin' as a religious phenomenon of the utmost complexity" (154). The nature of sin is illustrated by many of the stories of the OT (cf. Childs 1986: 201; Fischer, Getty, and Schreiter 1996: 916-17). It is particularly significant that in these narratives neither the founding fathers Abraham and Jacob, nor the great leader Moses, nor the kings David and Solomon are depicted as plaster saints; they are human beings with human weaknesses and failings. As Solomon remarks, "There is no one who does not sin" (1 Kgs 8:46; cf. Eccl 7:20). Indeed, throughout Scripture there runs the paradox that the closer individuals come to God, the more they become aware of their sinfulness and of the gap that separates sinful humanity from a holy God. It is when Isaiah, in the temple, becomes aware that he is standing in the very presence of the LORD of hosts that he cries out, "Woe is me! I am lost, for I am a man of unclean lips, and I live among a people of unclean lips!" (Isa 6:5). The prophets' call to repentance presupposes a deep sinfulness on the part of the people. Thus Jeremiah declares, "The sin of Judah is written with an iron pen; with a diamond point it is engraved on the tablet of their hearts. . . . The heart is devious above all else; it is perverse" (Jer 17:1, 9).

In the Psalms the writer is often identified with "the righteous"; this is not, however, a claim to be morally perfect, but rather to stand in a basically right relationship with God (see von Rad 1962: 381). Other psalms reveal a deepened awareness of human sinfulness.

> The LORD looks down from heaven on humankind
> > to see if there are any who are wise,
> > who seek after God.
> They have all gone astray, they are all alike perverse;
> > there is no one who does good,
> > no, not one. (14:2-3; cf. 53:1-3)

The essential sinfulness of human nature is revealed especially in the group of seven psalms that have been traditionally classified as "penitential psalms" (6; 32; 38; 51; 102; 130; 143); what they have in common is the fact that "the affliction from which suppliants plead for deliverance is a deep sense of guilt" (B. W. Anderson 1983: 93).

> For I know my transgressions,
> > and my sin is ever before me,

says the writer of Ps 51 (v. 3), who goes on to acknowledge:

> Against you, you alone [i.e., God], have I sinned
> > and done what is evil in your sight. . . .
> Indeed, I was born guilty,

a sinner when my mother conceived me.

> (vv. 4-5; cf. Job 25:4, and see Gelin and Descamps 1964: 28-29)

"This sin is not a matter of occasional deviation from the right way, but of *the consistent outcome of a natural tendency of his being,* which is already planted in him by the inheritance passed on to him at his birth. Here we have such a clear confession of original sin . . . that the spiritual affinity with Gen. 3 is incontestable" (Eichrodt 1967: 411).

c. The Nature of Sin

i. Sin as Rebellion

The most basic understanding of sin is as a rebellion of human beings against God. Typically this is most graphically illustrated by a story, the story of Gen 3 where Adam and Eve are tempted to distrust and rebel against God. "Man sins because he wishes vainly to assert his autonomy over against God" (Porteous 1962b: 244). With great insight this story captures the true nature of sin and speaks to human beings in all ages (cf. 2-1.5). The story of Israel from the exodus onward is in many ways one of continuous rebellion against God; "you have been rebellious against the LORD as long as he has known you," charges Moses in Deut 9:24. Despite God's provision for them in the wilderness, Israel "sinned still more against him, / rebelling against the Most High in the desert" (Ps 78:17; cf. Ps 106; Ezek 20:8). The Israelites are depicted as continually "murmuring" (*lûn* = "murmur, complain") against their leaders, especially Moses (Exod 15:24; 16:2; Num 14:2), and against God himself (Exod 16:7-8; Num 14:27; 17:5; cf. Deut 1:27; Ps 106:25). The English translations "murmur" (KJV, RSV), "grumble" (NIV), or "complain" (NRSV) do not do justice to these narratives; as Coats (1968) has shown, "the murmuring motif is not designed to express a disgruntled complaint. Quite the contrary, it describes an open rebellion" (249). The Deuteronomic History depicts the period after the settlement and throughout the monarchy as a time of repeated rebellion culminating in the disaster of exile. The prophets repeatedly highlight Israel's rebellion: "I reared children and brought them up," God says in Isa 1:2, "but they have rebelled against me." The people of Judah are those "whose hearts turn away from the LORD" (Jer 17:5). Jerusalem, declared Ezekiel, "has rebelled against my ordinances and my statutes, becoming more wicked than the nations and the countries all around her" (5:6). Indeed, not only Israel but all nations "stubbornly follow their own evil will" (Jer 3:17; cf. 9:13; 16:12; etc.).

Pesha', usually translated "transgression," and the verb *pāsha'* frequently signify sin as rebellion. Sin on this view is basically sin against God; it "was comprehended as a *conscious and responsible act,* by which Man rebelled against the unconditional authority of God in order to decide for himself what way he should take, and to make God's gifts serve his own ego" (Eichrodt 1967: 383). It is for this reason that *idolatry* is so strongly condemned in the OT, for the essence of sin is worshiping something other than the one true God. While sin usually *results* in a wrong relationship to one's fellow human beings, sin *originates* in a wrong relationship with God, so that the psalmist can say to God, "Against you, you alone, have I sinned" (Ps 51:4; cf. Gelin and Descamps 1964: 16).

ii. Sin as Disobedience

Gen 3 also shows how distrust and rebellion result in *disobedience;* the man and the woman proceed to disobey God's command not to eat of the tree of the knowledge of good and evil (Gen 2:16-17; 3:6). If the Torah sets forth the lifestyle to be followed by God's people, then the narratives that follow the giving of the Torah show how the people constantly disobey and break God's law. Moses anticipates this in Deut 31:27-29: "I know well how rebellious and stubborn you are. . . . For I know that after my death you will surely act corruptly, turning aside from the way that I have commanded you." Both the historical and the prophetic books constitute a catalogue of Israel's disobedience of God's Torah. The most frequently used word for sin is *chāṭā'* (verb), *chaṭṭā'th* (noun), which has the basic sense of missing the mark (see Judg 20:16), i.e., failing to conform to a norm. *'āwōn,* usually translated "iniquity," derives from a root that probably means to stray from the path; "always implied in the use of this word . . . is the agent's awareness of the culpability of his action" (Eichrodt 1967: 381). It is vital to remember, however, that "sin according to the Old Testament is not a deviation from some abstract moral standard, an unfortunate miscalculation, but an offence directed against Yahweh himself" (Childs 1992: 574).

Disobedience implies freedom to obey or disobey God's commandments, yet it is an observable fact that while some do obey, it appears inevitable that many will not. In the late OT period reflection on this paradox surfaces. Thus *Sir* 15:11-15 strongly affirms free will:

> Do not say, "It was the Lord's doing that I fell away." . . .
> Do not say, "It was he who led me astray." . . .
> It was he who created humankind in the beginning,
>   and he left them in the power of their own free choice.
> If you choose, you can keep the commandments,
>   and to act faithfully is a matter of your own choice.

Yet 33:10-15 equally affirms that God determines the division of humankind into righteous and wicked (see Schnelle 1996: 80-81):

All human beings come from the ground. . . .
In the fullness of his knowledge the Lord distinguished them
    and appointed their different ways.
Some he blessed and exalted, . . .
    but some he cursed and brought low. . . .
Like clay in the hand of the potter,
    to be molded as he pleases,
so all are in the hand of their Maker,
    to be given whatever he decides.
Good is the opposite of evil, . . .
    so the sinner is the opposite of the godly.
Look at all the works of the Most High;
    they come in pairs, one the opposite of the other.

iii. Sin as Folly

Another angle of approach is found in the Wisdom Literature, where sin is often identified as folly, the opposite of wisdom. "The fool" (represented by a variety of Hebrew terms; see Blank 1962b: 303) is frequently characterized in the Wisdom Books: "whoever utters slander is a fool" (Prov 10:18); the fool "takes no pleasure in understanding" (18:2); "doing wrong is like sport to a fool" (10:23); and so on. While Wisdom is personified in female terms (1-1.4b.ii), there is a corresponding figure, Dame Folly, who also makes her appeal to human beings (9:13-18), and folly can be seen as ingrained in human nature: "Folly is bound up in the heart of a boy" (22:15). Since "the fear of the Lord is the beginning of wisdom" (9:10), folly is at root a failure to reverence God, but it is often portrayed in more practical terms as a rejection of the lessons of experience or of the advice of parents and elders. Fools fail to take account of the consequences of their actions, and so they often learn the hard way (cf. 10:13; 18:6; 19:29; *Sir* 22:9-12).

16-1.3. JUDGMENT

Sin is seen as bringing with it certain inevitable consequences.

a. The Lord Is Our Judge

In the OT judgment is an important human activity. To judge *(shāphat)* or render judgment/justice *(mishpāt)* involves considerably more than delivering a verdict in a court of law. In the book of Judges the "judges" are leaders, rulers, and above all deliverers of their people (e.g., 3:10). Kings judge the people; what this involves is well illustrated by the judgment of Solomon in 1 Kgs 3:16-28. Solomon had prayed for "an understanding mind to govern *(lishpōt)* your people, able to discern between good and evil" (v. 9), and when he was able to determine which of the two women was telling the truth and which was lying, "all Israel . . . stood in awe of the king, because they perceived that the wisdom of God was in him, to execute justice *(mishpāṭ)*" (v. 28). Judging involves more than simply handing down a legal decision. "The judge not only discovered what was right, but acted on it. . . . Basically judgment is the process whereby one discerns between the right and the wrong *and takes action as a result*. . . . He who does *mishpāṭ* seeks out the wrongdoer to punish him, and the righteous to vindicate his cause" (Morris 1960: 17). Thus in the book of *Susanna*, Daniel judges the wicked elders and thereby saves Susanna's life. "Doing *mishpāṭ*" involves especially defending and helping the weak, the poor, and the defenseless (Isa 1:17).

In the OT God is portrayed as "a God of justice *(mishpāṭ)*" (Isa 30:18), "the Judge of all the earth" (Gen 18:25; cf. Ps 94:2; see also 18-1.4). God judges not only his people Israel, but also all humankind:

> He judges the world with righteousness;
>   he judges the peoples with equity. (Ps 9:8)

God judges wickedness and oppression (Deut 32:41; Jer 1:16), but he is a God of steadfast love, faithfulness, and righteousness as well as of justice (Ps 36:5-6). His judgment "is a blend of reliability and clemency, of law and love" (Morris 1960: 21).

In the earlier stages of Israel's history especially, it is the nation that is held responsible and that comes under God's judgment. But individual human beings are also responsible before God. The canonical OT at the outset shows God passing judgment on Adam and Eve. They may represent humankind, but they are also portrayed as individuals.

A stronger stress on individual responsibility is found in Jer 31:29-30, and similarly but at greater length in Ezek 18, where the prophet uses repetition to drive home the message that "the soul that sins shall die" (v. 4 RSV).

b. Judgment in This Life

In the OT generally, God's judgment is thought of as operating primarily in this present life. Characteristic is what has been called "the piety-prosperity equation": those who are pious, faithful, and obedient will be rewarded in this world with long life, health and happiness, and victory over their enemies. Conversely, God's judgment will fall on the impious in the form of this-worldly misfortunes. In other words, God acts in judgment *within history* (cf. 3-1.3c). This view is found particularly in Deuteronomy, and it underlies the Deuteronomic History (Joshua through 2 Kings), but it is also found in the Psalms (e.g., Ps 1) and Wisdom (e.g., Prov 10:27), and to some extent in the Prophets. God's blessing falls on those who trust and obey him; the opposite of blessing is curse, and the two ways are nowhere more vividly portrayed than in Deut 28. "The central religious dogma of the Deuteronomic theologians is the scheme of sowing and reaping, of reward and punishment — the dogma of retributive justice" (Beker 1987: 31). On this view nations are judged through defeat by enemies or being carried off into exile. Individuals are judged by loss of health, family, possessions — everything that makes life worth living.

c. Sin and Death

In the story of Gen 3 the rebellion and sin of Adam and Eve does not lead to death immediately; they are expelled from the garden, not struck dead. But it is significant that in leaving the garden they also leave behind access to the tree of life. Sin leads to separation from God, who is the source of life. There is little theoretical discussion of this in the OT, though in the Deuterocanon, *Wis* 2:24 teaches that

> through the devil's envy death entered the world,
>   and those who belong to his company experience it.

(see more fully, 20-2.2)

16-1.4. ANXIETY

The Bible also sees human life as characterized by anxiety. The word "anxiety" is not frequent in English translations of the OT, but the reality is represented by a number of Hebrew words (see P. E. Davies 1962: 154), including *dᵉʾāgâ* and *yᵉhābh*, both of which are translated in the LXX by *merimna* = "anxiety, worry, care." Moreover, the reality is often present, particularly in narratives, even when the specific terminology is absent.

"Anxiety" covers a spectrum that ranges from concern through worry to distress; at the far end of the spectrum it shades over into dread, fear, and terror. "Fear" in the Bible, it should be noted, is ambiguous (cf. Terrien 1962); it can refer to a natural reaction to a threat such as the Syrian-Ephraimite coalition of which King Ahaz stood in dread (Isa 7:4), but it can also be used in a positive sense of "the fear of the Lord," signifying the awe, reverence, and respect that are God's due (see 17-1.3c).

To some extent the OT sees it as natural that "anxiety weighs down the human heart" (Prov 12:25). Sickness and the taunts of enemies cause the psalmist to lie awake at night (Ps 102:7). Life is uncertain and often under threat so that anxiety can be caused by famine (Ezek 4:16-17), the prospect of oppression (Ps 49:5), or enemy attack (Mic 1:12; 2 *Macc* 15:19). Family life brings its own worries (*Sir* 42:9; *Tob* 10:3), but then so does barrenness (1 Sam 1:16). Anxiety and fear are common in the face of suffering of all kinds (see below, 16-1.5), and in the face of death (see 20-2.5).

In part the OT sees anxiety as an inevitable feature of the human condition. But it can also see it as a symptom of lack of faith and trust in God. Thus anxiety is particularly characteristic of the wicked (Job 15:24; Ps 73:18-19; Isa 33:14; see Sacks 1988: 782). Wisdom sees the folly of anxiety that "brings on premature old age" (*Sir* 30:24). Faith as it finds expression in the Psalms calls on the believer not to fret over the injustices of this life (37:1) or to spend the day "eating the bread of anxious toil" (127:2), but to cast one's burden on the Lord (55:22).

16-1.5. SUFFERING

a. The Problem of Suffering

Throughout the OT the various writers wrestle with the problem of human suffering. The Bible is above all an honest book. It does not seek to evade a question basic to human existence yet one to which there so often seems to be no answer at all. While it affirms faith in God, it is well aware of how that faith can be sorely tried by the experience of suffering.

Human suffering forms much of the background of the "psalms of lament" that constitute the largest single category of Psalms. While these psalms cannot be subject to rigid classification, most scholars find it helpful to distinguish between "community laments" and "individual laments" (cf. B. W. Anderson 1983: 70; see 3-2.1a for the distinction and for a discussion of community laments). Individual laments generally follow the broad pattern found also in community laments: a *cry to God*, the *lament/complaint* proper describing the situation faced by the psalmist, a *petition* or appeal to God for help, an *expression of trust in God*, and sometimes a *vow to praise God*. Individual laments have already been discussed in 9-1.2 and 10-1.1 under the rubric of "The Servant Psalms." But they are relevant not just to the experience of Moses or the great prophets; they speak to the human condition and raise the fundamental question of human suffering. Originally used in the setting of temple worship, they came to be used in synagogue and church, in private as well as in public. They are "prayers of troubled saints" (Kelley 1984), and anyone can identify with the suffering and the anguish of the psalmist, as well as with the expression of hope and confidence with which these psalms usually conclude. They do not abandon faith in God, but in the face of suffering they frequently cry out to the God who appears to have forgotten his servant (Ps 13:1), or gone to sleep (44:23), or gone into hiding (10:1; 89:46).

It is important to distinguish different types of suffering in the OT (cf. the detailed analysis in Gerstenberger and Schrage 1980: 22-102; also Scharbert and Schmid 1981: 890; B. D. Smith 1996). Where suffering is caused by other human beings, especially fellow Israelites, e.g., in the form of oppression and injustice, the Torah and the Prophets, as part of their advocacy of social justice, call for the relief of such suffering (see 19-1.3c). Similarly, although medical science was still at a rudimentary stage, the OT approves whatever can be done to relieve pain and suffering caused by illness (see 20-1.3).

The main focus of the OT, however, is on suffering over which there is no control, e.g., that caused by famine, drought, disease for which there is no cure, war, etc. It is these types of suffering that raise the most difficult questions, especially when they afflict the righteous.

b. The Traditional View

The view that is most strongly represented in the OT is that suffering is a consequence of sin (see Simundson 1980: 17-41). According to the piety-prosperity equation (above, 16-1.3b), those who obey God prosper while those who disobey him can expect to suffer in this life. It is a short step from such a view to concluding that when a person does suffer in this life — from poor health, poverty, bereavement, etc. — then that person must have sinned against God. The curses of Deut 28:15-68, portrayed as the penalty of disobedience, include a terrible catalogue of individual suffering:

> The LORD will afflict you with the boils of Egypt, with ulcers, scurvy, and itch, of which you cannot be healed. The LORD will afflict you with madness, blindness, and confusion of mind. . . . You shall become engaged to a woman, but another man shall lie with her. You shall build a house, but not live in it. You shall plant a vineyard, but not enjoy its fruit. . . . Your sons and daughters shall be given to another people. . . . The LORD will strike you on the knees and on the legs with grievous boils of which you cannot be healed, from the sole of your foot to the crown of your head. (vv. 27-35)

This view affirms that there is a God who is just and actively involved in human affairs. Since it knows nothing of a life beyond death, it holds that goodness must be rewarded and evil punished in this life. While this theory helped Israel understand its national history (the exile, for example, being seen as punishment for the nation's sins), it was clearly less successful at the individual level.

c. Challenges to the Traditional View

The traditional view that all suffering is the penalty of sin does not go unchallenged in the OT. One challenge is constituted by the recognition that being a faithful servant of God does *not* exempt such persons from suffering, but in fact often involves them deeply in it. Ideally all Israel, the people of God, are called to serve God and thus to suffer, but this ideal is most clearly embodied in faithful individuals such as a Moses or a Jeremiah (see the fuller discussion in 9-1). "In the Bible every man called by God, from Moses onwards, is called to suffering and to submit to God's will." Indeed, the more righteous and faithful the servant, the more that person is likely to suffer: "his very identification with the cause of God, his submission to the will of God, involves him through acute sensibility in suffering of a different order from the physical suffering of his fellow-men, though he may well have to endure that also" (Leaney 1963: 286).

Connected with this is the view that suffering should be seen not as a punishment but as a form of *discipline,* for as a father may have to discipline his children for their own good, so God may discipline even his most faithful servants. This view is particularly characteristic of the Wisdom Literature:

> My child, do not despise the LORD's discipline
> or be weary of his reproof.
> (Prov 3:11; but cf. also Ps 94:12; Jer 10:24; 31:18)

Connected with this also is the interpretation of suffering as *vicarious* found in 2 Isaiah (see Simundson 1980: 63-79). According to Isa 40:2, the community of exiles in Babylon "has received from the LORD's hand / double for all her sins." The exiles have suffered not just for their own sins, but for the sake of others, for suffering can be vicarious and redemptive. This is expressed in the Servant Songs (cf. 9-1.3), where the suffering of the Servant (in the first instance, the faithful remnant of God's people) is borne for the transgressions of others, that they might be made whole (53:4-5).

The traditional view is also seriously challenged particularly in the book of Job, and to a lesser extent in Ecclesiastes (cf. Beker 1987: 38-41).

Job consists of one of the most powerful portrayals anywhere in world literature of an individual wrestling with the problem of suffering and of faith in God; it is a tale of "spirituality under duress" (Terrien 1978: 361). While dramatic in form, it is perhaps best regarded as "a 'closet drama' intended to be read rather than acted" (Ryken 1987a: 343). Apart from the prose prologue (Job 1–2) and epilogue (42:7-17), it is also poetic in form. Thus it does not present any sustained or systematic argument; rather it portrays characters in conflict and draws the reader into discussion and debate. Many scholars have explored the book from a variety of approaches without exhausting its meaning (see

Terrien, 361-73; Simundson 1980: 81-101; Milazzo 1991: 114-23; Brueggemann 1997: 386-93).

The book poses the problem of human suffering in a more direct way than any other book of the Bible. Job "was blameless and upright, one who feared God and turned away from evil" (1:1), and accordingly was blessed with family and worldly goods. In a series of devastating blows, he loses all that he has (1:13-19), and then is himself stricken with a terrible disease, "loathsome sores . . . from the sole of his foot to the crown of his head," precisely one of the curses that is to fall on those who do not obey the Lord according to Deut 28:35! Job cries out to God and against God:

> Why do you hide your face,
>   and count me as your enemy? (13:24)

The question posed by the book is thus, "Why do bad things happen to good people?"

A canonical BT will at the outset ignore the many critical theories that seek to eliminate parts of the book as "secondary" or to rearrange the text; it is the book in its final canonical form with which we have to wrestle (cf. Childs 1979: 532, 542-43). This does not mean that Job necessarily presents one consistent viewpoint; on the contrary, it offers a number of complementary approaches (cf. 533, 543). The prose epilogue with its "happy ending" suggests one approach. "The LORD blessed the latter days of Job" (42:12); he ended up with twice as much wealth as he had originally. In the light of this, the message of the book may be seen as: have patience, for *while in the short run the righteous suffer, in the long run they are rewarded* (cf. 16-2.5a). But in the light of the radical questioning that penetrates the rest of the book, this seems a simplistic solution. In the book it is Job's three "friends" who represent the traditional solution of the OT in general and of Wisdom in particular: since Job suffers, it is obvious that he must have committed some grievous secret sin. It is clear that *one* purpose of the book is "to contest the theory that suffering is a sign of divine punishment and presupposes sin on the part of the sufferer" (Childs, 531). Much of the irony of the drama arises from the fact that the "friends" continue to spout "orthodoxy" while the reader knows it is totally inadequate as a way of understanding Job's situation (cf. Ryken 1987a: 343). Nevertheless, in a total canonical context, the epilogue is not to be set aside; it suggests that suffering is never the last word, though for the NT that hope may be fulfilled only beyond this earthly life (see 16-4.5).

The prose prologue offers a different set of insights. The reader is told what the characters in the drama do not know: the Satan (cf. 4-1.5) suggests that Job only fears God for what he can get out of it. Take away all he has and see whether Job really fears God for nothing (1:9). So the Satan is permitted by God to strike Job's possessions and family, and then Job himself. This, too, clearly denies the piety-prosperity equation. Suffering is not necessarily a punishment;

there are times when God, while not directly sending suffering, permits it as *a test of faith*. Job's faith is severely tried but ultimately triumphs. This view is echoed in *Wis* 3:5, where it is said of the righteous,

> Having been disciplined a little, they will receive great good,
> because God tested them and found them worthy of himself.

Another approach recognizes the theme of *the limits of human wisdom and reason*. This is seen in the inadequacy of the "friends'" advice, especially in chapter 28, which stresses the inaccessibility of Wisdom:

> But where shall wisdom be found? . . .
> Mortals do not know the way to it. . . .
> It is hidden from the eyes of all living. (vv. 12-13, 21)

When God finally appears to Job out of the whirlwind (38:1), it is not to provide him with "answers." Instead Job is given a tour of the marvels and mysteries of creation, and is asked how a mere human being could possibly understand how the whole universe is run. Job discovers that his God is too small. "Insisting that his concept of God account for his actual life experiences, Job discovered in the living God a vastness, mystery and power which had been lost completely in the closely formulated tenets of his religious establishment" (Hanson 1978: 13). It is not for Job to question God; God questions Job (38:3; 40:7). Human wisdom cannot understand all life's mysteries or provide all the answers, but people can still trust in the God who created and controls the universe, even when they do not fully understand (cf. B. D. Smith 1996: 752).

Chapters 40 and 41 offer yet another insight into the mystery of suffering and of evil in the world. The two creatures Behemoth and Leviathan are not the hippopotamus and the crocodile but belong to the dragon of chaos/evil tradition (see 4-1.3c). The monsters are fierce and beyond human control, yet God created them and God controls them. Job is asked:

> Can you draw out Leviathan with a fishhook . . . ?
> Can you put a rope in its nose,
> or pierce its jaw with a hook? (41:1-2)

The implication is that God has the dragon on a leash, almost like a pet (41:3-11). Despite appearances to the contrary, *God is in control of the forces of evil*; they are allowed to go so far, but no farther.

Finally, there is much to be said for seeing the real climax of the book not in the prose epilogue but in the conclusion of the poetic dialogues in 42:1-6. After enduring suffering and crying out against God, Job finally admits, "I have uttered what I did not understand" (v. 3), and then confesses:

I had heard of you by the hearing of the ear,
    but now my eye sees you. (v. 5)

Job may have been blameless and upright, but his faith had been conventional and secondhand. As a result of what he had been through, *his faith in God is not simply restored but reemerges at a much deeper level,* based now not on hearsay but on a direct personal experience of God; "Job now discovers a living encounter and communion with God beyond the limits of conventional piety" (Gladson 1993: 236). In one sense Job is not given any answers to his questions, but in another sense he discovers that God himself is the answer.

Each of these approaches has its own validity, and together they indicate something of the profound insights of the book of Job into the mystery of human suffering.

Ecclesiastes is in some ways a more questioning book, though also less profound than Job (cf. Milazzo 1991: 123-36, and see further 17-1.3d). What it does have in common with Job is a questioning of the piety-prosperity equation, which, for the author, simply does not accord with the facts of life. "There is a vanity that takes place on earth, that there are righteous people who are treated according to the conduct of the wicked, and there are wicked people who are treated according to the conduct of the righteous" (8:14; cf. 7:15). The writer counsels acceptance and enjoyment of life despite its limitations (3:12-13; cf. 2:24; 9:7-10), but from a canonical perspective the book's main value is to underline the inadequacy of the traditional view of suffering and thus point toward more satisfactory approaches including those of the NT.

Old Testament: Promise

16-2. THERE IS NONE THAT DOES GOOD

Pessimism regarding human nature is the backdrop against which the promise of a new way shines even brighter. In prophets like Jeremiah and Ezekiel we find a recognition that only a radical change in human nature will permit a right relationship between God and his people in the new age. In a certain tension with this are passages that reveal a deepened awareness of human sin and a pessimism as to whether human nature will ever change.

16-2.1. HUMAN NATURE

Since sin is deeply rooted in human nature, real change in the relationship between sinful human beings and a holy God must involve radical change in that nature. In Jeremiah and Ezekiel, therefore, "the prophetic hope for a better future also included anthropological changes, a transformation of human beings which would finally make obedience possible" (Gowan 1986: 69). This comes to expression in the promises of a new "heart" and a new "spirit."

For Jeremiah,

> The heart is deceitful above all things,
> and desperately corrupt. (17:9 RSV)

But in 24:7 God promises his people, "I will give them a heart to know that I am the Lord . . . for they shall return to me with their whole heart." In the prophecy of a new covenant (cf. 11-2.3), God promises, "I will put my law *within them,* and I will write it *on their hearts*" (31:33).

But it is Ezekiel especially who foresees a profound change in human nature. In 18:31 the prophet calls on the people to "get yourselves a new heart and a new spirit!" In 11:19 it is God who promises that when he restores his scattered people, "I will give them one *heart,* and put a new *spirit* within them; I will remove the *heart of stone* from their flesh and give them a *heart of flesh.*" 36:25-27 makes it clear that the human spirit will change only when it is cleansed and empowered by the divine Spirit (cf. 5-2.3).

16-2.2. SIN

In tension with promises of a change in human nature are some passages that appear to question whether the sinfulness of human beings will ever change. Thus, at one point Hosea declares:

> O Ephraim, you have played the whore;
> Israel is defiled.
> Their deeds do not permit them
> to return to their God.
> For the spirit of whoredom is within them,
> and they do not know the Lord. (5:3-4)

Israel's sin has gone beyond the point where repentance and therefore divine forgiveness are possible.

Jeremiah sees no way in which the impending judgment on Jerusalem can be averted, and he asks in despair,

> Can Ethiopians change their skin
> or leopards their spots?
> Then also you can do good
> who are accustomed to do evil. (13:23)

16-2.3. JUDGMENT

As already noted, the OT speaks frequently of a future judgment (cf. Morris 1960: 24), both within history (prophetic eschatology — see 3-2.3) and beyond history (apocalyptic eschatology — see 2-2.3). Judgment will fall on God's own people:

> I will judge you according to your ways,
>   and punish you for all your abominations (Ezek 7:8),

but will also extend to all humankind:

> For he is coming to judge the earth.
> He will judge the world with righteousness,
>   and the peoples with his truth. (Ps 96:13)

In prophetic eschatology judgment tends to fall on the *nation,* and thus on the individual only as part of the nation. With the emergence of apocalyptic eschatology, the idea of a final judgment that will be more a judgment of *individuals* emerges. According to Dan 12:2, "Many of those who sleep in the dust of the earth shall awake, some to everlasting life, and some to shame and everlasting contempt." Similarly, in the picture of the judgment in *Wis* 4:20–5:23, a division is made between the righteous and the unrighteous (cf. 3:18). The book of Isaiah ends with a warning to those who rebel against God that may suggest a kind of "hell" awaiting the unrighteous: "For their worm shall not die, their fire shall not be quenched, and they shall be an abhorrence to all flesh" (66:24; cf. *Jdt* 16:17; *Sir* 7:17).

The martyrology of 2 *Macc* 7 presents a different understanding of judgment. The fourth brother to die expresses hope in God's gift of resurrection, but tells his tormentors, "For you there will be no resurrection to life!" (v. 14). The view expressed here is of conditional immortality: the righteous will receive new life beyond death, whereas the unrighteous will not (see further, 16-4.3d.iii). This accords with OT passages that speak not of everlasting punishment but rather of the ultimate destruction of the wicked:

> Let sinners be consumed from the earth,
>   and let the wicked be no more. (Ps 104:35; cf. 37:1-2; 145:20)

> See, the day is coming, burning like an oven, when all the arrogant and all evildoers will be stubble; the day that comes shall burn them up, says the LORD of hosts, so that it will leave them neither root nor branch. (Mal 4:1)

16-2.4. ANXIETY

As we have seen, OT eschatology is marked not by a superficial optimism but by a realistic recognition that the forces that threaten life and cause anxiety and fear will not gradually disappear but if anything will intensify before the final triumph of God's kingdom (cf. 3-2.2; 4-2.2). Nevertheless, those who put their trust in God can face the future, whatever it may bring, without anxiety or fear.

> Strengthen the weak hands,
> > and make firm the feeble knees.
> Say to those who are of a fearful heart,
> > "Be strong, do not fear!
> Here is your God. . . .
> > He will come and save you." (Isa 35:3-4; cf. 41:10; 43:5; Jer 30:10)

In *2 Esdr* 2:27 God's faithful people are told, "Do not be anxious, for when the day of tribulation and anguish comes, others shall weep and be sorrowful, but you shall rejoice and have abundance."

16-2.5. SUFFERING

Although the OT wrestles with the problem of suffering mainly in terms of this present world and this present life, at one or two points it does reach out toward an eschatological solution.

a. The Prophetic Solution

The typical prophetic response is "Wait!" God's people may be suffering now, but God will act and put matters right, within the historical process, in due time. As noted above (16-1.5c), the prose conclusion of Job adopts this approach. Frequently God's promised action seems to be delayed so that the advice of the prophet is often that of Habakkuk: "If it seems to tarry, wait for it" (Hab 2:3).

b. The Apocalyptic Solution

The apocalyptic viewpoint looks beyond history and expects a new age that will be free from suffering (see Gerstenberger and Schrage 1980: 111-13). In that age "The Lord GOD will wipe away tears from all faces" (Isa 25:8); "sorrow and sighing shall flee away" (35:10); "no more shall the sound of weeping be heard in it

[Jerusalem], / or the cry of distress" (65:19). The book of Daniel exemplifies the apocalyptic solution: it expects suffering to increase, but suffering can be endured because of the hope of the final apocalyptic defeat of evil. "There shall be a time of anguish, such as has never occurred since nations first came into existence. But at that time your people shall be delivered" (12:1). "Suffering is endurable for the apocalypticists, such as Daniel, because they believe that God will vindicate their undeserved suffering and will soon achieve a final and complete triumph over the hostile powers that thwart God's redemptive purpose for Israel" (Beker 1987: 41). Until the end there is an interim period during which suffering can be seen as refining, purifying, and cleansing the righteous (Dan 11:35; 12:10).

New Testament: Fulfillment

16-3. ALL ARE UNDER THE POWER OF SIN

16-3.1. HUMAN NATURE

a. Characteristics of New Testament Anthropology

Unlike the OT, the NT does not begin with a picture of the human predicament (as in Gen 1–11; see above, 16-1.2a); it begins with the four Gospels' accounts of the Christ event. As is the case with the OT, it does not present a theoretical or neatly packaged "doctrine of man" (cf. F. C. Grant 1950: 160). Nevertheless, the NT assumes and accepts the OT estimate of the human condition, while also expanding and deepening it. This is particularly true of Paul, who, especially in Romans, comes closest to providing a systematic discussion, though it is going a bit too far to say that he expounds "a thoroughly thought-out doctrine of man" (Käsemann 1971: 1).

As in the OT, NT scholars have often approached this topic by means of a study of the "anthropological terms" employed. The same provisos apply here as did for the OT: there is some value in this approach in terms of clearing the ground and warning against modern misinterpretations. But the use of the various terms is very flexible; there can be considerable overlap of meaning; and rigid definitions are simply not possible. Though NT anthropology has been accused of tending toward dualism, in fact it retains the basic biblical view of the essential unity of human beings. As in the OT, the NT does not conceive of human beings as consisting of two (body/soul) or three (body/mind/spirit) or more component parts. 1 Thess 5:23, for example, is not to be taken as implying a tripartite division: "May your *spirit* and *soul* and *body* be kept sound"; here "Paul is merely emphasizing that the sanctifying work of God concerns the whole person" (Schnelle 1996: 104; cf. Whiteley 1964: 37-38). A person is basically a unity that can be viewed from different perspectives, and it is these to which the various anthropological terms apply. Here too the "word study" approach has value, but it needs to be followed by study of the major aspects of the human condition as these are understood in the NT.

b. The Main Anthropological Terms

The NT view of the human body is similar to that of the OT, and like the OT it can refer to it in terms of "flesh" *(sarx* = OT *bāsār).* The expression "flesh and blood" or "all flesh" can simply be the equivalent of "human beings" (Matt 16:17; John 17:2 RSV). Regularly *sarx* refers to the human body (Luke 24:39; Acts 2:31; 1 Pet 3:18). That body, of course, is subject to illness (Mark 5:29) and decay, and 1 Pet 1:24 directly quotes Isa 40:6-9 to the effect that "all flesh is grass." These texts refer to flesh in a good or at least neutral sense, but in other passages flesh has a bad connotation, so much so that the NT has been accused of harboring a "dualism" that is quite foreign to the OT. This is particularly the case where "flesh" *(sarx)* is contrasted with "spirit" *(pneuma).* Jesus himself, in Gethsemane, warned Peter to watch and pray, for "the spirit indeed is willing, but the flesh is weak" (Matt 26:41//Mark 14:38); here flesh is not evil, but it does provide a point of entry for temptation. In John's Gospel Jesus contrasts what is born of the flesh and what is born of the Spirit (3:6), and says that while the Spirit gives life, "the flesh is useless" (6:63). Any idea, however, that the flesh in and of itself is evil or the source of evil is negated by the strong emphasis in the Johannine literature on the fact that Jesus himself "became flesh" (John 1:14; 1 John 4:2; 2 John 7; cf. also Heb 2:14; 5:7).

Paul also contrasts "flesh" and "spirit" (Rom 8:1-17; Gal 5:16-25; Phil 3:3), but his usage is in some ways distinctive. He too can use *sarx* in a neutral sense meaning human beings generally (Rom 3:20; Gal 1:16), the physical body (1 Cor 5:3), or with reference to bodily weakness or pain (2 Cor 12:7; Gal 4:13). But he frequently uses it to mean what is bound up with this world and this age. To be "of the flesh" (Rom 7:14; 1 Cor 3:3), or to live "after the flesh," means to live as if this world and this life is all there is, in effect therefore ignoring God and rejecting the claims of God. In this sense *sarx* becomes a bad word. In Rom 7:14 Paul says, "I am of the flesh, sold into slavery under sin"; here *sarx* "becomes the epitome of a life separated from God and rebelling against God" (Schnelle 1996: 61). Despite this, it remains true to say that Paul "nowhere betrays the outlook of the metaphysical dualist" (F. C. Grant 1950). Evil does not reside in matter or in the physical body; "for St. Paul sin is not a taint due to 'flesh' *(sarx)* or body *(sōma)* which is inherently evil, but is due to wrong willing by the whole personality, though this wrong willing often takes place in the sphere of flesh" (Whiteley 1964: 32). "The flesh" for Paul does not describe a *part* of a human being; it describes the *whole* of a person insofar as he or she rebels against God and rejects the claims of God. Here we may recall that Paul shares John's belief in the incarnation; Jesus lived on earth in a "fleshly body" (Col 1:22). "The sinfulness of the *sarx* does not belong to it simply because it is bodily, earthly existence" (Kümmel 1963: 41-42). Paul lists "the works of the flesh" in Gal 5:19-21, but he does not imply that sin has its root in the flesh. Nor does his list consist of what a modern reader might understand by "the sins of the flesh"; although the list includes sexual sins, two-thirds of the terms do not refer to this but denote various forms of breakdown of human behavior, e.g., enmity, strife, jealousy, anger, etc. It is somewhat bewildering to discover that Paul can say both that believers continue to live in the flesh (2 Cor 10:3) and that they are no longer in the flesh (cf. Thiselton 1975: 676)! More precisely, believers live "in the flesh" but not "according to the flesh." To sum up, "flesh" is used by Paul in two senses: *sarx* as neutral denotes human beings living in the world; *sarx* as evil denotes human beings living for the world.

Unlike the OT, the NT does have a separate word for "body" *(sōma)*. It can refer simply to the physical body (Mark 5:29; Jas 2:16), consisting of various "members" (see Schütz, Wibbing, and Motyer 1975: 229-32, 239-41). Since the physical body inevitably dies, *sōma* can refer to a corpse (Matt 27:58; Luke 17:37). Here again, however, Pauline usage is distinctive and deserves careful study (see Schnelle 1996: 55-59). To some extent Paul's use of *sōma* and *sarx* overlaps. He can use *sōma* in a neutral sense meaning the physical body (1 Cor 13:3; Gal 6:17). Occasionally he can even use it in a bad sense like that of *sarx,* in expressions such as "body of sin" (Rom 6:6) or "body of death" (7:24), and in Col 2:11 he talks of "putting off the body *(sōma)* of the flesh *(sarx)*." But *sōma* can have a good meaning that *sarx* never has. Paul can affirm that "the body is meant . . . for the Lord," "your bodies are members of Christ," and "your body is a temple of the Holy Spirit" (1 Cor 6:13, 15, 19). Here Paul means something more than merely the physical body: *sōma* denotes "the outward, visible, concrete manifestation of the individual person" (F. C. Grant 1950: 163); "man as a whole, man as a person" (Schütz, Wibbing, and Motyer, 235); or "the comprehensive expression of the human self" (Schnelle, 57). Thus *sōma* can be used to mean the self: when Paul says "present your bodies *(sōmata)* as a living sacrifice" (Rom 12:1), what he is saying in effect is "offer your very selves" (NEB). The difference between *sarx* and *sōma* is shown particularly by the fact that the *sarx* does not survive death; "flesh and blood cannot inherit the kingdom of God" (1 Cor 15:50). There is no resurrection of the *sarx,* but there is a resurrection of the *sōma,* for the earthly body will be transformed by God into a spiritual, heavenly body (15:42-57; see further, 20-4.4b).

The term *psychē* is roughly the equivalent of the OT *nephesh,* and refers to the life principle in both animals and human beings, and in some contexts to earthly life itself. Traditionally it has been translated "soul," and while in some cases that might be appropriate (Matt 10:28; Heb 6:19; 1 Pet 2:11), generally it is not. *Psychē* can mean one's life (Mark 10:45; John 10:11; Phil 2:30), and in some texts is virtually the equivalent of the self: "What shall it profit a man, if he shall gain the whole world, and lose his own soul?" (Mark 8:36 KJV) can be rendered "What does a man gain by winning the whole world at the cost of his true self?" (NEB). But *psychē* tends to refer to this life, so that the adjective *psychikos* means "pertaining to the life of the natural world" and can be contrasted with *pneumatikos* or "spiritual" (1 Cor 15:44). Thus it can refer to "unspiritual" persons (2:14) and to "worldly" people (Jude 19).

The term *kardia*, usually translated "heart," is roughly the equivalent of the OT *lēv*, and refers to the center and source of the whole inner life, with its thinking (2 Cor 4:6) and volition (Rom 2:15) as well as emotions, wishes, and desires (1:24). Jesus emphasizes the heart as the center of human motivation: "Out of the heart come evil intentions . . ." (Matt 15:19; cf. 5:28). But those who respond to God's grace can become "pure in heart" (5:8). The heart can be "hard and impenitent" (Rom 2:5), but it is also with the heart that one believes (10:10), and God's love can be poured into our hearts through the Holy Spirit (5:5).

While *kardia* can be used to refer to what we would call the mind, unlike the OT the NT does have a separate word for the mind, *nous*. It denotes the understanding and the intellect, and is the seat of reason in contrast to emotion (1 Cor 14:14-15). It can also refer to an attitude or way of thinking (Rom 12:2). As Whiteley (1964) points out, *nous* "is not as such a privileged part or rather aspect of man" (43). Thus it is possible to have "a debased mind" (Rom 1:28), though it is also possible for the mind to be renewed "so that you may discern what is the will of God" (12:2).

The term *pneuma*, usually translated "spirit," can (like the OT *rûach*) also mean "wind" (John 3:8) and "breath" (2 Thess 2:8). In the NT it is used especially of the Holy Spirit (see 5-3), but as in the OT, human beings have a spirit also (see 1 Cor 2:11, where Paul draws an analogy between the two). *Pneuma* denotes the life or vital force, what gives life to the body, so that "the body without the spirit is dead" (Jas 2:26). To yield up the spirit means to die (Matt 27:50), but a few NT texts speak of "spirits" as people living on in a future life (Heb 12:23; 1 Pet 3:19). In addition, *pneuma* can mean "the source and seat of insight, feeling and will" (Arndt and Gingrich 1957: 681). It is that aspect of a person which is most open to the divine Spirit (Matt 5:3; Rom 8:16); however, "the *pneuma* unique to each person individually . . . is not removed by the Spirit of God or of Christ but is taken up and transformed" (Schnelle 1996: 46).

Finally, as in the OT, strong emotions can be connected not with the heart but with the intestines. Thus *splanchna* = "the inward parts" (KJV, usually "bowels") is used of the seat of the emotions such as love, sympathy, compassion, and longing (Phil 1:8; Col 3:12).

16-3.2. SIN

a. Creation and Fall

As in the OT, the NT understanding of human nature is grounded in its belief in God as creator (see the fuller discussion in 2-3). Though it lacks anything comparable to the major, poetic OT passages on creation, the NT clearly assumes and accepts the OT proclamation of God as creator. It assumes therefore that all human beings, whether they acknowledge it or not, owe their life and their very existence to God: "In him we live and move and have our being" (Acts 17:28).

The NT also assumes that human beings are created in the image of God and that this image has been defaced by sin, but it goes beyond the OT in asserting that only through Christ, who is the true image of God, can the image be restored to human beings (see 2-3.2b).

More so than the OT, the NT sees human beings as "a good thing gone wrong." Unlike the OT, the NT does go back to the story of the fall in Gen 3 and draw out its implications for an understanding of human nature. In the light of what God has done for humankind in Christ, it brings out in a new way the true nature and extent of human sinfulness.

b. All Have Sinned

The NT builds on the OT understanding of human sinfulness (above, 16-1.2), but expands and deepens it. Everywhere in the NT the universality of human sin is taken for granted. Jesus assumes that all human beings are sinners (Matt 7:11; Luke 13:1-5; John 8:7; cf. Kümmel 1963: 19-31; Gelin and Descamps 1964: 63-89). He took up John the Baptist's call to repentance (Mark 1:15). He came "to call not the righteous but sinners to repentance" (Luke 5:32), taught his followers to pray for forgiveness (Matt 6:12), and himself pronounced the forgiveness of sins (Mark 2:10). Sin, he taught, is found not just in outward acts but in the inner motivation (Matt 5:17-48). Jesus assumed throughout his preaching and teaching that "before God human beings can know themselves only as sinners" (Schnelle 1996: 25). Paul is the most systematic in his approach, especially in the discussion of Rom 1:18–3:20. His conclusion is set out in 3:9-20 and summarized in 3:9: "All, both Jews and Greeks, are under the power of sin." According to 1 John 1:8, "If we say that we have no sin, we deceive ourselves, and the truth is not in us." The author of Hebrews is equally conscious of "the sin that clings so closely" (12:1).

c. The Nature of Sin

The NT understands sin in two fundamental ways. On the one hand, like the OT, it emphasizes human responsibility: the root of sin lies in rebellion against God, and it issues in disobedience and folly. On the other hand, however, the NT also sees sin as a power that enslaves human beings, linking it with Satan and the powers of evil, and with the original sin of the ancestors of the human race.

i. As in the OT, sin is basically rebellion against God. In the parable of the prodigal son (Luke 15:11-32), the son rebels against the father and goes his own way. For Paul it is an observable fact that though created by God, human beings worship and serve the creature rather than the Creator, and like the OT he sees idolatry, the worship of anything less than the one true God, as the root of all sin (Rom 1:18-23). From one point of view Paul's contribution to the understanding of the human condition can be said to be "a tremendous deepening of the conception of human responsibility" (F. C. Grant 1950: 174). The author of Hebrews warns his readers not to be rebellious like the Israelites in the wilderness (3:7-18).

Rebellion against God issues in a lifestyle that is contrary to God's will for his children. Jesus holds people responsible for their actions; for him "sin is a deliberate, wilful, evil deed" (McCasland 1962: 247). Paul's analysis in Rom 1 and 2 shows how, although Jews have the revelation of God's will in the Torah and Gentiles know God's ethical demands through conscience (cf. 18-3.3e.ii), both Jews and Gentiles disobey and fail to keep God's law.

Though the understanding of sin as folly is not as prominent as in the OT, it is also found in the NT. Jesus, for example, contrasts the wise and foolish men who built their houses on differing foundations (Matt 7:24-27). He characterizes the person who builds his life on material things but ignores God as a fool (Luke 12:20). What the world regards as "wisdom" is in effect folly, while paradoxically it is the "folly" of preaching that manifests the divine wisdom (1 Cor 1:18-31). Those who live godless lives demonstrate their folly (2 Tim 3:9).

ii. The NT also links sin with the power of evil that lies outside of human beings (for the NT understanding of Satan and the powers of evil, see 4-3). What is merely hinted at by the role of the serpent in Gen 3 (cf. *Wis* 2:23-24), is made explicit in the NT: sin is the result of the onslaught of Satan. Jesus saw human beings as in the grip of the devil (John 8:44) and held that "everyone who commits sin is a slave to sin" (8:34). For Paul, too, humans are enslaved to Satan and to the principalities and powers. He frequently speaks of "sin" in the singular in a way that suggests it should be spelled with a capital S, for it is a power to which human beings are subject (Rom 6:17; cf. Gelin and Descamps 1964: 57). The helplessness of human beings in the face of the power of sin is brought out by Paul in a key passage, Rom 7:14-25. The basic problem of human nature is not that of not knowing what is right, for even when people know what is right they do wrong: "I do not do the good I want, but the evil I do not want is what I do" (v. 19). Despite the use of "I" throughout this passage, which has led some commentators to see it as strongly autobiographical, it is best seen as part of Paul's general analysis of the human condition (cf. Childs 1992: 582-83). As noted above, sin in part consists of disobedience of God's law. In some texts, surprisingly, Paul sees "law" itself almost as an evil power that causes sin and enslaves human beings (cf. Rom 7:5-13, and see more fully 18-3.3b).

Paul's analysis of sin is carried a stage further in those passages where he traces human sinfulness back to Adam, the ancestor of the human race (see Whiteley 1964: 45-53). As noted in 7-3.4a, in Rom 5 and 1 Cor 15 Paul employs a form of typology, drawing out a parallel between Adam and Christ. It is a typology, however, in which the *contrast* is more important than the *comparison*. What the two have in common is that they are representative figures: Adam represents humanity in rebellion against God, whereas Christ represents the new humanity (cf. Sabourin 1973: 70; Childs 1992: 583-84). Thus Paul says that "sin came into the world through one man" (Rom 5:12), and "by the one man's disobedience the many were made sinners *(hamartōloi katestathēsan hoi polloi)*" (5:19). "In Adam" human beings are under the dominion of sin and death (1 Cor 15:21-22). On this view, "Adam and Eve did not sin for themselves alone, but, from their privileged position as the first, originally sinless couple, act as representatives for the human race. Since then, sin, sinfulness, and the consequences of sin have marred all. Every child of Adam encounters a race marked by sin, condemnation and death (Rom. 5:12-21)" (Doriani 1996: 736).

The two fundamental ways in which the NT views human sin stand in considerable tension with one another (cf. the foreshadowing of this in the late OT period in *Sirach;* see above, 16-1.2c.ii). The rebellion/disobedience/folly model stresses human responsibility and choice, whereas the enslavement-to-Satan-and-sin/inheritance-of-Adam's-sin model on its own is highly deterministic. The tension is greatest when the two views are directly juxtaposed, as in John 8:44 where Jesus says, "You are from your father the devil, and you choose to do your father's desires," or in Rom 5:12 where Paul says, "Sin came into the world through one man [Adam], and death came through sin, and so death spread to all because all have sinned"; here "sin is at once both fate and an act" (Schnelle 1996: 64). Of course, the central message of the NT is that through the Christ event and especially Jesus' atoning death on the cross, the power of sin has been defeated and a new humanity has come into existence. "Whether it is depicted as individual acts or as a universal power threatening all humankind, sin is everywhere prevalent and is overcome only in union with Jesus through a faith that confesses him to be the Christ" (Fischer, Getty, and Schreiter 1996: 921). There remains, however, the tension between summoning people to decide and accept the gospel and recognizing that salvation is purely a gift of God's grace. A canonical BT must strive to do justice to *both* emphases and, as in the closely related issue of predestination and free will (see 11-3.2b), must affirm what to human minds remains a paradox.

16-3.3. JUDGMENT

As in the OT, sin is seen as bringing with it certain inevitable consequences. Judgment continues to be a major theme in the NT. God is "the one who judges all people impartially according to their deeds" (1 Pet 1:17). Judgment cannot be dismissed as a later or peripheral theme in the NT; nowhere is it more prominent than in the teaching (especially the parables) of Jesus himself.

In the OT it is primarily the nation that is judged. "In the New Testament, while social and communal responsibility is not overlooked, the emphasis in judgment is on what the individual does or does not do" (Morris 1960: 49).

a. The Wrath of God/the Lamb

Judgment stems from the attitude of the holy God to sin, an attitude frequently described in the NT as "wrath" *(orgē)*. Like John the Baptist (Matt 3:7), Jesus warned of the wrath to come (Luke 21:23; John 3:36). Paul can talk about "the wrath *(orgē)* of God" which is "revealed from heaven against all ungodliness and wickedness" (Rom 1:18; the term is frequent in Paul), and the writer of Revelation refers to "the wrath of the Lamb" (6:16). The modern mind is often uncomfortable with talk of "wrath." In the NT it does not denote an unreasonable emotion; God does not "get mad" and lose his temper. He is not capricious and unpredictable like the pagan gods (cf. Beker 1987: 59). "If there are those who reject him and thereby bring upon themselves his wrath, they reject not the cosmic sadist whose obstacle race they have failed to complete, but the one who in his love has offered himself to all mankind. And it is he who will confront us at the judgment" (Travis 1986: 53).

Dodd argued that in Paul "wrath" does not really have its root in God (1959: 47-50). The phrase "wrath of God," he claimed, occurs only three times in Paul (Rom 1:18; Col 3:6; Eph 5:6), and the verb *orgizō* = "to be angry" is never used with God as subject. Dodd's conclusion was that wrath does not describe "the attitude of God to man" but rather "an inevitable process of cause and effect in a moral universe" (50). Such a view, however, is not in accordance with the NT understanding; "we can rationalize the idea in that way, if we like, but it would be a mistake to suppose that the NT writers did so" (A. Richardson 1958: 76). While sin inevitably brings certain consequences, "The God of the New Testament does not sit back and let 'natural' laws bring about the defeat of evil: He is actively opposed to evil in every shape and form. . . . It is difficult to see what meaning can be attached to an 'impersonal process' (as applied to moral affairs) in a universe where God is all-powerful and omnipresent. . . . The wrath of God is a necessary consequence of his holiness" (Morris 1960: 70-71). On the other hand, of course, talk of God's judgment and wrath must never be divorced from what the NT as a whole says about God's attitude to the sinner. After a detailed review of all the relevant Pauline passages, Whiteley (1964) concludes that "in all cases *orgē* refers to what [God] will do or is already doing. It must be emphasized, however, that 'wrath' is the action of a personal God Who hates sin. He is far from being 'emotionally' neutral, but loves sinners" (69).

b. Now Is the Judgment

In the NT judgment is primarily a future event (see below, 16-4.3). But it is also something that takes place here and now.

Judgment as a present reality is especially stressed in John's Gospel: "Now is the judgment" (12:31). While it is true that the primary purpose of Christ's coming was "not to judge the world, but to save the world" (12:47; cf. 3:17), nevertheless Jesus can also say, "I came into this world for judgment" (9:39). Jesus' ministry provokes a *krisis,* a judgment or separation, for even now a person is judged in accordance with how he or she reacts to the claims of Christ: "This is the judgment, that the light has come into the world, and people loved darkness rather than light because their deeds were evil" (3:19).

Paul also sees God's judgment at work in the present in a variety of ways. The wrath of God even now falls on the ungodly and the wicked (Rom 1:18). Paul sees one form of present judgment in God's "giving up" (*paradidōmi* = "hand over, deliver") those who rebel against him "to a debased mind and to things that should not be done" (1:28); impurity and depravity, as it were, become their own punishment. God's judgment is present within the Corinthian church, disciplining believers (1 Cor 11:32; cf. 2 Thess 1:5). The state too can be an agent of God's wrath in the present (Rom 13:4-5).

"By the choices we make, by the way we respond when confronted by Christ and his gospel, we bring judgment on ourselves" (Travis 1986: 53). Present judgment is an anticipation of the final judgment (see 16-4.3); but as long as people live, they have an opportunity to repent and turn to God.

c. Sin and Death

More so than in the OT the NT makes a strong connection between sin and death. Paul takes over from the OT the view that death is a consequence of Adam's sin (Rom 5:15; see 20-4.2c). But for Paul death means basically separation from God. "To set the mind on the flesh is death, but to set the mind on the Spirit is life and peace" (8:6). It follows that people can be alive or dead now, in the present. Paul writes to Christian converts in Ephesians, "Even when we were dead through our trespasses, [God] made us alive together with Christ" (2:5; cf. Rom 6:11). See further, 20-3.1.

16-3.4. ANXIETY

Like the OT, the NT also sees the human condition as characterized by anxiety. It employs a vocabulary that includes *merimna* (anxiety, worry, care), *merimnaō* (to be anxious or concerned), and *amerimnos* (free from anxiety). Older translations such as the KJV obscure the meaning of several passages by employing the word "care," which has changed its meaning in English. Thus in Phil 4:6 (KJV) Paul tells his readers, "Be careful for nothing." In modern usage it is generally a wise thing to be "careful," but of course what Paul really meant was, "Do not worry about anything" (TEV, NRSV, CEV) or "Do not be anxious about anything" (NIV). (In a couple texts Paul uses *merimnaō* not in the sense of being anxious but of being genuinely concerned for others; see 1 Cor 12:25; Phil 2:20.)

As in the OT, the NT recognizes that anxiety covers a spectrum of emotions that at one end shades over into dread and fear. In the NT also, "fear" is used in two senses: negatively, in relation to a threat, as when Joseph feared to return to a Judea ruled by Herod Archelaus (Matt 2:22), and positively, as an appropriate "fear of the Lord" (Luke 1:50; 2 Cor 5:11).

Again like the OT, the NT to some extent sees anxiety "as the natural reaction of man to poverty, hunger and other troubles which befall him in his daily life. Oppressed by the burdens laid upon him, man imagines himself delivered to a fate before which he stands powerless" (Goetzmann 1975: 277). Everyone is subject to "the cares of the world" (Matt 13:22), and is tempted to find false security in riches (Mark 4:19) or to find escape in "dissipation and drunkenness" (Luke 21:34). Family responsibilities can cause anxiety (Luke 2:48; 1 Cor 7:32-34), and despite his own admonitions (1 Cor 7:32; Phil 4:6), Paul confesses to being "under daily pressure because of my anxiety for all the churches" (2 Cor 11:28; cf. Phil 2:28).

More so than the OT, however, the NT, and especially Jesus himself, sees anxiety as a sign of lack of faith in God's providential care. For Jesus "anxiety is a subtle insinuation that God is either unable or disinclined to see to our welfare" (Enlow 1996: 28). In the Sermon on the Mount (Matt 6:25-34//Luke 12:22-31), "Jesus' teaching on anxiety strikes a new and radical note, for he outlaws anxiety and brands it as pagan and worldly" (P. E. Davies 1962: 155; cf. Schnelle 1996: 12). He tells his followers, "Do not worry about your life, what you will eat or what you will drink, or about your body, what you will wear" (Matt 6:25). Anxiety is caused by getting one's priorities wrong: it is conquered by seeking first God's kingdom and righteousness, for when that is done, God will provide for all one's needs (6:33). Similarly Martha was "worried and distracted by many things," whereas in fact only one thing was really necessary, i.e., listening to and obeying the teaching of Jesus (Luke 10:38-42; see Goetzmann 1975: 278). In a similar vein Peter advises his readers: "Cast all your anxiety on him [God], because he cares for you" (1 Pet 5:7).

16-3.5. SUFFERING

As in the OT, suffering covers a broad spectrum (see the discussion in Gerstenberger and Schrage 1980: 155-63). Like the OT, the NT recognizes the existence of suffering that is capable of being relieved and suffering for which there is no remedy. While it calls for social justice (see 19-3.3c), there was much less opportunity than in ancient Israel for the earliest Christian communities to influence or change society. Nevertheless, believers are called to relieve suffering wherever this is possible (cf. Matt 25:31-46; Luke 10:30-37; Jas 2:15-16; 1 John 3:17). The NT emphasizes that sickness and disease are not God's will for his children and calls on the church to continue Jesus' ministry of healing (see 20-3.3).

While some passages in the NT correlate sin and suffering, especially sickness (Matt 9:1-8; Luke 18:29-30; Acts 5:1-11; James 5:16), perhaps the most striking feature of the NT's approach is its rejection of any sweeping, simplistic answers along piety-prosperity lines. In Luke 13:1-5 Jesus refers to two recent disasters in which a number of people had lost their lives, the massacre of some Galileans by the Romans and the collapse of a tower; he specifically rejects any idea that the victims must have been worse sinners than anyone else (see Gerstenberger and Schrage 1980: 228-29). John 9, the story of the man blind from birth, raises the question in very pointed fashion. When an infant is born with a handicap, whose fault is it, the child's (hardly possible at such an age) or the parents' (no doubt an answer given by some)? Jesus' response to the question is a firm "neither." Linked with this is the fact that in some passages of the NT not God but Satan is said to be the originator of suffering (Luke 13:16; Acts 10:38; 2 Cor 12:7).

The fact is that in the NT as a whole, and not least in the teaching of Jesus, the OT theme of the suffering of God's righteous servants (16-1.5c) is picked up and the piety-prosperity equation is virtually reversed. Following Jesus may well bring suffering rather than long life, good health, and material rewards (Matt 10:17-23; 24:9; Mark 13:9-11; Luke 21:12-19; cf. Scharbert and Schmid 1981: 894-95). Jesus does not say (as parts of the OT say), "Blessed are the rich," but rather "Blessed are you who are poor" (Luke 6:20). He tells people to take up their cross and follow him (Mark 8:34 and //s).

In the NT, following Christ can lead on occasion to martyrdom, as in the case of Stephen (Acts 7:54-60) and Antipas (Rev 2:13). Paul's letters vividly reveal the sufferings that he endured as a faithful servant of Christ (2 Cor 11:23-33; 12:10). In Phil 1:29 he tells the Philippians that God "has graciously granted you the privilege not only of believing in Christ, but of suffering for him as well." Paul can see this as a sharing in the redemptive suffering of Christ himself (see Piper 1962c: 452), and can even rejoice in his sufferings (Col 1:24; cf. Matt 5:12). Similarly Peter tells his readers to "rejoice insofar as you are sharing Christ's sufferings"; he is speaking of suffering "as a Christian" and not for some crime committed (1 Pet 4:13-16). 1 Pet 2:18-25 is addressed in the first instance to slaves, but its teaching may readily be extended to all Christians: by enduring unjust suffering believers are following in the steps of Christ, the Suffering Servant (on this passage, see Osborne 1983). Hebrews cites OT precedents for this kind of suffering (11:35-38; see Gerstenberger and Schrage 1980: 146-49). Suffering for the name of Jesus (Mark 13:13; John 15:21; 1 Pet 4:14; Rev 2:13) can be a powerful form of Christian witness.

With the OT the NT can see suffering as a test (Jas 1:2-3; 1 Pet 1:6-9; 4:12) or as a form of discipline (Heb 12:3-11), and Paul points out how it can have positive results: "Suffering produces endurance, and endurance produces character, and character produces hope" (Rom 5:3-5). In the face of suffering, what is needed is *hypomonē,* or "patient endurance" (Rom 5:3; 2 Cor 1:6; Heb 10:36; 12:1; Jas 1:3-4; Rev 1:9; 2:3; 3:10; etc.). Suffering can also be better endured when it is shared, and within the Christian community "if one member suffers, all suffer together with it" (1 Cor 12:26). "Belonging to Christ and his body rescues one from isolation even in suffering" (Gerstenberger and Schrage 1980: 255). To share Christ's sufferings means, like him, identifying with and reaching out in compassion to those who suffer (cf. G. G. Hull 1991).

But the most distinctive contribution of the NT is brought to a focus in the suffering and death of Jesus himself (see Piper 1962c: 452). Christ is consistently portrayed in the NT as sinless, and certainly he was totally innocent of the charges brought against him (cf. 9-3.2). Thus the piety-prosperity equation is completely shattered, and the cross provides the extreme example of undeserved suffering. Yet in accordance with Isa 53, Christ's suffering is not meaningless but is rather vicarious and redemptive. Most of all, faith in the incarnation affirms that God is not remote from human existence and human suffering but in Christ has entered into it.

New Testament: Consummation

16-4. THE COMING JUDGMENT

16-4.1. HUMAN NATURE

Human nature will not change short of the final consummation. Until the last judgment human beings will continue to be divided into evildoers and righteous (Rev 22:11).

16-4.2. SIN

The sinfulness of human nature will persist. Indeed, the period between the present and the final end will see an intensification of evil (see more fully, 4-4).

16-4.3. JUDGMENT

The NT makes central the expectation which is just emerging in the late OT (16-3.3) that all persons must face future judgment. This firm belief pervades the entire NT.

a. The Day of Judgment

The imminence of the judgment was a major theme in the preaching of John the Baptist (cf. Scobie 1964: chap. 5); "Even now," he declared, "the ax is lying at the root of the trees" (Matt 3:10//Luke 3:9). In light of this, John called on his hearers to repent, be baptized, and live righteous lives. The Coming One of whom John spoke would baptize not only with the gift of the Holy Spirit, but also with the fire of judgment (Matt 3:11//Luke 3:16; cf. 5-3.1b). For the Gospel writers, that coming one was Jesus, and future judgment continued to be a major theme in Jesus' teaching, especially in many of his parables. On one count twelve of Jesus' thirty-six longer parables depict the last judgment (Ewert 1980: 121). All peoples will be gathered before the judgment throne of the Son of Man (Matt 25:32), and everyone will have to give an account of their lives (12:36-37). Like John, Jesus spoke of judgment in terms of fire (7:19; 25:41). A final judgment is clearly asserted in John 5:29 (cf. 1 John 4:17). According to Acts, it was a major feature of early Christian preaching (10:42; 17:31; 24:25).

Picking up the OT expression, Paul equates "the day of the Lord" (see 2-4.3) with the day of judgment (1 Thess 5:2; 1 Cor 5:5; etc.). He can also refer to "the day of wrath" (Rom 2:5) or simply "the day" (2:16; 1 Cor 3:13). On that day "we will all stand before the judgment seat of God" (Rom 14:10). For Hebrews "eternal judgment" is one of the fundamentals of the faith (6:1-2; cf. 10:27; 12:23). James reminds his readers that "there is one lawgiver and judge who is able to save and to destroy" (4:12; cf. 5:9). At the last day God will "execute judgment on all" (Jude 15). All people "will have to give an accounting to him who stands ready to judge the living and the dead" (1 Pet 4:5). Judgment is a recurring theme in the book of Revelation, and the final judgment is portrayed in graphic terms, especially in 20:11-15 when all the dead stand before God's throne and the books are opened.

This all-pervasive emphasis on a last judgment "stresses man's accountability and the certainty that justice will finally triumph over all the wrongs which are part and parcel of life here and now" (Morris 1960: 72). Final judgment is closely linked to present judgment (above, 16-3.3b): "The final judgment means God's underlining and ratification of the relationship towards him which we have chosen in this life. If we have fellowship with God now, we shall enter into a fuller experience of his presence then. If we do not know him now, we shall not know him then." Heaven and hell are not so much future reward and punishment as "the logical outcome of our relationship to God in this life" (Travis 1986: 54).

b. The Role of Christ

A distinctive feature of the expectation of the judgment in the NT is the role to be played by Christ as *the agent of God's judgment.* In Matt 25:31 the judge is the Son of Man (= Christ). According to Acts 10:42, Christ "is the one ordained by God as judge of the living and the dead" (cf. 17:31), and 2 Cor 5:10 declares that "all of us must appear before the judgment seat of Christ." Similarly in John 5:22, the Father "has given all judgment to the Son." Hence the last day can be referred to as "the day of our Lord Jesus Christ" (1 Cor 1:8).

Christ's role in the judgment does not make it any less the judgment of God. Paul speaks equally of "the judgment seat of God" (Rom 14:10) and "the judgment seat of Christ" (2 Cor 5:10). Sinners will have to face "God's wrath" (John 3:36) but also "the wrath of the Lamb" (Rev 6:16). That this involves no contradiction is seen most clearly in Rom 2:16, where Paul speaks of "the day when . . . God, through Jesus Christ, will judge the secret thoughts of all" (cf. John 5:22; Acts 17:31).

Thus, while the judgment is to be taken with the utmost seriousness, for believers the fact that Christ is the judge is a ground of hope. "Who is to condemn? It is Christ Jesus, who died, yes, who was raised, who is at the right hand of God, who indeed intercedes for us" (Rom 8:34; cf. Heb 6:10; 1 John 4:17).

c. The Criterion of Judgment

Throughout the NT the criterion of judgment is "deeds" or "works." Those who are condemned in the judgment are "evildoers" (Matt 13:41). Nowhere are the criteria for judgment spelled out more clearly than in Jesus' vision of the sheep and the goats; people will be judged on the basis of their behavior toward the hungry, thirsty, strangers, naked, sick, and imprisoned (25:31-46). According to 1 Pet 1:17, all people will be judged "impartially according to their deeds." In John's vision of the judgment, "books were opened. . . . And the dead were judged according to their works, as recorded in the books" (Rev 20:12).

This emphasis on judgment on the basis of how a person has lived is also found in Paul: God, he says, "will repay according to each one's deeds" (Rom 2:6; cf. vv. 7-8), "for all of us must appear before the judgment seat of Christ, so that each may receive recompense for what has been done in the body, whether good or evil" (2 Cor 5:10). For many, such texts pose a major problem in light of the typical Pauline emphasis that no one will be justified by works, but only by grace, through faith in Christ, who saves us from the wrath of God (Rom 5:9;

1 Thess 5:9; cf. 18-3.3b). How can believers be *both* justified by faith *and* judged by works? N. M. Watson's (1983) careful analysis of the apparently conflicting texts helpfully emphasizes that Paul's letters are addressed to different audiences: "the message of justification to those like the Galatians who were overscrupulous, fearfully and meticulously keeping the law in order to earn salvation, and the warning of judgment to those like the Corinthians who were living in the illusion that they were free to do whatever they wished" (214). Even where the emphasis falls on judgment, however, "there are indications in these passages that Paul does not intend the message of judgment to be his last word to his readers but rather as the word they need to hear so long as they remain in a state of illusion" (216). The dominant emphasis in Paul remains on the fact that sinful human beings cannot be freed from their sinful nature by their own efforts so as to be acquitted at the judgment.

> The only one who can hope for such a pardon . . . is the one to whom God the creator grants, as an act of free grace, a new nature in righteousness and the spiritual ability to do what is right, and then establishes at the judgment an advocate at his or her side, against whom no accuser can appear. According to Paul, this is precisely what happens in Christ. By virtue of the atoning death of Jesus, sinners obtain liberation from sin and acquire a new nature in righteousness (cf. 2 Cor. 5:17, 21). The Spirit then enables the Christian to fulfil the just requirement of the Law (Gal. 5:18, 22ff.; Rom. 8:4ff.). And finally, Christ, the one who was given over to death and then raised "for us," steps in at the final judgment as an advocate for those who believe (cf. Rom. 8:34; Heb. 7:25; 9:24; 1 John 2:1f.; Rev. 3:5). (Stuhlmacher 1994: 47; cf. Travis 1986: 53-54)

d. The Fate of the Unrighteous

The reward of the righteous in the future life is clearly affirmed in the NT (see further, 20-4). The fate of the unrighteous has occasioned much discussion and controversy (see the various views, along with critiques, presented in Crockett 1992). Basically there are three main options.

i. *Universalism* is the belief that ultimately all persons will be saved (see Toon 1986: 183-97; Fudge 1994: 199-206); it is as old as Origen (ca. 185–ca. 254) and has found numerous supporters in modern times. Proponents of this view point especially to some texts that use the word "all": "all Israel will be saved" (Rom 11:26); "God has imprisoned all in disobedience so that he may be merciful to all" (11:32); "for as all die in Adam, so all will be made alive in Christ" (1 Cor 15:22; cf. John 12:32; Rom 5:18). They also appeal to the pictures of the final reconciliation of all things (Eph 1:10; Col 1:19-20), and "the time of universal restoration" (*apokatastasis*, Acts 3:21, but see 3:23). It is very doubtful, however, if these few texts can bear the theological weight that is put upon them (see commentaries; Ewert 1980: 141-45). God may *desire* the salvation of all (1 Tim 2:4; 2 Pet 3:9), and in principle Christ may have died for the sins of the whole world (1 John 2:2; cf. Heb 2:9), but people are saved only when they respond in faith. Universalism tends to depend more on theological arguments; e.g., if God is love and God is all-powerful, then ultimately nothing can thwart God's purpose that is to save all humankind.

Universalism can be held only by ignoring the considerable biblical evidence for a *final separation*. According to Dan 12:2, some go to everlasting life, some to everlasting shame. Nowhere is this more clearly portrayed than in the teaching of Jesus, including some of his most striking parables, such as the wheat and the weeds (Matt 13:24-30), the good and the bad catch (13:47-50), the sheep and the goats (25:31-46), and Luke 16:19-31 where, we are told, between Dives and Lazarus, after death, "a great chasm has been fixed" (v. 26). In John 5:28-29 Jesus distinguishes clearly between "the resurrection of life" and "the resurrection of condemnation." Paul too envisages a final judgment in which "each may receive recompense for what has been done in the body, whether good or evil" (2 Cor 5:10; cf. 2 Thess 1:7-9). In the judgment scene of Rev 20:11-15, a separation is made depending on whether or not one's name is written in the book of life. This body of evidence makes it clear that universalism cannot be considered truly biblical.

A variant of out-and-out universalism accepts the biblical evidence for separation and for the punishment of the unrighteous, but sees the punishment in terms of an interim state of "purgatory" (see Toon 1986: 109-36; Hayes in Crockett 1992: 91-118). On this view either all, or at least some, of those whose sins disqualify them from heaven experience a purifying fire that eventually purges them of their sins and allows them to enter heaven. Fire, it is argued, can be a symbol of refining, not just destruction (cf. Zech 13:9; Mal 3:2; 1 Cor 3:12-15). There is, however, no convincing scriptural basis for the belief in purgatory (see Ewert 1980: 61; Crockett 1992: 119-26); it is the product of (Western, Roman Catholic) church tradition. It has been generally rejected by Protestants, particularly because they have seen it as implying that salvation has in some sense to be merited, whereas according to Scripture salvation can only be the free gift of God.

ii. We noted above the clear biblical evidence for a *separation* of righteous and unrighteous after death. The most common view has been that the unrighteous are condemned to *eternal punishment* in hell (see Walvoord in Crockett 1992: 11-28). It is in the teaching of Jesus that we find almost all the references to "Gehenna," usually translated as "hell" (Gk. *geenna;* Aram. *gēhinnām;* Heb. *gē hinnōm*). The word originally signified a valley just south of Jerusalem, the site of a pagan shrine and of child sacrifices (Jer 7:31), on that account desecrated by King Josiah (2 Kgs 23:10). Jeremiah saw it as the site of God's future judgment on his people (Jer 7:32; 19:6). Evidently, because of its associations, it became the city dump of Jerusalem, where garbage was perpetually burned (Ewert 1980:

133; Fudge 1994: 96-99). By NT times the term had come to signify the place of eschatological punishment of the wicked (Michl 1981b: 370). Hades (Gk. *ha(i)-dēs* = Heb. *sheʾôl*), though sometimes translated "hell," signifies in the OT the underworld or abode of the dead, with no connotation of reward or punishment (see more fully, 20-2.3). Hades is used in this sense also in the NT (Matt 16:18; Acts 2:27, 31; Rev 1:18; 20:13), the single exception being Luke 16:23, where it refers to a place of future torment.

The NT is generally restrained in its description of hell (cf. Bietenhard 1976a: 209), in distinction from both rabbinic literature and later Christian writers. To be sure, it is a place where there will be "weeping and gnashing of teeth" (Matt 8:12; cf. Luke 6:25). The most common image is that of *fire*. John the Baptist proclaimed a coming judgment by fire (Matt 3:10). Jesus refers to the "Gehenna of fire" (5:22; 18:9), "the unquenchable fire" (*to pyr to asbeston,* Mark 9:43), "the furnace *(kaminos)* of fire" (Matt 13:42). Revelation has a series of references to "the lake of fire," the ultimate destination of the beast and the false prophet (19:20), the devil (20:10), Death and Hades (20:14), but also of sinners (20:15; 21:8). Fire, on this view, is understood as a means of torture, and this is certainly so in the case of Dives, who after death "was being tormented" *(huparchōn en basanois)* and was "in agony in these flames" (Luke 16:23-24).

The other common image is that of *darkness*. Jesus talks of those who will be consigned to "outer darkness *(to skotos to exōteron)*" (Matt 8:12; 22:13; 25:30), while 2 Pet 2:17 (cf. Jude 13) refers to "deepest darkness."

That the punishment of hell is everlasting is suggested particularly by the use of the adjective *aiōnios*, generally translated "eternal" or "everlasting" and understood as referring to endless time (see Walvoord in Crockett 1992: 23-27). Thus, for example, in the parable of the sheep and the goats, the "goats" are told, "Depart from me into the eternal fire *(to pyr to aiōnion)* prepared for the devil and his angels" (Matt 25:41). Eternal punishment is also envisaged in Rev 14:10-11, where those who worship the beast "will be tormented with fire. . . . And the smoke of their torment goes up forever and ever" (cf. also Dan 12:2; Matt 18:8; Heb 6:2; Rev 20:10).

Arguments that hell must be taken "literally" (cf. Walvoord in Crockett 1992: 28) are largely beside the point. All language referring to realities beyond human experience is bound to be metaphorical or symbolic; the unknown can only be described in terms of the known. That this is true of the NT picture of hell is suggested especially by the fact that the two main images are not literally compatible: if an eternal fire burns in Gehenna, it can hardly be a place of total darkness (cf. Crockett, 30)! These images are symbolic, but symbols are a very powerful means of conveying truth, and the symbols of fire and darkness each in their own way point to the dreadful reality of the fate of the unrighteous (see Toon 1986: 489, 106; Crockett, 43-76).

However uncongenial to modern interpreters, this body of evidence cannot lightly be set aside.

iii. There is also, however, considerable biblical evidence for what is generally referred to as *conditional immortality* (see Pinnock in Crockett 1992: 135-66; Fudge 1994); this has been defined as "the doctrine that states that human beings are not inherently immortal, but rather have immortality conferred upon them as part of the experience of salvation" (T. Gray 1996: 14). On this view, after the resurrection and judgment only the righteous enter eternal life; the unrighteous simply pass out of existence (hence this is also known as "annihilationism"). We have noted that this view appears already in 2 *Macc* 7 (see above, 16-2.3).

The fate of the unrighteous, it is pointed out, is frequently pictured in terms of *exclusion* from the blessings of the new age. They will fail to gain admittance to the eschatological banquet (Luke 13:22-30; cf. Matt 25:12). Paul's view is that those who follow the works of the flesh "will not inherit the kingdom of God" (Gal 5:19-21; cf. 1 Cor 6:9; Eph 5:5). In Rev 22:15 the wicked find themselves outside the holy city. The metaphor of darkness, it can be argued, points in the same direction: God is light, and to be consigned to outer darkness is to be excluded from the blessings of the light.

More specifically there are texts that speak of the *annihilation* of the wicked (cf. the OT examples cited above in 16-2.3). Their fate can be described as "destruction" *(olethros);* according to 2 Thess 1:9, the unrighteous "will suffer the punishment of eternal destruction, separated from the presence of the Lord and from the glory of his might" (cf. 1 Thess 5:3; 1 Tim 6:9). Jesus counsels, "Fear him who can destroy *(apolesai)* both soul and body in hell" (Matt 10:28), and says that the fate of those who do not believe is to perish (John 3:16; 17:12; *apollumai* = "perish"); Paul refers to unbelievers as "those who are perishing *(hoi apollumenoi)*" (1 Cor 1:18; 2 Thess 2:10). Other texts use the term *apōleia:* "the gate is wide . . . that leads to destruction" (Matt 7:13); Judas is called "the son of perdition" (*ho huios tēs apōleias,* John 17:12 RSV); 2 Pet 3:7 speaks of the "destruction of the godless" (cf. Phil 3:19; 1 Tim 6:9; Heb 10:39). While the metaphor of fire may signify torture, it can be argued that it more naturally suggests total destruction. If the model for Gehenna is the city garbage dump with its perpetual fires, then it most readily points to the destruction of what is regarded as totally useless (cf. Matt 13:30; John 15:6). The metaphor of the worm that never dies (Mark 9:48), derived from Isa 66:24 (see above, 16-2.3), while it is difficult to reconcile with the metaphor of fire, probably points in the same direction (cf. Michl 1981b: 370).

This position, it can also be argued, is more consistent with the biblical view of the future life (see 20-4.3) which is *not* based on the immortality of the soul but on the resurrection of the righteous to eternal life. "Since in the biblical view men are not naturally immortal, and the gift of immortality or eternal life is conditional upon faith in Christ, those who do not have such faith will not receive immortality. They will simply cease to be" (Travis 1986: 54; cf. Pinnock in Crockett 1992: 147-49; Fudge 1994: 21-40). In support of this view it can be argued that according to the NT, only God possesses immortality (1 Tim 6:16; cf. T. Gray 1996: 16).

A major objection to conditional immortality is constituted by those texts that use the term *aiōnios* and describe the fate of the unrighteous as "eternal" or "everlasting" punishment (e.g., Matt 25:46; see above under ii.). Against this it has been argued that *aiōnios* properly means "pertaining to the (new) *aiōn*," i.e., the new age (see A. Richardson 1958: 13-16; and 20-3.1). In other words, it is used in a qualitative rather than a quantitative sense (see Fudge 1994: 73-74); *zōē aiōnios* means not "everlasting life" in a temporal sense, but "the life of the age to come." Similarly *kolasis aiōnios* (Matt 25:46) means not "everlasting punishment," but the punishment that will be meted out in the new age.

There is thus biblical evidence for both eternal punishment and conditional immortality, and it is not easy to champion one view against the other without disregarding a significant body of texts.

16-4.4. ANXIETY

Even more than the OT, the NT recognizes that the forces that call forth anxiety and fear will remain, and indeed intensify, as long as history lasts (see 3-4.2). The time before the end, as the book of Revelation amply attests, will be marked by tribulation and persecution of the faithful.

While Jesus warned his disciples to expect opposition and persecution in the future, he counseled them not to be anxious about what they will say when put on trial before the authorities (Matt 10:17-20//Mark 13:9-11//Luke 21:12-15). Mark's version of the saying brings out the fact that anxiety is basically worry about what will happen in the future: "Do not be anxious beforehand *(mē promerimnate)*" (13:11). The tribulation that precedes the end will be a time to be on guard against "the worries of this life" (Luke 21:34-36). Only with the final consummation will God's people be free from anxiety and fear.

16-4.5. SUFFERING

The ultimate solution to the problem of suffering that the NT advances is the eschatological one: suffering will be eliminated at the final consummation (see Gerstenberger and Schrage 1980: 218-24). In Jesus' teaching, those who suffer in this life will be rewarded in the next: "Blessed are you when people revile you and persecute you. . . . Rejoice and be glad, for your reward is great in heaven" (Matt 5:11-12; cf. Luke 16:19-31). In John 16:20-22 Jesus speaks of a coming time of pain and mourning, but beyond that of a time of joy at his parousia. Paul declares: "I consider that the sufferings of this present time are not worth comparing with the glory about to be revealed to us" (Rom 8:18; cf. 8:31-39), and he assures the Corinthians that "this slight momentary affliction is preparing us for an eternal weight of glory" (2 Cor 4:17). Peter anticipates a "fiery ordeal" (1 Pet 4:12), but he encourages his readers by pointing to the final consummation: "After you have suffered for a little while, the God of all grace . . . will himself restore, support, strengthen, and establish you" (5:10).

More than any other book, Revelation provides the apocalyptic solution (cf. Beker 1987: 52-54). On the one hand it is realistic in its anticipation of intensified suffering of the faithful (cf. 3-4.2); on the other hand it calls for faithful endurance and grounds this in the hope of the final victory of God. In its vision of the future, Revelation lays a strong emphasis on the final vindication of the martyrs. Already the multitude of martyrs, white-robed, serve God in heaven (Rev 7; note esp. v. 14); in Rev 20 they will reign with Christ for a thousand years prior to the final defeat of evil (cf. 3-4.4b). 21:4 echoes and reinforces the promises of Isa 25:8, 35:10, and 65:19 (Revelation adds "pain"):

> He [God] will wipe every tear from their eyes.
> Death will be no more;
> mourning and crying and pain will be no more,
> for the first things have passed away.

16-5. THE HUMAN CONDITION: THEOLOGICAL REFLECTIONS

1. One traditional definition of theology has been "a consistent view of God, man, and the world." The main focus of BT must be on God: on God's activity in creation and in history, and above all on what God has done in and through the Christ event. This, however, has implications for an understanding of human nature. It has been argued above that while what has been traditionally called "the biblical doctrine of man" or "biblical anthropology" is not presented in Scripture in a systematic or theoretical fashion, nevertheless the Bible does have a consistent though also developing and deepening understanding of the human condition; that understanding therefore has a legitimate place in BT. This does not mean that anthropology takes center stage. Bultmann's discussion of Pauline theology consists of two parts, "Man Prior to the Revelation of Faith" and "Man under Faith" (1952: 190-352); brilliant though the treatment may be in some respects, focusing basically on "man" and on the individual distorts the perspective of the NT (see the critique in Schnelle 1996: 6-10, and also the assessment in Käsemann 1971). For Christian theology it is also imperative that its understanding of human nature not be derived from modern philosophy, psychology, sociology, or any other source, but rather from Scripture, and specifically from the biblical understanding of God. "Man-talk and God-talk

are closely related and only possible as they are related to one another. . . . It is critical that anthropology be considered from a biblical perspective" (Schultz 1996: 602).

2. Both OT and NT employ a range of "anthropological" terms. The actual terminology was no doubt, in both cases, shared with the surrounding culture, but what counts for BT is the way the terms are employed in Scripture itself. It is important not to import meanings into the terms that they may have held in the ancient Near Eastern or Hellenistic worlds. It is even more important not to read these terms in the light of what "flesh," "soul," "heart," and so on may suggest to a modern reader, for that can be highly misleading. A careful study of the use and meaning of the anthropological terms in their biblical context, therefore, clears the way for broader study of the biblical assessment of the human condition. The use of *sarx* (flesh) in Paul is a case in point. The citing of individual texts out of context could easily suggest a form of dualism. In the centuries immediately following the NT, the Christian church struggled against the highly dualistic faith/philosophy of Gnosticism. The common assumption is that Christianity won that struggle, yet the question has been asked, "Did Gnosticism win after all?" Dualistic ideas did enter Christianity so that this world, matter, the human body, sexual relations, and so on all came to be viewed as essentially evil and the source of sin, whereas only what is of the "spirit" is good. This is a major deviation from the biblical view, and only a careful study of biblical anthropology can correct it. Some Christian theologians have spoken of the "total depravity" of humankind. While this is hardly a happy choice of words, what the doctrine really intends to convey is the view that no part of a human being is unaffected by sin. It is not that the flesh is evil while the heart, mind, soul, and spirit are essentially good: all are tainted by sin and therefore in need of redemption.

3. The Bible's estimate of human nature is both higher and lower than most nonbiblical faiths and philosophies. Human beings are the crown of creation, made only a little lower than the angels, yet they are also rebellious, disobedient, and foolish sinners! The Christian church has been accused of introducing a much darker picture of human nature than is found in the OT, this being reflected in the essential optimism of Judaism as against the essential pessimism of Christianity (cf. Gowan 1986: 78). This is at best a half-truth. We have seen that the OT recognizes the universality and seriousness of human sin. While the account of the fall in Gen 3 is not referred to anywhere else in the OT, its canonical position makes it of central importance; it sheds light on all that follows and is in turn to be read in the light of what follows, including the NT identification of the serpent with Satan. The NT, it is true, deepens and expands the OT view. The idea found in some modern liberal thought that Jesus believed in the essential goodness of human beings — in contrast to Paul, who was obsessed with sin — simply does not accord with the evidence of the Gospels (cf. Childs 1992: 579). The most penetrating analysis of the human condi-

tion in Scripture is found in Paul. Historically, it is quite possible that Paul's view of human nature was developed "backwards"; he did not begin with fixed views on the human condition, but rather, reflection on Christ's death on the cross and the cost of redemption led him to a deeper understanding of the nature and extent of human sinfulness. Be that as it may, Paul's view is best described not as pessimistic but as realistic, and it forms the essential backdrop for the proclamation of the good news. The paradoxical nature of the NT understanding of human sin has been noted above. "Sin" is a power, associated with Satan and the other powers that enslave human beings, yet it is also something for which human beings are responsible. "We are born into a world conditioned by Adam's sin and by the accumulated sins of others; we are *involved in* and *influenced by* that world; and our lives are often shaped by the ongoing consequences of human sinfulness. But we are *guilty of* — and therefore morally and spiritually *responsible for* — our own actual sins, and not the sins of others" (Cronk 1982: 45). While the tension between the two views of sin appears paradoxical, it is nevertheless true both to the biblical witness and to human experience. The biblical emphasis on human sinfulness is of course uncongenial to much of modern thought, which frequently oscillates between optimism and despair, but at the outset of a new millennium it may fairly be claimed that the biblical analysis of the human condition is as relevant as ever (cf. Schnelle 1996: 145-49).

4. If the frank recognition of human sin is uncongenial to the modern mind, then belief in divine judgment is even more so. Yet we have seen that judgment is a pervasive theme throughout Scripture. If judgment in this life and within history predominates in the OT, future judgment is the main emphasis in the NT, though what happens at the final judgment is seen as a ratification of the judgment that takes place in the present. The biblical picture of a final separation followed by everlasting rewards and punishments has caused problems not only for critics of the Christian faith but also for sincere believers; universalism is not only a popular modern option, it has a long history, despite the fact that it goes against significant parts of the biblical evidence. To some extent, what people have reacted to is not the biblical teaching, which is on the whole restrained, but the elaboration of the pictures of hell found in patristic and especially medieval Christianity, to say nothing of Protestant sermons like Jonathan Edwards's "Sinners in the Hands of an Angry God" that dangled their hearers over the fires of hell and sought to "scare people into the kingdom of God" in a way quite inconsistent with the NT (cf. Pinnock in Crockett 1992: 138-40). Nevertheless, the NT does clearly point to a separation after death. Where the evidence is capable of being interpreted in more than one way is in relation to the final fate of the unrighteous. Over against the more traditional view of unending conscious torment, which many believers think depicts God as a cosmic sadist, there is considerable biblical evidence favoring conditional immortality. The fact that in the second half of the twentieth century a number of

conservative evangelical scholars, holding a high view of the inspiration of Scripture, came out in favor of this view suggests that it must be given very careful consideration (cf. T. Gray 1996: 14-15). Whatever conclusion is drawn, it remains true that for the Bible people's attitudes and actions here on earth have momentous eternal consequences.

5. Anxiety is a characteristic of the human condition in every age, not least our own. Behind "the stresses and strains of modern life" lie deeper anxieties caused by the search for meaning in life, by feelings of guilt, by the threat of disease and death, and by the prospect of what, if anything, lies beyond death. The Bible is well aware of all these aspects of the human condition, though of course the biblical analysis forms the backdrop for what it has to say about faith and hope. Biblical faith acknowledges as legitimate concerns for life and health and for an adequate provision of the material necessities of life. It is when people make these things their first concern and thus become burdened with anxiety that they need to be told, "Do not worry about your life. . . . Strive first for the kingdom of God and his righteousness, and all these things will be given to you as well" (Matt 6:25, 33).

6. Suffering constitutes probably the most enduring riddle of human existence. Despite the advances of modern science, technology, and medicine, suffering is as much as ever part of the human lot (cf. Gerstenberger and Schrage 1980: 130-31). Modern means of communication have actually made people more vividly aware of suffering (e.g., famine, earthquakes, genocide, ethnic cleansing), and have thus made it even more of a problem for many (cf. Beker 1987: 14, 16). Today, many view the world in "apocalyptic" terms, sharing the biblical view of the pervasiveness of evil and suffering but abandoning its hope of the victory of good over evil at a final consummation (cf. the discussion in Beker, 17-23). Suffering, however, is not just a modern concern (cf. Milazzo 1991: 27-28), and the Bible, in both Old and New Testaments, acknowledges the problem and wrestles with it.

Suffering is particularly a problem for those who believe in God; if God does not exist, then suffering is simply one aspect of a life that is essentially meaningless. For believers, however, undeserved suffering can be very difficult to reconcile with the God of the Bible. In the face of the death of a young child through cancer or the indiscriminate slaughter caused by an earthquake, believers ask, "How can a loving God allow this to happen?" Surely, if God is all-loving, he cannot be all-powerful, or if he is all-powerful, he cannot be all-loving. The question that underlies the book of Job echoes down through the ages: "Why do bad things happen to good people?" The book of Job is the prime example both of the seriousness with which the Bible takes the problem and of its reluctance to jump in and offer easy answers. It is true that both Old and New Testaments suggest ways of seeking to understand suffering: as a challenge to action, as a test of faith, as a form of discipline, as an opportunity for witness, as a sharing in the vicarious, redemptive suffering of Christ. But Scripture is realistic in acknowledging that suffering will remain part of the human lot as long as history lasts, and in the NT the comfort it offers rests primarily on the hope of the final, apocalyptic victory over all the powers that oppress humankind. Perhaps the most important insight offered by Scripture is the view, hinted at in the OT but more fully developed in the NT, that God is not a remote spectator of human suffering. He is all-loving but not all-powerful in the sense that he can and will simply flatten everything and anything that opposes his will. God's power is above all the power of love, and this is often manifest in apparent weakness. Above all, the NT affirms that God was in Christ, sharing in the suffering of the world and taking it upon himself. "Our God knows our pain because he has been there with us. We live in the hope that, eventually, he will take the suffering away. In the meantime, we know that we have a God who weeps with us, who hears and understands our cries of pain, who is completely approachable even when we walk through the valley of the shadow of death. To believe in such a God is enough" (Simundson 1980: 141).

CHAPTER 17

Faith and Hope

Old Testament: Proclamation

17-1. TRUST IN THE LORD

God's people are called to turn from their own evil ways and to walk in God's way, but throughout Scripture this is seen as something made possible only by God himself. The biblical view of the human condition has been characterized as pessimistic though also realistic (see chap. 16). Balancing this, of course, and more than balancing it, is the good news of God's plan of salvation for humankind, and especially, in the NT, the "gospel," or good news, of what God has done in Christ. The Bible emphasizes throughout the priority of divine grace (cf. 1-3.1b); in all his dealings with humankind it is God who takes the initiative. Divine grace, however, always calls forth *a human response.*

There is considerable continuity between OT and NT in their view of that human response. Since *sin* is the barrier that separates humankind from God (cf. 16-1.2; 16-3.2), the human response to God's grace must begin with a recognition of that sin, a recognition that "we have all turned to our own way" (Isa 53:6), and hence with *repentance,* for only then can God's *forgiveness* be received. Repentance means turning *from* sin; the other side of the coin is turning *to* God and walking in his ways. An essential component of this on the human side is *faith* or trust in God. The result is a new or restored relationship with God, frequently described in Scripture as *"knowing"* God, in the sense of entering into a close personal relationship with him. Such a relationship is nourished, above all, by the life of *prayer.*

There are also, however, some significant differences between OT and NT. The OT is addressed to God's people, Israel, who have already experienced his saving power and have been called into a covenant relationship with him (11-1). Israel frequently goes astray and hence needs to be called to repent, i.e., to turn away from their sins. But they are called not so much to *turn* to the Lord as to *return* to the Lord; this is emphasized by the fact that the one verb *shûbh* (lit. "turn") does duty for both types of "turning."

In the NT, however, in the light of the Christ event, the inauguration of the kingdom of God, and the dawning of the new age, *all* human beings — Jews and Gentiles alike — are called upon to repent and to turn to the Lord in a new and radical way. The human response to the gospel involves "conversion," a total transformation of the self that includes a dying to the old way of life and a rebirth to the new. "Faith" acquires a new importance and takes on new dimensions of meaning as the means of accepting and appropriating the new life offered in Christ.

17-1.1. REPENTANCE AND FORGIVENESS

Human sin drives a wedge between Israel and God, but the LORD is not only a holy God, he is a God who is willing to forgive in order to restore his people to a right relationship with himself. A recurring OT formula asserts both the serious and far-reaching consequences of sin and God's willingness to forgive, for he is

> The LORD, the LORD,
> a God merciful and gracious,
> slow to anger,
> and abounding in steadfast love and faithfulness,
> keeping steadfast love for the thousandth generation,
> forgiving iniquity and transgression and sin,
> yet by no means clearing the guilty,
> but visiting the iniquity of the parents
> upon the children
> and the children's children,
> to the third and fourth generation.
> (Exod 34:6-7; cf. 20:5-6; Deut 5:9-10; Neh 9:17; Ps 86:15; Joel 2:13)

Provision for the forgiveness of sin is made to some degree through the sacrificial system (see 14-1.5b), though it is not confined to it, and the prophets in particular emphasize the ineffectiveness of sacrifices unless they are accompanied by confession of sin and genuine repentance (see 14-1.5b.iv).

It is because God's people Israel so often rebel against the Lord and disobey him, hence incurring his judgment, that they have to be repeatedly called upon to repent. Repentance involves being sorry for one's sins, and this can be expressed by the verb *nicham* (be sorry, repent), as when Job says,

> I despise myself,
> and *repent* in dust and ashes. (Job 42:6)

But by far the most common word for "repent" is *shûbh* (LXX *epistrephō*), meaning "turn," i.e., turn from evil. "Turn now, all of you from your evil way, and amend your ways and your doings" (Jer 18:11); "repent and turn from all your transgressions; otherwise iniquity will be your ruin" (Ezek 18:30). Such pleas are typical of much of the message of the prophets, who "called for the type of true conversion which would bring every aspect of Israel's life into life-giving contact with the grace and power of Jahweh" (Sklba 1981: 73). Their concern was for "the maintenance of an existing covenant relationship through continual 'turning' from evil to God, a process in which both God and the individual (or more typically the community as a whole) have a part" (France 1993: 294). The metaphor of "turning" underlines that this is not simply a matter of a change of mind but is also a change in behavior; people are called to

> remove the evil of your doings
> from before my eyes. (Isa 1:16)

The first step in repentance is recognition of one's faults. Thus David in the Bathsheba incident was brought to the point where he cried out, "I have sinned against the LORD" (2 Sam 12:13). The Deuteronomic Historian ascribes the disasters that befell God's people to their failure to repent: "The LORD warned Israel and Judah . . . 'Turn from your evil ways and keep my commandments and my statutes, in accordance with all the law that I commanded your ancestors and that I sent to you by my servants the prophets.' They would not listen but were stubborn, as their ancestors had been, who did not believe in the LORD their God. They despised his statutes, and his covenant that he made with their ancestors, and the warnings that he gave them" (2 Kgs 17:13-15). Repentance involves confession of sin and prayer for God's forgiveness. God is ready to forgive sin, but forgiveness is conditional on repentance: "When your people Israel, having sinned against you, . . . confess your name, pray and plead with you in this house, then hear in heaven [and] forgive the sin of your people Israel" (1 Kgs 8:33-34). Failure to repent makes God's forgiveness impossible (Ps 7:12), but when people repent God is more than ready to forgive:

> Let the wicked forsake their way,
>   and the unrighteous their thoughts;
> let them return to the LORD, that he may have mercy on them,
>   and to our God, for he will abundantly pardon.
> (Isa 55:7; cf. Jer 18:8; Mal 3:7)

Repentance is a *response* to God's gracious offer, but, as the prophets discovered, the stubborn sinfulness of the people often prevented them from repenting and therefore from receiving God's forgiveness. The inevitability of this is stressed in Isaiah's call, where God tells him sarcastically to say to the people:

"Keep listening, but do not comprehend;
keep looking, but do not understand."
Make the mind of this people dull,
    and stop their ears,
    and shut their eyes,
so that they may not look with their eyes,
    and listen with their ears,
and comprehend with their minds,
    and turn *(wāshābh)* and be healed. (6:9-10)

In the OT it is frequently the *nation* that is called to repentance. Yet repentance must also be personal. Jeremiah says to the inhabitants of Jerusalem, "Turn now, *all of you* from your evil way" (Jer 18:11), and stresses that repentance must be from the heart (3:10). "The prophets emphasize that man's relation to God is personal, and that sin roots in a wrong relationship to God. Repentance also is personal: it is a reorientation of the entire person and a return to Yahweh" (Quanbeck 1962: 34).

Although "turning" is a human response, according to the OT it is God who makes it possible. Paradoxically, "it is God who turns us to Him, and man, who has turned away from God, is turned back by God himself" (Schniewind 1952: 269). God's people can pray, "Lord, turn us back to you, and we shall come back" (Lam 5:21 REB). Occasionally God can be said to "turn" Israel back, as in Ps 80:3 where the people pray, "Restore us *(hªshîbhēnû),* O God" (cf. Jer 31:18). With the exception of Jonah 3:10, where the people of Nineveh "turned from their evil ways," all the uses of *shûbh* refer to God's covenant people.

Repentance can be *symbolized* in the OT in quite dramatic ways, such as fasting (Joel 2:12), rending one's garments (2 Kgs 19:1), and wearing sackcloth and ashes (Job 42:6; 2 Kgs 19:1; in 1 Kgs 21:27 Ahab does all three).

17-1.2. RETURN TO THE LORD

The word *shûbh* is used both of turning *from* sin and turning *to* the LORD. In practice the two meanings often blend; they are separated here only for the purposes of discussion. While the call to turn to the LORD is found throughout the OT, it is especially typical of the prophets, for whom turning *from* evil must also involve turning to, or rather *returning to,* God:

Let the wicked forsake their way, . . .
let them return to the LORD.
               (Isa 55:7; cf. 2 Chr 30:6, 9; Jer 3:14, 22; Lam 3:40)

Come, let us return to the LORD;
    for it is he who has torn, and he will heal us. (Hos 6:1)

A passage such as Joel 2:12-13 well illustrates what lies at the heart of so much of the prophetic message:

> Yet even now, says the LORD,
>   return to me with all your heart,
> with fasting, with weeping, and with mourning;
>   rend your hearts and not your clothing.
> Return to the LORD, your God,
>   for he is gracious and merciful.

"This text," writes Witherup (1994), "shows that the call to return to God is a strong exhortation to effect a dramatic turnabout in life. It is to be a redirection toward God, accompanied by visible symbolic actions, but rooted more profoundly in a fundamental, internal change of heart. At the centre of the motivation for such a substantial change is recognition of the need for turning from evil and returning to a deep trust in the mercy of God" (9-10).

"Returning" in the OT is not the same as what is commonly called "conversion" in the NT (see below, 17-3.2a), but it does often involve a *call to decision,* a call not just to repent of past sin but also to make a new commitment to the Lord. Moses called the people to decision: "I have set before you life and death, blessings and curses. Choose life" (Deut 30:19). Similarly Joshua had to summon the people to "choose this day whom you will serve" (Josh 24:15). There is no more dramatic scene than the contest between the prophet Elijah and the prophets of Baal atop Mount Carmel. "How long will you go limping with two different opinions?" Elijah demanded of the people. "If the LORD is God, follow him; but if Baal, then follow him" (1 Kgs 18:21). The prophets in many a crisis situation called on the people to decide to return to the Lord (Isa 44:22; Jer 3:12). The Wisdom Literature in its own, less dramatic way is constantly calling on its readers to decide: to choose wisdom and reject folly, to choose the fear of the LORD (Prov 1:29) and reject the way of the wicked (3:31).

17-1.3. FAITH AND DOUBT

In the NT "faith" *(pistis)* is a key word in expressing the individual's response to God. The fact that words for "faith" and "believe" are not common in the OT must not blind us to the fact that the reality of faith is there, in the form of personal trust and commitment to the Lord. When the writer to the Hebrews wished to draw up a roll call of faith, he had no difficulty citing a whole series of men and women from the OT whose lives were characterized by what he understood as "faith" (11:4-40). This is one of the clearest examples of the limitations of the "word study" approach; the absence of the noun "faith" in the concordance does not mean the absence of faith from the characters of the OT (contra J. Barr 1999: 257, who sees the place given to faith in some OT theologies as a "Christianizing" of the OT).

a. Examples of Faith

While the OT does not give an abstract definition of "faith," it does illustrate faith in many narratives (see the discussion under "Stories about Faith" in Hermisson and Lohse 1981: 10-46).

The classic case is Abraham, who in response to God's call, "Go from your country and your kindred . . ." (Gen 12:1), ventured forth in faith, "not knowing where he was going" (Heb 11:8). Faith here is closely linked with obedience: "So Abram went, as the LORD had told him" (Gen 12:4). Despite the impossibility of having a child in extreme old age, Abraham nevertheless trusted God to bring this about (15:6; cf. Rom 4; Heb 11:11-12). Many have rightly seen in the story of the binding of Isaac (Gen 22:1-19) a supreme instance of faith: "Was not Abraham found faithful when tested, and it was reckoned to him as righteousness?" (*1 Macc* 2:52; cf. *Sir* 44:20). The Abraham narratives present him as "*the type of the faithful,* the man who takes his stand on the promises of God, and who lives by his assurance of God's will, whatever appearances may suggest to the contrary" (Eichrodt 1967: 278; cf. von Rad 1962: 171).

The note of faith and trust permeates many of the Psalms, especially those that are generally classified as "songs of faith" or "songs of trust" (11; 16; 23; 62; 91; 121; 131; see B. W. Anderson 1983: 205-15). While these psalms may originally have had a place in the worship of the temple, they are suitable for use by believers in any circumstances. The best known of these is Ps 23, a psalm which "by virtue of its profound simplicity and matchless beauty . . . has touched the hearts of countless people down through the centuries" (Anderson, 206; cf. Hermisson and Lohse 1981: 60-62). In vv. 1-4 the psalmist expresses faith in God as the Good Shepherd who cares for his sheep, while in vv. 5-6 the metaphor shifts only slightly to God as the host who offers the traditional hospitality of his tent to the desert traveler. Many psalms of lament also conclude with an expression of faith; thus, for example, Ps 13, an individual lament that begins with the despairing cry, "How long, O LORD?" ends with the confident assertion:

> But I trusted in your steadfast love;
>   my heart shall rejoice in your salvation. (v. 5)

Again and again the prophets, especially in their oracles of deliverance and salvation, called on God's people to have faith and to trust that God would indeed bring these things to pass. Dan 1–6 provides a series of illustrations of faith in action, of which the best known are the three men in the fiery furnace

(Dan 3) and Daniel in the lions' den (Dan 6); in both cases faith in God in seemingly impossible circumstances is vindicated.

b. Believing in God

Though not common, the verb *'āman* (Hiph'il), from a root meaning to be firm or secure, is used of people believing or trusting in God (see J. M. Ward 1976: 329); in the LXX it is translated by *pisteuō*, which becomes the NT word for "believe," "have faith" (see below, 17-3.3a). According to Gen 15:6, Abraham "believed the LORD; and the LORD reckoned it to him as righteousness"; "Abraham's faith involved both a trust in God, and a belief in the divine promise as true *(fides qua* and *fides quae),* in spite of God's word appearing quite impossible according to human experience" (Childs 1992: 597; cf. Ward, 330-31; Hermisson and Lohse 1981: 21-30). Because of his faith, God accepted Abraham into a right relationship with himself. After the crossing of the sea, the people "believed in the LORD and in his servant Moses" (Exod 14:31b), though subsequently their faith often wavered (Num 14:11; Ps 78:32).

The prophet Isaiah counseled King Ahaz,

> If you do not stand firm in faith,
> you shall not stand at all.
> (Isa 7:9; see commentaries on the wordplay involved)

In face of the Assyrian threat Isaiah counsels, "One who trusts will not panic" (28:16), and gives the assurance:

> In returning and rest you shall be saved;
> in quietness and in trust shall be your strength. (30:15)

Salvation will not depend on frantic human efforts or on political intrigue, but on a calm trust in the LORD (cf. Childs 1992: 598). Isaiah, comments Stuhlmacher (1994), is the first to speak of faith "as a way of behavior in which one unreservedly and exclusively depends on and has dealings with God, his promises, and his will" (76). In face of the apparent inactivity of God, the prophet Habakkuk counsels waiting, and affirms that "the righteous live by their faith" (2:4; *'ᵉmûnâ* here can be read either as "faith" or "faithfulness").

Akin to *'āman* is *bāṭach,* meaning "trust." Hezekiah, we are told, "trusted in the LORD the God of Israel" (2 Kgs 18:5). The word is frequently used in the Psalms to express trust in God (9:10; 21:7; 22:5; etc.). The opposite of such trust is fear (56:4; Isa 12:2; cf. Brueggemann 1997: 468).

c. The Fear of the Lord

One of the most basic ways of expressing the response of persons to God in the OT is by the use of the verb *yārē'* = "to fear," or the noun *yir'â* = "fear" (of the Lord). This expression is found especially in the patriarchal narratives, in the rest of the Pentateuch (it is a key expression in Deuteronomy), in the Psalms, and in Wisdom. It denotes an attitude of "fear" in the sense of reverence or respect. "Essentially it represents the basic and proper stance of mortals before the divine" (Barré 1981: 42).

In Gen 22 Abraham's faith and obedience are commended because, as the angel says, "now I know that you fear God" (v. 12). In response to the destruction of the Egyptians at the sea, "the people *feared* the LORD" (Exod 14:31). Fearing God is emphasized especially in Deuteronomy. It can mean to be loyal to God and serve only him, as in 10:20: "You shall *fear* the LORD your God; him alone you shall worship; to him you shall hold fast." However, as Kaiser (1978) points out, "this fear was not a worked-up feeling of some numinous awe, but it was the result of hearing, learning, and responding to God's Word" (169). Thus it also involves obedience to God: "Therefore keep the commandments of the LORD your God, by walking in his ways and by *fearing* him" (Deut 8:6; cf. Lev 25:17). Similarly in Psalms, those who fear God are not only those who trust in him (33:18; 145:19), but those who also obey him (112:1; 119:63).

While wisdom is based on observation and experience, nevertheless the fear of the Lord is a fundamental principle of the Wisdom Literature in its canonical form. That "the fear of the LORD is the beginning of knowledge" is laid down at the outset of Proverbs, and is a recurring refrain (1:7; cf. 2:5; 9:10; 14:26; 15:33; 19:23; cf. also *Sir* 1:27; 19:20). The summation of Ecclesiastes is, "Fear God, and keep his commandments" (12:13). In Job, the Hymn to Wisdom (Job 28) climaxes in the saying,

> Truly, the fear of the Lord, that is wisdom;
>   and to depart from evil is understanding. (28:28)

Thus for the Wisdom writers, reverence and respect for God was the basis of true wisdom without which "humanity was destitute of effective leadership and bankrupt in its appreciation or apprehension of God, man and things" (Kaiser 1978: 171).

d. Doubt and Despair

While the OT constantly calls on people to trust in God and to love and obey him, it also has a lot to say about doubt and despair. Davidson (1968) has pointed out that a survey of several leading OT theologies reveals a curious fact:

"While there are abundant references to 'faith,' its nature and meaning, 'doubt' is conspicuous by its absence" (41). In point of fact, questioning of God has a major place in the OT. It is certainly found in the individual laments of the Psalter, in which the writer frequently calls out in doubt and despair (see 3-2.1a; 16-1.4). It is found also in the Prophets. Even the stalwart Elijah is revealed to us as a man not immune from depression and doubt of God's purposes; forced to flee by the threats of Queen Jezebel, he made his way to the wilderness where "he asked that he might die" and cried out, "It is enough; now, O LORD, take away my life, for I am no better than my ancestors" (1 Kgs 19:4). In a remarkable series of poetic passages (Jer 11:18-23; 12:1-6; 15:10-21; 17:12-18; 18:18-23; 20:7-18) generally referred to as "The Confessions of Jeremiah," the prophet Jeremiah bares his soul and reveals the inner struggle and anguish he endured as he tackled what often seemed to be a hopeless task (see von Rad 1965: 201-6). The six poems seem to mirror a growing doubt and despair, culminating in the accusation that God has deceived him (20:7) and the cursing of the day he was born (20:14-15); yet even in the midst of this, there is embedded an expression of confidence in God (20:11-13).

But questioning of God in the Wisdom Literature is given its freest expression in Job (see 16-1.5c) and especially in Ecclesiastes (see Terrien 1978: 373-80; Brueggemann 1997: 393-98). Surprise is often expressed that a book as apparently skeptical, if not agnostic, as Ecclesiastes should find a place in the Bible, and the epilogue (12:9-14) is commonly regarded as a "happy ending" tacked on to try to salvage a work that got into the canon because of its assumed authorship by Solomon (see Childs 1979: 584-86).

The author of Ecclesiastes does not have the same problem as Job; as far as we can determine, he is healthy and prosperous. His concern is not with the meaning of suffering but with the meaning of life. Unlike Job, he does not suffer, he does not pray to God, and God does not speak to him. Yet in some ways his doubts are more radical.

While parts of the book echo conventional Wisdom, the keynote that is struck at the very outset is remarkably negative: "Vanity of vanities! . . . All is vanity" (1:2). Vanity (hebhel) means a breath or vapor, hence that which does not last or is worthless, empty, or futile. The author challenges many of the assumptions of orthodox piety. To those who say "Trust in God and all life's problems will be solved," he comes close to agnosticism when he says that "even though those who are wise claim to know [the work of God], they cannot find it out" (8:17; cf. 11:5). To those who say "The righteous always prosper," he strongly denies the piety-prosperity equation (7:15; 8:14; cf. 16-1.5c). To those who might say "The wrongs of this world will be righted in the world to come," he is agnostic regarding a future life: "Who knows whether the human spirit goes upward?" (3:21; see 3:19-21; and cf. 2:15-16; 9:2-3). His advice to accept life and make the best of it, "There is nothing better for mortals than to eat and drink, and find enjoyment in their toil" (2:24; cf. 3:12-13; 9:7-10), sounds not unlike Epicureanism.

But it is possible to interpret the book at least in part as a commentary on what happens when one refuses to give God chief place in one's life. True satisfaction cannot be found in pleasure (2:1-3), possessions (2:4-8), work (2:9-11), or even wisdom (1:12-18; 2:12-17). Ryken (1984) suggests, from a literary viewpoint, that the author employs *the quest motif:* "as readers, we accompany the speaker as he recalls his quest to find meaning in life" and we learn of "the dead ends he pursued" (126). Ryken also sees the structural principle of the book as *a dialectical system of opposites.* When the author describes the futility of life "under the sun" *(tachath hashshāmesh),* "that is, life lived by purely human or earthly standards," he is "not offering his final verdict on life," for the negative sections of the book are balanced by positive ones throughout, and not just at the end (127). Hence the book in fact underlines a basic biblical theme: "Life lived by purely earthly or human standards, without faith in God and supernatural values, is meaningless and futile" (Ryken 1987a: 320; cf. also Ryken and Longman 1993: 268-80). As a Wisdom Book, Ecclesiastes ignores salvation/judgment history and says nothing of exodus, covenant, or Torah; it can thus be seen as fulfilling a negative function by demonstrating the futility of life apart from divine redemption.

The fact remains that just as the book of Job allows the expression of radical doubts regarding the traditional view of suffering (cf. 16-1.5c), so Ecclesiastes allows doubt and even agnosticism to find expression. Certainly in both books there is a tension or dialectic between faith and doubt.

17-1.4. KNOWING GOD

Those who return to God in faith and obedience enter into fellowship and communion with him. One of the most common ways of expressing this in the OT is by saying that God's people "know" him (generally by use of the verb *yāda'* = "know"; noun *da'ath* = "knowledge, understanding, wisdom"; see Piper 1962a: 42-44).

Because God has made himself known to his people, they know that the Lord is great (Ps 100:3), that he is the only God (135:5; Isa 45:6), and that he calls them by name (Isa 45:3). At a more personal level, the individual can say, "This I know, that God is for me" (Ps 56:9), and "I know that it will be well with those who fear God" (Eccl 8:12).

yāda', however, does not merely denote an intellectual knowledge; rather it involves a very close and intimate personal relationship. (To "know" human beings can mean to have sexual relations with them; e.g., Gen 4:1 — "the man knew his wife Eve, and she conceived.") In the Prophets, to know God "means above all *a practical and active recognition of God, confession or gratitude*" (Botterweck and Zimmermann 1981: 472-73). Thus in Hos 13:4 God can say, "You know no God but me"; this does not mean that Israel was not aware of claims that were made for other (pagan) gods, but rather that Israel is bound in a close relationship to the LORD only. For Hosea the "knowledge of God" (4:1; 6:6) is "no mere theoretical knowledge of God's nature and will but the practical application of a relationship of love and trust, as this is seen at its loveliest in the association of a true wife and her husband" (Eichrodt 1967: 291). Of course, God knows his people before they know him (Ps 139:4; Jer 12:3; Ezek 11:5).

Ideally therefore, God's people "know" him in this sense (cf. Ps 9:10; Jer 9:24), though in the OT as a whole, more often than not the complaint is that Israel does *not* know God as they ought:

> The ox knows its owner,
>   and the donkey its master's crib;
>   but Israel does not know. (Isa 1:3)

"They do not know me, says the LORD" (Jer 9:3; cf. Isa 45:5; Jer 2:8; Hos 5:4). Consideration of texts like these suggests that "moral decline is intimately connected with this absence of the knowledge of God" (Botterweck and Zimmermann 1981: 473).

"Knowing" God has practical consequences; those who truly know God seek to serve and obey him, so that to know God is to know his ways (Ps 25:4; Jer 5:4) and his ordinances (Ps 147:20). Knowing God means championing the cause of the poor and needy (Jer 22:16). To know God is also to love him, and God's people are called to respond to God's love by loving him (*'āhēbh* = "love"). The response of love is stressed particularly in Deuteronomy, Hosea, and Jeremiah. Judaism rightly has seen in the Shema (Deut 6:5) the clearest formulation of the response that God expects from his people: "You shall love (*'āhabhtā*) the LORD your God with all your heart, and with all your soul, and with all your might" (cf. 10:12; 11:13; etc.). In this key passage "the demand for love to God is set out in such a way as to show the supreme importance which the Deuteronomists attached to it" (Clements 1968: 82). Deuteronomy stresses God's prior love for Israel: "Because he loved (*'āhabh*) your ancestors, he chose their descendants after them," and delivered them at the exodus (4:37; cf. 7:8; 10:15). Israel's love for God therefore is a response to his love for them. The context of Deut 6:5 suggests a close link between love for God and obedience. Parallels between the Shema and the Wisdom Literature show that the basic picture is of God as a father and Israel as son, or God as teacher and Israel as the pupil. The love of God that is commanded is akin to "filial obedience, reverential love, or *pietas*" (McKay 1972: 435). It is often objected that it is difficult to command love, if love is thought of as a spontaneous emotion. But the love that is required of Israel "is seen in reverential fear, in loyalty, and in obedience" (McCarthy 1965: 145); it is the obedient love that constitutes Israel's obligation under the covenant.

God's steadfast love (*chesedh;* cf. 11-1.3f) in upholding the covenant calls for a like response from Israel. In Hos 6:6 God declares, "I desire steadfast love and not sacrifice"; that is, loyalty to the covenant is more important than any religious ritual (cf. 12:6). Love for God can often be expressed in worship (e.g., Ps 116:1-2).

17-1.5. PERSONAL PRAYER

One of the most important ways in which God's people respond to him is by means of prayer, and the Bible has much to say on the necessity and value of personal prayer.

a. Public Prayer and Personal Prayer

As we have already noted, prayer was an important element in the public worship of God (14-1.5a.i; 14-3.5b.i) — in the earlier sanctuaries, in the temple, in the synagogue, and in the developing liturgy of the early church. It is helpful, for the purpose of discussion, to separate public and private prayer. But of course, they cannot always be clearly differentiated; they are certainly not in mutual opposition, and the Bible indicates that the one must feed the other. A good example is the Psalms. Originally they must have been written by individuals (traditionally many of them by David). They came to be used in the public, corporate worship of the temple, the synagogue, and the church. Yet again and again over the centuries, they have been read and appropriated by individuals in their personal devotions.

b. Teaching and Example

The OT offers remarkably little in the way of formal teaching on personal prayer. What it does do repeatedly is portray individuals at prayer, and it frequently cites actual examples of personal prayers (cf. Peskett 1990: 19-21).

Abraham is portrayed as a person of prayer, e.g., in his intercession for Sodom in Gen 18:22-33. Jacob throws himself on God's mercy in the prayer quoted in 32:9-12, and in 32:22-32 he wrestles with God in prayer all night. Moses is an outstanding example of a person of prayer, not least in his prayers on behalf of the people (e.g., Exod 32:30-32; see W. Harrington 1980: 9-10). Other examples of prayers include those of David in 2 Sam 7:18-29 and of Solomon in 1 Kgs 3:5-14, where he wisely asks not for long life, riches, or the lives of his enemies, but for "an understanding mind." An intense interest in personal prayer marks the deuterocanonical books (see N. B. Johnson 1948). *Tobit* has been called "an impressive treatise on prayer" (Harrington, 52). Significantly the deuterocanonical *Additions to Esther* includes prayers of Mordecai and Esther (there are no prayers in the original Esther). Prayer is important also in *Susanna* (see *Sus* 42-44). *Prayer of Manasseh,* which presupposes the account of Manasseh's repentance in 2 Chr 33:10-19, "is a worthy example of post-exilic piety. . . . If even *Manasseh . . .* could, having turned back to the Lord, feel confident of salvation, there is hope for any and every sinner" (Harrington, 31). *2 Macc* 12:43-45 mentions prayer for the dead, and 15:12-16 refers to prayer by the dead (Jeremiah, Onias) for the living.

c. The Theology of Prayer

Despite the lack of formal teaching on prayer, the wealth of examples of personal prayer in the OT allows us to outline some of the main features of a theology of prayer.

i. Dialogue with God

While there are technical terms for prayer, used especially in relation to prayer in public worship, it is significant that individual prayer is often described using the regular words for "say" and "speak" or "cry out"; the use of such vocabulary in relation to prayer "suggests its character as a *conversation or dialogue with God*" (P. D. Miller 1994: 461). This need not be initiated from the human side: God may open the conversation by calling, "Abraham, Abraham!" (Gen 22:11), "Moses, Moses!" (Exod 3:4), or "Samuel! Samuel!" (1 Sam 3:4). While prayer may be defined as "talking with God," it should also involve listening to God. When God spoke to Samuel, wise old Eli's advice to the lad was to respond, "Speak, LORD, for your servant is listening" (3:9). In many OT examples of prayer God speaks, giving direction and guidance, or calling the listener to a particular task. Again and again the OT assures the individual member of God's people that the Lord is only too willing to enter into this dialogue; he is the hearer and the answerer of prayer. "The LORD hears when I call to him" (Ps 4:3b). "The Bible does not present an art of prayer; it presents the God of prayer, the God who calls before we answer and answers before we call (Isa. 65:24)" (Clowney 1990: 136). It is because God is above all a personal God, who enters into a personal relationship with his people, that this dialogue with God through prayer is possible.

ii. Language

While one must beware of sweeping generalizations, one of the main impressions one gets of personal prayer in the OT is its ease and naturalness. "What may surprise us Christians is the naturalness of the prayer of Israel. Old Testament men and women spoke straightforwardly to their God. And they turned to him with a refreshing boldness. Theirs is no God of terror but a God who is very personal and very near" (W. Harrington 1980: ix). Note, for example, the boldness of Abraham's prayer in Gen 18:22-33, and of Moses' in Ex 33:12-13.

iii. Types of Prayer

The main types of prayer found in public worship (14-1.5a.i) are appropriate to personal prayer also. Since prayer is dialogue with God, it is appropriate that individuals come into God's presence with praise and thanksgiving (see P. D. Miller 1994: 178-232); examples are found in the Psalter, especially in individual psalms of thanksgiving and in hymns of praise. Confession of sin is an essential element (see Miller, 244-61); examples are found in the penitential psalms (see 16-1.2b), such as Ps 51. While prayer is far from asking God for what we want, nevertheless prayers of petition have their place (see Miller, 55-134); the Psalms are full of prayers for help and deliverance, for forgiveness and healing, for God's guidance and blessing. As the story of Solomon in 1 Kgs 3 illustrates, one of the most important things to pray for is wisdom (cf. Ps 90:12; *Wis* 9:4; see Vawter 1975). The OT also provides many examples of individual prayers of intercession (see Miller, 262-80); Moses and the prophets are frequently found praying for the people. To these we could add, as an essential element of prayer, a reverent and expectant silence in which one waits to hear God speak.

iv. Unanswered Prayer

Despite the assurances that God hears prayer, there are some passages in the OT which declare that God will not answer prayer, and some startling examples of "unanswered" prayer.

One aspect of the teaching of the prophets is that under some circumstances God will not answer prayer:

> When you stretch out your hands,
>   I will hide my eyes from you;
> even though you make many prayers,
>   I will not listen. (Isa 1:15; cf. Mic 3:4)

This saying from Isaiah is part of a passage (1:10-17) that condemns a worship divorced from repentance and obedience. Prayer is not a means of turning on God's favor like a tap, regardless of the lifestyle of those praying to God.

The OT includes two striking examples of "unanswered" prayer (cf. Buck 1975: 109). Near the end of his life, Moses prayed that he might be allowed to enter the Promised Land (Deut 3:25). The prayer was refused; Moses was allowed to see the land but not to enter it (3:26-27; cf. 32:48-52; 34:1-4). According to 2 Sam 12, the child born to David and Bathsheba fell sick and David prayed for his recovery (v. 16). His prayer was not answered and the child died a week later. Both stories illustrate the fact that in the Bible prayer is not a way of controlling or manipulating God; rather, as a dialogue with God, it involves listening, ascertaining the will of God, and conforming to it.

Old Testament: Promise

17-2. A NEW HEART I WILL GIVE YOU

The OT is only too well aware of the failings of God's people: their failures truly to repent, to return to the Lord, to trust him, to know him, and to commune with him in prayer. As it looks to the future and the dawning of a new age, the OT is mindful of the deep sinfulness of human nature (cf. 16-1.2). Human beings are powerless to save themselves: human nature itself must be changed, and that is something only God can do. In the OT it is also something God promises to do, and that is ground for hope.

17-2.1. MY HOPE IS IN YOU

Despite its pessimism about human nature, the OT looks forward to the future with hope (on the various Hebrew words, see Minear 1962: 640-41; Hoffmann 1975: 239; and the listing of all the relevant texts in Moule 1963b: 58-67).

The term "hope" is used in two basic ways in BT. As noted at the outset of this study (E-3; 1-2.1b), the OT not only *proclaims* what God has done in the past, it also looks forward to what God *promises* to do in the future. What on God's side is given as promise, on the human side is experienced as hope. The "OT hope" can refer therefore to the *content* of that hope: God's promise of the coming of his kingdom, of the coming of a Messiah, of the inauguration of a new covenant, of the final victory over evil, and so on (see D. A. Hubbard 1983). Hope in this sense is an essential component part of BT, and thus the second section of each chapter of this book deals with some aspect of the OT hope.

The other side of "hope" is the *attitude* of those who trust in the promises of God. Like faith, it is not something that can be proved rationally; it involves commitment and trust. *Hope, we may say, is faith in the future tense.*

The two meanings of hope are, of course, closely connected. The source of hope is God; it is the LORD himself who is the "hope of Israel" (Jer 14:8). "God alone is the hope of the individual, the covenant community, and of the whole creation" (H. R. White 1981: 3). The hope of the individual is grounded in the hope that God holds out to humanity and to his people (see 1-2.1b; cf. Wolff 1974: 152; Brueggemann 1997: 476-85).

Hope finds expression at many points in the OT, especially in the Psalms. Many of the psalms of lament end on a note of hope and expectation.

> And now, O Lord, what do I wait for?
>   My hope is in you. (39:7)

> I wait for the LORD, my soul waits,
>   and in his word I hope. (130:5; cf. 42:5, 11; 43:5; 119:81)

However, there are times when the lamp of hope burns low (cf. 69:3). The theme of hope is also found in the Prophets (Isa 40:31; 64:4; Jer 17:13; Mic 7:7) and in Wisdom (Prov 20:22). "Thus hope is not a subsidiary theme in the Old Testament. On the contrary, it is indissolubly linked with Yahweh as the God of the patriarchs and prophets, the God of the threats and promises that he has proclaimed, the God of great changes and of final salvation; but equally with the God of all who pray and with the God of the wise" (Wolff 1974: 153).

Minear helpfully distinguishes four aspects of hope as an attitude of believers in the OT (1962: 641). It involves "a trust in God, through which one commits his cause to the Lord . . . and lives in serenity and peace under his present protection" (e.g., Job 11:18); "a ready eagerness to take refuge in him from one's foes, and to rely on him for speedy deliverance" (e.g., Ps 65:5); "the confident expectation of good, of future gladness which becomes the occasion for present rejoicing" (e.g., Prov 10:28); and "a waiting in patience and courage for the Lord to bring his salvation" (e.g., Ps 119:114, 166).

17-2.2. CAUSE US TO RETURN

There is hope for the future only if God's people repent and return to him (Isa 1:27). Deuteronomy foresees a time when in their distress God's people will return to him and heed him (4:30; cf. Jer 30:10; Hos 3:5). As Hos 14:4-7 makes clear, it is in response to God's love and healing power that the people will repent and return. The role of the returning Elijah (cf. 6-2.4) will be to call the people to repentance: "He will turn the hearts of parents to their children and the hearts of children to their parents" (Mal 4:6).

Though repentance is a human response, yet in a sense only God can enable his people to return to him. While at times God's future deliverance appears to be conditional on Israel's repentance, elsewhere the order is reversed and it is God's future deliverance that will trigger Israel's repentance and return to the Lord. In Isa 37:29 God says,

> I will turn you back on the way
>   by which you came.

And in Jer 24:7 he promises, "I will give them a heart to know that I am the LORD . . . for they shall return to me with their whole heart"; i.e., God will provide the new heart that will make returning possible (cf. also Isa 44:22; Ezek 36:26-31; and see Gowan 1986: 63-64).

17-2.3. I WILL PUT THE FEAR OF ME IN THEIR HEARTS

Among the major prophets especially, the conviction develops that if God's people are to have faith in him in their hearts, then human nature itself must be radically transformed (cf. 16-2.1).

According to Jer 32:39-41, God promises, "I will give them one heart and one way, that they may fear me for all time. . . . I will put the fear of me in their hearts, so that they may not turn from me." This transformation must be the work of God himself: "A new heart I will give you, and a new spirit I will put within you" (Ezek 36:26; cf. 11:19; 18:31; Jer 24:7).

17-2.4. THEY SHALL ALL KNOW ME

The OT promises that the new order will be marked by a closer communion of God's people with him, based on a restoration of the relationship of mutual "knowing" that has been God's will and intention all along.

Ezekiel repeatedly speaks of God's future action (mainly in judgment) with the added comment, "then you shall know that I am the LORD" (6:7; etc.). As part of the promise of a new covenant (see 11-2.3), God gives the assurance to his people that "No longer shall they teach one another, or say to each other, 'Know the LORD,' for they shall all know me, from the least of them to the greatest" (Jer 31:34). "Therefore my people shall know my name; therefore in that day they shall know that it is I who speak" (Isa 52:6; cf. Hos 2:20; Joel 2:27).

In the new age the knowledge of God will not be limited to Israel,

> for the earth will be full of the knowledge of the LORD
>   as the waters cover the sea.
>   (Isa 11:9; cf. Hab 2:14; Isa 19:21; Jer 16:21; see 12-2.4)

17-2.5. I WILL HEAR YOU

Whatever the future holds, God promises to hear the prayers of those who cry to him. "Then when you call upon me and come and pray to me, I will hear you" (Jer 29:12). In the new age God will even anticipate the needs of his faithful people:

Before they call I will answer,
while they are yet speaking I will hear. (Isa 65:24)

New Testament: Fulfillment

17-3. REPENT AND BELIEVE

The NT emphasizes even more strongly than the OT the priority of divine grace; both Testaments present the same basic pattern, according to which any thought or action on the human side can only come as a response to what God has already done.

17-3.1. REPENTANCE AND FORGIVENESS

The NT agrees with the OT in seeing sin as the barrier that separates human beings from God, but it also proclaims that in the Christ event, and especially through Jesus' death and resurrection, God has in a final, unique, and decisive way made atonement for human sin, and thus made possible for all humankind forgiveness of sin and reconciliation with God (see 9-3.4). The gospel of forgiveness and reconciliation, however, calls for a response on the human side that must begin with repentance.

The NT word for "repent," *metanoeō* (noun *metanoia* = "repentance"), by derivation means to "change one's mind," but it would be a mistake to suppose that the change referred to is merely intellectual (cf. Laubach, Goetzmann, and Beker 1975: 358). The contexts in which the word is used in the NT show a strong carryover from the broader OT connotations: repentance involves not only turning *from* sin but also turning *to* God, not only a change of mind and heart but also a change of life (cf. Schniewind 1952: 270; Sklba 1981: 67; Witherup 1994: 19).

The call to repent is first heard on the lips of John the Baptist as he fulfills the prophecy of the returning Elijah, who calls for repentance in the light of the breaking in of the new age (Luke 1:17; Matt 11:14; 17:10-13; Acts 13:24; see above, 17-2.2). According to Matthew, his message was "Repent, for the kingdom of heaven has come near" (3:2), and he called on his hearers to "bear fruit worthy of repentance" (3:8).

The core of Jesus' message, according to Mark 1:15, was "repent, and believe in the good news." As in the OT, God's forgiveness is conditional on repentance (Luke 13:1-5). Yet Jesus' message does not constitute a threat, but rather good news. In him God's kingdom is already breaking in. In him God's grace is present and active, so that he reaches out, even to the outcasts of society, calling "not the righteous but sinners to repentance" (Luke 5:32). Luke shows a special interest in the themes of repentance, forgiveness, and conversion, nowhere more so than in Luke 15 where he brings together the parables of the lost sheep, the lost coin, and the lost son. The rejoicing over the recovery of the lost sheep and coin parallels the joy in heaven over "one sinner who repents" (vv. 7, 10). The parable of the lost son (vv. 11-32) is a classic example of the power of a story to challenge the hearer/reader. "No other parable portrays more poignantly that God operates a lost and found department, and yet none of the typical vocabulary of conversion, repentance, or returning appears! Instead, Luke allows the power of the story itself to communicate its message" (Witherup 1994: 48). In compelling fashion the story focuses on the erring son who "came to himself *(eis heauton de elthōn)*" and recognized his sins (vv. 17-18), and even more on the waiting father who runs out to welcome him home (vv. 20-24).

According to Mark 6:12, when Jesus dispatched the Twelve, "they went out and proclaimed that all should repent." The risen Christ, appearing to his disciples, pointed them to the Scriptures that foretold the Messiah's suffering and resurrection, and directed that "repentance and forgiveness of sins is to be proclaimed in his name to all nations" (Luke 24:46-47). Thus the call to repent was carried over directly into the earliest Christian preaching, as in Peter's sermon on the Day of Pentecost: "Repent, and be baptized . . ." (Acts 2:38; cf. 8:22). It is Jesus' death and resurrection that makes possible the call to repentance and the offer of forgiveness of sins (5:31). As in the OT, turning *from* sin (repentance) is the presupposition of turning *to* God (conversion) (3:19; 26:20). And as in the OT, while people are called to repent and respond to God's gracious offer, stubborn sinfulness often prevents this happening. The sarcastic comment of Isa 6:9 (see above, 17-1.1) about people's failure to "turn" and be healed is repeated in the NT by Jesus himself in Matt 13:13-15 (cf. Mark 4:12; Luke 8:10) and John 12:40, as well as by Paul (Acts 28:26-27; cf. Rom 11:8).

Actual references to "repentance" occur infrequently in Paul and not at all in John. This may be in part because these writers "have clearly merged the call to repentance with that to faith" (Schnackenburg 1968: 559). But also, whereas Acts highlights the missionary preaching of the early church, Paul and John address believers who are already members of Christian communities, and they focus therefore on the new life in Christ (cf. Quanbeck 1962: 34; Laubach, Goetzmann, and Beker 1975: 359). However, though the terminology of repentance may be lacking, the strong elements of ethical exhortation in the Pauline and Johannine epistles make it clear that turning from sin and turning to God must be an ongoing process in the lives of believers. One book that does explicitly recognize the need for ongoing repentance is Revelation: John calls, e.g., on the members of the church at Ephesus: "Remember then from what you have fallen; repent, and do the works you did at first" (2:5; cf. the repeated calls to repent in 2:16; 3:3, 19).

In some tension with this is the view found in the Epistle to the Hebrews.

It is true that "repentance from dead works and faith toward God" are regarded as belonging to "the basic teaching about Christ" (6:1), but the author goes on to declare that "it is impossible to restore again to repentance those who have once been enlightened . . . and then have fallen away" (6:4, 6). This rigorist attitude reappears in 10:26, which warns that "if we willfully persist in sin after having received the knowledge of the truth, there no longer remains a sacrifice for sins," while 12:16-17 alludes to the bad example of Esau, who "found no chance to repent." These texts appear to say that after their initial repentance and conversion, believers cannot receive forgiveness for "postbaptismal sin." What becomes of the need for ongoing repentance? On this view, what hope would there have been for Peter, who betrayed his Lord after being his disciple for several years? The impact of these texts may be softened somewhat if they refer not to all sins, but only to some form of very serious sin. We may compare the distinction made in 1 John 5:16-17 between sins that are "unto death *(pros thanaton)*" and sins that are "not unto death" (John, however, provides no definition of what later came to be termed "mortal sin" and "venial sin"). It may be that what these passages have in mind is "high-handed" sin (cf. Num 15:30; this suits Heb 10:26), or else apostasy, i.e., the deliberate public denial of the Christian faith (this suits Heb 6:4-6; see commentaries). Whatever their exact reference, these texts certainly function as warnings against "cheap grace," but they have to be balanced against the dominant NT view that turning from sin is part of an ongoing process whereby believers develop toward maturity (see below, 17-4.2, and cf. Witherup 1994: 100-102).

17-3.2. TURN TO THE LORD

a. Conversion

When a person becomes a Christian believer, modern English usage generally refers to this as "conversion." It comes as a surprise to many that the noun "conversion" (= *epistrophē*) occurs only once in the NT, in Acts 15:3 where Paul and Barnabas "reported the conversion of the Gentiles." However, the corresponding verb is frequently used: *epistrephō* means literally to turn, or turn around, and it corresponds to the OT *shûbh* in the sense of turning *to* the Lord (see above, 17-1.2). As in the OT, "true turning to God follows upon repentance and belief" (Marsh 1962: 678). Thus Peter can call on the people of Jerusalem to "repent therefore, and turn to God" (Acts 3:19). *Epistrephō* is the standard NT term for turning to the gospel message on the part of both Jews (3:19; 9:35) and Gentiles (11:21; 15:19; 1 Thess 1:9; 1 Pet 2:25). It makes clear that for the NT conversion "means a fundamentally new turning of the human will to God, a return home from blindness and error to the Saviour of all" (Laubach, Goetzmann, and Beker 1975: 355). Paul's retrospective summary of the message he preached makes clear the continuity with the OT prophetic message: after his Damascus road experience he declared to Jews and Gentiles "that they should repent and turn to God and do deeds consistent with repentance" (Acts 26:20).

Some have held that a clear distinction must be made between those who were Jews and accepted the gospel and those who were Gentiles with a pagan background. France distinguishes between "insider conversion," i.e., returning to one's own religious tradition, and "outsider conversion," i.e., transferring from one religious tradition (or none) to another. The OT prophets definitely worked for an insider conversion, calling on God's people to return to the original covenant relationship with God. In the NT, when Gentiles respond to the gospel, this is clearly an outsider conversion, for they "turned to God from idols" (1 Thess 1:9; cf. Acts 14:15). It might be claimed that acceptance of the gospel by Jews should be classified insider conversion; they were not required to turn from idols, for they already worshiped the one true God. At this point, however, the insider/outsider distinction breaks down. Jews were not simply called to return to loyalty to the covenant; despite strong elements of continuity, in the call to recognize Jesus as the Messiah and to recognize in the Christ event the inbreaking of the new order, they were being challenged to make a decision and make a commitment in the face of something radically new (cf. France 1993: 298 n. 10).

Jesus' own message of the kingdom of God was proclaimed in a way that challenged his hearers to decision and commitment. Entering the kingdom is the most important decision a person can make; as the parables of the treasure hidden in a field and the pearl of great price (Matt 13:44-46) suggest, it is worth any sacrifice (cf. Blomberg 1990: 279); Jeremias (1963) stresses that it is the joy of the discovery that prompts "the unreserved surrender of what is most valuable" (201). Jesus' parables often ended with a challenge: "Let anyone with ears to hear listen!" (Mark 4:9). "No one," he said, "can serve two masters" (Matt 6:24); people must decide whom they will serve, and whether to build their lives on rock or on sand (7:24-27). He sent out the Twelve to proclaim the good news, recognizing that some would welcome them and some would not (10:7, 14-15).

Acts portrays the proclamation (*kerygma;* see 1-3.1b) of the gospel by the earliest preachers and the varying response it received (on conversion in Acts, see Witherup 1994: 57-73). Most light is shed on the nature of conversion to Christianity in the early church by the *narratives* of Acts. While there are some references to the conversion of large numbers (2:41; 4:4), it is doubtful if these were really "mass conversions" in the later sense (cf. France 1993: 306). The main focus in Acts is on the conversion of individuals such as the Ethiopian eunuch (8:27-39), Cornelius (chap. 10), Sergius Paulus (13:7-12), Lydia (16:14-15), the Philippian jailor (16:27-34), and of course Paul (9:1-9; cf. 22:4-16; 26:9-18). In one sense these conversions are deeply personal, but they also have a strong corporate dimension; turning to God is closely linked with baptism (2:41; 8:38; 9:18; 10:48; 16:33), and hence with incorporation into the believing community.

b. New Birth

For the NT, conversion in the sense of "turning" means something more than and different from what the OT means by "returning" to God (above, 17-1.2). With the inbreaking of the kingdom of God in the ministry of Jesus, and the inauguration of the new order by the Christ event, repentance and conversion are the preconditions for a radical change in people's lives.

Jesus summoned people to make a radical break with their past lives, characterized by sin and self-centeredness, and to make a fresh start that constitutes a whole new life. "Those who want to save their life will lose it, and those who lose their life for my sake, and for the sake of the gospel, will save it" (Mark 8:35). People must totally change the direction of their lives and, as it were, start over again: "Whoever does not receive the kingdom of God as a little child will never enter it" (10:15). The nature of the new life is most clearly brought out by Jesus in his encounter with Nicodemus in John 3 (see Toon 1987: 13-15, 26-29; Witherup 1994: 78-81). As "a leader of the Jews" (v. 1) and "a teacher of Israel" (v. 10), Nicodemus represents God's people Israel. But in Jesus he confronts the Son of Man (v. 13), God's only Son (v. 16), the one who brings the kingdom of God (v. 3). Confronted with the new order, Nicodemus is told by Jesus, "You must be born again/from above *(dei humas gennēthēnai anōthen)*" (vv. 3, 7). The Greek word *anōthen* has a double meaning, either "again" or "from above," and while "from above" is more in accordance with Johannine usage (cf. J. M. Robinson 1962b: 24), both meanings are probably intended here. Nicodemus takes it literally and asks how anyone could enter a second time into his mother's womb (v. 4). Jesus responds by saying that the new birth of which he speaks involves being born "of water and Spirit" (v. 5). In addition to one's natural birth, it is necessary to be born of the Spirit, i.e., to receive the divine gift of the Holy Spirit from above; the outward sign of this transformation is the "water" of baptism. It is important to note that when Jesus says "*You* must be born again/from above," "the word *you* is in the plural and so it is not only Nicodemus but all Jews who are being addressed by Jesus" (Toon, 28). Rebirth has a corporate as well as an individual aspect: all Israelites are called upon to receive the new birth and, through baptism, enter the community of the new Israel.

In the Johannine literature the new birth becomes the standard way of describing the change that takes place within people as they pass from the old to the new order. To all who received Christ, "he gave power to become children of God, who were born, not of blood or of the will of the flesh or of the will of man, but of God" (John 1:12-13). Those who turn to God in Christ and believe in him are "born of God" (1 John 3:9; 4:7; 5:1, 18).

In a similar fashion Peter declares that God "has given us a new birth" through Christ's resurrection (1 Pet 1:3; *anagennaō* = "beget again, cause to be born again"). Believers "have been born anew, not of perishable but of imperishable seed, through the living and enduring word of God" (1:23; cf. John 1:13 for the contrast with natural human birth). Jas 1:18 says God "gave us birth by the word of truth" (*apokueō* = "give birth to"). Both Peter and James highlight the fact that the new birth is brought about by the "word," i.e., the proclamation of the gospel.

Paul also speaks of the new life in Christ in terms of a radical new beginning. Baptism, the outward sign of entry into the new community, symbolizes a *dying* to the old life and a *rising* to the new life in Christ. The symbolism would be more vivid for his readers if, as is probable, baptism was by total immersion with the candidate literally going down under the water and rising again from it. Paul says, "All of us who have been baptized into Christ Jesus were baptized into his death[.] Therefore we have been buried with him by baptism into death, so that, just as Christ was raised from the dead by the glory of the Father, so we too might walk in newness of life" (Rom 6:3-4). Paul's distinctive emphasis is that the transformation of the believer parallels the death and resurrection of Christ. The transition from the old to the new order, brought about by the Christ event, is reenacted, as it were, in each individual believer. This involves both death and resurrection: believers have died to the old sinful life (Rom 6:6-7, 11; Eph 2:5; Col 2:20; 3:3), and they have been "raised with Christ" (Col 3:1) to "newness of life" (Rom 6:4). Of course, the typical already/not yet tension remains so that in one sense the believer's resurrection still lies in the future (cf. Rom 6:5).

Titus 3:5 introduces a distinctive term for the new birth symbolized in baptism. God saved us, this text tells us, "according to his mercy, through the washing of rebirth and renewal by the Holy Spirit." *Palingenesia*, which is used only here and in Matt 19:28 (see below, 17-4.4), means literally "rebirth" or "regeneration."

The idea of rebirth or regeneration was common in the Hellenistic world (see J. M. Robinson 1962b: 25-26), and some critical scholars hold that it was imported from there into Christianity, at a relatively late date. Against this it can be argued that since birth is a universal human experience, the image could well have been used by Jesus and the early church (cf. Toon 1987: 28-29). BT, however, is not concerned with tracing historical origins but with how the image is used in the NT, and there it is indissolubly linked with the Christ event.

Of the other images used for the transition from the old to the new life, the most striking is that of the transfer of a person from the sphere of darkness to that of light: converts "turn from darkness to light" (Acts 26:18), "for once you were darkness, but now in the Lord you are light" (Eph 5:8; cf. 2 Cor 4:6; 1 Pet 2:9). In the Johannine writings especially, people are confronted with a choice between darkness and light (John 3:19-21; 1 John 1:5-7), and are called to "believe in the light" (John 12:36) and "walk in the light" (1 John 1:7).

Despite distinctive emphases, there is a strong basic unity in the NT's view of the transition to the new life. A radical change is involved: people must, in addition to their natural birth, receive a second, spiritual birth (John, Peter); they must die to their old life and rise to the new (Paul). This happens in response to the preaching of the Word, and is the work of God who "begets" believers, through the power of the Holy Spirit. The new birth involves incorporation into the church, the new Israel, the outward sign of which is baptism.

17-3.3. FAITH AND DOUBT

The call to have faith/believe plays a major role in the NT's understanding of the response of the individual to the grace of God.

a. Faith

The NT uses the verb *pisteuō* = "to believe, believe in, trust, have faith," and the noun *pistis* = "faithfulness; trust, confidence, faith; a body of faith or belief, doctrine." The expression to "receive" or "accept" Christ *(lambanō* or *paralambanō)* comes close in meaning to *pisteuō* (John 1:11; 5:43; 13:20; Col 2:6).

In his preaching Jesus called for faith: "Repent, and believe *(pisteuete)* in the gospel" (Mark 1:15). For Jesus faith is basically faith in God, with whom all things are possible (9:23; 14:36; cf. Stuhlmacher 1994). Faith, according to Jesus, can move mountains (11:23 and //s). He was quick to commend faith wherever it manifested itself: "Not even in Israel have I found such faith" (Matt 8:10 RSV). Faith plays an important role in Jesus' healings: "Your faith has made you well" (Mark 5:34). In this sense it may be defined as "the hoping expectation with which a person in need turns to Jesus and asks for help" (Hermisson and Lohse 1981: 116). Faith may have to surmount discouragement, as in the story of the blind beggar (Mark 10:47-52 and //s) where "many sternly ordered him to be quiet, but he cried out even more loudly." "This narrative focuses on the blind man who is thereby presented as a model of faith in Jesus in spite of discouragement, and as one who eagerly answers the call of the Master and follows him in the way of discipleship" (W. Harrington 1980: 131). While in the Synoptics faith is primarily faith in God, by implication it is also faith in Jesus as the one in and through whom God is acting in a unique way.

In the Johannine literature the noun *pistis* is lacking, with the solitary exception of 1 John 5:4: "This is the victory that conquers the world, our faith." But the verb *pisteuō* is frequent and is a key term. The purpose of writing John's Gospel, says the author, is "that you may come to believe that Jesus is the Messiah, the Son of God, and that through believing you may have life in his name" (20:31). What is implicit in the Synoptics is made explicit in John; Jesus calls for faith not only in God but also in himself: "Believe in God, believe also in me" (14:1). To believe in Jesus is to believe in God (12:44) and to believe that God sent him (5:24). Whoever believes in Jesus receives the gift of eternal life (3:15-16). While some texts in John's Gospel suggest that Jesus' miracles ("signs") evoked faith (e.g., 2:11; cf. 6:14), in 4:48 ("Unless you see signs and wonders you will not believe") Jesus characterizes this at best as an imperfect kind of faith (see Schnackenburg 1968: 571). Thomas represents the view that "seeing is believing" (20:25), but Jesus says, "Blessed are those who have not seen and yet have come to believe" (20:29).

After Easter the church called for faith in Jesus as the one in and through whom God had inaugurated the new age. In response to the preaching of the gospel, "many of those who heard the word believed" (Acts 4:4; cf. 11:21). While faith involves individual decision, for the early church it always also has a corporate dimension: "Only the individual person can give the answer of faith by which the gospel is accepted. However, by means of this answer he also becomes a member of the community which assembles as the people of God, and he belongs to the convocation of believers" (Hermisson and Lohse 1981: 112).

Faith is central for Paul and may be defined as the total response of the individual to the gospel (see Stuhlmacher 1994). "The gospel," Paul declares, "is the power of God for salvation to everyone who has faith. . . . For in it the righteousness of God is revealed through faith for faith; as it is written, 'The one who is righteous will live by faith'" (Rom 1:16-17, quoting an adapted form of Hab 2:4). He tells the Galatians, "You are all children of God through faith" (3:26). The people of God are constituted not by those physically descended from Abraham, but by those who share the kind of faith that Abraham had (Rom 4:16-25; Gal 3:6-9; see Hermisson and Lohse 1981: 138-44). For Paul, however, faith is basically "faith in Jesus Christ" (Rom 3:22; Gal 2:16, 20; Phil 3:9; Col 1:4). Attempts have been made to show that the phrase *pistis Iēsou Xristou* (e.g., Rom 3:22) should be taken as a subjective genitive meaning "through the faithfulness of Jesus Christ" (see Torrance 1957), and this has been much debated (see J. Reumann 1976: 332-33). On balance, however, in the context of Paul's theology as a whole, it seems best to take it as an objective genitive meaning "faith (i.e., by believers) in Jesus Christ."

Paul emphasizes the role of faith in relation to "justification *(dikaiosynē)*" or "being justified *(dikaioō)*" (see 3-3; 9-3.4b), i.e., being accepted into a right relationship with God on the basis of what God has done in Christ, especially through his atoning death. It will be recalled that Luther took the phrase "justification by faith" as a key to Pauline theology and indeed to NT theology as a whole (cf. B-2). While Paul emphasized that justification is an act of sheer grace, he also recognized that grace has to be received in order to become operative in a person's life. For Paul this takes place through *faith* that involves trust, commitment, and obedience. Hence Paul's typical formula: "A person is justified not by the works of the law but through faith in Jesus Christ" (Gal 2:16). It will be clear that to speak of "justification *by* faith" seriously misrepresents Paul. Persons are not accepted by God *because* of their faith; that would make faith a precondition, a "work" in Pauline terminology. Faith is merely the channel through which God's grace is received, and in a mysterious way even faith itself is a gift from God. Eph 2:8 summarizes the Pauline position concisely: "By grace you have been saved through faith, and this is not your own doing; it is the gift of God." Thus Paul's understanding is more accurately defined as "justification *by* grace *through* faith" (cf. Ziesler 1990: 83-85). On the relationship between faith and works, see further 18-3.

A contrast has often been drawn in NT theology between "faith in" (personal trust in Christ) and "faith that" (acceptance of certain beliefs); in Paul's letters (i.e., the "genuine" or earlier ones), it is held, faith is faith in Christ in the sense of personal trust, commitment, and obedience. It is generally held that there is a shift in the Pastoral Epistles toward "faith that," i.e., more of an emphasis on the content of the faith that is to be passed on from one generation to another (cf. Childs 1992: 610-11). Thus Timothy is said to be "nourished on the words of the faith and of the sound teaching that you have followed" (1 Tim 4:6); here "the faith" (note the definite article) seems to be closely parallel to "the sound teaching" (cf. 1:10-11; Titus 1:4). But too strong a contrast must not be drawn, for even in the earlier Pauline letters faith is not only "faith in" but also "faith that." For Paul faith presupposed the basic proclamation *(kerygma)* of the Christian message that he received from the earliest Christian communities (1 Cor 15:3), particularly as that focused on the death and resurrection of Christ. Faith therefore includes "believing *that*" God raised Christ from the dead (Rom 10:9; 1 Thess 4:14), even though it is primarily believing *in* Christ. Childs (1992) summarizes by saying that "faith in Paul is the acceptance of the kerygma, but not in the intellectual sense of simply holding facts to be true. Rather, it is to be seized by an act of God which has been demonstrated by his raising Christ from the dead. . . . For Paul, faith is not just a noetic acknowledgment of what God has done in Jesus Christ, but a passionate, life-determining act of reception which serves as a condition for partaking of God's gracious benefits" (606-8). In the Pastorals there is undoubtedly a shift of emphasis, but it is important to note that Paulines and Pastorals balance one another within the canon; "faith in" cannot exist without some kind of "faith that"; in order to trust personally in Christ it is necessary to know something about Christ.

"Faith" is a key word in Hebrews, and 11:1 gives the only formal definition in the NT: "Faith is the assurance of things hoped for, the conviction of things not seen." Faith looks both to the future, to the final consummation, and above, to the unseen world where God already reigns. In practical terms faith involves particularly trust in and obedience to God; this is illustrated especially in the "roll call of faith" in 11:4-40. The author does not speak of believing in Christ, but he does see Christ as "the pioneer and perfecter of our faith" (12:2), i.e., "the exemplar and the facilitator of faith" (Hamm 1990: 286; see the whole article for a fuller discussion of faith in Hebrews).

b. Doubt

Not only does the NT appear to have less to say than the OT on the subject of doubt, there are a number of passages that clearly condemn doubt. There are no books comparable to Job or Ecclesiastes; the message of the gospel rings out with a new note of confidence that calls for faith and commitment rather than for doubt or even questioning. Jesus condemns doubt: "If you have faith and do not doubt," you can move mountains (Matt 21:21). He asks his disciples in astonishment, "Why did you doubt?" (14:31). Similarly James counsels: "Ask in faith, never doubting, for the one who doubts is like a wave of the sea, driven and tossed by the wind" (Jas 1:6-8).

Yet there are indications that Jesus, as part of his total identification with the human condition, wrestled with doubts in his temptations (Matt 4:1-11; Luke 4:1-13), in the Garden of Gethsemane (Mark 14:32-42 and //s), and on the cross (Matt 27:46//Mark 15:34). One story in Mark's Gospel provides a classic statement of the faith/doubt dialectic — the man who cried out to Jesus, "I believe; help my unbelief!" (9:24). The story also suggests that even faith is in a sense a gift of God, not a human accomplishment. In John's Gospel the story of "Doubting Thomas" (20:24-29) also recognizes a dialectic between faith and doubt.

17-3.4. KNOWING CHRIST

Faith brings the believer into a close relationship with the God who is revealed in Christ. This can be expressed in a variety of ways in the NT.

The NT echoes the language of the OT in speaking of the believer "knowing" God (*ginōskō* = "know"; *gnōsis* = "knowledge"). But the knowledge of God is radically reinterpreted in the light of the Christ event: through Christ believers can come to know what God is really like, and through Christ they are enabled to enter into a close personal relationship with God (cf. Piper 1962a: 45).

Jesus claims to mediate the true knowledge of God: "All things have been handed over to me by my Father; and no one knows the Son except the Father, and no one knows the Father except the Son and anyone to whom the Son chooses to reveal him" (Matt 11:27//Luke 10:22). "Jesus is, in a unique sense, the revealer of the Father since he alone 'knows' the Father as the Father 'knows' him" (Botterweck and Zimmermann 1981: 475). This claim is more frequently found in John's Gospel, where Jesus assures his disciples that a true knowledge of God comes through him: "If you know me, you will know my Father also," he tells them, and when Philip demands to see the Father, he responds, "Whoever has seen me has seen the Father" (14:7-9). Jesus reveals God because he alone truly knows God (7:29; cf. 8:55), and God knows him (10:15). Jesus, however, does not merely reveal the Father but enables believers to know God: "This is eternal life, that they may know you, the only true God, and Jesus Christ whom you have sent" (17:3). 1 John frequently echoes the language of "knowing" but emphasizes in particular that such knowledge must issue in ethical living: "Whoever says, 'I have come to know him,' but does not obey his commandments, is a liar" (2:4).

For Paul, believers are those who "have come to know God, or rather to be known by God" (Gal 4:9). He speaks of knowing God (1 Cor 15:34; 2 Cor 4:6; 10:5; Col 1:10), but also of knowing Christ; all else pales before "the surpassing value of knowing Christ Jesus my Lord" (Phil 3:8; cf. Eph 4:13; also 2 Pet 1:2-3, 8; 2:20; 3:18). Believers can be said to be "filled with all knowledge" (Rom 15:14; cf. 1 Cor 1:5). Some of Paul's references to knowledge *(gnōsis)*, however, have a polemical setting (cf. 1 Tim 6:20). In 1 Corinthians especially, he appears to be countering a group that claimed to have a special *gnōsis* (8:1-2; see commentaries for reconstruction of the historical situation and the identity of Paul's opponents). In response he stresses that true knowledge is a gift of the Spirit (12:8; cf. 14:6), and that to have "all knowledge" without love is of no avail (13:2).

Another way Paul speaks of the close personal relationship between believers and Christ is by saying that they are "in Christ": "If anyone is in Christ, there is a new creation" (2 Cor 5:17). Paul thinks in terms of a mutual indwelling; as well as speaking of the believer being in Christ, he also speaks of Christ being in the believer. "It is no longer I who live," he can declare, "but it is Christ who lives *in me*" (Gal 2:20). He says to the Romans that "Christ is in you" (Rom 8:10; this appears to be very close to what he says in the previous verse, that "the Spirit of God dwells in you"). As Ziesler (1990) puts it, for Paul "believers *exist* in Christ, but Christ is *active* in believers" (50). These expressions point to a close personal relationship between Christ and the believer, but as noted earlier (11-3.4c), in these texts Paul is thinking not just in individualistic but also in corporate terms. To be "in Christ" also means to be a member of the body of Christ, the church: "We, who are many, are one body *in Christ,* and individually we are members one of another" (Rom 12:5). Thus it is hardly correct to speak of a "mystical union" between the believer and Christ or to suggest that Paul's thought can be classified as a form of "mysticism."

In John's Gospel Jesus also speaks of the relationship between the believer and himself as a mutual "abiding" *(menō en* = "remain, continue, abide in"): "Abide in me as I abide in you" (15:4); to some degree this parallels Jesus' own relationship with the Father, since he speaks of the Father abiding in him (14:10). This relationship will continue beyond Jesus' death because Jesus promises his disciples that the Spirit will abide with them (14:17). Though a close and intimate personal relationship is thus indicated, here again it is doubtful whether it can be said to have "an indubitably mystical element" (contra Munzer 1978: 225), for "abiding" has its corporate dimension also. It is as the members of the community share the Eucharist that Christ abides in them, and they in him (6:56). Believers are members of the church, branches that abide in the vine because only then can they produce fruit (15:1-11).

The Johannine Epistles echo the language of abiding (1 John 2:24; cf. 2 John 9); believers know they abide in Christ, and he in them, "because he has given us of his Spirit" (1 John 4:13). 1 John is particularly concerned with how to determine whether a person truly abides in Christ. Those who abide in Christ, it says, will walk as he walked (2:6), will obey his commandments (3:24), will confess that Jesus is the Son of God (4:15), and will abide in love (4:16).

As in the OT, to know God is also to love him: "Whoever does not love does not know God" (1 John 4:8; cf. 5:2). The NT emphasizes above all the *prior* love of God: "We love because he first loved us" (4:19), as well as the fact that love for God is meaningless unless it issues in the love of others.

In response to a question as to which commandment is the first of all, Jesus reiterated the Shema of Deut 6:4-5 (above, 17-1.4) (Mark 12:30 and //s): "You shall love the Lord your God with all your heart, and with all your soul, and with all your mind, and with all your strength," coupling with it the command to love your neighbor as yourself (= Lev 19:18). God demands and deserves our undivided love (Matt 6:24; cf. Luke 11:42). In John's Gospel Jesus emphasizes the priority of the divine love that calls forth love in response: "As the Father has loved me, so I have loved you; abide in my love" (15:9). To love God is to love Christ also (8:42). Paul also stresses the priority of God's love: "God proves his love for us in that while we were still sinners Christ died for us" (Rom 5:8; cf. 8:39; Eph 2:4; 3:19 speaks of the love of Christ); but this love calls forth a response, and believers are "those who love God" (Rom 8:28) or have "an undying love for our Lord Jesus Christ" (Eph 6:24). According to Jas 2:5, God has promised his kingdom to those who love him. 1 John, as noted above, also speaks of believers loving God in response to God's love: "In this is love, not that we loved God but that he loved us" (4:10). Such love is valueless and meaningless unless it is reflected in love for others; 4:20 says in the bluntest possible way: "Those who say, 'I love God,' and hate their brothers or sisters, are liars" (cf. 3:17).

17-3.5. PERSONAL PRAYER

In the NT, as in the OT, prayer is the lifeblood of the relationship between God and people (cf. W. Harrington 1980: 93). The NT opens with figures like Anna who "never left the temple but worshiped there with fasting and prayer night and day" (Luke 2:37), and ends in the book of Revelation with the prayers of the saints rising up to God (5:8; 8:3-4).

a. Public Prayer and Personal Prayer

The NT has less to say about public prayer than the OT, since the liturgical life of the church was still at an early stage of development (cf. 14-3.5). But here too it is clear that public and private prayer are mutually supportive. The line between the two may not always be clearly drawn, especially if those scholars are right who hold that in the NT epistles the authors sometimes draw upon liturgical materials used in the early Christian communities (cf. Cullmann 1995: 71)

b. The Example and Teaching of Jesus

Within the NT Jesus' own example and teaching on prayer hold a special place. The Gospels underline the place of prayer in Jesus' own life (see Jeremias 1967: 66-78). To him it meant taking time to be alone with God, and seeking to know God's will for his life. At the outset of his ministry, according to Mark, "in the morning, while it was still very dark," Jesus "got up and went out to a deserted place, and there he prayed" (1:35). Mark 6:46//Matt 14:23 and Luke 6:12 all speak of Jesus withdrawing to the hills to pray, and suggest that this was a regular practice. These passages make clear that Jesus' "consciousness of his mission, his total submission to the Father were deepened in solitary prayer, in the silence of nature" (Hamman 1971: 86). Luke in particular stresses Jesus' prayer life, citing many examples of Jesus at prayer not found in the other Gospels (see O'Brien 1973: 113-16). Specific prayers of Jesus are quoted on eight occasions, five in the Synoptics and three in John (Matt 11:25-26//Luke 10:21-22; Matt 26:39//Mark 14:36//Luke 22:42; 23:34; Matt 27:46//Mark 15:34; Luke 23:46; John 11:41-42; 12:27-28; 17:1-26 — Jesus' "High Priestly Prayer").

In the OT, as we have seen, there are numerous examples of prayer but very little actual teaching on prayer. In the NT, by way of contrast, prayer is an important theme in Jesus' ministry of teaching (cf. P. D. Miller 1994: 307). Matthew has gathered an important block of material on this subject in the Sermon on the Mount (6:5-15). But here again, most material is found in Luke, in particular in the parables of the friend at midnight (11:5-8), the unjust judge (18:1-8), and the Pharisee and the publican (18:9-14).

A special place is held by the prayer that Jesus gave to his disciples as a model (on the Lord's Prayer, see "The Lord's Prayer in the Light of Recent Research" in Jeremias 1967: 82-107; J. R. W. Stott 1978: 142-52; Clowney 1990: 159-65; P. D. Miller 1994: 328-35; Cullmann 1995: 37-69). The Lord's Prayer is found in different contexts and in slightly different forms in Matt 6:9-13 (the fuller form) and Luke 11:2-4 (see Jeremias, 85-94; Cullmann, 39). According to Luke, it was given in response to a request from a disciple who asked, "Lord, teach us to pray" (11:1-2). While it is true that we are not to convert it "into a mantra and mumble a hundred 'paternosters' as steps on a ladder to heaven" (Clowney, 159), nevertheless the Lucan setting does suggest that the prayer was given to be memorized and repeated. On the other hand, in Matthew it is presented more as a model prayer; when the disciples pray, they are to do so "in this way *(houtōs)*" (6:9). Both emphases are thus present in the canon.

The Lord's Prayer is a simple, direct, confident prayer with three petitions which relate to God: that God's name (i.e., God himself) be reverenced, that his kingdom come, and that his will be done. There is much to be said for the suggestion (first made by Origen) that the phrase "on earth as it is in heaven" (Matt 6:10) applies to each of these three petitions (cf. J. R. W. Stott 1978: 147; Cullmann 1995: 50). These are followed by three petitions relating to our own needs: for provision for material needs one day at a time, for forgiveness of our sins "as we hereby forgive our debtors" (so Jeremias 1967: 102), and for deliverance from the attacks of the evil one (Satan).

c. The Early Church

The book of Acts continues Luke's special interest in prayer and demonstrates how the early church heeded and obeyed the teaching of Jesus. Prayer precedes all the main stages of the church's development (e.g., 1:24-25; 6:6; 10:9-16; 12:5; 13:3; 14:23; 20:36). A series of incidents in Acts clearly parallels events in Luke's Gospel: in both, prayer precedes the descent of the Holy Spirit (Luke 3:21//Acts 1:14; cf. Acts 8:15-17) and also the selection of apostles (Luke 6:12//Acts 1:24-25), while the dying Stephen's prayer committing himself to God and prayer for his executioners parallel those of Jesus (Acts 7:59//Luke 23:46; Acts 7:60//Luke 23:34; see O'Brien 1973: 122).

The epistles also bear testimony to the key role of prayer in the life of the church. Paul refers to his own prayer life, for example, when he says, "We give thanks to God always for you all, constantly mentioning you in our prayers" (1 Thess 1:2 RSV; cf. Rom 1:9; Phil 1:3-4; Col 1:3), and he urges the readers of the same letter to "pray without ceasing" (1 Thess 5:17; cf. Rom 12:12). A considerable amount of the material in the epistles (especially those of Paul) could be classified as prayer (cf. Coggan 1967: 95-167; Stanley 1973; D. Peterson 1990). Wiles (1974) has made a special study of Paul's intercessory prayers.

d. The Theology of Prayer

i. Dialogue with God

As in the OT, prayer is essentially dialogue with God. God himself may open the conversation, as when he called, "Saul, Saul" (Acts 9:4), and went on to change the whole direction of his life. Even more so than the OT, the NT emphasizes God's willingness to enter into dialogue. Jesus' own easy and intimate access to the Father was something he sought to share with his disciples. He encouraged people to pray: "Ask, and it will be given you; search, and you will find; knock, and the door will be opened for you" (Matt 7:7//Luke 11:9). His parabolic teaching uses the "how much more" technique. If an unjust judge will vindicate a widow who keeps pestering him, how much more will God vindicate his people who cry to him for help (Luke 18:1-8)? If a householder, snug in bed, will eventually get up to answer the need of a neighbor, how much more will God respond to the requests of his people (11:5-8; cf. the argument in Matt 7:9-11//Luke 11:11-13)? In the farewell discourses in John, Jesus assures his disciples that "the Father will give you whatever you ask in my name" (15:16; see Cullmann 1995: 98-106). Texts such as these do not mean that believers can ask for and receive whatever they want. For Jesus, prayer involved seeking to know and do God's will. He himself prayed, and taught others to pray, "Your will be done" (Matt 6:10; Luke 22:42).

The theme of access to God is particularly stressed in Hebrews. Because of Jesus' high-priestly ministry, "let us therefore approach the throne of grace with boldness, so that we may receive mercy and find grace to help in time of need" (4:16). Christ's sacrificial death has opened up a "new and living way" to God, so "let us approach with a true heart in full assurance of faith" (10:20, 22).

Paul stresses the role of the Spirit in prayer (see Cullmann 1995: 72-80). "The Spirit helps us in our weakness; for we do not know how to pray as we ought, but that very Spirit intercedes with sighs too deep for words" (Rom 8:26). "Man is irrevocably human and his aspirations often fight a losing battle with his natural weakness. The Spirit comes to his help, adding to man's prayer his own intercession which transcends human frailty" (W. Harrington 1980: 160). It is through the agency of the Spirit that believers can address God with the intimate family title of "Abba! Father!" (Rom 8:14-16; Gal 4:6).

In the NT prayer is generally addressed to God as Father (e.g., Matt 6:9; Eph 3:14), "through" Christ (e.g., Rom 1:8; Heb 13:15) or "in the name of" Christ (e.g., Eph 5:20; John 14:13), in the Spirit (e.g., Eph 6:18; Jude 20). It is quite legitimate therefore to speak of "the trinitarian character of Christian prayer" (see P. D. Miller 1994: 314-21).

ii. Language

The language of Jesus' prayers is simple, direct, and addressed to one who can be called "Father." Seven of the eight recorded prayers of Jesus begin with the word "Father" (the only exception is Matt 27:46//Mark 15:34, but of course, this is a quotation of Ps 22:1). Mark 14:36 shows that the original Aramaic word used by Jesus in prayer was *Abba* (cf. 1-3.4a; 8-5.1). As Jeremias (1967) has shown, this word that comes from the intimate family circle was not used in contemporary Jewish prayers. Jesus' use of it in all his prayers reveals that "he spoke to God as a child to its father, simply, inwardly, confidently" (62); his use of it in the Lord's Prayer shows that he encouraged and enabled his followers to approach God in a similar way (97), and the actual Aramaic word *Abba* was retained in the prayer language of the early church (Rom 8:15; Gal 4:6). Jesus also commended brevity in prayer: "When you are praying, do not heap up empty phrases as the

Gentiles do; for they think that they will be heard because of their many words. Do not be like them, for your Father knows what you need before you ask him" (Matt 6:7-8; cf. Mark 12:40//Luke 20:47). Here again Jesus practiced what he preached: six of his eight recorded prayers consist of one sentence.

iii. Types of Prayer

The main types of prayer (cf. 14-1.5a.i) are represented in personal prayers in the NT (see D. Peterson 1990: 87-93). It is appropriate to enter God's presence with *praise* and *thanksgiving*. Jesus gave thanks to God (Matt 11:25; Mark 14:22); prayers of thanksgiving are specially commended by Paul (Col 3:17), and are found near the start of most epistles (Galatians is the striking exception in Paul's letters). Prayers of *confession* are well illustrated in the parable of the Pharisee and the publican, where the latter prays, "God, be merciful to me, a sinner!" (Luke 18:9-14). Prayers of *petition* are illustrated in the Lord's Prayer, and are frequent, especially in Paul's letters. Jesus prayed for his disciples and taught them to pray for others, even their enemies (Matt 5:43-45). Paul constantly prayed for his churches, typically that they might know God's will (Col 1:9; cf. 4:12; Phil 1:9-10), and prayers of *intercession* are specially commended in 1 Tim 2:1 (see P. D. Miller 1994: 325-27 on prayers of intercession in the NT).

iv. Unanswered Prayer

The NT also contains some striking examples of "unanswered prayer" (cf. above, 17-1.5c.iv). In Gethsemane Jesus prayed that he might be spared suffering and death: "Abba, Father, for you all things are possible; remove this cup from me" (Mark 14:36). This prayer was not granted; the cup of suffering was not removed, and Jesus went to the cross. John 12:27-28a provides a close parallel in substance, if not in wording: "Now my soul is troubled. And what should I say — 'Father, save me from this hour'? No, it is for this reason that I have come to this hour. Father, glorify your name" (cf. P. D. Miller 1994: 322). In 2 Cor 12:7-9 Paul tells of praying for the removal of a thorn or stake *(skolops)* in the flesh, probably a recurring, painful, physical illness: "Three times I appealed to the Lord about this, that it would leave me," but this did not happen (see 20-3.3). These passages make a vital contribution to the theology of prayer; as Miller says, "in these examples . . . Christian prayer begins to be shaped by a theology of the cross" (323). Jesus' prayer in Gethsemane is a model one; along with Paul's prayer it demonstrates that it is not wrong to pray to avoid suffering, yet all prayers must be qualified by what follows — "nevertheless not my will, but thine, be done" (Luke 22:42 RSV); "access to God in prayer implies that we seek to do the will of God" (Clowney 1990: 148). The essence of prayer is not getting God to do what we want, but learning to do what God wants, i.e., discovering and submitting to the will of God (cf. Cullmann 1995: 32-34).

New Testament: Consummation

17-4. PRESS ON TOWARD THE GOAL

The NT brings the good news that the promises and hopes of the OT have been fulfilled. Human nature can be changed: human beings can turn to God, in Jesus Christ, through the Holy Spirit, and can experience the new life of the new order. Nevertheless, as we have constantly seen, the NT is characterized throughout by the already/not yet tension. Therefore it also looks forward in hope to the final goal of creation and of history, and to the final consummation when faith will be replaced by sight.

17-4.1. A LIVING HOPE

For this reason "hope" plays a major role in the NT. The word for hope is *elpis* (verb *elpizō*; see Hoffmann 1975: 241; for cognate words meaning "expect," "wait for," see 244-46; for a listing of all relevant texts, see Moule 1963b: 67-71). As in the OT, hope has a double meaning. It signifies the *content* of what God promises his people, that for which they hope: the coming of God's kingdom in power and glory, the parousia of Christ, the final victory over Satan and all the powers of evil, the resurrection and the gift of eternal life. This "forward look" is an essential part of NT faith, and so the fourth section of each chapter of this book deals with some aspect of the NT hope (cf. E-3; 1-4.1). The other side of hope is the *attitude* of Christian believers who trust in the promises of God. The two meanings of course are closely connected. The attitude of hope is grounded in what God has already done in Jesus Christ (1 Pet 1:3, 21), and in the promises he has made (Acts 26:6). God is "the God of hope" who can make believers "abound in hope by the power of the Holy Spirit" (Rom 15:13; cf. Acts 24:15).

According to the NT, "hope is an essential feature of authentic Christian life" (Schlier 1968: 142). Eph 2:12 refers to the time before its readers became believers when they were "without Christ . . . having no hope and without God in the world." Especially in face of death, Christians are not to grieve "as others do who have no hope" (1 Thess 4:13).

The vocabulary of hope is largely absent from the Gospels, though what the word designates is present. With dramatic irony the two disciples on the walk to Emmaus say of Jesus, "We had hoped that he was the one to redeem Israel" (Luke 24:21). The later writers of the NT look back to the Christ event, to the redemption that he won, and find in that the ground of hope. Hope plays a major role in Paul's thought (cf. Minear 1962: 641-42); he groups together faith, hope, and love as the central marks of the life of believers (1 Cor 13:13; 1 Thess 1:3; 5:8; cf. Rom 5:1-5). 1 Peter has been called "the epistle of hope," so important is the theme of "a living hope" to it (see esp. 1:3-5). Hebrews links hope closely with faith (cf. Ewert 1980: 179), as in its famous definition "faith is the assurance of things hoped for . . ." (11:1). The fact that the words *elpis* and *elpizō* are lacking from the book of Revelation underscores the limitations of a "word study" approach (cf. A. Barr 1950a: 68), for no book of the NT does more to hold up the hope of God's final victory and to encourage believers through that hope.

Hope is essentially forward looking; it confidently expects what it cannot at present see. "For in hope we were saved. Now hope that is seen is not hope. For who hopes for what is seen? But if we hope for what we do not see, we wait for it with patience" (Rom 8:24). Hope, the NT recognizes, does not necessarily come easily; it has to surmount barriers. Paul speaks of Abraham "hoping against hope" (4:18); i.e., "against what human judgment of the future declared to be impossible he set the hope given him through God's promise" (Hoffmann 1975: 243; cf. Hermisson and Lohse 1981: 147-48). There is much in human experience, such as suffering and death, that contradicts hope. "We can see that hope in the NT sense does not mean to ignore such an obstacle to hope. To hope is not to dream" (Schlier 1968: 149; cf. Moule 1963b: 17-18). Thus in Rom 5:2-5 Paul explains that those who have been justified "boast in our hope of sharing the glory of God. And not only that, but we also boast in our sufferings, knowing that suffering produces endurance, and endurance produces character, and character produces hope, and hope does not disappoint us, because God's love has been poured into our hearts through the Holy Spirit that has been given to us." Hope involves waiting, and waiting requires patience (cf. 8:24; 15:4; Jas 5:7-8); thus it may truly be said that "In the New Testament . . . patience is an auxiliary virtue to hope" (Bauer 1981a: 378).

H. R. White (1981) contends that in the NT "hope is inherently trinitarian" (4). Hope focuses on Christ: "the hope of glory" is "Christ in you" (Col 1:27), and in 1 Tim 1:1 he is referred to simply as "Christ Jesus our hope." Yet the NT can also say, "We have our hope set on the living God" (4:10; cf. 1 Pet 1:21). And in face of obstacles, it is in particular the presence of the Holy Spirit that makes hope possible: "May the God of hope fill you with all joy and peace in believing, so that you may abound in hope by the power of the Holy Spirit" (Rom 15:13). As Moule (1963b) puts it, "the present tense of hope is the Holy Spirit in the Christian Church" (35-36).

17-4.2. DEVELOPMENT TOWARD MATURITY

Hope looks to the future, and the ultimate goal of the Christian life lies at the final consummation. But the NT stresses that in this life there can be development and progress toward that goal, and in this sense too the Christian life has a forward look. In Phil 3:12-14 Paul admits that he has not yet reached the goal, "but I press on to make it my own. . . . This one thing I do: forgetting what lies behind and straining forward to what lies ahead, I press on toward the goal for the prize of the heavenly call of God in Christ Jesus."

Just as the beginning of the Christian life is spoken of as a new birth, so converts can be seen as "babes" or "infants" *(nēpioi)* who need to grow up and advance toward maturity. Thus Paul says the Corinthians were "infants in Christ" whom he fed "with milk, not solid food," and he complains that they are still not ready for solid food (1 Cor 3:1-3). Hebrews employs exactly the same analogy, and makes the same complaint: "Though by this time you ought to be teachers, you need someone to teach you again the basic elements of the oracles of God. You need milk, not solid food" (5:12).

The goal of the Christian life is to become *teleios,* a word traditionally translated as "perfect." This suggests a highly unrealistic ideal, but most modern translations more accurately render it as "mature" (noun *teleiotēs* = "maturity"). Thus Paul says to the Corinthians, "Do not be children in your thinking; be babes in evil, but in thinking be mature" (1 Cor 14:20 RSV; NRSV translates *teleioi* as "adults"). The particular context here suggests that a mature Christian is one who can assess a situation in a responsible way and decide on priorities. Another mark of maturity is that a person is well educated in the faith. Col 1:28 speaks about "teaching everyone in all wisdom, so that we may present everyone mature in Christ," and according to Heb 5:12, the mature Christian ought to be able to teach others. A further mark of progress is moral maturity (Matt 5:48; 19:21; Jas 3:2). Christians are mature when their lives are controlled by love that, according to Col 3:14 (AT), is "the bond of maturity *(sundesmos tēs teleiotētos).*" Christ himself is the pattern and norm of maturity; the aim of the Christian life is to attain "to maturity, to the measure of the full stature of Christ" (Eph 4:13).

All of us, says Paul, "seeing the glory of the Lord . . . are being transformed into the same image from one degree of glory to another" (2 Cor 3:18). This is essentially a process by which believers move toward a goal, even if that goal can be fully and finally attained only when the faithful join their Lord in glory.

17-4.3. WE SHALL SEE HIM

Throughout this life, according to the NT, faith and hope are the keys to the Christian life. But at the final consummation faith and hope will be replaced by sight (on this theme, see already 1-4.4; 8-4.1).

In ancient times mirrors did not give the clear image we associate with them today. Paul employs the comparison of the unclear mirror in 1 Cor 13:12 when he declares that "now we see in a mirror, dimly, but then we will see face to face. Now I know only in part; then I will know fully, even as I have been fully known." 1 John 3:2 expresses a similar confidence: "Beloved, we are God's children now; what we will be has not yet been revealed. What we do know is this:

when he is revealed, we will be like him, for we will see him as he is." We can hardly conceive what it will mean to know God fully, to experience

> What no eye has seen, nor ear heard,
>> nor the human heart conceived,
> what God has prepared for those who love him,

though we do have a foretaste through the Spirit (1 Cor 2:9; cf. Isa 64:4).

17-4.4. THE RENEWAL OF ALL THINGS

The ultimate goal of the individual is full communion with God in the company of God's people. The NT visions of the future, as we have seen (cf. 11-4.1), are strongly corporate in nature, yet the final consummation will also be a time when each individual finds true fulfillment.

For the NT this will happen only at the final consummation. It is noteworthy that Jesus speaks of that consummation in terms of "regeneration" (*palingenesia;* cf. above, 17-3.2b). "At the renewal of all things *(en tē(i) palingenesia(i))*" believers will share Christ's rule and inherit eternal life (Matt 19:28-29). Not only individuals and not only God's people will be "born again," but also all creation (cf. 2-4.4b). Thus, according to the NT, "personal regeneration is part of a cosmic activity by God which involves the whole created order and provides the Christian community with wonderful promises in which to rest" (Toon 1987: 49).

17-4.5. THE PRAYERS OF ALL THE SAINTS

Prior to the final consummation the faithful pray for the coming of God's kingdom. Jesus taught his disciples to pray "Your kingdom come" (Matt 6:10//Luke 11:2). At the present time angels bear the prayers of the saints to God's throne (Rev 5:8; 8:3-4).

At the final consummation, however, there is no mention of prayer, for the faithful enjoy unbroken communion and fellowship with God.

17-5. FAITH AND HOPE: THEOLOGICAL REFLECTIONS

1. Some of the concerns of this chapter, such as the tension between faith and doubt and the place of personal prayer, have not often found a place within BT, perhaps because they are considered more the province of pastoral theology. It

is essential, however, for BT to reflect the entire range of concerns of the biblical material itself.

2. As noted at the outset (17-1), there is considerable continuity between OT and NT in their understanding of the human response to God's grace: both call for repentance in order to receive God's forgiveness, for a turning to the Lord, for faith, and for a close personal relationship with God. But there are also significant differences. The OT is addressed to God's people Israel, who stand in covenant relationship with him. Children who are born into the covenant are regarded as members of God's people from birth, the outward sign of this being circumcision. When they go astray, the people of Israel are typically called to *return* to the Lord. The NT arises out of the ministry of Jesus and the preaching of the early church. The proclamation of the breaking in of the kingdom and of the inauguration of the new order through the Christ event is addressed to all — Jews and Gentiles alike. In keeping with its more radical view of human sinfulness, the NT calls for a radical response: no one by nature or by birth stands in a right relationship to God; this can happen only through the grace of God, in Jesus Christ, through the Holy Spirit. Therefore, not just repentance and faith in God are called for, but also faith in Christ as the one who ushers in the new age, conversion, and a radical change that amounts to a new birth. Given the circumstances of the beginnings of Christianity, this message and this demand are addressed to those who can hear and understand and make their own conscious decisions. Those who accept the message are baptized and incorporated into the Christian community, where they begin their growth in grace. This is the paradigm that prevailed in the early years of the church, and it has also characterized Christian missions to non-Christian societies all down the centuries. It may also become more common in the "post-Christian" West as people with no Christian background accept the Christian message.

Beginning in the early centuries, however, another paradigm developed as children were born into Christian homes and brought up in the faith. The church was seen as a covenant community, in keeping with the OT pattern; children born into the covenant were seen as members of God's people from birth, the outward sign of this being baptism, the NT equivalent of circumcision (on infant baptism, see 14-3.4b). As this became the norm, the church associated regeneration with infant baptism: children of believing parents, who are born into the believing community, are "born again" through baptism, though it is only gradually as they grow up that they experience the working of the Holy Spirit in their lives. When they attain an appropriate age, they can "confirm" the decision made by their parents. Despite their criticisms of the medieval church, the main Reformers retained this basic pattern. In reaction to this paradigm, however, the evangelical revival, followed by many modern "evangelistic" movements (see Toon 1987: 156-82), came to emphasize the necessity of a personal decision, of "conversion" and of being "born again," as a conscious and more or less instantaneous experience on the part of those who have reached years of discretion. Even those already baptized as infants must undergo "believers' baptism" (contrary to the practice and belief of mainline churches, for whom more than one baptism is contrary to Scripture). The two understandings of baptism, conversion, and regeneration continue, in tension with one another, to the present day. The "evangelistic" view can claim NT support and rightly emphasizes the need for personal transformation and personal commitment, but it runs the risk of excessive individualism and of making salvation dependent on human decision rather than on the grace of God that can work in many ways, including through the birth of children into Christian homes and families. The view that regeneration can accompany infant baptism recognizes the priority of grace and the corporate nature of the Christian faith, but it runs the risk of condoning a nominal Christianity, and of undervaluing the need for personal decision and commitment.

3. Those groups that emphasize the need for a conscious experience of "conversion" usually think of this as sudden, and in some cases do not consider the experience valid unless the person concerned can name the exact day, if not the hour, of his or her "conversion." In this connection, Paul's experience on the Damascus road is often taken as a paradigm of sudden conversion. By contrast, however, it is notoriously difficult to pinpoint when Peter was converted; his "faith journey" had its ups and downs. No one type of experience is presented in the NT as the norm to which every single believer must conform. What is important is turning from sin, believing in Christ, and entering upon a life of discipleship, not exactly when and how this happens. For the NT salvation does not depend on personal experience but on the grace of God and on the operation of the Holy Spirit. It is noteworthy that although Paul's call/conversion is narrated three times over in Acts (Acts 9; 22; 26), Paul himself is reluctant to speak about his own religious experience and does so only when his apostolic authority is at stake (Gal 1:13-17; 2 Cor 11:16–12:13; cf. Witherup 1994: 88-93). His gospel was based on what God had done in Christ, not on his own personal experience. Furthermore, as we have also noted (above, 17-4.2), for the NT conversion is only the beginning of the Christian life; it is followed by a long process of progressing toward maturity.

4. The centrality of faith is underlined in all parts of the NT, and while the vocabulary is mainly lacking from the OT, the reality is there, more often in narrative than in abstract discussion or definition. A notable OT contribution is the recognition of the dialectic between faith and doubt, especially in the books of Job and Ecclesiastes. Not only is there a tension within these books, but they also contribute to a canonical dialectic. The very inclusion of writings within the canon that give such strong expression to doubt and skepticism is in itself profoundly significant. They do not negate those parts of the Bible that proclaim a confident faith in God, but with their realism they add a dimension of depth to the total biblical picture. For this reason they deserve greater atten-

tion and fuller discussion than they have hitherto been accorded in most works of BT.

5. Prayer permeates the whole of Scripture and is the lifeblood of believers' relationship with God; as P. D. Miller (1994) argues, "prayer and faith are interwoven into a single whole" (1). Both OT and NT encourage prayer and emphasize God's willingness to hear prayer. Christians pray "in the name" of Jesus, for it is through Christ that believers have access to the Father, and they are promised the aid of the Holy Spirit when they pray. Many people, however, even church members, have problems with personal prayer and find great difficulty in praying (cf. Cullmann 1995: 1-13). Some have theoretical problems ("If God already knows what we need, why pray to him?"); for others the problems are more practical, particularly relating to what is perceived as "unanswered prayer." Behind this often lies an immature and imperfect understanding of the true nature of prayer. The many biblical assurances that God hears and answers prayer must be read in the light of a well-rounded BT of prayer. In the Bible, "the essence of all prayer is that it is a conversation with God as the partner" (Cullmann, 17). Thus it includes praise and thanksgiving, and also confession of sin and seeking God's forgiveness, as well as petition and intercession. Moreover, like any true dialogue, it involves listening as well as speaking, for it is through listening that one learns God's will and thus can seek to conform to it. Praying "in the name" of Jesus also means that requests should be in accordance with the will of God as revealed in Jesus. The examples of "unanswered prayer" cited from both OT and NT remind us of the true nature of prayer. Reflection suggests that it is not really appropriate to label the prayers of Moses and David (above, 17-1.5c.iv) "unanswered prayers"; God answered both prayers, but in these specific cases, for reasons best known to God, the answer was no. In the case of Jesus and of Paul (above, 17-3.5d.iv), it is also not accurate to speak of "unanswered" prayer. As Jesus' model prayer in Gethsemane shows, prayer is not getting God to do what the believer wants; it is getting the believer to learn, accept, and do what God wants (cf. John 12:27-28). In Paul's case, while his illness was not healed, nevertheless his prayer was answered, and he in fact records God's answer: "He said to me, 'My grace is sufficient for you, for my power is made perfect in weakness'" (2 Cor 12:9). The answer was, in effect, "No, I will not spare you the suffering, but yes, I will give you the strength to overcome it."

6. While "hope" has been discussed here as part of the human response to the grace of God, it should be recalled that in this BT the second and fourth sections of each chapter deal with the content of both the OT and NT hope. The hopes of the OT are partially fulfilled in the NT with the inauguration of the new order, but Christians still have their sights set on the future, especially on the hope of the final consummation.

The beginning of a new millennium sees much ambivalence regarding the future. For many, pessimism seems to be the order of the day. Others, however, still cling to "the belief in progress," despite all the twentieth century did to dispel that myth. There is a tenacious streak in human nature, and others again simply "hope against hope," citing perhaps the old Latin tag *dum spiro, spero,* "while I breathe, I hope" or "where there's life, there's hope." Christian hope is based neither on a tenuous belief in the perfectibility of human nature nor on blind optimism; it is above all *realistic* (cf. H. R. White 1981: 65). The Bible presents a "*theology* of hope" grounded in God. What D. A. Hubbard (1983) says of hope in the OT is equally true of the NT: "In a society filled by immanental hope of social engineering, of human potential, of political revolution, we need to hear the great themes of Old Testament hope. Our hope is in the Lord, who is also our salvation; all other hope is hopeless" (58). Biblical hope is grounded both in what God has done in the past, especially in the Christ event, and in what he still promises to do in the future. "Christian hope does not have its roots in the changing circumstances of life in which hopes and dreams are often shattered and buried. Rather, it springs . . . from the deep conviction that God is the Lord of history" and "that in Christ God has in fact intervened and brought in his kingdom" (Ewert 1980: 173). While the NT sees the possibility of limited progress within history (cf. 3-4.4), its main ground for hope is the promised victory over evil and all that is opposed to God at the final consummation. Christians thus live between past and present, between memory and hope. It is both because of what God has done and because of what he promises to do that believers "have this hope, a sure and steadfast anchor of the soul" (Heb 6:19).

CHAPTER 18

God's Commandments

Old Testament: Proclamation

18-1. LOVE ME AND KEEP MY COMMANDMENTS

Throughout Scripture there is a constant emphasis on the fact that if people truly know and love God, then they must walk in his ways. "Biblical ethics" refers to that *way of life* appropriate to the human family (the created order) and especially to the people of God (the historical order).

18-1.1. THE THEOLOGICAL BASIS OF ETHICS

a. Ethics as Response

As we saw in chapter 17, divine grace calls forth a human response, in terms of repentance, returning to the Lord, and faith, that leads to truly "knowing" God. To *know* God, however, is also to *obey* him and to walk in his ways (see 17-1.4). In the OT ethics is to be understood as a part — a very important part — of the response of God's people to his grace and goodness.

This is evident not just from individual laws or sayings but from the very context and structure of OT ethical teaching. Thus the Decalogue begins with a declaration of what God has done for Israel *before* it sets forth what Israel is to do for God: "I am the LORD your God, who brought you out of the land of Egypt, out of the house of slavery; you shall have no other gods before me" (Exod 20:2-3; Deut 5:6-7). As Brueggemann (1997) puts it, "The God who commands is the God who delivers" (184). The book of Deuteronomy can be seen as an expanded version of the same pattern, with chapters 1–3 giving a résumé of God's care for Israel before going on to say, "So now, Israel, give heed to the statutes and ordinances that I am teaching you to observe" (4:1). Thus "for ancient Israel, the basic motive for ethical action of a particular kind is the obligation to respond to the activity of God on her behalf. Human conduct is called to be an answer to what God has done and promised" (Fletcher 1971: 52).

Biblical ethics is grounded in what God has done for humankind and especially for his people. It is also grounded in the very nature of God himself (cf. C. J. H. Wright 1983: 26-28). In the OT "the power of the good rests entirely on the recognition of God as the One who is good. Of moral behaviour for the sake of an abstract good there is none" (Eichrodt 1967: 316). A recurring formula in the OT is "You shall be holy *(qᵉdhōshîm),* for I the LORD your God am holy *(qādhôsh)*" (Lev 19:2; etc.). The basic meaning of *qādhôsh* is "separate," "set apart," or "sacred." God's servants, especially the priests, are said to be "holy" (21:7-8), i.e., set apart for God's service, but God's people as a whole are also holy: "For you are a people holy to the LORD your God" (Deut 7:6; cf. 14:2), and they can be referred to as "holy ones" or "saints" *(qᵉdhōshîm;* LXX *hagioi,* from *hagios* = "holy"; Pss 16:3; 34:9). In the OT, as applied to God's people, holiness has strong ethical implications. "The important thing to note is that a certain obedience, a certain way of life is demanded from the people because of what is known about God. In other words, the ethical norm is brought into intimate relationship with the revealed character of God" (Davidson 1959: 376).

b. Ethics and Community

While the OT knows of ethical norms applicable to all humankind (below, 18-1.3), in the OT ethics is primarily concerned with the response of *Israel,* the people called by God to serve him (cf. 11-1). Individuals, of course, are called to serve and obey God, but only in the context of the wider covenant community. It is the *community* of Israel that is called to be holy, i.e., set apart from other nations. One of the most important ways in which they are set apart is through being the recipients of God's commandments: "What other great nation has statutes and ordinances as just as this entire law that I am setting before you today?" (Deut 4:8).

Israel is called to be "a priestly kingdom and a holy nation" (Exod 19:6); as priests their task is to represent God to the nations of the world and to embody his holiness in their way of life. As the servant of the Lord (cf. 9-1.3d), Israel is to be a "light to the nations" (Isa 42:6) and to model for them the way of life that is God's will for all humankind. As C. J. H. Wright (1983) puts it, Israel's "very existence and character as a society were to be a witness to God, a model or paradigm of his holiness expressed in the social life of a redeemed community" (43). This remains true however much, in actual fact, Israel failed to live up to its calling.

c. God's Commandments

The way of life to be followed by God's people is based not on abstract "laws" or "rules," but on what God commands, i.e., on the revealed will of God; in the OT "devotion to God involves morality; morality is obedience to the will of God" (Crook 1990: 56; cf. Eichrodt 1966: 313). The terminology of "command" (verb *tsāwāh*) and "commandment" *(mitswâh)* runs throughout Exodus-Deuteronomy. The Torah consists of "the commandments of the LORD" (Deut 10:13). God speaks of "my commandments" (Exod 20:6). Moses can be said to give commandments, but only in the sense that he mediates God's commands: "If you obey the commandments of the LORD your God that I [Moses] am commanding you today . . ." (Deut 30:16).

Though the terminology is less frequent in the prophets, their message is based on what God commands (e.g., Jer 1:7, 17; Dan 9:4-5; Zech 1:6; Mal 4:4). Much of the message of the prophets could be summed up in the cry, "O that you had paid attention to my commandments!" (Isa 48:18).

In the Wisdom Literature, though there is no reference to the commandments of the Torah, wisdom nevertheless is based on the commandments of the wise:

> My child, if you accept my words,
> and treasure up my commandments. . . . (Prov 2:1)

The concluding advice of Ecclesiastes is, "Fear God, and keep his commandments" (12:13; cf. Job 23:12).

d. Sayings: Principles, Precepts, and Prescriptions

The way in which God's will is conveyed to his people in the OT varies considerably, and is embodied in both sayings and narrative.

Classification of ethical sayings material can hardly be separated from hermeneutical discussion of how the material is to be understood and applied today. Numerous systems of classification have been proposed (see the surveys in Long 1965; Gustafson 1970: 439-47; Birch and Rasmussen 1976: 21-24; Hays 1996: 208-9), but very broadly speaking two main approaches have been taken.

On the one hand, traditionally many have sought to find ethical *laws* in Scripture, i.e., specific rules, commands, directions, or prescriptions. This approach appeals to those who want specific guidance, but it has come under heavy criticism on the grounds that it ignores both the diversity within the biblical material and the extent to which it is historically conditioned.

On the other hand, Scripture has been seen as the source of ethical *principles,* or ideals. The advantage of this approach is that it recognizes the gap between biblical times and today, yet holds that there are basic biblical principles that can be applied in new situations. This view has been criticized on the grounds that biblical ethical material usually does not present vague ideals but very concrete advice in specific situations.

Careful study of *all* the ethical sayings material in Scripture suggests that the question must not be posed in either-or terms. Rather, the biblical material presents a broad *spectrum* that ranges all the way from general ethical *principles* at the one extreme to very specific *prescriptions* at the other, with what may be termed *precepts* coming somewhere in the middle. In adopting this terminology, it must be stressed that there is no question of neatly pigeonholing all biblical ethical sayings material into three categories. These terms are merely a convenient way of indicating *points on a spectrum* and highlighting the *range of material found in Scripture;* they may be illustrated with reference to the main types of ethical material found in Torah, Prophets, and Wisdom.

At one extreme, there *are* texts that lay down *broad ethical principles,* grounded in the theological proclamation of the OT. For example, "You shall love your neighbor as yourself" (Lev 19:18); or

> Let justice roll down like waters,
>   and righteousness like an ever-flowing stream (Amos 5:24);

or "Righteousness exalts a nation" (Prov 14:34). Despite the aversion of many scholars to speaking of ethical "principles," this terminology does seem appropriate to such texts. They are not impersonal principles but are grounded in the will of God; and of course, the OT constantly insists that they are to be put into practice in concrete situations.

Somewhere in the middle of the spectrum are what may be termed *precepts,* general moral laws that *do* prescribe particular modes of conduct. For example, "Honor your father and your mother" (Exod 20:12); or the command to "defend the orphan, / plead for the widow" (Isa 1:17); or the advice that the wise person is one who speaks the truth (Prov 12:17).

At the other extreme are very specific *prescriptions,* applicable in particular sets of circumstances (see Goldingay 1981: 51). For example, Deut 22:8 lays down that "When you build a new house, you shall make a parapet for your roof." Amos condemns an act of ethnic cleansing carried out by Gaza (Amos 1:6). Wisdom also can be specific: "A false balance is an abomination to the LORD" (Prov 11:1).

While principles, precepts, and prescriptions represent points on a spectrum, nevertheless some such distinction is of fundamental importance for the understanding and interpretation of biblical ethics.

Principles may indicate the roots of ethics in theology and give inspiring general direction, but they do not provide instructions on a specific mode of conduct to be followed. It is the task therefore of the believing community today to determine how these biblical principles are to be applied in the modern world.

Precepts lie between principles and prescriptions. They deal with laws of human conduct that can be applied in many different situations, and as exemplified in the second table of the Decalogue, for example, they probably come closest to commands that can be transferred directly to the modern world.

Prescriptions do give very direct guidance on what to do in specific sets of circumstances, but for that reason they are limited in their application, since the situations faced by people today may be very different. Nevertheless, they are always based on underlying ethical, and ultimately theological, principles.

e. Narrative: Paradigms

While ethical directions are generally embodied in some kind of sayings material, it has long been suggested that biblical *narrative* can also have ethical implications. In particular, OT narratives have traditionally been seen as highlighting moral qualities in individual characters — for example, "the peaceableness and unselfishness which stand out in a figure like Abraham, the honour and sincerity for lack of which misfortune dogs the hard life story of Jacob, the forgiveness and placability which are accentuated in Joseph" (Eichrodt 1967: 321-22).

The use of narrative material for ethical purposes, however, poses a number of problems (see Goldingay 1981: 39-41). Firstly, most biblical narratives are remarkably free of moralizing comments; if there is an ethical interpretation, that is largely left to the readers (cf. Childs 1992: 679-80). Secondly, it is often doubtful to what extent OT narratives are intended to offer ethical examples. In the Deuteronomic History of Joshua through 2 Kings, Israel is more often depicted as straying from God's way than following it. As far as individuals are concerned, it has often been observed that the Bible does not depict even its heroes and heroines as plaster saints. This has always been seen by many as a major problem; witness, for example, the whole chapter that Kaiser devotes to the morally offensive character and acts of men and women in the Old Testament (1983: 270-83). Of course, narratives that depict a bad example can function as ethical warnings: in such cases as the story of David and Bathsheba (2 Sam 11–12) and Naboth's vineyard (1 Kgs 21), the behavior of David and of Ahab is clearly intended not as a positive but as a negative example. Thirdly, narratives always deal with very specific historical situations. Some scholars argue that such situations are so culturally conditioned that there is no way they can offer ethical guidance to people living two or three thousand years later in a totally different cultural situation.

Against this, however, are those who believe that modern interpreters can and must look for some kind of *analogy* between the situation portrayed in a biblical narrative and the situation they face today. On this view, for example, "those actions of persons and groups are to be judged morally wrong which are similar to actions that are judged to be wrong or against God's will under similar circumstances in Scripture" (Gustafson 1970: 442). A number of recent writers have suggested that narratives interpreted in this way can be seen as "paradigms." As C. J. H. Wright (1983) explains, "a paradigm is something used as a model or example for other cases where a basic principle remains unchanged, though details differ . . . a paradigm is not so much imitated as applied" (43). W. Janzen (1994) has advocated "a paradigmatic approach" to OT ethics, and has identified five paradigms — familial, priestly, wisdom, royal, and prophetic — of which the familial is the dominant one. He defines "paradigm" quite broadly as "a personally and holistically conceived image of a model (e.g. a wise person, good king) that imprints itself immediately and nonconceptually on the characters and actions of those who hold it" (27-28). For those who think OT ethics consists of laws or rules, this is a helpful corrective, but Janzen tends to go to the opposite extreme; he does not take sufficient account of the ambiguity of many narratives, and he undervalues the central role of ethical *teaching,* especially of the Torah (focused in the Decalogue), in OT ethics.

The position adopted here is that some biblical narratives can certainly be seen as paradigmatic (either positively or negatively), though this approach needs to be used with caution. In light of the qualifications outlined above, a wise principle would seem to be that in terms of ethical guidance, narrative material should be interpreted in the light of sayings material rather than vice versa.

f. Visionary and Pragmatic Ethics

Despite the fact that the OT provides ethical principles (stated or implied) that ought to be applied in specific situations, there remains a tension between these high ideals, sometimes referred to as "visionary ethics," and the realities of the actual situations in which the ethical principles were to be applied. Israel was a small nation in the wider ancient Near East, and social, economic, and political pressures set certain parameters within which even Israel had to operate, so that what we often find is what is sometimes referred to as "pragmatic ethics."

On the one hand, Israel is called to be different from the nations, and some practices common in the ancient Near East, such as cultic prostitution, witchcraft, and child sacrifice, are totally prohibited. On the other hand, as C. J. H. Wright (1983) points out, "some customs and practices common in the ancient world were tolerated within Israel, without explicit divine command or sanction, but with a developing theological critique which regarded them as falling short of God's highest standards. The customs in question were then regulated by legal safeguards in such a way as to soften or eliminate their worst effects" (175-76).

Practices and institutions mentioned in the law codes and ethical teaching of the OT but not directly commanded by God include polygamy (see 19-1.2d.i), divorce (see 19-1.2d.ii), and slavery (see 19-1.3c.i). The OT accepts these institutions as inevitable and concentrates mainly on mitigating their effects. Thus, for example, "the aim of the OT law on slavery may . . . be seen as seeking to make slavery work with as little injustice as possible" (Goldingay 1981: 59).

18-1.2. ETHICAL NORMS: THE HISTORICAL ORDER

Considerable parts of the OT contain ethical direction given specifically to God's people Israel (the historical order); this is found in the Torah and in the Prophets.

a. Torah

The term "Torah" *(tôrâh)* has traditionally been translated into English as "law" (cf. LXX *nomos*). It can indeed be used in the singular (Exod 24:12; Lev 11:46), or in the plural (*tôrōth;* Lev 26:46; Neh 9:13) of what may fairly be called "laws"; equivalents include "commandments" *(mitswōth),* "statutes" *(chuqîm),* and "ordinances" *(mishpātîm)* (cf. Deut 6:1). In light of the fact that "law" can have a negative ("legalistic") connotation for many Christians, it is frequently pointed out that the root *yrh* means to "point" or "show," and hence to "direct," "teach," or "instruct"; some therefore prefer to translate *tôrâh* as "direction," "instruction," or "teaching." The term "Torah" also came to be applied to the first five books of the Old Testament (Genesis, Exodus, Leviticus, Numbers, and Deuteronomy), or the Pentateuch, which of course contain narrative material as well as laws or teaching. By extension "Torah" could also be used to refer to the Prophets (cf. 1 Cor 14:21) and the Writings (cf. John 10:34). The context must determine in what sense the term "Torah" is used.

BT cannot be based on the many speculative and often contradictory theories (from Wellhausen onward) regarding the development of Israel's laws and the composition of the Torah (cf. Goldingay 1981: 44-47; Richardson and Westerholm 1991: 19-43), but only on the Torah in its canonical form.

i. The Context of Torah

In the Pentateuch, narrative and law are interwoven (see C. J. H. Wright 1983: 21-24; cf. above, 18-1.1a, on ethics as response). "It is extremely significant . . . that the promulgation of the specific laws which go to make up the Old Testament code of conduct is closely and constantly bound up with the record of what God has done for Israel" (T. W. Manson 1960: 19), or as Levenson (1980) puts it, "the story authenticates the statutes" (19). Specifically, Torah represents Israel's obligations under the covenant (cf. 11-1.3c). "When God demands the obedience of the twelve tribes, this is no arbitrary demand; it is based on the covenant in which he has declared Israel to be his own possession. Thus it is only in relation to the covenant that the significance of the commandments of God can be fully understood" (Kraus 1958: 25). Israel did not earn God's favor by keeping the Torah. In the OT, as in the NT, grace precedes law (cf. J. A. Sanders 1975: 373, 381; Goldingay 1981: 44). "The torah was thus not an instrument of salvation — that had already taken place — but a characterization of life-principles reflecting the state or quality of the sacred people, a living thank offering to the God of their salvation" (J. M. Myers 1975: 83; cf. Eichrodt 1966: 311). Torah is thus not a burden placed on Israel but a gift designed to lead God's people in the way of life. "The LORD commanded us to observe all these statutes, to fear the LORD our God, for our lasting good, so as to keep us alive, as is now the case" (Deut 6:24; cf. 10:13). The Torah is "God's gift, showing how men can enjoy to the full the benefits of life and possessions which are also divinely given" (Clements 1968: 59).

This view of Torah is found in the "Torah Psalms" (see B. W. Anderson 1983: 219-22): Ps 1, which pronounces blessed those who delight in the Torah of the Lord (v. 2), Ps 19:7-14 ("The [Torah] of the LORD is perfect, / reviving the soul"), and especially the long (alphabetical acrostic) Ps 119, which praises the Torah at length, the author of which exclaims, "Oh, how I love your law!" (v. 97). These psalms, situated at strategic locations in the canonical Psalter, demonstrate that Israel's piety, based on Torah, "is a glad obedience to the commands of Yahweh, enacted in full confidence that such obedience produces a life of joy, well-being, and blessing" (Brueggemann 1997: 198).

ii. Torah as God-Given

One of the most striking features of the Torah is the way in which, at least in its final canonical form, the entire body of teaching and law is presented as being revealed by God, through Moses, to the people of Israel. Especially surprising is the absence of any laws from kings such as David or Solomon (cf. J. A. Sanders 1972: 27). Historical criticism, it is true, has seriously questioned the traditional view. Most critical scholars assume that many of the laws are of a later date but were read back into the Mosaic period, and also that many laws were adopted (and adapted) by the Israelites from the Canaanites (cf. von Rad 1962: 33). This view is linked by some with a distinction made between *apodictic* (or absolute) law and *casuistic* (or case) law. Apodictic law is characterized by direct categorical commands in the second person, e.g., "You shall have no other gods before me" (Exod 20:3). Casuistic law is characterized by a clause beginning with "if" or "when" that defines a certain set of circumstances, followed by the ruling as to what to do in these circumstances. Some have argued that apodictic law is unique to the OT, and is more likely to represent the original law given through Moses, whereas casuistic or case law was built up by legal precedents over many years and then (retroactively) attributed to Moses. From a literary point of view, it is a help to distinguish apodictic and casuistic law (see L. L. Thompson 1978: 147-48), but further research has seriously called in question whether apodictic law was unique to Israel (cf. Sanders, 34). Moreover, just because a body of material takes the form of case law is not in and of itself sufficient to deny its origin in the time of Moses; the view that the Torah was not all given at one time but arose partly in response to new situations, is not absent from the Pentateuch (see Num 9:6-14; 15:23).

Whatever may be the case historically, the canonical arrangement has profound theological significance. It gives expression to the view that ethical principles and moral norms are not of human origin but ultimately are God-given (cf. Davidson 1959: 376-77; Eichrodt 1961: 75). "By ascribing all normative law to Moses, the canonical Pentateuch has made laws into personal commandments" (Levenson 1985: 50).

iii. The Structure of Torah

In the sense of directions or laws as distinct from the narrative framework, Torah is found in Exodus, Leviticus, and Deuteronomy. The material consists of a mass of laws, varying greatly in nature — civil, social, moral, cultic — often without any apparent order or sequence. Broadly speaking, four main blocks of material can be distinguished (cf. C. J. H. Wright 1983: 148-51).

1. Pride of place goes to the *Decalogue* (*ʿᵃsereth hadᵉbhārīm* = "the Ten Words"; Exod 34:28; Deut 4:13) or *Ten Commandments* (see Harrelson 1980; Childs 1986: 63-83; R. F. Collins 1986: 49-97; 1992; P. D. Miller 1989) that are embedded in the covenant narrative of Exod 19–24 at 20:1-17; a second version is found in Deut 5:6-21. On the enumeration of the commandments in the varying Jewish and Christian traditions, see Harrelson, 45-48. The paramount importance of the Decalogue is emphasized in two ways. In both Exodus (20:22) and Deuteronomy (4:10; 5:22) it is presented as the direct address of God to the people, whereas all the other laws are given via Moses (cf. Miller, 230-31). Secondly, in Deuteronomy (unlike in Exodus) the Decalogue stands alone as the basis of the covenant (Deut 4:13; 5:22); the other laws are given later in an address by Moses (see Nicholson 1977).

According to Exod 32:15-16, the Ten Commandments were written, by God himself, on two tablets of stone. Whether the division corresponds to the two tablets of the Law or not, the first four commandments (20:3-11) deal with the people's relationship with God while the second group of six (20:12-17) deal with relations between people (see von Rad 1962: 191). The Ten Commandments thus reveal both God's *nature* and God's *will* (Gese 1981a: 65). Typically the ethical follows, and is dependent on the theological.

The literary context clearly shows that the Decalogue is the basic constitution of Israel, the provisions of which are then elaborated in the other laws of the Pentateuch (see P. D. Miller 1989: 235-42). Attention is frequently drawn to the fact that eight out of the ten commandments are negative in form. In part this is because they basically set boundaries to Israel's behavior, but they also enshrine positive values — the values of family, human life, property, truthfulness and justice in human relations (cf. R. F. Collins 1986: 62). Indeed, they can be seen as a basic charter of human rights (cf. Harrelson 1980: 186-93).

2. The Decalogue is followed by the *Book of the Covenant* (Exod 24:7), an anthology of various laws found in 20:22–23:33. These, along with the Decalogue, form the basis of the covenant between God and Israel that is then ratified in Exod 24.

3. Other material follows in the rest of Exodus and Leviticus. Critical scholars seek to differentiate various codes, of differing dates, particularly the *"Holiness Code"* of Lev 17–26, but in the final canonical form these have been woven together.

4. *Deuteronomy* (*deutero* = "second"; *nom-* = "law") is the "second law," a restatement of the Torah in a highly characteristic hortatory style that has been characterized as "a wooing and imploring form of address" (von Rad 1962: 220); the whole of the book takes the form of Moses' farewell address to the people of Israel (see further, Clements 1968; Gese 1981a: 69-72).

iv. Characteristics of Torah

Torah, as noted above, should not be construed as "law" in a legalistic sense. As "teaching" or "instruction," it constitutes guidelines for the "way of life" of God's people (cf. Stuhlmacher 1986: 111-12). Far from being narrowly legalistic, its main concern is for people, not least for the weak and defenseless members of society. For example, Exod 22:26-27 states, "If you take your neighbor's cloak in pawn, you shall restore it before the sun goes down; for it may be your neighbor's only clothing to use as cover; in what else shall that person sleep?" Significantly v. 27 adds, "And if your neighbor cries out to me [i.e., to God], I will listen, for I am compassionate." In comparison with other ancient Near Eastern law codes, in the Torah "the value of human life is recognized as incomparably greater than all material values. The dominant feature throughout is respect for the rights of everything that has a human face" (Eichrodt 1967: 321; cf. T. W. Manson 1960: 35).

This aspect of Torah is seen in the so-called motive clauses (Gemser 1953; Kaiser 1983: 239-43) attached to some laws. A strong note of compassion for the oppressed and underprivileged is connected with the exodus event; because a compassionate God delivered his people from slavery and affliction in Egypt, they in turn are to show compassion for the downtrodden and afflicted. A compassionate God demands compassion from his people (cf. P. D. Hanson 1982:

22). A basic principle is laid down in Exod 23:9 — "You shall not oppress a resident alien; you know the heart of an alien, for you were aliens in the land of Egypt." Israel ought to be able to sympathize with the downtrodden and therefore be motivated to help them (cf. Lev 19:33-34; Deut 5:15).

Another basic motivating ethical principle is that all God's people are brothers and sisters, members of one family, and are to be treated accordingly. This is stressed especially in Deuteronomy: "If there is among you a poor man, one of your brethren, in any of your towns . . . you shall not harden your heart or shut your hand against your poor brother" (15:7 RSV; cf. 15:11; 23:19; Lev 25:35-38). Even a Hebrew man or woman sold as a slave is still "your brother" (Deut 15:12-18 RSV). "Brother" is closely related to "neighbor": "You shall not hate your brother in your heart. . . . You shall not take vengeance or bear any grudge against the sons of your own people, but you shall love your neighbor as yourself" (Lev 19:17-18 RSV). Here both "brother" and "neighbor" clearly refer to fellow Israelites, but it should be noted that vv. 33-34 extend the basic principle to strangers.

v. Sanctions

While the primary appeal is to covenant obedience, insofar as it functions as a civil and criminal code of law, Torah also provides for penalties for offenses. Many sanctions are based on the principle of exact compensation, the *lex talionis:* "If any harm follows, then you shall give life for life, eye for eye, tooth for tooth, hand for hand, foot for foot, burn for burn, wound for wound, stripe for stripe" (Exod 21:23-24). "An eye for an eye" is frequently criticized as being exceedingly harsh. But it should be remembered that originally the *lex talionis* limited retribution to one life for one life, not seven or seventy-seven (cf. Gen 4:24), something still not unknown in the modern world. Moreover, "an eye for an eye" is a basic principle, not a specific prescription. The law is to be administered by judges who must decide how the principle is to apply in individual cases. In practice the "retaliation" was often commuted to financial compensation. Significantly, and in marked contrast to modern practice, no provision is made for *imprisonment* as a punishment (cf. C. J. H. Wright 1983: 165-66).

The most extreme sanction is *the death penalty.* Gen 9:6 grounds this in the created order, in God's command to Noah:

> Whoever sheds the blood of a human,
>> by a human shall that person's blood be shed;
> for in his own image
>> God made humankind.

Since human beings are made in the image of God, human life is infinitely precious and the taking of human life is the most serious crime imaginable (cf.

Kaiser 1983: 165-67). In the Torah the death penalty is laid down for some seventeen offenses, most of which can be classified as offenses against God, against the family, and against the human person (cf. Lillie 1968: 453). Significantly, "in the Old Testament no crime against property warrants capital punishment. Once again, the point is that life is sacred, not things" (Kaiser, 92). In the OT understanding of capital punishment there are elements of retribution (Exod 21:23), deterrence (Deut 13:10-11), and expiation (cf. Num 35:33) (Lillie 1968).

The provisions for capital punishment in the OT are not as harsh as they might at first appear (cf. Van Ness 1987). The death penalty was not imposed for unpremeditated or unintentional killing (Num 35:22-28). Moreover, a murderer could be convicted only on the testimony of two witnesses (35:30), "a condition unmet in today's courts, where circumstantial evidence plays an important role" (Shelley 1984: 16). The provision that the eyewitnesses must be the first to participate in the execution (Deut 17:7) would also in practice limit the application of the death penalty. Kaiser (1983) holds that only for premeditated murder was "a 'ransom' or a 'substitute' payment unacceptable (Num. 35:31), but presumably all the other capital offenses could be commuted as the judges determined" (92; see, however, C. J. H. Wright 1983: 164).

Within the totality of the canon of the OT there is a tension between these laws and the principle enunciated in Ezek 33:11 that the Lord has "no pleasure in the death of the wicked"; his desire is that "the wicked turn from their ways and live," a principle that is demonstrated in a number of important OT narratives. *Cain,* the first murderer, was not struck dead by God but was protected by him (Gen 4:15); *Joseph's brothers* were guilty of the capital offense of kidnapping, but Joseph forgave them; *Moses* was a murderer (Exod 2:11-15), yet God saw fit to use him as one of his greatest servants; *David* was guilty of two capital offenses, adultery and murder, yet God accepted his repentance and forgave him (2 Sam 12:13). Thus, if the legal sanctions of the Torah declare that for certain offenses people are deserving of death, the narrative of God's dealing with his people balances this by an emphasis on God's forgiveness and redeeming love.

Significantly, punishment involving bodily mutilation, common in the ancient Near East, is almost entirely lacking in the OT (cf. Eichrodt 1961: 78-79).

b. Prophetic Ethics

i. Thus Says the LORD

The prophets proclaimed a God-given message (cf. 6-1.4) that was delivered in specific historical situations, and their proclamation had a strong ethical content (see W. Janzen 1994: 154-76; Brueggemann 1997: 644-46). Through the prophetic message God "summons all the members of the nation to renounce their sinful self-will, and to place themselves without reserve at the disposal of the claims of the divine will" (Eichrodt 1967: 327). While the prophets recognized the value of worship, they strongly attacked rites without righteousness (cf. 14-1.5b.iv).

Specific ethical teaching is most frequently found in oracles of judgment. For example, the oracle of judgment against Israel in Amos 2:6-16 consists of (a) the accusation of particular sins (vv. 6-8), (b) an appeal to salvation history (vv. 9-12), and (c) the pronouncement of judgment (vv. 13-16). It is the accusation that reveals the moral standards by which the people are being judged; in this case they are accused of oppression of the poor and sexual immorality. While the prophets could make general appeals to avoid evil and do good, they usually expressed their appeals in terms of specific requirements; "prophetic ethics is most itself when it is most concrete" (Muilenburg 1961: 76).

The prophets addressed all segments of Israelite society and beyond, so their ethical message covers a very wide range. They turned a powerful searchlight on the society in which they lived, exposing those with power and privilege and giving a voice to the poor, the powerless, the oppressed, and the marginalized. "The prophetic task in such a social world is to maintain a destabilizing presence, so that the system is not equated with reality, so that alternatives are thinkable, and so that the absolute claims of the system can be criticized" (Brueggemann 1994: 223). They spoke out against kings (2 Sam 12:1-12; Hos 8:4), royal officials (Hos 7:5), political leaders (Isa 30:1-7), the rich and powerful (Amos 5:11; 6:4-6), those who administer justice (Isa 5:23; Mic 7:3), and the religious leaders (Amos 7:10-17), as well as the people generally. Moreover, their message frequently reached beyond Israel to condemn the sins of surrounding nations; on the prophetic "oracles against the nations," see 12-2.2.

ii. Prophecy, Covenant, and Torah

According to Hos 6:6, what God demands first and foremost is *chesedh* ("steadfast love" or "covenant love"; see 11-1.3f):

> For I desire steadfast love and not sacrifice,
>   the knowledge of God rather than burnt offerings.

Even when they do not specifically employ the word "covenant," the prophets generally assume the covenant relationship as the basis of Israel's ethical obligation (see L. L. Thompson 1978: 188-89). The relationship was created by the prior saving acts of God. The basic appeal is to the exodus/wilderness/conquest tradition, e.g., in Jeremiah, Ezekiel, Hosea, Amos, and Micah. Isa 1–39 appeals only to the David/Jerusalem traditions; 2 Isaiah combines the two.

Israel's obligations under the covenant are spelled out in the Torah, and while the prophets seldom explicitly quote the Torah, their oracles of judgment in effect say to Israel, "You have forgotten the law of your God" (Hos 4:6). Their specific ethical demands frequently overlap very closely those of the Torah, especially the Decalogue: "Will you steal, murder, commit adultery, swear falsely, make offerings to Baal, and go after other gods . . . ?" (Jer 7:9; cf. Hos 4:2). This is vividly illustrated in the story of Naboth's vineyard (1 Kgs 21). To the presumptions of royal power and privilege that Jezebel brought from Phoenicia, Elijah brings the demands of the covenant with its commandments against coveting, false witness, and murder, and its understanding of Land as a gift from God (cf. Brueggemann 1994: 239-42). While the prophets upheld the provisions of the law, they strongly criticized those who perverted the legal system and undermined the spirit of the law even while obeying its letter (cf. Isa 10:1-2).

Torah and prophecy are thus not to be set against one another as alternative sources of ethical norms. In Deut 18:15-20 future prophets are seen as successors to Moses, and Mosaic Torah is presented as the standard by which prophets must be judged. "The prophets maintained a continuing source of divine *torah* for Israel, but this did not render the Mosaic *torah* unnecessary. On the contrary the prophets presumed it, and confirmed its authority. Thus, in the view of the Deuteronomists, the prophets were given by God to confirm the truth and authority of the Mosaic revelation" (Clements 1968: 65).

In some respects the ethical teaching of the prophets may be regarded as more advanced, but the difference should not be exaggerated; there are many "prophetic" elements in the Torah. "While we would agree that there is to be found in the prophets a deepening of insights in respect to many essential matters, nevertheless we would contend that there is no 'ethics of the prophets' which does not depend for its foundations on the revelation of God's command in the primal events of Israel's history" (Fletcher 1971: 50). For example, in Isa 1:10 God calls on the Israelites to "listen to the teaching *(tôrâh)* of our God." Specifically this means:

> Learn to do good;
> seek justice,
>   rescue the oppressed,
> defend the orphan,
>   plead for the widow. (1:17)

Such calls are typical of the prophets (cf. Jer 22:3; Ezek 22:7), but they are equally typical of the laws of the Torah (Exod 22:21-22; Deut 10:18; 24:17; etc.; cf. Hammershaimb 1959: 80-83). Whatever the historical relationship between Torah (especially Deuteronomy) and the Prophets, in their canonical form they have much ethical material in common.

iii. Sanctions

The prophets declare that when Israel repeatedly disobeys God's laws and breaks the covenant, there comes a point when God will pass judgment upon them. Though typical of the Prophets, such a view is already found in the Torah itself (Deut 4:25-27; 30:15-20). In terms of "prophetic eschatology" this is generally a this-worldly judgment, carried out by foreign nations whom God uses for his purposes (cf. 3-2.3). For the most part the prophets dealt with the nation as a unit. The nation, they declared, would prosper or be punished depending on its moral health. But in prophets such as Jeremiah and Ezekiel we see also an emphasis on individual ethical responsibility (Jer 31:29-30; Ezek 18).

18-1.3. ETHICAL NORMS: THE CREATED ORDER

The OT knows of ethical claims binding on all humankind, not just those revealed to Israel through Moses and the Prophets.

a. Creation Ethics

OT ethics are not only "a response to the activity of the redeemer God," but "they are also a response to the creator God, embody a conformity to the pattern of natural order, and apply as much outside as inside Israel" (Goldingay 1981: 42-43). Adam and Eve, representing humankind, are called upon to obey God. At the very outset of the biblical story there is an emphasis on the fact that all human beings know what God requires of them, even if there is also a strong tendency to rebel and disobey God. This insight runs like a thread through the OT. In the created order God provides certain ordinances (marriage, the family, society, the state) for the well-being of all humankind, and all persons recognize the obligations entailed in these ordinances (cf. Barclay 1990: 72). The story of the flood assumes that all people have some knowledge of God's moral law when it condemns humankind for its wickedness (Gen 6:5). The story of Noah and of the covenant with Noah and his descendants (9:9) assumes that certain basic moral principles are binding on all humankind. Ethical norms are assumed in the prophetic oracles against the nations. Amos, for example, condemns the surrounding nations for a series of crimes (Amos 1–2), thereby assuming that all peoples recognize and are obliged to follow a general moral law (cf. Barton 1979: 3-4); these peoples are condemned for what von Rad (1965) calls "breaches of the unwritten law of international relations" (135). The prophets, says Brueggemann (1997), "enunciate the claim that under the aegis of Yahweh's sovereignty, there is a kind of international law or code of human standards that seems to anticipate the Helsinki Accords of 1975 in a rough way, a code that requires every nation to act in civility and humaneness toward others. Any affront of this standard is taken to be an act of autonomy, arrogance, and self-sufficiency, which flies in the face of Yahweh's governance" (503). References to conduct being "an outrage" (*nᵉbhālâ*) and something that "ought not to be done" *(kēn lōʼ yēʽāseh)* indicate a type of community ethical standard that is widely recognized apart from the laws of the Torah (see Gen 34:7; cf. Judg 19:23; 20:6; 2 Sam 13:12; Jer 29:23; see Eichrodt 1967: 317-19).

Thus, without specifically spelling it out, the OT assumes the existence of a universal moral law, binding on all humankind, apart from the Torah revealed by God to Israel.

b. Wisdom Ethics

A large portion of the Wisdom Literature consists of ethical teaching and advice (Prov 10–31; *Sirach; Wisdom*). Wisdom can also be conveyed through narrative, such as the Joseph story in Gen 37–50 that provides a paradigm of wisdom in action (cf. W. Janzen 1994: 125-26; and see 3-1.3d). Wisdom ethics are the product of observation and experience; they represent the accumulated wisdom of society. Wisdom can be gained from contemplating nature (e.g., Prov 6:6-8), but especially human society (e.g., 13:1). "By the long-term observation of recurring patterns of human behaviour, wisdom teachers have sorted out the limits of freedom and the shape of acceptable behaviour, beyond which conduct dare not go without bringing hurt to self and to others" (Brueggemann 1997: 337). Solomon's judgment in the case of the two prostitutes (1 Kgs 3:16-28) is a classic case of wisdom in the sense of ability to make the right decision in a difficult case.

Of course, ultimately wisdom comes from God, because God has created all things through Wisdom and has implanted the preexistent divine Wisdom in the universe (cf. 8-1.4). But obviously Wisdom gives a much greater place to human responsibility and cooperation. This aspect has been stressed especially by Brueggemann (1972), who contends that Wisdom affirms that "man has primary responsibility for his destiny"; "man is able to choose wisely and decide responsibly" (20). Over against theologies that stress the fallenness of human nature, Wisdom offers a foundation for "a theology of responsibility" (61). In the succession narrative (2 Sam 9–1 Kgs 2), which shows strong links with Wisdom, history is viewed as essentially a human enterprise and people have to make their own choices and accept the consequences (90). This emphasis is a valid one, but two points need to be noted. Firstly, Wisdom is one element within the total canonical mix; it has to be held in balance with Torah ethics and prophetic ethics. Secondly, as we have already seen (8-1.4c), in the late OT Torah and Wisdom, originally independent of one another, are brought together (cf. Gese 1981a: 79-80). Sirach, for example, equates Wisdom with "the law that Moses commanded us" (*Sir* 24:23). Here Torah is set in the context not of salvation history but of the created order that is permeated by the divinely given Wisdom.

J. D. Levenson has pointed out that even within the canonical OT, Torah can be linked with the created order through the language of Wisdom. In Deut 4:6, for example, Moses tells the people that they must observe the statutes diligently, "for this will show your wisdom and discernment to the peoples, who, when they hear all these statutes, will say, 'Surely this great nation is a wise and discerning people!'" In Wisdom Psalms such as Ps 119:89-93, "the laws the created order observes are . . . associated with the Torah," so that "in this theology, law is most closely associated not with the sudden and terrifying theophany on Sinai . . . but with the predictable and reassuring self-revelation of creation" (Levenson 1980: 28-29). Torah and creation are similarly linked in Ps 19. Such passages suggest that "biblical Israel believed the will of God to be known not only through history but also through what we moderns call nature" (32). Thus, within the totality of the canon, Torah and Wisdom, the ethics of the historical order and the ethics of the created order, are not regarded as ultimately opposed to one another, for both ultimately come from God.

The motivation of Wisdom ethics is assumed rather than stated: Wisdom is better than folly. Wisdom can only make her appeal to human beings (Prov 8:1-5); it is up to people to decide how they respond. What the wise person gives typically is "advice" or "counsel" (noun *ʿētsâ;* verb *yāʿats* = "advise, counsel"); it is up to the recipient to accept or reject it, as for example in the account of King Rehoboam taking counsel with Solomon's seasoned advisers (1 Kgs 12:6-14). "Such counsel does not demand obedience, but it asks to be tested: it appeals to the judgment of the hearer; it is intended to be understood, and to make decisions easier" (von Rad 1962: 434).

Wisdom does have its own sanctions. These are at times expressed rather crudely in terms of the piety-prosperity equation (cf. 16-1.3b): wise conduct will be repaid by long life, health, and prosperity, and folly by the opposite (Prov 10:3, 27). But elsewhere it is recognized that wisdom leads to life — to a full and satisfying and blessed existence — while folly leads to destruction and death. Occasionally a specifically religious sanction can be invoked:

> A false balance is an abomination to the LORD,
>   but an accurate weight is his delight. (Prov 11:1)

18-1.4. RIGHTEOUSNESS AND JUSTICE

In the ethical vocabulary of the OT, "righteous" *(tsāddîq)* and "righteousness" *(tsᵉdhāqâh)* are key terms. We have already seen that in the OT God is a righteous God or a God of righteousness, and that basic to the biblical understanding of righteousness is the concept of relationship (see 3-1.1).

The OT, as we have also seen, recognizes the basic sinfulness of human beings (16-1.2), so that no one in and of oneself is righteous: "Surely there is no one on earth so righteous as to do good without ever sinning" (Eccl 7:20). In Deut 9:6 the Israelites are reminded "that the LORD your God is not giving you this good land to occupy because of your righteousness; for you are a stubborn people."

God, however, calls human beings, and especially the people of Israel, into a right relationship with himself, and on this basis they can be called "righteous." Thus Noah "was a righteous man" because he "walked with God" (Gen 6:9). Abraham "believed the LORD; and the LORD reckoned it to him as righteousness" (15:6). A righteous person *(tsāddîq)* is one who lives in a right relationship with God, but the OT insists that "man's faithfulness to the relationship had to prove itself in recognizing the commandments and keeping them" (von Rad 1962: 381). As Moses tells the people, "It will be righteousness for us *(ts^edāqâ tih^eyeh-lānû),* if we are careful to do all this commandment before the LORD our God, as he has commanded us" (Deut 6:25 RSV).

The righteous, or those who stand in a right relationship with God, are called to live in a right relationship with others, so that here too "righteousness" is very much a matter of relationships and of fulfilling the demands of whatever relationship one finds oneself in. In the OT therefore, "righteousness is a state of integrity in relation to God and one's fellowman, expressing itself in one's acts and speech. Even as the Lord is righteous in his creative, sustaining, and salvific acts, so people are expected to act and speak in such a way that righteousness is evident and is advanced" (Elwell 1988e: 1861). The opposite of the "righteous" are the "wicked" *(r^eshā'îm)* who renounce God (Ps 10:3-4) and do not serve the Lord (Mal 3:18; Ps 1), and therefore come under God's judgment (Jer 23:19).

Along with the demand for righteousness is often found the demand for "justice" *(mishpāṯ),* as in the famous call of Amos 5:24,

> Let justice *(mishpāṯ)* roll down like waters,
>   and righteousness *(ts^edāqâ)* like an ever-flowing stream,

or Isaiah's complaint that the LORD

> expected justice,
>   but saw bloodshed;
> righteousness,
>   but heard a cry! (Isa 5:7; see commentaries on the wordplay involved)

Between the two words there can be a considerable overlap of meaning. As we have seen (16-1.3a), *mishpāṯ,* from *shāphaṯ* = "to judge," can mean judgment, but since in the OT a judge does not simply hand down a legal decision but also acts to put things right, *mishpāṭ* comes to mean justice in the sense of defending and helping the oppressed and the defenseless. Seeking justice means ceasing to do evil *(ra')*, learning to do good *(tôbh),* rescuing the oppressed, defending the orphan, and pleading for the widow (Isa 1:16-17). As such, it is a central demand of the prophets:

> What does the LORD require of you
> but to do justice, and to love kindness,
>   and to walk humbly with your God? (Mic 6:8)

According to Prov 21:15,

> When justice is done, it is a joy to the righteous,
>   but dismay to evildoers.

The promotion of righteousness and justice is a key function of the ideal king (see Ps 72:1-2).

18-1.5. WORLD-AFFIRMING OR WORLD-DENYING?

a. World-Affirming

OT ethics are basically world-affirming. This world is essentially good (Gen 1), and all God's gifts are given for humankind to enjoy (cf. 2-1.2f). God provides

> wine to gladden the human heart,
> oil to make the face shine,
>   and bread to strengthen the human heart. (Ps 104:15)

"Eating and drinking, taking one's enjoyment, in a word, every material blessing that enhanced the quality of life, were accepted in a simple thankfulness from Jahweh's hand." When prophets condemn wealth and luxury, "it can only have been extreme indulgence which necessitated the raising of such complaints about the enjoyment of material things" (von Rad 1965: 137). All the good things of this life are gifts from God and are to be enjoyed, provided always that they are used in accordance with God's will.

b. Ascetic Strains

A couple of ascetic strains in the OT are the exceptions that prove the rule.

The *Rechabites* were a small group that traced their origins back to Jehonadab, the son of Rechab (2 Kgs 10:15-28), a fervent Yahwist. Jer 35:6-10 shows that they followed a rule that involved abstinence from wine, rejection of houses in favor of living in tents, and the rejection of agriculture; such practices are "the essence of nomadism" (Pope 1962b: 15). Their outlook reflects a rejection of the settlement, and a desire to turn back the clock and return to the period of wilderness wanderings. Jeremiah respected the Rechabites for sticking to their principles, but he did not regard these principles as binding on all God's people.

Nazirites were persons who took a special vow that involved abstinence from wine (Amos 2:12), leaving the hair uncut, and avoidance of contact with the dead and with all unclean food (J. A. Montgomery 1932: 203-5; Eichrodt 1961: 303-6; Rylaarsdam 1962). Their regulations bear some resemblance to those applying to the holy war (see 19-1.5a). Num 6 envisages a temporary Nazirite vow, but the story of Samson (Judg 13–16) features one who was a life-long Nazirite. The vow allowed persons to dedicate themselves to God in a special way, usually for a limited period of time.

The OT strongly affirms human sexuality (see 19-1.2a.i), and sexual abstinence is required only rarely, for a limited time, and for special reasons.

c. Fasting

Fasting is not a regular practice in the OT, but people did fast on certain special occasions. This might be in preparation for a revelation from God, on the principle that "fasting must precede divine illumination" (J. A. Montgomery 1932: 188), as in the case of Moses (Exod 34:28; Deut 9:9, 18) and Daniel (Dan 9:3). Fasting was also a sign of mourning (1 Sam 31:13). But more usually it was a sign of humility and of repentance, either individual (2 Sam 12:16) or national (1 Sam 7:6; Jonah 3:5). Times of severe crisis could provoke a national fast (Joel 1:14). Fasts could be proclaimed on an occasional basis (1 Kgs 21:9; Jer 36:9), but after the exile they were observed more regularly (Zech 7). National fasting was mainly associated with the annual Day of Atonement ritual (Lev 16:29-30; 23:26-32), where it served as "an expression of penitence accompanying Israel's solemn confession of her sins and the ritual through which atonement was sought" (H. H. Guthrie 1962: 243). By NT times the Day of Atonement was referred to as "the Fast" (Acts 27:9).

Fasting is a form of self-discipline, of humbling the soul, as in Ps 35:13, "I afflicted myself with fasting." Fasting and prayer came to be closely associated (Dan 9:3; *Jdt* 4:9; *Tob* 12:8). Like any practice that consists of outward acts, fasting can be abused, and it is abuse of the practice that is condemned, e.g., in Isa 58:3-5. Fasting is of no avail unless it is symbolic of a turning from sin:

> So if one fasts for his sins,
> and goes again and does the same things,
> who will listen to his prayer? (*Sir* 34:26)

Tob 12:8 stresses that fasting is not an alternative to good works: "Prayer with fasting is good, but better than both is almsgiving with righteousness" (cf. also Zech 7).

In NT times fasting was seen as a mark of special piety (Luke 2:37); it was practiced by the disciples of John the Baptist and by the Pharisees (Mark 2:18).

Old Testament: Promise

18-2. I WILL PUT MY LAW WITHIN THEM

18-2.1. ETHICS AND ESCHATOLOGY

Throughout the OT there is a deep consciousness of how humankind as a whole and God's people in particular fail to live as God would have them live. It is not surprising therefore that eschatological expectation should have a strong ethical content. The new age will see the defeat of the powers of evil (cf. 4-2.5), the judgment of the wicked (cf. 16-2.3), and the ushering in of a new age of righteousness. It is those who are set apart to the service of God, "the holy ones (Aram. *qaddîshîn;* RSV 'saints') of the Most High," who will inherit the coming kingdom (Dan 7:18, 22).

18-2.2. TORAH AND PROPHECY IN THE NEW ORDER

a. Torah in the New Order

Torah represents the guidelines to be followed by Israel as their side of the covenant relationship with God. But again and again Israel failed to live up to the Torah and hence broke the covenant. This forms the background of the promise of a new covenant and a new Torah in the new age.

Jeremiah's vision of a new covenant and Torah (31:31-34; see 11-2.3) is deliberately contrasted with the Sinai covenant and Torah: "It will not be like the covenant that I made with their ancestors when I took them by the hand to bring them out of the land of Egypt — a covenant that they broke" (v. 32). God promises that under the new covenant, "I will put my law *(tôrâh)* within them, and I will write it on their hearts" (v. 33; cf. also Ezek 36:26-28). The question is frequently raised: In what respect will the new covenant and Torah be new? A frequent answer is that it will be an inner, spiritual law, written not on tablets of stone but on people's hearts (Jer 31:33). This is an important feature of the new Torah, though it should be noted that an emphasis on obeying the law from the heart is found in Deuteronomy, part of the original Torah: "Keep these words that I am commanding you today in your heart" (6:6; cf. 11:18; 30:11-14; cf. also Pss 37:31; 40:8). Jer 31 does suggest that the Torah of the new age will be new in some sense, "yet not utterly divorced from the old Torah" (W. D. Davies 1952: 28).

The key to the *new* Torah is found in other passages where it appears in the context of *the promised eschatological ingathering of the Gentiles.* In Isa 2:2-4// Mic 4:1-4 (see 12-2.4a) the promise is made:

> Out of Zion shall go forth the law *(tôrâh),*
>> and the word of the LORD from Jerusalem. (Isa 2:3 RSV; Mic 4:2 RSV)

Here it is "all the nations" and "many peoples" who will stream to Mount Zion to be instructed by the eschatological Torah. Similarly, in Isa 51:4 (RSV) God says,

> Listen to me, my people,
>> and give ear to me, my nation;
> for a law *(tôrâh)* will go forth from me,
>> and my justice *(mishpāṭî)* for *a light to the peoples.*

This indicates that what will be new about the new Torah will be the fact that it will be a law that will not be for Israel only but for all humankind. It will therefore lack those features that are designed to *separate* Israel from the nations of the world (the ritual laws), and emphasize those (moral) laws that all peoples can obey. It will be in tune with God's original intention of extending his salvation to all humankind. Gese and Stuhlmacher refer to this eschatological law as the "Zion torah" (cf. Isa 2:3), in contrast to the "Sinai torah." "The Zion torah," says Stuhlmacher (1986), "brings to eschatological completion what was expressed in the Sinai torah only in historical provisionality" (115). Because it will be addressed to Gentiles, "the Zion Torah is more than just a quantitative expansion of the Sinai Torah" (Gese 1981a: 82).

In these texts it is God himself who will deliver the eschatological Torah to the Gentiles. The first Servant Song (Isa 42:1-7; cf. 9-1.3), however, portrays the Servant as having a mission to the Gentiles (cf. 12-2.5a):

> He will bring forth justice *(mishpāṭ)* to the nations. . . .
> He will not fail . . .
>> till he has established justice in the earth;
>> and the coastlands wait for his law *(lᵉtôrāthô,* i.e., for his Torah).
>>>> (vv. 1, 4 RSV)

While this at one level portrays the task of God's people Israel as the servant of the LORD, at another level it points to the role of a *future* messianic figure (see

9-2) who will be "a light to the nations" (v. 6) and whose task will include taking to them the messianic Torah (cf. W. D. Davies 1952: 29-34).

b. Prophecy in the New Order

As we have seen (6-2.4), toward the end of the OT period prophecy was believed to have ceased; the word of God was no longer directly proclaimed.

> The time is surely coming, says the Lord GOD,
>   when I will send a famine on the land;
> not a famine of bread, or a thirst for water,
>   but of hearing the words of the LORD. (Amos 8:11)

It is against this background that the expectation of a future rebirth of prophecy is to be read; see Joel 2:28 (cf. 5-2.3). As we have seen, one form of messianic expectation looked for the coming of an eschatological prophet (see 6-2.4). In the new age God's people will once again receive prophetic guidance.

18-2.3. WISDOM IN THE NEW ORDER

As already noted, wisdom is not an eschatological subject as a general rule; it is a means for guiding God's people now. Isa 33:5-6, however, lists wisdom among the gifts that God will bestow in the new age when he will fill "Zion with justice and righteousness . . . abundance of salvation, *wisdom,* and knowledge." And in Jer 23:5 the messianic king, or "righteous Branch," is one who will "deal wisely."

18-2.4. RIGHTEOUSNESS AND JUSTICE

Israel's failures to be true to the covenant relationship form the background of prophetic visions of the new order. The lack of righteousness and justice in the present (Isa 1:21; 5:7; 59:9; Jer 22:13) is the foil for visions of a new age when God's Spirit will be poured out and

> justice will dwell in the wilderness,
>   and righteousness abide in the fruitful field.
>   (Isa 32:16; cf. 45:8; 61:11; Hos 2:19)

The holy city, representing the community of God's people (cf. 13-2.4), will be transformed:

Afterward you shall be called the city of righteousness,
    the faithful city. (Isa 1:26; cf. Jer 31:23)

Zechariah envisages the ingathering of God's people to Jerusalem, where "they shall be my people and I will be their God, in faithfulness and in righteousness" (8:8).

Messianic prophecies in particular (cf. 6-2) have a strong ethical content. The future king will establish peace "with justice and with righteousness" (Isa 9:7);

    with righteousness he shall judge the poor,
        and decide with equity for the meek of the earth. (11:4)

He will be

    a ruler who seeks justice
        and is swift to do what is right. (16:5)

Jeremiah looks forward to the time when God "will raise up for David a righteous Branch, and he shall reign as king and deal wisely, and shall execute justice and righteousness in the land" (23:5; cf. 33:15). Of the promised Servant of the LORD, it is said that he will "bring forth justice to the nations" (Isa 42:1; cf. vv. 3-4).

18-2.5. WORLD-AFFIRMING OR WORLD-DENYING?

Fasting is a response to the human weakness and sin that characterize the present age; it will have no place, however, when the new age dawns. In Zech 7 a delegation from Bethel comes to the temple to ask whether they should continue to "mourn and practice abstinence in the fifth month" (v. 3), evidently referring to a regular fast that marked the destruction of the temple. They are answered in two ways. Zech 7:8-14 reminds them that the most important religious observance consists of righteous living. Zech 8 switches to an apocalyptic vision of the new order, part of which takes up the question of fasting by promising that the various fasts "shall be seasons of joy and gladness, and cheerful festivals for the house of Judah: therefore love truth and peace" (v. 19). In other words, not only will the fasting for the destruction of the temple become superfluous, but there will be no place for fasting at all, as the messianic age will be characterized by gladness and rejoicing.

New Testament: Fulfillment

18-3. A NEW COMMANDMENT

"New Testament ethics" refers to the way of living appropriate to the new people of God into which all the peoples of the earth are called.

18-3.1. THE THEOLOGICAL BASIS OF ETHICS

a. Ethics as Response

As in the OT, so also in the NT, ethics can be understood only in a theological context; the lifestyle of God's people is a response to the grace and goodness of God. For Christians, "theology comes before ethics and controls it because Christian moral action is fundamentally a grateful response to what God has done for us in Christ" (Spohn 1996: 29). In chapter 17 we saw how the NT, in the light of the Christ event, calls for repentance, conversion, new birth, faith, knowing God, and abiding in Christ. The gospel is the power of God to transform human beings, but the NT constantly emphasizes that this transformation is meaningless unless it has a strong ethical dimension (cf. 17-3.4).

We catch an echo of a basic OT principle (see above, 18-1.1a) in Jesus' ethical teaching: "Be perfect, therefore, as your heavenly Father is perfect" (Matt 5:48), or in Luke's version, "Be merciful, just as your Father is merciful" (Luke 6:36). Ethics, in other words, is grounded in the nature of God himself. The actual OT formula (Lev 19:2) is quoted in 1 Pet 1:15-16: "As he who called you is holy, be holy yourselves in all your conduct; for it is written, 'You shall be holy, for I am holy.'" In the NT believers are termed "saints" (*hagioi* = "holy ones"; *hagios* = "holy"; e.g., Acts 9:13; Rom 8:27; Eph 1:15; Heb 6:10; Rev 5:8). The church is thereby identified as the eschatological community, the saints of the Most High destined to inherit the kingdom (Dan 7:18, 22; see above, 18-2.1). While "sanctification" *(hagiasmos)* by derivation means being set apart in the service of God, an essential component in the NT is moral growth (Rom 6:19, 22; 1 Thess 4:3), inspired by the Spirit (2 Thess 2:13). Believers are said to have been "sanctified" (*hagiazō* = "make holy, consecrate, sanctify"), yet they are also "called to be saints" (1 Cor 1:2). This highlights a feature of the ethical language of the NT that corresponds to the frequently recurring already/not yet tension. In this connection scholars refer to the "indicative/imperative" tension; a *statement* about the Christian life is paired with a *command* or *exhortation*. Thus Paul tells the Galatians that they "live by the Spirit," yet also exhorts them to be "guided by the Spirit" (Gal 5:25). He tells the Romans that they have "died to sin," yet goes on to exhort them to "not let sin exercise dominion in your mortal bodies" (Rom 6:2, 12). Such texts show that "the new life of the believer exists in a tension determined by the 'already' of the new creation and the 'not yet' of the final consummation" (Lohse 1991: 110). NT Christians are far from "plaster saints," and therefore they have to be exhorted to become what they are destined to be, or paradoxically, to become what they already are.

In this process the Holy Spirit plays a key role. According to John 16:13, Jesus had promised his disciples the guidance of the Spirit/Paraclete after his departure. The Spirit gives ethical guidance to Christians, though not apart from the norms provided by the teaching and example of Christ, for it is the Spirit's function to bring these to the remembrance of believers (14:26). For Paul the Spirit is the dynamic motivating the Christian life, and producing in the lives of believers "the fruit of the Spirit" (Gal 5:22). Life in the Spirit frees believers from a legalistic approach to ethical questions (Rom 7:6; 2 Cor 3:6). Sanctification is not a once-for-all event but "a progressive and life-long process of moral and spiritual growth" aided by the Holy Spirit (Cronk 1982: 220; see 220-23 on the Orthodox understanding of the role of the Holy Spirit).

The basic pattern of ethics as the response to what God has done is found throughout the NT. Thus in the Synoptics, Jesus' ethical teaching is given only after his proclamation of the nearness of the kingdom; it is "kingdom ethics" and sketches the lifestyle appropriate to those who enter the kingdom. As Lohse points out, the Sermon on the Mount begins with the gracious promises of the Beatitudes; the demands that follow are to be read in the light of these promises (1991: 72). Several epistles follow the pattern of a theological section, expounding the meaning and significance of the Christ event, followed by an ethical section expounding the way of life appropriate to God's people. This structure is evident in:

	Theological	*Ethical*
Romans	1–8	12–15:3
Galatians	1–4	5–6
Ephesians	1–3	4–6
1 Peter	1–2:10	2:11–5

Note especially the transition point in Rom 12:1 that forms the hinge of the epistle: "I appeal to you therefore *(oun),* . . . by the mercies of God. . . ." A different pattern is found in Hebrews; here too theology and ethics go hand in hand, but structurally they appear in alternating blocks throughout the work.

b. Ethics and Community

Jesus' proclamation of the inbreaking of the kingdom of God is inextricably bound up with his creation of a new community, the eschatological Israel (see 11-3). Thus "Jesus' ethics was a 'code' of discipleship for renewed Israel" (Wiebe

1991: 39). In the NT God's call is not just to individuals. "Sanctification" is understood in corporate and not just individual terms; it is the new *community* that is called to be "a holy nation" (1 Pet 2:9), i.e., a people set apart from the surrounding society and culture by the unique quality of its way of life.

Several scholars have helpfully picked up the modern terminology of a "counterculture" and applied it to the community addressed in the NT, as well as to the contemporary Christian church, indicating the type of community it is called to be if it is to be faithful to the witness of Scripture. J. R. W. Stott entitles his study of the message of the Sermon on the Mount *Christian Counter-Culture* (1978; see p. 16). In the NT, says Hays (1996), "the church is a countercultural community of discipleship, and this community is the primary addressee of God's imperatives" (196).

c. Keep My Commandments

As in the OT, ethics in the NT does not involve conformity to an abstract norm, but obedience to the will of a personal God. Jesus unambiguously affirms an ethic that is based on what God commands. He quotes "the commandments" as authoritative (Matt 19:17), and affirms the commandments of Torah and prophets (5:17-20). The supreme commandments are those to love God and one's neighbor, for they sum up the Torah and the prophets (22:34-40). Attempts to replace "the commandment of God" with "human tradition" are condemned (Mark 7:6-8).

Paul can declare that for Christians "obeying the commandments of God is everything" (1 Cor 7:19), and he can on occasion quote "a command of the Lord" (14:37). The Pastorals are thus not inconsistent with Paul when they exhort Christians "to keep the commandment" (1 Tim 6:14). Yet for Paul "commandments" bear the same ambiguity as does "law"; divorced from God's grace, they can be viewed in a more negative light (see below, 18-3.3b).

The terminology of "commandments" is equally strong in the Johannine books, though here the emphasis shifts to the commandments given by Jesus himself (cf. Esser 1975: 337). "If you love me," Jesus tells his disciples, "you will keep my commandments" (John 14:15). Jesus' "commandments" can be summed up in one: "This is my commandment, that you love one another as I have loved you" (15:12). In 13:34 this is referred to as a "new commandment"; it is new in the sense that it has been uniquely exemplified by Jesus himself (cf. 1 John 2:7-8). Jesus in his turn obeys the Father's commandments (John 10:18). In Revelation the faithful are "those who keep the commandments of God" (12:17; 14:12).

d. Sayings: Principles, Precepts, and Prescriptions

Like the OT, the NT contains a considerable variety of ethical teaching, embodied in both sayings and narrative material.

Here too it is helpful to locate sayings on a spectrum ranging from broad ethical principles to very specific prescriptions, with what may be termed precepts occupying the middle ground.

Ethical *principles* tend to coalesce around the command to love one's neighbor (Mark 12:31) and to love others as Christ has loved us (John 15:12). Such principles are binding on all believers, but it remains to be determined what is entailed in each specific case. In the middle of the spectrum the NT provides ethical *precepts,* particularly through its reaffirmation of the second table of the Decalogue (e.g., Mark 10:19). Other parts of the NT provide *prescriptions* geared to very specific situations. In 1 Corinthians Paul responds to a whole series of particular inquiries relating to events in the Corinthian congregation at that time. In 1 Cor 11:2-16, for example, he directs women to cover their heads while leading public worship. This particular piece of advice is doubtless to be understood in connection with the social and cultural situation in Corinth at that time. The task of biblical ethics is to determine what basic ethical principle is being applied by Paul here, so that contemporary Christians can seek to determine how that principle may be applied in the very different social and cultural situation of our own day.

e. Narrative: Paradigms

In addition to ethical sayings material, as in the OT, so in the NT, *narrative* can have ethical implications, though there is considerably less narrative material in the NT. Some of the same qualifications also apply. Narratives are generally presented without providing any explicit moral interpretation. NT Christians were not plaster saints either, and are quite capable of offering bad examples (e.g., Ananias in Acts 5:1-6). As in the case of the OT, there are those who would argue that the situations depicted in the NT are so culturally conditioned that they can offer no guidance to Christians two thousand years later who face a quite different situation.

Against this, however, there appears to be a greater readiness in the NT to regard events or characters as having paradigmatic significance for ethics. Church leaders may model conduct for believers: the readers of Hebrews are told, "Remember your leaders, those who spoke the word of God to you; consider the outcome of their way of life, and imitate their faith" (13:7). Paul in particular is not averse to offering his own conduct as a model: "Be imitators of me," he tells the Corinthians (1 Cor 4:16; cf. 10:31–11:1; 1 Thess 1:6). In Phil 3:17-19 he couples a command to imitate both himself and "those who live according to the example you have in us" with a warning against those he obviously considers to be setting a bad example. These texts do warrant us looking to NT narratives in which Paul or other characters appear, and seeking to find in them "paradigms" in the sense defined by Hays (1996), who sees them as "stories or summary accounts of characters who model exemplary conduct (or negative paradigms: characters who model reprehensible conduct)" (209).

In the NT a unique place is held by the Gospel narratives of the ministry of Jesus. Not only Jesus' teaching but also his example is presented in the NT as an ethical norm (cf. Webster 1986), and indeed the life and example of Christ constitute the supreme paradigm for believers (cf. Crook 1990: 74-75). In the Gospels this theme is made most explicit in John when Jesus washes the disciples' feet and then tells them, "I have set you an example, that you also should do as I have done to you" (13:15). As Spohn (1996: 97) points out, "the narrative of the foot-washing acts out parabolically" Jesus' words that follow in 13:34: "I give you a new commandment, that you love one another. Just as I have loved you, you also should love one another." Jesus' sufferings are seen as an example that his disciples are called upon to follow: "If any want to become my followers, let them deny themselves and take up their cross and follow me" (Mark 8:34). Mark's Gospel in particular emphasizes the *cost* of discipleship (see 9-3.4d).

Paul can speak of becoming an "imitator" *(mimētēs)* of the Lord (1 Thess 1:6; cf. Rom 15:2-3; 1 Cor 11:1; Eph 5:1-2), and on one or two occasions he appealed to Jesus' example, especially in the Christ hymn of Phil 2:5f.: "Let the same mind be in you that was in Christ Jesus. . . ." Here Jesus' humility and unselfishness are held up as examples of the qualities needed to help restore unity and harmony among the Philippians. It has been argued that the hymn refers to the example of the preexistent Christ, not the earthly Jesus (whom Paul did not know); but the author of the (probably pre-Pauline) hymn can hardly have been uninfluenced by early oral traditions of the ministry of Jesus. With this passage may be compared Paul's declaration in 1 Cor 2:16 that "we have the mind of Christ." Paul reiterates Jesus' emphasis on the cost of discipleship, and indeed for Paul, as Hays (1996) puts it, *"Jesus' death on a cross is the paradigm for faithfulness in this world"* (197). "Knowing" Christ means "the sharing of his sufferings by becoming like him in his death" (Phil 3:10).

Much of the uniqueness and power of Jesus as an ethical figure derives from the congruity of his life and his ethical teaching. His teaching on forgiveness of enemies (Matt 5:43-47), for example, is matched by his own practice (Luke 23:34; cf. Acts 7:60, which shows Stephen following his Master's example). "It is difficult to find anything in the way of positive instruction in the Sermon on the Mount that cannot be parallelled in the actual conduct of the Preacher of the Sermon. Whatever else may be true of the Sermon on the Mount, it is not a sermon that says 'Do as I say and not as I do'" (T. W. Manson 1960: 53).

Jesus' *parables* constitute a special class of narrative that has paradigmatic ethical significance (see Spohn 1996: 89-93). This is particularly the case with those, preserved in Luke's Gospel, often classified as "example stories," such as the parables of the Good Samaritan (10:25-37), the rich fool (12:16-21), the rich man and Lazarus (16:19-31), and the Pharisee and the publican (18:9-14). Those who follow Jesus are not expected slavishly to imitate these examples, but they are called to "go and do likewise *(homoiōs)*" (10:37).

f. Visionary and Pragmatic Ethics

Like the OT, the NT provides ethical principles (stated or implied) that ought to be applied in specific situations, yet there remains a tension between these high ideals, or "visionary ethics," and the realities of the actual situations in which the ethical principles were to be applied. The early Christian church consisted of tiny communities scattered throughout the Roman Empire in the eastern Mediterranean. Inevitably social, economic, and political pressures set certain parameters within which even the church had to operate, so that what we can find is what is sometimes referred to as "pragmatic ethics." Some scholars tend to see in the teaching (and practice) of Jesus a purely visionary ethic that proceeded to get progressively watered down in the pragmatic ethics of the early Christian communities of the first and second centuries. While there may be some truth in this, the fact is that the tension between visionary and pragmatic runs through the whole of the NT. Examples may be found in the NT treatment of divorce (see 19-3.2d.ii), the status of women (see 19-3.3c.ii), and slavery (see 19-3.3c.i).

18-3.2. THE NEW ORDER: JESUS

In the ethics of the new order, Jesus plays the leading role as both teacher and example.

a. Jesus' Ethical Teaching

Jesus' ethical teaching is preserved primarily in the Gospels, especially the Synoptics; there is little specific ethical teaching in John. Matthew has collected an anthology of Jesus' ethical teaching in the Sermon on the Mount (Matt 5–7). Fragments of Jesus' teaching are preserved in the epistles (e.g., Rom 12:14-21; 1 Cor 7:10; Jas 5:12; see Lohse 1991: 26-29) and in Acts 20:35.

b. The Old and the New

To what extent did Jesus bring a new ethic and to what extent did he reiterate and reinforce that of the OT?

i. Judaism and Torah

The interpretation of what the NT says about Torah/Law was controlled for many years by certain assumptions. It is important to make a distinction here between "legalism" and "works righteousness." Any religion (Christianity is no exception!) that involves rites and ceremonies, laws and customs is open to the danger of "legalism" in the sense of emphasizing the *letter* of the law while neglecting its *spirit*, of focusing on the minutiae of observances rather than applying its great ethical principles. The OT prophets attacked the legalism of their day (see 18-1.2b). In the Gospels Jesus attacks the legalism of the scribes and Pharisees: "For you tithe mint, dill, and cummin, and have neglected the weightier matters of the law: justice and mercy and faith" (Matt 23:23). He accused them of finding (technically legal) ways of evading the true intent of the Law (Mark 7:9-13). Historically, the best of the Pharisees in Jesus' day would doubtless have agreed with such criticisms.

But the Judaism of the late OT and intertestamental period has long been accused of more than this. Influenced especially by the views of Luther (see Richardson and Westerholm 1991: 58-60), Protestant scholarship developed the theory that in this period Judaism strayed from its original path and became a religion of "works righteousness," in which pious Jews sought to observe every detail of the Torah in order to acquire merit and thus to *earn* salvation. This became "critical orthodoxy," copied in the nineteenth and twentieth centuries from one textbook to another and espoused even by scholars of the stature of Bultmann, who characterized the Judaism of Jesus' day as "a piety which endeavors to win God's favor by the toil of minutely fulfilling the Law's stipulations" (1952: 11; see further, Richardson and Westerholm, 60-63). This view, however, was seriously challenged in the last third of the twentieth century. In 1963 K. Stendahl published an article demonstrating that Paul has been misinterpreted through being read through Lutheran spectacles. In 1977 E. P. Sanders published *Paul and Palestinian Judaism,* a massive study which showed that in the surviving literature of Palestinian Judaism there is little or no evidence that the Judaism of Paul's day was a religion of works righteousness. It was rather, he suggested, "covenantal nomism," a view in fundamental agreement with the OT understanding of Law *(nomos)* and covenant. After delivering the Israelites in the exodus event, God took the initiative and graciously offered to enter into covenant with them, without their having in any way earned or deserved it. The Torah is a gift from God to show Israel the lifestyle within the covenant. In Sanders's terms, the Law has nothing to do with "getting in" to the covenant, though observing it is related to "staying in" the covenant. Sanders's view has been widely discussed (see Ziesler 1990: 104-7; Richardson and Westerholm, 63-72), and his basic position accepted by many scholars. It certainly is a much-needed corrective, though it is not clear that it fully and adequately explains Paul's view of the Law (see further below, 18-3.3b).

ii. Jesus and Torah

The key text for Jesus' relation to the Torah is Matt 5:17, strategically situated in the first part of the Sermon on the Mount, the first summary of Jesus' ethical teaching found within the canon of the NT. Jesus says, "Do not think that I have come to abolish the law. . . . I have come not to abolish but to fulfill." At first sight this suggests that Jesus endorsed the Torah in its entirety (cf. 5:18-20), and some critical scholars have held that this was indeed Jesus' view, while others have held that it represents the view of a conservative Jewish faction within the early church that has been ascribed to Jesus. Due weight, however, must be accorded to the claim that Jesus "fulfills" the Torah (*plēroō* = "fill up, complete, fulfill"). The broader context of this saying in Matthew's Gospel depicts Jesus as the second Moses (see 6-3.1a), and hence as the Messiah who brings the eschatological Torah (above, 18-2.2a; cf. W. D. Davies 1952: 92, contra Banks 1975: 185). Study of the actual content of Jesus' ethical teaching shows that he "fulfills" the Torah in two ways.

Firstly, Jesus fulfills or completes the Torah by making its moral laws even more demanding. In the antitheses of the Sermon on the Mount (Matt 5:21-48), he teaches that not only is murder wrong, but so are anger and hatred (vv. 21-26); not only is adultery wrong, but so is lust in the heart (vv. 27-30). Ethical motivation is found in the heart (Mark 7:18-23), and in switching the focus from outward actions to inner motivation Jesus is seen as the bearer of the eschatological Torah that will truly be written on the heart (Jer 31:33; see above, 18-2.2a; cf. C. J. H. Wright 1983: 160). The discussion of divorce in Mark 10:2-9 (and //s) shows Jesus undercutting the Mosaic legislation in order to declare the true will of God. For Jesus, "the divine law remained the true expression of God's will for Israel," but he "radicalized the law by confronting the hearer with the true intent of God's word" (Childs 1992: 692). Jesus' ethical teaching has been well characterized as a demand for "radical obedience." It is in this context that Jesus criticized any and all forms of legalism that undermined the true intent of the law. And it is in this sense that Jesus requires that his followers' righteousness exceed even that of the scribes and Pharisees (Matt 5:20). Stuhlmacher (1986) is therefore justified in claiming that "the critique, deepening, and focussing of the law that appear together in Jesus become most readily understandable if Jesus appeared with the claim that as the Son of man/Messiah inaugurating the eschatological reign of God he was also the messianic fulfiller of the torah. In and with Jesus the eschatological reality of the Zion torah is made manifest" (119).

Secondly, Jesus focuses entirely on the *ethical* teaching of the Torah at the expense of the *ritual* and *ceremonial* (cf. Crook 1990: 68-69). Of course, the terms "ethical" and "ritual" do not appear in any lexicon or concordance of the NT, and no such *theoretical* distinction is found in Jesus' teaching; the distinction is a *practical* one borne out by analysis of the entire relevant body of material in the Gospels. For example, in response to the "rich young ruler" (Matt 19:16-30//Mark 10:17-31//Luke 18:18-30), Jesus reaffirms the second (i.e., ethical) table of the Decalogue (cf. Mark 7:9-13; see R. H. Fuller 1989: 244-46). He sums up the law (Matt 22:34-40; Mark 12:28-34) by selecting two key commandments: love of God (Deut 6:5) and love of neighbor (Lev 19:18; see Lohse 1991: 52-59). In giving the basic ethical principle of the Golden Rule, "Do to others as you would have them do to you" (Matt 7:12//Luke 6:31), Jesus declares (in Matthew's version) that "this is *the law* and the prophets." The rule in its negative form was known in Judaism (cf. *Tob* 4:15; see Beck 1962a); Jesus states it as a positive ethical principle that embodies the essence of the Torah. As noted above, it is the *ethical* demands of the law that Jesus makes more demanding.

Jesus' reinforcement of these ethical demands is matched by a strong de-emphasis of the ritual and ceremonial demands. Technically he broke the Sabbath on many occasions in order to meet human need. His teaching on cleanness and uncleanness in Mark 7:1-23 virtually did away with the food laws. By touching lepers (in order to heal them) he again broke the ritual law. His saying, "Let the dead bury their own dead" (Matt 8:22), would have shocked observant Jews (cf. Wiebe 1991: 33).

In effect, therefore, Jesus' "fulfilling" of the law constitutes a new righteousness that is available for all humankind, not just for those bound by the ritual and ceremonial requirements of the Torah. The prologue of the Sermon on the Mount (Matt 5:1-2), with its emphasis on Jesus ascending the mountain and providing an authoritative reinterpretation of the law, points forward to the conclusion of the Gospel where Jesus again meets with his disciples on a mountain and bids them go and make disciples of all nations, "teaching them to obey everything that I have commanded you" (28:19-20); the messianic law is thus for all nations (see Lohse 1991: 63). In this sense also, therefore, Jesus does not merely repeat or reinforce the Sinai law but brings the eschatological Zion law promised for the new age (above, 18-2.2a).

The emphasis in John's Gospel is considerably different from that found in the Synoptics, yet ultimately it is not in conflict with it. Jesus inaugurates the new age that succeeds the age of the law: "The law indeed was given through Moses; grace and truth came through Jesus Christ" (1:17). This does not mean the abolition of the ethical teaching of Torah, however; in 8:11 Jesus confirms the validity of the commandment against adultery, though to the offender he offers forgiveness and a fresh start. The commandments of God are now summed up in a "new commandment, that you love one another"; this is new, and radical, and extraordinarily demanding, for it requires a love to match that of Jesus himself: "Just as I have loved you, you also should love one another" (13:34). The ethical emphasis of John's Gospel must be seen in its canonical context, where it does not contradict but rather complements the fuller ethical teaching of Jesus in the Synoptics.

iii. Jesus and Prophecy

Jesus also stands in the prophetic tradition (see more fully, 6-3.4), and this is evident in his ethical teaching (cf. W. Janzen 1994: 198-200). He did not come to abolish the prophets (Matt 5:17). His attacks on legalism are very much in line with those of the prophets. Like them, he denounced even the rulers of his day, calling Herod Antipas "that fox" (Luke 13:31-32). He quotes with approval the key text from the prophet Hosea: "I desire mercy, not sacrifice" (Matt 9:13; 12:7 = Hos 6:6). His demand for "justice and mercy and faith" (Matt 23:23) echoes Mic 6:8:

> What does the LORD require of you
> but to do justice, and to love kindness,
> and to walk humbly with your God?

As noted above, in teaching the Golden Rule he sees it as a summary of *the prophets* as well as of the Torah.

iv. Jesus and Wisdom

The role of Jesus as an ethical teacher has always been recognized (see 6-3.5). In the closing decades of the twentieth century the renaissance of Wisdom studies led to a fresh examination of the relationship between Jesus and the Wisdom tradition (cf. Conzelmann 1976: 958; W. Janzen 1994: 195-96). That Jesus should be seen as a teacher of Wisdom is scarcely surprising; in his hometown the people were astounded at his teaching and asked, "Where did this man get this wisdom?" (Matt 13:54), while the conclusion of the Sermon on the Mount comes with Jesus saying that "everyone then who hears these words of mine and acts on them will be like a wise man who built his house on rock" (7:24).

Formal affinities have been noted between Jesus' teaching and the Wisdom tradition (several scholars have found this to be true especially in Q, the hypothetical common source of Matthew and Luke, but their observations are pertinent quite apart from the validity of the Q hypothesis). Beardslee (1970), for example, has demonstrated the presence of Wisdom elements in Jesus' parables (the parable of the wedding banquet in Luke 14:7-11 is based on Prov 25:6-7), and especially in his proverbs with their use of antithesis (e.g., Mark 10:43-44), paradox (e.g., Luke 17:33), and hyperbole (e.g., Mark 10:25). Borg (1992) also notes the Wisdom character of Jesus' parables as well as his use of "aphorisms," by which he means "the short metaphorical sayings of Jesus, including beatitudes, nature sayings, and what are sometimes called proverbs. Compact, memorable and evocative, they are crystallizations of insight" (807).

In content Jesus' teaching scarcely follows the well-worn paths of traditional and conventional Wisdom, such as that found in Proverbs. Rather, most scholars emphasize how Jesus' teaching aimed to subvert traditional beliefs and values. Beardslee (1970) argues that in his use of parables Jesus uses "familiar experience of every day to jolt the reader into a new insight" (69), while Borg (1992) suggests that "the narrow way which leads to life is the alternative wisdom of Jesus. At its heart is an alternative image of reality, an alternative path, and an alternative paradigm for behaviour" (808).

These insights are valuable provided it is not suggested that Jesus was *merely* "a teacher of wisdom" (so Borg 1992: 806); if he were only that, his subsequent influence would be impossible to explain. Two points need to be noted here. First, as already noted (8-3.4), Wisdom is a christological category; Luke portrays Jesus as the eschatological envoy of Wisdom, while Matthew more directly identifies Jesus with Wisdom incarnate. In the OT tradition Solomon is the very personification of Wisdom, but with Jesus "something greater than Solomon is here!" (Matt 12:42). Secondly, the Wisdom elements in Jesus' teaching must not be separated from his authoritative reinterpretation of the Torah nor his claim to fulfill the message of the prophets, nor can they be separated from his proclamation of the kingdom. Jesus' ethics are "kingdom ethics," and Jesus claims that the kingdom is not only future but also present in his own words and deeds, a claim that has far-reaching christological consequences.

c. Sanctions

Jesus' teaching avoids immediate sanctions. John's Gospel sums up the attitude of Jesus during his ministry when it says, "God did not send the Son into the world to condemn the world, but in order that the world might be saved through him" (3:17). On the other hand, Jesus did retain strong eschatological sanctions (see 18-4.2).

Special importance attaches to Jesus' view of capital punishment. In the episode of the woman taken in adultery (John 8:2-11), Jesus recognizes adultery as sin but refuses to approve the sanction of capital punishment specified under the Torah. His attitude, it may be held, was "completely harmonious with everything else that he taught about the worth of every individual in the sight of God, about forgiveness, and about the possibility of reformation of character and conduct" (Crook 1990: 211). Jesus himself went on to become a victim (probably the most famous ever) of capital punishment; yet he died praying for his executioners: "Father, forgive them; for they do not know what they are doing" (Luke 23:34). Thus Jesus clearly aligns himself not with the Torah's demand for capital punishment but rather with the other strand in the OT that emphasizes God's forgiving and redeeming love (above, 18-1.2a.v).

18-3.3. THE NEW ORDER: THE CHURCH

Ethical teaching played a major role in the early Christian church, and it occupies considerable space in the NT outside the Gospels, especially in the Epistles.

a. The Historical Order: Torah in the Early Church

A key issue in the early church was the relation of its ethical teaching to the Law of Moses. Within the earliest Christian community there were clearly two views. The group led by Peter and then by James, and identified in Acts as "the Hebrews" (6:1), were evidently content as Jews to continue to observe all the requirements of the Torah. However, the "Hellenists," led initially by Stephen, held a more radical view, more in accordance with the radical views of Jesus himself. Stephen was accused of speaking against Moses and against the Law (6:11, 13). It was the Hellenists who were the first to appreciate the significance of the Christ event as the inauguration of the new age, the time for the eschatological reunion of North and South (see 11-3.5b) and the eschatological ingathering of the Gentiles (see 12-3.4), and hence for the acceptance of Gentiles without the requirements of the ritual law (on the origins of the Gentile mission, see more fully 12-3.2; 12-3.3). The Hellenists established the church at Antioch that became the base of the Gentile mission and that found its greatest champion in Paul. The key issue at the "Council of Jerusalem" in Acts 15 was whether, with the "Judaizers," to require of Gentile converts circumcision and full observance of the Torah, or whether, with Paul and Barnabas, to accept Gentiles without requiring observance of the whole ritual law. The council, including Peter and even James, decided in favor of Paul's view of the Law, though for a time problems remained regarding how Jewish Christians and Gentile Christians could coexist (see 12-3.2).

b. The Historical Order: Torah in Paul

Paul's understanding of the Law is a pivotal question for Pauline theology and indeed for BT generally, and has been the subject of extensive and lively debate (cf. Westerholm 1988).

No progress can be made until it is realized that Paul uses the term "law" (*nomos*) in at least six senses. The meaning in any given text can be determined only by the *context,* and by the relationship between the individual text and Paul's thought as a whole. It is crucial to distinguish these different senses.

i. Firstly, Paul can use *nomos* to refer to a *principle* that governs one's actions, as in Rom 7:21: "I find it to be a *law* that when I want to do what is good, evil lies close at hand."

ii. Secondly, Paul can use *nomos* to refer to the *Pentateuch,* as in Rom 3:21 when he refers to "the law and the prophets." He frequently quotes from the Pentateuch as inspired Scripture, and sees God's promise to Abraham in Genesis as of fundamental importance (cf. 12-3.4b).

iii. Thirdly, Paul can speak of the Gentiles having *a law written on their hearts.* Though they do not know the OT Torah, through conscience they do have a knowledge of God's moral law (Rom 2:14-16; see further below, 18-3.3e).

iv. Fourthly, Paul can use *nomos* of the Torah, delivered by God, through Moses, at Mount Sinai, including all its "laws," religious, cultic, civil, and moral (cf. Rom 9:4). Paul's attitude to law in this sense can appear very negative. He insists that believers are justified or accepted into a right relationship with God "not by doing the works of the law, because no one will be justified by the works of the law" (Gal 2:16). It was in conjunction with statements such as this that biblical scholars for many years assumed that Paul's polemic was directed at contemporary Judaism on the grounds that it was a religion of "works righteousness" (see above, 18-3.2b.i). If this is a misrepresentation, and if Palestinian Judaism was still basically a religion of "covenantal nomism," against whom was Paul's polemic directed? The *context* of much of Paul's discussion of the law is his conflict with the "Judaizers," those in the early church who demanded that Gentile converts, in order to become Christians, had first of all to become Jews by being circumcised and taking on all the obligations of the Jewish ceremonial and ritual law.

The Judaizers had failed to grasp what Paul saw as the very basis of the gospel, the fact that with the Christ event the new age had dawned and the era of the law had come to an end. With the inauguration of the new order the eschatological promises of the OT were being fulfilled: the Spirit was poured out on all God's people and the eschatological ingathering of the Gentiles had begun (see 12-3.4). This had happened entirely due to God's grace demonstrated in the Christ event, especially in the atoning death and triumphant resurrection of Jesus. God's righteousness, his acting to put things right for sinful humanity, was based on grace, and the gospel message was open to all, Jews and Gentiles alike, *with no preconditions.* When Paul says justification is not by "works of law," he is therefore thinking primarily of such things as circumcision and the food laws, which the Judaizers *did* demand as a precondition for Gentiles to be accepted.

Dunn has argued (1990: 191-94) that a careful study of Paul's letters shows that what he opposed was (1) circumcision, (2) the food laws, and (3) the observance of Jewish feasts (cf. Gal 4:10). These were not to be demanded of Gentile converts as a precondition of acceptance into the Christian community. Thus "his denial that justification is from works of law is, more precisely, a denial that justification depends on circumcision or on observance of the Jewish purity and food taboos" (191). These are prime examples of the ritual laws that served to separate Israel from the nations and mark Israel as God's covenant people. But in the new age they could no longer apply, for now all persons, Jew and Gentile, could be part of God's people, participating in the new covenant. As Dunn points out, this does not mean that Paul is opposed to "ritual" on principle; what were baptism and the Lord's Supper but Christian rituals (198)? It is these particular OT rituals he objects to because they symbolize the (now outdated) position that only Israel is God's covenant people.

If the question is raised, "Why then the law?" (Gal 3:19), Paul's answer is a thoroughly salvation-historical one. The law *did* have a role to play, a very important role, but *only in the period from Moses to Christ,* the period during which God used Israel to prepare for the coming of Christ. In Gal 3:24 (RSV) Paul says, "The law was our custodian *(paidagōgos)* until Christ came." *Paidagōgos* does not mean "schoolmaster" (KJV), but refers to a slave whose duty it was to escort the son of the house to and from school, protecting him from harm. So the law served the purpose of protecting Israel. Circumcision and the food laws, for example, kept Israel apart from the nations, protecting against the danger of assimilation and thus preserving the promises of the coming of a new age. It is clear then that Paul does not attack the whole law, but only the ritual and ceremonial laws that served a purpose in their day but now no longer apply. Much has been made of Rom 10:4, where Paul says, "Christ is the end *(telos)* of the law." Clearly *telos* does not here mean "end" in the sense that the whole law is abolished or done away with. It means "end" in the sense of goal or completion: Christ fulfills the law and completes its original intention (cf. J. A. Sanders 1975: 382). Rom 10:4 states: "Christ is the end of the law *so that there may be righteousness for everyone who believes,"* and as Paul goes on to show (v. 12), that means Jews *and* Gentiles. Thus for Paul, "Christ is the goal of the law to everyone who believes, because the ultimate goal of the law is that all nations are to be blessed in Abraham" (G. E. Howard 1969: 337).

v. Fifthly, while the above salvation-historical approach explains much of what Paul says about the law, it does not fully explain another strand in his thought that surfaces especially in Romans and Galatians. Paul's most negative view of the law is found in Rom 7, and here he is not thinking of circumcision and other ritual laws that were of temporary validity, for as his main illustration he takes the tenth commandment, "You shall not covet" (Rom 7:7 = Exod 20:17// Deut 5:21), a *moral* law that he considers still valid for all Christians (see Rom 13:9). Such moral laws are seen by Paul in Rom 7 in a surprisingly negative light. Law in the sense of the commandments of God's moral law can serve to *reveal* sin: "I would not have known what it is to covet if the law had not said, 'You shall not covet'" (Rom 7:7; cf. Gal 3:19). In fact, Paul virtually says that the law in this sense *causes* sin: "While we were living in the flesh, our sinful passions, *aroused by the law,* were at work in our members to bear fruit for death" (Rom 7:5), though he goes on to explain that law simply provides an opportunity for "sin" to lead people astray (7:7-13). Ziesler (1990) suggests that for Paul "the Law enables sin to be seen in its true nature as disobedience to God (Rom 7:13). It works rather like a poultice, bringing to the surface poison which can thus be recognized and dealt with" (107-8). In this negative sense law can be spoken of as a power that enslaves people (Rom 7:6; Gal 3:23). In these passages the context demands that we take *nomos* to mean something like *the demands of God's moral law thought of apart from the grace of God.*

The historical question of why Paul should have this negative view of the moral law is difficult if not impossible to answer, though there are a number of possible explanations. As noted above, the work of E. P. Sanders and others has shown that it does not reflect the outlook of Palestinian Judaism as that is witnessed to in the surviving literature; it is conceivable, however, that Paul encountered such a view somewhere in the Hellenistic Judaism of the Diaspora. Alternatively, an explanation may be sought in Paul's personal experience; some have linked it with what follows in Rom 7:14-25, but it is far from clear that this passage is autobiographical and refers to Paul's preconversion life (cf. 16-3.2c.ii, and see the discussion in Westerholm 1988: 53-64). More probably, Paul's views were linked with his Damascus road experience. He had been a zealous Jew observing the Torah in every detail (Gal 1:14; Phil 3:6), yet he had failed to recognize Jesus as the Messiah and had persecuted the church (1 Cor 15:9). He was not saved by the law; he was saved by divine intervention, by an act of God's grace, which revealed to him that the new age had dawned in Christ and that he was called to take part in the ingathering of the Gentiles. In addition, in speaking of the law in this sense, Paul was probably reflecting on Israel's history. Although Torah is not a way of earning God's favor, the maintenance of the covenant does depend on keeping the law so that the line between "getting in" and "staying in" (in Sanders's terms) could become a thin one (see Hagner 1997: 26). OT history, especially from the exile onward, is marked by "a growing awareness of the failure of the nation, the community of faith, and the individual in their existence before Yahweh. This very awareness corresponds to the insight into the human need for renewal and into the provisionality of the law of Moses from Sinai, an insight that emerged repeatedly from Jeremiah and Ezekiel on" (Stuhlmacher 1986: 114). Linked with this must surely have been Paul's estimate of the extent and seriousness of *human sin* (see 16-3.2c). Historically it is possible, as some scholars have suggested, that Paul's thought developed "backwards." He did not begin with a negative view of Judaism; it was his growing understanding of the cross as an atonement for human sin that led him to realize the inadequacy of any other route to salvation (cf. Richardson and Westerholm 1991: 70).

BT, of course, must not be dependent on any particular historical reconstruction. The fact remains that Paul can view the moral law negatively, but only apart from God's grace. That grace, for Paul, has now been manifest in the

Christ event, especially Jesus' death and resurrection, which enables believers to enter a right relationship with God, in the fellowship of the church, and empowers them through the Holy Spirit to live in accordance with God's commandments.

vi. This brings us to the sixth sense in which Paul uses the word "law." Although Christian living is "the fruit of the Spirit" (Gal 5:22-25) and can be summed up in the commandment to love one's neighbor (Rom 13:10; Gal 5:14), this does not mean that law plays no role in Christian ethics. Insofar as Torah is the revelation of God's will, "the law is holy, and the commandment is holy and just and good" (Rom 7:12). Paul can speak of being "under Christ's law" (1 Cor 9:21), of fulfilling "the law of Christ" (Gal 6:2), and of "the law of the Spirit of life" (Rom 8:2). He can also say, "Circumcision is nothing, and uncircumcision is nothing; but *obeying the commandments of God* is everything" (1 Cor 7:19). Through Christ's atoning death the power of sin has been broken "so that *the just requirement of the law* might be fulfilled in us" (Rom 8:4). As Dunn (1990) points out, "Paul is as little opposed to the law *per se* as he is to good works *per se*. It is the law understood in terms of *works,* as a Jewish prerogative and national monopoly, to which he takes exception" (200).

Thus, in giving ethical direction Paul specifically quotes "the commandments" in the form of the second table of the Decalogue (Rom 13:9; cf. 7:7; Eph 6:2-3). The sins listed in 1 Tim 1:8-10 allude to commandments five through nine in the canonical order (R. H. Fuller 1989: 254). Like Jesus, he sees the ethical commandments as summed up in the saying, "Love your neighbor as yourself" (Rom 13:9; Gal 5:14). Even when he does not specifically quote the law in giving ethical advice, it is clear that Paul regards the *content* of the law as binding on Christians in moral matters. Thus in 1 Cor 5:1-5 he deals with a case of incest, behavior that he condemns in no uncertain fashion. He could have appealed to the Torah (Lev 18:8), but prefers instead to refer to "sexual immorality . . . of a kind that is not found even among pagans" (1 Cor 5:1). In other words, instead of quoting the Sinai Torah, he quotes the law written in the hearts of all human beings in such a way as to indicate that it still guides the behavior of Christians.

For Paul, therefore, law still has a role for believers (cf. Hagner 1997: 27), but it is the "messianic Torah *(ton nomon tou Christou)*" (Gal 6:2 AT; cf. W. D. Davies 1952: 92), the eschatological Zion law promised in the Prophets, i.e., the Sinai law shorn of those ritual elements that exclude Gentiles (cf. 18-2.2a), the law as affirmed and deepened by Jesus. Paul's view is thus fundamentally in agreement and in continuity with that of Jesus (above, 18-3.2b.ii). Though he does not employ the terms "ritual" and "moral," it is precisely the ritual requirements of the Sinai law (circumcision, food laws, etc.) that Paul sees as no longer valid, and it is precisely the moral content of Zion law that is reaffirmed in a new way for Christian believers (cf. Cronk 1982: 210). "The 'torah of Christ' has its center in the love command and in the fundamental demands of the

Decalogue; in this torah of Christ the spiritual intention of the Torah from Sinai reaches its goal" (Stuhlmacher 1986: 125). Its role is akin to the original role of Torah: it serves as a guide, directing God's people. The law of Christ is not to be followed legalistically; obedience is empowered by the Spirit and motivated by love.

c. The Historical Order: Torah in the Rest of the New Testament

Law is much less an issue in the later books of the NT, though what they say on the subject is consistent with the main strand of NT teaching that runs from Jesus through Paul.

Of all the books of the NT, the Epistle to the Hebrews is the one that works out in greatest detail the Christian evaluation of the OT ritual and ceremonial law. It had its place, but basically it foreshadowed Christ as the great High Priest, and Christ's death as the supreme sacrifice for sin that has now rendered the whole system based on animal sacrifice obsolete. In this sense, with the Christ event, "there is necessarily a change in the law as well" (Heb 7:12). This does not mean, however, that the ethical requirements of the law no longer apply to Christians, as 13:1-5 shows.

1 John clarifies the ethical position of John's Gospel. Christian discipleship involves obeying Christ's commandments (1 John 2:3; 3:22). What Christ commands is in one sense "an old commandment" (2:7), and John leaves his readers in no doubt that, in accordance with the ethical teaching of the Torah, it involves caring for the poor and needy in the most practical way possible (3:17; 4:20-21). Yet Christ's commandment is also new, partly because of its demand for radical obedience: John echoes Jesus' teaching that hatred in the heart is the equivalent of murder (3:11-15). It is new also because it is reinterpreted by the one who has inaugurated the new age (2:8).

The Epistle of James consists virtually entirely of ethical exhortation, and for its author the life of believers must conform to law, though for him it is "the royal law" (2:8) and "the law of liberty" (1:25; 2:12). For many, James raises serious problems regarding the consistency of the ethical teaching of the NT (see Childs 1984: 438-43). In 2:14-26 he uses the terms "faith," "works," and "justified" in a way that on the surface appears to contradict Paul's use of the same terminology. James's key point is that faith without works is dead (2:17, 26), and he expresses this by saying, "You see that a person is justified by works and not by faith alone" (2:24). This sounds at odds with Paul's claim that "a person is justified by faith apart from works prescribed by the law" (Rom 3:28; cf. Gal 2:16), and the contrast is sharpened by the fact that both writers quote the example of Abraham to prove their point, Paul claiming Abraham was justified by faith (Rom 4; Gal 3:6-9) and James that he was justified by works (Jas 2:21)!

The historical question of the relationship between James and Paul is not the prime concern of BT, though it seems unlikely that James knew Paul directly, and was more probably reacting to a misunderstanding or misrepresentation of Paul's views. What is clear is that Paul and James are addressing quite different questions: "Paul is asking about the relation between the divine and the human in acquiring salvation. James is asking about the relation between the profession of faith and action consonant with it" (Childs 1984: 442). The main point to note is that Paul and James do not mean the same thing by either "works" or "faith." Paul denies that a person can attain a right relationship with God through "works of law *(erga nomou),*" i.e., either the observance of the Jewish ritual law or the observance of moral rules with the thought that they can earn salvation; salvation depends entirely on God's grace. By "works" James simply means good deeds, the ethical living that must be the outcome of faith in God. With this Paul would not disagree; for him, we may say, justification is *by grace, through faith,* but also *for works* (see esp. Eph 2:8-10). Similarly, by "faith" James means intellectual assent to the proposition that God exists, something that even the demons accept (Jas 2:19); Paul would certainly agree that this is not enough, and for him faith is something far more, including acceptance of the gospel message and entering into a totally new, living and dynamic relationship with God. Finally, though both James and Paul cite Abraham, they are thinking of different episodes in the life of the patriarch. Paul alludes to Gen 15 where God promises Abraham a son, a striking example of faith as trust that God can accomplish what is humanly impossible. James on the other hand refers to Gen 22, an example of how Abraham's willingness even to sacrifice his son Isaac demonstrated how far he was prepared to go to put his faith into practice. Thus Paul and James do not contradict one another, mainly because they are not in direct dialogue at all. Nevertheless, it is highly significant that James found a place in the canon alongside the letters of Paul. Theologically he is not in the same league as Paul, yet his letter is a healthy reminder that Christian faith must express itself in ethical living, something with which Paul would agree despite the fact that some of Paul's statements, taken out of context, might suggest otherwise (see 2 Pet 3:16).

d. The Historical Order: The Rebirth of Prophecy

The ethics of the early church stand in continuity with the prophetic ethics of the OT, just as did those of Jesus.

The inauguration of the new age saw the rebirth of prophecy in accordance with the promise of the OT and in association with the giving of the Spirit (Acts 2:17). The book of Acts testifies to the presence of prophets and prophetesses in the early church, as do Paul's letters (see more fully, 15-3.3c). Since prophets delivered Spirit-inspired utterances, it is a fair assumption that this included ethical advice and exhortation. The best example of prophecy in the NT is the book of Revelation, which is explicitly designated by the writer as prophecy (1:3). The letters to the seven churches (Rev 2–3) include ethical exhortation.

e. The Created Order: Sources of Ethical Norms

Like the OT, the NT recognizes a knowledge of ethical norms in the created order, i.e., outside of the OT and the tradition of Jesus' teaching and example.

i. The Universal Moral Law

There is not a total discontinuity between Christian ethics and the best of non-Christian ethics. The clearest recognition of this comes in Rom 2:14-16: "When Gentiles, who do not possess the law, do instinctively what the law requires, these, though not having the law, are a law to themselves. They show that what the law requires is written on their hearts, to which their own conscience also bears witness; and their conflicting thoughts will accuse or perhaps excuse them on the day when, according to my gospel, God, through Jesus Christ, will judge the secret thoughts of all." There has been much debate as to whether Paul, speaking here of the moral law written on the heart, recognizes the existence of a "natural law," especially since he says that Gentiles do what the law requires "by nature *(physis)*." But Paul certainly does not mean by *physis* what the Stoics meant; for him *physis* can only be an aspect of God's created order. It is more accurate to think in terms of a "general revelation" (cf. 2-3.3). What Paul recognizes is "the existence of a universal moral law, in the sense of a form of divinely bestowed ethical wisdom shared by all mankind" (Greenwood 1971: 267).

ii. Conscience

Paul links this universal moral law with "conscience" (*syneidēsis* = "consciousness, moral consciousness"; verb *synoida* = "share knowledge with, know oneself, be conscious"). The term is unknown in the OT but was common currency in NT times in Greek and Latin authors, and in Hellenistic Judaism (see W. D. Davies 1962a: 671-72), where it designates a faculty, characteristic of all human beings, that passes judgment, generally on specific acts of wrongdoing committed by the person concerned. In the NT it is used primarily by Paul (including the Pastorals), but is also found in Acts, Hebrews, and 1 Peter. The broad context of the NT references to conscience shows that "in the conscience it is the demand of God that comes to expression" (Lohse 1991: 91).

It has been argued that in the NT, following Hellenistic usage, conscience means basically "remorse" and its sole function is to condemn a wrong act after it has been committed (so Whiteley 1964: 210). But this is too narrow a definition. If conscience tells one that disobedience to the state is wrong (Rom 13:5), then it also tells one that obedience to the state is right. And even if conscience passes judgment after the event, people are capable of learning from conscience how they ought to act in the future. Thus, while conscience does indeed condemn wrong acts (Rom 13:5; 1 Cor 8:7; Heb 10:2, 22), more broadly it indicates both right and wrong (Rom 2:15: "accuse" and "excuse"), so that those who do right have "a clear conscience" (Acts 23:1; 24:16; cf. 2 Cor 1:12; 1 Tim 1:19; Heb 13:18; 1 Pet 3:16). Of course, the guidance of conscience can be rejected (1 Tim 1:19; 4:2). While conscience normally passes judgment on one's own conduct, 2 Cor 4:2 suggests it also passes judgment on others (but see also 1 Cor 10:29).

In his discussion of food offered to idols in 1 Cor 8 and 10, Paul recognizes that some have a weak conscience (cf. W. D. Davies 1962a: 674-75). Conscience, in fact, can become corrupted (Titus 1:15). Significantly in Rom 9:1 Paul links conscience with the operation of the Holy Spirit; thus for Paul, "open to corrupting influences as it is, conscience is to be quickened by the Spirit and itself enlightened by Christ" (Davies, 675).

iii. Wisdom

Elements of Wisdom teaching have been identified in the NT epistles. Paul, for example, can quote Prov 25:21-22 in the ethical advice he gives in Rom 12:20. It is more typical of Paul to contrast the message of the cross with human wisdom, as he does in 1 Cor 1–2, though even here he concedes that "among the mature we do speak wisdom" (2:6). On the use of Wisdom as a christological category in Paul, see 8-3.4.

The one book of the NT that most clearly belongs to the genre of Wisdom is the Epistle of James, which consists virtually entirely of ethical advice and exhortation. "The entire letter of James," Conzelmann (1976) has written, "is a wisdom document in parenetic style" that "documents the extent to which Christianity was able to retain Jewish wisdom" (960). Entirely in keeping with the OT view, "the letter of James depicts wisdom as a practical understanding of the will of God, an understanding which enables a man to live at peace with the Lord and with his fellow man" (Cronk 1982: 235). For James, "the wisdom from above is first pure, then peaceable, gentle, willing to yield, full of mercy and good fruits, without a trace of partiality or hypocrisy" (Jas 3:17).

Wisdom elements in the epistles, however, have been integrated into the broader framework of Christ-centered NT ethics, and James (as argued above, 18-3.3c) must be read in its canonical context, especially in relation to the ethical teaching of Paul.

f. The Household Codes

A distinctive pattern of ethical teaching is found in Col 3:18–4:1 and Eph 5:21–6:9, where advice is given concerning three pairs of relationships: husbands/wives, parents/children, and masters/slaves. A similar pattern is found in 1 Tim 2:8-15, 6:1-2, Titus 2:3-10, and 1 Pet 2:18–3:7 (though these deal with husbands/wives, masters/slaves only). Luther labeled these passages *haustafeln* ("house tables," i.e., tables or lists of duties for members of households); in English they are generally referred to as "household codes."

Many scholars hold that historically these codes were borrowed from similar material current in the ancient world, and thus are not really distinctively Christian (see Verhey 1984: 67). This view is linked with the perception that the codes are ultraconservative. Since a striking feature is the demand that one party "submit to" *(hypotassō)* or "obey" *(hypakouō)* the other, they are viewed as assuming and perpetuating the inferiority, if not the abuse, of wives, children, and slaves. In fact, the closest parallels are found not in Stoicism (Seneca, Epictetus, Diogenes Laertius) but in Jewish writers (Philo, Josephus), and if there was borrowing it probably came via Hellenistic Judaism (cf. Selwyn 1947: 438; Lillie 1975: 181). The point to be stressed, however, is that even if the codes include borrowed material, it is certainly also true that they were taken over only with significant modification (see esp. J. H. Yoder 1972).

From the viewpoint of BT, of course, the codes are to be read in their canonical and Christian context. When this is done, three of their features deserve special notice.

Firstly, the most striking feature of the NT codes is the fact that *all duties are reciprocal.* Stoic codes were typically directed to the individual man/husband/father/master (cf. Lohse 1991: 142), but in the NT each partner in the pair is treated as a moral agent (J. H. Yoder 1972: 174) and has a duty toward the other. In fact, the Ephesian code begins, *"Be subject to one another (hupotassomenoi allēlois) . . ."* (5:21). This is indeed, to borrow Yoder's phrase, "revolutionary subordination" (163, 181). Each partner is to surrender any thought of selfish domination and genuinely care for the other (cf. also Eph 6:9; 1 Pet 5:5).

Secondly, all relationships are to be conducted *"in the Lord."* References to the Lord (Christ/Master) permeate the codes (eight references in Colossians, twelve in Ephesians). As Schrage (1988) says, "these formulas are not simply tacked on like labels to indicate that the *haustafeln* are Christian. Instead, these admonitions . . . are set in the framework of the lordship of Jesus Christ" (252). If relationships are truly conducted "in the Lord," in the spirit of Christ, this of course would rule out any thought of domination or abuse. For example, the husband's attitude to his wife is to be comparable to that of Christ to the church (Eph 5:25). It can also be argued that the recurring appeal to the Lord "is a reminder that in Christ Jesus there is neither male nor female, but all are one in him" (Lohse 1991: 142; cf. Verhey 1984: 69). Note that Col 3:11, with its reference to the essential unity of all in Christ (cf. Gal 3:28), occurs just before the household code.

Thirdly, it should be noted that the codes are to be read in the context of Christian love *(agapē)*. Particularly striking is the command to husbands to love their wives (Eph 5:25; Col 3:19; cf. Titus 2:4; 1 Pet 3:8). In both Ephesians and Colossians the lead-in to the code urges the readers to "walk in love" (Eph 5:2 RSV) and to "clothe yourselves with love" (Col 3:14); the codes illustrate how that love is to be applied. Thus "women and men, children and parents, slaves and masters are addressed in terms of their mutual responsibility that is to be expressed in their love for each other" (Lohse 1991: 142).

To a certain extent the codes can be seen as examples of pragmatic ethics; they accept the existing structure of society and direct Christians how to live in a social order they are powerless to change (Lillie 1975: 183; Lohse 1991: 141). But they can also be seen as examples of visionary ethics, containing the seeds of change, and embodying specifically Christian principles capable of transforming the relationships and indeed the whole social order from within.

g. Sanctions

For the early church eschatological sanctions continue to play an important role in ethics (see further, 18-4.1). There are also indications of the beginnings of a system of church discipline that operates in cases of serious infractions of ethical norms. The regulations of Matt 18:15-17 are an indication of this, and 1 Cor 5:1-5 shows Paul dealing with a serious violation of Christian ethical standards in the church at Corinth.

The NT witnesses to capital punishment as a Jewish (Matt 15:4; John 8:1-11; Acts 7:58; cf. Acts 6:11 and Lev 24:16), and also a Roman (Matt 10:38 and //s; Jesus' crucifixion) practice. The early Christians were in no position to carry out capital punishment themselves, so the issue does not arise directly in the NT. The story of Ananias and Sapphira (Acts 5:1-11) is certainly to be seen as an example of divine judgment, but it is hardly relevant to the question of capital punishment in society (the church did not execute them, and the crime they had committed was not even liable to the death penalty according to the OT). Paul has been seen as endorsing the death penalty by the Roman state in Rom 13:4, where he declares that the state is God's servant. "If you do what is wrong, you should be afraid, for the authority does not bear the sword in vain! It is the servant of God to execute wrath on the wrongdoer." The "sword" could be taken as referring to the death penalty (cf. Acts 25:11), but if, as seems likely, the context in Romans is the growing Zealot movement, then the reference is more probably to the use of police or military to maintain law and order.

18-3.4. RIGHTEOUSNESS AND JUSTICE

The NT has a more fully developed ethical vocabulary than the OT. As the promised Messiah, Jesus is the one who brings God's righteousness, enabling people to live in a right relationship with God and calling on them, as a consequence, to live in a right relationship with others. While the NT does not lay down new laws, it is concerned to spell out the character of righteous living and it does this in part through lists of virtues and vices, the greatest of the Christian virtues being love.

a. The Righteousness of God Is Revealed

"Righteousness" *(dikaiosynē = ts^edhāqâh)* is an important theme, especially in Matthew's Gospel. John the Baptist, as the one who prepared for Jesus, came "in the way of righteousness" (21:32). Jesus calls people to enter the kingdom and to live the life of righteousness that this entails (6:33). Because of his emphasis on inner motivation (above, 18-3.2b.ii), Jesus demands that his followers' righteousness exceed that of the scribes and Pharisees (5:20).

As the promised Messiah and the Servant of the Lord (cf. above, 18-2.4), Jesus proclaims justice *(krisis = mishpāṭ)* to the nations (12:18-21 = Isa 42:1-4), and in true prophetic fashion he denounces those who neglect the most important aspects of God's Torah, including justice (Matt 23:23).

The most developed reflection on the theme of righteousness in the NT is found in Paul (see 17-3.3). In the light of the Christ event, he underlines even more strongly than the OT that no human being can claim a righteousness of his or her own: "There is no one who is righteous, not even one" (Rom 3:10). In the gospel, however, the righteousness of God is revealed (1:17). Through Christ, especially through his atoning death and triumphant resurrection, believers are "justified," i.e., accepted into a right relationship with God (see above, 18-3.3b and 17-3.3). That relationship of course must issue in righteous living: justification is by grace, through faith, for works (cf. above, 18-3.3c). Those who have died to sin and risen to the new life in Christ are called to present themselves to God "as instruments of righteousness" (Rom 6:13; cf. 1 Tim 6:11).

b. Lists of Virtues and Vices

If there is a reluctance to enact laws and rules for the Christian community, in Paul's letters (including the Pastorals) in particular there seems to be a strongly felt need to spell out in no uncertain terms the types of behavior and of character that are, and are not, consistent with Christian ethics. There is a vocabulary of virtues and vices that finds expression especially in various "ethical lists" (see Seitz 1962: 138-39; Lohse 1991: 83-88).

Jesus cites a list of evils that come from the heart (Matt 15:19//Mark 7:21-22), and lists of vices precede or follow and act as a foil for the household codes. Col 3:5-9 (preceding the code in 3:18–4:1), for example, lists fornication, impurity, passion, evil desire, greed, anger, wrath, malice, slander, abusive language, and lying; cf. Eph 5:3-5 (preceding the code in 5:21–6:9), 1 Tim 1:9-10 (preceding the code in 2:8-15), Titus 3:3 (following the code in 2:3-10), and 1 Pet 4:3 (following the code in 2:18–3:7). Other lists are found in Rom 1:29-31, 1 Cor 5:10-11, 6:9-10, and 2 Tim 3:2-7 (see F. C. Grant 1950: 176-82). Contrasting lists of virtues and vices are found especially in Gal 5:19-23, where Paul contrasts "the works of the flesh" (see 16-3.1b) — fornication, impurity, licentiousness, idolatry, sorcery, enmities, strife, jealousy, anger, quarrels, dissensions, factions, envy, drunkenness, carousing — with "the fruit of the Spirit" — love, joy, peace, patience, kindness, generosity, faithfulness, gentleness, and self-control. A similar list of virtues in Col 3:12-14 follows the list of vices in 3:5-9.

Grant (1950: 180) notes that the NT lists more vices than virtues. The vices are seen as typical of the pagan society on which converts have turned their backs (Rom 1:29-31; 1 Cor 5:10; Col 3:7; Titus 3:3; 1 Pet 4:3), and as an insurmountable barrier to inheriting God's kingdom (1 Cor 6:9; Eph 5:5); hence the felt need constantly to warn against them.

Some scholars hold that the ethical terminology, perhaps even actual lists, were derived historically from Stoicism and/or Hellenistic Judaism. The point is debatable, but in any case, even if borrowing of terminology did take place, the terms were infused with new meaning in their NT context.

c. The Greatest Is Love

In the ethical material of the NT one quality stands out among all others, that of "love." Love is frequently and rightly identified as "the central imperative" of biblical ethics (cf. Crook 1990: 69-72, 79-80). The verb *agapaō* is more common than the noun *agapē;* the less common verb *phileō* is also used, without any perceptible difference in meaning (see G. Johnston 1962: 169). *Agapaō* and *phileō* are two of several Greek words for "love," but the noun *agapē* is rare in Greek (though it is used in the LXX to translate the Hebrew *'ahᵃbhâ* = "love"). The meaning of the NT terms is not to be sought in etymology or in previous usage but rather in their use in the NT itself, where they designate the response of believers to God's love manifested in Christ. As already noted (17-3.4), the NT stresses that love for God is meaningless unless it issues in the love of others. Jesus called for both love of God and love of neighbor as the supreme marks of those who entered the kingdom he proclaimed (Mark 12:30-34; cf. above, 18-3.2b.ii). His understanding of love is illumined especially by his call to love not merely one's neighbor but even one's enemy (Matt 5:43-44); such love reflects the love of God poured out on the undeserving (5:45-48). John's Gospel amplifies Jesus' teaching on love: "I give you a new commandment, that you love one another. Just as I have loved you, you also should love one another" (13:34). Thus "it is the quality of Christ's graciously condescending, sacrificial love that is to be the model for that of his disciples in their relations with each other" (Johnston, 177).

Love occupies a central place in Paul's ethical teaching that climaxes in the great "Hymn to Love" of 1 Cor 13 with its portrait of love in action (vv. 4-6), its affirmation of love's enduring nature (vv. 8-12), and its prioritizing of love over all other gifts (vv. 1-3), including faith and hope (v. 13). Consistently Paul lists love as the premier Christian quality (Gal 5:22; Col 3:14; 1 Tim 1:5; 4:12). Love is the fulfilling of the law (Rom 13:8-10). As in John, Christian love mirrors that of Christ: "Live in love, as Christ loved us" (Eph 5:2).

1 John sums up the teaching of John's Gospel as "God is love *(ho theos agapē estin),* and those who abide in love abide in God" (4:16). For James also, love of neighbor sums up the law (2:8), and while it may not have the same centrality as in Paul and John, love is commended, e.g., in Heb 10:24, 13:1, 1 Pet 2:17, and Rev 2:4.

Following the classic study by Nygren (*Agape and Eros,* revised ET 1953), the love of which the NT speaks has been seen as essentially love not on the basis of merit (in contrast to *erōs,* love on the basis of the qualities of the one loved), but rather unmerited love, reflecting God's love, in Christ, for sinners. It may be defined therefore as "pure, disinterested, self-sacrificing love, like the love of the Saviour himself" (A. Barr 1950b: 425). Love is commanded in the NT not because it is a natural affection (something impossible to command), but because it is the appropriate, Spirit-empowered response to the divine love.

Jesus taught (and practiced) love for all (Luke 10:29-37), even enemies (Matt 5:44). It has been objected that in the NT as a whole love is essentially love for the other members of one's own community, love for "one another" (John 13:34), love for "the family of believers" (1 Pet 2:17). Paul still mirrors Jesus' attitude (Rom 12:14; cf. 1 Pet 3:9), but hostility and persecution in the later NT period no doubt made communities more inward-looking. While it is true that charity must begin at home, for Christian ethics it is always Jesus' own teaching and practice that must constitute the norm.

18-3.5. WORLD-AFFIRMING OR WORLD-DENYING?

a. World-Affirming

Like OT ethics, NT ethics is basically world-affirming. John the Baptist represented the more ascetic strain in Judaism (Mark 1:6), but in this matter he acts as a foil to Jesus. His disciples fasted while those of Jesus did not (2:18-20 and //s). Jesus not only affirmed the goodness of God's creation, he attended feasts (Luke 5:29; 11:37; 14:1) and weddings (John 2), and his behavior was such that his enemies accused him of being "a glutton and a drunkard" (Matt 11:19).

The early church encountered forms of asceticism in the "false teachings" that it battled. In face of these it continued to affirm the essential goodness of creation. Thus 1 Timothy condemns those who "forbid marriage and demand abstinence from foods, which God created to be received with thanksgiving," and goes on to affirm that "everything created by God is good, and nothing is to be rejected, provided it is received with thanksgiving" (4:3-5). Hence the famous advice, "No longer drink only water, but take a little wine for the sake of your stomach and your frequent ailments" (5:23).

b. Ascetic Strains

Are there also ascetic strains in the NT? The portrait of John the Baptist may not be intended to be a negative one. The saying of Jesus in Matt 19:12 about some who are eunuchs for the sake of the kingdom of heaven might be seen as approval for celibacy; if so, it would be for a voluntary celibacy (see further, 19-3.2c). In 1 Cor 7 Paul accepts the institution of marriage. He sees advantages in some people (like himself) remaining unmarried in order to be free to serve the Lord (vv. 32-35), but there is no hint of this as a requirement to be made binding on Christians; each person has his or her own particular gift from God. In vv. 25-26, as a personal opinion, he counsels virgins not to marry "in view of the present crisis *(dia tēn enestōsan anankēn)*"; like Jeremiah, this is not due to a devaluation of marriage but to a special set of circumstances (cf. J. A. Montgomery 1932: 198, 200).

c. Fasting

One form of asceticism calls for special mention (see esp. Wimmer 1982). Jesus fasted while in the wilderness during his temptations, presumably as a way of disciplining himself for his struggle with Satan (Matt 4:2; Luke 4:2). He condemned fasting if done as a public display of piety, but accepted it as a private practice seen only by God (Matt 6:16-18; Luke 18:12). In Mark 2:18-20 and //s, the dawning of the kingdom in Jesus' ministry is likened to a wedding, the least appropriate occasion on which to fast; yet after Jesus' departure, fasting will be in order (see H. H. Guthrie 1962: 244). The only NT references to fasting in the early church, however, are in conjunction with prayer in Acts 13:2-3 and 14:23.

Fasting is not an end in itself, but it can be a means toward a deeper and more dedicated Christian life. Believers need to learn how to deny self, and they constantly need to be purified of selfishness and egotism: "fasting has its place in this process of purification . . . but it must be rooted in love, coming from it and leading toward it" (Wimmer 1982: 112).

New Testament: Consummation

18-4. THOSE WHO KEEP THE COMMANDMENTS

18-4.1. ETHICS AND ESCHATOLOGY

In the NT ethics and eschatology are closely linked (see Lohse 1991: 39-47). This life is lived in the light of the promise of the final consummation. At present believers live in the moral darkness of this age, but they are exhorted by Paul in Rom 13:11-14: "Let us then lay aside the works of darkness and put on the armor of light; let us live honorably as in the day." The light of the final consummation sheds its light backward, as it were, into the present darkness. In the area of ethics, as elsewhere, there is a tension between the "already" and the "not yet." While justification and sanctification are basically present experiences, the coming of God's kingdom of righteousness, love, and peace still lies in the future so that Paul can say that "through the Spirit, by faith, we eagerly wait for the hope of righteousness" (Gal 5:5).

18-4.2. THE LAST JUDGMENT

The expectation of a future judgment is found throughout the NT, not least in the teaching and parables of Jesus (for fuller discussion of the last judgment, see 16-4.3). Pictures of the final judgment have a strong ethical emphasis, and Paul represents the general NT view when he says that God "will repay according to each one's deeds" (Rom 2:6; see the discussion in 16-4.3c). Nowhere is this more clearly illustrated than in the vision of the sheep and the goats (Matt 25:31-46), where it is how a person has treated the hungry, the thirsty, the stranger, the naked, the sick, and the prisoner in this life that determines his or her final destiny.

18-4.3. NOTHING UNCLEAN SHALL ENTER

Only at the final consummation will all that is contrary to the will of God and all that is evil be finally eliminated (see also 19-4). Paul makes it clear that "wrongdoers will not inherit the kingdom of God" (1 Cor 6:9; cf. Gal 5:21; Eph

5:5), and according to Rev 21:27, "Nothing unclean will enter it [the holy city], nor anyone who practices abomination or falsehood."

18-4.4. THE POWER OF HIS RESURRECTION

In keeping with the already/not yet tension typical of the NT, God's kingdom is already breaking in and is experienced in advance. For Paul the power of Christ's resurrection can be experienced even in the midst of suffering. According to the NT, *the church embodies the power of the resurrection in the midst of a not-yet-redeemed world*" (Hays 1996: 198). It is possible therefore to advance toward moral as well as spiritual maturity (cf. 17-4.2), like the believers in Thyatira whose "last works are greater than the first" (Rev 2:19; cf. 1 Thess 4:1, 10).

18-4.5. FAST AND FEAST

In the NT, as in the OT, there is a tension between fasting and feasting. So long as the present age, characterized by human weakness and sin, continues, there is a place for fasting. The presence of Christ who is the Bridegroom, however, anticipates the final consummation where there will be no place for fasting (Mark 2:19) but God's people will celebrate "the marriage supper of the Lamb" (Rev 19:9; cf. 14-4.5b).

18-5. GOD'S COMMANDMENTS: THEOLOGICAL REFLECTIONS

1. Considerable portions of both OT and NT are devoted to ethical matters, yet the field of biblical ethics has until relatively recently tended to be sadly neglected. For many years theologians and ethicists looked in vain for comprehensive and helpful treatments of biblical ethics on the part of biblical theologians. Fortunately the closing decades of the twentieth century saw a change, with a new emphasis on discussion of methodology and new treatments of OT and NT ethics. In determining an appropriate structure for a BT, we have argued that biblical ethics must be treated as an integral part of BT (see E-4.4) precisely because in Scripture itself, theology and ethics are so closely related.

2. Society today faces many perplexing ethical issues. The Christian community, as part of that wider society, is distinguished by the fact that it looks to the word of God in Scripture to provide normative guidance in ethical as well as theological matters. Modern ethical discussion and decision making must of

course take other factors into account; frequently these have been classified under the headings of tradition, reason, and experience. Ethical decisions are not made in a vacuum, but always in particular situations, and various modern disciplines such as sociology, psychology, and medicine may help in understanding and analyzing the situation. Nevertheless, the situation itself cannot provide the ethical norm; in ethics as well as in theology, most Christians accept that the *norm* is to be found in the word of God in Scripture.

3. This raises hermeneutical questions of great complexity and difficulty, to which there are no easy or simple solutions (cf., e.g., Lindars 1973; Longenecker 1984: 1-28; Barclay 1990; Kaiser 1992). Certainly there can be no simplistic appeal to "the biblical answer" or to isolated proof texts (cf. Sleeper 1968: 457). As many scholars are quick to point out, the problems facing those seeking ethical guidance from the Bible are formidable. The biblical material itself is historically conditioned; it is highly diverse (see Barton 1978) and has been, and continues to be, subject to highly diverse interpretations (see Hays 1996: 1-3). A great gap separates biblical times from today, and some pressing modern issues are not even mentioned in the Bible (cf. Goldingay 1981: 52). This has led some to declare that we cannot expect to discover biblical answers to modern ethical dilemmas: "The New Testament offers no encouragement to any expectation of finding in it specific moral direction" (Moule 1963a: 371). Others, however, while acknowledging the difficulties, have turned in more positive fashion to the discussion and formulation of hermeneutical procedures for moving from the biblical text to the contemporary situation. The result has been a wide range of proposals; see, for example, the surveys in Birch and Rasmussen 1976: 45-78; Swartley 1983: 205-10; Verhey 1984: 154-56; Hays, 215-90.

One of the most comprehensive and helpful proposals is that of Hays, who outlines the "fourfold task" of NT ethics (1996: 3-7; the methodology can readily be expanded to cover *biblical* ethics). (a) The *descriptive* task involves careful exegetical study of each book of the Bible and each author in their own historical context without any premature attempts at harmonization. Essential as this is, it must not be supposed that there can be any such thing as a neutral, impartial description of biblical ethics. As with BT, all scholars bring to the text their own presuppositions (cf. Sleeper 1968: 446), and, as Hays himself recognizes (Hays, 8), the descriptive and synthetic tasks cannot be divorced from hermeneutical concerns. (b) The *synthetic* task involves developing an overall understanding of biblical ethics and seeking to discover what elements of unity exist amidst the diversity. Here it is important to move from a historical to a *canonical* approach, and this is the prime task of a biblical ethics that is a part of BT (cf. Birch and Rasmussen 1976: 161-84). (c) The *hermeneutical* task involves establishing the method whereby one moves from the biblical text, understood as a canonical whole, to the modern world (see the discussion in Hays, 208-316). (d) Finally, the *pragmatic* task involves the making of ethical decisions (and living them out) by individual believers and by the Christian community in the very specific circumstances they face.

4. In their discussion of the hermeneutical task, a number of scholars have pointed to the role of Scripture in *shaping character* and in *shaping community,* and these are valid insights. Birch and Rasmussen (1976) argue that "the most effective and crucial impact of the Bible in Christian ethics is that of shaping the moral identity of the Christian and of the church" (104). Ethical decisions are made by believers, imperfect human beings to be sure, yet also people who are "called to be saints." Those who know themselves as having been redeemed by Christ, whose faith is nurtured by Scripture reading and study, and who prayerfully seek the guidance of the Holy Spirit ought to be, above all others, sensitive and responsible moral agents.

In light of the typical biblical individual/community dialectic, it is equally if not more important to appreciate the role of Scripture in shaping community. We have noted in both OT (18-1.1b) and NT (18-3.1b) that it is primarily the community of God's people that is called to be holy. Scripture suggests three ways in which Christian ethics must be practiced in a community context. Firstly, the church must be a *deliberative community* where ethical issues (especially difficult ones) can be discussed in a corporate context. Birch and Rasmussen (1976: 125) emphasize the role of the church as shaper of moral identity, bearer of moral tradition, and community of moral deliberation (cf. Swartley 1983: 215; Cahill 1990: 384). Secondly, the church must be a *witnessing community;* like Israel, it must be "a light to the nations," or as Jesus put it, "the light of the world" (Matt 5:14), embodying the values it proclaims in its own life, for all the world to see. Thirdly, the church must be a *supportive community,* not only helping individual members think their way through difficult ethical issues but offering them ongoing support, through the fellowship (*koinōnia;* see 11-3.5d) of the church as they live with the consequences of their decisions.

Valid though these points are, it is important to appreciate that Christian character and Christian community, while providing the essential *context* for ethical decision making and ethical living, do not in and of themselves provide the *content* of Christian ethical norms. These have to be derived from Scripture itself.

5. Christian ethical norms are to be derived from both sayings and narrative material in Scripture. We have emphasized the importance of recognizing the wide variety of types of sayings material and suggested that this can be seen in terms of a spectrum ranging from broad ethical principles to very specific prescriptions, with what may be termed precepts occupying the middle ground (above, 18-1.1d; 18-3.1d). On this spectrum it is the precepts, as embodied for example in the ethical table of the Decalogue, that most readily lend themselves to more or less direct application in the modern situation. The Bible *does* offer specific ethical laws in such areas as murder, adultery, stealing, and lying. More often, however, the norms of Scripture are embodied in what are best described

as "ethical principles." Despite the aversion of some scholars to using this terminology, it must be strongly affirmed first of all that Scripture *does* provide many examples of broad ethical principles, and secondly, that whenever Scripture offers specific prescriptive advice (as it often does), that advice, however much it may be geared to particular historical circumstances, is always based on an underlying ethical principle. The task of biblical ethics, therefore, very frequently is to study specific biblical injunctions, identify the underlying principles, then seek to understand how these principles can be applied in different circumstances today (cf. Kaiser 1992: 291).

An example will help to make this procedure clear. We noted (18-1.1d) as an example of a prescription the law of Deut 22:8 requiring the building of a parapet on the roof of a new house. This assumes a culture where most houses have flat roofs, a circumstance that did prevail in ancient Israel but does not exist in many parts of the world today. The law, however, is clearly based on a belief in the sanctity of human life, and on the conviction that each member of the community is responsible for the health and safety of other members. These are principles that can be applied in any society or culture. Scripture itself provides a precedent for deriving principles from specific prescriptions. Deut 25:4 rules that "you shall not muzzle an ox while it is treading out the grain," a prescription based on the humane treatment of animals and obviously directly relevant only in a particular type of agricultural community. In the NT, however, this verse is quoted in 1 Cor 9:9 and 1 Tim 5:18 to support the right of apostles and elders to receive recompense for the work they do; here the basic underlying principle of fair treatment and recompense has been applied in a situation quite different from that originally envisaged in Deuteronomy.

No suggestion is made here that the identification and application of biblical ethical principles is easy; the claim is rather that this is the most basic hermeneutical procedure in using Scripture as the guide for Christian ethics today. As Longenecker (1984) puts it,

> what we have in the New Testament is a *declaration* of the gospel and the ethical principles that derive from the gospel, and a *description* of how that proclamation and its principles were put into practice in various situations during the apostolic period. Its proclamation and principles . . . are to be taken as normative. The way that proclamation and its principles were put into practice in the first century, however, should be understood as signposts at the beginning of a journey which point out the path to be followed if we are to apply that same gospel in our day. (27)

6. We have noted that narrative, as well as sayings material, can provide ethical norms. Events in the history of God's dealings with his people and characters portrayed in biblical narratives can function as "paradigms" (see above, 18-1.1e; 18-3.1e), so that while there is no question of directly imitating the bibli-

cal examples, modern interpreters can look for some kind of *analogy* between the situation portrayed in the narrative and the situation they face today. The "creative transfer" this involves may be far from easy and usually requires the use of what has been termed "analogical imagination" (cf. Spohn 1996: 100). As suggested above, this "paradigmatic" approach has to be employed with caution. Great care has to be taken in determining which narratives are to be regarded as paradigmatic. For example, "Why not imitate Samson's destruction of the Philistines by terrorist tactics rather than Moses' deliverance of the people from slavery, since both are found in canonical Scripture?" (Spohn, 120). The paradigmatic approach is most relevant in relation to the Gospel portraits of Jesus which suggest that not only Jesus' teaching but also his example is to be regarded as normative (above, 18-3.1e; cf. 9-3.4d). Paul urges the Philippians to "let the same mind be in you that was in Christ Jesus" (Phil 2:5), and in Christian spirituality and ethics there is a long tradition based on *imitatio Christi* (the imitation of Christ). In the last decade of the twentieth century, many Christians facing ethical dilemmas sought to approach them by asking, "What would Jesus do?" Even in the case of Jesus, however, not every aspect of his life (e.g., celibacy, wandering lifestyle) is necessarily binding on all believers. There is also a danger, as Webster (1986) points out, that talk of imitating Christ can be connected with a deficient Christology: "the language of imitation often appears to envisage Jesus Christ as simply an exemplar whose work is the revelation of the perfect love of God for men and the demonstration of a perfect human response to that love" (102-3). The imitation of Christ has to be seen in the context of the total biblical view of "ethics as response." Believers are not justified by works, but they are justified for works, and one form that those works can take is the imitation of the attitudes and actions of Christ.

7. The place of "law" continues to be a matter of major debate and dispute in biblical ethics. There are those who contend that in the NT any form of ethics based on law is abolished. Jesus, they point out, felt free to break the law, and according to Paul, "Christ is the end of the law" (Rom 10:4), so that "if you are led by the Spirit, you are not subject to the law" (Gal 5:18). The requirements of the law are summed up in the injunction to "love your neighbor as yourself" (Mark 12:28-31; Gal 5:14; quoting Lev 19:18), so that all Christians have to do is to ask in any given situation what it means to love one's neighbor. A variant of this approach is to say that, according to the NT, the only ethical norm is "love" *(agapē),* so that in any given situation all one has to ask is what is the loving thing to do. Some would emphasize the importance of seeking the guidance of the Holy Spirit in applying the ideal of love.

This approach is obviously biblically based, yet it can easily lead to a form of "situation ethics" in which the content of the Christian's ethical obligation is determined in a very subjective fashion (cf. Hays 1996: 202). While rightly emphasizing certain aspects of biblical ethics, it ignores an important element. Both Jesus and Paul, as we have seen (18-3.2b.ii; 18-3.3b), made a clear de facto distinction between the ritual or ceremonial Torah, which is abolished by the Christ event, and the moral laws of the Torah that remain binding, constituting the eschatological (or "Zion") Torah that is for all people in the new age. Thus, as we have noted, both Jesus and Paul clearly regard the second table of the Decalogue as still binding. As Calvin argued, law retains a threefold purpose in Christian ethics: it serves to convict human beings of sin, to restrain human sinfulness through fear of consequences, and positively to instruct believers in the will of God (*Institutes* 2.7.12). "Love your neighbor as yourself" summarizes the moral law of the OT, but it does not replace its detailed ethical injunctions. Christians are indeed to be motivated by love and guided by the Spirit, but in their understanding of the will of God the moral law, that is, the eschatological law for all peoples, continues to play an important role.

8. We have noted that the ethical material in Scripture is primarily directed toward the people of God, Israel in the OT and the early Christian church in the NT. We have also seen, however, that both OT and NT recognize the existence of a God-given universal moral law (18-1.3; 18-3.3e; for a summary of recent discussion of "natural law" in relation to Scripture, see Spohn 1996: 38-55). There is continuity between the general revelation of God's nature and purpose in the created order and his revelation to Israel and the church in the historical order. Yet biblical ethics goes beyond the universal moral law in two main ways.

Firstly, biblical ethics are more encompassing and more demanding. Torah, prophecy, and Wisdom make the most extensive demands on all aspects of the life of individuals and of society. This is especially true in the NT, where the basis of its ethical teaching lies in Jesus' demand for "radical obedience" (18-3.2b.ii) and where following the Christian way involves taking up one's cross and following Christ (18-3.2d).

Secondly, biblical ethics are closely related to BT. In both OT and NT, ethics are always a response to what God has already done (18-1.1a; 18-3.1a). "We love because he first loved us" (1 John 4:19). Christians possess an ethical motivation and a source of ethical power not available to those who have not accepted the message of the gospel and are not members of the Christian community.

This can raise difficult problems for Christian ethics. On the one hand, believers will feel compelled to support the application of the highest ethical standards in the society in which they live, even when that is basically a post-Constantinian, secular society. On the other hand, Christians may have to realize that the point may come where they do not have a right to impose their standards on others who do not share the Christian community's faith and theological presuppositions.

9. Biblical faith in both OT and NT must be classified as basically world-affirming, not world-denying (18-1.5; 18-3.5). Yet there are ascetic strains, represented in the OT by the Rechabites and Nazirites, and in the NT by John the

Baptist and his disciples. These groups stand as a warning against compromise with the prevailing culture, and against the dangers of materialism and over-indulgence. Moreover, while the NT accepts the OT view of the goodness of creation, it also calls believers, as already noted, to "radical obedience" and to denial of self in the service of God and others. Contemporary Christianity must find a balance between these two emphases, but given the prevailing climate, at least in the West, it is perhaps the note of self-denial (however unpopular that may be) that needs to be sounded at the present time.

10. Talk of radical obedience and self-denial raises a major question posed by biblical ethics, especially by the teaching and example of Jesus: Is the ethic of Jesus really practicable, or does it set before people an unattainable ideal?

In efforts to deal with this objection, various interpretations of Jesus' ethical teaching have been offered (cf. Lohse 1991: 64-67). It has been seen as a law that serves to show how far short we fall of God's demands and how impossible it is for us to save ourselves; as a "higher morality" binding in its totality only on the minority who choose to follow the "religious" or monastic life; as an "interim ethic" that Jesus intended only for the short period before the end of all things; as an ideal that people can at least aim at even if they cannot attain to it; or as an ethic purely for personal morality but not to be applied in public or political life. None of these interpretations really accord well with the evidence of the Gospels which strongly suggests that Jesus did intend his teaching to be taken seriously by his followers. He admitted that "it is easier for a camel to go through the eye of a needle than for someone who is rich to enter the kingdom of God." When his hearers objected, "Then who can be saved?" Jesus replied, "What is impossible for mortals is possible for God" (Luke 18:18-30). The Sermon on the Mount, in its canonical context, is not a list of impossible demands; in his anthology of Jesus' ethical instruction Matthew "is presenting the teachings of Jesus to a Christian community which both remembers the life, death and resurrection of God's Messiah, and also continues to experience the presence of the resurrected Lord" (Childs 1984: 75). Christians are called to love as they have first been loved, to follow God's commandments, and, empowered by the Spirit, to base their lives on the teaching and example of Jesus, knowing that with God all things are indeed possible.

CHAPTER 19

Love Your Neighbor

Old Testament: Proclamation

19-1. YOU SHALL LOVE YOUR NEIGHBOR

To follow God's way is to seek to obey his commandments in every area of life. The ethical direction that is given in Scripture, however, is seldom ordered in systematic fashion. Any survey of biblical ethics is thus forced to adopt some scheme for organizing the material. The format adopted here begins by looking at the individual person and moves outward in widening circles to consider the family, society, the state, and finally the international scene.

19-1.1. THE INDIVIDUAL

a. The Individual and Society

We have repeatedly noted the dialectic between individual and society that runs through the Bible (see E-5.2). Individuals are important, but no person exists solely as an individual; they are also part of a family, of the society in which they live, and of the whole human family.

b. Reverence for Human Life

The taking of human life is forbidden by the sixth commandment, "You shall not murder" (Exod 20:13), a *precept* that is as specific and as applicable today as it was in the time of Moses. Behind this, and other biblical laws, however, stand two closely related *principles* that are capable of wider application.

The first is *the sanctity of each individual human life*. In Gen 9:6 the universal prohibition of murder is grounded in the creation of human beings in the image of God. It is because God is the Creator not just of "humankind" but of each individual human being (see 16-1.2a), and has endowed each human being with personhood and the ability to live in a personal relationship with God and with other humans (see 2-1.3c), that each human life is precious.

The second is the principle that *all life is in God's hands.* God is the source of human life (Gen 2:7), and God is the sustainer of human life (see 2-1.2b). Both the giving and the taking of life are ultimately in God's hands (Deut 32:39; 1 Sam 2:6; Ps 104:27-30). As Job put it after the loss of his sons and daughters, "The LORD gave, and the LORD has taken away; blessed be the name of the LORD" (Job 1:21). It is always right to pray and work for healing (see 20-1.3), but deliberately to end a human life is to usurp a divine prerogative and in effect to put oneself in the place of God, something that in the OT is of the essence of human sin.

i. Murder

The deliberate taking of another human life is condemned in the strongest terms both in the Noahide laws that apply to all humankind (Gen 9:6; the created order) and in the sixth commandment, "You shall not murder *(lō' tirtsāch)*" (Exod 20:13//Deut 5:17; the historical order; cf. also Exod 21:12; Deut 27:24). That this is the correct translation rather than "Thou shalt not kill" (KJV) is shown not only by linguistic considerations (see Kaiser 1983: 90, 164), but even more by the broader context of the OT that not only sanctions the taking of animal life (e.g., in the sacrificial system) but also, in certain circumstances prescribed by God, the taking of human life, e.g., by capital punishment or in war (cf. Harrelson 1980: 107-8; on capital punishment see 18-1.2a.v; 18-3.2c; 18-3.3g; on war see 19-1.5b; 19-3.5). The fact that accidental killing or manslaughter is recognized as a separate case (Exod 21:13-14; Num 35:16-34; Deut 19:4-13) shows that what the sixth commandment refers to is deliberate, premeditated murder.

Along with the prohibition of actual murder goes the condemnation of *violence* directed against human beings. God's judgment in the flood was provoked by the fact that "the earth was corrupt in God's sight, and the earth was filled with violence" (Gen 6:11). The law accepts the reality of personal violence and in pragmatic fashion seeks to deal with its consequences (e.g., in Exod 21:18-32; see Kaiser 1983: 101-5). The prophets equally condemn the vicious circle of violence in which "bloodshed follows bloodshed" (Hos 4:2).

The OT also encourages society to be proactive in relation to human life: see, for example, the laws relating to dangerous animals (Exod 21:28-32) and to the need to build parapets on flat roofs (Deut 22:8).

ii. Abortion

In contrast to the specific condemnation of murder and violence, the OT has nothing directly to say about abortion, the killing of the unborn, probably because such a practice would have been unthinkable for God's people. The OT does affirm that children are a gift and a blessing from God (Ps 127:3-5), and it regards the killing of children with special horror (e.g., Exod 1:16-17, 22; Lev 18:21; Jer 7:31-32; Ezek 16:20-21; Mic 6:7). Significantly, the OT also sees God as active in the creation of human beings from the time of conception. It is God who brings about conception in such cases as Sarah, Leah, Rachel, Ruth, and Hannah; these examples "demonstrate that birth is considered a co-creative process involving man, woman and God" (Hoffmeier 1987: 55). The author of Ps 139 speaks of God's knowledge of and care for him from conception onward:

> For it was you who formed my inward parts;
>   you knit me together in my mother's womb. . . .
>   My frame was not hidden from you,
> when I was being made in secret. . . .
> Your eyes beheld my unformed substance (*gōlem* = "embryo").
> (vv. 13, 15-16)

It is God who forms the fetus in the womb (Job 10:8-12; 31:15; Jer 1:5). Such passages show "a profound respect for life in the prenatal stage" (Bullock 1987: 68). The OT does not debate in any theoretical way whether a fetus is a "person," but it does depict the fetus as the work of God and the object of his knowledge, love, and care, and hence its destruction must be considered contrary to the will of God.

Exod 21:22-25 is a difficult text (see Kaiser 1983: 102-4, 170-72; Hoffmeier 1987: 57-61; J. J. Davis 1993: 136-37), but it almost certainly refers to harm done to an unborn child, in which case it shows that the child in the womb is regarded as a person (see Hays 1996: 446-47; contra Crook 1990: 132). The LXX has a significant variant that draws a distinction between a fetus that is and a fetus that is not "fully formed" (see Gorman 1982: 35), but such a distinction is not supported anywhere else in Scripture.

iii. Suicide

Nowhere in the OT is there any law or precept directly relating to the taking of one's own life. A few suicides are narrated, the most famous being King Saul, who, amidst the rout of his army by the Philistines, killed himself, followed by his armor-bearer, who had refused to kill the king (1 Sam 31). Zimri took his life in somewhat similar circumstances (1 Kgs 16:15-19). In Judg 9:52-54 the fatally wounded Abimelech has his armor-bearer kill him so that it would not be said that he was killed by a woman. With these may be compared Razis in 2 *Macc* 14:37-46, who, hard pressed by enemy troops, took his own life at the third attempt. The context of all these cases is war. A thin line divides them from Samson, who pulled down the house in which he was imprisoned, killing more Philistines by his death than he had in his life (Judg 16:28-31); this might be seen as taking his own life, but he has more in common with military heroes who risk and if need be give their own lives in order to defeat the enemy. Quite different from all of these is the case of the royal counselor Ahithophel; when his advice was rejected, he "went off home to his own city . . . set his house in order, and hanged himself" (2 Sam 17:23). In *Tob* 3:10 Sarah contemplates suicide but is deterred by the shame it would bring to her father; this is the one clear evidence of the social disapproval of suicide.

These deaths are all presented as tragic, but it is true to say that "suicide per se was not condemned by the biblical writers or by the community for whom their writings were to become sacred scripture" (Clemons 1990: 19; cf. Erickson and Bowers 1976: 19). Nor was a particular stigma attached to those taking their own lives; it is noteworthy that in three cases (Samson, Saul, and Ahithophel), it is specifically stated that the persons were given burial. Razis is even said to have preferred "to die nobly rather than to fall into the hands of sinners" (2 *Macc* 14:42), but then the account of his death is virtually a martyrology (*NOAB*, AP: 256).

On the other hand, nowhere is suicide recommended or encouraged. The number of cases is very small, and in all but one case the context is war.

iv. Euthanasia

The OT has even less to say about euthanasia or "assisted suicide." In the case of Saul, his request to his armor-bearer to kill him was denied; Abimelech's request was granted. But the Bible passes no judgment on either of these incidents, both of which are set in the context of battle with an enemy. More broadly, however, the OT sees human life as a gift entrusted to human beings by God, so that "the fundamental distinction between Creator and created sets limits on our freedom. . . . No one can ever claim total mastery over creation, including one's life" (Gula 1995: 13). Moreover, it could be argued that the sixth commandment, "You shall not murder" (Exod 20:13), which prohibits the deliberate taking of human life, would apply to ending the lives even of those who are ill, suffering, or elderly (cf. Crook 1990: 147).

19-1.2. THE FAMILY

So much of the ethical material of the Bible (including narrative) is devoted to relations within the family unit that it seems not unfair to say "the profoundest conception underlying the ethical teaching of both testaments is that of the family" (F. C. Grant 1950: 314). The Hebrew term *mishpāchâ,* usually translated "family," can significantly also be used of the wider clan, or tribe, or even of the whole nation (as in Amos 3:2 — "You only have I known / of all the families of the earth"). The term *bayith,* "house" or "household," corresponds more to the family unit; in OT times this would generally be an "extended family," including several generations along with servants or slaves and perhaps "aliens," though the development of cities led to smaller family units (see Perkin 1988: 767-68, and cf. Rodd 1967: 22-23). It is clear that "the family played an important part in Hebrew thought and affairs. It formed the base on which the social structure was built up; its indistinguishable merging into the wider sense of clan or tribe indicates how it affected the political life of the whole nation" (MacLeod 1963: 292). W. Janzen (1994: 26-54) emphasizes the key role of the "familial paradigm" in OT ethics and cites the story of Abraham and Lot in Gen 13 as an example of a paradigmatic narrative: Abraham's nonassertive disposition and willingness to deny himself (even if they are somewhat exceptional) help restore peace within the extended family (9-12).

a. The Biblical Affirmation of Sexuality

In the light of later misunderstandings and misrepresentations, the biblical affirmation of human sexuality can hardly be overemphasized. According to the first creation account, human beings are the crown of creation, and the distinction between the sexes (Gen 1:27) is the work of the Creator who pronounces everything he has made "very good" (1:31). The second account shows how humanity is incomplete apart from a loving relationship between husband and wife. It is not good for man to be alone, and a partner can be found only through the creation of woman (see R. F. Collins 1986: 157-59). Sexuality is strongly affirmed in a book like Ruth, perhaps the only biblical narrative that deals with the theme of romantic love (Ryken 1987a: 124-25). While one purpose of sex is the procreation of children (cf. Gen 1:28), it also promotes mutual pleasure, companionship, and love within the marriage relationship (cf. 2:18-23; 18:12; Prov 5:15-19; see Harrelson 1980: 125).

The most complete celebration of human sexuality in the OT is found in the Song of Songs (or Song of Solomon), an anthology of love poetry that employs a variety of erotic imagery and includes, for example, four poems (4:1-5; 5:10-15; 6:4-7; 7:1-5) of the genre known as the "wasf" (Carr 1993: 286-87) or "emblematic blazon," i.e., verses praising the beauty of one's beloved "by cataloguing his or her attractive features and comparing them to objects or emblems in nature" (Ryken 1987a: 283). Both Jewish rabbis and Christian Fathers dealt with this work by allegorizing it (see Childs 1979: 571, 574; Gollwitzer 1979: 15-20; Carr, 281-83), interpreting even the smallest details as referring to the relationship between God and Israel or between Christ and the church (or the individual human soul). This approach is not totally without merit since in Scripture the relationship between God and people is likened to that between husband and wife (see 11-1.4; 11-3.4a), and the relationships do shed light on each other (Gollwitzer, 22).

Nevertheless, the consensus of modern biblical scholarship (anticipated by Luther) strongly favors a literal approach that sees these poems as "love songs which simply extol love between the sexes" (R. F. Collins 1986: 165). The Song of Songs "celebrates human sexuality as a fact of life, God-given, to be enjoyed within the confines of a permanent committed relationship" (Carr 1993: 294). In contrast to so much in the Western literary tradition, "here the poetry is pure, uninhibited, sensuous without a trace of sensuality or lust" (Henn 1970: 88). It is wrong, however, to assume that what the Song of Songs refers to is extramarital sex (Kaiser 1983: 193-94; contra Gollwitzer 1979: 29-31). For one thing, one of the most widely accepted views of the origin of the work is that it consists of a song cycle designed to be sung at a *wedding* feast (see Collins, 165). Secondly, literary analysis suggests that the book has a chiastic structure so that the central section 4:16–5:1 in effect represents the consummation of the partners' love (see Carr, 291-94). And finally, of course, the book has to be read in its total canonical context in which sexual relations are approved only within marriage; thus "the Song is wisdom's reflection on the joyful and mysterious nature of love between a man and a woman within the institution of marriage" (Childs 1979: 575).

In the OT sexual abstinence is required only rarely, and then only for a limited time and for special reasons. It was required of the people as a preparation for the Sinai theophany (Exod 19:14-15). Warriors engaged in the holy war (19-1.5b) abstained from sex as a sign of their total dedication to the LORD for the duration of the campaign (1 Sam 21:5; 2 Sam 11:11).

b. Sexual Relations outside Marriage

All forms of sexual relationships outside of marriage are condemned in the OT. Some such relationships were not only tolerated among Israel's neighbors but even functioned as part of their religion, as the frequent references to cult prostitutes (female and male) demonstrate. Israel is called to be radically different from her neighbors; Lev 18 prefaces a list of forbidden sexual relations with the injunction, "You shall not do as they do in the land of Egypt, where you lived, and you shall not do as they do in the land of Canaan" (v. 3).

i. Adultery

This is the most strongly condemned; the seventh commandment of the Decalogue (Exod 20:14; Deut 5:18; cf. Lev 18:20) is a precept explicitly forbidding adultery. Lev 20:10 provides the death penalty for the offense. In OT times, however, a double standard operated in relation to this commandment. A married *man* committed adultery only by having sex with the wife of another man; sexual relations with a prostitute, a slave girl, or an unmarried woman were not considered adultery. For a married *woman,* however, sexual relations with any man other than her husband constituted adultery (see Harrelson 1980: 123; R. F. Collins 1986: 170).

ii. Prostitution

Surprisingly little is said specifically about prostitution in the OT. Participation in sacred prostitution, characteristic of the surrounding culture, is roundly condemned (Deut 23:17), as is the participation of Israelite girls in prostitution in Lev 19:29, but some OT references could be interpreted as tolerating the practice (e.g., the story of Judah and Tamar in Gen 38:12-26 and the story of Rahab in Josh 2). Explicit condemnation of liaisons with "the loose woman" is found in the Wisdom Literature; "to court this kind of woman and to indulge in sexual sin is to flirt with death itself (Prov. 2:18-19) and social disgrace (Prov. 6:26, 32-35)" (Kaiser 1983: 155; cf. Prov 5:1-14; 7:1-27; 9:13-18). If to some extent prostitution was tolerated, this has to be seen as an example of pragmatic ethics, and in the light of the total canonical context "must be judged as forming a blight on the commitment of the ancient Hebrews to the ideal of monogamy" (Grenz 1990: 83).

iii. Bestiality

This is strongly condemned (Exod 22:19; Deut 27:21) for both men and women (Lev 18:23). In God's plan sex relates to the deepest of human relationships, whereas an animal cannot be a true partner of a human being (Gen 2:20; cf. Kaiser 1983: 195-96; R. F. Collins 1986: 172).

iv. Homosexuality

OT references to homosexual practice are few, probably because such practices were virtually absent from ancient Israel (Scroggs 1983: 70). Suggestions that the relationships between David and Jonathan and Ruth and Naomi were homosexual in nature have no basis in the biblical text (cf. Pope 1976: 416-17; Bonnington and Fyall 1996: 9). In the story of Gen 19 (the men of Sodom; cf. also the story of Judg 19, the men of Gibeah) the reference is to homosexual assault (cf. Bartlett 1977: 134-35; J. J. Davis 1993: 103-4; contra D. S. Bailey 1955: 4f.), though of course what was intended was a gang rape. This is regarded as a sin, but not the only sin of Sodom (cf. Ezek 16:49-50; Jer 23:14; *Sir* 16:8; *Wis* 10:6-8). More relevant is the clear precept prohibiting homosexual practice in Lev 18:22:

"You shall not lie with a male as with a woman; it is an abomination" (there is no technical term for homosexual practice in Hebrew; the LXX provides a fairly close translation, *meta arsenos ou koimēthēsē(i) koitēn gynaikos,* lit. "with a male you shall not lie the bed of a woman"). Lev 20:13 repeats this law with the addition of the death penalty. The context of these prohibitions is a moral one, next to prohibitions of adultery and incest, and they therefore cannot be taken as referring merely to male cultic prostitution (cf. J. G. Taylor 1995: 5). The reference is to male homosexual practice only. No mention is made of the age of those involved, but since 20:13 holds those involved as equally responsible, the reference must be to consenting partners. The classification of homosexual practice as an "abomination *(tôʿēbbâh)*" puts it in the category of actions and attitudes characteristic of the pagan "inhabitants of the land" that defile the Land and are "incompatible with the holiness of Yahweh" (Bonnington and Fyall 1996: 12; cf. Lev 18:24-30).

The converse of these laws is the positive assertion, especially in the creation accounts, that it is heterosexual relations that are intended by God (cf. below, d). God created human beings male and female (Gen 1:27); in the second creation account a suitable partner for the man is found only with the creation of the woman (2:18-25). Thus, as J. R. W. Stott (1985) puts it, "Scripture defines the marriage God instituted in terms of heterosexual monogamy. . . . Scripture envisages no other kind of marriage or sexual intercourse, for God provided no alternative" (25).

c. Celibacy

Celibacy is rare in the OT (cf. 15-1.5a), and occurs only in exceptional circumstances. In Jer 16:2 the prophet is commanded not to take a wife, though "the prohibition was not a prohibition of marriage as such" but was related to "a historical situation and was a judgment on it." The fact remains, however, "that at least one prophet, among the greatest, ministered as a single person" (Stagg 1977: 11).

d. Husband and Wife

Like all God's good gifts, sexuality is to be used in accordance with God's will for humankind. In the OT marriage is seen as the God-given norm. The creation accounts in particular make it clear that sex should bind husband and wife together in the family relationship, not only within Israel but within the whole created order (cf. Kaiser 1983). God created male and female for each other (Gen 1:27-28); "therefore a man leaves his father and his mother and clings to his wife, and they become one flesh" (2:24). "The description of the creation of the first human pair indicates that the husband-wife relationship is to be seen as the primary expression of the God-given human drive to bonding and thus to community" (Grenz 1990: 45).

i. Marriage

For the OT the lifelong union of husband and wife is the basis of family life. Laws governing this relationship are found in the Torah, and much is also said about marriage indirectly in the narrative portions of the OT. Modern critical scholarship has explored in detail the legal and sociological situation presupposed by the biblical references to marriage, emphasizing the "patriarchal" nature of society (see Perkin 1988: 769). In keeping with the social and economic conditions of the time, many of the laws suggest that the wife was legally a possession of her husband (cf. Exod 20:17). Yet in the OT "the wife is never a mere possession, chattel, or solely a child-bearer" (Kaiser 1983: 155). Deut 22:13-19 shows that the power of a husband was not absolute; in the event of an unjust accusation against his wife, the husband was subject to discipline by "the elders of the city." A good wife is a gift from the Lord (Prov 18:22; 19:14). Marriage can be spoken of as a covenant (2:17; Mal 2:14), a term that suggests mutual obligations. Moreover, the OT provides many examples of loving and mutually fulfilling relationships between husbands and wives (Gen 24:67; 29:20; 1 Sam 1:8). The story of Ruth has been characterized as "a celebration of the ideal of wedded romantic love" (Ryken 1987a: 124). Significantly the God/Israel relationship is frequently compared to that of husband and wife (see Grenz 1990: 47-48; and cf. 11-1.4).

What emerges in the OT is the ideal of monogamy. Polygamy was practiced in the patriarchal period through to the time of the settlement, but beyond that only by the kings David and Solomon, who constitute a special case. Polygamy is an example of pragmatic ethics, a practice that was tolerated (for a limited period of time) but never required. It was probably practiced to ensure the survival of the family at a time of very high infant mortality, and in the case of kings to ensure a male successor to the throne (see Rodd 1967: 22). Significantly the ideal of monogamy is established in Gen 2:24, at the outset of canonical Scripture. It is assumed in the Law (Deut 28:54, 56) and in the Prophets (Jer 5:8; 6:11; Mal 2:14) and upheld in the Wisdom Literature (Prov 5:18; Eccl 9:9); see especially Prov 31:10-31, which celebrates a mature and lasting marriage relationship in which each partner makes a distinctive contribution.

The Torah prohibits sexual relations and hence marriage with anyone "near of kin" (Lev 18:6); the forbidden degrees are listed in 18:6-18 (cf. Deut 27:20, 23). Those guilty of incest "shall be cut off from their people" (Lev 18:29).

ii. Divorce

Divorce is another example of OT pragmatic ethics. It is a practice that is not commanded by the Torah (see Kaiser 1983: 200-201); it is tolerated and is regulated, particularly to safeguard the position of the woman. The key passage, Deut 24:1-4, assumes that only the husband can initiate divorce proceedings, but for the protection of the wife divorce must be for a specific, stated reason; a prescribed legal procedure must be followed; and the woman must be given a "bill of divorce" certifying her status (cf. Jer 3:8). Deut 24 permits the woman to remarry but strongly forbids, in the event of her again being divorced or of her being widowed, a remarriage with her first husband, thus outlawing what Wolff terms "a capricious to-ing and fro-ing" (1974: 175). The grounds for divorce are not specifically stated; the husband can divorce the wife if "he has found some indecency (*'erwath dābhār*) in her" (Deut 24:1 RSV; on possible meanings of the term, see J. J. Davis 1993: 84). *Sir* 25:25-26 comes closest to advocating divorce; if an "evil wife . . . does not go as you direct, / separate her from yourself," literally, "cut her off from your flesh," i.e., terminate the "one flesh" (Gen 2:24) union.

The Deut 24 legislation does not hold up an ideal; it recognizes that "conditions that are to be put down to human failure and which have become unbearable should not be given permanence" (Wolff 1974: 175). God's will and intention for marriage is clearly a lifelong union of one husband and one wife. Mal 2:13-16 speaks of God as the witness to the marriage covenant "between you and the wife of your youth, to whom you have been faithless, though she is your companion and your wife by covenant" (v. 14). The word for "companion" (*chᵃbhereth*) is the only use of the feminine form in the OT; the masculine "is normally used of men to designate their equality with one another. To use this term for a wife suggests that she is not a piece of property that may be discarded at will; she is an equal and is to be treated as such — as a covenant partner" (Garland 1987: 420). The passage goes on to warn, "So look to yourselves, and do not let anyone be faithless to the wife of his youth. *For I hate divorce,* says the LORD, the God of Israel" (vv. 15-16).

e. Parents and Children

i. Be Fruitful and Multiply

Throughout the Bible children are regarded as one of the greatest blessings that God can bestow. On creating humankind, male and female, God said to them, "Be fruitful and multiply . . ." (Gen 1:28). While having children is not the only purpose of marriage (cf. Grenz 1990: 53-54), it is an important part of God's intention for humankind and for creation. Children — and children's children — bring joy and blessing. God's promise to the patriarchs and matriarchs is that their descendants will be as numerous as the stars in heaven and the sand of the sea (Gen 15:5; 22:17; cf. 24:60). Of all the Canaanite customs, the one the Israelites looked upon with greatest revulsion was the practice of child sacrifice (cf. Deut 12:31; Jer 7:31).

ii. The Duties of Parents

According to the OT, the relationship between parents and children involves mutual obligations. Parents are responsible for the care and nurture of their children, for teaching and training them to take their place in society, and most important of all for bringing them up in the way of the Lord. Children are to be given a role in worship: in the Passover service, for example, they are to ask the question, "What do you mean by this observance?" (Exod 12:26). Immediately following the key passage in Deut 6:4-5, known as the "Shema" (see 1-1.1), the Israelites are told, "Keep these words that I am commanding you today in your heart. Recite them to your children and talk about them when you are at home and when you are away, when you lie down and when you rise" (vv. 6-7). The Wisdom Literature is largely family-oriented (cf. Clements 1992), and provides examples of a wide range of experience-based practical advice that was passed on from one generation to the next. It sees a role for discipline (Prov 13:24; 23:13-14), but even more for example (Job 5:4). The bringing up of children is the responsibility of both father and mother (Prov 1:8; 6:20; cf. the proverb quoted in Ezek 16:44, "Like mother, like daughter," and see Clements, 136-40).

iii. The Duties of Children

Children for their part owe respect and obedience to their parents. The importance of this is emphasized by the precept "Honor your father and your mother, so that your days may be long in the land that the LORD your God is giving you" (the fifth commandment, Exod 20:12; Deut 5:16 has a slightly expanded form; cf. *Sir* 7:27-28). In Lev 19:3 the order of parents is reversed: "You shall each revere your mother and father." This commandment has in view adults caring for aged parents, but it certainly applies also to children from their youngest years up. Disobedient children bring grief to their parents (Prov 10:1; 15:20; etc.), and the Torah provides harsh penalties for children who are "stubborn and rebellious" (Deut 21:18-21). Legally children were completely subject to the father, but this did not prevent children from being well loved (Perkin 1988: 771). Few scenes are more moving than Jacob's grief at the reported death of his son Joseph (Gen 37:35), or King David's grief at the loss of his son Absalom (2 Sam 18:33).

iv. The Elderly

The Bible frankly recognizes the shortness of human life (Ps 39:5). The Genesis prehistory, it is true, knows of some who lived to an exceptional old age, the oldest being Methuselah (Gen 5:27); this may be connected with the view that length of days is a reward for exceptional piety (cf. Prov 3:2; 10:27). Gen 6:3, however, marks a turning point; thereafter 120 years is to be the absolute maximum age. Given what we know of life expectancy in OT times, the traditional "threescore and ten" years of Ps 90:10 (RSV) would be for most a *maximum* rather than an *average* life span (see Blank 1962a: 55; Wolff 1974: 118-19). Old age brings with it failing strength (Ps 71:9; this psalm reflects the viewpoint of an elderly person), failing eyesight (Gen 27:1; 1 Sam 3:2), and loss of other faculties (2 Sam 19:35). Eccl 12:1-7 is a poetic allegory of the onset of old age (see Ryken 1987a: 327-28); it gives "a sober analysis of how with increasing age the powers, the senses and all the manifestations of life become weaker and weaker" (Wolff, 124).

In OT times the elderly lived as part of the extended family, and various OT passages suggest the tensions that could arise and the abuse to which the elderly might be subject. Children who show contempt for parents are strongly denounced (Prov 30:17), and in the Torah both verbal abuse (Exod 21:17; cf. Prov 20:20) and physical abuse (Exod 21:15) of parents are punishable by the death penalty. The context "suggests that the parents are aged or frail and have become a nuisance to the active adults who would very much like to be relieved of further responsibility for such aged ones" (Harrelson 1980: 94; cf. J. G. Harris 1987: 31).

The other side of the coin is the strong emphasis on the need to care for the elderly. While the fifth commandment, "Honor your father and your mother, so that your days may be long in the land that the LORD your God is giving you" (Exod 20:12; cf. Deut 5:16), certainly applies to young children, it originally probably applied even more to adults caring for their aged parents (see Harrelson 1980: 93; R. F. Collins 1986: 88-89). This commandment in effect "states that children must grant full significance to parents even when they may be losing physical and economic indications of importance" (J. G. Harris 1987: 62). Special care is demanded for *widows,* who in old age would constitute a particularly vulnerable group (Deut 14:29; 24:17; Isa 1:17; etc.). The OT is concerned not just that the aged receive the material necessities of life, but that they receive dignity and respect: "You shall rise before the aged, and defer to the old; and you shall fear your God: I am the LORD" (Lev 19:32). This point receives particular emphasis in the Wisdom Books:

> My child, help your father in his old age,
>   and do not grieve him as long as he lives;
> even if his mind fails, be patient with him;
>   because you have all your faculties do not despise him. (*Sir* 3:12-13)

Old age has its compensations. Length of days and long experience can bring wisdom (Job 32:7; cf. Deut 32:7), and the elderly can act as advisers (1 Kgs 12:6). The blessing of the aged is believed to have special power (Gen 27; Deut 33). Old age can still be a creative time of life (Ps 92:12-15), and in the OT, at least on occasion, God accomplished great things through characters such as Abraham, Sarah, and Moses when they were very advanced in years. Above all, the Bible depicts a God who cares for all his people, to the very oldest. When human strength fails, God can be a source of strength (Isa 40:29, 31), and his promise is:

> Even to your old age I am he,
>   even when you turn gray I will carry you. (46:4)

19-1.3. SOCIETY

Individuals and families exist in the wider setting of society, and much of the ethical material in the OT is concerned with God's demand for righteousness and justice (see 18-1.4) in society. In this section we first consider what the OT says about *economic justice,* then what it says about *social justice.* Obviously these two areas are closely related; they are separated here merely for the purposes of discussion.

a. The Setting

The OT, written over a period of about a thousand years, reflects a great *diversity* of economic and social situations. Disciplines such as archaeology and sociology assist the historian in reconstructing these situations, thereby shedding invaluable light on the *background* of the OT.

Not all periods of OT history, however, are of equal significance for biblical ethics. The seminomadism of the patriarchal period, the wilderness wanderings after the exodus, and the two-century period under the judges that at times came close to anarchy are not generally regarded in the OT as paradigms for social ethics (see, however, 18-1.5b). Basically three situations are ethically significant (cf. also below, 19-1.4, on the state).

i. The Exodus Deliverance

Various forms of liberation theology have drawn attention to the paradigmatic significance of the exodus (see Spohn 1996: 56-68). God's deliverance of Israel from Egypt demonstrates that he is on the side of the poor and the oppressed, and thus that his people are called to work for the liberation of those who are oppressed in any way.

ii. Israel's Existence as an Independent State

Torah, though given in the wilderness, represents God's guidelines for living in the Land. The opportunity to apply these guidelines came primarily in the period of the monarchy (including the divided monarchy), when God's people constituted an independent, self-governing state. This is the situation addressed by the preexilic prophets, and to a lesser extent by Wisdom. The narrative of the Historical Books and the preaching of the prophets, of course, amply document Israel's failures to be true to the covenant and to obey the economic and social laws of the Torah.

iii. Israel's Existence under Foreign Empires

Following the exile God's people lived under a succession of great powers that severely restricted the extent to which they could control their own economic and social affairs. Conditions varied under the different empires, but basically the ethical options available were limited within the parameters set by the ruling power. This situation is reflected in historical books such as Ezra, Nehemiah, Esther, *Judith,* 1 and 2 *Maccabees;* in the postexilic prophets (especially in Daniel); and to some extent in Wisdom.

b. Economic Justice

i. The Source of Wealth

The economic well-being of society depends on resources that ultimately are supplied by God the Creator (cf. Young 1962b: 818). In the created order God bestows wealth through entrusting the earth with all its resources to humankind (Gen 1:28-30; cf. 2-1.3). In the historical order God bestows the Land of Canaan on his people Israel (cf. 13-1.2).

These are good gifts of God to his people. Creation with all its resources is "very good" (Gen 1:31), and the Land is a good land, flowing with milk and honey (Exod 3:8). Wealth and possessions are given by God to humankind for their enjoyment (Eccl 5:19). But these resources are only entrusted to human beings, who are the *stewards* of God's gifts and are to use them in accordance with the will of the Creator (see 2-1.3b). The Israelites are told, "The land shall not be sold in perpetuity, *for the land is mine;* with me you are but aliens and tenants" (Lev 25:23). All the resources of the Land — its abundant water supply, its plentiful produce, the iron and copper ore in the ground — are *given* by God to his people (Deut 8:7-10). The danger is that exploitation of these resources and the ensuing prosperity will make people forget their total dependence on God: "When you have eaten your fill and have built fine houses and live in them, and when your herds and flocks have multiplied, and your silver and gold is multiplied, and all that you have is multiplied, then do not exalt yourself, forgetting the Lord your God. . . . Do not say to yourself, 'My power and the might of my own hand have gotten me this wealth.' But remember the Lord your God, for it is he who gives you power to get wealth" (8:12-14, 17-18).

ii. The Production of Wealth

God has placed humankind on earth to use the resources he provides in a responsible way and for the benefit of all. "God owns the earth but has entrusted it into the keeping of mankind whom he has equipped for the task and whom he holds accountable for his trusteeship" (C. J. H. Wright 1983: 68). Human beings are called to be coworkers with God. God himself works: the universe is the work of his fingers (Ps 8:3), and when it was complete, "God rested from all the work that he had done in creation" (Gen 2:3). In Gen 1 human beings are created to subdue the earth and to have dominion over all animal and vegetable life (vv. 26-30; cf. 2-1.3b), a task that certainly implies work. This is made explicit in the second creation account where people are put into the Garden of Eden "to till it and keep it" (2:15). Work is thus an essential part of God's plan for humankind; it is not a punishment imposed as a result of the fall (A. Richardson 1952: 23). The creation narratives clearly show that "God's intention from the very beginning was that people should find joy, fulfillment, and blessing in the fact and constancy of work" (Kaiser 1983: 150). "Work is not, therefore, as it is regarded elsewhere in antiquity, a curse or the miserable lot of slaves, but a task assigned by God" (Eichrodt 1967: 128).

The fall, to be sure, distorts the nature of work so that it becomes toilsome and frustrating (Gen 3:17-19; cf. C. J. H. Wright 1983: 71). Nevertheless, work continues to be part of the order ordained by God (Exod 20:9; Ps 104:23); the rich who live in idleness are condemned (Amos 6:4-7). "Broadly speaking, we may say that no stigma is attached to being a 'worker' in the Old Testament; on the contrary, it is expected that every man will have his proper work to do" (A. Richardson 1952: 21). The OT defends the rights of workers: laborers deserve their wages (Jer 22:13), and are to be promptly paid (Lev 19:13; Deut 24:14-15). Malachi classifies "those who oppress the hired workers in their wages" with sorcerers and adulterers (3:5). On the other hand, work is not the whole of life, and rest from labor every seventh day (Exod 20:8-11//Deut 5:12-15; see 14-1.2) puts work in perspective; humankind's first task is to serve God.

The Wisdom Literature develops a distinctive "work ethic" that commends hard work and condemns sloth (Prov 6:6-11; 10:4; 13:4; 24:30-34; Eccl 10:18; cf. Wolff 1974: 131). Work can be fulfilling: "There is nothing better for mortals than to . . . find enjoyment in their toil" (Eccl 2:24; cf. 3:22; 5:18-19). On the other hand, when work and the acquisition of wealth become the *sole* aim of existence, then life becomes empty and meaningless (2:4-11; cf. 4:7-8).

iii. The Distribution of Wealth

Both the resources of the Land and the resultant wealth are to be shared among all God's people. For modern readers one of the most boring sections of the OT is Josh 13–21, chapters that consist almost entirely of geographical lists. But to the Israelites these chapters enshrined a fundamental principle: each of the twelve tribes, and each family within each tribe, received its own "inheritance" (*nachᵃlâh* = "possession, property, inheritance"). The freedom, dignity, and worth of each family were to be ensured by their possession of a portion of the Land sufficient to provide for their needs (cf. C. J. H. Wright 1983: 76).

The ownership of private property is thus assumed and accepted in the OT. The eighth commandment, "You shall not steal" (Exod 20:15; Deut 5:19), is a precept that forbids taking property that belongs to another. "The ancient Israelites did recognize, as did their neighbours, that goods were an extension of the life of the family and that the rights of communities, families and individuals necessarily involved their right to maintain those goods" (Harrelson 1980: 135). Moreover, one strand in OT thought sees wealth, at least within certain limits, as a reward for righteousness (cf. 16-1.3b). Wisdom pragmatically recognizes that wealth provides security (Prov 13:8; 18:11) and "brings many friends" (19:4), though it also holds that "treasures gained by wickedness do not profit" (10:2).

What may at first sight appear to be a contrary trend is found in the Torah where laws protect the rights of the poor (Lev 19:9-10; Deut 14:28-29), and especially in the Prophets where we frequently meet condemnation of the rich (Amos 8:4-8; Isa 5:8-10; Mic 3:1-3) and championing of the poor (Jer 22:13-17). What is condemned, however, is not wealth or the ownership of property as such, but rather the acquisition of wealth at the expense of one's fellow human beings, i.e., the unequal and unfair division of God-given resources and the resultant wealth. In Amos 5:11, for example, luxurious houses and large estates are condemned because they are built by trampling upon the poor (cf. L. T. Johnson 1981: 95). The acquisition of property is condemned especially when it violates the original equitable division of God's Land among God's people (1 Kgs 21; Isa 5:8). "Throughout Israel's history stern warnings are directed against those who strive for wealth through greed, trickery and treachery" (Young 1962b: 818).

The desire to acquire more property and possessions can become an insatiable thirst that leads to the distortion of all values (Eccl 5:10-17). It is clear that "the biblical pattern of the holy life can never lead us to make the aim of our lives the securing of material possessions and wealth; pleasing God and enjoying him is to be the goal" (Kaiser 1983: 210). Covetousness is a major form of sin, condemned in the tenth commandment (Exod 20:17; Deut 5:21), which "has in view a hankering after the goods of others . . . and doing so in such a way as to be drawn by lust or unwholesome desire into making plans to take these as one's own" (Harrelson 1980: 136). Covetousness is graphically illustrated in the story of Achan (Josh 7:21), and is condemned not only in the Torah but equally in Wisdom (e.g., Prov 21:26) and in the Prophets (e.g., Mic 2:2).

The implied principle underlying the OT view of economic justice is thus an essentially *egalitarian* one: every family should have enough wealth to provide for their needs, but they should not accumulate excessive wealth at the expense of others. The OT realistically portrays the ways in which this norm broke down, especially from the time of the divided monarchy onward. The rich got richer and the poor got poorer; debts accumulated, and when these could not be paid the debtors sold their land, and then their families and themselves into slavery (cf. below, 19-1.3c.i). In the Torah, therefore, and especially in the Prophets there is a major concern for *the poor*. Likewise there is a concern for two other economically disadvantaged groups: *widows and orphans*, who had no male breadwinner to provide for them, and *resident aliens* (*gēr* = "stranger, sojourner, resident alien"; see 12-1.3b), who as outsiders had no "inheritance" in the Land in the first place (see Patterson 1973). "Widows, orphans and sojourners were or could easily become disenfranchised members of society in the ancient Near East: without protection of husband, father or free citizen, these three classes of society would have had few means of livelihood or juridical protection. The destitute (poor) likewise had severe difficulty providing for themselves or their families" (Engelhard 1980: 5). The Torah seeks to provide for these members of society in very practical ways, by supplying food for them (Lev 19:9-10; Exod 23:10-11; Deut 14:28-29), giving interest-free loans (Exod 22:25; Lev 25:35-37), and welcoming them at the major feasts (Deut 16:9-15). God's people are called to tithe (give one tenth of their wealth annually), in part for the support of the needy (Deut 14:28, 29; 26:12). Although ideally "there will . . . be no one in need among you" (15:4), the Torah is realistic enough to recognize that "there will never cease to be some in need on the earth" and that therefore each Israelite must "open your hand to the poor and needy neighbor in your land" (15:11). A similar concern for these groups appears in Wisdom (Job 24:3-4; Prov 14:31; 15:25; 19:17; 22:22) and in the Psalms (68:5; 82:3-4). The prophets thunder against those who mistreat them (e.g., Isa 1:23; Jer 7:5-7; Ezek 22:6-7). The preaching of the prophets must often seem to be negative and condemnatory, but it also constituted an ongoing call to society to reform its basic economic structures.

It is in this context that the prohibition of taking interest on loans (Exod 22:25; Lev 25:35-37; Deut 23:19-20) is to be understood. As these texts make clear, the reference is not to raising capital for commercial ventures but to helping out a fellow Israelite in need (cf. C. J. H. Wright 1983: 84); they are not, therefore, to be regarded as precepts applicable in a quite different modern situation. The basic principle here is that "loans and their repayments must never worsen the plight of the destitute" (Blomberg 1999: 42; cf. Wolff 1974: 187).

iv. Fair Dealing

As part of its vision of a just society, the OT calls for honesty and truthfulness in all human relationships. Behind the specific prescriptions forbidding the use of dishonest weights and measures in the Torah (Lev 19:35-36; Deut 25:13-16) and in Wisdom (Prov 11:1; 20:10) lies the basic principle of honesty in all commercial dealings: "God's call to holiness demands that both buyer and seller be fair and responsible" (Kaiser 1983: 213).

This can be seen as the application of an even broader principle of truthfulness that lies behind the ninth commandment, "You shall not bear false witness against your neighbor" (Exod 20:16//Deut 5:20). It may well be the case that originally "this commandment has in view the public testimony of individuals before the judges, in social and commercial dealings, and in gatherings for public worship where evildoers were publicly accused and where false accusation could be devastating" (Harrelson 1980: 143). Jezebel's plot to have Naboth killed provides a powerful negative paradigm of the consequences of false witness (1 Kgs 21:8-14). But the commandment is clearly of broader application and may be extended to all instances of what Proverbs calls "a lying tongue" (6:17; 12:19). The underlying general principle is set forth in 12:22:

> Lying lips are an abomination to the LORD,
>   but those who act faithfully are his delight.

c. Social Justice

Within the OT understanding of social ethics there is a considerable tension. On the one hand there is a strongly egalitarian element. A basic principle is that all human beings are created in the image of God, and each human life is therefore sacred (cf. above, 19-1.1b). In the previous section we saw a strong emphasis on the right of *all* God's people to receive a fair share of the economic resources he provides. On the other hand the OT provides ample evidence that in Israelite society all persons were not equal in status. As a matter of pragmatic ethics (cf. 18-1.1f), standards that generally prevailed in the ancient Near East were accepted in Israel also, though in modified form. Here we consider three aspects of social ethics: the institution of slavery, the role of women in society, and the OT attitude to race and culture.

i. Slavery

Slavery was universal in the ancient Near East, and Israel shared the practice with her neighbors, though with some very significant differences (see Zimmerli 1976; Kaiser 1983: 98-100). Persons could become slaves through capture in war, or through being forced to sell family members and finally themselves for debt (see Mendelsohn 1962: 384-85). While the OT nowhere commands or legislates slavery, it does assume and accept its existence (cf. Prov 29:19, 21) in the spirit of pragmatic ethics. This acceptance is, however, significantly modified by provisions, especially in the Torah, for regulating the practice and ensuring that it is administered in a humane fashion. Within Israel slaves were accorded "a degree of status, rights and protection unheard of elsewhere" (C. J. H. Wright 1983: 179). If slaves were physically injured by their master, they were to be given their freedom (Exod 21:26-27; these laws, however, do assume the right of masters to inflict corporal punishment). Slaves enjoy equal protection under the Sabbath law that guarantees one day's rest in seven (Exod 20:10; Deut 5:14). They are regarded as part of the religious community, participating in its festivals (Exod 12:44; Deut 16:11-14). Even more significant is the fact that Israelite slavery was not permanent. Israelite slaves were to be freed after six years' service unless they voluntarily chose to continue serving their master (Exod 21:2-6). A slave freed in these circumstances would be in a precarious economic position. Deut 15:12-18 has a more humane version of the Exodus law that differs from it in two ways: protection is extended equally to both male and female slaves, and the master is commanded not to let slaves go empty-handed but to "provide liberally" for them. 23:15-16 goes beyond this and in effect challenges the whole existence of slavery; it contains the extraordinary provision that runaway slaves are not to be given up, a law that is unique in the ancient Near East (Wolff 1974: 202). In the case of a runaway slave, "Israel's law not only allowed his freedom, it *commanded* his protection" (Wright, 181).

The motive for such laws and for the humane treatment of slaves generally lies in the fact that the Israelites themselves were once slaves: "Remember that you were a slave in the land of Egypt, and the Lord your God redeemed you" (Deut 15:15). From a salvation-historical perspective, therefore, the very institution of slavery is undercut. It is also called in question from the perspective of the created order. Particularly significant is Job's comment in the context of a reference to his male and female slaves:

> Did not he who made me in the womb make them?
> And did not one fashion us in the womb? (Job 31:15; cf. vv. 13-15)

C. J. H. Wright (1983) points out that the first reference to slavery in the Bible, in Gen 9:25-27, is in the context of a curse, which suggests that "slavery is seen as unnatural, fallen and accursed, in no way an essential and unchangeable part of the 'nature of things'" (182). Thus, although the OT accepts slavery, it legislates for a humane treatment of slaves and comes close to abolishing Israelite slavery.

ii. The Status of Women

The role and status of women in the OT is revealed not only in many of the laws of the Torah but also in numerous narratives that reflect the basic attitude of society. The OT has generally been seen as endorsing a patriarchal type of society in which the status of women was clearly inferior (see Fiorenza 1976: 39-47). More recently the question has arisen as to how far the biblical material is patriarchal, and how far the patriarchalism has been in the eyes of the (until recently, almost entirely male) later interpreters of Scripture (cf. L. M. Russell 1976: 15).

The first three chapters of Genesis are of crucial importance, and nowhere is the reevaluation of the evidence more significant than here. For example, the fact that man is created first in the Gen 2 account, and woman last, has traditionally been taken to show the inferiority of women. But in Gen 1 it is humankind that is created last, as the crown of creation! If "the best comes last" is the rule in Gen 1, why not also in Gen 2? Thus it can be convincingly argued that "The Yahwist account moves to its climax, not its decline, in the creation of women" (Trible 1973: 36). To give another example, in Gen 2:18 woman is created to be man's *ʿēzer*, translated by KJV as "an help meet" (NRSV "helper") and traditionally understood to denote a subordinate or inferior. Yet *ʿēzer* does not suggest either inferiority or superiority; it is often used of God as the helper of his people (Deut 33:7; etc.). Trible (1973) well characterizes the biblical usage: "God is the helper superior to man; the animals are helpers inferior to man; woman is the helper equal to man" (36; cf. Sakenfeld 1975: 224; Terrien 1973: 324). The Gen 2 story has frequently been emphasized to the neglect of the Gen 1 account that canonically comes first, and that pictures the climax of creation when "God created humankind in his image . . . male and female he created them" (1:27). Here, clearly "male and female are created together and equally in the image of God," while in the following verses "both male and female participate equally in their assignment within creation. There is no domination of male over female, but only of both together over the creatures" (Sakenfeld, 224; cf. Trible 1978: 18; Crook 1990: 185). Thus "there is no hint that woman has a subordinate status in the description of her creation" (Otwell 1977: 15).

If Gen 1 and 2 represent the divine intention for the basic equality of men and women, Gen 3 portrays the results of human sin and disobedience, and the consequent distortion of all human relationships (see esp. vv. 16-19). These verses "are not commands for structuring life. To the contrary, they show how intolerable existence has become as it stands between creation and redemption" (Trible 1978: 123; cf. Sakenfeld 1975: 226; Fiorenza 1976: 49).

Despite these distortions arising from human sin, the fact remains that women play a greater role in the OT than is often realized (cf. Otwell 1977: 193-94; Dewey 1976: 62f.). Recent studies have noted the contributions of Sarah, Rebekah, Leah and Rachel, the women in the exodus story, Ruth and Naomi, Hannah, Esther, Judith, Susanna, and so on. Women are often accorded a high place in the Wisdom Literature (Terrien 1973: 328; Scobie 1984b: 46). We have already noted that while excluded from the hereditary male priesthood and the eldership, women could be called to the charismatic ministries of the prophets and the wise (see 15-1.5b).

While all this provides a new perspective on the role of women, it does not alter the fact that in OT times society was generally patriarchal. For all her life a woman was legally under the protection of but also subject to a man, be it father, husband, or other family member. In fact, it has to be conceded that in a sinful society there are records of the abuse of women, including what Trible has termed "Stories of Terror" (referring to the stories of Hagar, Jephthah's daughter, the Levite's concubine, and Tamar; see Trible 1984).

An important concern of feminist biblical scholarship has been the role of language. At one level this has been concerned with the effects of male language in reference to God (on this complex issue, see 1-1.4b.ii). At another level it has been concerned with the use of "inclusive language" when the biblical text does not intend to be gender-specific, an approach that is increasingly reflected in recently revised modern translations (e.g., NRSV, REB).

iii. Race and Culture

The OT basically views all races and cultures as equal in God's sight. All human beings are created in the image of God (Gen 1:26-27; cf. Haselden 1964: 169-70), and all humankind is descended from Adam, and in particular from Noah. Gen 10 provides a "table of the nations" that traces the descent of the seventy nations of the world from the three sons of Noah — Shem, Ham, and Japheth. The table emphasizes the essential unity of humankind, and the classification is based on the known geographical distribution of the nations, not on race (see von Rad 1962: 161; cf. Speiser 1962: 236). If Gen 10 emphasizes the equality of all races and nations as created by God, Gen 11 emphasizes that they are equally in rebellion against God and hence at odds with one another.

Gen 9:20-29 has been used in defense of an antiblack racism. In this strange episode (see commentaries) Ham commits an offense against his drunken and naked father Noah, whereas his two brothers Shem and Japheth act to save their father's honor. As a result Noah pronounces a curse, not on Ham, but on Ham's son Canaan, who was to be a slave to Shem and Japheth. Ham, or Canaan, it has been claimed, was the ancestor of the black races who are thus inferior to, and destined to be slaves of, the other races. In fact, in the OT Canaan is the ancestor of the "Canaanites," indigenous inhabitants of the Land when the Israelites arrived, who were seen by the Israelites as morally corrupt; the view that they were ancestors of the black races is absolutely without foundation.

The OT shows no trace of discrimination on the basis of race or color. The black Ethiopian Ebed-melech (in biblical times "Ethiopian" referred to black

Africans; cf. Jer 13:23, and see P. Frost 1991: 1), who saved Jeremiah's life (Jer 38:7-13), was a court official and was assured that God would save him (39:15-17). Despite the claim that "black is beautiful," it is not clear that the reference to the bride in Cant 1:5-6 is to be taken in a racial sense (see commentaries); but at least it shows no prejudice against dark-skinned persons.

Israel is not listed in the table of nations, though the descent of Abram is traced from Shem in Gen 11:10-32. The choice of Abraham and Israel in no way implies a superiority of that group, whether racial, religious, cultural, or otherwise. Election is purely by grace (11-1.2a) and is directed toward the ultimate salvation of all humankind (12-1.1). Although the Israelites traced their descent from the twelve sons of Jacob/Israel, the later Israel was by no means racially "pure" (see 12-1.3a). It was a people (*'am*) rather than a nation (*gôy*), and God's choice of Israel was not "simply a matter of God arbitrarily picking out one nation or race from the rest. Rather, he called into being a community of people who would then live among the nations to serve his purpose" (C. J. H. Wright 1983: 109). God's care for Israel in salvation history does not involve a denial of his care for other nations (see 12-1.1).

19-1.4. THE STATE

a. The Setting

The OT reflects a great diversity of political situations (for a more detailed analysis, see C. J. H. Wright 1990: 4-9). Broadly speaking, we may discern two main types of relationships between the religious community of Israel and the state.

In one type *Israel is an independent state.* Historically we see this emerging in the centuries following the entry of Israel into the Land. The loose confederation of tribes in the period of the judges proved inadequate for national defense and the preservation of law and order: "In those days there was no king in Israel; all the people did what was right in their own eyes" (Judg 21:25). Hence it is only with the emergence of the monarchy under Saul, and particularly of a hereditary monarchy under David, that we can speak of an Israelite "state." This state continued under Solomon and through the period of the divided monarchy until the Assyrian conquest of the North in the eighth century B.C. and the fall of Judah in the south to the Babylonians in 597/86 (see 3-1.2d). Thereafter Israel was independent again only for a brief century under the Maccabees (see 3-1.2g).

The other type of relationship is one in which Israel is *subject to a foreign political power.* Israel first emerges, in the book of Exodus, as a community subject to a hostile state, that of the Egyptians. Then, after the period of the monarchy, Israel lost its political independence and lived under a series of foreign empires: Babylonian, Persian, Ptolemaic, Seleucid, and Roman.

b. Israel and the State

Despite these diverse political situations, existing over a period of many centuries, it is possible to discern certain broad principles governing the relationship between Israel and the state.

i. The OT witnesses agree that *the state is an institution ordained by God.* This is most obvious in the case of the independent Israelite state that is inseparably linked with the *monarchy* established by God (on which, see more fully 6-1.2). It is not too anachronistic to speak of the "divine right" of kings. The monarch is the Lord's "anointed"/"messiah," chosen and appointed by God, not divine by nature but adopted as God's son. The political and religious establishments work hand in glove as the account of Solomon's coronation shows: Zadok the priest anoints the king, and the people shout, "Long live King Solomon!" (1 Kgs 1:39). The political and religious communities are assumed to be identical: Israel is both a political and a religious unit with the king at its head. The state is divinely established and the people, for religious reasons, are required to obey the king, who in turn is responsible for the safety and well-being of his people. The Torah, especially insofar as it constitutes a code of civil law (see 18-1.2a.v), envisages a state that exists to restrain the violence and sinfulness of human nature and is authorized to administer appropriate penalties and deterrents through a duly constituted legal system. Similarly, we find in the Wisdom Literature "the assumption that the king holds office legitimately, that he is to be regarded as an instrument of just order and truth, and that his ability to wield power and to punish wrongdoers are part of a divinely ordained pattern of order" (Clements 1992: 96; see Prov 16:10, 12-15; 24:21).

The OT is prepared to see not only Israel but *all* states as divinely appointed institutions. It is by divine Wisdom that kings reign (Prov 8:15-16), and according to *Sir* 17:17, God "appointed a ruler for every nation." *Wis* 6:3 tells the rulers of the world that

> your dominion was given you from the Lord,
> and your sovereignty from the Most High.

Wisdom therefore counsels obedience to the state:

> My child, fear the LORD and the king,
> and do not disobey either of them. (Prov 24:21)

The prophets can be remarkably positive toward even such "pagan" regimes as the Babylonians and the Persians: Jeremiah advises the exiles in Babylon to "seek the welfare of the city where I have sent you into exile, and pray to the LORD on its behalf, for in its welfare you will find your welfare" (29:7), and 2 Isaiah is prepared to recognize the Persian king Cyrus as God's "messiah" in that particular historical situation (Isa 45:1).

ii. The OT equally agrees, however, that *the power of the state is not absolute.* The promonarchic view that culminated in the "royal theology" (see 6-1.2b) stands in tension with an older antimonarchic view that regards Israel as a theocracy, a view that finds classic expression in the reply of Gideon to those who would make him king: "I will not rule over you, and my son will not rule over you; the LORD will rule over you" (Judg 8:23). After the establishment of kings, this suspicion of monarchy takes the form of a prophetic critique of the state. The OT is only too well aware of the existence of "wicked rulers . . . who contrive mischief by statute" (Ps 94:20), and the Historical Books provide many examples of "bad kings." Such heads of state are by no means immune from criticism. Two paradigmatic narratives vividly illustrate this approach. One is the story of David and Bathsheba where the prophet Nathan, despite holding a position as court prophet, rebukes the king for his misdeeds (2 Sam 11–12). The story of Naboth's vineyard (1 Kgs 21) is similar in character: the prophet Elijah denounces King Ahab and Queen Jezebel and prophesies the divine judgment that will fall upon them. Here we see the "prophetic" function of religion in relation to the state, based on the belief that the state, embodied in and represented by the king, does not have absolute God-given powers. A Solomon or an Ahab rules only within certain limits, that is to say, only insofar as he obeys the divine law (cf. W. Janzen 1994: 17-19); as C. J. H. Wright (1990) puts it, "the prophets subordinated Zion to Sinai" (7). The same principle is enshrined in the Deuteronomic "law of the king" (Deut 17:14-20); the power and authority of the state are subject to God's Torah. Thus, unlike the political situation elsewhere in the ancient Near East, Israel was not to have an "absolute monarchy." Similarly, the supreme power of the king is judged by the criterion of wisdom. Solomon, in some ways the ideal OT ruler, is commended because, given the chance to write a blank check, he chose to ask God for wisdom: "Give your servant therefore an understanding mind to govern your people, able to discern between good and evil" (1 Kgs 3:9; cf. 16-1.3a; 18-1.3b; and see Clements 1992: 104-9). On the other hand, Wisdom recognizes that "a ruler who lacks understanding is a cruel oppressor" (Prov 28:16; cf. 16:12; 29:2), and it is a great evil when "folly is set in many high places" (Eccl 10:6). *Sir* 10:3 recognizes that

> an undisciplined king ruins his people,
>> but a city becomes fit to live in through the understanding
>>> of its rulers.

The OT sees not only Israel but all states as bound by the moral order established by God (cf. 18-1.3a). It is the God-given task of rulers to "decree what is just" (Prov 8:15); when they fail to do this, they become subject to God's judgment (see 12-1.2; 12-2.2). It is precisely because the authority of rulers is God-given that they will be judged when they do not

> . . . rule rightly,
> or keep the law,
> or walk according to the purpose of God. (*Wis* 6:4)

iii. What is to be *the response of God's people* when faced with an unjust state? The prophetic critique demonstrates that such a state cannot command the obedience of the faithful. The refusal of the Hebrew midwives to carry out Pharaoh's command to kill all Hebrew male babies (Exod 1:15-17) has often been seen as a paradigm for obeying God rather than human authority (cf. J. J. Davis 1993: 191-92). The book of Daniel reflects the dilemma faced by God's people living in a pagan state; Daniel is prepared to serve such a state (cf. 1:5; 8:27), but only up to a certain point, after which he is called to disobey a state that goes beyond its God-given mandate (Dan 6; cf. C. J. H. Wright 1990: 9).

The question can be raised as to whether opposition to a king who disobeys God may be carried beyond criticism and passive disobedience to violent revolution aimed at overthrowing a government and replacing it with another. The OT certainly speaks of *God's* power to overthrow unjust states: He "deposes kings and sets up kings" (Dan 2:21; cf. Job 12:18), and it can be argued that "God uses human instruments to accomplish his purposes" (J. J. Davis 1993: 202). Moreover, it provides examples of this, such as the rebellion and secession of the North in 1 Kgs 12, sparked by the prophet Ahijah (11:29-39), and the bloody revolution under Jehu, who had been anointed by Elisha (2 Kgs 9). The Maccabean revolt (*1 and 2 Maccabees;* see 3-1.2g) provides a clear example of armed rebellion undertaken for religious reasons (whether it is termed a "revolt" or a "war of liberation" is a matter of semantics). The Maccabean period, however, illustrates how quickly religious principles can be compromised (see *1 Macc* 2:32-41), and how in due course political power corrupts. It should be noted that while the book of Daniel provides paradigms of disobedience, it provides none of armed revolution: *God* will bring in his kingdom, and the task of the faithful is to watch and pray.

19-1.5. INTERNATIONAL AFFAIRS

The OT is concerned not only with Israel but with all the nations of humankind, many of which Israel interacts with at one time or another. The relation of Israel as God's people to the other peoples of the earth has been discussed in 12-1. Here we focus on one crucial issue: the question of war and peace. Some of the problems that arise here overlap with those discussed in the previous section on the state.

a. Holy War

The attitude of the OT to war constitutes a major problem for biblical ethics (cf. Gelston 1964: 325). It is not just that the Historical Books are full of wars and bloodshed; the LORD himself is depicted as a divine Warrior who calls Israel to wage holy war against her enemies.

The patriarchs generally lived at peace with their neighbors (Swartley 1983: 115), though Abraham's defeat of a coalition of kings in order to rescue his nephew Lot is the exception that proves the rule (Gen 14). In the deliverance of Israel from Egypt that includes the defeat and destruction of Pharaoh's army, it is the Lord, the divine Warrior, who fights for the Israelites and liberates them:

> The LORD is a warrior (*îsh milchāmâh* = "a man of battle");
> the LORD is his name. (Exod 15:3)

During the wilderness period the Israelites were forced to fight enemies who blocked their way (17:8-13), and the entry into the Promised Land was achieved, at least in part, by armed conquest. Once settled in the Land, Israel had to defend itself against invaders. The book of Judges sees this type of war as fully justified, and the Israelite tribes won spectacular victories over superior forces, provided that they relied on the LORD and fought in accordance with his instructions (cf. Gideon's victory over the Midianites in Judg 7–8). Having secured the nation's boundaries, however, David embarked on the conquest of surrounding nations (2 Sam 8:1-6; see Lind 1980: 114-20). During the period of the divided monarchy, Israel and Judah constantly fought against outside enemies, and occasionally with each other. The North eventually fell as a result of war with the Assyrians, and Judah as a result of war with the Babylonians. The later Maccabean revolt may be viewed either as a rebellion within the (Seleucid) state or as a war of liberation (cf. above, 19-1.4b.iii).

Following the influential work of von Rad, *Der Heilige Krieg im alten Israel*, 1958 (ET 1991, *Holy War in Ancient Israel*), it has been common to see behind many OT narratives an ideology of "holy war" (see Craigie 1978: 48-49; Gross 1981; Eller 1981: 46-62). Laws governing the conduct of holy war are found in Deut 20. The term "holy war" does not appear in the OT, which speaks rather of "the wars of the LORD (*milch\u1d43môth YHWH*)" (Num 21:14; 1 Sam 18:17). The term was introduced by Schwally on the analogy of the Muslim jihad (cf. Ollenburger in von Rad 1991: 5-6), and can be accepted as appropriate. Holy war is characterized by a group of features, not all of which necessarily appear in every instance (see von Rad 1991: 41-51).

Such war is waged at the direction of the LORD (Judg 20:23), who often appoints the charismatic leader (Deut 31:7-8; Judg 6:11-18). The soldiers must be volunteers (Judg 3:27-28), totally dedicated men (Deut 20:5-9; Judg 7:3) who are consecrated (Josh 3:5) and willing to accept temporary discipline, including abstinence from sexual relations (1 Sam 21:5; 2 Sam 11:11). Victory comes from the LORD (Deut 20:4), as the defeat of vastly superior forces demonstrates (cf. Judg 7:2-8; 1 Sam 14:6-15), and the LORD gives the enemy into the hands of Israel (Josh 8:1; Judg 4:7; 1 Sam 14:12). Israel is called not to fear, but to trust the LORD for victory (Exod 14:13; Deut 20:1; Josh 8:1; Judg 7:3). He is

> the LORD, strong and mighty,
> the LORD, mighty in battle. (Ps 24:8)

The purpose of such war is that God's people may have rest and peace in the Land; it is not for selfish gain, and the taking of booty is generally prohibited (cf. Josh 6:18; 7:1). Moreover, holy war "looks beyond the day of battle to the time of peace which the victorious conclusion of hostilities will bring" (Toombs 1962b: 798; cf. Hanson 1984: 347-49). The LORD "is a God whose moral purpose is consistently bent on delivering the oppressed and punishing the oppressor" (W. Janzen 1972: 161). Nevertheless, since holy war was exemplified in the conquest of Canaan and the slaughter of existing inhabitants (Deut 20:16-18), it can hardly be claimed that the holy wars were always defensive in character (contra Gross 1981: 959).

Some scholars seek to blunt the force of the holy war ideology.

i. One approach is to emphasize that it is the LORD who fights, rather than Israel. This is true of the exodus, which for that reason makes a poor paradigm for wars of liberation; Moses tells the Israelites, "The LORD will fight for you, and you have only to keep still" (Exod 14:14). Thus "the great defeat of Egypt which reverberates all through the Bible was a weaponless victory" (Enz 1972: 52; cf. Lind 1980: 24-31). But this is *not* true of the many subsequent wars fought by Israel at the LORD's command.

ii. Another approach has been to deny the historicity of much of the "conquest," seeing it rather as a "settlement," if not a "peasant revolt" (cf. Birch 1985: 1118; on Gottwald's view, see C-3), and especially seeing the whole idea of the slaughter of the existing inhabitants of the Land as a later invention. But hypothetical reconstructions of the conquest are a very insecure foundation on which to build, and the fact remains that holy war, including the extermination of enemies, constitutes an important feature of the canonical text. The prophets, and especially the NT, bring a very different view of war, but "as responsible historians and theologians, we must accept Israel's involvement in war, holocaust, and slaughter" (P. D. Miller 1965: 43).

b. Peace, Peace, Where There Is No Peace

A considerably different perspective on war emerges in the Prophets.

i. While the early prophets tended to support the holy war (2 Kgs 13:14-19), the later prophets become increasingly critical. The kings in particular are criticized, though this tends to be because they depart from the holy war ideology and put their trust not in the LORD but in the might of their own standing armies and/or in foreign alliances (Isa 30:1-2; 31:1; Hos 10:13). Moreover, the historical narratives suggest that David and some later kings "fought wars not in Yahweh's cause of defending the weak and impoverished against the oppressors but in careless adventures aimed at adding territory and wealth to their kingdoms" (Hanson 1984: 351). The essence of the prophetic objection is that the kings "take God's prerogative to decide over war and peace and his instrument to act in the world into their own hands" (von Waldow 1984: 38).

ii. With the major prophets comes a radical reversal of the earlier understanding of war. Instead of foretelling victory over Israel's enemies, they declare that a sinful nation will be defeated at the hands of its enemies (Amos 2:13-16; Jer 7:13-15), whom God will use as agents of his judgment (cf. 3-1.3c). The most striking instance of this comes when Jeremiah not only foretells the fall of Jerusalem to the Babylonians but also counsels surrender to them. For this "pacifist" stance, he is accused of un-Israelite activities and almost loses his life (Jer 38:1-6).

iii. Part of the prophetic critique of the state (cf. above, 19-1.4b) involves a deeper understanding of what is meant by peace (*shālôm;* on peace in the OT, see more fully 20-1.2, also Birch 1985: 1115-16). Peace is far more than the absence of war; it involves harmony within society and above all is linked with righteousness and justice. In the OT "Peace cannot exist without justice and neither can survive long under oppression" (Dearman 1983: 9).

Old Testament: Promise

19-2. EVERYONE WILL INVITE HIS NEIGHBOR

The promise of a new order includes the vision of a community in which all relationships will be ordered aright.

19-2.1. THE INDIVIDUAL

For the vision of the future of the individual in OT eschatology, see the discussion in 17-2.

19-2.2. THE FAMILY

In the eschatological intensification of evil (cf. 4-2.1), human relationships will deteriorate, especially within the family:

> The people will be oppressed,
>   everyone by another . . .
> the youth will be insolent to the elder. (Isa 3:5)

Micah sees the signs of the end in the fact that

> the son treats the father with contempt,
>   the daughter rises up against her mother,
> the daughter-in-law against her mother-in-law;
>   your enemies are members of your own household. (7:6; cf. Lam 5:12)

The new age, on the other hand, will see the restoration of intergenerational harmony. It will be the task of the returning Elijah to "turn the hearts of parents to their children and the hearts of children to their parents" (Mal 4:6). Zech 8:4-5 has a particularly beautiful vision of young and old living side by side in a renewed Jerusalem: "Old men and old women shall again sit in the streets of Jerusalem, each with staff in hand because of their great age. And the streets of the city shall be full of boys and girls playing in its streets." In Isaiah's vision of paradise restored with its reconciliation between humans and the beasts, "a little child" occupies an important place (11:6). In Joel's vision (cf. 5-2.3) the Spirit will be poured out upon all without distinction: male and female, young and old, master and slave (2:28-29).

19-2.3. SOCIETY

a. A New Society

The messianic age will be an age of righteousness (cf. 18-2.4). In the ideal future, wealth will be evenly distributed. Ezek 40–48, which envisages an equal division of land among all twelve tribes in the new community, is an idealized recapitulation of the original division of the Land (see 13-2.3). The Prophets envisage an ideal future when no one will be rich but all will have sufficient for their needs, sitting "under their own vines and under their own fig trees" (Mic 4:4). Wealth will be shared in an atmosphere of social harmony: "In that day, says the LORD of hosts, every one of you will invite his neighbor under his vine and under his fig tree" (Zech 3:10 RSV). In the new age distinctions of social class and sex will be abolished:

Even on the male and female slaves,
in those days, I will pour out my spirit. (Joel 2:29)

With the eschatological ingathering of the Gentiles (see 12-2.4), all peoples, without distinction of race, will be welcomed into God's kingdom.

b. Sabbatical and Jubilee Years

We have already noted the concern in the law and the prophets for the economically disadvantaged members of society. Another solution to these problems is proposed in legislation in the Torah. Employing the first division of time referred to in Scripture, the *seven*-day week (Gen 1), the laws of the Sabbatical and Jubilee Years call for a fresh start, at regular periods in the future, that would break the cycle of debt and poverty, deliver people from economic enslavement, and bring about a more egalitarian and just society.

The *Sabbatical Year* laws that are found in Exod 21:2-6, 23:10-11, Lev 25:1-7, and Deut 15:1-18 call for three types of action every seventh year. (1) The law of Exod 21:2-6 and (with significant modifications; see Ringe 1985: 21-22) Deut 15:12-18 calls for the release of Hebrew slaves. (2) Deut 15:1-11 requires the remission of all debts. (3) Exod 23:10-11 and Lev 25:1-7 stipulate that the land is to lie fallow; thus even nature is included in the seventh-year release, though the main purpose of this law is humanitarian ("so that the poor of your people may eat" — Exod 23:11). (2) and (3) envisage a seven-year cycle, whereas in (1) the seventh year appears to be calculated from the time a person was sold into slavery. While the Sabbatical Years may have been calculated (cf. Wacholder 1973), it is unclear how far these laws were actually put into practice. Jer 34:8-22 recounts how when the Babylonians were advancing on Jerusalem (ca. 588 B.C.), King Zedekiah "made a covenant with all the people in Jerusalem to make a proclamation of liberty *(derôr)* to them, that all should set free their Hebrew slaves" (vv. 8-9), presumably as a demonstration of faithfulness to God. The owners obeyed but took their slaves back again (evidently when the Babylonian threat passed), an action that brought forth a thunderous denunciation from Jeremiah. The prophet quotes the sabbatical law of Deut 15:12 in a way which suggests that the law had not been observed (Jer 34:14). According to Neh 5:10-13, Nehemiah required the cancellation of debts that were causing people to be sold into slavery; this, too, simply underlines the lack of a regular observance of the Sabbatical Year (*1 Macc* 6:49, 53 does refer to an observance of "a sabbatical year for the land," but there is no mention of provisions relating to debt and slavery).

The *Jubilee Year* comes in the fiftieth year following seven weeks of years (7 × 7 = 49 + 1 = 50), and detailed legislation is found in Lev 25:8-55 (see Milgrom 1997). On the Day of Atonement the trumpet is to be sounded throughout the land, and "you shall proclaim liberty *(dᵉrôr)* throughout the land to all its inhabitants" (v. 10). The laws call for the land to lie fallow, the release of slaves, and a return of people to their own property and families (hence the cancellation of debts). The basis of such legislation is the recognition that the Land belongs to God (v. 23), and that property should remain within the families to whom it was originally granted. The laws on slavery are particularly far-reaching, and vv. 39-43 in effect prohibit Israelite slavery altogether: "If any who are dependent on you become so impoverished that they sell themselves to you, you shall not make them serve as slaves. They shall remain with you as hired or bound laborers." The Israelites, God declares, "are my servants, whom I brought out of the land of Egypt; they shall not be sold as slaves are sold" (v. 42). It is inconceivable that brother should be the slave of brother (cf. Van der Ploeg 1972: 81-82).

It is putting it mildly to say that "if they had actually been observed, the collection of Jubilee laws would have had a sweeping impact on the social and political life of any community governed by them" (Ringe 1985: 27). "The legislation associated with the year of jubilee," as Fager (1993) remarks, "presents the most radical program for continuous social reform to be found in the Old Testament" (12; cf. Brueggemann 1997: 189-90); in fact, it "presents a vision of social and economic reform unsurpassed in the ancient Near East" (Gnuse 1985: 43). It has been suggested that the Jubilee was intended to be a once-only event, but the text indicates a recurring fifty-year cycle (see Lev 25:15). There is, however, no account in the OT of the Jubilee Year ever having been observed (cf. Wacholder 1973: 154; Gnuse 1985: 46-47; Fager 1993: 34-36).

Jubilee imagery resurfaces in Isa 61:1-2:

> The spirit of the Lord GOD is upon me,
> because the LORD has anointed me;
> he has sent me to bring good news to the oppressed,
> to bind up the brokenhearted,
> to proclaim liberty *(dᵉrôr)* to the captives,
> and release to the prisoners;
> to proclaim the year of the LORD's favor,
> and the day of vengeance of our God.

Originally the herald of the Jubilee may have been the prophet himself (there are some parallels with the Servant Songs). But the fact that the herald is endowed with God's Spirit and "anointed" and "sent" by God suggests a more messianic figure. Here the Jubilee has become an image of the eschatological reign of God that will at some point in the future be ushered in by God's chosen Servant. The Jubilee can thus be seen as prefiguring the dawn of the kingdom of God. As Kaiser (1983) points out, "since the Jubilee was proclaimed on the day of Atonement (Lev. 25:9), the removal of sin on *Yom Kippur* made possible the restored relationship between God and his people, and looked forward to the kingdom of peace and liberty in the *eschaton* as pictured in the Jubilee" (218).

The sabbatical and jubilee laws held up before Israel an ideal for society. They reminded God's people that "to confess God as sovereign includes caring for the poor and granting freedom to those trapped in a continuous cycle of indebtedness" (Ringe 1985: 28). But the laws called for such radical economic and social changes that they came to be associated not with the present order but with the time when God would bring in his new order.

19-2.4. THE STATE

After the collapse of the Maccabean kingdom and the eastward expansion of Rome, there was no longer any question of an independent Israelite state; God's people were subject to a foreign power, the power of Rome. In the late OT period and down into NT times, three basic attitudes to the state emerged (cf. A. Y. Collins 1977: 242-45).

i. One reflects the OT view that all states are ordained by God and, when they act as servants of God, deserve *the respect and obedience of the faithful.* Under the Romans conditions may not be ideal, but the best policy is a pragmatic one of making the best of it (cf. Schrage 1988: 108). In NT times it was the priestly party of the Sadducees that exemplified this attitude; they were willing to collaborate with the Romans in return for limited self-government, primarily in religious matters, and particularly for retention of their priestly powers and privileges. Broadly speaking, the Pharisees may be classified in this category also. While the name Pharisees probably means "the separated ones," they did not withdraw from society; they saw themselves as separate from the majority who failed to live in strict accordance with Torah, but they were prepared, however reluctantly, to live with the political setup under the Romans provided they were allowed religious freedom so that they might devote their time and energy to studying and living in accordance with God's Torah.

ii. A second attitude picks up another strand from the OT that sees armed resistance to a godless power as justified, and therefore aims to restore the former national state by *armed rebellion* against the existing political authorities. Memories of the successful Maccabean revolt no doubt inspired various groups in NT times such as the four thousand "assassins" (*sikarioi* = "dagger men," "assassins," comparable to our "terrorists," at least from the Roman point of view) mentioned in Acts 21:38 (see commentaries). In NT times there were those, sometimes referred to as the "Zealots," who favored this option that represents a reversion to the ideology of the "holy war," and who advocated armed rebellion against Rome, doubtless combining this with various forms of nationalistic messianic expectation.

iii. A third attitude goes beyond what is found in most of the OT, and is represented by *apocalyptic* (cf. 2-2.1b) with its much more negative assessment of worldly political regimes, which are symbolized by beasts. All human states are evil, and therefore the only hope is for a cosmic catastrophe when God will intervene in human history, overthrow all pagan powers, and usher in the kingdom of God. Since all human states are evil, the policy of believers is one of total withdrawal from the political process; their attitude toward the pagan empire is one of passive resistance, and their role is simply to watch and pray for the coming of the end. Such groups were probably inspired by the concept of the faithful remnant (cf. 11-2.2a); while evil reigns in the world, the majority of God's people are unfaithful, but a minority at least will keep the faith until God intervenes. An implication of this policy of nonresistance is that some of the faithful may suffer martyrdom (see 1 *Macc* 1:50-64). This view is exemplified in the book of Daniel. Although they are not mentioned in the NT by name, historically the Essenes and the monastic community that produced the Dead Sea Scrolls are to be classified here also. In the NT itself, this view is represented up to a point by John the Baptist.

19-2.5. INTERNATIONAL AFFAIRS

On the relationship between Israel and the other nations of humankind in OT eschatology, see 12-2. Here we focus on the question of war and peace.

a. The Age of Peace

Peace is an important element in the hopes and expectations of the prophets, who envisage a time when war will be no more. God promises through Hosea, "I will abolish the bow, the sword, and war from the land" (2:18). After centuries of warfare and the trauma of exile, the prophets promise a time when God's "covenant of peace" will be restored (Isa 54:9-10; cf. 52:7; Jer 32:36-41; Ezek 39:25-29). With their strongly ethical emphasis, the prophets recognize that peace and justice are closely linked: "The effect of righteousness will be peace" (Isa 32:17).

In association with the expectation of the eschatological ingathering of the Gentiles (see 12-2.4), we find an inspiring vision of a time of universal peace. Many peoples and nations will come to Zion, and God

> shall judge between the nations,
>   and shall arbitrate for many peoples;
> they shall beat their swords into plowshares,
>   and their spears into pruning hooks;

nation shall not lift up sword against nation,
neither shall they learn war any more. (Isa 2:4//Mic 4:3)

Behind these visions lies the assumption that "war is a violation of God's order of creation and as such war is sin"; they are "the prophetic way of saying that, at the end of days, Yahveh will restore the old order of creation of Gen 1 with one undivided human race in unity under God" (von Waldow 1984: 33, 40).

b. The Prince of Peace

The hope for peace in the future is associated with the new Servant of God. According to Isa 9:6, the coming Davidic ruler will be "Prince of Peace." Zechariah envisions a peaceful king,

humble and riding on a donkey. . . .
I will cut off the chariot from Ephraim
and the war horse from Jerusalem;
and the battle bow shall be cut off,
and he shall command peace to the nations. (9:9-10)

c. The Persistence of War

In tension with the promise of a future age of peace, however, are other prophecies that look for the continuation of war. Wars are the consequence of human sin; therefore, as long as history lasts there will be wars. Some prophecies actually look for an eschatological reversal when Israel will defeat its enemies. Thus in Zech 12:6 Judah will devour the peoples round about. Joel 3:9-10 even reverses the prophecy of Isa 2:4:

Prepare war,
stir up the warriors. . . .
Beat your plowshares into swords,
and your pruning hooks into spears.

Apocalyptic eschatology sees history in terms of a continuing series of world empires that will wage war and oppress God's people (Dan 2; 7).

d. The Last Battle

This tension is finally resolved in apocalyptic eschatology that transposes the idea of holy war into that of a final battle in which all that is evil and opposed to God will be defeated, and thus war will come to an end (cf. Gross 1981: 960; and see more fully, 4-2.3 and 4-2.5).

New Testament: Fulfillment

19-3. YOU SHALL LOVE YOUR NEIGHBOR

Despite being more limited in scope and size than the OT, the NT provides ethical guidance and direction on a wide range of issues.

19-3.1. THE INDIVIDUAL

a. The Individual and Society

It is often claimed that the NT is more concerned with the individual and that NT ethics therefore are more individual ethics. There is no doubting the value that is set upon the individual in the NT, but the individual is also always a member of the Christian community, the body of Christ, and NT ethics has much to say about interpersonal relations within the community. It is true that in the circumstances of the earliest decades of the Christian church believers and communities had very little if any influence on the social or economic or political affairs of the wider society in which they lived; still less did they exert any influence at the international level. Nevertheless, the NT sees Christians and the church set in the midst of the world, in relation to the surrounding society, to the state and to the wider world of nations, and it does offer guidance and direction in these areas also.

b. Reverence for Human Life

The NT assumes and accepts the basic ethical principles of the OT, including the sanctity of each human life and that all life is in God's hands. God's care extends to all his creation, even the humblest sparrow, but human beings are of more value in God's eyes than many sparrows (Matt 10:29-31; cf. 12:12). This is underlined not only by Jesus' teaching but even more by his example. For Jesus, "every individual is of infinite worth and is to be treated with respect. The reports of his work show that he made no distinction between people: men and women, Jews and Gentiles, righteous people and sinners were all respected as individuals, as people with whom God was concerned" (Crook 1990: 74). The value of each human life is underlined by the fact that "while we still were sinners Christ died for us" (Rom 5:8).

i. Murder

The sixth commandment prohibiting the deliberate taking of human life is reaffirmed by Jesus (Mark 10:19 and //s), Paul (Rom 13:9), and James (2:11). Jesus, however, reinterprets the commandment by internalizing it and radicalizing it (cf. 18-3.2b.ii): not only is murder wrong, but so too are the anger and verbal abuse that can lead to it (Matt 5:21-26; cf. Mark 7:21-22). For those who enter the kingdom hatred is to be replaced by love, even love of enemies (Matt 5:43-47), and retaliation is to be replaced by nonviolence (5:38-42). The emphasis on inner motivation is matched elsewhere in the NT in the lists of vices that include, e.g., "enmities, strife, jealousy, anger, quarrels, dissensions, factions, envy" (Gal 5:20-21), and "anger, wrath, malice, slander, and abusive language" (Col 3:8), i.e., the inward attitudes that can lead to violence and even to murder.

That believers are called to live by these high standards in their personal lives is beyond doubt. Where these texts have been subject to varying interpretations is over whether they apply to the state as well as to the individual, or whether the state has both a right and a duty to use force to restrain evil and maintain law and order; on this see below, 19-3.4.

ii. Abortion

Again there is no direct reference to this topic, one that must have been familiar to readers of the NT as abortion was widely practiced in the Greco-Roman world (Gorman 1982: 24-32; 1987: 74-75). The silence is thus not due to ignorance but rather to the early church's acceptance and continuation of OT norms that make such a practice virtually unthinkable. As in the OT, children are regarded as a gift and blessing from God (Mark 10:13-16 and //s; John 16:21), and the killing of children is regarded with particular horror (Matt 2:16-18; Acts 7:19). As in the OT, God is seen as active in the creation of human beings from the time of conception (Luke 1:24-25, 39-44). It is significant that the same word *(brephos)* is used for Elizabeth's unborn "child" in Luke 1:41, 44 as is used of the newborn baby of 2:12, and for that matter of the children brought to be blessed by Jesus in 18:15. It is clear that the biblical view is that "the fetus is human and therefore to be accorded the same protection to life granted every other human being" (Waltke 1976: 13).

iii. Suicide

Like the OT, the NT says nothing directly on this subject. It does contain perhaps the most famous of all suicides, that of Judas Iscariot, who, after betraying

Jesus, in remorse went and hanged himself (Matt 27:3-5; see Acts 1:18 for a variant version of his end). While Judas is clearly held responsible for sending Jesus to his death, no judgment is passed in the NT on the manner of his own death. In Acts 16:27 the Philippian jailor "drew his sword and was about to kill himself" but was restrained by Paul.

Quite separate from suicide is the willingness to sacrifice one's life for the sake of others, of which the supreme example is Jesus himself. Christians may be called to follow their Master's example (cf. 9-3.4d), and in extreme cases loyalty to the faith may result in martyrdom.

iv. Euthanasia

The NT has little to add on the question of euthanasia. It certainly reaffirms the sixth commandment, and here again this could be taken to prohibit ending the lives of the ill, suffering, or elderly. On the other hand, the NT also sees Jesus' ministry as a paradigm of mercy and compassion, and much more than the OT is concerned with bringing healing to the sick (see 20-1.3), though it also speaks of the grace of God that can enable persons to endure trials and suffering (2 Cor 12:10; Jas 1:2-4; 1 Pet 1:6-9).

19-3.2. THE FAMILY

As in the OT, the family continues to occupy a central place in NT ethics: "If . . . we are to isolate one idea that is more basic to New Testament ethics than the rest, it will be the idea of the family" (F. C. Grant 1950: 315). The most common term used is *oikos* = "house, household," which signifies an extended family. Acts recounts the conversion of a whole *oikos* on a number of occasions (10:2, 24, 44-48; 16:15, 31-34; 18:8). It is significant that the language of the family is extended to the church, in which God is the father, believers are brothers and sisters, and Christ the elder brother (Rom 8:29) (cf. 11-3.4a).

Jesus upheld the OT ethic of the family. He saw marriage as the lifelong union of one man and one woman, and divorce as contrary to the will of God. He quoted the commandments to honor parents and against adultery. His parables show a deep appreciation of family life (cf. I. Ellis 1985: 178), and the Gospels note his fondness for children. Even on the cross he was concerned to see that his own mother would be cared for (John 19:26-27).

Yet there is another strain in Jesus' teaching that seems at first glance to devalue the family. During his ministry Jesus' own family were not among his followers (John 7:5). According to Mark 3:21, Jesus' family *(hoi par' autou)* at one point tried to restrain him. A little later, told that his mother, brothers, and sisters were asking for him, Jesus looked at those around him and said, "Here are my mother and my brothers! Whoever does the will of God is my brother and sister and mother" (Mark 3:34-35 and //s). Somewhat in line with this is the "hard saying" of Luke 14:26-27//Matt 10:37-39: "Whoever comes to me and does not hate father and mother, wife and children, brothers and sisters, yes, and even life itself, cannot be my disciple." This (the Lucan) version is probably the more original, though Matthew is doubtless correct in interpreting it to mean, "Whoever loves father or mother *more than me* is not worthy of me. . . ." This saying, like the Mark 3 incident, shows that while Jesus valued the family highly, for him it was not the greatest good. If persons are forced to choose, they must give their allegiance to God and his kingdom above even the closest human ties. The community of the kingdom transcends all others (cf. Harrisville 1969: 437).

Another "hard saying" in Matt 10:34-36//Luke 12:51-53 seems to anticipate situations that did arise in the early church when some believers were forced to choose between faith and family: "Do not think that I have come to bring peace to the earth; I have not come to bring peace, but a sword" (Luke has "division" in place of "sword").

> For I have come to set a man against his father,
> and a daughter against her mother,
> and a daughter-in-law against her mother-in-law;
> and one's foes will be members of one's own household. (Matt 10:35-36)

Seen in the broader context of Jesus' teaching, this saying does not mean that it was Jesus' *purpose* to divide and break up families, but rather where there is unyielding opposition to the gospel on the part of some family members, the unfortunate *result* may be such a disruption. Such opposition and disruption are signs of the eschatological intensification of the battle between good and evil, as the quotation of Mic 7:6 (see above, 19-2.2) in Matt 10:35-36 shows. In the period before the end believers may even be betrayed and handed over to death by members of their family (Mark 13:12-13 and //s).

These passages must not be glossed over, but neither must they be isolated from the broader context of Jesus' reaffirmation of the family as a God-given institution (cf. I. Ellis 1985).

a. The NT Affirmation of Sexuality

The NT generally accepts and follows the OT's positive evaluation of sexual relationships and their relation to family life. Nowhere in the NT is human sexuality regarded as evil. It is, however, a divine gift, to be used in the way God intends.

b. Sexual Relations outside Marriage

The NT leaves no room for doubt that God's will and intention is that sexual relations be confined to lifelong, monogamous unions of husband and wife.

i. Adultery

The seventh commandment is a precept clearly reaffirmed by Jesus (Matt 19:18 and //s), Paul (Rom 13:9), and James (2:11). Jesus not only condemns the outward act, but also the lustful thought that potentially can lead to adultery (Matt 5:27-28; cf. Mark 7:21; and 2 Pet 2:14). In the case of the woman taken in adultery (John 8:1-11), Jesus does not condemn the woman, but he does say to her, "From now on do not sin again."

ii. Fornication

"Fornication" *(porneia)* is distinguished from adultery (Matt 15:19), but it can be used of "every kind of unlawful sexual intercourse" (Arndt and Gingrich 1957: 699); it is strongly condemned in 1 Cor 6:9, 13, 18, and its prohibition was a basic rule of the church (Acts 15:20, 29). Here too Jesus condemned not just the outward act but also the inward thought and intention, "for it is from within, from the human heart, that evil intentions come," including "fornication" (Mark 7:21//Matt 15:19).

iii. Prostitution

According to the Gospels, Jesus' ministry extended to prostitutes (Matt 21:31); he reached out to them, not because he approved of what they did, but because he saw them as sinners in need of forgiveness and redemption (Luke 7:48). Paul explicitly condemns sex with a prostitute in 1 Cor 6:15-16: the intimate personal union this involves is totally inconsistent with the believer's personal union with Christ. The author of Hebrews advises believers, "Let marriage be held in honor by all, and let the marriage bed be kept undefiled; for God will judge fornicators and adulterers" (13:4).

iv. Homosexuality

The early church spread into the Greco-Roman world where homosexual practice was common (Furnish 1985: 59) but by no means universally accepted (J. J. Davis 1993: 96). While it often took the form of a relation between an older and a younger man, other forms of relationship were also known. In Rom 1:18-32 Paul, as part of his analysis of humankind apart from God, condemns idolatry, one result of which he believes is that God has given up the pagan world to impurity.

While this involves "every kind of wickedness" (v. 29), prominent in the sins that Paul lists is both male and female homosexual practice. "Their women exchanged natural intercourse for unnatural, and in the same way also the men, giving up natural intercourse with women, were consumed with passion for one another. Men committed shameless acts with men and received in their own persons the due penalty for their error" (vv. 26-27). Homosexual practice is thus a lifestyle based on disregard of "God's decree" (v. 32), and it is contrary to nature (*para physin;* v. 26), though for Paul "nature" would mean "the natural order of things that God had established" (J. R. W. Stott 1985: 26). The context does not support the view that Paul was referring to the practice of homosexuality by heterosexuals, or to pederasty; rather, "it is clear that in Romans 1:26-27 Paul condemned homosexuality as a perversion of God's design for human sexual relations" (Malick 1993a: 340; cf. Bonnington and Fyall 1996: 19-21). In 1 Cor 6:9-11 Paul lists among the unrighteous who "will not inherit the kingdom of God," *malakoi* and *arsenokoitai.* The latter word recurs in a similar context in 1 Tim 1:10. *Malakoi* means literally "soft," and hence "effeminate." It can apply to those who take the passive role in homosexual relationships, but there are no grounds for restricting it to pederasty (so Malick 1993a; contra Scroggs 1983: 65). The second term, however, which some would render "sodomites" (RSV, NRSV), has no prior usage in Greek. It clearly echoes the Greek of Lev 18:22 and 20:13 in the LXX (*arsēn* = "male," and *koitē* = "bed"), so that *arsenokoitēs* literally means "one who goes to bed with a male" (cf. Malick 1993b: 482-87). There is no evidence that the term was restricted to pederasty; beyond doubt, the NT here repeats the Leviticus condemnation of all male same-sex relations (cf. J. G. Taylor 1995: 6-7; Hays 1996: 382-83). The converse of these prohibitions is the NT's positive affirmation, following that of the OT, that "God has made man and woman for one another and that our sexual desires rightly find fulfillment within heterosexual marriage" (Hays, 390; cf. Mark 10:6-9; 1 Cor 7:2; Eph 5:22-33).

c. Celibacy

More so than the OT, the NT recognizes that celibacy is an option that some may voluntarily choose (cf. 18-3.5b). Jesus' saying in Matt 19:10-12 about some who "have made themselves eunuchs for the sake of the kingdom of heaven" suggests that some may accept celibacy for the sake of the kingdom. The words are a statement, not a command, and hence at best represent an option that some may choose; they show that "Jesus affirmed the right to personal choice between marriage and remaining single" (Stagg 1977: 16). Schrage (1988) concludes that the text "represents Jesus as having decided to remain celibate for the sake of the kingdom" (93). Paul was almost certainly unmarried (cf. 1 Cor 9:5), and he sees both marriage and celibacy as gifts from God (7:7). He recognizes marriage as established by God and affirms its essential goodness (R. F.

Collins 1986: 199), but he also sees celibacy as an option in certain circumstances (7:32-35); it allows unmarried men or women to be "free from anxieties," i.e., family responsibilities, and hence able to devote all their time and energies to serving the Lord (see Schrage, 229). Paul's own very active career as a missionary serves as an example of this. The NT as a whole suggests that the celibacy of Jesus and Paul may serve as a paradigm for *some*, though not the majority of believers.

d. Husband and Wife

i. Marriage

The NT upholds the OT view that marriage is ordained by God. Jesus specifically quoted both the first creation account, "God made them male and female" (cf. Gen 1:27), and the second account, "For this reason a man shall leave his father and mother and be joined to his wife, and the two shall become one flesh" (cf. Gen 2:24). Significantly Jesus adds, "Therefore what God has joined together, let no one separate" (Mark 10:6-9//Matt 19:4-6). This shows that "faithful relationship in marriage is the demand of the Gospel, as well as that of the Creator" (R. F. Collins 1986: 187; cf. Scroggs 1976: 576). Jesus clearly taught that "according to the design of the Creator marriage consists of the monogamous union of a male and a female in a lifelong commitment to one another which is to be characterized by fidelity" (Grenz 1990: 44). Jesus' presence at the wedding in Cana of Galilee (John 2) has traditionally and quite rightly been seen as his blessing of the institution of marriage. Paul also quotes Gen 2:24 in 1 Cor 6:16 and Eph 5:31, and he assumes marriage as a God-given institution (cf. 1 Cor 7:2). 1 Timothy assumes that bishops and deacons are married (3:2, 12), and in 4:3-4 false teachers who "forbid marriage" are condemned on the grounds that "everything created by God is good."

Paul's advice to husbands and wives in 1 Cor 7:3-5 shows that for Paul, "in marriage Christian men and women have mutual rights and obligations. They are equally responsible to serve the needs of the other. They are moreover expected to form decisions by mutual consent" (Tetlow and Tetlow 1983: 64). More detailed treatment of the marriage relationship is found in the household codes. Eph 5:22-33, Col 3:18-19, and 1 Pet 3:1-7 give directions to husbands and wives; Titus 2:4-5 is incomplete, giving directions to wives only. These passages are to be interpreted in the light of the three main features of the codes identified in 18-3.3f. Firstly, the main emphasis is on *mutual* obligations and on *mutual* submission (Eph 5:21). Secondly, the marriage relationship is to be "in the Lord" (Col 3:18; Eph 5:22, 25). While marriage is a universal human institution, for Christian partners it is based on their common acceptance of Jesus as Lord; thus "marriage is authentically Christian only when it is based on God's call of two persons to enter into a covenant relationship of marriage with each other and in their common Lord" (Tetlow and Tetlow, 25). Thirdly, the relationship is to be characterized by love, and husbands are specifically told to love their wives (Col 3:19; Eph 5:25). The Ephesians passage is unique because of the introduction of the comparison between the husband/wife relationship and that between Christ and the church (5:25-32). Thus, "by use of the single verb *agapan* to describe both the husband's love for his wife and Christ's love for the Church, the author of Ephesians implies that the marital love of Christian spouses participates in the love of Christ for the Church" (R. F. Collins 1986: 203; on the church as the bride of Christ, see also 11-3.4a).

There is no direct reference to the prohibited degrees of marriage in the NT, though Paul does deal with a reported case of incest at Corinth in 1 Cor 5:1-5. For Paul such a relationship is beyond doubt contrary to the will of God (see 18-3.3b.vi).

ii. Divorce

Within the NT teaching on divorce, two divergent emphases are present. In Mark 10:2-12 (//Luke 16:18) Jesus is questioned on the subject, and declares that the legislation of Deut 24 (above, 19-1.2d.ii) was given "because of your hardness of heart." Quoting Gen 1:27 and 2:24, Jesus goes on to declare the indissolubility of marriage: "Therefore what God has joined together, let no one separate." Remarriage after divorce amounts to adultery. Thus, in response to the Pharisees, Jesus "raised the question to the level of the unconditional will of God. God's intention for marriage was that it be a lifelong commitment" (Garland 1987: 422). The concluding verses (Mark 10:11-12) contain two further revolutionary ideas. Firstly, if a man divorces his wife and marries another, says Jesus, he "commits adultery against her *(moichatai ep' autēn)*"; this is impossible in the OT, where a man can commit adultery only against another married man. Secondly, Jesus recognizes that a woman can divorce her husband, something impossible under OT law (but possible according to Roman law; cf. 1 Cor 7:13). In both these respects Jesus *puts man and woman on an equal footing* (cf. Hays 1996: 352). The prohibition by Jesus of divorce is echoed by Paul in 1 Cor 7:10-11 in one of his rare quotations from Jesus' teaching. Paul does recognize separation as a possibility, but in that case there is no possibility of remarriage.

Matt 19:3-9, however, has an account parallel to that of Mark 10:2-12; in it, and also in 5:32, Matthew has a version of Jesus' saying that contains the so-called "saving clause": "Whoever divorces his wife, *except for unchastity (mē epi porneia(i))*, and marries another commits adultery." *Porneia* is usually taken to refer to adultery here, but it can be used of any type of unlawful sexual activity (see Keener 1991: 28-33; J. J. Davis 1993: 87). Whatever the exact reference, in this version of Jesus' saying the prohibition of divorce is not absolute; an exception is recognized.

e. Parents and Children

In the NT, as in the OT, children are regarded as one of the greatest blessings bestowed by God. Jesus speaks of a mother who experiences "the joy of having brought a human being into the world" (John 16:21). He himself displayed a special fondness for children (Mark 9:36), and when the disciples tried to turn away children brought to him, Jesus "took them up in his arms, laid his hands on them, and blessed them" (10:16). The relationship of parents and children is one of the topics dealt with in the household codes; here again attention needs to be paid to the three specifically Christian features of the codes (see 18-3.3f).

i. Duties of Parents

In the household codes all duties are reciprocal; parents therefore have duties to children. They are admonished, negatively, not to provoke their children (Col 3:21; Eph 6:4), and positively to "bring them up in the discipline *(paideia)* and instruction *(nouthesia)* of the Lord" (Eph 6:4). *Paideia* means training, usually with an element of discipline involved, but that training is to be in the children's best interests, and not such as would discourage them. The relationship of parents to children is governed by their relationship to the Lord (6:1, 4; Col 3:20), while the broader context is that of acting in Christian love. That the instruction of children would include teaching based on Scripture is suggested by Paul's remarks to Timothy concerning the "sincere faith" Timothy inherited from his Jewish mother and grandmother (2 Tim 1:5), a faith grounded in his instruction "from childhood" in "the sacred writings," i.e., the Hebrew Scriptures (3:15). In the Pastorals both bishops and deacons are to manage their children and their households well (1 Tim 3:4, 12; cf. Titus 1:6). In the ancient world children were often regarded as economic assets (in the absence of a welfare state, they must support their parents in their old age). Writing to the Corinthians, Paul says, "I will not be a burden, because I do not want what is yours but you; for children ought not to lay up for their parents, but parents for their children" (2 Cor 12:14). This is a significant comment which teaches that from a Christian point of view parents are to do what is best for their children, rather than just regarding them as economic assets.

ii. Duties of Children

The commandment to "honor your father and your mother" (Exod 20:12; Deut 5:16) is reaffirmed by Jesus (Mark 10:19 and //s), and also by Paul, who underlines its importance by referring to it as the first commandment with a promise attached (Eph 6:2). Significantly he modifies the wording so as to detach the promise from the Land and give it a universal significance: "so that . . . you may live long on the earth" (cf. Kaiser 1983: 157). In the household codes children are urged to obey their parents because this is right (Eph 6:1) and because "this is your acceptable duty in the Lord" (Col 3:20; cf. Rom 1:30).

iii. The Elderly

The new people of God embraces all age groups, and from the beginning the aged are given a place of honor. The prominence of the elderly in the Lucan birth narratives is particularly striking: both Zechariah and Elizabeth were "getting on in years" (1:7), and the infant Jesus was blessed by the aged Simeon (2:25-35) and recognized by the eighty-four-year-old Anna (2:36-38).

Jesus in his teaching continues the OT concern for the elderly as a vulnerable group, showing a special sympathy for the plight of widows (Luke 4:25-26; Mark 12:41-44). On two occasions he quotes the fifth commandment: in Mark 7:9-13 where he strongly condemns using a religious vow as a pretext for not supporting mother and father, and in Matt 19:16-22 (and //s) where he affirms its validity to the "rich young ruler." In both cases Jesus is clearly addressing *adults* and emphasizing their duty to provide for elderly parents (see R. F. Collins 1986: 89-92).

With the Day of Pentecost the Spirit is poured out on all God's people without discrimination so that the prophecy of Joel is fulfilled: now is the time when not only "your young men shall see visions" but also "your old men shall dream dreams" (Acts 2:17 = Joel 2:28). The early church continued the concern of the OT and of Jesus for the elderly, especially for widows (Acts 6:1; 1 Tim 5:3-16, see 15-3.5b; Jas 1:27). The household codes deal with the relation between parents and children (cf. previous two sections), and this includes the obligation of adults to care for elderly parents (cf. R. F. Collins 1986: 92-95; J. G. Harris 1987: 85); see especially Eph 6:2-3, where the fifth commandment is quoted yet again.

19-3.3. SOCIETY

a. The Setting

The NT, written over a much shorter period of time than the OT, reflects a more limited range of economic and social conditions. Jesus' ministry takes place largely in the rural or small-town setting of Galilee, a small part of a Roman province. The later NT is set mainly in various cities of the eastern portion of the Roman Empire. Research into both these settings, aided by archaeological discoveries and sociological analysis, has shed much light on the *background* of the NT.

This setting reflects what is familiar from the latter part of the OT. As a small minority located within various provinces and cities of the Roman Empire, the early church had no power to influence economic and social policy. In its ethical decision making it had to work within strict parameters over which it had no control. As a religious community, however, it did enjoy a limited freedom to order its own life, not only in religious but to some extent in economic and especially social matters.

b. Economic Justice

i. The Source of Wealth

The NT assumes and accepts the OT understanding of God as the creator of all things and therefore as the one who provides the resources necessary to sustain life (see more fully, 2-3.1). In the NT, however, the focus shifts away from the Land as God's gift to Israel (see 13-3) to a more universal emphasis on the earth and its resources as God's gift to all humankind (see C. J. H. Wright 1983: 92-94). Sunshine and rain, the essentials for crops to grow, are God's gifts lavished on all humankind (Matt 5:45). The miracle of growth is something beyond human comprehension (Mark 4:27-28), and therefore something that comes from God. All the good gifts enjoyed by humans come from God above (Jas 1:17).

ii. The Production of Wealth

The NT, like the OT, recognizes that human beings are called by God to cooperate with him in using the resources he provides to create wealth for the good of all humankind. Hence, as in the OT, *work* is evaluated positively. The parables of Jesus frequently allude to employers and employees. It is assumed that everyone will work for a living and will be given the opportunity to work. In Luke 10:7 Jesus quotes with approval a popular proverb, "The laborer deserves to be paid." On the other hand, when work and the acquisition of wealth become the *sole* purpose of life, the results can be disastrous (12:16-21).

Unlike some sectors of Greco-Roman society (Schrage 1988: 230) but in line with the OT, daily work is given a very positive evaluation in the NT; "there is no suggestion of contempt for manual work as among the Greeks" (D. Guthrie 1981: 940). Jesus worked with his own hands as a carpenter (Mark 6:3): "hard, physical labor was not beneath the dignity of the Son of God" (Elwell 1988i: 2161). Peter worked as a fisherman (Mark 1:16), and Paul as a tentmaker (Acts 18:3; 20:34; cf. 2 Cor 12:14; 1 Thess 2:9). Faced with some for whom apocalyptic enthusiasm was a ready excuse for giving up work, Paul insisted that the Thessalonians "work with your hands, as we directed you" (1 Thess 4:11), and pointedly declares that "anyone unwilling to work should not eat" (2 Thess 3:10). Daily work obviously permits people to provide for themselves and not be a burden on others. Eph 4:28 adds a further motive:

"Thieves must give up stealing; rather let them labor and work honestly with their own hands, so as to have something to share with the needy."

The NT also views work in another light. While it is necessary and legitimate to work in order to provide for one's own needs and the needs of others, for believers the greatest satisfaction comes from doing the Lord's work. Jesus regarded his ministry as the "work" God had given him to do (John 4:34; 5:17; 17:4), and his followers are called to do "the work of the Lord" (1 Cor 16:10). Paul can speak of himself as "toiling" in God's service (Col 1:29), of associates as "fellow workers" (Phil 4:3 RSV; 1 Thess 3:2; cf. A. Richardson 1952: 31), and he calls on the Corinthians to excel in the work of the Lord "because you know that in the Lord your labor is not in vain" (1 Cor 15:58).

iii. The Distribution of Wealth

Faced with a society distorted by social and economic injustice, Jesus stands firmly within the OT Torah and prophetic traditions. He goes further, however, insofar as he claims that in a sense the kingdom of God is inaugurated in his ministry (see 1-3.1a). Jubilee themes (above, 19-2.3b) are echoed in the Gospels. Luke 4:16-30 tells of how Jesus, in the synagogue at Nazareth, read from Isa 61:1-2 (cf. also 58:6) and presented it as a manifesto for his ministry, albeit one that provoked a hostile reaction from the inhabitants of his hometown. The good news that is preached is the proclamation of "release" *(aphesis,* in LXX = *d^{e}rôr)* to the poor, the captives, the blind, and the oppressed. These terms are echoed throughout Luke, and indeed in all the Gospels. The promise of the Jubilee is fulfilled *now,* in Jesus' ministry: "Go and tell John what you hear and see: the blind receive their sight, the lame walk, the lepers are cleansed, the deaf hear, the dead are raised, and the poor have good news brought to them" (Matt 11:4-5//Luke 7:22). In his healings, in his exorcisms, and in his acceptance of sinners Jesus sets people free. "In Christ people are met by the healing, freeing, redeeming presence of God at their point of greatest pain" (Ringe 1985: 92).

Jesus, however, modifies the Jubilee theme in three significant ways. Firstly, he detaches it from the Land, a theme that figures nowhere in his teaching (see 13-3.2a; cf. Nicole 1997: 53). Secondly, he places it in the context of outreach to the Gentiles, thereby giving it a universal setting (Luke 4:25-27; cf. 12-3.1, and see Nicole, 54). Thirdly, he shifts the primary focus to release from sin. First and foremost Jesus brought liberation from sin *(aphesis* also means "forgiveness"). Sin can be pictured as a "debt" that is owed; Jesus brings the Jubilee that cancels these debts (cf. Matt 6:12, "forgive us our debts"; see also 18:23-35, the parable of the unforgiving servant). Nevertheless, having been ransomed, healed, restored, forgiven, Jesus' followers are to take his liberating power out into society. This includes a mandate to work for justice, to realize the aims and goals of the Jubilee.

This means that on the one hand Jesus shows a special concern for the "poor" that stands the piety-prosperity equation (16-1.3b) on its head. According to Luke 6:20, Jesus pronounced a blessing on the "poor"; according to Matt 5:3, on "the poor in spirit." The difference between these is not as great as might at first appear. Jesus recognized the special needs of those who were literally poor, those who were ill, those who were possessed, those who were the outcasts of society — in short, those who because they lacked wealth, power, and privilege were in a better position to recognize their own weakness and vulnerability and hence their need of God's help (cf. Ringe 1985: 50-64; Schrage 1988: 101).

On the other hand, it involves a condemnation of the rich. The rich are condemned where their riches are amassed at the expense of the poor. The parable of the rich man and Lazarus (Luke 16:19-31) shows a sympathy with the poor to match anything found in the Prophets, and with its grim reminder of the eternal consequences of behavior here on earth, it constitutes a clarion call for economic justice (see L. T. Johnson 1981: 15). But the rich are also condemned because, even more clearly than the prophets, Jesus sees how easily riches can become a false god: "Jesus is frankly pessimistic about the ability of men who possess wealth to escape being beholden to it" (Young 1962b: 819). "No one can serve two masters," he declares. "You cannot serve God and wealth (Gk. *mamōnas* = Aram. *mâmôn*)" (Matt 6:24//Luke 16:13; see Hengel 1974: 24; Schrage 1988: 102). Matt 6:19-21 demands a choice between earthly treasures and heavenly treasures: "For where your treasure is, there your heart will be also." In a memorable phrase Jesus declares that "it is easier for a camel to go through the eye of a needle than for someone who is rich to enter the kingdom of God" (Mark 10:25). Some have seen Jesus as demanding from all his followers a complete renunciation of property and wealth, and he certainly practiced such a renunciation himself (Matt 8:20//Luke 9:58). He counseled the rich young ruler to sell all that he had and give it to the poor, though the man found the demand too much and "went away grieving, for he had many possessions" (Mark 10:22). This advice, however, was directed to a particular person in whose case evidently riches had become an idol preventing him from putting God first (cf. Cranfield 1951: 309). On the other hand, Zacchaeus made restitution to all he had defrauded and gave half his possessions to the poor (Luke 19:1-10), thereby finding salvation — freedom from sin, and from selfishness. For the majority of his followers Jesus accepted the need for a moderate amount of wealth to provide for the necessities of life (cf. Hengel, 27). To all such Jesus gave two types of directions. Firstly, he sought to help people see wealth in proper perspective. The parable of the rich fool (Luke 12:16-21) underlines the transience of earthly riches. People are not to be consumed by anxiety about material things; if they get their priorities straight and seek God's kingdom and righteousness first, "all these things will be given to you as well" (Matt 6:25-33). Secondly, those who have the means are to give to the poor. Again and again almsgiving is commended (5:42; 6:2-4; Luke 14:13; 19:8). Jesus criticizes the abuse of tithing, not the practice itself (Matt 23:23; Luke 18:12).

The early church continued Jesus' attitude to riches. Excessive wealth is condemned as a false god (Rom 1:29; 1 Cor 5:10; Col 3:5; Eph 5:5; Rev 3:17). In 2 Cor 8 and 9 Paul sets out the principles of Christian giving: it is to be generous (8:2), in proportion to means (8:3), in response to Christ's giving of himself (8:8), voluntary (9:5), cheerful (9:7), and to the glory of God (9:13). It is not money but the love of money that is the root of all evil (1 Tim 6:9-10). James in particular continues the OT prophetic condemnation of the rich who acquire wealth by paying inadequate wages and spend it in luxury and pleasure (5:1-6); he condemns especially making distinctions within the local community favoring the rich at the expense of the poor (2:1-7). The general pattern is that of acceptance of moderate wealth when it is used in accordance with God's purposes. The sharing of wealth in the early Jerusalem community (Acts 2:44-45; cf. 4:32, 34-37) appears to have been spontaneous and voluntary (it is quite misleading to refer to it as a form of "communism"). In the short term it did not free the community from anxiety about riches (cf. 6:1), and in the long term it proved incapable of providing an adequate economic base for the community (see L. T. Johnson 1981: 119-32). Luke probably idealizes the earliest period, but in the NT as a whole it is not seen as a paradigm for later Christian communities (cf. Hengel 1974: 35; D. Guthrie 1981: 944). Jesus' call for freedom from anxiety about riches is continued (Phil 4:12-13; 1 Cor 7:30; 1 Tim 6:6-9), as is the charge to care for the poor (Acts 9:36; 10:2; 1 Tim 6:18; cf. Paul's collection for the Jerusalem church).

iv. Fair Dealing

The NT reinforces the OT's call for honesty and truthfulness in all human relationships. The ninth commandment, forbidding false witness, is reiterated by Jesus (Matt 19:18 and //s), and the condemnations of Jesus (Matt 26:60-61) and of Stephen (Acts 6:13-14) provide powerful negative paradigms of the consequences of false witness. Typically Jesus identifies the source of false witness in the heart (Matt 15:19) and calls for an absolute truthfulness in daily life that does not need to be backed up by the swearing of oaths: for the citizens of the kingdom their "Yes" should mean "Yes" and their "No" mean "No" (5:33-37; cf. Jas 5:12). Paul exhorts believers, "Putting away falsehood, let all of us speak the truth to our neighbors, for we are members of one another" (Eph 4:25), although he also reminds them of the necessity of "speaking the truth in love" (4:15).

c. Social Justice

In some respects there is an even greater tension in the NT than in the OT in the area of social ethics. The NT can be read in such a way as to suggest that the early church opposed social change. Slaves became Christians, but they remained slaves; women became Christians, but their inferior position in society did not change; Christianity accepted people of all races, but made no attempt to change racial attitudes in society generally. On the other hand, not only did Christianity accept the element in the OT that sees all human beings as equal in the sight of God; in the light of the Christ event it articulated a radically new vision of a society in which all are equal. This vision is grounded in the ministry of Jesus, who reached out and brought healing and salvation to all members of society, not least to those normally treated as outcasts. The theological understanding of this vision was worked out especially by Paul, and is most clearly expressed in the revolutionary ethical principle found in 1 Cor 12:13, Col 3:11, and in its fullest form in Gal 3:28: "There is no longer Jew or Greek, there is no longer slave or free, there is no longer male and female; for all of you are one in Christ Jesus." Since salvation depends entirely on God's grace made known in Jesus Christ, all human distinctions are relativized. The only requirement on the human side is faith, and the new community of the body of Christ is open to all on the basis of faith alone and accepts all believers into its fellowship on a basis of complete equality.

It can be argued that this vision did find expression, at least to some extent, within the early Christian community; the church made little or no impact on the wider society for the simple reason that it constituted a tiny minority within the Roman Empire with no more power to influence social policy than it had to influence economic policy. Nevertheless, within the NT itself there remains tension between the visionary and the pragmatic understandings of social ethics, and this fact raises difficult hermeneutical problems for Christian ethics that persist to this day.

Here we consider the three areas referred to in the formula of Gal 3:28: slavery, the status of women, and race and culture (cf. above, 19-1.3c).

i. Slavery

What the NT says about slavery has to be seen against the background of a Greco-Roman world in which the economy depended on slavery that existed on a massive scale (cf. Rollins 1976: 830; Longenecker 1984: 48-49). Jesus' mission, according to Luke 4:18-19 (quoting Isa 61:1-2), is to bring the Jubilee, "to proclaim release to the captives . . . to let the oppressed go free," and he brought healing to all, including slaves (Luke 7:2), on an equal basis. Paul articulates the basic principle that those who belong to the new Israel and to the new humanity are all equally sinners and equally in need of God's grace, so that human distinctions no longer apply. "For in the one Spirit we were all baptized into one body — Jews or Greeks, *slaves or free*" (1 Cor 12:13; cf. Gal 3:28; Col 3:11).

Nowhere in the NT, however, is there any call for the abolition of slavery. The expectation of the parousia may have played a role here, but the most important factor for Paul, and for the rest of the NT, was a purely pragmatic one. The church, a tiny community in a huge empire, had no power whatsoever to abolish slavery. Any moves in that direction would have branded the church as a subversive movement and threatened its very existence (cf. Longenecker 1984: 54). Thus most of the NT advice pertains to what to do given the situation that existed at the time. In 1 Cor 7:17-24 Paul applies to slaves his pragmatic principle: "Let each of you lead the life that the Lord has assigned, to which God called you." In the household codes (see 18-3.3f.) slaves are exhorted to obey their masters and to work honestly and well (Col 3:22-25; Eph 6:5; cf. 1 Tim 6:1-2; Titus 2:9-10; 1 Pet 2:18). In keeping with the distinctive Christian tone of the codes, the relationship is a reciprocal one, and in Ephesians and Colossians masters have duties to slaves: they are not to threaten them (Eph 6:9) but are to treat them justly and fairly (Col 4:1). Here again, all relationships are to be "in the Lord" and masters are to remember that they have to answer to a Master in heaven. Moreover, as in the case of other relationships, the instructions on masters and slaves are set in the general context of the need for all relationships to be governed by Christian love.

The most revealing light on the Christian view of slavery is shed by the letter to Philemon. Paul obeys the law by returning the runaway slave Onesimus to his master. Whatever Paul intended to happen to Onesimus, the really significant thing is that Philemon is urged to take him back "no longer as a slave but more than a slave, a beloved brother . . . both in the flesh and in the Lord" (Phlm 16). "Rather than engaging in a head-on confrontation with slavery, Paul sought to elevate the quality of personal relationships within existing structures of society" (Longenecker 1984: 59).

ii. The Status of Women

As in the case of the OT, there has also been widespread debate concerning the status of women in the NT. Here again we see a strong tension between the visionary and the pragmatic. The NT evidence has to be assessed in the first place against the background of Palestinian and Greco-Roman society, in which the role and status of women were generally severely restricted (Witherington 1984: 1-10; Kee 1992: 225-28; but see also Burrus 1992: 239-40; Longenecker 1984: 70-74). The early church was powerless to change that society, and it had to determine in a pragmatic way how to live within it.

But the early church also had a vision of the essential equality of male and female. That vision certainly had its origin in Jesus himself, and his attitudes and behavior toward women constitute the paradigm for Christians. Viewed against the background of contemporary society, says Schrage (1988), "Jesus' words and actions appear downright revolutionary . . . in word and in deed Jesus brought to an end the inferior status of women" (91). The Gospel narratives indicate that time and again Jesus spoke with women, healed them, and accepted them on an equal footing with men: the Syrophoenician woman (Matt 15:21-28//Mark 7:24-30) serves as a model of faith; Mary is the recipient of Jesus' teaching (Luke 10:39; cf. Stephens 1980: 34); the Samaritan woman is engaged in a long dialogue during which Jesus reveals his messiahship (John 4; cf. Dewey 1976: 69f.). "By the mere fact of granting women the right to learn the Good News of the Kingdom and to participate in his ministry, Jesus imparted to women a new dignity and role" (Longenecker 1984: 77; cf. Crook 1990: 184). Women play a major role in Jesus' parables (see Witherington 1984: 35-44). Women follow Jesus to the cross and play a key role in the resurrection narratives. This vision is implemented in part in the early church. An expanded role for women is emphasized particularly in Luke-Acts (Stephens, 106f.; Kee 1992: 233-35). It is noteworthy how often both men and women are mentioned as constituting the membership of early Christian congregations (Acts 5:14; 8:3; 9:2; 17:12).

There has been much controversy over the attitude of Paul to women, and some have seen him as the ultimate male chauvinist whose pernicious influence continues to this day. Others have argued that "Paul is early Christianity's greatest champion — second only to Jesus himself — in proclaiming full equality of the sexes in marriage and in the Church" (Cleary 1980: 82; cf. P. J. Ford 1975), though a verdict such as this is often qualified by the exclusion of the Pastoral Epistles (and sometimes 1 Cor 14:33-35) from the material regarded as Pauline (cf. Hall 1974). It is Paul who enunciates the basic principle that "there is no longer male and female" (Gal 3:28), and we have already seen how women ministered in the early church, especially in the Pauline congregations, though later this ministry was apparently restricted for pragmatic reasons (see 15-3.5b). Similarly we have seen how the advice to wives in the household codes, though set in a pragmatic framework, enshrines a vision of marriage based on mutual submission, enriched by love, and lived "in the Lord" (see 18-3.3f; 19-3.2d.i).

iii. Race and Culture

The NT world was divided along racial and cultural lines. Jews divided everyone into Jews and Gentiles; Greeks divided the world into Greeks and "barbarians," those who were culturally beyond the pale.

According to the NT, the Christ event inaugurates the new age; the time for the eschatological ingathering of the Gentiles has dawned, and the church is commissioned to make disciples of all nations (see more fully, 12-3). Christianity broke down the division between Jews and Gentiles, and people of all races and cultures were welcomed into the fellowship of the early Christian community. Jesus' attitude to Samaritans (considered by Jews as racially impure) shows his disregard for racial barriers (Luke 9:51-56; 17:11-19; cf. 11-3.5b); his parable of the Good Samaritan (10:25-37) redefines the term "neighbor" in a way that excludes all forms of national or racial prejudice. The book of Acts depicts the gospel spreading to people of many nationalities, with all persons being accepted equally on the basis of faith. This is underlined especially in Acts 8 where the gospel is accepted first by Samaritans, then by the black Ethiopian court official (cf. P. Frost 1991: 1). According to Paul, through his death Christ reconciled Jew and Gentile and "has made both groups into one and has broken down the dividing wall, that is, the hostility between us" (Eph 2:14). In the key text of Gal 3:28, Paul declares the basic principle that "there is no longer Jew or Greek." Paul underlines this in Col 3:11 by the addition to "Greek and Jew, circumcised and uncircumcised," of "barbarian, Scythian"; the Scythian was regarded as "the barbarian's barbarian" (Haselden 1964: 192), the extreme example of savagery. "By only a slight extension of the principle we may also say that the gospel lays on Christians the necessity of treating all people impartially, regardless of race or culture" (Longenecker 1984: 34). Another approach is found in Acts 17, where, in Paul's address to the Athenians, he says of God that "from one ancestor he made all nations to inhabit the whole earth" (v. 26). Here the essential unity of humankind is grounded not in redemption but in creation: all humankind, descended "from one ancestor," i.e., Adam, are equally created by God (cf. Haselden, 188).

It may fairly be claimed that in its acceptance of all races on a completely equal basis, Christianity brought something radically new. "In a world of widespread national mistrust and racial rivalries, the NT view of total equality stands out in stark contrast" (D. Guthrie 1981: 952).

Despite its overwhelming emphasis on the equality of all races before God, however, there is another aspect of the NT that came under increasing scrutiny in the second half of the twentieth century. The NT bears witness to a growing rift and to a growing hostility between the emerging Christian church and Judaism (see 11-3.2c). NT references to Jews and Judaism, it has been claimed, are either anti-Semitic or provided a ready platform for later anti-Semitism (see Cook 1991). Hence the NT itself harbors an implicit if not explicit form of racism, which had horrendous consequences in later centuries.

John's Gospel has been singled out, especially because of its use of the term "the Jews" *(hoi Ioudaioi)* to denote Jesus' adversaries (see more fully, 4-3.2a); many critical scholars see the Gospel as the product of a late-first-century Christian community in conflict with the synagogue. As early as 1 Thess 2:14, however, Paul can speak of the suffering of the early Palestinian Christian communities at the hands of "the Jews." Matthew's Gospel comes closest to the view that because of the Jewish rejection of Jesus as the Messiah, the church *replaces* Israel (see Hays 1996: 421-24). The verse most often cited as the basis for anti-Semitism is Matt 27:25, where "the people as a whole *(pas ho laos),*" in demanding Jesus' crucifixion, say, "His blood be on us and on our children!" Paul, on the other hand, wrestles with the problem of why so many of God's people have rejected the Messiah, but refuses to conclude that Israel has been ultimately rejected (Rom 9–11; see more fully, 11-3.2c).

As far as the death of Jesus is concerned, the NT makes it clear that historically this was brought about not by the Jewish people as a whole, but by a small group of Jewish leaders, and not least by the (Gentile) Roman governor, Pilate. The Jesus who was mocked, beaten, and tortured to death by Gentiles "is a *victim*, not a *protagonist*, of anti-Semitism" (Bromiley 1967: 549).

19-3.4. THE STATE

a. The Setting

Everything the NT says about the state has to be understood in terms of the Roman Empire; within this general context, however, three more specific political situations are to be distinguished.

Firstly, the ministry of Jesus and the earliest period of the Christian church (see Acts 1–8) are set in *Palestine,* an area ruled either by kings appointed by the Romans, such as Herod the Great and his son Herod Antipas (who ruled Galilee from 4 B.C. to A.D. 39), or directly by procurators (or prefects), as was the case with Judea for most of the period from A.D. 6 to 66. Judea, far too small to be a province on its own, was attached to the Province of Syria. Jesus could not be ignorant of or ignore the Sadducees and the Pharisees who each in their own way were prepared to accept the present political situation, the nationalists who advocated armed rebellion against the Romans, or the apocalyptic dreamers who tended to withdraw from society and await God's imminent intervention.

Secondly, as the early church expanded into the eastern Mediterranean basin, it encountered the state mainly in the form of local magistrates of cities granted limited self-government by Rome, and occasionally in the form of provincial governors. Christianity met with no official opposition from the empire because, at least until the mid-60s, the Roman authorities apparently did not differentiate clearly between Jews and Christians; hence Christians were able to shelter under the umbrella of Judaism, an officially recognized religion. It was during this period, however, that the nationalists in Judea found increasing support, a trend that culminated in the Great Revolt of 66-70, resulting in the capture of Jerusalem and the destruction of the temple. In the late 50s and early 60s, therefore, a movement originating in Palestine was bound to be viewed with growing suspicion.

A third period, beginning in the mid-60s, sees a radical change in the attitude of the state to the church, and is marked by sporadic and local persecution. Best known is the attack on Roman Christians under Nero in 64; the main evidence for this comes from the Roman historian Tacitus (*Annals* 15.44), but it falls well within the NT period. Further persecution of the church by Rome in Asia Minor (probably ca. 95 under Domitian) is the setting for the book of Revelation.

b. The Kingdom of God and the Kingdoms of This World

Virtually all scholars agree that Jesus' primary interest was not political; his task was to proclaim *the kingdom of God.* We have seen that while Jesus certainly affirmed a *future,* final, apocalyptic triumph of God's kingdom, what was most characteristic in his preaching and teaching was the claim that the kingdom was also *present* and was being inaugurated in his own ministry (see 1-3.1a). This kingdom is radically different from all earthly states. Jesus brings out the contrast when he says, "The kings of the Gentiles lord it over them; and those in authority over them are called benefactors. But not so with you; rather the greatest among you must become like the youngest, and the leader like one who serves" (Luke 22:25-26 and //s). The contrast is presented most sharply in John 18:36, where Jesus says to Pilate, "My kingdom is not from this world. If my kingdom were from this world, my followers would be fighting to keep me from being handed over to the Jews. But as it is, my kingdom is not from here." This does not mean that the kingdom of which Jesus speaks has nothing to do with serving God in this world; it does mean that his kingdom is not worldly in its *methods* (cf. N. T. Wright 1990: 13). The Sermon on the Mount (Matt 5–7) is generally seen as the manifesto of this "countercultural" kingdom (cf. 18-3.1b), and in relation to the state attention usually focuses on 5:38-48 (see Hays 1996: 319-29 on the interpretation of this key passage). Contrary to the OT *lex talionis* ("an eye for an eye, and a tooth for a tooth"), Jesus counsels nonresistance. Behind the prescriptions of 5:39-42 to turn the other cheek, give away your cloak, go the second mile, and lend freely lies the basic principle of nonretaliation. The passage climaxes in the call not to hate but to love one's enemies (vv. 43-48; on this, see Klassen 1984: 84-92). These verses constitute the climax of the "antitheses" of the Sermon on the Mount that make the laws of the Torah more demanding and that require of those who enter the kingdom "radical obedience" (see 18-3.2b.ii). Matching this is Jesus' call to forgive one's enemies, not seven times, but indefinitely (18:21-22; see Klassen, 29). Only through forgiveness and love can the vicious circle of hatred and violence be broken. Jesus' teaching on such matters is matched by his conduct: he himself consistently refused to use violence, and his counsel to forgive is matched by his own forgiveness of those who crucified him (on the treatment of enemies, see the fuller discussion in 4-3.2b).

The early church continued Jesus' teaching on nonviolence and nonretaliation as a code of conduct for believers. Christians are to seek to live in peace with all people — "if it is possible, so far as it depends on you, live peaceably with all" — and they are to refrain from vengeance (Rom 12:14-21; cf. Heb 12:14; 1 Pet 3:9-12).

c. Church and State

The Sermon on the Mount is addressed to Jesus' "disciples" (Matt 5:1), and with its radical demands produced only astonishment from the "crowds" (7:28). The key hermeneutical question is how this teaching of Jesus relates to the question of the state. Can the conduct that is required of those who enter the kingdom of God also be required of those who rule the kingdoms of this world? To answer this question we must avoid focusing narrowly on one passage and must consider the teaching of Jesus, and of the NT, as a whole. When we do this, it can be seen that the NT view of the state is in fundamental accord with that of the OT.

i. Firstly, *the state is seen as an institution ordained by God.* Jesus' view of the state comes closest to that of the Pharisees. The classic passage is found in Matt 22:15-22//Mark 12:13-17//Luke 20:20-26. When someone asked Jesus, "Is it lawful to pay taxes to the emperor, or not?" this was a trick question, for the extreme nationalists believed payment of taxes to the Romans was a betrayal of their national heritage. Jesus' response was to ask the questioners for a coin and ask whose image it bore. By producing the coin from their own pocket and answering "Caesar's," the questioners were forced by Jesus to admit that they carried and used Roman money; they took advantage of the law and order, peace and prosperity made possible by Roman rule. In saying "Render to Caesar the things that are Caesar's," Jesus in effect says that if the questioners take advantage of the benefits of Roman rule, they must be prepared to pay for them through taxation (cf. Cranfield 1962: 178; Schlier 1968: 231-32). Jesus' answer "affirms the validity of the claims of both Caesar and God upon the individual" (Crook 1990: 195); the state, even if it is a pagan one, has certain legitimate functions, and followers of Jesus owe the state a certain loyalty, though one that pales in comparison with the obligation to render to God the things that are God's.

Despite Jesus' call to his own disciples to practice nonviolence, the Gospels do recognize the right of *the state* to use arms to maintain law and order. According to Luke 3:14, John the Baptist gave advice to soldiers *(strateuomenoi)*, probably engaged more in police duties, thereby recognizing the validity of their role provided they did not abuse their authority. Jesus accepted a Roman centurion with no indication that he saw anything wrong with the man serving in the Roman army (Matt 8:5//Luke 7:2). In Matthew and Mark it is a Roman centurion who makes a key christological confession at the foot of the cross (Matt 27:54//Mark 15:39). Jesus' relationship to the state takes an altogether different turn in the passion narrative, yet even in this situation Jesus confirms that the authority of the state is God-given (John 19:11; cf. Barrett 1972a: 10-11).

Acts and the Epistles also show an appreciation for the state when it is carrying out its God-given task of maintaining order. The Roman centurion Cornelius is a notable example of a Gentile convert to Christianity (Acts 10–11), but, as in the case of Jesus' acceptance of a centurion, there is no hint of disapproval of the duties he carries out. Acts shows how Paul as a Roman citizen was able to travel freely in the empire without opposition by the Roman authorities, and in 23:16-35 we get a very favorable picture of the Roman officers who stepped in and used armed Roman soldiers to save Paul's life. In Acts one of Luke's purposes is to stress that the coexistence of the Roman state and the Christian church is a practical possibility (see Schlier 1968: 226; Barrett 1972a: 5).

The NT's positive assessment of the state finds clearest expression in Rom 13:1-7 (on Rom 13, see Bruce 1984; Furnish 1985: 117-34; Schrage 1988: 235-39; Lohse 1991: 132-34). As Furnish has argued, the immediate occasion for Paul's advice was probably his desire to disassociate the church from movements protesting certain Roman taxes around A.D. 58; Paul's main prescription is that Christians must pay all taxes (Rom 13:6-7). But, as many commentators agree, the passage also reflects Paul's personal experience, as a Roman citizen, of traveling through the eastern portion of the empire as a Christian missionary. Paul "shared the gratitude of most provincials for Roman peace, order, justice and administration, which had made possible his missionary journeyings, frequently rescued him from the violence of mobs, and often restrained social evils" (R. E. O. White 1979: 183). Paul's advice to the Roman Christians is: "Let every person be subject to the governing authorities; for there is no authority except from God, and those authorities that exist have been instituted by God." The word "authorities" *(exousiai)* here clearly refers to human authorities, i.e., the Roman government, as the injunction to pay taxes to them shows. In the NT, however, the term generally refers to the cosmic "principalities and powers" (cf. 4-3.5). Cullmann (1957) argues that Paul calls on believers to be subject to the "invisible powers" that lie behind the state, but only insofar as these powers have been subjected to Christ (see 65-70, 95-114; contra Bruce, 87-89). As long as these powers "remain in bondage to Christ . . . they stand in God's order. Therefore it is proper to be subject to them to the extent that they stay within their limits; for to that extent they are God's servants and have indeed sound judgment over good and evil" (Cullmann, 69). Thus, though the state belongs to this passing age, it is nevertheless God's servant (Rom 13:4 *diakonos;* Rom 13:6 *leitourgoi*). Paul recognizes two possible motives for obeying the state: one is fear of punishment, but the other is "because of conscience" (13:5), i.e., because one knows that this is the right thing to do. A similar view of the state underlies the reference in 2 Thess 2:6-7 to the "restraining" of the power of the "lawless one" presently at work in the world; the restraining power referred to here is almost certainly the power of the Roman Empire (cf. Bruce, 91, and see more fully, 4-4.4a). The same assumption underlies the direction in 1 Tim 2:1-4 that prayers be offered "for kings and all who are in high positions, so that we may lead a quiet and peaceable life in all godliness and dignity" (cf. also Titus 3:1). Similarly in 1 Pet 2:13-17 readers are told to "accept the authority of every human institution, whether of the emperor as supreme, or of governors, as sent by him to punish those who do wrong and to praise those who do right."

ii. Secondly, the NT affirms that *the power of the state is not absolute.* Jesus counsels giving to Caesar what is Caesar's, but very definitely not what is God's. He does not hesitate to speak of the divine judgment that will fall on a state that does not conform to God's way (cf. 3-4.3), nor does he hesitate to criticize a king by calling Herod Antipas "that fox" (Luke 13:32). The passion narratives show the state's abuse of its power; when the state brushes aside the question of truth (John 18:38), it oversteps the bounds of its legitimate authority and a horrendous miscarriage of justice results (see Schlier 1968: 215-24).

The opening chapters of Acts depict the earliest Jerusalem community in conflict with the same Jewish authorities that opposed Jesus. Peter and John were arrested and brought before the Sanhedrin, which attempted to silence them (4:1-18); Peter's response was to assert: "Whether it is right in God's sight to listen to you rather than to God, you must judge" (4:19). The same principle was reiterated by Peter after his second arrest and appearance before the Sanhedrin, when he declared, "We must obey God rather than any human authority" (5:29).

While Paul's advice in Rom 13 has often been interpreted as a call to unquestioning obedience to any state, however corrupt, this was clearly not his intention. "Paul's point is not the maximalist one that whatever governments do must be right and that whatever they enact must be obeyed, but the solid if minimalist one that God wants human society to be ordered; that being Christian does not release one from the complex obligations of this order; and that one must therefore submit, at least in general, to those entrusted with enforcing this order" (N. T. Wright 1990: 15). The passage makes clear that what Paul is talking about is basically a just state, one of the main functions of which is to restrain wrongdoing and maintain law and order (cf. Crook 1990: 197). It is authorized by God to "bear the sword" (Rom 13:4), the symbol of "the military power of Rome, which Paul knew was capable of putting down rebellion, keeping the sea lanes free of pirates and the highways free of brigands" (Furnish 1985: 128). The clear implication is that obedience is due to the state *only when it acts as God's servant.* "Paul is not thinking here of a case in which there could be a conflict of conscience in which the Christian could be compelled to choose between obeying God and obeying human authorities — in which case the Christian must choose the former" (Lohse 1991: 134).

Paul's teaching in Rom 13 is often contrasted with Rev 13, but the historical backgrounds of these two passages are completely different. Behind Rev 13 lies the demand of the state for worship of the emperor, and the claim of Domitian to be *Dominus et Deus,* "Lord and God" (see Schrage 1988: 343). When the state and the head of state put themselves in the place of God, they are no longer servants of God. The "powers" behind the state then become demonic and are intent on destroying the church, hence in Rev 13 the Roman Empire and the organization enforcing emperor worship are symbolized by beasts (cf. Cullmann 1957: 71-85; Schlier 1968; Talbert 1994: 51-59).

iii. What is to be *the response of God's people* when faced with an unjust state? It is clear that the NT, like the OT, does not counsel obedience to a state that fails to function as God's servant. A more difficult question, however, is whether it ever sanctions armed rebellion against a corrupt and unjust state.

In Jesus' day this was a major issue in Palestine. Despite some attempts that have been made to prove otherwise, the Gospels make it abundantly clear that Jesus totally rejected the revolutionary movement and its advocacy of armed rebellion (so Cullmann 1970; Hengel 1971; Klassen 1984: 96-102; contra Brandon 1967). Advice to go the second mile if pressed into service by the Romans (Matt 5:41) or to love one's enemies (5:44) would have been anathema to the revolutionaries. Jesus himself both preached (5:38-48) and practiced nonviolence, and declared that "all who take the sword will perish by the sword" (26:52). Individual texts must be seen in the light of the total Gospel context. In Matt 10:34, "I have not come to bring peace, but a sword," the sword is metaphorical, as the Lucan parallel clearly shows when it renders the text, "No, I tell you, but rather division," i.e., Jesus' message may even divide families (cf. above, 19-3.2, and see Hays 1996: 332-33). In Luke 22:36, "The one who has no sword must sell his cloak and buy one," the sword may again be metaphorical, or more probably refers to the carrying of a weapon for self-defense on long and dangerous journeys. Nor can the cleansing of the temple by any stretch of the imagination be pictured as an assault upon or occupation of the temple courts; this would have required a large armed force and would immediately have been strongly resisted by Roman troops stationed nearby (cf. Furnish 1984: 369).

There can be no doubt that behind the admonitions of Paul and Peter to be subject to the Roman state there lay a desire to disassociate Christianity from any revolutionary movements that advocated violence against the state. Even in the very difficult situation that lies behind the book of Revelation there is no hint of a "liberation theology" in the sense of justifying armed rebellion against a corrupt and oppressive regime. Believers are called upon to resist the state, but it is a *passive, nonviolent* resistance to which they are called, a resistance that will require some to be martyrs, a resistance that is inspired by faith in the final apocalyptic defeat of evil and triumph of God (see A. Y. Collins 1977: 246-52).

19-3.5. INTERNATIONAL AFFAIRS

On the relationship between the church, as the new Israel, and the nations of humankind, see 12-3. Here we focus on the NT view of war and peace.

a. War and Peace

If war be defined as armed conflict between sovereign states, then, in striking contrast to the OT, the NT has very little to say directly on this topic (cf. Crook 1990: 216-18). Jesus and the early church existed entirely within the bounds of the Roman Empire, and the issues that arise are therefore more those of church and state (see previous section) than of war and peace.

i. The Zealot Option

The question of the use of armed force in the NT arises primarily in relation to the nationalist or Zealot option advocated by those who called for an armed rising against Rome. From the point of view of Rome, this would be an internal rebellion against the state, though doubtless from the point of view of the Zealots it would be a war of liberation, in fact a new, divinely sanctioned "holy war."

We have already seen that Jesus totally rejected the Zealot option, and that while Paul did not advocate unquestioning obedience to the state, his advice to the church at Rome was motivated in part by a desire to disassociate the church from the Jewish nationalist movement that was gathering strength in the late 50s (see above, 19-3.4). It should be recalled also that while the NT sees Jesus as the fulfillment of the promise of a royal Messiah, that category is radically reinterpreted and shorn of all nationalist and military connotations (see 6-3.2, and cf. Enz 1972: 69-78). As a matter of history, what is known as either "The Great Revolt" or "The Jewish War" from A.D. 66 to 70 was a total disaster for the Jewish people. It provides a perfect example of Jesus' maxim that "all who take the sword will perish by the sword" (Matt 26:52); it resulted not only in the capture of Jerusalem and the destruction of the temple, accompanied by huge loss of life, but also in the total loss of political independence of the Jews for almost two thousand years.

The other side of the coin, however, is the NT's recognition of the right and indeed the duty of the state to restrain evil and anarchy and to uphold law and order, by force if necessary (above, 19-3.4c). It might be argued that the principles laid down in the NT would support Rome's maintaining an army to protect its borders from barbarian attacks and in this way maintain the Roman peace, but that NT principles would not support wars of aggression designed to enlarge its borders; these, however, are issues that simply do not arise in the NT.

ii. He Is Our Peace

The NT as a whole tackles the question of war and peace at a completely different level. War is basically one of the most horrific consequences of human sin. James puts his finger on the problem when he says, "What causes wars, and what causes fightings among you? Is it not your passions that are at war in your members? You desire and you do not have; so you kill. And you covet and cannot obtain; so you fight and wage war" (4:1-2 RSV). "The ultimate causes of war are not to be found in the social and economic circumstances external to man, but within man himself" (J. J. Davis 1993: 208). The message of the gospel is that sin itself has been dealt with through the atoning death and triumphant resurrection of Christ. His sacrifice accomplishes reconciliation between a holy God and a sinful humanity, and hence also makes possible reconciliation among all peoples, nations, and races of humankind (see 9-3.4b). Paul can say of Christ that "he is our peace" because he "has broken down the dividing wall" between Jews and Gentiles (Eph 2:14). It is this "gospel of peace" (6:15) that the church is called to take to the whole world (on the NT understanding of peace, see more fully 20-3.2).

iii. Love Your Enemies

Those who enter the kingdom and belong to God's people are called to be "peacemakers" (Matt 5:9). Their methods are not based on armed force, but on nonretaliation, nonviolence, forgiveness, and love of enemies (see above, 19-3.4b). While Jesus' teaching appears to envisage primarily the sphere of interpersonal relations, the underlying ethical principles are equally applicable at a national and international level.

b. The Weapons of Our Warfare

The OT "holy war" or war against the forces opposed to God reappears in the NT, transposed into a different key (cf. Toombs 1962b: 801). Jesus is seen as the leader of the forces of good, locked in battle with the forces of evil. A major theme of the Gospels is the war between Jesus and Satan and the demons (see more fully, 4-3.3b; 4-3.4b), a war that climaxes in the defeat of evil through the death and resurrection of Christ. By using language derived from the divine Warrior tradition, the NT is saying that "no enslaving power whether personal, societal or cosmic can ultimately stand before the triumph of the crucified and risen Lord" (Dearman 1983: 12).

This warfare carries over into the Christian church that is called, not to a literal warfare, but to the struggle with Satan and the powers of evil. Paul interprets the Christian life in terms of a war, though "we do not wage war according to human standards; for the weapons of our warfare are not merely human" (2 Cor 10:3-4). In Eph 6:10-17 Paul urges his readers to "put on the whole armor of God" for the battle against the cosmic powers of evil (cf. 4-3.5c). Military terminology is also characteristic of the Pastorals: Timothy is urged to "fight the good fight" (1 Tim 1:18) and be "a good soldier of Christ Jesus" (2 Tim 2:3).

New Testament: Consummation

19-4. NOTHING UNCLEAN SHALL ENTER

Only at the final consummation will all that is morally wrong and contrary to the will of God finally be eliminated. In his description of the holy city John says, "But nothing unclean will enter it, nor anyone who practices abomination or falsehood, but only those who are written in the Lamb's book of life" (Rev 21:27).

19-4.1. THE INDIVIDUAL

For the vision of the future of the individual in NT eschatology, see the discussion in 17-4.

19-4.2. THE FAMILY

In the NT visions of the final consummation the family unit fades from view and is replaced by a more corporate vision of the whole family of God; see more fully, 11-4.

19-4.3. SOCIETY

a. The Eschatological Reversal

The NT recognizes the gross injustices that prevail in society in the present age. It views these, however, in the light of the eschatological reversal that the new age will bring. The positions of rich and poor will be reversed in the world to come: Lazarus will be in the bosom of Abraham while the rich man will be excluded from the kingdom (Luke 16:19-26). In the coming age the rich man will fade away (Jas 1:9-11). The ideal to which the NT looks forward, however, is not an earthly paradise but a heavenly kingdom. Jesus' advice is not to focus one's life on the acquisition of more and more material wealth, but so to live that you lay up for yourself "treasures in heaven" (Matt 6:19-21//Luke 12:33-34; Matt 19:21//Mark 10:21//Luke 18:22).

b. The Great Jubilee

The book of Revelation reflects the pattern of the Jubilee in its structure that (excluding prologue and epilogue) is composed of seven sets of seven: seven churches (1:9–3:22), seven seals (4:1–8:1), seven trumpets (8:2–11:19), seven portents (12:1–14:20), seven bowls (15:1–16:21), seven visions (17:1–19:10), and seven judgments (19:11–20:15) (see L. L. Thompson 1969: 332-34). The final consummation that comes after these sequences (21:1–22:5), i.e., after 7 × 7 = 49, therefore marks the Jubilee, when all the powers that enslave human beings will be fully and finally defeated.

19-4.4. THE STATE

While the OT may look for the restoration of an ideal state in terms of prophetic eschatology, the NT vision of the final consummation is pictured in more apocalyptic terms. The period prior to the end will see the intensification of evil (cf. 4-4.2), and one form this will take is conflict between church and state, and the harassment and persecution of believers by the state (on this, see more fully 3-4.2). With the final consummation all earthly political regimes will come to an end and be replaced by the kingdom of God and the holy city of Rev 21–22, which is essentially a heavenly city (21:2). Yet there is not total discontinuity with what is best in the states of this world. The anticipatory vision of 11:15 declares,

> The kingdom of the world has become the kingdom of our Lord
>   and of his Messiah,
> and he will reign forever and ever,

and the concluding vision of the city illumined by God himself foretells that "the nations will walk by its light, and the kings of the earth will bring their glory into it" (21:24). This vision of the incorporation of what is best in the kingdoms of this world into the kingdom of God means that Christians see "not only the ultimate limitation but also the ultimate promise under which the states and governments of history stand" (Cranfield 1962: 192).

19-4.5. INTERNATIONAL AFFAIRS

a. Wars and Rumors of Wars

We have seen (4-4.2) that as the NT contemplates the future it warns that evil will increase rather than decrease in the period before the final consummation. It will be a time of "wars and rumors of wars" that will test the faith of God's people (Mark 13:7-13). In the vision of Rev 6:3-4 John sees a rider on a red horse take peace from the earth (cf. also 9:7-11). This is not to say that the NT condones war, but simply that it looks to the future with an honest and courageous realism.

b. The Last Battle

At another level the NT sees the battles between Christ and Satan continuing until the final consummation. History will culminate in a climactic struggle between the forces of good and the forces of evil (cf. 4-4.5). The Christ who will destroy the lawless one with the breath of his mouth (2 Thess 2:8) and lead the armies of heaven to victory over the beast (Rev 19:11-21) can indeed be seen as the divine Warrior (cf. Stevens 1983), but his weapons are not of this world. Christ is the one who, as the conquering Lion, will finally defeat the forces of evil. But it is never forgotten that his triumph comes through his sacrificial death; he is also the sacrificial Lamb (Rev 5:6).

19-5. LOVE YOUR NEIGHBOR: THEOLOGICAL REFLECTIONS

19-5.1. THE INDIVIDUAL

a. Reverence for Life

Many modern ethical dilemmas revolve around the life of the individual. Developments in medical science have brought issues such as abortion and euthanasia to the forefront of contemporary ethical discussion where they occupy a prominence that is certainly not accorded them in the biblical material. The identification of the basic biblical principles is therefore of paramount importance. The principles of the sanctity of each individual human life and that all life is in God's hands, it should be noted, are thoroughly *theological*. We can speak of "the sanctity of human life" or, in the phrase made famous by Albert Schweitzer, "reverence for life," but this terminology cannot be separated from its grounding in what the OT says about God. "There was in ancient Israel," Harrelson (1980) points out, "no notion of the sanctity of human life in and of itself. . . . Human life has its basic meaning in relation to God's own purpose for life and not in the sheer fact of life itself" (116). It will hardly be surprising if those who do not accept the basic theological beliefs underlying these principles arrive at ethical conclusions different from those who do. This raises difficult questions regarding how far Christians can expect or demand that a basically secular society be governed by Christian ethical standards.

b. Murder and Violence

The twentieth century probably saw more disregard for human life and for basic human rights than any previous century. The toll of human life, from the

Armenian massacres in the early part of the century, through the Holocaust, to the genocides in Rwanda, Kosovo, and elsewhere, is so horrendous that it numbs the imagination. Such events show that where there is no respect for God, there is no respect for human life, and they show too the power of evil that continues until the final consummation (cf. 4-4). The Christian community is called to witness to the sanctity of human life by teaching and example. Unfortunately, in history the church has used violence and murder for its own ends, for example, in the Inquisition. Even in modern times instances of physical and sexual abuse in church-run homes, as well as the tacit approval of policies of racism and nationalism that inevitably lead to violence, constitute some of the darkest stains on the church's witness to the world.

c. Abortion

The question of "abortion on demand" emerged in the closing decades of the twentieth century as one of society's most contentious issues, with rival groups supporting "prolife" and "prochoice" positions (see Grenz 1990: 135-38). The prohibition of murder and the biblical principles of the sanctity of human life and of all life being in the hands of God are certainly relevant here (cf. Harrelson 1980: 115-16), but they do not address the key issue of whether the fetus is to be regarded as a person (does life begin at conception or at birth?). There are, however, biblical texts that clearly portray God as active in the creation of human beings from the time of conception, and that regard the fetus as human (above, 19-1.1b.ii; 19-3.1b.ii; contra B. W. Harrison 1983: 70, who dismisses these texts and holds that "the ancient moral ethos reflected in Scripture is not always noble by our moral standards and has been superseded by a more adequate morality at some stages in later human history"). The fact that very early Christian writings outside the NT (*Didache, Epistle of Barnabas;* see J. J. Davis 1993: 119) explicitly condemn abortion may be seen as confirming that this is the correct interpretation of the biblical material. Scripture therefore provides no sanction for abortion on demand, the only exception being cases where the principle of the sanctity of the life of the unborn conflicts with an equally biblical principle, e.g., where the life of the mother is threatened. Abortion provides an excellent example of the community as a context for Christian ethics, as Hays's fine discussion shows (1996: 456-60). There are alternatives to abortion (cf. Crook 1990: 134), and the Christian community ought to be able to assist persons wrestling with this issue, and even more, ought to be willing to provide help and support to those who reject abortion but have difficulty coping with the consequences.

d. Suicide

In the Bible suicide is nowhere commended. It may fairly be argued that the precept forbidding the deliberate taking of human life applies here also (cf. Harrelson 1980: 120), and certainly the principle of the sanctity of human life is relevant. J. J. Davis (1993), who cites the cases of Saul, Ahithophel, Zimri, and Judas, contends that "every instance of suicide in the Bible is directly associated with the person's spiritual collapse" (170); nevertheless, it remains true that there is no specific biblical prohibition of suicide (cf. Young 1962a: 454). In the rare cases where suicide is recounted, it is seen not as an unforgivable sin but as a terrible tragedy. There is no biblical basis for the kind of condemnation of suicide found in later Christian tradition (see Clemons 1990: 75f.), nor for the denial of burial to suicides. Neither is there any basis for any encouragement of suicide, or for any "right" to take one's own life. In face of even the most terrible trials, the Bible urges not the taking of one's own life but patience, faith, and trust in the God who does not allow anyone to be tested beyond what he or she can bear. The Christian community must do everything it can to prevent suicide by addressing the conditions, especially in certain population groups (teenagers, native communities), that contribute toward this tragedy.

e. Euthanasia

Another of the most contentious of modern ethical issues is "euthanasia" (*eu* = "good"; *thanatos* = "death"), whether in the form of "assisted suicide" (providing the means whereby a person can take his or her own life) or of "mercy killing" (the deliberate ending of another person's life), in cases where someone is so seriously ill or injured or suffering that there is no reasonable prospect of recovery. Paradoxically, modern medical science has in some ways increased the chances of a prolonged if not also painful death (see Crook 1990: 144-45). Since there is minimal reference to this subject in the Bible, a decision must be made on broadly based biblical principles rather than by appealing to specific texts (see Erickson and Bowers 1976). The problem is that such principles may conflict. Those who favor euthanasia see it as an act of mercy and appeal to the biblical portrayal of God as a God of mercy and especially to Jesus as a paradigm of compassion for the sick and suffering (see Duntley 1991; Gula 1995: 36-40). But against this must be placed the principle of the sanctity of human life, and especially the belief that to decide who may and who may not live is in effect to "play God"; Scripture does not support the modern view that people are autonomous beings who have a right completely to control their own destiny (see Gula, 8-20). Texts that speak of God enabling believers to endure trials and sufferings are also relevant. In practice, the decision as to how to balance these principles may be an agonizing one. On the basis of the biblical material the dominant principle would seem to be the sanctity of human life, though many Christians believe that Scripture is not at odds with the distinction between "active" and "passive" euthanasia: it is wrong to administer medication or treatment designed to bring about a person's death, but it is not wrong in extreme cases, where there is no hope of recovery, to withhold extraordinary treatment or procedures designed merely to prolong physical life (see Duntley, 1135; Gula, 21-32). In all cases Scripture would support the view that every effort should be made to relieve human pain and suffering.

f. Prochoice or Prolife

Ethical conduct is possible only where there is a choice to be made. Nevertheless, the Bible does not support the "right" to choose life or death for oneself or another; its concern is with discerning and doing God's will. The biblical viewpoint can much more readily be described as "prolife," and the point is well made that this ought to involve not only opposition to all forms of the denial of the right to life, but also positive action to preserve life (e.g., medical research, improved sanitation, preventative medicine, highway safety, gun control, etc.; cf. Granberg 1982: 563).

19-5.2. THE FAMILY

a. The Centrality of the Family

Family life at the turn of the millennium is frequently declared to be "in crisis" or "under siege." For some, the phrase "family values" has become a matter of mockery and derision, and traditional standards and values are being challenged in an unprecedented way (cf. Crook 1990: 102-6). In the Bible, however, as we have seen, the family occupies a central place, grounded as it is in the created order as well as in God's revelation to his own people.

b. Sexuality

Closely linked to its view of the family is the biblical estimate of sexuality as one of God's gifts, something to be celebrated (above, 19-1.2a), yet also something to be enjoyed and used in accordance with the will of God. Christian sexual ethics have suffered untold harm from dualistic views (probably gnostic in origin) that infiltrated the church in the early centuries, leading to a devaluation of the human body and human sexuality, the linking of the sex act to the transmission of original sin, and the elevation of celibacy as a lifestyle superior to marriage for those who would be truly "religious." Over the centuries Christian attitudes to sex have often been legalistic, hypocritical, and lacking in compassion. If such views continued through Victorian times, the twentieth century saw the pendulum gradually swinging to the opposite extreme with the church, in some cases, compromising its ideals in conformity to pressures from an increasingly permissive society. BT and biblical ethics have an important role to play in helping the Christian community articulate a healthy and balanced sexual ethic based on truly biblical principles rather than on conformity to the latest trends in contemporary society.

c. Marriage

In its view of sexual relations the Bible recognizes only two valid options: marriage or celibacy (cf. Grenz 1990: 43). The NT views celibacy as a possibility that some may choose, recognizing that this is God's will for them. Celibacy may free some persons to devote themselves wholeheartedly to the Lord, in which case it is to be accepted as a gift from God, though it is in no sense a superior way. The norm for the majority of people, however, is marriage, defined as a lifelong monogamous union. All other forms of premarital or extramarital sex are seen as contrary to the will of God. These are high standards, and they may well run counter to what is "natural" to many people. They are not presented in Scripture, however, as an "ideal" simply to aim at, but as a standard attainable with God's help that promotes the happiness and well-being of both individuals and society. As R. F. Collins (1986) points out, "the different outcomes of the encounter between Joseph and Potiphar's wife (Gen 39) and that between David and Bathsheba (2 Sam 11) indicate well that human sexuality is not an awesome force over which man has no control." These stories "clearly proclaim that man is responsible for the way in which he uses his sexuality" (167). When people, including members of the church, fail to live up to these standards, they must be treated with kindness and compassion, and assured of God's forgiveness and redeeming power that is always available to those who repent. But faithfulness to biblical norms will not allow compromising of the standards themselves.

d. Divorce

The biblical *ideal* of marriage is the lifelong union of one man and one woman. As an example of pragmatic ethics, however, divorce is tolerated and regulated in the OT, though nowhere commanded or commended. Malachi sets forth the basic principle that marriage is a lifelong covenant (2:14-16), and Jesus reaffirms this as the will of God (Mark 10:2-12; cf. 1 Cor 7:10-11). However, in a striking example of diversity, if not of contradiction within Scripture, Matthew twice quotes Jesus' saying on divorce with the "saving clause" (19-3.2d.ii). Many critical scholars solve the problem by assuming that the Mark/Paul version is the earliest and the authentic one; the Matthean version is a product of the early church, which found Jesus' absolute prohibition of divorce too demanding and softened it (Soulen 1969: 448-49; Stock 1978: 24-30). The change may have been influenced by rabbinic debates on the subject. Those for whom such an explanation is not acceptable have spent much ingenuity trying to reconcile the two sets of texts (see Keener 1991: 28-31). Perhaps *porneia* refers to premarital sex, only discovered after the marriage (cf. Marshall 1975: 506); or perhaps it refers to marriage within the prohibited degrees (Garland 1987: 425). Some Christian traditions see the Matthean sayings as sanctioning separation (but not divorce, and therefore not remarriage). These explanations seem forced, and it is best to recognize the existence of two traditions in tension with one another. In one Jesus declares the absolute divine will: divorce is not part of God's will or intention. This is the basic principle, seen in terms of visionary ethics. The other tradition reflects the pragmatic side of NT ethics. While divorce is contrary to God's will and is to be avoided if in any way possible, nevertheless there may come a point when a marriage has obviously broken down completely and where, as an exception to the general rule, divorce may be permitted as the best thing that can happen in the circumstances (see Grenz 1990: 109-10). In such cases remarriage is possible, even for the so-called guilty party (cf. J. J. Davis 1993: 89-90; contra Keener, 37, 49, 109); Jesus' attitude to sinners provides a paradigm whereby forgiveness and a fresh start are always possible, conditional on true repentance. In other words, this is a prime example of the visionary-pragmatic dialectic in NT ethics (cf. 18-3.1f). Willingness to recognize divorce as a tragic necessity must not deflect attention from the Bible's vision of marriage as a lifelong union, especially in the situation prevailing in some Western societies where close to 50 percent of marriages are destined to end in divorce. Christians need to emphasize that marriage is a God-given institution, to ensure that those entering marriage receive wise counseling and adequate preparation, and to provide, through the Christian community, ongoing support to couples and families (cf. Hays 1996: 372).

e. Homosexuality

This topic does not warrant a separate discussion on the basis of the relatively few biblical references, but in the latter part of the twentieth century it became a highly contentious and divisive issue, particularly in relation to the ordination of practicing homosexuals, in part because it constitutes a crucial test case on the authority of Scripture (see Bonnington and Fyall 1996: 5). Although much still remains unclear about the causes and nature of homosexuality, today a clear distinction is drawn between homosexual *orientation* and homosexual *behavior*. It is widely accepted that for some people (variously estimated at from 3 to 10 percent) homosexuality is an innate trait over which they have no control. In reaction to widespread discrimination and laws against homosexuals, some modern secular states are moving in various ways to grant them "equal rights" (see Crook 1990: 117-20). The Bible knows nothing of the modern distinction between orientation and behavior. What it clearly condemns is homosexual *practice*. For Christians who advocate the recognition and even the blessing of homosexual unions, two approaches are possible. One is to question the biblical evidence, or to claim that it does not refer to "committed" relations between consenting adults. The other, perhaps more honest approach is to acknowledge, as e.g. Bartlett (1977) does, that "all the specific texts which mention homosexual practices in the Bible condemn those practices," but to hold that "a literal interpretation of Scripture is an [in]adequate guide to Christian ethical conduct — an unchristian guide in fact" (141-42; cf. Sheppard 1985). On this approach the modern view that homosexuality is an innate trait takes precedence; for some, homosexuality is "natural," and failure to treat practicing homosexuals equally, in the state or in the church, constitutes a denial of basic human rights. The problem here is that the key biblical passages are ethical in content and context, and are clearly intended as *precepts* to be followed. If these precepts are rejected, it may be argued, why not, for example, approve incestuous relationships between consenting adults, providing that they are loving and provide "self-fulfillment"? No one can choose his or her orientation, but people can choose their behavior. Biblical standards are not based on doing what is "natural"; they often demand behavior that is contrary to sinful human nature and that requires (with God's help) great self-discipline. As Grenz (1990) points out, "ethics is not merely a condoning of what comes naturally. . . . Even though some researchers conclude that males are naturally promiscuous, this supposedly natural inclination does not set aside the biblical ethic of fidelity" (206). Those therefore who hold that biblical norms take priority in ethical matters see homosexual *practice* as contrary to the will of God, though it is no worse a sin than any other. The Christian community, if it follows biblical guidelines, will cleanse itself of any homophobia that singles out one group in society and treats them with discrimination and even violence; to those of homosexual orientation who elect the biblical prescription of celibacy, it will offer complete acceptance; to those who do not conform to the biblical standard, it will hold out the gospel offer of forgiveness and redemption (as it must to all humankind), and it will offer help and support to persons who face extremely difficult choices regarding their lifestyle (see J. G. Taylor 1995: 4-9; Hays 1996: 400-403). Here again, in the context of modern secular states, Christians cannot impose their demanding ethic on society as a whole, but they do have a right to uphold and practice their own standards.

f. Family Relationships

From time to time critics have accused Jesus of subverting the OT view of the family, believing this view was reinstated in early Christianity, especially in the household codes (cf. I. Ellis 1985: 173). But as we have seen (19-3.2), Jesus' "hard sayings" on the family are not to be read in isolation but are to be balanced by others that show his deep appreciation for the family. Jesus does teach that the family is not an ultimate good in and of itself; families can be highly selfish and inward-looking units (even the Mafia has its own "family values"!). The challenge today is to apply the biblical principles in such a way as to encourage and support the development of truly *Christian* families.

This raises difficult hermeneutical problems. Scripture does reflect in part the surrounding society that was generally "patriarchal," with the husband as the head of the house, the wife expected to be submissive to her husband, and the children expected to be submissive to parents. Nevertheless, this is not the whole picture. In the OT we see a vision of loving relationships between husband and wife and parents and children, based on mutual love, understanding, and respect. This vision emerges more clearly in the NT, not least because of Jesus' own attitude to women and children. Despite their pragmatic aspect, the household codes' teaching on family relations is to be seen primarily in terms of their distinctive emphases on mutual obligations and mutual submission, conducting all relationships "in the Lord," and infusing these relationships with Christian love. The codes must also be seen in their total canonical context. In Gen 1 and 2 man and woman are created equal, for partnership with one another; it is the entry of sin in Gen 3 that distorts this relationship and brings about the subordination of women (v. 16). In Christ sin is overcome and God's original intention that marriage be a "community of equality and mutuality" is restored (see Tetlow and Tetlow 1983: 41-83). Where this underlying principle is recognized, and where family relationships are truly "in the Lord" and controlled by Christian love, all forms of abuse, violence, dominance, and coercion are completely precluded. Social and economic changes in the twentieth century opened up new possibilities for family life, and the church is challenged to discover new models for family living (cf. Ruether 1983), based on the application of the basic biblical principles in new and changing circumstances.

g. The Elderly

In biblical times the elderly generally survived as part of an extended family, or not at all. The situation envisaged is therefore considerably different from that which prevails today, at least in most Western societies, where the elderly are encouraged to live on their own as long as possible, and when that is no longer the case are often cared for in institutions (seniors' homes, nursing homes), something that did not exist in biblical times. Nevertheless, the basic biblical principles remain valid: the strong condemnation of all forms of abuse (physical or mental) of the elderly, and the strong emphasis on the obligation of adults to care for their aged parents so that not only are they provided with the necessities of life, but they are also treated with dignity and respect. Churches have often led the way in providing homes for the elderly, and many continue through such homes to exercise a valuable ministry to those in their declining years. From a biblical perspective, however, the isolation of the elderly from the rest of society is far from ideal. Believers are challenged to find ways of integrating the elderly into church and society, thus anticipating in the present the prophetic vision of the new age that will be marked by intergenerational harmony (above, 19-2.2).

19-5.3. SOCIETY

The Bible, and especially the OT, has a great deal to say about the economic and social aspects of society, but most of it seems so remote from the "global village" of the third millennium, linked by jet planes and the Internet, with its economies increasingly dominated by multinational corporations and its pressing social problems, that many, even Christians, see the Bible as having little or no relevance to the contemporary situation. On the other hand, basic human nature does not change, and when we discover that the Bible does deal with such issues as, e.g., the use of natural resources, finding satisfaction in one's work, the oppression of the poor, the status of women, and racial discrimination, it does not seem quite so remote.

There is, of course, no question of directly transposing biblical directions to the very different economic and social conditions of today (see J. G. Janzen 1973). But the Bible does embody ethical principles that can be applied in changed circumstances. This, of course, involves the Christian community in the difficult and exacting task of analyzing and seeking to understand the economic and social problems of today, then of deliberating as to how biblical principles can and should be applied in present circumstances.

Ethical norms in this area are found primarily in the Torah, in the Prophets as they applied the basic principles of Torah to the concrete situations of their day, and to a lesser extent in Wisdom. It is true that much of the material applies to Israel in its life in the Land. But Israel can be seen as a paradigm of the Christian community that is open to all nations, and indeed of the whole human community. As C. J. H. Wright (1983) says, "We are justified . . . in taking the social and economic laws and institutions of Israel and using them as models for our own ethical task in the wider world of modern-day secular society. In the economic sphere, the Old Testament paradigms provide us with *objectives* without requiring a *literal* transposition of ancient Israelite practice. . . .

But at the same time the paradigmatic approach compels us to wrestle seriously with the texts themselves in order fully to understand the models we are seeking to apply" (89). The NT accepts the basic principles of the OT but reinterprets them in the light of the Christ event that inaugurates the kingdom of God and the Jubilee, even if it realistically acknowledges that economic and social justice can only be imperfectly realized this side of the final consummation.

a. Economic Justice

The fundamental biblical principle in this area is that just as the Land was God's gift to Israel, so the whole earth is God's gracious gift to human beings who are but stewards of what is entrusted to them. There are no such things as "natural resources," only God-given resources that are to be used in accordance with God's will for the mutual benefit of all humankind. The Bible recognizes the private ownership of property, but "property is always held in trust and . . . people are responsible to God for the use they make of property" (Crook 1990: 230). This of course runs totally counter to the outlook of so much of modern secular society which assumes that the earth is there to be exploited. Even when the need for conservation is recognized, the motives are still essentially selfish.

The consistent biblical view is that "the possession and careful use of private property is not against God's order of things. . . . Only the arrogance, idolatry, and selfish use of wealth are condemned in Scripture" (Kaiser 1983: 220). The biblical attitude towards wealth is basically one of moderation: "the avoidance of extremes of wealth and poverty is a consistent, recurring biblical mandate" (Blomberg 1999: 68; Blomberg's study of "a biblical theology of material possessions" takes its title *Neither Poverty nor Riches* from Prov 30:8).

The Bible sees work not as a tiresome necessity but as a calling from God, and it affirms the value of all useful and productive work. It does not directly address the modern problem of unemployment, nor the complex problems of labor-management relations, but it may be said to be in keeping with biblical principles to affirm the right of all persons to work, to receive a fair return for their labor, and to enjoy both fair working conditions and adequate rest (cf. C. J. H. Wright 1983: 69, 80; Crook 1990: 239-41). The NT stresses the value of doing the work of the Lord: some of the greatest satisfaction in life is to be derived from *voluntary* work, in the service of the church or of fellow human beings in need.

It is in regard to the distribution of wealth that biblical principles clash most radically with the assumptions that underlie almost all modern economies. Both Old and New Testaments consistently call for the sharing of wealth with the less fortunate members of society. The NT urges generous voluntary giving rather than setting rules; many Christians find the OT principle of the tithe a helpful guideline (see Blomberg 1999: 248). In the capitalist economies of

Europe and North America, to varying degrees some provision is made to assist the economically disadvantaged, yet wealth is very unevenly distributed and a huge and widening gap still separates rich and poor. On a world scale the end of colonialism in the twentieth century did not see an end to the economic exploitation of the Third World. The gap between rich (and nominally Christian, or ex-Christian) and poor countries widened, with much of the Third World mired in unpayable debts. The exodus paradigm, the laws of the Torah, the protests of the Prophets, and the attitude of Jesus all combine to proclaim a God who is on the side of the poor and the oppressed, and who calls his people to a radical critique of contemporary society and to a firm commitment to economic justice.

The Christian response has often been debated in terms of "evangelism" or "social (and economic) action." Liberal churches de-emphasized or abandoned evangelism to focus on a "social gospel" and medical/educational/economic aid. Conservative churches focused on evangelism at home and abroad, and greatly neglected social action. From the point of view of biblical ethics, this is a false polarity. Whatever the church does is to be done in the name of Christ and as a witness to the gospel, yet such witness is meaningless unless it is translated into practical care and concern for all who are in need (see the discussion in Sider 1981: 45-68).

It is easy to despair of ever implementing biblical principles in the harsh realities of today's dog-eat-dog economic world. The church is called at least to embody these principles within its own community as an example to the world. But it is called also to reach out into that wider world. A project such as Jubilee 2000 shows that even the most idealistic biblical principles such as the forgiveness of Third World debt can be seen as a realistic and humane alternative to the existing situation.

The call for honesty and truthfulness in all relationships is also one that goes against the grain of much that is taken for granted in the modern world. Not only in courts of law, but in every sphere from advertising to politics (cf. Harrelson 1980: 144-45), Christians are called to expose false witness and to show an example of truthfulness in action.

b. Social Justice

We have noted in the OT, and especially in the NT, a considerable tension between the pragmatic and the visionary approaches to social ethics. Even when we recognize the radical nature of the principle embodied in Gal 3:28, it must be noted that this vision can be interpreted in two ways (see Stendahl 1966: 32-35). One way consists of affirming that in the light of the Christ event all persons are equal "in the sight of God" *(coram Deo);* this does not mean, however, that they are to be accorded equality within the structures of the church, and still less within the structures of society. The other interpretation affirms that equality means little or nothing unless it does find expression in the structures of the church and ultimately within the structures of society, and that the church therefore, as and when opportunity arises, is called to translate its vision into structural change.

It may be argued that the NT church followed the first way, though it can be urged that it did this from necessity, not conviction. But the matter is not so simple. Of the three relationships in Gal 3:28, Paul focused most of his attention on "Jew and Greek," and, as Stendahl (1966) argues, "there can be no doubt that Paul did everything in his power to apply this principle in the actual life of his congregations" (33). He insisted, for example, in the dispute with Peter at Antioch (Gal 2:11-14), that it was *not* enough simply to acknowledge that Gentiles could be admitted to the church; racial equality had to be *real* and it had to be translated into practice in terms of table fellowship. Paul did affirm and probably practiced equality of men and women within the church, though historically it seems that these gains were largely relinquished in the late NT and following period as the church found it pragmatic to conform to the standards of surrounding society. Slaves were accepted as equals within the Christian fellowship, but the first-century situation made anything beyond this impossible.

Nevertheless, the NT vision remained. The equality of Jew and Greek was implemented (after a struggle) in the early church (though the later church was capable of relapsing into racism). The equality of slave and free had to wait until the eighteenth and nineteenth centuries. The struggle for equality of male and female was still in progress at the end of the twentieth century.

c. Slavery

Slavery may not be considered a major ethical issue today, though it must not be assumed that slavery no longer exists, either in its traditional form or in the guise of forced labor, child labor, and forced prostitution: "modern slaves might be children weaving carpets" (Ucko 1997: 6). The issue has particular significance, however, as a *test case in hermeneutics* that dominated much ethical discussion in the nineteenth century (cf. Swartley 1983; K. Giles 1994). It provides one of the clearest illustrations of the need to distinguish between pragmatic and visionary ethics.

The OT accepts slavery, yet, as noted above, the institution is significantly modified, not only by provisions for the humane treatment of slaves, but by underlying theological and ethical principles that point toward equality and freedom. The OT attitude to slavery is at least potentially revolutionary (cf. Wolff 1973: 260), though it may be going too far to say that "it sowed a seed which in later times did contribute to its final and universal abolition" (Van der Ploeg

1972: 87). That seed is found rather in the NT, which lays down the basic ethical principle that in Christ there is neither slave nor free. The letter to Philemon illustrates both sides of the biblical tension. At one level it is pragmatic, since Paul returns the runaway slave to his master, yet it also sets forth basic theological and moral principles (cf. W. J. Richardson 1968). The designation of a slave as a brother lays the foundation for the ultimate abolition of the institution of slavery; the tragedy is that it took so long for Christians to implement the NT vision.

d. The Status of Women

In the course of the twentieth century, changing social patterns, a growing awareness of the many forms of discrimination suffered by women, and the emergence of the women's liberation movement (see Crook 1990: 174-83) resulted in the question of the role and status of women becoming a major issue in BT. This is an example of how a contemporary issue has prompted a fresh look at Scripture and a reevaluation of the biblical evidence. The rise of feminist theology, often seen as a form of liberation theology (see Spohn 1996: 68-76), has raised some serious questions regarding biblical teaching and biblical hermeneutics. Of particular significance has been the belated entry into the field of women biblical scholars who have brought fresh perspectives and have advocated new approaches (cf. Sakenfeld 1975: 223; see also Perdue 1994: 197-227).

It has to be conceded that the OT reflects in pragmatic fashion the prevailing patriarchal social norms, but only up to a point. As noted above (19-1.3c.ii), at least some patriarchal interpretation has been read *into* the text. Within the NT itself there is clearly a tension between passages which affirm the principle of equality in Christ and those which provide evidence that (for pragmatic reasons) implementation of this principle was limited (see esp. 1 Tim 2:9-15). The task of the contemporary interpreter of Scripture is not simply to quote texts in isolation, but in effect to do what the NT writers do: determine the basic principles that arise from the gospel, and then seek to determine how these principles should be applied in the very changed circumstances that face Christians today (cf. R. K. Johnston 1978: 236-39; cf. Boucher 1969: 50). Of the three pairs of relationships in Gal 3:28, it is in the area of the full equality of the sexes that the church has been slowest to implement the basic biblical principle.

e. Race and Culture

At the dawn of the third millennium it unfortunately remains true that in many parts of the world ethnic and cultural minorities find themselves subject to stereotyping, to prejudice, to discrimination, and even to horrific forms of violence such as ethnic cleansing and genocide (see Crook 1990: 152-61). It is even more unfortunate that sometimes professing Christians are involved in promoting and perpetuating such attitudes and actions. The Bible teaches the equality of all people before God (see Crook, 165-68), and it is one of the great tragedies of Christianity that a movement that initially broke down the barriers not only between Jews and Gentiles but also among all races should later in its history be tainted by racism. Two forms of racism in particular have claimed a basis in Scripture.

Prejudice against *blacks,* as noted above, is completely unbiblical. The view that Ham, or one of his sons, was black and cursed by God is not found in the Bible, but unfortunately it is found in rabbinic Judaism, from whence it passed into medieval Christianity, where it was revived in the fifteenth and sixteenth centuries and used to justify black slavery and the slave trade (see P. Frost 1991: 3, 9-10). Even after the abolition of slavery, continuing antiblack racial prejudice, discrimination, and segregation remain one of the worst blots on the witness of Christianity.

The question of whether the NT provides a basis for later *anti-Semitism* is more difficult. The NT texts have to be read against the background of Jewish persecution of the early church (Gal 1:13; 1 Thess 2:14), which could result in imprisonment (Acts 4–5) and death (Stephen: Acts 6–7). We must remember also that Jesus himself, all the earliest Christians, and all the writers of the NT (with the exception of Luke) were Jews. The conflicts reflected in the NT still took place within a Jewish context, so that the NT criticisms of Judaism (like those of the OT prophets) were essentially still criticism *from within* (cf. Hays 1996: 429). If Jesus attacked the Pharisees, it was because he sympathized with them and felt that they of all people should be ready to respond to his message. Even after his conversion Paul continued to identify himself as a Pharisee (Acts 23:6; cf. Phil 3:5). John's Gospel comes from a Jewish-Christian community. The problem is that in later centuries, when the church had become overwhelmingly Gentile, the writings of the NT came to be read in an *anti*-Jewish fashion.

The failure of the majority of the Jewish people to accept Jesus as Messiah caused a variety of reactions within the early Christian church. The NT believes that God has chosen the church rather than the Jewish people as his instrument to take the message of salvation to all humankind, but that does not mean that he has abandoned the Jewish people. In his agonizing discussion of this matter in Rom 9–11 (see more fully, 11-3.2c), Paul's final word is his belief that "all Israel will be saved" (11:26). Hays (1996) has proposed that Paul's position "ought to be judged determinative for Christian attitudes and actions toward the Jewish people, and that the other New Testament writings must be either interpreted or critiqued within this Pauline framework" (430).

Strictly speaking, neither the NT nor the later church (at least until modern times) can be accused of "anti-Semitism"; the opposition to, and even hatred of, Jews was based on *religious* and not *racial* motivation. This does nothing to lessen the horrors of the Crusades, when Jews in Europe and the Holy Land were slaughtered as "Christ-killers," or the subsequent horrors of the Inquisition. Christian anti-Judaism, further exemplified in Luther (cf. his 1542 tract *Concerning the Jews and Their Lies*), contributed to the ghettos of Europe and the pogroms of Russia, and provided the climate in which anti-Semitism in the strict sense could arise and flourish. Nietzsche (1844-1900) and Houston Stewart Chamberlain (1855-1927) provided the "scientific" basis for the racial anti-Semitism that led to Nazism and the Holocaust, and that persists to this day in "Holocaust denial," vandalism of synagogues, attacks on Jews, and so on.

Nowhere does Scripture justify racial or cultural prejudice or discrimination; it views all peoples as equal in God's sight — equally sinners in need of grace, and equally called to be part of a new humanity. The church is called to repent of the racism it has so often harbored and promoted, and to embody the biblical norm of a truly interracial society (cf. Hays 1996: 441).

19-5.4. THE STATE

Most modern states, e.g., Western democracies, represent very different forms of government from those encountered in Scripture, and obviously modern political problems cannot be solved by quoting individual biblical texts. Yet it must not be concluded that the Bible is irrelevant to the relationship between believers (or the church) and the modern state (see Crook 1990: 198-204). Every passage in Scripture that refers to the state has to be read in the first instance against its historical background. Since that background varied drastically over the centuries, the first impression of the biblical view of the state is one of great diversity, and clearly great care has to be taken in applying biblical texts to modern situations (cf. C. J. H. Wright 1990: 9). Yet each passage has also to be read in relation to the canonical whole, and it is precisely attention to the historical backgrounds that permits the perception of at least certain consistent broad principles that lie behind the biblical view of the state, principles that continue to be applicable today.

Firstly, the Bible *does not sanction withdrawal from the state*. The OT is basically world-affirming, not world-denying, and in it we find people from Joseph to Daniel who are called to serve pagan states, though only within certain limits. Although in the NT there is a greater awareness of the powers of evil at work in the world and in the state, the NT does not counsel monastic withdrawal or the abrogation of all responsibilities to the state. The believer has an obligation to "render to Caesar the things that are Caesar's," and where circumstances permit, this may include "informed participation in the process of the making and the enforcing of laws and policies" (Crook 1990: 199). Christians are called to serve God in the real world, and the Bible knows nothing of the adage that "religion and politics don't mix" (cf. N. T. Wright 1990: 11).

Secondly, the Bible recognizes that *the state has God-given powers and authority*. It is "one of the provisions made by God for the well-being of his creation" (Barrett 1972a: 19). According to Scripture, "the bearers of political power exercise the functions of the office not on the basis of its having been founded and agreed upon by human beings, but by God's will — whether they are aware of it or not" (Lohse 1991: 131). At this point the biblical view that the authority of the state derives from God is in sharp contrast to much modern political philosophy, according to which the authority of the state derives from the people.

Thirdly, *the state does not have an absolute power;* it retains its authority only when it carries out its God-given functions and serves the good of those it governs. As noted above, a consistent principle runs through both OT and NT; the biblical understanding "of the authority of the state recognizes that no human authority is absolute. All authorities are ultimately subject to God, from whom their authority derives" (J. J. Davis 1993: 192). Governments are called by God to "rule rightly" and keep God's law (*Wis* 6:4); they are God's servants for "good" (Rom 13:4), sent by God "to punish those who do wrong and to praise those who do right" (1 Pet 2:14). "The state's task is . . . first and foremost to defend and promote what is good. Besides upholding justice and promoting what is good, the organs of the state are charged with protecting its citizens against what is evil. The state, in other words, has the function of maintaining order and preventing chaos" (Schrage 1988: 237). The state exists to restrain anarchy and evildoing, and to promote peace, prosperity, and the welfare of its citizens. Both Jesus himself and the later NT recognize that the state has a right and a duty to employ force when necessary so as to maintain the order without which the life of the state could not continue. It is in this context that biblical writers from Jeremiah to Paul call on believers to cooperate with the state, even if it is a pagan one: God can work through a Babylonian or a Roman empire. Even in a modern secular state, therefore, believers have a duty to pay their taxes, and where possible and appropriate to participate in the political process.

The duty of the state to maintain order stands in tension with Jesus' teaching on nonretaliation and nonviolence and with his call to love and to forgive enemies; yet both these emphases are found within canonical Scripture, and both must be affirmed by BT. The Bible recognizes the sinfulness of human nature and the violence that is so deeply ingrained in human beings. Through the institution of the state, God works to restrain evil and violence and create the conditions that make all life, including the life of the church, possible. According to Paul, "it is God's purpose that the state should, by restraining the chaotic tendencies of men's self-assertion, maintain those outward conditions under which the Gospel may be preached to all and sundry without hindrance" (Cranfield 1962: 179-80). Insofar as the kingdom of God is a present reality, it is embodied in a community that is called to deal with human sin through the proclamation of the gospel, and through preaching and practicing love, forgiveness, reconciliation, and nonretaliation, for only so in the long run can the vicious circle of violence and hatred be broken. Church and state therefore each have their God-given tasks and their own spheres of service.

Fourthly, the Bible warns that *when the state goes beyond its God-assigned limits and authority, it may become demonic.* Cullmann in particular has shown how the apparently different NT attitudes toward the state are by no means contradictory. Believers are urged to render to Caesar what is Caesar's and to be subject to the governing authorities, so long as the state is basically just and carrying out its God-assigned tasks. But when the state exceeds these limits, the church is called upon to exercise a prophetic function and provide a critique of the state. We see this not only in the OT prophetic critique of the state, but also in the NT where only what is rightfully Caesar's is to be rendered to Caesar. The Christian approach to the state will be informed by the biblical understanding of human nature that recognizes how easily and how often individuals and groups act out of selfishness and self-interest. The advice to be "subject" *(hypotassō)* to the governing authorities (Rom 13:1; Titus 3:1) cannot, in the total NT context, be taken to mean blind, unquestioning obedience. "That, whenever the civil ruler's commands conflict with the commandments of God, the Christian 'must obey God rather than men' (Acts 5.29) is in the New Testament everywhere presupposed" (Cranfield 1962: 182). Scripture knows nothing of the principle that "religion and politics don't mix"; it encourages and demands a prophetic critique of the state when the state transgresses its God-given limits. When the state not only exceeds these limits but (as in the situation that lies behind Revelation) claims the ultimate loyalty and total obedience of its subjects, that is to say, claims not only what is Caesar's but also what is God's, then the situation changes drastically. When the state becomes, in modern terminology, "totalitarian," when it ceases to be the servant of God and becomes demonic (cf. Schlier 1968: 235), then believers must resist and are justified in disobeying the state (see the discussion in J. J. Davis 1993: 196-98, "Criteria for Justified Acts of Civil Disobedience").

The duty of Christians to become involved in political action and actively to oppose an unjust state has been powerfully articulated by various forms of "liberation theology" which have contended that "the God of the Bible wants to be understood, and wants to be obeyed, in political, economic terms" (J. H. Yoder 1985: 59). Such an approach can be accepted only with reservations. Liberation theology in practice has made considerable use of Marxist thought and has frequently advocated some form of state socialism. The experience, e.g., of Eastern Europe under Communism does not suggest that this is the best route to a just and humane society, and in any case, biblical authority cannot be invoked to support one particular political system. Some (though not all) forms of liberation theology have advocated carrying resistance to a corrupt and unjust state to the point of armed rebellion. Historically such action has often been seen by Christians as justifiable (as a last resort). While there are undoubtedly paradigms for this in the OT, it is difficult to see how the principles underlying the NT sanction this option for believers.

Thus, while Scripture does not advocate any particular form of political government, it does provide certain basic principles capable of being applied in widely varying circumstances.

19-5.5. INTERNATIONAL AFFAIRS

The issue of war and peace poses a major issue for biblical ethics. The twentieth century saw more wars than any other previous century, and advances in science and technology have simply increased the power of nations to maim and injure and destroy their enemies. Fear of a nuclear conflict may have been a deterrent to a third world war, but has in no way diminished the myriad of local conflicts.

The earlier part of the OT clearly sanctions war as a means toward the conquest and defense of the Promised Land. We are not dealing here with institutions, such as slavery, polygamy, and divorce, that are to be accepted in pragmatic fashion as inevitable, even though they are not commanded or required by God. In the OT God is the divine Warrior who not only destroys the Egyptian army at the Red Sea but *commands* Israel to exterminate the Canaanites (Num 21:3; Deut 20:17-18) and utterly destroy the Amalekites (1 Sam 15). The wars against Israel's enemies are "holy wars" or "wars of the LORD." Against this, of course, has to be balanced the prophetic critique of later wars and the splendid prophetic visions of a new age when nations will beat their swords into plowshares.

Basically, however, the biblical evidence has to be interpreted in terms of "progressive revelation." The norm for Christians has to be found in the NT where the "holy war" of the OT becomes a type of the battle between good and evil, where the "divine Warrior" is the Christ who dies on a cross forgiving his enemies, and where God's people are called to fight against evil and injustice, not with worldly weapons, but with "the whole armor of God."

This does not solve the difficult problems that arise in the modern world. When we are faced with forces of evil and injustice on an international scale (e.g., as in the rise of Hitler and the Nazis), is war always wrong, or is the use of force to restrain evil permitted and even required as a last resort?

The so-called pacifist approach focuses on Jesus' teaching in the Sermon on the Mount and makes a powerful appeal to Jesus himself as a paradigm; it counsels in effect withdrawal from participation in the state and the bearing of an often costly witness to the way of nonviolence (see the challenging discussion in Hays 1996: 339-44). This tradition has a long and noble history, exemplified in groups such as Mennonites and Quakers that have made notable contributions to peace.

What has been the majority tradition has problems in taking Jesus' teaching literally and especially in transposing it to the international scene (cf. J. J. Davis 1993: 210-13). The key hermeneutical question is whether Jesus' teaching on nonviolence can be applied to states, especially those in the modern world that are to all intents and purposes secular. Clearly Christians must do all they can to promote international goodwill and understanding, and to remove the global injustices that are so often the causes of war. Wars are always evil, and always involve the suffering and death of innocent civilians as well as combatants. The issue remains, however, as to whether there may be situations in which going to war may be *the lesser of two evils;* i.e., whether there may be such a thing as a "just war," or rather a "justified war" (cf. Crook 1990: 218, and the discussion entitled "The Just War Tradition" in Davis, 214-18). Granted that it is only too easy for a nation to "justify" war, and that many so-called just wars have not in fact conformed with the criteria for a just war laid down by Augustine and others, nevertheless there may be situations where war can act to restrain an even greater evil.

The NT, as we have seen, does understand the state as having a God-given right and duty to restrain evil by force, if necessary. The problem has always been how to transpose this function to the international scene, though the second half of the twentieth century saw at least halting efforts to do this under the auspices of the United Nations ("peacekeeping" has been notably more successful than "peacemaking"). The NT obviously requires Christians first and foremost to work and pray for peace, to oppose oppression and injustice that are the basic causes of war, and in their own life as the church to model a world community that transcends national barriers. It cannot be said, however, that as a canonical whole Scripture rules out the use of force by the international community, as a last resort, to restrain evil in extreme cases such as aggression, genocide, and ethnic cleansing.

CHAPTER 20

Life

Old Testament: Proclamation

20-1. THE LAND OF THE LIVING

A "way," by definition, always leads to a destination, and in Scripture the Way of the Lord leads to *life* — life that, according to the NT, will be experienced in its fullness only beyond death, but also a quality of life that God's people experience in the here and now. One of the most surprising things about the OT is how little it has to say about life after death. Its attention is focused on what it frequently refers to as "the land of the living." "The Bible," Brueggemann (1985a) has said, "offers us a way of understanding the world in a fresh perspective, a perspective that leads to life, joy and wholeness" (9).

20-1.1. THE AFFIRMATION OF LIFE

According to the OT, God is the giver and sustainer of human life (*chayyîm* = "life"; *chāyāh* = "to live"). When God created the first human being out of the dust of the ground, he "breathed into his nostrils the breath of life *(nishmath chayyîm)*" (Gen 2:7), and all life depends on the sustaining power of God's Spirit (Job 34:14-15; cf. Piper 1962b: 125). Human life, however, is limited, and each person has his or her allotted span (see below, 20-2.1, 2).

Again and again in the OT this life is seen as a wonderful gift bestowed by God, and above all as a gift that is to be *enjoyed*. Long life is certainly prized (e.g., Prov 3:16; 1 Kgs 3:10-14) and is sometimes seen as a reward of the righteous (see below, 20-2.2d), but the emphasis is generally much more on the *quality* of life. "To the Israelites . . . the sheer vitality, concreteness and diversity of life were a source of the utmost delight" (Link 1976: 478). True life is more than length of days, prosperity, and material blessings: "One does not live by bread alone, but by every word that comes from the mouth of the LORD" (Deut 8:3). It is "the living God" (5:26; etc.) who gives meaning to life, and "life in its fullness is possible only through union with God" (Schmitt 1981: 500).

The Torah presents people with the way to life, by which it means life in the here and now: "You shall keep my statutes and my ordinances; by doing so one shall live" (Lev 18:5). Torah confronts people with a choice: "See, I have set before you today life and prosperity, death and adversity. If you obey the commandments of the LORD your God . . . then you shall live" (Deut 30:15-16). This passage goes on to spell out what "life" means: "I have set before you life and death, blessings and curses. Choose life so that you and your descendants may live, loving the LORD your God, obeying him, and holding fast to him; for that means life to you" (30:19-20). In other words, fullness of life is found primarily in fellowship with and obedience to God. In 32:46-47 Moses exhorts the Israelites diligently to observe all the words of the Torah, for, he says, "This is no trifling matter for you, but rather your very life."

The Prophets also present people with the way to life:

> For thus says the LORD to the house of Israel:
> Seek me and live. (Amos 5:4)

Jeremiah repeats the Deuteronomic call to choose either the way of life or the way of death (21:8). According to Ezekiel, repentance and obedience will deliver a wicked person from death, and this is what God desires: "Have I any pleasure in the death of the wicked, says the Lord GOD, and not rather that they should turn from their ways and live?" (18:23; cf. 18:28; 33:14-16).

Wisdom too claims to be "a tree of life to those who lay hold of her" (Prov 3:18), and whoever finds Wisdom finds life (8:35; see "Wisdom as the Path of Life" in Clements 1992: 77-80). Wisdom offers practical guidance for living a happy and fulfilling life in this world, though it does not forget that the fear of the LORD is the beginning of wisdom (cf. 18-1.3b). For the psalmist God is "the fountain of life" (Ps 36:9), and true life is to be found in God's word (119:93).

20-1.2. PEACE

Life in its fullness is characterized by "peace" or *shālôm,* a word that is extremely difficult to translate into English. The root meaning is "completeness" or "wholeness" (verb *shālēm* = "be complete, be sound"), and *shālôm* can mean health, security, well-being, and salvation as well as peace. It thus denotes something much more than simply the absence of conflict. "The fundamental idea is totality. . . . Anything that contributes to this wholeness makes for *shalom.* Anything that stands in the way disrupts *shalom*" (D. J. Harris 1970: 14). *Shālôm* is basically a gift from God, not a human attainment (cf. Launderville, Tambasco, and Wadell 1996: 709). "I will grant peace in the land," says God, "and you shall lie down, and no one shall make you afraid" (Lev 26:6; cf. Pss 4:8; 29:11). The Aaronic blessing (Num 6:24-26; see below, 20-1.4c) calls upon God to grant its recipients "peace," which overlaps in meaning with "blessing"; here "peace" seems to be used "in the widest sense to include every divine blessing," and it "combines the supreme good of fellowship with God with the blessings of earthly life" (Eichrodt 1967: 358).

Individuals can certainly experience *shālôm* in the OT (cf. Good 1962c: 705). The psalmist is confident that God

> will deliver my soul in *shālôm*
> from the battle that I wage. (Ps 55:18 RSV)

Keeping the commandments of Wisdom will bring "length of days . . . and abundant *shālôm*" (Prov 3:2). "Peace" is used as a greeting, either in meeting someone — "Peace be to you" (1 Sam 25:6) — or in parting from someone — "Go in peace" (1:17) — because the greatest thing one person can wish for another is God's peace.

But in the OT *shālôm* is almost always *communal* rather than merely individual, for peace exists only when God's people live in a harmonious relationship with God, and with others. "If an individual has *shalom*, he has health, wholeness, soundness and integrity. As he lives in harmonious relationship with his family, this contributes to *shalom*. The wider the covenant of peace extends, the more all-inclusive is *shalom*" (D. J. Harris 1970: 18). God's covenant with his people is a "covenant of peace" (Isa 54:10) because it is the framework within which Israel can live in a harmonious relationship with God. In other words, "Shalom describes the intactness and well-being of a community" (Duchrow and Liedke 1989: 114). In worship this comes to expression in the "peace offering" *(shelem)* where sacrifice and a common meal symbolize right relationships with both God and one's fellow worshipers (see 14-1.5b.ii).

Peace can mean the end of hostilities (Judg 21:13) or the absence of war (1 Sam 16:4-5), and in some cases can refer to material well-being; in Jer 33:6 and Ps 73:3, for example, the NRSV translates *shālôm* as "prosperity" (cf. P. B. Yoder 1987: 11-13). More typically, however, *shālôm* involves harmonious relationships, and thus a condition of true peace is obedience to God:

> O that you had harkened to my commandments!
> Then your peace would have been like a river. (Isa 48:18 RSV)

"Great peace have those who love your law" (Ps 119:165). A number of scholars have quite rightly drawn attention to the strong emphasis, especially in the Prophets, on the fact that *peace cannot coexist with injustice* (see Brueggemann 1976b: 18-19; Yoder, 13-15; Duchrow and Liedke 1989: 120-21). Thus Jeremiah condemns those who are "greedy for unjust gain," saying,

> They have treated the wound of my people carelessly,
>> saying "Peace, peace,"
>> when there is no peace. (6:13-14)

When obedience is lacking, *shālôm* is destroyed, so that God can say in Jer 16:5, "I have taken away my peace from this people." In particular, *shālôm* is often linked to the two closely related terms "righteousness" *(ts^edhāqâ)* and "justice" *(mishpāṭ)* (on these, see 18-1.4). Where there is no justice, there can be no true peace (Isa 59:8; cf. Zech 8:16). In relation to peace in this sense, God's people are called to be proactive; they are to

> depart from evil, and do good;
>> *seek peace, and pursue it.* (Ps 34:14)

Paradoxically, peace is both a gift that only God can bestow and a task to which his people are called (cf. Brueggemann, 85-94).

While peace can be enjoyed by God's people now, it will be experienced in its fullness only in the promised new age. God's purpose for the future is to bring good, not evil, to his people: "I know the plans I have for you, says the LORD, plans for welfare *(shālôm)* and not for evil, to give you a future and a hope" (Jer 29:11 RSV). OT eschatology, however, it will be recalled (see 4-2), expects not gradual progress toward peace but rather an intensification of the opposition to God, so that the age of peace lies only beyond the final defeat of evil and all the powers opposed to God (see 19-2.5b). At the end, when God bestows his promised salvation, "he will speak peace to his people" (Ps 85:8). One of the titles of the Davidic Messiah is "Prince of Peace" (Isa 9:6), and Ps 72 (interpreted as a messianic psalm; see 6-2.2) prays of the messianic king: "In his days may righteousness flourish / and peace abound" (v. 7). Ezekiel looks forward to a "covenant of *shālôm*" that God will make with his people in the new age (34:25; 37:26; cf. 11-2.3); God's peace will encompass even the created order, and God's people will sleep securely knowing that they will experience "showers of blessing." In one of Isaiah's greatest visions, the eschatological outpouring of the Spirit is linked with both the renewal of creation and the establishment of justice and righteousness, the result of which will be true *shālôm;* he looks for a time when

> the Spirit is poured upon us from on high,
>> and the wilderness becomes a fruitful field,
>> and the fruitful field is deemed a forest.
> Then justice will dwell in the wilderness,
>> and righteousness abide in the fruitful field.
> And the effect of righteousness will be peace,
>> and the result of righteousness, quietness and trust for ever.
>>> (32:15-17 RSV)

20-1.3. HEALING

A common threat to fullness of life, and even to life itself, is sickness. The OT is never concerned simply with the "spiritual" state of individuals, but rather with their total well-being. It regards the all-round health of the individual, within a healthy society, as a most important part of God's gift of life.

The OT refers to a great variety of illnesses, but it is not always possible to make an exact medical identification (Wolff 1974: 143-44). There are graphic descriptions of the experience of illness (e.g., Job 33:19-22), especially in the psalms of lament (e.g., Ps 41:5-7, which describes the pain not only of physical distress but also of social rejection).

The Torah provides guidelines for the life of God's people in all its aspects, including public health. While this legislation is primarily cultic, it also embodies "preventive medicine" to a certain extent (cf. R. K. Harrison 1962: 542-46). The institution of the Sabbath, for example, constitutes a recognition that "the body requires regular periods of rest" (543). Laws relating to food and water, to washings, and to sanitation would help prevent disease.

One strand in OT thought connects illness with sin (cf. 16-1.5b). In the classic statement of the piety-prosperity equation in Deut 28, the terrible consequences of not obeying the Lord include various diseases: "The LORD will strike you on the knees and on the legs with grievous boils of which you cannot be healed, from the sole of your foot to the crown of your head" (v. 35; cf. vv. 21-22, 27-29; Lev 26:16). The same point is frequently made in narrative: Miriam is punished with "leprosy" (Num 12:10); the people are punished by a plague (Num 25). Prayers for healing often assume a connection between illness and guilt:

> There is no soundness in my flesh
>   because of your indignation;
> there is no health in my bones
>   because of my sin. (Ps 38:3)

Suppression of guilt and failure to confess sin can sap health and strength:

> When I declared not my sin, my body wasted away
>   through my groaning all day long. (32:3 RSV)

But running contrary to this line of thought, as in the case of suffering generally (see 16-1.5c), is another which refuses to accept the simple formula that wickedness leads to ill health, and conversely that those who suffer disease are necessarily being punished by God. This issue is a major one in Job (see Seybold and Mueller 1981: 59-60, 78-85; and cf. 16-1.5c), and the Satan, in his second attempt to break Job, "inflicted loathsome sores on Job from the sole of his foot to the crown of his head" (2:7). The wording clearly echoes Deut 28:35, and

Job's "friends" were quick to draw the obvious, but wrong, conclusions. The reader knows that Job is upright and that the illness is a test of Job's faith that God permits. The Servant of Isa 53 is described in terms that suggest a physical affliction; his contemporaries deemed him "stricken, struck down by God, and afflicted" (v. 4), but the song reveals that he suffers not for his own sins but for the sins of others (cf. Seybold and Mueller, 76-78).

There are only a few traces in the OT of another possible cause of illness: the operation of evil powers. Saul's illness is ascribed to "an evil spirit" that is nevertheless said to be "from the LORD" (1 Sam 16:14-16). 2 Sam 4:4 reminds us that natural causes could also be recognized: the fact that Mephibosheth was a cripple was due to an accident when his nurse dropped the five-year-old boy.

Whatever the cause of ill health, the OT generally proclaims the LORD as the healing God: "I am the LORD who heals you," God assures the Israelites (Exod 15:26; cf. Deut 7:15), while Ps 103:3-4 blesses the LORD as the one

> who forgives all your iniquity,
>> who heals all your diseases.

Psalms of lament frequently end by giving thanks for deliverance from ill health (e.g., Pss 32; 116; cf. 107:17-22). Narratives such as the cures of Naaman (2 Kgs 5) and of King Hezekiah (20:1-11; Isa 38) demonstrate God's healing power. Little is said about the limits of healing, but obviously there were cases where healing was not in accordance with God's plan, and this simply had to be accepted. In 2 Sam 12, for example, David prayed for his infant son when he fell sick, yet the child died and David had to accept this (vv. 20, 23; see 17-1.5c.iv). There are times when sickness simply has to be endured:

> The human spirit will endure sickness;
>> but a broken spirit — who can bear? (Prov 18:14)

Lev 19:14 accepts the existence of people with disabilities, and forbids mistreating them: "You shall not revile the deaf or put a stumbling block before the blind."

In the OT, belief in God as the one "who heals all your diseases" might be seen as excluding recourse to any form of human medical assistance. In 2 Chr 16:12-13 we read of the severe illness of King Asa that resulted in his death: "His disease became severe; yet even in his disease he did not seek the LORD, but sought help from physicians." As Clements (1992) points out, "This report is one of the relatively few to indicate that there existed in Israel a class of physicians which was separate from the cultus. It further demonstrates that to resort to such persons for help was looked upon as a betrayal of loyalty to the Lord God of Israel, and so was viewed as a form of apostasy" (71). It may be argued, however, that Asa is condemned not so much for seeking the help of doctors as for failing to seek the help of the LORD. It is noteworthy that in the case of King Hezekiah, while he in the first place prayed to God for healing, his recovery also involved the application of a poultice to the boil (2 Kgs 20:3, 7); this suggests that seeking God's help is not incompatible with using whatever medical techniques are available (cf. Wolff 1974: 145).

Practical commonsense wisdom, based on experience and observation, leads to life and hence also to healing. Proverbs knows the importance of avoiding stress in personal relations:

> A tranquil mind gives life to the flesh,
> > but passion makes the bones rot (14:30);

the value of a sense of humor:

> A cheerful heart is a good medicine,
> > but a downcast spirit dries up the bones (17:22);

and above all the need to put God first:

> Fear the LORD, and turn away from evil.
> It will be a healing for your flesh
> > and a refreshment for your body. (3:7-8)

It was doubtless this practical approach to healing that led the Wisdom tradition to welcome new developments in medical science when these became available in the Hellenistic period (see Seybold and Mueller 1981: 98-100; Clements 1992: 92-93). *Sir* 38:1-15 reflects a Hellenistic background and has a very positive evaluation of both the medical and pharmaceutical professions. God is the source of healing, but he uses doctors and confers on them the gift of healing:

> Honor physicians for their services,
> > for the Lord created them;
> for their gift of healing comes from the Most High. (vv. 1-2)

Likewise,

> the Lord created medicines out of the earth,
> > and the sensible will not despise them. (v. 4)

When someone is ill, the first thing to do is to pray to the Lord for healing (v. 9), but then "give the physician his place" (v. 12). Doctors (as well as patients) pray to God for success in diagnosis and in healing (v. 14). There is thus no incompatibility between praying to God for healing and enlisting the services of the medical profession.

While God's healing power can be experienced in the present, it will be manifested in a special way in the messianic age:

> On that day the deaf shall hear
> > the words of a scroll,
> and out of their gloom and darkness
> > the eyes of the blind shall see. (Isa 29:18; cf. 32:3-4)

35:5-6 adds to the cure of the deaf and the blind the healing of the lame and the dumb:

> Then the eyes of the blind shall be opened,
> > and the ears of the deaf unstopped;
> then the lame shall leap like a deer,
> > and the tongue of the speechless sing for joy.

In Ezekiel's symbolic eschatological vision of paradise restored (see 13-2.3), the life-giving stream from the new temple produces all kinds of trees, the leaves of which will be "for healing" (47:12).

20-1.4. BLESSING

A comprehensive term for God's goodness to people in this life is "blessing" (*bᵉrākhâ* = "blessing"; *bārakh* = "to bless"; see Mowvley 1965: 74); the word may mean either the conveying of a gift or the gift itself. Blessing is in fact understood in the OT in a fourfold way.

a. The LORD, Our God, Has Blessed Us

God is the source of every blessing, and in his grace and goodness he blesses his people. "I will command my blessing upon you," he promises (Lev 25:21 RSV). In the OT blessing often refers to material blessings, especially when these are part of the continuing flow of life: birth of children, fertility of crops and herds, defeat of enemies, long life, health and happiness. The opposite of "blessing" is "curse" (*qᵉlālâ* = "curse"; *'ārûr* = "cursed"), and this involves all kinds of material disasters. "An essential part of the covenant God made with Israel at Mt Sinai was the promise of blessings for keeping the covenant and curses for breaking it" (Elwell 1988c: 560), and nowhere is this more dramatically illustrated than in Deut 28, which first lists the blessings that will come upon God's people if they diligently keep his commandments (vv. 1-14), but then lists the curses that will overtake them if they disobey (vv. 15-68). But God also blesses his people by being present with them (Gen 26:3, 28-29; Deut 2:7) and granting them his Spirit (Judg 13:24-25; Isa 44:3). "Fertility, prosperity in anything to which the blessed one puts his hand, well-being, riches, crops and the presence of God or his Spirit — these form its [blessing's] content" (Mowvley 1965: 79). It will be recalled that Westermann in particular has called attention to the OT's witness not only to "the saving God" who acts in history, but also to "the blessing God" who acts in creation (cf. 3-1.3e). "Deliverance is experienced in events that represent God's intervention. Blessing is a continuing activity of God" (Westermann 1978: 4). In addition to God's "mighty acts," "God's work with his people includes things manifested not in deeds but in processes that are usually regarded as 'unhistorical' — the growth and multiplying of the people and the effects of the forces that preserve their physical life . . . growth, prosperity, and success in all their forms" (6). As P. D. Miller (1975) points out, the recognition of "blessing" is important "for counterbalancing a too heavy kerygmatic theology or emphasis on the mighty acts of God. Such a theological thrust puts God heavily on the boundaries, in the gaps, in extraordinary events rather than at the centre of everyday life" (251); blessing, by contrast, concerns "the ongoing, steady regular work of God to provide and care for life, to insure its context" (248).

The activity of the blessing God figures prominently in the Wisdom Literature (see Westermann 1978: 37-40), which focuses not on "salvation history" but on discerning God's ways in creation and in society. The nature of God's blessing lies at the heart of the book of Job (see 16-1.5c); the book questions a too simple correlation of piety and earthly blessings and points forward to the NT understanding of blessing that can be independent of external circumstances.

God's blessing is promised especially to his covenant people, but it will be recalled that in a key passage, at the outset of salvation history, God promises not only that Abraham will be blessed but that through his descendants God's blessing will be channeled to all humankind (Gen 12:2-3; see 12-1.1).

b. Bless the LORD, O My Soul

In response, God's people "bless" him for all that they receive; i.e., they give him thanks and praise. The blessing of God in this sense is a frequent theme in the book of Psalms:

> Blessed (bārûkh, LXX eulogētos) be the LORD,
> for he has heard the sound of my pleadings. (28:6)

> I will bless the LORD at all times;
> his praise shall continually be in my mouth. (34:1)

c. Bless Me, O My Father

People may also bless other people, though since God is the source of all blessing, what they are really doing is asking God's blessing on others. Blessing "is something which is dependent on God who himself alone can give or withhold it. Men can only transmit blessing as He permits it or commands it" (Mowvley 1965: 75). Especially common is the blessing of a father (at the end of his life) on his children. The story of Jacob cheating Esau out of their father Isaac's blessing (Gen 27) illustrates both the importance of the father's blessing and the fact that, once given, it cannot be reversed. At the dedication of the temple King Solomon blesses the people (1 Kgs 8:14, 55), and in his prayer he praises both the saving God and the blessing God (cf. Westermann 1978: 30 n. 19).

Blessing forms an important part of worship and is therefore particularly a function of the priests (Deut 10:8; 21:5). Ps 115:14-15, for example, is probably a blessing pronounced on the worshipers by a priest:

> May the LORD give you increase,
>   both you and your children.
> May you be blessed by the LORD,
>   who made heaven and earth.

According to Lev 9:22, at the conclusion of worship "Aaron lifted his hands toward the people and blessed them." The blessing comes at the end of worship, for it "is to go with those who receive it, out into their life outside the times of worship" (Westermann 1978: 43). The "Aaronic Blessing" with which Aaron and his sons (i.e., the priests) are to bless the people is found in Num 6:24-26:

> The LORD bless you and keep you;
>   the LORD make his face to shine upon you, and be gracious to you;
>   the LORD lift up his countenance upon you, and give you peace.

Such a blessing is regarded in the OT as being powerful and effective, yet it is not a magic formula. The repetition of "the LORD" at the start of each line here again "gives emphasis to the fact that Yahweh is the one who is the dispenser of blessing" (P. D. Miller 1975: 249, 244).

d. Blessed Are Those

The English word "blessed" is also used to translate a quite distinct, though not unrelated, Hebrew idiom. The term *'ash^{e}rê* (only in plural construct) introduces an exclamation meaning "O the blessedness of!" or "O the happiness of!" The LXX renders *'ash^{e}rê* by *makarios,* hence such exclamations can be termed in English "makarisms," or more frequently "beatitudes" (Lat. *beatus* = "happy, blessed"). The idiom follows a more or less set pattern (see W. Janzen 1965: 217) consisting of (1) the exclamation *'ash*ᵉ*rê*, (2) a clause describing the person(s) pronounced blessed, and (3) a statement giving the basis for the pronouncement. The formula is always applied to people (never to God, and never to oneself) either in the singular, e.g. "Blessed is the man *('ash*ᵉ*rê hā'îsh)* / who walks not in the counsel of the wicked" (Ps 1:1 RSV), or in the plural, e.g. "Blessed are all *('ash*ᵉ*rê kol)* who take refuge in him [the LORD]" (2:11 RSV).

The *basis* for such pronouncements is very similar to "blessing." Ps 144:9-15, for example, gives a list of this-worldly blessings: deliverance from enemies, sons and daughters, full barns and abundant flocks, peace and security, then exclaims,

> Blessed are the people of whom this is true;
> blessed are the people whose God is the LORD. (v. 15 NIV)

Other blessings, however, include taking refuge in the LORD (34:8), receiving God's forgiveness (32:1), delighting in God's Torah (1:2), doing righteousness (106:3), and finding wisdom (Prov 3:13; *Sir* 25:10). *Sir* 25:7-10, it should be noted, brings together a series of nine beatitudes. In other words, *"receipt of that which blessing has to bestow qualifies a person or group to be called AŠRÈ"* (W. Janzen 1965: 223).

The *'ash*ᵉ*rê* formula, however, does not *convey* a blessing. It reflects rather the stance of a bystander who observes and declares the blessedness of certain types of people. Nevertheless, Guelich (1976) is surely correct in observing that "the declaration comes almost as a challenge for the hearers to join the ranks of the 'blessed' by meeting the implicit demands of the statement" (416-17). In the OT people are almost always pronounced "blessed" in the present (cf. Mowry 1962: 370), but in the late OT we see the emergence of the *apocalyptic makarism* that pronounces blessed the faithful who persevere until the coming of the new age (Dan 12:12). They may suffer now, but they will be rewarded in the future:

> Happy are those who love you. . . .
> Happy also are all people who grieve with you
>   because of your afflictions;
> for they will rejoice with you
>   and witness all your glory forever. (*Tob* 13:14)

20-1.5. JOY

Throughout the OT the experience of God's life, peace, healing, and blessing is the ground for rejoicing. The idea of joy is expressed through a rich vocabulary (see D. Harvey 1962: 1000), and is demonstrated, for example, by shouting, singing, dancing, and through the medium of music.

Joy is occasioned primarily by this-worldly blessings such as a successful harvest (Isa 9:3; cf. Joel 1:16), victory over enemies (1 Sam 18:6; Ps 31:7-8), a wedding (*Tob* 11:17-18), or having a family (Ps 113:9). The Wisdom Literature, however, cautions against a joy that depends only on material prosperity, and warns that "the end of joy is grief" (Prov 14:13). True joy is grounded in the Lord (Ps 149:2), and in his word (19:8; Jer 15:16), and above all through living in fellowship with God:

> You show me the path of life.
> In your presence there is fullness of joy;
> in your right hand are pleasures forevermore. (Ps 16:11)

Joy is a natural response to all that the faithful have received from the Lord:

> I will greatly rejoice in the Lord,
> my whole being shall exult in my God;
> for he has clothed me with the garments of salvation,
> he has covered me with the robe of righteousness. (Isa 61:10)

Rejoicing is frequently associated with public worship, particularly at Passover (2 Chr 30:21; Ezra 6:22; *1 Esdr* 7:14) and at the other feasts (Deut 16:11; Neh 8:17; Esth 8:17; *1 Macc* 4:59), and with the worship of the temple (Ps 122:1), and it is no coincidence that the theme of joy runs throughout the book of Psalms (9:1-2; 33:1-3; 95:1-2; etc.). Not only God's people but all creation is called upon to rejoice in the Lord (19:5; 96:11; 97:1).

While joy is found in life here and now, it will also be a marked feature of the new age when God's people will "be glad and rejoice in his salvation" (Isa 25:9; cf. 49:13; 56:7; 61:3). The note of rejoicing resounds throughout the "Book of Consolation" (Jer 30–31), where God promises his people that in the coming new age:

> Then shall the young women rejoice in the dance,
> and the young men and the old shall be merry.
> I will turn their mourning into joy,
> I will comfort them, and give them gladness for sorrow. (31:13)

The coming of the messianic King will be a cause for rejoicing (Zech 9:9). The prophet Habakkuk, despite the desolation of the present, looks to the future and confidently affirms:

> Yet will I rejoice in the Lord;
> I will exult in the God of my salvation. (3:18)

Thus rejoicing in the OT "not only testifies to past experiences of God's salvation; it also exults in his faithful dealings which are still future . . . and which the believer sees ensured by Yahweh" (Beyreuther and Finkenrath 1976: 353).

Old Testament: Promise

20-2. YOUR DEAD SHALL LIVE

Only in the context of its basic emphasis on "the land of the living" does the OT look at death and raise the question of what lies beyond it.

20-2.1. THE FACT OF DEATH

The OT in no way seeks to evade the reality of death, but rather refers to it in straightforward terms without any euphemism (Wolff 1974: 103). "We must all die; we are like water spilled on the ground, which cannot be gathered up" (2 Sam 14:14; cf. Josh 23:14; Ps 49:20; *Sir* 14:17). Human life, at best, covers a brief span (Ps 39:5). The "three score and ten" years of Ps 90:10 (RSV) would be much more of a maximum than an average age span in biblical times (Wolff, 119). Life and death are in God's hands, for "the LORD kills and brings to life" (1 Sam 2:6). Both Elijah (1 Kgs 17:17-24) and Elisha (2 Kgs 4:18-37) are credited with raising young people from the dead, but "what is involved there is a temporary and not a final liberation from the power of death" (Kaiser and Lohse 1981: 28; cf. also 2 Kgs 13:20-21).

20-2.2. THE UNDERSTANDING OF DEATH

a. The Key Passage

For the OT understanding of death, Gen 2–3 is a key passage; as always, BT must be based on the canonical text, not on reconstructions of a hypothetical original. The story of the Garden of Eden tells of two trees. One is the tree of the knowledge of good and evil (cf. 2-1.5a), the eating of which was forbidden on pain of death (2:16-17). The other is "the tree of life" (2:9); the couple were not prohibited from eating this tree, though 3:22 makes it clear that they did not do so. God expels humankind from the garden as a result of their rebellion and disobedience "lest [man] put forth his hand and take also of the tree of life, and eat, and live for ever" (3:22 RSV). In other words, the potential for eternal life was there, but expulsion from the sphere of the tree of life brought about the inevitability of death.

b. Spiritual Death

Although the penalty for eating from the tree of the knowledge of good and evil was death (Gen 2:17), it is noteworthy that when the first couple do eat of this tree they are not struck dead; though expelled from the garden, they continue to live for many years thereafter. The "death" referred to is thus not primarily physical death but rather a spiritual death that results from alienation from God. In distrusting and disobeying God, humankind has already passed from life to death. The rest of the prologue of Genesis (Gen 1–11) depicts how death quickly spreads to all aspects of human life and culture.

As we have seen above, the OT's primary concern is with life in this world, life as a present reality; the reverse of this is death in this world, death as a present reality. "Death" is frequently used in the OT "as a metaphor for those things which detract from life as Yahweh intends it, among them illness, persecution, despair and non-participation in the life of the covenant community"; it is "used to describe the various conditions which detract from the full potential which Yahweh intended for his creatures" (L. R. Bailey 1979: 39-40).

Just as "life" is an option open to God's people in the present, so inevitably the other option is "death": "See, I have set before you today life and prosperity, death and adversity" (Deut 30:15). To refuse God's gracious offer is to opt for the sphere of death here and now:

> Before each person are life and death,
> and whichever one chooses will be given. (*Sir* 15:17)

c. Sin and Death

As a result of their rebellion and disobedience, the first humans face spiritual death now and the prospect of physical death in due course. The rest of the OT has remarkably little to say about the link between sin and death; for the most part it is content to accept the reality of physical death as the inevitable boundary of each human existence and to concentrate almost entirely on the choice between life and death in the present (cf. Brueggemann 1976a: 220).

It is the later Wisdom Literature that returns to reflect upon the implications of the Genesis story. The book of *Wisdom* stresses that death was not part of God's original plan for creation:

> God did not make death,
> and he does not delight in the death of the living.
> For he created all things so that they might exist. (1:13-14)

As we have seen (4-1.5), it is Wisdom that first connects the serpent of Gen 3 with the devil, who thus becomes the one really responsible for death:

> For God created us for incorruption,
> and made us in the image of his own eternity,
> but through the devil's envy death entered the world,
> and those who belong to his company experience it. (2:23-24)

Sirach also refers to the decree, "You must die!" (14:17), and the link between sin and death (25:24).

d. Length of Days

In keeping with the piety-prosperity equation (cf. 16-1.3b), a correlation is often made in the OT between the kind of life a person lives and the length of that life. Righteousness is held to be rewarded with long life, while conversely wickedness results in life being cut short. Prov 10:27 puts this view in a nutshell:

> The fear of the LORD prolongs life,
> but the years of the wicked will be short.
>
> (cf. 10:21; Job 22:15-16; 36:13-14; Ps 55:23)

The long lives of some persons before the flood (Gen 5) reflect a view of that period as an ideal age. After the flood an absolute upper limit of 120 years is established (6:3).

Once again, this part of the piety-prosperity equation is questioned, nowhere more so than in Ecclesiastes, where the author declares: "In my vain life I have seen everything; there are righteous people who perish in their righteousness, and there are wicked people who prolong their life in their evildoing" (7:15). His conclusion is that "the same fate comes to all" (9:2).

In the late OT period the death of martyrs raised the problem in a particularly acute form.

20-2.3. THE LAND OF DARKNESS: SHEOL

One of the most fundamental human questions is what happens to the individual after death. Despite the OT's emphasis on life in the present, it does raise this question: "If mortals die, will they live again?" (Job 14:14). Two basic answers are found, standing in considerable tension one with another. The dominant view is that after death individuals go to Sheol (*sheʾôl*), a colorless, shadowy underworld where they are cut off from all that makes life worth living, including even the presence of God himself.

a. The Place of the Dead

The most common designation for the place of the dead is *sheʾôl*, the etymology of which is uncertain (Jacob 1958: 302 n. 1). The main cognate terms are the Pit *(shachath, bôr)* and Abaddon *(ʾabhaddôn;* from a root meaning destruction or ruin).

It appears to be thought of as a netherworld, in or below the earth; at death people go *down* to Sheol:

> But you are brought down to Sheol,
> to the depths of the Pit. (Isa 14:15; cf. Job 7:9; Ps 86:13)

Typically it is portrayed as a place of gloom and darkness:

> You have put me in the depths of the Pit,
> in the regions dark and deep. (Ps 88:6)

> Let me alone, that I may find a little comfort
> before I go, never to return,
> to the land of gloom and deep darkness,
> the land of gloom and chaos,
> where light is like darkness. (Job 10:20-22)

b. The Shadows

After death the physical body decays (Job 34:15; *Sir* 19:3). What survives death is not so much one part of the person, a "soul" or "spirit," but rather a kind of shadowy remnant of the total person, "the person reduced to its weakest possible state" (L. R. Bailey 1979: 46). In some parts of the OT people after death are referred to as *rephāʾîm* = "shades, shadows" (Isa 14:9; Ps 88:10; Prov 2:18).

In Sheol the shades lead what is generally thought of as a virtual nonexistence. Stricken with a severe illness, the author of Ps 39 begs God to hear his prayer "before I depart and am no more" (v. 13). According to Isa 26:14,

> The dead do not live;
> shades do not arise —
> because you have punished and destroyed them,
> and wiped out all memory of them.

Eccl 9:10 declares that "there is no work or thought or knowledge or wisdom in Sheol." In some texts a kind of half existence seems to be implied, as in Isa 14, which says to the king of Babylon as he descends to the place of the dead:

Sheol beneath is stirred up
    to meet you when you come;
it rouses the shades to greet you. . . .
All of them will speak
    and say to you:
"You too have become as weak as we!" (vv. 9-10; cf. L. R. Bailey 1979: 47)

There is a terrible finality about a person's going to Sheol:

As the cloud fades and vanishes,
    so those who go down to Sheol do not come up;
they return no more to their houses,
    nor do their places know them any more. (Job 7:9-10)

c. Cut Off from God

Worst of all, Sheol is a place where a person is cut off from God. The writer of Ps 88 says he is

like those forsaken among the dead,
    like the slain that lie in the grave,
like those whom *you remember no more,*
    for *they are cut off from your hand.* (vv. 4-5; cf. vv. 10-12)

"This defines the dead as beings who have been expelled from Yahweh's sphere of influence" (Wolff 1974: 106). God is the Lord of life, so his sphere is that of the living rather than the dead. As King Hezekiah put it in his prayer:

Sheol cannot thank you,
    death cannot praise you;
those who go down to the Pit cannot hope
    for your faithfulness.
The living, the living, they thank you,
    as I do this day. (Isa 38:18-19)

Such texts suggest that "for the member of the community of Israel, the dead were beyond his interest for they had ceased to live and praise Yahweh" (J. B. Burns 1973: 339).

d. Communicating with the Dead

Although the cult of the dead was common in the ancient Near East (L. R. Bailey 1979: 32), all communication with the dead is strictly forbidden in the OT. Deut 18:9-11 classes such communication with "the abhorrent practices" of the surrounding nations (cf. Lev 19:31; 20:6). Equally strong is the condemnation of mediums or wizards who would participate in such practices (Lev 20:27; Isa 8:19).

It is true that one striking example of communication with the dead is recorded in the story of King Saul and the medium of Endor (1 Sam 28:7-25); ironically, it was Saul who had "expelled the mediums and the wizards from the land" (28:3). What the story really shows is that "nothing is to be expected from the spirits of the dead beyond what has been witnessed to by living messengers" (Wolff 1974: 104). The purpose of trying to contact the dead in OT times was not to resume communion with departed loved ones, but to receive guidance. The only true source of guidance (beyond fellow human beings) is God. It is foolish to seek help from the dead rather than from the living God.

e. Their Name Shall Live

Where this view of Sheol prevails, there is comfort in the belief that a person does live on in his "name," either through his descendants or through the memory of his righteous deeds. Thus Boaz marries Ruth "to maintain the dead man's name on his inheritance" (Ruth 4:10), while the point of levirate marriage is that a man may have an heir even after his death, "so that his name may not be blotted out of Israel" (Deut 25:6).

According to Prov 10:7,

> The memory of the righteous is a blessing,
>> but the name of the wicked will rot.

Sir 44:14 says of the righteous dead:

> Their bodies are buried in peace,
>> but their name lives on generation after generation.

20-2.4. THE PROMISE OF LIGHT: RESURRECTION

While the dominant view is that after death individuals go to Sheol, within the OT an inner dynamic is to be observed that leads to the emergence of a belief in a future resurrection. Two main factors bring this about: the growing conviction that the life of fellowship with God experienced now cannot be broken even by death, and the growing conviction that God's purposes must eventually triumph. Historically, it is possible that belief in a future resurrection arose at least in part under the influence of Iranian religion (cf. Birkeland 1949: 74-76). BT, however, is not concerned with origins, but with the form the belief takes in the canonical text.

a. The Presence of God

The understanding of Sheol as a sphere of existence cut off from God and therefore from life runs counter to some basic OT affirmations regarding God (cf. Wolff 1974: 107). Ps 139 gives clearest expression to the view that there can be no place where the presence of God cannot be found:

> Where can I go from your spirit?
>> Or where can I flee from your presence?
> If I ascend to heaven, you are there;
>> *if I make my bed in Sheol, you are there.* (vv. 7-8)

The conviction that the close fellowship between God and his servants cannot be broken even by death lies behind two exceptional individual cases in which God snatches persons from death: Enoch (Gen 5:24) and Elijah (2 Kgs 2:1-12) (cf. 10-1.3). In these accounts "there appear momentary glimpses of a possible overcoming of death" (Schmitt 1981: 183).

b. Resurrection

If God is creator and ruler, can even death thwart his purposes? In the context of prophetic eschatology, as we have seen (10-2.1; 11-2.2b), such texts as Hos 6:1-2 and Ezek 37:1-14 promise a future resurrection of *the nation* (cf. Birkeland 1949: 73-74).

Isa 65:17-25 combines features of prophetic and apocalyptic eschatology and may be regarded as a transitional passage. It says of the new Jerusalem:

> No more shall there be in it
>> an infant that lives but a few days,
>> or an old person who does not live out a lifetime;
> for one who dies at a hundred years will be considered a youth. (v. 20)

The hope here, however, is more for a prolongation and enhancement of life on earth than a life beyond death.

It is only in a few texts which are expressions of apocalyptic eschatology that a genuine hope for individuals emerges in the form of belief in a future resurrection. In the context of the eschatological victory banquet, Isa 25:7-8 declares:

> And he will destroy on this mountain
>> the shroud that is cast over all peoples,
>> the sheet that is spread over all nations;
>> he will swallow up death forever.
> Then the Lord GOD will wipe away the tears from all faces.

Sheol is often described as "swallowing up" persons (Num 16:32; Ps 69:15; Prov 1:12); here the tables are turned and it is death itself that will be swallowed up.

Although Isa 26:19 has been read by some as referring to national resurrection (see Gaster 1962a: 40; L. R. Bailey 1979: 71), it seems more natural to read it with 25:7-8 as a reference to resurrection from the dead (cf. Gese 1981a: 55-56):

> Your dead shall live, their corpses shall rise.
>> O dwellers in the dust, awake and sing for joy!
> For your dew is a radiant dew,
>> and the earth will give birth to those long dead.

There is no ambiguity about Dan 12:2-3, a text that presents the full apocalyptic picture of a general resurrection, combined with a final judgment: "Many of those who sleep in the dust of the earth shall awake, some to everlasting life, and some to shame and everlasting contempt. Those who are wise shall shine like the brightness of the sky, and those who lead many to righteousness, like the stars forever and ever." While these verses may echo Isa 26:19 (cf. Nickelsburg 1972: 18-19), they go further in speaking not simply of a resurrection of the righteous but of a *general* resurrection that precedes a judgment in which righteous and unrighteous are consigned to their separate fates. On future judgment in the OT, see more fully 16-2.3. The comparison of the resurrected righteous with stars in Dan 12:3 suggests that what is envisaged is not a literal, physical resurrection, but rather some form of existence akin to that of the angels (cf. 8:10, where stars are equated with angels; see B. F. Meyer 1989: 111).

Isa 26 and Dan 12 assume some kind of intermediate state described as a "sleep" (Dan 12:2; cf. Ps 13:3), from which the dead shall "awake" (Isa 26:19) to participate in the judgment and resurrection (cf. D. Alexander 1986: 45).

In the Deuterocanon, belief in a future individual resurrection resolves the otherwise unbearable problem of the Maccabean martyrs. In the horrendous tale of the martyrdom of a mother and her seven sons in 2 *Macc* 7, the second son addresses the king, "You accursed wretch, you dismiss us from this present life, but the King of the universe will raise us up to *an everlasting renewal of life,*

because we have died for his laws" (v. 9; cf. vv. 11, 14, 23, 29, 36). "Significantly
different from the Daniel stories where the heroes are rescued at the brink of
death, here the brothers are rescued and vindicated in spite of and after death"
(Nickelsburg 1976: 349).

Although references to a future life have been seen in the book of Job, this
is unlikely on the basis of the Hebrew text (see commentaries, esp. on Job 19:25-
26). The Septuagint, however, reflecting the continuing development of the
biblical tradition, introduces clear references to a future resurrection (see Gard
1954). In 14:14 where Job asks wistfully, "If a man die, shall he live again?" (RSV),
the LXX reads

> For if a man dies, *he will live,*
> having completed the days of his life;
> I will abide until I be born again *(palin genōmai).*

At the conclusion of the book, the LXX adds to v. 17, "and it has been written
that he [Job] will rise up again with those whom the Lord raises up."

2 *Maccabees* and the LXX version of Job confirm what is known from
noncanonical sources, that belief in a future resurrection came to be accepted
by some, though not all, Jews in the two centuries before Christ. The NT witnesses to the fact that such a belief was one of the distinguishing marks of the
Pharisees. The story of Acts 23:6-8 highlights the distinction between Sadducees and Pharisees: "The Sadducees say that there is no resurrection, or angel,
or spirit; but the Pharisees acknowledge all three" (cf. Matt 22:23).

c. Immortality

The problem of the death of the righteous lies behind the discussion of life after
death in *Wisdom of Solomon* 1–6 (see esp. 2:10-22; cf. Nickelsburg 1972: 48-92;
Kaiser and Lohse 1981: 12-20). Because the term "immortality" *(athanasia)* is
used (3:4; 6:18; 8:17; 15:3), the claim is often made that in *Wisdom* the biblical
view of resurrection has been displaced by the Greek view of the immortality of
the soul. But if by the "immortality of the soul" is meant a belief that all persons
are endowed with a soul or spirit that automatically survives physical death,
then this certainly does not represent the view of *Wisdom,* a work that adheres
to the basic biblical view. Human beings were created for incorruption
(aphtharsia),

> but through the devil's envy death entered the world,
> and those who belong to his company experience it. (2:23-24)

Immortality is not the lot of all human beings, but only of the righteous:

> But the righteous live forever,
> and their reward is with the Lord. (5:15; cf. 4:7)

The unrighteous, on the other hand, invite death by the error of their lives (1:12).

Little is said about the judgment and the separation of the righteous from the wicked (cf. Nickelsburg 1972: 88-89). According to 3:1, "the souls of the righteous are in the hand of God," and it is possible that the author envisages judgment taking place upon the death of the individual, when the righteous souls would receive immortality. But the author can also speak of "the day of judgment" (3:18; cf. 3:13; 4:6), which suggests an eschatology akin to that of Dan 12. Either way, it is important to note that in *Wisdom* "immortality and life are not inherent in the soul. The person — or his soul — acquires life or death as a result of his actions in this life. Therefore it is the soul of only the righteous that is immortal. . . . In the Wisdom of Solomon, Greek immortality language has garbed what is basically a Jewish two-way theology, which elsewhere speaks in terms not of immortality, but of life and death" (Nickelsburg, 179). Thus *Wisdom* adheres to the basic biblical view and anticipates the hope of immortality that is more fully and accurately set forth in the NT (see 20-4.4d).

20-2.5. ATTITUDES TO DEATH

A fear of death is natural to all humankind. All people, observes *Sirach*, of whatever station in life, have "anxious thought of the day of their death" (40:2). In the book of Job Bildad calls death "the king of terrors" (18:14). Yet most texts that display such an attitude come from contexts in which a person is threatened with an early death (e.g., 1 Sam 15:32; Isa 38:10). Against them are to be balanced other passages that show an acceptance of death, especially when it occurs at "a good old age" (e.g., 1 Chr 29:28; Gen 46:30).

Grief at the death of someone dear is a natural reaction; despite the advanced age at which he died, "the Israelites wept for Moses in the plains of Moab thirty days" (Deut 34:8). The death of a child or young person is particularly an occasion for grief (Gen 21:16; 2 Sam 18:33; Amos 8:10). In such cases acceptance is difficult and requires the faith of Job, who even on learning of the death of his sons and daughters could say: "The LORD gave, and the LORD has taken away; blessed be the name of the LORD" (Job 1:21).

One of the functions of the psalms of lament is to assist people in coping with grief. Brueggemann (1977a: 265) has drawn some interesting comparisons — and contrasts — between the form of the OT lament and the five elements of the death-grief process (denial, anger, bargaining, depression, acceptance). What distinguishes the OT approach to grief is that it is dealt with in the context of the covenant community. However anguished the cry, it is a cry of a member of God's people to the Lord, and the OT lament typically ends not on a note of mere resignation but rather on a note of affirmation of faith and even praise of God. Pagan practices in which grief finds extreme expression (including forms of self-mutilation) are strongly prohibited (Lev 19:28; Deut 14:1).

It is important that the dead be given a decent burial (1 Sam 31:8-13; 2 Sam 21:10-14), yet relatively little importance is attached to graves in the OT (cf. Wolff 1974: 100-102). The tomb of the patriarchs and matriarchs is well known (Gen 23; etc.), but the site of David's burial is not precisely given (1 Kgs 2:10), and the fact that Moses' burial place is unknown is especially emphasized (Deut 34:6); this is probably to discourage any revering of graves as shrines. A rich official, Shebna, is condemned for having prepared an overelaborate tomb for himself (Isa 22:15-16), and there is no place for elaborate funeral services; the embalming of Jacob and his great funeral procession (Gen 50:2-3, 7-9) are exceptional and reflect Egyptian, not Israelite, custom.

Only once, in the Deuterocanon, is there any mention of prayer for the dead. In 2 *Macc* 12:39-45 Judas and his men pray for their dead comrades, "praying that the sin that had been committed might be wholly blotted out." They also collected money and sent it to Jerusalem so that sacrifice might be offered to make atonement for the dead, "so that they might be delivered from their sin" (12:43, 45).

New Testament: Fulfillment

20-3. FROM DEATH TO LIFE

The NT proclaims Christ as the conqueror of death, and holds out the promise of life beyond death for believers. Nevertheless, in keeping with the OT, it also constantly affirms life here and now.

20-3.1. THE AFFIRMATION OF LIFE

The NT shares the OT's faith in God as "the living God" (Matt 16:16; Rom 9:26; etc.), the one who "has life" (John 5:26; *zōē* = "life"). God is the giver and sustainer of life (Acts 17:25, 28) who will provide the necessities of life to those who trust in him (Matt 6:25-33). Unlike the OT, however, the NT sees life in this world in the light of what is variously called "the life to come (*zōē tēs mellousēs*)" (1 Tim 4:8), "eternal life (*zōē aiōnios*)" (Matt 19:16; etc.), or simply "life *(zōē)*" (Mark 9:43; etc.). The NT agrees with the OT in believing that *true* life is to be found in fellowship with God, but goes beyond the OT in holding out the firm promise and hope that "life" in this sense is a gift God will bestow on believers beyond death. This is what Jesus is referring to when he talks simply about entering into "life *(zōē)*" (Mark 9:43, 45). "The fact that the future life is occasionally referred to by the use of *zōē* alone, i.e. without any qualifying phrase . . . indicates that such life is regarded as real and true, the very life of God himself" (Link 1976: 481). For a discussion of the NT understanding of the future life, see more fully below, 20-4.3, 4.

In keeping, however, with the already/not yet tension that characterizes so much of the NT, the life of the age to come can already, to some degree at least, *be experienced here and now.* This is indicated by the very term "eternal life." *Aiōnios* can mean "endless" or "of unending duration," or "eternal" in the sense of "without beginning or end." Life beyond death will not be subject to the kind of limitation that is so characteristic of our life here on earth. But *aiōnios* also means "pertaining to the *aiōn*," i.e., the "age" to come (cf. Mark 10:30; see 16-4.3d), the new age that has already been inaugurated with the Christ event. The primary reference, therefore, is not to life of mere endless duration but rather to the distinctive *quality* of life (see W. F. Howard 1943: 190-91). *Zōē aiōnios* means "the life of the new age": something believers will inherit beyond death, yet also a quality of life they can experience here and now.

For Jesus, entering into life and entering the kingdom of God are virtually the same thing (cf. Mark 9:43 and 9:47; John 3:5 and 3:36; see A. Richardson 1958: 74; R. W. Thomas 1968: 203). As the kingdom is not only future but is also inaugurated in the ministry of Jesus (see 1-3.1a), so life can be found in Jesus here and now. Jesus quotes the Deut 8:3 saying about not living by bread alone (Matt 4:4); life is found now in obedience to God's word. In the parable of the lost son (Luke 15:11-32), the prodigal, when he leaves his father, is said to be "dead," but when he returns to his father's house is "alive again" (v. 24); true life is found only in fellowship with God.

Life as a present possession is particularly stressed in John's Gospel (see Kaiser and Lohse 1981: 144-50), though here too the already/not yet tension is maintained (see D-2.9). In 5:25-29 Jesus speaks of a *future* "resurrection of life" (and also of condemnation), but in v. 25 he says, "The hour *is coming, and is now here,* when the dead will hear the voice of the Son of God, and those who hear will live." In other words, the life of the age to come is available to believers, through Christ, here and now (cf. Ewert 1980: 166). Thus Jesus can say, "Whoever believes in the Son *has (echei)* eternal life" (3:36), or, in a variant formulation, "Anyone who hears my word and believes him who sent me *has* eternal life" and "*has* passed from death to life" (5:24). This life is closely linked with faith in God and especially with faith in Christ, who is "the bread of life" (6:35), "the resurrection and the life" (11:25), and "the way, and the truth, and the life" (14:6). "This is eternal life," Jesus says in 17:3, "that they may know you, the only true God, and Jesus Christ whom you have sent." In these Johannine texts, "life" is a term rich in meaning: "For John life is the all-inclusive concept of salvation. It takes in everything which the Saviour of the World sent by God brings to men" (Schmitt 1981: 501).

The Gospel's understanding of life as a present possession as well as a future hope is underlined and amplified by the author of 1 John, who writes, "God gave us eternal life, and this life is in his Son. Whoever has the Son has life; whoever does not have the Son of God does not have life" (5:11-12). Believers *know* that they have this life if they love one another (3:14-17).

In Paul the tension between life as a future promise and life as a present possibility is particularly marked (cf. Piper 1962b: 129-30; Link 1976: 481). "Eternal life" is a future gift (Rom 2:7; Gal 6:8), but in another sense believers have already passed from death to life. This is linked in the closest possible way on the one hand with the Christ event, and on the other hand with baptism. In an important passage, Rom 6:1-11, Paul speaks of believers having been baptized into Christ's death (v. 3), "so that, just as Christ was raised from the dead . . . we too might walk in newness of life" (v. 4). He seems to think of this new life as still primarily future: "if we have been united with him in a death like his, we will certainly be united with him in a resurrection like his" (v. 5), yet he concludes the passage by saying, "so you also must consider yourselves dead to sin and alive to God in Christ Jesus" (v. 11). That life is a present reality is more clearly emphasized in Eph 2:5-6, which declares that God "made us alive together with Christ . . . and raised us up with him" (cf. Col 2:12; 3:1); here there is no doubt that believers have already been raised with Christ. Moreover, for Paul, life in the here and now is inspired by the Spirit, and if "to set the mind on the flesh is death," then "to set the mind on the Spirit is life and peace" (Rom 8:6; cf. 1 Tim 6:12).

20-3.2. PEACE

As in the OT, peace *(eirēnē)* is one of God's greatest gifts, and one that can be enjoyed here and now. Study of the Greek background of *eirēnē* is not particularly helpful; however, the word is used in the LXX to translate *shālôm*, and we must expect a strong carryover from the OT understanding with its connotations of wholeness, health, salvation, and harmonious relationships (cf. P. B. Yoder 1987: 19; Launderville, Tambasco, and Wadell 1996: 711). This is clear from what the Gospels say about Jesus and peace. Luke sees Jesus' coming as guiding God's people in the way of peace (1:79; cf. 2:14). Peace is one of the greatest things that can be bestowed upon a person and, as in the OT, Jesus uses "peace" as a greeting. For example, he says, "Go in peace," to a woman he has restored to health and wholeness (Mark 5:34), and to another who has been restored to a right relationship with God through forgiveness of sin (Luke 7:50). Although Jesus is here employing the common Jewish greeting of "peace," "it is clear . . . that as he used it, and as he expected his disciples to use it, it was much more than a merely conventional salutation. With the word of peace went the actual bestowal of peace" (Mitton 1962: 706).

Christians are to follow Jesus' example in bestowing peace in the form of a greeting (Matt 10:12-13; cf. Jas 2:16). Particularly noteworthy is the frequent use of "peace" (usually coupled with "grace") in the opening greetings of epistles (e.g., Rom 1:7; 1 Cor 1:3; 1 Pet 1:2; 2 John 3; Rev 1:4).

For the early Christians, looking back on the Christ event, peace is first and foremost peace with God, made possible through Christ. God is "the God of peace" (Rom 15:33; Heb 13:20), and the Christian message itself can be termed "the gospel of peace" (Eph 6:15; cf. Acts 10:36). It is since we are justified through faith that "we have peace with God through our Lord Jesus Christ" (Rom 5:1; cf. Col 1:20).

The Christian peace is not to be assessed by the standards of this world; indeed, in the NT peace is more paradoxical than in the OT, and the emphasis shifts more to an inner peace that is independent of external circumstances. Thus, while Jesus bestows peace he can also say, "I have not come to bring peace, but a sword" (Matt 10:34//Luke 12:51; cf. 19-3.2), for believers may face division within their own families. In John Jesus says to his disciples, "Peace I leave with you; my peace I give to you. I do not give to you as the world gives" (14:27). "This is not a placid peace. Peace here is not the absence of trouble" (D. J. Harris 1970: 41). Paul assures the Philippians that "the peace of God, which surpasses all understanding, will guard your hearts and your minds in Christ Jesus" (Phil 4:7; cf. Col 3:15). In such passages *eirēnē* means something akin to what we mean by "peace of mind" (cf. Mitton 1962: 706).

However, because peace means living in a right relationship with God, it also means peace between people. In a secular sense it can mean the cessation of hostilities (Luke 14:32; Acts 12:20), but for Christians it means much more. Jesus' followers are to be "peacemakers" (Matt 5:9), restoring harmonious relations between people (cf. Mark 9:50). *Eirēnē* refers to harmony between husband and wife (1 Cor 7:15), within the Christian community (2 Cor 13:11; Eph 4:3), and more generally to peace "with all," at least as far as that depends on believers (Rom 12:18; cf. Heb 12:14). Paul defines the kingdom as "righteousness and peace and joy in the Holy Spirit," and on this basis exhorts his readers, "Let us then pursue what makes for peace and for mutual upbuilding" (Rom 14:17, 19). The death of Christ brings about peace especially between Jews and Gentiles. Christ "is our peace; in his flesh he has made both groups into one and has broken down the dividing wall, that is, the hostility between us" (Eph 2:14). "The thought of reconciliation carries with it the implication of breaking down the dividing wall of hostility between man and man" (D. J. Harris 1970: 46; cf. Duchrow and Liedke 1989: 130). Thus, according to the NT, "Christians are peacemakers working to reconcile all men and women in Christ because it is through that activity that they best imitate God and carry forward what God began in Christ and continues in the Spirit" (Launderville, Tambasco, and Wadell 1996: 714). As in the OT, peace is meaningless without a concern for justice in society and practical help for those in need, a point made in typically forceful fashion by James: "If a brother or sister is naked and lacks daily food, and one of you says to them, 'Go in peace; keep warm and eat your fill,' and yet you do not supply their bodily needs, what is the good of that?" (Jas 2:15-16). Similarly Peter calls on Christians to be proactive in seeking the biblical type of peace that cannot coexist with injustice in society:

> Let them turn away from evil and do good;
>> let them seek peace and pursue it. (1 Pet 3:11, quoting Ps 34:14)

In keeping with biblical eschatology that sees an ongoing struggle between good and evil as long as history lasts, true peace — for individuals, for society, and for nations — will finally be attained only in the new age with the defeat of all the powers opposed to God (cf. 19-4.5).

20-3.3. HEALING

Sickness is no less a threat to life in the NT than in the OT, but the new order brings a new healing power and a new attitude to illness. The concern of the NT, especially that of Jesus himself, for *the whole person* echoes and amplifies that of the OT. When the Gospels talk of a person being "saved" ($s\bar{o}(i)z\bar{o}$ = "save, preserve, rescue, heal"), that salvation is frequently physical as well as mental and spiritual (see Mark 5:28, 34; 6:56; 10:52; etc.; cf. Wilkinson 1971: 334).

The NT recognizes the existence of many different types of diseases, and vividly portrays the plight of the sick. There is nothing in the NT to correspond to the Torah health regulations. On one occasion Jesus did instruct ten healed lepers to go and show themselves to the priests in conformity with that legislation (Luke 17:14), but more striking are Jesus' *violations* of the laws of cleanness. Instead of segregating lepers from society, he reached out to heal them, and by touching them (Mark 1:41) technically broke the law. He accepted the touch of a woman with a hemorrhage (5:27), though Torah forbids contact with those discharging blood. By taking Jairus's daughter by the hand (5:41), he was technically becoming unclean by touching a corpse. The ritual law regarded God as holy, the author of life and health; therefore anything associated with death or disease had to be kept apart. Jesus too saw God as the author of life and health, but he broke through the barrier of uncleanness to *bring* life and health to the sick and the suffering (cf. G. J. Wenham 1982: 124-26). In his healing ministry he identified himself with the sick in the spirit of the Suffering Servant (see Matt 8:17, quoting Isa 53:4, "He took our infirmities and bore our diseases").

The NT recognizes that in some cases sin can be a factor in causing illness, and healing can be linked with forgiveness of sin (Mark 2:5; 1 Cor 11:30; Jas 5:15-16). Two factors, however, radically modify any simplistic sin-sickness equation (cf. Wilkinson 1971: 333). One is Jesus' explicit rejection of any necessary connection between sin and illness in John 9:1-3. The disciples echo the traditional view in asking, "Rabbi, who sinned, this man or his parents, that he was born blind?" Jesus answered, "Neither this man nor his parents sinned; he was born blind so that God's works might be revealed in him." A second factor is the attribution, especially in the Synoptic Gospels, of certain disorders to Satan and to evil powers, "demons," or "evil"/"unclean" spirits that "possess" a person (see 4-3.4); in such cases illness is never connected with sin but is viewed as the result of external forces of evil.

In the new order the healing power of God is focused in a dramatic new way in the ministry of Jesus, and continues to operate in the early church.

Exorcisms and healings constitute a major part of Jesus' ministry according to the Gospels; see the twofold summaries in Mark 1:32, 34; 3:10-11; 6:13; Luke 6:17-18; 7:21 (cf. A. Richardson 1941: 59-60; Seybold and Mueller 1981: 149). Mark's Gospel has the highest proportion of healings. John, on the other hand, is highly selective and narrates only three cures (4:46-54; 5:1-9; 9:1-7); he is concerned to bring out their deeper meaning, and sees them as "signs" *(sēmeia)* that reveal Christ's glory and evoke faith (see Wilkinson 1967: 451).

i. Exorcisms have already been discussed in 4-3.4, where it was noted that they constitute a major feature of Jesus' ministry in the Synoptics (there are no exorcisms in John). They are clearly distinguished from physical healings, and the symptoms described are mostly those that today would be associated with various forms of mental illness. The saying on the return of the unclean spirit (Matt 12:43-45//Luke 11:24-26) points to the need not simply for expelling demons but for replacing them with a more powerful force. Exorcisms can meet resistance, and demons can convulse persons in a last-minute, desperate effort to harm them (Mark 1:26; 9:26). An exorcism is generally accomplished by a sharp word of command (1:25), and its result is that the afflicted person is restored to "his right mind" (5:15).

ii. Healings, as distinct from exorcisms, are found in all four Gospels, which provide examples of the cure by Jesus of a variety of types of illnesses, with leprosy, blindness, and paralysis being the most common (Seybold and Mueller 1981: 138-48). Jesus heals the sick with a word of command (Mark 5:34) and often through touching the sufferer (Luke 5:13; 22:51). Form critics have noted that healing stories generally follow a standardized, threefold pattern, consisting of (1) a description of the illness, (2) an account of the cure, and (3) a report of the results that attest the reality of the cure (see R. H. Fuller 1963: 33). This in no way impugns the historicity of the accounts, for the structure is not an "artificial form imposed on the material, but the natural way in which an event such as a miracle might be described" (Wilkinson 1967: 444).

In many healings, though not all, the faith of the sick person plays a significant role (Seybold and Mueller 1981: 158-65). Faith is a reaching out for help (Mark 5:27-28). Despite the saying "Your faith has made you well" (5:34), the Gospels make it clear that faith is not the *source* of the healing. Jesus' healings are "mighty works" or "deeds of power" *(dynameis)*, i.e., demonstrations of the healing power of God (cf. John 3:2). In most cases faith is a *means* of receiving this healing power; note, however, that in some instances the faith is that of family (Mark 7:24-30) or friends (2:3-12). On Jesus' part, healings are expressions of his love and compassion for those in need. Jesus' motive for healing is expressed in the phrase "moved with compassion" (Matt 20:34; cf. Luke 7:13; *splanchnizomai* = "have pity, sympathy, compassion").

Jesus' exorcisms and healings are seen in the Gospels as signs of the inbreaking of God's kingdom. The exorcisms are understood in terms of a battle between the forces of Satan and the forces of God; only a power opposed to Satan and stronger than he can cast out his agents (Mark 3:22-27 and //s), but the stronger power of God's kingdom is present in and through Jesus (cf. Matt 12:28//Luke 11:20). The new age in which the deaf hear, the blind see, the dumb speak, and the lame walk (see above, 20-1.3) is now here; Jesus' healings "are not just 'wonders' but are signs that the day of salvation promised in the OT has begun to dawn" (Gowan 1986: 95; cf. A. Richardson 1941: 38-40; R. H. Fuller 1963: 41). Unlike John, the Synoptics use the term "signs" *(sēmeia)* only in a bad sense: "An evil and adulterous generation asks for a sign" (Matt 12:39). In the Synoptics "signs" mean spectacular stunts, designed to *compel* belief. Behind the difference in terminology, however, the Synoptics and John are in basic agreement. In the Synoptics Jesus' exorcisms and healings are signs of the inbreaking of the kingdom — for those who have eyes to see (Richardson, 46-49; cf. 3-4.2) — while in John the "signs" are not proofs but rather challenges to faith.

Acts and the Epistles make it clear that exorcisms and healing continued in the early church. A link between Jesus and the church is found in the mission charge to his disciples in which they are commanded to heal (Matt 10:1, 8; Mark 6:7; Luke 9:1-2); while the charge has a specific historical setting, the Twelve are seen as modeling the type of ministry that will be continued by the church (contra Wilkinson 1974: 313-20). Visitation of the sick is one of the criteria for inheriting the kingdom (Matt 25:36). In the longer ending of Mark the risen Christ says future believers "will lay their hands on the sick, and they will recover" (16:18). In John 14:12 Jesus promises that believers will do the works he does, and in fact even greater ones. In Acts both Peter (3:1-10; 5:15) and Paul (14:8-10; 28:8-9) engage in healing. In 1 Cor 12:9, 28 Paul refers to "gifts of healing" in a way that assumes their existence in the church. Christian healers did not claim to heal the sick by their own power or piety (Acts 3:12); they healed "in the name of Jesus Christ of Nazareth" (3:6). The laying on of hands could be employed in healing (9:12, 17; 28:8).

Jas 5:13-18 gives us a revealing glimpse of the healing ministry of the early church (see Wilkinson 1971). The sick are to be anointed with oil (v. 14; cf. Mark 6:13); this may be symbolic, though the healing properties of oil are attested in the NT (Luke 10:34). The main emphasis is on *prayer*, especially corporate prayer. No fewer than four types of prayers are distinguished: prayer by the sick person (Jas 5:13), prayer by the elders who are representatives of the church (v. 14), prayer by believers for each other (v. 16), and prayer by a righteous person (vv. 16-18).

The people who populate the pages of the Gospels had little or no contact with doctors, although Mark 5:26 does record a disparaging remark regarding the woman who "had endured much under many physicians, and had spent all that she had; and she was no better, but rather grew worse." A totally different estimate of the medical profession is suggested by Paul's reference to "Luke, the beloved physician" (Col 4:14). Clearly there is no thought here of any conflict between the healing ministry of the church and the work of the medical profession.

Despite its emphasis on healing, the NT also recognizes that it may not always be God's will that a person be cured of his or her illness. Paul mentions a "physical infirmity" that played some role in his first visit to the Galatians (Gal 4:13; see commentaries for suggestions on the nature of the illness). This may or may not have been the same ailment alluded to in 2 Cor 12:7-10, where Paul describes some painful recurring illness from which he suffered as a "thorn in the flesh" (see Seybold and Mueller 1981: 171-82). Paul tells of how he three times asked God to take this away, but God's reply was, "My grace is sufficient for you, for my power is made perfect in weakness." It was not God's will that Paul should be healed of his disease; God could accomplish more by demonstrating his power through Paul's weakness (cf. 17-3.5d.iv). In 2 Tim 4:20 Paul comments that he left Trophimus ill in Miletus, while in 1 Tim 5:23 he advises Timothy to "no longer drink only water, but take a little wine for the sake of your stomach and your frequent ailments." These two colleagues of Paul, like Paul himself, evidently suffered ongoing health problems from which they were not healed. In Timothy's case Paul gives sensible advice on coping with illness based on the limited medical knowledge of the time.

20-3.4. BLESSING

As in the OT, "blessing" (*eulogia*; *eulogeō* = "to bless") can refer to all the good gifts received from God in this life, but in the NT the emphasis shifts from material to spiritual blessings.

a. God Has Blessed Us

The NT assumes more than it restates the OT view that all blessings come from God (cf. Jas 1:17). For example, rain that falls on the earth, making it fertile and fruitful, is assumed to be a blessing sent from God (Heb 6:7). The NT emphasis, however, is on spiritual blessings rather than on material prosperity and security: God "has blessed us in Christ with *every spiritual blessing* in the heavenly places" (Eph 1:3; see 3-3.3e). In fact, in the NT "there is a decidedly new formulation in which the word *blessing* characterizes God's saving activity in Christ" (Westermann 1978: 66). God's people have been blessed by the sending to them of his Servant, Jesus (Acts 3:26), in fulfillment of the promise to Abraham (Gen 12:2; cf. Gal 3:9), and God's greatest blessing, now available to all humankind, is to be found in Christ (cf. Rom 15:29). Those who are blessed by the Father will inherit the kingdom (Matt 25:34).

b. Blessed Be God

In response, God's people "bless" him for what they receive. When the aged Simeon saw the boy Jesus, "he took him up in his arms and blessed God" (Luke 2:28 RSV). Blessing God can take the form of an exclamation: "Blessed be the God and Father of our Lord Jesus Christ" (Eph 1:3). God is to be thanked for daily provisions in the form of a "blessing" before a meal (cf. Mark 6:41). Jesus teaches the importance of this by means of example, at the feeding of the crowds (Mark 6:41 and //s), at the Last Supper (14:22), and at the meal at Emmaus (Luke 24:30). Blessing finds a place in Christian worship, for at the Lord's Supper the church follows Jesus' example in blessing the bread and wine. The cup of wine is "the cup of blessing that we bless" (1 Cor 10:16).

c. He Blessed Them

People may bless other people, in effect asking God's blessing upon them. Thus Jesus blessed young children (Mark 10:13-16), and also his own disciples (Luke 24:50-51). Believers are called upon to bless even their enemies (Luke 6:28; 1 Pet 3:9; Rom 12:14).

d. Blessed Are Those

The NT also employs the idiom of the makarism or beatitude (cf. above, 20-1.4d), by which a person or persons are pronounced blessed or happy (see Mowry 1962: 370-71). For example, when a woman exclaimed to Jesus, "Blessed *(makaria)* is the womb that bore you and the breasts that nursed you!" he responded, "Blessed *(makarioi)* rather are those who hear the word of God and obey it!" (Luke 11:27-28). In Rom 14:22 Paul declares, "Blessed are those who have no reason to condemn themselves," while the book of Revelation has a series of *seven* beatitudes beginning with 1:3, "Blessed is the one who reads aloud the words of the prophecy, and blessed are those who hear and who keep what is written in it" (see also 14:13; 16:15; 19:9; 20:6; 22:7, 14).

Most significant, however, are *the* Beatitudes, the series of Jesus' pronouncements found in Matt 5:3-12 with partial parallels in Luke 6:20-23. There are differences of form and content (see commentaries; Mowry 1962; Guelich 1976), but Matthew's version is fuller, with nine beatitudes, and is also the one that accords most closely with the OT idiom. Jesus, of course, is not referring to nine separate groups of people (cf. J. R. W. Stott 1978: 31); the Beatitudes are addressed to those who respond to his message, and the first clause of each pronouncement (e.g., "Blessed are the poor in spirit") refers to some aspect of their character, while the second (e.g., "for theirs is the kingdom of heaven") describes some aspect of their blessedness. Is that blessedness experienced now, or only in the future? The Beatitudes certainly recall the apocalyptic makarism, and Matt 5:4, "Blessed are those who mourn, for they will be comforted," is reminiscent of *Tob* 13:14. The wording, however, varies between present and future, and the reference to the kingdom in Matt 5:3 and 5:10 suggests that this question poses a false alternative. The blessedness that Jesus' followers will enjoy in the coming kingdom can be experienced in anticipation here and now: "we enjoy the firstfruits now; the full harvest is yet to come" (Stott, 35).

The form of the Beatitudes has led some to see them as "entrance requirements" for the kingdom: only those who display all the qualities listed will be admitted. But it is vital to see the Beatitudes in their wider canonical context: they are addressed to those who have responded to Jesus' proclamation and inauguration of the kingdom. They are to be seen "in the dynamic context of proclamation and response"; "the future blessing (salvation) is so announced to the hearer in Jesus' word of authority that the hearer becomes a new person through Jesus' summons, a person called by God and therefore blessed" (Guelich 1976: 433, quoting from Schweizer, *NTS* 19 [1973]: 126).

The Beatitudes above all demonstrate the paradoxical nature of blessing in the NT. In some ways they turn the OT idea of blessing upside down. It is not the rich but the poor who are blessed (Matt 5:3; Luke 6:20), not the well fed but the hungry (Matt 5:6; Luke 6:21). True blessing is found in spite of — in fact, almost because of — suffering and persecution (Matt 5:10-12). Thus "the NT beatitudes stress the eschatological joy of participating in the kingdom of God, rather than rewards for this earthly life" (Mowry 1962: 370).

20-3.5. JOY

As in the OT, God's gifts of life, peace, healing, and blessing are the grounds for believers' rejoicing (*chairō* = "rejoice"; *chara* = "joy"; *agalliaomai* = "exult, be overjoyed"; *agalliasis* = "exultation"; on these and other cognate terms, see Beyreuther and Finkenrath 1976; Morrice 1984: 19-81). As Ewert (1980) remarks, "the note of joy is struck everywhere in the New Testament from the outbursts of song at the birth of Jesus to the hallelujah choruses of the Apocalypse" (169).

"Rejoice always," Paul exhorts the Thessalonians (1 Thess 5:16), while to the Philippians he says, "Rejoice in the Lord always; again I will say, Rejoice" (Phil 4:4). While joy may be occasioned by such things as fruitful seasons (Acts 14:17) or a reunion with friends (1 Cor 16:17), in the NT the prime cause of rejoicing is the Christ event; indeed, "the whole NT message as the proclamation of God's saving work in Christ is a message of joy" (Beyreuther and Finkenrath 1976: 357). Joy is the reaction to Jesus' birth (Luke 2:10 — "good news of great joy for all the people"), to his mighty works (13:17; 19:37), to his resurrection (Matt 28:8; John 20:20), and to his ascension (Luke 24:52). Hearing the word of the gospel brings joy (Matt 13:20, 44). According to Acts 13:52, "the disciples were filled with joy and with the Holy Spirit." As in the OT, joy is expressed particularly in corporate worship; in the earliest Jerusalem community, "exultant joy and thanksgiving were prominent characteristics of all its members as they attended the temple daily and as they met for eucharistic worship in private homes. Their very meals were festivals of exultation (Acts 2:46)" (Morrice 1984: 22). Believers also find joy in the compassionate service of those in need (Rom 12:8), and Paul reminds the Corinthians that "God loves a cheerful giver" (2 Cor 9:7, quoting Prov 22:8 LXX). In the Johannine literature there is a special emphasis on the *fullness* of joy that Christ can bestow: "I have said these things to you," declares Jesus to his disciples, "so that my joy may be in you, and that your joy may be complete *(plērōthē(i))*" (John 15:11; cf. 16:24; 17:13; 1 John 1:4; see Beyreuther and Finkenrath, 359; Morrice, 107-8).

A deeper note enters the NT understanding of joy, however, for believers are frequently called upon to rejoice in the midst of suffering (cf. D. Harvey 1962: 1001; Beilner 1981: 441). Jesus calls on his followers to rejoice in persecution (Matt 5:11-12; cf. Acts 5:41), and in Acts 16:25 we find Paul and Silas living out this truth as they sing hymns in prison at midnight (cf. 16:34). The paradox of joy even in the midst of weakness (2 Cor 13:9), sorrow (6:10), and suffering (Col 1:24) is brought out most sharply in the Pauline Epistles (see Beyreuther and Finkenrath 1976: 359-61). The secret lies in the fact that the believer rejoices "in the Lord *(en kyriō(i))*" (Phil 3:1; 4:4), and that joy is one of the fruits of the Spirit (Gal 5:22; cf. Rom 14:17; 1 Thess 1:6). Such joy is not only individual, but can be shared by the Christian community (cf. 2 Cor 2:3; Phil 2:17). "Whenever you face trials of any kind," counsels James, "consider it nothing but joy" (1:2; cf. 1 Pet 1:6; 4:13).

Believers are sustained in present trials through the assurance of fullness of joy in the new age. The faithful servant will receive the invitation, "Enter into the joy of your master" (Matt 25:21; cf. Luke 10:20). Believers are called to follow in the footsteps of their Lord, who "for the sake of the joy that was set before him endured the cross" (Heb 12:2). The eschatological banquet is a symbol of joy (Rev 19:7; see more fully, 14-4.5b). God, Jude assures his readers, will "make you stand without blemish in the presence of his glory with rejoicing (*agalliasis* = 'exultation'; KJV 'exceeding joy')" (v. 24). Thus "joy is at the same time pledge, possession, and essential part of that day when the redeemed will praise God: 'Let us rejoice and exult . . . , for the marriage of the Lamb has come' (Rev 19:7)" (Beilner 1981: 442).

New Testament: Consummation

20-4. YOU WILL LIVE ALSO

Compared with the OT, the NT reveals a considerable shift of emphasis in regard to belief in life after death; this shift is brought about by the Christ event and its consequences.

20-4.1. THE FACT OF DEATH

Like the OT, the NT frankly faces the reality of physical death. It is God "alone who has immortality" (1 Tim 6:16); human beings are those who are "mortal" (Rom 6:12; Heb 7:8). "It is appointed for mortals to die once, and after that the judgment" (Heb 9:27). In fact, in the NT there is always the possibility that loyalty to one's faith may cost one's life (Rev 2:10; 12:11), as in the cases of Stephen (Acts 7:54-60), Paul (21:13; cf. 2 Cor 4:11-12; Phil 1:21), Peter (John 21:18-19), and Antipas (Rev 2:13) (cf. 16-3.5). No one knows when one's life may come to an end (Luke 12:16-21).

20-4.2. THE UNDERSTANDING OF DEATH

The NT in part echoes what the OT says about death, but in a number of important ways its understanding of death goes beyond that of the OT.

a. Spiritual Death

Like the OT (above, 20-2.2b), the NT recognizes that just as life can be experienced here and now (20-3.1), so can death. Those who rebel against and depart from the Father enter into the sphere of death, like the prodigal son, of whom it was said, "This brother of yours *was dead* and has come to life" (Luke 15:32). For John, "whoever does not love abides in death" (1 John 3:14). In Paul "death" is used "in the widest possible metaphoric use of the term: as everything within creation which deviates from the Creator's design" (L. R. Bailey 1979: 88). "To set the mind on the flesh is death" (Rom 8:6), and apart from Christ a person is "dead through the trespasses and sins" (Eph 2:1-2; cf. Rom 7:9-10, 24). Even for the most committed Christian there is a sense in which "death is at work in us" (cf. 2 Cor 4:10-12).

b. The Power of Death

The OT, with its strong insistence on the LORD as the only God, largely rejects the idea of any rival power, and therefore of any power representing the forces of death. In the NT, however, there is a much clearer and fuller recognition of a personal adversary and of powers opposed to God (see 4-3). Hence in the NT death is linked with Satan. Death and Hades can be personified (Rev 1:18; 6:8; 20:13-14), and Death is regarded as an enemy, the last of the powers opposing God to be destroyed (1 Cor 15:26).

c. Sin and Death

More clearly than the OT, the NT affirms a connection between sin and physical death. In Romans and 1 Corinthians Paul takes up the interpretation of Gen 3 found in *Wis* 1–2. "Many died through the one man's [i.e., Adam's] trespass. . . . The judgment following one trespass brought condemnation. . . . One man's trespass led to condemnation for all" (Rom 5:15-18); hence "the wages of sin is death" (6:23). "Death came through a human being," i.e., Adam (1 Cor 15:21-22), and "the sting of death is sin" (15:56), for sin makes one liable to the judgment.

d. Length of Days

While the NT is not entirely free of the view that human sinfulness can result in life being cut short (cf. the death of Herod Agrippa in Acts 12:20-23), nevertheless it generally abandons such an idea. The death of Jesus himself is a striking illustration of the fact that "the good die young."

20-4.3. BECAUSE HE LIVES

The NT is characterized by a firm and confident faith that for believers the life they have begun to experience here and now will continue, but in fuller measure, beyond physical death.

a. The Teaching of Jesus

Although it is not the *teaching* of Jesus that constitutes the cornerstone of the NT's view of life after death, Jesus in his ministry did clearly and unambiguously align himself with the Pharisees and accepted their belief in a future resurrection (cf. above, 20-2.4b). He can readily refer in a saying, the main point of which lies elsewhere, to "the resurrection of the righteous" (Luke 14:14). More explicit and detailed is the story of the rich man and Lazarus (16:19-31), in which the two main characters both survive physical death: Lazarus is "carried by the angels to Abraham's bosom," while the rich man finds himself "in Hades *(en tō(i) ha(i)dē(i))*, being in torment" (vv. 22-23 RSV). The theme of a future judgment assumes that of a general resurrection, to be followed by rewards and punishments (Matt 10:28//Luke 12:4-5; Matt 25:31-46). John's Gospel is as clear on this as the Synoptics: "The hour is coming when all who are in their graves will hear his voice and will come out — those who have done good, to the resurrection of life, and those who have done evil, to the resurrection of condemnation" (5:28-29). On the future judgment, see more fully 16-4.3.

Jesus' most explicit teaching comes in response to a trick question posed by representatives of the Sadducees (Mark 12:18-27//Matt 22:23-33//Luke 20:27-40; see Kaiser and Lohse 1981: 124-25). They cite the case of a woman who, following the levirate law (Deut 25:5-6), is married in turn to seven brothers, and ask, "In the resurrection whose wife will she be?" Brushing aside this attempt to make the belief appear ludicrous, Jesus affirms that people do indeed rise from the dead and declares, "And as for the dead being raised, have you not read in the book of Moses, in the story about the bush, how God said to him, 'I am the God of Abraham, the God of Isaac, and the God of Jacob'? He is God not of the dead, but of the living; you are quite wrong" (Mark 12:26-27). Jesus quotes Exod 3:6, the words of God to Moses at the burning bush. By that time Abraham, Isaac, and Jacob were long dead, but God uses the present tense and says, "*I am* the God of Abraham...." For Jesus this implies that the close personal relationship that existed between God and each of the patriarchs was of such a nature that it could not be broken by death; hence they must have continued to live beyond death in fellowship with God.

It may fairly be said that in Jesus' teaching, "while a resurrection of the dead is assumed . . . it is not stressed in such a fashion as to deprecate the importance of this life" (L. R. Bailey 1979: 92).

b. Raising the Dead

On three occasions the Gospels tell of how Jesus in his ministry raised individuals from the dead, demonstrating a power that is greater than death: the raising of Jairus's daughter (Matt 9:18-19, 23-26//Mark 5:22-24, 35-43//Luke 8:40-42,

49-56); the raising of the widow of Nain's son (Luke 7:11-17); and the raising of Lazarus (John 11:1-44). It is significant that in his response to the question of John the Baptist, Jesus not only calls attention to his healings, but also to the fact that "the dead are raised" (Matt 11:5//Luke 7:22); the clear implication is that these are signs of the dawning of the new age. The accounts of Jesus raising the dead also echo the stories of Elijah and Elisha (cf. above, 20-2.1), but at best the OT prophets are types of the prophetic Messiah who has appeared in the person of Jesus. Implicitly Jesus' miracles have a significance far beyond the temporary restoration of some individuals to life. It is clear that "the Evangelists undoubtedly held that He Who had raised Jairus's Daughter, the Widow's Son and Lazarus would likewise raise all those who had died in Him; these miracles were but the signs of the greater resurrection which He would accomplish on His return in glory" (A. Richardson 1941: 75). What is *implicit* in the Synoptic stories becomes very *explicit* in John. John 11 is a pivotal chapter in the Gospel, and both points forward to Jesus' impending death (v. 51) and resurrection and also presents Jesus as the one who will grant resurrection and life to those who believe. The raising of Lazarus "was a sign of Christ's power over death itself and is thus a confirmation of the universal resurrection of the dead, which has been made possible in and through the Lord's own glorious resurrection" (Cronk 1982: 183). The key verses, located in the center of the narrative, are 25 and 26, where Jesus says, "I am the resurrection and the life. Those who believe in me, even though they die, will live, and everyone who lives and believes in me will never die." The three Gospel accounts of the raising of the dead thus constitute "a pledge of the conquest of death by Jesus" (Ewert 1980: 96).

c. The Resurrection of Christ and the Resurrection of Believers

The distinctive NT view of life after death is focused in Jesus' own death and resurrection; it is his victory over death that guarantees and assures believers of their coming victory. As part of the earliest Christian preaching, the apostles proclaimed that "*in Jesus* there is the resurrection of the dead" (Acts 4:2). When Paul arrived in Athens, he proclaimed to the philosophers "Jesus and the resurrection" (17:18; cf. v. 32).

Paul, it is true, was willing to identify himself as a Pharisee and thus a believer in the resurrection, but this was in exceptional circumstances, before a Jewish audience (23:6; cf. also 24:15; see Bruce 1971: 457). In his epistles, without exception, Paul grounds faith in a future resurrection of believers in Jesus' death and resurrection. Thus in Rom 5 Paul argues that death came into the world through Adam's sin, but Christ's death and resurrection have reversed this process: "Just as one man's trespass led to condemnation for all, so one man's act of righteousness leads to justification and life for all" (v. 18; cf. v. 21). As a result, "death is no longer an irrational tragedy clamouring for solution, but a recognized enemy over whom victory can be won in the power of Christ. The decisive battle has already been fought; the final triumph is no longer in doubt" (R. W. Thomas 1968: 209).

Paul's whole argument in 1 Cor 15 depends on the assumption that there is a very close link between Christ's resurrection and the resurrection of believers: "If Christ has not been raised, your faith is futile. . . . Then those also who have fallen asleep in Christ have perished" (vv. 17-18; see vv. 12-19). "Christ has been raised from the dead, the first fruits *(aparchē)* of those who have died" (v. 20); as the "first fruits" represent the whole harvest, so Christ's resurrection represents, anticipates, and guarantees the resurrection of believers (cf. M. J. Harris 1983: 109-12). Because he is the inclusive representative of humanity (cf. 7-3.3b), "when Christ now is called the firstfruits, this is meant to say that as the Resurrected One he stands for the whole of humanity. With Christ's resurrection, the resurrection of the dead has already begun" (Kaiser and Lohse 1981: 134). Christ is the "firstborn from the dead" *(prōtotokos ek tōn nekrōn* — Col 1:18; cf. Rev 1:5). He "abolished death and brought life and immortality to light through the gospel" (2 Tim 1:10). Christ's victory over the devil (cf. 9-3.4a) was at the same time a victory over death (cf. Heb 2:14-15). Thus it is Christ's resurrection that is the basis of the Christian's "living hope" (1 Pet 1:3-4). Christ now has "the keys of Death and of Hades" (Rev 1:18).

Here we encounter once again the typical NT already/not yet tension. So long as the old order continues, the fact of physical death remains — for believers, as for all humankind. The final defeat and elimination of the power of Death will come only at the final consummation (1 Cor 15:24-26). At that time Death and Hades will be thrown into the lake of fire (Rev 20:14) and "death will be no more" (21:4).

20-4.4. HOW ARE THE DEAD RAISED?

For many people the assurance of a future life is not enough; they seek fuller information and, like the interlocutor in 1 Cor 15:35, ask, "How are the dead raised? With what kind of body do they come?" Although Paul calls such a questioner a "fool," he does take the question seriously and attempts to answer it (vv. 36-50). Other passages in Paul and elsewhere in the NT also address this question, though only in a limited way.

a. Two Scenarios

The NT presents two alternative eschatological scenarios and two alternative ways of understanding what happens at the death of the individual.

i. At the Last Trumpet

One timetable associates the resurrection with the apocalyptic events of the final consummation, following the parousia and the last judgment. Thus the vision of the sheep and the goats (Matt 25:31-46) depicts the coming of the Son of Man followed by the judgment, at which people are assigned their final destinations, the righteous going to "eternal life." Apparently, even at a very early stage the question had arisen in the Thessalonian church: If the resurrection takes place at the final consummation, what happens to those who die before then? In answering this question Paul provides in 1 Thess 4:13-18 an apocalyptic timetable, according to which the Lord himself will descend (= parousia), the dead in Christ will rise first, those still alive will rise to meet the Lord, and "we will be with the Lord forever." In other words, those who have already died will be at no disadvantage; all believers will share the same resurrection life. In v. 17 Paul says that those who are alive at the time of the parousia "will be caught up (*harpagēsometha*) in the clouds . . . to meet the Lord." The use here of the verb *harpazō*, meaning snatch or seize, has led some to term this event the "rapture" (Lat. *rapio, raptum* = "snatch, seize"). As has already been noted (3-5.5; 7-5.6), there is no biblical basis for detaching the so-called rapture foreseen in 1 Thess 4:17 from the other events of the final consummation, including the parousia and the last judgment, and inserting an interval between the two; this is to impose on the NT an apocalyptic timetable that has no warrant in the biblical material itself.

A similar apocalyptic context for the resurrection is assumed in 1 Corinthians, though with fewer details: "We will not all die, but we will all be changed, in a moment, in the twinkling of an eye, at the last trumpet. For the trumpet will sound, and the dead will be raised imperishable, and we will be changed" (15:51-52).

The book of Revelation is unique in envisaging *two* resurrections. At the millennium (cf. 3-4.4b) the martyrs are raised and reign with Christ for the thousand years: "They came to life and reigned with Christ a thousand years. . . . This is *the first resurrection*" (20:4-5). Everyone other than the martyrs awaits the final resurrection and judgment (20:11-15).

A natural question that arises in connection with this scenario is: What happens to believers who die between the time of their death and the final consummation? The NT repeatedly says of those who have died that they have "fallen asleep" (Matt 27:52; John 11:11; Acts 7:60; 13:36; 1 Thess 4:13; 2 Pet 2:3). This would be in line with one strand in Jewish thought (see 2 *Esdr* 7:32). Some see this as little other than a euphemism for "they died" (see Whiteley 1964: 262-69), but taken at face value it suggests that on death individuals enter a state of sleep, i.e., unconsciousness, in which they remain until the day of resurrection.

ii. Today . . . in Paradise

The second view found in the NT is that the righteous enter the future state immediately upon death. This view would be compatible with another strand in Jewish thought (see 2 *Esdr* 7:75-101). In Jesus' story of Dives and Lazarus, the two men who die go immediately to Abraham's bosom and Hades respectively (Luke 16:19-31). On the cross Jesus assures the dying criminal: "Today you will be with me in Paradise" (Luke 23:43). In Phil 1:21-23 Paul does not know whether he prefers to die now or live longer. "I am hard pressed between the two: my desire is to depart and be with Christ." This seems to imply an immediate entering upon the future state at death. Something of the same understanding may underlie the discussion of the future life in 2 Cor 5:1-5; Paul's preference for being "away from the body and at home with the Lord" (5:8; cf. 5:6) may suggest that the transition takes place at death (cf. M. J. Harris 1983: 98-101). Some have seen here evidence of a development in Paul's thought, with the earlier scenario being replaced, as Paul's own death drew nearer, by the second scenario. The theory of a development of Paul's thought (that would have had to take place over a relatively short period of time) is less popular today than it once was (cf. Whiteley 1964: 248; B. F. Meyer 1989). The fact remains that two differing scenarios stand side by side in the canonical text, and both are part of the canonical witness.

iii. Resolving the Tension?

Various attempts have been made to reconcile the two scenarios. Those passages that refer to going to Abraham's bosom/Paradise/being with Christ could be taken to refer to an intermediate state, to be followed at the end by the resurrection (so M. J. Harris 1983: 134-35). Against this it must be noted that (a) none of these passages contain any reference to the resurrection as a still-future event; (b) all these passages refer in their own way to the final state (what more could a still-future resurrection bring?); (c) if these passages refer to an intermediate state, they are difficult to reconcile with those texts that speak of the period prior to the resurrection as a sleep. It is best to acknowledge the presence within the canon of two scenarios and not attempt a forced reconciliation of them.

b. A Spiritual Body

Historically, it is likely that within the Judaism of NT times a variety of views existed regarding the nature of the future life. Some no doubt accepted a very literal belief in a resurrection of the actual physical body. This probably lay behind the Sadducees' question to Jesus about whose wife the woman would be in the resurrection. Jesus, however, clearly rejects the premise on which the question was based. "Is not this the reason you are wrong, that you know neither the scriptures nor the power of God? For when they rise from the dead, they neither marry nor are given in marriage, but are *like angels in heaven*" (Mark 12:24-25 and //s). "This contrast suggests that the resurrection body will be without sexual passions or procreative powers, not that the resurrected righteous will be sexless (since sexual identity is an essential part of personality, and personality is retained in the resurrection)" (M. J. Harris 1983: 123). There will indeed be a future resurrection, but the future life cannot be pictured simply as a continuation of our present physical existence; God will provide us with a transformed mode of existence that will not be subject to the limitations of this present life. Jesus' view is thus akin to that found in Dan 12:3 (cf. above, 20-2.4b).

Paul's classic discussion in 1 Cor 15:35-50 is entirely in line with Jesus' teaching. As a good Jew, "Paul evidently could not contemplate immortality apart from resurrection; for him a body of some kind was essential to personality" (Bruce 1971: 469). Thus, by the use of analogies (seed/fruit, human/animal bodies, and terrestrial/celestial bodies) he teaches that there will be a resurrection of the "body," *but the physical body will be transformed into a spiritual body.* It is not the physical human flesh, the *sarx,* that survives; Paul clearly states that "flesh *(sarx)* and blood cannot inherit the kingdom of God" (1 Cor 15:50). It is a *sōma* which survives, though a *sōma pneumatikon,* a "spiritual body" (15:44), which, unlike the physical body, is imperishable and is characterized by glory and power (15:42-43). The resurrection body of believers is analogous to the resurrection body of Christ; hence we await a Savior who "will change our lowly body to be like his glorious body" (Phil 3:20-21 RSV). Similarly in 2 Cor 5:1, "the earthly tent" (the physical body) will be replaced by "a building from God" (the spiritual body). Death involves being both "unclothed" and being "further clothed" (5:4).

The NT is thus consistent in affirming that at the resurrection God will provide believers with an appropriate form of existence, a "spiritual body." As "spiritual" *(pneumatikon),* it will be free from weakness, infirmity, and decay. As a "body" *(sōma),* it will be in continuity with our present existence, and will ensure the continuance of the individual personality.

c. With Christ

As has frequently been observed, the NT is on the whole remarkably reticent in its description of the future state. The main exception is the book of Revelation, which does speak of heaven using a rich variety of imagery and symbolism.

The future state can be referred to concisely as being "with Christ" (Luke 23:43 — "with me"; 1 Thess 4:17 — "with the Lord"; Phil 1:23 — "with Christ"). The best clue as to the nature of the life hereafter is the nature of that abundant life "in Christ" that Christians experience here and now.

The Spirit serves as a first installment of what is to come hereafter (see 5-4). Of all the gifts of the Spirit, the most enduring and hence the one that will be most characteristic of the future life is love *(agapē)* (1 Cor 13:8-13).

Three times in the NT the future state is termed "Paradise" (Luke 23:43; 2 Cor 12:3; Rev 2:7). The Greek *paradeisos* is a loanword from the Persian meaning a garden. The Rev 2:7 reference certainly indicates an allusion to Gen 2–3. The final state of humankind will be like the original situation in the Garden of Eden before the rebellion against God and the intrusion of sin. The original fellowship between humankind and God will be restored, and the faithful will at last have access to the tree of life (Rev 2:7).

In John 14:2 Jesus assures his disciples that "in my Father's house there are many dwelling places *(monai)*." *Monē* can mean a room, dwelling place, and also a resting place for a traveler on a journey. But any speculation about progress in the future life or an ascent to God through many stages (typical of some forms of gnosticism) has no basis in the NT (cf. Ewert 1980: 148-49).

It is important to note that the NT images of the future life generally have a strongly *corporate* element. Believers will participate in the eschatological banquet (see 14-4.5b), sharing it with the patriarchs (Matt 8:11). The picture of Lazarus after death in "Abraham's bosom *(eis ton kolpon Abraam)*" (Luke 16:22-23) may be associated with the same image: when we recall that at the Last Supper the Beloved Disciple reclined "on Jesus' bosom *(en tō(i) kolpō(i) tou Iēsou)*" (John 13:23 KJV), Lazarus is probably pictured as reclining at table with Abraham, i.e., in the eschatological banquet (cf. Ewert 1980: 153). Similarly, Rev 19 pictures the great eschatological wedding feast. The key symbol in the book of Revelation, the holy city, new Jerusalem, is essentially a corporate one. In Rev 21–22 John combines elements drawn from Gen 2 (the river of the water of life, the tree of life) with the expectation of the heavenly/eschatological Jerusalem (for a fuller discussion, see 13-4.2). At the center of the vision is the presence of God with his *people* (21:3). Balancing this, however, we may note that the letters to the seven churches each conclude with a word directed to faithful *individual* members of the churches: they are promised a share in the blessings of the closing vision (see, e.g., 2:10; cf. Beasley-Murray 1974: 85).

When all is said and done, the NT remains reticent about the future life and regards its nature as a mystery but dimly comprehended in this life: now "we see in a mirror, dimly" (1 Cor 13:12).

d. Immortality

The NT belief in resurrection is frequently and rightly contrasted with belief in the "immortality of the soul," in the sense that every person is endowed with a soul or spirit that automatically survives beyond death (cf. Cullmann 1958, and see above, 20-2.4). But as M. J. Harris (1983: chaps. 7, 8) has pointed out, the NT does use two words that can be translated "immortality," *athanasia* = "not subject to death," and *aphtharsia* (adjective *aphthartos*) = "not subject to corruption." Although in a sense God alone has immortality (1 Tim 6:16), nevertheless Christ "abolished death and brought life and immortality *(aphtharsia)* to light through the gospel" (2 Tim 1:10). As a result of Christ's victory over death, immortality becomes a possibility for those who believe the gospel. Hence at the resurrection, "the dead will be raised imperishable *(aphthartoi)*" (1 Cor 15:52), i.e., those who are believers will receive from God the gift of immortality by entering into life that is subject to neither death nor decay (Rom 2:7; 1 Cor 9:25; 15:53-54; 1 Pet 1:4).

There is no contradiction in speaking of the Christian hope for a future life in terms of both "resurrection" and "immortality." "The two concepts," as Harris (1983) has shown, "are complementary. A resurrection transformation of the type described in the New Testament guarantees that immortality is personal rather than ideal, racial or pantheistic, is corporate rather than individualistic, and is somatic rather than spiritual. On the other hand, NT teaching about immortality guarantees that resurrection is a continuing state rather than simply a single event, is a permanent rather than a temporary condition, and is a transformed state constantly sustained by God's life and power" (239-40).

20-4.5. ATTITUDES TO DEATH

To fear death is natural, but Christians know that Christ partook of human nature in order to "free those who all their lives were held in slavery by the fear of death" (Heb 2:15). In the face of death, believers are not to "grieve as others do who have no hope"; in their faith they have the source of mutual comfort (1 Thess 4:13, 18).

Although death is regarded as an enemy power and is associated with Satan, Christians are assured of victory; death, along with the other powers, has been defeated so that believers can be sure that "neither death, nor life . . . will be able to separate us from the love of God in Christ Jesus our Lord" (Rom 8:38-39; cf. 1 Cor 15:57).

In its recognition of the need for decent burial, the early church followed Jewish custom (Mark 15:46; 16:1; Acts 5:6, 9-10; 8:2).

The NT knows nothing of prayers for the dead. Those who have died are in the hands of a merciful God, the God and Father of our Lord Jesus Christ.

20-5. LIFE: THEOLOGICAL REFLECTIONS

1. It is a classic criticism of Christianity that it is concerned with "pie in the sky by and by," and hence by implication devalues life here on earth and ignores its

problems and injustices. Against any such view the OT constitutes a powerful antidote. Here is an area in which a truly *biblical* theology is essential. The NT does not cancel out what the OT has to say about life here and now; it supplements it. Here, if anywhere, what both OT and NT have to say has to be taken into consideration and held in balance.

The basic question of the OT, it has often been noted, is not "Do you believe in life *after* death?" but "Do you believe in life *before* death?" Throughout the OT there is a ringing affirmation of life in this world: of life that is the gift of God, of life that is to be lived in accordance with the will of God, and above all of life that is to be lived in fellowship with God if it is to be enjoyed to the full. In the NT the emphasis certainly shifts, but the NT does not cancel out the OT's affirmation of life in the here and now. It does add a new dimension to it, especially in Paul and John, where true life is found in Christ and is both a present possession and a future hope. In both Testaments "life" is a term rich in meaning that overlaps with the themes of peace, healing, blessing, and joy.

2. One of the greatest goods in this life is *shālôm:* health, wholeness, harmony, well-being of both individuals and society. In Christian piety "peace with God" has often been understood in highly individualistic terms, as an "inner peace":

Peace, perfect peace, in this dark world of sin?
The blood of Jesus whispers peace within.

This is not wrong, for the NT does speak of an inner peace that the world cannot give and cannot take away (above, 20-3.2). However, "peace" has to be seen in its total biblical context. For the NT, as for the OT, it is never purely individual; it always involves not just absence of conflict, but the health, wholeness, and well-being of the *society* of which the individual is part. Brueggemann (1976b) has written that *shālôm,* on the biblical understanding, "conveys a sense of personal wholeness in a community of justice and caring that addresses itself to the needs of all humanity and all creation" (185; cf. Launderville, Tambasco, and Wadell 1996: 713). In the Bible *shālôm* is essentially communal in nature and cannot be separated from God's demand for justice in society; "shalom making is working for just and health giving relationships between people and nations" (P. B. Yoder 1987: 15). Thus Christians who genuinely seek peace are called to work toward "reduction of violence between human beings and non-human creation, between human beings, and between the nations. Whenever violence is successfully reduced, there will be space for new life" (Duchrow and Liedke 1989: 147). On the other hand, the Bible does not teach that social action will automatically produce peace. The greatest barrier to peace is human sinfulness, and for the NT it is those who have found peace with God through forgiveness and justification that are then called to work for peace and justice in society.

3. In Scripture an important aspect of "life" is God's gift of healing. The point is frequently made, and rightly so, that the Bible does not separate the healing of body, mind, and spirit; it is concerned not with "soul salvation" but with "whole salvation." The salvation that Jesus brought included the healing of the sick via both exorcisms and physical healings. In many of Jesus' healings faith played a role, but modern attempts to explain this as merely the power of autosuggestion are wide of the mark. As A. Richardson (1941) points out, "the Gospel miracles of healing are not examples of 'faith-cures,' and attempts to explain them along these lines are far removed from the spirit of the Gospels" (63; cf. R. H. Fuller 1963: 42). Healing is accomplished by the power of God, though it is received *through* faith in most cases. Some have seen gifts of healing as abnormal phenomena, designed, as it were, to launch Christianity into the world but confined to the apostolic age. The NT does not support this view: Jesus' followers are commissioned to carry out a ministry of healing with no restrictions attached. In point of fact, the healing ministry of Jesus has been seen down through the centuries as a clear indication that all forms of disease, mental illness, and disability are contrary to the will of God, and hence as the great charter of Christian service to the sick, the handicapped, and the mentally ill. From the monastic hospitals of medieval times, through modern medical missions, to many contemporary healing ministries (see Wilkinson 1974: 325-28) the church has sought to obey Jesus' command to "heal the sick" (Matt 10:8 RSV).

Two points deserve careful notice. The first is that the Bible sees no conflict between prayer to God for healing and employing the services of a physician. Although *Sirach* is a deuterocanonical work, its insight that all healing comes from God is thoroughly in accord with the rest of Scripture. Its advice to pray for healing and then seek the best medical attention available provides a model that is as valid today as ever. Seeking medical help is not a sign of lack of faith, and the whole history of modern medical missions demonstrates how Christian faith and medical science can complement each other. BT can play an important role in recovering the holistic approach to healing that is characteristic of Scripture. As Wilkinson (1971) points out, it is unfortunate that the rise of modern medical science "coincided with the dominance of Cartesian dualism in philosophy with the result that medicine and the Church went their separate ways, the one to deal with the body and the other to deal with the soul. This separation has led to a great impoverishment of the work of both, and it is time that a truer perspective was restored to the situation and medicine and the Church seen as two parts of the whole instead of two opposed or unrelated wholes" (341-42).

The second point is that while the Bible emphasizes the healing power of God, it also recognizes that physical healing is not God's will in every case. Here, as always, it is important to consider the full range of the canonical evidence, and we noted both OT and NT examples of cases where physical healing did not take place. These examples show that it is never wrong to pray for healing, but also that prayer does not mean people demanding from God what they want but rather discerning the will of God for their lives (cf. 17-3.5d.iv). God always answers prayer, but sometimes, as in the case of Paul's "thorn in the flesh," the answer may involve not physical healing but grace and strength to cope with physical weakness.

Exorcism poses particularly difficult problems, and these were discussed in 4-5.4. Here we further note that two basic interpretations of the biblical material are possible. One asserts the reality of demon possession as a cause of forms of mental illness and supports the modern use of exorcism. McAll (a British consultant psychiatrist) advocates this position, emphasizing that the patient's family and friends should be involved, and that the patient should be led to a growing relationship with Jesus Christ in the context of the local Christian community (McAll 1975). M. Wilson (1975) warns of the dangers of this approach and sees Jesus' acceptance of demon possession as evidence of true incarnation: Jesus accepted the views current in his day. He stresses that whether exorcism is employed, or modern methods of healing, "recovery takes place only when the particular help is undergirded by a strong group or congregational life which is founded upon life's normality" (295). In the light of the BT of healing outlined above, it may be urged that prayer should play a central role, including prayer to be delivered from whatever powers of evil and disorder threaten physical, mental, and spiritual health, but that modern methods of healing should not be seen as replacing but rather complementing prayer, in the recognition that all true healing ultimately comes from God.

4. In the biblical understanding of "life," the blessings bestowed by God play an important role. The theme of blessing, however, is marked by a certain tension within canonical Scripture. The OT emphasizes God's ongoing activity in the whole of life and his gracious provision of material blessings in the form of fertility, progeny, security, long life, health, and happiness. It must not be forgotten, of course, that the OT also sees fellowship with God and life in obedience to his commandments as the greatest of blessings.

The NT, however, displays a considerable change of emphasis away from this-worldly blessings toward spiritual blessings, which can be anticipated now but experienced in full only in the coming kingdom. This raises a problem of translation. The makarism formula is often translated "O the happiness of . . ." or "Happy are . . ." "Happy," however, is not the best translation if it suggests a subjective feeling (cf. J. R. W. Stott 1978: 33) or the contentment that comes when all is well. Believers can be "blessed" by God even in the midst of persecution, for their state is grounded in God and not subject to the varying fortunes of this life. The two canonical emphases must somehow be held together: the NT understanding of blessing does not cancel out the OT but goes beyond it and puts it in a new perspective.

Blessing plays an important role in worship, especially the concluding blessing, a practice continued in the Christian church. As Westermann (1978) points out, "the blessing is a bridge that joins what happens in worship to what takes place outside. What has happened there is imparted to those who now leave one another to return to their daily lives" (106). Those who gather for worship know that God's blessing goes with them into their daily lives whatever may befall them there.

5. Throughout Scripture God's gifts of life, peace, healing, and blessing bring to believers a deep and lasting joy. The OT points especially to rejoicing as a mark of the corporate worship of God: worship is not intended to be solemn or dreary, but rather characterized by joyful praise, in which all creation joins. If the OT looks forward to the joy of God's eschatological salvation, the NT declares that the age of salvation has dawned, an age marked by rejoicing even in the midst of suffering and tribulation. For the NT too, however, joy has a forward look as Christians anticipate entering into the joy of their Lord at the final consummation. "The fact that the New Testament is the most joyful book in the world," Morrice (1984) asserts, "must have implications for us today. . . . Christian joy . . . should find expression in revitalized worship. . . . Again, it affects our daily life and work in the world. . . . For the Christian, pain and suffering are transformed, while service for others is given a new dimension, for we live for Christ and rejoice in his service" (154).

6. It has often been observed that in the nineteenth century the taboo subject, never mentioned in polite conversation, was sex, whereas in the twentieth century it was death. According to Gatch (1969), "the twentieth century has had a curious reticence about discussing, defining, and even facing death" (4). The Bible has no such reticence: both OT and NT speak openly and frankly about the fact of death. Scripture makes no bones about the finality of death, and it very clearly forbids any kind of "spiritualism" that tries to communicate with the dead (something that apparently still has a fascination for some people). The subject is touched on in the story of Saul and the medium of Endor, but by no stretch of the imagination can this one episode be viewed as providing biblical sanction for the practice of necromancy or spiritualism (cf. L. R. Bailey 1979: 33).

One of the surprises of BT is that the OT, for the most part, has no developed view of a future life; its focus, as we have seen, is largely on "life before death," and it was apparently content for many centuries to consign the dead to the virtual nonlife of Sheol. In one or two passages, however, it does look forward to a future resurrection, and we know that this tradition was developed in the two centuries before Jesus and formed a part of the faith of the Pharisees, a faith that was shared by Jesus and Paul.

The NT, however, does not simply continue the Pharisees' belief in a future resurrection. It grounds its clear and confident hope of the continuation of life beyond the grave in the death and resurrection of Christ. This confidence is coupled with a certain reticence to go into details about the future life. The NT, it has been observed, has little to say about the temperature of hell or the furniture of heaven. When it does venture into this area it inevitably makes use of analogies, which of course must not be pushed too far. Moreover, it has frankly to be acknowledged that it is difficult to fit everything the NT says about the future life into one consistent picture. It is best to recognize within the NT two scenarios. According to one, upon death people enter a state of sleep, from which they will be awakened at the final consummation and participate in the judgment and resurrection. According to the other view, people enter into their final state immediately upon death. The fact of two scenarios should not cause undue concern: even modern science employs two parallel theories to explain the nature of light (a wave theory and a particle theory). In any case, the difference between the two views should not be exaggerated. On the first view, from the perspective of the individual, if the intermediate period is a period of sleep, i.e., unconsciousness, then what individuals *experience* hardly differs from what they experience according to the second view. What we have are two different ways of saying that death is basically a falling asleep and an awakening to the future state.

An essential feature of the biblical view is that it looks for a *resurrection* of the dead. The continuation of life beyond the grave is not automatic; it is a gift conferred by God. The biblical view is not based, as was the Greek (Platonic) view (see Gatch 1969: 26-34), on the belief that every human being possesses a soul that is immortal, and that on death the soul continues in some form of future life. Such a view did in time enter Christianity, and many assume to this day that this is the orthodox Christian view. In biblical thought, however, human beings do not possess an immortal soul; the biblical writers see human beings basically as a unity, not in terms of separate parts (cf. 16-1.1; 16-3.1), and they would have great difficulty in thinking of a soul surviving without some kind of body. For the NT, what happens — be it at death or at the final consummation — is that God raises up believers and provides them with a "spiritual body," an appropriate form for their new existence. Belief in "the resurrection of the body" (one of the clauses of the Apostles' Creed) does *not* involve a literalistic view of a resumed physical existence (hence fears over what happens to those whose bodies are disfigured in accidents, or are cremated, are groundless). On the other hand, the provision of a spiritual *sōma* gives assurance of continuity with a person's earthly existence and the survival of the complete personality. "So far from involving a mystical absorption of individual personalities into the one Person, or a pantheistic absorption of the many into the One, the Christian hope entails the retention — intact — of personhood" (M. J. Harris 1983: 127).

Eternal life is a *gift* of God bestowed upon his people, not a natural endowment. For believers it begins here on earth, and life in Christ, in the Spirit, and in the fellowship of the church are but anticipations of the life that will continue beyond death. For believers death is still an enemy, but one that can be faced without fear. There may be much that remains a mystery about the future life, but the most important thing the NT teaches is that beyond death believers will be "with Christ"; if they know that, they know all they need to know.

Outline of Part II

CHAPTER 1: THE LIVING GOD

Outline of Part II

CHAPTER 2: THE LORD OF CREATION

OLD TESTAMENT: PROCLAMATION	NEW TESTAMENT: FULFILLMENT
2-1. **GOD CREATED THE HEAVENS AND THE EARTH**	2-3. **A NEW CREATION**
2-1.1. THE CREATED ORDER	2-3.1. THE GOD WHO MADE THE WORLD
a. Genesis 1–11	
b. Psalms	
c. Second Isaiah	
d. Wisdom	
2-1.2. CREATOR AND SUSTAINER	2-3.2. THE COSMIC CHRIST
a. In the Beginning	a. All Things Were Made by Him
b. Continuous Creation	b. Christ Who Is the Image of God
c. Cyclic Time	c. To Reconcile All Things
d. Creation and Chaos	
e. Ex Nihilo?	
f. God Saw That It Was Good	
2-1.3. LET THEM HAVE DOMINION	2-3.3. IN THE THINGS THAT HAVE BEEN MADE
a. Humankind as the Crown of Creation	
b. The Relation of Humankind to Creation	
c. In the Image of God	
2-1.4. CREATION THEOLOGY	2-3.4. THE CORRUPTION OF CREATION
a. The Heavens Declare the Glory of God	
b. Creation and Culture	
c. Every Living Thing	
2-1.5. THE CORRUPTION OF CREATION	2-3.5. REALIZED ESCHATOLOGY: A NEW CREATION
a. Human Society	a. We Have Seen His Star
b. The Physical Universe	b. With the Beasts
	c. Even Wind and Sea Obey Him
	d. Behold the New Has Come

OLD TESTAMENT: PROMISE	NEW TESTAMENT: CONSUMMATION
2-2. **NEW HEAVENS AND A NEW EARTH**	2-4. **NEW HEAVENS AND A NEW EARTH**
2-2.1. APOCALYPTIC ESCHATOLOGY: THE END OF HISTORY	2-4.1. APOCALYPTIC ESCHATOLOGY: THE END OF HISTORY
a. The Place of Apocalyptic in the Old Testament	
b. Characteristics of Apocalyptic Eschatology	
2-2.2. SIGNS OF THE TIMES: COSMIC UPHEAVALS	2-4.2. SIGNS OF THE TIMES: COSMIC UPHEAVALS
2-2.3. THE DAY OF THE LORD: COSMIC JUDGMENT	2-4.3. THE DAY OF THE LORD: COSMIC JUDGMENT
2-2.4. ALL THINGS NEW: COSMIC SALVATION	2-4.4. ALL THINGS NEW: COSMIC SALVATION
a. Paradise Restored	a. New Heavens and a New Earth
b. The Wolf and the Lamb	b. Paradise Restored
c. New Heavens and a New Earth	
2-2.5. THE TIME OF THE END	2-4.5. THE TIME OF THE END

2-5. THE LORD OF CREATION: THEOLOGICAL REFLECTIONS

OUTLINE OF PART II

CHAPTER 3: THE LORD OF HISTORY

OLD TESTAMENT: PROCLAMATION

3-1. **I WILL CALL TO MIND THE DEEDS OF THE LORD**

3-1.1. SALVATION HISTORY
   a. Linear Time
   b. Historical Sequences
   c. Historical Summaries
   d. Salvation History Psalms

3-1.2. THE STORY LINE
   a. The Patriarchal Period: God Calls the Ancestors of His People
   b. The Exodus Event: God Delivers His People
   c. The Entry: God Settles His People in the Land
   d. The Monarchy: God Rules His People through Kings
   e. The Exile: God Disciplines His People
   f. The Return: God Restores His People
   g. The Maccabees: God Again Delivers His People

3-1.3. GOD ACTS IN HISTORY
   a. Divine Intervention
   b. Divinely Inspired Leadership
   c. Judgment/Salvation
   d. Providence
   e. Blessing
   f. Suffering Love

3-1.4. GOD SPEAKS IN HISTORY
   a. Receiving God's Revelation
   b. Recognizing God's Activity

3-1.5. REMEMBER THE FORMER THINGS

NEW TESTAMENT: FULFILLMENT

3-3. **WE ARE WITNESSES TO ALL THAT HE DID**

3-3.1. THE CLIMAX OF SALVATION HISTORY

3-3.2. THE STORY LINE
   a. John the Baptist
   b. The Christ Event
   c. The Early Church

3-3.3. GOD ACTS IN HISTORY
   a. Divine Intervention
   b. Divinely Inspired Leadership
   c. Judgment/Salvation
   d. Providence
   e. Blessing
   f. Suffering Love

3-3.4. GOD SPEAKS IN HISTORY

3-3.5. DO THIS IN REMEMBRANCE OF ME

OLD TESTAMENT: PROMISE

3-2. **I WILL RESTORE THE FORTUNES OF MY PEOPLE**

3-2.1. PROPHETIC ESCHATOLOGY: THE END IN HISTORY
   a. The Psalms of Lament
   b. The Book of Lamentations

3-2.2. SIGNS OF THE TIMES: A TIME OF ANGUISH

3-2.3. JUDGMENT IN HISTORY

3-2.4. SALVATION IN HISTORY
   a. A New Exodus
   b. Restoration of the Davidic Kingdom

3-2.5. THE TIME OF THE END

NEW TESTAMENT: CONSUMMATION

3-4. **THE END WILL NOT FOLLOW IMMEDIATELY**

3-4.1. PROPHETIC ESCHATOLOGY: THE END IN HISTORY

3-4.2. SIGNS OF THE TIMES: TRIALS AND TRIBULATIONS

3-4.3. JUDGMENT IN HISTORY
   a. Judgment on Jerusalem
   b. Judgment on Rome

3-4.4. SALVATION IN HISTORY
   a. The Worldwide Preaching of the Gospel
   b. The Millennium

3-4.5. THE TIME OF THE END

3-5. THE LORD OF HISTORY: THEOLOGICAL REFLECTIONS

Outline of Part II

CHAPTER 4: THE ADVERSARY

OLD TESTAMENT: PROCLAMATION

4-1. OUR ADVERSARIES
4-1.1. WHAT THWARTS GOD'S PURPOSES?
4-1.2. THE HISTORICAL ORDER

  a. Historical Adversaries
  b. Personal Adversaries
  c. Treatment of Enemies

4-1.3. THE CREATED ORDER: POWERS OF CHAOS
  a. Creation and Conflict

  b. Here Shall Your Proud Waves Be Stopped
  c. You Broke the Heads of the Dragons

4-1.4. THE CREATED ORDER: POWERS OF EVIL

4-1.5. THE CREATED ORDER: THE ADVERSARY

NEW TESTAMENT: FULFILLMENT

4-3. OUR ADVERSARY, THE DEVIL
4-3.1. D-DAY AND V-DAY
4-3.2. ADVERSARIES IN THE HISTORICAL ORDER
  a. Historical Adversaries
  b. Treatment of Enemies

4-3.3. THE CREATED ORDER: SATAN

  a. That Ancient Serpent Who Is the Devil and Satan
  b. I Saw Satan Fall
  c. The Devil Prowls Around

4-3.4. THE CREATED ORDER: DEMONS
  a. All Who Were Possessed with Demons
  b. They Fell Down before Him
  c. He Gave Them Authority over Unclean Spirits

4-3.5. THE CREATED ORDER: POWERS
  a. The Spiritual Forces of Evil
  b. Triumphing over Them
  c. Who Shall Separate Us?

OLD TESTAMENT: PROMISE

4-2. WRATH TO HIS ADVERSARIES
4-2.1. INTENSIFICATION OF OPPOSITION AND FINAL VICTORY
4-2.2. THE HISTORICAL ORDER: INTENSIFICATION
4-2.3. THE HISTORICAL ORDER: VICTORY
  a. Their Dominion Shall Be Taken Away
  b. They Shall Be Put to Shame
4-2.4. THE CREATED ORDER: INTENSIFICATION

4-2.5. THE CREATED ORDER: VICTORY

NEW TESTAMENT: CONSUMMATION

4-4. THE ANTI-CHRIST
4-4.1. INTENSIFICATION OF OPPOSITION AND FINAL VICTORY
4-4.2. THE HISTORICAL ORDER: INTENSIFICATION
4-4.3. THE HISTORICAL ORDER: VICTORY

4-4.4. THE CREATED ORDER: INTENSIFICATION
  a. The Anti-Christ
  b. Satan Will Be Loosed
4-4.5. THE CREATED ORDER: VICTORY
  a. Victory over the Powers
  b. Victory over the Antichrist
  c. Victory over Satan
  d. No More Sea/Night

4-5. THE ADVERSARY: THEOLOGICAL REFLECTIONS

OUTLINE OF PART II

CHAPTER 5: THE SPIRIT

OLD TESTAMENT: PROCLAMATION

5-1. **THE SPIRIT OF THE LORD**
5-1.1. WHITHER SHALL I GO FROM YOUR SPIRIT?
  a. Wind, Breath, Spirit
  b. God as Spirit
  c. His Holy Spirit
5-1.2. THE CREATED ORDER: CREATION

5-1.3. THE CREATED ORDER: WISDOM

5-1.4. THE HISTORICAL ORDER: DIVINE CARE

5-1.5. THE HISTORICAL ORDER: HUMAN LEADERSHIP
  a. Ecstasy
  b. Prophecy
  c. Transferring of the Spirit

NEW TESTAMENT: FULFILLMENT

5-3. **ALL FILLED WITH THE HOLY SPIRIT**
5-3.1. THE PROMISE OF THE SPIRIT

  a. The Lucan Infancy Narrative
  b. John the Baptist

5-3.2. JESUS AND THE SPIRIT
  a. The Teaching of Jesus
    i. The Help of the Spirit
    ii. The Blasphemy against the Holy Spirit
  b. The Spirit of the Lord Is upon Me
5-3.3. THE GIVING OF THE SPIRIT
  a. All Were Given the One Spirit to Drink
  b. The Rush of a Mighty Wind
  c. Receive the Holy Spirit
    i. The Paraclete
    ii. He Breathed on Them
    iii. Worship in Spirit
5-3.4. THE GIFTS OF THE SPIRIT
  a. Varieties of Gifts
  b. The Gift of Tongues
  c. Testing the Spirits
    i. Test Everything
    ii. Give Me This Power
    iii. Do Not Believe Every Spirit
5-3.5. SPIRIT, SON, AND FATHER

  a. The Holy Spirit
  b. Spirit of God/Spirit of Christ

OLD TESTAMENT: PROMISE

5-2. **I WILL POUR OUT MY SPIRIT**
5-2.1. BY THE SPIRIT OF THE LORD
5-2.2. THE PROMISE OF THE SPIRIT
5-2.3. THE SPIRIT AND GOD'S PEOPLE
5-2.4. THE SPIRIT AND GOD'S SERVANT
5-2.5. THE SPIRIT AND A NEW CREATION

NEW TESTAMENT: CONSUMMATION

5-4. **HIS SPIRIT AS A GUARANTEE**
5-4.1. I WAS IN THE SPIRIT
5-4.2. HE HAS GIVEN US HIS SPIRIT
5-4.3. THE SPIRIT AS THE FIRST INSTALMENT
5-4.4. THE SPIRIT AS THE FIRST FRUITS
5-4.5. THE SPIRIT AS A SEAL

5-5. THE SPIRIT: THEOLOGICAL REFLECTIONS

Outline of Part II

CHAPTER 6. THE MESSIAH

OUTLINE OF PART II

CHAPTER 7: THE SON OF MAN

OLD TESTAMENT: PROCLAMATION

7-1. SON OF MAN, I SEND YOU
7-1.1. THE SON OF MAN PROBLEM

7-1.2. ADAM AND MANKIND
7-1.3. ANGEL OR HUMAN BEING

7-1.4. MEN AND WOMEN OF GOD

7-1.5. O SON OF MAN

NEW TESTAMENT: FULFILLMENT

7-3. BEHOLD, THE SON OF MAN
7-3.1. THE SON OF MAN IN THE SYNOPTIC GOSPELS
7-3.2. THE SON OF MAN IN JOHN'S GOSPEL
7-3.3. THE THEOLOGICAL PROCLAMATION
   a. Jesus Is the Inclusive Representative of God's People
   b. Jesus Is the Inclusive Representative of Humanity
   c. The Son of Man Has Authority
   d. The Path to Glory Leads through Suffering
7-3.4. THE SECOND ADAM
   a. Christ and Adam
   b. The Christ Hymn of Philippians 2
   c. The Son of Man in Hebrews
7-3.5. THE EXALTED SON OF MAN

OLD TESTAMENT: PROMISE

7-2. ONE LIKE A SON OF MAN
7-2.1. WITH THE CLOUDS OF HEAVEN
7-2.2. THE ADAM CONNECTION

7-2.3. AN INDIVIDUAL ESCHATOLOGICAL FIGURE
7-2.4. LIKE THE FIGURE OF A MAN
7-2.5. THE IDEAL HUMAN BEING

NEW TESTAMENT: CONSUMMATION

7-4. ONE LIKE A SON OF MAN
7-4.1. THE PAROUSIA
7-4.2. THE PAROUSIA IN THE TEACHING OF JESUS
7-4.3. THE PAROUSIA IN THE CHURCH'S EXPECTATION
7-4.4. FIRST AND SECOND COMING
7-4.5. EVEN SO, COME

7-5. THE SON OF MAN: THEOLOGICAL REFLECTIONS

OUTLINE OF PART II

CHAPTER 9: THE SERVANT'S SUFFERING

Outline of Part II

CHAPTER 10: THE SERVANT'S VINDICATION

OLD TESTAMENT: PROCLAMATION

10-1. **THEY SHALL NOT PREVAIL AGAINST YOU**
10-1.1. ASSURANCE OF FINAL TRIUMPH
    a. The Servant Psalms
    b. The Servant Songs

10-1.2. GOD WHO RAISES THE DEAD

10-1.3. GOD TOOK HIM
    a. Enoch
    b. Elijah
10-1.4. THE VINDICATING GOD: LORD
10-1.5. THE VINDICATING GOD: SAVIOR

NEW TESTAMENT: FULFILLMENT

10-3. **GOD HAS HIGHLY EXALTED HIM**
10-3.1. RESURRECTION
    a. The New Testament Proclamation
      i. Narrative Proclamation
      ii. Theological Proclamation
    b. The Significance of the Resurrection
      i. An Act of God
      ii. The Climax of the Christ Event
      iii. A Challenge to Faith
      iv. A Call to Commitment
      v. A Guarantee of the Resurrection of Believers
    c. The Easter Event
      i. The Empty Tomb
      ii. The Appearances
      iii. The Nature of Christ's Resurrection Body
10-3.2. ASCENSION
    a. The New Testament Proclamation
    b. The Significance of the Ascension
10-3.3. AT GOD'S RIGHT HAND
    a. The Claims of the New Testament
    b. Theological Significance
10-3.4. JESUS CHRIST IS LORD
10-3.5. THE SAVIOR OF THE WORLD

OLD TESTAMENT: PROMISE

10-2. **A PORTION WITH THE GREAT**
10-2.1. GOD'S PEOPLE WILL RISE
10-2.2. GOD'S SERVANTS WILL RISE

NEW TESTAMENT: CONSUMMATION

10-4. **OUR LORD, COME!**
10-4.1. JESUS WILL COME IN THE SAME WAY
10-4.2. MARANA THA
10-4.3. WE AWAIT A SAVIOR

10-5. THE SERVANT'S VINDICATION: THEOLOGICAL REFLECTIONS

OUTLINE OF PART II

CHAPTER 11: THE COVENANT COMMUNITY

Outline of Part II

CHAPTER 12: THE NATIONS

OLD TESTAMENT: PROCLAMATION

12-1. AMONG THE NATIONS
12-1.1. THE GOD OF THE NATIONS

12-1.2. THE SINS OF THE NATIONS
12-1.3. THE STRANGER WITHIN YOUR GATES
    a. A Mixed Crowd
    b. The Stranger/Resident Alien
    c. A Classic Case: Ruth
12-1.4. PROSELYTES

12-1.5. EXCLUSIVISM

NEW TESTAMENT: FULFILLMENT

12-3. MAKE DISCIPLES OF ALL NATIONS
12-3.1. SERVANT TO THE CIRCUMCISED
    a. Condemnation of Pharisaic Proselytizing
    b. Jesus' Mission to Israel
    c. The Eschatological Ingathering
    d. Jesus' Acceptance of Gentiles
    e. Universal, Not Nationalistic
12-3.2. KEEP THE LAW OF MOSES
12-3.3. A DOOR OF FAITH TO THE GENTILES
    a. The Origins of the Gentile Mission
    b. The Development of the Gentile Mission
12-3.4. THAT EVERY KNEE SHOULD BOW
    a. The Theology of Mission: A Light to the Gentiles
        i. Present rather than Future
        ii. The Church rather than God
        iii. Centrifugal rather than Centripetal
    b. The Pauline Theology of Mission
    c. Theologies of Mission
12-3.5. DO THE WORK OF AN EVANGELIST

OLD TESTAMENT: PROMISE

12-2. ALL THE NATIONS SHALL COME

12-2.1. THE GOD OF THE NATIONS
12-2.2. THE JUDGMENT OF THE NATIONS
12-2.3. THE ESCHATOLOGICAL REVERSAL
    a. The Homage of the Nations
    b. The Service of the Nations
    c. The Tribute of the Nations
12-2.4. THE INGATHERING OF THE NATIONS
    a. Every Knee Shall Bow
        i. The Instruction of the Nations
        ii. The Worship of the Nations
        iii. The Salvation of the Nations
    b. A Blessing in the Midst
    c. Nations Shall Come
        i. The Ingathering of the Nations Is an Eschatological Event
        ii. The Ingathering Will Be the Work of God, Not of Israel
        iii. The Nations Will Come to Israel, Not Israel to the Nations
12-2.5. A LIGHT TO THE NATIONS
    a. Isaiah
    b. Jonah
    c. Psalms

NEW TESTAMENT: CONSUMMATION

12-4. A GREAT MULTITUDE FROM EVERY NATION

12-4.1. THE GOD OF THE NATIONS
12-4.2. THE NATIONS RAGE
12-4.3. TO ALL THE NATIONS

12-4.4. THE JUDGMENT OF THE NATIONS

12-4.5. THE FINAL INGATHERING OF THE NATIONS

12-5. THE NATIONS: THEOLOGICAL REFLECTIONS

OUTLINE OF PART II

CHAPTER 13: LAND AND CITY

Outline of Part II

CHAPTER 14: WORSHIP

OLD TESTAMENT: PROCLAMATION

14-1. **O COME, LET US WORSHIP**
14-1.1. WHERE GOD IS WORSHIPPED
  a. The Story of Where God Is Worshipped
    i. The Patriarchs
    ii. The Wilderness Period
    iii. The Settlement
    iv. The Jerusalem Temple
    v. Reformation and Centralization
    vi. Destruction and Rebuilding
    vii. Desecration and Rededication
  b. The Understanding of Where God Is
    Worshipped
14-1.2. WHEN GOD IS WORSHIPPED:
    THE SABBATH
14-1.3. WHEN GOD IS WORSHIPPED:
    THE FESTIVALS
14-1.4. HOW GOD IS WORSHIPPED:
    PREPARATION
  a. Circumcision
  b. Purification
14-1.5. HOW GOD IS WORSHIPPED:
    COMING BEFORE THE LORD
  a. Elements of Worship
    i. Prayer
    ii. Praise
    iii. Scripture Reading
    iv. Preaching
    v. Almsgiving
  b. Sacrifice
    i. The OT Accounts
    ii. Types of Sacrifice
    iii. The Meaning of Sacrifice
    iv. The Prophetic Critique of Sacrifice

NEW TESTAMENT: FULFILLMENT

14-3. **WORSHIP IN SPIRIT AND IN TRUTH**
14-3.1. WHERE GOD IS WORSHIPPED
  a. Jesus and the Temple
  b. The Church as the New Temple
  c. The Heavenly Temple
  d. Your Synagogue
  e. The Church in Your House

14-3.2. WHEN GOD IS WORSHIPPED: THE
    SABBATH
14-3.3. WHEN GOD IS WORSHIPPED: THE
    FESTIVALS
14-3.4. HOW GOD IS WORSHIPPED:
    PREPARATION
  a. Circumcision
  b. Baptism
14-3.5. HOW GOD IS WORSHIPPED: COMING
    TOGETHER
  a. Sacrifice
  b. Elements of Worship
    i. Prayer
    ii. Praise
    iii. Scripture Reading
    iv. Preaching
    v. Almsgiving
  c. The Lord's Supper

OLD TESTAMENT: PROMISE

14-2. **ALL PEOPLE SHALL COME TO WORSHIP**
14-2.1. WHERE GOD IS WORSHIPPED
  a. The New Temple
    i. Prophetic Visions of a Rebuilt Temple
    ii. Apocalyptic Visions of an Eschatological
      Sanctuary
  b. The Heavenly Temple
14-2.2. WHEN GOD IS WORSHIPPED:
    THE SABBATH
14-2.3. WHEN GOD IS WORSHIPPED:
    THE FESTIVALS
14-2.4. HOW GOD IS WORSHIPPED:
    PREPARATION
14-2.5. HOW GOD IS WORSHIPPED:
    COMING BEFORE THE LORD

NEW TESTAMENT: CONSUMMATION

14-4. **THEY FALL DOWN AND WORSHIP**
14-4.1. I SAW NO TEMPLE

14-4.2. UNCEASING PRAISE: THE SABBATH REST

14-4.3. UNCEASING PRAISE: NO NEED OF SUN
    OR MOON
14-4.4. THEY HAVE WASHED THEIR ROBES

14-4.5. HIS SERVANTS SHALL WORSHIP HIM
  a. Elements of Worship
    i. The Prayers of the Saints
    ii. The Songs of the Redeemed
    iii. The Reading of the Scroll
    iv. The Proclamation of the Word
  b. The Marriage Supper of the Lamb

14-5. WORSHIP: THEOLOGICAL REFLECTIONS

OUTLINE OF PART II

CHAPTER 15: MINISTRY

Outline of Part II

CHAPTER 16: THE HUMAN CONDITION

OUTLINE OF PART II

CHAPTER 17: FAITH AND HOPE

OLD TESTAMENT: PROCLAMATION

17-1. **TRUST IN THE LORD**
17-1.1. REPENTANCE AND FORGIVENESS
17-1.2. RETURN TO THE LORD

17-1.3. FAITH AND DOUBT
    a. Examples of Faith
    b. Believing in God
    c. The Fear of the Lord
    d. Doubt and Despair
17-1.4. KNOWING GOD
17-1.5. PERSONAL PRAYER
    a. Public Prayer and Personal Prayer
    b. Teaching and Example
    c. The Theology of Prayer
       i. Dialogue with God
      ii. Language
     iii. Types of Prayer
     iv. Unanswered Prayer

NEW TESTAMENT: FULFILLMENT

17-3. **REPENT AND BELIEVE**
17-3.1. REPENTANCE AND FORGIVENESS
17-3.2. TURN TO THE LORD
    a. Conversion
    b. New Birth
17-3.3. FAITH AND DOUBT
    a. Faith
    b. Doubt

17-3.4. KNOWING CHRIST
17-3.5. PERSONAL PRAYER
    a. Public Prayer and Personal Prayer
    b. The Example and Teaching of Jesus
    c. The Early Church
    d. The Theology of Prayer
       i. Dialogue with God
      ii. Language
     iii. Types of Prayer
     iv. Unanswered Prayer

OLD TESTAMENT: PROMISE

17-2. **A NEW HEART I WILL GIVE YOU**
17-2.1. MY HOPE IS IN YOU
17-2.2. CAUSE US TO RETURN
17-2.3. I WILL PUT THE FEAR OF ME IN THEIR
    HEARTS
17-2.4. THEY SHALL ALL KNOW ME
17-2.5. I WILL HEAR YOU

NEW TESTAMENT: CONSUMMATION

17-4. **PRESS ON TOWARD THE GOAL**
17-4.1. A LIVING HOPE
17-4.2. DEVELOPMENT TOWARDS MATURITY
17-4.3. WE SHALL SEE HIM

17-4.4. THE RENEWAL OF ALL THINGS
17-4.5. THE PRAYERS OF ALL THE SAINTS

17-5. FAITH AND HOPE: THEOLOGICAL REFLECTIONS

CHAPTER 18: GOD'S COMMANDMENTS

OUTLINE OF PART II

CHAPTER 19: LOVE YOUR NEIGHBOR

OLD TESTAMENT: PROCLAMATION

19-1. **YOU SHALL LOVE YOUR NEIGHBOR**
19-1.1. THE INDIVIDUAL
  a. The Individual and Society
  b. Reverence For Human Life
    i. Murder
    ii. Abortion
    iii. Suicide
    iv. Euthanasia
19-1.2. THE FAMILY
  a. The Biblical Affirmation of Sexuality
  b. Sexual Relations outside Marriage
    i. Adultery
    ii. Prostitution
    iii. Bestiality
    iv. Homosexuality
  c. Celibacy
  d. Husband and Wife
    i. Marriage
    ii. Divorce
  e. Parents and Children
    i. Be Fruitful and Multiply
    ii. The Duties of Parents
    iii. The Duties of Children
    iv. The Elderly
19-1.3. SOCIETY
  a. The Setting
  b. Economic Justice
    i. The Source of Wealth
    ii. The Production of Wealth
    iii. The Distribution of Wealth
    iv. Fair Dealing
  c. Social Justice
    i. Slavery
    ii. The Status of Women
    iii. Race and Culture
19-1.4. THE STATE
  a. The Setting
  b. Israel and the State

19-1.5. INTERNATIONAL AFFAIRS
  a. Holy War
  b. Peace, Peace, Where There Is No Peace

NEW TESTAMENT: FULFILLMENT

19-3. **YOU SHALL LOVE YOUR NEIGHBOR**
19-3.1. THE INDIVIDUAL
  a. The Individual and Society
  b. Reverence for Human Life
    i. Murder
    ii. Abortion
    iii. Suicide
    iv. Euthanasia
19-3.2. THE FAMILY
  a. The NT Affirmation of Sexuality
  b. Sexual Relations outside Marriage
    i. Adultery
    ii. Fornication
    iii. Prostitution
    iv. Homosexuality
  c. Celibacy
  d. Husband and Wife
    i. Marriage
    ii. Divorce
  e. Parents and Children
    i. Duties of Parents
    ii. Duties of Children
    iii. The Elderly
19-3.3. SOCIETY
  a. The Setting
  b. Economic Justice
    i. The Source of Wealth
    ii. The Production of Wealth
    iii. The Distribution of Wealth
    iv. Fair Dealing
  c. Social Justice
    i. Slavery
    ii. The Status of Women
    iii. Race and Culture
19-3.4. THE STATE
  a. The Setting
  b. The Kingdom of God and the Kingdoms of This World
  c. Church and State
19-3.5. INTERNATIONAL AFFAIRS
  a. War and Peace
  b. The Weapons of Our Warfare

OLD TESTAMENT: PROMISE

19-2. **EVERYONE WILL INVITE HIS NEIGHBOR**
19-2.1. THE INDIVIDUAL
19-2.2. THE FAMILY
19-2.3. SOCIETY
  a. A New Society
  b. Sabbatical and Jubilee Years
19-2.4. THE STATE
19-2.5. INTERNATIONAL AFFAIRS
  a. The Age of Peace
  b. The Prince of Peace
  c. The Persistence of War
  d. The Last Battle

NEW TESTAMENT: CONSUMMATION

19-4. **NOTHING UNCLEAN SHALL ENTER**
19-4.1. THE INDIVIDUAL
19-4.2. THE FAMILY
19-4.3. SOCIETY
  a. The Eschatological Reversal
  b. The Great Jubilee
19-4.4. THE STATE
19-4.5. INTERNATIONAL AFFAIRS
  a. Wars and Rumors of Wars
  b. The Last Battle

Outline of Part II

OUTLINE OF PART II

CHAPTER 20: LIFE

OLD TESTAMENT: PROCLAMATION

20-1.   **THE LAND OF THE LIVING**
20-1.1. THE AFFIRMATION OF LIFE
20-1.2. PEACE
20-1.3. HEALING
20-1.4. BLESSING
    a. The Lᴏʀᴅ, Our God, Has Blessed Us
    b. Bless the Lᴏʀᴅ, O My Soul
    c. Bless Me, O My Father
    d. Blessed Are Those
20-1.5. JOY

NEW TESTAMENT: FULFILLMENT

20-3.   **FROM DEATH TO LIFE**
20-3.1. THE AFFIRMATION OF LIFE
20-3.2. PEACE
20-3.3. HEALING
20-3.4. BLESSING
    a. God Has Blessed Us
    b. Blessed Be God
    c. He Blessed Them
    d. Blessed Are Those
20-3.5. JOY

OLD TESTAMENT: PROMISE

20-2.   **YOUR DEAD SHALL LIVE**
20-2.1. THE FACT OF DEATH
20-2.2. THE UNDERSTANDING OF DEATH
    a. The Key Passage
    b. Spiritual Death
    c. Sin and Death
    d. Length of Days
20-2.3. THE LAND OF DARKNESS: SHEOL
    a. The Place of the Dead
    b. The Shadows
    c. Cut Off from God
    d. Communicating with the Dead
    e. Their Name Shall Live
20-2.4. THE PROMISE OF LIGHT:
    RESURRECTION
    a. The Presence of God
    b. Resurrection
    c. Immortality
20-2.5. ATTITUDES TO DEATH

NEW TESTAMENT: CONSUMMATION

20-4.   **YOU WILL LIVE ALSO**
20-4.1. THE FACT OF DEATH
20-4.2. THE UNDERSTANDING OF DEATH
    a. Spiritual Death
    b. The Power of Death
    c. Sin and Death
    d. Length of Days
20-4.3. BECAUSE HE LIVES
    a. The Teaching of Jesus
    b. Raising the Dead
    c. The Resurrection of Christ and the
       Resurrection of Believers
20-4.4. HOW ARE THE DEAD RAISED?
    a. Two Scenarios
    b. A Spiritual Body
    c. With Christ
    d. Immortality
20-4.5. ATTITUDES TO DEATH

20-5. LIFE: THEOLOGICAL REFLECTIONS

Bibliography

Abba, R.
1962a   "Expiation" and "Propitiation." In *IDB*, 2:200-201; 3:920-21.
1962b   "Priests and Levites." In *IDB*, 3:876-89.
1977   "The Origin and Significance of Hebrew Sacrifice." *BTB* 7: 123-38.

Achtemeier, E.
1962a   "Righteousness in the NT." In *IDB*, 4:91-99.
1962b   "Righteousness in the OT." In *IDB*, 4:80-85.
1993   "Why God Is Not Mother." *CT*, 16 August, 17-23.

Ackerman, J. S.
1982   "Joseph, Judah, and Jacob." In *Literary Interpretations of Biblical Narratives, II*, edited by K. R. R. Gros Louis, 85-113. Nashville: Abingdon.

Adams, E. W.
1996   "Resurrection." In *EDBT*, 676-79.

Ahern, B.
1947   "The Indwelling Spirit, Pledge of Our Inheritance (Eph. 1:14)." *CBQ* 9: 179-89.

Alexander, D.
1986   "The Old Testament View of Life after Death." *Them* 11: 41-46.

Alexander, T. D.
1998   "Royal Expectations in Genesis to Kings: Their Importance for Biblical Theology." *TynB* 49: 191-212.

Alfaro, J. I.
1978   "The Land — Stewardship." *BTB* 8: 51-66.

Allen, D. W.
1959   "Christ's Teaching about Missions." *IRM* 48: 157-67.

Allen, E. L.
1956   "Jesus and Moses in the New Testament." *ExpT* 67: 104-6.

Allen, L. C.

1992   "Images of Israel: The People of God in the Prophets." In *Studies in Old Testament Theology*, edited by R. L. Hubbard et al., 149-68. Dallas: Word.

Allison, D. C.

1993   *The New Moses: A Matthean Typology*. Minneapolis: Fortress.

Alsup, J. E.

1962   "Theophany in the NT." In *IDBSup*, 898-900.

Anderson, B. W.

1957   "The Place of Shechem in the Bible." *BA* 20: 10-19.

1962a   "God, Names of." In *IDB*, 2:407-17.

1962b   "Hosts, Host of Heaven." In *IDB*, 2:654-56.

1962c   "Lord." In *IDB*, 3:150-51.

1963   "The New Covenant and the Old." In *The Old Testament and Christian Faith*, edited by B. W. Anderson, 225-42. New York: Harper & Row.

1967   *Creation versus Chaos: The Reinterpretation of Mythical Symbolism in the Bible*. New York: Association.

1978   "From Analysis to Synthesis: The Interpretation of Genesis 1–11." *JBL* 97: 23-39.

1983   *Out of the Depths: The Psalms Speak for Us Today*. 2nd ed. Philadelphia: Westminster.

1995   "Standing on God's Promises: Covenant and Continuity in Biblical Theology." In *Biblical Theology: Problems and Perspectives*, edited by S. J. Kraftchick et al., 145-54. Nashville: Abingdon.

Anderson, B. W., ed.

1962   *Israel's Prophetic Heritage*. New York: Harper & Row.

1969   *The Old Testament and Christian Faith*. New York: Harper & Row.

1984   *Creation in the Old Testament*. Philadelphia: Fortress.

Anderson, G. H., ed.

1961   *The Theology of the Christian Mission*. New York: McGraw-Hill.

Anderson, G. W.

1965   "Enemies and Evildoers in the Book of Psalms." *BJRL* 48: 18-29.

1971   "The History of Biblical Interpretation." In *ICB*, 971-77.

Andreasen, N.-E.

1974   "Recent Studies of the Old Testament Sabbath: Some Observations." *ZAW* 86: 453-69.

Antwi, D. J.

1991   "Did Jesus Consider His Death to Be an Atoning Sacrifice?" *Int* 45: 17-28.

Argyle, A. W.

1955   "The Ascension." *ExpT* 66: 240-42.

1965   *God in the New Testament*. London: Hodder & Stoughton.

Arias, M.
1991   "Rethinking the Great Commission." *ThTo* 47: 410-18.

Arndt, W. F., and F. W. Gingrich
1957   *A Greek-English Lexicon of the New Testament and Other Early Christian Literature.* Chicago: University of Chicago Press.

Bailey, D. S.
1955   *Homosexuality and the Western Christian Tradition.* London: Longmans, Green.

Bailey, L. R.
1979   *Biblical Perspectives on Death.* Philadelphia: Fortress.

Baker, D. L.
1976   *Two Testaments: One Bible.* Downers Grove, Ill.: InterVarsity.

Baker, J.
1965   "Moses and the Burning Bush." *ExpT* 76: 307-8.

Bakken, N. K.
1968   "The New Humanity: Christ and the Modern Age. A Study Centering in the Christ-Hymn: Philippians 2:6-11." *Int* 22: 71-82.

Balchin, J. F.
1982   "Paul, Wisdom and Christ." In *Christ the Lord,* edited by H. H. Rowdon, 204-19. Downers Grove, Ill.: InterVarsity.

Baltzer, K.
1965   "The Meaning of the Temple in the Lukan Writings." *HTR* 58: 263-77.
1968   "Considerations Regarding the Office and Calling of the Prophet." *HTR* 61: 567-81.

Banks, R.
1975   "The Eschatological Role of the Law in Pre- and Post-Christian Jewish Thought." In *Reconciliation and Hope: New Testament Essays on Atonement and Eschatology,* 173-85. Grand Rapids: Eerdmans.

Barclay, O. R.
1990   "The Theology of Social Ethics: A Survey of Current Positions." *EQ* 62: 63-86.

Barr, A.
1950a   "'Hope' (ἘΛΠΙ΄Σ, ἘΛΠΙ΄ΖΩ) in the New Testament." *SJT* 3: 68-77.
1950b   "Love in the Church: A Study of First Corinthians, Chapter 13." *SJT* 3: 416-25.

Barr, J.
1961   *The Semantics of Biblical Language.* London: Oxford University Press.
1963   "Revelation through History in the Old Testament and Modern Thought." *Int* 17: 193-205.

1968 "The Image of God in the Book of Genesis — a Study of Terminology." *BJRL* 51: 11-26.

1972 "Man and Nature — the Ecological Controversy and the Old Testament." *BJRL* 55: 9-32.

1974 "Trends and Prospects in Biblical Theology." *JTS* 25: 265-82.

1988 "The Theological Case against Biblical Theology." In *Canon, Theology, and Old Testament Interpretation*, edited by G. M. Tucker et al., 3-19. Philadelphia: Fortress.

1993 *Biblical Faith and Natural Theology.* Oxford: Clarendon.

1999 *The Concept of Biblical Theology: An Old Testament Perspective.* Minneapolis: Fortress.

Barré, M. L.
1981 "'Fear of God' and the World View of Wisdom." *BTB* 11: 41-43.

Barrett, C. K.
1947 *The Holy Spirit and the Gospel Tradition.* London: SPCK.
1950 "The Holy Spirit in the Fourth Gospel." *JTS* 1: 1-15.
1955 "The Lamb of God." *NTS* 1: 210-18.
1962 *From First Adam to Last: A Study in Pauline Theology.* London: Adam & Charles Black.
1972a *New Testament Essays.* London: SPCK.
1972b *The Signs of an Apostle.* Philadelphia: Fortress.
1985 *Church, Ministry, and Sacraments in the New Testament.* Grand Rapids: Eerdmans.

Barrois, G. A.
1974 *The Face of Christ in the Old Testament.* Crestwood, N.Y.: St. Vladimir's Seminary Press.
1980 *Jesus Christ and the Temple.* Crestwood, N.Y.: St. Vladimir's Seminary Press.

Bartels, K. H.
1978 "Remember, Remembrance." In *DNTT*, 3:230-47.

Barth, M.
1958 "A Chapter on the Church — the Body of Christ." *Int* 12: 131-56.

Bartlett, D.
1977 "A Biblical Perspective on Homosexuality." *Fnds* 20: 133-47.

Barton, J.
1978 "Understanding Old Testament Ethics." *JSOT* 9: 44-64.
1979 "Natural Law and Poetic Justice in the Old Testament." *JTS* 30: 1-14.

Bassler, J. M.
1992 "God (God in the NT)." In *ABD*, 2:1049-55.

Bater, B. R.
1969 "Towards a More Biblical View of the Resurrection." *Int* 23: 47-65.

Bauer, J. B.
1981a   "Hope." In *EBT*, 376-79.
1981b   "Redemption." In *EBT*, 738-41.
1981c   "Saviour." In *EBT*, 812-13.

Beardslee, W. A.
1970   "Uses of the Proverb in the Synoptic Gospels." *Int* 24: 61-73.

Beare, F. W.
1958   "The Risen Christ Bestows the Spirit: A Study of John 20:19-23." *CJT* 4: 95-100.
1964   "Speaking with Tongues: A Critical Survey of the New Testament Evidence." *JBL* 83: 229-46.

Beasley-Murray, G. R.
1974   "The Contribution of the Book of Revelation to the Christian Belief in Immortality." *SJT* 27: 76-93.

Beck, D. M.
1962a   "Golden Rule, The." In *IDB*, 2:438.
1962b   "Transfiguration." In *IDB*, 4:686-87.

Becker, J.
1980   *Messianic Expectation in the Old Testament.* Philadelphia: Fortress.

Becker, O.
1975   "Covenant." In *DNTT*, 1:365-75.

Becker, V.
1976   "Gospel, Evangelize, Evangelist." In *DNTT*, 2:107-15.

Beckwith, R. T.
1980   "Canon of the Old Testament." In *IBD*, 1:235-38.
1985   *The Old Testament Canon of the New Testament Church.* Grand Rapids: Eerdmans.

Beckwith, R. T., and W. Stott
1980   *The Christian Sunday: A Biblical and Historical Study.* Grand Rapids: Baker.

Behm, J.
1964   "Arrabōn." In *TDNT*, 1:475.

Beilner, W.
1981   "Joy." In *EBT*, 438-42.

Beker, J. C.
1958   "Aspects of the Holy Spirit in Paul." *USQR* 14: 3-16.
1980   *Paul the Apostle: The Triumph of God in Life and Thought.* Philadelphia: Fortress.

1987   *Suffering and Hope: The Biblical Vision and the Human Predicament.*
            Philadelphia: Fortress.

Bender, H. S.
1962   *These Are My People: The Nature of the Church and Its Discipleship according to the New Testament.* Scottdale, Pa.: Herald.

Benjamin, H. S.
1976   "Pneuma in John and Paul: A Comparative Study of the Term with Particular Reference to the Holy Spirit." *BTB* 6: 27-48.

Bergant, D., J. A. Fischer, and J. R. Halstead
1996   "Humankind." In *CPDBT,* 449-55.

Berkhof, H.
1977   *Christ and the Powers.* 2nd ed. Scottdale, Pa.: Herald.

Berry, R. W.
1982   "The Beginning." *ThTo* 39: 249-59.

Best, E.
1960   "Spiritual Sacrifice: General Priesthood in the New Testament." *Int* 14: 273-99.
1984   "The Revelation to Evangelize the Gentiles." *JTS* 35: 1-30.
1993   *Interpreting Christ.* Edinburgh: T. & T. Clark.

Betz, O.
1962   "Biblical Theology, History of." In *IDB,* 1:432-37.

Beyer, H. W.
1965   "Kanōn." In *TDNT,* 3:596-602.

Beyreuther, E., and G. Finkenrath
1976   "Joy, Rejoice." In *DNTT,* 2:352-61.

Bietenhard, H.
1953   "The Millennial Hope in the Early Church." *SJT* 6: 12-30.
1976a   "Hell, Abyss, Hades, Gehenna, Lower Regions." In *DNTT,* 2:205-10.
1976b   "Lord, Master." In *DNTT,* 2:508-20.

Bietenhard, H., C. Brown, and J. S. Wright
1978   "Satan, Beelzebul, Devil, Exorcism." In *DNTT,* 3:468-77.

Birch, B. C.
1980   "Tradition, Canon and Biblical Theology." *HBT* 2: 113-25.
1984   "Biblical Hermeneutics in Recent Discussion: Old Testament." *RSRev* 10: 1-7.
1985   "Old Testament Foundations for Peacemaking in the Nuclear Age." *CCen* 102: 1115-19.

Birch, B. C., and L. L. Rasmussen
1976   *Bible and Ethics in Christian Life.* Minneapolis: Augsburg.

Birch, C., and L. Vischer
1997   *Living with the Animals: The Community of God's Creatures.* Geneva: World Council of Churches.

Birdsall, J. N.
1980   "Canon of the New Testament." In *IBD*, 1:240-45.

Birkeland, H.
1949   "The Belief in the Resurrection of the Dead in the Old Testament." *ST* 3: 60-78.

Black, M.
1962   "Scribe." In *IDB*, 4:246-48.

Blackman, E. C.
1962   "Reconciliation, Reconcile." In *IDB*, 4:16-17.

Blair, E. P.
1961   "An Appeal to Remembrance: The Memory Motif in Deuteronomy." *Int* 51: 41-47.

Blank, S. H.
1962a   "Age, Old." In *IDB*, 1:54-55.
1962b   "Folly." In *IDB*, 2:303-4.

Blauw, J.
1962   *The Missionary Nature of the Church.* New York: McGraw-Hill.

Bloch, A. P.
1978   *The Biblical and Historical Background of the Jewish Holy Days.* New York: Ktav.

Blomberg, C. L.
1990   *Interpreting the Parables.* Leicester: Apollos.
1996   "Holy Spirit" and "Holy Spirit, Gifts of." In *EDBT*, 344-48, 348-51.
1999   *Neither Poverty nor Riches: A Biblical Theology of Material Possessions.* Grand Rapids: Eerdmans.

Bonnington, M., and B. Fyall
1996   *Homosexuality and the Bible.* Cambridge: Grove.

Borg, M. J.
1992   "Jesus, Teaching of." In *ABD*, 3:804-12.

Bornemann, R.
1991   "Toward a Biblical Theology." In *The Promise and Practice of Biblical Theology,* edited by J. Reumann, 117-28. Minneapolis: Fortress.

Bornkamm, G.
1968   "*Presbys,* etc." In *TDNT,* 6:651-83.

Borsch, F. H.
1992   "Further Reflections on 'The Son of Man': The Origins and Development of the Title." In *The Messiah: Developments in Earliest Judaism and Christianity,* edited by J. H. Charlesworth, 130-44. Minneapolis: Fortress.

Bossmann, D.
1979   "Ezra's Marriage Reform: Israel Redefined." *BTB* 9: 32-38.

Botterweck, G. J., and H. Zimmermann
1981   "Knowledge of God." In *EBT,* 472-78.

Boucher, M.
1969   "Some Unexplored Parallels to I Cor 11, 11-12 and Gal 3, 28: The NT on the Role of Women." *CBQ* 31: 50-58.

Bourke, M. M.
1968   "Reflections on Church Order in the New Testament." *CBQ* 30: 493-511.

Bousset, W.
1970   *Kyrios Christos.* ET. Nashville: Abingdon.

Bowers, P.
1987   "Fulfilling the Gospel: The Scope of the Pauline Mission." *JETS* 30: 185-98.

Bowman, A. L.
1992   "Women in Ministry: An Exegetical Study of 1 Timothy 2:11-15." *BS* 149: 193-213.

Bowman, J. W.
1962   "Armageddon." In *IDB,* 1:226-27.

Brandon, S. G. F.
1967   *Jesus and the Zealots: A Study of the Political Factor in Primitive Christianity.* Manchester: Manchester University Press.

Branick, V. P.
1989   *The House Church in the Writings of Paul.* Wilmington, Del.: Michael Glazier.

Bratcher, R. G.
1975   "'The Jews' in the Gospel of John." *BibT* 26: 401-9.

Bratsiotis, N. P.
1974   "'ish." In *TDOT,* 1:222-35.

Braude, W. G.
1940   *Jewish Proselytizing in the First Five Centuries of the Common Era.* Providence: Brown University Press.

Bray, G. L.

1996   *Biblical Interpretation: Past and Present.* Leicester: InterVarsity.

Bright, J.

1953   *The Kingdom of God.* Nashville: Abingdon.

Brockington, L. H.

1945   "The Presence of God: A Study of the Use of the Term 'Glory of Yahweh.'" *ExpT* 57: 21-25.

Bromiley, G. W.

1967   "Who Says the New Testament Is Anti-Semitic?" *CT* 11: 548-49.

Brooks, O. S.

1987   *Baptism in the New Testament: The Drama of Decision.* Peabody, Mass.: Hendrickson.

Brown, C.

1976   "Chilias." In *DNTT,* 2:697-704.

Brown, C., H.-G. Link, and H. Vorländer

1978   "Reconciliation, Restoration, Propitiation, Atonement." In *DNTT,* 3:145-76.

Brown, R. E.

1966   "EGŌ EIMI — 'I AM.'" In *The Gospel according to John (i–xii),* app. IV, 533-38. Garden City, N.Y.: Doubleday.

1967   "The Paraclete in the Fourth Gospel." *NTS* 13: 113-32.

1971   "Jesus and Elisha." *Perspective* 12: 85-104.

1973   *The Virginal Conception and Bodily Resurrection of Jesus.* New York: Paulist.

1994   *An Introduction to New Testament Christology.* New York: Paulist.

Brown, R. E., et al., eds.

1973   *Peter in the New Testament.* Minneapolis: Augsburg.

1978   *Mary in the New Testament.* Philadelphia: Fortress.

Brownlee, W. H.

1977   "The Ineffable Name of God." *BASOR* 226: 39-46.

Bruce, F. F.

1963   "The Holy Spirit in the Acts of the Apostles." *Int* 27: 166-83.

1968   "Paul and Jerusalem." *TynB* 19: 3-25.

1969   *The New Testament Development of Old Testament Themes.* Grand Rapids: Eerdmans.

1971   "Paul on Immortality." *SJT* 24: 457-72.

1982   "The Background to the Son of Man Sayings." In *Christ the Lord,* edited by H. H. Rowdon, 50-70. Downers Grove, Ill.: InterVarsity.

1984   "Paul and 'the Powers That Be.'" *BJRL* 66, no. 2, pp. 78-96.

Brueggemann, W.

1968   "The Kerygma of the Deuteronomic Historian." *Int* 22: 387-402.

1969   "King in the Kingdom of Things." *CCen* 86: 1165-66.

1972   *In Man We Trust: The Neglected Side of Biblical Faith.* Atlanta: John Knox.

1974   "From Hurt to Joy, from Death to Life." *Int* 28: 3-19.

1976a   "Death, Theology of." In *IDBSup*, 219-22.

1976b   *Living toward a Vision: Biblical Reflections on Shalom.* Philadelphia: United Church Press.

1977a   "The Formfulness of Grief." *Int* 31: 263-75.

1977b   *The Land.* Philadelphia: Fortress.

1985a   *The Bible Makes Sense.* Atlanta: John Knox.

1985b   "A Shape for Old Testament Theology, I: Structure Legitimation" and "A Shape for Old Testament Theology, II: Embrace of Pain." *CBQ* 47: 28-46, 395-415.

1994   *A Social Reading of the Old Testament: Prophetic Approaches to Israel's Communal Life.* Minneapolis: Fortress.

1995   "A Shattered Transcendence? Exile and Restoration." In *Biblical Theology: Problems and Perspectives,* edited by S. J. Kraftchick et al., 169-82. Nashville: Abingdon.

1996   "The Loss and Recovery of 'Creation' in Old Testament Theology." *ThTo* 53: 177-90.

1997   *Theology of the Old Testament: Testimony, Dispute, Advocacy.* Minneapolis: Fortress.

Buck, F.

1975   "Prayer in the Old Testament." In *Word and Spirit,* edited by J. Plevnik, 61-110. Willowdale: Regis College.

Buckwalter, H. D.

1996   "Virgin Birth" and "Word." In *EDBT,* 799-802, 828-31.

Bullock, C. H.

1987   "Abortion and Old Testament Prophetic and Poetic Literature." In *Abortion: A Christian Understanding and Response,* edited by J. K. Hoffmeier, 65-71. Grand Rapids: Baker.

Bultmann, R.

1952   *Theology of the New Testament.* Vol. 1. New York: Scribner.

1953   "New Testament and Mythology." In *Kerygma and Myth,* edited by H. W. Bartsch, 1-44. London: SPCK.

1955   *Theology of the New Testament.* Vol. 2. New York: Scribner.

1963   "Prophecy and Fulfilment." In *Essays on Old Testament Interpretation,* edited by C. Westermann, 50-75. London: SCM Press.

Burns, J. B.

1973   "The Mythology of Death in the Old Testament." *SJT* 26: 327-40.

Burns, R. J.

1987   *Has the Lord Indeed Spoken Only through Moses? A Study of the Biblical Portrait of Miriam.* Atlanta: Scholars.

Burrows, M.

1946a   *An Outline of Biblical Theology.* Philadelphia: Westminster.

1946b   "The Task of Biblical Theology." *JBR* 14: 13-15.

Burrus, V.

1992   "Blurring the Boundaries: A Response to Howard C. Kee." *ThTo* 49: 239-42.

Bush, F. W.

1992   "Images of Israel: The People of God in the Torah." In *Studies in Old Testament Theology,* edited by R. L. Hubbard et al., 99-115. Dallas: Word.

Buzzard, A.

1992   "The Kingdom of God in the Twentieth-Century Discussion and the Light of Scripture." *EQ* 64: 99-115.

Cady, S., M. Ronan, and H. Taussig

1986   *Sophia: The Future of Feminist Spirituality.* San Francisco: Harper & Row.

Cahill, L. S.

1990   "The New Testament and Ethics: Communities of Social Change." *Int* 44: 383-95.

Caird, G. B.

1956a   "Expository Problems: The Transfiguration." *ExpT* 67: 291-94.

1956b   *Principalities and Powers: A Study of Pauline Theology.* Oxford: Clarendon.

1957   "Expository Problems: Predestination — Romans ix.–xi." *ExpT* 68: 324-27.

1980   *The Language and Imagery of the Bible.* Philadelphia: Westminster.

1994   *New Testament Theology.* New York: Oxford University Press.

Callan, T.

1996   "Son of Man." In *CPDBT,* 936-39.

Campbell, A.

1992   "Do the Work of an Evangelist." *EQ* 64: 117-29.

1993   "The Elders of the Jerusalem Church." *JTS* 44: 511-28.

Campbell, J. C.

1950   "God's People and the Remnant." *SJT* 3: 78-85.

Campbell, J. Y.

1948   "The Origin and Meaning of the Christian Use of the Word EKKLESIA." *JTS* 49: 130-42.

BIBLIOGRAPHY

Carr, G. L.
1993   "Song of Songs." In *A Complete Literary Guide to the Bible,* edited by
            L. Ryken and T. Longman, 281-95. Grand Rapids: Zondervan.

Carson, D. A.
1981   *Divine Sovereignty and Human Responsibility: Biblical Perspectives in Ten-
            sion.* London: Marshall, Morgan & Scott.

Carson, D. A., ed.
1982   *From Sabbath to Lord's Day: A Biblical, Historical, and Theological Investi-
            gation.* Grand Rapids: Zondervan.
1990   *Teach Us to Pray: Prayer in the Bible and the World.* Exeter: Paternoster.

Cazelles, H.
1966   "The Unity of the Bible and the People of God." *Scr* 18: 1-10.

Cazelles, H., and F. Mussner
1970   "Servant of the Lord." In *EBT,* 839-44.

Chapman, C.
1992   *Whose Promised Land?* Oxford: Lion.

Charlesworth, J. H., ed.
1992   *The Messiah: Developments in Earliest Judaism and Christianity.* Minne-
            apolis: Fortress.

Childs, B. S.
1959   "The Enemy from the North and the Chaos Tradition." *JBL* 78: 187-98.
1962   *Memory and Tradition in Israel.* London: SCM Press.
1970   *Biblical Theology in Crisis.* Philadelphia: Westminster.
1979   *Introduction to the Old Testament as Scripture.* Philadelphia: Fortress.
1982   "Some Reflections on the Search for a Biblical Theology." *HBT* 4: 1-12.
1984   *The New Testament as Canon.* London: SCM Press.
1986   *Old Testament Theology in a Canonical Context.* Philadelphia: Fortress.
1992   *Biblical Theology of the Old and New Testaments: Theological Reflection on
            the Christian Bible.* Minneapolis: Fortress.

Chilton, B.
1996   "The Son of Man — Who Was He?" *BRev* 12, no. 4, pp. 34-39, 45-47.

Christensen, D. L.
1993   "The Center of the First Testament within the Canonical Process." *BTB*
            23: 48-53.

Ciholas, P.
1981   "Son of Man in the Synoptic Gospels." *BTB* 11: 17-20.

Clark, K. W.
1947   "The Gentile Bias in Matthew." *JBL* 66: 165-72.

Cleary, F. X.

1980   "Women in the New Testament: St. Paul and the Early Pauline Churches."
          BTB 10: 78-82.

Clements, R. E.

1968   *God's Chosen People: A Theological Interpretation of the Book of Deuteron-*
          omy. Valley Forge, Pa.: Judson.

1992   *Wisdom in Theology.* Grand Rapids: Eerdmans.

Clemons, J. T.

1990   *What Does the Bible Say about Suicide?* Minneapolis: Augsburg.

Clifford, R. J.

1980   "Psalm 89: A Lament over the Davidic Ruler's Continued Failure." *HTR*
          73: 35-47.

Clines, D. J. A.

1980   "Story and Poem: The Old Testament as Literature and as Scripture." *Int*
          34: 115-27.

Clouse, R. G., ed.

1977   *The Meaning of the Millennium: Four Views.* Downers Grove, Ill.:
          InterVarsity.

Clowney, E. P.

1990   "A Biblical Theology of Prayer." In *Teach Us to Pray: Prayer in the Bible*
          and the World, edited by D. A. Carson, 136-73. Exeter: Paternoster.

Coats, G. W.

1968   *Rebellion in the Wilderness: The Murmuring Motif in the Wilderness Tra-*
          ditions of the Old Testament. Nashville: Abingdon.

1973   "The Joseph Story and Ancient Wisdom: A Reappraisal." *CBQ* 35: 285-97.

Coenen, L.

1975   "Bishop, Presbyter, Elder." In *DNTT,* 1:188-201.

Coggan, F. D.

1967   *The Prayers of the New Testament.* Washington, D.C.: Carpus.

Cohn, R. L.

1981   *The Shape of Sacred Space: Four Biblical Studies.* Chico, Calif.: Scholars.

Collins, A. Y.

1977   "The Political Perspective of the Revelation to John." *JBL* 96: 241-56.

Collins, J. J.

1979   "The 'Historical' Nature of the Old Testament in Recent Biblical Theol-
          ogy." *CBQ* 41: 185-204.

1990   "Is a Critical Biblical Theology Possible?" In *The Hebrew Bible and Its In-*
          terpreters, edited by W. H. Propp et al., 1-17. Winona Lake, Ind.:
          Eisenbrauns.

Collins, R. F.
1983   *Introduction to the New Testament.* Garden City, N.Y.: Doubleday.
1986   *Christian Morality: Biblical Foundations.* Notre Dame, Ind.: University of Notre Dame Press.
1992   "Ten Commandments." In *ABD*, 6:383-87.

Conrad, J.
1980   "*Zāqēn*, etc." In *TDOT*, 4:122-31.

Conzelmann, H.
1960   *The Theology of St. Luke.* London: Faber & Faber.
1970   "History and Theology in the Passion Narratives of the Synoptic Gospels." *Int* 24: 178-97.
1976   "Wisdom in the NT." In *IDBSup*, 956-60.

Cook, M.
1991   "The New Testament: Confronting Its Impact on Jewish-Christian Relations." In *Introduction to Jewish Christian Relations,* edited by M. Shermis and A. Zannoni, 34-62. New York: Paulist.

Cooke, G.
1961   "The Israelite King as Son of God." *ZAW* 73: 202-25.
1964   "The Sons of (the) God(s)." *ZAW* 76: 22-47.

Cousar, C. B.
1990   *A Theology of the Cross: The Death of Jesus in the Pauline Letters.* Minneapolis: Fortress.

Craigie, P.
1978   *The Problem of War in the Old Testament.* Grand Rapids: Eerdmans.

Cranfield, C. E. B.
1951   "Riches and the Kingdom of God: St. Mark 10.17-31." *SJT* 4: 302-13.
1962   "The Christian's Political Responsibility according to the New Testament." *SJT* 15: 176-92.
1988   "Some Reflections on the Subject of the Virgin Birth." *SJT* 41: 177-89.

Crawford, R. G.
1972   "The Resurrection of Christ." *Theol* 75: 170-76.

Creager, H. L.
1974   "The Divine Image." In *A Light unto My Path,* edited by H. N. Bream et al., 103-18. Philadelphia: Temple University Press.

Crenshaw, J. L.
1976   "Wisdom in the OT." In *IDBSup*, 952-56.
1977   "In Search of Divine Presence: Some Remarks Preliminary to a Theology of Wisdom." *RevExp* 74: 353-69.
1978   *Gerhard Von Rad.* Waco, Tex.: Word.
1981   *Old Testament Wisdom.* Atlanta: John Knox.

Crockett, W., ed.

1992   *Four Views on Hell.* Grand Rapids: Zondervan.

Crollius, A. A. R.

1974   "DeReK in the Psalms." *BTB* 4: 312-17.

Cronk, G.

1982   *The Message of the Bible: An Orthodox Christian Response.* Crestwood, N.Y.: St. Vladimir's Seminary Press.

Crook, R. H.

1990   *An Introduction to Christian Ethics.* Englewood Cliffs, N.J.: Prentice-Hall.

Cross, F. M.

1983   "The Epic Traditions of Early Israel." In *The Poet and the Historian: Essays in Literary and Historical Biblical Criticism,* edited by R. E. Friedman, 13-39. Chico, Calif.: Scholars.

Cullmann, O.

1950   *Baptism in the New Testament.* London: SCM Press.

1953   *Early Christian Worship.* London: SCM Press.

1956   *The Early Church.* London: SCM Press.

1957   *The State in the New Testament.* London: SCM Press.

1958   *The Immortality of the Soul or the Resurrection of the Dead?* London: Epworth.

1961   "Eschatology and Missions in the New Testament." In *The Theology of the Christian Mission,* edited by G. H. Anderson, 42-54. New York: McGraw-Hill.

1962   *Christ and Time.* 2nd ed. London: SCM Press.

1963   *The Christology of the New Testament.* 2nd ed. London: SCM Press.

1967   *Salvation in History.* London: SCM Press.

1970   *Jesus and the Revolutionaries.* New York: Harper.

1995   *Prayer in the New Testament.* Minneapolis: Fortress.

Culpepper, R. H.

1966   *Interpreting the Atonement.* Grand Rapids: Eerdmans.

Cuming, G. J.

1949   "The Jews in the Fourth Gospel." *ExpT* 60: 290-92.

Daly, R. J.

1978   "The New Testament Concept of Christian Sacrificial Activity." *BTB* 8: 99-107.

Danell, G. A.

1953   "The Idea of God's People in the Bible." In *The Root of the Vine: Essays in Biblical Theology,* edited by A. Fridrichsen, 23-36. New York: Philosophical Library.

Daniélou, J.

1961   *The Ministry of Women in the Early Church.* London: Faith Press.

1970   "Millenarianism." In *EBT,* 582-84.

Davey, F. N.

1961   "The Gospel according to St. John and the Christian Mission." In *The Theology of the Christian Mission,* edited by G. H. Anderson, 152-63. New York: McGraw-Hill.

Davidson, R.

1959   "Some Aspects of the Old Testament Contribution to the Pattern of Christian Ethics." *SJT* 12: 373-87.

1966   "Faith and History in the Old Testament." *ExpT* 77: 100-104.

1968   "Some Aspects of the Theological Significance of Doubt in the Old Testament." *ASTI* 7: 41-52.

Davies, G. H.

1962a   "Glory" and "Theophany." In *IDB,* 2:401-3; 4:619-20.

1962b   "Memorial, Memory." In *IDB,* 3:344-46.

Davies, H.

1967   "The Ark of the Covenant." *ASTI* 5: 30-47.

Davies, J. G.

1953   "The Primary Meaning of ΠΑΡΑΚΛΗΤΟΣ." *JTS* 4: 35-38.

Davies, P. E.

1962   "Anxiety." In *IDB,* 1:154-55.

Davies, W. D.

1952   *Torah in the Messianic Age and/or the Age to Come.* Philadelphia: Society of Biblical Literature.

1962a   "Conscience." In *IDB,* 1:671-76.

1962b   "A Normative Pattern of Church Life in the New Testament?" and "Light on the Ministry from the New Testament." In *Christian Origins and Judaism,* 199-229, 231-45. London: Darton, Longman & Todd.

1974   *The Gospel and the Land: Early Christianity and Jewish Territorial Doctrine.* Berkeley: University of California Press.

1984   "The Territorial Dimension of Judaism." In *Jewish and Pauline Studies,* 49-71. Philadelphia: Fortress.

Davis, C.

1982   "The Theological Career of Historical Criticism of the Bible." *Cross Currents* 32: 267-84.

Davis, J. J.

1993   *Evangelical Ethics: Issues Facing the Church Today.* Phillipsburg, N.J.: Presbyterian and Reformed.

Dearman, J. A.

1983   "The Problem of War in the Old Testament: War, Peace and Justice." *Austin Seminary Bulletin* 99: 5-14.

DeGuglielmo, A.

1957   "The Fertility of the Land in the Messianic Prophecies." *CBQ* 19: 306-11.

Deissler, A., and R. Schnackenburg

1981   "God." In *EBT,* 298-316.

Delorme, J., et al.

1964   *The Eucharist in the New Testament: A Symposium.* Baltimore: Helicon.

Dempster, S.

1997   "An 'Extraordinary Fact': *Torah and Temple* and the Contours of the Hebrew Canon." Parts 1 and 2. *TynB* 48: 23-56, 191-218.

Dentan, R. C.

1962   "Redeem, Redeemer, Redemption." In *IDB,* 4:21-22.

1963   *Preface to Old Testament Theology.* 2nd ed. New York: Seabury Press.

Deutsch, R.

1972   "The Biblical Concept of the 'People of God.'" *SAJT* 13: 4-12.

De Vaux, R.

1971   "Is It Possible to Write a 'Theology of the Old Testament'?" In *The Bible and the Ancient Near East,* 49-62. London: Darton, Longman & Todd.

Dewey, J.

1976   "Images of Women." In *The Liberating Word: A Guide to Nonsexist Interpretation of the Bible,* edited by L. M. Russell, 62-79. Philadelphia: Westminster.

DeWitt, C. B., ed.

1991   *The Environment and the Christian: What Does the New Testament Say about the Environment?* Grand Rapids: Baker.

Dobbie, R.

1962   "The Biblical Foundation of the Mission of the Church — II. The New Testament." *IRM* 51: 281-90.

Dodd, C. H.

1930   "Jesus as Teacher and Prophet." In *Mysterium Christi,* edited by G. K. A. Bell et al., 53-66. London: Longmans, Green & Co.

1936   *The Apostolic Preaching and Its Developments.* London: Hodder.

1952   *According to the Scriptures.* London: James Nisbet.

1959   *The Epistle of Paul to the Romans.* London: Collins.

Doriani, D.

1996   "Sin." In *EDBT,* 736-39.

Doughty, D. J.

1973　　"The Priority of ΧΑΡΙΣ: An Investigation of the Theological Language of Paul." *NTS* 19: 163-80.

DuBose, F. M.

1983　　*God Who Sends: A Fresh Quest for Biblical Mission.* Nashville: Broadman.

Duchrow, U., and G. Liedke

1989　　*Shalom: Biblical Perspectives on Creation, Justice, and Peace.* Geneva: World Council of Churches.

Duling, D. C.

1992　　"Kingdom of God, Kingdom of Heaven." In *ABD*, 4:49-69.

Dumas, A.

1975　　"The Ecological Crisis and the Doctrine of Creation." *Ecumenical Review* 27: 24-35.

Dumbrell, W. J.

1984　　*Covenant and Creation: A Theology of Old Testament Covenants.* Nashville: Nelson.

1985　　*The End of the Beginning: Revelation 21–22 and the Old Testament.* Grand Rapids: Baker.

Dunn, J. D. G.

1970　　*Baptism in the Holy Spirit: A Re-examination of the New Testament Teaching on the Gift of the Spirit in Relation to Pentecostalism Today.* London: SCM Press.

1980　　*Christology in the Making: A New Testament Inquiry into the Origins of the Doctrine of the Incarnation.* Philadelphia: Westminster.

1990　　*Jesus, Paul, and the Law: Studies in Mark and Galatians.* London: SPCK.

1997　　"He Will Come Again." *Int* 51: 42-56.

Dunn, J. G. D., and J. P. Mackay

1987　　*New Testament Theology in Dialogue.* London: SPCK.

Duntley, M. A.

1991　　"Covenantal Ethics and Care for the Dying." *CCen* 108: 1135-37.

Durham, J. I.

1984　　"The King as 'Messiah' in the Psalms." *RevExp* 81: 425-35.

Dyrness, W.

1979　　*Themes in Old Testament Theology.* Downers Grove, Ill.: InterVarsity.

1992　　"Environmental Ethics and the Covenant of Hosea 2." In *Studies in Old Testament Theology,* edited by R. L. Hubbard et al., 263-78. Dallas: Word.

Eakins, J. K.

1977　　"Moses." *RevExp* 74: 461-71.

Ebeling, G.

1963 "The Meaning of 'Biblical Theology.'" In *Word and Faith*, 79-97. Philadelphia: Fortress.

Eichrodt, W.

1961 *Theology of the Old Testament*. Vol. 1. Philadelphia: Westminster.

1966 "Covenant and Law: Thoughts on Recent Discussion." *Int* 20: 302-21.

1967 *Theology of the Old Testament*. Vol. 2. Philadelphia: Westminster.

1984 "In the Beginning: A Contribution to the Interpretation of the First Word of the Bible." In *Creation in the Old Testament*, edited by B. W. Anderson, 65-73. Philadelphia: Fortress.

Eisenhower, W. D.

1988 "Your Devil Is Too Small." *CT* 33 (15 July): 24-26.

Eissfeldt, O.

1956 "El and Yahweh." *JSS* 1: 25-37.

1962 "The Promise of Grace to David in Isaiah 55:1-5." In *Israel's Prophetic Heritage*, edited by B. W. Anderson, 196-207. New York: Harper & Row.

Elder, W. H.

1977 "The Passover." *RevExp* 74: 511-22.

Eller, V.

1981 *War and Peace: From Genesis to Revelation*. Scottdale, Pa.: Herald.

Ellis, E. E.

1974 "'Spiritual' Gifts in the Pauline Community." *NTS* 20: 128-44.

1976 "Prophecy in the Early Church." In *IDBSup*, 700-701.

Ellis, I.

1985 "Jesus and the Subversive Family." *SJT* 38: 173-88.

Ellisen, S. A.

1991 *Who Owns the Land?* Portland, Oreg.: Multnomah.

Elwell, W. A.

1988a "Church." In *BEB*, 1:458-61.

1988b "Second Coming of Christ." In *BEB*, 2:1918-22.

Elwell, W. A., ed.

1988c "Curse, Cursed." In *BEB*, 1:560-61.

1988d "Demon, Demon Possession" and "Satan." In *BEB*, 1:610-12; 2:1907-8.

1988e "Righteousness." In *BEB*, 1860-62.

1988f "Savior." In *BEB*, 2:1911-12.

1988g "Son of God" and "Virgin Birth of Jesus." In *BEB*, 2:1981-83; 2:2124-26.

1988h "Tabernacle, Temple." In *BEB*, 2:2015-28.

1988i "Work, Biblical View of." In *BEB*, 2:2161-63.

Engelhard, D. H.

1980 "The Lord's Motivated Concern for the Underprivileged." *CTJ* 15: 5-26.

Engelsman, J. C.
1979   *The Feminine Dimension of the Divine.* Philadelphia: Westminster.

Enlow, R. E.
1996   "Anxiety." In *EDBT,* 28.

Enz, J. J.
1972   *The Christian and Warfare: The Roots of Pacifism in the Old Testament.* Scottdale, Pa.: Herald.

Erickson, M. J., and I. E. Bowers
1976   "Euthanasia and Christian Ethics." *JETS* 19: 15-24.

Esser, H. H., et al.
1975   "Command, Order." In *DNTT,* 1:330-43.

Evans, G. R.
1991   *The Language and Logic of the Bible: The Earlier Middle Ages.* New York: Cambridge University Press.

Evans, O. E.
1957   "The Unforgivable Sin." *ExpT* 68: 240-44.

Everson, A. J.
1979   "The Days of Yahweh." *JBL* 93: 329-37.

Ewert, D.
1980   *And Then Comes the End.* Scottdale, Pa.: Herald.
1983   *The Holy Spirit in the New Testament.* Kitchener, Ontario: Herald.

Fackre, G.
1983   "Narrative Theology: An Overview." *Int* 37: 340-53.

Fager, J. A.
1993   *Land Tenure and the Biblical Jubilee: Uncovering Hebrew Ethics through the Sociology of Knowledge.* JSOTSup 155. Sheffield: JSOT.

Faierstein, M. M.
1981   "Why Do the Scribes Say That Elijah Must Come First?" *JBL* 100: 75-86.

Fannon, P.
1967   "A Theology of the Old Testament — Is It Possible?" *Scr* 19: 46-53.

Fee, G. D.
1994   *God's Empowering Presence: The Holy Spirit in the Letters of Paul.* Peabody, Mass.: Hendrickson.

Fensham, F. C.
1971   "The Covenant as Giving Expression to the Relationship between Old and New Testament." *TynB* 22: 82-94.

Fiorenza, E. S.
1976   "Interpreting Patriarchal Traditions." In *The Liberating Word: A Guide to Nonsexist Interpretation of the Bible*, edited by L. M. Russell, 39-61. Philadelphia: Westminster.

Fischer, J. A., M. A. Getty, and R. J. Schreiter
1996   "Sin." In *CPDBT*, 916-23.

Fish, S. E.
1980   *Is There a Text in This Class? The Authority of Interpretive Communities.* Cambridge: Harvard University Press.

Fisher, M. C.
1988   "Servant of the Lord." In *BEB*, 2:1927-28.

Fletcher, V.
1971   "The Shape of the Old Testament Ethics." *SJT* 24: 47-73.

Ford, J. M.
1992   "Millennium." In *ABD*, 4:832-34.

Ford, P. J.
1975   "Paul the Apostle: Male Chauvinist?" *BTB* 5: 302-11.

Forestell, J. T.
1975   "Jesus and the Paraclete in the Gospel of John." In *Word and Spirit*, edited by J. Plevnik, 151-97. Willowdale: Regis College.

Fortna, R. T.
1974   "Theological Use of Locale in the Fourth Gospel." *ATRSup* 3: 58-95.

Foulkes, F.
1996   "Death of Christ." In *EDBT*, 156-60.

Fraine, J. D.
1965   *Adam and the Family of Man.* Staten Island, N.Y.: Alba House.

France, R. T.
1968   "The Servant of the Lord in the Teaching of Jesus." *TynB* 19: 26-52.
1982   "The Worship of Jesus: A Neglected Factor in Christological Debate." In *Christ the Lord*, edited by H. H. Rowdon, 17-36. Downers Grove, Ill.: InterVarsity.
1993   "Conversion in the Bible." *EQ* 65: 291-310.

Franklin, E.
1970   "The Ascension and the Eschatology of Luke-Acts." *SJT* 23: 191-200.

Freed, E. D.
1967   "The Son of Man in the Fourth Gospel." *JBL* 86: 402-9.

Freedman, D. N.
1960   "The Name of the God of Moses." *JBL* 79: 151-56.

Fretheim, T. E.

1984   *The Suffering of God: An Old Testament Perspective.* Philadelphia: Fortress.

1987   "Nature's Praise of God in the Psalms." *Ex Auditu* 3: 16-30.

Fridrichsen, A., ed.

1953   *The Root of the Vine: Essays in Biblical Theology.* New York: Philosophical Library.

Fritsch, C. T.

1955   "God Was with Him: A Theological Study of the Joseph Narrative." *Int* 9: 21-34.

Frizzell, L. E.

1980   *God and His Temple: Reflections on Professor Samuel Terrien's "The Elusive Presence: Toward a New Biblical Theology."* South Orange, N.J.: Seton Hall University, Institute of Judeo-Christian Studies.

Froelich, K.

1971   "The Ecology of Creation." *ThTo* 27: 263-76.

Froelich, K., ed.

1985   *Biblical Interpretation in the Early Church.* Philadelphia: Fortress.

Frost, P.

1991   "Attitudes toward Blacks in the Early Christian Era." *SCent* 8: 1-11.

Frost, S. B.

1962   "Psalm 22: An Exposition." *CJT* 8: 102-15.

1963   *Patriarchs and Prophets.* Montreal: McGill University.

Frye, N.

1981   *The Great Code: The Bible and Literature.* Toronto: Academie.

Fudge, E. W.

1994   *The Fire That Consumes: The Biblical Case for Conditional Immortality.* Carlisle, Pa.: Paternoster.

Fuller, D. P.

1992   "The Importance of a Unity of the Bible." In *Studies in Old Testament Theology,* edited by R. L. Hubbard et al., 63-75. Dallas: Word.

Fuller, R. H.

1963   *Interpreting the Miracles.* London: SCM Press.

1969   *The Foundations of New Testament Christology.* London: Collins.

1971   *The Formation of the Resurrection Narratives.* New York: Macmillan.

1989   "The Decalogue in the New Testament." *Int* 43: 243-55.

Furnish, V. P.

1981   "Theology and Ministry in the Pauline Letters." In *A Biblical Basis for*

Ministry, edited by E. E. Shelp and R. Sutherland, 101-44. Philadelphia: Westminster.
1984   "War and Peace in the New Testament." *Int* 38: 363-79.
1985   *The Moral Teaching of Paul: Selected Issues.* 2nd ed. Nashville: Abingdon.

Gadamer, H.-G.
1975   *Truth and Method.* New York: Seabury Press.

Gamble, H. Y.
1985   *The New Testament Canon: Its Making and Meaning.* Philadelphia: Fortress.

Gammie, J. G.
1989   *Holiness in Israel.* Minneapolis: Fortress.

Gard, D. H.
1954   "The Concept of the Future Life according to the Greek Translator of the Book of Job." *JBL* 73: 137-43.

Garland, D. E.
1987   "A Biblical View of Divorce." *RevExp* 84: 419-32.

Garrett, D. A.
1996   "Feasts and Festivals of Israel." In *EDBT,* 249-55.

Gaster, T. H.
1962a   "Resurrection." In *IDB,* 4:39-43.
1962b   "Satan." In *IDB,* 4:224-28.

Gatch, M. M.
1969   *Death: Meaning and Mortality in Christian Thought and Contemporary Culture.* New York: Seabury Press.

Gelin, A., and A. Descamps
1964   *Sin in the Bible.* New York: Desclée.

Gelston, A.
1964   "The Wars of Israel." *SJT* 17: 325-31.

Gemser, B.
1953   "The Importance of the Motive Clause in Old Testament Law." VTSup, 1:50-66.

Gerstenberger, E. S., and W. Schrage
1980   *Suffering.* Nashville: Abingdon.

Gese, H.
1981a   *Essays on Biblical Theology.* Minneapolis: Augsburg.
1981b   "Wisdom, Son of Man, and the Origins of Christology: The Consistent Development of Biblical Theology." *HBT* 3: 23-57.

Giles, K.

1994   "The Biblical Argument for Slavery: Can the Bible Mislead? A Case Study in Hermeneutics." *EQ* 66: 3-17.

Giles, P.

1975   "The Son of Man in the Epistle to the Hebrews." *ExpT* 86: 328-32.

Gilkey, L. B.

1961   "Cosmology, Ontology, and the Travail of Biblical Language." *JR* 41: 194-205.

Gilmour, S.

1963-64   "Pastoral Care in the New Testament Church." *NTS* 10: 393-98.

Gladson, J. A.

1993   "Job." In *A Complete Literary Guide to the Bible,* edited by L. Ryken and T. Longman, 230-44. Grand Rapids: Zondervan.

Glasson, T. F.

1945   *The Second Advent: The Origin of the New Testament Doctrine.* London: Epworth.

1963   *Moses in the Fourth Gospel.* London: SCM Press.

Gleason, R. W.

1964   *Yahweh the God of the Old Testament.* Englewood Cliffs, N.J.: Prentice-Hall.

Gnuse, R.

1985   "Jubilee Legislation in Leviticus: Israel's Vision of Social Reform." *BTB* 15: 43-48.

Goetzmann, J.

1975   "Care, Anxiety." In *DNTT,* 1:276-78.

Goldingay, J.

1975   "The Chronicler as a Theologian." *BTB* 5: 99-126.

1981   *Approaches to Old Testament Interpretation.* Downers Grove, Ill.: InterVarsity.

1987   *Theological Diversity and the Authority of the Old Testament.* Grand Rapids: Eerdmans.

Goldsworthy, G.

1981   *Gospel and Kingdom: A Christian Interpretation of the Old Testament.* Exeter: Paternoster.

1987   *Gospel and Wisdom.* Exeter: Paternoster.

1991   *According to Plan: The Unfolding Revelation of God in the Bible.* Leicester: InterVarsity.

Gollwitzer, H.

1979   *Song of Love: A Biblical Understanding of Sex.* Philadelphia: Fortress.

Good, E. M.
 1962a   "Jealousy." In *IDB*, 2:806-7.
 1962b   "Love in the OT." In *IDB*, 3:164-68.
 1962c   "Peace in the OT." In *IDB*, 3:704-6.

Gordon, C. H.
 1966   "Leviathan: Symbol of Evil." In *Biblical Motifs*, edited by A. Altmann, 1-9. Cambridge: Harvard University Press.

Gorman, M. J.
 1982   *Abortion and the Early Church.* Downers Grove, Ill.: InterVarsity.
 1987   "Abortion and the New Testament." In *Abortion: A Christian Understanding and Response*, edited by J. K. Hoffmeier, 73-85. Grand Rapids: Baker.

Goshen-Gottstein, M.
 1987   "Tanakh Theology: The Religion of the Old Testament and the Place of Jewish Biblical Theology." In *Ancient Israelite Religion*, edited by P. D. Miller et al. Philadelphia: Fortress.

Gottwald, N. K.
 1962   *Studies in the Book of Lamentations.* London: SCM Press.
 1997   "The Biblical Jubilee: In Whose Interests?" In *The Jubilee Challenge: Utopia or Possibility? Jewish and Christian Insights*, edited by H. Ucko, 33-40. Geneva: World Council of Churches.

Gowan, D. E.
 1986   *Eschatology in the Old Testament.* Philadelphia: Fortress.

Granberg, D.
 1982   "What Does It Mean to Be 'Pro-Life'?" *CCen* 99: 562-66.

Grant, F. C.
 1950   *An Introduction to New Testament Thought.* New York: Abingdon.

Grant, R. M.
 1952   "History of the Interpretation of the Bible, I. Ancient Period." In *IB*, 1:106-14.
 1984   *A Short History of the Interpretation of the Bible.* 2nd ed. New York: Macmillan.

Grassi, J.
 1964-65   "Ezekiel xxxvii.1-14 and the New Testament." *NTS* 11: 162-64.

Gray, J.
 1962   "Idol" and "Idolatry." In *IDB*, 2:673-75, 675-78.

Gray, T.
 1996   "Destroyed For Ever: An Examination of the Debates concerning Annihilation and Conditional Immortality." *Them* 21 (January): 14-18.

Grayston, K.
  1981   "The Meaning of PARAKLETOS." *JSNT* 13: 67-82.

Greenberg, M.
  1984   "The Design and Themes of Ezekiel's Program of Restoration." *Int* 38: 181-208.

Greenwood, D.
  1971   "Saint Paul and Natural Law." *BTB* 1: 262-79.

Grenz, S.
  1990   *Sexual Ethics: A Biblical Perspective.* Dallas: Word.

Groh, D. E.
  1990   "Montanism." In *EEC*, 622-23.

Gross, H.
  1981   "War." In *EBT*, 958-61.

Gryson, R.
  1976   *The Ministry of Women in the Early Church.* Collegeville, Minn.: Liturgical Press.

Guelich, R.
  1976   "The Matthean Beatitudes: 'Entrance-Requirements' or Eschatological Blessing?" *JBL* 95: 415-34.

Gula, R.
  1995   *Euthanasia: Moral and Pastoral Perspectives.* Mahwah, N.J.: Paulist.

Gulley, N. R.
  1992   "Ascension of Christ." In *ABD*, 1:472-73.

Gundry, R. H.
  1966   "'Ecstatic Utterance' (N.E.B.)?" *JTS* 17: 299-307.

Gunkel, H.
  1984   "The Influence of Babylonian Mythology upon the Biblical Creation Story." In *Creation in the Old Testament*, edited by B. W. Anderson, 25-52. Philadelphia: Fortress.

Gustafson, J. M.
  1970   "The Place of Scripture in Christian Ethics: A Methodological Study." *Int* 24: 430-55.

Guthrie, D.
  1981   *New Testament Theology.* Downers Grove, Ill.: InterVarsity.

Guthrie, H. H.
  1962   "Fast, Fasting." In *IDB*, 241-44.

Habel, N.

1972 "The Symbolism of Wisdom in Proverbs 1–9." *Int* 26: 131-57.

1995 *The Land Is Mine: Six Biblical Ideologies.* Minneapolis: Fortress.

Haenchen, E.

1970 "History and Interpretation in the Johannine Passion Narrative." *Int* 24: 198-219.

Hagner, D. A.

1985 "Biblical Theology and Preaching." *ExpT* 96: 137-41.

1997 "Balancing the Old and the New: The Law of Moses in Matthew and Paul." *Int* 55: 20-30.

Hahn, F.

1965 *Mission in the New Testament.* London, SCM Press.

1969 *The Titles of Jesus in Christology: Their History in Early Christianity.* London: Lutterworth.

1973 *The Worship of the Early Church.* Philadelphia: Fortress.

1980 "The Confession of the One God in the New Testament." *HBT* 2: 69-84.

Hall, B.

1974 "Paul and Women." *ThTo* 31: 50-55.

Hamerton-Kelly, R. G.

1970 "The Temple and the Origins of Jewish Apocalyptic." *VT* 20: 1-15.

1973 *Pre-existence, Wisdom, and the Son of Man: A Study in the Idea of Pre-existence in the New Testament.* Cambridge: Cambridge University Press.

Hamilton, V. P.

1992 "Satan." In *ABD*, 5:985-89.

Hamm, D.

1990 "Faith in the Epistle to the Hebrews: The Jesus Factor." *CBQ* 52: 270-91.

Hamman, A.

1971 *Prayer: The New Testament.* Chicago: Franciscan Herald.

Hammershaimb, E.

1959 "On the Ethics of the Old Testament Prophets." VTSup, 7:75-101.

Hannay, T.

1950 "The Temple." *SJT* 3: 278-87.

Hanson, P. D.

1971 "Old Testament Apocalyptic Reexamined." *Int* 25: 454-79.

1978 *Dynamic Transcendence.* Philadelphia: Fortress.

1979 *The Dawn of Apocalyptic: The Historical and Sociological Roots of Jewish Apocalyptic Eschatology.* 2nd ed. Philadelphia: Fortress.

1980 "The Responsibility of Biblical Theology to Communities of Faith." *ThTo* 37: 39-50.

1982   *The Diversity of Scripture: A Theological Interpretation.* Philadelphia: Fortress.
1984   "War and Peace in the Hebrew Bible." *Int* 38: 341-62.
1986   *The People Called: The Growth of Community in the Bible.* San Francisco: Harper & Row.
1987   *Old Testament Apocalyptic.* Nashville: Abingdon.

Hare, D. R. A., and D. J. Harrington
1975   "'Make Disciples of All the Gentiles' (Mt 28:19)." *CBQ* 37: 359-69.

Harkness, G., and C. F. Kraft
1976   *Biblical Backgrounds of the Middle East Conflict.* Nashville: Abingdon.

Harner, P. B.
1967   "Creation Faith in Deutero-Isaiah." *VT* 17: 298-306.

Haroutunian, J.
1956   "The Doctrine of the Ascension: A Study of the New Testament Teaching." *Int* 10: 270-81.

Harrelson, W.
1980   *The Ten Commandments and Human Rights.* Philadelphia: Fortress.

Harrington, D. J.
1980   *God's People in Christ: New Testament Perspectives on the Church and Judaism.* Philadelphia: Fortress.

Harrington, W.
1973   *The Path of Biblical Theology.* Dublin: Gill & Macmillan.
1980   *The Bible's Ways of Prayer.* Wilmington, Del.: Michael Glazier.

Harris, D. J.
1970   *The Biblical Concept of Peace: Shalom.* Grand Rapids: Baker.

Harris, J. G.
1987   *Biblical Perspectives on Aging: God and the Elderly.* Philadelphia: Fortress.

Harris, M. J.
1983   *Raised Immortal: Resurrection and Immortality in the New Testament.* London: Marshall, Morgan & Scott.

Harrison, B. W.
1983   *Our Right to Choose: Toward a New Ethic of Abortion.* Boston: Beacon Press.

Harrison, R. K.
1962   "Healing, Health." In *IDB*, 2:541-48.
1996   "Angel." In *EDBT*, 21-23.

Harrisville, R. A.
1969   "Jesus and the Family." *Int* 23: 425-38.

Harvey, A. E.
1974   "Elders." *JTS* 25: 318-32.

Harvey, D.
1962   "Joy." In *IDB*, 2:1000-1001.

Harvey, J.
1971   "The New Diachronic Biblical Theology of the Old Testament." *BTB* 1: 5-29.

Hasel, G. F.
1972   *The Remnant: The History and Theology of the Remnant Idea from Genesis to Isaiah.* Berrien Springs, Mich.: Andrews University Press.
1978   *New Testament Theology: Basic Issues in the Current Debate.* Grand Rapids: Eerdmans.
1982   "Biblical Theology: Then, Now, and Tomorrow." *HBT* 4: 61-93.
1984   "The Relationship between Biblical Theology and Systematic Theology." *TrJ* 5: 113-27.
1991   *Old Testament Theology: Basic Issues in the Current Debate.* 4th ed. Grand Rapids: Eerdmans.
1994   "The Nature of Biblical Theology: Recent Trends and Issues." *AUSS* 32: 203-15.

Haselden, K.
1964   *The Racial Problem in Christian Perspective.* New York: Harper.

Hay, D. M.
1990   "Moses through New Testament Spectacles." *Int* 44: 240-52.

Hayes, J. H.
1963   "The Tradition of Zion's Inviolability." *JBL* 82: 419-26.

Hayes, J. H., and F. Prussner
1984   *Old Testament Theology: Its History and Development.* Atlanta: John Knox.

Hays, R. B.
1996   *The Moral Vision of the New Testament: A Contemporary Introduction to New Testament Ethics.* San Francisco: Harper.

Hayter, M.
1987   *The New Eve in Christ: The Use and Abuse of the Bible in the Debate about Women in the Church.* Grand Rapids: Eerdmans.

Hedlund, R. E.
1991   *The Mission of the Church in the World.* Grand Rapids: Baker.

Heinisch, P.
1955   *Theology of the Old Testament.* Collegeville, Minn.: Liturgical Press.

Hendry, G. S.

1971   "The Eclipse of Creation." *ThTo* 28: 406-25.

Hengel, M.

1971   *Was Jesus a Revolutionist?* Philadelphia: Fortress.

1974   *Property and Riches in the Early Church.* London: SCM Press.

1976   *The Son of God: The Origin of Christology and the History of Jewish-Hellenistic Religion.* Philadelphia: Fortress.

1981   *The Atonement: The Origins of the Doctrine in the New Testament.* Philadelphia: Fortress.

Henn, T. R.

1970   *The Bible as Literature.* London: Lutterworth.

Hennecke, E.

1963   *New Testament Apocrypha.* Philadelphia: Westminster.

Hermisson, H.-J.

1984   "Observations on the Creation Theology in Wisdom." In *Creation in the Old Testament,* edited by B. W. Anderson, 118-34. Philadelphia: Fortress.

Hermisson, H.-J., and E. Lohse

1981   *Faith.* Nashville: Abingdon.

Heron, A.

1983   *The Holy Spirit.* Philadelphia: Westminster.

Hess, K.

1978   "Serve, Deacon, Worship." In *DNTT,* 3:544-53.

Hiers, R. H.

1971   "Purification of the Temple: Preparation for the Kingdom of God." *JBL* 90: 82-90.

1974   "Satan, Demons and the Kingdom of God." *SJT* 27: 35-47.

Higgins, A. J. B.

1946   "Jesus as Prophet." *ExpT* 57: 292-94.

1952   *The Lord's Supper in the New Testament.* London: SCM Press.

1953   "Priest and Messiah." *VT* 3: 321-36.

1964   *Jesus and the Son of Man.* Philadelphia: Fortress.

Hill, D.

1967   "The Request of Zebedee's Sons and the Johannine *Doxa*-Theme." *NTS* 13: 281-85.

1972   "Prophecy and Prophets in the Revelation of St John." *NTS* 18: 401-18.

Hillers, D. R.

1969   *Covenant: The History of a Biblical Idea.* Baltimore: Johns Hopkins University Press.

Hinson, E. G.

1992   "Historical and Theological Perspectives on Satan." *RevExp* 89: 475-87.

Hobbs, T. R., and P. K. Jackson

1991   "The Enemy in the Psalms." *BTB* 21: 22-29.

Hoekema, A. A.

1972   *Holy Spirit Baptism.* Exeter: Paternoster.

Hoffmann, E.

1975   "Hope, Expectation." In *DNTT*, 2:238-46.

Hoffmeier, J. K., ed.

1987   *Abortion: A Christian Understanding and Response.* Grand Rapids: Baker.

Høgenhaven, J.

1988   *Problems and Prospects of Old Testament Theology.* Sheffield: Sheffield Academic.

Hogg, W. R.

1988   "Psalm 22 and Christian Mission: A Reflection." *IRM* 77: 238-46.

Hooker, M. D.

1959   *Jesus and the Servant.* London: SPCK.

1967   *The Son of Man in Mark.* Montreal: McGill University Press.

1974   "The Johannine Prologue and the Messianic Secret." *NTS* 21: 40-58.

1978   "Interchange and Atonement." *BJRL* 60: 462-81.

1979   "Is the Son of Man Problem Really Insoluble?" In *Text and Interpretation: Studies in the New Testament Presented to Matthew Black,* edited by E. Best and R. M. Wilson, 155-68. Cambridge: Cambridge University Press.

1982   "Trial and Tribulation in Mark XIII." *BJRL* 65: 78-99.

1994   *Not Ashamed of the Gospel: New Testament Interpretations of the Death of Christ.* Carlisle, Pa.: Paternoster.

Horn, F. W.

1992   "Holy Spirit." In *ABD*, 3:260-80.

Horst, F.

1950   "Face to Face: The Biblical Doctrine of the Image of God." *Int* 4: 259-70.

Horvath, T.

1979   *The Sacrificial Interpretation of Jesus' Achievement in the New Testament.* New York: Philosophical Library.

Houlden, J. L.

1973   *Ethics and the New Testament.* Harmondsworth: Penguin Books.

Houlden, L.

1986   "Is the Bible Still There?" *Theol* 89: 87-89.

Howard, G. E.
1969   "Christ the End of the Law: The Meaning of Romans 10:4ff." *JBL* 88: 331-37.

Howard, W. F.
1943   *Christianity according to St. John.* London: Duckworth.

Hubbard, B. J.
1974   *The Matthean Redaction of a Primitive Apostolic Commissioning: An Exegesis of Matthew 28:16-20.* Missoula, Mont.: Scholars.

Hubbard, D. A.
1983   "Hope in the Old Testament." *TynB* 34: 33-59.

Hubbard, R. L.
1988   *The Book of Ruth.* Grand Rapids: Eerdmans.

Hubbard, R. L., et al., eds.
1992   *Studies in Old Testament Theology.* Dallas: Word.

Huffmon, H. B.
1965   "The Exodus, Sinai, and the Credo." *CBQ* 27: 101-13.
1969   "The Israel of God." *Int* 23: 66-77.

Hull, G. G.
1991   "Your Pain in My Heart." *CT* 35 (11 February): 26-28.

Hull, J. M.
1976   "Exorcism in the NT." In *IDBSup*, 312-14.

Hultgren, A. J.
1979   *Jesus and His Adversaries: The Form and Function of the Conflict Stories in the Synoptic Tradition.* Minneapolis: Augsburg.

Hurtado, L.
1988   *One God, One Lord: Early Christian Devotion and Ancient Jewish Monotheism.* London: SCM Press.

Jacob, E.
1958   *The Theology of the Old Testament.* New York: Harper & Row.

Jacobs, L.
1971   "Halakhah." In *EncJud*, 7:1155-66.

Jansen, W.
1973   "Geography of Faith: A Christian Perspective on the Meaning of Places." *SR* 3: 166-84.

Janzen, J. G.
1973   "The Bible and Our Social Institutions: A Theoretical Perspective." *Int* 27: 327-50.

Janzen, W.

1965   "'*AŠRÊ* in the Old Testament." *HTR* 58: 215-26.

1972   "War in the Old Testament." *Mennonite Quarterly Review* 46: 155-66.

1992   "Land." In *ABD*, 143-54.

1994   *Old Testament Ethics: A Paradigmatic Approach.* Louisville: Westminster/ John Knox.

Jay, E. G.

1981   "From Presbyter-Bishops to Bishops and Presbyters." *SCent* 1: 125-62.

Jeremias, J.

1958   *Jesus' Promise to the Nations.* London: SCM Press.

1962   "Theophany in the OT." In *IDBSup*, 896-98.

1963   *The Parables of Jesus.* London: SCM Press.

1966   *The Eucharistic Words of Jesus.* London: SCM Press.

1967   *The Prayers of Jesus.* London: SCM Press.

1971   *New Testament Theology, Part One.* London: SCM Press.

Jodock, D.

1990   "The Reciprocity between Scripture and Theology: The Role of Scripture in Contemporary Theological Reflection." *Int* 44: 369-82.

Johnson, L. T.

1981   *Sharing Possessions: Mandate and Symbol of Faith.* Philadelphia: Fortress.

Johnson, N. B.

1948   *Prayer in Apocrypha and Pseudepigrapha.* Philadelphia: SBL.

Johnson, R. F.

1962   "Moses." In *IDB*, 3:440-50.

Johnson, S. E.

1962   "Lord (Christ)." In *IDB*, 3:151.

Johnson, S. L.

1967   "The Transfiguration of Christ." *BS* 124: 133-43.

Johnston, G.

1943   *The Doctrine of the Church in the New Testament.* Cambridge: Cambridge University Press.

1962   "Love in the NT." In *IDB*, 3:168-78.

1963   "Minister." In *DB*, 661-62.

1970   *The Spirit-Paraclete in the Gospel of John.* Cambridge: Cambridge University Press.

Johnston, R. K.

1978   "The Role of Women in the Church and Home: An Evangelical Testcase in Hermeneutics." In *Scripture, Tradition, and Interpretation*, edited by W. W. Gasque and W. S. Lasor. Grand Rapids: Eerdmans.

1992   "Images for Today: Learning from Old Testament Wisdom." In *Studies in*

Old Testament Theology, edited by R. L. Hubbard et al., 223-39. Dallas: Word.

Joines, K. R.
1975   "The Serpent in Gen 3." *ZAW* 87: 1-11.

Jones, D.
1955   "*Anamnesis* in the LXX and the Interpretation of 1 Cor. xi.25." *JTS* 6: 183-91.

Jones, J. D.
1981   "Humans and Animals: Compassion and Dominion." *ATR* 63: 259-72.

Kaiser, O., and E. Lohse
1981   *Death and Life.* Nashville: Abingdon.

Kaiser, W. C.
1978   *Toward an Old Testament Theology.* Grand Rapids: Zondervan.
1983   *Toward Old Testament Ethics.* Grand Rapids: Zondervan.
1992   "New Approaches to Old Testament Ethics." *JETS* 35: 289-97.
1995   *The Messiah in the Old Testament.* Grand Rapids: Zondervan.

Kamlah, E., J. D. G. Dunn, and C. Brown
1978   "Spirit, Holy Spirit." In *DNTT,* 3:689-709.

Kane, J. H.
1976   *Christian Missions in Biblical Perspective.* Grand Rapids: Baker.

Käsemann, E.
1969   "The Beginnings of Christian Theology." In *New Testament Questions of Today,* 82-107. Philadelphia: Fortress.
1971   *Perspectives on Paul.* Philadelphia: Fortress.
1973   "The Problem of a New Testament Theology." *NTS* 19: 235-45.
1984   *The Wandering People of God: An Investigation of the Letter to the Hebrews.* Minneapolis: Augsburg.

Kaufman, G.
1968   "On the Meaning of 'Act of God.'" *HTR* 61: 175-201.

Kee, H. C.
1968   "The Terminology of Mark's Exorcism Stories." *NTS* 14: 232-46.
1980   *Christian Origins in Sociological Perspective: Methods and Resources.* Philadelphia: Westminster.
1992   "The Changing Role of Women in the Early Christian World." *ThTo* 49: 225-38.

Keegan, T. J.
1985   *Interpreting the Bible: A Popular Introduction to Biblical Hermeneutics.* New York: Paulist.

Keener, C. S.
1991   *And Marries Another: Divorce and Remarriage in the Teaching of the New Testament.* Peabody, Mass.: Hendrickson.

Kelley, P. H.
1984   "Prayers of Troubled Saints." *RevExp* 81: 377-83.

Keown, G. L.
1987   "Messianism in the Book of Malachi." *RevExp* 84: 443-51.

Kepler, T. S.
1963   *The Meaning and the Mystery of the Resurrection.* New York: Association.

Kesich, V.
1965   *The Passion of Christ.* Crestwood, N.Y.: St. Vladimir's Seminary Press.

Kiddle, M.
1934   "The Death of Jesus and the Admission of the Gentiles in St. Mark." *JTS* 35: 45-50.
1935   "The Admission of the Gentiles in St. Luke's Gospel and Acts." *JTS* 36: 160-73.

Kingsbury, J. D.
1975   "The Title 'Kyrios' in Matthew's Gospel." *JBL* 94: 246-55.

Kittel, G., et al.
1964   "*Angelos,* etc." In *TDNT,* 1:74-87.

Klassen, W.
1984   *Love of Enemies: The Way to Peace.* Philadelphia: Fortress.

Klatzker, D.
1983   "The Holy Land in Jewish-Christian Dialogue." *USQR* 38: 193-201.

Klauck, H.-J.
1992   "Lord's Supper." In *ABD,* 4:362-72.

Klein, G.
1972   "The Biblical Understanding of 'The Kingdom of God.'" *Int* 26: 387-418.

Knierim, R. P.
1981   "Cosmos and History in Israel's Theology." *HBT* 3: 59-123.
1984   "The Task of Old Testament Theology." *HBT* 6: 25-57.

Knight, D. A.
1980   "Canon and the History of Tradition: A Critique of Brevard S. Childs' *Introduction to the Old Testament as Scripture.*" *HBT* 2: 127-49.

Knight, G. A. F.
1966   "The Protestant World and Mariology." *SJT* 19: 55-73.
1983   *I Am, This Is My Name: The God of the Bible and the Religions of Man.* Grand Rapids: Eerdmans.

Knight, G. W.
1981   "The Ordination of Women: No." *CT* 25: 260-63.
1984   "*ΑΥΘΕΝΤΕΩ* in Reference to Women in 1 Timothy 2:12." *NTS* 30: 143-57.

Knox, J.
1957   *The Early Church and the Coming Great Church.* London: Epworth.
1964   "Romans 15:14-33 and Paul's Conception of His Apostolic Mission." *JBL* 83: 1-11.

Koch, K.
1972   *The Rediscovery of Apocalyptic.* London: SCM Press.
1978   "*Derekh*, etc." In *TDOT*, 3:270-93.

Koch, R.
1981a   "Ascension." In *EBT*, 37-42.
1981b   "Spirit." In *EBT*, 869-89.

Koenig, J.
1978   *Charismata: God's Gifts for God's People.* Philadelphia: Westminster.

Kraft, C. F.
1963   "Child, Children." In *DB*, 133-34.

Kraftchick, S. J., et al., eds.
1995   *Biblical Theology: Problems and Perspectives.* Nashville: Abingdon.

Kraus, H.-J.
1958   *The People of God in the Old Testament.* New York: Association.
1966   *Worship in Ancient Israel: A Cultic History of the Old Testament.* Oxford: Blackwell.
1986   *Theology of the Psalms.* Minneapolis: Augsburg.

Kuemmerlin-McLean, J. E.
1992   "Demons: Old Testament." In *ABD*, 2:138-40.

Kuhn, K. G.
1968   "Prosēlytos." In *TDNT*, 6:727-45.

Kümmel, W. G.
1963   *Man in the New Testament.* London: Epworth.

Kürzinger, J.
1970   "Virgin Birth." In *EBT*, 939-45.

Ladd, G. E.
1962   "The Kingdom of God — Reign or Realm?" *JBL* 81: 230-38.
1974   *The Presence of the Future: The Eschatology of Biblical Realism.* Grand Rapids: Eerdmans.
1981   "New Testament Apocalyptic." *RevExp* 78: 205-9.
1993   *A Theology of the New Testament.* 2nd ed. Grand Rapids: Eerdmans.

Landes, G. M.
1958   "Shall We Neglect the Angels?" *USQR* 14, no. 4, pp. 19-25.

Langton, E.
1949   *Essentials of Demonology.* London: Epworth.

Laubach, F., J. Goetzmann, and U. Beker
1975   "Conversion, Penitence, Repentance, Proselyte." In *DNTT,* 1:353-62.

Launderville, D., A. J. Tambasco, and P. J. Wadell
1996   "Peace." In *CPDBT,* 709-14.

Laurin, R. B.
1977   "Tradition and Canon." In *Tradition and Theology in the Old Testament,* edited by D. A. Knight, 261-74. Philadelphia: Fortress.

Laurin, R. B., ed.
1970   *Contemporary Old Testament Theologians.* Valley Forge, Pa.: Judson.

Lawson, J.
1948   *The Biblical Theology of St. Irenaeus.* London: Epworth.

Lazareth, W. H., ed.
1982   *Baptism, Eucharist, and Ministry.* Geneva: World Council of Churches.

Leaney, A. R. C.
1963   "The Eschatological Significance of Human Suffering in the Old Testament and in the Dead Sea Scrolls." *SJT* 16: 286-96.

Leenhardt, F. J.
1964   *Two Biblical Faiths: Protestant and Catholic.* London: Lutterworth.

Leitch, J. W.
1966   "Lord Also of the Sabbath." *SJT* 19: 426-33.

Leivestadt, R.
1972   "Exit the Apocalyptic Son of Man." *NTS* 18: 243-67.

Lemaire, A.
1973   "The Ministries in the New Testament: Recent Research." *BTB* 3: 133-66.

Lemke, W. E.
1982   "Revelation through History in Recent Biblical Theology." *Int* 36: 34-46.
1989   "Is Old Testament Theology an Essentially Christian Theological Discipline?" *HBT* 11: 59-71.

Levenson, J. D.
1980   "The Theologies of Commandment in Biblical Israel." *HTR* 73: 17-33.
1985   *Sinai and Zion: An Entry into the Jewish Bible.* Minneapolis: Winston.
1987   "Why Jews Are Not Interested in Biblical Theology." In *Judaic Perspectives on Ancient Israel,* edited by J. Neusner et al., 281-307. Philadelphia: Fortress.

Lewis, J. O.

1977   "The Ark and the Tent." *RevExp* 74: 537-48.

Lewis, J. P.

1964   "What Do We Mean by Jabneh?" *JBR* 32: 125-32.

Lightfoot, R. H.

1937   *Locality and Doctrine in the Gospels.* New York: Harper.

Lightstone, J. N.

1988   *Society, the Sacred, and Scripture in Ancient Judaism.* Waterloo, Ontario: Wilfred Laurier.

Lillie, W.

1968   "Towards a Biblical Doctrine of Punishment." *SJT* 21: 449-61.

1975   "The Pauline House-Tables." *ExpT* 86: 179-83.

Lind, M. C.

1980   *Yahweh Is a Warrior: The Theology of Warfare in Ancient Israel.* Scottdale: Herald.

Lindars, B.

1973   "The Bible and Christian Ethics." *Theol* 76: 180-89.

1975   "Re-enter the Apocalyptic Son of Man." *NTS* 22: 52-72.

1976   "Word and Sacrament in the Fourth Gospel." *SJT* 29: 49-63.

Lindblom, J.

1962   *Prophecy in Ancient Israel.* Philadelphia: Fortress.

Lindeskog, G.

1953   "The Theology of Creation in the Old and New Testaments." In *The Root of the Vine: Essays in Biblical Theology,* edited by A. Fridrichsen, 1-22. New York: Philosophical Library.

Lindhagen, C.

1956   "Important Hypotheses Reconsidered: IX. The Servant of the Lord." *ExpT* 67: 279-83, 300-302.

Lindsell, H.

1975   "Spiritual Gifts: A Biblical Perspective on What They Are and Who Has Them." *CT* 19: 675-77.

Ling, T.

1961   *The Significance of Satan: New Testament Demonology and Its Contemporary Relevance.* London: SPCK.

Link, H.-G.

1976   "Life." In *DNTT,* 2:474-84.

Linzey, A., and T. Regan

1988   *Animals and Christianity: A Book of Readings.* New York: Crossroad.

Lohfink, G.
1984   *Jesus and Community: The Social Dimension of the Christian Faith.* Philadelphia: Fortress.

Lohmeyer, E.
1962   *Lord of the Temple.* Richmond: John Knox.

Lohse, E.
1991   *Theological Ethics of the New Testament.* Minneapolis: Augsburg Fortress.

Long, E. L.
1965   "The Use of the Bible in Christian Ethics: A Look at Basic Options." *Int* 19: 149-62.

Longenecker, R. N.
1984   *New Testament Social Ethics for Today.* Grand Rapids: Eerdmans.

Longman, T.
1987   *Literary Approaches to Biblical Interpretation.* Grand Rapids: Zondervan.

Lotz, D.
1988   "Peter's Wider Understanding of God's Will: Acts 10:34-48." *IRM* 77: 201-7.

Lowe, M.
1976   "Who Were the ΙΟΥΔΑΙΟΙ?" *NovT* 18: 101-30.

MacGregor, G. H. C.
1954-55   "Principalities and Powers: The Cosmic Background of Paul's Thought." *NTS* 1: 17-28.

MacHaffie, B. J.
1986   "Women and the Early Churches." In *Her Story: Women in the Christian Tradition,* 23-41. Philadelphia: Fortress.

Machen, J. G.
1930   *The Virgin Birth of Christ.* New York: Harper & Row.

MacLeod, A. G.
1963   "Family." In *DB,* 291-93.

MacRae, G. W.
1973   "Whom Heaven Must Receive until the Time: Reflections on the Christology of Acts." *Int* 27: 151-65.

Maddox, R. L.
1968   "The Function of the Son of Man according to the Synoptic Gospels." *NTS* 15: 47-74.
1985   "Contemporary Hermeneutic Philosophy and Theological Studies." *RelS* 21: 517-29.

Maertens, T.

1966   *The Spirit of God in Scripture.* Montreal: Palm.

Maier, G.

1977   *The End of the Historical-Critical Method.* St. Louis: Concordia.

Malick, D. E.

1993a   "The Condemnation of Homosexuality in Romans 1:26-27." *BS* 15: 327-40.

1993b   "The Condemnation of Homosexuality in 1 Corinthians 6:9." *BS* 15: 479-92.

Maly, E. H.

1975   "Creation in the New Testament." In *Biblical Studies in Contemporary Thought,* edited by M. Ward, 104-12. Burlington, Vt.: Trinity College Biblical Institute.

Mánek, J.

1957   "The Apostle Paul and the Empty Tomb." *NovT* 2: 276-80.

Manson, T. W.

1935   "The Son of Man." In his *The Teaching of Jesus,* 211-34. Cambridge: Cambridge University Press.

1950a   "The New Testament Basis of the Doctrine of the Church." *JEH* 1: 1-11.

1950b   "The Son of Man in Daniel, Enoch and the Gospels." *BJRL* 32: 171-93.

1960   *Ethics and the Gospel.* London: SCM Press.

1963   "The Johannine Logos Doctrine." In *On Paul and John,* edited by M. Black, 136-59. London: SCM Press.

1964   *Only to the House of Israel? Jesus and the Non-Jews.* Philadelphia: Fortress.

Manson, W.

1953a   "The Biblical Doctrine of Mission." *IRM* 42: 257-65.

1953b   "Mission and Eschatology." *IRM* 42: 390-97.

Marcel, P.

1953   *The Biblical Doctrine of Infant Baptism: Sacrament of the Covenant of Grace.* London: Clarke.

March, W. E.

1994   *Israel and the Politics of Land: A Theological Case Study.* Louisville: Westminster/John Knox.

Marcus, J.

1988   "Entering into the Kingly Power of God." *JBL* 109: 663-75.

Marks, J. H.

1972   "God's Holy People." *ThTo* 29: 22-33.

Markus, R. A.

1957   "Presuppositions of the Typological Approach to Scripture." *CQR* 158: 442-51.

Marsh, J.

1962   "Conversion." In *IDB*, 1:678.

Marshall, I. H.

1967   "The Divine Sonship of Jesus." *Int* 21: 87-103.

1970a   *Luke: Historian and Theologian.* Grand Rapids: Zondervan.

1970b   "The Son of Man in Contemporary Debate." *EQ* 42: 67-87.

1973   "The Biblical Use of the Word 'Ekklesia.'" *ExpT* 84: 359-64.

1975   "Divorce." In *DNTT*, 1:505-7.

1982   "Incarnational Christology in the New Testament." In *Christ the Lord*, edited by H. H. Rowdon, 1-16. Downers Grove, Ill.: InterVarsity.

1985   "The Hope of a New Age: The Kingdom of God in the New Testament." *Them* 11: 5-15.

Martens, E.

1977   "Tackling Old Testament Theology." *JETS* 20: 123-32.

1981   *God's Design: A Focus on Old Testament Theology.* Grand Rapids: Baker.

1996   "God, Names of." In *EDBT*, 297-300.

Martin, R. P.

1974   *Worship in the Early Church.* Grand Rapids: Eerdmans.

1979   *The Family and the Fellowship: New Testament Images of the Church.* Grand Rapids: Eerdmans.

1992   "Gifts, Spiritual." In *ABD*, 2:1015-18.

Martin-Achard, R.

1962   *A Light to the Nations: A Study of the Old Testament Concept of Israel's Mission to the World.* Edinburgh: Oliver & Boyd.

Martyn, J. L.

1976   "We Have Found Elijah." In *Jews, Greeks, and Christians: Religious Cultures in Late Antiquity*, edited by R. Hamerton-Kelly et al., 181-219. Leiden: Brill.

Marxsen, W.

1969a   *The Beginnings of Christology: A Study of Its Problems.* Philadelphia: Fortress.

1969b   *Mark the Evangelist: Studies in the Redaction History of the Gospel.* Nashville: Abingdon.

1970   *The Resurrection of Jesus of Nazareth.* Philadelphia: Fortress.

1990   *Jesus and Easter: Did God Raise the Historical Jesus from the Dead?* Nashville: Abingdon.

Matthey, J.

1980   "The Great Commission according to Matthew." *IRM* 69: 161-73.

May, H. G.

1955   "Some Cosmic Connotations of MAYIM RABBÎM, 'Many Waters.'" *JBL* 74: 9-21.

May, P.

1959   "Towards a Biblical Theology of Missions." *IJT* 8: 21-28.

Mayer, R., and C. Brown

1978   "Scripture, Writing." In *DNTT*, 3:482-97.

Mayers, R. B.

1987   *Evangelical Perspectives: Toward a Biblical Balance.* Lanham, Md.: University Press of America.

McAll, R. K.

1975   "The Ministry of Deliverance." *ExpT* 86: 296-98.

McArthur, H. K.

1962a   "Parousia." In *IDB*, 3:658-61.

1962b   "Second Coming." In *IDB*, 4:261.

McBride, S. D.

1990   "Transcendent Authority: The Role of Moses in Old Testament Traditions." *Int* 44: 229-39.

McCann, J. C.

1993   *A Theological Introduction to the Book of Psalms.* Nashville: Abingdon.

McCarthy, D. J.

1965   "Notes on the Love of God in Deuteronomy and the Father-Son Relationship between Yahweh and Israel." *CBQ* 27: 144-47.

McCasland, S. V.

1958   "The Way." *JBL* 77: 222-30.

1962   "Man, Nature of, in the NT." In *IDB*, 3:246-50.

McConville, J. G.

1979   "God's 'Name' and God's 'Glory.'" *TynB* 30: 149-63.

1992   "Jerusalem in the Old Testament." In *Jerusalem Past and Present in the Purposes of God,* edited by P. W. L. Walker, 21-51. Cambridge: Tyndale House.

McCoy, C. S.

1963   "Johannes Cocceius: Federal Theologian." *SJT* 16: 352-70.

McDonald, L. M.

1988   *The Formation of the Christian Biblical Canon.* Nashville: Abingdon.

McGrath, A.

1985   "The Moral Theory of the Atonement." *SJT* 38: 205-20.

McKay, J. W.

1972   "Man's Love for God in Deuteronomy and the Father/Teacher—Son/Pupil Relationship." *VT* 22: 426-35.

McKelvey, R. J.
1969   *The New Temple: The Church in the New Testament.* Oxford: Oxford University Press.

McKenzie, J. L.
1952   "God and Nature in the Old Testament." *CBQ* 14: 18-39, 124-45.
1959   "The Elders in the Old Testament." *Bib* 40: 522-40.
1974   *A Theology of the Old Testament.* Garden City, N.Y.: Doubleday.

McKim, D. D.
1992   "The Grand Farewell." *CT* 36 (18 May): 36-37.

McKnight, S.
1990   *A Light among the Gentiles: Jewish Missionary Activity in the Second Temple Period.* Minneapolis: Fortress.
1996   "Blasphemy against the Holy Spirit." In *EDBT*, 67-69.

McLelland, J. C.
1957   "Covenant Theology — a Re-evaluation." *CJT* 3: 182-88.

McNeill, J. T.
1952   "History of the Interpretation of the Bible, II. Medieval and Reformation Period." In *IB*, 1:115-26.

Meeks, W. A.
1966   "Galilee and Judaea in the Fourth Gospel." *JBL* 85: 159-69.
1976   "Moses in the NT." In *IDBSup*, 605-7.

Menard, J. E.
1957   "*Pais Theou* as Messianic Title in the Book of Acts." *CBQ* 19: 83-92.

Mendelsohn, I.
1962   "Slavery in the OT." In *IDB*, 4:383-91.

Mendenhall, G. E.
1962   "Covenant." In *IDB*, 1:714-23.

Metzger, B. M.
1957   *An Introduction to the Apocrypha.* Oxford: Oxford University Press.
1991   "Introduction to the Apocryphal/Deuterocanonical Books." In *NOAB*, AP: iii-xii.

Meyer, B. F.
1965   "Jesus and the Remnant of Israel." *JBL* 84: 123-30.
1989   *Critical Realism and the New Testament.* Allison Park, Pa.: Pickwick.
1993   "The Temple: Symbol Central to Biblical Theology." *Greg* 74: 223-40.

Meyer, P. W.
1979   "The Holy Spirit in the Pauline Letters: A Contextual Exploration." *Int* 33: 3-18.

Michel, O.

1978   "*Pais Theou*, Servant of God." In *DNTT*, 3:607-13.

Michl, J.

1981a   "Demon." In *EBT*, 191-96.

1981b   "Hell." In *EBT*, 369-71.

Miethe, T. L., ed.

1987   *Did Jesus Rise from the Dead? The Resurrection Debate.* San Francisco: Harper & Row.

Migliore, D. L.

1976   "How Historical Is the Resurrection? (A Dialogue)." *ThTo* 33: 5-14.

Milazzo, G. T.

1991   *The Protest and the Silence: Suffering, Death, and Biblical Theology.* Minneapolis: Fortress.

Milgrom, J.

1963   "The Biblical Diet Laws as an Ethical System." *Int* 17: 288-301.

1997   "Leviticus 25 and Some Postulates of the Jubilee." In *The Jubilee Challenge: Utopia or Possibility? Jewish and Christian Insights*, edited by H. Ucko, 28-32. Geneva: World Council of Churches.

Miller, D. G.

1961   "Pauline Motives for the Christian Mission." In *The Theology of the Christian Mission*, edited by G. H. Anderson, 72-84. New York: McGraw-Hill.

Miller, J. W.

1989   *Biblical Faith and Fathering: Why We Call God Father.* New York: Paulist.

1994   *The Origins of the Bible: Rethinking Canon History.* New York: Paulist.

Miller, P. D.

1965   "God the Warrior: A Problem in Biblical Interpretation and Apologetics." *Int* 19: 39-46.

1969   "The Gift of God: The Deuteronomic Theology of the Land." *Int* 23: 451-61.

1975   "The Blessing of God: An Interpretation of Numbers 6:22-27." *Int* 29: 240-51.

1989   "The Place of the Decalogue in the Old Testament and Its Law." *Int* 43: 229-42.

1994   *They Cried to the Lord: The Form and Theology of Biblical Prayer.* Minneapolis: Fortress.

1995   "Creation and Covenant." In *Biblical Theology: Problems and Perspectives*, edited by S. J. Kraftchick et al., 155-68. Nashville: Abingdon.

Minear, P. S.

1960   *Images of the Church in the New Testament.* Philadelphia: Westminster.

1962   "Hope." In *IDB*, 2:640-43.

1983   "Holy People, Holy Land, Holy City: The Genesis and Genius of Christian Attitudes." *Int* 37: 18-31.

Mitton, C. L.
1962   "Peace in the NT." In *IDB*, 3:706.

Molin, G.
1981a   "Glory." In *EBT*, 292-98.
1981b   "Vocation." In *EBT*, 954-58.

Mollenkott, V. R.
1983   *The Divine Feminine: The Biblical Imagery of God as Female.* New York: Crossroad.

Montgomery, J. A.
1932   "Ascetic Strains in Early Judaism." *JBL* 51: 183-213.

Montgomery, J. W.
1962   "Wisdom as Gift: The Wisdom Concept in Relation to Biblical Messianism." *Int* 16: 43-57.

Moo, D. J.
1984   "Jesus and the Authority of the Mosaic Law." *JSNT* 20: 3-49.

Moody, D.
1962   "Virgin Birth." In *IDB*, 4:789-91.
1965   "Charismatic and Official Ministries." *Int* 19: 168-81.
1968   *Spirit of the Living God.* Philadelphia: Westminster.

Moore, A. L.
1966   *The Parousia in the New Testament.* Leiden: Brill.

Morgan, R.
1973   *The Nature of New Testament Theology.* London: SCM Press.
1979   "The Hermeneutical Significance of Four Gospels." *Int* 33: 376-88.
1981   *Wisdom in the Old Testament Traditions.* Atlanta: John Knox.
1987   "Gabler's Bicentenary." *ExpT* 98: 164-68.
1995   "New Testament Theology." In *Biblical Theology: Problems and Perspectives,* edited by S. J. Kraftchick et al., 104-30. Nashville: Abingdon.

Morrice, W. G.
1984   *Joy in the New Testament.* Exeter: Paternoster.

Morris, L.
1952   "The Biblical Use of the Term 'Blood.'" *JTS* 3: 216-27.
1960   *The Biblical Doctrine of Judgment.* Grand Rapids: Eerdmans.
1965   *The Cross in the New Testament.* Grand Rapids: Eerdmans.
1986   *New Testament Theology.* Grand Rapids: Academie.

Most, W. G.
1967   "A Biblical Theology of Redemption in a Covenant Framework." *CBQ* 29:
            1-19.

Mott, S. C.
1982   *Biblical Ethics and Social Change.* New York: Oxford University Press.

Moule, C. F. D.
1957   "Expository Problems: The Ascension — Acts i.9." *ExpT* 68: 205-9.
1961   *Worship in the New Testament.* Richmond: John Knox.
1963a   "Important Moral Issues. Prolegomena: The New Testament and Moral
            Decisions." *ExpT* 74: 370-73.
1963b   *The Meaning of Hope: A Biblical Exposition with Concordance.* Philadel-
            phia: Fortress.
1964   *Man and Nature in the New Testament: Some Reflections on Biblical Ecol-
            ogy.* Philadelphia: Facet.
1968   *The Significance of the Message of the Resurrection for Faith in Jesus Christ.*
            London: SCM Press.
1978   *The Holy Spirit.* Grand Rapids: Eerdmans.

Mowinckel, S.
1962   *The Psalms in Israel's Worship.* 2 vols. New York: Abingdon.

Mowry, L.
1962   "Beatitudes." In *IDB,* 1:369-71.

Mowvley, H.
1965   "The Concept and Content of 'Blessing' in the Old Testament." *BibT* 16:
            74-80.

Muilenburg, J.
1961   *The Way of Israel: Biblical Faith and Ethics.* New York: Harper & Row.
1965   "Abraham and the Nations: Blessing and World History." *Int* 19:387-98.

Müller, M.
1993   "The Septuagint as the Bible of the New Testament Church." *Scandina-
            vian Journal of the Old Testament* 7: 194-207.

Munzer, K.
1978   "Remain." In *DNTT,* 3:223-26.

Murphy, R. E.
1994   "Wisdom Literature and Biblical Theology." *BTB* 24: 4-7.

Murray, R.
1975   "New Wine in Old Wineskins: XII. Firstfruits." *ExpT* 86: 164-68.

Myers, C. D.
1995   "The Persistence of Apocalyptic Thought in New Testament Theology."
            In *Biblical Theology: Problems and Perspectives,* edited by S. J. Kraftchick
            et al., 209-21. Nashville: Abingdon.

Myers, J. M.

1975   *Grace and Torah.* Philadelphia: Fortress.

Nations, A. L.

1983   "Historical Criticism and the Current Methodological Crisis." *SJT* 36: 59-71.

Navone, J.

1973   "Three Aspects of the Lucan Theology of History." *BTB* 3: 115-32.

Nestle, E., K. Aland, et al.

1979   *Novum Testamentum Graece.* Stuttgart: Deutsche Bibelstiftung.

Newman, C. C.

1992   *Paul's Glory-Christology: Tradition and Rhetoric.* Leiden: Brill.

Newman, R. C.

1976   "The Council of Jamnia and the Old Testament Canon." *WTJ* 38: 319-49.

Newsom, C. A.

1992   "Angels (OLD TESTAMENT)." In *ABD,* 1:248-53.

Nicholson, E. W.

1977   "The Decalogue as the Direct Address of God." *VT* 27: 422-33.

1986   *God and His People: Covenant and Theology in the Old Testament.* Oxford: Clarendon.

Nickelsburg, G. W. E.

1972   *Resurrection, Immortality, and Eternal Life in Intertestamental Judaism.* Cambridge: Harvard University Press.

1976   "Future Life in Intertestamental Literature." In *IDBSup,* 348-51.

1992   "Son of Man." In *ABD,* 6:137-50.

Nickle, K. F.

1966   *The Collection: A Study in Paul's Strategy.* London: SCM Press.

Nicole, J.

1997   "The Jubilee: Some Christian Understandings throughout History." In *The Jubilee Challenge: Utopia or Possibility? Jewish and Christian Insights,* edited by H. Ucko, 53-58. Geneva: World Council of Churches.

Nineham, D. E., ed.

1963   *The Church's Use of the Bible: Past and Present.* London: SPCK.

Niven, W. D.

1953   *Reformation Principles after Four Centuries,* 13-22. Glasgow: Church of Scotland.

Nixon, R. E.

1963   *The Exodus in the New Testament.* London: Tyndale.

North, C. R.
1950   "Sacrifice." In *TWBB*, 206-14.
1962   "Servant of the Lord, The." In *IDB*, 4:292-94.

North, R.
1963   "The Theology of the Chronicler." *JBL* 82: 369-81.

Obersteiner, J.
1981   "Messianism." In *EBT*, 575-82.

O'Brien, P. T.
1973   "Prayer in Luke-Acts." *TynB* 24: 111-27.

O'Collins, G. G.
1993   *The Resurrection of Jesus Christ: Some Contemporary Issues.* Milwaukee: Marquette University Press.

Okure, T.
1988   *The Johannine Approach to Mission: A Contextual Study of John 4:1-42.* Tübingen: J. C. B. Mohr.

Ollenburger, B. C.
1985   "Biblical Theology: Situating the Discipline." In *Understanding the Word*, edited by J. T. Butler, 37-62. Sheffield: JSOT.

Omanson, R. L.
1986   "The Role of Women in the New Testament Church." *RevExp* 83: 15-25.

Orlinsky, H. M.
1986   "The Biblical Concept of the Land of Israel: Cornerstone of the Covenant between God and Israel." In *The Land of Israel: Jewish Perspectives*, edited by L. A. Hoffman, 27-64. Notre Dame, Ind.: University of Notre Dame Press.

O'Rourke, J. J.
1968   "The Hymns of the Apocalypse." *CBQ* 30: 399-409.

Ortlund, R. C.
1996   *Whoredom: God's Unfaithful Wife in Biblical Theology.* Grand Rapids: Eerdmans.

Osborne, T. P.
1983   "Guide Lines for Christian Suffering: A Source-Critical and Theological Study of 1 Peter 2:21-25." *Bib* 64: 381-408.

O'Toole, R. F.
1979   "Luke's Understanding of Jesus' Resurrection-Ascension-Exaltation." *BTB* 9: 106-14.

Otto, E., and T. Schramm
1980   *Festival and Joy.* Nashville: Abingdon.

Otwell, J. H.
1977   *And Sarah Laughed: The Status of Women in the Old Testament.* Philadelphia: Westminster.

Packer, J.
1991   "Let's Stop Making Women Presbyters." *CT* 35: 18-21.

Pamment, M.
1981   "Moses and Elijah in the Story of the Transfiguration." *ExpT* 92: 338-39.

Panikulam, G.
1979   *Koinōnia in the New Testament: A Dynamic Expression of Christian Life.* Rome: Biblical Institute Press.

Parke-Taylor, G. H.
1975   *Yahweh: The Divine Name in the Bible.* Waterloo, Ontario: Wilfred Laurier University Press.

Parnham, F. S.
1972   "Moses the Meek." *EQ* 44: 103-6.

Parratt, J. K.
1971   "The Holy Spirit and Baptism: Part I. The Gospels and the Acts of the Apostles" and "The Holy Spirit and Baptism: Part II. The Pauline Evidence." *ExpT* 82: 231-35, 266-71.

Patrick, D.
1981   *The Rendering of God in the Old Testament.* Philadelphia: Fortress.

Patterson, R. D.
1973   "The Widow, the Orphan, and the Poor in the Old Testament and the Extra-biblical Literature." *BS* 130: 223-34.
1993   "Old Testament Prophecy." In *A Complete Literary Guide to the Bible,* edited by L. Ryken and T. Longman, 296-309. Grand Rapids: Zondervan.

Payne, D. F.
1961   "The Everlasting Covenant." *TynB* 7-8: 10-16.

Perdue, L. G.
1994   *The Collapse of History: Reconstructing Old Testament Theology.* Minneapolis: Fortress.

Perkin, H. W.
1988   "Family Life and Relations." In *BEB,* 1:767-73.

Perrin, N., and D. C. Duling
1982   *The New Testament: An Introduction.* New York: Harcourt Brace Jovanovich.

Perry, M.
1990   "Taking Satan Seriously." *ExpT* 101: 105-12.

Perry, V.

1976   "Problem Passages of the New Testament: Does the New Testament Call Jesus God?" *ExpT* 87: 214-15.

Peskett, H.

1990   "Prayer in the Old Testament Outside the Psalms." In *Teach Us to Pray: Prayer in the Bible and the World,* edited by D. A. Carson, 19-34. Exeter: Paternoster.

Peters, G. W.

1972   *A Biblical Theology of Missions.* Chicago: Moody.

Peterson, D.

1990   "Prayer in Paul's Writings." In *Teach Us to Pray: Prayer in the Bible and the World,* edited by D. A. Carson, 84-101. Exeter: Paternoster.

1992   *Engaging with God: A Biblical Theology of Worship.* Leicester: Apollos.

Peterson, E.

1964   *The Angels and the Liturgy.* New York: Herder & Herder.

Pinnock, C. H.

1989   "Climbing Out of a Swamp: The Evangelical Struggle to Understand the Creation Texts." *Int* 43: 143-55.

Pinto, E.

1974   "Jesus as the Son of God in the Gospels." *BTB* 4: 75-93.

Piper, O. A.

1951   "The Apocalypse of St. John and the Liturgy of the Ancient Church." *CH* 20: 10-22.

1957   "Unchanging Promises: Exodus in the New Testament." *Int* 11: 3-22.

1962a   "Knowledge." In *IDB,* 3:42-48.

1962b   "Life." In *IDB,* 3:124-30.

1962c   "Suffering and Evil." In *IDB,* 4:450-53.

1964   "The Virgin Birth: The Meaning of the Gospel Accounts." *Int* 18: 131-48.

Pittenger, N.

1969   "On Miracle: II, B. The Virgin Birth." *ExpT* 80: 147-48.

Placher, W. C.

1999   "Christ Takes Our Place: Rethinking Atonement." *Int* 53: 5-20.

Plevnik, J., ed.

1975   *Word and Spirit.* Willowdale: Regis College, 1975.

Pokorny, P.

1993   "The Problem of Biblical Theology." *HBT* 15: 83-94.

Pope, M. H.

1962a   "Proselyte." In *IDB,* 3:921-31.

1962b   "Rechab." In *IDB,* 4:14-16.

1976   "Homosexuality." In *IDBSup* 415-17.

Porteous, N.
1962a   "Image of God." In *IDB*, 2:682-85.
1962b   "Man, Nature of, in the OT." In *IDB*, 3:242-46.
1967   "Jerusalem-Zion: The Growth of a Symbol." In *Living the Mystery*, 93-111. Oxford: Blackwell.

Porter, J. R.
1965   "The Legal Aspects of the Concept of 'Corporate Personality' in the Old Testament." *VT* 15: 361-80.

Prager, M.
1981   "Satan." In *EBT*, 808-12.

Preuss, H. D.
1995   *Old Testament Theology*. Vol. 1. New York and Evanston, Ill.: Harper & Row.
1996   *Old Testament Theology*. Vol. 2. New York and Evanston, Ill.: Harper & Row.

Priest, J.
1992   "A Note on the Messianic Banquet." In *The Messiah: Developments in Earliest Judaism and Christianity*, edited by J. H. Charlesworth, 222-38. Minneapolis: Fortress.

Quanbeck, W. A.
1962   "Repentance." In *IDB*, 4:33-34.

Rabe, V. W.
1967   "Israelite Opposition to the Temple." *CBQ* 29: 228-33.

Rae, F. J.
1955   "The Two Circles of Faith." *ExpT* 66: 212-15.

Redford, D. B.
1970   *A Study of the Biblical Story of Joseph (Genesis 37–50)*. Leiden: Brill.

Reese, D. G.
1992   "Demons: New Testament." In *ABD*, 2:140-42.

Reese, J. M.
1981   "Christ as Wisdom Incarnate: Wiser than Solomon, Loftier than Lady Wisdom." *BTB* 11: 44-47.

Reid, J. K. S.
1955   *The Biblical Doctrine of Ministry*. Edinburgh: Oliver & Boyd.
1957   *The Authority of Scripture: A Study of the Reformation and Post-Reformation Understanding of the Bible*. London: Methuen.

Rendtorff, R.
1968   *Men of the Old Testament.* London: SCM Press.
1988   "Must 'Biblical Theology' Be Christian Theology?" *BRev* 4: 40-43.
1989   "'Covenant' as a Structuring Concept in Genesis and Exodus." *JBL* 108: 385-93.
1993   *Canon and Theology: Overtures to an Old Testament Theology.* Minneapolis: Fortress.

Rétif, A., and P. Lamarche
1966   *The Salvation of the Gentiles and the Prophets.* Baltimore: Helicon.

Reumann, J.
1976   "Faith, Faithfulness in the NT." In *IDBSup,* 332-35.

Reumann, J., ed.
1991   *The Promise and Practice of Biblical Theology.* Minneapolis: Fortress.

Reumann, J. H. P.
1974   "Psalm 22 at the Cross: Lament and Thanksgiving for Jesus Christ." *Int* 28: 39-58.

Reumann, W.
1966   "The Gospel of the Righteousness of God: Pauline Reinterpretation in Romans 3:21-31." *Int* 20: 432-52.

Reventlow, H. G.
1985   *Problems of Old Testament Theology in the Twentieth Century.* Philadelphia: Fortress.
1986   *Problems of Biblical Theology in the Twentieth Century.* Philadelphia: Fortress.
1992   "Theology (Biblical), History of." In *ABD,* 6:483-505.

Rhodes, A. B.
1977   "Israel's Prophets as Intercessors." In *Scripture in History and Theology,* edited by A. L. Merrill and T. W. Overholt, 107-28. Pittsburgh: Pickwick.

Richardson, A.
1941   *The Miracle-Stories of the Gospels.* London: SCM Press.
1952   *The Biblical Doctrine of Work.* London: SCM Press.
1958   *An Introduction to the Theology of the New Testament.* London: SCM Press.

Richardson, P.
1969   *Israel in the Apostolic Church.* Cambridge: University Press.

Richardson, P., and S. Westerholm, eds.
1991   *Law in Religious Communities in the Roman Period: The Debate over Torah and Nomos in Post-biblical Judaism and Early Christianity.* Waterloo, Ontario: Wilfred Laurier.

Richardson, W. J.

1968   "Principle and Context in the Ethics of the Epistle to Philemon." *Int* 22: 301-16.

Riesenfeld, H.

1953   "The Ministry in the New Testament." In *The Root of the Vine: Essays in Biblical Theology,* edited by A. Fridrichsen, 96-127. New York: Philosophical Library.

Riggans, W.

1995   "The Parousia: Getting Our Terms Right." *Them* 21 (October): 14-16.

Ringe, S. H.

1985   *Jesus, Liberation, and the Biblical Jubilee: Images for Ethics and Christology.* Philadelphia: Fortress.

Ringgren, H.

1947   *Word and Wisdom: Studies in the Hypostatization of Divine Qualities and Functions in the Ancient Near East.* Lund: Hakan Ohlssons Boktryckeri.

1956   *The Messiah in the Old Testament.* London: SCM Press.

Rist, M.

1962a   "Antichrist" and "Dualism." In *IDB,* 1:140-43, 873.

1962b   "Millennium." In *IDB,* 3:381-82.

Roberts, J. J. M.

1973   "The Davidic Origin of the Zion Tradition." *JBL* 92: 329-44.

1992   "The Old Testament Contribution to Messianic Expectations." In *The Messiah: Developments in Earliest Judaism and Christianity,* edited by J. H. Charlesworth, 39-51. Minneapolis: Fortress.

Robertson, P.

1971   "The Outlook for Biblical Theology." In *Toward a Theology for the Future,* edited by D. F. Wells and C. H. Pinnock, 65-91. Carol Stream, Ill.: Creation House.

Robinson, H. W.

1944   "The Council of Yahweh." *JTS* 45: 151-57.

1955   *The Cross in the Old Testament.* London: SCM Press.

1980   *Corporate Personality in Ancient Israel.* 2nd ed. Philadelphia: Fortress.

Robinson, J. A. T.

1957   *Jesus and His Coming: The Emergence of a Doctrine.* London: SCM Press.

1962   "Resurrection in the NT." In *IDB,* 4:43-53.

Robinson, J. M.

1962a   "Descent into Hades." In *IDB,* 1:826-28.

1962b   "Regeneration." In *IDB,* 4:24-29.

Robinson, R. B.
1991   "Narrative Theology and Biblical Theology." In *The Promise and Practice of Biblical Theology,* edited by J. Reumann, 129-42. Minneapolis: Fortress.

Rodd, C. S.
1967   "The Family in the Old Testament." *BibT* 18: 19-26.

Rogers, C. L.
1993   "The Davidic Covenant in the Gospels." *BS* 15: 458-78.

Rogerson, J.
1970   "The Hebrew Conception of Corporate Personality: A Re-examination." *JTS* 21: 1-16.

Rogerson, J., B. Lindars, and C. Rowland
1988   *A History of Christian Theology.* Vol. 2, *The Study and Use of the Bible.* Grand Rapids: Eerdmans.

Rollins, W. G.
1976   "Slavery in the NT." In *IDBSup,* 830-32.

Roon, A. von
1974   "The Relation between Christ and the Wisdom of God according to Paul." *NovT* 16: 207-39.

Rordorf, W.
1968   *Sunday: The History of the Day of Rest and Worship in the Earliest Centuries of the Christian Church.* Philadelphia: Westminster.

Ross, J. F.
1962   "The Prophet as Yahweh's Messenger." In *Israel's Prophetic Heritage,* edited by B. W. Anderson, 98-107. New York: Harper & Row.

Ross, J. M.
1954   "The Decline of the Devil." *ExpT* 66: 58-61.
1979   "The Status of the Apocrypha." *Theol* 82: 183-91.

Roth, C.
1960   "The Cleansing of the Temple and Zechariah xiv.21." *NovT* 4: 174-81.

Roth, W. M. W.
1964   "The Anonymity of the Suffering Servant." *JBL* 83: 171-79.

Rowdon, H. H., ed.
1982   *Christ the Lord.* Downers Grove, Ill.: InterVarsity.

Rowley, H. H.
1945   *The Missionary Message of the Old Testament.* London: Carey Kingsgate.
1950a   *The Biblical Doctrine of Election.* London: Lutterworth.
1950b   "The Suffering Servant and the Davidic Messiah." *OS* 8: 100-136.
1953   *The Unity of the Bible.* London: Carey Kingsgate.

1967 *Worship in Ancient Israel: Its Forms and Meaning.* Philadelphia: Fortress.

Ruether, R. R.
1979 *Mary, the Feminine Face of the Church.* London: SCM Press.
1983 "An Unrealized Revolution: Searching Scripture for a Model of the Family." *CCris* 43: 399-404.

Russell, D. S.
1964 *The Method and Message of Jewish Apocalyptic.* Philadelphia: Westminster.

Russell, L. M., ed.
1976 *The Liberating Word: A Guide to Nonsexist Interpretation of the Bible.* Philadelphia: Westminster.

Ryken, L.
1984 *How to Read the Bible as Literature.* Grand Rapids: Zondervan.
1987a *Words of Delight: A Literary Introduction to the Bible.* Grand Rapids: Baker.
1987b *Words of Life: A Literary Introduction to the New Testament.* Grand Rapids: Baker.
1993 "The Bible as Literature: A Brief History." In *A Complete Literary Guide to the Bible,* edited by L. Ryken and T. Longman, 49-68. Grand Rapids: Zondervan.

Ryken, L., and T. Longman, eds.
1993 *A Complete Literary Guide to the Bible.* Grand Rapids: Zondervan.

Rylaarsdam, J. C.
1946 *Revelation in Jewish Wisdom Literature.* Chicago: University of Chicago Press.
1962 "Nazirite." In *IDB,* 3:526-27.

Sabourin, L.
1973 "Original Sin Reappraised." *BTB* 3: 51-81.
1977 "The Coming of the Son of Man (Matt 10:23b)." *BTB* 7: 5-11.

Sacks, S. D.
1988 "Fear." In *BEB,* 1:781-83.

Sahlin, H.
1953 "The New Exodus of Salvation according to St. Paul." In *The Root of the Vine: Essays in Biblical Theology,* edited by A. Fridrichsen, 81-95. New York: Philosophical Library.

Sakenfeld, K. D.
1975 "The Bible and Women: Bane or Blessing?" *ThTo* 32: 222-33.

Sanders, E. P.
1977 *Paul and Palestinian Judaism: A Comparison of Patterns of Religion.* London: SCM Press.

Sanders, J.

1991   *No Other Name: An Investigation into the Destiny of the Unevangelized.* Grand Rapids: Eerdmans.

Sanders, J. A.

1962   "Enemy." In *IDB*, 2:101.

1972   *Torah and Canon.* Philadelphia: Fortress.

1975   "Torah and Christ." *Int* 29: 372-90.

1980   "Canonical Context and Canonical Criticism." *HBT* 2: 173-97.

1984   *Canon and Community: A Guide to Canonical Criticism.* Philadelphia: Fortress.

1992   "Canon: Hebrew Bible." In *ABD*, 1:837-52.

Sandnes, K. O.

1994   "The Death of Jesus for Human Sins: The Historical Basis for a Theological Concept." *Them* 20: 20-23.

Sandys-Wunsch, J.

1980   "G. T. Zachariä's Contribution to Biblical Theology." *ZAW* 92: 1-23.

1981   "Spinoza — the First Biblical Theologian." *ZAW* 93: 327-41.

Sandys-Wunsch, J., and L. Eldredge

1980   "J. P. Gabler and the Distinction between Biblical and Dogmatic Theology; Translation, Commentary, and Discussion of His Originality." *SJT* 33: 133-58.

Santmire, H. P.

1985   "The Liberation of Nature: Lynn White's Challenge Anew." *CCen* 102: 530-33.

Sauer, A. von Rohr

1974   "Ecological Notes from the Old Testament." In *A Light unto My Path*, edited by H. N. Bream et al., 421-34. Philadelphia: Temple University Press.

Saunders, E. W.

1976   "Resurrection in the NT." In *IDBSup*, 739-41.

Sawyer, J. F. A.

1993   *Prophecy and the Biblical Prophets.* New York: Oxford University Press.

Scalise, C. J.

1996   *From Scripture to Theology: A Canonical Journey into Hermeneutics.* Downers Grove, Ill.: InterVarsity.

Scalise, P. J.

1986   "Women in Ministry: Reclaiming Our Old Testament Heritage." *RevExp* 83: 7-13.

Scharbert, J., and J. Schmid

1981   "Suffering." In *EBT*, 890-97.

Schelkle, K. H.

1971-78   *Theology of the New Testament.* 4 vols. Collegeville, Minn.: Liturgical Press.

Schippers, R.

1975   "Persecution, Tribulation, Affliction." In *DNTT,* 805-9.

Schlier, H.

1961   *Principalities and Powers in the New Testament.* New York: Herder & Herder; Montreal: Palm.

1968   *The Relevance of the New Testament.* New York: Herder & Herder.

Schmidt, H. H.

1984   "Creation, Righteousness, and Salvation: 'Creation Theology' as the Broad Horizon of Biblical Theology." In *Creation in the Old Testament,* edited by B. W. Anderson, 102-17. Philadelphia: Fortress.

Schmithals, W.

1975   *The Apocalyptic Movement: Introduction and Interpretation.* Nashville: Abingdon.

Schmitt, E.

1981   "Death" and "Life." In *EBT,* 181-84, 499-503.

Schnackenburg, R.

1968   "The Notion of Faith in the Fourth Gospel." In *The Gospel according to St. John,* 1:558-75. Freiburg: Herder.

Schneider, J., and C. Brown

1978   "Sōtēr." In *DNTT,* 3:216-21.

Schneider, S.

1985   "Church and Biblical Scholarship in Dialogue." *ThTo* 42: 353-58.

Schnelle, U.

1996   *The Human Condition: Anthropology in the Teachings of Jesus, Paul, and John.* Minneapolis: Fortress.

Schniewind, J.

1952   "The Biblical Doctrine of Conversion." *SJT* 5: 267-81.

Schrage, W.

1988   *The Ethics of the New Testament.* Philadelphia: Fortress.

Schultz, C.

1996   "Person, Personhood." In *EDBT,* 602-4.

Schumaker, M.

1980   *Appreciating Our Good Earth: Toward a Pertinent Theology of Nature.* Kingston: Queen's Theological College.

Schütz, H. G., S. Wibbing, and J. A. Motyer

1975   "Body, Member, Limb." In *DNTT*, 1:229-42.

Schweizer, E.

1961   *Church Order in the New Testament*. London: SCM Press.

1980   *The Holy Spirit*. Philadelphia: Fortress.

Scobie, C. H. H.

1963   "Apocryphal New Testament." In *DB*, 41-45.

1964   *John the Baptist*. London: SCM Press.

1970   "Paul and the Universal Mission of the Church." *Crux* 8: 10-17.

1976   "North and South: Tension and Reconciliation in Biblical History." In *Biblical Studies in Honour of William Barclay*, edited by J. R. McKay and J. F. Miller, 87-98, 203-8. London: Collins.

1982   "Johannine Geography." *SR* 11: 77-84.

1984a   "Jesus or Paul? The Origin of the Universal Mission of the Christian Church." In *From Jesus to Paul*, edited by P. Richardson and J. C. Hurd, 47-60. Waterloo, Ontario: Wilfred Laurier University Press.

1984b   "The Place of Wisdom in Biblical Theology." *BTB* 14: 43-48.

1991a   "The Challenge of Biblical Theology." *TynB* 42.1: 31-61.

1991b   "The Structure of Biblical Theology." *TynB* 42.2: 163-94.

1992a   "Three Twentieth Century Biblical Theologies." *HBT* 14: 51-69.

1992b   "Israel and the Nations: An Essay in Biblical Theology." *TynB* 43: 283-305.

Scroggs, R.

1966   *The Last Adam: A Study in Pauline Anthropology*. Oxford: Blackwell.

1976   "Marriage in the NT." In *IDBSup*, 576-77.

1983   *The New Testament and Homosexuality: Contextual Background for Contemporary Debate*. Philadelphia: Fortress.

Scullion, J. J.

1992   "God (God in the OT)." In *ABD*, 2:1041-48.

Seitz, O. J. F.

1962   "Lists, Ethical." In *IDB*, 3:137-39.

Selwyn, E. G.

1947   "Particular Relationships: The Social Code (SUBIECTI)." In *The First Epistle of St. Peter*, 419-39. London: Macmillan.

1969   "On I Peter III.18–IV.6." In *The First Epistle of Peter*, 314-62. London: Macmillan.

Senior, D., and C. Stuhlmueller

1983   *The Biblical Foundations for Mission*. Grand Rapids: Eerdmans.

Seybold, K., and U. B. Mueller

1981   *Sickness and Healing*. Nashville: Abingdon.

Shaw, J. M.

1990   *The Pilgrim People of God: Recovering a Biblical Motif.* Minneapolis: Augsburg.

Shed, R. P.

1964   *Man in Community: A Study of St. Paul's Application of Old Testament and Early Jewish Conceptions of Human Solidarity.* Grand Rapids: Eerdmans.

Shelley, M.

1984   "The Death Penalty: Two Sides of a Growing Issue." *CT* 28 (2 March): 14-17.

Shelp, E. E., and R. Sutherland, eds.

1981   *A Biblical Basis for Ministry.* Philadelphia: Westminster.

Shepherd, M. H.

1962   "Evangelist." In *IDB,* 2:181.

Sheppard, G. T.

1985   "The Use of Scripture within the Christian Ethical Debate concerning Same-Sex Oriented Persons." *USQR* 40: 13-35.

Shoemaker, M. H.

1996   "Priest, Christ as." In *EDBT,* 631-32.

Sider, R. J., ed.

1981   *Evangelicals and Development: Toward a Theology of Social Change.* Exeter: Paternoster.

Simundson, D. J.

1980   *Faith under Fire: Biblical Interpretations of Suffering.* Minneapolis: Augsburg.

Sklba, R. J.

1981   "The Call to New Beginnings: A Biblical Theology of Conversion." *BTB* 11: 67-73.

Slane, C. J.

1996   "Sabbath." In *EDBT,* 697-99.

Sleeper, C. F.

1968   "Ethics as a Context for Biblical Interpretation." *Int* 22: 443-60.

Smalley, S. S.

1969   "The Johannine Son of Man Sayings." *NTS* 15: 278-301.

Smart, J. D.

1960   *The Rebirth of Ministry: A Study of the Biblical Character of the Church's Ministry.* Philadelphia: Westminster.

1979   *The Past, Present, and Future of Biblical Theology.* Philadelphia: Westminster.

Smith, B. D.
1996   "Suffering." In *EDBT,* 749-52.

Smith, D. M.
1974   "Glossolalia and Other Spiritual Gifts in a New Testament Perspective." *Int* 28: 307-20.
1981   "Theology and Ministry in John." In *A Biblical Basis for Ministry,* edited by E. E. Shelp and R. Sutherland, 186-228. Philadelphia: Westminster.

Smith, R.
1952   "The Relevance of the Old Testament for the Doctrine of the Church." *SJT* 5: 14-23.

Sonne, I.
1962   "Synagogue." In *IDB,* 4:476-91.

Soulen, R. N.
1969   "Marriage and Divorce: A Problem in New Testament Interpretation." *Int* 23: 439-50.
1978   "Matthean Divorce Texts." *BTB* 8: 24-33.

Souter, A., and C. S. C. Williams
1954   *The Text and Canon of the New Testament.* 2nd ed. London: Duckworth.

Speiser, E. A.
1962   "Man, Ethnic Divisions of." In *IDB,* 3:235-42.

Spencer, A. D. B.
1974   "Eve at Ephesus: Should Women Be Ordained as Pastors according to the First Letter to Timothy 2:11-15?" *JETS* 17: 215-22.

Sperling, D.
1976   "Navel of the Earth." In *IDBSup,* 621-23.

Spina, F. W.
1982   "Canonical Criticism: Childs versus Sanders." In *Interpreting God's Word for Today: An Inquiry into Hermeneutics from a Biblical Theological Perspective,* edited by W. McCown and J. E. Massey, 165-94. Anderson, Ind.: Warner.

Spohn, W. C.
1996   *What Are They Saying about Scripture and Ethics?* New York: Paulist.

Spriggs, D. G.
1974   *Two Old Testament Theologies.* London: SCM Press.

Stagg, F.
1962   *New Testament Theology.* Nashville: Broadman.

1977   "Biblical Perspectives on the Single Person." *RevExp* 74: 5-19.

Stählin, G.

1956   "'On the Third Day': The Easter Traditions of the Primitive Church." *Int* 10: 282-99.

1974   "Chēra." In *TDNT*, 9:440-65.

Stander, H. F.

1990   "Marcion." In *EEC*, 568-69.

Stanley, D. M.

1973   *Boasting in the Lord: The Phenomenon of Prayer in St. Paul.* New York: Paulist.

Stauffer, E.

1955   *New Testament Theology.* London: SCM Press.

Steele, D. A.

1986   *Images of Leadership and Authority for the Church: Biblical Principles and Secular Models.* Lanham, Md.: University Press of America.

Steffen, L.

1990   "Casting the First Stone." *CCris* 50: 11-16.

Stein, R. H.

1996   "Kingdom of God." In *EDBT*, 451-54.

Steinmetz, D. C.

1980   "The Superiority of Pre-critical Exegesis." *ThTo* 37: 27-38.

Stemberger, G.

1974   "Galilee — Land of Salvation?" In *The Gospel and the Land: Early Christianity and Jewish Territorial Doctrine,* by W. D. Davies, app. IV, 409-38. Berkeley: University of California Press.

Stempvoort, P. A. van

1958   "The Interpretation of the Ascension in Luke and Acts." *NTS* 5: 30-42.

Stendahl, K.

1962   "Biblical Theology, Contemporary." In *IDB*, 1:418-32.

1963   "The Apostle Paul and the Introspective Conscience of the West." *HTR* 56: 199-215.

1966   *The Bible and the Role of Women: A Case Study in Hermeneutics.* Philadelphia: Fortress.

1977   "Glossolalia and the Charismatic Movement." In *God's Christ and His People,* edited by J. Jervell et al., 122-31. Oslo: Universitetsforlaget.

Stephens, S.

1980   *A New Testament View of Women.* Nashville: Broadman.

Stevens, B. A.

1983   "Jesus as the Divine Warrior." *ExpT* 94: 326-29.

Stewart, A.

1898   "Bible." In *HDB*, 1:286-99.

Stewart, J. S.

1951   "On a Neglected Emphasis in New Testament Theology." *SJT* 4: 292-301.

Stewart, R. A.

1967   "The Sinless High-Priest." *NTS* 14: 126-35.

1971   "The Synagogue." *EQ* 43: 36-46.

Stock, A.

1978   "Matthean Divorce Texts." *BTB* 8: 24-33.

Stott, J. R. W.

1978   *Christian Counter-Culture: The Message of the Sermon on the Mount.* Downers Grove, Ill.: InterVarsity.

1985   "Homosexual Marriage: Why Same-Sex Partnerships Are Not a Christian Option." *CT* 29 (22 November): 21-28.

Stott, W.

1978   "Sabbath, Lord's Day." In *DNTT*, 3:405-15.

Stouffer, A. H.

1981   "The Ordination of Women: Yes." *CT* 25: 256-59.

Stuhlmacher, P.

1977   *Historical Criticism and Theological Interpretation of Scripture.* Philadelphia: Fortress.

1978   "Adolf Schlatter's Interpretation of Scripture." *NTS* 24: 433-46.

1979   "The Gospel of Reconciliation in Christ — Basic Features and Issues of a Biblical Theology of the New Testament." *HBT* 1: 161-90.

1986   *Reconciliation, Law, and Righteousness: Essays in Biblical Theology.* Philadelphia: Fortress.

1987   "The Ecological Crisis as a Challenge for Biblical Theology." *Ex Auditu* 3: 1-15.

1994   *Paul's Letter to the Romans: A Commentary.* Edinburgh: T. & T. Clark.

1995   *How to Do Biblical Theology.* Allison Park, Pa.: Pickwick.

Suggs, M. J.

1970   *Wisdom, Christology, and Law in Matthew's Gospel.* Cambridge: Harvard University Press.

Sundberg, A. C.

1964   *The Old Testament of the Early Church.* Cambridge: Harvard University Press.

1968   "The 'Old Testament': A Christian Canon." *CBQ* 30: 143-55.

1975   "The Bible Canon and the Christian Doctrine of Inspiration." *Int* 29: 352-71.

Swain, C. W.
1963   "'For Our Sins': The Image of Sacrifice in the Thought of the Apostle Paul." *Int* 17: 131-39.

Swartley, W. M.
1983   *Slavery, Sabbath, War, and Women.* Scottdale, Pa.: Herald.

Sweet, J. P. M.
1967   "A Sign for Unbelievers: Paul's Attitude to Glossolalia." *NTS* 13: 240-57.

Swetnam, J.
1974   "Why Was Jeremiah's New Covenant New?" VTSup 26: 111-15.

Sykes, M. H.
1960   "The Eucharist as 'Anamnesis.'" *ExpT* 71: 115-18.

Takahashi, M.
1966   "An Oriental's Approach to the Problems of Angelology." *ZAW* 78: 343-50.

Talbert, C. H.
1994   *The Apocalypse: A Reading of the Revelation of John.* Louisville: Westminster/John Knox.

Talmon, S.
1971   "The Biblical Concept of Jerusalem." *JES* 8: 300-316.
1977   "The 'Navel of the Earth' and the Comparative Method." In *Scripture in History and Theology,* edited by A. L. Merrill and T. W. Overholt, 243-68. Pittsburgh: Pickwick.

Tate, M. E.
1981   "Promising Paths toward Biblical Theology." *RevExp* 78: 169-85.
1992   "Satan in the Old Testament." *RevExp* 89: 461-74.
1994   "The Comprehensive Nature of Salvation in Biblical Perspective." *RevExp* 91: 469-85.

Tate, W. R.
1991   *Biblical Interpretation: An Integrated Approach.* Peabody, Mass.: Hendrickson.

Taylor, J. G.
1995   "The Bible and Homosexuality." *Them* 21 (October): 4-9.

Taylor, V.
1920   *The Historical Evidence for the Virgin Birth.* Oxford: Clarendon.
1953   *The Names of Jesus.* London: Macmillan.
1956   *The Cross of Christ.* London: Macmillan.
1962   "Does the New Testament Call Jesus God?" *ExpT* 73: 16-118.

Teeple, H. M.
1957   *The Mosaic Eschatological Prophet.* Philadelphia: Society of Biblical Literature.
1965   "The Origin of the Son of Man Christology." *JBL* 84: 213-58.

Terrien, S. L.
1952   "History of the Interpretation of the Bible, III: Modern Period." In *IB,* 1:127-41.
1962   "Fear." In *IDB,* 2:256-60.
1973   "Toward a Biblical Theology of Womanhood." *RelLife* 42: 322-33.
1978   *The Elusive Presence: Toward a New Biblical Theology.* New York and San Francisco: Harper & Row.
1981   "The Play of Wisdom: Turning Point in Biblical Theology." *HBT* 3: 125-53.

Tetlow, E. M., and L. M. Tetlow
1983   *Partners in Service: Toward a Biblical Theology of Christian Marriage.* Lanham, Md.: University Press of America.

Thiselton, A. C.
1975   "Flesh." In *DNTT,* 1:671-82.
1980   *The Two Horizons: New Testament Hermeneutics and Philosophical Description with Special Reference to Heidegger, Bultmann, Gadamer, and Wittgenstein.* Grand Rapids: Eerdmans.

Thomas, O. C., ed.
1983   *God's Activity in the World: The Contemporary Problem.* Chico, Calif.: Scholars.

Thomas, R. W.
1968   "The Meaning of the Terms 'Life' and 'Death' in the Fourth Gospel and in Paul." *SJT* 21: 199-212.

Thompson, J. W.
1971   "The Gentile Mission as an Eschatological Necessity." *RQ* 14: 18-27.

Thompson, L. L.
1969   "Cult and Eschatology in the Apocalypse of John." *JR* 49: 330-50.
1978   *Introducing Biblical Literature: A More Fantastic Country.* Englewood Cliffs, N.J.: Prentice-Hall.

Thomson, J. G. S. S.
1955   "The Shepherd-Ruler Concept in the OT and Its Application in the NT." *SJT* 8: 406-18.

Thurian, M.
1963   *Mary, Mother of the Lord, Figure of the Church.* London: Faith Press.

Thurston, B. B.
1989   *The Widows: A Women's Ministry in the Early Church.* Minneapolis: Fortress.

Tiede, D. L.
1990   *Jesus and the Future.* New York: Cambridge University Press.

Tobin, T. H.
1992   "Logos." In *ABD*, 4:348-56.

Tödt, H. E.
1963   *The Son of Man in the Synoptic Tradition.* London: SCM Press.

Toombs, L. E.
1962a   "Throne." In *IDB*, 4:636-37.
1962b   "War, Ideas of." In *IDB*, 4:796-801.

Toon, P.
1984   *The Ascension of Our Lord.* Nashville: Nelson.
1986   *Heaven and Hell: A Biblical and Theological Overview.* Nashville: Nelson.
1987   *Born Again: A Biblical and Theological Study of Regeneration.* Grand Rapids: Baker.
1996   "Lord's Supper, the." In *EDBT*, 491-94.

Torrance, T. F.
1957   "One Aspect of the Biblical Conception of Faith." *ExpT* 68: 111-14.

Tostengard, S.
1992   "Psalm 22." *Int* 44: 167-70.

Trafton, J. L.
1996   "Lord's Day, the." In *EDBT*, 488-89.

Travis, S. H.
1986   "The Problem of Judgment." *Them* 11: 52-57.

Trible, P.
1973   "Depatriarchalizing in Biblical Interpretation." *JAAR* 41: 30-48.
1976   "God, Nature of, in the Old Testament." In *IDBSup*, 368-69.
1978   *God and the Rhetoric of Sexuality.* Philadelphia: Fortress.
1984   *Texts of Terror: Literary-Feminist Readings of Biblical Narratives.* Philadelphia: Fortress.

Trites, A. A.
1994   *The Transfiguration of Christ: A Hinge of Holy History.* Hantsport, Nova Scotia: Lancelot.

Trotter, A. H.
1996a   "Ascension of Jesus Christ." In *EDBT*, 39-40.
1996b   "Atonement." In *EDBT*, 43-45.

Tsevat, M.
1972   "The Basic Meaning of the Biblical Sabbath." *ZAW* 84: 447-59.
1986   "Theology of the Old Testament — a Jewish View." *HBT* 8: 33-50.

Tuckett, C. M.
1992   "Atonement in the NT." In *ABD*, 1:518-22.

Tugwell, S.
1973   "The Gift of Tongues in the New Testament." *ExpT* 84: 137-40.

Turner, H. E. W.
1956   "The Virgin Birth." *ExpT* 68: 12-17.

Turner, M. M. B.
1982   "The Spirit of Christ and Christology." In *Christ the Lord,* edited by H. H. Rowdon, 168-90. Downers Grove, Ill.: InterVarsity.

Turro, J. C., and R. E. Brown
1968   "Canonicity." In *JBC,* 515-34.

Ucko, H., ed.
1997   *The Jubilee Challenge: Utopia or Possibility? Jewish and Christian Insights.* Geneva: World Council of Churches.

Ury, M. W.
1996   "Holy, Holiness." In *EDBT,* 340-44.

Van der Ploeg, J. P. M.
1972   "Slavery in the Old Testament." VTSup, 22:72-87.

Van Ness, D. W.
1987   "Punishable by Death." *CT* 31 (10 July): 24-27.

Vawter, B.
1975   "Postexilic Prayer and Hope." *CBQ* 37: 460-70.

Verhey, A.
1984   *The Great Reversal: Ethics and the New Testament.* Grand Rapids: Eerdmans.
1992   "Remember, Remembrance." In *ABD,* 5:667-69.

Verhoef, P. A.
1970   "Some Thoughts on the Present-Day Situation in Biblical Theology." *WTJ* 33: 1-19.

Verkuyl, J.
1978   *Contemporary Missiology.* Grand Rapids: Eerdmans.

Vermes, G.
1967   "The Use of *BR NSH/BR NSH*' in Jewish Aramaic." In *An Aramaic Approach to the Gospels and Acts,* edited by M. Black, 310-30. 3rd ed. Oxford: Clarendon.

Verseput, D. J.
1987   "The Role and Meaning of the 'Son of God' Title in Matthew's Gospel." *NTS* 33: 532-56.

Viering, F., ed.

1970   "Understanding the Death of Jesus." *Int* 24: 139-50.

Vischer, W.

1949a   *The Witness of the Old Testament to Christ.* London: Lutterworth.

1949b   "Words and the Word: The Anthropomorphisms of the Biblical Revelation." *Int* 3: 3-18.

Vogels, W.

1998   "Trends in Biblical Theology." *Theology Digest* 45: 123-28.

Von Rad, G.

1962   *Theology of the Old Testament.* Vol. 1. New York and Evanston, Ill.: Harper & Row.

1965   *Theology of the Old Testament.* Vol. 2. New York and Evanston, Ill.: Harper & Row.

1966   *The Problem of the Hexateuch and Other Essays.* Edinburgh: Oliver & Boyd.

1972   *Wisdom in Israel.* London: SCM Press.

1984   "The Theological Problem of the Old Testament Doctrine of Creation." In *Creation in the Old Testament,* edited by B. W. Anderson, 53-64. Philadelphia: Fortress.

1991   *Holy War in Ancient Israel.* Grand Rapids: Eerdmans.

Von Wahlde, U. C.

1982   "The Johannine 'Jews': A Critical Survey." *NTS* 28: 33-60.

Von Waldow, H. E.

1974   "Israel and Her Land: Some Theological Considerations." In *A Light unto My Path,* edited by H. N. Bream et al., 493-508. Philadelphia: Temple University Press.

1984   "The Concept of War in the Old Testament." *HBT* 6: 27-48.

Vos, G.

1948   *Biblical Theology: Old and New Testaments.* Grand Rapids: Eerdmans.

Vriezen, T. C.

1953   "Prophecy and Eschatology." VTSup, 199-229.

1970   *An Outline of Old Testament Theology.* Oxford: Blackwell.

Wacholder, B. Z.

1973   "The Calendar of Sabbatical Cycles during the Second Temple and the Early Rabbinic Period." *HUCA* 44: 153-96.

Wainwright, A.

1982   *Beyond Biblical Criticism: Encountering Jesus in Scripture.* London: SPCK.

Wainwright, G.

1981   *Eucharist and Eschatology.* New York: Oxford University Press.

Walker, P. W. L., ed.

1992   *Jerusalem Past and Present in the Purposes of God.* Cambridge: Tyndale House.

Walker, W. O.

1969   "Postcrucifixion Appearances and Christian Origins." *JBL* 88: 157-65.

1972   "The Origin of the Son of Man Concept as Applied to Jesus." *JBL* 91: 482-90.

1983   "The Son of Man: Some Recent Developments." *CBQ* 45: 584-607.

Walker-Jones, A. W.

1989   "The Role of Theological Imagination in Biblical Theology." *HBT* 11: 73-97.

Wallace, H. N.

1992   "Adam." In *ABD*, 1:62-64.

Wallace, R.

1981   *The Atoning Death of Christ.* Westchester, Ill.: Crossway.

Waltke, B. K.

1976   "Reflections from the Old Testament on Abortion." *JETS* 19: 3-13.

Ward, J. M.

1976   "Faith, Faithfulness in the OT." In *IDBSup*, 329-32.

1991   *Thus Says the Lord: The Message of the Prophets.* Nashville: Abingdon.

Ward, W. E.

1977   "Towards a Biblical Theology." *RevExp* 74: 371-87.

Ware, T.

1969   *The Orthodox Church.* Harmondsworth: Penguin.

Watson, D. F.

1992   "Angels (NEW TESTAMENT)." In *ABD*, 1:253-55.

Watson, F.

1997   *Text and Truth: Redefining Biblical Theology.* Grand Rapids: Eerdmans.

Watson, N. M.

1983   "Justified by Faith, Judged by Works — an Antinomy?" *NTS* 29: 209-21.

Watson, P. S.

1962   "The Nature and Function of Biblical Theology." *ExpT* 73: 195-200.

Watts, J. D. W.

1956   "The People of God: A Study of the Doctrine in the Pentateuch." *ExpT* 67: 232-37.

Webber, R. E.

1982   *Worship Old and New.* Grand Rapids: Zondervan.

Weber, H.-R.

1989   *Power: Focus for a Biblical Theology.* New York: World Council of Churches.

Webster, J. B.

1986   "The Imitation of Christ." *TynB* 37: 95-120.

Wedderburn, A. J. M.

1985   "Paul and Jesus: The Problem of Continuity." *SJT* 38: 189-203.

Weinfeld, M.

1983   "Zion and Jerusalem as Religious and Political Capital: Ideology and Utopia." In *The Poet and the Historian: Essays in Literary and Historical Biblical Criticism,* edited by R. E. Friedman, 75-115. Chico, Calif.: Scholars.

Wenham, D.

1982   "'This Generation Will Not Pass . . .': A Study of Jesus' Future Expectation in Mark 13." In *Christ the Lord,* edited by H. H. Rowdon, 127-50. Downers Grove, Ill.: InterVarsity.

Wenham, G. J.

1981   "The Theology of Unclean Food." *EQ* 53: 6-15.

1982   "Christ's Healing Ministry and His Attitude to the Law." In *Christ the Lord,* edited by H. H. Rowdon, 115-26. Downers Grove, Ill.: InterVarsity.

Wernberg-Möller, P.

1960   "Is There an Old Testament Theology?" *HibJ* 59: 21-29.

Westerholm, S.

1988   *Israel's Law and the Church's Faith: Paul and His Recent Interpreters.* Grand Rapids: Eerdmans.

Westermann, C.

1963a   *Essays on Old Testament Interpretation.* London: SCM Press.

1963b   "God and His Creation." *USQR* 18: 197-209.

1963c   "God and His People: The Church in the Old Testament." *Int* 17: 259-70.

1965   *The Praise of God in the Psalms.* Richmond: John Knox.

1969   "The Way of Promise through the Old Testament." In *The Old Testament and Christian Faith,* edited by B. W. Anderson, 200-224. New York: Harper & Row.

1972   *Beginning and End in the Bible.* Philadelphia: Fortress.

1974   *Creation.* Philadelphia: Fortress.

1978   *Blessing: In the Bible and in the Life of the Church.* Philadelphia: Fortress.

1979   *What Does the Old Testament Say about God?* Atlanta: John Knox.

1980   *The Psalms: Structure, Content, and Message.* Minneapolis: Augsburg.

1982   *The Elements of Old Testament Theology.* Atlanta: John Knox.

Wharton, J. A.

1981   "Theology and Ministry in the Hebrew Scriptures." In *A Biblical Basis for*

Ministry, edited by E. E. Shelp and R. Sutherland, 17-71. Philadelphia: Westminster.

Whitaker, D.
1970   "What Happened to the Body of Jesus? A Speculation." *ExpT* 81: 307-10.

White, H. R.
1981   *The Meaning and Significance of Christian Hope.* New York: Vantage Books.

White, L.
1967   "The Historical Roots of Our Ecological Crisis." *Science* 155: 1203-7.

White, R. E. O.
1979   *Biblical Ethics.* Atlanta: John Knox.
1996   "Baptize, Baptism." In *EDBT,* 50-53.

Whiteley, D. E. H.
1964   *The Theology of St. Paul.* Oxford: Blackwell.

Whybray, R. N.
1968   *The Succession Narrative: A Study of II Sam. 9–20 and I Kings 1 and 2.* London: SCM Press.

Wiebe, B.
1991   "Messianic Ethics: Response to the Kingdom of God." *Int* 45: 29-42.

Wilckens, U.
1978   *Resurrection. Biblical Testimony to the Resurrection: An Historical Examination and Explanation.* Atlanta: John Knox.

Wilcoxen, J. A.
1968   "Some Anthropocentric Aspects of Israel's Sacred History." *JR* 48: 333-50.

Wiles, G. P.
1974   *Paul's Intercessory Prayers: The Significance of the Intercessory Prayer Passages in the Letters of St. Paul.* Cambridge: University Press.

Wilken, R. L.
1988   "Byzantine Palestine: A Christian Holy Land." *BA* 51: 214-17, 233-37.
1992   *The Land Called Holy: Palestine in Christian History and Thought.* New Haven: Yale University Press.

Wilkinson, J.
1967   "A Study of Healing in the Gospel according to John." *SJT* 20: 442-61.
1971   "Healing in the Epistle of James." *SJT* 24: 326-45.
1974   "The Mission Charge to the Twelve and Modern Medical Missions." *SJT* 27: 313-28.

Williams, C. G.

1974   "Ecstaticism in Hebrew Prophecy and Christian Glossolalia." *SR* 3: 320-38.

Williamson, G. A.

1965   *Eusebius: The History of the Church from Christ to Constantine.* Harmondsworth: Penguin Books.

Wilson, M.

1975   "Exorcism: A Clinical/Pastoral Practice Which Raises Serious Questions." *ExpT* 86: 292-95.

Wilson, S. G.

1973   *The Gentiles and the Gentile Mission in Luke-Acts.* Cambridge: Cambridge University Press.

Wimmer, J. F.

1982   *Fasting in the New Testament: A Study in Biblical Theology.* New York: Paulist.

Wink, W.

1973   *The Bible in Human Transformation: Toward a New Paradigm for Biblical Study.* Philadelphia: Fortress.

1984   *Naming the Powers: The Language of Power in the New Testament.* Philadelphia: Fortress.

1986   *Unmasking the Powers: The Invisible Forces That Determine Human Existence.* Philadelphia: Fortress.

1992   *Engaging the Powers: Discernment and Resistance in a World of Domination.* Minneapolis: Fortress.

Winn, A. C.

1981   *A Sense of Mission: Guidance from the Gospel of John.* Philadelphia: Westminster.

Winward, S. F.

1969   *A Guide to the Prophets.* Atlanta: John Knox.

Witherington, B.

1984   *Women in the Ministry of Jesus: A Study of Jesus' Attitudes to Women and Their Roles as Reflected in His Earthly Life.* New York: Cambridge University Press.

Witherup, R. D.

1994   *Conversion in the New Testament.* Collegeville, Minn.: Liturgical Press.

Wolff, H. W.

1972   "The Day of Rest in the Old Testament." *CTM* 43: 498-506.

1973   "Masters and Slaves: On Overcoming Class-Struggle in the Old Testament." *Int* 27: 259-72.

1974   *Anthropology of the Old Testament.* London: SCM Press.

Wolverton, W. I.

1963   "The Psalmists' Belief in God's Presence." *CJT* 9: 82-94.

Wood, C. M.

1981   *The Formation of Christian Understanding.* Philadelphia: Westminster.

Wood, J. D.

1958   *The Interpretation of the Bible.* London: Duckworth.

Woods, G. N.

1991   *Biblical Backgrounds of the Troubled Middle East.* Nashville: Gospel Advocate.

Worgul, G. S.

1982   "People of God, Body of Christ: Pauline Ecclesiological Contrasts." *BTB* 12: 24-28.

Wright, C. J. H.

1983   *An Eye for an Eye: The Place of Old Testament Ethics Today.* Downers Grove, Ill.: InterVarsity.

1990   "The People of God and the State in the Old Testament." *Them* 16 (October/November): 4-10.

1992   "A Christian Approach to Old Testament Prophecy concerning Israel." In *Jerusalem Past and Present in the Purposes of God,* edited by P. W. L. Walker, 1-19. Cambridge: Tyndale House.

Wright, D. F., ed.

1989   *Chosen by God: Mary in Evangelical Perspective.* London: Marshall Pickering.

Wright, G. E.

1939   "The Good Shepherd." *BA* 2: 44-48.

1952   *God Who Acts: Biblical Theology as Recital.* London: SCM Press.

1961   "The Old Testament Basis for the Christian Mission." In *The Theology of the Christian Mission,* edited by G. H. Anderson, 17-30. New York: McGraw-Hill.

Wright, J. S.

1978   "The Virgin Birth." In *DNTT,* 3:660-64.

Wright, N. T.

1990   "The New Testament and the 'State.'" *Them* 16 (October/November): 11-17.

1992   "Jerusalem in the New Testament." In *Jerusalem Past and Present in the Purposes of God,* edited by P. W. L. Walker, 53-77. Cambridge: Tyndale House.

Yates, R.

1974   "The Antichrist." *EQ* 46: 42-50.

Yoder, J. H.

1972   *The Politics of Jesus.* Grand Rapids: Eerdmans.

1985   "Biblical Roots of Liberation Theology." *Grail* 1: 55-74.

Yoder, P. B.

1987   *Shalom: The Bible's Word for Salvation, Justice, and Peace.* Newton, Kans.: Faith and Life.

Young, F. W.

1949   "Jesus the Prophet: A Re-examination." *JBL* 68: 285-99.

1962a   "Suicide." In *IDB*, 4:453-54.

1962b   "Wealth." In *IDB*, 4:818-19.

Zehr, P. M.

1981   *God Dwells with His People: A Study of Israel's Ancient Tabernacle.* Scottdale, Pa.: Herald.

Ziesler, J. A.

1972   *The Meaning of Righteousness in Paul: A Linguistic and Theological Enquiry.* Cambridge: Cambridge University Press.

1990   *Pauline Christianity.* 2nd ed. New York: Oxford University Press.

Zimmerli, W.

1964   "The Place and Limit of the Wisdom in the Framework of the Old Testament Theology." *SJT* 17: 146-58.

1976   "Slavery in the OT." In *IDBSup*, 829-30.

1978   *Old Testament Theology in Outline.* Atlanta: John Knox.

1985   "The 'Land' in the Pre-exilic and early Post-exilic Prophets." In *Understanding the Word*, edited by J. T. Butler et al., 247-62. Sheffield: JSOT Press.

Zimmerli, W., and J. Jeremias

1957   *The Servant of God.* London: SCM Press.

Index of Authors

Index of Subjects